Praise for *Choosing the Ri...*

"By far the best college guide in America . . . *Choosing the Right C...*
is the right college for you, not what is the 'best' college by some formula for f...
universities. In addition to a very thorough examination of the academic realities at these institutions, it goes into the social atmosphere, which can make or break the whole college experience."
—**Thomas Sowell**, nationally syndicated columnist

"*Choosing the Right College* is aimed at exposing the political biases of academe, the prevalence of permissive sex, and the lack of core curriculums to prospective students and their parents."
—*New York Times*

"American parents (and students) have long needed a reliable 'review' of our nation's universities so they can be sure they will not be supporting the systematic destruction of the values, faith, and worldview they have spent so many years building up. *Choosing the Right College* is the right book for them." —**Cal Thomas**, nationally syndicated columnist

"If you're looking at the big-name schools, this [guide] will be of great value in helping you decide which one is for you." —*New York Post*

"An excellent guide for students and parents—and probably the best available for a certain kind of student and parent." —*National Review*

"An essential purchase for anyone seeking to make an informed choice concerning a college education."
—*First Things*

"If prospective students and their families want a critical look at what is taught at America's most powerful and celebrated schools, *Choosing the Right College* may be their only guide." —*World*

"A valuable tool that asks more probing questions and provides far more significant answers than the typical college guide." —**Michael Medved**, nationally syndicated radio host

"Perhaps the most refreshing feature of *Choosing the Right College* is that it looks beyond the 'usual suspects' to find great, unsung colleges." —*Fresno Bee*

"An essential reference for prospective students and their parents." —*Homeschool Magazine*

"To parents like me, this wise and informative book is a rich blessing." —**William Murchison**, syndicated columnist

"An indispensable guide for anyone who wants to make an informed and intelligent choice about one of the most important—and expensive—decisions most of us will ever make." —**Roger Kimball**, author of *Tenured Radicals: How Politics Has Corrupted Our Higher Education*

Choosing the Right College
2014–15

The Inside Scoop on Elite Schools and Outstanding Lesser-Known Institutions

Intercollegiate Studies Institute

ISI
BOOKS

Wilmington, Delaware

Choosing the Right College is made possible in part by the generosity of Mr. Gilbert I. Collins, Mr. and Mrs. Richard Gaby, and the Grover Hermann Foundation.

Cataloguing-in-Publication data is on file with the Library of Congress and available upon request. ISBN: 9781610170772.

52477931 09/13

Published by: ISI Books
Intercollegiate Studies Institute
3901 Centerville Road
Wilmington, DE 19807-1938
www.isibooks.org

Credits for images used in *Choosing the Right College* are listed at www.CollegeGuide.org.

Contents

Contents

BLUE COLLAR IVIES:
An Elite Education on a Shoestring   245

Contents

Foreword

You Can Thrive in College

by Thomas E. Woods Jr.

In the age of the Internet, people often assume that all the information they need can be found online. And one can indeed find online information about various colleges. But a college website is going to tell you only what the administration wants you to hear, and I can't imagine that online college reviews by third parties could be as systematic as the book you hold in your hands. Practically every aspect of university life that a potential student would want to investigate can be found within these pages: academic life, core curricula (if any) in the Western tradition, sports, demographics, faculty, student life, housing, study-abroad opportunities, overall strengths and weaknesses, and interesting miscellanea.

Naturally, I couldn't help flipping ahead to the entry for Harvard, where I spent my own undergraduate years. Things have changed a bit since I was there, but I certainly recognize the institution this book describes. People have sometimes wondered how I could have spent four years at Harvard without winding up a sloganeering automaton, slavishly following chic opinion. My own experience as an undergraduate, which helps to answer that question, might be of some interest to students who wonder how they'll survive four years in a hostile milieu, and to parents who are justifiably concerned that eighteen years of raising decent and sensible children may go down the drain in just four.

I came from a relatively conservative, old Massachusetts town, one of the few in which the now-forgotten James Rappaport had defeated Senator John Kerry. I wasn't fully prepared for what I encountered in Cambridge.

On my way to the dining hall every night as a freshman I passed by people selling the *Workers Vanguard*, a communist newspaper. I was genuinely stunned. I felt compelled to engage them in conversation. I actually thought I could make them abandon their position if I described to them what had actually happened in the wake of the Bolshevik Revolution and challenged what Vladimir Brovkin, my professor for twentieth-century Russia, called the "good Lenin, bad Stalin" myth. I didn't make much headway, but the whole experience got me reading more and more history—which, to my surprise, eventually became my major. (You read that right: I owe my career to communism.)

In 1991, during my sophomore year, I even attended a meeting of the organization that published *Workers Vanguard*: the Friends of the Spartacus Youth Club. The Soviet Union was falling apart by that time. The speaker passed around a hat asking for donations to keep the worker's paradise together. Where that $18.32 went is anyone's guess, but no one seemed to find this a peculiar request. The Bolshevik Revolution had ushered in "the freest society in the history of the world," the speaker told us, so it was urgent that we preserve those gains.

In my second semester, one professor required that books for his course be purchased at a store called Revolution Books. Inside, portraits of some of history's greatest mass murderers adorned the walls. I decided I would find the books elsewhere.

I kept my sanity by joining student groups, including a student publication, where I could expect to find like-minded people around whom I didn't have to justify myself and with whom I could feel politically at ease. We were just preaching to the choir, some said. Maybe so. But the choir does need to be preached to from time to time, and in so doing we helped both ourselves and others—who, when they saw what we were writing and saying, realized they were not alone.

My experience is proof positive that with the proper formation and the help of a support network on campus, a nonleftist can not only survive but even thrive at a modern American university. The strange things I encountered in Cambridge did not cause me to abandon everything I held dear and promptly adopt the official line of fashionable opinion. To the contrary, it encouraged me to become all the more attached to and consistent in my views. Whatever these people were, I decided, I wanted to be pretty much the opposite.

Bizarre as some of my experiences surely were, it would be a mistake to suggest that those four years were a waste of time or yielded me nothing but leftist propaganda. To be sure, in our day every educated person must to some extent be an autodidact. But even in our university system, shot through with problems though it is, determined students can still get a good education from scholars who have made genuine contributions to the sum total of human knowledge. Quality and standards can still be found, and good work is still rewarded. And that is one of the ways this book can help you: it pinpoints who the great scholars are, what the great programs are, which courses highlight an institution's strengths, what kinds of extracurricular enrichment you can pursue, and much else.

In my own days as a college professor, I taught a good many adult students in my night classes. Nearly all of them were unusually industrious, and many told me they wished they had seized the opportunities before them the first time they tried making their way through college. This was rather a pleasant contrast with so many of the comatose eighteen-year-olds we faculty had to endure.

You have the chance to do things right the first time, to understand the nature of the opportunity before you and to seize everything it has to offer. The book you hold in your hands can play a key role in one of life's critical decisions, and I am delighted to commend it to you.

Thomas E. Woods Jr. is the *New York Times* bestselling author of eleven books. A senior fellow of the Ludwig von Mises Institute, Woods holds a bachelor's degree in history from Harvard and his master's, MPhil, and PhD from Columbia University.

Introduction

The Most Expensive Decision You'll Ever Make

by John Zmirak

Going off to college is an amazing privilege, a onetime opportunity to stretch your soul, toughen your mind, make lifelong friends, and find your vocation in life. But picking the right school and then navigating the college experience once you're there is not easy. There are many wrong decisions just waiting for you. Think of this guide as a mentor that can warn you away from the worst of them. There are pockets of toxic ideology and large swathes of boring mediocrity at most universities, but it's possible to pick a healthy, tasty meal from the vast buffet that steams before you. There's real meat among the glistening piles of Spam. It's up to you to choose it. And we're here to help.

The sad truth is that students need this help now more than ever. Things are much more chaotic—and costly—at today's colleges and universities than they were even a decade ago. The explosion of online education opportunities, as laid out in Richard Bishirjian's essay (page xxvii), may offer some people the chance to opt out of a bricks-and-mortar school. But most of you will indeed be marching off to college, if for no other reason than that employers generally treat a bachelor's degree as a minimum requirement. The challenge is to get the most out of college that you can. This book shows you how to do it.

To help you make one of the most important, and expensive, decisions of your life, the Intercollegiate Studies Institute (ISI) has used its team of journalists and a network of thousands of student and faculty contacts to dig beneath the rosy reports that colleges include on their websites and in their glossy brochures. Even other college guides won't tell you about the vast array of problems you can expect to encounter once you get on a college campus—*after* having plunked down all that tuition.

But you can prepare yourself. With *Choosing the Right College*, ISI exposes the problems endemic at many schools and shows you how to avoid them.

THE PROBLEM: Colleges are too expensive. Tuition has been skyrocketing for years, rising much faster than the rate of inflation—and faster than most family's incomes too. And all that extra money isn't going to an improved educational experience. Costs have been jacked up by salaries for useless administrators ("diversity" consultants and sports media flacks), lavish accommodations that approximate three-star hotels, and pricey distractions like "rec centers" and luxurious gym equipment. These costs are masked by loans you'll still be repaying when you're fifty—and since they are owed to the government, they are as sacrosanct as tax debt: no bankruptcy, no escape.

THE ISI SOLUTION: We get into the numbers, telling you which schools deliver bang for the buck and which don't. For starters, we reveal the key numbers most college admissions officers don't like to talk about—such as the average student-loan burden carried by recent graduates, how high (or low) a percentage of students get need-based financial aid, and what portion of students manage to graduate in four years or even six years.

But that's not all. We're excited to introduce a brand-new section called **"Blue Collar Ivies."** Here we profile the best *low-cost* colleges in every state, guiding students to the top programs and teachers they have to offer. Turn to page 245 to find an affordable college near you and insider tips on how to get a real education there.

THE PROBLEM: Universities emphasize research at the expense of teaching. They let their most learned faculty teach very rarely so they can crank out books and articles, and consign the paying students to adjuncts or grad students.

THE ISI SOLUTION: We tell you where teaching is still a priority—and which professors in particular you should seek out. We find out how accessible teachers are, according to students—and how smart and hardworking students are, according to teachers. We also ask how important is teaching (as opposed to publishing research papers) in deciding whether a teacher gets tenure and keeps his job. And we name the best teachers in a wide variety of departments. It's easy to forget, amid all the many distractions of college life, but the heart of the whole collegiate endeavor is really lodged in human encounters: between devoted teachers and willing students, and between one intellectually curious student and another. If a school (or a department within one) neglects the classroom experience, it's probably worthwhile for you to look elsewhere.

Things that make a difference as to whether teaching is strong or not include the amount of teaching—and grading—done by actual professors as opposed to graduate teaching assistants. Another factor is the average size of introductory and advanced classes in various majors. We report all that.

THE PROBLEM: Too many college majors fail to offer a *real* education. These days, many students are receiving not an education but only shallow preparation for a career in an industry that might disappear in ten years. At many schools, you won't find a solid curriculum that ensures that their students come out as culturally literate citizens with any business voting in U.S. elections. Colleges long ago threw out the prescribed courses in English literature, Renaissance art, and European and U.S. history that every liberal arts student used to take.

THE ISI SOLUTION: We investigate each school's "general education" requirements to see whether they add up to a real liberal arts education—and show you how to put your education together yourself when the requirements fall short. What kinds of classes does a school demand of every student, regardless of major? Do those classes form a true liberal arts education? Where they don't, we offer an eight-course "Suggested Core Curriculum" drawn from the course catalog of that particular school. (For the rationale behind these choices, see "Finding and Following the Core" on page xix.) In it we pick out one current course in each of the following critical subjects:

1. *Classical literature in translation.* Homer, Cicero, Caesar—the fun stuff that ends up in footnotes to all subsequent Western literature.
2. *Ancient philosophy.* Plato, Aristotle, all the way up through Boethius. Lay down the intellectual bedrock before you start on the sheetrock.
3. *The Bible.* Be careful about the professor here. You want your beliefs deepened and questioned, not put through a blender.
4. *Christian thought before 1500.* Here's your chance to read Augustine and Aquinas and appreciate the source of all the "social capital" we moderns are busy squandering.
5. *Modern political theory.* Where we went wrong, starting with Hobbes, up through Rousseau, Marx, and Mill. Make sure you bring along the antidotes, in the forms of Burke, Mises, and *The Federalist Papers.*
6. *Shakespeare.* Avoid classes that mention "race," "class," or "gender." They'll just ruin the Bard for you. And don't be afraid to rent DVDs in addition to reading—the plays were meant to be seen.
7. *U.S. history before 1865.* Our nation wasn't founded by Rosa Parks, no matter what they teach in high school.
8. *Nineteenth-century European intellectual history.* Most of the madness we're still suffering through today—from feminism to radical environmentalism to multiculturalism—is a dumbed-down version of nineteenth-century errors. Read the addled geniuses who inspired contemporary maniacs and learn how to spot false premises in seconds, instead of decades.

Take these eight courses at almost any school and you'll have a solid foundation for learning in your major, and for ongoing reading and learning for the rest of your life.

THE PROBLEM: Colleges offer dozens—sometimes hundreds—of different majors. They can't all do an equally good job in every field. But since each department wants to blow its own horn (and writes its own website), it's hard to tell from college literature which programs are weak and which are strong.

THE ISI SOLUTION: We identify the best and worst programs at each school—based on inside information from faculty and current students. The faculty at a school know which departments the school has really gotten behind—and so will students' future employers. Teachers are also aware of which disciplines are really weak, with limited (or unskilled) faculty, few course offerings, and no national reputation. You deserve to know whether the school you are considering offers worthy programs in the subjects that interest you—so we find that out, from sources on the ground. We locate business internships, research opportunities in the sciences, and dual-enrollment programs that allow students to make progress toward advanced degrees while they are still undergrads.

To tighten our scrutiny, we take a kind of core sample at each school—checking out the quality of the courses required in three key disciplines: English, history, and political science. Must English majors take a course in Shakespeare? In any literature written before 1800, or even 1950? Do history majors have to study the United States before 1865? Before 1945? Must political science majors understand the U.S. Constitution and the principles underlying it? Or can they take all their classes in Marxist meta-analysis of postcolonial Asia? You'll be surprised at some of the answers we turn up. We also sample the kinds of electives offered to see how trendy, politicized, or obscure they are—or whether they are worthy choices that advance a student's mastery of a subject.

THE PROBLEM: Some of the most affordable schools are also huge and largely mediocre. It's hard to find out if they have any worthwhile options.

THE ISI SOLUTION: We point you to the pockets of excellence that exist even at universities that are otherwise deeply flawed. Often there are fine opportunities in the form of an honors or a Great Books program. You might have to apply for it separately and keep up a certain GPA. But such programs typically offer smaller classes with real professors (instead of grad students), better readings, and more challenging work. Often they include extras like honors housing (where it's quiet enough to get that extra reading done), off-campus trips, and chances to network and lay the groundwork for that all-important first job. We find these programs and recommend them.

THE PROBLEM: At some schools, teachers or administrators try to bully or indoctrinate students into towing a narrow, "politically correct" line on intellectual, moral, and religious issues.

THE ISI SOLUTION: "Red Light" means stop; "Green Light" means go. We find out from students and teachers how free they feel in the classroom and on campus to express a wide range of opinions. We also document abuses of free speech and free association by faculty and administrators. Such abuses are rampant on many campuses, from unpunished thefts of conservative student newspapers, to schools forcing Christian groups to accept non-Christian members, to raunchy sex activists officially sponsored on campus. At some schools, you might have to keep your opinions to yourself—unless they mirror the teacher's. At others, you'll even have to watch what you write on Facebook or post on your dorm room door, lest you violate the vague speech code and commit "harassment." In many departments, teachers choose course topics and readings based on their own notion of what's "progressive" and infuse even the most traditional of subject matters (including, in one case we document, Ancient Greek grammar) with the politics of multiculturalism and diversity—code words for anti-Western, and typically anti-Judeo-Christian, ideology. We report the most significant events and sum up the political atmosphere at each school with ISI's unique "traffic light" feature—giving each school a Green, Yellow, or Red Light rating.

THE PROBLEM: Schools pay lip service to diversity and multiculturalism but don't do much to nurture a genuine appreciation of the variety of human experience. Despite making mantras of the words *diversity* and *multiculturalism*, many colleges don't require a foreign language of students or encourage study abroad. A real respect for cultural differences is best gained by learning the languages other people actually speak and visiting them where they live.

THE ISI SOLUTION: We find out how extensive each school's foreign language requirements and study-abroad options are. This analysis includes the quality and range of the programs themselves. In the case of study abroad, we highlight both credit and non-credit programs.

THE PROBLEM: Many college dorms are unsanitary hellholes or sinkholes of booze and vice. But schools don't exactly tell you about that when you're applying. By the time a student figures this out, it's already too late.

THE ISI SOLUTION: We make the best recommendations for living arrangements based on feedback from current students. We interview students about their living conditions and the extent of the "party atmosphere" at each school. The substance abuse, noise, and hookup culture in some dormitories can make life unsupportable for earnest students with traditional mores. We locate substance-free, honors, and off-campus alternatives.

THE PROBLEM: Too many students gain the "freshman fifteen" and become couch potatoes.

THE ISI SOLUTION: We look into how well each school keeps the balance of body and mind. We start by examining how good the sports programs are at each college. We also report on those colleges where sports mania has become the pretext for substance abuse or public disorder. Where intercollegiate sports have essentially become professionalized, serving as revenue generators for a school, we locate club teams and other alternatives—including wilderness activities. Since we are embodied minds, not angels, it's important that schools encourage physical health and activity.

THE PROBLEM: At some schools, virtually all the political clubs promote the same agenda. Even the chaplaincies depart from the creeds they're supposed to represent.

THE ISI SOLUTION: We look for groups where like-minded people can come together for support, learning, and fellowship. This includes not only clubs devoted to political or philosophical debate but also religious organizations and ministries. We even try to determine, where we can, how faithful those ministries are to their stated creeds. And when those ministries fall short, we seek out local houses of worship that keep the faith.

THE PROBLEM: Some schools have a serious crime problem. Not every school sits on some idyllic mountaintop, like the University of the South. Many are plunked down in the middle of major cities, and some are inundated with crime that spills over from troubled neighborhoods.

THE ISI SOLUTION: We report the truth and offer student and faculty advice on how to stay safe at each school. Using statistics that it took an act of Congress to make some schools report, we flag which schools have an ongoing crime problem, recount how secure students say they feel, and offer their street-savvy tips on how to stay safe on and off campus.

We have made exhaustive efforts, working with many professional journalists and thousands of student and faculty contacts, to make this year's guide the most informative, accurate, and readable resource for students and parents looking at colleges. We're confident that with the help of this guide, you can avoid all the hidden land mines (including tens of thousands of dollars in unnecessary debt).

For all the problems that plague higher education today, you can—with a little guidance—still make college the rich and challenging journey that it should be for every student.

John Zmirak, editor in chief of *Choosing the Right College* and CollegeGuide.org, received a BA from Yale University and a PhD in English from Louisiana State University. He has taught at LSU, Tulane, and the Thomas More College of Liberal Arts. The author of several books, Zmirak has worked extensively as a journalist, writing for publications ranging from *USA Today* to *Investor's Business Daily*. He lives in his native New York City.

Finding and Following the Core

by Mark C. Henrie

Faithfully following the strictures of the contemporary ideology of multicultural diversity, American university curricula today resemble a dazzling cafeteria indifferently presided over by an amiable and indulgent nutritionist. There are succulent offerings to suit every taste, and the intellectual gourmand can only regret that he has but four years to sample the fare. Never in history have there existed institutions providing such an array of fields of study—from Sanskrit to quantum mechanics, from neoclassical microeconomic theory to Jungian psychology, from the study of medieval folklore to the study of 1950s billboards. Everything that can repay study is studied, however small the dividend.

But as every parent knows, children seldom choose to eat what's good for them. They seem irresistibly drawn to high-fat foods and sugary desserts. Or sometimes they develop a fixation upon one particular dish and will eat no others. Parents do what they can to ensure a balanced diet, and in years past the university, standing in loco parentis, likewise made sure that the bill of fare, the courses required for graduation, were also "balanced." Various dimensions of intellectual virtue were each given their due: the basic cultural knowledge by which an educated man situates himself in history, a broad exposure to various methods of inquiry, the mastery and command that are the fruit of disciplinary specialization. Programmatically, this balance was achieved by a core curriculum in the literary, philosophical, and artistic monuments of Western civilization; a diverse set of requirements in general education; and a carefully structured course of studies in a major.

Things are rather different today, for we live in an era when the idea of a university—and therefore the university's institutional expression—has been transformed by the cultural currents that erupted in the 1960s. Although it is still possible to acquire a genuinely fine liberal arts education at many colleges and universities (and this guide shows you how), the 1960s generation has had a deleterious impact on the American university. That generation rebelled against their parents, and so against the very idea of anyone or anything standing in loco parentis. Enthusiasts for various forms of Marxist and post-Marxist critique, they understood themselves not as inquirers standing on the shoulders of giants but rather as change agents striving to overcome an inheritance of injustice. Like Thrasymachus in Plato's *Republic*, their sense of outraged injustice drove them to the moral relativism we now call postmodernism. But this very relativism led only to the dead end of self-contradiction, for it required them to deny that there could be any true standard of justice by which injustice could be admitted. Famously, they enjoined themselves to trust no one over thirty: obviously, the great works of the Western tradition, hundreds and thousands of years old, could not be trusted. They were instead to be deconstructed. Locked into an indiscriminate stance of questioning authority, they found themselves at length well over thirty and in the awkward position of being university authorities. What have been the effects on the curriculum?

The major

The system of majors still flourishes, but outside the natural sciences, the structured sequencing of courses within the major—one course building upon another and probing to a deeper level—has been largely abandoned. For reasons associated with careerism, professors today are often more committed to their research than to their teaching obligations, and so they resist or reject a "rigid" curricular plan that would make frequent and irregular sabbaticals difficult. Moreover, faculty themselves have fundamental disagreements about the very nature of their disciplines and so find it impossible to reach a consensus about the "end" toward which a course of studies should be directed. The faculty's solution has been to avoid direction.

Students in a major are thus largely free to pick and choose as they please and as the current course offerings allow. Consequently, many students experience their major in a rather aimless way: the major does not "progress" or "culminate" in anything. Graduating students often do not understand themselves to have achieved even preliminary mastery of a discipline. Whereas "critical" methods of teaching and learning have been pushed forward to earlier and earlier years of study, mastery of a discipline (in fields outside the natural sciences) has been pushed back to graduate school.

General-education and distribution requirements

A system of distribution and other general-education requirements also persists. Commonly, students will find that they are required to reach a certain proficiency in a foreign language, to demonstrate command of written English, and to take a prescribed number of courses in a range of fields of study. Sometimes these last, "distribution," requirements are vague: for example, they might prescribe twelve credits each from the sciences, humanities, and social sciences. Sometimes the requirements are more specific: for example, two courses in math, one in the physical sciences and one in the life sciences, a course in history, a course in a non-Western subject, etc.

The theoretical justification for requirements in general education is broad exposure to various bodies of knowledge and approaches to understanding. There is an echo here of John Henry Newman's argument in his famous book *The Idea of a University* that a university is "a place of teaching universal knowledge" and that failure to take the measure of all areas of inquiry results in a kind of deformity of the intellect. Some students may grumble at these requirements, which take them away from pursuing their major subject with single-mindedness: in the university cafeteria, they want nothing but the lime Jell-O. Frequently, faculty members sympathize with such complaints. After all, the professors have themselves undertaken graduate studies in increasingly narrow fields. But Newman's argument about the humane value of broad learning remains compelling. Students should approach their general-education requirements as a serious opportunity for intellectual growth.

Consider, for example, the requirement of mastery in a foreign language. Americans are notoriously bad at foreign languages; ambitious students may fear that their GPAs will suffer in language courses. But it really is true that some thoughts are better expressed in one language than another. Acquiring a foreign language can open up whole new worlds, and when kept up, a foreign language is a possession for life. Similarly, it is only through distribution requirements that the "two cultures" of science and the humanities are forced to engage each other in the modern university. Without this encounter, the student of the sciences risks falling into a value-free technological imperialism. Without this encounter, the student of the humanities risks falling into an antiquarian idyll, cut off from one of the major currents of the modern world.

There is also a simply practical advantage to distribution requirements. Today about two-thirds of all students will change their major during their college career; many will change more than once. What students will "be" in life is almost certainly not what they thought they would "be" when they set off for college. Distribution requirements offer an opportunity to view the world from different intellectual perspectives. Who knows but that an unexpected horizon may prove to correspond to the heart's deepest desires?

The core curriculum

It is the core curriculum, a survey of the great works of Western civilization, that has fared the worst in the curricular reforms of the past generation. With few exceptions, the core curriculum has been simply eliminated from American higher education. Those of a suspecting cast of mind may speculate that this change has occurred for structural reasons. Following the model of the natural sciences, PhDs in the humanities are awarded for original "contributions to knowledge." But the great works of Western culture have been studied for centuries. What genuinely "new" insights can be gleaned there? Have aspiring PhDs perhaps turned, in desperation, to other subjects in which there is still something "original" to be said? If so, how can they be expected to teach the Great Books, which were not their subject of study? But then, the elimination of the core is also surely the result of a moral rejection: the generation of the 1960s, which admired the Viet Cong and cheered U.S. defeat in Southeast Asia, viewed their own civilizational tradition as a legacy not to be honored but to be overcome. The "privileging" of the great books of the West therefore had to end.

A more positive justification for the demise of the core is frequently given, however. To prepare students for the Multicultural World of Tomorrow, it is said, college must expose them to the diversity of world cultures. A merely Western curriculum would be parochial, a failure of liberal learning. Moreover, since our modern or postmodern technological civilization is characterized by rapid change, it is more important to be exposed to "approaches to knowledge," to "learn how to learn," than it is to acquire any particular body of knowledge. Education then becomes nothing but the cultivation of abstract instrumental rationality, divorced from any content and divorced from any end. Consistent with these arguments, many universities now call their distribution requirements a "core curriculum." They claim to have undergone curricular development rather than curricular demise.

As a practical matter, this multicultural transformation of the curriculum can have two curious results. In the worst cases, what passes for a multicultural curriculum is nothing but a peculiar kind of Western echo chamber. Students are given over to studying Marxist critics in contemporary Algeria and neo-Marxist critics in contemporary Brazil and post-Marxist critics in contemporary France. All that is really learned are variations on the "critique of ideologies"—a legacy of one great Western mind, that of Karl Marx. In other cases, however, students really are exposed to the high cultures and great works of non-Western societies—but their encounter with Western high culture remains slight. We thus are presented with the spectacle of many students today who habitually associate high ideals, profound insight, and wisdom with every culture but their own.

What, then, is the abiding justification for the traditional core curriculum in Western civilization? Why is it a major premise of this guide that a university lacking a core curriculum is educationally deficient—even as we stand at the dawn of the Multicultural World of Tomorrow? The purpose of the core is not to inculcate any kind of Western chauvinism, certainly not any ethnocentrism that would prevent a student from exploring and learning from non-Western cultures. Indeed, one expects that it will be precisely those who have delved most thoughtfully into the wisdom of the Occident who will be in a position to learn the most from the wisdom of the Orient—rather like Matteo Ricci and the other Jesuits who encountered Chinese civilization with such sympathetic results in the sixteenth century. Lacking a foundation in the depths of our own civilization, a student can approach another as little more than a tourist.

There are really two arguments for the traditional core. They concern the importance of high culture and the importance of history.

High culture

A not-uncommon sight on a university campus during freshman week is a group of students sitting on the grass in the evening, one with a guitar, singing together the theme songs of vintage television sitcoms. In a society as diverse as twenty-first-century America, this is to be expected: television is one of the few things that young people from all walks of life have in common. But what are we to think when the same scene is repeated at senior week, four years later? Has higher education done its job when the only common references of those with a baccalaureate degree remain those of merely popular culture?

The core curriculum is the place in university studies where one encounters what Matthew Arnold called "the best which has been thought and said." Such a view of education is hierarchical, discriminating, judgmental: it reflects the fact that the high can be distinguished from the low, and the further understanding that the high can comprehend the low, whereas the low can never take the measure of the high. By spending time with the best, with the highest expressions and reflections of a culture, the mind of the student is equipped for its own ascent. Without such an effort, the student remains trapped in the unreflective everyday presumptions of the current culture: the student remains trapped in clichés. The high culture of the traditional core curriculum is therefore liberating, as befits the liberal arts.

Throughout history there have been countless thinkers, poets, writers, and artists; the vast majority of all their labor has been lost, and most of them have been entirely forgotten. What survives are the truly great works that have been held in consistently high esteem through the changing circumstances of time and place. Thus, the traditional canon of Great Books—the common possession of educated men and women across the centuries of Western history—is not an arbitrary list, nor does the canon reflect relations of "power"; rather, as Louise Cowan has observed, the classics of a civilization "select themselves" by virtue of their superior insight. The presumptions and presuppositions of our lives, which lie so deep in us that we can scarcely recognize them, are in the great works made available for inspection and inquiry. High culture is a matter not of snobbish refinement but of superior understanding.

It is here that the core curriculum is indispensable. For every student brings to college a preliminary "enculturation"—we have all by the age of eighteen absorbed certain perspectives, insights, narratives, stereotypes, and values that communicate themselves to us in the prevailing popular culture. This enculturation is the common possession of a generation, whatever the diversity of their family backgrounds by class or ethnicity. But the artifacts of popular culture are always mere reflections of the possibilities glimpsed and made possible by works of high culture. The traditional core curriculum provides a student with access to that high culture; its higher "enculturation" provides a student with a vantage point from which he can grasp the meaning and implications of his everyday cultural presumptions. And he begins to hold something in common with the educated men and women of past ages; they become his peers.

One of the peculiar presumptions of our time is that novelty is good: social and technological transformations have given us a prejudice against tradition and in favor of "originality." But it is the great works of the traditional canon that constitute the record of true originality: that is why they have survived. Only by becoming familiar with them are we enabled to recognize just how derivative is much of what now passes as original insight. A university that does not orient its students to high culture effectively commits itself to a project of deculturation, and thereby traps its students in a kind of permanent adolescence.

History

George Santayana famously asserted that those who do not remember the past are condemned to repeat it. Centuries earlier, Cicero observed that to know nothing of the world before one's birth is to remain always a child. These cautionary aphorisms are perfectly and pointedly true, and in the first instance they constitute one justification for the historical studies undertaken in a core curriculum. Practically speaking, there is wisdom to be found in experience. This wisdom is never more fully appreciated than when we experience the consequences of our actions at firsthand. But because human affairs exhibit certain recurring patterns, knowledge of history provides a stock of experiences at secondhand from which more general "lessons" may be drawn as well—at least by those with ears to hear and eyes to see.

Nevertheless, these admonitions of Santayana and Cicero do not constitute the truly decisive historical reason for embarking on the traditional core curriculum. After all, insofar as human affairs exhibit patterns, and insofar as we approach history merely in search of the generally applicable "laws" or "rules" of human interaction, one may as well find one's stock of lessons in any given civilization as in any other. Anyone's history would be as good as anyone else's. It is because the contemporary academic mind views the matter in just this social-scientific way that it is necessarily driven to understand the traditional core curriculum's Western focus as nothing but the result of chauvinism or laziness.

But the core curriculum's particular emphasis on Western history is not the result either of ethnocentrism or of sloth. The core curriculum does mean to value history in itself, not just the "laws" that are abstracted from its examples. How so?

All of us are born into a natural world governed by laws not of our making. Some of these laws are the laws of human nature and of human interaction, laws that apply in every time and place. But all of us are also born into the historical world at a particular time, and there is a certain unrepeatable (and unpredictable) quality to each historical moment, the result of free human choices. What is more, the historical moment we inhabit now is the outcome, in part, of the contingent history of our particular community, both recently and more remotely. To answer the first question of every true inquirer—What is going on here?—it is necessary to uncover the historical narrative of the present: that is, it is necessary to answer the question, What is going on now? To answer this question in any profound sense, it is necessary to understand the historical narrative of one's own civilization—to understand, as well, what was going on then.

Consequently, the traditional core curriculum is not simply the study of the great books of the Western world isolated from their historical contexts; rather, that study proceeds side by side with an inquiry that locates those works in history. While the great works articulate the great human possibilities, not all human possibilities are equally available to us today. In effect, to understand the meaning of that relative availability (and unavailability) is to understand one's place in the stream of history, and this is the second argument for undertaking a core curriculum.

Typically, when a core curriculum has been poorly constructed, it reads history in a Whiggish way, or "progressively." In the Whig narrative, Western history tells the simple tale of how the world has progressed ever upward until it reaches its high point, the present (and in particular, me). Moreover, such a facile historical sense anticipates a future that is a straight-line extrapolation of the present. When the core is structured well, however, it leaves open the question of whether the present is the outcome of progress or decline. (The truth, it has been said, is that things are always getting both better and worse at the same time.) A student who has learned the deep historical lessons of a core curriculum is as alert to the possibilities of historical transformation just ahead as he is to the possibility of continuity.

Today it is extremely common for a college student to reach the end of four years of study with all requirements met but with a profound sense of disorientation and confusion, even disappointment. What's it all about? Usually, there will have been no sense of progression in the student's plan of study, no sense of mastery, no perspective touching deeply on many connected subjects that might serve as the basis for ever-deeper inquiry with the passing of the years. There will have been no ascent to a truly higher culture and no cultivation of historical consciousness.

What a lost opportunity!

The bad news is that it is most unlikely that we will see a return of the core curriculum in the next generation, and certainly not in time to benefit most of the readers of this guide. The good news is that much of the substance of the old core is still available, scattered across various courses in the departments. The eight courses that may constitute a "core of one's own" are here listed for each of the colleges covered in this guide (excepting only those schools that still offer a true core); the rationale for these eight courses—what each contributes to the comprehensive perspective of the core—is given in my book *A Student's Guide to the Core Curriculum* (ISI Books). Thanks to the elective system, the benefits of the core are not entirely beyond reach. The very best dishes are still available in the contemporary university cafeteria: you simply have to choose them. Alas, that may entail occasionally passing on the chocolate cheesecake.

A curriculum is a "course"—like the course that is run by a river. A curriculum should take you somewhere. After four years of college, a graduating senior should be a different and better person than his former self, the matriculating freshman. Instead, most students today find themselves merely lost at sea, swamped by the roiling waters of various intellectual enthusiasms. Undertaking the discipline of a "voluntary" core curriculum today offers a student the prospect for the most profound of transformations—and the most delightful of journeys.

Mark C. Henrie holds degrees from Dartmouth, Cambridge, and Harvard. He is the author of *A Student's Guide to the Core Curriculum* (ISI Books), chief academic officer at the Intercollegiate Studies Institute, and executive editor of *Modern Age*.

Online Learning

What You Need to Know about New Alternatives to Traditional Education

by Richard J. Bishirjian

If you've purchased this book, you're clearly looking for the right educational option, either for yourself or for someone you love. And if you've explored the profiles included here, you have doubtless noticed a few salient truths about American universities today:

- They have moved, in terms of politics, culture, and moral standards, very far from where they used to be—and from the values that many of you treasure.
- These institutions have built cocoons of esoteric research and obscure ideology that are insulated from any reality test by the cushion of permanent tenure—lifelong job security for higher-level faculty. (Nice work if you can get it.) Meanwhile, younger scholars who haven't become insiders drift from low-paid part-time job to job.
- These schools are phenomenally expensive, with prices rising much, much higher than inflation, and students shouldering ever-mounting levels of debt even as their job prospects upon graduation grow increasingly uncertain.

These factors and others add up to an education industry in crisis. Universities are no longer serving the social purposes for which they were founded, and they are far too expensive to survive much longer in their current form. The numbers just don't add up.

Since the economic crisis began in 2008, a major shift in the behavior of education consumers has begun. Across the landscape of traditional higher education, many students previously enrolled in expensive, four-year bricks-and-mortar colleges are shifting to two-year public community colleges or less expensive public universities, or they are dropping out of school altogether. At the same time, financially strapped states and municipalities are reducing their support for public education and, in many cases, hiking tuition.

Students who enroll in community colleges to knock off two years of college before advancing to four-year state universities find overcrowded classrooms, overworked instructors, heightened emphasis on vocational studies, and less emphasis on general education. A "four-year" college education at a public institution too often takes *six years*—that's two years' lost wages, plus extra debt—because students cannot complete degree-program requirements any sooner. The courses they need are simply not offered often enough.

Religious or conservative parents will want to consider sending their children to a college that upholds their beliefs. Others who simply want their children to get a "good education" will look for institutions that have high academic and admission standards. And all parents want an education for their children that they can afford. That, of course, is not easy to find. Good colleges tend to be costly, compelling many middle-class parents to seek relief in public colleges and universities. Unfortunately, many public colleges and universities have all the problems we associate with government institutions like the Postal Service—inefficiency, bureaucracy, and the pressure to lower standards. They are also rife with the same toxic ideologies we find in elite, expensive institutions.

Yorktown University, an online academy centered on traditional educational and moral values—where I serve as president—recently participated in a study of Texas public higher education and reported on Florida public institutions. Our findings are not encouraging. Although Texas and especially Florida public colleges are inexpensive, they lack many of the qualities we value most in education. Community colleges have low retention and high student-loan default rates. Public four-year universities do not impose general-education requirements sufficient to guarantee that graduates are culturally literate citizens. And very few faculty members anywhere identify themselves as "conservative"—creating a radical political imbalance that is unrepresentative of the true diversity of opinion in America.

As *Forbes* magazine reported in November 2012:

> There are colleges—including many community colleges—that are at capacity in certain core classes due to budgetary constraints. In fact, according to a recent College Board report, state and local funding for public higher education per student fell by 21 percent from 2000 to 2010, and continues to decline. A recent *Los Angeles Times* article described how last fall, nearly 70,000 California community college students had to attend two or more different schools to take their required classes. A survey by the Chancellor's office of the California Community College System in August 2012 revealed that course sections have been reduced by 24%, and more than 472,000 of the system's 2.4 million students were put on waiting lists for fall classes. Students at these institutions often have to wait 2–3 years to fulfill their degree requirements.

Something has to give. Traditional education stands today where the Big Three auto companies did in the early 1980s: fat, happy, and totally unsustainable. And there are competitors waiting in the wings: the explosive intellectual and informational opportunities offered via the Internet.

The move to online education

By offering vocational degree programs that enable students to obtain employment and working adults to earn promotions and higher pay, proprietary education companies such as Capella University, American Public University, and Northcentral University have demonstrated that there is a market for Internet-based programs. Other institutions, including the University of Phoenix, Strayer University, DeVry University, Walden University, Keiser University, Full Sail, ITT, and Embry-Riddle Aeronautical University, offer classroom-based instruction in vocational areas. If a student is inclined to become a computer programmer, production supervisor for entertainment companies, or airplane technician, there are any number of schools where he may learn the skills for employment in these industries.

Working adults dealing with time, work, and family constraints find that attendance at bricks-and-mortar institutions is very difficult. Until recently, most traditional colleges did not hold Saturday or evening classes. That explains why working adults make up more than 75 percent of enrollments at proprietary institutions.

But what about students who want something like a traditional liberal arts education? I'm happy to say that the online options are good and getting better each year.

In the next five to ten years, the percentage of college-age students earning some college via the Internet will increase exponentially. The University of Phoenix, which started as a classroom-based institution and then grew enrollments via the Internet, is run like a business, so some of the ideological nonsense is absent. American Public University (which began as "American Military University") offers courses in military history and other subjects that most colleges disdain. These and others are fully accredited, which means that when a student decides she wants to spend the final two years at a traditional college, her associate of arts degree and most of the academic credits earned will transfer. High school students can earn college credits online via "Dual Credit" or "Early College" programs at certain public colleges. And full four-year college programs awarding bachelor's degrees are becoming more common at traditional institutions with online programs, including Grand Canyon, Liberty, Bellevue, Regent, and other regionally accredited universities.

Pros and cons

Parents and students will wonder if something is lost by studying online. That cannot be denied. Based on thirteen years of experience administering online programs, I can confidently affirm that "distance learning" via the Internet is not a substitute for classroom instruction and real-time engagement with instructors. Still, online education can provide quite a lot. With five or twenty-five students, most Internet course delivery systems easily organize course content and provide a network by which students may engage in discussions with instructors via threaded e-mail comments, ask questions, and submit assignments for grading.

Internet higher education should be seen as an alternative when circumstances do not permit taking the traditional track. Unfortunately, American higher education is so rife with ideological pressures—as amply documented in the red and yellow traffic lights that appear throughout this book—that savvy students and parents may want to explore the alternatives.

The current wisdom is that a bachelor of arts degree from a traditional college or university is an absolute necessity for any non-blue-collar job. (Indeed, this perception may be the only thing keeping many mediocre institutions in business.) Education critics such as Charles Murray and Peter Thiel have questioned how long employers will continue to limit their hiring to people who have slogged through four to six years of increasingly ideological and esoteric courses and saddled themselves with debt.

At the same time, online universities are pushing hard at the gates of academic "respectability," and hundreds of thousands of students are learning from lectures presented free online by an increasing number of traditional universities. One company, Coursera, is developing online courses with dozens of respected schools, including Brown, Caltech, Columbia, Duke, Georgia Tech, Johns Hopkins, Princeton, Rice, Stanford, the University of Michigan, the University of Pennsylvania, the University of Virginia, and Vanderbilt.

These and other colleges have taken the first tentative steps to leverage the latest development in Internet-based course delivery technology: massive open online courses (MOOCs). MOOC platforms like Coursera, Udacity, Udemy, and edX (founded by Harvard and MIT) offer courses for free and without qualifying those who access them. No pricing barriers or previous education requirements block enrollments, and most are idealistic attempts to open the doors to the acquisition of knowledge to any and all. As Coursera puts it, "We envision a future where the top universities are educating not only thousands of students, but millions." By the spring of 2013, Coursera claimed to have enrolled some three million students. Udacity's first class, "Introduction to Artificial Intelligence," enrolled 160,000 students in more than 190 countries. Numbers like those mean that MOOCs will have an impact and may, eventually, batter down the creaky gates of traditional academia—for better or worse. College as we know it is an institution with medieval roots and nineteenth-century practices, trying to charge late-twentieth-century prices to twenty-first-century consumers. It's over, or about to be.

Access to education is endangered by forces that drive private college tuition beyond the ability of many to pay and that challenge the states to continue to subsidize public education at previous levels. These conditions suggest that we may soon see a radical change in how higher education is delivered and priced. In the meantime, online education can serve as a good alternative for students who cannot find—or cannot afford—a college where their moral and educational goals are taken seriously. In ten years, online college study may seem as ordinary as homeschooling does today.

Richard J. Bishirjian is a businessman and educator who holds a PhD in government and international studies from the University of Notre Dame. In 2000 he founded Yorktown University, which offers not-for-credit college-level courses at Educourse.net.

Choosing the Right College
2014–15

Amherst College

Amherst, Massachusetts • www.amherst.edu

Self-Directed Studies

Founded in 1821 as a school for New England's elite, Amherst College is still one of the most prestigious liberal arts colleges in America. It is also one of the most univocally liberal. The college no longer maintains a core curriculum or even distribution requirements. As one professor says, "The most impressive part of Amherst is the intellectual caliber of the faculty and student body. The most disappointing things about Amherst are its cultural degeneration (as shown by its 'Orgasm Workshops'), arrogance, elitism, and stifling political correctness."

Academic Life: Could I but ride indefinite

Amherst's once-impressive curriculum was abolished in 1967 in favor of the current laissez-faire approach. The administration claims that its current laxity "ensures that each student in every classroom is there by choice." By sophomore year, the student selects a major area of study and an adviser within that field. This system, however, does increase the risk that a student will be "made in his liberal adviser's image," one undergrad warns. Recently, the college has made an effort to revamp pre-major advising because of many complaints.

The institution has also turned toward an emphasis on writing and quantitative reasoning; absent core requirements, students had been passing through the college without sharpening such skills.

The only academic regulation that dictates a student's curriculum is within his major field of study. Most programs at Amherst require between seven and nine courses, usually built around the fundamental topics of the discipline. Yet the various majors can have acutely different requirements.

Economics majors must complete nine courses; in addition, students must pass a comprehensive examination before they can receive their degrees. Students must take three core theory classes, with a "suggested" order. At least two of the nine required courses must be upper-level courses.

English majors complete 10 courses for the major, but students are completely free to choose which ones. In other words, the English department requires no course work in the history of the language, Shakespeare, or even British or American literature. Students may instead opt for courses in film studies, creative writing, cultural studies, or gender studies. There are no senior honors courses as there are in some other majors.

The history department requires nine courses, including four "in an individually chosen area of concentration." All majors are required to take a seminar involving a major research paper. Students must take a course in three of the six listed geographical regions: the U.S., Europe, Asia, Africa and Diaspora, Latin America and the Caribbean, and the Middle East. Further, students must take two courses in either pre-1800 history or pre-1800 history and comparative history. This means a history major could emerge without having studied the American Founding or the Civil War.

The political science department's requirements include one course in each of the following areas: Institutions and Law: states, institutions, parties, political economy, the law and public policy; Society and Culture: civil society, social movements, rights and identities, cultural politics; Global: war, peace, diplomacy, foreign policy and globalization studies; Political Theory: power, norms, and justice. Courses in this department are sometimes infused with teachers' personal views. "One professor referred to *Forrest Gump* as a work of Reaganite propaganda," a student reports.

Students seem to work hard at Amherst, especially if they are in the sciences. One physics major says that he and his classmates spend between four and six hours a night studying: "Although the workload is demanding, it is not usually burdensome. Most of the work is engaging and interesting."

Faculty are thick on the ground; the school enjoys an outstanding student-teacher ratio of 8 to 1, and the average Amherst class has only 16 students. In such an environment, teacher-student interaction is, happily, inevitable.

Says one student: "The political science department is one of Amherst's best. Most of the professors in the department are both experts in their fields and very accessible. Also, for a small school, it has a wide range of courses. The philosophy department is also excellent. The professors I've had are remarkably intelligent, and the small class sizes are helpful. The Classics department has even smaller class sizes than does philosophy, and the community of students and faculty is very close-knit. I've had only one science class, but I've heard biology, chemistry, neuroscience, and physics are all excellent as well."

One outstanding professor at Amherst is Hadley Arkes. "He is a great antidote to the political correctness on campus; his Colloquium on the American Founding series brings speakers to campus that would otherwise be marginalized," says a student. Other highly recommended teachers include Javier Corrales, Pavel Machala, and William Taubman in political science; Jonathan Vogel in philosophy; Walter Nicholson, Frank Westhoff, and Geoffrey Woglom in economics; Allen Guttmann, William Pritchard, and David Sofield in English; Rebecca Sinos in Classics; and N. Gordon Levin in American studies and history. One student says of Levin,

CAMPUS POLITICS: RED LIGHT

The dominant political ideology at Amherst is evident in the classroom and in every department, although bias varies by class and professor. Reports one student: "Many courses in English and history are hotbeds of postcolonialism, feminism, cultural relativism, revisionist history, and other postmodern fads, though there are certain gem courses that can be found in each department. My worst experience at Amherst was with an American studies professor. In the course of a semester-long freshman seminar, rather than reading Plato and Locke to discuss eternal questions as addressed in legendary works, we learned about 'growing up in America.' Over these three months, we discussed racial identity (after which the professor concluded that Clarence Thomas was 'denying his blackness'), heard that guns were destroying America, and read a book titled *Ain't No Makin' It in a Low Income Neighborhood*. The thesis of the book is that hard work is futile for low-income minorities."

Amherst has a thriving and highly visible Democratic club, but the school's Republican population is minuscule. At one point there was an alternative, conservative newspaper, *The Spectator*, but it has since gone defunct. The school sponsors an annual production of *The Vagina Monologues* and has 11 "activism" clubs, such as the Feminist Alliance and the (gay) Pride Alliance. There is a small, resurgent College Republicans chapter, and some students find refuge from the dominant atmosphere in the Amherst Christian Fellowship.

"He resists revisionist histories for reading and assigns noted scholars like Kissinger and Beschloss."

"About 40 percent of the school studies abroad. . . . There are plenty of opportunities," a student reports. The school hosts an annual event that brings many of the overseas programs to campus so students can easily compare them. The website lists approved programs in Brazil, China, Costa Rica, Egypt, France, Germany, Greece, India, Italy, Japan, Mali, Turkey, Russia, Spain, and Tanzania, among others.

Amherst offers a limited range of language majors: Chinese, French, German, classical Greek and Latin, Japanese, Russian, Spanish, and classes in Arabic. Others may be studied at neighboring colleges.

Student Life: Industrious angels

The Amherst campus spreads over 1,000 acres. Campus facilities include the Robert Frost Library (with more than 900,000 volumes), and the renovated Mead Art Museum, which houses more than 18,000 works.

Amherst, Massachusetts, a town of more than 37,000 people, lies in the central part of the state, some 90 minutes west of Boston and three hours north of New York City. The town of Amherst "has a historic downtown that is well-lit, well-kept, and has a good collection of shops and restaurants," says one student. "There is not that much to do in the town, but for people interested in going to college in the country, yet who do not want to be cut off from the world, Amherst is a pretty good compromise." A bus system provides regular free transportation among the surrounding towns.

A professor says, "The most impressive part of Amherst is the intellectual caliber of the faculty and student body. The most disappointing things are its cultural degeneration, arrogance, elitism, and stifling political correctness."

Some 97 percent of Amherst students live in the 37 dorms on campus. All freshmen must live on campus, and are housed together. Housing is decided by a lottery system, using class-based rankings, and is guaranteed for four years. Three dorms have been dubbed "quiet, studying" dorms, and one dorm has been dubbed the "thesis-writing" dorm. Dorms are all coed, and bathrooms are usually shared by floor, unless one has a suite.

Amherst offers students a choice of 37 residential housing options. While all buildings are coed, some dorms do offer single-sex floors. On coed floors with only one bathroom, students vote on whether the bathroom will also be coed (most vote in favor). Out of deference to radical mores, members of opposite sexes are allowed to share rooms at Amherst. Some space is also allocated for "theme housing" in which like-minded students live together to explore a foreign language, black culture, or health and wellness.

The college prohibits the Greek system on campus. But Amherst's students are hardly shy when it comes to partying. "Dorm life can be summarized as follows: drinking, drinking, and more drinking. Residential counselors are pretty inactive. The only real function they serve in non-freshman dorms is to bill students for dorm damage," says one student. Theme parties—such as one called "Pimps and Hos"—are well known for sexual abandon. One student describes these parties as "meat markets." Amherst College also sponsors a weekly alcohol-free shindig called The Amherst Party (TAP for short), which is usually well attended.

There are some 140 student organizations on campus, the largest are the *Amherst Student* (the weekly student newspaper), Association of Amherst Students (Student Government), Amherst College Outing Club, Amherst College Diversity Coalition, and numerous musical groups. The school also has a radio station, WAMH. The college hosts the Argentine Tango club, Asian Students Association, Much Ado about Knitting, Amherst Political Union, Amherst Dance, and Students for Justice in Palestine, to name a few. Not surprisingly, groups like Pride Alliance (for homosexual rights) and the Amherst College Democrats are thriving, but there is not a single Republican group or politically conservative organization on campus.

As a whole, the students at Amherst are not very politically active. While there are speakers, lectures, and debates, students at Amherst have a reputation for placing their interests elsewhere. Still, the culture on campus is very liberal, and, as with everywhere else, the LGBTQ group is trying very hard to make the college a welcoming place for people with varying sexual orientations.

Amherst offers 27 Division III sports programs. Amherst came first in the 2010 National Collegiate Scouting Association Power Rankings for academic and athletic performance. The college is a member of the New England Small College Athletic Conference with 10 other schools. Some 32 percent of Amherst students participate in varsity sports, and more than 80 percent take part in club and intramural sports.

About 40 percent of the students in the Amherst class of 2015 identify themselves as "students of color." Currently, Amherst has more male than female students—no mean feat these days, when men are becoming ever scarcer on college campuses. Students in the class of 2015 hail from 41 states, plus D.C., Puerto Rico, Guam, and 23 foreign countries.

A large part of the student body is Jewish, and the campus has an active (and activist) Hillel group. A Newman Club and a Christian Fellowship exist on campus; the latter is a chapter of InterVarsity Fellowship and holds weekly meetings. Down the street at UMASS–Amherst is a large and lively Newman Center for Catholic students.

SUGGESTED CORE

1. European Studies 121, Readings in the European Tradition I or Classical Studies 123, Greek Civilization
2. Philosophy 217, Ancient Philosophy
3. Religion 263/273, Ancient Israel/Christian Scriptures
4. Religion 275, History of Christianity—The Early Years
5. Political Science 480, Contemporary Political Theory
6. English 338, Shakespeare
7. History 453, Era of the American Revolution
8. Religion 278, Christianity, Philosophy, and History in the 19th Century

The crime figures for Amherst are unremarkable, except for the fact that, in the latest year figures are available, there were 16 sex offenses—15 of them forcible sexual offenses. There was also one aggravated assault, and 13 burglaries on campus in 2011. All Amherst residential halls are secured with digital combination locks. One student says that although the campus is safe overall, certain areas of Amherst are "not completely desirable." For instance, the University of Massachusetts' Frat Row, right down the street from the college, is not a safe place for walking alone at night.

Amherst is pricey; during the 2011–12 school year, it listed a comprehensive fee (including room and board) of $53,370. However, the school practices need-blind admissions and provides aid to more than 60 percent of students, meeting the need of most admitted students. Recently, because of the financial aid, the school says that students are graduating with less debt than in the past—although it does not provide the numbers to prove this.

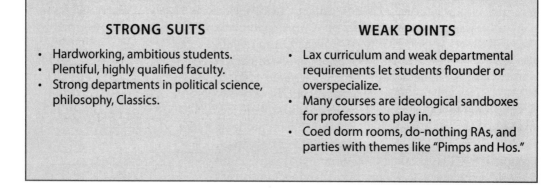

STRONG SUITS	WEAK POINTS
• Hardworking, ambitious students. • Plentiful, highly qualified faculty. • Strong departments in political science, philosophy, Classics.	• Lax curriculum and weak departmental requirements let students flounder or overspecialize. • Many courses are ideological sandboxes for professors to play in. • Coed dorm rooms, do-nothing RAs, and parties with themes like "Pimps and Hos."

Ave Maria University

Ave Maria, Florida • www.avemaria.edu

Fresh, Hot, and Crusty

Founded in 2002 by pizza magnate and philanthropist Thomas Monaghan as an alternative to secularized Catholic universities, Ave Maria University sits in a blank spot on the map of Florida, around which Monaghan has planned a profit-making development of an entire town called Ave Maria. Faculty report that they are optimistic about the school and praise the "academic freedom" they enjoy, within the gladly accepted parameters of Catholic orthodoxy. Students sound enthusiastic about their classes and speak highly of their skilled teachers, whose course loads are light enough that they can offer each student significant personal attention.

Academic Life: From the heart of the church

Ave Maria provides not only a core program steeped in the classical liberal arts; it also offers majors such as biology, mathematics, and economics, as well as preprofessional studies that allow students to earn certificates in business, prelaw, and premedicine. The school also trains future organists and choir directors in its Department of Sacred Music. Summer programs offer intensive courses in languages such as Greek and Latin.

VITAL STATISTICS

Religious affiliation: *Roman Catholic*
Total enrollment: *987*
Total undergraduates: *886*
SAT CR/Verbal midrange: *530*
SAT Math midrange: *520*
ACT midrange: *23*
Applicants: *1,242*
Applicants accepted: *65%*
Accepted applicants who enrolled: *31%*
Tuition (general/out of state): *$21,496*
Tuition (in state): *N/A*
Room and board: *$8,841*
Freshman retention rate: *72%*
Graduation rate (4 yrs.): *45%*
Graduation rate (6 yrs.): *52%*
Courses with fewer than 20 students: *45%*
Student-faculty ratio: *15:1*
Courses taught by graduate students: *2%*
Students living on campus: *95%*
Students in fraternities: *none*
Students in sororities: *none*
Students receiving need-based financial aid: *85%*
Avg. student-loan debt of a recent graduating class: *not provided*
Most popular majors: *biology, business administration, theology*
Guaranteed housing for 4 years? *yes*

The very solid core curriculum consists of about 16 classes and includes three theology, three philosophy, two Western civilization, two literary tradition, and elementary and intermediate Latin courses, with two classes in either biology, chemistry, or physics, and an American studies class, and a math class.

The theology department is widely viewed by students as one of the university's strongest. Favorite teachers include Fr. Matthew Lamb, William Riordan, and Marc Guerra. Students praise them for their "enthusiasm" and "love for theology."

Philosophy is cited as another solid major. Students cite the "excellent approach" taken by Maria Fedoryka. Courses in this department include classic subjects such as "Plato and Aristotle" and studies of St. Thomas Aquinas and John Henry Newman, but also "Recent Philosophy" and "Modern and Contemporary Philosophy."

The literature department, headed by Michael Raiger, includes courses such as "Early Modern Literature," "American Literature," and "Twentieth Century Literature"—a class that at Ave Maria includes, alongside James Joyce and T. S. Eliot, such unjustly neglected Catholic authors as Evelyn Waugh and G. K. Chesterton. Aside from the core courses, the literature major requires classes in medieval literature, Shakespeare, romanticism, American literature, the novel, early modern literature, twentieth-century literature, and senior seminars.

Colin Barr is chairman of the history department, which focuses on the story and civilization of the Christian West. Two core courses are required, as well as a historiography class, a seminar, and an American civilization class. Otherwise, six electives are necessary in a range of classes from ancient and medieval, European, and American history.

The politics major requires "Intro to Political Thought," "Comparative Politics," "American Civilization," "International Relations," "American Government," "Catholic Political Thought," "Constitutional Law," a senior seminar, and two electives in various areas. Some recent electives were "American Foreign Policy" and "Internship in Politics."

The newer Department of Sacred Music, headed by Dr. Timothy McDonnell, centers squarely on the traditions that grew up around the

Roman Catholic liturgy and includes classes such as "Heritage of Sacred Music," "Choral Conducting," and "Gregorian Chant."

Recommended teachers in other departments include chemistry professor James Peliska, who is cited as a good mentor for premed students; "influential" mathematics teacher Michael Marsalli; and economics chair Gabriel Martinez, who is praised for sharing with students an understanding of both the practical and the ethical aspects of business. This squares well with one of university founder Monaghan's aspirations: in addition to the school, he founded Legatus, a national organization of Catholic businessmen devoted to the spiritual formation of Catholic business leaders.

Amid these solid academic departments, there lingers turmoil from the school's troubled founding in Michigan and sudden move to Florida—which embittered many at Ave. The university's administrative staff suffers from high turnover, as members resign unexpectedly or are quietly released. Students report that administration members are keenly aware of their public perception in the academic community, which leads to an excessive concern (in one student's words) for "trying not to look 'fringe.'" Some higher-ups at the school are described by students as "paranoid" and "controlling," while lower-level staff members are reportedly "friendly and helpful" but "tight-lipped"—citing fears of dismissal.

Teachers we contacted describe themselves as contented and are reluctant to criticize university staff or the university—although several acknowledge unspecified "difficulties" within the administration. But one faculty member insists that "although the next few years will also have their own troubles, I think that the faculty and staff that we have now are optimistic and hardworking, the more so because we have hoped high and endured."

Despite these growing pains, the school keeps its promise about the type of education it offers. Its students enjoy the facilities of a university as well as the intimacy of a small liberal arts college with a highly qualified faculty. The student-faculty ratio is a middling 15 to 1, and the average class size is 17. Although a significant portion of the faculty is young, 81 percent of the full-time faculty possess a doctorate.

Students report an excellent relationship with faculty members. One undergrad cites "professors who are very concerned about their individual students and willing to dedicate a great deal of time and effort to helping them grasp the material." Another noted that his

---

CAMPUS POLITICS: GREEN LIGHT

Ave Maria University combines a strong curriculum with a spirit of "joyful fidelity to the Magisterium of the Catholic Church." Unlike the vast majority of American Catholic colleges, Ave Maria follows the Vatican directive *Ex Corde Ecclesiae* and arranges for its theology faculty to obtain a *mandatum* (mandate) from the local bishop, affirming their adherence to official church teaching. The college faculty publicly offers a Profession of Faith and an Oath of Fidelity to the Church at the beginning of every academic year.

Whatever its growing pains, Ave Maria provides a wholesome and hopeful environment for deeply committed Catholics to obtain a liberal arts education among like-minded people. Non-Catholics or dissenting Catholics would likely find the environment somewhat stifling—especially given the school's geographical isolation.

SUGGESTED CORE

The core curriculum required for liberal arts students suffices.

teachers reach beyond the classroom, to assist with students' spiritual and personal formation. "There is a great deal of nonacademic camaraderie between the students and the faculty, staff and their families."

First-year students are assigned an adviser from among the full-time faculty. Then, if a student picks a major in which his adviser does not teach, he may get a different adviser within that field.

The university also offers a graduate program in theology and two highly praised study-abroad programs—at Ave Maria's campus in Nicaragua and a program in Rome, Italy. The university has a Language Learning Center that provides computer-based support for university classes in French, Greek and Latin, and Spanish. It also supplies supplementary materials for the study of Arabic, Chinese, French, German, Greek and Latin, Italian, Russian, and Spanish. Both study-abroad programs are conducted in English.

Student Life: Tropical chastity

The new (2007) Ave Maria campus boasts a large three-story academic building, with new offices for the faculty, classrooms, a lecture hall, and state-of-the-art science labs. The school also has a shiny new student center featuring a cafeteria, game rooms, a big (and aggressively ugly) chapel, a ballroom, and offices. The newly constructed Canizaro Library has 200,000 volumes, with a capacity for twice as many.

The campus has five single-sex dorms—two for women, three for men—with a total capacity of about 1,150 students. Intervisitation in common areas of the dorms is permitted from 9:00 a.m. to 1:00 a.m. Sundays through Thursdays, and 9:00 a.m. to 2:00 a.m. on weekends. One student reports she is satisfied with the limitations, noting that "it allows interaction with members of a different sex, while creating a healthy atmosphere that encourages chastity." Another student reports, "The RAs are very nice and very approachable, and there is a great dorm life. Everyone knows each other and talks." Some 77 percent of undergraduate students live on campus, and the dorms are reputedly excellent. Full-time students are required to live on campus unless they are 23 years of age or live with immediate family. Off-campus housing is less expensive than living in the residence halls, but it really varies depending on whether they live with family.

> A student says that "professors are very concerned about their individual students and willing to dedicate a great deal of time and effort to helping them grasp the material." Teachers reach beyond the classroom to assist with students' spiritual and personal formation.

Some students report that it's "difficult to find things to do" on the weekends, noting that Naples, Florida, is a 45-minute drive away. The town offers shopping, dining, and entertainment, as well as many golf courses and white beaches. Some students travel to the Everglades National Park for recreational activity.

Student organizations on campus include yearbook and drama clubs; the Knights of Columbus; and various faith outreach groups, including Communion and Liberation. There is a College Republicans chapter (but no College Democrats) as well as a Students for Life group. New athletic facilities support a football field, two soccer fields, a baseball diamond, basketball courts, and tennis courts. An ice skating club exists too.

Other activities on campus include dances throughout the year, concerts, and intramural sports. The university supports intercollegiate women's basketball, soccer, and volleyball, while men's intercollegiate sports include basketball and soccer.

Spiritual opportunities at the university include daily Mass in both the Ordinary and Extraordinary form (Latin), and Divine Office (lauds, vespers, and compline). The Blessed Sacrament is reserved in each residence hall. Priests are available for confession and spiritual direction. The university is named for the Archangel Gabriel's greeting to the Virgin, and Marian devotions are numerous. Students pray the Angelus each day at noon and 6:00 p.m., and there is a community-wide Rosary walk every evening.

Security patrols the campus at all times, and students report it to be "very safe." In 2011 there were no crimes reported on campus. In 2010 the only crimes reported on campus were two robberies.

Tuition for 2010–11 was $21,496, while housing and meals added up to $8,841. Eighty-five percent of students received need-based financial aid.

STRONG SUITS	WEAK POINTS
• Intense dedication to the school's religious identity and mission. • Serious liberal arts requirements that make learning Western Civ mandatory. • Solid departments emphasizing core competencies. • An emphasis on business and preprofessional training missing at most other start-up religious colleges.	• Geographic isolation, in a newly founded map-dot town in a tropical climate. • Limited entertainment and social activities. • Students speak of some "paranoid" and "controlling" administrators.

Barnard College

New York, New York • www.barnard.edu

Columbia's Little Sister

Founded in 1889, the all-female Barnard College is recognized as one of the top liberal arts colleges in the country. Columbia, located just across the street, has been coed for nearly three decades, but Barnard remains single sex and financially independent from Columbia. Barnard students may take from Columbia University as many or as few courses as they desire. Only Columbia's "core" courses are off-limits, which is a shame, since they're the best thing offered at either school.

One Barnard student says, "Most semesters, the majority of my classes are across the street. I study in Butler [Columbia's history and humanities library] every day, and most of my friends are Columbia students. . . . Columbia is a really good resource and is one of the major reasons I don't go crazy at Barnard." A suffocating atmosphere of radical feminism pervades this women's college. Barnard president Debora Spar opined in a January 4, 2009, *Washington Post* op-ed that the worldwide financial meltdown could have been averted had women, rather than "rich, white, middle-aged guys," been at the helm. We wish that courses in logic were part of Barnard's degree requirements.

Academic Life: Crossing the street

Each incoming Barnard student takes a first-year seminar in which she learns writing and speaking skills in a small-group environment. Every student must prepare a semester- or yearlong project or thesis within her major. Across the curriculum, and especially in the humanities, instructors emphasize good writing and communication skills. Seminars are limited to 16 students and emphasize reading and writing. Most math and science courses must be taken at Columbia, as Barnard offers very few classes in these subjects.

Barnard students can easily sign up for most of Columbia's classes. New York City also offers many opportunities for research, internships, and transfer credit from area colleges and universities. For instance, students can major in music by taking courses from Barnard as well as Juilliard and the Manhattan School of Music.

The Barnard advising system is superb. Each student is assigned a professor from the department of her proposed major as an adviser. These are often helpful, with last-minute advice on papers. All students must visit their advisers at least once a semester for approval of the advisee's course load.

Barnard's student-faculty ratio is 9 to 1, which helps students see a lot of their professors. Some of the best professors, according to students, are Rajiv Sethi and Sharon Harrison in economics; Anne Lake Prescott in English; Joel Kaye, Herb Sloan, and Robert McCaughey in history; Alan Gabbey in philosophy; and Kimberly Zisk Marten and Richard Pious in political science. Novelist Mary Gordon also teaches, and students agree that her classes are superb. Graduate students do not lead classes at Barnard.

Barnard's strongest departments include English, psychology, political science, economics, history, and biology. Besides its respected English faculty, the school "excels in teaching writing," reports an insider. In addition to her "Critical Writing" class, the Barnard English major must take two courses in pre-19th-century literature as well as "The English Colloquium," a two-semester introduction to literature of the Renaissance and the Enlightenment. (Students may substitute appropriate courses—for

VITAL STATISTICS

Religious affiliation: *none*
Total enrollment: *2,390*
Total undergraduates: *2,390*
SAT CR/Verbal midrange: *630–730*
SAT Math midrange: *620–710*
ACT midrange: *28–31*
Applicants: *5,440*
Applicants accepted: *23%*
Accepted applicants who enrolled: *49.3%*
Tuition (general/out of state): *$41,850*
Tuition (in state): *N/A*
Room and board: *$13,810*
Freshman retention rate: *94%*
Graduation rate (4 yrs.): *84%*
Graduation rate (6 yrs.): *92%*
Courses with fewer than 20 students: *72%*
Student-faculty ratio: *9:1*
Courses taught by graduate students: *none*
Students living on campus: *90%*
Students in fraternities: *N/A*
Students in sororities: *N/A*
Students receiving need-based financial aid: *39%*
Avg. student-loan debt of a recent graduating class: *$17,416*
Most popular majors: *English, psychology, political science.*
Guaranteed housing for 4 years? *yes*

CAMPUS POLITICS: RED LIGHT

Barnard's radicalism is so pervasive that most students have, according to one professor, "no awareness that what they're being taught are varieties of leftism. They're just different aspects of the truth, since there is no alternative ever contemplated. Perhaps the best illustration of this are casual (as well as administration-backed) references in class and conversation to 'activism' as another unquestioned good. Naturally, said activism does not include working for the Republican Party or the Heritage Foundation! If the only perspectives one offers are variants of leftism, then the choice is simple: become 'active' in a leftist cause of one sort or another, or else 'apathetically' confine your leftist ideas to the classroom and don't do anything to put them into action."

The most active contingent of Barnard student life appears to be the gay community. "Barnard's and Columbia's campuses offer tons of ways to get involved in queer activism and social life," declares Barnard's website. Indeed. There are at least nine very outspoken homosexual organizations on campus. Queer Awareness Month (QuAM) sponsors a monthly "Casual Crossdressing" during which undergrads attend class and mince about campus in drag. On December 3, 2010, Queer Alliance hosted the Vagina Ball in Barnard Hall wherein many students dressed up as various parts of female genitalia.

instance, one on Shakespeare.) English majors must also choose three other advanced electives and two senior seminars. Allowing for heavy doses of feminism, many of the courses seem solid and interesting.

The Barnard history major is strongly geared toward developing a senior research paper of 30 to 50 pages, written as part of a two-term project. Majors must complete 11 classes in the major, including eight in a specific concentration area (for example, medieval history). They must also take three introductory history classes. Two of these must be in one's subject area of concentration. Most of the introductory history courses are substantive. However, a Barnard history major might well graduate without ever learning anything about the United States.

The political science major calls for nine courses, including introductory classes in at least three of the four areas of the field (U.S. government, international relations, comparative government, and political theory). A major must also take two colloquia (which include 25-to-30-page research papers) and a one-term senior research seminar. Still, it is possible to complete the major without learning the basics of U.S. government.

Weaker departments, students report, include economics, which one student says was "famous for being Marxist," while another says that her economics courses were a "joke at Barnard, but great at Columbia. At Barnard I never attended and got good grades." Observes a professor: "Teaching is taken very seriously, but the small size of some of the departments may be an issue. Here's an example: the political science department's 'Plato to NATO' course is taught by a Gandhi scholar—although, to be fair, he is respectful of Western thinkers."

Barnard is not an environment in which conservatives feel comfortable. A professor says that he was shocked by the climate at Barnard: "There's a casualness and thoughtlessness and partisanship to the political correctness that's more extreme. At a place like Harvard, people know that you may not agree with them about every one of the liberal shibboleths. At Barnard they simply don't understand that." As one student observes, "It's just assumed that you should be a radical feminist." Another politicized major is human rights studies, an interdisciplinary program. This is often pursued as part of a combined major with political science, as is women's studies.

One student opines, "Undeniably, this school has major problems with political correctness and blatant bias toward liberal—even communist—positions. I tried majoring in political science and then in history, but grew frustrated with these 100 percent leftist departments. The English courses I've taken were just as bad: Marxist, feminist, race-conscious—you name it. We actually read *The Communist Manifesto* in 'First-Year English.' When I tried to defend capitalism in class, the professor called me into her office for a private meeting. 'Surely, you have to admit that capitalism is a brutal system,' she insisted. I refused, and we argued at length. I ended up with a low grade in the class."

Barnard provides instruction in French, German, Greek and Latin, Italian, Russian, and Spanish, but other languages must be studied at Columbia. Barnard offers study-abroad programs in more than 45 countries, as well as off-campus study programs in the U.S. Barnard's programs partner with some famous universities like Oxford and Heidelberg, but also with colleges in less obvious places like Morocco, Niger, and Nepal.

Student Life: They say the neon lights are bright

Most of Barnard's pedestrian-friendly campus is clustered between Broadway and Claremont Avenues. The main structures are Milbank Hall (which houses several administrative offices and academic departments), and Barnard Hall (which holds classrooms, a gym, and a swimming pool). The Quad, a group of four residence halls with a courtyard in the center, is where most first-year students live. Students need only cross Broadway to get to Columbia. A series of underground tunnels connect buildings and halls around the Barnard campus.

A professor says that "there's a casualness and thoughtlessness and partisanship to the political correctness."

Students say that living in Manhattan is one of the greatest advantages of attending the school. The Upper West Side has a number of lively bars, which (students report) strictly enforce alcohol laws, and the drinking scene, compared to other colleges, is mild.

The college sponsors annual student events, including spring and winter festivals and Founder's Day. There is a plethora of diverse (and bizarre) student clubs and organizations on campus, including the AAA (Asian American Alliance), BOSS (Black Organization of Soul Sisters), Bach Society, Caribbean Students Organization, Dance Dance Revolution Club, Psychology Club, a television station, and Q—a group that "promotes the visibility of lesbian, gay, bisexual, transgender, intersex, queer, questioning, two spirit, genderqueer,

SUGGESTED CORE

1. Classical Literature W4300x, Classical Tradition
2. Philosophy V2101x, History of Philosophy I: Pre-Socratics through Augustine
3. Religion V3501x/V3120y, Hebrew Bible/Introduction to the New Testament
4. Religion V2105x, Christianity or Religion V3140y, Early Christianity
5. Political Science V1013y, Political Theory
6. English BC3163x/3164y, Shakespeare I or II
7. History BC1401x, Survey of American Civilization to the Civil War
8. Philosophy V2301y, History of Philosophy III: Kant to Nietzsche

pansexual, omnisexual, and allied women at Barnard and Columbia." Trust us, they're already pretty visible. And don't try sporting that pro-life button if you want to make many friends.

There is a thriving Orthodox Jewish community on campus, and the cafeteria offers kosher food. It also offers special dining hours during Ramadan. Students of faith can find numerous synagogues and churches (including the stunning Episcopal Cathedral of St. John the Divine) within easy walking distance. The Catholic community at Barnard and Columbia, hosted at the nearby Church of Notre Dame, is said to be especially vibrant.

Barnard lacks the close-knit atmosphere that other all-women colleges like Bryn Mawr and Mount Holyoke boast. In fact, Barnard's "all-women" status makes little practical difference. One student says that 90 percent of her classes are coed, as are her extracurricular activities—and so are some of the dorms (at Columbia, where Barnard students are allowed to live). "I wouldn't say the fact that Barnard is a women's school has too much effect on my social life, although I do wish that there were more guys around sometimes," she says. "Girls can be catty!"

The Barnard student body is composed of 2,390 undergraduates from 53 countries and nearly every state, with approximately 29 percent coming from New York State. Barnard has fewer international students than do most schools because it has little financial aid to offer them, but an admissions counselor says Barnard has a huge immigrant population.

About 90 percent of Barnard students live in 12 Barnard residence halls and four Columbia residence halls, where some live in coed dorms with Columbia students. First-year students are housed together in freshman-only dormitories or floors. Barnard guarantees housing for all four years—no small feat in Manhattan.

Students at Barnard and Columbia play together in 16 NCAA Division I and Ivy League varsity teams, and also team up in more than 30 club sports.

Barnard is intent on preventing crime. The gates to the Barnard campus are closely guarded, and there are guard posts on every block. In 2011 Barnard reported one forcible sexual offense and five burglaries on campus. It's worth noting that New York is now the safest large city in America and has been rated in surveys as the friendliest.

Barnard is as pricey as any of the Seven Sisters, with 2012–13 tuition at $41,850. Room and board were listed at $13,810. However, its financial aid is generous; admissions are need blind, and the school guarantees to meet a student's full financial need. Some 50 percent of students are currently receiving need-based financial aid, and the average indebtedness of a recent graduate was $17,416.

STRONG SUITS	WEAK POINTS
• Superb advising system. • Abundant, elite professors. • Excellent writing program, with some famous writers on staff. • Access to courses and facilities at "brother" school Columbia University. • It's in *New York City*.	• Pervasive, doctrinaire leftism pervades every nook and cranny of campus. • Small departments force professors to teach far outside their specialties. • Intense, outspoken, one-sided activism— for instance, there are nine separate gay organizations on campus, and almost no conservative groups.

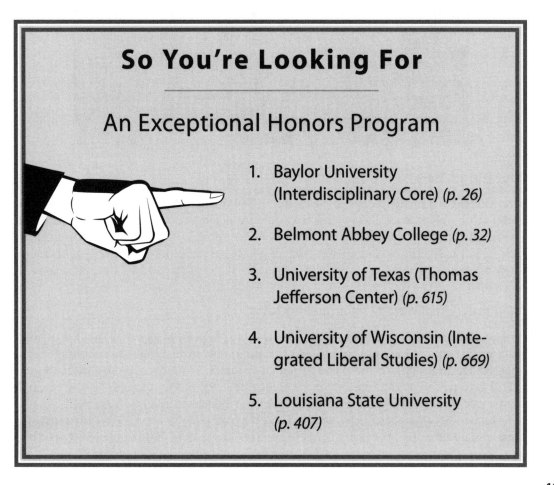

So You're Looking For

An Exceptional Honors Program

1. Baylor University (Interdisciplinary Core) *(p. 26)*

2. Belmont Abbey College *(p. 32)*

3. University of Texas (Thomas Jefferson Center) *(p. 615)*

4. University of Wisconsin (Integrated Liberal Studies) *(p. 669)*

5. Louisiana State University *(p. 407)*

Bates College

Lewiston, Maine • www.bates.edu

Educating Liberals

Bates College sits on 109 acres, 35 miles north of Portland, Maine. While it carries on a tradition of academic excellence and is known for a tolerant atmosphere, the school has also adopted the lax curriculum and pervasive leftist politics that characterize most other colleges in the Northeast. But a Bates student can receive a sound education—if he knows where to look.

Academic Life: Short term and long term

With a student body of around 1,700, Bates has all the advantages of a small, teaching-centered institution. Even the largest lecture halls are intimate enough to encourage questions. No teaching assistants lead undergraduate courses. Professors devote almost all their attention to teaching, and most are quite accessible. Even in the sciences, faculty research complements course work and comes rarely at the expense of students.

Like most other liberal arts colleges, Bates has long since given up on requiring its students to acquire "core" knowledge by taking courses in Western culture, literature, and history. Bates students can graduate without ever having taken a course in philosophy, English, history, or a foreign language—and that's more freedom than anybody needs. Still, most of the classes offered at Bates are academically solid, and students are known for intellectual curiosity

Bates is particularly strong in the sciences, and even the brightest students majoring in math, chemistry, biology, or physics feel challenged. A chemistry major says that when she tells people her course of study, their "first reaction is to cringe." The Bates science program has distinguished itself from those at other small liberal arts colleges in New England and brings in millions of dollars in research grants.

One of the virtues that Bates hopes will attract generous donors is its fine reputation for teaching. Strong departments include English, history, political science, psychology, and those in the hard sciences. Students praise Sanford Freedman for his Shakespeare class: "He requires students to read fast but carefully, really scrutinizing the texts," says one.

The philosophy major includes a goodly number of serious offerings, including "Contemporary Moral Disputes," "Philosophy of Law," and "Moral Philosophy" with David Cummiskey. Says a student, "Students pore over Supreme Court writings and philosophical commentary to work their way through the principles of law. They read Aristotle, Locke, Mill, Hobbes, and Hume."

Students also praise courses in history, politics, and economics. Medievalist Michael Jones is called "an amazing lecturer," while historian John Cole "is good-humored and very tolerant." Bill Corlett is a Marxist political science teacher whom students recommend as an open-minded teacher. Students also laud math professor Pallavi Jayawant, who reportedly "finds a way to make every student 'get it.' She is always willing to help, and easy to reach." Another beloved professor is Mark Okrent, chair of the philosophy department, known for "enthusiasm and teaching classes very clearly." John Corrie, known as "the most enthusiastic professor on campus," delights in teaching music and conducting the choir. Heidi Taylor, professor of sociology, wins praise for being open-minded to many points of view and shows that she "will stick up for students whose ideas put them in the minority."

VITAL STATISTICS

Religious affiliation: *none*
Total enrollment: *1,769*
Total undergraduates: *1,769*
SAT CR/Verbal midrange: *630–710*
SAT Math midrange: *620–710*
ACT midrange: *not provided*
ACT composite: *29–31*
Applicants: *5,196*
Applicants accepted: *1,405 (27%)*
Accepted applicants who enrolled: *502 (35%)*
Tuition (general/out of state): *$57,350 (comprehensive)*
Tuition (in state): *N/A*
Room and board: *N/A*
Freshman retention rate: *93%*
Graduation rate (4 yrs.): *87%*
Graduation rate (6 yrs.): *92%*
Courses with fewer than 20 students: *64%*
Student-faculty ratio: *10:1*
Courses taught by graduate students: *none*
Students living on campus: *93%*
Students in fraternities: *N/A*
Students in sororities: *N/A*
Students receiving need-based financial aid: *42%*
Avg. student-loan debt of a recent graduating class: *$20,706*
Most popular majors: *economics, political science, psychology*
Guaranteed housing for 4 years? *yes*

CAMPUS POLITICS: YELLOW LIGHT

Bates students of all political persuasions agree that the campus leans decidedly to the left. As one student says, "Bates is definitely left-leaning, and that is putting it mildly. But most teachers conduct classes with a fairly high level of political balance." Faculty have even been known to inject political opinions into seemingly harmless classes like "Cellular and Molecular Biology" and to have anti-Republican posters on office doors. On issues of religion, a student says, "Very few professors openly talk about their faith, but many are glad to talk about their lack of it."

The Bates Republican Club is much more active on campus than it used to be, sponsoring conferences and speakers—including, in 2012, Bay Buchanan, Phyllis Schlafly, and Dinesh D'Souza. Back in 2005, the club helped to pass an Academic Bill of Rights, which declared that political and religious beliefs should not be singled out for ridicule, that students should not be forced to express a certain point of view in assignments, and that university funds should not be used for one-sided conferences. Contrarily, Bates incorporated a "Pledge of Social Responsibility" into its 2010 graduation ceremony, in which all soon-to-be-graduates stand up and recite, "I, [student's name], pledge to explore and take into account the social and environmental consequences of any job I consider and will try to improve these aspects of any organizations for which I work."

Other excellent professors include Jen Koviach-Côté in chemistry; Amy Bradfield Douglass and Todd Kahan in psychology; Stephanie Richards in biology; Dolores O'Higgins in classical and medieval studies; Stephanie Kelley-Romano in rhetoric; and Paul Kuritz in theater.

Some "fluff" classes can be found in the disciplines of religion and women and gender studies. The anthropology department is said to be quite hostile toward conservative viewpoints.

Bates seniors spend their final semester, and sometimes an entire year, working on a thesis, either conducting new research or preparing for a performance. As one student told the school newspaper, "It gave my major a real meaning. It was a nice finale to my Bates education." For many, completing such an impressive project as undergraduates makes the prospect of graduate school less intimidating.

The English department requires its majors to take 11 courses in the subject with at least three covering literature composed before 1800. However, many of the department's offerings sound depressingly recondite—such as "Constructing Sexuality in the Enlightenment," "Sexuality in Victorian Literature," "Black Feminist Literary Theory and Practice," and "Afrofuturism." A Bates English grad need not read Shakespeare, Chaucer, or Milton, but if he does, it will likely be through a jaundiced lens.

The history major requires a "short course" in historical methods, two classes in the history of East Asia or Latin America, one introductory survey class, five classes in a "concentration area," and a senior thesis. The possible concentration areas are: East Asia, Latin America, Europe, the United States, and premodern history. So a Bates history major could graduate without taking a single class on U.S. or European history. In the politics major, a student must take 11 courses, including five in a concentration area. He must also complete a senior essay. There is no course required on the American political system or Constitution.

Professors are well-integrated into the Bates community, and it is not uncommon for a student to have dinner with a professor or to become a personal friend of his family. "I was on a first-name basis with all my professors and got to know them well," a foreign language major says. Students report that advisers are helpful; one student says that hers "provided not only academic advice but also advice on my future decisions and other interests in my life that weren't necessarily academic." Independent study courses are quite popular, and students often work closely with professors either to explore a subject not offered in a traditional course or to perform new research.

Bates offers programs for those studying Chinese, French, German, Ancient Greek, Latin, Japanese, Russian, and Spanish. Study abroad is extraordinarily popular, with 60 percent of juniors, and smaller percentages from other years, participating. The college sponsors a fall semester program in St. Petersburg, Russia, but Bates students travel all over the world through other colleges.

Student Life: Outing club

Bates College is the lone intellectual hot spot in the working class New England mill town of Lewiston, Maine. The campus is the undisputed center of student life. The college guarantees housing for all four years and requires students to live on campus, except by special permission.

Food on campus is mostly organic and tasty. Attractive new residence halls opened in September 2007 and look like hotels compared to the older dorms, which "are so old and quaint—it's like going back in time," marvels one resident.

Outside the classroom, most students participate in club and varsity sports, many engage in performing arts, and almost all take part in one of more than 100 student-run clubs or organizations. About 40 percent of students take on career internships, and more than two-thirds of recent graduates enroll in graduate study within 10 years of graduation. The Bates Museum of Art specializes in Maine artists, but in April and May, studio art majors showcase their works there. The annual Gala is a college-wide formal featuring a live orchestra or band. Bates brings in a number of lecturers each year, although, one student complains, these aren't often conservative speakers.

A student reports: "Bates is definitely left leaning, but most teachers conduct classes with a fairly high level of political balance."

Most of the dormitories are coed, but some have single-sex floors. In some coed suites, students of opposite sexes might share a common bathroom. Students also have an alcohol-free living option and designated quiet houses and halls. Freshmen all live together in doubles, triples, or quads, with every 15 or so students matched with a junior adviser. Some of these advisers are now complaining about their jobs. Says one, "I serve as a residence life staff member, and I am paid to ensure that students are safe and most important (from the

SUGGESTED CORE

1. History 108/109, Roman Civilization: The Republic/ The Empire
2. Classical and Medieval Studies 271, Ancient Greek Philosophy
3. Religious Studies 235/236, Introduction to the Hebrew Bible/New Testament
4. Religious Studies 242, History of Christian Thought II: The Emergence of Modernity
5. Politics 191, Western Political Theory
6. English 213/214, Shakespeare
7. History 140/141, Origins of the New Nation, 1500–1820/America in the Age of Civil War
8. Philosophy 273, Philosophy in the 19th Century

college's perspective) politically correct. [We] go through hours of training in dealing with the many situations that arise in dorm life, but most training focuses on dealing with racist/biased speech and messages that may make different people uncomfortable for any reason."

Everything at Bates emphasizes the school's close-knit community atmosphere. Says a student: "The best aspect of Bates is that there are lots of different kinds of intelligent people. They really expanded my beliefs." Life at Bates is said to revolve around the residences, the site of most cerebration and celebration alike. The close college community becomes even closer on typical weekend nights, when many students resort to tippling. Says one dorm resident, "Security is very lax about drinking beer, though a recent effort has been made to eliminate all hard alcohol from the premises." The school is applying increasing pressure to diminish alcohol consumption; one tactic tried was to have a "guilty by association" policy, whereby students in the same room with anyone possessing hard alcohol were subject to the same penalties as their host.

Opportunities for students to express their political views are available in the Democrat and Republican clubs. Both groups like to liven things up by bringing provocative speakers to the school. Overall, students are tolerant of differing views, and vocally biased professors are in the minority. One conservative student insists, "If you can back your view up with empirical evidence, it will be accepted."

Bates Outing Club is the most popular extracurricular organization; in fact, students are automatically registered as members when they arrive on campus. The club allows students to borrow backpacks, bikes, and tents at no cost, and it sponsors outings to the beach, mountains, and Maine ski resorts several times each semester.

Bates is a very athletic campus, with around 60 percent of the student body participating in intramural sports. One-third of Bates students are varsity members of one of the Bobcats' thirty intercollegiate teams, which compete in the New England Small College Athletic Conference (NESCAC) against teams such as Amherst, Bowdoin, Colby, and Tufts. Bates has excellent athletic facilities for a school its size, including an indoor track and an ice arena.

Religion isn't a major priority for Bates students—most would prefer to study or ski. The school's head chaplain, William Blaine-Wallace, who impresses students with his "enthusiasm and friendly spirit," was one of the first Episcopalian clergy to officiate in same-sex marriages in Boston. Bates Christian Fellowship holds Bible studies and prayer services each week. The school also hosts Hillel and a Catholic Student Community Center.

Tradition-oriented Catholic students might wish to check out the Latin Mass offered at Lewiston's gorgeous Basilica of Saints Peter and Paul.

Lewiston is a tough town for the college. At one point, Bates College was surrounded by razor wire to keep out undesirable Lewistonians. The school's previous president tore down the fences to promote better college-community interaction. This may or may not have worked; excessive student drinking causes friction with unfriendly townsfolk, and in May 2010 a call to the police for aid to a drunken student resulted in a fight between students and the police, in which an officer's leg was broken. Still, violence inflicted by or on students is very rare; in 2011 Bates reported 14 burglaries, six sexual assaults, and one case of arson.

Bates does not list a separate cost for tuition, room, and board, but its comprehensive fee in 2011–12 came to a whopping $57,350. One student reports that "financial aid at Bates is very fair. It was my reason for attending the college, and the aid they gave is almost entirely composed of grants." Forty-two percent of students received need-based aid, and the average student-loan debt of a recent graduate was $20,706.

STRONG SUITS	WEAK POINTS
• Strong teaching, especially in the sciences.	• The lax curriculum leaves students to construct their own educations.
• Many solid, foundational courses are offered.	• A heavily secular atmosphere; religious life is mostly off campus.
• An intense intellectual atmosphere.	• The town where it's located is a battered rust-belt community with few cultural opportunities.
• Wonderful opportunities for outdoors exploration and fitness.	

Baylor University

Waco, Texas • www.baylor.edu

The Protestant Notre Dame?

Baylor, the world's largest Baptist university, was founded 168 years ago by Baptist missionaries, but unlike many of America's most prestigious universities, Baylor has strengthened its commitment to the faith of its founders. Baylor's Baptist tradition informs its academic programs and the social life of its students in increasingly significant and academically rigorous ways. In fact, Baylor seeks to inculcate in its students an understanding of the harmony between faith and understanding and to show them that they need not choose between academic excellence and Christian devotion. While many schools have dumbed down their academic standards, Baylor has strengthened its own.

Last year, Baylor completed an ambitious 10-year plan, "Baylor 2012," demonstrating its commitment both to the life of the mind and to the life of faith. The plan pledged to seek new levels of national prominence and Christian academic excellence and to become, as many put it, a "Protestant Notre Dame." Baylor 2012 included plans to hire high-profile Christian faculty, to increase commitments to research and teaching, to erect more and better academic facilities, to support athletic programs with integrity, and to add doctoral programs. Despite some initial resistance (the president who introduced it was forced out of office), most of the plan's goals seem to have been largely achieved. One professor suggests that many in the Baylor family are just exhausted from the battles of the past several years and are less likely to cause trouble. The political situation has also improved, as many of the faculty hired at the start of the 2012 plan have now been tenured.

Academic Life: Faith and knowledge

While it does not insist on a traditional core, Baylor's solid curriculum dictates more than half of a student's course work. Of course, a few students enroll in less-demanding classes such as the geology class "Earthquakes and Other Natural Disasters" (a.k.a. "Shake and Bake") to boost their GPAs, but faculty advising is generally solid at Baylor, and students who select their courses wisely can get a great education.

Some students choose to satisfy their general-studies requirements through the Baylor Interdisciplinary Core (BIC), under the auspices of the Honors College (which also includes an honors program for students across the disciplines as well as the Great Texts major). The BIC is not a major but rather replaces the general-education requirements of the university (and includes 44 total hours of course work). Students in the BIC undertake a coherent and integrated interdisciplinary course of study that emphasizes reading primary sources (such as the Bible, the *Analects*, and Plato's dialogues) from Eastern and Western traditions in their proper historical order. The BIC curriculum is made up of five sequences of courses: World Cultures, World of Rhetoric, Social World, Natural World, and the Examined Life. The courses are team taught by professors from diverse disciplines; however, some students complain that BIC professors are forced to teach material unfamiliar to them.

Like the BIC, the Scholars Program (UNSC) replaces the university general-education requirements, but the UNSC is also a major and is less structured than the BIC. Students in the UNSC program are required to take only five courses: two introductory religion courses and a rigorous three-course sequence of Great Texts courses (ancient, medieval, and modern). Aside from those courses, students are free to select any courses to craft their own major; they might combine courses in music and biology, for example. Each student's selection of courses

VITAL STATISTICS

Religious affiliation: *Protestant (Baptist)*
Total enrollment: *15,364*
Total undergraduates: *12,918*
SAT CR/Verbal midrange: *550–660*
SAT Math midrange: *570–670*
ACT midrange: *24–29*
Applicants: *27,828*
Applicants accepted: *61%*
Accepted applicants who enrolled: *19%*
Tuition (general/out of state): *$35,972*
Tuition (in state): *N/A*
Room and board: *$11,372*
Freshman retention rate: *87%*
Graduation rate (4 yrs.): *54%*
Graduation rate (6 yrs.): *75%*
Courses with fewer than 20 students: *49%*
Student-faculty ratio: *15:1*
Courses taught by graduate students: *12%*
Students living on campus: *39%*
Students in fraternities: *13%*
Students in sororities: *21%*
Students receiving need-based financial aid: *62%*
Avg. student-loan debt of a recent graduating class: *$40,000*
Most popular majors: *biology, business/marketing, communications*
Guaranteed housing for 4 years? *no*

is unique, and the program succeeds because of its outstanding advisers, who meet often with students and require them to take well-rounded schedules. One liberal arts student reports being "required" by her adviser to take calculus. In addition to taking classes, UNSC students must also compose a reading list of significant texts in the Western canon and complete a one-hour exit interview on it with the director of the program and other professors. Finally, UNSC students are required to research, write, and defend a senior thesis. The program is rigorous, and students typically go on to graduate school, medical school, or law school. One student says, "I would recommend this program to all students with an ardent curiosity and strong work ethic who desire a truly well-rounded undergraduate education that will prepare them for any and all careers to follow."

The major fields of study are likewise intellectually serious. Baylor students select from a broad range of generally solid departments; there are 144 undergraduate degree programs as well as 77 master's programs and 32 doctoral programs. Students speak highly of Classics, biology, philosophy, business, nursing, law, and music. The premed program and engineering school are highly regarded nationally, as is Baylor's entrepreneurship program.

English majors must take four intermediate courses in British and American literature (out of five solid choices), advanced courses in the history of British literature, one upper-level class in American literature, and two English electives (such as "Oxford Christians" or "The Contemporary Novel"). They cannot graduate without encountering Shakespeare.

History majors must take introductions to world history and the history of the United States; choose two additional American history courses; two courses in African, Asian, Latin American, or Middle Eastern history; two European history courses; and one general history elective (such as "Cultural and Intellectual History of Modern Europe" or "History of Gender in Latin America").

Baylor's political science department has sound requirements. The department proudly notes on its website: "Political Science students at Baylor learn about American political history and institutions, study the development of our constitutional law from the founding era to the latest Supreme Court decision, master the techniques of rigorous political analysis, examine the causes and effects of political change around the world, and survey the writings of great philosophers (such as Plato, Aristotle, Hobbes, and Locke)."

Students report that faculty research—encouraged by the 2012 plan—is not detracting from teaching, and some faculty find ways to involve undergraduates in their research. The current student-faculty ratio is 15 to 1, and students maintain that professors find plenty of time to spend with each of their students. One reports, "I have never had a professor with whom I did not have some meaningful or helpful conversation outside of class." It is not uncommon for professors to have students over to their houses, and eight professors have even moved right into the campus dormitories with their families through Baylor's faculty-in-residence program. Professors teach almost all courses, although students say graduate teaching assistants sometimes run labs or weekly discussion sections.

Baylor has been on a hiring spree, giving preference to those scholars for whom faith and scholarship are integrally related. The quality of the faculty members is quite high, particularly within the Honors College. The growing list of fine professors at Baylor includes David Corey, David Nichols, and Mary Nichols in political science; Julie Sweet in history; Phillip Donnelly and Ralph Wood in English; Michael Beaty, Robert Baird, Francis Beckwith, C. Stephen Evans, James Marcum, and Robert Roberts in philosophy; Michael Foley, Douglas Henry, Thomas Hibbs, David L. Jeffrey, Robert Miner, and Sarah-Jane Murray in the Honors College; Julia Dyson Hejduk, Jeff Fish, and Alden Smith in Classics; Robyn Driskell in sociology; Robin Wallace in music history and literature; Joseph McKinney in economics; Bennie Ward in physics; and John A. Dunbar in geology.

> A highly intellectual Baptist university, Baylor fosters mentoring. A student says, "I have never had a professor with whom I did not have some meaningful or helpful conversation outside of class."

Baylor offers a great many study-abroad options spanning six continents, with programs in 27 European countries, plus more than 20 programs outside Europe. Baylor does not, however, offer programs in any Middle Eastern country (although it does offer one in Turkey). Baylor offers courses in Arabic, Chinese, French, German, Greek and Latin, Hebrew, Italian, Japanese, Korean, Portuguese, Russian, Spanish, and Swahili.

Student Life: As perceived by Texas Baptists

In 2004 Baylor began requiring all incoming freshmen to live on campus. To make this possible, the university completed several large, attractive residential facilities and renovated several others; Baylor's goal was to have 50 percent of students in residence halls by 2012 but had reached only 39 percent in 2013. Qualified students have the option of living in one of two popular residential colleges: the Honors College residences or Brooks Hall. A senior in the honors residence reports, "There is hardly a resident whom I do not know and who would not be willing to discuss big ideas, play music, or pick up a Frisbee with me.... Students who live here share an eagerness for study, and yet also know how to have fun and grow together as a community." Both residential colleges host regular dinners, lectures

SUGGESTED CORE

1. Classics 3301/3302, Roman Civilization/Greek Civilization
2. Philosophy 3310, History of Philosophy: Classical
3. Religion 4305/4315, Topics in Old Testament/New Testament Studies
4. Religion 4352/4353, History of Christian Theology I/II
5. Political Science 3373, Western Political Thought: Modern
6. English 4324, Shakespeare: Selected Plays
7. History 2365, History of the United States to 1877
8. History 4339, Cultural and Intellectual History of Modern Europe or Philosophy 3312, History of Philosophy: Modern European Philosophy

(with "world-class speakers," according to one student), teas, and activities to build a community among the students, faculty, and chaplains who live together there.

Men and women live in separate residence halls, except for in a few living areas for married students, and university policies limit intervisitation to certain hours: 1:00 p.m. to 10:00 p.m. Sunday through Thursday and 1:00 p.m. to midnight on Friday and Saturday. Students report that these policies are enforced and infractions are punished. Baylor prohibits alcohol in all residences and smoking in all university buildings. One student claims that "alcohol is present just as it is on any campus," but another suggests that drinking at Baylor is more moderate than that found at secular universities. Baylor policy requires school officials to inform parents when their children violate alcohol laws or rules.

Students may find some of these regulations intrusive, but Baylor expects that each student "will conduct himself or herself in accordance with Christian principles as commonly perceived by Texas Baptists." The school is serious about maintaining a Christian community, and students must attend two semesters of mandatory twice-weekly chapel services to graduate. On Mondays at chapel, the speaker could be anyone from a religious rapper to a Christian movie critic. Chapels on Wednesdays are worship services with varied music. An optional weekly 15-minute prayer service is held in a chapel in one of the honors dorms. Optional prayer services are also held in the Robbins chapel, a peaceful space with beautiful stained-glass windows attached to the Brooks Hall dormitory. These and several other prayer gardens and chapels around campus aim to stimulate impromptu meditation and prayer. Numerous Christian denominations flourish at Baylor, with Catholics the second-largest group after Baptists.

Many university traditions center on Baylor athletics. The Baylor Line, organized by freshmen, helps welcome the football team to the field by waving flags. The student body also names "yell leaders" who lead fans in organized cheers. And at every homecoming, fans remember the "Immortal Ten," basketball players who died in a 1927 train wreck. The green-and-gold-clad Baylor Bears play a huge role in student life, and affection is high for the Baylor mascots, three small black bears housed in a new visitor-friendly living environment at the center of campus. Competing in the powerful NCAA Division I, Big 12 Conference, Baylor achieved the holy grail of sports awards when quarterback Robert Griffin won the Heisman Trophy in 2011, the same year his football team finished 12th in the nation. Baylor also won the 2012 national championship in women's basketball, led by the country's best-known female college basketball player, 6'8" center Brittney Griner. The school also excels in less costly pursuits like golf and track and field.

Most students spend their time outside class studying and engaging in apolitical extracurricular groups. There are more than 270 chartered student organizations, and more than 80 percent of Baylor students are involved in at least one student organization. About half of Baylor students participate in the university's popular intramurals program. Baylor's chapter of Habitat for Humanity, the first in the country, is extremely popular, as are mission trips sponsored by Baptist Student Ministries. The campus is home to a strong Greek community, including 12 fraternities and eight sororities (none of which are allowed to maintain residences).

Although violent crime is not common in Waco, the area around the Baylor campus has relatively high levels of reported property crimes. In 2011 Baylor reported one aggravated assault, 11 burglaries, and one stolen car.

Tuition at Baylor for the 2012–13 academic year was $35,972, and room and board approximately $11,372. The university offers an installment plan to help with the cost of tuition, and 62 percent of students received need-based financial assistance. The average debt of Baylor graduates approached a whopping $40,000 a few years ago, and the school has since stopped providing this information to the public.

STRONG SUITS	WEAK POINTS
• Recent expansions of faculty have drawn top-notch scholars from across the country.	• High tuition and high student debt.
• The school is strongly attached to its Baptist vision and mission.	• Faculty in honors programs must sometimes teach outside their specialties.
• A wholesome campus environment with many fun traditions.	• Waco, Texas, is not everyone's cup of tea; high-culture options are limited.
• A solid curriculum that ensures every graduate has an intellectual foundation.	

Belmont Abbey College

Belmont, North Carolina • www.belmontabbeycollege.edu

The Rule

Founded in 1876 by the Order of St. Benedict, Belmont Abbey is one of a small band of Catholic colleges that still adheres closely to its mission and identity. The monastic community continues to serve as the bulwark of the college. Benedictines sponsor the school, serve on its board of trustees, and teach. Theology faculty affirm their fidelity to church teaching and seek out a mandate ("*mandatum*") from the local bishop.

Academic Life: Monks and motorsports

Belmont's core curriculum, beginning with the First-Year Symposium, introduces students to the knowledge, values, traditions, and academic culture characteristic of a Catholic, Benedictine liberal arts education.

At Belmont, teaching is of paramount importance, and many faculty have received honors for the quality of their instruction. More than 80 percent of faculty members hold doctoral degrees in their subjects. All professors carry a four-course load. As a result, a teacher writes, "There does not appear to be much time for research." Another professor mourns that "our teachers are very busy preparing classes, grading papers, and attending meetings. These are the pressures which diminish the vigor of debate and (unfortunately) make philosophic and political discussion sometimes difficult to find time for."

One student says: "Teachers in accounting are remarkable for their hard work and clear articulation of concepts. Teachers in the theology department are exemplars of Christian virtue and take a keen and involved interest in all aspects of student life. Members of the business, psychology, and biology departments are indefatigable. . . . Students under their care and instruction have made remarkable progress as behavioral psychologists and natural scientists. There is a palpable collegiality."

The senior faculty members of the English department are known for their strong commitment to teaching. Requirements for majors are solid, calling for 12 literature courses, including "Literature of the English Renaissance," "Restoration and Eighteenth-Century British Literature," "Shakespeare: Tragedies," and "Literary Criticism." In addition, the major requires foreign language study and additional classes in the humanities division and general electives.

One professor says that the Department of Government and Political Philosophy is "particularly strong due to the broad educational grounding of its members . . . steeped in the study of primary texts. The American Government concentration places special importance upon the study of the American Founding and critical moments in American political history: to the Declaration of Independence, the American Constitution, the Federalist Papers, Lincoln's speeches, and Progressive writings." Trendy classes do not get in the way. "Novelty is not big on this campus," says a professor. "There are no feminist, ethnic, or gay and lesbian studies here."

Biology is a department noted for its family atmosphere, its excellent teaching, and its rigorous courses.

Theology majors become well-acquainted with the Catholic tradition, sources say.

Admirably, the history department requires majors to take two survey courses each in "World Civilization" and "United States History," plus seven more intermediate-level courses and three seminars, as well as foreign language study, "Introduction to Computers," general

VITAL STATISTICS

Religious affiliation: *Roman Catholic*
Total enrollment: *1,706*
Total undergraduates: *1,706*
SAT CR/Verbal midrange: *420–560*
SAT Math midrange: *450–570*
ACT midrange: *20–24*
Applicants: *1,843*
Applicants accepted: *64%*
Accepted applicants who enrolled: *26%*
Tuition (general/out of state): *$27,622*
Tuition (in state): *N/A*
Room and board: *$10,094–10,774*
Freshman retention rate: *63%*
Graduation rate (4 yrs.): *32%*
Graduation rate (6 yrs.): *39%*
Courses with fewer than 20 students: *96%*
Student-faculty ratio: *16:1*
Courses taught by graduate students: *none*
Students living on campus: *43%*
Students in fraternities: *6%*
Students in sororities: *5%*
Students receiving need-based financial aid: *84%*
Avg. student-loan debt of a recent graduating class: *$21,602*
Most popular majors: *biology, business management, elementary education*
Guaranteed housing for 4 years? *yes*

CAMPUS POLITICS: GREEN LIGHT

There is a widespread atmosphere of acceptance and inclusion on campus. Administrators relate that "students will find that we Catholics at Belmont are peculiarly open to discussion; if we are all seeking truth together, there should be no problem wherever we're going." That commitment to open inquiry is substantial: Belmont Abbey continues to impress those looking for a faithful Catholic environment. Recently, the school eliminated health care coverage for procedures and devices—such as abortion, contraception, and sterilization—that violate church teachings. It has fought back against the Obama administration mandate requiring that all employers offer such coverage, with a high-profile lawsuit (filed along with many other religious institutions) that is likely to reach the U.S. Supreme Court. Yet just 55 or 60 percent of students at the college identify as Catholics, and the school's ability to balance its Catholic commitments with an approach that welcomes non-Catholics is a testament to its strength.

One teacher says, "Belmont is a comfortable mix of everything from orthodox Catholics to open atheists. This has provided wonderful interreligious discussions inside and outside of the classroom." His colleague agrees: "There is no department where conservative or religious students would feel unwelcome....While there are liberal-minded and conservative-minded professors here, they do not impose their personal ideologies in the classroom." Yet another faculty member relates, "I am not Catholic, and I have felt welcome in all circumstances on campus. And to my knowledge, students do not feel excluded because of their faith, or lack of it."

electives, and upper-level classes in English and theology.

The school has taken advantage of its location near NASCAR's headquarters to create a Motorsports Management Program—the first four-year business degree of its kind. It is swiftly growing in size and prestige. A participant writes, "The board of directors is basically a 'who's who' of motorsports. The contacts that can be made in the industry are unlike anything else. Also, the internships that are required are incredible opportunities."

The Honors Institute at the Abbey provides students with up to $20,000 in scholarships annually and allows them to work with faculty on independent study projects and to engage in cultural activities outside the classroom. A student must maintain a minimum GPA of 3.5 to remain in the program. One of these 14 honors students exclaims, "The Honors Institute here at Belmont is wonderful! It is not for the fainthearted, however! We concentrate on Plato, Aristophanes, Aquinas, Aristotle, Augustine, Bacon, Hobbes, Machiavelli. At no or minimal cost, we attend arts events throughout the semester, such as operas, ballets, and concerts." Honors professors receive high reviews from colleagues and students alike. Says one faculty member, "I have been impressed with the care and professionalism that Dr. Gene Thuot brings to the honors program he directs."

Teachers praised by students include Elizabeth Baker, Sheila Reilly, and Robert Tompkins in biology; Simon Donoghue in theater; Mary Ellen Weir in English; Jane Russell, OSF, and David Williams in theology; Stephen Brosnan in mathematics and physics; and Angela Blackwood in accounting.

First-Year Symposium instructors serve as primary academic advisers for students. After a student declares a major, a professor from within the department will become his adviser. Each semester, the student must meet with him to discuss his choice of course work. Students find the Academic Resource Center very useful. The center offers tutoring by faculty and peers for a number of courses across the academic disciplines.

Despite a student-faculty ratio of 16 to 1, only 4 percent of classes contain more than 20 students, and the school maintains an average class size of 17. Strong relationships are fostered between professors and their charges. A professor says that John Henry Newman's motto, "heart speaks to heart," could describe faculty-student relationships at the Abbey.

While the language studies program offers no majors, introductory and intermediate courses are taught in Spanish, French, Italian, and Latin. The school provides language-intensive studies overseas, as well as an International Leadership Semester in Rome and the School of Field Studies.

Student Life: Snowball fights with monks

Students overwhelmingly report that Belmont Abbey is a welcoming place, in part thanks to the hospitality of its ubiquitous monks. One student remarks, "Something that I've found very neat is the way the monks are so involved with the school. They are regularly walking around campus, eating with us in the cafeteria, or sitting in on a few of our classes."

One teacher says, "Belmont is a comfortable mix of everything from orthodox Catholics to open atheists. This has provided wonderful interreligious discussions inside and outside the classroom."

Says another, "The Benedictine commitment to hospitality affects everyone, even if you aren't Catholic. It's all about meeting each person as if he were Christ. Everyone here is trying to treat people that way, living so that 'in all things, God may be glorified.' And that means, for instance, trying to keep the bathrooms clean!"

A teacher says, "The student is encouraged to come here and learn how to be a good person in every way, to seek excellence in virtue . . . and to make the most of what they have been given. The emphasis at Belmont is on a balance of all the elements that make up the human person."

The quaint town of Belmont (pop. 15,000) is 10 miles west and across the Catawba River from Charlotte, the largest city in the Carolinas and the "melting pot" of the South. Belmont is located two hours from the Great Smoky Mountains and four hours from the North Carolina coast.

The Abbey's 650-acre wooded campus is home to the Belmont Abbey Monastery, the Saint Joseph Adoration Chapel, the Lourdes Grotto, and the Abbey Basilica. Most of the Gothic Revival buildings were designed and built by the monks themselves in the 19th century.

For many of the students, the 20 or so monks on campus are confessors, counselors, mentors, and friends who make the college a "real home away from home," as a student

SUGGESTED CORE

1. English 201, World Literature (*closest match*)
2. Honors 288, History of Ideas I (Classical and Christian Perspectives)
3. Theology 105, Introduction to Scripture
4. Honors 240, Classics of Christian Theology & Spirituality or Political Science 402, Medieval Political Philosophy
5. Political Science 403, Early Modern Political Philosophy
6. English 410/411, Shakespeare: Tragedies/ Comedies
7. History 203, U.S. History, 1492–1877
8. Honors 289, History of Ideas II (Modern Perspectives) or Political Science 404, Late Modern Political Philosophy

reports. A senior wrote in *The Crusader* student newspaper, "I love the fact that we get to learn from, take classes with, go on retreats with, eat with, watch basketball games with, laugh at, get into snowball fights with, cheer for, and mourn with the monks."

A resident remarks, "It's a beautiful campus, with brick Gothic architecture, lush landscaping, yet you can see Charlotte on the horizon." Says another insider, "There's lots to like here. It's a unique, warm, and friendly place, full of very nice people; there's a real atmosphere of peace, harmony, and spiritual goodness. The location is superb and physically beautiful; it's right off the highway and close to shopping centers and cultural events, but also has lovely architecture, tall old trees, and the charm of a little town."

All unmarried, full-time students must live on campus unless they live within commuting distance with a parent or legal guardian, or they are older than 22 when they begin classes or are enrolled as an Adult Degree Program student.

Housing includes three residence halls and a four-building apartment complex where men and women live on separate floors. Overnight guests in student housing can stay only with students of the same sex. Intervisitation hours are limited. A student comments, "The resident assistants are very helpful and do a very good job."

Extramarital sexual activity is forbidden by the school, and violators of the policy face punishments, which can include expulsion.

Only 5 percent of women and 6 percent of men belong to one of the four sororities and three fraternities.

At Belmont Abbey, alcohol is not permitted in public areas of residence halls, in the two halls primarily designated housing for first-year and second-year students, or outside on campus grounds; however, 21-year-old students are free to imbibe in their rooms. Kegs and grain alcohol are prohibited, as are any devices or activities that have the primary purpose of consuming alcohol quickly to achieve inebriation.

The Campus Activities Board sponsors social weekends, dances, theatrical performers, comedians, musical performers, coffeehouse artists, lectures, and other special events. Students gather frequently at the Holy Grounds coffee shop for socializing.

A sophomore remarks, "There's a lot of fun community service events, plenty of intramural sports to choose from, Greek life, households . . . and if they don't have a particular group, they'll probably help you form it."

The monks gather in the Abbey Basilica to pray the canonical hours or celebrate Mass four times a day. The students are under the spiritual care of the monks, eucharistic adoration is available daily, and confession every day except Sunday. Each year a group of faculty, staff, monks, and students attend the March for Life in Washington. The Felix Hintemeyer Catholic Leadership Award provides full scholarships for qualifying students.

The Belmont Abbey College Crusaders participate in the NCAA Division II Conference Carolinas. Abbey Athletics consists of 19 varsity teams and two men's junior varsity teams (baseball and basketball). The Crusaders compete at the varsity level in men's and women's lacrosse, basketball, cross-country, golf, soccer, baseball/softball, tennis, track and field, and volleyball. Additionally, men may wrestle. The renovated Wheeler Athletic Center has a new fitness center, an athletic training facility, and auxiliary gyms.

In 2011 the school reported 17 burglaries as the only crimes on campus.

Tuition in 2012–13 was $27,622 for entering students, with room and board ranging from $10,094 to $10,774. Some 84 percent of students at the college received need-based financial aid. Students in 2011 graduated with an average of $21,602 in loans.

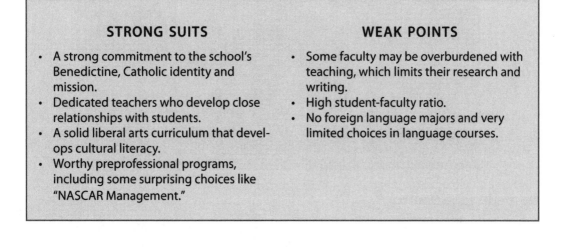

STRONG SUITS	WEAK POINTS
• A strong commitment to the school's Benedictine, Catholic identity and mission.	• Some faculty may be overburdened with teaching, which limits their research and writing.
• Dedicated teachers who develop close relationships with students.	• High student-faculty ratio.
• A solid liberal arts curriculum that develops cultural literacy.	• No foreign language majors and very limited choices in language courses.
• Worthy preprofessional programs, including some surprising choices like "NASCAR Management."	

Berry College

Rome, Georgia • www.berry.edu

Nestled in the South

Founded in 1902, Berry became a four-year college in 1930. Berry boasts a fine, committed faculty, and one that is less afflicted with postmodern pathologies than the staff at better-known colleges. Particularly impressive is the refreshing campus climate, where students are friendly and professors for the most part care about their students' educations.

Academic Life: Diamonds in the kudzu

Berry College's general-education requirements are weak. The most politicized classes, sources report, are the two required English composition courses (English 101 and 102) and the mandatory class, "Introduction to Speech." One faculty member says the English composition sequence is where "virtually all the professors favor students who adopt their views. Not surprisingly, these courses are the least popular at Berry." Fortunately, that's the worst curricular silliness you'll likely find at Berry; there are so far no school-wide requirements at Berry for gender, multicultural, or diversity studies.

The religion and philosophy department offers a "solid curriculum based on the study of the great books of the Western philosophical canon," says a professor. Says another,

"There's a strange kind of academic freedom that comes from being neither a state school nor a denominational school—in combination with a relatively diverse but still very liberal faculty and basically conservative students. It's one of the few places where both sides of *Roe v. Wade* can be discussed in class." Majors take an introductory class, a course in critical thinking or symbolic logic, and one course each in ancient/medieval philosophy and modern philosophy. This curriculum provides a solid overview of the discipline and "successfully avoids the twin perils of an overly analytic approach that ignores the history of the subject and of trendy Continental postmodernism," the professor adds. "The religion-in-life program is especially vital," says one professor who reports that he finds "faith flourishing" there.

The small history department at Berry wins accolades. As one professor tells us, "Courses that may not be so fashionable elsewhere (for example, military history) are offered regularly." Another says the department "has almost no 'social history' and is strong in both American and medieval." Here majors are required to take strong survey courses in "World History to 1550," "World History since 1550," "American History to 1877," "American History since 1877," and "Historiography," plus three upper-level electives in both American and European and/or world history.

The English department is said to be plagued with political correctness; there is a required multicultural literature class, and some determined professors use any and all teaching material to promote their private agendas, students report. However, the department offers many solid courses, and the requirements for a major are quite comprehensive and traditional. English majors must complete an introductory course and a course on the "Western Literary Tradition," as well as one class each in pre-1800 British and post-1800 British literature, American literature, multicultural literature, and a senior-level class ("Studies in Cinema," "Studies in Southern Literature," "Studies in Genre," for example).

According to one faculty member, there are a number of excellent teachers in the government and international studies department. Students should seek out the courses that focus on "philosophy, the connections between religion and politics, [and]

VITAL STATISTICS

Religious affiliation: *none*
Total enrollment: *2,166*
Total undergraduates: *2,041*
SAT CR/Verbal midrange: *520–630*
SAT Math midrange: *510–620*
ACT midrange: *composite 24–29*
Applicants: *3,485*
Applicants accepted: *66%*
Accepted applicants who enrolled: *27%*
Tuition (general/out of state) and fees: *$27,650*
Tuition (in state): *N/A*
Room and board: *$9,679*
Freshman retention rate: *75%*
Graduation rate (4 yrs.): *54%*
Graduation rate (6 yrs.): *61%*
Courses with fewer than 20 students: *58%*
Student-faculty ratio: *13:1*
Courses taught by graduate students: *none*
Students living on campus: *86%*
Students in fraternities: *N/A*
Students in sororities: *N/A*
Students receiving need-based financial aid: *95%*
Avg. student-loan debt of a recent graduating class: *$20,611*
Most popular majors: *animal science, communications, psychology*
Guaranteed housing for 4 years? *yes*

the American Founding." Students majoring in government must complete a departmental curriculum that includes "American National Government" and "Ancient Political Philosophy" in addition to several other worthy courses.

In the sciences, the physics department is particularly strong, with faculty members who are active researchers as well as devoted teachers. "They approach physics as an integral part of the liberal arts," says a Berry professor. The college's first-rate program in animal science boasts a high student acceptance rate into veterinary school and is one of Berry's most popular majors. A professor in another department calls Berry's animal science program "the best in the country connected with a four-year college."

Weaker areas at Berry include the education program, which is also one of the school's most popular majors. It is "good at placing graduates in schools but has the same problems and deficiencies as education schools elsewhere," says a faculty member. Marketing and management in the business school contain "the highest concentration of deadwood at the college," says a teacher. Other disciplines in the business school, such as economics and accounting, get higher marks.

Another strong program is the communications department, which is both academically sound and politically diverse, a professor tells us. Berry also offers preprofessional classes in dentistry, law, medicine, pharmacy, and veterinary medicine; however, faculty members tell us that students majoring in the humanities tend to be much more intellectually curious than their preprofessional peers.

With just 2,041 undergraduates, Berry College can offer a student-faculty ratio of 13 to 1. As a professor explains, "Faculty here tend to 'be around' and to give students lots of attention. The result is we have 'high maintenance' students—in the good sense, and there's a real academic culture here." At least one student agrees, "Trust me, it would be hard to find a more helpful and willing bunch of professors."

Highly praised professors include Peter Lawler and Eric Sands in government; Chaitram Singh and Kirsten Taylor in international relations; Jonathan Atkins and Larry Marvin in history; Bob Frank ("a legendary teacher") and Randy Richardson ("one of the country's best forensics coaches") in communications; Thomas Carnes in accounting; and Michael Papazian in philosophy.

The most willing students can be found in the college's honors program, which requires an ongoing 3.5 GPA. One faculty member says the honors program is particularly strong at the freshman level, when students are required to complete two three-credit honors colloquia. The first is "Perennial Questions," which focuses on the Great Books and ideas of the West. "My students read Aristophanes, Sophocles, Plato, and the Bible," says a professor. The second colloquium is called "Democracy and Its Friendly Critics" and concentrates on the American Founding and the writings of de Tocqueville. An honors student says this course made "a great use of literature to help us build our understanding of democratic society." Additionally, honors students take three seminars together (most of which fulfill general-education requirements) and then, as juniors and seniors, two honors thesis courses that culminate in a traditional research paper or some other "performative effort." Seniors defend their theses during their last semester at Berry.

> The religion and philosophy programs at this secular school offer a "solid curriculum based on the study of the great books of the Western philosophical canon," a professor says.

The honors program provides a distinctive exchange opportunity at the University of Glasgow, where students take "The Ideas and Influences of the Scottish Enlightenment" as well as two or three classes in their major or minor. Other study-abroad programs are offered around the world, from Egypt to New Zealand. Berry also helps students find international internships in a number of subject areas and service opportunities around the world.

When it comes to foreign languages, the school is very limited: Berry offers only Spanish, French, and German. Students majoring in foreign languages are strongly encouraged to study abroad in France, Germany, Spain, or Central or South America.

Student Life: Chicken people

The deer outnumber the students at Berry College on the largest contiguous campus out in the country, with more than 26,000 acres of mostly forest land. The enormous campus is ideal for outdoorsy students. Many of the buildings on campus are stately stone structures modeled on those at Oxford.

Berry has more than deer. It also has "chicken people." That's the campus term for those fortunate students who have gotten scholarships from WinShape, the charitable foundation of the Chick-fil-A restaurants. At Berry, 125 students receive a $4,000 per year scholarship toward the cost of tuition. (Berry often supplements the scholarship with additional aid.) The grant requires attendance at weekly meetings, participation at regular leadership discussion groups and in community service, and the practice of a "Christian lifestyle." Although Chick-fil-A work experience is no longer required for recipients, it is preferred.

Berry College students must attend a minimum of 24 cultural events (three per

SUGGESTED CORE

1. English 337, Western Literary Tradition (*closest match*)
2. Philosophy 351, Ancient and Medieval Philosophy
3. Religion 101/102, Interpreting the Old Testament/ New Testament
4. Religion 103, Introduction to Christian Theology or Government 318, Ancient Political Philosophy (*closest match*)
5. Government 319, Modern Political Philosophy
6. English 401WI, Shakespeare
7. History 205, American History to 1877
8. Philosophy 357, Later Modern Philosophy (*closest match*)

semester) to qualify for graduation. Qualifying events include concerts, plays, lectures, panel discussions, debates, convocations, and poetry readings. Students say that there is always something worth doing on campus—get-togethers, concerts, campus activities, and club meetings.

A number of academic and professional organizations add to the Berry curriculum. The school hosts the Astronomical Society, Block and Bridle club for animal science students, Forensic Union for debaters, Model United Nations, and Politics and Law Society. Campus media groups include the *Cabin Log* yearbook, *Campus Carrier* newspaper, *Ramifications* literary magazine, and Viking Fusion multimedia group, which maintains a news and entertainment website.

The college does sponsor a few multicultural organizations (a Black Student Alliance, Hispanic culture group, and international club) and several political organizations: Amnesty International, College Republicans and Young Democrats, EMPOWER women's group, and Students Against Violating the Earth all have a presence on campus. Performing arts groups include the College Theater Company, men's and women's singing ensembles, and a women's dance team.

In the summer of 2009, Berry College became a provisional member of the NCAA Division III, and the college now holds dual membership in both the NCAA and the NAIA. The Berry College Vikings and Lady Vikings play in blue and silver on 17 different teams. The school's Society of Outdoor Life and Exploration program offers climbing, caving, and hiking excursions for free or at nominal cost.

Although it is not a distinctly Christian school, Berry retains its initial commitment to "the furthering of Christian values." The school pledges "an interdenominational, ecumenical approach to Christian faith and values," and most religious opportunities at Berry are Christian. The Baptist Student Union, Canterbury Club Episcopal group, Catholic Student Association (which provides a weekly Mass), Fellowship of Christian Athletes, Presbyterian Student Fellowship, and Wesley Foundation all meet regularly, as does the school's Jewish Study Group. Three picturesque chapels are maintained on campus, and Mount Berry Church meets weekly with college chaplain Dale McConkey serving as pastor.

No Greek life exists, and the entire campus is dry. Students are not forbidden to drink off campus, but opportunities are generally limited to of-age upperclassmen, who can frequent the few restaurants and bars in nearby Rome. Many students report that the college borders on being a "suitcase school," where people pack up and go home on weekends.

Though Berry College is a relatively small school, it still offers a wide variety of residential options, from traditional dormitory halls to a log-cabin cottage that houses 17 women. Thomas Berry Hall (for women) includes two-, three-, four-, and six-bedroom suites, most of which have full kitchens. The newest, Audrey B. Morgan Residence Hall and Deerfield Hall, include scenic views and outdoor fireplaces. The school's 16 townhouses, popular with upperclassmen, can accommodate 187 students. Most residential halls are single sex, although one coed hall is available. Berry College is a residential school, and students are required to live on campus; the only exceptions are seniors and students whose families live within 40 miles.

It's not surprising that crime is infrequent at this secluded school. A Berry student made headlines in 2010 for "attempted aggravated child molestation," but this was a shocking exception. In 2011 there were reports of five burglaries, one motor vehicle theft, and one forcible sex offense.

Tuition at Berry College ran $27,650 in 2012–13, plus an average room and board of $9,679. Nearly every single Berry student receives some type of aid, averaging $10,700, and the average student-loan debt carried by a Berry graduate is $20,611.

STRONG SUITS	WEAK POINTS
• Highly qualified faculty committed to teaching first.	• English department is said to be highly politicized, infused with multiculturalism.
• Most "core" course options are solid and foundational, not esoteric or politicized.	• Education, marketing, and management departments are academically weak— but much too popular.
• The physics department is highly regarded, and the veterinary science program is one of the nation's finest.	• Isolated location; there are literally more deer than people on campus.
• Plenty of religiously committed but nonstodgy students offer support and encouragement, plus outreach opportunities.	

Boston College

Chestnut Hill, Massachusetts • www.bc.edu

Jesuit Brahmin

Boston College, founded by the Jesuits in 1863, has recently focused on the fundamentals of liberal education and slowly but steadily rededicated itself to the school's Catholic identity. Despite its overall political and theological liberalism, ambitious students eager to attend an elite college with an ongoing faith tradition in a historic American city ought to consider BC.

Academic Life: Four years BC

Boston College is widely known for fostering first-rate classroom discussions and close relationships between teachers and students. "Professors here have teaching as their prime motivating factor," a student says. "Very few are here for just research and publishing. Faculty members jump at the chance to interact with students."

For an institution of its size, BC does a decent job of requiring a basic liberal arts education. Says a teacher, "The Jesuit presence . . . continues to influence the way in which the 'great questions' are introduced and discussed, and there is clearly a sense that the purpose of a university is to shape the character of students by encouraging the discussion of serious things by serious people." Trendy or ideological courses are far outnumbered by solid, traditional classes.

The worthiest academic choice at BC is its honors program. Freshmen and sophomores take a six-credit course titled "The Western Cultural Tradition." Reading only primary texts, students in this course begin with ancient Greek literature and philosophy and end with major cultural, historical, and philosophical works of modernity. As juniors, students take an advanced seminar called "The Twentieth Century and the Tradition." Seniors in the honors program end their BC years by writing a senior thesis or by participating in an integrative seminar.

The College of Arts and Sciences offers the Perspectives program, a four-year interdisciplinary program "grounded in the great texts of Western Culture that seeks to integrate the humanities and natural sciences." All four Perspectives courses are yearlong and double credit, with an evening class component, and each fulfills certain core requirements. One faculty member says the Perspectives program is a popular way for students to fulfill their core requirements.

The Boston College Core also includes a two-term survey of modern history, a two-course sequence in theology, and a math course. Moreover, undergraduates must also demonstrate proficiency in a foreign language.

The PULSE Program for Service Learning, run by the philosophy department, operates in a manner similar to that of Perspectives, using some of the same texts, but it focuses more on ethics and politics. In addition to performing the course work, students in the program are placed with a service organization within the Boston community, where they work throughout the year.

Some of the strongest departments at BC are in the traditional liberal arts disciplines, such as philosophy—where the university's Catholic heritage is central, more so than in the theology department. "Philosophy takes its Catholic character seriously," says one professor, "and this informs its hiring and its course offerings," such as courses in Catholic apologetics. Noteworthy faculty members include Richard Cobb-Stevens (emeritus); Joseph Flanagan, SJ; Jorge L.A. Garcia; Gary Michael Gurtler, SJ; Richard Kearney; famous apologetics author Peter Kreeft; and Ronald Tacelli, SJ.

VITAL STATISTICS

Religious affiliation: *Roman Catholic*
Total enrollment: *14,513*
Total undergraduates: *9,088*
SAT CR/Verbal midrange: *610–700*
SAT Math midrange: *640–730*
ACT midrange: *29–32*
Applicants: *32,974*
Applicants accepted: *29%*
Accepted applicants who enrolled: *25%*
Tuition (general/out of state): *$43,878*
Tuition (in state): *N/A*
Room and board: *$12,608 (average)*
Freshman retention rate: *91%*
Graduation rate (4 yrs.): *91%*
Graduation rate (6 yrs.): *91%*
Courses with fewer than 20 students: *48%*
Student-faculty ratio: *14:1*
Courses taught by graduate students: *not provided*
Students living on campus: *80%*
Students in fraternities: *N/A*
Students in sororities: *N/A*
Students receiving financial aid: *70%*
Avg. student-loan debt of a recent graduating class: *$30,998*
Most popular majors: *communications, economics, finance*
Guaranteed housing for 4 years? *no*

CAMPUS POLITICS: GREEN LIGHT

Boston College is one of the Jesuit colleges that has long been vexed by secularizers and heretics, but unlike most of its peer institutions, it is moving in the right direction—slowly but inexorably, with the clear support of the current administration. For instance, BC returned crucifixes and other Catholic images to its classrooms after decades of their absence. (They were taken down under the excuse that federal aid to the college demanded it. Which was, of course, a lie.) This return of Jesus to Jesuit classrooms came by direct request of the college's president, Rev. William P. Leahy, SJ, according to the *Boston College Observer*. "Bravo for Boston College!" says Patrick J. Reilly, president of the Cardinal Newman Society, a Catholic campus watchdog organization. "For Catholics, outward signs, symbols, and practices of our faith are an important part of relating to God in a material world."

Unsurprisingly, a number of faculty responded with outrage. "I can hardly imagine a more effective way to denigrate the faculty of an educational institution. If that has been the purpose of the administration of Boston College, I congratulate them, as they have succeeded brilliantly," sniffed the chairman of the chemistry department, reports the *Observer*. At least one professor, the paper said, is "refusing to teach in classrooms adorned by a crucifix even if he should have to move his class to a different room at his own expense." But the days when Boston College employed radical feminist Mary Daly—who refused to teach male students in her women's studies classes—are long over. Daly left BC in 1999, and this mortal coil in 2010.

Another outstanding department at BC is political science, where, according to one professor, students will find "a seriousness about the study of politics in its broader theoretical and historical context, and a very strong commitment to undergraduate and graduate teaching." The department's requirements are solid, including courses in American politics, comparative politics, international politics, and political theory. Distinguished teachers here include Nasser Behnegar, Christopher Bruell, Robert K. Faulkner, Christopher J. Kelly, Marc Landy, R. Shep Melnick, Susan Shell, Peter Skerry, and widely read liberal commentator Alan Wolfe.

The English department has broad, detailed requirements. Beginning with the class of 2015, requirements for its majors include a freshman writing course and 33 credits from the department itself. These must include Studies in Poetry and Studies in Narrative, usually taken in sequence in the sophomore year. Majors are also required to take nine credits in British or American literature, pre-1900. The final required course is Theories and Methods of Interpretation, which emphasizes disciplinary approaches to literary and cultural study.

The history department has also changed its requirements, beginning with the class of 2014. Students must take two history core classes and two U.S. history survey courses. They must also take a course in the study and writing of history and two non-Western history classes. Additionally, majors must take four upper-division courses. Those not writing a thesis must include a senior colloquium or a senior seminar in their upper-division course mix.

Students report that BC's theology department is disappointing, in part because "it has placed a lot of emphasis on interreligious dialogue," says a former student familiar with the program. Expect plenty of courses like "Liberation Christology" and "Women and the Church." One bonus for theology students is BC's membership in the Boston Theological Institute, a consortium of theology faculties primarily in the Boston-Newton-Cambridge area that allows advanced students to take classes at Harvard Divinity School, Gordon-Conwell Theological Seminary, the Boston University School of Theology, and other schools. Students taking theology at BC should seek out Stephen F. Brown; David Hollenbach, SJ; Frederick Lawrence; John J. Paris, SJ; Margaret A. Schatkin; and Thomas E. Wangler, our sources report.

Boston College's philosophy department "takes its Catholic character seriously," says one professor, "and this informs its hiring and its course offerings." But theology places too much "emphasis on inter-religious dialogue," says a student.

Other highly recommended faculty across the college include Michael J. Connolly in Slavic and Eastern languages, Thomas Epstein in the honors program, Thomas C. Chiles in biology, Michael Barry in finance, and Avner Ash, Gerard E. Keough (Emeritus), and Mark Reeder in mathematics.

Overall, besides philosophy and political science, the school's strongest disciplines are economics, biology, chemistry, physics, and history. One professor says the English department is generally solid but possesses "significant weaknesses." The finance department also has a fine reputation; the associate dean of the school of management told the *Boston College Chronicle* that the rising number of finance majors "is the fruit of a 'virtuous circle' of renowned faculty raising the stature of a department from which employers want to pluck talented graduates." The natural science departments have grown stronger in recent years, and the university offers plenty of opportunities to do real and worthy research in laboratory environments.

Weaker departments, students report, include the Lynch School of Education and the sociology department. The latter, says one student, "is at the center of leftist activism on campus and should be avoided." The description for one sociology course, "Gender and Society," promises to "examine gender primarily as a social and structural construct." Another student describes courses on "child development, gender, et cetera" at the education school as "watered-down and liberal."

"Professors are quite approachable," says a student. The school's collegiality and good student-teacher ratio of 14 to 1 make possible close student-faculty relationships. Before entering Boston College, each student is paired with a faculty member who advises him; once he declares a major, he gets a professor within the chosen department.

Over the past decade or so, Boston College has grown to become a serious research university, and as one faculty member tells us, "This has placed inevitable strains on the perennial conflict between research and teaching." He explains, "Excellence in teaching is expected. Nonetheless, hiring and promotion decisions continue to emphasize the publication of books, or the equivalent, and faculty are always aware of the competing demands on their time."

Among the languages offered at BC are Arabic, Bulgarian, Chinese, French, German, Greek and Latin, Hebrew, Italian, Japanese, Polish, Portuguese, Russian, Spanish and Turkish. Students can elect majors in Classics, French, German, Italian, Spanish, and Russian. Around 40 percent of BC undergraduates travel abroad in one of the 66 academic partnerships in any of 27 countries.

Student Life: View from the Heights

Boston offers splendid opportunities for the thousands of students attending more than 80 colleges in the area. The college offers 31 dormitories, with freshmen housed on the school's Newton Campus (a one-and-a-half-mile bus ride from the main campus) or the Upper Campus. More than 80 percent of undergraduates live in university housing. Residence halls separate men and women by floor. There are no single-sex dorms available, and while the housing office says that members of the opposite sex cannot stay in residence halls overnight, that rule is not strictly enforced.

Strong drink is readily available and joyously consumed at BC, but the administration has been cracking down on alcohol abuse, making it harder for underage students to obtain alcohol. For the most part, BC undergrads "are intellectually focused and serious about their studies," says one student. "At the same time, studies do not dominate their lives; they know how to let loose and have an active social life."

With about 130 registered undergraduate student organizations at BC to choose from, students should have no trouble finding clubs to fit their interests. BC has no fraternities or sororities. Student news publications include the twice-weekly *Heights* and the biweekly *Observer*, which defends Catholic orthodoxy and conservative principles on campus. BC has a vibrant music and arts scene, featuring jazz, classical, a cappella, folk, gospel, and swing.

In 2010, as in years past, the student government promoted on-campus events for National Coming Out Week. The campus gay, lesbian, and bisexual group is not sanctioned by the administration—unlike Allies, a campus "gay-straight alliance." BC's student guide was recently revised to state that any event featuring a speaker opposed to Catholic doctrine must be balanced by a speaker who affirms church teaching.

Boston College is not as uniformly liberal as most big-name colleges are these days, says a professor. "There is a definite conservative voice on the campus that university officials make no effort to discourage," he says. One notable exception occurred just a few days before a campus production of the *Vagina Monologues*, when the university held a campus-wide debate over the merits and shortcomings of the play—which in one scene celebrates the statutory rape of a young girl by an older woman. According to *The Observer*, the debate was heavily slanted in favor of the play: the five panelists included three tenured professors plus the executive director of the play. The lone voice opposing the play was a sophomore student. In their defense, the organizers of the debate claimed they could not find any faculty members who would speak against holding the *Monologues* on campus. If true, this speaks rather poorly for the school.

About 70 percent of Boston College students identify themselves as Catholic, but their degree of involvement in religious activities varies. Opportunities abound for student participation, including daily liturgies, small faith-sharing communities (CURA and Salt and Light), and student clubs. The Campus Ministry office offers ecumenical and Catholic worship services. It sponsors service programs such as 4Boston, whose volunteers work at shelters, lunch kitchens, schools, youth centers, hospitals, and live-in facilities. Catholic students who adhere to official church teaching should seek out the St. Thomas More Society, an orthodox Catholic student group, while those attached to traditional liturgies should attend the weekly Latin Mass offered at Boston's Cathedral of the Holy Cross.

The university fields 12 Division I varsity teams for men and 15 for women. The Boston College Eagles are particularly strong in basketball, football, and hockey. The university consistently ranks among the best in the nation in terms of Division I student-athlete graduation rates; its football team has one of the highest graduation rates of any Division I-A program in the country. The $27 million, 72,000-square-foot Yawkey Athletics Center opened in spring 2005, and the Newton Campus Field Hockey Complex was completed that fall.

Boston College's proximity to a major city makes it an occasional target for criminals. In 2011, the university reported seven forcible sex offenses, one aggravated assault, eight burglaries, and three stolen cars.

Boston College is an elite experience—a fact reflected in its price. Tuition and fees in 2012–13 were $43,878. Room and board were $12,608. Some 70 percent of the student body receives financial aid, while the university pledges to meet 100 percent of a student's financial need. Still, more than half the student body borrows money to pay for college, and the average student in the 2012 graduating class had $30,998 in student-loan debt.

STRONG SUITS	WEAK POINTS
• Elite, semi-Ivy reputation. • Trendy courses are far outnumbered by solid, traditional fare. • A first-rate Great Books–centered honors program. • Graduates in finance have a fast track to jobs in big Boston firms. • Terrific political science department.	• Aging, disgruntled, dissenting Catholics still prominent in some departments. • High tuition and high average student debt. • Education and sociology departments are mediocre hotbeds of radical activism.

Boston University

Boston, Massachusetts • www.bu.edu

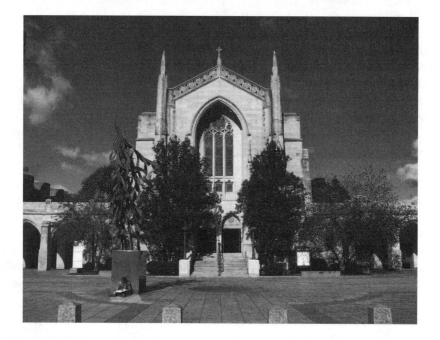

Keeping Faith

Founded in 1869 out of a former Vermont Bible college, Boston University is now the nation's fourth-largest private university. Thanks to the lasting work of the late John Silber (the former president whose policies seem largely intact for now), Boston University offers a true (if optional) core curriculum, providing students who seek it with the foundations of a liberal arts education. Serious students will choose to take the core's small, faculty-led seminars that explore the best works of literature, art and music, and social, religious, scientific, and philosophical thought.

Academic Life: Methodical ex-Methodists

BU offers more than 250 majors and minors. One student says that "selecting a major can be a bit overwhelming if you are undecided." Ambitious students should apply for an honors program in the College of Arts and Sciences, which consists of four special classes, one per semester, on liberal arts subjects with the college's best faculty. Students enjoy special activities and trips, especially involving the fine arts, and an annual lecture conducted by notable speakers. Honors classes may count toward fulfillment of core curriculum requirements.

Each full-time student has an adviser with whom to construct a particular program and with a choice of major receives advising in collaboration with that department. The advising program "is not very good unless you put effort into it," one student says.

The English department requires 11 courses, including literary analysis; a literature seminar; two surveys in British literature; a class on "Major Authors"; advanced-level courses in both early American literature and literary criticism; and a mandatory "diversity" class. Sadly, the department does not require a course centered on Shakespeare. But he is covered in surveys, and most of the department's courses focus on important writers and their works, not on ideology.

The history department offers a general major, along with specialty tracks, such as the U.S.A./Canada, European, world/regional history, and intellectual/cultural history. Students in the general-history program are required to take one course each in American, European, world, and premodern history. In addition, history majors must take the class "The Historian's Craft" and at least two seminars in any historical area.

Political science majors must take 11 courses, including a choice of three at the introductory level from a selection of five offerings in American politics, public policy, comparative politics, international relations, and political theory.

"One of the legacies of John Silber is the awarding of substantial prizes for excellence in teaching, awarded with much fanfare at commencement," says a professor. One English major says that "most professors that I've encountered are really willing to help you. Every professor has office hours, and if you make an effort they'll take an interest in you." Graduate students teach some introductory courses each year and lead almost all discussion and laboratory sections. One student warns, "Science TAs are often foreign and barely speak English." But "by your junior year, nearly all interaction is with professors," says another student.

Boston University has an impressive array of well-known scholars and writers. Students and faculty alike recommend noted conservative commentator Andrew Bacevich in international relations; William R. Keylor, Igor Lukes, and Nina Silber in

VITAL STATISTICS

Religious affiliation: *none*
Total enrollment: *32,439*
Total undergraduates: *18,140*
SAT CR/Verbal midrange: *570–670*
SAT Math midrange: *610–700*
ACT midrange: *26–30*
Applicants: *41,802*
Applicants accepted: *49%*
Accepted applicants who enrolled: *19%*
Tuition (general/out of state): *$42,994*
Tuition (in state): *N/A*
Room and board: *$13,190*
Freshman retention rate: *91%*
Graduation rate (4 yrs.): *80%*
Graduation rate (6 yrs.): *85%*
Courses with fewer than 20 students: *55%*
Student-faculty ratio: *13:1*
Courses taught by graduate students: *not provided*
Students living on campus: *80%*
Students in fraternities: *3%*
Students in sororities: *7%*
Students receiving need-based financial aid: *44%*
Avg. student-loan debt of a recent graduating class: *$36,488*
Most popular majors: *business/marketing, social sciences, journalism*
Guaranteed housing for 4 years? *yes*

CAMPUS POLITICS: GREEN LIGHT

Politics are not entirely absent from BU's classrooms. But things could be much, much worse. One conservative student says that liberal professors usually present both sides equally and fairly and welcome debate in class—even though some show their political prejudices by presenting the opposing viewpoint "so terribly that it looks pathetic." Says a professor, "One of the things I like about BU is that this is an institution that is always trying to get better. We are not afraid of self-criticism. There is no such thing as a 'political line' that dominates. My sense is that the BU faculty contains a healthy range of viewpoints."

In general, the students at BU seem more interested than the faculty in political activism and protest. One faculty member says that the student body is "less politicized and less politically active than seems to be the case elsewhere," and another says "much more of their energy goes into community service projects than into politics."

history; Charles Glenn in education; Roye Wates in music; Christopher Ricks, Robert Wexelblatt, and (*Night* author) Elie Wiesel in humanities; Robert Pinsky, Charles Rzepka, Christopher Martin, and Rosanna Warren in English; Charles Griswold, Krzysztof Michalski, and David Roochnik in philosophy; James J. Collins in engineering; Dorothy S. Clark and Michael Elasmar in communications; Sheldon Glashow in physics; Walter Clemens (emeritus), Walter D. Connor, and Sofía Pérez in political science; and David Eckel in religion.

Overall, the best departments are economics, biomedical engineering, philosophy, earth sciences, mathematics, and English. International relations, with a top-notch faculty, is one of the fastest growing majors. Reportedly, the most politicized departments are psychology and sociology, women's studies, and African American studies—in each of which some professors equate scholarship with activism.

Faculty members in the core curriculum program are known for being "scholarly, academic, and not biased at all," a student says. Another agreed that the program is "pretty evenhanded. 'Intro to Philosophy' is divided into Western and Eastern traditions so you get appropriate exposure to the classics." A professor adds that the core "is generally respectful of Western heritage and institutions, much more so than similar courses in other selective colleges."

In education, BU has a "commitment to forming teachers with solid liberal arts formations," says one professor. The School of Education has forged mutually beneficial links with inner-city schools in Boston and public schools in neighboring Chelsea.

The College of Communication hosts a number of learning laboratories. Among them are PRLab, AdLab, and BUTV10, "student-run production facilities that manage real-world public relations, advertising, and television campaigns," says the BU catalog.

Each year, nearly 2,300 students participate in study-abroad programs of BU in locations in 40 cities, throughout 27 countries, on six continents. Says a student: "BU has a phenomenal study-abroad program. I did two semesters in London and got to work in Parliament as a science adviser." BU also has an auxiliary campus in Washington, D.C., for students interested in government internships, and an auxiliary campus in Los Angeles focused on film and TV apprenticeships.

BU offers a large array of foreign languages, including Arabic, Chinese, French, German,

Greek (Classical and Modern), Hebrew, Hindi-Urdu, Italian, Japanese, Korean, Latin, Persian, Portuguese, Russian, Spanish, Turkish, and a number of African languages.

SUGGESTED CORE

The College of Arts and Sciences' Core Curriculum option suffices.

Student Life: Heart of the city

Boston is not so much a college town as a town full of colleges. To study and live in a city so rich in American history and culture is an education in itself. The campus is close to Fenway Park, home of the Red Sox. With easy access to Boston's rail-based mass transit system, "the T," the entire city is available for exploration.

Freshmen are required to live on campus, and Boston University guarantees four years of on-campus housing. According to one student, "For a school of this size, the housing is impressive; an eclectic mix of remodeled brownstone walk-ups on Bay State Road and modern high-rise towers on West Campus." Most freshmen live in large dormitories and can choose to live on single-sex floors or wings, single-sex dormitories, single-occupancy dorm rooms, specialty floors organized around academic interests, or apartment-style residences. The dorms at BU are all coed, but men and women are usually in separate sections with their own bathrooms.

Upperclassmen may opt for smaller residences, including one of more than 100 brownstones, some of which overlook the Charles River. Many of these residences are used as specialty houses where students with common academic or social interests—a foreign language, philosophy, engineering, writing, music, community service, or hospitality administration, for example—can live together. Students in the Wellness House, for instance, agree to forgo drugs, alcohol, and smoking.

A professor states that the core curriculum "is generally respectful of Western heritage and institutions, much more so than similar courses in other selective colleges."

In recent years, record numbers of Boston University students have sought on-campus housing, making competition for the most popular residences even fiercer.

There are more than 500 registered student clubs and organizations at BU, including many social, ethnic, and preprofessional groups, as well as both College Democrats and College Republicans and ACLU and Right to Life chapters. There are also 22 religious clubs that run the gamut from the Evangelical Real Life to the Zen Community. Marsh Chapel houses some dozen chaplains of various faiths and multiple weekly religious services.

The student-run *Daily Free Press* boasts the fourth-largest print run of Boston's daily newspapers; in addition to campus news, it reports on city, state, and national news. BU is a major force in the local arts scene. Notable arts organizations at BU include the Huntington Theatre Company, a professional theater in residence that is regarded as Boston's best.

The university is one of only a handful of schools nationwide offering its students ROTC programs in all three services: Army, Navy, and Air Force.

BU sports a College Republican club of a hundred or so members, but as a whole the student body does not seem to be overly politically active. Uniquely, at BU some people complain that the administration is more conservative than the students.

The university fields 23 NCAA Division I varsity sports, 13 for women and 10 for men, although there is no varsity baseball team. The Terrier's men's ice hockey team is almost always in the running for the NCAA title, and BU takes pride in sending more players to the NHL than any other college or university. Each semester, more than 7,000 students choose from 15 intramural and 33 club sports, ranging from sailing to the ever-popular ice broomball. According to one student, "The new athletic center is state of the art and includes a climbing wall, lazy river, and ice rink that doubles as one of the largest concert venues in the city." The Boathouse, one of the country's best rowing centers, is located along the banks of the Charles River, site of the international Head of the Charles regatta each fall.

While a no-drinking policy is strictly kept in the dorms, there is a party scene at BU, most of it off campus. There are frat parties, with 3 percent of men enrolled in a fraternity and 7 percent of women in a sorority. However, with BU's curriculum, parties do not seem to overwhelm schoolwork.

According to one student, "The crime rate is often secondary to student carelessness. There were a series of assaults late at night on students returning to campus from bars/parties." In response, the university has significantly improved late-night transportation options. In 2011 the school also reported 58 burglaries, six forcible sex offenses, two robberies, two aggravated assaults, and two car thefts.

Tuition for BU in 2012–13 was $42,994, plus $13,190 (minimum) for room and board. Admissions are need blind, but the school does not guarantee it will cover the full financial need for all applicants. Forty-four percent of students received need-based financial aid. The average recent graduate who borrowed emerged with a daunting $36,488 in student debt.

STRONG SUITS	WEAK POINTS
• An excellent (if optional) core curriculum sequence. • Political balance in the classroom and on campus. • Accessible, helpful teachers. • Good programs in economics, biomedical engineering, philosophy, earth sciences, mathematics, English, and international relations.	• Graduate teaching assistants lead some introductory classes—not always in comprehensible English. • Politicized programs in psychology and sociology, women's studies, and African American studies. • High tuition and high average student debt.

Bowdoin College

Brunswick, Maine • www.bowdoin.edu

Cold Comforts

This fabled New England liberal arts college founded in 1794 does a decent job of living up to its reputation. At Bowdoin, students really do discuss ideas with their professors and classmates. The campus is indeed gorgeous in any season, although "it's really cold in winter!" shivers one student. Campus election polls continue to reveal a left-wing dominance, but outside the classroom the college has seen an emergence of a more balanced debate. Still, academic life is the highest priority at Bowdoin, whose students by and large graduate as well-informed and well-read citizens of the republic. And that's saying a lot.

Academic Life: Remembering Maine

In lieu of a core curriculum, Bowdoin students complete a series of broad distribution requirements in the following fields: mathematical, computational, or statistical reasoning; inquiry in the natural sciences; international perspectives; visual and performing arts; and the diversity category called "Exploring Social Differences." The choice of eligible courses in each field is broad and rather lax, allowing students to pursue either foundational subjects or idiosyncratic curiosity.

VITAL STATISTICS

Religious affiliation: *none*
Total enrollment: *1,778*
Total undergraduates: *1,778*
SAT CR/Verbal midrange:
    670–750
SAT Math midrange:
    660–740
ACT midrange: *30–33*
Applicants: *6,554*
Applicants accepted: *16%*
Accepted applicants who
    enrolled: *46%*
Tuition (general/out of
    state): *$44,118*
Tuition (in state): *N/A*
Room and board: *$12,010*
Freshman retention rate:
    96%
Graduation rate (4 yrs.): *88%*
Graduation rate (6 yrs.): *92%*
Courses with fewer than 20
    students: *68%*
Student-faculty ratio: *9:1*
Courses taught by graduate
    students: *none*
Students living on campus:
    92%
Students in fraternities:
    none
Students in sororities: *none*
Students receiving need-
    based financial aid: *46%*
Avg. student-loan debt of a
    recent graduating class:
    $17,569
Most popular majors:
    *government, economics,
    biology*
Guaranteed housing for 4
    years? *no*

During orientation, each freshman is assigned a premajor faculty adviser with similar academic interests; once he declares a major, the student switches to a faculty member in his department. Thanks to these advisers, students who seek help get it. And seek it they should, because the curriculum itself provides little guidance. Students could theoretically graduate by taking courses such as "Music of the Caribbean" and "Lawn Boy Meets Valley Girl: Gender and the Suburbs" and nearly skipping American or Western history, art, and literature altogether.

Bowdoin's most salient virtue is its commitment to teaching over research and publishing. Bowdoin encourages its faculty members to spend most of their time in the classroom, and students report that faculty are extraordinarily accessible and sincerely concerned with their education. Says one student, "The best aspect of Bowdoin is the professors and how they interact with the students. They are friends as well as mentors, and students have dinner and go bowling with them." If a student is having trouble in class, odds are that the Bowdoin professor will invite him to office hours. To give faculty time for teaching and advising, Bowdoin limits professors' loads to just two courses per semester and maintains the student-faculty ratio at an excellent 9 to 1, which allows for very intimate classroom settings. Many courses are presented in cozy seminars. Over 60 percent of students participate in at least one independent study course, working closely with a professor. Freshman seminars, meant to help newcomers hone their academic skills, are required; students may choose from topics such as "Living in the Sixteenth Century," a philosophy course on "Love," and the gender and women's studies department's "Lesbian Personae" as well as the rather specialized "Queer Gardens." There are no graduate students at Bowdoin and hence no graduate teaching assistants. In foreign language classes, upperclassmen—mostly native speakers—sometimes lead discussion classes and run the language lab.

On the whole, courses at Bowdoin are rigorous, and students report that earning good grades demands a genuine commitment to learning. However, there are some notoriously easy courses and in some departments grades are inflated. Good grades in social science courses are much easier to come by than in the quantitative sciences. The best departments at Bowdoin are government, economics, and some of the hard sciences.

In the government department, all majors must take classes in four fields: American government, comparative politics, political theory, and international relations. Classes on the U.S. Constitution and American political philosophy are required. Other courses range from "Classical Political Philosophy" to "The Politics of Ethnicity."

History majors do not have to take a single Western civilization or American history class but must take at least four courses in either African, East Asian, Latin American, or South Asian history.

While its English faculty offers some fashionable courses in feminist and ethnic literature, it also serves up more traditional fare. English majors take 10 required courses, at least three of which must focus on pre-1800 British or Irish literature, and one must be chosen from "literature of the Americas." Bowdoin does not offer English composition courses, but the college does make an effort— a successful one, most students say—to continue its strong rhetorical tradition with the Bowdoin Writing Project, a peer tutoring program that links qualified students with those who would like to improve their writing.

Faculty most often lauded by Bowdoin students are Paul N. Franco, Jean M. Yarbrough, Richard E. Morgan, Christian P. Potholm II, and Allen L. Springer in government; Thomas Baumgarte and Stephen Naculich in physics; Gregory P. DeCoster, Guillermo Herrera, and B. Zorina Khan in economics; John C. Holt in religion; Steven R. Cerf in German; Robert K. Greenlee in music; William C. VanderWolk in French; and Sarah F. McMahon and Patrick J. Rael in history. One student calls Greenlee a "genius," while Franco and Yarbrough are mentioned again and again as excellent government theory professors. Bowdoin students also highly praise Richard Morgan, some calling him "awesome" and "very learned, a great lecturer with a wealth of knowledge." Greg DeCoster is "so engaged and enthusiastic about his topic [economics], you could listen to him for hours."

The faculty at Bowdoin are predominantly leftist. One alumnus—otherwise a huge fan of the college, who "hated to leave"—admits that "the worst aspect of the college is

CAMPUS POLITICS: YELLOW LIGHT

Outside the classroom, perhaps the most obvious political manifestations on campus arise from the Women's Resource Center. The center offers exclusively feminist fare, including information on student internships with the abortion provider Planned Parenthood. Other groups include environmental organizations, the College Democrats, and the Bowdoin Queer-Straight Alliance, which sponsors events like the annual Drag Ball.

An informal survey exploring the party affiliations of Bowdoin teachers and administrators showed that Democrats outnumber Republicans by 23 to 1. However, student views are more intellectually diverse, although another informal poll disclosed 76 percent of the student body voted for Obama in 2012 (down from 84 percent in 2008). The Bowdoin College Republicans are exceptionally active and visible and seek to ensure that conservative students have a voice on campus. For the most part, students of various political stripes feel secure enough to voice their opinions. Says one undergraduate, "Though a student may possess a minority opinion, anyone can find a support system here."

that it's like 90 percent liberal. Instead of the rather superficial diversity they try to achieve merely culturally, I wish Bowdoin cultivated more diversity of opinion." The *Bowdoin Orient* reported on November 2, 2012, that 76 percent of Bowdoin's students intended to vote for Obama, concluding "that the Bowdoin student body leans significantly left of both the nation and the state of Maine." The college has also garnered criticism for its encroachment on free speech in the form of a vaguely worded ban on jokes and stories "experienced by others as harassing." Another student agreed, "There is an overall intolerance of differences of opinion; Bowdoin is very politically correct." Indeed, he says that the religion department "has an open disrespect for traditional Catholic faith," as evidenced by such courses as "Christian Sexual Ethics" taught by a militant feminist whose academic research focuses on "the theological commitments of Marxist philosopher Theodor Adorno." She also teaches the basic "Theories about Religion" course, described as "a historical overview of religion's interpretation and explanation."

O ne student laments there "is an overall intolerance of differences of opinion." He notes that the religion course "Christian Sexual Ethics" is taught by a militant feminist whose specialty is neo-Marxism.

Bowdoin is host to the Gay and Lesbian Studies and Women and Gender Studies departments, and according to students we consulted, some faculty in the anthropology, sociology, and African studies departments are also known to inject politics into the classroom. On the other hand, students report that the college's president, Barry Mills, is known as fair-minded toward people of diverse opinions. However, a recent push to diversify Bowdoin's professor base was focused entirely on hiring more professors of different ethnic backgrounds—rather than intellectual or political viewpoints.

Bowdoin's study-abroad programs are solid and quite popular; more than half the student body chooses to study off campus. "It's pretty expensive but so worth it," one participant reports. "I appreciated having the easier classes so we could enjoy our surroundings." Bowdoin offers study-abroad programs all over the globe. The foreign language programs at Bowdoin are praiseworthy, offering instruction in nine languages: Chinese, French, German, Greek and Latin, Italian, Japanese, Russian, and Spanish.

Student Life: Outward bound

Over 90 percent of the student body chooses to live in one of the college's residential spaces, which include singles, doubles, and suites in houses and dormitories. First-year students live together in separate dorms with upperclassmen residential advisers on each floor. Bowdoin offers no single-sex dormitories, and many students may find that members of the opposite sex live right next door; however, in the freshman "bricks," four out of the six floors are single sex. There are no coed rooms, but bathrooms can be coed, if so ordered by house vote. Freshmen normally live in triples, whereas upperclassman may live in apartments or off campus. "Bowdoin has the best first-year housing of any college I've ever seen, with plenty of room for privacy and space," says one alumna. Some dorms that hadn't been updated since 1911 were recently renovated. There are also several substance-free dormitories available on campus, where even alcohol is prohibited. "The dorms are awesome; they provide unique living options," says a student. "One dorm, Cole Tower, is the second-tallest building in Maine. It has sixteen stories; you can see the ocean!"

Many students told us how "friendly" the typical Bowdoin student is. "I have met so many great people here: bright and very accepting," reports one. However, others complain about the lack of ethnic diversity. "This is one of the whitest campuses in America," groans one student. Somehow, Bowdoin students muddle through. No doubt it helps that, as one student says, "Everyone is accepted and made to feel welcome. There is no climate of snobbery at all."

In 2000 the Bowdoin administration abolished fraternities. Now the college assigns each freshman to a college house, each with its own set of residence halls, parties, and other social events. There is no structured socialization beyond the freshman year.

Given that half of partygoers are under 21, the administration has chosen to shift legal risks onto students themselves, requiring that a student "host" sign for every keg at a party; if any alcohol-related injuries occur, the student is held responsible. Social clubs have also been opened in freestanding houses, where the college attempts to teach students how to hold responsible parties. This has been moderately successful, changing the focus away from "beer blasts."

Bowdoin is a small college in a tightly knit New England community. Nevertheless, of the three elite Maine liberal arts colleges (Bates and Colby are the others), Bowdoin probably has the most social options available. Many activities center on sports teams. Most students at the school are involved in sports: varsity or intramural. "I came here for the hockey!" exclaims one. "I love how athletics and academics coexist here." The Bowdoin Polar Bears are Division III and highly competitive in 13 men's and 16 women's sports teams.

Bowdoin hosts both College Republicans and College Democrats, the latter being more entrenched on this predominantly liberal campus. But the College Republicans have been very active in making their views heard on campus in recent years. "One important role that we can play is engaging the prevalent liberal sentiment and philosophy intellectually.

SUGGESTED CORE

1. Classics 102, Introduction to Ancient Greek Culture, or History 202, Ancient Rome
2. Philosophy 111, Ancient Philosophy
3. Religion 215/216, The Hebrew Bible in Its World/ The New Testament in Its World
4. History 110, Medieval, Renaissance, and Reformation Europe (*closest match*)
5. Government and Legal Studies 241, Modern Political Philosophy or Philosophy 112, Modern Philosophy
6. English 210/211/212, Shakespeare's Comedies and Romances/Tragedies and Roman Plays/History Plays
7. History 231, Colonial America and the Atlantic World, 1607–1763
8. Government and Legal Studies 244, Liberalism and Its Critics

We are going to do our best to bring conservative ideas into the Bowdoin community," explained former CR president Steven Robinson to the *Bowdoin Orient*. He added that "it's troublesome that you can count the number of conservative professors here on one hand. The College Republicans would like to see an increase of intellectual diversity and more honest discussion of social and political issues." They are certainly doing their part in hosting conservative speakers, conferences, and meetings on campus and in growing their membership in recent years.

One student says, "Spirituality is practically nonexistent at Bowdoin." Another admits, "Students here are generally proud of their aspirituality." Brunswick is home to churches of most major denominations, but students are said to attend mostly on major holidays. Student religious groups include the Catholic Student Union, the Bowdoin Christian Fellowship, and a strong Hillel club.

Students report that the college does an excellent job of providing intellectual and artistic stimuli on campus, hosting frequent lectures, many political speakers, and a number of cultural events. By far the most popular organization is the Outing Club, which gives students the chance to explore the bucolic regions of Maine and northern New England. Says one wistful alumnus, "I loved the Bowdoin lifestyle. It is such a beautiful location on the coast of Maine, with a marvelous natural landscape. The atmosphere is studious but relaxed; sometimes the college is called 'Camp Bowdoin.' It felt like it."

Bowdoin's rural location provides, not surprisingly, for a very safe environment. Says an insider, "The town is full of old folks and tenured professors. I'm safe." Statistics show that violent crime on or around campus is rare; substance abuse is certainly present, although incidents have diminished in recent years. In 2011 the school reported seven forcible sex offenses and 11 counts of burglary on campus.

Bowdoin's tuition in 2012–13 was $44,118, and room and board added up to $12,010. Forty-six percent of all students received need-based aid and the average indebtedness of recent graduates was a modest $17,569.

STRONG SUITS	WEAK POINTS
• Faculty who value teaching over research and work closely with students.	• Weak requirements for general education.
• Solid requirements in key departments like English and government.	• A very secular, almost antireligious bias among most students.
• Plenty of activities on campus, both cultural and athletic.	• Several highly politicized departments—including religion.
• Despite the school's elite status, a friendly, nonsnobbish social atmosphere.	• No dorms are single sex, and some bathrooms are coed.

Brandeis University

Waltham, Massachusetts • www.brandeis.edu

New and Improved

Founded in 1948, Brandeis has accomplished a great deal in less than 70 years. Its undergraduates are exposed to excellent teaching in the humanities, sciences, and liberal arts in general, and the university is well regarded as a research institution. Sponsored by the American Jewish community in the wake of World War II, Brandeis began as and remains a nonsectarian institution. Students on campus describe it as an open community enriched by its diverse population rather than one obsessed with the ideology of diversity.

Academic Life: The right to be left alone

Like most schools these days, Brandeis eschews a real core curriculum and merely asks its students to select a few courses from broad categories. "If someone really wants to avoid a subject, it's far from impossible," says a student. Another says, "Brandeis will not tell you what you should think. And it will most definitely not choose your courses for you." One professor insists, "The curriculum here is well structured so that students take a good mixture of courses that are necessary fundamentals and fun electives, as well as being exposed to new ideas in their fields of study."

VITAL STATISTICS

Religious affiliation: *none*
Total enrollment: *5,828*
Total undergraduates: *3,504*
SAT CR/Verbal midrange: *600–710*
SAT Math midrange: *630–740*
ACT midrange: *28–32*
Applicants: *8,917*
Applicants accepted: *40%*
Accepted applicants who enrolled: *24%*
Tuition (general/out of state): *$42,682*
Tuition (in state): *N/A*
Room and board: *$12,256*
Freshman retention rate: *93%*
Graduation rate (4 yrs.): *87%*
Graduation rate (6 yrs.): *91%*
Courses with fewer than 20 students: *61%*
Student-faculty ratio: *10:1*
Courses taught by graduate students: *not provided*
Students living on campus: *81%*
Students in fraternities: *N/A*
Students in sororities: *N/A*
Students receiving need-based financial aid: *51%*
Avg. student-loan debt of a recent graduating class: *$21,351*
Most popular majors: *social sciences, business/marketing, biological/life sciences*
Guaranteed housing for 4 years? *no*

Each freshman is assigned an adviser (a faculty member or administrator) upon arrival and must consult with him before registering. The student gets a new faculty adviser when he selects a major, but isn't required to meet with him. "Most people I know honestly saw no need for their advisers," one student says. Students report that there are ways to slide by without even brushing against laboratory science or math. If you intend to study science, one student warns that the department is "overly focused on premed students." However, says one student, "The classes here are challenging in any discipline you study. The tests will ask you to think, not simply list facts. And you will get to know the library pretty well."

Ambitious students should explore Brandeis's excellent interdisciplinary major in European cultural studies (ECS), the best option on campus for obtaining a traditional liberal arts education. The major requires study of European literature along with "fine arts, history, music, philosophy, politics, sociology, and theater arts" and is intended "for those students who feel intellectually adventurous."

English majors must take an introductory course, two classes in pre-1800 English literature, two classes in post-1800 English literature, and a course each in two of the following three categories: literary theory, media/film, and multicultural literature/world Anglophone, plus three electives. Post-1800 classes seem less rigorous: "Literature and Medicine," "Queer Readings," and "Adolescent Literature from Grimm to Voldemort" are typical classes.

History majors must complete nine courses in history, including one pre-1800, one post-1800, one U.S., one European, and one non-Western. One of the classes "must require a substantial research paper." It would be easy to skip the American Founding and Civil War.

The politics major calls for nine classes, with at least one each in political theory, American politics, comparative politics, and international politics. Sadly, classes like "Social Movements in American Politics" and "Race, Inequality, and Social Policy" can fulfill the American politics requirements.

One undergrad notes that professors' personal politics "intrude in the classroom, to no end in—you would never guess—the politics department. I've also heard some in the economics and classical studies departments. ...One conservative told me that whenever he raised his hand, the professor would address him as 'Republican.'" Says a student, "I've found Brandeis to have both altered and reinforced the viewpoints I had when I entered. ...My conservative ideology is now [even more] firmly rooted in the concept of the free market—and I have realized the necessity of granting spheres of privacy in individual life." Brandeis has done a good job of keeping politics out of most classrooms and promoting solid teaching along with research, but some departments and courses are weaker than others. A new program called Social Justice and Social Policy (SJSP), which offers a minor, is "basically a bunch of really liberal sociology classes and the like," a student says. Brandeis's sociology and politics departments are also noteworthy for their politicization.

In all, Brandeis offers 43 majors and 45 minors. Students list as among the strongest Near Eastern and Judaic studies (said by some to be the best in the country), English and American literature, classical studies, the sciences, history, and politics.

Students single out as among the best professors at Brandeis: Thomas Pochapsky in chemistry; Mary Campbell, Billy Flesch, Michael "Timo" Gilmore, and Caren Irr in English and American literature; Leonard Muellner in Classics; Susan Dibble, Marya Lowry, and Janet Morrison in theater; Jerry Cohen in American studies; Gordie Fellman in sociology; Ray Jackendoff (emeritus) in linguistics and cognitive science; Graham Campbell and Susan Lichtman in fine arts; and Robert J. Art in international relations. In history, students laud David Hackett Fischer (a Pulitzer Prize–winning author) as "an amazing lecturer, truly dedicated to teaching," and call professor emeritus John Schrecker "accessible and eloquent." Students also praise Mike Coiner as "everyone's favorite economics professor, more adept at distilling economic theory to hundreds of students than anyone else at Brandeis."

CAMPUS POLITICS: YELLOW LIGHT

The Foundation for Individual Rights in Education has consistently criticized Brandeis for its free-speech policies—reporting on its website of a professor who told his Latin American politics class that "wetbacks" was a discriminatory term used against Mexican immigrants. A student took offense at the use of the word and anonymously reported Professor Hindley for using "inappropriate, racial" language. Hindley, a well-known liberal and professor of almost 50 years, was not granted a hearing, allowed to be defended by the rest of his students (who understood that he used the term educationally), or even formally notified of the charges against him. Rather, he was threatened with termination, informed that a monitor would be present in his classes for the rest of the term, and ordered to attend sensitivity training. He refused, and Brandeis did its best to ignore the media fallout but kept the "sensitivity" monitor in Hindley's classes and has still failed to clear his name, simply declaring the matter "closed."

Still, there has been pushback by conservatives on campus, who in 2012 successfully sponsored a talk on radical Islam by David Horowitz—whom censorious leftists have prevented from speaking at many other colleges. According to the student-run *Brandeis Hoot* newspaper, his talk was provocative but received respectfully by curious students of varying political persuasions.

Students report no problems with registering for classes or with talking to teachers. "Professors are very accessible," says a student. In larger courses, professors deliver lectures, leaving teaching assistants to conduct discussion sections occasionally. One faculty member says, "Students are very highly motivated and curious. They often come by to discuss their ideas." Another professor says, "My classes have a high percentage of students engaged intellectually. I am never bored by the seminars I teach." The number one priority at Brandeis is academics," says one student matter-of-factly.

One professor strongly recommends the university's study-abroad programs, observing: "The kids come back glowing." The university offers 350 such programs in 70 countries, and nearly half of Brandeis's juniors study abroad. Any student receiving need-based financial aid is eligible to apply for a Brandeis Scholarship for Study Abroad.

Brandeis offers courses in Arabic, Chinese, French, German, Greek and Latin, Hebrew, Italian, Japanese, Russian, Spanish, and (a rare option) Yiddish.

Student Life: World religions

Waltham, Massachusetts, is nine miles west of cultural metropolis Boston, and the suburb has a variety of restaurants, interesting old buildings, and independent theaters. "It's definitely not a party school," says one student. "Don't be fooled by the school's proximity to Boston," says another. "Most students spend nights and weekends studying. If you do get out, it will probably be only as far as the highly suburbanized Harvard Square." But a third student says, "Brandeis is what you make of it. The school pours money into hundreds of student clubs and organizations that are constantly organizing events, dances, concerts, et cetera. I guarantee you that there is not a single weekend during the school year when the event calendar is completely empty." Students who do find time to get off campus can take the free school shuttle from Waltham to Boston.

One student concludes: "Brandeis is essentially a breeding ground for lawyers and doctors."

A professor says, "At Brandeis there's a special tradition of concern which people are mindful of. You're always supposed to ask yourself, 'Are we serving social justice? In our courses? In our treatment of each other?'" Yet, in the end, according to a student, "Brandeis is essentially a breeding ground for lawyers and doctors," and ultimately, "The coolest thing about the place is getting an awesome job after college."

Recent speakers on campus have addressed political topics from a number of different viewpoints in the past few years: Noam Chomsky, Dinesh D'Souza, (the late) Christopher Hitchens, congressman Barney Frank, and former senator Bill Bradley, among others.

University higher-ups occasionally discuss "diversifying" the campus, meaning in most cases that they would like to hire more professors "of color." But the real push on campus for multiculturalism comes from students. One student admits that his peers "lack a certain open-mindedness" to opposing viewpoints. Besides groups representing ethnic minorities—many of which are primarily social networks—there are a number of leftist student political groups, including Brandeis Labor Coalition, Feminist Majority Leadership Alliance, and Students for a Democratic Society. There are no conservative groups of similar size or stature; College Republicans are essentially a social organization, but Brandeis also features a Tea Party chapter, and the Libertarian-Conservative Union.

Brandeis hosts a variety of intramural and club sports for both men and women (including basketball, equestrian sports, gymnastics, aikido, fencing, volleyball, and tennis) to fill in the gaps in Brandeis's intercollegiate athletic program, which includes nine varsity teams for men and 10 for women. Athletic facilities for all students include a pool, racket sports courts, a gymnasium, and a track.

The Judges, as the school's teams are known, compete in blue and white at the NCAA Division III. "Athletes in general are considered a minority and sometimes feel marginalized," says one student. "Most kids simply don't have the time to invest in sports. They read books and write papers."

> **SUGGESTED CORE**
>
> 1. Humanities 10a, The Western Canon
> 2. Philosophy 161a or 162b, Plato/Aristotle
> 3. Near Eastern and Judaic Studies 111a/130a, The Hebrew Bible/New Testament
> 4. Near Eastern and Judaic Studies 128a, Introduction to Christianity
> 5. Politics 182a, Liberal Political Thought
> 6. English 33a, Shakespeare
> 7. History 51a, History of the United States: 1607–1865
> 8. History 192b, Romantic and Existential Political Thought

Students generally comment on the remarkable religious tolerance that prevails at the school. Religious groups include Orthodox, Conservative, and Reform organizations for Jews, as well as Chabad and Hillel. Two Buddhist clubs; an umbrella group for Hindus, Jains, and Sikhs; a Muslim Students Association; and the Brandeis Interfaith Group round out Baptist, Orthodox, and Catholic organizations.

The school's brainy, egalitarian gestalt may be indicated by the administration's prohibition on fraternities and sororities. A few nonrecognized fraternities and sororities do exist, but students by and large praise the absence of Greek life on campus.

Freshmen and sophomores are guaranteed spots in campus dorms, which are said to be adequate but not luxurious. Brandeis's dorms are all coed, but some floors are single sex. The school currently hosts three Common Cause Communities—a philanthropic Alternative Spring Break floor for sophomores; a Substance Awareness for Everyday (SAFE) floor for juniors; and the Balanced Living House for seniors, who focus on healthy living and sponsor programs encouraging good health.

One female student observes, "Dorm life is amusing and enjoyable. After freshman year you can live in suites. There are no female or male dorms. The freshman dorms are usually single sex by floor, though some are coed. Bathrooms are typically single sex, although when someone is drunk it doesn't matter." Sophomores or upperclassmen living on mixed-gender floors may opt for sex-neutral housing, where students may choose a roommate regardless of either person's sex. The school does discourage couples from living together.

All but four dorms are officially dry, and students say resident advisers will intervene to stop excessive noise. The school's alcohol policy is quite lenient, and the "wet" dorms allow alcohol for people of drinking age. At the school's Stein Restaurant, beer is on the menu alongside burgers and pasta. While the campus grounds themselves are quite nice, "the buildings are a bit of a mix and match," says one student. "Some are weird. Some are very ugly."

Brandeis's campus is quite safe: in 2011, the school reported two forcible sex offenses, three burglaries, one robbery, and one motor vehicle theft on campus. Students report that they feel secure at the school. "Waltham is not a crime-ridden city, and there's always a late-night bus service. Safety is hardly your major concern," says one student.

Brandeis is pricey but generous. Tuition for 2012–13 was $42,682, and room and board $12,256. However, Brandeis's admissions decisions are need blind. Some 51 percent of students received need-based aid, and Brandeis met 82 percent of their demonstrated need. The average Brandeis student graduated with $21,351 in debt.

STRONG SUITS	WEAK POINTS
• Academically intense, ambitious students. • Accessible, helpful faculty. • An excellent program in Western Civ called European Cultural Studies. • Despite the overall liberalism of the campus, mostly nonpoliticized classes.	• Thanks to lax requirements, science and math are easy for non-majors to avoid. • A few more-partisan departments, such as sociology and political science. • A paucity of conservative students and groups.

Brown University

Providence, Rhode Island • www.brown.edu

Amateur Architects

Founded in 1764, Brown University boasts many fine teachers and intellectually curious students. What it lacks is a curriculum. Not only is there no core; there are no distribution, language, math, or science requirements. Brown provides a fascinating, tempting environment that "may be daunting for students who need more structure," according to one undergrad. Brown has a "commitment to undergraduate freedom," says the school's literature, and its students are "architects of their courses of study." Call us old fogies, but we prefer to rely on builders with a little more expertise.

Brown's small academic departments offer fewer course choices than at other schools. A student might not be able to get into the most popular classes until his senior year, if then. The school's social and political atmosphere are at the "progressive" cutting edge even of the Ivy League, which more reserved or traditional students should keep in mind before applying.

Academic Life: You get to put it together

Brown is proud of its laissez-faire approach. As one student says, "Brown has a diverse and unique liberal arts education to offer. If you're not up for the task of crafting your own

VITAL STATISTICS

Religious affiliation: *none*
Total enrollment: *8,808*
Total undergraduates: *6,402*
SAT CR/Verbal midrange:
  660–750
SAT Math midrange:
  680–770
ACT midrange: *29–33*
Applicants: *30,944*
Applicants accepted: *9.6%*
Accepted applicants who
  enrolled: *55.8%*
Tuition (general/out of
  state): *$42,808*
Tuition (in state): *N/A*
Room and board: *$12,208*
Freshman retention rate:
  98%
Graduation rate (4 yrs.): *83%*
Graduation rate (6 yrs.): *95%*
Courses with fewer than 20
  students: *68%*
Student-faculty ratio: *9:1*
Courses taught by graduate
  students: *not provided*
Students living on campus:
  78%
Students in fraternities: *not
  provided*
Students in sororities: *not
  provided*
Students receiving need-
  based financial aid: *46%*
Avg. student-loan debt of a
  recent graduating class:
  $20,455
Most popular majors:
  *economics, biological
  sciences, international
  relations*
Guaranteed housing for 4
  years? *yes*

educational curriculum, advising is available." Another student lauds Brown's approach: "Students are free to attend graduate-level courses. There is a level of respect between the faculty and students. . . . Even as freshmen, students have the opportunity to work on graduate-level research projects with renowned faculty." Another agrees, "Brown is great because it has no general-ed requirements. It means you can pursue what you love and dally in your curiosities."

Students can take or avoid any class. Theoretically, students can graduate from Brown without ever having taken American or world history, a foreign language, English, economics, philosophy, or a single science course. One student admits that there are some who feel at sea. However, "Brown has actively worked to improve academic advising and has made significant strides with the Meiklejohn Advising Program, which pairs up freshmen with upperclassmen mentors," this student says. "In short, if you're lost at Brown, there are plenty of resources to guide you." As freshmen, Brown students are assigned two "advising partners": an upperclassman "peer adviser" and a faculty member who guides the student through first-year courses and pre-major choices. Once students have declared a concentration, they work with faculty advisers in their departments.

Departments and concentrations often require students to take a core of fundamental courses. A student majoring in Classics (a strong department at Brown) completes eight courses, including one in Greek or Latin, two semesters of Greek or Roman history, and five other electives. Comparative literature and geology get strong marks for teaching, as do applied math and international relations. The philosophy department takes a sober, earnest approach to Continental philosophy. The hard sciences are serious and highly regarded by those who choose to study them.

English majors are required to take a class in literary theory, but not a Shakespeare course, although one is offered as an elective. The history department includes a broad survey of introductory courses, including American and world history, in its major requirements; however, a basic Western civilization class is not even available. The political science department is one of the five largest concentrations in undergraduate enrollment, and the program is excellent, requiring all majors to take courses in American politics, political theory, and international and comparative politics.

Brown students are effusive about their favorite teachers, such as the popular Stephen T. McGarvey in epidemiology, who teaches the acclaimed course "The Burden of Disease in Developing Countries." Brian Hayden in psychology is "phenomenal," according to a student, while another says that Susan Ashbrook Harvey's lectures in religious studies "feel like story time. She really cares about her students." Political science professor John Tomasi "is doing an outstanding job with the Political Theory Project, which exposes students to classical political philosophy; it's very popular," says an undergrad. Others offer praise for Matthew Zimmt in chemistry and Barrett Hazeltine (emeritus) in engineering.

The weakest and most politicized departments are the usual suspects. Africana studies, the gender and sexuality department, the race and ethnicity program in American studies, and the urban studies program should be actively avoided, sources say.

Professors are accessible, students report. "My favorite aspect of Brown is the overall sense that administrators care about undergraduates and their experiences," says one. "At Brown's peer schools, such as Harvard or Yale, I don't think that's the case." Another student points to the helpful attitude of teachers: "If you enjoy learning and want to continue to do so, Brown is the place for you. You will be encouraged to achieve more through inspiration and individual passion."

CAMPUS POLITICS: YELLOW LIGHT

As at most New England colleges, conservatives are in the minority and for that reason can garner a reputation for being silent and sullen. As one student complains, "I believe that, in response to the question 'Why don't you participate in voter registration initiatives?' the College Republicans replied, 'We would only be registering Democrats, so why bother?'" Another self-described "mildly liberal" student opines that conservatives are actually too quiet on campus; they shouldn't be so shy, he thinks. "I feel that most of the Brown students I know are willing and interested to hear other intelligent viewpoints."

But change is in the air. As *FrontPage Magazine* reports: "A new generation of students has resurrected the Right. This nascent conservative community even publishes its own monthly magazine, the *Brown Spectator*." The paper is funded by the Foundation for Intellectual Diversity at Brown, founded by recent alumni, and in a recent edition featured an interview with the president of Brown—suggesting that the paper does not have the pariah status conservative journals sometimes gain at other schools (see Dartmouth). The foundation also publishes *Closing Remarks*, a Christian literary and arts magazine. Several right-of-center groups, such as Students for Liberty and the College Republicans, have taken their place in Brown's marketplace of ideas.

A current student says, "Overall, Brown's freedom allows you to seek the type of education you want. Conservative complaints about Brown are largely exaggerated. It is very easy to get a solid education at Brown, join religious groups, and take part in conservative activity if you seek it out. As a conservative at Brown, I am very happy with the overall experience."

Grade inflation is an issue at Brown, as at most schools these days. Much of the blame can be placed on the university's sloppy grading system, which does not include pluses or minuses. Brown continues to debate this grading system; the faculty voted on it as recently as 2006, making the decision at the time to keep the current grading system.

Brown offers students a wide selection of foreign languages to study, including Akkadian, Arabic, Chinese, Czech, German, Greek and Latin, French, Classical and Modern Hebrew, Hindi/Urdu, Italian, Japanese, Korean, Persian, Portuguese, Russian, and Spanish. The university also sponsors many excellent study-abroad programs, to places such as Brazil, Cuba, France, Germany, Hong Kong, India, Ireland, Italy, Japan, Spain, and the United Kingdom. Approximately 600 Brown undergraduates study outside the United States each year.

Student Life: Diverse dorms, sizzling social life

Brown is an urban school, and students can be seen milling up and down Thayer Street, visiting shops and restaurants. Providence offers virtually nowhere to park. Students walk, bike, or take buses and trams up the cobbled paths and through historic archways.

Students find themselves caught up in a lovely city of manageable proportions and can meet a variety of people, if they take the time. The town offers plenty of interesting food spots, including a plethora of ethnic restaurants. The area surrounding the campus caters to students and their eccentricities, and there are all manner of trendy shops. The campus is divided into five main areas. The largest is East Campus, but Pembroke Quad houses the most students. Residence halls are located no more than a six- or seven-minute walk from classes. The university does not offer single-sex dorms but allows students to opt for same-sex floors in coed residence halls. Students who choose same-sex floors are targeted with "educational programming" that is "designed to help residents explore women's and men's issues through events focused on gender." Most of the Greek organizations are also single sex and occupy dormitory space.

Brown has no core curriculum and no distribution requirements. It's a fascinating, tempting environment that "may be daunting for students who need more structure," an undergrad says.

The university offers virtually every type of living option, including suites and apartments, theme houses, and traditional dormitories. Coed or "gender-neutral" bathrooms and rooms are standard; Brown's housing website states that "residence-hall, room, and roommate assignments are made without regard to race, color, creed, sexual orientation, or nation origin."

Currently, 78 percent of students live on campus, where, according to one undergrad, they are "lightly supervised by Resident Counselors as freshmen and Community Assistants thereafter. Neither of these positions comes with any power to enforce rules;

they merely sell condoms and ask politely that we pay for them."

Brown is reputed to be more of a party school than the other Ivies. Indeed, Brown students enjoy the standard college drinking scene, found mainly at private parties rather than fraternities. Students discuss politics in the cafeteria and read the main student newspaper, the *Brown Daily Herald*—a decent paper for news coverage. The *Brown Noser*, founded in 2006, claims to be "Brown University's oldest satirical newspaper" where "most of what you read is false."

Protests, which crop up frequently and for almost any reason, also prop up the school's reputation for leftism and rampant political correctness. A student reporter says, "If I hear gibberish being screamed from the Main Green, I grab my video camera, and I run as quickly as I can to see what sort of inane cause we are fighting for today." The student comments that such protests happen mainly during the warmer months. "The same people are involved in every single protest. For these students, it seems that protesting has become a pastime." Says one student, "Lots of people are liberal, yes. They are not raging liberals, they engage in peaceful protest and start initiatives in the hope of changing their community. As for conservative students, they are completely welcome. They are far less active on campus, which is no one's fault but their own."

SUGGESTED CORE
1. Classics 1210/1310, Greek History I/Roman History I
2. Philosophy 350, Ancient Philosophy
3. Judaic Studies 470, The Hebrew Bible and the History of Ancient Israel and Religious Studies 400, New Testament and the Beginnings of Christianity
4. Religious Studies 110, Christianity
5. Political Science 110, Introduction to Political Thought
6. English 400A, Introduction to Shakespeare
7. History 510, American History to 1877
8. History 170, Great Modern European Thinkers or History 1220, European Intellectual and Cultural History: Exploring the Modern, 1880–1914

Brown's Queer Alliance hosts an annual "SexPowerGod" dance that gives students a chance to explore their sexual proclivities in a "sober, sane, safe and consensual environment," say event planners. So safe, in fact, that one year 24 students required medical attention after the event. None of the university's Department of Public Safety officers are allowed in; attendees rely on student monitors, who look out for any nonconsensual activity. Students are not allowed to be intoxicated when they arrive, and no alcohol is sold at the event, but the event boasts other attractions: a "booty box," free lubricant, consensual-sex patrols, and "sex techno." One year, the dance had a surprise guest: an undercover Fox News reporter, Jesse Watters, who described the event as "pure debauchery" and reported hearing people having sex in the bathrooms. According to the *Brown Alumni Magazine*, "the annual dance has widespread appeal among students, many of whom use it as an opportunity to drink too much and wear almost nothing." In the same vein, every fall the Watermyn House, part of the Brown Association for Cooperative Housing, throws the invitation-only "Naked Party." Then there's the "Naked Doughnut Run" at the end of each semester, wherein various student groups walk naked through the libraries to offer donuts to students studying for exams.

By way of violent contrast, Brown is very close to dozens of old Catholic churches and one large Catholic college, Providence. (Rhode Island is statistically one of the most Roman

Catholic states in the union.) The Catholic group on campus holds popular events and hosts outreach programs and solid lecturers. There are a variety of other faith groups on campus—from Imani to Quakers—and "all are welcoming," says a student. There is only one actual chapel on campus, Manning, which is on the second floor above the anthropology museum. Mass is celebrated there three times during the week and twice on Sundays.

Sports at Brown take a backseat compared to their prominence at other Ivies, especially basketball-friendly Princeton and Penn. In fact, Brown's teams have improved markedly in recent years. Brown fields 37 varsity teams, and the university also has some 20 club sports and an intramural program featuring flag football, Ultimate Frisbee, tennis, ice hockey, and other pursuits.

The school is less than half a mile from the Rhode Island School of Design (RISD, pronounced "ris-dee"), where students can register for art classes and receive course credit. Musical groups and campus dance groups perform frequently.

There are many artistic and cultural groups among the more than 300 student organizations, including student theater, a popular student-run radio station, and a wide variety of community and social outreach programs. Says one exhausted student, "There is so much to do at Brown . . . students complain that there is not enough time in the day to attend all the student-run activities they would like to." There are new clubs starting all the time. An insider says, "Due to the student-led nature of the campus, there is a large emphasis on innovation and planning new events. The Brown social scene is very much alive and vibrant."

Crime on campus is not bad for an urban school: in 2011 there were 32 burglaries, one aggravated assault, one robbery, and seven forcible sex offenses on campus.

Like the other Ivies, Brown is astronomically expensive, with 2012–13 tuition at $42,808, and $12,208 for room and board. Brown reverted (after a budget-induced hiatus) to need-blind admissions in 2007, but it does not (unlike most other Ivies) guarantee to meet a candidate's full demonstrated need. Considering the cost, recent graduates' average indebtedness of $20,455 is quite moderate.

STRONG SUITS	WEAK POINTS
• Elite teachers and smart fellow students.	• Absolutely no general-ed requirements; students can be dilettantes.
• Excellent programs in the hard sciences, Classics, philosophy, comparative literature, and international relations.	• All courses can be taken pass/fail.
• Revamped and now effective advising program.	• More of a party atmosphere than most Ivies.
• Set in a beautiful town with several other colleges, and many arts, cultural, and dining options.	• Coed rooms and bathrooms.
	• Aggressive, raunchy sex activism on campus.

Bryn Mawr College

Bryn Mawr, Pennsylvania • www.brynmawr.edu

The Smart Sister on the High Hill

Bryn Mawr College was founded in 1885, became the first women's school to offer graduate programs, and remains the only such institution to offer a wide range of advanced degrees. But while most of its individual courses and majors are strong, the college's curriculum is frail and sickly, and leftist political opinions permeate course offerings, content, and classroom discussion. If a conservative student is unwilling to live in such a hostile climate, she should look elsewhere.

Academic Life: Global queer cinema

Bryn Mawr's distribution requirements do not demand a true breadth of study. One faculty member says, "It would be worse if we didn't have such serious girls, but, undeniably, the program of study is pretty vague." Bryn Mawr does prescribe a full slate of rigorous courses for almost all its majors and boasts a distinguished faculty. The typical student is earnest about her studies; many opt to spend weekends in the library. "Everyone here really works," one student says. "I have a friend on the debate team. When she told me what the attitude of students at the schools she competed with—like Harvard and Yale—were toward attending

VITAL STATISTICS

Religious affiliation: *none*
Total enrollment: *1,785*
Total undergraduates: *1,313*
SAT CR/Verbal midrange:
  600–710
SAT Math midrange:
  600–720
ACT midrange: *26–31*
Applicants: *2,335*
Applicants accepted: *46%*
Accepted applicants who
  enrolled: *33%*
Tuition (general/out of
  state): *$42,246*
Tuition (in state): *N/A*
Room and board: *$13,340*
Freshman retention rate:
  90%
Graduation rate (4 yrs.): *82%*
Graduation rate (6 yrs.): *87%*
Courses with fewer than 20
  students: *68%*
Student-faculty ratio: *8:1*
Courses taught by graduate
  students: *none*
Students living on campus:
  95%
Students in fraternities: *N/A*
Students in sororities: *N/A*
Students receiving need-
  based financial aid: *59%*
Avg. student-loan debt of a
  recent graduating class:
  $22,830
Most popular majors: *biol-
  ogy, English, psychology*
Guaranteed housing for 4
  years? *yes*

class, I thought she was kidding." Another student adds, "It's not just the premeds who work in the lab courses. People think it's important. Why else come?" It may be indicative that mathematics is a popular undergraduate major.

One of the main features of Bryn Mawr academic life is the strength of the relationships that develop between faculty members and students. Such relationships grow naturally, thanks to the school's small size. Class sizes range from around 30 (for introductory courses) to just three (for senior-level topical seminars). Many students say that professors treat them as younger colleagues. Students visit their professors regularly, often discussing subjects unrelated to class. Faculty members view teaching—not publishing or research—as their main responsibility. "If you go meet with a professor at their office," one student reports, "there's almost always this good, inviting energy. They don't try to make you sweat for recommendation letters." Another student says, "There's a lot of personal attention—not only from the faculty but from the deans and from your adviser."

There are graduate students at Bryn Mawr who teach no courses but sometimes lead laboratory sections. Upon entry to Bryn Mawr, students are assigned a college dean as an adviser. After the student declares a major, she chooses a faculty adviser from her department.

Some of the many excellent professors at Bryn Mawr include Catherine Conybeare and Radcliffe Edmonds in Classics; Robert J. Dostal and Christine Koggel in philosophy; Peter M. Briggs in English; Jeremy Elkins and Stephen Salkever in political science; and Nathan Daniel Wright in sociology.

Bryn Mawr has had great success in the sciences. "My bio professors all really cared about whether we understood what we were doing in lab, and all the math professors I have had, you could understand," reports one science major. Professors from outside the department concur that "Bryn Mawr has consistently excellent science programs." Of all women awarded PhDs in physics, more began their educations at Bryn Mawr than at any other liberal arts school. At Bryn Mawr, students in the sciences work closely with professors on research projects, gaining valuable experience and strengthening academic relationships with faculty members. Moreover, the science departments offer an escape from the feminist ideology that saturates most aspects of campus life.

A veteran professor particularly recommends the Classics, political science, and philosophy departments. Another popular major is English, though many of the course titles suggest a trendy emphasis on women authors. For undergrads there are whole courses devoted to figures like Virginia Woolf and Toni Morrison. Classes like "Topics in Film Studies: Global Queer Cinema" and "Gender and Technology" dominate the department's course catalog.

The philosophy department, though small, consists of professors who are "strong scholars and are attentive to students," according to one faculty member. The philosophy and political science departments offer strong introductory courses that "teach the intellectual history of the West"—more so than the history department, students note. The polisci major must take "Introduction to American Politics" and "Introduction to Political Philosophy: Ancient and Early Modern," while the history major is not even offered—much less required to take—a basic Western civilization class. The art history department is strong, emphasizing the classical tradition, and giving students opportunities to study abroad.

CAMPUS POLITICS: RED LIGHT

At Bryn Mawr, the line between academic and political life is thin and permeable, even in many classrooms. Faculty members and students alike generally assume that contemporary feminism is an unqualified good and that no one at Bryn Mawr would question such a view. For example, one student complains that "feminist views are generally considered a given." We were unable to find a single conservative organization listed at Bryn Mawr, though there were plenty of groups along the lines of Taboo, which "provides a safe space for . . . students to discuss issues relating to alternative sexualities and lifestyles. Our topics include BDSM, polyamory, swinging, the sex industry, sex positivism, sexual spirituality, and more." In a positive development, when the Foundation for Individual Rights in Education (FIRE) complained in 2010 that Bryn Mawr's sexual harassment code was a serious threat to freedom of speech and academic discourse on campus, the school changed it—largely satisfying FIRE's concerns.

Standard, leftist views are reinforced in courses such as the sociology offering "Social Inequality," which will provide an "introduction to the major sociological theories of gender, racial-ethnic and class inequality . . . including the role of the upper class(es), inequality between and within families, in the work place and in the educational system," reports the catalog. Weirder perhaps is a course called "The Sociology of AIDS," which attempts to explain the "social construction of the disease."

Many of the college's humanities course offerings are dedicated to the exploration of feminist issues or the politics of victimhood. Not so unusual, for instance, is the anthropology department's "Childhood in the African Experience," which provides a "gendered perspective on selected topics in the experiences of children and youth in Africa concerning indigenous cultural practices such as initiation ceremonies and sexual orientation." Students report that in such courses and in others, professors often make little attempt to conceal their political opinions—and that they are not above proselytizing. Office doors have political cartoons and leftist bumper stickers, making visits awkward for conservative students.

Bryn Mawr admissions policies put a high priority on having a racially diverse student body; about 25 percent of recent classes have come from minority groups. Once a student is admitted, a panoply of ethnic-based programming awaits her. "Voices of Color," an orientation event held each April, is a "multicultural experience" during which admitted students learn that—surprise!—Bryn Mawr is a diverse and welcoming place for racial minorities. As if to make that point, students of African or Hispanic descent are given the chance to live . . . in separate residence halls.

The college's honor code and self-governance system are crucial to the school's identity; the college website says Bryn Mawr was the first college in the United States to "give students responsibility not only for enforcing rules of behavior upon themselves, but also for deciding what those rules should be." Faculty and peers trust that Bryn Mawr students are committed to honesty, and as a result students can schedule their own final exams and may take tests home.

> One student says that "coming out as a person of faith at Bryn Mawr" is like "coming out as a homo- or bisexual."

The relationship between Bryn Mawr and its Philadelphia Main Line neighbor, Haverford College, is essential to academic life at both schools. Bryn Mawr students are free to take courses at either college and can even major in a discipline at Haverford not offered at Bryn Mawr. If a desired course is not offered at either campus, a student can enroll at Swarthmore College or the University of Pennsylvania. A limited number of courses at nearby Villanova University are also available to Bryn Mawr students. Bryn Mawr's proximity and close connection to these colleges allow students to seek greater depth in their studies and to encounter views that may not be discussed at their own college. Frequent shuttle vans run among the campuses, and students who request a book typically receive it the next day.

An impressive one-third of Bryn Mawr students spend at least a semester abroad at some point, and students speak highly of the school's programs in more than a dozen foreign countries on several continents. At home, Bryn Mawr offers foreign language classes in French, German, Latin and Greek, Hebrew, Italian, Russian, and Spanish.

Student Life: Athena, clean bathrooms, and Wicca

Some 11 miles west of Philadelphia, the college sits in the village of Bryn Mawr—which is Welsh for "high hill." Its magnificent 135-acre suburban campus offers many comfortable dorms. (That may be why 95 percent of Bryn Mawr students live on campus.) First-year students live together in their own halls, but upperclassmen are housed close by.

Bryn Mawr women enjoy athletics—actually competing, not merely watching. A charter member of the Centennial Conference and the only women's college in the conference, Bryn Mawr sponsors a variety of varsity intercollegiate sports: badminton, basketball, cross-country, crew, field hockey, lacrosse, soccer, swimming, tennis, track and field, and volleyball. The college also sponsors varsity club rugby, and students at Bryn Mawr and Haverford have formed bi-college equestrian and Ultimate Frisbee clubs.

One of the most vocal groups on campus is the Rainbow Alliance, a homosexual group whose membership has been mercifully declining steadily since the 1998–99 school year, when—as one student claims—almost half the student body belonged to it. The school hosts College Democrats and a fledgling chapter of College Republicans, but the most popular political causes on campus concern feminism and the environment. The school's political activists often participate in Philadelphia's many protests and rallies. Many of the events on campus deal with body image and ways in which women can purportedly become more comfortable with their own. For instance, a decades-old tradition of dancing around the May Pole in white dresses now has its intentionally nonphallic feminist counterpart: a dance around the May Hole.

Speaking of heathen rites, in addition to the ordinary run of religious organizations—Catholic, Protestant, Jewish, Muslim, and Quaker—Bryn Mawr features Athena's Circle, "a student Pagan group" for "Wiccans, Greco-Roman and Egyptian reconstructionists, Goddess-worshippers, Buddhists, and other magical people" who "worship during full moons, dark moons, solstices, equinoxes, and the other Wiccan Sabbats." Some followers of more mainstream Western creeds reportedly feel awkward on campus. Father John Ames, Catholic chaplain, told the Bryn Mawr alumnae bulletin that "some Catholic Bryn Mawr students have conveyed that speaking and living with religious moral convictions can be difficult." One student was a little blunter. The bulletin cited Kristin Henry '01, who "compared 'coming out' as a person of faith at Bryn Mawr with coming out as a homo- or bisexual."

Students who show up at Bryn Mawr not understanding the mores of its student body may be in for a surprise. "It took me a while to realize that other women were pursuing me," a student acknowledges. "When I did get it, it was a bit of a shock. I mean I've never felt harassed. But it definitely happens."

Bryn Mawr is an all-women's school, but many students don't even notice the difference—with men on campus for classes, frequent buses to and from Haverford and Swarthmore, and countless opportunities to interact with the opposite sex. (Bryn Mawr students can even live in coed dormitories at Haverford.) One student says that while she sees men all the time in classes at Haverford, and she and many of her friends have boyfriends at

SUGGESTED CORE

1. Classical Studies B205/B207, Greek History/Early Rome
2. Philosophy B101, Happiness and Reality in Ancient Thought
3. Religion H118/H122, Hebrew Bible: Literary Text and Historical Context/Introduction to the New Testament
4. Religion H124, Introduction to Christian Thought
5. Political Science B231, Introduction to Political Philosophy: Modern
6. English B225, Shakespeare
7. History B201, American History: Settlement to Civil War
8. Philosophy B204, Readings in German Intellectual History

area colleges, Bryn Mawr is an escape from testosterone. "In some ways you do feel more comfortable. There's less sense of competition and that you have to dress or act a certain way," she says.

Weekends spent in the library are quite common, and sometimes even expected. As one student puts it, "They tell us about all the women PhDs we've produced, and they want us to know we're expected to carry on the tradition."

The college and its surrounding affluent suburb experience little crime. During 2009, 10 burglaries and two forcible sex offenses were reported on campus. To guarantee student safety, the college patrols the campus 24 hours a day.

Bryn Mawr offers a rare and privileged environment, and exacts a concomitant price: tuition in 2012–13 was $42,246, and room and board $13,340. The school no longer offers need-blind admission. Still, 59 percent of all undergraduates received need-based financial aid, and the average student-loan debt of a recent graduate was $22,830.

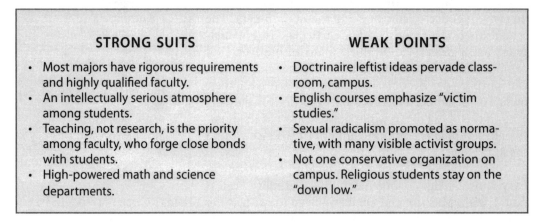

STRONG SUITS	WEAK POINTS
• Most majors have rigorous requirements and highly qualified faculty. • An intellectually serious atmosphere among students. • Teaching, not research, is the priority among faculty, who forge close bonds with students. • High-powered math and science departments.	• Doctrinaire leftist ideas pervade classroom, campus. • English courses emphasize "victim studies." • Sexual radicalism promoted as normative, with many visible activist groups. • Not one conservative organization on campus. Religious students stay on the "down low."

Bucknell University

Lewisburg, Pennsylvania • www.bucknell.edu

Best of Both?

Bucknell University was founded in 1846. It bills itself as both a professional university and a liberal arts college that offers the best of both worlds. If Bucknell suffers from a severe strain of obsessive political correctness, it also boasts strong academic programs, faculty members who enjoy teaching, and plenty of opportunities for students to get involved in research or study abroad. Bucknell students can earn a solid liberal arts education, but they'll have to be intent on attaining one, since the curriculum is riddled with loopholes, and it's up to the student to avoid them.

Academic Life: Plenty of monkeys

The university's two colleges—Arts and Sciences, and Engineering—enroll 3,500 undergraduates. About 80 percent study in Arts and Sciences, which offers 47 majors and 62 minors. (Many Bucknell students combine majors and minors.) The College of Engineering is much smaller, enrolling about 600 students, and offers a more research-based curriculum in computer science and the engineering fields.

The college ranks 32nd among national liberal arts colleges and fifth for most

VITAL STATISTICS

Religious affiliation: *none*
Total enrollment: *3,635*
Total undergraduates: *3,554*
SAT CR/Verbal midrange:
 570/590–680/690
SAT Math midrange:
 620–710
ACT midrange: *28–31*
Applicants: *7,940*
Applicants accepted: *28%*
Accepted applicants who
 enrolled: *42%*
Tuition (general/out of
 state): *$45,132*
Tuition (in state): *N/A*
Room and board: *$10,812*
Freshman retention rate:
 95%
Graduation rate (4 yrs.): *86%*
Graduation rate (6 yrs.): *91%*
Courses with fewer than 20
 students: *58%*
Student-faculty ratio: *9:1*
Courses taught by graduate
 students: *none*
Students living on campus:
 86%
Students in fraternities: *39%*
Students in sororities: *43%*
Students receiving need-
 based financial aid: *42%*
Avg. student-loan debt of a
 recent graduating class:
 $21,000
Most popular majors: *eco-
 nomics, biology, English*
Guaranteed housing for 4
 years? *yes*

beautiful schools. The College of Engineering is ranked as the ninth best undergraduate engineering program among schools without PhD programs.

Bucknell does not have a core curriculum across the board, but beginning with the class of 2014, the College of Arts and Sciences has instituted a core curriculum that specifies four types of requirements: Intellectual Skills, including a foundational seminar and lab sciences; Tools for Critical Engagement, including ideologically charged classes on diversity in the U.S., environmental, and global topics; Disciplinary Perspectives, which involves courses on the arts and humanities, natural science and mathematics, and social sciences; and Disciplinary Depth, which involves academic conventions of writing and speaking and completes the requirements of a particular major. The student is free to experiment with specialized or trendy courses while still mastering this common core of knowledge and skills. Bucknell honors programs are consigned to the different departments, involving independent study under an adviser, completion of an honors thesis or creative project, and an oral examination. However, there is no college-wide honors program and no Great Books program.

The university's advising program is only what students make of it. For an Arts and Sciences student, the instructor in the required "foundations seminar" will be his academic adviser for the first two years, after which he may choose another.

Some of Bucknell's most risible classes are, not surprisingly, to be found in the women's and gender studies department. There are also a few dubious course offerings in the international relations major—"Gender in International Relations," for example—but these are less pervasive than they were in the past. Bucknell also offers a minor in the grim-sounding discipline "peace studies."

The College of Engineering at Bucknell is reputedly strong, as are the theater, dance, and music programs. Also well regarded are its environmental, ecology, and evolution studies programs.

Although the English department has some of the school's best-liked and most-respected professors, it has no clear plan of study. Students may choose one of three concentrations: literary studies, creative writing, and film/media studies. One could well graduate with an English degree without having ever read Shakespeare, Donne, Milton, or Tennyson. The department also offers dollops of toxic fluff, such as "Gender and Sexuality in America" and "Gender and Film."

History majors choose two of seven elective clusters: American, European, non-Western, intellectual, political and economic, social, and science and medicine. At least eight courses are needed, and no more than six classes can be in a single field. In spite of an abundance of respected teachers, there is no guarantee that a graduate majoring in the subject will have learned about such basic material as the American Founding or the Renaissance, and there are plenty of politicized-sounding courses. But a sound and motivated student who chooses well can still get a solid formation.

Political science majors take four "core courses" in American politics and policy, political theory, comparative politics, and international relations. Many electives seem inflected with trendy campus politics; however, the major requirements seem solid.

Professors are lauded for their accessibility outside of class. Bucknell works hard to retain close interpersonal contact between students and professors. Professors, not graduate students, teach all courses.

For freshmen, Bucknell's residential colleges combine classroom and cocurricular activities. Students enrolled in a choice of seven theme-based houses live together, attend a course together, and participate in an hour-long discussion each week. The Social Justice and the Global colleges are the most partisan at the university. One example is the Social Justice College: "Examine topics including poverty, inequality, health care, immigration, LGBT issues and civil rights." Students say that most professors present such issues from a monochromatically leftist viewpoint. According to one student, "My professors—like a lot of professors—told us that we could say anything we wanted in class, if we were being respectful. But it turned out that we were supposed to regurgitate the liberal ideology we were being fed."

CAMPUS POLITICS: RED LIGHT

Bucknell has for many years running received a "red light" from the Foundation for Individual Rights in Education (FIRE), which named Bucknell one of the 12 worst schools for free speech in America. The worst incidents occurred in 2009, when the university prevented conservative students on three separate occasions from engaging in satire. Forbidden topics included the Obama administration's stimulus plan and affirmative action. Students were not allowed to engage in a "diversity bake sale" meant to satirize unequal admissions policies for students of different races. FIRE reported that the Bucknell conservative students stood at "Bucknell's student center and passed out fake dollar bills with President Obama's face on the front and the sentence 'Obama's stimulus plan makes your money as worthless as monopoly money' on the back. One hour into this symbolic protest, Bucknell administrator Judith L. Mickanis approached the students and told them that they were 'busted,' that they were 'soliciting' without prior approval, and that their activity was equivalent to handing out Bibles." Closing ranks and stonewalling, university administrators refused to allow FIRE to purchase an ad in a student newspaper criticizing these abuses of free speech. In 2010 FIRE wrote its third letter of appeal to the school's new president, noting that the policies used to punish students for free speech remained in place.

On a brighter note, Bucknell has plenty of monkeys. One of Bucknell's unique features is the psychology department's primate laboratory. Created in the 1960s, the student-dubbed "Monkey House" is home to colonies of Hamadryas baboons, macaques, squirrel monkeys, and capuchin monkeys. Undergraduate and graduate students observe the animals for research, and some courses include regular field trips to the center.

The university's best departments are said to be engineering, computer science, economics, physics, mathematics, English, chemistry, animal behavior, ecology, and accounting. Professors students name as the school's best teachers include Elizabeth Armstrong in East Asian studies; Morgan Benowitz-Fredericks and Kate Toner in biology; Katie Hays in English; Ned Ladd in astronomy; Robert A. Stockland Jr. and Eric Tillman in chemistry; John Enyeart in history; Scott Meinke and Michael James in political science; Richard Fleming and Peter Groff in philosophy; Mary Beth Gray in geology; Christopher S. Magee and Geoff Schneider in economics; and William R. Gruver in management.

> Says a professor: "Our students are not overwhelmingly intellectually curious. Most Bucknell students are more interested, frankly, in their Greek organizations, or their athletic teams, or their social lives."

As for weak areas, one faculty member says, "We offer a bunch of education classes. I think these people are mostly earnest, but the classes have no place at a serious school. Then there's peace studies. I'd rather not say what I think of that." One student reports ideological bias in a "Pre-Modern Europe" history class, noting that the professor "focused so much on how women and minorities were oppressed that I feel we didn't cover enough of the big events."

Last year, more than 300 students at Bucknell studied abroad at some 130 international educational sites on every inhabited continent. Some 45 percent of Bucknell students participate in a study-abroad program.

Beginning with the incoming class of 2014, there is no foreign language requirement at Bucknell. However, prerequisites for admission to Bucknell include two years of foreign language in high school. The school does offer classes in American Sign Language, Arabic, Chinese, French, German, Greek and Latin, Hebrew, Japanese, Russian, and Spanish.

Student Life: It's Greek to them

Lewisburg, Pennsylvania, offers students a pleasing balance between peaceful beauty and university culture. The town's main drag, Market Street, is a quaint, tree-lined avenue replete with more than 40 boutiques, restaurants, and bars. But town-gown relations are strained. Lewisburg residents are said to regard Bucknell students as "spoiled brats" who crowd the bars and siphon off cheap housing, while Bucknell students—many of whom graduated from elite northeastern private schools—complain about the town's provincialism.

Bucknell guarantees on-campus housing for all undergraduates. Some 87 percent of the student body lives in the school's residence halls, apartments, and special interest, theme, or fraternity houses. Though men can live in fraternity houses, sorority members are housed in Hunt Hall, an all-women dormitory. Most other residence halls are coed by floor, meaning that men often live right next door to women. There are no coed rooms or bathrooms, except in apartments and special interest houses.

Student life at Bucknell is dominated by the Greek system. More than half of Bucknell upper-class students are members of one of the 11 fraternities or eight sororities. The university has begun instituting standards for Greek admission, including higher GPAs, more educational programming, required community service hours, and an external review process. It is still reportedly easy to get into a fraternity or sorority, however. Says one professor, "Our students are not overwhelmingly intellectually curious. Most Bucknell students are more interested, frankly, in their Greek organizations, or their athletic teams, or their social lives, or all of the above than in books and ideas."

Arts groups include poetry slams, hip-hop dance, and theater. There are four undergraduate a capella groups. *The Bucknellian* is Bucknell's weekly student newspaper (the school, blessedly, does not have a journalism department). The Calvin and Hobbes group provides the campus with substance-free activities, while KRAID, a video game club, invites students to skip parties and instead socialize as first-person shooters. (Dumbledore's Army is a substance-free group for Harry Potter fans, as you might have guessed.) Bucknell has both College Republican and Democratic clubs. The campus offers ROTC, appropriately named the "Bison Battalion."

A full-time Protestant chaplain, Catholic priest, and Jewish rabbi provide weekly religious services at Rooke Chapel. Also offered are weekly Pentecostal, Quaker, and Orthodox services, and weekly "mindfulness meditation." There are quite a few Christian devotional and outreach groups on campus.

For many years each February, the Office of Lesbian, Gay, Bisexual, and Transgender Awareness promoted its annual "National Freedom to Marry Week." It now offers a Day of Silence for the LGBT community and a Drag Ball. The university-funded office provides T-shirts and buttons and sends out an e-mail to all students asking them to take a specific political stance in support of gay marriage. The left-leaning Bucknell Caucus for Economic Justice includes several professors from the economics department and concentrates on issues like the living wage.

The Bucknell University Conservatives Club (BUCC), which calls for "lively discussion" based on "freedom, liberty, and personal responsibility," has been tirelessly active

SUGGESTED CORE

1. Classics 221, Heroic Epic or Humanities 128, Myth, Reason, Faith
2. Philosophy 205, Greek Philosophy
3. Religion 105, Introduction to the Bible
4. Religion 223, History of Western Religious Thought
5. Political Science 251, History of Western Political Thought II: Machiavelli to Bentham
6. English 257, Shakespeare
7. History 111, Introduction to U.S. History I or History 219, Antebellum America, and History 112, Introduction to U.S. History II
8. History 268, European Intellectual History II

at Bucknell. The left is feeling the pain: "It seems like a lot of the liberal student groups' activities solely consist of complaining about the conservatives' club," says one student. The BUCC presents its ideas through its popular magazine, *The Counterweight*.

At Bucknell, athletics are a priority. In addition to 23 clubs and 17 regular-season intramural sports (and more than 40 teams), Bucknell supports 12 teams for men and 13 teams for women in its Division I athletic program. The Bucknell Bisons compete in the Patriot League in 27 sports. Bucknell's student-athlete graduation rate is among the highest nationwide, according to the NCAA.

The bacchanalian parties hosted by fraternities and sororities have attracted persistent attention from the liability-conscious administration. In an effort to stem the tide of reckless drinking (alcohol poisoning, acts of violence, and DUI) by students, an emergency alcohol policy was implemented back in 2003. The policy, based on a disciplinary point system, bans hard liquor. It provides the severest sanctions—including a semester leave—for minors and legal-age students who violate liquor laws or regulations. The university also initiated a mandatory alcohol education program for incoming freshmen—"Alcohol 101"—taught by professors and staff. Students say that this has increased the "coolness" factor for drinking but reduced the amount of dangerous and extreme insobriety. "There's not as much of the students puking on the lawns as at some schools, but obviously drinking hasn't stopped," says one graduating senior.

In 2011, Bucknell reported five forcible sexual assaults, eight aggravated assaults, 22 burglaries, and three acts of arson.

Bucknell is a pricey adventure. Tuition for 2012–13 was $45,132, with an average cost of $10,812 for room and board. Some 42 percent of students get need-based financial aid. The average student-loan debt of a recent graduate is around $21,000.

STRONG SUITS	WEAK POINTS
• Very strong engineering program. • Solid faculty in the hard sciences, English, history, the performing and graphic arts. • Respected evolution studies major, with a famous primate lab on campus.	• A strong party atmosphere pervades the powerful Greek system on campus. • No honors or Great Books options offered. • Weak general-education requirements. • Repeated abuses by administrators of students' right to free speech.

California Institute of Technology

Pasadena, California • www.caltech.edu

Math Camp

Caltech was founded in 1891 as Throop University but in 1920 was renamed the California Institute of Technology. Caltech now calls itself the "world's best playground for math, science, and engineering." So far, faculty and alumni have been awarded 31 Nobel Prizes, 66 have won the National Medal of Science or Technology, and 110 have been elected to the National Academies. Where Caltech imposes a core curriculum, it is in mathematics and the sciences, while offering a respectable number of liberal arts courses. The institution wastes little time on ideology, in or out of the classroom.

Caltech provides a thorough, balanced grounding in a variety of scientific disciplines, rather than encouraging early specialization. As one student says, "It would not be far wrong to consider the program a 'liberal sciences education.'"

Academic Life: The liberal sciences

The school's science core is so rigorous that a student in engineering says, "I know enough math and physics to totally switch into those areas." These requirements are in addition to those of a student's major (called an "option" at Caltech—it's one of the few things they get

VITAL STATISTICS

Religious affiliation: *none*
Total enrollment: *2,231*
Total undergraduates: *978*
SAT CR/Verbal midrange:
700–770
SAT Math midrange:
770–800
ACT midrange: *33–35*
Applicants: *5,225*
Applicants accepted: *13%*
Accepted applicants who
enrolled: *37%*
Tuition (general/out of
state): *$39,588*
Tuition (in state): *N/A*
Room and board: *$12,084*
Freshman retention rate:
98%
Graduation rate (4 yrs.): *73%*
Graduation rate (6 yrs.): *89%*
Courses with fewer than 20
students: *64%*
Student-faculty ratio: *3:1*
Courses taught by graduate
students: *none*
Students living on campus:
95%
Students in fraternities: *N/A*
Students in sororities: *N/A*
Students receiving need-
based financial aid
54–58%
Avg. student-loan debt of a
recent graduating class:
$13,442
Most popular majors:
*engineering, mathematics,
physical science*
Guaranteed housing for 4
years? *yes*

to choose). Of the 26 options that lead to a BS degree, several are divided further into "areas of study" or "concentrations." Those who opt for engineering and applied science may concentrate in mechanical engineering, for example. Students choosing this discipline also face a "core" set of courses, including a required seminar; one out of three applied math courses; 12 specific mechanical engineering courses; and two semesters of labs. Mechanical engineers get to pick a grand total of two electives in their field.

Students get guidance from their faculty advisers—professors assigned to them when they choose an option. The Career Development Center provides useful professional placement advice, while the Ombuds Office explains and interprets university policies. However, a student says that "most students don't take advantage of these services, because they listen to the upperclassmen instead."

The university is arranged into seven divisions, six of which are scientific: biology; chemistry and chemical engineering; engineering and applied science; geological and planetary science; physics, mathematics, and astronomy; and the independent studies program. The seventh division is humanities and social science. Few go to Caltech to major in the traditional liberal arts; as one recent alumnus says, "People who go to 'tech' to study anything outside the sciences are doing themselves a disservice." Still, such students have six options: business economics and management; economics; history; history and philosophy of science; social science; and literature. In literature, course choices seem solid and traditional. Required history courses include "American History," "European Civilization," and, not surprisingly, "Introduction to the History of Science." Multicultural courses are available, such as "Race Matters: Transatlantic Perspectives" and "Ethnic Visions." Political science courses are particularly weak, almost completely scanting political philosophy or the U.S. Constitution.

Free-speech restrictions are not a problem on the Caltech campus, inside class or out. "As a rule, I'd say all the professors make themselves available to their students and are open to new viewpoints," one faculty member says. "Given, of course, that the viewpoints are backed up with some sort of thought."

NASA's Jet Propulsion Lab, the leading U.S. center for the robotic exploration of the solar system, is now administered by Caltech. Among its many top-flight research projects is the agency's Infrared Processing and Analysis Center. The Beckman Institute conducts research in chemistry and biology, while the SIRTF Science Center supports NASA's infrared Spitzer Space Telescope. The university also hosts the Laboratory for Molecular Sciences and the Materials and Process Simulation Center. Caltech owns and operates the Palomar Observatory in north San Diego County and sponsors (with NASA and the University of California) the W. M. Keck Observatory in Hawaii.

Students use these facilities as part of their class work, in the production of their senior theses, and in the course of their campus jobs. Students also have plenty of opportunities to participate in research projects with their professors. "So many profs need help," says one student, that "each student has the opportunity to develop cutting-edge research during his undergraduate career." Summer Undergraduate Research Fellowships (SURF) fund about 75 research proposals each year.

Students are seen as the future of the university—and a critical part of its present, especially in the collaborative, labor-intensive, and highly remunerative world of laboratory science. The average Caltech professor brings in $600,000 to $700,000 a year in grant money. This funding is the university's lifeblood.

Even apart from collaborating with them on research, students have no trouble getting attention from their instructors. Professors teach most classes, with teaching assistants leading discussion sessions. The ratio of undergrads to faculty is an astounding 3 to 1. The faculty is as distinguished a lot as one is likely to find anywhere, with five Nobel winners on staff. Students especially like the teaching styles of Niles Pierce in mathematics; Steven Frautschi (emeritus) in physics; Axel Scherer in electrical engineering; and Christopher Earls Brennen (emeritus), Fred E. C. Culick (emeritus), Vice Provost Melany Hunt, and Richard Murray in mechanical engineering.

One faculty member says that it is impossible to single out the best disciplines, since "we have so many Nobelists, National Medal winners, and so on in all the departments."

CAMPUS POLITICS: GREEN LIGHT

Caltech does not have a reputation as a politicized campus. Despite this, Caltech students are not disengaged by any stretch of the imagination and are far from passively subservient in their "apprenticeships." In recent years students have repeatedly galvanized themselves to action on matters directly pertaining to their own needs and those of the university. This mostly has centered on nonpolitical, school-related issues with a direct impact on students.

The "Social Activism Speakers Series" brings primarily left-wing speakers to campus. The program says it is "organized by a committee of undergraduates, graduates, and staff as well as community members. We work closely with other groups on campus such as the Caltech Y and the Caltech Democratic Club. This kind of collaboration ensures that we bring important and relevant issues to the campus."

The Foundation for Individual Rights in Education has given Caltech a "red light" on issues of free expression because of an all-encompassing and dangerously vague "harassment" code that unduly restricts free speech.

This isn't gross immodesty, just a statement of fact. It is fair to say, however, that physics, engineering, chemistry, astronomy, and biology are very strong in every respect. Departments in the humanities and social sciences do not quite match the quality of the engineering and hard science departments.

Academic pursuits are governed by the university's honor system. Most exams are take-home and none are proctored, and collaboration is encouraged on most homework. Students routinely get keys to research facilities and can use them day or night. Discussions of the honor system form part of freshman orientation.

> Working with so many Nobelists and National Medal winners, "each student has the opportunity to develop cutting-edge research during his undergraduate career."

Grades at Caltech are not inflated—if anything, they're deflated. "I think the average GPA is 3.2, and the students work really hard for that," says a senior. "For instance, most classes have one homework set a week, and that set could last 10 hours or more. The least time I've spent on a homework set would have to be four to five hours, but usually I'm working a lot longer." Rumor has it that some grad schools automatically add up to 0.7 points to the GPAs of Caltech students when considering them for admission. And if grad schools aren't doing that, they should be.

The school sponsors six study-abroad programs—Cambridge Scholars Program, Copenhagen Scholars Program, Ecole Polytechnique Scholars Program, Edinburgh Scholars Program, London Scholars Program, and Melbourne Scholars Program. Students must apply during their sophomore or junior year for acceptance during their junior or senior year.

Caltech's foreign language offerings are slim, but solid, and include Chinese, French, German, Japanese, and Spanish.

Student Life: The sorcerers' apprentices

Caltech is no party school, nor will it ever be mistaken for a country club. Since Caltech runs mostly on the overhead expense deductions from faculty grant money, the incentive for improving student accommodations is limited. However, graduates will also be at the top of the pecking order when it comes to grad-school admissions or employment.

Multiculturalism and quotas apparently play little role in hiring decisions and a very small one in admissions; the Caltech full-time faculty is only 16 percent female and about 13 percent minority, and the student body is a mere 1 percent African American, but a whopping 40 percent Asian American. This failure to be sufficiently "progressive" has not gone unnoticed. A recent university report concluded, "In essence, to achieve its full potential, Caltech needs to hire more women faculty, be more proactive in nurturing its junior faculty, and make itself friendlier to the working family."

Caltech is only 11 miles away from Los Angeles, so students have plenty of choices for out-of-class activities—if they can find time for them.

There is a religious presence at Caltech, including Hillel, Mandarin Christian Fellowship, and Muslim Students Association. Catholic students are served by the Newman Center, and the Caltech Christian Fellowship assists Protestants. Lacking a chapel at Caltech, members of these communities conduct services in various on-campus facilities. For Episcopalians looking for something traditional, Our Savior in neighboring San Gabriel will be more to their liking than nearby All Saints. Catholic students should look into St. Therese of Lisieux Parish in nearby Alhambra, which offers Sunday Latin Masses with Gregorian chant.

In leading the studious life, Caltech students find a supportive community. As one student says, "Teachers are absolutely more collaborative than competitive.... Caltech is a challenge, but we want everyone to make it through. Support is completely mutual." Indeed, a remarkable 98 percent of freshmen return the following year. Students are required to live on campus for their first two years, usually in one of eight coed houses. Caltech does not provide any on-campus single-sex dorms, but according to a housing assistant, the office makes an off-campus residence available for women each year. Some on-campus community houses do have coed bathrooms, and a housing official says there are a few coed dorm rooms on campus as well.

Each on-campus residence houses from 65 to 100 students of all different classes. House members dine together and often play intramural sports as a team; in addition, study groups often form from the houses. Campus housing is guaranteed for four years, and some students remain in the same house for their entire careers. Others can enter a lottery for off-campus, university-owned housing, next door to campus.

There is no "typical" Caltech student. "We have a lot of pranksters, clubbers, partiers, video gamers, and the occasional athlete," a student says. The student government group, Associated Students of the California Institute of Technology, publishes *little t* (the title comes from the proper way to write Caltech—"Cal Tech" is wrong), a guide for campus living. There are around a hundred registered student groups, most of them nonpolitical (many of them science-related), covering all types of interests, including performing arts, religion, and recreation. However, while the left-leaning Caltech Progressive Coalition appears to be flourishing, the College Republicans are defunct.

There is an extremely lively gay group at Caltech called PRISM. On their website they feature "Coming Out" stories. One recent entry preens: "The student support networks are eager to show that they are true LGBT 'allies.' Many straight faculty, staff, and fellow students are equally eager to show their support. While there may always be a few idiots or a few fossils who just aren't retiring soon enough, I've discovered that the Caltech community is generally very open-minded."

SUGGESTED CORE

1. English 118, Classical Mythology or English 116, Milton and the Epic Tradition
2. Humanities 3a, European Civilization: The Classical and Medieval Worlds
3. No suitable course
4. Philosophy 103, Medieval Philosophy
5. Philosophy 151, 18th-Century Philosophy: Locke to Kant or Philosophy 186, Political Philosophy
6. English 114ab, Shakespeare
7. Humanities/History 2, American History
8. Humanities 3c, European Civilization: Modern Europe

Some Caltech students—though apparently not many—can even play sports at the NCAA Division III level. Caltech has nine varsity teams for men and eight for women, and while we'd hate to jump to any stereotypical conclusions, it took 201 games and many years before the men's soccer team finally won—once, in 2009. Men's basketball boasts a 259-game losing streak, with the decisive win against Bard in 2007, the first victory since 1996. The women's basketball team's most successful season to date was 2006–7, when it won two games. The men's football team, on the other hand, has remained undefeated since 1993—when the program was eliminated.

The grandest tradition at Caltech is Ditch Day, a fixture since 1921. On this day seniors leave campus. In days past, undergraduates attempted to trash their rooms—filling them with sand, gluing furniture to the ceiling, even disassembling cars or cement mixers and reassembling them in the rooms. These days, seniors still "ditch" their classes but now prevent any property damage (which they would have to pay for) by providing the undergraduates with elaborate games and puzzles. The webpage says it best: "It's a peculiarly [Caltech] kind of fun."

Apart from this officially sanctioned vandalism, Caltech's Pasadena campus is remarkably safe. One burglary and one liquor law violation were the only reported crimes on campus in 2011.

Caltech is fairly pricey—though cheaper than comparable Ivies—with 2012–13 tuition and fees at $39,588 and room and board at $12,084. The school practices need-blind admissions and guarantees to meet the full financial need of students who enroll. On average, between 54 percent and 58 percent of Caltech undergraduate students received need-based assistance, and their average debt upon graduation was a stunningly low $13,442.

STRONG SUITS	WEAK POINTS
• Many of the top scientists in the world teach here. • Elite, high-achieving students eager to delve into real research as undergrads. • Very extensive opportunities to do hands-on work that can lead to rapid career advancement. • Small classes taught by distinguished professors, not teaching assistants. • Solid courses in most humanities. • A mostly open, nonactivist political environment.	• Nonscience options are comparatively anemic. • Almost no courses on political philosophy or American government. • All dorms and some bathrooms are coed.

Carnegie Mellon University

Pittsburgh, Pennsylvania • www.cmu.edu

Nerves of Steel

Founded by industrialist and philanthropist Andrew Carnegie in 1900 as a "first-class technical school" for the sons of local steel-mill workers, and merged in 1967 with the Mellon Institute of Industrial Research, Carnegie Mellon University is widely renowned for its academic excellence and international leadership in technological advances and research work. CMU is also well regarded as a global research facility and a widely recognized leader in computer science, robotics, and engineering. With almost 12,569 students and 5,000 faculty and staff, CMU is large, even crowded, but the college is rising to the challenge. The vast majority of CMU students are very serious about their work and put in long hours outside class. There is comparatively little interest in social and political issues on campus.

Academic Life: How do you get to Carnegie Hall?

Engineering students in the Carnegie Institute of Technology boast that they learn not just by traditional classroom and textbook study but also by doing the "fun stuff," including interactive research opportunities—wiring robots, designing Ferris wheels, and building steam engines. CMU introduces students to "industrial experiences" by teaching them

VITAL STATISTICS

Religious affiliation: *none*
Total enrollment: *12,569*
Total undergraduates: *6,178*
SAT CR/Verbal midrange:
630–730
SAT Math midrange:
680–780
ACT midrange: *29–35*
Applicants: *16,257*
Applicants accepted: *30%*
Accepted applicants who
enrolled: *28%*
Tuition (general/out of
state): *$44,880*
Tuition (in state): *N/A*
Room and board: *$11,550*
Freshman retention rate:
95.7%
Graduation rate (4 yrs.): *71%*
Graduation rate (6 yrs.): *87%*
Courses with fewer than 20
students: *69%*
Student-faculty ratio: *10:1*
Courses taught by graduate
students: *not provided*
Students living on campus:
61%
Students in fraternities: *12%*
Students in sororities: *13%*
Students receiving need-
based financial aid: *56%*
Avg. student-loan debt of a
recent graduating class:
$29,303
Most popular majors: *com-
munications, computer
science, engineering*
Guaranteed housing for 4
years? *no*

about customer needs, competitive markets, and manufacturing. One professor believes that a unique "mixture of creativity, practical problem solving, and innovation" is what makes a Carnegie Mellon education distinctive. For example, CMU engineering students are continually refining the video simulation HazMat HotZone, which trains emergency responders (such as the New York City Fire Department) how to react under catastrophic circumstances. In the past, CMU robots developed for Three Mile Island's nuclear meltdown were used at Russia's disaster at Chernobyl.

Students also have the option of combining their scientific know-how with philosophical insights by participating in the liberal arts programs of the College of Humanities and Social Sciences—or by working simultaneously for the bachelor of science and arts (BSA). The drama and music departments also have outstanding reputations. The College of Humanities and Social Sciences contains a limited number of smallish departments: economics, English, history, modern languages, philosophy, psychology, social and decision sciences, and statistics. Most of them have two tracks: a more traditional "disciplinary" major (economics or philosophy, for instance) and a more specialized "professional" major (usually a compound name, like logic and computation, psychology and biological sciences, or policy and management).

Undergraduates in all schools take some general-education classes in composition, the arts, history, math, humanities, and social sciences. In the College of Humanities and Social Sciences, students are presented, as one professor says, "with a broad range of course offerings." What is more, "faculty in this department are constantly publishing and doing new research." But placing the highest priority on new, innovative research in the sciences doesn't translate so well in the history department, resulting in classes like "Family and Gender in Russian History" and "Photography, the First 100 Years: 1839–1939," instead of fundamental Western civilization or basic American history classes. This tendency is painfully evident in the history major requirements. In addition to an introductory research class and the multicultural campus-wide general-education requirement "Global Histories," there are only three required courses for history majors: "The Development of American Culture," which is more of a sociology class; one "regional" course, with options like "Mayan America"; and one non-U.S. class, such as "Modern China." History majors may fulfill their remaining requirements with classes like "Food, Culture, and Power: A History of Eating" and "Extreme Ethnicity."

One student says of the philosophy department: "For those interested in other fields but who would like also to study philosophy, this major is one of the easier ones to complete. For those who want to make philosophy their primary field of study, they run into the problems of limited class selection biased toward logic and computational philosophy, in a small, relatively new department."

There is no political science department per se, but a Social and Decision Sciences department, which offers degrees in decision science, international relations and politics, and policy and management. Majors are not required to take classes in either the U.S. Constitution or political philosophy of any kind (though a few such electives are offered)—reinforcing CMU's emphasis on the practical, the "how" of getting something done, at the expense of learning the "whys" that guide a person in making the right decisions.

CAMPUS POLITICS: GREEN LIGHT

Carnegie Mellon's rather grinding workload and preprofessional atmosphere dampen most campus activism, and the school is known for relative tolerance of various political viewpoints. Most CMU people we consulted agreed that theirs is a largely apolitical campus; people are just too busy in the lab or studio to go marching for a cause. One student says, "CMU is very proud of its diversity. This means that there are religious beliefs and political leanings of all kinds, but they're uniformly downplayed as personal choices and opinions."

Occasional troubling incidents, however, do take place on campus—not that most people seem to notice. For instance, AB Films, a division of CMU's Activities board, has been known to show pornographic movies. CMU's official response was that while it is not "consistent with our values as a university community, it is not prohibited by university policy."

In 2012 an article in the liberal *Huffington Post* lauded CMU as one of the "best colleges for free speech" in America.

Few students attend Carnegie Mellon to major in English, and with good reason. The English department is more politicized than most, stressing the importance of diversity and multiculturalism "by teaching the overlooked works of women and writers of color alongside well-known authors . . . by teaching film, television, and other storytelling media alongside conventional texts," according to its website. A Shakespeare course is not required but is offered as an elective alongside classes like "Post-Race Culture."

Students craving a traditional liberal arts education should apply to the Humanities Scholar Program. Most Scholar participants agree to live in the same dorm in a "cluster," fostering community and discussion. They attend a seminar class together each semester for the first two years. In the third year, students prepare a research proposal as prologue to their fourth-year capstone project. Students report that the program teachers are enthusiastic. One participant lauds the "higher degree of academic dedication, which is assisted by the small-group dynamic that is cultivated."

Incoming freshmen in the humanities/social science college are assigned to one of just four academic advisers at the Academic Advisory Center. Once a student declares a major, he is offered a faculty adviser from his department—but meetings with advisers are optional. Since many students do not declare majors until the middle of the sophomore year, four advisers for the entire college is wholly inadequate, students complain.

Carnegie Mellon is not the best option for students seeking to use their college years as a period of soul-searching; rather, it is for those who are pretty sure what they want to study, especially if they seek a career in science or the fine arts. Students cannot experiment or dabble much in different disciplines before choosing majors. Transfer between colleges can be difficult, and changing majors may delay graduation.

Professors at CMU are said to teach nearly all classes, and students express satisfaction with the quality of teaching. One student says that he felt constantly challenged by professors who, for the most part, were enthusiastic. There are occasional complaints that certain faculty members are inaccessible. But most students indicate that professors are, on the whole, genuinely interested in getting to know their students. As one professor notes, "Research is emphasized, but we are putting progressive emphasis on teaching." Among the best professors at CMU are Kiron Skinner in political science; business school dean Bob Dammon in finance; Bruce Armitage and Garry Warnock in chemistry; Alex John London in philosophy; and Bob Dalton (emeritus) and Finn Kydland, a Nobel Prize winner, in economics.

> A sked to name one of CMU's traditions, one professor responds: "Working hard. I wouldn't characterize this as a party school by any means."

Students of all disciplines participate in the university's strong study-abroad program. Carnegie Mellon sponsors several university-wide exchange programs in Chile, Hong Kong, Israel, Japan, Mexico, Singapore, and Switzerland; has branch campuses in Australia and Qatar; and a partnership with CyLab in Seoul, Korea. Individual departments also offer exchanges overseas.

Although it is weak in Classics, CMU features a nationally respected modern language department. Students can take a major or minor in Chinese, European studies, French and Francophone studies, German, Hispanic studies, Japanese, or linguistics.

Student Life: Finding time

To a large extent, the character of student life at Carnegie Mellon derives from the school's demanding curriculum and particular strengths. Asked to name one of Carnegie Mellon's traditions, one professor responds, "Working hard . . . I wouldn't characterize this as a party school by any means."

The school has a reputation for having a student body of "nerds" and "geeks." There certainly isn't much of a fan base for the school's athletics teams. The student body is rather indifferent to intercollegiate athletics and often ignores CMU athletics in order to cheer for the Steelers. Some students complain that there is virtually no school spirit at CMU. The Tartans (a nickname that honors the school's Scottish founder) field 17 varsity athletic teams and are members of the NCAA Division III University Athletic Association.

First-year students are required to buy a meal plan. Student housing both on and off campus is available to all students over the age of 17. On-campus housing is located just a few minutes' walk from academic buildings, while the Oakland Community Apartments is about a five- or 10-minute walk and is served by the college's shuttle service. Almost all freshmen—currently 99 percent—live on campus in college-affiliated housing, typically in standard double or triple rooms. Most dormitories are coed, but the university also offers some single-sex dorms as well as plenty of smoke-free buildings and floors, not to mention New House, a new "green" dormitory designed to conserve energy. There are no coed bathrooms or dorm rooms in the residence halls. There are ample fraternities (18) and sororities (eight) that offer housing throughout the chic Pittsburgh neighborhoods of Oakland, Shadyside, and Squirrel Hill.

> ## SUGGESTED CORE
>
> 1. English 76–221, Studies in Classical Literature: Books You Should Have Read by Now
> 2. Philosophy 80–250, Ancient Philosophy
> 3. No suitable course
> 4. History 79–350, Early Christianity
> 5. Philosophy 80–135/80–235, Introduction to Political Philosophy/Political Philosophy
> 6. English 76–245/76–247, Shakespeare: Histories and Tragedies/Comedies and Romances
> 7. History 79–247, The Civil War Era, 1848–1877 (*closest match*)
> 8. Philosophy 80–253, Continental Philosophy

Some 61 percent of the undergraduate student body live on campus. Most students and professors carp about the abominable quality of campus food, so health buffs and foodies spend Saturday mornings shopping in the Strip District downtown. The city's inadequate downtown subway and poor bus system make the campus shuttle or a car the preferred mode of transport for most students. Public parking is reasonably cheap throughout Pittsburgh.

The university hovers at about 58 percent male, while the engineering school is almost 70 percent male. This makes CMU a refreshing exception to the trend at most colleges in America, where women have begun to outnumber men (in many places) by a ratio of 60 percent to 40 percent.

A healthy Greek system exists at CMU; approximately 12 percent of male undergraduate students enter one of the 18 fraternities, while approximately 13 percent of female undergrads are members of the school's eight sororities. Undergrads can also join a vast number of student organizations—including political groups from all across the spectrum. The College Republicans and Respect Life are especially popular among conservative students. Many of the 240 student organizations center on ethnicity, such as Multicultural Alliance, Muslim Student Association, and Young African Leaders Alliance. There is also a designated branch of the Student Life department dedicated exclusively to sexual orientation issues for the campus homosexual group, ALLIES. Other clubs and organizations include orchestra, mock trial, photography, astronomy, ballroom dance, prelaw, poker, Big Brothers/Big Sisters, and Habitat for Humanity.

On a more traditional note, the school offers many religiously oriented clubs, including organizations for Baptist, Catholic, Episcopal, Jewish, Lutheran, Methodist, Mormon, and Orthodox students, as well as the Asian Christian Fellowship, Christians on Campus, and InterVarsity Christian Fellowship. Pittsburgh is known as the city of a thousand churches; there are many churches of virtually every denomination and faith around CMU's campus. The imposing St. Boniface Church, a short drive from campus, offers Latin Mass on Sundays with a chant choir. Catholic undergrads should seek out the excellent study group FOCUS.

The crime rate in Pittsburgh is low, a fact which is reflected on campus: 21 burglaries were reported in 2011, along with four forcible sex offenses, two aggravated assaults, and one arson.

Carnegie Mellon may have been founded by a philanthropist, but it isn't free. Tuition was $44,880 in 2012–13, with room and board $11,550. Some 56 percent of undergraduates received need-based financial aid and graduated with an average debt of $29,303.

STRONG SUITS	WEAK POINTS
• Very strong science, technology, and engineering programs. • Good options in drama and music. • Tech students do hands-on work—wiring robots, designing Ferris wheels, building steam engines, refining emergency simulation software. • A diverse political environment, with many religiously oriented clubs. • A pleasant campus in a very livable city, Pittsburgh.	• Smallish, limited offerings in economics, English, history, modern languages, philosophy, psychology, social sciences, and statistics. • New research drives too many of the course options in the humanities, displacing essential surveys in favor of esoteric classes. • No political science department and few political philosophy courses offered. • English department focused on media, pop culture, ideological issues.

Catholic University of America

Washington, D.C. • www.cua.edu

Change and . . . Continuity?

Founded by the bishops of the United States and chartered by Pope Leo XIII in 1887, the Catholic University of America is this country's only pontifically sponsored school. In the past two years, CUA has moved even more strongly in the direction of affirming its Catholic identity—for instance, by reinstating single-sex dorms. Its strong academics and comparatively solid religious base make it a competitive choice for students who care about the Catholic educational tradition and who prefer to study at a large, mainstream university.

Academic Life: Intellectual genealogy

CUA offers 72 bachelor's degree programs in six schools: arts and sciences, architecture and planning, engineering, music, philosophy, and nursing, which is ranked as one of the best in the country. One outstanding option is the honors program, which a professor calls "a fine opportunity to gain a genuine liberal arts education, especially with its director, Dr. Michael Mack." Two of the sequences in the honors program, The Christian Tradition and An Aristotelian Studium, if taken together offer one of the best liberal arts preparations available in America, grounded in primary texts centered on the most important questions any student will encounter in his life. Any CUA student would do well to enroll. According to students, other strong departments include politics, philosophy, history, and English.

Catholic University imposes a stronger set of distribution requirements than most schools. One student boasts, "My curriculum in politics and philosophy (double major) and minor in theology is nothing but studying the Great Books from those subjects. Especially for philosophy, everything is taught directly from the sources themselves." Another student claims, however, that some of the distribution requirements are actually weaker than they appear. The religion requirement, for instance, can be met "without ever having to do anything more substantial than a few 'reflection' papers—the sort of thing that begins with the words 'I feel.'"

Religion majors can concentrate in biblical studies, Roman Catholic studies, religious development and religious education, or religion and culture. The quality and fidelity of classes vary with the professors, sources say. They recommend students ask around to find out which are rigorous and orthodox. One former instructor commented that "it is sad to admit, but most heterodoxy was to be found in the school of religious studies." A graduate instructor commented, "The seminarians enrolled in my Latin class regretted that CUA's pontifical status required that they study Latin. Their preference was—if any foreign language—German so that they would have greater access to 'progressive' theologians."

Politics is considered one of the strongest departments for undergraduates and is particularly solid in political theory. As one student comments: "The opportunities provided by being in D.C. are amazing for politics majors." However, one student warns of only "limited offerings for undergraduates" in American political philosophy, especially the Constitution. Still, poli-sci majors are required to take introductory classes in the U.S. Constitution and American political theory. Students say the best faculty members in the department are Phil Henderson, John Kromkowski, James O'Leary, Claes Ryn, and David Walsh. One professor claims that the "politics department is quite strong for those who care about a real liberal-arts-oriented education, rather than the trendy behavioral studies that have polluted political science almost everywhere else." Another professor laments that the world politics concentration is weak. An exclusive and exciting option available for political science students at CUA is the study-abroad program wherein a student may intern for a semester or summer at the British Parliament at Westminster, the Irish Parliament in Dublin, or the EU Parliament in Brussels, an opportunity a student calls "a politics major's dream."

The academic pride and flagship school of CUA is its School of Philosophy, which is highly regarded nationwide for its programs in classical and medieval thought. Professors V. Bradley Lewis, Timothy Noone, Matthias Vorwerk, Tobias Hoffman, David Thayer, and Kevin White are named as some of the best in the school, along with Robert Sokolowski, who specializes in phenomenology, and John F. Wippel, an expert on Aquinas and metaphysics. Regis Armstrong on Franciscan theology, Joseph Capizzi in moral theology and ethics, and William Loewe in Christology are also purported to be outstanding.

Other notable professors in the university include Michael Mack (famous on campus for his Shakespeare class), Ernest Suarez, Christopher Wheatley, Rosemary Winslow, and Stephen Wright in English; Virgil Nemoianu in comparative literature and philosophy; Mario Ortiz in Spanish; Sarah Ferrario in Classics; and Katherine L. Jansen and Jerry Z. Muller in history.

CAMPUS POLITICS: GREEN LIGHT

In recent years Catholic University has had a markedly more traditional atmosphere than most Catholic-founded colleges. One professor says, "There's little-to-no PC stuff around here." A student agrees that in the classroom "CUA is great at encouraging debate. Dissent is usually encouraged. There is perhaps some condescension toward conservative students but not usually anything beyond that." One alumnus said, "Many of my teachers were moderate liberals—obviously so. Occasionally we were required to do absurd things like avoid using BC and AD, and instead use BCE and CE, but for the most part, even the politically correct faculty were demanding scholars and interested in genuine discussion and serious reading."

Says one student of the political atmosphere on campus, "Generally everyone knows this is a conservative campus, even though some pockets of strong liberals endure. The College Republicans dominate student life in the political sense, and in numbers the College Democrats are always at a loss to compete with Republican efforts and the general attitude on campus."

Scholar Harold Bloom listed Catholic University's English department as one of the few in the country with exceptionally high standards of teaching and scholarship. The requirements for an English major are excellent, including "History of English Literature" I and II, "Intensive Readings in Lyric, Drama, and Narrative," "Chaucer and His Age," and "Plays of Shakespeare." As one student testifies, "Teaching and scholarship are important. The more liberal literary ideologies are almost nonexistent in the classroom."

The history department, on the other hand, is weaker, offering an overabundance of "diversity" and multicultural classes. The major requirements reflect this trend as well, although students must take two foundational world civilization courses to graduate with a history degree.

Graduate students regularly teach introductory courses, especially in the social sciences and foreign language courses. The university says it closely monitors them for quality control and trains them with a pedagogy class. One professor notes, "For a research-oriented university, our teaching loads are high. The number of professors who nonetheless work hard at their teaching is noticeable." A student confirms this, saying that "teachers have always been accessible enough for me."

Class sizes—once you get past the introductory courses—are usually small, with an average of 17 students. Small groups encourage discussion and faculty-student interaction. Class participation is often part of a student's grade, especially in seminars.

Every freshman has two advisers, an academic and a first-year adviser. The academic adviser is in the major department, so students are encouraged to make an early, tentative choice of major.

A student says, "My curriculum in politics and philosophy and theology is nothing but studying the Great Books from those subjects."

Science majors complain that the chemistry and biology departments lack adequate, modern facilities. Students and faculty alike say that music and drama are especially strong programs at Catholic University and that modern languages is the weakest.

CUA offers many study-abroad opportunities through its CUAbroad department. The flagship programs in Rome and Oxford are the most popular, but many students decide to study at the school's 17 other affiliate programs in Argentina, Australia, Chile, China, Ecuador, France, Germany, Greece, India, Ireland, Japan, Mexico, Morocco, New Zealand, Poland, South Africa, and Spain.

On campus, students are offered foreign language classes in Arabic, French, German, Greek and Latin, Hebrew, Italian, and Spanish.

Student Life: In the city, but not of it

Catholic University adjoins the massive Shrine of the Immaculate Conception, the Dominican House, the Washington Theological College, and the U.S. Council of Catholic Bishops. CUA students—largely East Coast, Catholic, parochial-schooled, and middle- and upper-middle class—tend to take their college careers seriously. Nevertheless, they find time to take part in the life of the nation's capital. CUA is a mere three Metro stops from the city's rail hub, Union Station.

Most students are required to live on campus for the first two years of school. CUA began in fall 2011 to restore single-sex dorms for all incoming students. This brave, counter-cultural decision should do much to improve student life at CUA. In the "wellness" dorm, students pledge to go without alcohol. Students are not allowed to have guests of the opposite sex past midnight on weeknights and 2:00 a.m. on weekends. However, the campus newspaper, *The Tower*, says of this policy: "Nobody abides by its intent or letter, including resident assistants. Enforcing this rule would have a catastrophic effect on both the academic and social lives of students." According to one student, with the exception of orientation lectures on the dangers associated with alcohol, drug use, and promiscuity, "moral formation seems to be left to the student rather than entrusted to the school." Aside from the rowdy dorm atmosphere, CUA's campus offers little in the way of a nightlife.

The university has over a hundred registered clubs, organizations, and professional societies, as well as one fraternity and one sorority. Some years back, a proposal for an approved gay and lesbian organization was narrowly defeated in student government. On the whole the student body tends to be more conservative than the faculty and staff, a graduate notes. Both College Democrats and College Republicans have chapters on campus.

Students are very active in campus ministry at CUA. Organizations like Habitat for Humanity, Knights of Columbus, and Students for Life bring students together for spiritual and charitable purposes, emphasizing the university's Catholic tradition. One student says that the school's Campus Ministry "offers a ton of activities and advice for all students to have a proper moral formation and religious formation: Theology on Tap, scripture studies, 'Renew' prayer groups, et cetera." While the immense National Shrine of the Immaculate Conception stands adjacent to campus, students also have access to Saint Vincent's Chapel and Caldwell Chapel for on-campus prayer.

CUA competes in the NCAA Division III, with 21 varsity sports teams, all called the Cardinals. The university also offers 11 club and 14 intramural sports, ranging from coed indoor soccer to racquetball and badminton.

A Metro stop at one corner of the campus provides easy access to the rest of the Washington area. One student says: "From volunteer-ushering at Ford's Theater to enjoying class trips to the National Gallery, from ice skating in the Sculpture Garden to walking the monuments at moonlight, D.C. has been an education and an adventure in itself."

While enjoyable and fascinating, Washington, D.C., is statistically the most violent city in the country. So escort services provided by Public Safety and the Safe Ride program take students home from late-night study sessions and parties. Still, campus crime statistics are fairly reassuring. In 2011 the school reported three forcible sex offenses, 10 burglaries, and one car theft.

Catholic University's tuition in 2012–13 was $36,320, with room and board totaling $14,274. The school does not practice need-blind admission or guarantee to meet a student's full financial need. Fifty-six percent of undergraduates received need-based financial aid, and the school refused to release the average indebtedness of its recent graduates.

SUGGESTED CORE

1. Comparative Literature 207, Masterpieces of Western Literature I
2. Philosophy 201, The Classical Mind: The Origin and Growth of Western Philosophy
3. Theology and Religious Studies 200/210, Introduction to the Old/Introduction to the New Testament
4. Theology and Religious Studies 220, Church through the Ages: Paul to Luther
5. Politics 360, Modern Political Thought
6. English 461/462, Plays of Shakespeare I/II
7. History 257, American History Survey I
8. History 341, Modern European Intellectual History II

STRONG SUITS	WEAK POINTS
• An increasing, countercultural commitment to its religious mission and identity. • Excellent, demanding honors program. • Solid, traditional programs in most disciplines—especially English, philosophy, political science, architecture (which teaches neoclassical design). • One of the top nursing programs in the U.S. • Politics students pursue excellent internships—easy to do, since the school is in the middle of Washington, D.C. • Recently restored single-sex dorms.	• Founded as a graduate institution, CUA uses too many graduate teaching assistants in classes. • Religion requirement too vague and can be satisfied with touchy-feely classes. • Not all faculty in religion classes are orthodox Catholics. • Worthy dorm policies are often left unenforced by RAs.

Centre College

Danville, Kentucky • www.centre.edu

Smack Dab in the Middle

Centre College is neither a trendy school overrun by contemporary ideologies, nor a deeply religious college informed by a particular denomination. (The school is officially Presbyterian.) Founded in 1819, Centre College has a long history of service to both Kentucky and the nation. Through required courses in the humanities and the "fundamental questions," students are at least exposed to the best ideas in the Western tradition and the important issues of faith and doubt. One student says of her experience: "Centre College is a wonderfully nurturing environment that cultivates lifelong learners who are civically active."

Academic Life: Solid Centre

Centre students face a rather structured set of general-education requirements. According to one professor, "These kids don't have to learn Latin and Greek, but most get a smattering of the basics."

Students are appointed general advisers—usually matched by interests—during their first and second years. Then they choose an adviser in their major department.

Requirements for the majors, especially in the humanities, are solid. Students majoring

VITAL STATISTICS

Religious affiliation: *Protestant (Presbyterian)*
Total enrollment: *1,337*
Total undergraduates: *1,337*
SAT CR/Verbal midrange: *570–690*
SAT Math midrange: *590–680*
ACT midrange: *26–31*
Applicants: *2,230*
Applicants accepted: *74%*
Accepted applicants who enrolled: *21%*
Tuition (general/out of state): *$43,800*
Tuition (in state): *N/A*
Room and board: *not provided*
Freshman retention rate: *94%*
Graduation rate (4 yrs.): *85%*
Graduation rate (6 yrs.): *82%*
Courses with fewer than 20 students: *53%*
Student-faculty ratio: *11:1*
Courses taught by graduate students: *none*
Students living on campus: *98%*
Students in fraternities: *39%*
Students in sororities: *37%*
Students receiving need-based financial aid: *67%*
Avg. student-loan debt of a recent graduating class: *$26,700*
Most popular majors: *history, psychology, social sciences*
Guaranteed housing for 4 years? *yes*

in English must explore literature from various centuries—including one course in Shakespeare. History majors must also take courses from different periods and places. Requirements, refreshingly, do include "Development of the United States" I and II. Most classes sound solid, apart from some electives, such as "Gender and Sexuality in Western Society." We're pleased to see that government majors are required to take "American Politics and Institutions."

Students would do well to ask around before signing up for courses in the religion department. One undergrad states that "the religion department is the weakest because of the inconsistency among professors." One student reports that she decided not to major in religion at Centre when she "discovered the professor teaching my class didn't think the Bible had any value other than anthropology. He isn't the only one who thinks like that, and I wasn't able to grit my teeth and get through it the way some students do."

Centre has a strong reputation in the sciences. One professor informs us that "biochemistry and molecular biology has an excellent track record for medical school acceptance. Its curriculum is rigorous and oriented toward developing laboratory skills. Their senior seminar is the strongest capstone experience in the college. Most students are heavily involved in some form of undergraduate research." The chemistry program also has had success in preparing students for graduate study and obtaining top summer lab internships.

Centre is a small school. The philosophy department lists just four faculty members, the history department 10, and the psychology department nine. A professor says, "All these programs are very small, so if there is any faculty turnover, things can change very quickly." By design, Centre's approach to education is interdisciplinary, and many classes are cross-listed with those in other departments. One student notes, "It lets you find out how interrelated learning truly is." If the courses offered are limited, most are rigorous. One student says, "There is no grade inflation. . . . Sometimes I wish I had gone to an easier school, but I know it's worth it." Another says, "It is very hard to fall through cracks here. Professors know and care about who you are and what you want to do."

The school offers students "the Centre Commitment," guaranteeing an internship, an opportunity to study abroad, and graduation within four years—or else they'll get a free year's study at the school. According to Centre, "Not once . . . have we had to pay for an additional year."

There are no teaching assistants at Centre, and the school does not require its professors to "publish or perish." Their main objective is to teach. A student says that "one of Centre's strongest aspects is the accessibility of professors." Another adds, "Professors are extremely helpful. I can always go to them after hours for any help I have with the class work."

One student says that the faculty's devotion to students makes Centre a "very transformative experience. . . . Before coming to Centre, I had no idea what my intellectual passions were."

Some of the best professors, students report, include Christine A. Shannon in math and computer science; J. Preston Miles in chemistry; Jane W. Joyce (emeritus) in classical studies; Stephen E. Asmus and Peggy Richey in biochemistry; Robert E. Martin (emeritus) in economics; C. Kenneth Keffer in French; Donna M. Plummer in education; Mark T. Lucas in English; Richard D. Axtell (also the college chaplain) in religion; Stephen R. Powell in art; Lori Hartmann-Mahmud in government; Dan Stroup in political science; and Michael Hamm and Clarence Wyatt in history.

CAMPUS POLITICS: YELLOW LIGHT

Classroom politics, students say, are generally kept to a minimum. One student says the campus has a fairly free exchange of ideas and remembers a few instances when the school itself encouraged political debate. However, a faculty member says it is rare that political ideas are actually exchanged. "Part of that is an inherently southern civility," he says, "and part of it is a student body that is generally rather conservative." While there are quite a few conservative students on campus, the faculty tends to be quite liberal. This has its impact on student life. A few years ago a group of students wished to form a pro-life group but were effectively blocked from doing so because not a single faculty member would agree to sponsor the group. Students reported that while there are pro-life faculty members, they were apparently afraid to sponsor the group for fear of reprisals from colleagues.

According to one teacher, "While I would characterize most of the faculty as being politically left of center, I have not heard of anyone pushing his or her personal agenda in the classroom. On the other hand, many of the reading and course assignments, particularly in the humanities and social sciences, appear to reflect the political views of the professors."

A student reports: "Our study-abroad program is very strong. Between 80 and 90 percent of each graduating class has studied abroad at least once." The school maintains its own facilities and professors in these foreign programs, so that "classes are very rigorous and take advantage of the location," a student says. The college operates residential programs in England, France, and Mexico as well as exchange programs with universities in China, Japan, and Northern Ireland. One student reports: "When Centre students go abroad, they are definitely more than tourists. When I traveled to Costa Rica, we lived with a family that had only one light bulb in the house, where we had to wake up every morning with the rooster and cook meals with the 'mom,' go out to the 'palms' to pick oranges, and come in by 1:00 p.m. every day, before the rains came, then sit on the porch with our 'dad' and pick the bad pieces of rice out of the pile." Since travel can be expensive, the school has an endowed fund to assist students with need-based aid to cover the extra cost.

Foreign languages taught at Centre include French, German, Greek (Ancient or New Testament), Hebrew (biblical), Japanese, Latin, Mandarin, and Spanish. Majors and minors are offered only in French, German, and Spanish.

Student Life: Biden twice

Built almost entirely in red brick, the Centre campus has many buildings listed in the National Register of Historic Places. According to a student, "There is a seal in front of Old Centre. If two students kiss on the seal at midnight, they will get married."

Sixty-one percent of the student body hails from Kentucky, but most tend to stay on campus on the weekends. Some 98 percent of Centre students live on campus, and students have several options for living arrangements, including traditional dormitories, suite-style living, and apartments. Most dorms are single-sex, although some upperclassman dorms are coed by floor. Visiting hours are strictly enforced, and visitors must use the public bathrooms. One student tells us, "About 10 percent of our student body applies every year to be a resident assistant. The application process is very rigorous." RAs are paid a minimal stipend, but competition for the positions is high. "Nobody's in it for the money," one RA says. "We genuinely want to help each other out."

Some students live in the Greek Park fraternity and sorority houses, but space is limited, and the houses are primarily used for social events. One student stressed that Centre students genuinely want to be on campus. "Everyone is so polite here," several students report.

One student calls the school a "very transformative experience. Before coming to Centre, I had no idea what my intellectual passions were."

One professor says, "The most distinctive feature of the life at Centre is civility. The faculty and the administration prize it. The culture encourages people to be polite and to prevent ideological, pedagogical, and intellectual differences from becoming personal. We certainly do have our disagreements and arguments here, but they rarely turn nasty. Faculty who join us from other institutions are amazed. Visitors who spend any time here at all almost always remark on it." The fraternities and sororities are also known for being friendly and welcoming.

Danville is a small town, and students tend to stick to campus and make their own fun. Just about every weekend sees frat parties, which are technically off campus, and all students are welcome. There is, of course, a certain amount of drinking at these events—however, students report that alcohol consumption is pretty moderate, even at frat parties.

Danville is a "moist" town—meaning there are no bars or liquor stores, although restaurants can serve alcohol.

Students report there is very little dating among students. Of course, there is no rule against such fraternizing (this isn't a military academy), but for some reason—perhaps the significant course workload—the dating life at Centre isn't much to write home about.

With more than a hundred student organizations on campus, undergrads can stay busy. Groups include Association of Women in Mathematics, Badminton Club, B-GLAD (Bisexuals, Gays, Lesbians and Allies for Dignity), Centre Cheerleading, and a variety of religious and special interest clubs.

Each year a wide variety of cultural events come to the college. Such "convocations" have included a speech by Justice Sandra Day O'Connor, concerts by the Boston Pops, and performances by the likes of Mikhail Baryshnikov. According to one student, "These convocations teach me so many things that I would not learn in the classroom." In 2000 and 2012, Centre College hosted the national vice-presidential debates.

There is an excellent turnout for home games in all sports. The school competes in 23 intercollegiate varsity sports, with 44 percent of the student population participating. There are also 15 intramural sports in which 80 percent of students participate. The school offers no athletic scholarships.

Centre's religious roots remain relevant. The department of religious affairs offers many opportunities for Bible study and fellowship throughout the year, with Wednesday night Centre Christian Fellowship meetings particularly well attended. According to one student, the college student body has a strong Catholic presence—but a rather weak on-campus group. Catholic students seeking something a little more traditional can find a daily and weekly Latin Mass in nearby Lexington, at St. Peter's Church.

Crime is infrequent at Centre. In 2011 the school reported one forcible sex offense and seven burglaries on campus.

Centre is a moderately priced school with tuition, room, and board costing a total of $43,800 for the 2012–13 school year. The college does its best to meet students' financial needs, and 67 percent of students received need-based financial assistance. The average indebtedness of a recent Centre graduate was $26,700.

SUGGESTED CORE

1. Humanities 110, Introduction to Humanities I (*closest match*)
2. Philosophy 210, Ancient Philosophy
3. Religion 110, Biblical History and Ideas
4. Religion 120, History of Christian Thought
5. Government 300/301, Western Political Theory I/II
6. English 301/302, Shakespeare I/II
7. History 230, Development of the United States I
8. Philosophy 330, 19th-Century Philosophy

STRONG SUITS

- Solid requirements for general education and key disciplines such as English, history, political science.
- Mostly traditional course offerings, non-politicized classrooms, and varied range of opinion on campus.
- Devoted teachers who are close to students; no graduate teaching assistants.
- A famously civil, friendly atmosphere on campus.

WEAK POINTS

- Religion department leans secularist, offending some students of faith.
- An absence of openly conservative faculty—not one was willing to sponsor a campus pro-life group, so it died.
- Social life and dating are said to be weak on campus; students may be too busy.

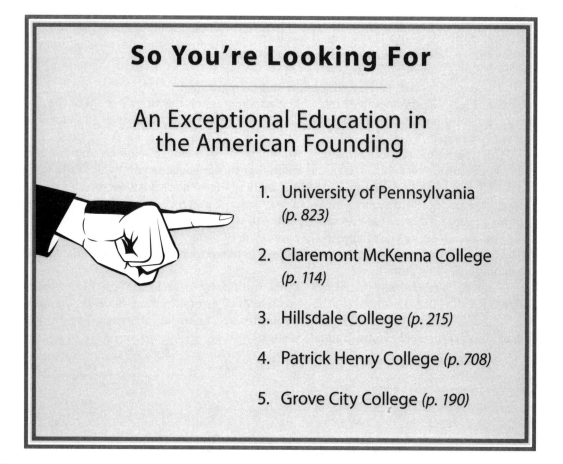

So You're Looking For

An Exceptional Education in the American Founding

1. University of Pennsylvania *(p. 823)*

2. Claremont McKenna College *(p. 114)*

3. Hillsdale College *(p. 215)*

4. Patrick Henry College *(p. 708)*

5. Grove City College *(p. 190)*

Christendom College

Front Royal, Virginia • www.christendom.edu

Back to the Middle Ages

Christendom College was founded in 1977 by a group of conservative Catholic academics. The entire faculty formally swears fidelity to Catholic teaching every year, and all classes are opened with prayer. This does not mean that the school feels like a seminary, however; students report that the school maintains an atmosphere of healthy debate and academic interchange within certain closely defined parameters of faith.

Academic Life: To form the whole person

The college seeks to give a student "the solid moral principles, core knowledge and skills, and intellectual flexibility suited to a liberally educated person," reports one professor. Another tells us that "Christendom does a great job in the liberal arts. There are few places that are better. Students will get a pretty solid grounding in the classics, in a setting that puts them in their context (i.e., not a Great Books approach)."

The college confers a bachelor of arts degree, with majors available in classical and early Christian studies, English, history, philosophy, political science and economics, and theology. Christendom also offers master's programs in theological and catechetical studies

VITAL STATISTICS

Religious affiliation: *Roman Catholic*
Total enrollment: *500*
Total undergraduates: *388*
SAT CR/Verbal midrange: *560–700*
SAT Math midrange: *510–640*
ACT midrange: *23–28*
Applicants: *300*
Applicants accepted: *80%*
Accepted applicants who enrolled: *51%*
Tuition (general/out of state): *$21,000*
Tuition (in state): *N/A*
Room and board: *$7,970*
Freshman retention rate: *83%*
Graduation rate (4 yrs.): *69%*
Graduation rate (6 yrs.): *70%*
Courses with fewer than 20 students: *59%*
Student-faculty ratio: *14:1*
Courses taught by graduate students: *N/A*
Students living on campus: *95%*
Students in fraternities: *N/A*
Students in sororities: *N/A*
Students receiving need-based financial aid: *51%*
Avg. student-loan debt of a recent graduating class: *$24,000*
Most popular majors: *history, philosophy, political science*
Guaranteed housing for 4 years? *yes*

through its Notre Dame Graduate School in Alexandria, Virginia.

One professor informs us that "the intellectual curiosity of the students is higher than at most schools. Because things relate to their faith, students want to know more than they normally would. That is a great thing." Another faculty member adds, "Learning here continues outside of the classroom. Discussions do not end in the classroom but continue through the course of a student's term."

Christendom College assigns each freshman a faculty adviser, but once the student picks a major, he is advised by that department chairman or his delegate.

Philosophy has long been and remains the most popular major. Within that department, students praise John Cuddeback, J. Michael Brown, and Steven Snyder. The department's classes are infused by the methods of St. Thomas Aquinas but also examine at length the works of modern and contemporary philosophers. According to one student, "The philosophy department has an amazing variety of professors who make the subject matter understandable, ranging from ancient and medieval to modern thinkers. The material helps to form your intellect to know truth and to be able to defend your faith."

History is also another well-populated major at the college; the school's leading founder was a historian. A providential view of history shapes the school's entire curriculum. One professor tells us that "history is the strongest major. It has professors who are the most interested in scholarship, and they are the most published." American history is required of majors, as are comprehensive surveys of the history of the West.

Literature courses study complete works rather than selections. The freshman at Christendom acquires writing and critical-reading skills through the study of the *Iliad, Odyssey, Aeneid,* and Aristotle's *Poetics.* Works by Milton, Dante, and T. S. Eliot round out the literature core. A course in Shakespeare is required.

Theology classes such as "Ascetical and Mystical Theology," "Theology and the Public Order," and "Latin Readings in St. Thomas Aquinas" build on the school's impressive core requirements in Catholic theology. One teacher whom students consistently praise is Eric Jenislawski.

In political science and economics (a single major), Christendom students speak highly of Patrick Bracy Bersnak (a favorite), Bernard Way, and William Luckey. Graduates in this major frequently opt for a career in politics in nearby Washington, D.C., or continue on to law school. One political science professor tells us, "The motto of the college is to restore all things in Christ. We think about the practical implications of that more than any other department. Political science is where the rubber hits the road." American government and politics are required of majors.

Christendom maintains an excellent classical and early Christian studies department. According to one professor, the department "has a number of exceptionally talented instructors in both Latin and Ancient Greek. Students have many opportunities to study a wide range of both pagan and Christian literature from antiquity through to the medieval period. Hebrew and Syriac occasionally supplement the course offerings. Several students have won national awards for their achievements in Latin and Ancient Greek."

All classes at Christendom are taught by professors rather than graduate students. Faculty members keep office hours and usually eat meals with students. Students report easy access to their professors: "The professors are extremely accessible. They make themselves available to students for anything," says a teacher.

CAMPUS POLITICS: GREEN LIGHT

Shield of Roses, a group of Christendom students, travels every Saturday to Washington, D.C., to pray at abortion clinics. On January 22 each year, classes are canceled so that students may participate in the March for Life in D.C. The college charters buses for the event, and the entire student body, along with the professors, must take part. (We'd like this universal participation much better if it were voluntary.)

Although one need not be Catholic to go to the school, it certainly helps. Non-Catholics, unless they are on the path to conversion, would probably feel uncomfortable. The overwhelming majority of students are serious Catholics, which serves as one of the strongest bonds in the community life of the college. Graduates report forming strong friendships that carry well beyond college years (and more than a few marriages). However, with a small student body, it is also true that, as one student warns, "everybody knows everybody. It's very dramatic sometimes when everybody knows what is going on in other people's lives."

One professor informs us that "while some faculty routinely publish books and articles, and others attend conferences or give lectures abroad, these activities are voluntary. Some faculty prefer to focus on teaching alone. The classroom performance of the professors is routinely evaluated, and teaching ability is a major consideration in hiring and retaining them."

"Christendom faculty and students share a common love of learning and of the church," says one professor. However, a professor adds, "political correctness does not exist on campus." Many issues remain open to debate. "The main factions on campus consist of Republicans, agrarians, libertarians, paleoconservatives, and *ancien régime* traditionalists. Sometimes debates between these groups enter into the classroom, but this is usually interesting rather than intrusive." Students report that they gather with their friends often to discuss issues outside of class. One says, "Sometimes I am drawn into a heated discussion with fellow students at an off-campus party about things as simple as the meaning of community, music, or economics."

One of the highlights for a Christendom student is the junior semester in Rome. "The semester in Rome was one of the greatest experiences of my life," says an enthusiastic student. "It was a spiritual, intellectual, cultural adventure." Another professor notes that there is room for improvement in the program: "Study abroad is very popular. I don't have the impression that it is the most academic thing. It is more holy tourism than a part of a liberal education."

The college has its weaknesses. The combined math and science department is sparse, with very few offerings. Modern languages are also reported to be comparatively anemic; French and Spanish are generally offered only through the intermediate level, while there is rudimentary Italian sufficient for the semester abroad in Rome.

A professor complains of a certain moralism among faculty, suggesting that "our distinct and irreplaceable contribution to the spiritual and moral lives of our students should be through the cultivation of their intellects. . . . If we do not force people to cultivate their intellect, then no one will."

Student Life: Everybody knows everybody

Christendom's campus outside Front Royal, Virginia, sits in a commuter city for the Washington, D.C., area. A modest collection of area bars and restaurants and a local movie theater constitute the main entertainments in town; however, cultural opportunities abound in Washington, D.C., about 75 miles away.

Moderate consumption of alcohol and tobacco are socially acceptable to most students, while illegal drug use is shunned. A strict policy banning the storage and use of alcohol on campus sends many student parties to surrounding properties or off-campus houses. "We do have our parties," says one student flatly, "but we try to drink within the realms of moderation." Punishment for breaking the alcohol policy is suspension from the campus. Illegal drug use results in expulsion.

A student praises numerous "professors who make the subject matter understandable. The material helps to form your intellect to know truth and defend your faith."

The campus also has a policy banning romantic displays of affection or "RDAs." However, "Most of the RAs know what it's like to date," says one student. "Unless it's a blatant disregard of the rules, they are not out to bust you." In tune with Catholic teaching, school rules strictly forbid the sort of recreational sexual activity found on many secular campuses—and the punishment for violations is significant, up to and including expulsion.

One student tells us, "There are RAs or proctors on every floor, and they are extremely fun and helpful in any circumstance. They are all great leaders and show an interest in each person under their care." Another student tells us that a few of the RAs look more to the letter than the spirit of the law and continually bust people for very minor infractions.

Church feast days are campus-wide holidays at Christendom, and classes are canceled on Holy Days of Obligation. Christendom's "zeal for Catholic culture" is apparent in its annual Medievalfest and Oktoberfest celebrations. A strict dress code enforces "a professional appearance" for students in class, with a strict modesty code banning all skirts that fall above the knee and thin-strapped tank tops. These modesty codes also apply to students outside of class, although "normal" attire such as jeans and T-shirts are acceptable.

> ### SUGGESTED CORE
>
> The school's required core curriculum suffices.

Christendom offers an abundance of spiritual opportunities. A full 15 percent of alumni go on to serve as priests and religious. Three college chaplains offer Mass two to three times a day and provide numerous opportunities for confession. Students speak admiringly of the spiritual direction offered at the school. Many students volunteer their time to join the Chapel Choir, which sings hymns for the campus Mass on Sunday and routinely travels to area parishes.

As a member of the United States Collegiate Athletic Association (USCAA), Christendom fields intercollegiate teams in men's and women's basketball, golf, and soccer; men's baseball and rugby; and women's volleyball and softball. Intramurals are popular among the students.

Dorms are single sex and *verboten* to the opposite sex. The men's and women's dorms are situated on opposite sides of the campus. Most of the student dorms are doubles, although some larger rooms are split into triples. Some 95 percent of the students live on campus.

So little crime occurs on campus that Christendom does not compile statistics, although students report a few thefts and the occasional rowdy drunk. Security guards monitor the campus during the night.

Tuition for the 2012–13 academic year was $21,000, and room and board were $7,970. Some 51 percent of students received need-based financial aid, and the average student-loan debt of a graduating student in 2009 (the last year available) was $24,000.

STRONG SUITS	WEAK POINTS
• Fierce commitment to its religious mission and intellectual heritage.	• Moral formation of students can trump education as a priority among some faculty.
• Strong core curriculum that guarantees a broad education, regardless of major.	• Very close, small-town environment with little privacy.
• High level of intellectual curiosity among students.	• Math, science, modern language programs are weak.
• Dedicated professors, small classes.	• Dominance of a single subculture can result in groupthink among students.
• A very friendly environment for conservative and devout students.	

Claremont Colleges

Claremont, California • www.claremont.edu

The Five Cs

The consortium known as the Claremont Colleges is a group of five undergraduate colleges and two graduate universities all located within one square mile in Claremont, California. Each of the Claremont colleges is distinct but draws upon the vast array of resources the group offers. The colleges share 12 campus buildings, athletic facilities and teams, a student newspaper, and plenty of social activities; therefore, a student can benefit from the strengths of the four other colleges, making the weaknesses at his own more bearable. Generally speaking, the Claremont colleges boast dedicated and accessible faculty members, first-class facilities, excellent academic programs, small classes, and an intimate intellectual and social community. The colleges' peaceful campuses are just 40 miles from the bustle of Los Angeles.

Academic Life: Prepare to work

It is generally accepted that Pomona, Claremont McKenna (CMC), and Harvey Mudd are the toughest of the Claremont colleges, while Scripps and Pitzer are less demanding. Students arriving at any of the colleges, however, need to be prepared to work. CMC's intellectually rigorous education draws enthusiastic reviews rather than groans and moans from its students. "It's a really solid education," says one. "It's very focused and very leadership oriented. I compare notes with friends back east at Ivy League schools and wouldn't trade my education at all. I think I'm very well served." Another student says, "We have a lot of general-education requirements, so that helps students get a breadth of knowledge."

Students meet with faculty advisers shortly after their arrival at any of Claremont's colleges, to plan their freshman course work. This system seems to be fairly effective.

CMC requires most students to complete a senior thesis under the direction of a faculty reader. Says one student, "I think it's wonderful because it really gives you the opportunity to take what you've learned over the past four years [and use it], and you have a reader whom you work with very closely."

Claremont's government and economics departments are top notch, and its international relations program is also highly regarded. "The government department is arguably the best in the country for providing a sound liberal arts education with a major in government," says one professor. Says another, "The economics and government faculties are outstanding. . . . Many faculty have had high-level Washington experience [as] presidential appointees, cabinet-secretary appointees, and extensive involvement in politics at the national and state levels." Yet another professor says, "The government department has a wide variety of approaches to the study of politics: political philosophy, political history, constitutional history and constitutional law, institutional history and analysis. This is not a department dominated by rational-choice modeling or multivariate regressions on minutiae." However, we note with alarm that government majors are not required to study the U.S. Constitution or governmental system.

Students report that the history discipline is the most politicized. "The focus is more on modern history," says one, "The program isn't what it could be." The colleges offer a fair range of classes, such as "Governing Rome: The History of the Roman Empire," "The Ancient Mediterranean," and "Late Antiquity and the

VITAL STATISTICS (CMC)

Religious affiliation: *none*
Total enrollment: *1,321*
Total undergraduates: *1,321*
SAT CR/Verbal midrange: *630–720*
SAT Math midrange: *670–760*
ACT midrange: *30–33*
Applicants: *4,412*
Applicants accepted: *14%*
Accepted applicants who enrolled: *49%*
Tuition (general/out of state): *$43,840*
Tuition (in state): *N/A*
Room and board: *$13,980*
Freshman retention rate: *96%*
Graduation rate (4 yrs.): *84%*
Graduation rate (6 yrs.): *91%*
Courses with fewer than 20 students: *82%*
Student-faculty ratio: *9:1*
Courses taught by graduate students: *none*
Students living on campus: *94%*
Students in fraternities: *5%*
Students in sororities: *N/A*
Students receiving need-based financial aid: *44%*
Avg. student-loan debt of a recent graduating class: *$9,915*
Most popular majors: *interdisciplinary studies, psychology, social sciences*
Guaranteed housing for 4 years? *yes*

CAMPUS POLITICS: GREEN LIGHT

Students at the Claremont colleges can join clubs that are either exclusive to one campus or available to students from all five. These clubs range from the Far Left to the Respectable Right. As one student says, "We take advantage of what goes on at other campuses, because in a sense we're all one campus." Student groups include College Republicans and College Democrats; a Debating Union; the Inter-Varsity Christian Fellowship; the James Madison Society, the Pro-Life Society; and *The Collage*, a weekly newspaper that serves students on all five campuses.

Political correctness certainly does have a foothold at the colleges; back in 2009 Pomona College banned its own official song, "Hail, Pomona, Hail!," after a college panel concluded that the song had originally—back in 1910—been written for a black-faced minstrel show. Having your official college song banned is a little like "having your baby shot in front of you," Carl Olson, a Pomona College alumnus, told the *Chronicle of Higher Education*.

Early Middle Ages." They also offer courses like "Queering the Renaissance" and "Modern Feminisms in East Asia," and allow history majors to skip, if they wish, the formative periods of American history.

The CMC literature department's offerings range widely, from "Dante, Shakespeare, and Dostoyevsky," "The Bible," and "Homer and Virgil," to "Gay and Lesbian Writers," "Black Politics and Literary Imagination," and "Paranoia in Modern Literature and Culture." One student tells us that conservatives should "beware this department." While it does have "sharp professors," he says, they are on the whole outspoken leftists. At Pomona, the English department is particularly strong. Scripps has excellent art, art history, and music departments. Pitzer's sociology department is highly regarded but incredibly politicized (to the left). Literature majors, alas, can emerge without taking a single course on Shakespeare.

Among the best faculty at CMC are Joseph M. Bessette, Mark Blitz, Charles R. Kesler, Chae-Jin (C. J.) Lee, Chris Nadon, James H. Nichols, John J. Pitney Jr., and Ralph A. Rossum in government; Eric Helland, Manfred Keil, and Marc Massoud in economics and accounting; Paul Hurley in philosophy; Robert Faggen, John Farrell, and Nicholas Warner in literature; and Newton Copp in biology. At Pitzer, look for Barry Sanders (emeritus) in the "History of Ideas" and Albert Wachtel in English. At Scripps, John Geerken (emeritus) in history and Michael Deane Lamkin (emeritus) in music are excellent. At Harvey Mudd, try Michael E. Orrison in mathematics and Stephen C. Adolph in biology.

Most classes—in all five schools—are small and inviting, allowing students to interact freely with their professors. Faculty-student closeness is impressive. "I can basically drop by their offices anytime," says one student. "I've had dinner with a number of their families, in fact. . . . We're at a teaching college." This closeness is "not merely a 'feel good' asset—it has practical benefits for students," says a professor.

"The use of TAs is minimal, and they are only used when there is an extraordinary demand for a certain class," one student says. "In these cases, [the college] may add a section taught by a TA from the Claremont Graduate University in addition to the already scheduled sections."

A multitude of learning opportunities are offered by some 11 research institutes. The Henry Salvatori Center for the Study of Individual Freedom focuses on "the study of political philosophy and freedom as it relates to American Constitutionalism and the American Founding." The Rose Institute of State and Local Government allows students to get involved with the political process. Harvey Mudd offers its students plenty of opportunities to gain research experience as summer interns working alongside faculty members. The school's Corporate Partnership program allows students to apply for scholarships from corporations such as Boeing, Dow, Motorola, and General Motors. Through the school's Clinic Program, corporations commission students to work on research projects throughout the school year and to present their research upon completion.

Students can participate in a semester of foreign study around the globe—from Kenya and Vietnam to Ecuador and Great Britain, or closer to home in Canada, Mexico, or the U.S. capital. One student says, "CMC's Washington, D.C., Program is great. Students have full-time internships and take a full-time course load. We have to arrange our own housing, internships, and survive basically on our own. It's a very hard semester, but my time in Washington was one of the most rewarding experiences of my college career."

Claremont McKenna College offers Arabic, French, Korean, and Spanish; other modern languages offered at the Claremont colleges include Chinese, Japanese, and Russian at Pomona, and Italian at Scripps. Latin and Greek are offered through Scripps's Classics department.

Student Life: The Bar Monkey

While the Claremont colleges share many resources, each has its own feel. One CMC student helpfully provides the following stereotypes: "Pomona: pretentious liberal intellectuals." (An alumnus adds that they tend to be "filled with guilt over their parents' success.")

> "It's very focused and very leadership oriented," says one student. "I compare notes with friends back east at Ivy League schools and I wouldn't trade."

The student continues, "Pitzer: hippies and 'crazy liberals.'" Another student muses, "Scripps: lesbians/bisexuals; artsy types. CMC: more conservative, beer-drinking, ambitious students. Mudd: math and science nerds; study a great deal and often have quirky habits such as unicycle riding." One student says, "There is definitely a feeling of individuality with respect to each school, but since so much is shared—classes, sports, facilities—there is also a feeling of overall commonality among the five Claremont colleges."

Claremont McKenna is "one of the most politically balanced schools in the country, with a good variety of views and healthy representation from among both liberals and conservatives," says a faculty member. A student says, "CMC is a very open environment both politically and religiously. Dialogue on both sides of political issues is open and fair. . . .

SUGGESTED CORE

1. Literature 98, News from the Delphic Oracle: Ancient Greek Literature and Culture
2. Philosophy 100A, Classical Philosophy
3. Literature 61, The Bible
4. Religious Studies 37, History of World Christianity
5. Literature 62/64/66, Shakespeare's Tragedies/Shakespeare's Histories and Romances/Shakespeare's Comedies
6. Government 80, Introduction to Political Philosophy
7. History 80, Early America: From Invasion to Civil War
8. History 132E, European Intellectual History or Philosophy 100D, 19th-Century Philosophy

For the most part, liberals and conservatives are happy to agree to disagree and argue points academically . . . political argument from both sides is embraced." A survey conducted by the *Claremont Independent*, a conservative student publication, found that around a third of CMC students identified themselves as conservatives. "We have to be one of the most evenly split colleges in the country," says one student. Further, another student notes, "Many professors are conservative, and nearly every professor I've had has either kept politics out of the classroom or been fair to both sides of an issue." CMC's political environment is healthy and open, and regardless of a student's political leanings, he will find his views taken seriously and thoughtfully. "We're a very politically conscious campus," says one student, "but dissenting from orthodoxy is not a problem." Another student says, "From whatever side you come from, you always have allies in the classroom."

"Pomona is very left-wing and ideological—almost to the point that conservative viewpoints are not tolerated," one student says. For the most part, Scripps College follows the trend of other small liberal arts schools for women. Many of its course offerings are presented from a feminist perspective, and Scripps students may find it hard to avoid them. Sometimes this slant backfires, however; the *Claremont Independent* quotes one rare Scripps traditionalist: "Being at Scripps made me more conservative. I had to defend myself, and it made me see the flaws of liberal arguments more. Scripps forced me to delineate my beliefs." Pitzer College seems to be even less balanced. One student calls Pitzer "hopelessly liberal." Owing to its engineering and hard-science bent, students say Harvey Mudd is mostly nonideological, since students there are likely to spend more time working on projects and internships than they are attending protests and political rallies.

Religious life at the Claremont Colleges is overseen by a joint Office of the Chaplains, based at McAlister Center, which maintains the Volunteer Service Center. Events and activities include Volunteer Study Break (recruiting evenings), canned food drives, the Oxfam Hunger Awareness Program, Community Service Awareness Week, Habitat for Humanity builds, tree planting, and alternative spring-break trips. Denominational activities are offered, an easy task given that the full-time chaplaincy staff includes a Catholic priest, a Protestant minister, and a rabbi. There are many congregations of various denominations in easy driving distance.

The town of Claremont is charitably described as "sedate," even boring, at least for college students. "There aren't your normal college-town things in Claremont," says one student. Despite the sleepy environs, "Everyone has fun to some degree because there's so much going on," a student says. There are dozens of student groups and plentiful athletic opportunities, and the close-knit atmosphere makes it easy to find and make friends. Students of the five colleges also share membership in other organizations, including Amnesty International; the traveling, competing Claremont Colleges Ballroom Dance Company; Claremont Colleges Fencing Club; the *Claremont Independent*; a debate union; Hillel; a Lesbian, Gay, and Bisexual Students' Union; and many other groups.

The Claremont colleges boast an impressive athletics program. Claremont McKenna, Harvey Mudd, and Scripps make up CMS athletics (Claremont, Mudd, Scripps). Students from these three colleges compete on varsity teams together. The men are known as the Stags, the women as the Athenas. Their archrivals are the Pomona-Pitzer Sagehens.

Except for three fraternities at Pomona, there is no Greek system on the campuses. Students are left to their own devices when it comes to partying, and the campus has dried up a little of late. "People drink, but not nearly as much as when I was a freshman," a student says. "The climate has changed, and people don't drink nearly as much—the keggers used to start on about Wednesday." However, another student says that "student life tends to revolve around alcohol consumption." Another student claims, "Drinking is almost a tradition here." However, another student reports that he has "felt no pressure to drink."

Science students at Harvey Mudd invented the Bar Monkey, an automated bartender that lets students type in the drink they desire. The Bar Monkey is now restricted to private use. The idea seems to be that it is better to have a wet campus with controlled conditions than to have students getting into trouble in bars. One student says, "Everybody is very laid back here, which is nice. The student council buys kegs for parties out of student fees."

Campus housing is abundant and adequate. All dorms are coed, but most floors and suites are separated by sex. Residence halls, only about two to three minutes away from each other, are mixed by class—freshmen often live next door to seniors. "Dorm life is a blast," says one student. "It feels kind of like a family." Across the five colleges, dorms are generally coed but with separated wings, floors, or suites. There are, however, some coed bathrooms.

In 2011 campus crime statistics from the five colleges counted 21 burglaries, one aggravated assault, five forcible sexual offenses, and three motor vehicle thefts.

Claremont McKenna College charged tuition of $43,840 in 2011–2012; room and board came to $13,980. Some 44 percent of students received need-based aid, and the average debt of a recent grad was $9,915. The numbers at the other four colleges are roughly comparable.

STRONG SUITS	WEAK POINTS
• Good general-education requirements. • Claremont McKenna's government, economics, and international relations programs are nationally famous. • Pomona's English department is highly praised by students. • Scripps has excellent art, art history, and music departments.	• History programs are more politicized, too focused on modern period. • Scripps, Pitzer, and Pomona colleges infused with standard academic leftist ideology, which emerges in classroom. • Most dorms are coed, and some have coed restrooms.

Colby College

Waterville, Maine • www.colby.edu

Some Assembly Required

Founded in 1813, Colby is one of three top-tier colleges in Maine—along with Bowdoin and Bates—and sometimes they're hard to tell apart. One Colby faculty member took a stab at it, though: "Bates is too liberal, and Bowdoin is too snotty." Well, that settles that. Like its peers, Colby offers small classes, close faculty-student interaction, strong study-abroad programs, a mostly considerate community atmosphere, and the surrounding beauty of Maine. Like most other elite schools, Colby has watered down its curriculum. So if a student does graduate with a solid liberal arts education, it's because he put it together himself.

Academic Life: See you at the buffet

A campus tour guide summed up the general-education mandates at Colby thus: "Take courses you're interested in, and you'll have no problem fulfilling the requirements." Indeed, Colby's distribution requirements are "so broadly defined that they hardly have much meaning," laments a professor. An incurious student could well emerge from Colby with little or no understanding of American history, philosophy, or literature—having instead knocked off his literature requirement (for instance) with courses like "Race and Gender in Shakespeare."

The required courses within some important departments remain solid, faculty members report. For instance, English majors still have to take three courses in pre-1800 English literature—which will usually include Shakespeare, although some students describe the English department as rather ideological, with "an inordinate emphasis on gender and sexuality in the course topics." History majors take two courses each in North American and European history, meaning they're likely to learn about the American Founding. A student reports, "The government department is outstanding: academically rigorous, professional, and grounded in the classics of political science." While government majors don't face a requirement that covers the American political system, course options are very strong. A student says of this discipline, "There is a general spirit of cooperation among [people of] various ideologies, and in recent years the chair of the department has passed back and forth between conservatives and liberals."

Other intellectually rigorous departments include economics, chemistry, mathematics, Classics, and history. The geology department is said to have "a very strong record of graduating successful geologists." The math department has a strong menu of courses, particularly "Mathematical Modeling," and the "Topics" courses for senior math majors, such as "Topics in Real Analysis" and "Topics in Abstract Algebra."

Freshmen are assigned faculty advisers who must approve their course choices, adding a minor, or switching majors. However, complains one faculty member, "This 'approval' often involves simply pressing a button on a webpage."

Students wax effusive about professors' dedication. One economics major says that she chose Colby precisely because of this: "When I visited Colby as a prospective student, an economics professor gave me her name and e-mail address," she says. "Now I'm majoring in economics, and I know every faculty member in the department. I come to office hours frequently, have dinner with them, and even babysit their kids." Another student says that professors often share books with their students, attend campus events, and "are very

VITAL STATISTICS

Religious affiliation: *none*
Total enrollment: *1,815*
Total undergraduates: *1,815*
SAT CR/Verbal midrange: *610–710*
SAT Math midrange: *630–710*
ACT midrange: *27–33*
Applicants: *5,241*
Applicants accepted: *29%*
Accepted applicants who enrolled: *31%*
Tuition (general/out of state): *$55,700 (comprehensive)*
Tuition (in state): *N/A*
Room and board: *N/A*
Freshman retention rate: *86%*
Graduation rate (4 yrs.): *86%*
Graduation rate (6 yrs.): *91%*
Courses with fewer than 20 students: *67%*
Student-faculty ratio: *10:1*
Courses taught by graduate students: *none*
Students living on campus: *95%*
Students in fraternities: *none*
Students in sororities: *none*
Students receiving need-based financial aid: *41%*
Avg. student-loan debt of a recent graduating class: *$22,367*
Most popular majors: *social sciences, multi/interdisciplinary studies, biology*
Guaranteed housing for 4 years? *yes*

CAMPUS POLITICS: YELLOW LIGHT

One professor says of Colby, "There are occasional reports of faculty making light of conservative student opinions or of treating them as nondiscussable, though it is unclear how pervasive this actually is." In fairness to the school, the professor says, "there are reports of at least one tenure denial having been motivated by this kind of behavior in class." Most Colby students are said to be fair-minded. One student gave a presentation on the abortion issue in a politics and religion class; he says that students were at first shocked by his pro-life stance, but when he "demonstrated that I could do the work and make the presentation go well, it defused some of the tension."

But other conservative students complain of the atmosphere in the Colby classroom. One reports that "the school encourages a social and political environment that demands absolute conformity to the status quo, to political correctness." Complaints have also been raised about the "first-year book" that is carefully discussed at student orientation; it is now always about "diversity" issues. One professor says that "the first-year 'wellness seminars' tend to focus on the usual liberal shibboleths." As for the faculty as a whole, it is said there is "a lot of liberal bias, some of it unconscious, that molds the actions of the administration, particularly when it comes to student affairs."

willing to use their contacts and knowledge to steer you into programs." A faculty member says, "Colby obsessively emphasizes good teaching, so one could quite easily have only great professors."

Academically, says one student, "Colby is fantastic. Professors are top notch, and most classes are small and well run." Another reports that "students who can take the pressure love their courses." For instance, Larissa J. Taylor's "Church History and Theology in Medieval Europe" is said to "give good insight into both the church's development and medieval society." Joseph R. Reisert in government is said to have a "strong grounding in the classic works of political thought." Guilain Denoeux, a State Department consultant, gives students "an in-depth understanding of international relations. His 'Politics of the Middle East' course is not to be missed." Anthony J. Corrado Jr. is a "campaign-finance guru who is well connected in Washington" and teaches students the practical aspects of American politics in courses such as "Interest Group Politics."

Two Classics professors, Joseph and Hanna Roisman, "teach all aspects of classical civilization, from Greek tragedy to Roman battle tactics, with enthusiasm and in-depth expertise." Professor Elizabeth D. Leonard is lauded as an expert on the Civil War. In geology, Robert E. Nelson ("Dr. Bob") makes a student "want to be a geology major. He's very, very inspiring!" Jeff Anderson in anthropology brings to bear "lots of first-hand knowledge, having lived with the Apache and Navajo." Government teachers are "strong, open-minded, and fun to argue with," says a student. "They appreciate a different point of view." The history department is also "getting stronger," as is biology. Other recommended professors include Otto K. Bretscher, Fernando Q. Gouvêa, Leo Livshits, and George Welch in mathematics; D. Whitney King in chemistry; Liam O'Brien in statistics; and David W. Findlay in economics.

Some students, however, are dissatisfied with humanities courses at Colby. One alumna reported: "There were two classes in four years in which I felt legitimately challenged and exposed to new material and perspectives. I wrote more papers about how literature made me 'feel' rather than . . . any sort of objective, quality/standard-based analysis." Other students disagree. Says one: "Colby really pushes you to think. It's like a mini Ivy." Another complains, "It's really, really intense, too much so. Plenty of students find it difficult to satisfy the requirements." Colby has its tough courses, as one student relates: "It can be hard to come from a high school where you may have been at the top to a college where you are average. You learn to challenge yourself."

The Farnham Writers' Center is staffed by students eager to help classmates with papers. During exam time, the center is open 24 hours a day for those pulling the inevitable all-nighter. Calculus After Hours assists students with math and is "dynamic, effective, and fun," say insiders.

Some programs are weaker. The religious studies department is largely staffed by feminists. Says one insider, "None of the faculty members in that department have any respect for tradition." In lieu of Christianity, most courses focus on women and feminism, film, non-Western religions, and sociological studies, such as "Contemporary Wicca: Formalists, Feminists, and Free Spirits." Sounds like an exorcism might be in order.

The interdisciplinary programs tend to be the most politicized: American studies; indigenous peoples of the Americas (a minor in the anthropology department); African and African American studies; and women's, gender, and sexuality studies. The philosophy and education departments have also been described as "given to trendy topics, such as issues related to gender and 'social justice.'"

A studio art major calls his department "pretty minimal," while another gripes that Colby is a "bad place to be an artist, musician, or just creative in general."

The school sponsors programs in Salamanca, Dijon, and St. Petersburg, among other locations. Still more options can be arranged through cooperating colleges—although one professor complains that "for some students it can become just a long vacation. It is up to the student to choose something worth doing." Language options on campus include East Asian studies, French, German, Greek and Latin, Italian, Jewish studies, Russian, and Spanish.

SUGGESTED CORE

1. Classics 138, Heroes of the World
2. Philosophy 231f, History of Ancient Greek Philosophy
3. Religion 143f/144s, Introduction to the Hebrew Bible/New Testament
4. Philosophy 373, History of Medieval Philosophy
5. Government 272, Modern Political Theory
6. English 412s, Global Shakespeares
7. History 131f, Survey of U.S. History to 1865
8. Philosophy 359f, 19th-Century Philosophy

Student Life: Green day

The 714-acre Colby campus is surrounded by lush scenery, and Colby has committed to becoming 100 percent "eco-friendly." Says one insider, "Everyone is very pro-environment here, as befits rural Maine. Dr. Thomas Tietenberg has done much to strengthen the environmental studies program here; it's a lot more than just singing songs and holding hands."

The campus is quaint and charming, with red-brick buildings separated by lush, verdant lawns. Downtown Waterville, Colby's hometown, is a 15-minute walk away, but students complain that outside of the usual fare of food and movies, the town offers very little. Sniffs one student, "Waterville is poor, white, and kind of stand-offish to Colby students."

"The administration is constantly pushing diversity, with activities like mandatory supper seminars designed to sensitize students," another student complains. "A lot of us nap in the back." Incessantly, the lead "news" article in the *Colby Echo* will spotlight some breach of multicultural dogma. The Colby Outdoor Orientation Trip (COOT) for freshmen now includes a diversity workshop, reports the *Echo*. Annual "Diversity Reports," on issues of race, gender, and sexual orientation, are mandatory for all academic departments. Some real diversity does exist on campus, thanks to scholarships that have substantially increased the number of international students. Reports one grateful professor, "These kids are really smart. Their presence has really improved the classroom, as their goal is to actually learn."

O ne student says, "Professors are top notch, and most classes are small and well run." Others complain of liberal bias.

Political and religious diversity are dicier propositions, students report. Says one Orthodox Jewish student, "It is close to impossible to be kosher at Colby and is also incredibly difficult for Muslim students." She complained that several professors violated university regulations by assigning midterms on Yom Kippur, while the kosher food options consist of "a small table with matzo, soup, and boiled eggs. Sometimes bagels."

Says one student, "There aren't very many of us conservatives on campus, and we do feel lonely in some sense, but not beleaguered or under pressure." Mostly, in fact, students seem "apathetic." One student sums up the atmosphere on campus: "Most students are preppy New Englanders, with a few hippies thrown in." Other groups include the Colby Democrats, Colby Republicans, Roosevelt Institution, Amnesty International, and the Eco-Reps (environmental). Nonpolitical groups—especially for outdoor activities—are many.

One professor comments, "The chapel is not at all central to the mainstream way of life here. In fact, few of my students know who Job is when I make the reference." Says a student, "Spiritual life here is mediocre all the way." The Colby Christian Fellowship is fairly vibrant, however, hosting prayer and Bible discussion groups. The Catholic Newman Council offers a variety of activities in addition to weekly services. A Hillel foundation and several other smaller religious organizations serve those of other faiths.

Some 95 percent of the student body lives on campus in residences mixing freshmen with upperclassmen. Most campus residences are centrally located dormitories, except for one apartment complex in which about a hundred seniors live. Colby offers no single-sex dormitories (or even single-sex floors), and students are bound to find themselves living next door to a member of the opposite sex. However, there are no coed dorm rooms or coed bathrooms. Men and women are permitted to share apartments as seniors. One living option is a quiet dorm, where residents and visitors must adhere to a 21-hour-a-day quiet rule. All dorms on campus are nonsmoking, and there are also alcohol-free and substance-free residences available, as well as a Spanish language house.

Colby has its own on-campus pub, which serves alcohol, and many students spend weekends drinking together in dorm rooms. The college attempts to provide alternatives to alcohol, and a hard liquor ban was implemented in the 2010–11 school year. Many students occupy their free time with activities in small niche clubs such as pottery or photography, politically oriented groups, or sports.

Colby is a very athletic campus, with a solid third of its students involved in some sport. Colby fields thirty-two varsity teams in the New England Small College Athletic Conference, and has seven club sports and numerous intramural sports. The Outing Club is the most active group on campus, organizing hiking, boating, skiing, and camping trips.

The college is fairly secluded from the town of Waterville. The only crimes reported on campus in 2011 were one forcible sex offense and six burglaries.

Colby doesn't come cheap; for 2012–13, tuition, room, and board (it's a package deal) cost $55,700. Beginning in 2008–9, Colby replaced all "packaged" loans (usually in the form of Perkins or Colby loans) with grants, meaning that students from now on can potentially graduate debt-free. Admissions are not need blind, but 41 percent of students received need-based aid. The average student-loan debt of a recent graduate was $22,367.

STRONG SUITS	WEAK POINTS
• Small classes, close faculty-student relations, strong study-abroad programs. • Mostly solid requirements and solid courses in key disciplines such as English, history—and government, an especially good program. • Strong departments in economics, chemistry, mathematics, Classics, geology. • Lovely campus and beautiful nature close by, beloved by outdoorsy students.	• Watered-down curriculum allows students to skip major areas of knowledge. • English department too fixated on ideology (i.e., "Race and Gender in Shakespeare"). • Broadly accepted political correctness encouraged by the administration. • Anemic spiritual life on campus and few students of faith.

Colgate University

Hamilton, New York • www.colgate.edu

A Glowing Student Body

Founded in 1819, Colgate University has long been a small, quality-oriented liberal arts college focusing on undergraduate education. With a very good student-faculty ratio, no teaching assistants, professors who care about student learning, and a faculty full of experienced scholars, at Colgate "the students are the faculty's main priorities, and advising them is a close second," says a student. According to one professor, "Colgate is still a place committed to a well-rounded kid who is smart, socially adept, and politically moderate. Kids have genuine intellectualism, but the school produces CEOs, not PhDs." Heavy-handed efforts by a past college administration to push leftist notions of "diversity" have planted seeds of political correctness at the college that have sprouted in ugly ways. As one professor warns, "diversity" courses may "corrupt" students "but not in the way you'd think." They are not brainwashed by flaky offerings from the Left. Instead, "They become cynical. Education becomes instrumental." Still, Colgate has many strengths and is worth a careful look.

Academic Life: The mental obstacle course

Colgate's core curriculum leaves major gaps in the education it requires of undergraduates. In particular, there is a dearth of history instruction covering the years AD 700–1700, while the formative period of Christendom is virtually skipped. One professor familiar with the university's introductory Western civilization course says that after a stint on ancient Greece and Rome, "There's nothing on Hellenism, medieval Christendom, the Reformation, the Renaissance—and then we get to the modern period."

Politics can intrude into the classroom. One student recalls a core class that was "supposed to be about Homer and the Bible. But the professor wanted to talk about [American foreign policy]. . . . There are plenty of liberal professors with agendas." The student adds that in the second semester core "Challenge of Modernity" class, "We read a lot of Virginia Woolf and W. E. B. DuBois. It seemed at times like they were trying to turn it into an anti-old-white-males class." But another student says that with the exception of one notorious professor, Colgate doesn't have the "horror stories that trickle out of other schools concerning the stifling of debate." Too often, first-year courses at Colgate take a narrowly 21st-century perspective and challenge the student to consider such hot-button issues as global warming, stem cell research, and AIDS before he has studied such foundational subjects as religion, philosophy, or Western history. According to one faculty veteran, the core is awful. "It's staffed by the faculty's husbands and wives, who are insufficiently employed, and by departments lacking enrollment." But the deft student can sidestep these dead ends. The first-rate Professor Barry Shain's popular introduction to political science has a huge waiting list and explicitly tries to fill in what other core offerings lack.

Until recently, ideological bias seemed mostly localized in the usual places—departments such as women's, Africana, and Latin American studies. However, the political virus is said to be infecting such traditional departments as philosophy and religion. For example,

VITAL STATISTICS

Religious affiliation: *none*
Total enrollment: *2,850*
Total undergraduates: *2,854*
SAT CR/Verbal midrange: *660–740*
SAT Math midrange: *670–750*
ACT midrange: *30–33*
Applicants: *7,798*
Applicants accepted: *29%*
Accepted applicants who enrolled: *33%*
Tuition (general/out of state): *$44,330*
Tuition (in state): *N/A*
Room and board: *$11,075*
Freshman retention rate: *95%*
Graduation rate (4 yrs.): *94%*
Graduation rate (6 yrs.): *90%*
Courses with fewer than 20 students: *64%*
Student-faculty ratio: *9:1*
Courses taught by graduate students: *none*
Students living on campus: *90%*
Students in fraternities: *14%*
Students in sororities: *17%*
Students receiving need-based financial aid: *40%*
Avg. student-loan debt of a recent graduating class: *$16,128*
Most popular majors *English, political science, economics*
Guaranteed housing for 4 years? *yes*

CAMPUS POLITICS: YELLOW LIGHT

A decade ago, Colgate decreed that all Greek houses had to be sold to the school and that any student who belonged to an unrecognized fraternity could face suspension or expulsion. Colgate now prohibits groups of more than eight students from living together without its approval. Only the school's Delta Kappa Epsilon chapter fought the move, but its lawsuit was dismissed by the New York State Supreme Court.

According to one professor, the frat houses are now "creatures of the university. Before, the frat boys competed to show off their masculine stupidity. Now they compete to do service projects for various charities. The administration's goal was androgynization. But the boys are still mostly boys and girls still mostly girls."

There is a thoughtful conservative presence on campus thanks to the Center for Freedom and Western Civilization, directed by Robert Kraynak, and the Philosophy, Politics, and Economics Institute, directed by Stanley Brubaker. Their existence bodes well for the future of free expression at Colgate and helps promote genuine intellectual diversity at the school.

students can fulfill one of their scant humanities requirements with "Philosophy and Feminisms," in which they study feminist, "womanist," and *mujerista* (don't ask) interpretations of politics. The course focuses on the "interconnections among oppressions," the (allegedly unique) political characteristics of violence against women, and the "barriers separating women and embodiment."

However, such courses can be avoided by the savvy student. "With care, you can skip the crackpots and get a great education, but you have to show initiative in selecting your courses," a faculty member observes.

Colgate's advising system does seem to do a fine job of guiding students, especially if they are lucky enough to receive help from a professor like the above mentor. Even before entering Colgate, students can ask for help from "prematriculation advisers," who help students choose their courses for the first semester. As freshmen, students turn to their first-year seminar instructors for guidance. These professors serve as advisers until students choose their majors and a faculty adviser from that department.

Unlike most colleges and universities, Colgate expects its students to take only four courses per semester. They may take five courses with special permission but are not allowed to enroll in more than that. The idea is to give students the chance to focus more closely on the courses they do take. Besides satisfying general-education requirements, students must also choose a major, where they will generally receive more structure. For instance, the English department requires its majors to take a broad range of courses. Unfortunately, it cut the survey course that exposes students to such canonical authors as Chaucer, Shakespeare, and Milton. History majors do not have to take American history before 1900. In this area, too, Colgate appears to be blindly following trends set by other, more prestigious schools.

There does seem to be a genuine commitment to teaching at Colgate. According to a professor, "Colgate is a place where teaching and research are equally balanced. And teaching is an important consideration in deciding on which professors get tenure." Another professor notes, "At Colgate there are no TAs. You have to grade all the papers." Indeed, graduate students do not teach courses at Colgate. Faculty members hold regular office hours, and most students take advantage of these. Colgate, says one student, offers "incredible accessibility to professors. . . . Only a handful of classes have more than 40 students. The largest (Psych 151) is limited to 150."

Colgate boasts some excellent departments, especially political science and economics. Some courses in political science are so beloved that the department often has hundreds of students on the waiting list to enroll in them. By contrast, according to one undergrad, some areas to skip are "peace and conflict studies, women's studies, and Africana and Latin American studies. Those are the three academic departments most looked down upon by students and faculty alike as being 'soft.' Courses there are generally to be avoided." Another student says that "English, religion, and women's studies are way too liberal and don't prepare students for reality."

A professor familiar with the mess that the religion department has become says, "You can take a course in African religion or Native American religion, but not in American working-class Protestantism." There is nothing on Calvin, for instance. And Catholicism is taught from a feminist perspective. Students warn that some professors in this department are "known for being closed-minded . . . and hostile to critical thinking. Students' opinions are worthless if they are in conflict with that of the professors."

If it's any consolation, the political science department is so strong, one professor can boast, "We probably teach more theology [here] than they do in the religion department. It's a top-flight department with four or five conservatives, and even those on the Left are very decent." (It does not, however, require that political science majors study American constitutional theory.)

A professor says, "Colgate kids have genuine intellectualism, but the school produces CEOs, not PhDs."

One teacher points to the "very good" philosophy and Classics departments and the school's strong programs in the natural sciences. He adds, "For students interested in hard science, Colgate might be a better choice than they think. There's more attention to undergrads than they'd find at a research institution and more chance to work with faculty on experiments." One student recommends, "If you're interested in natural sciences, economics, political science, or international relations, then Colgate is for you."

Students name the following faculty members as among the best at Colgate: Tim Byrnes, Fred Chernoff, Michael Johnston, Robert Kraynak, and seminal conservative scholar Barry Shain in political science; Stanley Brubaker in law and political science; Douglas Macdonald in international relations; Kay Johnston in education; Susan Cerasano, Margaret Maurer, and Jane Pinchin in English; Karen Harpp, Amy Leventer, and Paul Pinet in geology; Takao Kato, Jay Mandle, and Robert Turner in economics; David Dudrick in philosophy; Ray Douglas in history; Doug Johnson in psychology; Grace Ts'ao in accounting; and Thomas Balonek in physics and astronomy.

(see our Yellow Light)

SUGGESTED CORE

1. Classics 221, The Epic Voice and Its Echoes
2. Philosophy 301, Ancient Philosophy
3. Religion 208/209, Hebrew Bible/New Testament
4. Religion 301, The Christian Tradition
5. Political Science 260, Foundations of Political Thought
6. English 321/322, Shakespeare
7. History 103, American History to 1877
8. Political Science 385, Modernity and Its Conservative Critics

Students interested in study abroad may wish to consider the school's popular Geneva Study Group program, and Colgate offers study abroad on every continent except Africa, along with some interesting programs for specialists. "The London Economics Study Group, which Colgate has been running since 1962, studies the economy and economics of Britain and the European Community," the school reports. Closer to home, undergraduates can get "an insider's look at Washington, D.C., political life through the Washington Study Group."

Colgate offers foreign language majors in Chinese, French, German, Greek and Latin, Japanese, and Spanish.

Student Life: From *Animal House* to *Animal Farm*

Hamilton is a small town located about a half-hour southeast of Syracuse, New York. Most students stay on campus on weekends. With only 4,239 full-time residents, Hamilton's population almost doubles during the academic year. Students can easily walk to shops or restaurants or to the village green at the center of town, where the university hosts a college-town picnic at the start of each new year.

Colgate is largely a residential school, with more than 90 percent of students living in university-owned housing. The university guarantees housing for all four years. Students can choose single-sex or coed dormitory floors; no single-sex dorms are available. There are no coed dorm rooms for freshmen and sophomores, and all bathrooms are single sex. There is no intervisitation policy. Colgate offers a number of theme houses for first-year students and upperclassmen.

Colgate's Residential Education program has dramatically changed the student housing experience. Students are placed in housing specified by year and are required to participate in scheduled programs intended to produce a student body that is "forward thinking" and "progressive." This social engineering replaced the forcibly suppressed Greek system on campus (see our Yellow Light). Even without a Greek system on campus, Colgate students still know how to party, perhaps too well; in 2010 Colgate placed number nine in the Princeton Review's category "Most Beer Drinkers on Campus."

Devout students will find religious houses on campus. There is a Jewish Union, a Christian Fellowship, a Muslim group, and a Newman Center. More traditional Catholics may enjoy attending St. Mary's parish in Hamilton.

Activists hungry for extracurricular leftism may choose from an array of student organizations. Colgate's political organizations include grandly named groups like Advocates (queer/straight alliance) and the Sisters of the Round Table. Those who find these causes too general may choose from organizations such as African American Student Alliance, Students for Environmental Action, College Democrats, and even College Republicans. There is no conservative student paper.

In the area surrounding the university, outdoor activities abound. The Outdoor Education program is hugely popular with students, allowing them to rent backpacks, tents, and other outdoor equipment for a freshman Wilderness Adventure Program.

The university offers its students 29 club sports, in which 16 percent of the student body participates. For more serious athletes, the university's 25 varsity teams compete in the Patriot League (NCAA Division I) against schools like Army, Navy, and American University. Colgate is the smallest school in the country to compete in the NCAA's Division I-A.

Says one student, "Crime is no concern here. We're in the middle of cornfields." In 2011 the school reported one forcible sex offense and 18 burglaries.

Colgate's 2012–13 tuition was a hefty $44,330, with room and board averaging $11,075. Admissions are not need blind, but the school does meet the full financial need of those who get in. The school admits students, and offers aid, on a first-come, first-served basis. About 40 percent of Colgate undergraduates received some form of need-based aid, and the average student-loan debt of a recent graduate was $16,128.

STRONG SUITS	WEAK POINTS
• Professors (not teaching assistants) do all teaching and grading. • Good programs in the natural sciences, philosophy, Classics, economics, political science, and international relations. • A reasonable (if incomplete) core curriculum ensures students are better rounded than most.	• Administrative coercion of students. It seized all fraternities and threatened dissidents with expulsion. Frats were replaced by housing with "progressive" reeducation programs. • A strong drinking culture on campus. • Several weak or politicized departments, especially religion and English. • Core courses skip the Middle Ages and the Renaissance and are sometimes taught by underqualified, partisan faculty.

College of the Holy Cross

Worcester, Massachusetts • www.holycross.edu

Give Us Barabbas!

Founded in 1843, Holy Cross is the oldest Catholic college in New England. The college is committed to undergraduate teaching. But Holy Cross has shed most of its religious identity—enshrining in place of Christian doctrine a postmodern leftist orthodoxy. Nevertheless, a small number of committed conservatives on campus fight to defend what's left of the school's heritage of Catholic liberal arts education.

Academic Life: The traditional and the trendy

Sadly, the academic program at Holy Cross requires very little mandatory liberal arts course work—especially in philosophy, language, and religion, the very courses that once distinguished a Jesuit education. One student reports that "promiscuity has definitely decreased my junior and senior year"; this was not due to a crackdown or moral instruction from college administrators, however, but "because police have gotten incredibly strict off campus, so it prevents 'random hookups' from occurring."

Each student chooses courses to fulfill distribution requirements. For instance, he can satisfy his historical studies requirement by taking a course such as "Environmental

History"—and nothing else. But one professor insists, "Students who seek such a grounding can get it if they seek out professors for advice early in their HC career—ideally, e-mailing some of those recommended in this guide during the summer before their freshman year." Holy Cross's theology requirement allows students to study Islam, Buddhism, Hinduism, Confucianism, or Taoism instead of any Christian doctrine. Islamic studies is the most egregiously politicized program, with one professor publicly justifying Islamic jihad violence.

Each freshman is assigned to one of five thematic "clusters": Natural World, Divine, Self, Global Society, or Core Human Questions. Then students take a small-group seminar that falls under the theme. The Divine cluster, for instance, offers the seminars "From Heroes to Hemlock," "Scientists Argue about Gods," and "The Devil Made Me Do It," among others. These freshman seminars are limited to small groups, offering an intensive introductory academic experience. But few of them focus on fundamental issues and/or great texts, while some are devoted to narrow topics that become the occasion for leftist agitprop. One student's reading of a feminist author led her to decide that the Adam and Eve story was responsible for a supposedly negative view of women in Western civilization: "If in the Bible it had said that Adam had eaten the apple, starting at the very beginning of Christianity, people would have had a different view of women." The fact that Christians did not *write* the Book of Genesis seems to have escaped her notice.

The honors program is a brighter spot. In this intellectually serious, selective program, students explore themes in small classes. Sophomores begin by taking a team-taught course on "human nature." Professors from various departments explore the theme in natural sciences, social sciences, and the arts. As juniors, students select another honors-level seminar. Every senior writes a thesis, and the results of the research are published in-house and presented in a conference at the end of the year.

The college's list of degree programs includes a mix of the traditional and the trendy. Among the latter, perhaps the worst is the Center for Interdisciplinary and Special Studies, which offers students concentrations in such fields as women's and gender studies, peace and conflict studies, environmental studies, and Africana studies.

VITAL STATISTICS

Religious affiliation: *Roman Catholic*
Total enrollment: *2,891*
Total undergraduates: *2,891*
SAT CR/Verbal midrange: *600–690*
SAT Math midrange: *610–690*
ACT midrange: *29*
Applicants: *7,228*
Applicants accepted: *34%*
Accepted applicants who enrolled: *31%*
Tuition (general/out of state): *$43,400*
Tuition (in state): *N/A*
Room and board: *$11,730*
Freshman retention rate: *95%*
Graduation rate (4 yrs.): *89%*
Graduation rate (6 yrs.): *93%*
Courses with fewer than 20 students: *53%*
Student-faculty ratio: *10:1*
Courses taught by graduate students: *none*
Students living on campus: *91%*
Students in fraternities: *N/A*
Students in sororities: *N/A*
Students receiving need-based financial aid: *57%*
Avg. student-loan debt of a recent graduating class: *$26,567*
Most popular majors: *economics, psychology, English*
Guaranteed housing for 4 years? *yes*

CAMPUS POLITICS: RED LIGHT

Campus speakers have included some who show a callous disregard of Catholic teachings on central moral issues. Campus events reflect the college's overall leftist tilt. During the 2013 school year, they included a visit by the liberal, pro-abortion "Catholic" secretary of state, John Kerry, and the environmental activist and Second Amendment opponent Jenny Price.

In 2013 Holy Cross's Alternate College Theatre presented the appalling rock musical *Spring Awakening*, which covers the themes of child abuse, masturbation, teen pregnancy, abortion, homosexuality, rape, and suicide within its child and adolescent roles. Since 2002 Holy Cross and its Women's Forum have hosted performances of *The Vagina Monologues*, a play that, among other disturbing features, celebrates the lesbian statutory rape of a teenage girl. One student said that the administration "defended the play by turning to moral relativism and emotivism, despite other attempts to appeal to Catholic moral teachings and objective truth."

Although there are both College Republicans and College Democrats on campus, neither seems to be highly active at present. Of political life at the college, one professor tells us, "There is a highly pronounced leftist bias, though a small minority of conservatives is tolerated if it behaves." Indeed, programming organized by the administration has exhibited a decidedly partisan, left-wing tilt, students complain. As one contact puts it, "To a remarkable degree for a Catholic institution, the college features a considerable amount of gay/lesbian programming."

Students report that classes in many departments are taught with a political bent, usually from the left. However, says one, "While there are certainly some leftist professors who may stifle the viewpoints of conservatives or religious students, most professors are tolerant of other opinions. Therefore, even with some of the more liberal faculty, a conservative or religious student is generally free to voice his own opinion" without a negative impact on grades.

While the most politicized department is sociology, the history, religious studies, and English departments also trend sharply left. Of the English department, a professor says that, "while it has a few very strong faculty, it has unfortunately tended to replace teachers who were devoted to literary classics with others who are interested in race/class/gender." The religious studies department offers such courses as "Sexual Justice: A Social Ethic of Sexuality" and "Social Ethics," in which, according to the catalog, there will be "a Christian ethical evaluation of such issues as impoverishment and economic justice, racism, and First World/Two-Thirds World relations in the struggle against war and the search for peace."

The class deans are responsible for academic advising at Holy Cross, assigning each freshman a faculty adviser before enrollment. As soon as students declare a major, they are assigned faculty advisers in their major department.

English majors must take at least 10 courses above the first-year level, four of them chosen from seven possible periods: medieval; Renaissance; 18th-, 19th-, or 20th-century British; and 19th- or 20th-century American. A student cannot take more than three courses studying periods after the 1800s. Hence it would be hard for an English major to miss studying Shakespeare. The department also offers education and creative writing options.

History majors take at least 10 courses, including "The Historian's Craft" and two courses in premodern history, but requirements in American, European, and world history have been replaced by a four-course cluster in one of five "Thematic Concentrations." Some 2013 themes include "Gender in Public and Private Life" and "Race and Ethnicity."

Over the years, the political science department has distinguished itself as one of the finest in the country, taking a serious, historical, institutional, and philosophical approach to the discipline. Majors must take introductory courses in American government, political philosophy, comparative politics, and international relations, plus at least six upper-division courses. Outstanding faculty include David L. Schaefer, Donald R. Brand, Loren R. Cass, Daniel Klinghard, Vickie Langohr, B. Jeffrey Reno, Denise Schaeffer, and Ward J. Thomas.

What one professor says of the English department applies more broadly at Holy Cross: "While it has a few very strong faculty, it has unfortunately tended to replace teachers who were devoted to literary classics with others who are interested in race/class/gender."

Holy Cross has one of the largest, strongest undergraduate Classics programs in the country. One professor reports, "Students fall in love with the Classics." A major calls the department "first rate." Another student says: "Two professors in particular I would mention are Ellen E. Perry and Blaise J. Nagy. They not only go above and beyond the call of helping students to grow in Latin, ancient Greek, and ancient history; they also take students on trips to Italy on spring break so they can learn firsthand about the glory of the past." Other recommended professors in the department include John D. B. Hamilton and Thomas R. Martin. The Classics department hosts a chariot race on campus each year for local high school students.

Science and math studies seem strong at the school. The mathematics and computer science departments are also rigorous and respected.

One student says: "The professors are the best part of Holy Cross. Their doors are always open, they answer e-mails quickly, and they really want to get to know their students outside the classroom. I've taught a professor to dance for his daughter's wedding, I've had a traditional Hungarian meal at a professor's house, and I've debated with my professors about all manner of things: Milton, Verdi's *Requiem,* Catholicism, the Geneva Convention."

In departments besides those listed above, students and faculty name the following as excellent teachers: Jeffrey Bernstein, Lawrence E. Cahoone, Christopher A. Dustin, Kendy Hess, and Joseph P. Lawrence in philosophy; Robert K. Cording, James M. Kee, Jonathan D. Mulrooney, Lee Oser, and Helen M. Whall in English; David Schap and Robert Baumann in economics; Noel Cary in history; and Jessica Waldoff in music; Virginia Raguin in visual arts; Robert H. Garvey in physics; John F. Axelson, Mark Freeman, Charles M. Locurto, and Amy Wolfson in psychology; Robert Bertin in biology; Edward Isser and Steve Vineberg in theater; and Susan Sullivan in sociology.

The college currently offers study-abroad programs in Argentina, Australia, Cameroon, China, England, France, Germany, Greece, Ireland, Italy, Japan, Peru, Russia, Scotland, and Spain. In addition, there is a Washington Semester program in which students hold internship positions at various government, "public interest," and media organizations.

Besides Latin and Greek, Holy Cross offers classes in Arabic, Chinese, Italian, French, German, Spanish, Russian, and "American Sign Language and Deaf Studies." The latter includes course offerings such as "Deaf Literature" and "The Deaf Community: Language and Culture."

Student Life: The exorcism room

Worcester, Massachusetts, is a college town with more than 15 schools. Some 90 percent of the student body lives in the college's 11 residence halls, where space is guaranteed for four years. Though the sexes are separated by floor, all dormitories are coed. Quiet hours are in effect Sunday through Thursday 10:00 p.m. to 8:00 a.m. and Friday and Saturday midnight to 8:00 a.m. All guests must be registered, validated, and accompanied by a student at all times. Some rooms offer a view of the Fenwick clock tower, home of the Exorcism Room, where (according to legend) a long-ago exorcism ended in death.

A professor observes about the students: "Like most schools at its level, Holy Cross has a mix of some students genuinely motivated by intellectual curiosity and others just here for the fun and the degree. Certainly we have a significant number of intellectually serious, motivated students. But there is a large party crowd as well."

Holy Cross undergrads can choose from more than 120 student organizations, ranging from a ballroom dancing society to academic clubs like the Biology Society—and activist groups such as the ABiGaLe (Association of Bisexuals, Gays, and Lesbians) and Allies, a homosexual and bisexual advocacy association that operates with the college's blessing and funding.

Says one student: "While from the top down, things do not look good for the college's Catholic identity, there is a small group of committed Catholic students who are determined to spread the faith by witnessing to their peers." Worthy groups on campus include College Republicans and Students for Life. The *Fenwick Review,* a conservative student newspaper founded by Fr. Paul Scalia in 1992, publishes four or five issues each year. The administration met with protests when it tried to close down the newspaper for satirizing the notion of gay "marriage." The school has since relented, and the *Review* now flourishes.

While a mix of viewpoints can be found in the articles and editorials of the student weekly, *The Crusader,* readers should also be prepared to find faculty dismissing the teachings of the Catholic Church. In response to an article by a student defending traditional marriage, a religious studies professor wrote a letter condoning same-sex unions and criticizing "our society" and "many churches" that "still try to silence gay people."

Daily Mass is available at the St. Joseph Memorial Chapel and two other chapels. Says one student: "The chaplains try their hardest to attract students to Mass (there are two daily Masses and four Masses on the weekends), but they often resort to reducing the Catholic faith to 'social justice' or selling the celebration of the Eucharist as a useful way to 'de-stress' after a long week." The college also has Protestant and nondenominational services each Sunday and provides a Muslim prayer room. More traditional Catholic students should look into the weekly 10:30 a.m. Latin Mass at St. Paul the Apostle Parish in Warren.

The Holy Cross Crusaders compete in the Patriot League in 27 sports, 13 men's and 14 women's, and has one of the highest student-athlete graduation rates of any NCAA Division I school. Holy Cross also offers 22 club and 13 intramural sports teams that are wildly popular with students.

Like many colleges, Holy Cross has had trouble with student drinking, but the college has instituted a tough zero-tolerance policy that it strictly enforces. On the whole, the campus is perceived as very safe. In 2011 Holy Cross reported four forcible sex offenses, two aggravated assaults, and 14 burglaries. One student noted: "The lack of crime at Holy Cross is almost comical. An incident as small as the theft of a watch or wallet from an unlocked gym locker generates campus-wide safety alerts and a Herculean investigation from Public Safety."

In 2012–13 Holy Cross tuition was $43,400, and room and board $11,730. About 57 percent of the student body receives need-based financial aid. Admissions are need blind, and the school promises to meet 100 percent of a student's financial need. The average recent graduate of Holy Cross bears a student-loan debt of $26,567.

STRONG SUITS	WEAK POINTS
• A good honors program for students who choose it.	• A vapid, one-course religion requirement, which can be fulfilled with a class on sacred gardens.
• Most professors, regardless of their views, are fair to students who disagree.	• Anti-Western Islamic studies courses.
• Very fine Classics, political science, math, and science departments.	• Plenty of politicized disciplines, such as women's and gender studies, peace and conflict studies, environmental studies, and Africana studies.
• Highly qualified, responsive professors teach—not graduate students.	• Extensive gay activist and other socially libertine programming promoted by the administration.
• A strong, if small, Catholic "resistance" promoting orthodoxy on campus.	

Columbia University

New York, New York • www.columbia.edu

At the Top of the City

Columbia University in New York City was founded in 1754. The school became a national center of humane letters, which it has remained ever since, and was the first American college to grant medical degrees. Columbia has also passed along Western civilization and American history by means of the traditional liberal arts education it provides, as enshrined in its worthy (and sadly, almost unique) core curriculum—Columbia's single greatest strength—which remains in place despite a strongly, if not quite monolithically, leftist student body and faculty.

Academic Life: Uptown cosmopolitan

With some of the most respected scholars in the country on its faculty, Columbia's elite reputation is well deserved. This reputation is further justified by the university's require-ment that all undergraduates take a number of courses focused on the Western canon; this core dominates the course load for freshmen and sophomores and is popular among many students of different political stripes—who knew what they were getting into before they enrolled. "[The core courses] will stay with me for the rest of my life. . . . No one can graduate from Columbia without being well-rounded," said one undergrad. Indeed, Columbia is the only Ivy League college from which it is impossible to graduate without having read Homer, Shakespeare, and the Bible or having listened to Bach, Beethoven, and Mozart.

Columbia also has a number of very strong departments, mostly in the humanities and liberal arts, and history in particular. Among the department's famous faculty are Eric Foner, former president of the American Historical Association; Alan Brinkley, a popular historian; and Kenneth Jackson, former head of the New York Historical Society. Most courses offered are solid and free from the overt historical revisionism of political correctness. Unfortunately, history majors are not required to take American history courses before or after 1865, although they are offered.

English majors must complete 10 departmental courses, with three of these covering periods before 1800. These required classes must include one covering Shakespeare, plus another in British literature, one in American literature, one in English-language writing from outside the U.S. and U.K., one in drama, one in poetry, and one in prose or narrative. The requirements seem very flexible, but the English major coupled with the core classes guarantee a solid study of the Western canon of literature.

The political science major requirements are a little more vague. Majors must take two of three intro classes: "Intro to American Gov and Politics," "Intro to Comparative Politics," and "Intro to International Politics." Students must also take three classes in any of four subjects: American politics, comparative politics, international relations, or political theory, plus four other classes in other distinct subfields. The emphasis seems to be shifting toward contemporary workings of the American system rather than the founding or Constitution—with plenty of trendy choices concerning race, gender, environment, and the media in politics.

The controversial Middle Eastern, South Asian, and African Studies (commonly known as "MESAAS") department bears the stamp of the late leftist scholar Edward Said—a member of the Palestine Liberation Organization who supported armed violence against Israel. Jewish students have made repeated complaints that faculty in this

VITAL STATISTICS

Religious affiliation: *none*
Total enrollment: *28,211*
Total undergraduates: *8,103*
SAT CR/Verbal midrange: *690–780*
SAT Math midrange: *700–780*
ACT midrange: *32–35*
Applicants: *34,929*
Applicants accepted: *6.9%*
Accepted applicants who enrolled: *58%*
Tuition (general/out of state): *$45,028*
Tuition (in state): *N/A*
Room and board: *$11,496*
Freshman retention rate: *99%*
Graduation rate (4 yrs.): *94%*
Graduation rate (6 yrs.): *96%*
Courses with fewer than 20 students: *81%*
Student-faculty ratio: *7:1*
Courses taught by graduate students: *not provided*
Students living on campus: *95%*
Students in fraternities: *10%*
Students in sororities: *10%*
Students receiving need-based financial aid: *52%*
Avg. student-loan debt of a recent graduating class: *$12,500*
Most popular majors: *engineering, history, social sciences*
Guaranteed housing for 4 years? *yes*

CAMPUS POLITICS: YELLOW LIGHT

At Columbia, a tolerant and open-minded brand of liberalism is more or less regnant among the faculty. Most Columbia professors remain traditionalists when it comes to how and what they teach and how they approach their scholarship. The propagandistic African American studies, Middle East languages and cultures, and women's and gender studies departments are the exceptions. But keep in mind that these are small departments in a huge school.

Columbia was on the cutting edge when it came to gay rights, advocating the homosexual lifestyle even before Woodstock. The first support network for gay students was founded at Columbia in 1967 as Columbia's Student Homophile League, better known today as the Queer Alliance. Other popular activist groups include a local chapter of the International Socialist Organization, Columbia Atheists and Agnostics, Students for Choice, Students against Imperialism, Students for Economic and Environmental Justice, and the distinctive Conversio Virium: "Columbia University's Student BDSM Discussion Organization." The International Socialist Group is a particularly hard-to-avoid and unpleasant bunch that aggressively pursues students on "College Walk, demanding the U.S. let Iran get nuclear weapons or, alternately, physically attacking students at College Republican events," comments one undergrad.

department are biased toward Arab perspectives and that this had led to classroom incidents of anti-Semitism. On the positive side, the MESAAS program also features Turkish Nobel Prize–winning novelist and memoirist Orhan Pamuk, a humanities professor.

Besides the previously mentioned faculty, excellent teachers at Columbia include Carol N. Gluck and Simon Schama in history; Elaine Combs-Schilling in anthropology; Andrew Delbanco, Frances Negron-Muntaner, Michael Rosenthal, and James Shapiro in English; Richard Betts and Robert Leiberman in political science; Stephen Murray in art history; James E. G. Zetzel in Classics; Jeremy Dauber in Germanic languages and literature; David Helfand in astronomy; and Alessandra Casella in economics. One of the most rewarding courses, students report, is Kenneth T. Jackson's "History of the City of New York," which culminates in an exhilarating all-night bike ride, on which the professor leads the whole class through the city. Students seeking out the best professors can—and should—make use of the Columbia Underground Listing of Professor Ability (www.culpa.info) for its professor ratings by students.

The advising system is at best inadequate. Advising systems vary by department, and most do not assign students to specific faculty mentors. While the core classes are celebrated for their small class sizes and personalized attention, students have to seek out advisers on their own. One student makes a special point about this: "If you don't like your instructor or they're low-rated on CULPA, the smart thing may be to make a change in your schedule so you get someone else. But getting a change in your schedule can be time consuming with all the bureaucracy."

Usually, the more famous the professor, the less likely it is that he will grade any of a student's work over the course of a semester. Classes with well-known professors are lecture courses of up to 400 students, so while the university touts the fame of many of its professors, students may have trouble getting to know them. While all professors have office hours twice a week, unless students take the initiative, faculty members will rarely learn their names. Grade inflation varies by department. "As a rule of thumb," one senior says, "in hard-science classes grades are deflated, in social sciences they are left alone, in the humanities they are inflated, and in the arts they are all As." The student-faculty ratio is a stunning 7 to 1. Although professors conduct almost all classes, graduate students do teach—particularly the small "recitation" sections of 15 to 20 students that usually accompany large lecture courses, where assistants are responsible for the grading. Their quality is said to vary, sometimes dramatically. This is an issue especially for sections of foreign languages and, as at so many universities, math.

> An undergrad says that Columbia's core classes "will stay with me for the rest of my life. No one can graduate without being well-rounded."

The university offers many highly regarded junior-year-abroad programs, including a special program with Oxford and Cambridge and a popular study program in Berlin. The programs in Japan and China have greatly increased in popularity in the past couple of years. The college offers study-abroad programs to more than 40 countries, including Argentina, Australia, Brazil, France, Ghana, India, Italy, New Zealand, Russia, South Africa, and the United Kingdom.

The school offers foreign language majors in Classics, East Asian studies (Chinese, Japanese, Korean, Tibetan), French, German, Italian, Middle Eastern languages and literature (Arabic, Hebrew, Hindi), Portuguese, Russian, Slavic studies, and Yiddish studies. In addition, Columbia offers classes in Armenian, Bengali, Czech, Dutch, Farsi, Finnish, Hebrew, Hausa, Hindi, Polish, Punjabi, Romanian, Sanskrit, Serbo-Croatian, Swahili, Swedish, Tamil, Turkish (Modern and Ottoman), Ukrainian, Urdu, Vietnamese, Wolof, and Zulu.

Student Life: Annexing the neighborhood

Housing in New York City is notoriously expensive and hard to find, so it's not surprising that 95 percent of the Columbia student body lives on campus. All freshmen are required to live on campus, and Columbia guarantees housing to its undergraduates for all four years.

Dormitories are coed, but the university sets aside a few floors solely for men or women. Women students can also live at Barnard, which offers all-women residence halls. Columbia does have a few coed bathrooms, but students can easily avoid them. Some dorms, like other areas of New York, have had trouble with bedbugs and cockroaches. Apparently the dorm lottery is very hit or miss. Special-interest housing allows groups of students to live together in one of several townhouses. Quiet hours and noise regulations govern almost every dormitory. Sensitive students may have trouble getting these policies enforced, but

SUGGESTED CORE

Required core curriculum courses (such as Humanities C1001–C1002: "Masterpieces of Western Literature and Introduction to Contemporary Civilization 1101–1102") may be supplemented with the following:

1. Religion W4170, History of Christianity
2. English W3335x/W3336y, Shakespeare I/II
3. History BC1401, American Civilization to the Civil War

most students on campus do not view noise as a major problem. Although it is up to the discretion of the residence adviser, most floors offer some sort of "condom box," making contraception widely available to students. Likewise, some floors have signs that provide information on the "morning-after pill" and other "health" services.

A row of fraternity houses lines the two blocks just south of the university's increasingly chic Morningside Heights neighborhood, and the university does have a frat scene, although the school's frats are a bit more cosmopolitan than houses at many other schools. Students generally say that there is not much Greek life at Columbia and that it is very self-contained.

As part of orientation week, the university sponsors a number of tours to familiarize students with the city. One graduating senior says simply, "Don't miss the first-week tours. As someone from the Midwest who didn't know the city at all, I can say that it really made my first year in New York more comprehensible—and you meet a lot of your classmates at the same time." Informational sessions on the dangers of date rape are mandatory for all students. Selected freshmen also attend receptions segregated by race or interest, including the Black Students Reception and the Gay, Lesbian, and Transgender Students Reception. Reportedly, the purpose of all these talks is to indoctrinate students in the ubiquity of oppression. However, "They went over like a lead balloon" with freshmen, said one student.

The school has about 500 official student organizations, including the Artist Society, Brazilian Jiu-Jitsu, Chess Club, Club Sports, Columbia University Poker Club, Dance Marathon, Earth Coalition, Figure Skating, Gospel Choir, Haitian Students Association, Japan Club, Law School Student Senate, Multicultural Greek Council, Nightline (peer counseling), Sailing, Saving Mothers, and U.S. Military Veterans of Columbia University.

The politically active population on campus comprises only a minority of students, but it is an outspoken group with strong allies in student government and the faculty. There are around 40 politically active groups at the college, supposedly more than any other in the nation. Groups include the College Democrats, College Libertarians, the Columbia Political Union, and the College Republicans. For all the problems the school has had with truculent leftists, there are more conservatives at Columbia than one might think. The Columbia College Republicans currently boasts a membership of more than 500. Columbia has not had an ROTC program since 1969, however.

Devout students will find chaplains representing most common (and many uncommon) faiths. The friendly, active, and orthodox Catholic chaplaincy sponsors the highbrow Augustine Club, which features doctrinal discussions and lectures. The school also hosts a Hillel, a chapter of Campus Crusade for Christ, an Orthodox Christian Fellowship, a Muslim Students Association, a Ba'hai and a Buddhist organization, among many others.

Episcopalian students—and fans of exquisite architecture—should check out the nearby Cathedral of St. John the Divine.

But don't look for spiritual guidance in the religion department. When asked whether he believed in God, the chairman of the religion department and codirector of the Institute for Culture and Religious Life, Mark C. Taylor, replied, "Not in the traditional sense. God, or, in different terms, the divine, is the infinite creative process that is embodied in life itself. As such, the divine is the arising and passing that does not itself arise and pass away. This process is actualized in an infinite web of relations that is an emergent self-organizing network of networks extending from the natural and social to the technological and cultural dimensions of life." So at least we're clear about that.

The Columbia Lions, who compete—if that is the word—in the Ivy League, are known for their record losing streaks.

Columbia sits in a newly prosperous neighborhood in what is now the safest large city in America. Says one student, "People think we're living in Harlem. It's quite safe. I feel I'm in more danger visiting friends at other schools. I went to visit a friend at Oberlin. That was scary." In 2011 the school reported three forcible sex offenses—down from 14 in 2009, one robbery, four aggravated assaults, and 24 burglaries on campus.

Columbia students pay for their privileges: tuition in 2012–13 was $45,028, and room and board were $11,496. However, admissions are need blind, and the university promises to meet the full need of any student who gets in—and does so generously. About 50 percent of students received need-based financial aid. While the school has announced a "no loans" policy, the median student-loan debt of a recent graduating class was $12,500, according to the *Wall Street Journal*.

STRONG SUITS	WEAK POINTS
• One of the most comprehensive cores in the world. Every student learns Western and world cultures.	• Some trendy and politicized departments—especially Middle Eastern, South Asian, and African Studies, and political science.
• Stellar teachers and highly qualified fellow students.	• Weak advising and a Byzantine bureaucracy that drives students crazy.
• A vibrant social and cultural scene in New York City.	• Faculty, while often famous, are hands-off. Most interaction is with grad students, who sometimes teach.
• High-powered programs in hard sciences, humanities, history, English.	• Religion program marked by skepticism, secularism.
• Expansive options in study abroad and foreign languages—including many hard-to-find tongues.	• Aggressive, obnoxious leftist activism on campus.

Cornell University

Ithaca, New York • www.cornell.edu

Hybrid Vigor

Founded in 1865, Cornell is a unique and successful public-private partnership in American higher education. Students from New York majoring in technical subjects can receive an Ivy League education at a state university price. Cornell places heavy emphasis on research; the university stands in the top 20 institutions nationwide in research spending. Twenty-eight Rhodes scholars and more than 40 Nobel Prize winners have spent time as students or faculty at this school in remote upstate New York.

Arts and Sciences students are only a third of undergrads, and even among that third, the hard sciences have pride of place. Three decades of successful student radicalism have weakened the morale of the undergraduate liberal arts—inspiring neoconservative Allan Bloom to leave his Cornell post and write *The Closing of the American Mind*.

With so many good classes, professors, and programs, the university offers the chance for a stellar undergraduate experience. However, if you are a political or social conservative in the liberal arts, sources on campus suggest you prepare either to practice discretion or face conflict with intolerant fellow students.

Academic Life: Seven colleges, no waiting

Undergraduate Cornell is divided into seven colleges, three of which—Agriculture and Life Sciences, Industrial and Labor Relations, and Human Ecology—are sponsored by the state of New York. The rest are private colleges whose funds come from Cornell. The College of Arts and Sciences is the subject of this profile, although several of the others are well regarded—especially Engineering, Architecture, and Hotel Administration. If a student's interests lean toward life science or human ecology, he can qualify for the economical land-grant tuition rate.

Within the College of Arts and Sciences are 39 departments offering 42 majors and serving 4,100 undergraduates (out of some 14,158 students on campus). Students must fulfill a set of distribution requirements, but no courses are required by name—leading one faculty member to call Cornell's requirements "meaningless and arbitrary."

The two required freshman writing seminars, with just 15 to 20 students per section, draw the most praise. The university offers a hundred choices, "so whatever your interest, you'll find a cool class," says a student. "You will become a better writer by default. You'll be writing papers on a regular basis." Classes range from the traditional ("Greek Mythology") to the trivial ("Cigarette Cultures").

Since the distribution courses and electives can come from any undergraduate college, there are literally a thousand options at a student's disposal. The trick is whether a student can put together a coherent program of study that provides a grasp of Western civilization.

There are indeed thousands of solid courses at Cornell, and a few frivolous ones—many of which do not fulfill requirements. The school's faculty is top-notch and devoted to teaching. "Many of the faculty are widely renowned in their fields, have published the authoritative works, are heads of international institutions, and have done groundbreaking research. And these are the people teaching the intro courses to freshmen," a student says. "The best professors are the ones teaching the freshmen," says another. That may be because many faculty members who teach upper-level courses are more involved in research

VITAL STATISTICS

Religious affiliation: *none*
Total enrollment: *21,131*
Total undergraduates: *14,158*
SAT CR/Verbal midrange: *630–730*
SAT Math midrange: *660–770*
ACT midrange: *29–33*
Applicants: *37,808*
Applicants accepted: *18%*
Accepted applicants who enrolled: *51%*
Tuition (general/out of state): *$43,185*
Tuition (in state): *$27,045*
Room and board: *$13,104*
Freshman retention rate: *97%*
Graduation rate (4 yrs.): *87%*
Graduation rate (6 yrs.): *93%*
Courses with fewer than 20 students: *70%*
Student-faculty ratio: *8:1*
Courses taught by graduate students: *5%*
Students living on campus: *57%*
Students in fraternities: *27%*
Students in sororities: *22%*
Students receiving need-based financial aid: *50%*
Avg. student-loan debt of a recent graduating class: *$19,180*
Most popular majors: *agriculture, business/marketing, engineering*
Guaranteed housing for 4 years? *no*

CAMPUS POLITICS: YELLOW LIGHT

Although students and faculty do seem to lean left, as is commonplace in a university setting, a healthy conservative movement continues to flourish at Cornell. The long-embattled *Cornell Review* (the conservative student newspaper founded by, among others, Ann Coulter '84) is a frequent source of conflict. In repeated incidents, papers have been stolen, dumped, or burned. In recent years the paper has come under fire for publishing an article criticizing self-segregation in racially themed houses and a piece satirizing radical Muslims in the U.K. (the latter was written by an American Muslim). Calling the articles "offensive, ignorant, and . . . full of hate," the Student Assembly proposed a resolution to disaffiliate the paper from the university. Ironically, the purported goal of the Student Assembly is to promote the university's commitment to "a more diverse and inclusive campus."

As one student wrote in the *Daily Sun*, "Conservatives on campuses like Cornell's invariably find themselves in the ideological minority, as the majority of their peers rarely encounter, and often are openly hostile to, their political outlook. It's clear that in face of such widespread opposition, conservatives find themselves on the defensive with regards to their positions and feel obligated to constantly sharpen and publicize their arguments."

and publishing than they are in teaching. It is publications, not teaching skills, according to a full professor, that yield tenure here.

Fortunately, it is very rare for a graduate teaching assistant to be the sole instructor of a class, and students say that the TAs who deliver the occasional lecture and supervise section discussions are first-rate. Those sectional meetings can be important in survey courses that enroll up to 500 students. Cornell has one course, "Psychology 101," that, according to the school's website, is the world's largest lecture at 1,600 students and two TAs, with dozens of tutors to lead smaller groups.

Students select their own faculty academic advisers from their major departments. However, warns one undergrad, advisers vary in quality. "They can be great or completely ignorant, depending on the person. Do not trust your adviser with your academic career. Seek multiple sources of advice and information." The university has a Peer Advisor Program that pairs upperclassmen with new students. Advice includes "anything from campus resources to social life to dining options," according to the campus paper, the *Daily Sun*. The university also has a strong and well-advertised Career Office for both academic and career counseling. Students say that popular courses are hard to get into and can take up to three years to open up.

Many departments have outstanding teachers, and most Cornell faculty members are committed to undergraduate instruction and are available during office hours. Among the best are Isaac Kramnick, Theodore J. Lowi, and Elizabeth Sanders in government; John Najemy and Richard Polenberg in history; Gail Fine in philosophy; and Patricia Carden in Russian literature. A Hotel Administration school student also mentions Bill Carroll in microeconomics, noting that "not only does Professor Carroll present his curriculum in a clear and concise way, but he makes sure the students have fun learning, going as far as to hand out $20 bills to students in class during the lecture on Game Theory." Mark McCarthy's "Micro-Computing" was "voted by seniors the most practical course," while the law class taught by David Sherwyn is said to be "a ton of fun" with his stories of his days as a trial lawyer. He insists his students "never look at a situation without thinking of the legal repercussions ever again."

Cornell has some academically weak and polemical departments, including Africana studies and feminist, gender, and sexuality studies. Unfortunately, even the economics department is somewhat politicized. "There used to be a greater mix of political views," one longtime professor told the *Cornell American*, a conservative campus journal. "There was more interest in political debate. . . . Debate was more fun, and you got more out of it."

Major requirements seem a little lax. English students must take three courses in which more than half the material comes from before 1800—which would make it possible to miss out on Shakespeare, but not on the whole British literary tradition. History students must likewise take three courses set before 1800—of any region in the world, so it's quite possible for majors to miss the American Founding and Civil War. The government major has slightly better prerequisites, requiring two introductory classes and some electives in political philosophy and U.S. government.

> "**M**any of the faculty are widely renowned in their fields, have published the authoritative works, and have done groundbreaking research. And they are teaching the intro courses to freshmen," a student says.

Cornell students can study abroad literally anywhere in the world as long as their adviser and college approve it. Students have recently traveled to places as diverse as Argentina, China, Israel, Senegal, and South Africa, and students are not limited to academic institutions: programs may include field study, research, service work, an internship, or some combination thereof. About 500 students travel to 40 different countries each year, mostly as juniors, to study or work for a semester or two.

Over 50 foreign languages are taught on campus, from Cantonese and Czech to French and Italian. Cornell offers six Southeast Asian languages and intensive summer programs in languages like American Sign Language, Ancient Greek, Arabic, and Swahili. The school's FALCON program provides full-time language study in Chinese or Japanese, giving students three years' worth of instruction in a single year. Language courses often go hand in hand with majors in departments like China and Asia-Pacific Studies, German, Near Eastern Studies, Russian, and Spanish.

Student Life: Home to Ithaca

The winter weather is lousy, but the countryside is lovely, and "Ithaca itself is a thriving small city with great opportunities, nightlife, and restaurants," a student says. "You name it, it's available." At a university of Cornell's size, students can find plenty to fill up time outside the classroom. Students and their primary interests run the gamut, as one would

SUGGESTED CORE

1. Classics 2601/2612, The Greek Experience/The Roman Experience (*closest matches*)
2. Philosophy 2200, Ancient Philosophy
3. Religious Studies 2613/2629, The Bible in Context: An Introduction to the Hebrew Bible and New Testament/Introduction to New Testament and Other Early Christian Literature
4. Religious Studies 3150, Medieval Philosophy
5. Government 2605, Social and Political Philosophy or German Studies 4150, Marx, Freud, Nietzsche
6. English 2270, Shakespeare
7. History 1530, Introduction to American History I
8. History 3340, 19th-Century European Culture and Intellectual History or Philosophy 2220, Modern Philosophy

expect. "You can't label the students," one says. "I knew brains, stoners, athletes, artists, well-rounded and balanced students, drug addicts, alcoholics—they were all in the mix. On the whole, however, most students practiced the 'work hard, play hard' motto at Cornell. During the week, they studied, and then on the weekend they partied."

Cornell's Big Red athletes compete on 34 sports teams at the NCAA Division I level with an unofficial bear mascot. Students who are not varsity material can play sports through the largest intramural program in the Ivy League, with more than 30 leagues and tournaments to choose from.

Student organizations skew to social or cultural themes; more than two dozen chaplaincies on campus support Buddhist, Catholic, Hindu, Jewish, Muslim, and Protestant students. Religious services include African American worship, Chinese and Korean Christian churches, Cru (formerly Campus Crusade for Christ), Chabad, Humanist associations, InterVarsity Christian Fellowship, Mormons, the Navigators, Quakers, and Unitarian Universalist churches, along with Catholic Masses and mainline and evangelical Protestant services.

With 928 student organizations, Cornell students have options. Political groups include College Democrats and Republicans, as well as Amnesty International, Asian Pacific Americans for Action, the Cornell Progressive, Haven: the LGBTQ Student Union, the Islamic Alliance for Justice, and La Asociación Latina. The student-run *Daily Sun* includes among its alums E. B. White, Dick Schaap, Kurt Vonnegut Jr., and Frank Gannett. The *Sun* became the first collegiate member of the Associated Press in 1912.

With over 25 percent of the student body pledged, the Greek system is "the center of the social scene on campus," says the *Daily Sun*. According to a student, however, "there is a huge underground drug culture that pervades the Greek system."

The student body is a mixture of different types, but "the majority is rich white kids from Long Island and New York and the rest of the Northeast. . . . Most people are very competitive, ambitious, driven, and have connections from their parents. Most are well off, and many went to private school before Cornell," says a student.

The university guarantees housing only for students' first two years (all freshmen live on campus). Undergraduates choose their housing from dormitories, program houses, cooperative programs, and fraternities and sororities. Most "freshmen stay in North Campus, which has brand-new dorms and the best food in the nation," a student says. Freshmen can choose program houses as long as they are on North Campus. The *Daily Sun* reports that students housed in some of the older dorms are petitioning for renovation, citing poor heating, unsanitary bathrooms, and bedbugs among the list of complaints.

Residence halls are usually coed, but the university has a few single-sex dorms, even for those not in fraternities. There are no coed bathrooms or dorm rooms in residence halls, although dormitories do not have restricted visiting hours. "We're not a Christian school, and this isn't the 1950s," a student says. "General rules of respect and order are enforced by the resident adviser, but it depends on the RA. Some might not care about drinking or drugs in the dorm; some might."

The university received a perfect score of 5 (out of 5) on Campus Pride's "LGBT-Friendly Campus Climate Index," which rates schools on their policies regarding lesbian, gay, bisexual, and transgender issues.

Those who live at Cornell consider the campus quite safe. In 2011, four forcible sex offenses, one aggravated assault, and two burglaries were reported on campus.

Cornell's tuition system is unique. For a narrow range of students—those hailing from New York State who wish to study in the colleges of Agriculture and Life Sciences, Human Ecology, or Industrial and Labor Relations—tuition was only $27,045 in 2012–13. For all others, tuition was a more standard $43,185. Standard (double) room and traditional board were $13,104 for everyone. Admission is need blind, and the school promises to meet the full need of admitted students; it provides need-based aid to some 50 percent of students. Still, the student-loan debt of a recent graduate is $19,180.

STRONG SUITS	WEAK POINTS
• Highly qualified faculty who do most of the teaching and enjoy interacting with students outside class time. • Worthy programs in the hard sciences, with plenty of research on campus. • Good, effective freshman writing courses. • Special, low-tuition programs for certain schools: the colleges of Agriculture and Life Sciences, Human Ecology, and Industrial and Labor Relations.	• Popular courses are often oversubscribed, so students wait years to take them. • Several weak and/or polemical departments, such as Africana studies; feminist, gender, and sexuality studies; and even economics. • Outside of study time, a party atmosphere can reign in dorms—which have no restrictions on overnight guests. • Older dorms plagued by poor heating, unsanitary bathrooms, and bedbugs. • Vocal conservatives often feel they are under siege by their fellow students.

Dartmouth College

Hanover, New Hampshire • www.dartmouth.edu

Traditions Run Deep

Dartmouth College was founded in 1755. Its small size and geographical isolation have created a powerful camaraderie on campus and lasting loyalty among graduates. Perhaps as a result, many alumni of the school assist conservative undergraduates who resent the administration's efforts to reshape Dartmouth—for instance, by persecuting fraternities while supporting women's studies and gay programs, and deemphasizing the football program.

Dartmouth remains an institution beloved by its students and alumni and known for its rowdy Greek social life and close interaction between world-class faculty and students. "What most impresses me about Dartmouth is the genuine love for the school shared by the student body," says a student. "The Dartmouth spirit is powerful and enduring."

Academic Life: Parental guidance suggested

In lieu of a real core curriculum, Dartmouth imposes extensive but vague distributive requirements. According to one junior, some students "manipulate their course selections to boost GPAs. Many majors are not tremendously time intensive, so students are able to take a wide range of classes." Recently, Dartmouth modified its requirements to include a "Culture and

Identity" component. As a result, one student states, "one often has to bite the bullet and take a class on feminism, African American heritage, or any of a number of similar courses, which vary in tone from liberal to ridiculously liberal." But more traditional subject matter is still taught by distinguished scholars, if you seek them out.

The college offers more than 50 majors. Students may also choose to work toward a double major or to create their own fields of study. "The economics major is exceptionally strong and popular at Dartmouth," says an undergrad. "It gives students access to a superb faculty and a broad range of classes. But since the major is popular, lower and midlevel classes can be large and/or difficult to get into. The number of economics majors has doubled in the last 10 years, resulting in long waiting lists and crowded classrooms."

Not all courses are graded rigorously. In the spring of 2012, nearly half of classes had an A- average grade, and only three classes (one biology, one economics, and one Spanish) recorded an average grade of B-. Dartmouth transcripts now also include such information as the size of each class and the median grade.

Students aren't required to seek guidance, but the college does assign advisers to freshmen, and "many students seek informal advising from various professors and peers," one student explains. Another student asserts that "the interaction between accomplished professors and undergraduates at Dartmouth is unmatched by any of its peer institutions."

Many students also use the Student Assembly's online Professor/Course Review to help select courses. More help comes from the conservative *Dartmouth Review*, which offers candid, sometimes biting assessments. The *Review* publishes and distributes a Freshman Issue that includes articles on "worst and best professors" and "courses of note." Professors' accessibility is uniformly and enthusiastically praised by students. Professors, not teaching assistants, teach all courses. This is a major benefit that should not be taken for granted and isn't offered at every Ivy.

The most traditional and rigorous departments at Dartmouth according to students and professors are Classics, economics, history, and religion. Among the many excellent professors at Dartmouth are Jeffrey Hart (emeritus) and Barbara Will in English; Paul Christesen in

VITAL STATISTICS

Religious affiliation: *none*
Total enrollment: *5,987*
Total undergraduates: *4,196*
SAT CR/Verbal midrange: *670–780*
SAT Math midrange: *680–780*
ACT midrange: *30–34*
Applicants: *23,110*
Applicants accepted: *9.8%*
Accepted applicants who enrolled: *48.5%*
Tuition (general/out of state): *$43,782*
Tuition (in state): *N/A*
Room and board: *$12,954*
Freshman retention rate: *98%*
Graduation rate (4 yrs.): *88%*
Graduation rate (6 yrs.): *95%*
Courses with fewer than 20 students: *64%*
Student-faculty ratio: *8:1*
Courses taught by graduate students: *not provided*
Students living on campus: *86%*
Students in fraternities: *48%*
Students in sororities: *47%*
Students receiving need-based financial aid: *45%*
Avg. student-loan debt of a recent graduating class: *$18,130*
Most popular majors: *economics, government, psychology*
Guaranteed housing for 4 years? *no*

CAMPUS POLITICS: YELLOW LIGHT

Since 2005, when it abolished its unpopular speech code, Dartmouth has been praised as a haven of free student speech. The administration—once implacably hostile—has learned to live with the dissident *Dartmouth Review*, and a number of alumni-sponsored conservative initiatives are active on campus.

That doesn't mean things are always easy for them. Their fellow students aren't exactly welcoming. In 2012 pro-lifers at Dartmouth set up a display commemorating the victims of *Roe v. Wade*—in the form of 546 American flags, or one for each 100,000 aborted American children. This "cemetery of the innocents" was quickly defaced, according to the *Dartmouth Review*, and a Dartmouth student actually drove his Toyota Camry off the road and into the display, knocking over many of the flags. The student faced criminal charges for this action.

Classics; John Rassias in French (all foreign language classes at Dartmouth use the now famous Rassias method); Allen Koop and David Lagomarsino in history; Lucas Swaine in government; Colin Calloway in history and Native American studies; and Ehud Benor in religion.

According to one student, "The usual suspects for liberal departments are anthropology, geography, women and gender studies, and English. History fits into this category, because the professors teach history from a social perspective and ram the importance of social movements down your throat. The government department is surprisingly fair." Other students cited Latin American studies as a politicized discipline.

Dartmouth English majors must complete two classes on literature from before the mid-17th century, two from the mid-17th to the 19th century, and one class on 20th-century literature, as well as a criticism and theory class.

History majors must take classes in geographical areas (U.S. and Canada, Europe, non-Western, and interregional) and four classes that form a concentration like "The Black Radical Tradition in America" or "Modern Europe: The Twentieth Century."

Government majors, unfortunately, face even less-stringent requirements: they must simply take two courses at the introductory level, two seminar level courses, and six classes that form a concentration.

For more traditional perspectives, check out the Daniel Webster Project, which strives to bring "ancient and modern perspectives to bear on issues of permanent moral and political importance." By offering lectures, conferences, and symposia on the Dartmouth campus, the Daniel Webster Project adds both new and forgotten (i.e., conservative) voices to the intellectual life at Dartmouth. Such supplements are needed. As one alumnus says, "Dartmouth students are no longer required to read Shakespeare, Dante, Plato, or even to know the basic facts of American history."

Some 61 percent of Dartmouth undergraduates study abroad, making it number one among Ivy League schools in this category. Dartmouth students study off campus as close as Amherst or Vassar and in places as distant as Tokyo, the Cayman Islands, or Denmark.

Back on campus, three semesters of a foreign language are required; the school offers Arabic, Chinese, French, German, Greek and Latin, Hebrew, Italian, Japanese, Russian, Spanish, and Swahili.

Student Life: Sheepskin vs. pigskin

The New Hampshire town of Hanover and the 200-acre campus are surrounded by woodlands and mountains. Traditional residence halls and smaller social houses make up the nine residential communities that are home to around 86 percent of undergraduates. Nearly a third of the rooms are singles (most of which are assigned to upperclassmen), and many of the rooms have private or semiprivate bathrooms. There are a few single-sex floors but no single-sex dorms. Substance-free residences are available to students, as are "academic affinity programs," which include the offices of ethnic clubs and societies as well as theme houses in language, eco-consciousness, cooperative living, and religion.

Dartmouth has male, female, and coed leagues for more than 30 clubs and over 20 intramural sports. Dartmouth also fields 29 NCAA Division I intercollegiate teams. About 80 percent of students participate in athletics at Dartmouth. Dartmouth has no official mascot and is known as "Big Green," now that its "Indians" mascot has been deemed offensive.

The college is often referred to as "Camp Dartmouth" and the "conservative party school," according to TheDartmouth.com. (National Lampoon's *Animal House* was based on the stories of three Dartmouth fraternity members.) The long-flourishing Greek scene attracts about 48 percent of the eligible population—freshmen are not permitted to pledge—to join one of 28 fraternity, sorority, and three coed houses—despite the best efforts of the school to "henpeck them into submission through regulation," according to the *Review.* Journalistic accounts of disgusting hazing rituals have attracted scrutiny from the administration.

> **P**rofessors, not teaching assistants, teach all courses—and they forge close bonds with students.

Vocal conservatives have had some success in publicizing the gradual encroachment of political correctness into the college's academic and student life. The *Review,* with its constant calls for free speech, plays a large part in bringing unsavory issues to light, and the school administration does not always appreciate the favor. For its part, the paper has occasionally published juvenile, genuinely offensive pieces. Still, the *Review* has had a positive impact on the campus as a strident conservative voice and appears to be resurgent after a short period of decline. Other student-operated papers include the far-left *Dartmouth Radical* and the *Dartmouth* (the official school newspaper).

Dartmouth sustains a lively political debate. The Dartmouth College Democrats and the College Republicans are both active, and the Libertarian Party has recently become strong as well. A pro-life group, fitfully active, exists on campus. New Hampshire's first-in-the-nation primary status gives Dartmouth students unprecedented access to aspiring presidential nominees.

Two hundred student organizations mean that Dartmouth offers something for everyone, with numerous singing, dance, and music groups, and more than 20 publications and media outlets. Radio fans, too, find much to engage them at Dartmouth: WDCR and its sister station, WFRD, are the only completely student-run commercial broadcast stations in the United States.

SUGGESTED CORE

1. Classical Studies 5, The Heroic Vision: Epics of Greece and Rome
2. Philosophy 11, Ancient Philosophy
3. Religion 4/5, Religion of Israel: The Hebrew Bible/ Early Christianity: The New Testament
4. History 43, European Intellectual and Cultural History, 400–1300
5. Government 64, Modern Political Thought
6. English 24, Shakespeare I
7. History 10, Colonial America or History 20, American Thought and Culture to 1865
8. History 51, Modern European Intellectual History

Religious groups abound; more than 25 are represented in the directory. The Aquinas House offers a daily Mass, the Orthodox Christian Fellowship offers a weekly vespers service with discussion following, the Muslim prayer room in North Fairbanks Hall holds daily prayers, and various Jewish groups sponsor services. There is an active evangelical Alpha Omega student group, as well as Mormon and Buddhist gatherings. The Society of Friends has weekly meetings and monthly speakers.

When students free themselves from course work, they usually socialize in the dorms or social houses. One student claims that "beer pong is the most popular social activity on campus."

Crime reports from 2011 reveal 12 forcible sex offenses, six burglaries, and one case of arson. The campus includes 48 emergency phones, patrol by security officers, safety escorts, transportation help for sick and injured students, and security guards for social events.

Dartmouth is expensive but generous. Tuition for 2012–13 came in at $43,782, and $12,954 for room and board. Students are also required to own computers. Admissions are need blind, and the college guarantees to meet the full need of accepted students. Many students take out loans to pay for room, board, books, and incidentals, and the average student-loan debt of a recent graduate was $18,130.

STRONG SUITS

- Good programs in Classics, economics, history, government, and religion.
- Highly qualified teachers who work closely with students.
- Abundant religious groups and active conservative initiatives with alumni support.
- Excellent opportunities for study abroad.

WEAK POINTS

- No core curriculum and vague general-education requirements—including a diversity course.
- Several politicized departments, including anthropology, geography, women and gender studies, Latin American studies, and English.
- Rampant grade inflation.
- Aggressive attempts to control student life.
- Ongoing problems with hazing in fraternities.

Duke University

Durham, North Carolina • www.duke.edu

Eternal Union?

Founded in 1838 by Methodists and Quakers, then merged into Duke University, Duke maintains as its largest division the Trinity College of Arts and Sciences. A metal plaque in front of the Duke Chapel maintains that "the aims of Duke University are to assert a faith in the eternal union of knowledge and religion set forth in the teaching and character of Jesus Christ, the Son of God."

To those who know Duke firsthand, these words will ring bitterly hollow. Links to orthodox Christianity, long stretched thin, finally snapped when the Duke Chapel allowed homosexual "weddings" in 2000. The school still bears scars from the 2006 incident in which a local stripper falsely accused three Duke men's lacrosse players of rape, luring professors, administrators, and Duke president Richard Brodhead into outrageous denunciations of the wrongly accused athletes. One student reports that, "post-lacrosse case, the overall sentiment is that students are much less happy with Brodhead and his cronies." While Duke is a leader in many areas of scholarship and research, it slavishly follows the academic ideological trends of elite schools nationwide.

VITAL STATISTICS

Religious affiliation: *none*
Total enrollment: *15,427*
Total undergraduates: *6,680*
SAT CR/Verbal midrange: *680–780*
SAT Math midrange: *690–780*
ACT midrange: *31–34*
Applicants: *28,145*
Applicants accepted: *14%*
Accepted applicants who enrolled: *44%*
Tuition (general/out of state): *$44,101*
Tuition (in state): *N/A*
Room and board: *$11,770*
Freshman retention rate: *97%*
Graduation rate (4 yrs.): *88%*
Graduation rate (6 yrs.): *94%*
Courses with fewer than 20 students: *71%*
Student-faculty ratio: *8:1*
Courses taught by graduate students: *not provided*
Students living on campus: *82%*
Students in fraternities: *29%*
Students in sororities: *42%*
Students receiving need-based financial aid: *48%*
Avg. student-loan debt of a recent graduating class: *$21,713*
Most popular majors: *engineering, psychology, social sciences*
Guaranteed housing for 4 years? *yes*

Academic Life: Beautiful fragments

Duke has two undergraduate schools: the Pratt School of Engineering and the Trinity College of Arts and Sciences. Trinity undergraduates may choose one of two programs to attain a bachelor's degree. Program I is the more traditional and popular choice; its curriculum, revised in 2000, revolves around four interrelated sets of curricular requirements: Areas of Knowledge, Modes of Inquiry, Small Group Learning Experiences, and a student's major subject. None of these vague guidelines guarantees a traditional liberal arts education. Program II has still laxer core requirements but allows students to construct unorthodox programs of study, with faculty approval.

Individual majors impose further requirements. Philosophy majors, for instance, take two survey courses, "History of Ancient Philosophy" and "History of Modern Philosophy," both solid introductions. English majors must take at least one course in "Literary and Cultural Study" of the medieval and early modern period, the 18th and 19th centuries, and the modern and contemporary period. English majors are no longer required to take a course on a major author—Chaucer, Milton, or Shakespeare—as they had been in the past, but very few graduate without having taken one.

Political science remains one of the school's stronger departments. Standout teachers include Ruth Grant and Thomas Spragens Jr. in political theory; Peter D. Feaver in international relations; J. Peter Euben in political philosophy and ethics; and department chairman Michael C. Munger, who is a political economist. Albert F. Eldridge (emeritus) and Michael Gillespie are also favorites. One faculty member tells us that the department is weakest in American political institutions. Still, political science majors must take at least one course in American politics. According to numerous students, the excellent instruction in the political science department is offset by the great power wielded by graduate teaching assistants, many of whom reportedly have difficulties with the English language. Students speak highly of the Gerst Program in Political, Economic, and Humanistic Studies, which aims to foster student understanding in "the central importance of freedom for democratic government, moral responsibility, and economic and cultural life" and has freshmen in the program beginning with four courses that help introduce students to the tradition.

History majors are required to take just one introductory class and nine other courses, including classes in three of five geographic areas, a concentration of four classes in a theme like "emotions and the psychology of self" or military history, and a senior seminar. Recommended professors in history include Barry Gaspar, Bruce Kuniholm, and Timothy Tyson.

Other good teachers at Duke, according to students, include David Aers, James Applewhite (emeritus), Ian Baucom, Buford Jones, Michael Moses, Thomas Pfau, Deborah Pope, and Victor Strandberg in English; Diskin Clay (emeritus) in classical studies; Robert Brandon, Michael Ferejohn, Martin Golding, Alexander Rosenberg, and David Wong in philosophy; Mark Goodacre, who "resists a lot of disturbing trends in recent religious scholarship and is one of the few bright spots of the religion department"; and Craufurd Goodwin in economics. Thomas Nechyba, also in economics and the department chair, is described as a "true conservative with very strong values . . . and a hard grader." The economics department is one of the university's most respected, according to students and faculty; one student warns prospective students to beware of introductory classes: "They're generally used only to remove any students unqualified for the later classes."

CAMPUS POLITICS: RED LIGHT

In 2010 the Duke Women's Center canceled its "Discussion with a Duke Mother" event (sponsored by Duke Students for Life) when some students objected to the presence of a pro-life group in the Women's Center. Center director Ada Gregory stated that "mistakes were certainly made" and defended the pro-life group after the decision was exposed. However, Gregory found herself in the midst of controversy again in 2010 by supporting Duke's new "sexual misconduct" policy. According to the Foundation for Individual Rights in Education (FIRE), the policy "can render a student guilty of nonconsensual sex simply because he or she is considered 'powerful' on campus. . . . Duke's new policy transforms students of both sexes into unwitting rapists simply because of the 'atmosphere.'" FIRE summed up the policy in the *Washington Times* as follows: "At Duke, you can be a rapist without even knowing it."

Conservative students can be cheeky about responding to political correctness: in 2012 the Duke Federalist Society (based at its law school) tweaked liberal sensitivities by serving food from Chick-fil-A—a company being boycotted for its support of traditional marriage, according to *Campus Reform*.

As one student tells us, faculty and administrators are fixated on "race, gender, and class." The good news is that, except for some obviously radical classes, "Duke does a reasonably good job of keeping politics out of the classroom," as one student puts it, and many students and faculty agree. For the most part, teachers are fair, even if they are intensely left wing.

Duke's Sanford School of Public Policy is an extremely politicized enclave within the university; many professors there live within a "liberal cocoon," one student complains. The sociology program is also quite weak, and one faculty member reports that the department "has simply decided to sacrifice education in exchange for higher enrollments. The classes are rudimentary and political. The 'Markets and Management' program, housed in the department, is really a fraud and should be avoided by serious students."

Freshmen are assigned advisers based on their residence halls. Some students say that this causes problems, since computer science professors, for instance, have little guidance to offer students who want to major in philosophy. After declaring a major (usually in the sophomore year), a student takes a faculty adviser within that major. At that point, it is up to the student to take the initiative and gain all he can from the relationship. Unfortunately, most students visit advisers only once a semester, and that only to obtain a PIN necessary for online registration.

Students report that many professors are willing to have discussions and share meals outside office hours. With an impressive student-faculty ratio of 8 to 1, Duke students have a real opportunity to get to know their professors. Too few do, sources say. One undergrad reports that Duke students are "mostly there to get a ticket punched and attend some parties along the way." A professor agrees: "There are many people who are dedicated teachers. The students don't take enough advantage of this." Economics and public policy majors are known for being inordinately interested in padding their résumés, while premed students are notorious grade grubbers, an alumna says.

> One undergrad says that Duke students are "mostly there to get a ticket punched and attend some parties along the way."

Professors teach most courses, but graduate teaching assistants sometimes teach introductory classes and often grade exams. "Writing 20," Duke's one required course, is usually taught by graduate students, who decide course content and class discussion. One student says that this class is a "complete waste of time," often politicized by the instructors. Introductory freshman classes are often large (100 to 175 students), but by the junior and senior years, when most students are working on their majors, class sizes dwindle to a more manageable 25 or fewer.

Serious first-year students should consider Duke's Focus Program, where they'll have an opportunity to spend their first semester immersed in true academic life, studying, living, and socializing with other students in their same "cluster." One faculty member says the Focus programs "are the best way to start college and equal to the best programs anywhere else in America." The university offers about a dozen topics; "Visions of Freedom" and "The Power of Ideas" are the best, says another professor.

Duke offers a long list of study-abroad programs, and 45 percent of Trinity students participate in a program, most commonly with a semester in Australia, Italy, Spain, or the U.K. Programs are available around the world, from Costa Rica to Ghana. Marine biology courses are available along the North Carolina coast, as well as programs in New York (arts and media or financial markets) or Los Angeles.

Duke teaches language classes in Arabic, Balto-Finnic, Chinese, Croatian, French, German, Greek and Latin, Hebrew, Hindi, Hungarian, Italian, Japanese, Korean, Pashto,

Persian, Polish, Portuguese, Romanian, Russian, Serbian, Spanish, and Turkish.

Student Life: Are you Charlotte Simmons?

Duke University is located in Durham, North Carolina. Lately, the "Durham Renaissance" has spawned new bars and restaurants close to Duke's East Campus. Still, most students remain on campus, venturing into the surrounding bar and restaurant areas only if they are upperclassmen and have cars. Racial and economic tensions still run high between black residents and students at NC Central University and Duke.

Duke requires all students to live on campus for their first three years at the school. After freshman year, housing is chosen by lottery. Smoking is not allowed in any residence halls. Most dormitories are coed but divide the sexes by halls; there are no coed bathrooms. Single-sex floors are available for both male and female students. The university guarantees housing for all four years, but it is expensive. As a result, half of seniors move off campus. Substance-free and theme housing are available.

The school tries to be strict about substance abuse. Fraternities and sororities at Duke must hire a university-approved bartender for all their parties. Alcohol is forbidden on the freshman campus, and the policy is usually well enforced. Many students smoke marijuana, the only illegal drug in wide use at the school.

Duke has a plethora of student groups of all types, and students are welcome to create another one if the university doesn't already offer it. The university has a strong ROTC program, with Army, Navy, and Air Force options. Other popular student organizations are the daily newspaper, *The Chronicle*; community service activities through the Circle K; the InterVarsity Christian Fellowship; musical groups; and various cultural organizations. Since the 1980s Duke has had the continuous presence of a conservative newspaper, group, or magazine on campus, although the name, genre, and focus have changed several times. The university currently plays host to the Duke Conservative Union.

Religious organizations include the Lutheran Campus Ministry, Wesley Fellowship, Campus Crusade, Manna Christian Fellowship, Westminster Presbyterian Fellowship, Hillel, Cambridge Christian Fellowship, Muslim Student Association, Navigators, Unitarian Universalist Community, and the aforementioned InterVarsity. The campus also includes Jewish, Catholic, and Episcopalian centers.

Greek life is a big deal at Duke—over 42 percent of women and 29 percent of men belong to one of the 38 sororities and fraternities at Duke. Only fraternities have designated housing (they live in sections or floors of the dorms). The dedicated residential sections are

SUGGESTED CORE

1. Classical Studies 181S/284, Greek Civilization/Roman History
2. Philosophy 203, History of Ancient Philosophy
3. Religion 145/102, The Old Testament/Hebrew Bible, The New Testament
4. Religion 355, History of the Christian Church
5. Political Science 175D, Introduction to Political Philosophy
6. English 334/336/337, Shakespeare: Comedies/Romances, Shakespeare before 1600, Shakespeare after 1600
7. History 111A/111C, North America to 1760/The New Nation 1800–1860
8. Philosophy 201, History of Modern Philosophy

comprised mostly of sophomores, but some juniors and seniors choose to live in fraternity housing as well. The comingling of Greek and non-Greek students tends to have a leveling effect on cliques. Although some exclusive fraternities exist, most pre-rush-season parties are open and spill out of the residential halls.

According to some students, the student body has become segregated as a result of the administration's support for "diversity," and students of different races rarely mix after freshman year. Those students who choose to live in on-campus apartments, for instance, are usually black, while fraternities are mostly composed of upper-middle-class whites.

Although Duke has a reputation for leftism, the student body as a whole is largely apolitical. Studying, playing sports, getting drunk, and "hooking up" rank above political activism for most Dukies. Still, it's rare that a week at Duke passes without a task force report on racism, a panel on gender issues, a rally against sweatshops or the treatment of pickle-factory workers, or the like. As one conservative student says: "There are so many leftist causes on campus that, after a while, you stop noticing any of them."

In reality, "the only thing that brings everyone together is sports," says a student. In men's basketball (and increasingly women's), Duke is always a strong contender for the national championship. Men's basketball players are treated, it's said, as "gods" on campus. Students also participate in intercollegiate club sports, competing against other area colleges and universities on 38 teams.

Durham is prone to crime, though the university insists it is taking steps to reduce crime on campus even as stats worsen. Crime statistics in 2011 included one nonforcible and seven forcible sex offenses, two robberies, six aggravated assaults, 54 burglaries, nine car thefts, and two counts of arson on campus

Duke is a pricey adventure. Tuition for 2012–13 ran $44,101; room and board were around $11,770. However, admissions are need blind, and all admitted students are guaranteed sufficient aid. Some 48 percent of Duke students received need-based aid, and the average award was around $36,877. The average Duke student graduated with $21,713 in student-loan debt.

STRONG SUITS	WEAK POINTS
• Abundant resources and elite faculty.	• Administrators crazed by political correctness—see the lacrosse "rape" case.
• Excellent requirements for English, political science majors, each in a strong department.	• The School of Public Policy is a "liberal cocoon"; sociology has traded high standards for high enrollments.
• Distinctive offerings such as the Gerst and Focus programs that educate students in core knowledge.	• The required writing course is often taught by politicized graduate students and hence "a complete waste of time."
• Mostly fair teachers, regardless of ideology.	• Too many students are caught up in a sport and party culture.
• Strong ROTC program and numerous active conservative groups.	

Emory University

Atlanta, Georgia • www.emory.edu

For God and Mammon

Money won't buy everything, but you can't blame Emory for trying. Drawing on its substantial endowment ($5.4 billion as of 2011), Emory has made its students extremely comfortable. Faculty are plentiful and highly qualified, research opportunities and internships are available in nearly every discipline, and students can choose one of 70 majors. Money can buy a lot. Since Emory's main campus moved to Atlanta in 1919, the school has seen a steady shift in priorities. The liberal arts now play second fiddle to career-driven disciplines, and classroom discussions between students and professors have become less important than research. Late-night philosophical debates are rare; conversations on how to make money in investment banking are not.

Academic Life: New South

Emory imposes no core curriculum and has relatively anemic distribution mandates. Emory's "requirements are quite minimal and the 'fields' are very broadly defined," one professor says. "I'm sure it's quite easy to avoid courses that should be fundamental to a true liberal arts education. The laxness may be a blessing in disguise, however, insofar as students

VITAL STATISTICS

Religious affiliation: *none*
Total enrollment: *14,236*
Total undergraduates: *7,656*
SAT CR/Verbal midrange:
620–730
SAT Math midrange:
660–760
ACT midrange: *29–32*
Applicants: *17,493*
Applicants accepted: *27%*
Accepted applicants who
enrolled: *30%*
Tuition (general/out of
state): *$42,980*
Tuition (in state): *N/A*
Room and board: *$12,000*
Freshman retention rate:
95%
Graduation rate (4 yrs.): *83%*
Graduation rate (6 yrs.): *90%*
Courses with fewer than 20
students: *66%*
Student-faculty ratio: *7:1*
Courses taught by graduate
students: *not provided*
Students living on campus:
70%
Students in fraternities: *27%*
Students in sororities: *23%*
Students receiving need-
based financial aid: *49%*
Avg. student-loan debt of a
recent graduating class:
$28,076
Most popular majors: *busi-
ness/marketing, biology,
social sciences*
Guaranteed housing for 4
years? *no*

may avoid being forced by the college to take unserious or trendy classes."

Students should seek out the Program in Democracy and Citizenship, developed by Professor Mark Bauerlein and currently directed by Professor Harvey Klehr. The innovative program provides courses for freshmen, extracurricular events, and seminars intended to introduce students to the founding texts, arguments, and principles behind American democracy, capitalism, and culture. Professor Bauerlein created the program to "remedy the vacuousness of undergraduate knowledge of American foundations," gathering funding from the university and outside sources to sponsor traditional courses in the liberal arts.

Happily, Emory has pumped a good deal of its money into teaching. Classes are small, and almost all are taught by full-time faculty members—except most of the required freshman English courses, which are run by graduate students, meaning that where students arguably need the guidance of professors the most, Emory doesn't provide it. However, "professors are extremely open to helping students and getting to know them outside of class," says one student. Honors theses, independent study, and research projects allow students to interact with faculty members in more formal academic relationships. Professors are required to hold weekly office hours, and students often take advantage of them.

"Emory students are generally characterized by professional ambition more than by intellectual curiosity, and there is much obsession with grades (as opposed to the work required to get them)," says a professor. A colleague agrees: "Only a handful in a given year love the discussion of ideas for their own sake."

Over half of Emory students go on to graduate or professional school, and their undergraduate careers are often focused on landing at such a destination. One professor says, "Academics are taken seriously by a great many students, and the liberal arts, while under pressure, remain very strong."

Advising begins freshman year with faculty and peer advisers. Once a student declares a major, which he must by the end of sophomore year, he is assigned to a professor within that department. Advisers are usually helpful if students need them, but it is the student's responsibility to seek one out. "Students must use their good judgment, or the guidance of a good teacher, rather than depend on Emory for guidance," says one professor.

Among Emory's strongest departments are political science, psychology, English, history, anthropology, and biology. "Every professor in the philosophy department is great," a student says. However, one alum cautions: "I would advise undergrads to choose courses wisely. Much of what is taught will be biased toward a view that philosophy and truth have little to do with one another."

The English major calls for one course in British literature before 1660 and one after 1660, one course in American literature, and one course having an interdisciplinary or theoretical emphasis, with offerings such as "Postcolonial Literature" and "Literature and Religion."

The history department takes a traditional approach. Majors pursuing its General Studies track must take courses in American history before and after 1860; European history before and after 1750; and at least one non-Western world history class. Those outside this track may specialize and might miss most U.S. history.

Political science is less structured, with a broad list of classes that fulfill major requirements (from "Political Philosophy of Aristotle" and "The American Founding" to "Women and the Law" and "American Radicalism"). All poli-sci majors must take a class on the American political system; political methodology; one course each from the four fields of American politics, international politics, comparative government and politics, and political theory; and four electives.

Emory's undergraduate business college offers a distinctive bachelor's in business administration, which starts in junior year—allowing students to develop a solid liberal

CAMPUS POLITICS: YELLOW LIGHT

While the Emory administration and faculty lean further left than the student body, most faculty seem content and report the freedom to teach as they see fit. With a generous smattering of diehard progressive and traditional professors and a massive variety of course offerings, Emory is truly a place where any type of education may be attained.

The Foundation for Individual Rights in Education (FIRE) has warned students that Emory's speech codes forbid all negative stereotyping and "acts of intolerance," including "all 'use of epithets or names in a derogatory manner,'" a rule the U.S. Supreme Court has deemed unconstitutional. Emory has left the interpretation of what constitutes harassment, "demeaning depictions," intolerance, and derogatory speech in the hands of the Office of Resident Life and Student Conduct—and, in some cases, in the hands of the accuser. Because of this, FIRE warns, legitimate works of satire or parody could violate the university's speech codes.

FIRE reported that a 2011 plan to create a campus "free-speech zone" was intended to exclude "hateful" speech. FIRE also noted that such speech included everything from racist venom to religious objections to forms of sexual behavior or political legislation. Especially troubling was the position of the dean of students, Bridget Riordan, who said, "Hate messages are always a concern. That's why we've stuck with reservable space [in the past] so we know what student organization was [putting up material] and we could hold people accountable. If you have unreservable space and someone does it, you don't know how to hold that person accountable."

arts footing. While the business school has a strong reputation, economic studies at Emory are said to be less prestigious. The university retains a rigorous premed program.

Emory has almost as many graduate and professional school students as it does undergraduates. The powerful professional schools (and the campus presence of the Centers for Disease Control) can't be ignored, says one professor, "with the massive medical school tail sometimes wagging the dog."

Among the best teachers at Emory are Patrick Allitt and James Melton in history; Juan del Aguila (emeritus), Merle Black, Harvey Klehr, Randall Strahan, and Carrie R. Wickham in political science; Mark Bauerlein and Ron Schuchard in English; Marshall P. Duke in psychology; Donald Livingston and Donald Verene in philosophy; Timothy Dowd, Cathryn Johnson, and Frank Lechner in sociology; Arri Eisen in biology; and Paul Rubin in economics.

Forty percent of Emory students take their junior year or at least one semester abroad. Destinations literally span the globe, including Australia, Ecuador, Japan, Namibia, the Netherlands, Russia, and Scotland. Languages offered on campus include Arabic, Chinese, Dutch, French, German, Greek and Latin, Hebrew, Hindi, Italian, Japanese, Korean, Portuguese, Russian, Spanish, Tibetan, and Yiddish.

Student Life: The real thing

The visitor cannot help but be impressed by the expansive beauty of the largely traditional-looking campus. "It looks like a country club," says one student. "We have apartments, tennis courts, cafés. My parents think I'm getting spoiled." The Cox Computer Center offers rows and rows of equipment; some workstations have two large monitors for every computer. "There's almost no reason for a student to bring a computer to campus," says one student. A recent addition to student conveniences is Wi-Fi coverage over nearly the entire campus, including dorm rooms.

> "Emory students are generally characterized by professional ambition more than by intellectual curiosity, and there is much obsession with grades," says a professor.

Freshmen and sophomores are required to live on campus, since life on campus is convenient, traffic in Atlanta is horrible, and off-campus apartments can get expensive. Except for freshmen, who live together in traditional dormitories, Emory students usually enjoy suite-style residences or on-campus apartments close to most academic buildings. Emory offers three types of dormitories: single sex by floor; "grouped coed" floors, with stairwells or lobbies separating the sexes; and mixed coed floors. All bathrooms are separated by sex.

Students have practically every dining option available but only one kind of soft drink. One of the first gifts to Emory came in 1914 from the president of the Coca-Cola Company, and a large percentage of the endowment is still invested in the company.

Emory has no football team, and any attention paid to sports is usually directed toward the soccer and basketball teams or to intramurals, which are very popular. One professor says, "While 'school spirit' is not what it is at football factories, Emory does have a serious intercollegiate sports program that is among the best in Division III in the country. Sports plays the role it should in a serious academic institution." About 60 percent of the student body participates in intercollegiate, club, recreation, or intramural sports.

Few students explore Atlanta, though it's just a commuter rail ride away. Students can purchase reduced-rate tickets on campus to art exhibits and cultural performances throughout the city. Then there's the Michael C. Carlos Museum, Emory's on-campus art facility, with a fine permanent collection and diverse visiting exhibits each year.

Thirty-five percent of students are members of Emory's 15 fraternities and 11 sororities, and Greek organizations provide most of the activities for weekend social life. "Greek life is strong here, but it's not as intense as at most other schools," says one student. Parties and drinking are prevalent on campus. "Because the majority of students are affluent, they are able to buy a lot of alcohol and throw big parties," one student says. "But most students' primary goal is academics and grades—when those are satisfied, anything else goes."

The school offers an impressive variety of activities, from the Breakdance Club to the Rathskellar improvisation group; student government offers six associations and councils; cultural clubs include the Asian Christian Fellowship, the Persian Club, Thai Connection, and Chinese Calligraphy; and media clubs include magazines, journals, and papers like *Alloy* (the literary magazine), *Black Star* ("Emory's Microphone to the Black Community"), and the humor periodical *The Spoke*. There's also WMRE radio.

Emory hosts four political organizations: College Republicans, CSAmerica, Students for a Free Tibet, and the Young Democrats. The College Republicans were founded by Newt Gingrich in the early 1960s and have recently hosted Mitt Romney, Bob Barr, David Horowitz, and Jonah Goldberg. The Collegiate Society of America "encourages non-partisan political exploration in a social setting" through debate, dialogue, guest speakers, and political movies.

Emory's Cannon Chapel is the site of an ecumenical worship service every Sunday morning and a Catholic Mass and reception on Sundays and most Wednesdays. Religious student organizations abound and include the Baptist Student Union (BSU), Christian Fellowship, Episcopal Campus Ministry, Reformed University Fellowship, Greek Orthodox Campus Ministry, Catholic Campus Ministry, Wesley Fellowship, and many others. The Latter-day Saints, Jewish, Muslim, Hindu, Buddhist, and Baha'i communities all hold

SUGGESTED CORE

1. Classics 150–00P, Masterworks of Classical Literature
2. Philosophy 200, Ancient Greek and Medieval Philosophy
3. Religion 205/348, Biblical Literature/The New Testament in Its Context
4. Religion 311, Early and Medieval Christianity
5. Political Science 302, Modern Political Thought
6. English 311, Shakespeare
7. History 231, The Foundations of American Society to 1877
8. History 376, European Intellectual History: 1789–1880

services on campus. Although Emory is in the Bible Belt, it does not have the feel of a religious school. One philosophy graduate student says, however, that "there have been quite a few students who have renewed their spiritual life as a result of their interactions with professors."

Crime is a drawback for most other Atlanta schools, but Emory is located in the relatively safe Druid Hills neighborhood. Still, in 2011 the campus reported 12 forcible (and one nonforcible) sex offenses, eight burglaries, one aggravated assault, one robbery, one arson, and 10 stolen cars on campus.

Emory's price is as upscale as the experience it provides; in 2012–13, tuition was $42,980, while room and board averaged $12,000. Admissions are need blind, and Emory promises to offer full aid to accepted students. Forty-nine percent of students received need-based aid averaging $33,323, and the average student-loan debt of a recent graduate was $28,076.

STRONG SUITS	WEAK POINTS
• Plentiful, highly qualified faculty, research opportunities, and internships in nearly every discipline, and 70 majors.	• Students tend to be pragmatically preprofessional rather than intellectually curious.
• Classes are small, and almost all are taught by full-time faculty members.	• Unlike the business programs, economics is said to be rather weak.
• The stellar Program in Democracy and Citizenship, which explores American political philosophy.	• Vague and lax curricular requirements, allowing students to overspecialize—and many do.
• Serious-minded, ambitious students.	
• A broad range of political opinion, freely expressed.	

Fordham University

Bronx, New York • www.fordham.edu

A Jesuit Medley

Founded in 1841, Fordham was the first Catholic college in its region. Since then it has gained a distinguished academic reputation and offers nearly 50 majors. More than most Jesuit colleges, it has stayed connected to its liberal arts mission and (with exceptions) to its Catholic identity—making it a worthy option for ambitious, hardworking students. Fordham's academic culture is one of mutual respect. Even though many at Fordham regard ethnic and sexual "diversity" as a value in itself, liberal tolerance also extends to philosophical differences and grants traditionalists a place at the table—most of the time.

Academic Life: Dig for the treasures

Fordham's curriculum displays both breadth and rigor. Students describe the core classes as thorough and demanding. One undergraduate says, "I think Fordham has a great liberal arts education. . . . It is one of our strengths." Another says that the core "was the best part" of college life at Fordham. However, one student warns that because some course offerings have thematic titles, "teachers can teach almost anything," neglecting essential primary texts in some instances.

VITAL STATISTICS

Religious affiliation: *Roman Catholic*
Total enrollment: *15,189*
Total undergraduates: *8,427*
SAT CR/Verbal midrange: *570–680*
SAT Math midrange: *580–670*
ACT midrange: *26–30*
Applicants: *27,377*
Applicants accepted: *42%*
Accepted applicants who enrolled: *19%*
Tuition (general/out of state): *$41,732*
Tuition (in state): *N/A*
Room and board: *$15,374*
Freshman retention rate: *90%*
Graduation rate (4 yrs.): *74%*
Graduation rate (6 yrs.): *78%*
Courses with fewer than 20 students: *47%*
Student-faculty ratio: *14:1*
Courses taught by graduate students: *not provided*
Students living on campus: *49%*
Students in fraternities: *N/A*
Students in sororities: *N/A*
Students receiving need-based financial aid: *64%*
Avg. student-loan debt of a recent graduating class: *$38,151*
Most popular majors: *business, communications, psychology*
Guaranteed housing for 4 years? *no*

Fordham's honors program is highly competitive and worth applying for. Participation fulfills the university's core requirements—and goes well beyond them. Students are required to take 18 specific courses: an "Ancient Literature" class that examines "the Greek, Roman, and biblical texts which have played a central role in the definition of the Western tradition," and similar classes in ancient philosophy, ancient history, classical art, as well as in honors mathematics. Then students take classes in medieval literature and art, philosophy, and history; after that they move on to similar courses in the early-modern and contemporary periods. Juniors take a religion and an ethics class, while seniors write an honors thesis research project in their major field. This program is the single best option at Fordham.

One professor observes that the history, English, theology, and philosophy programs require introductory courses "that center directly on Western intellectual and cultural life." Of all the departments, philosophy garners the most praise for its emphasis on the great traditions of Christian thought. A good number of Jesuits teach here, infusing courses with their classical formation from extensive studies for the priesthood. Philosophy professors most often praised include Michael Baur; Christopher Cullen, SJ; and Joseph Koterski, SJ. The department is home to the American Catholic Philosophy Association, the Society for Medieval Logic and Metaphysics, and the Fordham Philosophical Society. According to one philosophy graduate student, "My conservative political views put me in the minority. But for the most part, I've found that others are respectful and willing to have rational discussions."

Right-leaning students are less positive about the political science department. One major says that she keeps a low profile as a conservative. Another undergraduate says that the stated views of his political science professors actually caused him to switch his major to history. On the other hand, poli-sci can boast several highly recommended teachers; one of them is William Baumgarth (who also teaches Classics). Students must take "Introduction to Politics" as well as an intermediate or advanced class from three of the four subfields: American politics, political theory, international politics, or comparative politics. Additionally,

Fordham requires an upper-level seminar and five intermediate or advanced electives.

History majors must take "Understanding Historical Change" (an upper-level seminar), four upper-level electives, and one advanced course each from medieval, European, American, and African/Asian/Latin American/Middle East history. "Historical Change" classes cover ancient Greece and Rome, medieval history, and early modern Europe, among others. While a history student could graduate from Fordham without any significant encounter with American history, Fordham is particularly strong in ancient and European history and offers an impressive breadth of innovative and fascinating courses. One conservative student in the department states that although he has not found philosophical allies there, his views are respected. The department teaches history as an academic subject, not as a pretext for activism. Highly recommended professors in history include Paul Cimbala, Richard F. Gyug, and Michael E. Latham.

Fordham's English department offers both a solid curriculum and reasonable electives. Majors must take three courses from selections that cover English literature up to 1800, including ample offerings in Chaucer, Shakespeare, Milton, and other greats. Among more contemporary courses, one finds electives like "American Catholic Women Writers."

The Fordham theology department is a mixed bag. One student notes that the required theology courses are often taught as world religion classes. Among other core requirements, all students must take two theology classes, the first in "faith and critical reason" and the second a course in "sacred texts and traditions" such as the Jewish scriptures, the New Testament, the Qur'an, and *The Divine Comedy*.

A much better choice for students interested in Catholic thought and culture is the school's stellar medieval studies program, which consistently draws many of the most talented students on campus. It offers a major, a minor, and graduate degrees up through the doctorate.

CAMPUS POLITICS: YELLOW LIGHT

While the student body seems evenly divided, and faculty span the broad range from dissenting ex-Catholics to orthodox representatives of the best in the Jesuit tradition, the Fordham administration has recently turned sharply in the direction of limiting free expression. In an appalling abuse of the college's speech code, the school apparently pressured the College Republicans into rescinding a 2012 invitation to columnist Ann Coulter to speak on campus. The college president went so far as to publicly denounce the group for inviting her in the first place: "To say that I am disappointed with the judgment and maturity of the College Republicans, however, would be a tremendous understatement. . . . [Coulter's] message is aimed squarely at the darker side of our nature."

The highly active and well-organized College Republicans—who far outnumber their Democrat counterparts—took the rebuke and arranged for another talk by the less provocative conservative George Will.

Shortly after the Coulter imbroglio, Fordham itself invited Princeton professor Peter Singer, who defends abortion, infanticide, and interspecies sex, to speak at a panel entitled "Christians and Other Animals."

Fordham's Catholic identity is still moderately strong, students feel. As one undergraduate says, "The school is a very Catholic place if you want it to be." One student, who entered the philosophy department in order to strengthen his faith and "go deeper into the thought of St. Thomas Aquinas," reports that his aspirations were "well supported" at Fordham. Another philosophy student says that "there are tremendous Catholic intellectuals at Fordham and an undergraduate can get an excellent Catholic education if he or she takes the right professors." He says that the priests he has met at Fordham are scholars "making something of philosophical ideas rather than cataloguing them."

The university as a whole, however, does not always live up to this ideal. One student says: "I don't think that the university makes enough of an effort to give a defensible account of the Faith. I rarely find a Fordham undergrad who can give me an intelligent explanation for why the church holds its moral positions." One Jesuit faculty member, proud of the job Fordham does in liberal arts education, concedes that it could go further in giving such an "account of the Faith." One graduate student says that the "proactive undergraduate can get a good grounding in the Catholic tradition" at Fordham.

One professor observes that the history, English, theology, and philosophy programs require introductory courses "that center directly on Western intellectual and cultural life."

Fordham offers extensive opportunities for study and travel abroad. Fordham maintains Global Outreach programs in the English-speaking world, and in Africa, Asia, Europe, and Latin America. Fordham also maintains an MBA program in Beijing with Peking University and has a new affiliation with Heythrop College in London. The Fordham University London Center provides semester-long study-abroad programs in theater and business. Fordham offers an impressive list of international semester-aboard programs in 150 countries around the world.

Foreign language options on campus include Arabic, French, German, Greek and Latin, Italian, Russian, and Spanish.

Student Life: Roses in the Bronx

Fordham University has an idyllic gothic campus in the Bronx, known as Rose Hill; another in the Westchester suburbs; and a third at Lincoln Center in Manhattan. A shuttle bus regularly runs from one campus to another, and students are free to choose classes from any of the three campuses.

Most dorms are coed, with single-sex floors or wings (and hence single-sex bathrooms). The curfew for visits from members of the opposite sex is a surprisingly late 3:30 a.m. Upperclassmen may live in university-owned apartments off campus, such as those in the Little Italy neighborhood nearby. The lovely Queens Court is the best dorm for serious students at Fordham. Those who choose it must sign a no-drinking and no-smoking pledge and apply via letter to the resident priest—the philosopher Rev. Joseph Koterski, SJ. It features nightly readings and performances by students.

Fordham does have a party culture. Students "are serious about having a good time but are also here for academics," says a student, while another counters that "the student body is overly focused on partying."

The Campus Ministry office advertises pastoral events, retreats, Mass schedules, and a weekly Bible study group. The campus chapel, which seats 500, is always full for the Sunday evening Mass. "I think our religious community is vibrant and growing every day," a student says. Another observes that "both the numerous Masses and the more numerous service opportunities provided by the campus ministry are very well attended."

There is a full-time Protestant chaplain on the staff of the Campus Ministry, as well as priests and lay members. Connections to Catholic, Protestant, Orthodox, Jewish, and Islamic congregations as well as 15 other diverse congregations can all be made through the office. Students in search of more traditional Catholic worship should investigate the Latin Mass at Church of Our Lady of Mount Carmel in the Bronx.

> ## SUGGESTED CORE
>
> 1. Classical Civilization 2000, Texts and Contexts: Myth in Greco-Roman Literature (*closest match*)
> 2. Philosophy 3501, Ancient Philosophy
> 3. Theology 3100/3200, Introduction to the Old Testament/Introduction to the New Testament
> 4. Theology 3330, Medieval Theology Texts and Philosophy 3552, Medieval Philosophy
> 5. Political Science 3412, Modern Political Thought
> 6. English 3206, Shakespeare
> 7. History 3775, The Early Republic
> 8. History 4575, History and Theory, or Philosophy 5002, 19th-Century Philosophy

Student athletes will find a strong program featuring a wide range of varsity sports: baseball, men's and women's basketball, football, golf, women's rowing, men's and women's soccer, women's softball, squash, men's and women's swimming and diving, men's and women's tennis, men's and women's cross-country, men's and women's indoor (and outdoor) track and field, volleyball, men's water polo, and cheerleading. Football is the school's most prominent sport; Fordham was Vince Lombardi's alma mater.

Other student activities range widely, from a campus chapter of Amnesty International to a College Republicans club, and an extensive array of ethnic and culturally based and pre-professional organizations. There are more than 100 student organizations, including Respect for Life, Pershing Rifles, Mock Trial, Hellenic Society, Ignatian Society, PRIDE Alliance (for gay students), and numerous academic, political, performance, and music organizations.

Students staff an award-winning NPR-affiliated radio station, WFUV, and the Fordham Nightly News program, and two undergraduate papers, *The Ram* and *The Observer* (one published at Rose Hill, the other at Lincoln Center). Other student publications include literary magazines *The Ampersand* (and its sister supplement, *The Vagabond*) and *The Kosmos*, while *the paper* is Rose Hill's alternative newspaper. Students also publish a law review and produce the Liberty Forum, a conservative media outlet consisting of a magazine, a blog, and a TV show.

Crime is not a major issue on Fordham's Rose Hill campus. In 2011 the school reported seven forcible sex offenses, 26 burglaries, two stolen cars, and one aggravated assault.

Fordham's price tag is on the high end for private colleges, with 2012–13 tuition running $41,732. Room and board averaged $15,374. According to the most recent data, 64 percent of undergraduates received institutional aid or scholarships averaging around $17,518. About three-quarters of students received grants or loans. The average cumulative indebtedness for degree recipients in 2010 was $38,151.

STRONG SUITS	WEAK POINTS
• Excellent core curriculum that focuses on the heart of Western civilization. • A slowly reviving attachment to its Jesuit, Catholic identity. • Good, traditional English and philosophy departments, with some excellent faculty in political science as well. • Many political voices on campus, from across the spectrum.	• This being a Jesuit school, the theology department is shaky, with a heavy emphasis on world religions rather than Catholicism. • An excessive party culture, with some heavy drinkers. • Some less-than-tolerant faculty—in political science, for example. • An administration that regulates student political speech—by conservatives (see "Campus Politics").

Georgetown University

Washington, D.C. • www.georgetown.edu

Ignatius Wept

Founded in an ill-starred year (1789), Georgetown University is one of the most prestigious American universities, and certainly the best-known school founded by Catholics. In its clamber to the top, however, Georgetown has shed most Catholic attributes. That faith now lives on as a kind of ghost that is rumored to haunt the premises. Whether that spirit may someday take on flesh again—or, more likely, be exorcised by some helpful Jesuit—is up to the leaders of the university.

Georgetown is still, formally, a Jesuit, Catholic institution. Its website states that in 2011 there were 59 members of the Jesuit community active at the school. But the university is religiously schizophrenic: it properly denied a pro-choice student group official recognition—but is so proud of the pro-abortion congressman Rev. Robert Drinan (a former faculty member) that Georgetown endowed a "human rights" chair in his name. While the medical school's hospital does not perform abortions, it is reported to have done research with embryonic stem cells. When American bishops condemned Notre Dame for conferring an honorary degree on President Obama in 2009, Georgetown responded by hosting the president on campus—covering up Catholic images at his request. Georgetown here showed once again its unseemly eagerness to render unto Caesar the things that are God's.

Academic Life: Philosophy *sí, sí*; theology *no, no*

Georgetown University has four graduate and professional schools (including law and medicine) and four undergraduate schools. The College of Arts and Sciences, the largest undergraduate division, offers more than 30 major programs—ranging from philosophy and Classics to an interdisciplinary major in women and gender studies—and 40 minor programs. To satisfy the college's general-education requirements, students must take at least two courses each in the humanities and writing, history, philosophy and theology, math and science, and the social sciences, and must also demonstrate "mastery of a foreign language through the intermediate level," according to the undergraduate bulletin.

The college has no core curriculum or Great Books program, and although serious courses are offered in most of Georgetown College's distribution areas, there are notable deficiencies in some of the freshman courses. A professor notes, for example, that in the key area of American government, "few faculty have the comprehensive knowledge of the system to do a good job." Similarly, "history has no one to teach a comprehensive course in Western Civ." On the other hand, says one teacher, "With guidance a student can get a good traditional liberal arts education, but guidance is essential." Serious freshmen should investigate the yearlong Liberal Arts Seminar, which incoming freshmen must apply to and which is limited to only 30 students.

Both history and government are among the most outstanding departments (and popular majors) at the university, according to both faculty and students. "We get a lot of the best people in these fields because they want to be in D.C.," says a faculty member. "Obviously, you have to choose carefully, but there are some superb instructors."

Government majors take 10 courses overall in the department, including four introductory courses, such as "International Relations," "U.S. Political Systems," "Elements of Political Theory," and "Comparative Political Systems." The department is notable for the quality of its faculty, with George W. Carey, Anthony Clark Arend, and Michael Bailey among the stars. Historically it has been known for its surprising number of conservative scholars, but that may be changing: the brilliant James Schall, SJ, recently retired, and Patrick J. Deneen left the school for a position at Notre Dame.

History majors are given a wide array of classes from which to fulfill the 11-class requirement. Three classes must cover any part of Africa, the Middle East, Latin America, or Asia, and three classes must cover Russia, Europe, or North America. In history, Roger Chickering (emeritus), Jo Ann Hoeppner Moran Cruz, and David J. Collins, SJ, are among the better teachers.

The most outstanding resource that Georgetown students should explore is the Tocqueville Forum on the Roots of American Democracy, whose purpose is to highlight "the two main roots of American democracy, Western political philosophy and the biblical and Christian religious tradition." Its founding director, Deneen, has left Georgetown, however.

Conversely, students should be wary of the school's Saudi-funded courses on Islam and the Middle East, which tend to paint Christians, Americans, and Israelis as perennial villains.

Philosophy is another highly respected department, with praise liberally offered for its graduate studies in bioethics. One well-regarded philosophy teacher is Mark Murphy. There are rigorous requirements for philosophy majors, such as "Ancient and Medieval Philosophy" and "History of Modern Philosophy," plus at least one four-credit "Text Seminar" and one course in logic.

In the English department, majors take a combination of courses with at least one Gateway Course, which features intensive writing. Beyond the gen-ed requirements and the Gateway courses, students need to take only seven additional upper-level English classes.

CAMPUS POLITICS: YELLOW LIGHT

Except for the indifferentism and heterodoxy that predominates in the theology department and the servile multiculturalism that dominates Islamic studies, plus the programs in sociology and women's studies, classrooms at Georgetown are mostly free of overt politicization. "In general, this is not a problem, to my knowledge," notes one longtime professor who also says, "On the whole, I don't detect any disparagement of Western civilization or our system of government or society in general." Political debate on campus "is free but not vigorous—there is a standard liberal slant," notes a professor, who continues: "My feeling is that this comes more from the students themselves than is imposed from above."

As for the school's Catholic identity, Georgetown's grip on it seems ever more tenuous. A group of prominent alumni, led by *Exorcist* author William Peter Blatty, are actually suing the school under canon law to force it to stop claiming any Catholic status. Blatty writes: "For 21 years now, Georgetown University has refused to comply with [papal instruction] *Ex Corde Ecclesiae* ("From the Heart of the Church"), and, therefore, with canon law. And it seems as if every month GU gives another scandal to the faithful! The most recent is Georgetown's obtuse invitation to Secretary Sebelius [a prominent supporter of legal abortion] to be a commencement speaker.

"Each of these scandals is proof of Georgetown's noncompliance with *Ex Corde Ecclesiae* and canon law. They are each inconsistent with a Catholic identity, and we all know it."

Students may skip Shakespeare for "Transnational Modernism" or enroll in interdisciplinary programs such as "Women and Gender Studies" or the "Lannan Center for Poetics and

Social Practice." English professor Paul Betz (emeritus), an expert on Wordsworth, gets plaudits from students; undergrads call him "exceptional," "inspiring," and "modest, a fine guy and a good teacher."

Scandalously, one of the weakest departments at Georgetown, as reported by students and faculty alike, is theology, which "is not exactly doctrinal—or logical," says one student. The student adds, "It's not just that they're not clearly Catholic. You really haven't a clue if they're even Christian." This department recently began offering a PhD in religious pluralism. Nor can any student escape exposure to this department, given the general-education requirement that students take two courses in theology—one of which must be either "Introduction to Biblical Literature" or "The Problem of God." These courses vary greatly "depending on which prof you get," reports a student. One theology teacher who is noted by students and professors alike as a standout: Rev. Stephen M. Fields.

> As for theology, one student says of his teachers that "it's not just that they're not clearly Catholic. You really haven't a clue if they're even Christian."

Georgetown places a high premium on research, often at the expense of teaching. Instructional quality varies widely. But despite its immense size and the presence of quite a few huge lecture classes, the school is well staffed. Including adjuncts, the school has approximately 2,173 faculty members, and the student-to-faculty ratio is a strong 12 to 1. Hence, even most intro classes are generally taught by regular faculty. Much of the grading, sources tell us, is done by TAs, and current students will oftentimes give tips on which TAs to avoid.

Georgetown attracts a fair share of blatantly careerist students. (President Bill Clinton is an alumnus.) "An impressive number of the kids come here for our name, and are thinking about law school from the day they arrive," says one professor. Another professor notes that some students are "superior, but most could be a lot more curious."

Many students participate in study-abroad programs. Georgetown offers opportunities to study in Argentina, Australia, Austria, Brazil, Chile, China, Dominican Republic, Ecuador, Egypt, England, France, Germany, Hungary, Ireland, Italy, Japan, Mexico, Poland, Russia, Scotland, Senegal, Spain, Switzerland, and Taiwan.

Foreign language courses are plentiful and rigorous at Georgetown. Majors are offered in Arabic, Chinese, French, German, Greek and Latin, Italian, Japanese, Portuguese, Russian, and Spanish. Minors are offered in most of those languages and in modern Greek and Hebrew. Courses in Korean and Turkish are also offered. Perhaps more important, an unusual number of the school's best-regarded faculty teach these classes. The Spanish department in particular receives positive responses from students.

Student Life: Top of the world

Georgetown University sits on a hilltop in Washington, D.C. Approximately 68 percent of undergraduates live in campus residential halls or in nearby university-owned apartments and townhouses. All freshmen and sophomores are required to live on campus. Housing for underclassmen tends not to be a problem. Residence halls are all coed, with some female-only floors. (The undergraduate student body is 55 percent female.)

Georgetown's main campus is about two miles from the White House and four miles from the Capitol. For nightlife, students frequent Georgetown itself, the fashionable Dupont Circle neighborhood, and above all the artsy Adams Morgan district. Most bars are said to be either a long walk or a short cab trip from campus—which, given D.C.'s still-high crime rate, is a real drawback.

Masses are held daily at Dahlgren Chapel, although more conservative students travel to Old St. Mary's church in Chinatown or the Cathedral of St. Matthew the Apostle. St. William's Chapel in Copley Hall is the site of Protestant services. Protestants compose about a fifth of Georgetown's student body; Catholics account for approximately half. The university also has Jewish and Muslim chaplains and student organizations.

Georgetown University does not recognize or allow on campus any fraternities or sororities other than service organizations. Because of the absence of frats, the most popular on-campus nightlife events are dorm parties. As the *Georgetown Voice* reports: "Upperclassmen throw everything from 'Guido Bros and Jersey Hos' ragers to post-basketball-game bashes. There's also a spirit of inclusiveness you don't get at Greek schools."

There are more than 200 official student organizations, including health and fitness clubs, ethnocultural groups (including an Armenian Students Association and Iranian Cultural Society), performing arts groups, and religious and political organizations. Student publications include the major, twice-weekly campus paper, *The Hoya*; the monthly *Georgetown Independent*; and a liberal publication, the *Georgetown Voice*. The university's sports teams are the Hoyas and participate in the NCAA's Division I. Georgetown competes in the Big East Conference in most NCAA sports. Intercollegiate men's and women's sports include basketball, track and field, lacrosse, cross-country, golf, sailing, soccer, tennis, and swimming and diving. There are also women's volleyball and field hockey teams and men's crew, football, and baseball. The men's basketball team remains extremely popular.

Serious crime is not unknown in the Georgetown neighborhood, but for the most part it is well policed and the campus is safe. The city's dangerous slums are physically remote from Georgetown's tony surroundings. In 2010 university police reported eight forcible sex offenses, one aggravated assault, one robbery, one vehicle theft, and 38 burglaries. The Department of Public Safety has become very conscientious about reporting crimes, and students may sign up to receive e-mail alerts of crimes in particular neighborhoods.

Annual tuition at Georgetown as of 2012–13 was $42,870, with room and board an additional $13,632. Georgetown University practices need-blind admissions and guarantees

> ### SUGGESTED CORE
>
> The Liberal Arts Seminars 001 through 006 in the Interdisciplinary Studies Program is an 18-credit series of courses that suffice for a somewhat abbreviated core.

to meet demonstrated student need. Approximately 41 percent of students received some form of scholarship or need-based financial aid. (To its credit, the school offers Air Force, Army, and Navy ROTC programs.) The average student-loan debt of a recent graduate was $25,315.

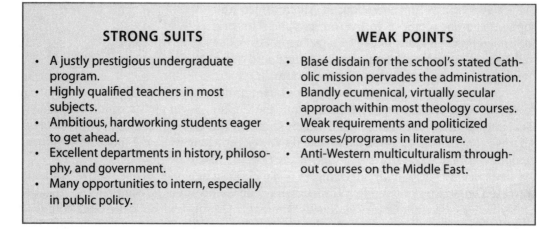

STRONG SUITS	WEAK POINTS
• A justly prestigious undergraduate program.	• Blasé disdain for the school's stated Catholic mission pervades the administration.
• Highly qualified teachers in most subjects.	• Blandly ecumenical, virtually secular approach within most theology courses.
• Ambitious, hardworking students eager to get ahead.	• Weak requirements and politicized courses/programs in literature.
• Excellent departments in history, philosophy, and government.	• Anti-Western multiculturalism throughout courses on the Middle East.
• Many opportunities to intern, especially in public policy.	

Gordon College

Wenham, Massachusetts • www.gordon.edu

Missionaries to New England

Founded in Boston in 1889 as a missionary training institute, Gordon College moved in 1955 to its current campus. Describing itself as New England's only traditional, nondenominational, Christian liberal arts college, Gordon aspires to teach the latest in science, philosophy, literature, and so forth, while working with the student's faith in Christ, not against it. The school maintains a rigorous scholastic atmosphere, small classes, and a moderately strong core curriculum, guaranteeing students a broad-based, faith-infused education. For intellectually serious Evangelical Christian students who wish to study in the snowy northeast, Gordon is the first place to apply.

Academic Life: Freedom within a framework

A faculty member reports that the "faculty, as well as the students, must articulate a basic Christian orthodoxy and a commitment to a vibrant intellectual life as Christians. . . . The 'Christian mind' is overtly encouraged in both students and faculty." He continues: "Our best students match up with anyone, something we've discovered from our years of experience sending people to Oxford. Our students tend to be serious, earnest, and diligent

VITAL STATISTICS

Religious affiliation: *nondenominational (Christian)*
Total enrollment: *1,909*
Total undergraduates: *1,580*
SAT CR/Verbal midrange: *510–646*
SAT Math midrange: *506–642*
ACT midrange: *23–29*
Applicants: *1,701*
Applicants accepted: *not provided*
Accepted applicants who enrolled: *not provided*
Tuition (general/out of state): *$32,230*
Tuition (in state): *N/A*
Room and board: *$9,430*
Freshman retention rate: *85%*
Graduation rate (4 yrs.): *60%*
Graduation rate (6 yrs.): *72%*
Courses with fewer than 20 students: *69%*
Student-faculty ratio: *13:1*
Courses taught by graduate students: *not provided*
Students living on campus: *89%*
Students in fraternities: *N/A*
Students in sororities: *N/A*
Students receiving need-based financial aid: *75%*
Avg. student-loan debt of a recent graduating class: *$34,919*
Most popular majors: *communications, English, psychology*
Guaranteed housing for 4 years? *yes*

without a lot of flash and dash. It may not attract headlines, but it's very satisfying in a classroom setting."

On top of a respectable core curriculum, the school offers the interdisciplinary honors program called the Jerusalem and Athens Forum—principally a Great Books course in the history of Christian thought and literature. The forum is something any prospective Gordon student should seriously consider. The readings consist of authors such as Aristotle, St. Benedict, Adam Smith, and Aldous Huxley. (They even read ISI's *A Student's Guide to Liberal Learning*, we're proud to note.) The program strives to help students reflect on the relationship between faith and intellect, deepen their own sense of vocation, and awaken their capacities for intellectual and moral leadership. All costs are covered by the program, which also gives students a stipend to help them subscribe to a scholarly periodical and pursue vocational exploration and career development. As one professor says, "The Jerusalem-Athens Forum is excellent and is our best on-campus program."

Gordon offers 38 majors across its five academic divisions: education, fine arts, humanities, natural sciences, and social sciences. The most popular majors are English, psychology, economics/business, Bible/youth ministry, and education. The school confers three separate undergraduate degrees: bachelor of science, bachelor of arts, and bachelor of music. While completing their academic programs, students have access to academic advisers who can guide them and approve their course selections.

Teaching at Gordon is said to be strong. One student says of his teachers: "Every professor I have had is willing to spend time talking with students after classes as well as during regular office hours. Many professors have lunch with students in the cafeteria, getting to know them personally as well as academically."

Some departments such as English, however, rely heavily on part-time faculty. This must limit the accessibility of some professors to their students. The English and the communications departments are said to be a bit weak due to aging teachers and the school's inability to hire full-time faculty. The chemistry department lacks equipment due to inadequate funding.

Quite a number of teachers come highly recommended. Gordon sources speak highly of Thomas Albert (Tal) Howard (director of the Center for Faith and Inquiry) and Steve Alter in history; Timothy Sherratt and Paul Brink in political science and studies; Bert Hodges in psychology; Stephen Smith and Bruce Webb in economics and business; Bruce Herman in art; Dorothy Boorse in biology; Thomas Brooks and David Rox in music; and Jennifer Hevelone-Harper, chair of the history department.

English majors take four courses in British and American literature (with at least one course in each), two in comparative/global literature, and three in rhetoric, theory, and/or composition. It would be possible for a student to graduate without studying Shakespeare, but that student would still have studied a variety of foundational authors. The English department offers a few politically charged courses like "Women's Literature," but most are good offerings of classic literature, from "Shakespeare" to "The Great American Novel."

History majors are required to take courses in ancient, medieval, and modern European history, United States history, and

CAMPUS POLITICS: GREEN LIGHT

All students at Gordon are required to adhere to the school's statement of faith, which asserts the essentials of Protestant orthodoxy. However, the statement is basic enough that Catholic or Eastern Orthodox students might feel comfortable with it as well. Gordon College states that it bases its beliefs and philosophy on the Bible but that it is not a "Bible college." One of its mottoes is "freedom within a framework." According to one faculty member, "Christian colleges come in all shapes and sizes. Please don't confuse us with places that are rather deliberately constructed to escape the challenges and responsibilities of contemporary life." The school says that its goal is not indoctrination but rather education based in doctrine. The school is described by one professor as "generally respectful of Western/Christian history but trying to globalize the curriculum a good bit."

also one course in the history of Asia, Africa, the Middle East, and Latin America. Within these requirements, there is freedom to choose specific courses, but most students would be exposed to essential topics of study, such as the American Founding and the Civil War.

Political studies majors must take a class that focuses on the U.S. Constitution, along with courses in American politics, comparative politics and international relations, and political theory. They are also encouraged to intern in public and private governmental settings.

Gordon's music program is outstanding. At this relatively small school one can earn a bachelor's degree in music, in performance, in music education, or a master's degree in music education. The school also hosts a nonprofit organization, Christians in the Visual Arts, dedicated to supporting and educating painters of faith.

By working with the Council of Christian Colleges and Universities, Gordon offers some impressive off-campus opportunities, including semester-long programs in the Holy Land, Uganda, and China. The Gordon in Oxford program is available to select juniors and seniors. French majors can study in Aix, while art students have access to the Gordon in Orvieto program, for an interdisciplinary course in the cultural history of the Renaissance and two classes in studio, history, or theory. According to one undergrad: "All students are encouraged to study abroad for a semester during their time at Gordon. While not required, a good amount of students do study abroad, in places like Israel, Italy, India, and others." Another program offers an integrated look at the Christian music industry, sending students to Nashville for a semester to use a recording studio, research song writing, develop a marketing plan, design a performance, and bring it all together with a capstone event—all in Music City USA.

Gordon offers majors in French, German, Spanish, and linguistics, and a minor in Mandarin Chinese. There are also classes offered in Italian, Latin, Biblical Greek, and Biblical Hebrew.

Student Life: Bird watching and the Bible

Gordon's location in Wenham is a fine compromise between urban and rural, situated on several hundred acres of woodlands. One student says, "The school is surrounded by woods and lakes, and the campus itself is by far the most beautifully groomed campus I have ever seen." There is enough countryside for students who like to hike, but Boston is less than an hour away, accessible by train from the nearby city of Manchester-by-the-Sea. For direct access right from Gordon, students can take the weekend shuttle bus to the Boston T's Orange line.

Of the 1,500 undergraduate students, most live in one of 10 dormitories. Students are required to live on campus unless they are married, live nearby, or are older than 23. Apartment-style buildings are reserved for upperclassmen, while the traditional dorms, usually triples, are for underclassmen. Not all dorms are segregated by sex, but male and female quarters are separated by a common area. During intervisitation, the school handbook warns, "doors must remain fully open and lights left on . . . and excessive or offensive displays of affection will not be acceptable." Resident assistants are expected to monitor interactions to avoid violations. Restrictions also apply to alcohol, dancing, and tobacco. In addition, the student handbook admonishes that pranks are to be respectful and courteous. There are no fraternities or sororities.

A teacher says that "the 'Christian mind' is overtly encouraged in both students and faculty."

The school places a healthy emphasis on sport. Its athletes, known as the "Fighting Scots," compete in basketball, baseball, track and field, cross-country, lacrosse, softball, field hockey, tennis, swimming, volleyball, and soccer. The athletic facilities also include the Bennett Athletics and Recreational Center, a 72,000-square-foot teaching and sporting venue with an outdoor rock gym and an indoor pool. The Brigham Athletic Complex is an artificial turf field for lacrosse and field hockey that is surrounded by an NCAA (Division III) caliber all-weather track. Intramural sports are encouraged. Sports camps for school-age boys and girls run all summer long on campus.

While reason dominates in the classroom, formation in faith is the ribbon that weaves throughout the texture of life at Gordon. All students are required to earn 30 Christian Life and Worship credits each semester, regardless of work schedule. (Married students and commuters have fewer requirements.) Credits, also called sessions, are earned by attending chapel services, the various convocations held each week, the annual college symposium, or the provost's film festival. The school proclaims that its goal is to "agree on the basics and show charity on the peripherals." Despite this irenicist attitude, students from a more liturgical church, such as Catholic or Orthodox, may find it difficult to fulfill both their own and the school's Sunday obligations. For those willing to travel, nearby Boston offers every kind of worship service imaginable.

Students at Gordon can participate in a variety of clubs, including some that focus on specific academic areas like biology, physics, German, and social work. Other clubs include Cornhole Team, Ultimate Frisbee, ModelScot Radio, Photography Club, and a theater club called By the 'Rood. The school hosts the College Republicans and Democrats, and Gordon's Human Rights Club focuses on the rights of the unborn. Interested students can take part in the student-run publications, which include an art and poetry journal, *Idiom*; *VOX*, a newsletter of student voices; and a student newspaper, *The Tartan*.

Gordon is a very safe school. In 2011 no crimes were reported on campus.

The school reports that the cost of discipleship in 2012–13 was $32,230, with room and board at $9,430. Several scholarship programs are available, but most of the students take some form of government loans. Some 75 percent of students received need-based financial aid, and the average student-loan debt of a recent graduating class was $34,919.

SUGGESTED CORE

1. English 262, Classical Literature
2. Philosophy 202, History of Philosophy I: Ancient through Medieval
3. Biblical Studies 101/103, Old Testament History, Literature, and Theology/ New Testament History, Literature, and Theology
4. Biblical Studies 308, Christian Theology
5. Political Studies 223, Theories of Politics (*closest match*)
6. English 372, Shakespeare
7. History 232, America 1492–1846
8. Philosophy 203/204, History of Philosophy II/III: Early Modern Philosophy/ Late Modern Philosophy

---

STRONG SUITS

- Good core curriculum, and excellent (though optional) Great Books program.
- Firm commitment to teaching and close student-faculty relationships.
- Solid requirements for key majors and mostly foundational course offerings.
- Outstanding music program and extensive study-abroad programs.
- A healthy balance of Christian commitment and intellectual ambition.

WEAK POINTS

- Some departments, such as English and communications, lean heavily on part-time faculty.
- Scientific equipment, for subjects such as chemistry, are aging or insufficient due to lack of funding.
- Significant chapel requirements can make it difficult for non-Protestants to attend their own services off campus.

Grinnell College

Grinnell, Iowa • www.grinnell.edu

Social Gospel, Lots of Capital

Founded in 1846, Grinnell began as self-consciously progressive, becoming the first college west of the Mississippi to grant degrees to both black students and women. Since then, the school has progressed very far to the left. Today it has a reputation as a place where granola crunchers and radicals of all varieties feel particularly comfortable. Grinnell imposes no curricular or distributional requirements beyond a first-year tutorial; no science, math, writing, or foreign language courses are required. Still, students with the motivation and preparation to structure their own studies could get an excellent liberal arts education at Grinnell.

Academic Life: Recommend it, and they will come

Whatever curricular course they choose, Grinnell students are expected to study hard. A professor says, "This is the rub and the shock for some students—they get into a course and find that the freedom ends there and they have to do what they are told." One science major notes, "There are a few less-serious classes, but not many. The most common such courses are in science for nonscience majors (such as physics for poets)." Another student says that "the course load here is extremely rigorous and requires excellent time-management skills; I personally have close to five hours of homework each night, which is about the average here."

The one required tutorial is designed to introduce students to professors and to college-level work. Most recently, students could pick among courses such as "Humanities I: The Ancient Greek World" or "M'm! M'm! Good! Food Choices and Their Consequences." The tutorial usually culminates with a research project. The professor with whom a student takes the tutorial also serves as his adviser until the student declares a major, when he gets a new faculty adviser from his major department. One teacher says the tutorial "usually ensures that students enroll in a balanced liberal arts curriculum for the first three semesters."

Some majors have serious requirements, while others allow inordinate flexibility. English majors, for instance, must take nine courses in all, with no single required class. To satisfy their early literature requirements, English majors choose one course in premodern literature (from two offered), one in British or postcolonial literature, and one in American literature. English students must also show proficiency in a foreign language. What students read and study in these courses varies by professor. However, one syllabus for "The Tradition of English Literature II," a course that covers English literature from the 17th through the 19th centuries, reveals that students study traditional fare: such as Wordsworth, Shelley, Austen, and Dickens.

Grinnell's political science majors take an introductory class, and others in American, comparative, and international politics. Some of the courses require a reading of the U.S. Constitution, but students could get by without being exposed to it.

In the Grinnell history major, students must take a minimum of 32 credits within the department. Eight of these credits must be upper division. No courses in U.S. history before 1900 are required. The department also recommends that students reach proficiency in a foreign language and in quantitative analysis. The syllabus for the basic course in early American history in fall 2009 included a number of secondary and politicized-sounding sources but not *The Federalist Papers* or the works of John Locke.

VITAL STATISTICS

Religious affiliation: *none*
Total enrollment: *1,693*
Total undergraduates: *1,693*
SAT CR/Verbal midrange: *600–720*
SAT Math midrange: *610–710*
ACT midrange: *28–32*
Applicants: *not provided*
Applicants accepted: *51%*
Accepted applicants who enrolled: *not provided*
Tuition (general/out of state): *$41,004*
Tuition (in state): *N/A*
Room and board: *$9,614*
Freshman retention rate: *94%*
Graduation rate (4 yrs.): *83%*
Graduation rate (6 yrs.): *not provided*
Courses with fewer than 20 students: *62%*
Student-faculty ratio: *9:1*
Courses taught by graduate students: *none*
Students living on campus: *88%*
Students in fraternities: *N/A*
Students in sororities: *N/A*
Students receiving need-based financial aid: *71%*
Avg. student-loan debt of a recent graduating class: *$15,720*
Most popular majors: *biology, literature/foreign languages, social sciences*
Guaranteed housing for 4 years? *yes*

CAMPUS POLITICS: RED LIGHT

A student says, "I do feel that there is often too much political correctness on campus, where students sometimes must think twice before expressing a thought that could in any way be perceived as insensitive to one of the many thousands of groups that could be considered a minority." The real minorities on campus are the conservatives, and the school's progressive atmosphere will not change anytime soon, as the administration is proud of its position at the forefront of progressive schools.

There is a small conservative community at Grinnell. The president of the College Republicans says, "We have nearly twenty people on our mailing list, which is kind of amazing given the very liberal leanings at this school." According to its website, the Grinnell College Republicans (whose mission is to "ensure the conservative voice is heard amidst the sea of liberal propaganda") recently became affiliated with the National College Republicans and "has been growing rapidly ever since." Another student says that, at Grinnell, "liberals feel very comfortable. Conservatives probably feel very out of place. Sometimes liberalism here feels a little like anticonservatism rather than its own set of beliefs."

In 2011 a campaign stop by Rep. Michele Bachmann was transformed by the arrival of a large group of Grinnell students, alerted by the school's College Democrats group. Rather than face the students—holding liberal signs—she turned what had been a speaking event into a private meeting with donors.

A professor says, "It is interesting that, with no requirements, math, science, and foreign language courses are filled to capacity." Still, one professor warns, "The college does not like to talk about the fair number [of students] who get by with a poorly rounded course of study and with the help of grade inflation." A student says, "Academic advising here is excellent, as advisers give very sound advice to students on what courses to take and also help in the career preparation of students."

At Grinnell, classes average about 17 students, and only 5 percent of classes have more than 30. The student-faculty ratio is an excellent 9 to 1. Because Grinnell is exclusively an undergraduate institution, there are no graduate teaching assistants. This lets Grinnell provide students with small classes and close interaction with faculty. In fact, according to one administrator, there is almost a master-apprentice relationship between professors and students, especially in the junior and senior years, when it is not uncommon for students to publish papers and attend conferences with their teachers.

"Professors are very accessible," a senior says. "All of them have regular office hours, and if a student is unable to make them, almost all professors are willing to set up some other appointment." Another student says, "If one needs to meet a professor, it's usually done the same day. The professors here know everyone in their classes by name, usually by the second day of class." For most faculty members, teaching is a clear priority over research or publishing. A professor says, "Good teaching is supposed to be, and rarely is not, the sine qua non of succeeding on the Grinnell faculty. But peer-approved scholarship appropriate to one's field is also a requirement for tenure."

"The professors here are the reason to come to Grinnell," a student says. Students name the following as some of the best on campus: Michael Cavanagh in English; Donna

Vinter, director of the highly recommended Grinnell-in-London program; Charles Duke in physics; Bruce Voyles in biology; Monessa Cummins and Sarah Purcell in history; Robert Grey, H. Wayne Moyer, Ira L. Strauber, and Barbara Trish in political science; David Campbell in environmental studies; and David Harrison and Philippe Moisan in French and Arabic.

The best departments—biology, history, political science, and English—are also among the most popular. The Classics department offers a solid and rigorous curriculum, attracting some of the best students in the college. The most ideologically fraught areas of study—no surprise—are Grinnell's 11 interdisciplinary concentrations, including gender and women's studies and sexual studies. One professor warns, "There are many courses, even outside these areas, that are politicized."

More religious or conservative students will sometimes feel uncomfortable in the Grinnell classroom. For example, some courses in the social sciences departments use Marxist-Leninist theory. (Why not try phrenology?) However, professors generally try to keep their politics outside the classroom. One conservative student says that while most students and faculty are "pretty far left," most of his professors "have been very good about teaching material from a wide range of viewpoints, many of which they disagreed with. The professors I've had also have always made it clear when they are talking about something they personally believe as opposed to established facts." Another student says, "Professors have told me personally they enjoy classes where conservatives are present, as it makes for a better discussion. I have never heard of any professors discriminating against students on the basis of their political beliefs."

> One conservative student says that while most students and faculty are "pretty far left," most of his professors "have been very good about teaching material from a wide range of viewpoints, many of which they disagreed with."

Free and open debate seems to be the rule. A student says, "I would say that, yes, this is a very liberal campus, and there are not a lot of conservative viewpoints in the faculty or in the student body. However, I would not say that a conservative (there are plenty of religious students here, and they are all very well accepted) would be uncomfortable in any classes I've taken unless they do not like to argue or don't have good ideological reasoning behind their views." On the other hand, many conservatives may find it more agreeable to keep their opinions to themselves.

Through the Mentored Advanced Project (MAP), the college provides extensive internships all over the world. Students studying French might spend a year in France living with local families, visiting museums, libraries, national monuments, and interning in Parisian schools. In fact, 55 to 60 percent of each year's graduating class participates in an off-campus study program in places as different as Washington, D.C., and Cairo, Egypt. Study of international issues receives great emphasis at Grinnell, with strong interdisciplinary

SUGGESTED CORE

1. Humanities 101-I, The Ancient Greek World (*closest match*)
2. Humanities 102-II, Roman and Early Christian Culture
3. Religious Studies 211/214, The Hebrew Bible/The Christian Scriptures
4. Religious Studies 213, Christian Traditions (*closest match*)
5. Philosophy 264, Political Theory II
6. English 121, Introduction to Shakespeare
7. History 211/212, Colonial and Revolutionary America, 1450–1788/Democracy in America, 1789–1848
8. Philosophy 234, 19th-Century Continental Philosophy

concentrations and a new Center for International Studies. The Grinnell Corps provides one-year service fellowships to new graduates in places including Greece, Macau, and Nepal. Grinnell offers majors in Arabic, Chinese, French, German, Japanese, Russian, and Spanish, and classes in Greek and Latin.

Student Life: Small town, U.S.A. . . . without the "gender binary"

Grinnell is an idyllic college town. The college hosts "Town and Gown" events several times each year to encourage students and employees to interact more with the Grinnell townsfolk. A student says, "Grinnell is in the middle of nowhere, and no one will try to hide that fact. That said, campus life here is fun because the school and student organizations have to put that much more work into making it fun. Plus, no one leaves on the weekends, so you always have the whole campus to get to know and enjoy."

Technically, all Grinnell students are required to live on campus. Each year, about 12 percent of the student body (mostly juniors and seniors) moves off campus. It's hard to see why: most of the college's dormitories house fewer than a hundred students, and students can request to live on either coed or single-sex floors (no dorms are single sex). Some residence halls have coed bathrooms, but only by unanimous consent of that floor. Grinnell now offers coed rooms in close to half of the dormitories as part of its push to provide environments "where the gender binary is not perpetuated." Nonsmoking dorms are available, and the college also offers three substance-free residence halls. The college provides five language houses for students looking to immerse themselves in the language and culture of a particular country, including China, France, Germany, Russia, and Spain. Most residential halls are locked at 10:00 p.m. and do not reopen until 6:00 a.m., but students can always enter by way of electronic access cards. To ease overcrowding and improve older facilities, the college recently opened four new residence halls. Grinnell has no Greek system.

The college reports more than 180 registered student clubs and organizations, from the Jugglers Union and the Ceramics group to the Quidditch club and Wild Turkeys Water Polo. The school hosts Grinnell College Campus Democrats and many other liberal organizations but few Republican or conservative political groups. There are several religious groups, including Catholic Student Association, Chalutzim, Muslim Student Association, Pagan Discussion Circle, and Unitarian Universalists.

There are also a number of other student movements dealing with racism, economic disparity, and cultural diversity. The Stonewall Resource Center (SRC) serves as a "confidential safe space to serve the campus's gay, lesbian, bisexual, and transgender, queer and questioning community and allies." In fact, Grinnell's whole campus is a "safe space" for these students, whose groups (along with other student organizations) receive considerable support from the college. The Princeton Review ranks Grinnell College as one of the top 20 most "queer-friendly" schools in the United States. On its webpage, SRC links to pertinent student groups at Grinnell: Stonewall Coalition (an umbrella group), Coming, Queer People of Color, BiFocal (for bisexual students), Lesbian Movie Night and Organized Procrastination (LMNOP), and the Queer Rainbow Super Team, which "plays games and has fun!" Another group, the Grinnell Monologues, provides the important service of "perform[ing] a collection of monologues about gender and genitalia."

Grinnell offers a panoply of athletic opportunities. The first intercollegiate football and baseball games west of the Mississippi were played in Grinnell, and the home teams won. Today the Grinnell Pioneers and its NCAA Division III athletic program field 18 varsity teams in the Midwest Athletic Conference, but there are no athletic scholarships at Grinnell. The college also has a well-developed intramural program and club sports for intercollegiate competition, the most popular of which are football, rugby, and Ultimate Frisbee.

Grinnell is a pretty safe place—like most of Iowa. In 2011 the school reported six forcible sex offenses, 22 burglaries, and one stolen car on campus.

Tuition for 2012–13 was $41,004 with an additional $9,614 for room and board. Grants and scholarships form the bulk of Grinnell's financial aid, which is awarded primarily on the basis of need and is not considered in admissions decisions. Some 71 percent of students get some need-based aid, and admissions are need blind. The average student-debt load of a recent graduate is about $15,720.

STRONG SUITS	WEAK POINTS
• Academic advising is excellent. • Small classes with dedicated, accessible teachers—not graduate students. • A serious workload—five hours of homework per night, as one student reports. • Even ideologically committed professors are said to be fair in teaching and grading.	• No curricular or distributional requirements (math, science, writing, foreign language) beyond a first-year tutorial. • Some coed bathrooms and dorm rooms, since the school opposes "the gender binary." • The school is "in the middle of nowhere," a student admits. • Almost unanimous commitment to political correctness and radical social mores. (There are Marxist/Leninist professors.)

Grove City College

Grove City, Pennsylvania • www.gcc.edu

Faith and Freedom

Founded in 1876 with ties to the Presbyterian Church, Grove City College today remains a bastion of traditional, Christian liberal arts education. Grove City is one of the most conservative colleges in the country—refusing to accept any federal funding, including federal student financial aid. As one recent student says, Grove City College remains "a rare breed of Christian college that seems to be nearing extinction in America. It upholds a Christian worldview and champions Western civilization."

Academic Life: Heritage

Grove City's humanities core curriculum is required of all students in both its School of Arts and Letters and School of Science and Engineering. These six courses focus on "America's religious, political, and economic heritage of individual freedom and responsibility and their part in the development of Western civilization."

The humanities core receives mixed reviews from students. One calls it "one of the highlights. All the classes are critically respectful of our Western heritage and do a very good job." Others, however, report that "students can get through the humanities core by taking only the easy, not-very-thoughtful professors" and that "the classes only skim the surface and neglect the intense, face-to-face, soul-searching encounters of the Great Books." Furthermore, "the same intellectual standards historically associated with the liberals arts are not equally applied to engineering/science/education students." The sources used in the humanities core—in most cases textbooks and selected excerpts, not full texts of classic works—may also leave something to be desired.

Another factor is the motivation of students themselves. One recent alum reports, "I am definitely a better person for having taken the harder professors and have learned a great deal of respect not only for American institutions but Western civilization as a whole." He cites Professors Jason R. Edwards, Joshua F. Drake, and Gillis Harp as excelling in the core program. Some professors suggest that too few students display genuine intellectual curiosity—and that too many teachers present a single perspective without examining alternatives.

Academic advising is intense and hands-on at Grove City, involving professors along with career counselors and staff of the student life office. The school says that its advising program is "thoroughly Christian and evangelical in character."

Teaching, rather than research and publishing, is the emphasis of all Grove City's departments. Professors are readily available for consultation outside of class. Faculty are generally devoted to the students and loyal to Grove City's mission. One student says, "Each professor has a unique viewpoint on life, but one thing they all share is a faith in Jesus Christ." Grove City College is overall quite politically conservative, a student says, "but there are definitely students who hold opposing points of view. The college brings in many guests and speakers who help foster an atmosphere of debate about different ideas."

Popular majors include engineering, business, and accounting—all of which, according to one professor, are highly regarded regionally and attract many potential employers for on-campus interviews. Mechanical, electrical, and computer engineering and biology/molecular biology are very popular as well. Among the best science professors are Michael Falcetta in chemistry, Dorian P. Yeager in computer science, and Dale L. McIntyre in math.

VITAL STATISTICS

Religious affiliation: *Protestant (Presbyterian)*
Total enrollment: *2,461*
Total undergraduates: *2,461*
SAT CR/Verbal midrange: *559–692*
SAT Math midrange: *560–677*
ACT midrange: *25–30*
Applicants: *1,592*
Applicants accepted: *76%*
Accepted applicants who enrolled: *51%*
Tuition (general/out of state): *$14,212*
Tuition (in state): *N/A*
Room and board: *$7,744*
Freshman retention rate: *91%*
Graduation rate (4 yrs.): *77%*
Graduation rate (6 yrs.): *83%*
Courses with fewer than 20 students: *47%*
Student-faculty ratio: *15:1*
Courses taught by graduate students: *none*
Students living on campus: *95%*
Students in fraternities: *13%*
Students in sororities: *11%*
Students receiving need-based financial aid: *42%*
Avg. student-loan debt of a recent graduating class: *$26,597*
Most popular majors: *biology, business/marketing, mechanical engineering*
Guaranteed housing for 4 years? *yes*

The political climate on campus is summed up by one insider thus: "Since Grove City is arguably the most conservative school in the nation, it is the liberals that may feel unwelcome. . . . The professors, however, do a very good job of keeping their politics out of the classroom. As with anything, there are exceptions, especially in political science and sociology. Professors are quite religious and do come from a variety of religious backgrounds, including Catholic, Anglican, Lutheran, Presbyterian, and other Christian denominations, so any religious student should feel right at home. . . . In terms of debate, the college encourages it as much as can be on a relatively homogenous campus. There is always a platform for dissenting views, and I have been in several classes where professors will encourage debate and accept any differing views."

Several students also pointed to the school's lack of racial diversity as a drawback: "The most disappointing thing about Grove City might be the lack of diversity in both race and thought among the student body," says one student.

The English department is praised by students and professors alike. One major says: "My experiences with my English classes have challenged me to wrestle with fundamental questions of humanity, to develop a critical mind, and to uphold truth and virtue in my own life." Appropriately, a course in Shakespeare is required of majors (as it is not at many elite colleges). Notables in this department include Eric A. Potter, Janice B. Brown, and H. C. Messer.

Political science has a strong conservative orientation and attracts students by its reputation. One major says that the department has "a distinguished reputation and excellent track record for placing its graduates in jobs, especially at 'movement' conservative institutions in Washington." American constitutional theory is required of majors. Marvin J. Folkertsma, Paul G. Kengor, and Michael L. Coulter are known to be exceptional instructors.

Students give high marks to the history department, especially professors Mark W. Graham, Andrew J. Mitchell, and chairman Gary S. Smith. Fittingly, majors must study American history before 1900. Options for concentrations include Latin American and modern Asian studies.

The economics department at Grove City also stands apart. For more than 35 years the department was led by Professor Hans Sennholz, a student of Ludwig von Mises—the leading exponent of the rigorously free-market "Austrian" school of economics. A strong Austrian influence is felt at Grove City to this day through professors Jeffrey M. Herbener (who extends hospitality to students through an "economics picnic" every summer) and Shawn R. Ritenour (described as "well loved and very challenging").

In religion, a recent grad says, "the majority of the faculty is fantastic. The bent of the department is decidedly Reformed and evangelical. . . . The systematic theology courses that I took were presented from a broad Protestant perspective; though the professor himself is solidly Presbyterian, he gave evenhanded explanations of various positions. Iain M. Duguid is an excellent teacher. T. David Gordon (a favorite with students for his liveliness) is a recognized scholar in Reformed circles and publishes some interesting books."

Possibly because of its religious orientation, the school's music department also excels, especially in organ (taught by Richard A. Konzen), and thanks to inspiring instruction by Paul A. Munson, Joshua F. Drake, and Beverly H. Carter, the required humanities music selection "is probably the only course where not one section is a dud."

A recent grad says, "I am definitely a better person for having taken the harder professors and have learned a great deal of respect not only for American institutions but Western civilization as a whole."

The most popular majors at Grove City are within the field of education, and indeed Grove City is renowned as a teacher-training school. "Education is easily the largest department," says one professor in another field, "and based on placement after graduation is the best program in Pennsylvania and essentially the nation. If you graduate from Grove City's education department, you are going to get hired." Even so, more than one student suggests that within Grove City the education department has "a reputation for being somewhat lackluster academically." A former education major characterizes the department as "weak," even though "education majors are unnecessarily overworked [with] tedious and banal projects and worksheets rather than intellectually challenging readings." An exception to this trend in the education department is Professor Jason Edwards, whose classes, according to one student, are "a shock to many freshmen. He challenges students to think deeply, and he's also a very thorough and hard paper grader." As for general science requirements, "These are good introductory courses that offer students an easy way to access the sciences even for those who are uninterested," a teacher says. Math, on the other hand, poses a greater hurdle, since "some of the toughest professors teach the lower-level math courses."

A good number of students study abroad. Particularly popular are the faculty-led trips, usually conducted during the first few weeks of January. In 2012–13 the school sponsored "Archeology, Anthropology and Artistry of France," taught in several cities across France. "A Literary Odyssey" and "C. S. Lewis" took students through Greece, Italy, and England.

Grove City is not strong in foreign languages. Serious language courses are in short supply, with only French and Spanish majors, and nonmajor courses offered in French, German, and Chinese. A recent graduate complains: "The classes are a joke and do not really prepare the students for a career in the language field."

Student Life: A Christian community

As Grove City's website points out, "Unlike many colleges and universities today, Grove City embraces a strong traditional and residential campus experience," with 95 percent of students living on campus. There are 10 residence halls—all of them single sex. "Dorm life is great," says a recent alum. "I had a fantastic experience and have made friendships on my freshman hall that will continue forever. I was able to stick with my freshman hall for all

SUGGESTED CORE

1. English 302, Classical Literature in Translation
2. Philosophy 334, Plato and Aristotle
3. Religion 211/212, Old Testament/New Testament Literature and History
4. Religion 341, Christendom and Reform or Philosophy 336, Augustine and Aquinas
5. Political Science 256, Modern Political Thought
6. English 351/352, Shakespeare I/II
7. History 251, United States Survey I
8. Humanities 201, Civilization and the Speculative Mind

four years of my college experience. The limitations are not bad at all and are easy to live with."

Alcohol is not allowed on campus, and there are limited hours for visitation between male and female students. Students speak well of the RAs. "The RAs are very friendly; they enforce the rules, but will make exceptions when necessary. I had five fantastic RAs that made my college experience great." Says one upperclassman: "My two RAs were both true men of God who helped me and the guys on my hall to grow spiritually and socially."

Outside the dorms, "the most impressive part of the campus is easily the architecture," says a student. "All the buildings follow a neo-Gothic pattern and match very well. They contribute greatly to the atmosphere."

Religion suffuses student life at Grove City, both formally and informally. Students are required to attend at least 16 chapel events each semester—scanning their student ID cards at the chapel door to prove it. Fraternities (13 percent of men are members) and sororities (11 percent of women belong) are Christian based and more like small-group fellowships than traditional Greek organizations. Many students contribute to international and community service causes.

Although the college retains its traditionally Protestant, Presbyterian flavor, a professor notes that "Catholics do not feel uncomfortable on the campus, and the Newman Club is very active." The faculty includes teachers from many faith traditions.

Grove City offers a range of sports teams, fraternities and sororities, and more than 130 other extracurricular organizations. The school hosts College Republicans, College Democrats, and College Libertarians. The Republicans are by far the most popular political group, and it bears mentioning that Grove City College does not have a single pro-abortion, homosexual, or feminist organization on campus.

There are 19 NCAA Division III sports at Grove City, which is a member of both the Presidents' Athletic Conference and the Eastern College Athletic Conference. Over half of Grove City's students participate in one or more of the college's 30 Intramural Sports and Club Sports programs—a statistic that prompted *Men's Fitness* magazine to name the college the seventh fittest college in the nation in 2006. The college also owns an AM and an FM radio station, which provide students with opportunities for broadcasting experience.

Serious crime is virtually unknown, both in the town and on campus; a recent graduate recalls, "I usually didn't lock my car and would often leave my laptop, books, and notes at a desk in the library for hours when I wasn't there." The school does not report crime stats.

Although it accepts no federal money, Grove City has been able to keep tuition and other costs far below the national average. Tuition in 2012–13 was $14,212 and room and board $7,744. Grove City offers both need-based and merit-based scholarships and works with PNC Bank to provide students with private in lieu of federal loans. Some 42 percent of students received need-based financial aid, and the average student-loan debt of a recent graduate was $26,597.

STRONG SUITS

- An ambitious core curriculum aimed at producing well-rounded students.
- Devoted, faith-driven teachers who focus on students, not research.
- Strong requirements and teaching in English, history, and political science.
- A very strong, principle-driven economics department committed to understanding the free market.
- Very strong music program.
- Single-sex housing and restricted intervisitation—which add to a wholesome campus atmosphere.

WEAK POINTS

- Core classes sometimes "just skim the surface," using excerpts from Great Books, not whole works.
- Some professors present just one side—in this case, the conservative side—of disputed questions.
- Weak offerings and courses in foreign languages.
- Limited facilities and resources for studying the hard sciences.

Hampden-Sydney College

Hampden-Sydney, Virginia • www.hsc.edu

The Alpha Male

Founded during the American Revolution, Hampden-Sydney College provides an excellent liberal arts education to its approximately 1,050 students. And all those students are men. Hampden-Sydney is one of only four remaining all-male institutions of higher education in America. Moreover, its curriculum has never been neutered. *Insight* magazine named Hampden-Sydney as one of the 15 finest schools that "still teach the fullness of the Western academic traditions."

Academic Life: Solid at the core

Hampden-Sydney provides a challenging curriculum that almost constitutes a traditional core. The heart of the Hampden-Sydney program is its Western culture requirement: three specific courses focusing on the West's classical beginnings and its development through the present. The courses include broad sketches of politics, art, religion, philosophy, and the intellectual history of Western society, and combine history with the reading of Great Books. "A professor may discuss the possibility that eternal truths or human nature exist, as well as taking the typical historicist approach so prevalent in the humanities and social sciences in most colleges," says one faculty member. Another professor who teaches one of these courses says, "In my Western Culture 101 class, students read the Bible, Homer's *Iliad*, Sophocles's *Oedipus Rex* and *Antigone*, Aristophanes's *The Clouds*, Plato's *Apology*, Aristotle's *Politics*, Plutarch's lives of Alcibiades and Caesar, and Augustine's *Confessions*." Another teacher says, "The core courses are serious—though, as anywhere, there are perceived differences in difficulty, depending on the instructor. To some degree, the differences are mitigated by the assessment procedure, which establishes common standards and goals." After taking the three courses in Western civilization, students then need two American studies courses, chosen from a short list of courses in the history, English, government and foreign affairs, and religion departments.

Hampden-Sydney's curriculum and faculty members encourage intellectual curiosity. "This semester we had nearly fifty students take a course on Plato and Aristotle," a professor says. "We had to open a new section of the course to accommodate the demand. So many students seem to be searching for something more than just careers."

Just as rigorous as these general requirements are the demands of major departments. The English major does require a "literature of difference" course—basically a cultural diversity requirement that has students choosing from options like "Introduction to African-American Literature," "Women and Literature," and "Multi-Ethnic American Literature." The good news is that the department still requires survey courses in both English and American literature, as well as a course in Shakespeare. The English department's offerings in ethnic literature, postcolonialism, and cinema are kept to a minimum. One English faculty member says, "Our department used to be more traditional than it is now. The trend is definitely in the direction of requiring less literature written before the twentieth century."

In the history department, majors need three courses in American history, three in European history, and two outside these areas, plus a colloquium. The U.S. requirement can be satisfied by classes like "American Intellectual History," not the bizarre history courses you find at many other liberal arts schools. However, students will also have to take a course from a different major to satisfy the requirement, and

VITAL STATISTICS

Religious affiliation: *Protestant (Presbyterian)*
Total enrollment: *1,057*
Total undergraduates: *1,057*
SAT CR/Verbal midrange: *480–610*
SAT Math midrange: *510–620*
ACT midrange: *21–27*
Applicants: *2,528*
Applicants accepted: *55%*
Accepted applicants who enrolled: *23%*
Tuition (general/out of state): *$35,570*
Tuition (in state): *N/A*
Room and board: *$11,166*
Freshman retention rate: *79%*
Graduation rate (4 yrs.): *63%*
Graduation rate (6 yrs.): *not provided*
Courses with fewer than 20 students: *74%*
Student-faculty ratio: *10:1*
Courses taught by graduate students: *none*
Students living on campus: *95%*
Students in fraternities: *34%*
Students in sororities: *N/A*
Students receiving need-based financial aid: *57%*
Avg. student-loan debt of a recent graduating class: *$27,740*
Most popular majors: *economics, history, political science/government*
Guaranteed housing for 4 years? *yes*

CAMPUS POLITICS: GREEN LIGHT

For the most part, politics—faculty or student—has a different flavor at Hampden-Sydney than at other liberal arts schools. Students do not protest or stage sit-ins, and only rarely do they organize for political causes. However, Hampden-Sydney men do tend to have strong political opinions. One senior says, "We don't protest here, but almost everyone has strong views."

Outside the classroom, the college political atmosphere is sometimes rather sedate. The one relatively liberal group is the College Democrats, which generally sticks to campaigning for candidates and squaring off with Republicans for debates. The Republican Society is dedicated to the study of American politics and "the philosophy of the Republican Party." Students have also organized the Society for the Preservation of Southern Heritage, dedicated to "the Constitution of the United States, a strong family unit, religious faith, courage, honor, and integrity." Except for a few explicitly political speakers, most guest lecturers are academics.

this class might be "Multi-Ethnic American Literature."

Professors and students say that English, modern languages, and history are more politicized than most other departments. Still, says one professor, "there is less nuttiness here than at most places. In our English courses, for example, texts are read and taught, not the latest literary theories." The English department offers four or five courses that sound more politicized, such as "Postcolonial Literature," but they are not the norm. Judging from the course catalog, the history department offers nothing but serious classes. "At Hampden-Sydney, there are no trendy departments," says another professor. "Everyone takes books and ideas very seriously. There are individual faculty members who present the 'latest' ideas, but generally in a sober and thought-provoking way." One student says, "The faculty is liberal, but I know several conservative professors. I have never had a professor try to push his/her beliefs on me or politicize the class." Other students disagree and report that some of their more outspoken professors do vent their own views in the classroom.

One of the strongest departments on campus is government and foreign affairs. At Hampden-Sydney, this department studies contemporary political problems in light of the writings of great Western and American political thinkers. Majors take a course on American government, another on modern governments around the world, and one in "Classical Political Philosophy." Students can then choose between several courses: "Medieval Political Philosophy," "Early Modern Political Philosophy," and "Modern Political Philosophy." Finally, all majors will complete "Pre-Thesis Seminar" and "Senior Seminar and Thesis" courses.

Classics, while small, has in the past been considered one of the college's best teaching departments. Many Hampden-Sydney students major in economics, and the department is reportedly strong. The science departments are also good; faculty single out chemistry as the strongest.

The faculty has a reputation for sensible research in traditional areas, with only a couple of professors recently undertaking scholarship in areas like popular culture, film, and women's studies. A senior faculty member says, "It would be hard to find a professor trying to indoctrinate in the classroom here."

Hampden-Sydney assigns each incoming student a faculty adviser and a peer adviser. In addition, to help new students adjust to college, Hampden-Sydney requires that its students take an advising seminar, which is taught by the faculty adviser and aided by the peer adviser. Once a student selects his major, he is assigned a faculty adviser within his department. Students must visit their advisers each semester before registering for courses.

Since Hampden-Sydney does not have graduate students, faculty teach all courses—none of which has more than 40 students. "Our professors are in their offices most of the time when they aren't teaching, so it's not a problem finding them," a government major says. "Most of my professors give out their home telephone numbers on the first day of class, and I have called

> "At Hampden-Sydney, there are no trendy departments," says a professor. "Everyone takes books and ideas very seriously. There are individual faculty members who present the 'latest' ideas, but generally in a sober and thought-provoking way."

them at home many times. I think that is one of the best aspects of Hampden-Sydney." Some of the best teachers at the college include David E. Marion and James F. Pontuso in government and foreign affairs; Anthony M. Carilli, Saranna R. Thornton, and Kenneth N. Townsend in economics; James A. Arieti in Classics; William A. Shear and Alexander J. Werth in biology; Victor N. Cabas Jr. and Susan P. Robbins in rhetoric; and Ralph S. Hattox and James Y. Simms Jr. in history.

Hampden-Sydney students value the small classes and personal attention they receive at the school. As one student recalls, professors "won't let you hide in the back" of a small class and fall asleep. Most classes are structured as a combination of lecture and seminar.

The study-abroad program sends students to all parts of the world, from Argentina to China. One of the grandest is the school's program at Oxford, in which a small group of students study Tudor-Stuart history and literature at St. Anne's College. The college offers majors in French, German, Greek and Latin, and Spanish.

Student Life: Live white males

Of course, the most distinctive thing about Hampden-Sydney is that there aren't any women in class. "Being all-male is nice during the week because you do not have to deal with dating or being distracted by a good-looking young woman," a student says. "You also have the chance to form a unique brotherhood with your fellow students." Another student who went to a coed high school says, "I get a better education in the all-male classroom. Class discussions are vastly improved because more students are willing to talk and share their opinions." School parties do attract women to campus each weekend, and many fraternities host dances and mixers with nearby sororities. A number of women's colleges that maintain a close social relationship with HSC are within driving distance. As a popular bumper

SUGGESTED CORE

1. Classical Studies 203, Greek Literature in Translation
2. Government and Foreign Affairs 310, Classical Political Philosophy
3. Religion 102, Introduction to Biblical Studies
4. Religion 221, History of Christian Thought I
5. Government and Foreign Affairs 413, Early Modern Political Philosophy
6. English 333/334, Shakespeare
7. History 111, United States I
8. Western Culture 103: 1800–Present

sticker reads, "I pay tuition to Sweet Briar, but my daughter goes to Hampden-Sydney." Longwood University, a coed school known primarily for teacher education, is only a few miles away and helps enliven the social scene. On weekends, students sometimes visit the University of Virginia, Virginia Tech, and North Carolina State, all within a comfortable drive. One student says, "There is normally something to do, but some weekends are slow, and Farmville is not a town with a nightlife."

Hampden-Sydney's rural, isolated setting helps bind the campus community together. Ninety-five percent of students live on campus, which is the locus of most social activity. The school provides a free guest house for visiting women, conveniently located on Fraternity Circle. Because of the school's honor code (see below), visitors are allowed to come and go as their hosts wish. The few students who choose to live off campus can opt for a college-owned cottage or (with permission) test their luck on the rental market. One of Hampden-Sydney's dormitories offers a substance-free floor.

The college is home to America's second-oldest collegiate debating club. Since 1789 the Union-Philanthropic Literary Society has served as an extracurricular intellectual forum for students. Its discussions also provide one of the few outlets for political controversy on campus. "Some faculty members grumbled when the boys debated whether feminism was killing free speech, but no one tried to stop the debate," says one professor. "We are pretty old-fashioned down here. We say mostly what we like, and we are pretty civil about the whole thing."

Student social life is heavily influenced by the Greek system, which includes eight social fraternities, one professional fraternity for chemistry and related majors, and 14 honors fraternities. More than a third of Hampden-Sydney men join these groups. But one nonmember says, "There is not a sharp division between Greeks and non-Greeks, as on some campuses." Aside from college-sponsored speeches and lectures, most social, musical, and cultural events revolve around the Greek houses; these events are usually open to the entire campus. Each spring, students participate in Greek Week, a campus-wide festival.

The Hampden-Sydney Tigers compete in 10 varsity sports in the NCAA Division III Old Dominion Athletic Conference—and Title IX obviously isn't a problem. Students have organized a few more intercollegiate club teams, including lacrosse and soccer. The school has a strong intramurals program in which over 70 percent of the student body participates.

Hampden-Sydney's biggest social event is the annual football game against the school's archrival, Randolph-Macon College. Tailgating before football games is a perennially popular activity. With a $2.5 million donation, Hampden-Sydney completed a new football stadium in time for the 2007 football season.

The college offers a number of Christian groups for interested students, and one member says the school is a "good place to grow in your faith because of growing campus ministry groups like the Baptist Student Union, InterVarsity, Chi Alpha Fellowship, Wesleyan Fellowship, and the Fellowship of Christian Athletes." However, he says, "the strong party culture provides a testing ground for a person's beliefs." The ministries and religion professors, as well as local churches, provide spiritual support. The on-campus College Presbyterian Church serves as the school chapel, where religious groups of various denominations hold services. Most students are Protestant, but Jewish and Catholic student groups exist.

Hampden-Sydney's academic and social excellence is founded on one of its oldest traditions: the honor code. Because one of the main goals of life, the school believes, is to live a "moral existence," the honor code assumes that all students will "behave as gentlemen" and will not lie, cheat, or steal. The system is administered by a court of student leaders, and service on the court is considered an honor. One former student, Stephen Colbert of Comedy Central's *Colbert Report,* insists that he still takes the honor code so seriously that decades after Hampden-Sydney, he can recite its text from memory. Faculty members affirm that the honor system works. Exams are not proctored, and, one professor says, "in my personal experience of forty years, never need to be."

Students and administrators say the honor code and the college's rural location are largely responsible for keeping the campus as safe as it is. In 2011 the school saw one sexual assault, two burglaries, and one arson case.

Tuition for 2012–13 was $35,570, and room and board $11,166. Some 57 percent of the student body receives need-based financial aid, and the average debt of a graduating student is $27,740. Unfortunately, Hampden-Sydney does not have the financial means to cover 100 percent of students' financial needs: in 2010 just 80 percent was met. However, the college recently completed a successful $100 million–plus campaign; among other things, it will help strengthen financial aid.

STRONG SUITS	WEAK POINTS
• One of a tiny handful of all-male colleges left in the U.S.	• All-male environment not for everyone.
• A vital esprit de corps built on an honor code that students take to heart.	• Thriving party culture.
• A core curriculum focused on the Great Books of Western civilization.	• Rural, isolated setting with few off-campus options.
• Intellectually curious, rather than careerist, students.	• Some English classes are apparently politicized.
• Excellence in most humanities, especially government and foreign affairs.	
• All classes taught by highly qualified teachers, not grad students.	

Harvard University

Cambridge, Massachusetts • www.harvard.edu

First

Harvard University was founded in 1636, and it is the oldest university in the United States. In recent decades, Harvard's once impressive core curriculum was dismantled, and the school morphed into the quintessential modern research university with its attendant specialization, premature professionalism, and political correctness. Nevertheless, with a $32 billion endowment (the largest in the world), unmatched library facilities, a faculty that consists of the cream skimmed off the best universities in the world, and students who have survived a highly selective admissions process, Harvard will remain a powerhouse of intellectual life for the foreseeable future.

Academic Life: Genius observed

One Harvard professor says, wryly: "Of course we have a core curriculum. It contains over 350 courses!" Actually, Harvard's core is a modest set of distribution requirements, directing students to mostly excellent courses—many of which, however, are rather narrow and specialized. As a result, "Students can, if they want to and are persistent, get a very good traditional education; it's also possible to waste a lot of time."

Students must take one course each in aesthetic and interpretive understanding; culture and belief; empirical and mathematical reasoning; ethical reasoning; science of living systems; science of the physical universe; societies of the world; and the U.S. in the world. This won't require Harvard students to master particular bodies of knowledge (such as American history or the plays of Shakespeare) but will at least force students to take classes outside their private, idiosyncratic interests.

Still, the Harvard catalog "is an astonishing document," says one graduate. "I don't know if any university in the world offers such an amazing array of courses on everything under the sun, most of them taught by serious, often outstanding scholars."

According to one professor, "Most Harvard students are very good at getting into Harvard. That requires a lot of skill and dedication—but not much curiosity. I'd characterize them, intellectually, as highly competitive but not very imaginative." One student says, "Most students at Harvard, while quite accomplished, are uninteresting—lacking intellectual curiosity, conversational skills, or in the worst cases general decency. The thing that separates them from other students is a pathological desire to succeed and to work as hard as they need to in order to do so. There are obviously many exceptions to this broad characterization, but I think it generally holds true."

Upon entering Harvard, each student is assigned a freshman-year faculty adviser and later on is assigned a concentration adviser (a faculty member or graduate student). "Advising is as varied as the advisers," says one student. "Most undergrads find that graduate student advisers know more than the faculty advisers, but it's very dependent on the person." One student says, "Although professors are required to hold one-hour-long office hours each week, their accessibility depends on how busy they are. However, many faculty also choose to participate as freshmen advisers, and thesis advisers to seniors, as well as advise students informally."

Graduate "teaching fellows" interact with undergraduates more than many faculty do. As a history major says, "Professors here must publish to keep their jobs." Students don't seem to mind the emphasis on research. As one observed, "How else would most of the major disciplines be taught by the leading scholars

VITAL STATISTICS

Religious affiliation: *none*
Total enrollment: *20,524*
Total undergraduates: *6,657*
SAT CR/Verbal midrange: *690–780*
SAT Math midrange: *700–800*
ACT midrange: *31–36*
Applicants: *34,303*
Applicants accepted: *6%*
Accepted applicants who enrolled: *80%*
Tuition (general/out of state): *$40,866*
Tuition (in state): *N/A*
Room and board: *$13,630*
Freshman retention rate: *97%*
Graduation rate (4 yrs.): *87%*
Graduation rate (6 yrs.): *97%*
Courses with fewer than 20 students: *87%*
Student-faculty ratio: *7:1*
Courses taught by graduate students: *1%*
Students living on campus: *98%*
Students in fraternities: *N/A*
Students in sororities: *N/A*
Students receiving need-based financial aid: *60%*
Avg. student-loan debt of a recent graduating class: *$11,000*
Most popular majors: *economics, government, psychology*
Guaranteed housing for 4 years? *yes*

CAMPUS POLITICS: YELLOW LIGHT

Harvard undergraduates face a gamut of university-mandated gender-neutral language requirements, sexual harassment policies, humorless affirmative action and sex tutorials, and sensitivity-training sessions.

RAs organize meetings between incoming freshmen and "peer contraceptive counselors," who distribute condoms and dental dams (don't ask). A student group called True Love Revolution (TLR) was founded in opposition to what former student copresident Justin S. Murray ('07) called Harvard's "hookup culture." The nonsectarian group is dedicated to the promotion of premarital chastity by distributing flyers and hosting seminars.

Conservative students do report that they have benefited greatly from having to defend their beliefs in class—and none have reported classroom harassment or punitive grading. As one graduate says, Harvard "retains a largeness of outlook that eclipses the more parochial liberalism of some people." On the other hand, many students find it difficult to communicate with certain segments of the student body because they consider Harvard's affirmative action policies downright divisive. "It creates a definite tension," says one source. "If you're a designated 'minority,' you spend your years as an undergraduate trying to prove to everyone else that you were one of the kids who got in based on merit."

in their fields?" TAs usually lead the weekly discussion sections that supplement lecture courses. "In some intro classes, graduate students do most of the teaching," another student says. In the opinion of one professor, "It has gotten to be conventional to split the professor's job into 'teaching' and 'research,' but for most of my colleagues these are external manifestations of a single underlying social process: we are trying to move the world of knowledge along and to bring our colleagues and students with us as we go."

The leftward tilt of Harvard's faculty is partly balanced by the presence of several stellar thinkers in the center or on the right, who help "sober the academic discourse and attitudes on campus," in the words of a student. Of course, dozens more Harvard professors are stars in their fields and for that reason are worth seeking out—although some are better teachers than others. Harvard undergrads are eager to praise certain challenging courses and professors, including Lino Pertile in Romance languages and literature; Robert Levin in music; Daniel Donoghue, Louis Menand, Daniel Albright, and Robert Kiely in English; James McCarthy in earth and planetary sciences; Thomas Scanlon in philosophy; Jon D. Levenson of the Divinity School; Peter Hall, Michael Sandel, and Stephen Rosen in government; Robert Barro and Martin Feldstein in economics; and Ann Blair, James Hankins, and Mark Kishlansky in history.

Students should seek out courses taught by the eminent professor of government Harvey Mansfield. One student referred to him as "the only direct advocate of conservative principles at Harvard."

The Classics department draws mixed reviews. But a recent graduate says it is possible to avoid the politicized classes that apply "structuralism to Herodotus and Thucydides" in favor of the more rigorous composition courses. She notes that one professor teaches in the great Germanic tradition of philology, demanding of his students not just correct grammar but Ciceronian style. The department also offers courses in ecclesiastical Latin and medieval/Byzantine Greek. Another student adds, "I could not study Latin at a better place, including a seminary."

In the English department, the first two terms of a student's English studies are spent in three "Common Ground" courses: "Arrivals" (earliest centuries of English literature), "Poets," and "Diffusions" (American literature). After these courses, students may make it up as they go, choosing electives. English honor students must take at least one foreign language literature course taught and read in the original language.

History majors may skip over fundamental American and European history courses but must take classes in historical analysis, Western history, non-Western history, and pre-modern history, in addition to one reading seminar and one research seminar.

In like fashion, the government department offers "a very flexible concentration," yet thankfully requires sophomores to take a half course in each of four subfields: political theory, comparative government, American government, and international relations. One student says the program "offers a wide range of courses from a variety of political and methodological perspectives. For undergraduates, political theory and international relations are the highlights. Courses in these fields tend to bring up real issues of political conflict and are least likely to get bogged down in technical disputes." Junior government majors participate in a research seminar, and seniors take a tutorial in which they have the option of writing a thesis.

The multicultural studies departments (for example, African studies, women's studies), as well as the religion, social studies, and language departments, are said to be heavily infused with a postmodern ideology. According to one student, "In courses in social studies, sociology, Af-Am, or WGS (women, gender, and sexuality), where the premise is a progressive notion of 'social justice,' politics cannot but help intrude into discussion, lecture, and ultimately grading. Religious students would do well to avoid the religion department, which is essentially taught by the Divinity School faculty, known for their lack of rigor and religion." Luckily, such programs are easy to avoid for a student with his ear to the ground.

Grade inflation is rampant in the humanities and social sciences—as opposed to "disciplines like economics and physics [which] are places where the professoriate still believes in the value of concepts like 'truth' and so are more likely to apply strict standards," a student says. As a result, one professor tells us, "Science students regularly do better in non-science courses than nonscience students do in science courses." That same professor adds, "Surely a teacher wants to mark the few best students with a grade that distinguishes them from all the rest in the top quarter, but at Harvard that's not possible."

Harvard has a rigorous honors program for each of its majors. To enter the honors program, a student must have a high GPA and be willing to write an extensive senior thesis. For the English major, for instance, students must have a GPA of 3.40 or higher. In junior year they will write a 20-page essay on a literary topic (there is also a creative writing option), and by the end of senior year they will have completed either a creative thesis or a researched thesis of 12,000–15,000 words.

Harvard's music, history, physics, mathematics, earth and planetary sciences, and other science departments are among the world's finest. Virtually all students agree that Harvard's research facilities and other resources are second to none and that the university's biological science programs are as rigorous as any in the world. According to one student, "just like almost everything else, the sciences are taught by the leading scholars in their fields." Furthermore, "Undergraduates have numerous opportunities to do cutting-edge research in the labs on both the medical campus and the School of Public Health campus," says a former biology instructor. "You can't take short cuts around research." Unfortunately, one of those areas of research now involves embryonic stem cells. Opportunities for study abroad abound at Harvard, which sends students to 10 countries in Africa, 14 in Latin America and the Caribbean, nine in Asia, 18 in Europe, and four in the Middle East, as well as to Australia and New Zealand. One of the programs allows students to attend the University of Edinburgh and work with the Scottish Parliament.

A graduate says, "I don't know if any university in the world offers such an amazing array of courses on everything under the sun." But weak general-education and major requirements mean "you can waste a lot of time."

Harvard offers a stunning array of foreign languages on campus: Amharic, Akkadian, Arabic, Aramaic, Armenian, Bamanakan, Bengali, Cape Verdean Creole, Catalan, Chichewa, Chinese, Czech, Danish, Dinka, Egyptian Hieroglyphs, English (Old and Middle), Finnish, French, German, Gikuyu, Greek (Ancient and Modern), Haitian Creole, Hausa, Hebrew, Hittite, Igbo, Indo-European, Iranian, Irish (Modern and Old), Italian, Japanese, Kinyarwanda, Korean, Latin, Luganda, Manchu, Mongolian, Nahuatl, Nepali, Norse (Old), Norwegian, Oromo, Pali, Persian, Polish, Portuguese, Russian, Sanskrit, Scottish Gaelic, Slavonic (Old Church), Somali, Spanish, Sumerian, Swahili, Swedish, Tamil, Thai, Tibetan, Tigrinya, Turkish, Twi, Ukrainian, Urdu-Hindi, Uyghur, Vietnamese, Welsh (Old, Middle, and Modern), Wolof, Xhosa, Yiddish, Yoruba, and Zulu.

Student Life: Parking in Harvard Yard

Campus life is centered around Harvard Yard during freshman year and a series of residential houses thereafter. Those houses serve as administrative units of the college as well as dormitories. Each house is presided over by a master—a senior faculty member who is responsible for guiding the social life and community of the house—and a resident dean, who oversees students in the house. Though students reside in same-sex suites, house floors (but not bathrooms) can be coed.

Harvard students do not have a reputation for bacchanalian excess, but alcohol and drug use is far from unknown, in the houses and elsewhere. Most Harvard students, however, are too ambitious to jeopardize their future with reckless carousing. Some, for instance, take to prayer. "A lot of students seem to become more religious at Harvard," one student says. "The Catholic Students Association runs a tight ship." Students attend

St. Paul's parish, which is adjacent to the campus. The Boston Boy Choir School sings each Sunday at the 11:00 a.m. Mass and is often joined by the adult choir.

There are no fraternities or sororities on campus, but there are more than 400 official student organizations that meet at the 50,000-square-foot Student Organization Center. In fact, Harvard caters to nearly as many extracurricular as intellectual interests—and does so with a distinctive style. As one student says, "Harvard's diversity is not always a bad thing. Everyone can find [his] flavor here." Harvard University athletics, intramurals, newspapers, and literary societies offer an unmatched variety of creative outlets and comfortable niches for students seeking a release from their studies. The most prestigious of these organizations are the *Harvard Crimson,* the justly famous *Harvard Lampoon,* Harvard's world-famous men's Glee Club, and the Hasty Pudding Club. "I sing madrigals, play sports, spend long hours in the dining hall," says one student. There is also a Harvard Republican Club and a Harvard Right to Life group, among many other conservative political and religious organizations, although they are greatly outnumbered by liberal groups.

The school fields 42 varsity teams, giving it the largest Division I program, according to the university. Harvard has excellent facilities for tennis, squash, and other recreational sports. There are numerous intramural teams, most of which are formed around the residential houses. The university estimates that over 75 percent of the student body participates, at some level, in athletic activities.

Although Harvard's Cambridge campus is moderately safe, students should not forget that they live in a large city bordering Boston. In 2011 the school reported 21 forcible sex offenses, seven aggravated assaults, one robbery, three car thefts, and 24 burglaries. Bicycles, wallets, and electronics—especially laptop computers—are the articles most frequently stolen.

Harvard's costs match its reputation. Tuition for 2012–13 was $40,866, with room and board at $13,630. Admission is need blind, and needy students are guaranteed all the aid they require. Some 60 percent of students received need-based financial aid, the average student-loan debt for recent graduates of the class of 2011 was just over $11,000, and two thirds of students now graduate debt-free. Harvard is gradually eliminating loans from its financial packages and replacing them with grants.

SUGGESTED CORE

1. Classical Studies 97a/97b, Greek Culture and Civilization/Roman Culture and Civilization
2. History 1300, Western Intellectual History: Greco-Roman Antiquity
3. Ancient Near East 120a/120b, Introduction to the Hebrew Bible and Old Testament 1/Introduction to the Hebrew Bible and Old Testament 2 and Religion 1400, Introduction to the New Testament: History and Interpretation
4. Religion 1402, Early Christian Thought 2: The Latin Tradition
5. Government 1061, The History of Modern Political Philosophy
6. Aesthetic and Interpretive Understanding 55, Shakespeare, The Early Plays and English 8hb, Four Shakespeare Plays
7. History 2400, Readings in Colonial and Revolutionary America—Proseminar
8. History 2320hf, Foundations of Modern European Intellectual History

STRONG SUITS

- Top scholars creamed off from universities around the world in almost every department.
- Among the best research and library facilities in existence.
- Rigorous honors programs.
- A vibrant, if small, religious and conservative subculture.
- Perhaps the largest array of foreign language courses available.

WEAK POINTS

- Students are often ambitious rather than curious, to the point of incivility.
- Professors more focused on research and publishing. Most student interaction is with graduate teaching assistants.
- Religion classes less than rigorous, mostly taught by faculty from the post-Christian Divinity School.
- Grade inflation rampant outside the hard sciences.
- An administration obsessed with promoting "safe sex" and libertine mores.

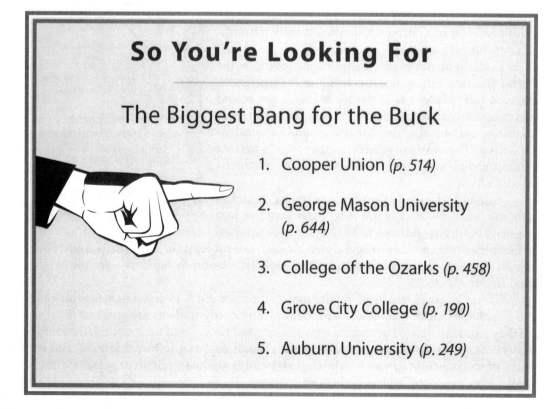

So You're Looking For

The Biggest Bang for the Buck

1. Cooper Union *(p. 514)*

2. George Mason University *(p. 644)*

3. College of the Ozarks *(p. 458)*

4. Grove City College *(p. 190)*

5. Auburn University *(p. 249)*

Haverford College

Haverford, Pennsylvania • www.haverford.edu

Fast Friends

Haverford was founded by the Religious Society of Friends in 1833. Haverford is not "officially" Quaker, but you hear a lot about the Quaker mind-set and principles at the college. This is felt most strongly in the school's honor code, the main point of which is to instill trust in one's professors, in one's classmates, and in oneself. One student says, "It really works! You are guaranteed to come out of here valuing honesty as the highest of virtues." Students make eye contact, leave their backpacks in the dining hall lobby while they eat, and leave their mailboxes wide open. It's a placid and familial school—no small virtue these days.

Unfortunately, some other traditional educational values, such as a solid curriculum, have fallen by the wayside. Haverford's reputation for academic excellence is well deserved, but, since we're being honest, the school's penchant for progressive politics and overwhelming price tag make it a tough sell for some.

Academic Life: Intense friends

Haverford's distribution requirements impose no real constraints on students—almost 80 different courses in the English department alone satisfy the humanities requirement, while more than 50 courses in political science could stand in for social sciences. As one professor put it, "A student seeking a 'traditional liberal education' can find that at Haverford. But he can also avoid it." One student says that the "best scholarship in almost every discipline is out there if you want to go and grab it. But if you don't, no one can really force you to."

The college attracts intellectually curious students, most of whom are eager to take a wide variety of courses. Unfortunately, their options include classes like "Sex, Gender, and Representation: An Introduction to Theories of Sexualities" and "Native American Music and Belief HU"—each of which fulfill basic humanities requirements. Even the natural sciences are dicey: one's sole science course could be "Disease and Discrimination," which "analyzes the nature of discrimination against individuals and groups with . . . diseases."

On the positive side, academic life at Haverford is not as politicized as at other schools. Haverford still offers many traditional courses and is one of only three top 10 liberal arts colleges to offer comprehensive surveys in English, history, and political science, as well as a history course in Western civilization. The history department offers courses in all the discipline's fundamental areas, as do the philosophy, religion, and English departments.

Sadly, the requirements for important majors are fairly loose. A student majoring in English must complete at least seven courses, at least two of them in works from before 1800. But he need not study any Shakespeare. Study of the American Founding is not required of history majors, and political science majors can graduate without covering the U.S. Constitution.

Still, academic life at Haverford is intense, say professors. One points to "many students here who are adventurous and do take courses merely to learn and not simply to get a good grade." Students expect to work every night during the week and during the day on weekends. "People here really want to learn, and they study hard," a student reports. And classes are rigorous: "It is virtually impossible to have a perfect GPA here, no matter how hard you work." Every student must complete a senior thesis, a comprehensive exam, or a special project paper or series of classes.

Students struggling with their papers can find assistance at the college's Writing Center, where student advisers offer advice and editing every evening, Sunday through Thursday.

Haverford benefits from a close relationship with its sister school, Bryn Mawr College, and nearby Swarthmore. Haverford students can take courses at the other two schools and even choose to major in a discipline offered only there. Haverford also offers a 3–2 engineering program in which students spend three years at Haverford and two at Caltech, emerging with degrees from both institutions.

Haverford is strongest in the sciences, particularly biology and chemistry, and the school boasts that it is one of only two undergraduate colleges in the country (along with Pomona College) to guarantee research opportunities for students in the sciences, the humanities, and the social sciences.

Among the most highly praised professors at Haverford are Linda Gerstein in history; Kimberly Benston, C. Stephen Finley, and Laura McGrane in English; Mark Gould in sociology; Kathleen Wright in philosophy; and Richard J. Ball in economics.

Faculty-student relationships at Haverford are about as close as one sees anywhere—and no wonder, with a luxurious student-faculty ratio of 8 to 1. A professor says that one of the school's greatest strengths is its "dedicated teachers across the board who spend a lot of time with students." Without a graduate program or the pressure to secure large grants, Haverford teachers can typically afford to invest more time and energy into teaching. However, one professor claims that "the administration's expectations of research have been rising." Students generally agree that professors are readily available for help, and not only during office hours: one student says his math professor "gave us her home phone number and told us to call her whenever we feel we are stuck on a problem for more than forty-five minutes—even if it is past midnight!" Each freshman is assigned both a faculty adviser and an upperclassman "peer adviser."

Haverford's honor code strengthens relationships between students and teachers. Students say they are amazed at the amount of trust faculty members place in them. "Cheating, plagiarism, and other dishonesty in the classroom are incredibly rare because students are

CAMPUS POLITICS: GREEN LIGHT

Haverford is by and large a liberal institution where you're not likely to run into many Quakers who are still within the bounds of Christian orthodoxy, like their founder, George Fox. One professor seemed to hit the nail on the head by characterizing the college as "soft left." Students and faculty tend to be "quite liberal socially," he averred, and for students "capitalism arouses as much suspicion as communism." Politics on campus, while clearly left leaning, seem fairly thoughtful. Above all, one insider said, "Haverford's way" is one that is both "polite and suffused with tolerance."

The College Republican group on campus, in its appeal for members, states: "At Haverford College, young conservatives are decidedly in the minority. We want to recruit like-minded conservative individuals in our club so that we can create a close-knit community which can offer a dissenting voice." One of the founders of the revived CR club told *The Clerk* (the student newspaper), "I know many conservative or Republican students are often scared or ashamed to speak up in class, so perhaps this will show them that it is okay to be a Republican."

not willing to break that trust," one says. Students can usually take exams home and complete them on their own time. One student reports that when he brought an exam home, his time ran out mid-sentence; he turned it in just like that. The honor code is student written and student run. Students who violate it are judged by peers on an honor council, and the most serious consequence of breaking the code is "separation," which is essentially a one-semester expulsion.

Aside from the plentiful academic options close to home, Haverford students can also benefit from educational partnerships further afield. The school's study-abroad program has been expanding of late, and 50 percent of students spend at least one semester abroad in foreign locales as diverse as Northern Ireland and South Africa. The big expansion has been due to grants from the Center for Peace and Global Citizenship (CPGC), which funds student internships in foreign places, as well as in inner cities in the U.S. Foreign languages offered at Haverford include Chinese, French, German, Greek and Latin, Italian, Japanese, Spanish, and Russian.

Student Life: Varsity cricket

The undergraduate population stands at around 1,198 students from 45 states and 38 countries, some 46 percent male and 54 percent female. Around 32 percent of Haverford students are members of a minority group (including international students), and the college is intent on admitting and retaining a more racially diverse student body. But one student complains that while "Haverford is sufficiently diverse racially and ethnically, and students are accepting of other cultures . . . we're not really diverse socioeconomically—we're all privileged and upper class."

> The college attracts intellectually curious students eager to take a wide variety of courses. Unfortunately, their options for core requirements include "Sex, Gender, and Representation" and "Disease and Discrimination."

In place of residential advisers, Haverford appoints CPs ("custom people") to show the first-year students the ropes and catechize them about the school's traditions. This arrangement dates back to the mid-1800s.

Quakerism encourages confronting problems through dialogue, and promotes reaching agreement by consensus. So things go at Haverford. When a dispute arises—something as minor as a hallmate playing music too loud or as major as whether the nation should go to war—students' first reaction is to face the other side and initiate a discussion.

Haverford, along with Bryn Mawr and Swarthmore, sponsors a summer orientation program for incoming minority freshmen. The Multicultural Scholars Program (MSP), originally known as Haverford's Minority Science Scholars Program, offers a bonanza of support services for minority students. For its size, Haverford has a plethora of minority student groups, among them Alliance of Latin American Students, Asian Students Association, Caribbean Essence Organization, Queer Discussion Group, and Women in Action, which focuses on "dialogue and activism regarding feminist issues." However, the school still has a ways to go toward attaining ideological diversity.

The student body supports the usual academic organizations, like Debate Team, Model UN, and the *Haverford Journal*. Far-out special interest groups, such as the Cornhole Ring of Champions and Haverford Hookah Club, stand in distinct contrast to their more sober counterparts, like the Chess Club, much as "innovative" spiritual groups like Athena's Circle (at sister school Bryn Mawr) darkly mimic more traditional counterparts like the Newman Catholic Campus Ministry.

The College Democrats seem to hold a comfortable hegemony over their competition, as the College Republicans club was formed in 2003 because of "an interest in demonstrating to the Haverford community that there is a diversity of political opinion on campus, and that it is okay not to conform to the political views often expressed by students, faculty, and the administration."

Haverford students confess that their school is not exactly an athletic powerhouse in the NCAA Division III Centennial Conference, where it competes with Swarthmore, Bryn Mawr, Franklin and Marshall, and Johns Hopkins, among others. Academics come first, and classes are scheduled so that students have no conflicts with practice. "We're not spectacular, but we always have a lot of fun," says one student, who ran for the track and cross-country teams without any previous experience.

> ## SUGGESTED CORE
>
> 1. Classics 1137, Hellenistic Roman Republic History
> 2. Philosophy 210/212/310, Plato/Aristotle/Topics in Ancient Greek and Roman Philosophy
> 3. Religion 118/122, Hebrew Bible: Literary Text and Historical Context/Introduction to the New Testament
> 4. Religion 206, History and Literature of Early Christianity
> 5. Political Science 231, Western Political Theory (Modern) (*offered at Bryn Mawr*)
> 6. English 225/325, Shakespeare: The Tragic and Beyond/Advanced Shakespeare
> 7. History 265/Political Science 276, American Colonial Encounters (*offered at Bryn Mawr*)/American Political Thought from Founding to Civil War (*closest matches*)
> 8. Philosophy 323, Topics in 19th-Century Philosophy

"On every team, there is an incredible range of abilities." Thirty-seven percent of students are varsity athletes. There are 21 varsity squads (but no football team). Haverford fields the only varsity cricket team in the nation; their competition comes from adult cricket leagues and club teams at area universities. The college also has a physical education requirement, which consists of six half-semester courses during a student's first two years at Haverford. So students are a physically fit lot. "At four o'clock every day, the library clears out and everybody is outside doing something. Haverford students are incredibly active," says a senior. The $28 million Douglas B. Gardner '83 Integrated Athletic Center and $1 million Johnson Track and Walton Field provide students with ample space to work off that freshman 15.

Haverford's multitude of options—traditional dormitories, single rooms in suite-style arrangements, on-campus apartments, and the dorms at Bryn Mawr—leaves students with virtually no reason to live off campus, and only about 2 percent do. At the beginning of each school year, students decide whether to make the bathrooms single-sex or coed, and for some reason students usually choose the coed route. There are no Greek organizations on campus.

As small as Haverford College is, there is still plenty to do. Regular buses to Bryn Mawr and Swarthmore colleges expand options even further. One student says that, in general, "Haverford students tend to think of 'Mawrtyrs' as weird—either gay or promiscuous. Swatties [Swarthmore students] are just weird and snobby." The party atmosphere is muted, with many students content to hang out with friends, play board games in Lunt Cafe, or attend the lectures and concerts held on campus every week. Fords against Boredom (FAB) sponsors free social events like midnight bowling, trips to Phillies games, a weekly film series, and the ever-popular mud wrestling.

Crime at Haverford appears to be decreasing. In 2011 the school reported three forcible sex offenses, two burglaries, and one aggravated assault. Drug and alcohol offenses crop up occasionally but not enough to think of Haverford as a party school, and blue-light emergency phones situated all over campus give students easy access to police.

Tuition for 2012–13 at Haverford was a stiff $43,310, plus $13,290 for room and board. Some 58 percent of undergraduates received financial aid, and the average student-loan debt upon graduation was $16,525.

STRONG SUITS	WEAK POINTS
• Though most faculty are liberal, many classes and the school atmosphere not politicized. • An open, friendly, honest, and cooperative atmosphere pervaded by mutual trust. • Highly qualified students and faculty. • Small classes and lots of close contact with professors; no graduate teaching assistants.	• Very weak general-education requirements; a student could miss cultural literacy in key subject matters. • Lax mandates for important majors such as English, history, and political science. Students can overspecialize and miss the basics. • An Ivy League tuition bill for a non-Ivy school.

Hillsdale College

Hillsdale, Michigan • www.hillsdale.edu

Reading in the Snow

Founded in 1844 by Free Will Baptists (though officially nonsectarian), Hillsdale College is fiercely independent—to the point of refusing federal aid that comes with federal strings. But the college has successfully raised money through private donors to provide financial aid, grants, and scholarships to students and has one of the lowest tuitions in the country for a liberal arts college. It also offers one of the most rigorous educations, in a distinctly conservative mode.

Academic Life: Rigor and Reagan

Thanks to its excellent core curriculum, the Western heritage forms the basis of every Hillsdale student's academic experience. Hillsdale offers 28 traditional majors in the humanities and natural sciences, seven interdisciplinary majors, nine preprofessional programs, and three business degrees—accounting, marketing/management, and financial management.

Most students spend their first two years fulfilling core requirements and exploring the different departments before declaring a major. Regardless of discipline, all Hillsdale

VITAL STATISTICS

Religious affiliation: *none*
Total enrollment: *1,400*
Total undergraduates: *1,400*
SAT CR/Verbal midrange: *630–740*
SAT Math midrange: *570–690*
ACT midrange: *26–32*
Applicants: *2,018*
Applicants accepted: *49%*
Accepted applicants who enrolled: *39%*
Tuition (general/out of state): *$21,390*
Tuition (in state): *N/A*
Room and board: *$8,640*
Freshman retention rate: *96%*
Graduation rate (4 yrs.): *72%*
Graduation rate (6 yrs.): *76%*
Courses with fewer than 20 students: *71%*
Student-faculty ratio: *10:1*
Courses taught by graduate students: *none*
Students living on campus: *80%*
Students in fraternities: *20%*
Students in sororities: *15%*
Students receiving need-based financial aid: *86%*
Avg. student-loan debt of a recent graduating class: *$18,500*
Most popular majors: *biology, physical science, social sciences*
Guaranteed housing for 4 years? *yes*

students must take a significant number of classes in language, literature, history, arts, political science, and the U.S. Constitution. As one teacher says, "Business majors take the same core as any other major, and thus come out able to think, speak, and write in a more coherent fashion than most business majors from other schools." Adds another faculty member: "The core is well thought out and well taught. The students know why they are here, and they are very much alive in the classroom. It is a joy to teach in such an environment."

The vibrant honors program at Hillsdale offers a heightened academic experience to qualified students. The students take special honors sections of the core curriculum, a one-credit honors seminar each semester, and in their senior year they complete and defend an interdisciplinary thesis. As a student says, the purpose of these seminars is to encourage "conversations that cross department boundaries," challenging and stretching motivated students. A maximum of 30 students, mostly freshmen, are accepted to the program each year— although it is possible to opt into the program later on.

Hillsdale's Center for Constructive Alternatives sponsors one of the largest college lecture series in America. "For a small school," says one student, "there are plenty of opportunities to be enriched."

The department of philosophy and religion has seen recent improvements. The school has bulked up its course offerings, and now, in addition to "Old Testament" and "History of Christian Thought," students can take a course in "Roman Catholic Theology" and "Introduction to Islam." One professor reports that, at Hillsdale, there is "a much greater exploration of the connections between philosophy and religion than happens in most departments." Highly praised teachers in this department include Donald Westblade, Peter Blum, Donald Turner, and Thomas Burke.

The English department is one of the strongest and most popular at Hillsdale, boasting excellent professors and fine courses. Some of the most beloved teachers include John Freeh, Daniel Sundahl, David Whalen, Justin Jackson, and Stephen Smith. According to a student, "Dr. Smith takes the time to thoroughly examine each piece of literature he presents in the classroom. The work is not easy but deeply rewarding." Shakespeare would be impossible for a major to miss.

Another popular major at Hillsdale is history. While the department is impressive in U.S. and European history, "the offerings with regard to Latin America, Africa, and Asia are scanty," a teacher says. According to the department's website, the history major must take nine courses beyond the two mandatory Western civilization freshman core courses, including three additional Western civilization classes and at least two American history courses. Recommended faculty include Mark Kalthoff, Paul Moreno, Thomas Conner, Paul Rahe, Richard Gamble, Bradley Birzer, and David Raney. Students in the history department are endearingly enthusiastic about their particular favorites. One recent alum says of Dr. Birzer, "He teaches his students what it means to be human through the material and by example, as well as the consequent duties and responsibilities we thus have to ourselves, our families, and each other."

While one professor says that "the strongest majors on campus are history and English," he also believes that "the professors from these disciplines are a central part of the freshman core. They tend to be popular with students and yet also academically demanding, and they help create the distinctive Hillsdale education."

CAMPUS POLITICS: GREEN LIGHT

Part of Hillsdale's strong national following stems from its well-known stance against federal encroachment into higher education. It circulates its high-minded newsletter, *Imprimis*, to more than one million readers—some of whom send support to keep the college growing.

Most students agree that the Hillsdale faculty encourage intelligent student comments and participation in class, regardless of a student's political viewpoint. One faculty member notes: "What is really most 'conservative' here is . . . the traditional nature of the academic program, the emphasis on substantive academic study, and extensive—not specialized—learning on the part of students, the importance education is understood to have in perpetuating a free republic . . . and the respect for the Western cultural and intellectual tradition." That said, an outspokenly leftist student would probably not feel comfortable at Hillsdale.

While education may be one of the smallest programs at Hillsdale, the department has recently created a new minor in classical education, which focuses on the medieval "trivium" and equips graduates to teach in many private schools where state certification is not required. The minor includes a teaching apprenticeship as well.

The music program is getting stronger every year, thriving in its home, the Howard Music Hall and Performance Center. Students and professors alike seem to take great pride in the program. One student happily reported that the performing arts encourage "diverse participation across campus," and her sentiments were seconded by a professor who boasted that "the music department has really taken off. We are getting conservatory-level students who want a liberal arts education, and the resulting quality of performance and program is genuinely impressive."

Political science is said to be "especially good in political theory and American government but could use some bolstering in foreign affairs," according to one teacher. The political science major takes a very impressive series of courses: "The U.S. Constitution,"

"American Political Thought," "Regimes: Classical and Modern," "Modern Political Philosophy" I and II, and "Introduction to American Foreign Policy," in addition to five electives. Highly praised teachers here include Mickey Craig and Kevin Portteus.

A professor says that "for tenure, successful teaching is a sine qua non. Nearly everyone on the faculty writes extensively, but everyone understands that we are here for the students, not vice versa."

Also recommended are Carmen Wyatt-Hayes in Spanish; Kirstin Kiledal in speech; Joseph Garnjobst and David Jones in Classics; Christopher Van Orman, Mark Nussbaum, and Lee Ann Baron in chemistry; Barbara Bushey, Anthony Frudakis, and Sam Knecht in art; and Kenneth Hayes in physics.

Thanks to a student-faculty ratio of 10 to 1, teachers and students are said to form strong relationships. One undergraduate fondly remembers an early encounter with a Hillsdale professor: "My first day of classes as a freshman, one of my professors strolled into the classroom, passed out the syllabus, reviewed it, and then pointed to the phone number at the top of the page, he said, 'Now, I realize that many of you are far from home, really far. This is my home phone number. My wife can cook. Please, feel free anytime you are feeling the grind, or just don't feel like eating at school, to give my home a call, and a place will be set at the dinner table for you.'"

Professors at Hillsdale tend to treat teaching as a privilege. One professor enthusiastically proclaims that "teaching is the place's raison d'être. For tenure, successful teaching is a sine qua non. . . . Nearly everyone on the faculty writes extensively, but everyone understands that we are here for the students, not vice versa." Comments a young faculty member, "I get a sense from my colleagues that every year the place gets better—new and better buildings, better students, new and lively colleagues."

Students eager to escape the midwestern cold can opt for one of Hillsdale's study-abroad programs, choosing among Oxford, England; Tours, France; Saarland or Würzburg, Germany; Seville, Spain; Córdoba, Argentina; St. Andrews, Scotland; or London, England. Hillsdale teaches a limited range of foreign languages: French, German, Greek and Latin, and Spanish.

Student Life: Buried in the dale

The rural, south-central Michigan town of Hillsdale (population 8,000) is sleepy and sits an hour from the nearest big city, Ann Arbor. As a result of the isolated location, however, the Hillsdale community is very close-knit, students report; they spend their nights and weekends primarily on campus, making their own fun or attending school-run activities. Many such activities are sponsored by Hillsdale's more than 70 registered student groups, such as the Christian Fellowship, Swing Club, Prodigy Ping-Pong Club, College Pep Band, Puppetry Club, some seven Greek houses, and 30 honors societies.

A faculty member observes, "Hillsdale is isolated, and the winter is cold. As a consequence, the college is an inward-looking community. The administration turns that to its advantage. The concerts, dances, and plays are really good and are really well attended; the number of speakers who pass through is astonishing. It is hard for me to do my teaching and my writing and to find the time to adequately exploit the place!"

While this is a decidedly nonsectarian school, two of the largest and most active student organizations are the Hillsdale Christian Fellowship and the Hillsdale Catholic Society. Each group hosts many social, volunteer, and religious activities for students.

One of the largest and busiest groups on campus is the College Republicans, which hosts debates and political speakers, participates in campaigns, and organizes trips to conventions around the state and in Washington, D.C. The Hillsdale CRs are very well known and respected in national political circles. While there is a College Democrats group on campus, it is very small and does not enjoy the same level of support from students or faculty.

Athletics also offer a relatively popular diversion for Hillsdale students—both the NCAA Division II varsity athletics and the competitive club sports leagues. Baseball and softball, men's and women's basketball, volleyball, track and field teams, women's swimming, and (of course) the football team are all popular parts of Hillsdale's student life. Because of the tight-knit nature of athletic teams and intensive hours of training together, there is some segregation between the athletes and the general student population.

There are seven Greek houses (four fraternities and three sororities), and they still serve as a hub of campus social activities. While frat parties and underage drinking are an occasional problem on campus, Hillsdale's Greek system is better known as a harmless and often exemplary system that provides fellowship and social, volunteer, and leadership opportunities to its members. Most houses have academic requirements for entrance.

While all the Greek houses offer a residency option for members, there are plenty of other housing choices. Most of Hillsdale's nearly 1,400 students live on campus or in nearby apartments. Juniors and seniors may apply for off-campus housing if they wish. There are 11 single-sex dorms scattered across Hillsdale's campus. The visitation policies have been extended recently, allowing more mixing between the sexes. Still, they are much more protective of privacy and modesty than the rules at most colleges, and students report that the visiting hours—as well as the alcohol and drug policies—are strictly enforced. Notes a female student, "Visitation is a drag, but you adapt to it quickly." Another says, "It's really nice to know that most mornings I don't have to worry about men being in the dorm to see me coming from the showers in my bathrobe."

SUGGESTED CORE

1. Classics 401/402, Greek Literature in Translation/Roman Literature in Translation
2. English 101–102, Freshman Rhetoric and Great Books I–II
3. Religion 211/212, Old/New Testament History and Literature
4. Religion 213, History of Christian Thought I
5. Political Science 212/213, Modern Political Philosophy I/II
6. English 401–02, Special Studies in British Literature: "Everybody's Shakespeare"
7. History 105, The American Heritage
8. Philosophy 217, 19th-Century Philosophy

The only coed dorm on campus is the Suites, an upperclassman residence with selective admittance and looser visitation hours and rules than other dorms. It features four singles arranged around a common room and kitchen. "The Suites have really improved the housing options for those who want to stay on campus their junior and senior years," says one student. "While we've had to deal with some initial problems with the construction of the building (leaky pipes and malfunctioning doors, thermostats, and phone jacks), overall I've loved living there."

One student says, "The RAs are very friendly and a great help to all students." Another reports, "Dorm life is a lot of fun. RAs are students, usually just a year or two older than residents, who tend to be very approachable and fun, and just happen to be in charge."

Hillsdale is said to be one of the safest college campuses in this guide, with no burglaries or aggravated assaults in recent years. (It does not report crime stats.) Still, students say fistfights with "townies" are not unheard of, especially for off-campus students. "Walk your girlfriends home after dark, guys," advises one student. As one undergrad says, "The average student taking the normal precautions has virtually nothing to fear." In fact, comments another student, most incidents on campus are student pranks.

Hillsdale's tuition for the 2012–13 academic year was $21,390, with room and board costing $8,640. Hillsdale College allocates more than $20 million to financial aid, resulting in an average aid package of nearly $16,000 per student. Some 86 percent of students get need-based aid. The average student-loan debt of a recent graduating class was a modest $18,500.

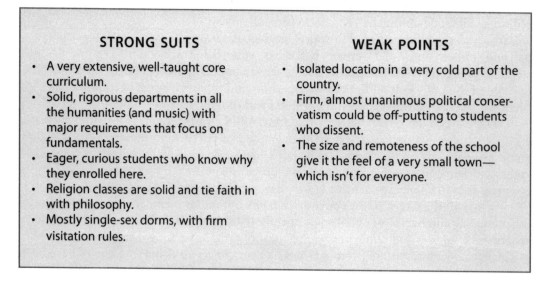

STRONG SUITS	WEAK POINTS
• A very extensive, well-taught core curriculum. • Solid, rigorous departments in all the humanities (and music) with major requirements that focus on fundamentals. • Eager, curious students who know why they enrolled here. • Religion classes are solid and tie faith in with philosophy. • Mostly single-sex dorms, with firm visitation rules.	• Isolated location in a very cold part of the country. • Firm, almost unanimous political conservatism could be off-putting to students who dissent. • The size and remoteness of the school give it the feel of a very small town—which isn't for everyone.

Johns Hopkins University

Baltimore, Maryland • www.jhu.edu

Life in the Lab

When Johns Hopkins University inaugurated Daniel Coit Gilman as president in 1876, Gilman asked, "What are we aiming at? The encouragement of research . . . and the advancement of individual scholars, who by their excellence will advance the sciences." Gilman's vision lives on at Johns Hopkins, the first research university of its kind and still one of the world's finest. But Hopkins's specialized focus has come at a cost. The school's emphasis on research leaves undergraduate teaching in the lurch, especially when it comes to general education. In a 2006 study of civic literacy on 50 of the nation's campuses, Johns Hopkins ranked dead last; its seniors knew considerably less about American history and institutions than did its freshmen.

On the other hand, many faculty members do use their research to complement their teaching, especially in the sciences and engineering, and 85 percent of undergraduates supplement their course work by participating in faculty research projects. Hopkins is for serious students who don't mind putting their social lives (and learning in the humanities) on hold for a few years so they can work with the best scholars in specialized fields. As one student says, "Prepare to spend four years studying, not making friends." And while the campus is largely apolitical, with students too busy grinding for grades to wave any

VITAL STATISTICS

Religious affiliation: *none*
Total enrollment: *6,838*
Total undergraduates: *4,997*
SAT CR/Verbal midrange:
    670–760
SAT Math midrange:
    690–790
ACT midrange: *30–34*
Applicants: *20,504*
Applicants accepted: *18%*
Accepted applicants who
    enrolled: *37%*
Tuition (general/out of
    state): *$42,280*
Tuition (in state): *N/A*
Room and board: *$12,962*
Freshman retention rate:
    97%
Graduation rate (4 yrs.): *83%*
Graduation rate (6 yrs.): *92%*
Courses with fewer than 20
    students: *66%*
Student-faculty ratio: *13:1*
Courses taught by graduate
    students: *not provided*
Students living on campus:
    56%
Students in fraternities: *22%*
Students in sororities: *26%*
Students receiving need-
    based financial aid: *46%*
Avg. student-loan debt of a
    recent graduating class:
    $24,307
Most popular majors:
    *biomedical engineering,
    international relations,
    public health studies*
Guaranteed housing for 4
    years? *no*

placards, there are occasional partisan conflicts on campus in which the administration consistently sides with the Left, earning Johns Hopkins one of the worst free-speech ratings in the country.

Academic Life: Darwin and Hobbes

Hopkins has made it clear from the beginning that it is primarily a research university, not a liberal arts college. Few students, particularly in the sciences, come to Hopkins to explore a variety of disciplines, but all are still required to take 30 credits outside their major. For humanities and social science students, 12 of those credits must be in math, science, or engineering; math, science, and engineering students must take 18 to 21 credits in the humanities or social sciences. Outside their major, however, students basically have free rein in deciding what remaining courses to take.

Each field has its own course requirements, of course. An English major, for example, must take two introductory courses outside the English department, one year of a foreign language at the intermediate level, and 10 courses in English. Worthy classes such as "American Literature to 1865" and "Shakespeare: Then and Now" are offered but not required.

The history department, one of the largest in the liberal arts at Johns Hopkins, is eclectic and uneven—some professors are much better than others. American history courses before and after 1865 are offered, but none are required; in fact, history majors may skip them and take instead courses like "History of Latin America," "History of Africa," and "History of East Asia." At least two courses must be outside a single geographic area (those studying American history must also take at least two courses set elsewhere in the world, for example).

The political science department, one of the first in the country, continues to be well respected in the field, especially in the areas of political theory and international relations. All poli-sci majors must take 13 courses in their major, with at least one course each in American politics, comparative politics, political theory, and international relations. Poli-sci students are required to study the U.S. Constitution and other fundamental topics, we are pleased to note. The most popular branch of the poli-sci department is international relations, perhaps in part because many of the classes are taught at the university's Paul H. Nitze School of Advanced International Studies in Washington, D.C. Many students choose to intern while in the nation's capital.

Besides the required two to four semesters of writing-intensive courses, students—especially those in the sciences—have little flexibility to pursue a real liberal arts education, as their semesters are filled with the requirements of their majors.

Most classrooms are free of extraneous politics. One finds, of course, the obligatory "gender"-fixated courses offered in several fields, but these are easily spotted and shunned. The only exceptions appear to be courses in the anthropology and sociology departments—disciplines that would prove quite uncomfortable for conservative students, according to our sources.

Undergraduates are intelligent and ambitious, sometimes to the degree of being antisocial, cutthroat competitors. In a physics lab, one alumnus says, some of the most overachieving students spent hours collecting iron filings, not because they needed so many samples but because they wanted to outdo their classmates. Another student says that professors lock organic chemistry labs to prevent students from sabotaging classmates' experiments. But if a student can survive such competition, a Johns Hopkins diploma is surely valuable. Alumni graduate and professional school acceptance rates are well above the national average. Hopkins tries to alleviate some student stress by "covering" the students' first-semester letter grades with a mark of "satisfactory" or "unsatisfactory." There is also a January term students can use as an extra-long vacation or to take an intensive interim course, thereby easing the strain in future semesters.

CAMPUS POLITICS: YELLOW LIGHT

With the student body largely focused on school work and making the grade, the average Hopkins student has little time for political activism. Students are typically either apolitical or apathetic. One student says that "while the campus has a slight leftist tendency because of the large number of students from Washington, D.C., and the northeastern states, politics just isn't a priority." One conservative student says there are "committed leftists here and there, but they are quite obvious and can easily be avoided."

The administration, on the other hand, has consistently earned Hopkins the worst possible free-speech rating from the Foundation for Individual Rights in Education (FIRE). Hopkins is one of only five schools on FIRE's Red Alert List, for having "acted with severe and ongoing disregard for the fundamental rights of their students and/or faculty members." Hopkins's nebulous speech code prohibits any "rude, disrespectful behavior," speech deemed "tasteless," or any written or spoken word that "breaches civility." The penalty for speech offenders is swift and severe, including school suspension, diversity workshops, community service, and dozens of multicultural book reports. A student suffered all these blows after posting a Halloween invitation on his Facebook page that the administration considered "tasteless."

In 2013 the JHU student government voted unanimously to deny recognition and funds to the student group Pro-Life Vanguard, comparing its members to white supremacists. It took national publicity and the threat of litigation to overturn this decision.

Many professors are top researchers vying for grants and awards. But persistent students should be able to find professors willing and eager to help with course work and to offer advice. "Every professor has office hours and almost all of them are friendly and helpful when students talk to them," a student says. "I had one professor who announced his office hours every lecture and told us that there was no need to do poorly in his class. . . . All we had to do was come in and talk to him." Another student says, "Students must show some initiative . . . but once [the professors] come to know you, they are generally most helpful." Professors teach almost all classes, but teaching assistants play a slightly greater role in engineering courses than they do in the humanities.

As one student says, "Prepare to spend four years studying, not making friends." Another reports, "Many people go to the library and practically live there. I'm in a very hard major, but I still find time to enjoy at least part of my Friday and Saturday."

One student calls the freshman advising program "atrocious," since students can avoid personal relationships with professors by using the Office of Academic Advising. After the first year, each student is assigned a faculty adviser, but another way to foster strong academic relationships with JHU faculty members is by taking advantage of one of the many research opportunities, especially in the sciences. For most research projects, students can even earn academic credit while preparing themselves for graduate school or a science-related career. The online registration procedures make it more difficult for students to choose the best courses, students tell us—and in some instances they have found themselves unable to take required courses in a timely manner and therefore graduate on time.

Students name the following as among the university's best undergraduate teachers in the liberal arts: Jeffrey Brooks, John Marshall, and William Rowe in history; William Connolly, Daniel Deudney, Eliot A. Cohen, and Richard Flathman (emeritus) in political science; Michael Fried in art history; Laurence M. Ball in economics; and Tristan Davies in the writing seminars. The science and engineering departments have a wide range of good professors, students say.

Hopkins is best known for its hard-science departments. The biology program was the nation's first; biology, biomedical engineering, neuroscience, and public health are some of the university's best. But JHU also maintains other excellent departments. The Romance language departments are all highly regarded, as are German and art history. A worthy option in the natural sciences allows students to create majors that bridge two or more academic disciplines—for example, biology and chemistry or physics and chemistry. In both area majors, students work closely with advisers to structure a four-year curriculum.

Only 16 percent of undergraduates study abroad, although Johns Hopkins offers programs in dozens of foreign locations. At home Hopkins students may choose to study Arabic, Chinese, French, German, Ancient Greek, Hebrew, Hindi, Italian, Japanese, Kiswahili, Korean, Modern Greek, Portuguese, Russian, Sanskrit, Spanish, Sumerian, and Yiddish.

Student Life: Hunker in the bunker

Johns Hopkins attracts some of the most academically focused students in the nation; therefore the school lacks most of the community atmosphere and entertainment options one finds at other colleges. "Social life is what you make of it," a biology major says.

Johns Hopkins currently has 10 residential halls, varying from single units to suites. All dormitories are coed, but there are no coed bathrooms or dorm rooms. Many students say they met most of their friends during their freshman year, when all live in dormitories on one residential quad where students leave their doors open and hallmates often drop by to say hello. Most sophomores, however, live in university-owned apartments, and social life suffers accordingly. The more intense students emerge, blinking, from their dorm rooms only to attend class or visit the library.

> **SUGGESTED CORE**
>
> 1. Great Books 360.133, Great Books at Hopkins
> 2. Philosophy 150.401, Greek Philosophy: Plato and His Predecessors
> 3. Jewish Studies Program 130.140, Hebrew Bible/Old Testament
> 4. No suitable course
> 5. Political Science 190.280, Classics of Political Thought
> 6. English 060.207, Shakespeare
> 7. History 100.112, Making America: Mastery and Freedom in British Mainland America 1607–1789 (*closest match*)
> 8. Philosophy 150.205, History of Modern Philosophy (*closest match*)

The Milton S. Eisenhower Library, an amazing resource, is built five stories underground so as not to be as tall as the revered Gilman Hall. Students say each floor becomes progressively quieter as you move downstairs; those studying on D level should expect annoyed stares at the slightest cough or crinkle of paper. "The Beach" is a green lawn behind the Eisenhower Library and bordering Charles Street, where students sunbathe and play soccer or Frisbee when the weather is pleasant. The Student Arts Center features a black-box theater, practice rooms, and arts and dance studios.

Hopkins boasts more than 360 student organizations, many of which are preprofessional societies or academic interest groups; others revolve around ethnicity, community service, media, sports, hobbies, the arts, and religious faith. A number of chaplaincies and student ministries serve Hopkins students of various creeds. The campus Hillel chapter is housed in the Smokler Center for Jewish Life, a four-level, 19,000-square-foot building. The Newman Center at JHU seems particularly solid, sponsoring talks on the theology of Pope Benedict XVI and on the Catholic *Catechism* and visits by members of faithful religious orders. Other active Christian groups include Catholic Community, Eastern Orthodox, Fellowship of Christian Athletes, and Agape Campus Christian Fellowship. The university estimates that a full 70 percent of students participate in at least one volunteer activity. Existing activist groups on campus, Left and Right, include the American Civil Liberties Union, Amnesty International, College Democrats, College Republicans, the NAACP, Students for Environmental Action, Pro-Life Vanguard (see "Campus Politics"), and Voice for Life.

Students who have attempted a bit of conservative activism have hit roadblocks from the administration. The *Carrollton Record* was founded by members of JHU's Republican club about 10 years ago. Shortly thereafter the Student Activities Council (SAC) decreed that publications must constitute their own student group and cannot fall under another group. Conservatives complained when *The Donkey,* a liberal student publication, was granted easy recognition as a student group and received school funds consistently denied the *Carrollton Record*. In fact, the paper has been unable either to obtain regular status as a student group or to receive student activities funding. The SAC has repeatedly changed the criteria for recognition and unfairly withheld funding from the paper, students complain.

About one-fourth of Hopkins students are involved in its 13 fraternities and eight sororities. One student says of the Greek system, "You can take it or leave it, and students can attend any of the campus fraternity parties." As for alcohol, one student says, "I think it's a lot less prevalent than in many other places, but it's here if you want it. There's a lot of stuff to do here, so there's no need to drink." But another humanities major says that, since the school has no social life, "students drink themselves to oblivion at one of the many frat parties. Most students still try to have a life when there is really no possibility of having one, and for this reason they are by and large miserable."

Varsity athletics do not play a significant role in Hopkins life and almost all varsity teams are Division III. One exception is lacrosse, the school's only Division I sport, and a national power. "Everybody goes to their games," says one student. "Lacrosse is huge." The admissions department says that 75 percent of the student body participates in sports—varsity, club, or intramural.

Hopkins's urban setting deters many students. The school has taken major steps in the last few years, however, to ensure the safety of its students. On-campus crime statistics for 2011 report one motor vehicle theft as the only incident.

Elite schools such as Johns Hopkins come at a premium price: tuition for 2012–13 was $42,280, with room and board at $12,962. Forty-six percent of undergraduates received need-based aid, and the average student-loan debt of recent graduates amounted to $24,307.

STRONG SUITS	WEAK POINTS
• First-rate programs in the hard sciences, engineering, political science, and foreign languages.	• Undergraduate teaching takes a back seat to research.
• Extensive opportunities for science students to work with professors on original research projects.	• The school's weak curriculum means that many students emerge as narrow specialists, uninformed about culture and civics.
• Little on-campus activism—students are too busy in the lab.	• Advising system is called "atrocious."
• Hardworking, ambitious students and leading researchers as professors.	• Relatively few liberal arts courses offered, with lax requirements for many majors.
	• Administration has terrible record on student free speech (see "Campus Politics").

Kenyon College

Gambier, Ohio • www.kenyon.edu

Ask Not for Whom

Every quarter hour, bells clang loudly from the Church of the Holy Spirit, resonating beyond the campus of Kenyon College, founded in 1824. "There's nothing better in Gambier than walking around the town on a warm Friday afternoon listening to the bells," recalls a graduate. However, the bells are now rung for different reasons. Over the past half decade or so, the bell has been tolled to mark solemnly the execution of criminals in the United States. This transformation of a venerable tradition into a political statement says quite a bit about what has happened to Kenyon College. However, one legacy that has survived untainted is Kenyon's devotion to hands-on instruction of students at a high academic level.

Academic Life: Ransoming Lowell

Kenyon College has no core curriculum but imposes instead some rather vague distribution requirements. More structure comes in one of the 31 majors—most in traditional disciplines, majors, or concentrations within 13 interdisciplinary programs, such as African American or women's and gender studies. A few students each year create their own interdisciplinary curricula and pursue "synoptic" majors.

One popular program that we highly recommend is the Integrated Program of Humane Studies (IPHS), which introduces students to classic (and other) texts of Western civilization in seminar-style tutorials. Over the course of a year, students study the Old Testament, then works of Plato, Virgil, Shakespeare, Aristotle, Nietzsche, Mann, Woolf, Kafka, Foucault, and others. After the first year, around a dozen students typically choose to concentrate in IPHS, taking courses such as "Dante's *Divine Comedy*" and "Modernism and Its Critics." Students attending Kenyon who seek a real liberal arts education should look no further than this department, which carries on the best of Kenyon's humanistic heritage.

Political science is highly respected among Kenyon faculty for the quality of its instruction and its commitment to exploring fundamental issues. The department provides an impressive yearlong freshman seminar, "Modern Quest for Justice," an introductory class that includes readings from the Bible, Thucydides, Tocqueville, Rousseau, and the American Founders. Political science majors are also required to take a course called "Liberal Democracy in America" and must choose another American politics course in addition to three courses in comparative politics and international relations. Students also take one upper-level seminar.

History majors face a rigorous program but not one that requires courses in U.S. history; students can choose European courses instead, and the study of non-Western history is strongly emphasized. Majors must complete a history senior exercise (see below) and write and defend a senior research paper. Honors students write an impressive 80-page independent study complete with maps, illustrations, bibliography, and footnotes.

Kenyon's English department is the school's largest—nearly a quarter of most graduating classes major in it. The English department was made famous by southern poet and critic John Crowe Ransom, who founded the *Kenyon Review*—which is still going strong. Many writers have attended Kenyon over the decades, including Robert Lowell, Peter Taylor, E. L. Doctorow, and William Gass. But the department has slipped since those glory days. Some students and professors now call it "overrated." Although solid courses like "Advanced Fiction Writing Workshop" and "Chaucer" still dominate the offerings, there is also now a marked emphasis on post-colonialist, postmodernist, and defiantly eccentric approaches to literature. Literary theory courses are required, but a course in Shakespeare, sadly, is not.

The college offers several science-related majors: biochemistry, biology, chemistry, molecular biology, neuroscience, physics, and environmental studies. The mathematics department is described as strong, with award-winning teachers. After completing courses taught only by professors (not graduate students), Kenyon's math and science students are said to find their way to good jobs after graduation.

Students and professors speak proudly of one Kenyon institution—the senior exercise, a departmental project or comprehensive exam that in most majors serves as the capstone of an undergraduate career. In the humanities and some social sciences, a student can satisfy the requirement by writing a chapter-length paper on a topic determined by his adviser. In other departments, such as economics and political science, majors take a comprehensive test. Any of these options serves as an excellent preparation for graduate school, and the college boasts that more than 70 percent of alumni find themselves studying for advanced degrees within five years.

Perhaps the students are inspired to emulate the devoted faculty they meet at Kenyon. "Students are our main 'business' in that we take them, their intellectual growth, and our teaching and learning seriously—intensely so," one teacher remarks. The faculty expects students to be enthusiastic about their educations and to crave learning for its own sake. Professors nurture students' intellects with constant book recommendations, additional reading assignments, and vigorous teaching. "We don't get caught up in rankings, future financial earnings, or prestige in general," says one student. "We immerse ourselves in learning."

CAMPUS POLITICS: YELLOW LIGHT

In any given year, the college typically has no more than 50 politically vocal students, usually of a liberal bent, sources tell us. The school hosts a group called ALSO (Allied Sexual Orientation), which is "dedicated to political activism regarding LGBT matters and heightening campus awareness of national queer issues." The Crozier Center for Women and the Snowden Multicultural Center also pursue liberal agendas. The Crozier Center annually sponsors Take Back the Night, a march protesting violence against women that students say usually turns into an orgy of rhetorical male bashing. For several years running it has hosted the inescapable *Vagina Monologues* and the Sex Workers Art Show, a traveling burlesque show staged by, uh, sex workers. Activists United is an umbrella organization that sponsors lectures concerning free trade, sweatshops, and the death penalty. The Crozier Center also publishes the journal *56%*, which is both liberal and racy.

Campus conservatives have hosted lectures by Bay Buchanan, Alan Keyes, and Ward Connerly in past years, typically through the fledgling College Republicans organization. One Kenyon conservative told the *Kenyon Collegian* in 2012: "I definitely feel pressure to identify solely Democratically. Some of the very reactionary, vocal liberals here make me feel like I'm doing something wrong because I'm not as upset about things as they are." Other students said that they feel more comfortable expressing their views on campus.

Upon entering the college, freshmen are paired with faculty advisers and upper-class counselors (UCC) in the same potential major who help ease the transition to college. "Without my adviser and UCC, choosing courses would have been a little overwhelming," says a recent alumnus. "Once admitted, students are given extraordinary support," reports one parent of a Kenyon undergrad, noting that her daughter's adviser mentored only five students. No one gets lost in the shuffle. Most classes meet around large conference tables.

Kenyon professors enjoy close relationships with students; according to a survey, 93 percent of freshmen have dined at a professor's house. Most professors are highly accessible and doggedly encourage students to visit them during office hours. One student says, "If you're not going to office hours, you're missing out on a wealth of knowledge." Students often crowd the hallways outside professors' offices during finals week.

According to a student, "We don't get caught up in rankings, future financial earnings, or prestige in general. We immerse ourselves in learning."

Kenyon students say they rarely encounter indoctrination in the classroom. Regardless of their beliefs, students usually feel comfortable enough to express varying viewpoints. "Politics stop at the classroom door," reports one undergrad. They don't necessarily stop at the door of a meeting room, however. Two professors report their distaste for what one calls the "unspoken agreements among many or most people that ensure the hiring of people who are politically acceptable." Another professor says that a "darker side to faculty relations in certain areas" is unavoidable. "A few of us are maintaining rational discourse as best we can," the teacher says. Professors with conservative sentiments are a distinct minority at Kenyon.

Science, mathematics, and music have at last come into their own at Kenyon, with recently built facilities and a strong emphasis on developing these disciplines.

The list of excellent professors at Kenyon is long. It includes Fred E. Baumann, John M. Elliott, Kirk R. Emmert (emeritus), Pamela K. Jensen, Joseph L. Klesner, David M. Rowe, and Stephen E. Van Holde in political science; Jennifer Clarvoe, Adele Davidson, William F. Klein, P. F. Kluge, Perry Lentz (emeritus), Sergei Lobanov-Rostovsky, and David Lynn in English; David E. Harrington and James P. Keeler in economics; K. Read Baldwin and Gregory P. Spaid in art; E. Raymond Heithaus (emeritus), Haruhiko Itagaki, and Joan L. Slonczewski in biology; Robert E. Bennett (emeritus) in Classics; Wendy MacLeod and Harlene Marley (emeritus) in dance, drama, and film; Matthew W. Maguire in history; Bradley Hartlaub and Judy Holdener (on sabbatical 2012–13) in mathematics; Natalia L. Olshanskaya in modern languages and literatures; Benjamin R. Locke in music; Juan De Pascuale and Joel F. Richeimer in philosophy; Frank C. Peiris and Paula C. Turner in physics; Allan Fenigstein and Michael P. Levine in psychology; and Royal W. F. Rhodes in religious studies.

Kenyon boasts a strong study-abroad program, sending students to sites across Europe, China, Japan, Russia, Latin America, and Africa. The college offers Greek and Latin, and eight modern languages: Arabic, Chinese, French, German, Italian, Japanese, Russian, and Spanish.

Student Life: Forty miles from Columbus

"There's obviously a lot to love about going to a school on a hill in the middle of Amish country, and there's obviously a lot to hate," says a recent alumnus. The college's 1,000-acre campus in Gambier, Ohio, is home to about 2,000 year-round residents—who are almost outnumbered by the students. The village has undergone little change since its founding, adding only a bank, two small inns, a nationally renowned bookstore, two coffee shops, a college bar, and a post office. Only two village buildings are not owned or operated by the college.

Kenyon is strictly residential, and nearly all students live in college housing and purchase the college board plan. A handful of seniors live off campus; most students enjoy the college apartments and dormitories. The housing market is tight in Gambier and Mount Vernon, a neighboring town of 16,135. There are resident halls for first-year students and for upper-class students. Students have the option of living on single-sex or coed floors; in suites, apartments, or smoking or nonsmoking dorms; and in substance-free housing. All residence-hall bathrooms are single sex, as are dorm rooms. Students can also apply for special-interest housing if, for instance, they want to live with the Black Student Union or an unrecognized sorority. Kenyon recently built a village green with 20 townhouses to house some 220 students.

There are more than 120 student clubs and organizations at Kenyon, ranging from the Art Club to the Chasers, which organizes rock and pop performances. Kenyon has both College Democrats and Republicans, although neither group seems to be terribly active. There are six religious groups on campus, five Christian and one Jewish: Canterbury Kenyon (Episcopal), Koinonia Open Programming Board, Newman Community (Catholic), Saturday Night Fellowship, Young Life, and Hillel. All groups are primarily dedicated to prayer and service, not political activism.

More lively are the student papers. The *Kenyon Collegian* is published weekly and reports on a variety of subjects. The *Kenyon Observer,* the school's student-run journal, is the oldest political magazine on campus. Once exclusively conservative, the *Observer* now features writing from all over the political spectrum. Students who have worked for the *Observer* have gone on to take prestige positions at *National Review* and *Forbes*.

Gambier is a quiet college town. For those who find the silence unnerving, the school offers a free shuttle to Mount Vernon and a cheap Saturday shuttle to Columbus. One student says, "The biggest fear one could face in Gambier is boredom." Students generally

---

SUGGESTED CORE

1. Integrated Program in the Humane Studies (IPHS) 325, The Epic in Antiquity
2. Philosophy 200, Ancient Philosophy or Political Science 220, Classical Quest for Justice
3. Religious Studies 310/225, Hebrew Scriptures/Old Testament; New Testament
4. Religious Studies 320, Medieval Christianity
5. Political Science 221, The Modern Quest for Justice
6. English 220, Studies in Shakespeare
7. History 101D, United States History, 1492–1865
8. Philosophy 215, 19th-Century Philosophy

work hard, but several professors remark that students' interest in writing well and reading more is quickly slipping. "Students do not read as much as they used to," one faculty member sighs.

While only one bar in Gambier serves alcoholic beverages until the legal closing hour (2 a.m.), the college's dozen fraternities and sororities do their part in hosting the student parties and dances that form the backbone of Kenyon's social life. College officials are said to be quite strict about underage drinking. The college employs several security officers to help enforce liquor laws to secure the safety of students.

Kenyon is a member of the NCAA Division III North Coast Athletic Conference, along with Oberlin, Ohio Wesleyan, Case Western Reserve, and archrival Denison University. Although the college offers 22 intercollegiate teams and several club and intramural teams, the school has a thin reputation for athletic prowess. Kenyon's swimming program is an exception: the men's team maintained the longest national championship streak in NCAA history—an impressive 26 years. Also impressive: the women's swimming team has won 19 straight conference titles. Other notable intercollegiate teams include women's tennis, men's soccer, and men's lacrosse. A $60 million Center for Fitness, Recreation, and Athletics opened in fall 2005.

Crime at Kenyon is rare. In 2011 the college reported three forcible sex offenses and two burglaries on campus.

Kenyon is on the pricey side, with 2012–13 tuition at $42,780, and room and board $10,340. Admission is not need blind, but students who get in are guaranteed financial aid to meet their full need. Fifty percent of students received need-based aid, and the average student-loan debt of a recent graduating class was $20,992.

STRONG SUITS	WEAK POINTS
• Professors are devoted to undergraduate teaching and work closely with students. • The Integrated Program of Humane Studies offers a Great Books education to students who want it. • Political science, history, English, and mathematics departments are particularly rigorous. • Kenyon's Senior Exercise demands graduate-level work and prepares students for advanced studies.	• Many politicized literature courses. • Faculty report that conservative job applicants are discreetly blackballed. • Weak general-education requirements undermine liberal arts learning.

Massachusetts Institute of Technology

Cambridge, Massachusetts • www.mit.edu

Whiz Kids

The Massachusetts Institute of Technology admitted its first students in 1865. From the start, the school stressed the importance of research; we've probably all benefited from something discovered or invented by an MIT scientist. Certainly, MIT excels in the sciences, especially engineering. However, even for those students who seek an education in the natural sciences, MIT requires enough course work in the humanities to permit, in addition, a decent introduction to the liberal arts. Rare liberal arts majors will find themselves in a rigorous program but must be aware of the science requirements—which, when mastered, make for a balanced and excellent education. Of the top schools in this guide, perhaps no other school can boast students who are so driven to accomplish things. "You won't find a cutthroat atmosphere here," says a student. "It's incredibly difficult, but your classmates are on your side."

Academic Life: Precision bearings

MIT comprises the following schools: Science; Engineering; Architecture and Planning; Humanities, Arts, and Social Sciences; the Sloan School of Management; and the Whitaker

VITAL STATISTICS

Religious affiliation: *none*
Total enrollment: *10,894*
Total undergraduates: *4,384*
SAT CR/Verbal midrange:
  670–770
SAT Math midrange:
  740–800
ACT midrange: *32–35*
Applicants: *12,443*
Applicants accepted: *11%*
Accepted applicants who
  enrolled: *64%*
Tuition (general/out of
  state): *$42,050*
Tuition (in state): *N/A*
Room and board: *$12,188*
Freshman retention rate:
  97%
Graduation rate (4 yrs.): *83%*
Graduation rate (6 yrs.): *91%*
Courses with fewer than 20
  students: *65%*
Student-faculty ratio: *7:1*
Courses taught by graduate
  students: *not provided*
Students living on campus:
  92%
Students in fraternities: *50%*
Students in sororities: *35%*
Students receiving need-
  based financial aid: *90%*
Avg. student-loan debt of a
  recent graduating class:
  $15,911
Most popular majors: *com-
  puter science, engineering,
  physical sciences*
Guaranteed housing for 4
  years? *yes*

College of Health Sciences and Technology. Each except the last accepts undergraduates. MIT is home to about 4,000 undergrads and 6,000 graduate students. The School of Humanities, Arts, and Social Sciences graduates fewer than a hundred students each year, with economics by far its most popular concentration, although the school offers 20 majors. Indeed, as one student told us, "The great secret of MIT is that it is a great place to study history, literature, music, and other liberal arts." Often, students will double major or minor in a humanities or social science program, combining with a science major.

MIT structures the better part of each freshman's schedule. Seventeen "Subjects" or courses make up the General Institute Requirements: six core courses from calculus, physics, chemistry, and biology to be completed in the first year, as well as one lab requirement (LAB); two Restrictive Electives in Science and Technology (REST); and eight humanities, arts, or social sciences courses ("HASS" requirements) as well as two communications requirements.

Students usually complete all General Institute Requirements by the end of their second year, the year during which they begin pursuing their majors (which are confusingly called "Courses" at MIT). Each undergraduate—even those in the humanities—is awarded an SB (really a bachelor of science) degree. Students have but little choice within the science requirements, and students assure us that nearly every course is solid and essential to future studies.

MIT offers a number of freshman programs, including five "learning communities," as an alternative to mainstream classes. Among these, the Concourse Program is very highly recommended for its attempt to integrate the humanities and science and help students choose wisely among nonscience courses. MIT is one of the few remaining campuses that offer ROTC programs in three branches of the military: Army, Navy/Marine Corps, and Air Force.

For help in navigating the curriculum, MIT assigns a faculty or staff adviser to each freshman. Students meet their advisers weekly in certain freshman seminars. When a student selects a major, an upperclassman in that department becomes his mentor. Students say that faculty are busy but willing to talk if you can find them at the right time. Persistence pays off.

Students attending MIT will surely have other helpers available, apart from their professors. Peer assistance here is incredibly strong. Says a student: "We're very collaborative here. We share. Basically, we have to work together if we're going to make it to graduation."

A normal MIT class is 12 units: three hours of class time, two hours in a discussion session, and seven study hours. How long students spend outside class varies, of course. "I know of several student geniuses here who basically just show up for the exam at the end of the semester," says a student. "I, however, spend fifty to sixty hours studying per week." The university places no limits on students' course loads. While a typical course load is around 48 to 60 units, one mechanical engineering major says, "120 units is not unheard of."

MIT is a work-intensive, challenging environment, especially for freshmen. Wisely, MIT gives first-semester freshmen only pass / fail grades. During the second semester, freshmen earn As, Bs, or Cs; if they get a D or an F, it will not appear on their transcripts. Very little grade inflation is reported at MIT.

MIT's Undergraduate Research Opportunities Program (UROP) is used by approximately 85 percent of undergrads at some point in their careers; it offers hundreds of varied opportunities for students to assist with ongoing faculty research projects. Participants spend six to 10 hours a week working for credit, for pay, or as volunteers—but the experience is priceless. "This school is filled with opportunities. Even as a freshman, you can plunge right into internships and research opportunities. My friends at Harvard couldn't believe it when I told them," says a student.

MIT has about 1,180 faculty members, supplemented by some 252 part-time instructors. Students are likely to be taught by a graduate student in some introductory courses. MIT puts its student-to-full-time-professor ratio at an exceptionally low 7 to 1 and claims that most faculty do teach undergraduates. As one professor says, "Unlike many Ivies or state schools, MIT offers an opportunity for any first-year student to take a class with a full professor." Sixty-five percent of the classes do not exceed 20 students, but MIT's lecture classes enroll hundreds of students. One sophomore told us, "My biology class (a required class) had more than 700 students. We couldn't even fit into the largest room on campus, so some of my classmates watched over a live-streaming video."

CAMPUS POLITICS: GREEN LIGHT

When asked about the state of free speech and political fairness at MIT, one professor noted that the students are argumentative and "love exploring every side of an issue." This teacher described the faculty's political views as "located across the spectrum from left to right," noting that "MIT sports one of the most contrarian of opponents of the global warming hypothesis, and a recently tenured molecular biologist who opposes embryonic stem cell research; it also sports the renowned Noam Chomsky, a former CIA director (and chemist), and a former (woman) secretary of the Air Force."

MIT does not boast many political activists among its students, who seem to hold a wide disparity of political ideas but don't spend time promoting them, rallying others to the cause, or demonstrating for them. They have too much work to do. One student tells us: "Instead of political activism, many students participate in social justice causes, fighting especially against poverty, hunger, and disabilities. MIT students tend to put their activism to work rather than to rallies."

Conservative students sometimes complain of unfair grading, especially when their views differ from their professors' on hot-button "social issues." Still, the overall atmosphere at MIT is said to be open minded, if sometimes narrowly utilitarian.

MIT has nine Nobel Prize winners on the faculty; in the institution's history, 78 members of the MIT community have won the Nobel Prize—most recently (2010) Professor Peter A. Diamond in economics. The current faculty also includes 17 MacArthur Fellows, 63 Guggenheim Fellows, and six Fulbright Scholars. Eleven present and former faculty members are winners of the Kyoto Prize. Attending MIT does not mean you'll be invited for tea at the home of a Nobel laureate. You won't. But you might contribute to one of their research projects and start to make a name in your field.

> "This school is filled with opportunities," says a student. "Even as a freshman, you can plunge right into internships and research opportunities. My friends at Harvard couldn't believe it when I told them."

Professors recommended by students include Daniel Kleitman (emeritus) in mathematics; Wolfgang Ketterle in physics; Patrick H. Winston in computer science; Alan V. Oppenheim, Harold Abelson, and Gerald Jay Sussman in electrical engineering and computer science; Richard R. Schrock in chemistry; Joseph M. Sussman in civil and environmental engineering; Diana Henderson in literature; Pauline R. Maier, Jeffrey S. Ravel, and William Broadhead in history; Sheila Widnall in aeronautics and astronautics; and Linda Rabieh and Lee Perlman in the Concourse program.

To fulfill the degree requirements toward a major in literature, students must take at least 10 subjects in literature, of which no more than three may be introductory courses and at least three must be seminars. Shakespeare would be hard to miss.

History majors must take four required courses: one topical seminar, a seminar in historical methods, a thesis tutorial, and a course in which students complete their thesis (final year of study). Additionally, the history major chooses six restricted electives. American history is not required.

The political science major must take both "Political Science Scope and Methods" and a "Political Science Laboratory" and must select one class from each of four fields: political philosophy or theory, United States politics, public policy, and international/comparative politics. They also complete three political science electives and a senior thesis (including a preparatory seminar). Study of the U.S. Constitution would seem hard to avoid.

In recent years, less than 20 percent of the MIT student body studies abroad. That is low compared with liberal arts colleges but high for engineering schools, where students tend to extend more effort in labs in the U.S. But the university does offer some excellent programs, such as the Cambridge-MIT exchange, and MIT-Madrid. Additional programs provide research and study opportunities in China (including Taiwan and Singapore), France, Germany, India, Italy, Japan, Mexico, and Spain. MIT offers three language majors: French, German, and Spanish. Minors are offered in these languages, and in Chinese and Japanese.

Student Life: Particles accelerating

MIT students who can find the time to raise their nose from their books and beakers have the fascinating city of Boston to explore. Students live in the cityscape of Cambridge, which stretches along the Charles River. Winters are hard in Boston, but thanks to an intricate tunneling system (second in the U.S. only to the Pentagon), MIT students rarely have to leave the warm indoors. "Once you figure it out, it can save you lots of chapped lips," says a student. Another interesting feature of the campus design is the Infinite Corridor: at 825 feet long it is the "longest corridor in the nation," according to MIT sources.

An abundance of extracurricular activities thrive at MIT: the school hosts an enormous number of exhibits, performances, and concerts each year, in addition to its own performing groups. According to one professor, "Much current student energy is dedicated to public service, international issues, and fun academic pursuits such as robotics." The university is home to 22 religious student organizations, with a majority of evangelical Christian groups from American Baptist to the United Church of Christ. The chaplaincy website also lists Muslim, Buddhist, and Hindu organizations, underlining the school's multicultural and multiethnic identity, according to the *Boston Globe*, which quotes a senior as saying, "When I came to MIT, I was expecting it to be full of nerds—people who don't really put together science and religion. I was really surprised—and still am—by the volume of Christian fellowship here." The Fellowship of Catholic University Students (FOCUS) and the Catholic chaplaincy are described as vibrant and faithful.

Among the many other student organizations are College Republicans and College Democrats, a pro-life group, the MIT Ski Team, Women's Water Polo and Volleyball, WMBR Radio (MIT's radio station), a Strategic Games Society, and *Stammtisch* (MIT's German conversation group). There is not much political activism on campus; most students are way too busy to engage in anything other than their studies.

Institute housing, as the dorms are called, is coed (except for the all-female McCormick Hall), though most dorms have "single-gender living areas," according to the school. There are no freshman dorms at MIT; to discourage age segregation, dorms are mixed so that freshmen can potentially live right next door to seniors. The summer before matriculating at MIT, students are sent a video detailing each of the 12 residence halls. Students rank their top choices, and MIT assigns them to a dorm based on their selections. "It's a high-stress environment here, so it helps to have a great living arrangement," says a student.

After their freshman year, students may live in fraternities, sororities, or independent

SUGGESTED CORE

1. Literature 21L.001, Foundations of Western Culture: Homer to Dante
2. Philosophy 24.01, Classics of Western Philosophy
3. Literature 21L.458, The Bible
4. History 21H.133, The Medieval World: 200–1500 (*closest match*)
5. Political Science 17.03, Introduction to Political Thought
6. Literature 21L.009/21L.010, Shakespeare: Global Shakespeares/Writing with Shakespeare
7. History 21H.101, American History to 1865
8. Literature 21L.002, Foundations of Western Culture: The Making of the Modern World

living groups (MIT has 33 combined), or in cooperative housing. Fraternity and sorority housing is located just on the other side of the Charles River, a short walk from campus. Living off campus is an option, but rent in and around Boston is prohibitively high; MIT says only about 8 percent of undergraduates elect to live off campus each year.

About 20 percent of MIT undergrads participate in intercollegiate athletics, while nearly 75 percent of students participate in intramurals (there are 18 sports) and informal recreation. Intramural offerings include bowling, dodgeball, and water polo. The school has 33 varsity teams and "provides the second most intercollegiate offerings among Division III institutions in America," according to the school.

The stunning Zesiger Sports and Fitness Center features an indoor track, ice arena, two pools, fitness floors, and more. "There's really something for everybody here," says a student. "You can choose rock climbing, ballroom dancing, archery, martial arts. You shouldn't have a problem finding something that interests you here." Every MIT student must also pass a hundred-yard swimming test, because, as one student conjectures, "We live next to the Charles River, and the wind could blow you in."

The school boasts a very active Greek life. Some 50 percent of the male student body are members of the 27 fraternities, while 35 percent of women belong to one of six sororities.

Given the workload they face, more than a few students turn to liquor as a sedative. The Campus Alcohol Advisory Board promotes responsible drinking on and off campus. Fraternities sometimes face problems with the Cambridge Licensing Commission, which can suspend residence permits for underage drinking.

The campus is fairly safe. Burglary (16 reports in 2011) and liquor law violations (38 in 2011) are the most common offenses. In 2011 MIT reported one motor vehicle theft, one aggravated assault, two robberies, and six forcible sex offenses on campus.

Tuition for 2012–13 was $42,050, plus an average $12,188 for room and board. Admissions are need blind, however, and the school guarantees that it will cover all demonstrated financial need. Approximately 90 percent of undergraduates received some kind of financial aid, and the average student-loan debt of a recent graduating class was a modest $15,911.

STRONG SUITS	WEAK POINTS
• Top-of-the-line programs in hard sciences, engineering, and technology.	• Limited options—and little time—for study of the liberal arts.
• Students dive into research with leading scientists, beginning their careers.	• Some enormous lecture classes (one had more than 700 students).
• The crushing workload makes students collaborative rather than competitive.	• Conservatives have complained of unfair grading.
• Politically diverse or neutral atmosphere on campus. People are too busy for activism.	• Narrow, scientific utilitarianism pervades discussion of ethical issues.
• Vital religious groups on campus with varied, worthy programs.	

Middlebury College

Middlebury, Vermont • www.middlebury.edu

Strong Language

Founded in 1800, Middlebury sits on what has been called New England's most beautiful campus. And it has many other virtues, amid its problems. One faculty member sums up the school this way: "The best aspect of Middlebury is the very high quality of teaching; from student evaluations, the students of Middlebury have great enthusiasm and respect for their teachers. The least favorable point is the minuscule representation of the conservative point of view among Middlebury faculty and the college as a whole." A student who holds alternative viewpoints must have courage and a strong backbone to flourish.

Academic Life: Pentecost—or Babel?

Middlebury may teach the liberal arts, but students are at liberty to choose which arts, thanks to the excessive flexibility of the curriculum. Middlebury also offers a sampling of obscure and trivial courses that can fulfill requirements. And while gaps in students' educations are certainly possible, they are not the norm. "A student who is extremely adept and savvy could probably avoid most of the 'fundamental' courses, but my experience is that they do not try to do that," says one teacher. Over the decades, Middlebury

VITAL STATISTICS

Religious affiliation: *none*
Total enrollment: *2,507*
Total undergraduates: *2,507*
SAT CR/Verbal midrange: *638–740*
SAT Math midrange: *640–740*
ACT midrange: *30–33*
Applicants: *8,533*
Applicants accepted: *18%*
Accepted applicants who enrolled: *43%*
Tuition (general/out of state): *$55,570 (comprehensive)*
Tuition (in state): *N/A*
Room and board: *N/A*
Freshman retention rate: *95%*
Graduation rate (4 yrs.): *83%*
Graduation rate (6 yrs.): *92%*
Courses with fewer than 20 students: *75%*
Student-faculty ratio: *9:1*
Courses taught by graduate students: *none*
Students living on campus: *97%*
Students in fraternities: *none*
Students in sororities: *none*
Students receiving need-based financial aid: *41%*
Avg. student-loan debt of a recent graduating class: *$20,514*
Most popular majors: *economics, English, political science*
Guaranteed housing for 4 years? *yes*

students have shown themselves inclined to take solid classes.

For the most part, the college steers clear of preprofessionalism, offering only the bachelor of arts degree, even for science majors. One professor reports that "this school is academically intense. Even those who major in the performing arts tend to do joint or double majors to cover a more traditional subject in depth.... We may not require that all our students read the Western canon, but we teach much of it, and we take it very seriously."

Insiders laud the close and frequent faculty-student interaction at Middlebury. "I know my teachers very well," a senior told us, "With very few exceptions, there are such great interactions, and the profs are completely approachable. Sometimes you'll even get 'call me at home' on a syllabus—so long as you don't call at eleven when they're putting their two-year-old to bed." Middlebury is the kind of school where students and faculty form intellectual relationships that last for years.

Freshmen are required to take one of several first-year seminars, which are intimate, interdisciplinary, discussion-oriented courses with an intensive writing component. Seminar instructors also serve as advisers for students until they declare majors. After completing the first-year seminar, each student completes a college writing course, which can be chosen from among a number of academic fields.

Teaching is by far the highest priority among faculty. Professors—not teaching assistants—teach every course. Highly recommended professors at Middlebury include Hang Du of the Chinese department, a native speaker known to present his courses "with clarity and understanding; he makes us feel at home." P. Frank Winkler of the physics department has taught at Middlebury for decades and engages students in his class with lively discussion topics. Jon Isham, director of environmental studies and professor of economics, according to one admirer, "presents his class in a clear, impartial manner, stressing the facts of the market and the realities of the business rather than the abstract theories that some professors prefer to teach." Other highly praised teachers include John Bertolini, John Elder (emeritus), Jay Parini, and David Price in English; Gregg Humphrey in education studies; Richard Wolfson in physics; Charles Nunley (emeritus) in French; and Paul Nelson (emeritus) and Allison Stanger in political science.

Middlebury is internationally known for its total-immersion foreign language programs, which bring in hundreds of students each summer. Middlebury offers majors in Arabic, Chinese, French, German, Greek and Latin, Italian, Japanese, Portuguese, Russian, and Spanish, and the school provides a number of courses in foreign literature in translation. The international studies major allows students to specialize in the language and culture of Africa, East Asia, South Asia, Europe, Latin America, Russia and Eastern Europe, or the Middle East. The department frequently sponsors lectures and symposiums. Sixty percent of each Middlebury junior class studies abroad each year, in more than 40 countries at more than 90 different programs and universities; the C. V. Starr–Middlebury Schools Abroad are in Argentina, Brazil, Chile, China, Egypt, France, Germany, Italy, Japan, Mexico, Russia, Spain, and Uruguay.

Although the language program is an important part of Middlebury College, "there are excellent programs across the curriculum," insists one professor. These include an esteemed Classics department and an academically diversified political science department. Another respected Middlebury program is the Bread Loaf School of English in nearby Ripton, Vermont (and three other campuses across the U.S. and the U.K.), which offers courses in literature and writing.

It should come as no surprise that this

CAMPUS POLITICS: YELLOW LIGHT

Many Middlebury students are involved in leftist activist groups and their various protests. Particularly active are the pro-choice and feminist organizations. Says one student: "There is no dialogue at all about the pro-choice issue. . . . Particularly disdained as well is the Christian viewpoint toward homosexuality. Those with conservative viewpoints are a silent minority who in general don't speak up for fear of losing friends."

There are signs that things may be looking up for the conservative minority at Middlebury. As one professor says, "There is a good Republican group on campus, a lively organization consisting of a small number of smart kids. However, I'd say about 95 percent of the faculty are leftist liberals, as is about 80 percent of the student body." Still, Middlebury is not as tolerant as campus literature claims.

In 2012 the Foundation for Individual Rights in Education warned of threats to free speech at Middlebury, noting that its harassment policy is so vaguely written that it could be used to suppress legitimate debate on controversial issues and that its policy on outside speakers burdens student sponsors with the job of maintaining order at meetings—thus granting a "heckler's veto" that could be used to keep unpopular ideas unspoken on campus.

small northeastern liberal arts college in a notably liberal state leans to the left. A faculty member contends, however, that "faculty and students support the discussion of controversial topics." But one student disagrees: "Any expression of conservative ideology on this campus draws either jeers or sneers, and I have many times felt very uncomfortable when four or five people at a time lambasted me for expressing even my most moderate positions. Though this is a racially and ethnically diverse school, there is only one accepted ideology." Another student reports, "This is a campus that swings far left. Liberal bias does creep into classrooms, particularly in the economics department." College Republicans complain that they were not invited to a question-and-answer luncheon for Chief Justice John Roberts when he came to address the school; they only heard about it through gossip, they claim, and wangled their way in at the last moment. The sole school newspaper, the *Middlebury Campus,* has a decidedly liberal slant.

Middlebury offers more courses in women's and gender studies than in economics. Because the women's studies department is interdisciplinary, many of these courses can, regrettably, fulfill several of the distribution requirements.

A professor tells us: "The best aspect of Middlebury is the very high quality of teaching. The least favorable point is the minuscule representation of the conservative point of view."

Fortunately, Middlebury's English faculty have largely resisted the ideological fashions that have ruined once-proud departments elsewhere. It is one of the few English programs that still requires its majors to take a course in Shakespeare. A National Association of Scholars study of liberal arts colleges' English departments concluded that "Middlebury offers a relatively well-structured major containing a high proportion of foundational courses." Still, there are problems. The department currently offers nine courses that claim to highlight the "problems" of sexuality and gender in literature, and some of even more questionable academic value, such as "Fictional Worlds," in which works to be studied include *The Matrix, Star Trek,* and *Dante's Inferno* (the video game, not the poem).

History majors are required to take one course in European history, one in American history, and one in the history of Asia, Africa, Latin America, the Middle East, or Russia/Soviet Union. Once these are taken care of—along with other requirements, such as two courses that deal primarily with the period before 1800—students can study "Listening to Brazilian Popular Music," "History of Mexican Food," and "American Empire."

Political science majors must complete three introductory courses chosen from four subcategories: political theory, American politics, comparative politics, and international relations. These could cover either classic political texts or "basic problems in American politics, such as race, gender, foreign policy, and education." Once these have been completed, the student may choose seven additional courses from a menu that includes "Local Green Politics," "Same Sex Marriage and the Law," and "Jihad vs. McWorld."

Apart from the courses that cover such things as "Topics in Reproductive Medicine" and "Bee Diversity and Ecology" in the biology department, and "Game of Go" in the mathematics department, Middlebury's math and science courses seem to be fairly straightforward.

Student Life: Uncommon commons

Upon entering the college, each "Midd" student is assigned to one of five "commons," which will serve as the center of the student's academic, social, and residential life. Every commons has its own faculty head, dean, coordinator, and residential advisers. Although housing is relatively inexpensive in Middlebury, the college is overwhelmingly residential: 97 percent of students live on campus. For the first two years, students are expected to live on campus. First-year students can choose to live on either a single-sex or a coed floor, but floors for upperclassmen are all coed. (There are no coed dorm rooms or bathrooms, however.) The college also has substance-free floors available for those who request them. One resident admits, "Dorm visitation rules have always been relatively lax."

Within the commons system, students have additional choices regarding living arrangements. Ethnic and themed houses "are fairly popular and also sponsor events," one student says. "If the Spanish house sponsors a party, there'll be sangria, awesome music, and people will come in hordes." As for dining, Middlebury operates its own food service and buys much of its food from local farmers and dairies.

To replace college fraternities, which were suppressed in 1990 for being "cliquish" and "exclusionary," the college offers six coed "social houses," which host parties, concerts, and other events. Binge drinking continues to be a problem. Students report that alcohol found its way even into the substance-free dorms. The Vermont liquor inspector has since cracked down on alcohol on campus. "Now," relates an insider, "there are no more alcoholic parties without a guest list. This leaves the freshmen to binge drink alone in their rooms."

Religious student groups, Bible discussions, and prayer meetings are available for students who want them, although few do. While admitting that religion is not very popular on campus, one insider allows, "Middlebury does cater to the religious student body relatively well." The Christian nondenominational group is very active but also, strangely, "very cliquey," says one student. "The Catholic group is more accepting, and they go to church together."

Other student organizations include, among many others: Amnesty International, the Bunker (a substance-free student-run venue), the Christian Orthodox Association, College Democrats, College Republicans, Feminist Action at Middlebury, Hillel (Jewish), Hindu Student Association, InterVarsity Christian Fellowship, Islamic Society, Midd East Action, Middlebury Musician's Guild, Middlebury Open Queer Alliance, Middlebury Student Quakers, Newman Club, Prajna Meditation Club, Prayz (nondenominational Christian),

---

SUGGESTED CORE

1. Classics and Classical Studies 150, Greek and Roman Epic Poetry
2. Philosophy 201, Ancient Greek Philosophy
3. Religion 280/281, Studies in Hebrew Bible/Studies in the New Testament
4. Religion 130, The Christian Tradition (*closest match*)
5. Political Science 318, Modern Political Philosophy
6. English 319/331/332, Shakespeare/Shakespeare's Comedies/Shakespeare's Histories
7. History 203, U.S. History 1492–1861
8. Philosophy 225, 19th-Century European Philosophy

Roosevelt Campus Network, Unitarian Universalists of Middlebury, Voices of Indigenous People, and organizations for the various languages.

Around half the student body participates in sports—varsity, club, or intramural. The Middlebury Panthers compete on 31 varsity teams in the NCAA Division III; since 1995, 30 of these have been championship teams. Recently, the men's tennis team won the NCAA championship. The college encourages fitness through a physical education requirement. The college's location in western Vermont gives students other athletic outlets as well; skiing is as popular in the winter as hiking, biking, and camping are in the other seasons.

The village of Middlebury is only a five-minute walk from campus. Students enjoy an abundance of restaurants and shops—many more than one would expect in a town of only about 8,000. Along with Middlebury's natural surroundings and the plentiful campus events, the presence of the town means that students rarely if ever have good reason to be bored.

Says one student: "I feel completely safe and secure on campus." A faculty member remarks that, "overall, the campus is pretty safe; there are some scattered incidents of a bike being stolen or a room broken into. The dorms have recently been locked, with entrance possible only through the use of a student card." In 2011 the school reported five forcible sexual assaults and 18 burglaries on campus.

Middlebury is a connoisseur's college, at a premium price. The "comprehensive" fee (including tuition, room and board, and health and other fees) for 2012–13 was $55,570. Some 41 percent of students received need-based aid. But the school admits students regardless of need and guarantees it will meet every student's demonstrated financial requirements. The average debt among students who took out loans was $20,514.

STRONG SUITS	WEAK POINTS
• Excellent teaching, all done by full-time faculty.	• Lax core requirements allow students to overspecialize and skip whole areas of knowledge.
• Students get close to professors, working with them, even feeling free to call them at home.	• Political bias often seeps into the classroom, marginalizing conservative students.
• First-rate programs in foreign languages (including Classics), political science, and English.	• Middlebury offers more courses in women's studies than in economics.
	• Binge drinking is not uncommon.

Blue Collar Ivies

An Elite Education on a Shoestring

"Blue Collar Ivies" is a brand-new addition to *Choosing the Right College*. We added this special section in recognition of the serious problems posed by college costs. The price of tuition has been skyrocketing for the past thirty years, far outstripping the rate of inflation—and the salaries of parents. (Experts call this phenomenon the "higher-education bubble" and are waiting for it to pop.) Meanwhile, jobs for new college graduates have become ever scarcer, with most starting annual salaries less than the amount each graduate owes (and many new graduates are unable to land full-time work at all). We won't barrage you with facts and figures, but here's a sobering one: according to the Project on Student Debt, students from the Class of 2011 who borrowed to gain their bachelor's degrees—that's two-thirds of graduates—emerged with an average of *$26,600* in student-loan debt.

And social analysts wonder why young people are delaying or simply avoiding marriage. There are doubtless cultural problems behind that, but money talks. If two average members of the Class of 2011 were to meet and marry tomorrow, they would start off life together owing $53,200—that's without a mortgage, before any kids. Let's not even talk about health insurance . . .

So clearly, cost is an essential factor to weigh in choosing the right college. A particular school may seem like a great fit for you, but if you're going to walk out of there carrying tens of thousands of dollars of debt, is it really the best choice? Maybe there are more affordable options where, with the right guidance and a little initiative, you can get a true education.

With college costs soaring, *Choosing the Right College* scoured the country to find the best *low-cost* educational options in America. We are excited to present the results, not only calling attention to these colleges but also providing detailed guidance on how to get a good education at each of them.

Among the Blue Collar Ivies profiled here are a number of schools that offer full-tuition scholarships to students, sometimes in return for full-time work on campus. Such schools were often established by wealthy benefactors to offer opportunities to the poor, like Kentucky's Alice Lloyd College. They are worth a careful look. But because these colleges can afford to be extremely selective, and some have income restrictions on whom they admit, we also profile *at least one public university in each of the fifty states*. Paying in-state tuition, you can attend at one-third or even one-fourth of what other students would pay.

The advantage of such a cost savings is obvious. And there really are excellent opportunities at most state universities. In these profiles, we point you to honors programs at state schools that often are nearly as rigorous as the options at elite private colleges. Some public institutions even offer Great Books programs; we tell you which ones. We highlight options for honors housing, which lets serious students escape the zoo atmosphere that pervades too many state college dorms. We also tell you about schools that have set up internship programs with local employers or enable science students to work closely with senior faculty in research.

Even outside these programs, the Blue Collar Ivies have many dedicated professors—frequently people whose own degrees come from the best schools in the country. Such teachers are often frustrated by the mediocrity and ideological pressure that prevails at state universities, and they uniformly report that they are delighted when eager, intellectually curious students seek them as mentors. You will find in every college profile some names of such professors. If you go to that college, contact them—even if they aren't in your major. Their advice will prove indispensable.

Of course, to thrive at many of these schools, you have to know how to find the gold amid all the tinsel. That's where we step in. While spotlighting outstanding programs at state universities, we also call attention to land mines you should avoid. We flag programs and departments that are directionless, underfunded, or flooded by radical activists (as many liberal arts departments sadly are), and we try to steer students to the strong ones. The good news is that state universities are so big, there is almost always some worthwhile path a proactive student can forge through the trackless forest. We find you that path, combing through each school's catalog to select a solid core curriculum of classes that will *guarantee a basic liberal arts education* to any student, regardless of major.

You won't find here any schools that are close to perfect. But if you follow the advice offered by the wise professors and savvy students who talked to our reporters, you will find a way to gain a solid, affordable education.

And if the state university where you live doesn't appeal to you, do not despair. Most states engage in some form of reciprocity with neighboring states, allowing students to gain significant discounts on tuition. You can find out which states offer which programs by looking at the following online resources:

The South: The Academic Common Market
www.sreb.org/page/1304/academic_common_market.html

The Midwest: The Midwest Student Exchange Program
http://msep.mhec.org/MidwestStudentExchangeProgram

The West: The Western Undergraduate Exchange
www.wiche.edu/wue

New England: The New England Regional Student Program
www.nebhe.org/programs-overview/rsp-tuition-break/overview/

If you live outside these regions, call the financial aid office of any state university to ask for guidance.

And now, let's look at the Blue Collar Ivies.

Auburn University

Auburn, Alabama • www.auburn.edu

Throwback

Founded as East Alabama Male College in 1859, Auburn University is in some ways a throwback to an earlier America: football is king, the Greeks rule the social scene, and political activism is next to nil. Auburn administrators emphasize preprofessional departments such as forestry, fisheries, information technology, and poultry science. Nonetheless, Auburn has a core curriculum that ensures that all students are at least exposed to more rarefied areas of inquiry than the migratory patterns of fish.

"Unlike most other universities, Auburn is conservative," says one instructor. Another adds, "It's just a very Christian, very professional atmosphere." According to a student, "The campus is gorgeous and the people are very southern. Everyone is very friendly."

Academic Life: Core all around

Auburn offers undergraduate degrees in more than 130 areas, including many highly specialized fields like forestry, aviation, and supply-chain management. While the university, thankfully, has retained a core curriculum, some professors say that the emphasis on the liberal arts has decreased. Unlike most schools in this guide, Auburn retains many elements

Blue Collar Ivy

VITAL STATISTICS

Religious affiliation: *none*
Total enrollment: *25,134*
Total undergraduates: *20,175*
SAT CR/Verbal midrange:
550–680
SAT Math midrange:
570–680
ACT midrange: *24–30*
Applicants: *18,323*
Applicants accepted: *70%*
Accepted applicants who
enrolled: *33%*
Tuition (general/out of
state): *$25,190*
Tuition (in state): *$9,446*
Room and board: *$10,606*
Freshman retention rate:
89%
Graduation rate (4 yrs.): *42%*
Graduation rate (6 yrs.): *68%*
Courses with fewer than 20
students: *26%*
Student-faculty ratio: *18:1*
Courses taught by graduate
students: *not provided*
Students living on campus:
19%
Students in fraternities: *23%*
Students in sororities: *35%*
Students receiving need-
based financial aid: *56%*
Avg. student-loan debt of a
recent graduating class:
$20,183
Most popular majors: *busi-
ness/marketing, educa-
tion, engineering*
Guaranteed housing for 4
years? *no*

of a traditional core curriculum, which it combines with respectable distribution requirements. According to one student, the core "takes up your first two years of study, but it really ensures that all students, regardless of major, get a well-rounded education in liberal arts, math, and science."

There are several truly excellent departments at Auburn, but most are outside the traditional liberal arts areas—preprofessional programs such as veterinary medicine, agriculture, forestry, architecture, and engineering are the strongest on campus.

The shining star at Auburn is its Department of Economics, which is based in the university's liberal arts college. The department boasts solid credentials and first-rate professors who understand the market economy. Majors must complete courses in macro- and microeconomics, math methods, international economics, econometrics, calculus, and statistics, as well as four electives and two foreign language classes. The economics degree has two tracks. The primary track requires students to complete a minor outside of economics. The quantitative track is for students with a strong interest in graduate studies and requires additional courses in mathematics and statistics. This department has on four occasions been included in the John Templeton Honor Roll for Free Enterprise Teaching. The nearby presence of the internationally known Ludwig von Mises Institute amplifies the appeal of Auburn to students with an interest in market economics and the philosophy of liberty.

The history and philosophy departments are among the strongest at Auburn (as is the College of Engineering). The history department does not provide much structure to its majors, requiring only "The Historian's Craft," two intermediate-, four upper-, and three advanced-level classes, each chosen from a short list. Students must also complete two foreign language courses, a class in public speaking, and a senior thesis project, as well as a number of liberal arts and history electives. Despite a lack of structure, by seeking advice from professors in the department, serious students can graduate with a thorough knowledge of the discipline.

The political science major follows a typical track, which requires the introductory class "American Government in a Multi-Cultural World," one class in political thought, and three courses chosen from comparative politics, international relations, public law and conflict resolution, and public administration. Students then opt to concentrate in an area like comparative politics or public administration.

English majors must take an introductory class, a literature course on "globalism, sustainability and diversity"—like "Survey of African-American Literature" or "Technology, Literacy, and Culture"—a linguistics or rhetoric class, and a critical theory class. Additionally, students seeking the English degree in literature are required to take upper-level literature classes in British, American, genre-focused, and author/topic-focused literature. Students could emerge without having studied Shakespeare.

Business is a popular major, though some faculty decry its rampant preprofessionalism. One student praises his education at the business school, saying that "the strongest point about the program was that professors were in touch with reality."

Professors to seek out at Auburn include Roger W. Garrison (emeritus) in economics; Daniel D. Butler in business; Kelly Bryant in architecture; Joey Shaw in agriculture; King "Ed" Williams in journalism; Mark Liles in biology; and James R. Barth in finance. Students report that "professors do not grade down conservative students," but some teachers do insist too strongly on their own views.

CAMPUS POLITICS: GREEN LIGHT

There seems to be little political bias, left or right, in the classroom at Auburn—which is quite an achievement. "There are good teachers and bad teachers," says one professor. "It's still possible to get a really good education at Auburn if you pick and choose." Another professor says that older faculty members tend to be less concerned with political agendas than are their younger peers. "They're hiring new, younger faculty members, and they bring the virus with them," he says. "But it's moving in the opposite way among students. The students are less politically correct, though they might be forced to mouth the words."

Auburn is best described politically as pleasant and noncontroversial. There are virtually no protests, no visible displays of angst, no significant groups of campus agitators. "There are very few leftists here," a conservative student says. "It's great, but sometimes it gets a little boring. There are no real wackos to fight with." The campus atmosphere is quite traditional. According to one student, "The typical student is preppy, courteous, and southern. It is a very friendly campus."

The university's Honors College, which selects some 600 freshmen from all the colleges and schools each year, is one of the university's outstanding programs. During their first two years, these students take six of their core courses together. Honors classes are small and designed to promote in-depth discussions with fellow students and faculty. They can earn a senior honors certificate either by writing a thesis or by taking four "honors participation courses," which supplement regular courses with extra writing or field work. The program comes with perks: honors students can live in separate residence halls and receive priority at registration, among other privileges.

In recent years, Auburn has dedicated millions of dollars to new research initiatives in transportation, information technology, food safety, biological sciences, fisheries and allied aquaculture, poultry science, and forestry and wildlife sciences.

One professor complains that football is "valued higher than academics, by the alumni, the administration, and everybody else. . . . Auburn is generally a party school, with athletics emphasized and academics downplayed and grade inflation like you wouldn't believe." According to one student, "You cannot go to Auburn if you do not like football."

Grade inflation and an emphasis on sports over liberal learning remain Auburn's most troubling flaws. Many students report little interaction with their professors. One science major informs us, "When I wanted to meet with my professors during office hours, I had problems finding them. However, e-mail always worked." Another student counters, "Professors here are very accessible. I have always been able to meet my professors outside of class. I have been taught by one graduate student, but there was also a professor who was helping to guide." Advising varies from college to college. Students in the College of Liberal Arts are invited to make appointments with nonfaculty advisers in the dean's office. Once a student has declared a major, he can meet with a faculty adviser within his department.

Graduate teaching assistants teach some undergraduate courses and most of the labs. Students can opt for professors by checking the class descriptions.

Many majors at Auburn require at least two semesters of foreign language study; the school offers Chinese, French, German, Greek and Latin, Italian, Japanese, Russian, and Spanish. Students looking for more intense language study can take advantage of one of Auburn's foreign language study-abroad programs in Costa Rica, Italy, Shanghai, Spain, or Vienna for summer study, and semester-long programs in Italy or Spain.

> "Unlike most other universities, Auburn is conservative," says one instructor. Another adds, "It's just a very Christian, very professional atmosphere." Auburn's two-year Core "ensures that all students, regardless of major, get a well-rounded education." But there are too many parties and there's a virtual cult of football.

Student Life: Sweet home Auburn

Auburn is the sort of place that generations attend in succession, where football runs deep in the blood. That game is the major focus of energy in the fall, culminating in the yearly showdown with Alabama, or perhaps a bowl game. The Auburn Tigers compete on 20 Division I teams, and their football team is Division I-A. The school is particularly strong in football, of course, as well as swimming and diving, women's basketball, and baseball. Auburn also offers club sports like sailing, water skiing, bass fishing, and lacrosse, as well as intramurals such as flag football, volleyball, and soccer.

Apart from athletics, fraternities and sororities dominate campus social life, and there have been some well-publicized incidents of hazing. About 23 percent of undergraduate men and 35 percent of undergraduate women belong to the Greek system, and many of the rest regularly attend weekend parties at Greek houses.

There are single-sex residence halls for women. In coed dorms, men and women are housed in separate wings or on alternating floors, and members of the opposite sex are not allowed to spend the night. Campus housing is in high demand. Only about 19 percent of students live on campus, but those who do seem to like it. One says, "Dorm life is great. Everyone loves living on the quad. The RAs are great people who try to connect with their residents."

Auburn offers hundreds of student clubs. There are around twenty-five religious organizations—mostly Protestant prayer groups and fellowships, but also a Catholic apostolate, a Jewish group, and a Mormon group. Media clubs include the award-winning *Auburn Plainsman* student newspaper, the *Southern Humanities Review*, the Eagle Eye TV News, and WEGL 91.1 FM. The politically minded student may join Democrat, Republican, or Libertarian groups, as well as the Young Americans for Liberty and Students for Life. There are also a number of service groups like Engineers without Borders; Habitat for Humanity; Best Buddies, which aids the mentally handicapped; and the Kadettes, who support the Army ROTC.

Auburn has some separate programs for nonwhite students, which some say serve to keep races segregated. Some programs border on the patronizing—such as the Minority Engineering Program, which provides "academic support services to entering minority engineering students," as well as tutoring and mentoring, according to university literature.

Students and professors describe the town of Auburn—known as the Loveliest Village on the Plain—as a university town that reflects the school's atmosphere. Some students claim there's little to do in Auburn, but others say the town is perfectly suited for study, research, dining, and relaxation. The town offers many excellent restaurants and historical sites.

The crime rate on campus is much lower than that for the surrounding community, which in turn is much lower than national rates. The 2011 crime statistics reported one forcible sex offense, two robberies, 22 burglaries, and three motor vehicle thefts on campus—among more than 25,000 students.

Auburn is quite reasonably priced—for a native. For 2012–13, in-state tuition was $9,446, while out-of-state was $25,190. Room and board amounted to $10,606. Some 56 percent of students received awards averaging half their demonstrated need, and the average student debt at graduation was about $20,183 for those who did borrow money (but most did not).

SUGGESTED CORE

1. Foreign Language Greek 3510/Latin 3510, Greek/Roman Literature and Culture in Translation
2. Philosophy 3330, History of Ancient Philosophy I
3. Religious Studies 1020/1030, Introduction to the Hebrew Scriptures/New Testament
4. Philosophy 3400, Medieval Philosophy
5. Political Science 3020, Introduction to Political Theory or Philosophy 3600, Political Philosophy
6. English 4610, Shakespeare
7. History 2010, Survey of United States History to 1877
8. History 5320 19th-Century Europe: 1815–1918

STRONG SUITS

- One of the few public universities with a good core curriculum.
- Excellent programs in philosophy, economics, history, veterinary medicine, agriculture, forestry, architecture, and engineering.
- Good honors program.
- Nonpoliticized classroom atmosphere in most departments.

WEAK POINTS

- An overemphasis on sports, socializing, and beer.
- The school pours resources into sciences but scants the liberal arts.
- Some undergraduate courses are taught by grad students, who also oversee labs.
- Professors don't always keep office hours, and some are inaccessible.
- Most students live off campus.

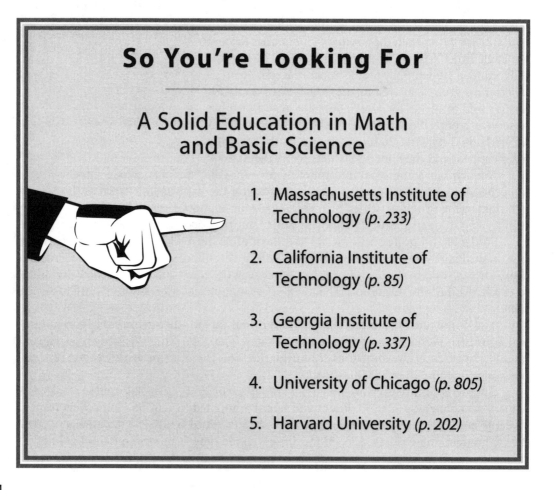

So You're Looking For

A Solid Education in Math and Basic Science

1. Massachusetts Institute of Technology *(p. 233)*

2. California Institute of Technology *(p. 85)*

3. Georgia Institute of Technology *(p. 337)*

4. University of Chicago *(p. 805)*

5. Harvard University *(p. 202)*

University of Alabama

Tuscaloosa, Alabama • www.ua.edu

A Sense of History

The University of Alabama is a public university with a rich history. Founded in 1831, it became a military school in 1860. By the end of the Civil War, Union troops had left only a few buildings standing on its Tuscaloosa campus, including the one the university president uses today as a residence.

It was about 100 years later that the university had its first sustained enrollment of black students. But that was not before Gov. George Wallace, himself an alumnus, put up a fight. Today, however, the university boasts of being "one of the top five public flagship universities in the nation in the enrollment of African-American students." They came to represent 12 percent of the student body in the 2011–12 academic year. The university had another first in November 2012, when Provost Judy Bonner became UA's first female president.

Academic Life: Philosophies of learning

The University of Alabama is like most other state universities, in that it imposes no core curriculum but only a set of general-education requirements—chosen from much too wide a set of parameters. If you want a real liberal arts education at Alabama, your best choice

255

VITAL STATISTICS

Religious affiliation: *none*
Total enrollment: *33,602*
Total undergraduates:
26,234
SAT CR/Verbal midrange:
500–620
SAT Math midrange:
495–640
ACT midrange: *22–29*
Applicants: *22,136*
Applicants accepted: *44%*
Accepted applicants who
enrolled: *59%*
Tuition (general/out of
state): *$11,850*
Tuition (in state): *$4,975*
Room and board: *$6,225*
Freshman retention rate:
87%
Graduation rate (4 yrs.): *37%*
Graduation rate (6 yrs.): *66%*
Courses with fewer than 20
students: *45%*
Student-faculty ratio: *19:1*
Courses taught by graduate
students: *11%*
Students living on campus:
28%
Students in fraternities: *22%*
Students in sororities: *33%*
Students receiving need-
based financial aid: *41%*
Avg. student-loan debt of a
recent graduating class:
$26,714
Most popular majors:
*business/marketing, com-
munications/journalism,
engineering*
Guaranteed housing for 4
years? *no*

is the Blount Undergraduate Initiative, which focuses on the classics of Western civilization, assigning such authors as Plato, St. Augustine, Galileo, Shakespeare, Jefferson, Madison, Dostoevsky, Yeats, and Faulkner. The university also has an Honors College that tries to enhance the undergraduate experience through "innovative academic experiences, advanced research opportunities, intercultural interactions and community service and leadership development," according to the university website. Students can major in any discipline.

"I would encourage anyone in the Honors College to get to know Dean [Shane] Sharpe," says one professor. Students at UA tend to find their teachers accessible, and teaching is given as much emphasis as research. "A faculty member must excel at both teaching and research to be awarded tenure," says an economics professor. "They are equally important. I am not personally aware of any instances where a terrible teacher was awarded tenure because he or she has an outstanding research record or brings in large sums of money. . . . At least in my department and college, most faculty have enough self-respect to try to do a good job in the classroom."

Professors and students we spoke to see as the strongest departments history, philosophy, American studies, biology, communications, public relations, electrical engineering, mechanical engineering, finance, nursing, law, and several areas in the Culverhouse College of Commerce (accounting; finance; economics; information systems, statistics. and management science).

As for history, the department provides "pretty good coverage" of American and European history, says one of its top professors. History majors must complete "Western Civilization to 1648" or "Comparative World Civilization," "Western Civ since 1648," "American Civilization to 1865" (and another course on post–Civil War America) and a research seminar offering training in historical methods and theory and culminating in a 15-page research paper. Although the department has "pretty high standards" and "some pretty fair-minded people," some of its younger teachers "are a little bit too enamored of the race-class-gender perspective," a teacher cautions. A professor outside the department feels there are a few faculty members "whose teaching is very politicized." Both the history and philosophy departments "require a lot of writing and logical reasoning," he observes.

The philosophy department is known as "pretty left of center," in one professor's words, "but I think it's a pretty rigorous department. They don't hand out a lot of As easily." One student warns that the department is made up almost entirely of professors who are atheists. "When we read philosophers who believed in a God, the professors offered some pretty serious spin," he said. Majors must take courses in deductive logic, ancient philosophy (from the pre-Socratics to the Skeptics), and early modern philosophy (Descartes and Kant). Then they may choose among courses such as symbolic logic; philosophy of mind; metaphysics; epistemology; philosophy of religion; ethics; philosophy of law; and mind, language, and reality.

The political science department is said to be solid, with strong points including four off-campus programs in Montgomery; Washington, D.C.; Belgium; and Sweden. "The International Relations faculty are probably the best researchers but have mixed reputations as teachers," says one professor. The department is small, he points out, and "a very high percentage of introductory-level classes in political science are taught by graduate students.... Because of its small size, there are fewer opportunities for political science majors to pursue independent research or thesis projects." Another professor reports that "most faculty members are fair-minded, but there are a few who I would caution conservative and Christian students to avoid."

The department offers majors in political science and international studies. Majors in the former must complete courses in American politics and choose among classes covering political theory, public administration, international relations, and comparative politics. Additional credits must be done in at least three subfields of poli-sci: American government, comparative politics, political theory, public administration, and international

CAMPUS POLITICS: GREEN LIGHT

At this culturally conservative school, there's some anecdotal evidence of political correctness interfering with the free expression of "unorthodox" viewpoints in several departments, including the gender and race studies, English, and education departments. "My recommendation is always try to engage what you're presenting," says one professor. "Don't just come in there with a holier-than-thou attitude like you know it all. Learn the argument you are presented with. Immerse yourself in what's offered to you."

Another professor feels that UA is the "darkest place, spiritually" in the state of Alabama, particularly in a department such as social work, which is characterized by a "very anti-Christian bent." Yet one of his colleagues says the university is "better than most schools about allowing students with dissenting points of view to express themselves." One professor in the College of Commerce pointed out that there are "many churchgoing faculty here."

Students themselves tend to be more conservative. "Being a poli-sci major, I can definitely pick up when politics does enter into the classroom," says one student. "But as far as the poli-sci department is concerned, I've always enjoyed the political discussions we have. There's a mix of conservative, moderate, and liberal professors, and I've never had any of them impose their views on the students."

relations. Special course offerings include one on southern politics. Only three political philosophy courses are offered.

An economics professor we surveyed said his department has a strong emphasis on microeconomics. The department offers a number of honors sections on principles of economics. "We participate in the University Scholars program [in which students can use a four-year undergraduate scholarship to earn a master's degree] and have two very good master's degree programs that do a very good job of placing students," he says. "At this time we are short on faculty, given the number of majors we have, so we are not able to offer as many electives as we would like." Gender and Race Studies (formerly Women's Studies) is, several professors agreed, UA's weakest department. "It's very ideological," says one. "If you don't toe a certain line, you're suspect." One teacher says that the courses offered by American Studies "sometimes seem a bit frivolous and politicized."

As for the English department, one professor finds it problematic. "They have a special system called No Credit, where you can keep repeating the course over and over. I think that's a bad system." He acknowledges that the department "does have some rigorous people" but others possess "the wrong ideological agendas," and some "will use their ideology to silence people." A Shakespeare course is not specifically required of English majors, though the Bard receives "serious treatment" in a required 200-level Brit lit course. Other course offerings include standard fare such as Chaucer, Milton, American literature, the Romantic period, 20th-century poetry, and linguistics.

> "I am not personally aware of any terrible teachers being awarded tenure," says an econ professor. "Most faculty have enough self-respect to do a good job in the classroom."

Weak departments, according to professors we surveyed, include education, health education, and foreign languages—which suffers, in one professor's estimation, from "too much infighting." One student finds weak teaching skills and thick foreign accents to affect the physics and computer science departments.

Aside from issues within specific departments, a trend that at least one professor sees as pervasive and harmful to education is what's called "active and collaborative learning." He explains: "Our young faculty is spending vast amounts of time putting together rubrics, matrixes, trying to measure collaborative and active learning," this professor says. "It's created an enormous amount of paperwork. There's not much emphasis on rigor or standards."

Recommended professors include David Beito, Steven Bunker, Lawrence Clayton, Howard Jones, George McClure, Michael Mendle, and Daniel Riches in history. George Rable, one professor notes, is "kind of a traditional Civil War historian." J. Norman Baldwin, Stephen Borrelli, Barbara Chotiner, and Utz McKnight get high marks in political science; so do Richard Richards in philosophy, James Cover in economics, Andrew Morriss in law, Bruce Barrett in statistics, and Ann Webb, director of the Emerging Scholars Program.

UA has a number of study-abroad programs. There are exchange programs at univer-

Alabama

sities in Australia, Austria, Belgium, China, Denmark, England, France, Germany, Italy, Japan, the Netherlands, Scotland, South Korea, Taiwan, and Wales. UA also collaborates with a variety of institutions abroad where Alabama students can study, do research, or intern. These include the Semester at Sea program, Consortium Institute of Management and Business Analysis, and Arcadia University School of Global Studies. The school offers courses in 28 foreign tongues, from Arabic to Vietnamese.

Student Life: Roll tide!

Football is big at Alabama—bigger perhaps than Bryant-Denny Stadium, which holds more than 101,000 fans. "Football season somehow lasts all year, and fans are extreme in their allegiance," says an undergrad. The Crimson Tide, led by head coach Nick Saban, has won 15 national championships, including the BCS championship against Notre Dame in 2013. Together with women's golf, gymnastics, and football, that gives the University

> **SUGGESTED CORE**
>
> 1. English 311–001, Classical Backgrounds
> 2. Philosophy 211, Ancient Philosophy
> 3. Religion 112, Introduction to New Testament
> 4. History 235, History of the Christian Church to 1500
> 5. Political Science 353, Modern Political Thought
> 6. English 333, Shakespeare
> 7. American Studies 485, American Experience: 1620–1865
> 8. History 212, European Social and Cultural History during the Long 19th Century

of Alabama a record of 22 NCAA championships. There are also several club sports, including baseball, crew, fishing, wheelchair basketball, cricket—and rugby, which was established in 1973 and makes it the longest active sports club on campus.

Not everyone at UA is athletic, though. The university was 13th on the Princeton Review's 2011 list of top party schools and eighth on its list of most hard-liquor drinkers. There is "plenty of underage alcohol consumption," says an undergrad. "That's probably the worst problem at my school, and not much is done to enforce drinking laws."

Almost as big as football at UA is the Greek system. More than 5,000 men and women are members of 56 fraternities and sororities. In late 2012 the university suspended all pledging activities by male fraternities amid allegations of hazing at some houses.

But there are plenty of other ways to socialize. There are some 250 student organizations one might join, such as Bama Students for Life, College Republicans, and Young Americans for Liberty. UA also has Army and Air Force ROTC.

The university requires all first-year students to live on campus. Only five of the 19 campus residence halls or complexes are single sex. Facilities such as Friedman Hall (part of the College of Commerce and Business Administration) and Harris Hall are coed with "community baths" or "shared baths." University policy prohibits "cohabitation" and "continual residing of two or more students or guests who are not roommates." Visitation hours are Sunday through Thursday 10 a.m.–12 a.m. and Friday and Saturday 10 a.m. to 2 a.m.

"I'd say there is definitely plenty of promiscuity on campus, based on conversations with classmates, but it's very possible to find a group of friends who are chaste," says an undergrad. "The university itself doesn't encourage chastity or abstinence, but individual students and organizations do." Also, "This is the Deep South," says an American studies major, "and most students care about their reputations. That's not to say that students don't hook up, but the culture on campus is generally conservative-leaning when it comes to sex."

Off-campus living is available, of course, and the university has resources to help students find appropriate housing. The university estimates that this could cost $615 to $790 monthly for a student living on his own, including rent and utilities.

For religious students, the university has many campus ministry groups, such as Campus Crusade for Christ, Orthodox Christian Fellowship, and active organizations of Catholics, Baptists, other Evangelical Christians, Jews, and others. "The work of campus ministries is everywhere," says a student. "Students are really involved with community service, social justice work, and church, but we still find plenty of time to take it easy and enjoy ourselves."

In general, students feel that the campus and surroundings are safe. "Crime is not a big concern in Tuscaloosa," says an undergrad. "Of course, there are parts of town that should be avoided at night, but what town doesn't have those parts? Near campus is very safe. If there is ever an incident on or near campus, UA notifies all students via our emergency alert system and provides updates until the situation is cleared." In 2011 there were 68 burglaries on campus, five robberies, three forcible sexual offenses, three aggravated assaults, two motor vehicle thefts, and one arson.

The university is a real bargain for native students, who paid only $4,975 in 2012–13—but was still competitive for out-of-staters at $11,850, with room and board at $6,225. Only 41 percent of students received need-based financial aid, and the average student-loan debt of a recent graduating class was an alarming $26,714.

STRONG SUITS	WEAK POINTS
• The Blount Undergraduate Initiative offers a Great Books education. • Good programs in history, philosophy, political science, American studies, biology, communications, public relations, electrical and mechanical engineering, finance, and nursing. • Many foreign language and study-abroad options. • A number of single-sex dorms available. • Many active chaplaincies and religious groups on campus.	• Distributional requirements very weak. • Philosophy majors may skip the entirety of Christian thought. • Younger faculty in humanities preoccupied with race/class/gender. • Excessive use of graduate teaching assistants. • Shaky programs in education, health education, foreign languages, physics, and computer science. • Drinking, hazing, hooking up too prevalent on campus.

University of Alaska

Anchorage, Alaska • www.uaa.alaska.edu

50 Shades of White

What began as classes in a high school building in 1954 is today Alaska's largest school, with 18,898 students. It quickly eclipsed the state's first university, in Fairbanks, thanks in part to its location in the largest Alaska city. (Anchorage is home to almost 300,000, while Fairbanks, the next largest city, has just 32,000 residents.) Today the school offers under-graduate degrees through six teaching units (the colleges of Education; Health and Social Welfare; Arts and Sciences; Business and Public Policy; the Community and Technical College; and the School of Engineering), as well as newly added graduate degrees in certain programs and joint doctoral degrees with other institutions. The university's past isn't entirely dead, though, as the school is still largely a commuter campus where more than half the undergrads are 25 or older.

Academic Life: Pick 49

General-education requirements at Alaska are soft and easy—a marked difference from the solid course material found in most majors. Students could easily graduate without studying any real literature or history (in fact, no history is required at all). These requirements start

VITAL STATISTICS

Religious affiliation: *none*
Total enrollment: *18,107*
Total undergraduates: *17,129*
SAT CR/Verbal midrange:
  430–580
SAT Math midrange:
  440–570
ACT midrange: *18–25*
Applicants: *4,312*
Applicants accepted: *3,433*
Accepted applicants who
  enrolled: *1,493*
Tuition (general/out of
  state): *$17,400*
Tuition (in state): *$4,950*
Room and board: *$9,827*
Freshman retention rate:
  73%
Graduation rate (4 yrs.): *25%*
Graduation rate (6 yrs.): *26%*
Courses with fewer than 20
  students: *53%*
Student-faculty ratio: *19:1*
Courses taught by graduate
  students: *not provided*
Students living on campus:
  34%
Students in fraternities: *14%*
Students in sororities: *15%*
Students receiving need-
  based financial aid: *65%*
Avg. student-loan debt of a
  recent graduating class:
  $24,396
Most popular majors:
  *business, history, health
  professions*
Guaranteed housing for 4
  years? *no*

off with promise in Tier I (basic college-level skills) with two required writing courses, but by Tier II ("a breadth of exposure to traditional academic disciplines") these have given way to Humanities and Fine Arts requirements that are all too easy to waste on narrowly focused courses. The most egregious is the Humanities requirement: a student needs two courses, but history, literature, philosophy, and logic are all lumped in the same category, and a student could choose none of the above and instead take two classes in American Sign Language or any other foreign language to fulfill the requirement. Likewise, the Social Sciences requirement lumps together disparate disciplines—psychology, sociology, anthropology, economics, business, political science—but despite the requirement that students take two courses in different disciplines, even the most dedicated of students are sure to miss a course or two in an important field. For Fine Arts, a student could choose to study the history of Western painting—or of jazz. While academic advising is not mandatory, faculty advisers are available for students who request them.

There is also, in many of the fields, a heavy offering of native Alaska courses ("Music of Alaska Natives and Indigenous Peoples of Northern Regions," "Alaska Native Perspectives," "Natives of Alaska," plus eight language courses) that could fulfill core requirements.

The honors program is little more than a few additional credits. Students do get "special leadership and internship opportunities, community involvement, and enhanced scholarship prospects." Students take one Enduring Books seminar (with selections like Rachel Carson's *Silent Spring* and William Whyte's *The Social Life of Small Urban Spaces*), one Social Science seminar, and guided volunteer service for credit. An Honors Thesis is required.

The best option for a solid education at Alaska is the excellent 49th State Fellows Program. Fellows take the regular honors core but also required courses in Western civilization, United States history, history of political philosophy, and macroeconomics. Students who complete this program will gain a traditional liberal arts background and a real understanding of American citizenship and culture. It's a magnet for conservative and religious students at Alaska. Political science professor James Muller, who helped found the program, is someone any intellectually ambitious student should seek out as a teacher and mentor.

Also of note is the University of Alaska Scholars Program, which offers the top 10 percent of all graduating seniors from Alaska high schools an $11,000 scholarship to any of the University of Alaska campuses.

Very few classes have more than 100 students, and the majority have 20 or fewer. With barely 1,000 graduate students, the good news is that professors teach most classes—which can be a point of contention among professors. "It's too much," says one professor. "Especially if you have a grant, it's too much teaching." Things may be changing, though. "Teaching is a HUGE part of UAA, but UAA is really trying to emphasize research more and more, and it is really giving some professors a mixed message about how to best spend their time," says a professor. A student complains, "It seems like professors are more interested in research than in students."

The university is also adding graduate programs. Available now are 26 graduate degree programs and a smattering of certificate programs, plus cooperative/collaborative MA and PhD programs with other universities.

CAMPUS POLITICS: GREEN LIGHT

As for classroom politics, one students says, "It's kind of liberal here." But the truth is, a pervasive lackadaisical attitude makes it difficult to find any politics at all. Even groups like Students for Life rest only on the work of one or two students and wane when those students graduate. "The biggest difference I have seen between UAA and other institutions I have worked at is the nature of the student," says a professor. "Very few of the students here are 18-to-22-year-olds who are full-time students. The majority of my students are older, were in the military, have families, full-time jobs, are beginning second careers, and commute to campus. They take six to ten years to graduate, and they take out lots of loans to do it. It is incredibly hard for me to see when students fail my class, sometimes multiple times, but so many of them just don't have the time to study." Or, understandably, to become political activists.

In addition to the 49th State initiative, the university offers other excellent programs, notably geomatics, engineering, psychology, biology, and geology. Also popular is the Aviation Technology Center, which offers associate degrees in air traffic control and professional piloting, as well as a BS in aviation technology. Weaker programs include the smaller departments in the College of Arts and Sciences.

Students report irritation with the strong and renowned College of Nursing because it has a huge waiting list. "It's frustrating," says one student. "You fulfill the requirements, then you sit around and wait." But one professor notes, "The state is spending considerable amounts of money in the entire Health College. This college will likely continue to grow as the need for health care in Alaska increases with the population. It is only likely to get stronger."

English requirements and options are strong and traditional, happily lacking most of the politically correct courses at other schools. Shakespeare is required of all students, regardless of whether they are pursuing the literature, rhetoric and language, or education option, and most courses focus on literature rather than political ideology.

History majors must complete 13 courses, mostly composed of Western history and

Blue Collar Ivy

worthy electives, including "Western Civilization" I and II, "History of the United States" I and II, "Historiography," a senior seminar, two non-Western history electives (examples include "The Rise, Fall, and Reinvention of the Samurai" and "Imperial Russian History"), and five upper-division history electives (examples are "Early Modern Europe: 1600–1789" and "Anglo-Saxons and Vikings").

Political Science offerings are solid. Devoid of trendy, politicized courses, the department is divided into five areas: comparative politics, international relations, political philosophy, American politics, and political behavior. Majors are required to take at least one course in each of these areas, to specialize in one of them, and to complete (among other courses) "Introduction to American Government," and "The American Political Tradition."

A student complains, "It seems like professors are more interested in research than in students."

Professors to seek out include Jim Pantaleone in physics; Connie Ambler, Joseph Nunnally, and Don Reardon in English; Stephanie Bauer in philosophy; Geran Tarr, Caroline Wilson, Robert Furilla, and Garry Davies in biology; John Petraitis and Claudia Lampman in psychology; Jeanne Borega and Sam Cook in mathematics; Guy Burnett in political science; Jeremy Tasch in geography; David Woodley and Ian Hartman in history; Shawnalee Whitney and Mark Bruner in communications; Zoelea Vey and Bart Tiernan in aviation; Gale Smoke in sociology; Kelly Shannon and Kimberly Pace in history; André Rosay in criminal justice; Edward Plastow in business; Kyle Hampton and Steve Jackstadt in economics; and Travis Hedwig in anthropology.

Students can major in French, German, Japanese, Russian, or Spanish. Courses are also offered in American Sign Language and Chinese, with plans to add a minor in Chinese soon.

UAA offers diverse study abroad, exchange programs, internships, and research opportunities in more than 55 countries, including Australia, Austria, Botswana, Costa Rica, Cuba, Denmark, Egypt, England, Fiji, France, Germany, Ghana, Hong Kong, Hungary, India, Israel, Japan, Malaysia, Mexico, Nicaragua, Peru, Poland, Qatar, Russia, Scotland, Spain, the United Arab Emirates, and Vietnam.

Student Life: On your own

The University of Alaska can be a quiet place, even with bustling Anchorage just three miles down the road. "This is not one of those campuses where people walk around handing out flyers, wanting you to sign petitions and sign up for stuff," says one student. "People mostly keep to themselves." This is reinforced by dorm life as well; the majority of the university's on-campus housing options are single-suite apartments with shared kitchens and living spaces, leading to a sense of isolation among students.

With a chronic on-campus housing shortage (just 946 beds) and constant complaints about parking, students would do well to apply early for on-campus options that include three residence halls and two apartment communities. Various floors and buildings are set up as Living Learning Communities, including halls for nursing, aviation and education majors, and honors students, among others.

The university does not offer coed or family housing but provides services to help students find off-campus residences. Other residence options include two sororities and two fraternities, which about 15 percent of students join. The university must approve events where alcoholic beverages will be served. The sale of alcoholic beverages at university-sanctioned events on campus is not permitted.

One of the most active groups on campus is Nihon Bunka (Japanese Culture) Club. Others include Model United Nations, College Republicans, College Democrats, Students for Life, and Young Americans for Liberty. There are also several groups focused on native students, including the Native Student Council. "The Alaska Native population brings a diverse set of ideas to campus, but often times they are not loud or outspoken, so their voices may not be heard," notes a professor. "But this is a wonderfully diverse campus with lots of ideas—many of them expressed weekly in the *Northern Light* student-run paper and also highlighted by different cultural events and clubs on campus."

Ice hockey and volleyball are among the most popular sporting events. The Seawolves, who compete in the Great Northwest Athletics Conference, field 11 varsity teams in men's and women's basketball, cross-country, skiing, and track and field; women's gymnastics and volleyball; and men's hockey. Options for intramural teams include coed basketball, volleyball, broomball, indoor soccer, and inner-tube water polo.

The Wells Fargo Sports Complex has a pool, ice rink, fitness center, dance studio and gymnasium, and track, but perhaps more important, it acts as a bridge from one end of the campus to the other, protecting students from the average nine-degree winter temperature.

Most campus-recognized chaplaincies are interdenominational in nature, and many are fairly quiet. InterVarsity Christian Fellowship is a growing organization, and True North Church and the Simple Truth both attract a fair number of students to Bible studies and group activities. But the fact remains that as a commuter and part-time campus, many students must find faith homes outside school.

In 2011 the university reported four forcible sex offenses, one robbery, one burglary, and two aggravated assaults on campus. However, the city of Anchorage has a crime rate twice the national median, and one student says, "I would never walk across campus alone at night."

Tuition is rising quickly (it more than doubled in the last 10 years) but remains a bargain for Alaska natives at $4,950, plus $832 in fees, for in-state students, and $17,400 for out-of-state students in 2012–13. Room and board added up to $9,827. Aid seems to be

SUGGESTED CORE

1. English A310, Ancient Literature (*closest match*)
2. Philosophy A211, History of Philosophy I
3. No suitable course offered
4. History A226, Medieval History (*closest match*)
5. Political Science A333, History of Political Philosophy II: Modern
6. English A424, Shakespeare
7. History A131, History of United States I
8. History A314, 19th-Century Europe

Alaska

generous; one administrator complains that students are using their student-loan money to finance "extravagant lifestyles." Some 65 percent of students received need-based financial aid, and the average debt of a recent graduate was $24,396.

STRONG SUITS	WEAK POINTS
• The 49th State Fellows Program offers a solid liberal arts education grounded in classic texts.	• General-education requirements are trivial and can be fulfilled with fluff courses.
• Extensive programs researching native Alaskan (aboriginal) culture.	• Popular nursing program is infamous for keeping students in limbo.
• Excellent, traditional requirements for English, history, political science majors.	• Honors program doesn't add much to ordinary requirements.
• Little interest in politics inside the classroom (or out).	• Little social life; most students seem to be busy, overworked loners.

University of Arizona

Tucson, Arizona • www.arizona.edu

Know When to Fold 'Em

The University of Arizona opened its doors in 1891 with a freshman class of six students. Today the school has more than 39,000 students and offers more than 150 majors—and it is expected to grow rapidly in future decades.

Although tuition has risen roughly 5 percent in the past two years, the legislature has reduced state funding to the point that university administrators have had to make serious program cuts at Arizona. "As part of budget issues in recent years, I believe our administration has trimmed [programs and departments] to a bare minimum," a professor says.

The combination of tight resources, weak curricular requirements, and standard-fare leftist campus politics make this a choice best considered by Arizonans seeking in-state tuition who can build their own core curriculum (with our help) and who are also willing to brave arguments in class with politicized teachers—or else keep their heads down.

Arizona residents may earn admission through the "assured admission process" if they "attend a regionally accredited high school, rank in the top 25 percent of their graduating class, and have no course work deficiencies as prescribed by the Arizona Board of Regents.

VITAL STATISTICS

Religious affiliation: *none*
Total enrollment: *39,236*
Total undergraduates:
30,665
SAT CR/Verbal midrange:
480–600
SAT Math midrange:
490–620
ACT midrange: *21–27*
Applicants: *32,227*
Applicants accepted: *69%*
Accepted applicants who
enrolled: *33%*
Tuition (general/out of
state): *$26,231*
Tuition (in state): *$10,035*
Room and board: *$9,714*
Freshman retention rate:
78%
Graduation rate (4 yrs.): *36%*
Graduation rate (6 yrs.): *61%*
Courses with fewer than 20
students: *35%*
Student-faculty ratio: *21:1*
Courses taught by graduate
students: *21%*
Students living on campus:
22%
Students in fraternities: *12%*
Students in sororities: *14%*
Students receiving need-
based financial aid: *48%*
Avg. student-loan debt of a
recent graduating class:
$21,247
Most popular majors:
*business/marketing, social
sciences, biology*
Guaranteed housing for 4
years? *no*

Academic Life: Avoid the mirages

The general-education requirements at Arizona are easy to satisfy with courses of uneven quality, which means that a fair number of students will waste their time in overspecialized or politicized classes. The wide choice of courses offered means that students who aren't vigilant could easily get sidetracked by lightweight courses that neither explore the Western tradition nor have any real-world application. New students should carefully read course descriptions, ask trusted upperclassmen for advice, and seek out some of the better faculty members (listed below).

Additional help for students comes from professors, who are eager to work with students if the students will seek them out. "It is easy for students to avoid faculty and advisers or get lost," a professor says. "But those students are never neglected who avail themselves of the opportunities to meet with advisers and faculty." An English professor says that there are "very strong opportunities for students to interact with faculty." Another professor says, "I have an open-door policy and try to have daily interaction with students in my classes and other students in our major."

The Faculty Fellows program has been helping students make the transition from high school and march on to graduation for thirty years. The college says that the Faculty Fellows program brings "all the richness of the school" together, allowing students to "connect with professors, instructors, librarians, and researchers on a personal level that might be overlooked in a university setting." There are currently 27 Faculty Fellows at different locations across campus. The goal, a professor says, is "to be more proactive in achieving faculty accessibility." As the college says, "Faculty Fellows take academics beyond the grade book and help [students] experience education through new avenues, such as hikes, cooking gourmet meals, and attending performances." The university helps Fellows with a small stipend.

Teaching assistants are a large part of the learning environment at Arizona, though the amount depends on the department. "There may be teaching assistants helping me, but I'm in charge and the class is mine," a business professor says. "In my college, we will use TAs in certain classes after they have proved effective in work with a faculty member, and as part of their PhD learning experience." Other departments do not use TAs as instructors, but as at most large schools, the introductory English writing courses required of all students are frequently taught by TAs. "My freshman year almost all my classes had a TA involved in some way, either teaching the class or leading the discussion groups," a liberal arts student told us. "Junior and senior years you see less of them."

According to students, politics intrude into the classroom on a regular basis, especially during election years. "In 2010 I had one professor who was constantly criticizing the Tea Party," says a student. "In 2012 nearly every professor I had made it known that he or she supported Obama."

Departments that shine at Arizona are almost invariably those in the sciences and the business school: optics, astronomy, chemistry, mining and geological engineering, and management information systems. In animal sciences, the equine and race track industry programs are strong, as are the veterinary science and microbiology programs. Agriculture education and Classics also get high marks.

CAMPUS POLITICS: YELLOW LIGHT

New York Times bestselling conservative author and 2010 Arizona graduate Katie Pavlich claims that "standing up for her conservative beliefs would lead to constant arguments with liberal professors," according to an interview in *Red Alert* magazine. The interview sparked many online discussions wherein current conservative Arizona students recounted similar experiences of being intimidated or ridiculed in the classroom by liberal professors.

The College of Social and Behavioral Sciences sponsored an "Immigration Week," including a "mock border wall" across campus that was intended "to interrupt the UA campus community's freedom of movement across the mall in order to dramatize the effects of U.S. immigration and border enforcement policies which dramatically limit access to safe transit across the US/Mexico border," according to the wall's sponsor, the UA student group *No Mas Muertes*.

The English department has an excellent set of requirements for its majors, consisting of six core courses (literary analysis; one survey of American and British literature to 1600 and one from 1600 to 1865; Shakespeare; a junior seminar; and a senior seminar) and six electives.

History majors must take 11 courses, including six classes distributed among at least three different geographical areas. Another course must cover one historical period (anywhere on earth) before 1500, and a senior capstone class is required. Students are given quite a bit of latitude in class choice; for example, both "Colonial America" and "Jews in American Film" fulfill one of the area requirements.

Political science majors must choose to specialize in one of six areas: American politics; ideas and methods; law and public policy; comparative politics; international relations; or foreign affairs. The requirements differ depending on area of specialization, but all students must take at least one class in each of the different areas, as well as six upper-division electives.

Teachers of note include David Soren, Mark Thatcher, Cynthia White, and Richard

Wilkinson (emeritus) in Classics; Roger Dahood, Larry Evers, Robert Houston, and Charles Scruggs in English; Kevin Kemper in journalism; William Schaffer in biology; Don McCarthy in astronomy; Gerald Swanson (emeritus) in economics; Donna Krawczyk in math; Suzanne Delaney in management; and Richard Eaton and Roger Nichols (emeritus) in history.

Studying abroad is very popular among Arizona undergraduates, and the school's busy Study Abroad and Foreign Exchange department "offers hundreds of programs in approximately 60 countries that range from four weeks to ten months," according to its website. Australia, Brazil, Chile, Cuba, Denmark, Germany, Ireland, Japan, Malaysia, Namibia, Russia, Singapore, Turkey, and United Arab Emirates are a few destinations offered in 2013.

At home, students can earn degrees in Chinese, French, German, Italian, Japanese, Latin, and Spanish.

Student Life: Stay on the sunny side

Just as students in the North would rather not have to deal with winter, Arizonans would just as soon skip summer—when Tucson broils and, as a student says, "life comes to a halt." Fortunately, summer sessions are optional. During the rest of the year, the climate is very pleasant. "Southern Arizona is a resort mecca," one professor says. "It's hard to find a more desirable location for a major university." Another says, "If students like sunshine and blue skies, our campus is the right place to be. Very few rainy and gray days seem to make all of us take a brighter view of life."

The campus itself is beautiful, with palm trees spread among a combination of southwestern-style redbrick buildings and more modern structures. There are 23 residence halls, but new entrants should apply for housing as early as possible, as rooms are snapped up quickly. Students are allowed to bring or rent a small fridge for their dorm rooms, and students can also bring their own microwave.

Students at Arizona are free to flourish or flounder. "It is easy for students to avoid faculty and advisers or get lost," a professor says.

Accommodation varies considerably at the University of Arizona. The popular Arizona-Sonora Hall is a double-tower, nine-story high-rise with triple-occupancy rooms that were remodeled a few years ago to include new furniture, bathrooms, and community areas. Many of the rooms at the Colonia de la Paz Hall overlook multiple courtyards, each with its own landscaping. The hall contains single-sex and coed wings, traditional double and single rooms, as well as a lounge and study, meeting, and recreational rooms. Female students might also want to consider Parker House, a hall that houses around 50 women, located near the UA Mall, Greek houses, and the UA Police headquarters. "Dorm life was fun and the facilities are really nice," a student tells us. "I lived in them my first two years and met a lot of great people." Some of the dorms have more of a party atmosphere than others, "but that's easy to avoid if you don't want to get involved," a student says. "The fraternities, on the other hand, are a continual party."

On campus are more than 50 Greek fraternities and sororities, overseen by four major governing councils. "The Greeks at UA are definitely the elite," says a student. "They have a big presence on campus." There are more than 500 student groups at Arizona, encompassing political, ethnic, literary, artistic, and other interests of every kind. Religious groups include Wildcats for Christ, Lutheran Student Fellowship, Alpha and Omega Christian Fellowship, Ambassadors for Christ, Catholic Newman Center Club, as well as the Episcopal Campus Ministry. The Jewish community is served by the Hillel Foundation and a chapter of Alpha Epsilon Phi, a Jewish-interest sorority. Lovers of architecture should visit the thriving San Xavier del Bac, a rococo Spanish mission that still runs as a Catholic parish at a nearby Indian reservation. It is one of the oldest, most beautiful churches in America.

The UA College Republicans are very busy on this liberal campus, holding well-attended weekly meetings as well as biweekly events. Students for Life has also been thriving since 2010, thanks to the persistence of the student members and the help of Foundation for Individual Rights in Education in forcing the administration to reverse course and grant the group official recognition and equal access to the university's resources.

On the literary front there is the *Persona* undergraduate magazine of art and literature and the *Red Ink* magazine covering all aspects of Native American culture. For the more kinetically inclined, there are also various performing arts clubs and jazz, tap, ballroom, hip hop, Latino, and even Mexican folkloric dance clubs. Four martial arts clubs (American Taekwondo Club, Shorin Ryu Karate, Bujinkan Martial Arts Club, and the Capoeira Club) are active on campus, as well as the Kyudo Club for those who want to practice the Japanese art of archery, and Ryuseiken Batto-do for students interested in traditional Japanese sword technique.

The Arizona Wildcats compete in the NCAA Division I and field teams in men's baseball, basketball, cross-country, football, golf, swimming and diving, tennis, and track and field (outdoor), as well as women's basketball, cross-country, golf, gymnastics, soccer, softball, swimming and diving, tennis, track and field (indoor and outdoor), and volleyball. "Sports are a really big deal here," says a student. "The weather is almost always beautiful, and everyone spends a lot of time outdoors." The men's basketball team is consistently one of the best in its division, making it to the NCAA tournament for 25 consecutive years. Baseball is also excellent, as are the men's and women's golf teams.

In light of the school's location in a medium-sized city and the size of its student body, crime is not a major issue at the University of Arizona. However, the school is not

SUGGESTED CORE

1. Classics 342, Homer
2. Philosophy 260, Ancient Philosophy
3. Religion 220A/220B, Literature of the Bible, Old Testament/New Testament
4. Religion 300, Christian Literature and Thought or Philosophy 261, Medieval Philosophy
5. Philosophy 262, Early Modern Philosophy
6. English 231, Shakespeare's Major Plays
7. History 442, History of American Society and Thought: Pre–Civil War
8. History 412a/b, European Intellectual History, 1600–Present/1870–Present

completely safe. In 2011 the school reported three forcible sexual offenses, two arsons, one murder, six stolen cars, and 43 burglaries on campus.

For local students, this school is a bargain. In 2012–13 Arizona resident tuition was a mere $10,035 per academic year, with room and board $9,714, but nonresidents paid $26,231 in tuition. Forty-eight percent of all undergraduates received some form of need-based financial aid, and the average student-loan debt of recent graduates amounted to $21,247.

STRONG SUITS	WEAK POINTS
• Good programs in optics, astronomy, chemistry, mining and geological engineering, agriculture education, Classics, and management information systems.	• Weak general-ed requirements that can be fulfilled with some trite courses.
• In animal sciences, the equine and race track industry programs are strong, as are the veterinary science and microbiology programs.	• It's easy for students to slip through the cracks (only 61 percent graduate in six years).
• Faculty Fellows program encourages teacher involvement with students.	• Many politicized professors, students report.
• Strong requirements for English major.	• History majors can skip the U.S. Founding, Civil War, etc.
• Comfortable, sane dorm life.	

University of Arkansas

Fayetteville, Arkansas • www.uark.edu

A Who's Who of Arkansas

Founded in 1871 by the state legislature as a land-grant college and state university, the University of Arkansas sits on 345 acres overlooking the Ozark Mountains. It was the first southern public institution to racially integrate, in 1948.

Today, the university consists of nine schools and colleges with more than 950 faculty members serving some 23,000 students. The names of various colleges and schools of the university reflect some of the more illustrious persons to have emerged from the state: the Clinton School of Public Service (both Bill Clinton and Hillary Rodham started their careers as faculty members here in the mid-1970s); the Dale Bumpers College of Agricultural, Food, and Life Sciences, for the former governor and U.S. senator; and the Fay Jones School of Architecture, for the famous apprentice of Frank Lloyd Wright. Sen. J. William Fulbright was an alumnus who went on to serve 30 years in the U.S. Senate as well as two years as president of the university. The university's College of Arts and Sciences is named for him. The Sam M. Walton College of Business is named for the Walmart patriarch. The university received a $300 million donation from the Walton Family Charitable Support Foundation in 2002. The funds were used to establish an honors college and create endowments for university libraries and professorships.

Blue Collar Ivy

VITAL STATISTICS

Religious affiliation: *none*

Total enrollment: *24,537*

Total undergraduates: *20,350*

SAT CR/Verbal midrange: *500–610*

SAT Math midrange: *520–630*

ACT midrange: *23–28*

Applicants: *16,749*

Applicants accepted: *63%*

Accepted applicants who enrolled: *27%*

Tuition (general/out of state): *$18,434*

Tuition (in state): *$7,554*

Room and board: *$8,672*

Freshman retention rate: *81%*

Graduation rate (4 yrs.): *35%*

Graduation rate (6 yrs.): *60%*

Courses with fewer than 20 students: *36%*

Student-faculty ratio: *19:1*

Courses taught by graduate students: *22%*

Students living on campus: *33%*

Students in fraternities: *17%*

Students in sororities: *26%*

Students receiving need-based financial aid: *47%*

Avg. student-loan debt of a recent graduating class: *$21,488*

Most popular majors: *business/marketing, social sciences, engineering*

Guaranteed housing for 4 years? *no*

Academic Life: Core knowledge

The University of Arkansas imposes no core curriculum but fairly lax general-education requirements—which can be satisfied from a list of mostly sane-sounding courses.

Professors we interviewed say the university strives to strike a balance between teaching and research. "We pride ourselves as a department and as a college in our strong teaching emphasis. We look seriously at teaching for tenure and promotion," says an English professor. "One cannot be tenured or promoted here on teaching alone, but one can, on occasion, be denied tenure/promotion if teaching is subpar." A professor in the agricultural college says there are "some excellent research efforts" at UA. Most classes have 20–29 students in them, with the average student-teacher ratio at 19–1.

About 22 percent of classes are taught by graduate teaching assistants. One arts and sciences undergrad reports that graduate students have taught most of her lower-level classes, but her professors in general "have been enormously helpful." Furthermore, "Most of my teachers do respond in a timely fashion or are available to speak to outside of class," says a psychological sciences senior. "The only graduate students I have had as teachers are in science labs or foreign language classes. Even in those cases, the graduate students were competent and beloved."

Some students complained about their teachers' accessibility. "Once you get them in a meeting with you, they are great, but they are quick to return to their caves after class, to read, I guess," laments an English major. "This has been the source of much frustration for me."

Teachers and students we spoke with see the strongest departments as history; English; drama; chemistry; physics; engineering; crop, soil, and environmental sciences; food sciences; animal sciences; poultry science; biological engineering; agricultural engineering; horticulture; psychological sciences; and the business college—which has a working replica of the NY Stock Exchange.

We're happy to report that Shakespeare is required of English majors, as are Medieval, Renaissance, and Restoration-period English lit courses.

Others requirements in this department include introduction to philosophy, surveys of world and American literature, African-American and southern literature, as well as literature in postcolonial areas of the world such as the Caribbean.

For history majors, a course in pre-1945 U.S. history is required. Other requirements include a choice from among introductions to African American studies, American studies, classical studies, European studies, international relations, Latin American studies, and Middle East studies. Other options provided to fulfill the upper-level-course requirements cover the history of Christianity, Islamic civilization, women and gender in Latin American history, and women and Christianity. History students also must select three credit hours in each of the following three geographical groups: Europe, including Britain and Russia; Africa, Asia, Latin America, Middle East, and Near East; and the United States. "At the moment, the history department has published more books than any department in the entire university," said a retired professor. Nevertheless, he says, "My erstwhile colleagues place a high premium on teaching." This professor also regards the philosophy department as solid.

"We have a left-leaning faculty and administration (more so in the arts and humanities than in the sciences)," reports an English professor. "In my own department, for example, we are strongly left-wing and teach courses in which gender, class, race, et cetera, are prominently featured. Having said that, however, I would emphasize that most (not all) of my colleagues would not cause a student's political or religious views to affect his/her grade. I wouldn't say that conservative students would feel 'unwelcome' in some classrooms, but in some departments (i.e.,

CAMPUS POLITICS: YELLOW LIGHT

Although the student body seems to be more conservative than those at other universities, administrators and professors tend to be liberal, and instances do occur where politics affect the classroom. "The problems we face as a public university is a nearly complete cultural control exerted by the secularist culture of academia," says a professor. "The secularist influence is deep and pervasive. . . . The culture which pervades the university here as elsewhere employs all aspects of the university to carry out a cultural agenda which is inimical to the foundations of our society."

An undergraduate active in her church near campus notes that Christian professors are "outnumbered." She said some of her professors have "openly mocked God and Jesus and the church." Says a professor: "Usually, the debate allowed is so constrained as to be laughable. Questions may be addressed such as 'How should our society and government mitigate the "problem" of climate change?' Obviously, there are so many assumptions made in the questions addressed that no meaningful discussion is ever intended."

The same approach is taken, he says, when the university asks how to combat "homophobia" on campus. "Where does one enter into this discussion in a meaningful manner?" he asks. "Are all objections to homosexual acts 'homophobia'? Are there some legitimate objections to such acts? I think faculty, staff, and students feel as if any attempts to truly address problems are going to be twisted in such a way as to make a thoughtful, intelligent, and kind person look mean and stupid."

political science, English, perhaps history, certainly sociology) they might feel that they are arguing against a prevailing orthodoxy. . . . In my opinion, we still have freedom of thought here."

A course in American political theory is required of political science majors. No political philosophy courses are required, and few appear to be offered.

Each of the university's colleges participates in the Honors College, which "is pretty rigorous," says a student. "They're good about making sure honors students have plenty of privileges and even their own study lounge, where you can get free printing, sodas, et cetera. The secretary there also cooks and bakes food and sets it out." Recent course offerings for honors students include "Quantum Reality and the Spiritual Quest," "Sacred Bodies, Sacred Spaces," and the "Arvest Fixed Income Securities" course, in which students manage a $5 million bond fund.

Students and teachers spoke of weaknesses in the departments of sociology, social work, communications, political science, math, and journalism, as well as of problems in the school's administration. One retired professor spoke of "a librarian who prides herself on 'clearing the book shelves' and transforming the library into an 'information center,'" for example. "She is an exceptionally pleasant person with no training in library science. She was hired to fill a 'diversity' slot."

> "In English, we are strongly left-wing and teach courses in which gender, class, race, et cetera, are prominently featured," says one professor.

Recommended teachers include Joseph Candido in English; Elliott West and Randall Woods in history; Brenda Zies in psychology; Peter Pulay and Roger Koeppe in chemistry; Laurent Bellaiche in physics; Michael and Jennie Popp in agricultural economics and agribusiness; Nilda Burgos, Paul Counce, and Mary Savin in crop, soil, and environmental sciences; Tom Costello in biological and agricultural engineering; Kevin Hall in civil engineering; and Kris Brye in poultry science.

Though the Ozark Mountains might not seem "cosmopolitan," the University of Arkansas does its best. One student admires the multicultural and international student programs on campus. "We have people here from more countries than you can count," she says. "There are consistently international events happening on campus as well as education about other cultures." At UA, a student can major in French, German, Greek and Latin, and Spanish, and take courses in Arabic, Chinese, Italian, Japanese, Russian, and Swahili.

There are student-exchange programs with universities in Austria, England, France, Japan, Korea, Morocco, and Spain, and study-abroad opportunities in Costa Rica, Ireland, Italy, and Scotland. Architecture students can study building styles in Mexico, and other students can go to Egypt to analyze skeletal material in a city built by Akhenaton. And the UA Classical Studies in Italy program takes students to Italy to compare the "social history, ideology and aesthetic development of art and architecture in classical Rome with its 'rediscovery' in the Renaissance."

Student Life: Easy to break rules

Single freshman under 21 are required to live in university residence halls, fraternity or sorority houses, or with their parents. Of the 18 campus residence halls, only a few are single sex. Halls have various hours for intersex visitation. Aside from the single-sex residence halls, arrangements vary. "In my dorm freshman year, floors were gendered, male, female, male, female, all the way to the top," a female student says. "This year, some floors are half girls, half guys, separated by an elevator bay. I don't think things get any closer than that." A student reports, "Any dorm visitor has to be escorted by someone from that dorm and has to leave by a set time of day specified in that dorm's policies."

A student said the culture of sexual promiscuity seems to be worst in fraternities and sororities. "It seems to me that the Greek system is bent on sex and alcohol and the occasional canned food drive," she says. She speaks of overhearing sorority sisters chatting about the prominent role sex plays in their lives, "and the sex they talk about in no way implies commitment. I know several girls who've gotten abortions, and several guys who've fathered children."

One senior who lived in a dorm during freshman year found that it was too easy for residents to break rules. Residents drank, even though they were underage, and "had boys on our floor at all hours," she reports. "They never got in trouble. Once at three A.M. I was in the bathroom and two drunk guys staggered in. It was terrifying."

But if there is promiscuity on campus, the student health center is there to help. It brings Planned Parenthood to campus for multiple events, such as "Wrap it Up!," a program about contraceptives. One student reports that at one such event, three women who worked in the health center, who were supposed to talk about "safe sex," ended up going on a "rant about pro-lifers and anti-abortion policies."

"On top of that, the health center refuses to pass out anything for our pregnancy center in town (which is upscale and reputable)," this student says. "They have one measly, outdated brochure on adoption, and otherwise refer to Planned Parenthood and have their literature. A past student who was in a sorority told me that when the nurse at the health center came back with her pregnancy test results, she began suggesting abortion places. When the woman suggested that she didn't think she would choose abortion, the nurse tossed prenatal vitamins at her and coldly left the room and didn't come back."

Yet there also seems to be a strong religious presence on campus, with prolific advertising of campus ministry gatherings and churches, a large Campus Crusade for Christ chapter, a highly active chapter of BYX (Brothers Under Christ), and in-house worship nights, where students gather in a private home for music, prayer, and praise. A Christian

SUGGESTED CORE

1. Greek 2013, Homer
2. Philosophy 4003, Ancient Greek Philosophy
3. English 3623, The Bible as Literature
4. Philosophy 4023, Medieval Philosophy
5. Philosophy 4033, Modern Philosophy—17th and 18th Centuries (closest match)
6. English 4303, Introduction to Shakespeare
7. History 4563, The Old South, 1607–1865
8. Philosophy 4043, 19th-Century Continental Philosophy

Blue Collar Ivy

student said the university's campus "fosters a strong Christian community, which is the backbone of social life on campus." Catholic students should seek out the Newman Club, which offers retreats, Bible studies, and weekly and daily Masses.

University sports teams compete nationally in 19 sports. The Razorbacks football team beat Kansas State in the 2012 Cotton Bowl.

There are more than 350 registered student organizations, including Army and Air Force ROTC, College Republicans, the Federalist Society, and Students for Life.

Crime does seem to be a concern at UA. There were 46 burglaries reported on campus in 2011, as well as 16 motor vehicle thefts, five forcible sex offenses, two aggravated assaults, and one robbery. The city of Fayetteville itself has an "aggressive rape percentage far above the nation's average," says one student. "There are plenty of sex offenders living around, too." The school seems to be trying to address the threat of rape, she says, teaching self-defense and setting up a "safe ride" system.

Tuition for native Arkansans was a bargain at $7,554 in 2012–13 (outsiders paid $18,434), and room and board only $8,672. Some 47 percent of students received need-based financial aid, and the average graduate bore a debt of $21,488.

STRONG SUITS	WEAK POINTS
• Heavy emphasis on teaching among faculty, who most students say are accessible.	• Lax general-education requirements let students dabble and flounder.
• Decent research opportunities for students.	• Some majors, like political science, have weak mandates for majors.
• Graduate students who teach are said to be helpful, while some are "beloved."	• Shaky departments of sociology, social work, communications, political science, math, and journalism.
• Rigorous, worthwhile honors program.	• Heavy school emphasis on diversity, sexual activism.
• Good study-abroad and foreign language options.	• Raunchy atmosphere in dorms, especially in the Greek houses.
• Many religious groups active on campus.	• Student health center rabidly pro-choice.
	• Significant crime near campus.

University of California at Berkeley

Berkeley, California • www.berkeley.edu

Barnum and Bailey, Step Aside!

Berkeley's reputation for student activism may have outlived the reality. Here, at the flagship campus of the University of California, student zeal since the 1960s has gradually veered from politics to preprofessionalism—leaving activism to a relatively small cadre of exhibitionists. Those who bump up against the residues of 1960s politics must stay academically focused, be ready to confront bureaucratic obstacles and political proselytizing, and retain a sense of humor. One insider says, "Politically, more students tend to be liberal than conservative, but most are politically apathetic. They're just here to get to their classes and get their degrees." It is not unusual for students to stay five years just to complete their graduation requirements.

Academic Life: Virtuosos and clowns

The College of Letters and Science (L&S) at Berkeley enrolls three-quarters of the school's undergraduate population. It offers more than 80 majors in 80 departments. Instead of a core, students in the college must complete vague distributional requirements. For instance, in arts and literature students can take "Avante-Garde Film" instead of more traditional

VITAL STATISTICS

Religious affiliation: *none*
Total enrollment: *36,142*
Total undergraduates:
    25,885
SAT CR/Verbal midrange:
    600–720
SAT Math midrange:
    650–770
ACT midrange: *26–34*
Applicants: *50,312*
Applicants accepted: *24%*
Accepted applicants who
    enrolled: *41%*
Tuition (general/out of
    state): *$36,802*
Tuition (in state): *$13,204*
Room and board: *$15,000*
Freshman retention rate:
    97%
Graduation rate (4 yrs.): *71%*
Graduation rate (6 yrs.): *90%*
Courses with fewer than 20
    students: *74%*
Student-faculty ratio: *17:1*
Courses taught by graduate
    students: *not provided*
Students living on campus:
    35%
Students in fraternities: *10%*
Students in sororities: *10%*
Students receiving need-
    based financial aid: *67%*
Avg. student-loan debt of a
    recent graduating class:
    $17,116
Most popular majors: *biol-
    ogy, engineering, social
    sciences*
Guaranteed housing for 4
    years? *no*

courses on American or British literature. Hundreds of courses fulfill the requirements in other areas. One professor maintains that "our students still graduate with a fine education," but with such broad requirements, the university does little to ensure it.

One professor says the economics, political science, history, and sociology departments are not politicized, and "in fact, they are among the best in the nation." The economics department promotes a variety of viewpoints. In political science, says one major, "I felt that for the most part, professors were very fair and objective in their presentation of the subject matter." He recommends Dan Schnur for his "incredible insight into both national and California politics."

History majors must take 12 classes, including surveys of American history, European history, any other world region's history, and an elective. Still, history majors could take all their upper-level classes on gender or race. The department is especially helpful for students who wish to pursue intellectual history, such as the history of science.

English majors must take three intensive survey courses in English literature, from Chaucer to the 20th century, an upper-division course in English literature before 1800, one upper-division seminar, and a course on Shakespeare (bravo!).

Poli-sci majors must "complete a total of eight upper-division courses," including one course each in "American Politics," "Comparative Politics," "Empirical Theory and Quantitative Methods," "Political Theory," and "International Relations." Students must also take three of the five introductory courses and one history course. Options include "History of Ancient and Medieval Political Thought" and "Racial and Ethnic Politics in the New American Century."

Students say that among the best professors are A. James Gregor in political science; Ann Swidler in sociology; Richard A. Muller and George F. Smoot (a Nobel laureate who still teaches undergraduates) in physics; Thomas Brady and David Hollinger in history; Ronald S. Stroud in Classics; David J. Vogel in business; and John R. Searle in philosophy. One student calls Searle her favorite professor: "He's a major influence on artificial intelligence/cognitive science and the closest thing to a conservative at Berkeley."

Classes are large but are mostly taught by professors. Weekly discussion sections, on the other hand, are led by graduate students—a typical arrangement at large universities. According to students, professors are available for meetings outside class. "If you take advantage of office hours, professors and graduate student instructors (GSIs) are very accessible. I got closest with my GSIs (mostly because they actually graded my work), and they were more than happy to write recommendation letters on my behalf if I asked them."

The university does not assign teachers to advise students before they have declared their majors. Instead, students consult the Office of Undergraduate Advising, staffed by professional advisers. Once a student has declared a major, he can visit an adviser within it, but even here the student does not have a specific faculty member to whom he is accountable.

Berkeley does sponsor an honors program, which according to one undergrad is "intense and basically only for those students who are highly motivated to do research." Professors will "individually mentor undergraduates as they write original theses over the school year."

The gender and women's studies department includes the usual dismal offerings: "Geographies of Race and Gender," "Transnational Feminisms," "Identities across Difference," "Alternate Sexualities in a Transnational World," and "Cultural Representations of Sexualities: Queer Literary Culture." One student cheerfully describes the department as "abominable."

Berkeley offers majors in French, German, Scandinavian languages, Slavic languages and literatures, and Spanish and Portuguese. Minors include French, German, and Spanish and Portuguese.

CAMPUS POLITICS: YELLOW LIGHT

The Berkeley political circus is not as scary as it looks. Here is one student's experience: "In my first semester at Cal, my psychology professor wanted to assure us that we would be safe in any campus psych experiments, and so she stated that, for example, we wouldn't go to an abortion clinic because there might be protestors who would throw rocks. I'm still not sure why she brought this up, but after class I talked to her about it and expressed my astonishment at such slander. She ended up retracting her comments and apologizing in the next class. Keep in mind that this class was held in Wheeler Auditorium, the largest lecture hall, and probably contained 600 to 700 people. I've found other professors to behave similarly. They might make extremely liberal remarks, but when called out on it, they are reasonable enough to take it back. This occurred especially when I took the class 'Mind, Language, and Politics' from Professor George Lakoff. He would state that conservatives simply don't care, they use fear to convince others, et cetera. But he welcomed an opposing opinion in the discussion-based classroom and even wrote me a letter of recommendation."

Surprisingly, amid the leftist organizations, Berkeley maintains a thriving and successful ROTC program, and the CIA and Department of Defense recruit from Berkeley during campus career fairs.

Still, conservative Berkeley students should expect some slings and arrows from the administration. In 2011 the chancellor of the university responded to the rampage of mentally unbalanced shooter Jared Loughner by blaming the killing on . . . opponents of illegal immigration.

Berkeley's Education Abroad Program offers semester-long, yearlong, and summer trips to more than 40 different countries.

Student Life: Conservatives push back

For those new to the Bay Area, a captivating escape beckons. Those "hills" rising up behind campus are really mountains, which lead into something nearly approaching high wilderness at the almost-2,000-foot summit. UC–Berkeley is not primarily a residential campus; it is mostly only freshmen who live in the university dorms. As at most large, urban universities, students usually move off campus into theme houses, Greek houses, or rental properties after their freshman year. Most residences are coed, but the university does have one all-female dorm and one all-male dorm. In many dorms, halls and even bathrooms are coed. There are no intervisitation restrictions to speak of. Theme houses are university-owned facilities in which students with common interests live together. For instance, a student can choose to live in the African American house; the gay, lesbian, bisexual, and transgender house; or the women in engineering and science house.

> Despite its radical reputation, UC Berkeley has many worthy programs and fewer bomb throwers nowadays than many other schools.

The student-run paper, the *Daily Californian*, covers news well, but compared to other university dailies, it sometimes lacks substance. Other publications available on campus include the *Socialist Worker* and the *California Patriot*, a monthly conservative magazine that has garnered national attention for its assessments of Berkeley's hard left.

According to Berkeley's catalog, the Center for Student Leadership recognizes more than 1,500 student organizations, "including fraternities and sororities and a variety of organizations that focus on the arts, academics, culture, politics, professions, publications, religion, sports, service and social issues."

Since Berkeley offers relatively low in-state tuition and reserves spots for California residents ("documented" or not) and squeezes outsiders, a large proportion of students (73 percent) come from that state. This means that Berkeley has a more parochial student body than do some other prestigious public universities.

Because classes are not often scheduled on Fridays, weekends at UC–Berkeley traditionally begin on Thursday evenings. Besides the dozens of bars and clubs in Berkeley, the school is also home to more than 60 Greek organizations, to which about 10 percent of undergraduates belong.

Religious life at UC–Berkeley is, to say the least, varied. In addition to various standard Christian, Jewish, Muslim, Buddhist, and Hindu groups, there are such distinctive organizations as Progressive Students of Faith, Network of Spiritual Progressives, and Students for a Nonreligious Ethos. The Catholic Newman Club is guided by the Paulists, and its chapel and liturgies are ultra-modern. It does host pro-life, devotional, and discussion events. The Orthodox Christian Fellowship offers a gateway to many ethnic parishes in the Bay Area. For Episcopalians, there is a standard Canterbury Group. More conservative Anglicans should attend the Chapel of Saint Joseph of Arimathea on Durant Street.

Berkeley fields 27 varsity athletic teams in the PAC-10 Conference. The Golden Bears maintain a heated rivalry with Stanford. The school also has a number of intramural offerings, with nine club sports and excellent facilities to accommodate them.

Berkeley is consistently among the top five universities in arrests for alcohol, drugs, and weapons. Crime statistics for 2011 show 14 motor vehicle thefts, nine robberies, seven assaults, 30 forcible sex offenses, 40 burglaries, and six cases of arson—all on campus. The university is so intermingled with the city of Berkeley that it is hard to insulate students from urban pathologies (or the city from pathological students). Crime is a problem on and off campus, although the university has tried to curb it with self-defense workshops, night escort services and shuttles, and round-the-clock patrols.

Berkeley is no longer quite the bargain it used to be, with 2012–13 tuition and fees for in-state students and illegal immigrants at $13,204 and expected to rise steeply. Americans from other states paid $36,802. Room and board were estimated by the school to be $15,000. Some 67 percent of students received need-based financial aid, and the average loan burden of a recent grad was a modest $17,116.

SUGGESTED CORE

1. Classics 10A, Intro Greek Civilization
2. Philosophy 25A, Ancient Philosophy
3. Religious Studies C119, The English Bible as Literature
4. History 275B, The Middle Ages
5. Political Science 112B, History of Political Theory
6. English 117B, Shakespeare
7. History 7A, The United States from Settlement to Civil War
8. History 164B, European Intellectual History from the Enlightenment to 1870

STRONG SUITS

- Good programs in economics, political science, history, and sociology.
- An intense, worthwhile honors program.
- Solid, foundational requirements in English, history, and political science.
- A huge array of student groups, including several conservative and many religious clubs.

WEAK POINTS

- Very weak general-ed requirements.
- A significant minority of students and faculty who are leftist activists, in and out of class.
- Coed bathrooms and even dorm rooms.
- Heavy crime around and even on campus.

University of California at Los Angeles

Los Angeles, California • www.ucla.edu

The Multi Cult

UCLA is often considered the most multicultural university in the country, and it's indeed delightful that the school has an ethnically diverse student body. What troubles us is its proliferation of ethnic studies programs, courses fixated on race, and segregated graduation ceremonies. UCLA is a highly polished, shattered mirror of postmodern American culture. But one of the mirror fragments—the heritage of Western thought—has recently been retrieved from the trash and polished up, becoming a focal point for a lively coterie of motivated students and faculty. It is treated mostly with the same tolerance and respect accorded the other cultural shards. In other words, conservative students at UCLA are now considered a minority deserving tolerance. Given the situation at many other schools, this is nothing to sneer at.

Academic Life: San Andreas faults

UCLA offers five undergraduate programs: the College of Letters and Science; the Henry Samueli School of Engineering and Applied Science; the School of the Arts and Architecture; the School of Nursing; and the School of Theater, Film, and Television. Letters and

Science is by far the largest of these. UCLA is on a quarter calendar (except for the law school), so students graduate having taken more (and shorter) courses than the typical college student. It is not always clear that this is a good thing.

The quality of a UCLA education depends heavily on the motivation and choices of the student. "I didn't want to take a philosophy class," admits a recent grad, "so I took one on Egyptian religion." Those seeking to avoid science can enroll in classes on "earthquakes, air pollution, dinosaurs, and astronomy." Still, one alum says that a course he took to meet the "literary cultural analysis" requirement for general education inadvertently introduced him to the subject that became his major, Classics. Says another pleased student, "It's a great school because if you're not sure of your major, there are a lot of options." On the other hand, "academic counseling is especially weak. I've been to the office five or six times and never really found the person who could tell me what I needed to know."

On a very hopeful note, law professor Daniel Lowenstein directs the Center for the Liberal Arts and Free Institutions. One of its purposes is to "assist and encourage students, faculty, and others to confront basic questions of the meaning of life, the nature of the cosmos and of human society, and the principles of right and wrong." It now offers courses including "Lincoln in His Own Words," "American Political Thought," "European Political Thought," "Introduction to Samuel Johnson," and "Justice and Public Responsibility in Literature." Taught by Lowenstein and Andrew Sabl, the offerings encourage "critical reading and writing," says a student. Sabl, furthermore, "could not have been better at bringing about balance in student discussion." Another student praises the one-unit "Fiat Lux" courses, one of which, she says, "ties Greek culture to American history." We highly recommend that all UCLA freshmen explore the center's offerings.

Some of the better teachers at UCLA include Sebastian Edwards in economics; Michael Allen, Edward Condren (emeritus), and Debora K. Shuger in English; Martie Haselton in psychology; Daniel Lowenstein (emeritus) in law; Ruth Bloch, Patrick Geary, Carlo Ginzburg (emeritus), and Richard Rouse (emeritus) in history; and Timothy Groseclose and Marc Trachtenberg in

VITAL STATISTICS

Religious affiliation: *none*
Total enrollment: *39,271*
Total undergraduates: *27,199*
SAT CR/Verbal midrange: *560–710*
SAT Math midrange: *610–740*
ACT midrange: *25–31*
Applicants: *72,000*
Applicants accepted: *25%*
Accepted applicants who enrolled: *35%*
Tuition (general/out of state): *$35,570*
Tuition (in state): *$12,692*
Room and board: *$14,232*
Freshman retention rate: *97%*
Graduation rate (4 yrs.): *68%*
Graduation rate (6 yrs.): *90%*
Courses with fewer than 20 students: *51%*
Student-faculty ratio: *15:1*
Courses taught by graduate students: *not provided*
Students living on campus: *45%*
Students in fraternities: *13%*
Students in sororities: *13%*
Students receiving need-based financial aid: *56%*
Avg. student-loan debt of a recent graduating class: *$18,814*
Most popular majors: *economics, psychology, history*
Guaranteed housing for 4 years? *no*

California

CAMPUS POLITICS: YELLOW LIGHT

It is sadly true that races and ethnicities at UCLA tend to segregate themselves, with the school's encouragement. UCLA even sponsors segregated graduation ceremonies. "Lavender Graduation" is a commencement ceremony for gay, lesbian, bisexual, and transgender students. "La Raza Graduation" is sponsored by MEChA, a Mexican racial-nationalist group with the motto "For the race, everything. Against the race, nothing." In its "Plan Espiritual de Aztlán," MEChA declares:

> In the spirit of a new people that is conscious not only of its proud historical heritage but also of the brutal "gringo" invasion of our territories, we, the Chicano inhabitants and civilizers of the northern land of Aztlán from whence came our forefathers, reclaiming the land of their birth and consecrating the determination of our people of the sun, declare that the call of our blood is our power, our responsibility, and our inevitable destiny.

In case you were wondering, this manifesto was not in fact translated directly from German in the 1930s.

In 2012 *Campus Reform* discovered that MEChA had received $100,000 in funding from UCLA in the previous academic year. It seems that the university relies on MEChA—whose goals include the annexation of the American Southwest by Mexico—to "support retention," by reaching out to students with low GPAs or who are "subject to dismissal."

political science. Trachtenberg has the largest fan club: "He is incredible—very rational, very balanced, very accessible, infectiously excited about his subject, and a true academic," says one student. "He is one of the founders of the Historical Society, an organization set up to counter the postmodern orthodoxy of the American Historical Association," says another.

The biology, chemistry, and economics departments are among the university's strongest, and the philosophy department is one of the best in the nation. Philosophy majors take 13 courses in the department, including three basic courses in Greek philosophy, medieval and early modern philosophy, and modern philosophy, plus seven other courses divided among the history of philosophy, logic and semantics, ethics and value theory, and metaphysics and epistemology. Students say Brian Copenhaver, Pamela Hieronymi, and Gavin Lawrence are particularly good in this department.

UCLA's Department of Film, Television, and Digital Media is considered the best in the country. It is also the most competitive. Those who gain admittance into the junior/senior program can take courses like "History of American Motion Picture," "Introduction to Animation," "Advanced Film and Television Producing Workshop for Producers, Writers, and Directors," "Intermediate Cinematography," and "Film Editing: Overview of History, Techniques, and Practice." This program is considered the front door for a career in the motion picture industry.

UCLA offers 125 majors in its five undergraduate schools, and many students choose to double major or earn minors. For students interested in research as undergraduates, UCLA is an excellent choice. The Student Research Program offers 90 slots each quarter in a wide range of projects. In addition to the experience, such research "is a good way to create close, long-lasting relationships with professors," a student says. The Undergraduate Research Center also supports student research in the humanities and social sciences every year.

Alarmingly, some of the larger lecture classes at UCLA enroll as many as 400 students. "In a class such as that, the one way to form a real relationship is to go to the professor's office hours and make yourself known by participating and asking questions," a student says. "It is not impossible to make an impression on a professor in a class of that size—it just requires some effort." Typically, professors teach larger courses and have graduate teaching assistants lead weekly discussion sections.

The university's advising program varies from department to department. The College of Letters and Science offers peer advising with "trained undergraduates." Once a student has declared a major, he can visit a faculty or staff adviser in that department. The Classics department, for instance, has one faculty member and one staff member to answer the questions of all the students majoring in the subject. There are also extra advising resources for athletes, honors students, and first-generation college students. Still, students we contacted described the school's advising resources as quite ineffective.

A far-from-atypical UCLA professor boasts in the course catalog that "issues of politics, religion, race, ethnicity, gender, and sexuality provide an overall framework of analysis in almost all my courses." Keep in mind that this is a *Classics* professor.

With smaller class sizes and distinguished faculty members, the university's Honors Collegium sounds promising at first hearing. But (with some exceptions, like those noted above in the new liberal education center) most of the seminars offered in the program focus on nonfoundational topics, with titles such as "Comparative Odysseys," "Practice and Ethics of Ethnographic Fieldwork," and "Secret Coups, Imperial Wars, and American Democracy since World War II." While the program gives freshmen the chance to get to know their professors and fellow students well, the price of participation is often a willingness to endure the program's dreary, heavy-handed ideological agenda.

UCLA has many ethnic studies departments: Afro-American studies; American Indian studies; Asian American studies; Chicana and Chicano studies; Islamic studies; Latin American Studies; and lesbian, gay, bisexual, and transgender studies. Many of these departments are politicized, mediocre, or both. But then you probably suspected that.

Even the more traditional departments have been colored by leftist politics. A Classics professor proudly proclaims in the course catalog that "issues of politics, religion, race, ethnicity, gender, and sexuality provide an overall framework of analysis in almost all my courses."

The political science department is also replete with ethnic offerings and does not seem to demand of majors a course in American constitutional theory. The history department is less trendy, it seems, but lacks a requirement that majors study 19th-century American

Blue Collar Ivy

history. Of key departments, English seems to have the most stringent major requirements, including two courses in Shakespeare, not to mention courses in Chaucer and Milton, and it seems to demand coverage in many periods.

UCLA has adopted what many multicult activists at the school have dreamed of for years—a diversity requirement for all undergrads.

Surprisingly, conservatives at UCLA seem fairly content. The "Academian Nut" section of the *Bruin Standard* (a conservative student publication) has made a habit of reporting on classroom abuses of conservatives. Aware that their off-topic comments might make their way into the campus spotlight, more politicized professors have been exercising self-restraint, students say. A writer for the paper says, "There's a little more pressure on them to stick to the subject." One conservative student avows, "I've been pretty impressed with how open others are. I have several liberal friends who are very supportive of the fact that I'm in the Bruin Republicans."

The best part of UCLA's emphasis on multiculturalism can be seen in its admirable foreign language offerings, which range from Arabic to Zulu, and include such hard-to-find tongues of interest to scholars as Catalan, Latin (Medieval, as well as Classical), and Venetic.

Not surprisingly, UCLA's study-abroad program is strong, with 250 programs in 35 countries, ranging from Argentina to Australia, Brazil to China, and Germany to Ghana. Students pay UCLA prices and earn UCLA credit while hitting the books in Paris or Rio.

Student Life: Off to see the wizard

Residential life at UCLA is mainly for freshmen. About 94 percent of all freshmen choose to live on campus, compared to only 45 percent of total undergraduates. The university guarantees housing for three years, provided students apply by the deadline. The university provides apartment and house-share listings and a roommate matching service, and maintains seven off-campus apartment buildings so students won't be left out in the warm. If a student does live on campus, he will find himself in one of four high-rise dormitories, in one of two buildings with residential suites, or (best of all) in one of two village-type apartment complexes. All on-campus dormitories are coed, but some have sex-segregated floors. Bathrooms are all single sex. There are no visitation restrictions. Writes one student: "I love the campus. West Coast weather with the East Coast Ivy League look. They plant flowers that smell nice. Little Chinese courtyards that you can rest and do homework in. Lots of little finds in buildings. They have strict rules about posting flyers, so that keeps things looking nice. There are no trash cans overflowing." One recent grad "loved" UCLA partly because of the "college-town feel" of Westwood, with its large old theaters like the Fox where big Hollywood premieres are held. Movie stars can sometimes be glimpsed flitting by.

Students say that alcohol is prevalent on and off campus but that drug use is not very popular or conspicuous. UCLA Housing has a zero-tolerance policy for drugs, but students are often seen drinking alcohol at campus parties. Off-campus fraternities and sororities have been steadily growing in popularity, and Fraternity Row swarms with parties, especially on Thursday nights. Besides the Greek system (to which 13 percent of students belong), other popular student organizations include community-service groups; activist and political groups such as CALPIRG (an environmental group that sponsors river and beach cleanups); groups devoted to voter registration and inner-city tutoring; and various campus media outlets. UCLA helps fund several ethnically oriented magazines, including *Al-Talib* (a Muslim paper); *Ha'Am* (Jewish); *La Gente* (Hispanic and Native American); *Nommo* (African); *Pacific Ties* (Asian); and *OutWrite* (gay, lesbian, transsexual, and transgender).

Maintaining muscle tone is as important to most UCLA students as is having a healthy tan. Athletics at UCLA are consequently very popular. In addition to 22 varsity teams (and a whopping 108 combined NCAA national titles, the most in the country), UCLA offers many opportunities for club and intramural sports. It has been three decades since the "Wizard of Westwood," John Wooden, held the reins of UCLA's men's basketball team and led them to win 10 NCAA titles. Since he retired, the team has managed to win only one—not good enough for the Bruins' fans. But coach Ben Howland took the team to consecutive Final Fours in 2006, 2007, and 2008, raising fans' hopes (and expectations) accordingly. Among fond UCLA traditions are football's Blue and Gold Week—complete with bonfire, concerts, and dancing; the midnight yell every night during finals week; and the "undie run" at midnight on Wednesday of finals week.

SUGGESTED CORE

1. Classics 142, Ancient Epic
2. Philosophy 100A, History of Greek Philosophy
3. English 111A/111B, Hebrew Bible in Translation/ Christian Biblical Texts in Translation
4. History 1B, Introduction to Western Civilization: Circa AD 843 to Circa 1715
5. Political Science 111B, Early Modern Political Theory from Hobbes to Bentham
6. English 90, Shakespeare
7. History 13A, History of the U.S. and Its Colonial Origins: Colonial Origins and First Nation Building Acts
8. History 122E, Cultural and Intellectual History of Modern Europe, 19th Century

Campus activism usually centers on the issues of race and ethnicity. UCLA can often seem like a haven for malcontents, with protests each week, chalked messages such as "Free Palestine" and "Living Wage Now" all over campus, and leftist student groups holding meetings nearly every night of the week. Although only a relatively small contingent of students actually stages these events, they do enjoy some official sanction and prestige.

Conservative students can try to stop them by joining the Bruin Republicans, whose membership numbers in the hundreds on this very liberal campus, where Democrats outnumber Republicans 15 to 1 in the faculty. The Bruin Republicans maintain an extremely lively schedule, with social events and guerilla theater—such as the "Affirmative-Action Bake Sale." The group also conducts outreach to local high school students and a wide variety of other activities.

Bruins seem divided—"about 50/50 between libertarians and traditionalists," says one insider, "so debate within the group is vigorous. And since we don't even agree on the issue, we can't even face off against the Bruin Democrats on abortion." Other right-leaning groups at UCLA include Bruins for Israel (said to be "huge") and Live Action (a pro-life group whose feisty past president Lila Rose appears on Fox News regularly).

The chaplaincy at UCLA offers clerics of every major faith, although not all these clergy appear to hew to the traditional morals of their respective faiths. For instance, the

University Catholic Chapel offers such attractions as Cornerstone, the LGBT (lesbian, gay, bisexual, transgendered) group. Devout students at UCLA might do well to find a conservative congregation somewhere outside the campus boundaries. Fortunately (especially for those with cars), there is a cornucopia of choices.

Crime on campus is becoming more of a concern, especially because of an increase in sex offenses. In 2011 the school reported two robberies, 118 burglaries, seven stolen cars, eight forcible sex offenses, and four aggravated assaults on campus.

Despite recent state budget hemorrhages, UCLA remains a pretty good bargain for students from California. In 2012–13 tuition for California residents and illegal immigrants was $12,692, compared to $35,570 for Americans from out of state. Room and board were $14,232. The school offers a dizzying array of scholarships, work-study programs, loans, and grants—and some 56 percent of students received need-based aid. The average loan burden of a recent grad was $18,814.

STRONG SUITS	WEAK POINTS
• The Center for the Liberal Arts and Free Institutions offers courses that provide a traditional humane education to those who seek it.	• Weak general-education requirements can often be knocked off with frivolous or ideological classes.
• The biology, chemistry, and economics departments are good, and the philosophy department is one of the best in the nation.	• Some enormous (400+) classes, where most interaction is with grad students.
• The Department of Film, Television, and Digital Media is the most famous such program on earth—and opens the doors to careers in media.	• Many politicized departments, including the various ethnic and sex-based studies majors, but also political science and history.
• Conservative groups, even pro-life pioneers, feel comfortable pushing back against the regnant leftism.	• Nearly continuous campus protests by a motley array of outraged activists.
	• Lots of drunken parties and significant campus crime.

University of California at Santa Barbara

Santa Barbara, California • www.ucsb.edu

Surf's Up

What is today the University of California at Santa Barbara (UCSB) was founded in 1909. Twice in the past decade, UCSB has been named one of *Newsweek*'s "twelve hottest American colleges." Five Nobel laureates and dozens of Fulbright and Guggenheim fellows on faculty attract such attention; so do 12 national state-of-the-art research centers. It also helps that students and teachers don't waste much of their time on radical politics. The school isn't near the beach; it's *on* the beach. (The university includes a weather report on its homepage.)

Academic Life: Science more than letters

Most of the almost 19,000 undergraduates at UCSB are attracted to the school's science-centered programs and the chance to participate in top-flight research, but Santa Barbara also has some good liberal arts departments. Although the university has no core curriculum, there are many substantial courses available that can help students gain a solid liberal arts foundation if they choose wisely.

    UCSB is known as a research institution, and its strengths accordingly lie in the

Blue Collar Ivy

VITAL STATISTICS

Religious affiliation: *none*
Total enrollment: *21,685*
Total undergraduates:
  18,620
SAT CR/Verbal midrange:
  550–670
SAT Math midrange:
  560–690
ACT midrange: *24–30*
Applicants: *55,249*
Applicants accepted: *45%*
Accepted applicants who
  enrolled: *17%*
Tuition (general/out of
  state): *$36,549*
Tuition (in state): *$13,671*
Room and board: *$13,275*
Freshman retention rate: *91%*
Graduation rate (4 yrs.): *67%*
Graduation rate (6 yrs.): *86%*
Courses with fewer than 20
  students: *47%*
Student-faculty ratio: *18:1*
Courses taught by graduate
  students: *not provided*
Students living on campus:
  33%
Students in fraternities: *8%*
Students in sororities: *13%*
Students receiving need-
  based financial aid: *55%*
Avg. student-loan debt of a
  recent graduating class:
  $18,627
Most popular majors:
  *business/marketing,
  communications, social
  sciences*
Guaranteed housing for 4
  years? *yes*

sciences. Several departments are among the best in the nation, especially physics, where four members of the physics faculty have won Nobel Prizes. More than 20 percent of undergraduates (including freshmen) participate in some form of research, and there are abundant opportunities—not just in the hard sciences but in the humanities and social sciences too—for those who seek them.

The humanities departments are excellent as well. Highly recommended professors are Apostolos Athanassakis, Robert Morstein-Marx, Robert Renehan, and Jo-Ann Shelton in Classics; Harold Drake in history; Christine Thomas in religious studies; and C. Anthony Anderson, Anthony Brueckner, and Matthew Hanser in philosophy.

Apart from instructors, students have plenty of other academic resources available. The UCSB Libraries are major research facilities with three million books and bound journals, and more than 500,000 sound recordings.

There are only a few politicized distractions in the curriculum—men in lab coats tend not to put up with them. "Strange and bizarre courses are very few, since UCSB mainly focuses on the hard sciences," says a student. For the most part, students can express their views without fear of reprisal. According to one student, because Santa Barbara is "predominantly a hard science school, there is a communal belief that everything has to test for validity, no matter who says it." But the few distractions, when they do occur, are glaringly obvious. The black and Chicano studies departments get most of their business by helping students fulfill a particular general-education requirement.

The film studies department is considered by some to be the best in the country and was given a big financial boost when alumnus Michael Douglas donated $1 million to the Carsey-Wolf Center for Film, Television, and New Media.

The Department of Religious Studies "is one of the major centers in North America for the study of religions," the school reports. It takes pride in having once employed the famed post-Christian theologian Paul Tillich. The department "houses the prestigious Capps Center for the Study of Ethics, Religion, and Public Life; maintains close ties with the Center for Middle Eastern Studies, [and] boasts several endowed chairs located within it—the XIV Dalai Lama Chair in Tibetan Studies, the Virgil Cordano Chair in Catholic Studies, and the Tipton Distinguished Visiting Chair in Catholic Studies." It's probably a good sign that a fair number of professors in the religious studies department earned degrees at the University of Chicago; several philosophy professors come from UCLA; and classical studies tends to hire from Berkeley and Harvard.

The English department's major requirements are excellent: "Introduction to Shakespeare," "Introduction to Literary Study," "English Literature from the Medieval Period to 1650," "English and American Literature from 1650 to 1789," and either two American literature classes covering 1789 to 1900 and 1900 to the present or two British literature classes covering 1789 to 1900 and 1900 to the present.

History majors are required to take two classes each in Western civilization, American history, and European history; one course in Asian, African, Latin American, or Middle Eastern history; and an additional class from any historical field.

The political science department insists that majors concentrate in one of four areas: American politics, comparative politics, international relations, or political theory. Half of all major classes must be from the selected concentration, and the remaining half from the other three areas. All majors are required to take at least one class on the U.S. Constitution and American political theory.

CAMPUS POLITICS: GREEN LIGHT

UCSB students think of their campus as politically inactive. "We tend not to get into political arguments with the general population, but rather find an intense debate among those involved in Associated Students [student government] or the campus administration," one says. "Our research comes first." The editorial pages of the student newspaper, the *Daily Nexus*, are mostly without the incendiary comments found at other schools, although the paper does engage in political issues by endorsing or opposing propositions from the state and commenting regularly on local Isla Vista news and events.

The student body's political apathy, however, doesn't stop the administration from attempting to discriminate against conservatives. In October 2011 the UCSB student government denied reimbursement to the College Republicans for the speaker's fee for conservative author David Horowitz, evidently because he stated the obvious fact that left-wing ideologues and Muslim extremists are infiltrating college classrooms. Once the Foundation for Individual Rights in Education (FIRE) became legally involved on the club's behalf, UCSB officials backed down and grudgingly acknowledged their "legal duty to provide equal funding for speakers regardless of their views," said FIRE's Adam Kissel.

For a student who knows what he would like to study and what courses to take to get there, the College of Creative Studies, dubbed "the graduate school for undergraduates," is an interesting alternative. With approximately 300 students, "the creative studies major is for talented students who are committed to advanced and independent work in one of the disciplines represented in the college," according to the catalog.

There is also an undergraduate College Honors Program, which earns a student a

Blue Collar Ivy

diploma with distinction as long as he maintains a B average. Some of the courses are graduate level, while some undergraduate courses may count for honors credit if students attend honors discussion groups. Honors students have access to the graduate student library, an honors study center, priority registration, special academic awards, field trips and research lectures, and a mentorship program that pairs honors upperclassmen with freshmen.

Students outside the honors program say the best advice comes from faculty advisers in their majors. Although there is a general-education advising office on the campus, "They can sometimes be helpful," a student warns, "but they don't always know the whole story. The professors have a better grasp."

Once in class, students can generally expect to find professors (in the upper-level courses) or lecturers (in the lower-level ones) doing their own teaching. Graduate teaching assistants handle some discussion sections and the grading in larger, lower-level courses. Class sizes for some general-education courses can range from 200 to 800. The average class size in lower-division classes is 52. Upper-division courses average 36 students. The overall student-faculty ratio is 18 to 1.

Despite the large classes, students are impressed with the faculty. They report that their professors are outstanding teachers and mentors with proven track records. "My professors have been the most important part of my education here and have encouraged me, guided me, taught me, and trained me," says one student. Another

S ince this is "predominantly a hard science school, there is a communal belief that everything has to test for validity, no matter who says it."

student calls her professors "amazing and helpful."

UCSB's Education Abroad Program hosts overseas programs in countries such as Argentina, Australia, Austria, Barbados, Brazil, Chile, China, Costa Rica, Czech Republic, Denmark, Egypt, England, France, Germany, Hong Kong, India, Ireland, Italy, Japan, Netherlands, New Zealand, Russia, South Africa, Spain, Tanzania, and Turkey. The UC system also hosts reciprocal programs in "over 100 institutions in approximately 30 countries," according to the school website.

At home, foreign language classes are offered in Arabic, Basque, Catalan, Chinese, Coptic, French, Galician, German, Greek, Hebrew, Hindi, Italian, Japanese, Korean, Latin, Portuguese, Russian, Sanskrit, Spanish, Syriac, Targumic Aramaic, Tibetan, and Yiddish.

Student Life: Sects on the beach

UCSB's buildings are arrayed above the Pacific Ocean on a spectacular point of land that also encompasses a lovely lagoon and includes four beaches with a view of the Santa Ynez Mountains. The university has completed the West Coast feel with a collection of "California modern" buildings of terra-cotta roofs set among lush greenery. "I find the buildings here express a certain exuberance and positive outlook that California had before the Vietnam War," a student says.

But you may not be able to live there. Only freshmen are guaranteed housing on campus. They live in standard dorm rooms and suites. All dorm floors are coed, and while the university offers special-interest floors (including floors dedicated to specific ethnic groups), not many students opt for them. There are no coed bathrooms or coed dorm rooms. Students of age can drink in the dorms but cannot do so in public or in a dorm room with more than five people present. A code of conduct for the dorms, including restrictions on overnight guests from off campus, is said to be strictly enforced. Upperclassmen may live off campus in university-owned apartments or they can rent from private owners in the community of Isla Vista—at most a five-minute walk to campus. About 67 percent of students live in private housing. Rental prices are steep (an average of $2,700 per month for a three-bedroom place), and many available apartments are complete dives, according to several stories in the campus newspaper, the *Daily Nexus*.

Hispanics comprise the largest minority group on campus, making up 24 percent of the student body. Some 16 percent are Asian, and 4 percent are black.

Associated Students (AS) distributes funding to almost 500 groups registered with the Office of Student Life. These organizations range from the conventional to the absurd—the Anime Club, the Black Quare, the Zen Sitting Group, Brothas from Otha Mothas (BFOM), and Students Stopping Rape all receive UCSB funds. Student government provides a number of other services, including a campus radio station, a magazine, a faculty and staff newspaper, a number of service committees, and a bike shop where students can borrow tools. The College Republicans claim some 300 members. The university has a handful of decidedly niche organizations, such as the Laughology, and multiple ethnic and multicultural clubs, but more clubs fall under the heading of "recreation" than any other category. The place is, after all, on the beach.

Greek life is rather sober, as "all Greek-lettered organizations are required to have alcohol-free social events," according to the university. Moreover, "hazing is absolutely forbidden."

St. Mark's Catholic Community is renowned for "innovative" liturgies and its mural of the "Cosmic Christ." The Episcopal Campus Ministry's motto is "Absolute faith is not a requirement at Saint Michael's. An open heart is." But Santa Barbara itself offers churches of all stripes. There are a great number of more or less solid religious groups on campus, ranging from InterVarsity Christian Fellowship (an evangelical organization), Hillel, the Islamic Peace Fellowship, the Orthodox Christian Fellowship, Sun Lotus (Nichiren Buddhists at UCSB), and the University Christian Fellowship.

More than 80 percent of students participate in UCSB's more than 700 intramural

SUGGESTED CORE

1. Classics 36, Ancient Epic
2. Philosophy 20A, History of Philosophy: From Thales to Aristotle
3. Religious Studies 115A/116A, Literature and Religion of the Hebrew Bible/The New Testament and Early Christianity
4. Philosophy 20B, History of Philosophy: Medievals to Rationalism
5. Political Science 188, Modern Political Theory
6. English 105B, Shakespeare: Later Plays
7. History 17A, The American People (Colonial through Jacksonian Era)
8. History 4C, Western Civilization (1714 CE to Present)

California

Blue Collar Ivy

and club sports, including equestrian polo, surfing, alpine racing, tennis, and squash. The school's athletic teams (the Gauchos) are quite active in the NCAA Big West Conference in 10 men's and 10 women's sports.

Isla Vista is a congested area with about 23,000 people living in 1.5 square miles; it is said to have the highest population density in California. A few years ago, the area was known as a continual party, with kegs of beer regularly "rolling up on skateboards," according to a student. The neighborhood still tends toward excess, and it is less safe than the campus itself, but police departments are becoming more involved in the community, and it's not the free-for-all it once was. The *Daily Nexus* contains a weekly police report, which recounts fairly regular instances of arrest for intoxication, inhalation, and aggression.

On-campus crime at UCSB is rather low, with petty theft the most common offense. In 2011 the school reported seven forcible sex offenses, one nonforcible sex offense, three aggravated assaults, 40 burglaries, one robbery, three cases of arson, and four stolen cars.

In 2012–13 California residents (and illegal aliens residing in California) paid $13,671 in tuition and required fees to attend UCSB. Out-of-state Americans paid $36,549. Room and board were a hefty $13,275. Fifty-five percent of all students received need-based aid, and the average loan burden of a recent grad was a moderate $18,627.

STRONG SUITS	WEAK POINTS
• Comparatively little ideology in the classroom: "Just the data, ma'am."	• Some enormous (800-student) classes.
• 20 percent of students take part in research with teachers.	• Politicized courses in the black and Chicano studies programs fulfill general-ed mandates.
• Excellent hard-science departments (especially Nobel-rich physics) and good programs in the humanities, political science, and film studies.	• General advising is weak.
• Highly qualified faculty who do all teaching (grad students lead discussion sections).	• Many bars and a good deal of drinking near campus.
• Comparatively wholesome dorm policies and a beautiful campus.	• Several chaplaincies are slackly heterodox.

United States Air Force Academy

Colorado Springs, Colorado • www.usafa.af.mil

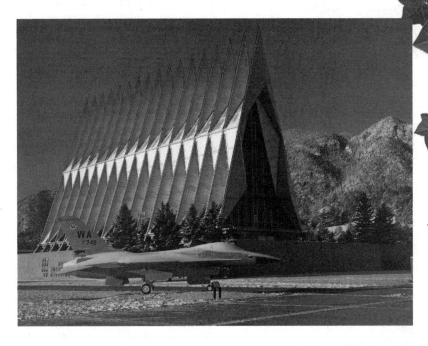

Into the Wild Blue Yonder

The U.S. Air Force Academy was founded in 1954. The architecture of the place was "Space Age," as "a living embodiment of the modernity of flying," the school reports. Today the faculty consists of around 540 military officers and civilian faculty. As one of its members notes, "All of our professors are dedicated to teaching and ensuring our cadets succeed academically. They are available at the cadets' request whenever extra instruction is needed. We do not have tenure for our professors." Faculty research and publications are not emphasized by the USAFA, and cadets are granted substantial attention from their teachers as they work their way through the school's rigorous curriculum.

Academic Life: Active duty

The Air Force Academy is state of the art in every way—just what one would expect in a school so given over, by necessity, to the mathematical and the technical. There are laboratories, observatories, and a library containing more than 1,744,000 volumes. As one cadet notes, "All students fly, all gain valuable survival training and character building education, and many have other opportunities such as jumping out of airplanes, flying propeller

Blue Collar Ivy

VITAL STATISTICS

Religious affiliation: *none*
Total enrollment: *4,413*
Total undergraduates: *4,413*
SAT CR/Verbal midrange:
 590–680
SAT Math midrange:
 630–710
ACT midrange: *28–33*
Applicants: *12,274*
Applicants accepted: *10%*
Accepted applicants who
 enrolled: *85%*
Tuition (general/out of
 state): *free*
Tuition (in state): *N/A*
Room and board: *free*
Freshman retention rate:
 90%
Graduation rate (4 yrs.): *76%*
Graduation rate (6 yrs.): *78%*
Courses with fewer than 20
 students: *100%*
Student-faculty ratio: *not
 provided*
Courses taught by graduate
 students: *not provided*
Students living on campus:
 100%
Students in fraternities:
 none
Students in sororities: *none*
Students receiving need-
 based financial aid: *N/A*
Avg. student-loan debt of a
 recent graduating class:
 N/A
Most popular majors:
 *business, engineering,
 management*
Guaranteed housing for 4
 years? *yes*

aircraft, and more. In addition, you gain the best leadership training in a college environment. You are in a solid academic environment with small classes and attentive professors."

Academy students are called "cadets." As at West Point and Annapolis, cadets are organized into a self-run corps, the 4,413-strong Cadet Wing. Although the school's curriculum is heavy on science and math, it is possible to gain a solid liberal arts education here, and the academy offers 32 majors. However, as much time and thought are put into developing both the cadet's personal character and leadership abilities as into his academic skills. The curriculum, extracurricular activities, and daily life all work in concert to create a well-rounded cadet. One staff member comments, "Development is the thread that binds all our programs—academic, athletic, and military—together. Hence, character development is part and parcel of every job requirement."

Each cadet, after commencement, is commissioned as an officer in the Air Force for at least five years. Upon entrance to the academy, each cadet swears on his honor to "support and defend the Constitution of the United States against all enemies, foreign and domestic." There is no room for conscientious objectors.

Criteria for acceptance are rigorous. As the academy's website says, "A well-rounded program of academic, leadership, and athletic preparation is important. You must also carefully consider whether you possess the characteristics of dedication to duty, desire to serve others, ability to accept discipline, morality, and the enjoyment of challenge." A nomination to the academy is essential. This must come from an applicant's U.S. senator, congressman, or the vice president. As one school insider warns, "It's tough to get into the academy, and even tougher to stay here."

The Center for Character and Leadership Development (CCLD) includes the Honor Division, which guides a cadet committee in administering the cadet Honor Code ("We will not lie, steal, or cheat nor tolerate among us anyone who does"). Those found guilty of violations will generally be expelled or placed on an intensive six-month-long honor probation program. The code is considered the "foundation" of cadets' "personal concept of professional ethics," and as such it is the "minimum standard of integrity." The CCLD holds four graduation requirement seminars per year, so that cadets gain greater insight into leadership and responsibility.

And, of course, the school calls for a highly technical core curriculum. Given that these are literally life-and-death topics for Air Force officers, the scientific courses are taught painstakingly and well. About 60 percent of a cadet's time in school is taken up by core courses, but all majors provide solid guidelines toward completing both academy and departmental requirements. Available majors include English, foreign-area studies, history, humanities, legal studies, political science, and social studies.

English majors at the USAFA are required to complete an impressive set of classes beyond the school's core curriculum. They substitute "Literary Criticism" and "Speech Communication" for "Literature and Intermediate Composition" and "Advanced Writing and Speaking." Additionally, they must take a Shakespeare class, pre-1780 and post-1780 British literature courses, and an introduction to American literature. They also complete a junior and senior English seminar, four semesters of foreign language, and six electives.

The history major calls for a similar structure: students take 11 history classes, including "Historiography and Methodology," "The Foundations of Modern America," and "The History of Modern America." They must also complete an AeroSpace History class and a course focusing on an area or time, like "History of Traditional East Asia," "Foundations of Middle Eastern History," or "Modern European History." Four of the five must be in American history or military history if a cadet wants an American history or military history designation on his diploma. Finally, a capstone course in American, military, or global history must be completed. Students are also required to take an elective from any area and complete four semesters of a foreign language.

CAMPUS POLITICS: GREEN LIGHT

There seems to be little ideology of any kind infusing course work at the academy. As one cadet states, "We have true academic freedom in our classrooms. Debate is highly encouraged but so is respect for opposing views. There are no 'campus politics' here that intrude into the classroom." In keeping with the traditions of the American military, there are no political clubs at the academy, although civic involvement is encouraged through volunteer community service.

However, CNS News reports a distressing incident of political correctness in January 2011, when the USAFA chaplain's office retracted an invitation to former Marine officer and Family Research Council president Tony Perkins after he criticized President Obama's repeal of the "Don't Ask, Don't Tell" policy regarding homosexuals in the military. Republican congressman Trent Franks, a member of the House Armed Services Committee, was outraged at the USAF and blasted it from Capitol Hill: "It is absolutely political correctness if, in the name of inclusiveness, we throw out someone who is a Christian or has a view that might be a little bit different than Mr. Obama's. Then we've dishonored the very service that fights to uphold and defend the Constitution."

No wonder some appointees of more liberal administrations are trying to rein in the USAF Academy; in 2012 the Alumni Factor conducted an issues survey of American college alumni. Graduates of the USAF Academy gave the most conservative answers; alumni of Reed College generated the most liberal.

Political science majors take an introductory course, a class in political theory, and the "Politics of National Security." They then select one course each from a short list in American government, international relations, and comparative politics. A capstone seminar completes the set curriculum, but cadets must also complete three political science electives, any social science or humanities class, and four semesters of foreign language study.

For the student looking for a broader liberal arts approach, the humanities major provides a creative option. Students pick a class each from English, fine arts, history, and military and strategic studies, in addition to a course called "Great Philosophers." They must also complete four humanities electives and four semesters of foreign language. One staff member comments: "Our core curriculum is heavily weighted toward math and science. However, we do have a vibrant liberal arts program with numerous liberal arts majors available. At graduation, however, all our cadets receive a bachelor of science degree, regardless of their major."

A student says: "The education is excellent, the friends you make there will remain friends for life, and you will test the limits of your mind and body."

There are, of course, a great many strictly military courses at the USAFA, as well as airmanship and aviation training sessions, designed to prepare the cadet for his career in the Air Force. Some courses include soaring or gliding and free-fall parachuting. In addition, all manner of military training is conducted year round.

According to several cadets who wrote in various online forums, the academy's education exceeds anything they expected. One cadet lauds the academy's "small class sizes, highly qualified instructors, and limitless opportunities to talk personally with your instructors and receive tutoring and extra instruction. You will have professors with PhDs willing to remain for one or two hours after class with you personally to help you with your work. None of the educators there are getting paid to do research [but] only to teach, meaning that 100 percent of their effort is focused on students. Keep in mind, however, that the academy is . . . both physically and mentally demanding to the point that many students are not able to handle it." Another cadet agrees: "The education is excellent, the friends you make there will remain friends for life, and you will test the limits of your mind and body. It will also probably be the hardest four years of your life, as it was for me."

Rather than traditional study-abroad programs, which would clash with the school's rigorous requirements, the USAFA provides cross-commissioning with other military academies—providing, say, an aspiring helicopter pilot a path to that coveted career in a less competitive branch of the military.

Foreign language courses are also required of all cadets—two semesters for technical majors, four for nontechnical majors. Cadets are encouraged to pursue "strategic languages" such as Arabic, Chinese, and Russian, although French, German, Japanese, Portuguese, and Spanish are also offered.

Student Life: Careful about the branding

Arrival at the Air Force Academy means exchanging civilian gear for a uniform, having one's hair cut, taking the oath, learning the lingo, and making the transition to military life. This is not the environment for edgy fashions. Piercings need to be removed before admission (nonremovable piercings are not allowed). The school warns, "Tattoos or brands must not be excessive. Nor may they contain inflammatory, obscene, racist, sexist, or similar content."

SUGGESTED CORE

The school's prescribed curriculum suffices as an abbreviated core.

Basic Cadet Training (BCT) starts six weeks before academics begin. Fresh arrivals at Colorado Springs are called "doolies" (from the Greek *doulos,* "slave"). Basic training—the academy's version of boot camp—is extremely challenging and meant to separate the wheat from the chaff. Often it results in lifelong friendships—and sometimes in a hasty departure.

In the first half of BCT, doolies are instructed in military customs and courtesies, the Honor Code, Air Force heritage, marching, and room inspection. The second portion of BCT takes place in Jack's Valley, a rugged, wooded area on the academy grounds. This training is particularly physical—among other things the cadet will learn small-unit tactics and proper use of firearms. He will also make his way through several rigorous training circuits: the assault course, obstacle course, and leadership reaction course. The BCT ends with the Acceptance Parade, which marks the doolies' entrance into the Cadet Wing and the commencement of the school year.

Drawn from the first-class (senior year) cadets, the Cadet Wing commander oversees four cadet group commanders, who in turn monitor the commanders and their staffs of 40 squadrons, each composed of about 110 cadets. Supervising these cadet officers are air officers—commanding and noncommissioned academy military trainers, who are located in each squadron and group.

Each year at the academy brings the cadets specific challenges. The fourth-class (freshman) cadet will end his first year "with an initial foundation of Air Force history, heritage, honor, discipline, drill, and followership skills." The third-class (sophomore) year includes learning survival, land navigation, and water-survival skills. The third summer involves practical training in Air Force military skills, as second-class cadet military training prepares the cadet to be a primary trainer of third- and fourth-class cadets. Life as an Air Force Academy cadet is a year-round experience, including summers; cadets generally get only three weeks of leave in the summer. The balance of their time is spent in a variety of training or education programs, or as the trainers of incoming new cadets.

Every cadet takes two physical education courses each semester; it is mandatory for him to participate in either intercollegiate (club or varsity) or intramural sports as well. There are more than 40 athletic teams available. Team sports are seen as a further part of the cadet's education, instilling in cadets "a sense of initiative, self-confidence, and the knowledge that they are part of something greater than themselves," says the school. Intercollegiate sports are strong, consistently competing in national championships—the school's boxing team has never ranked lower than second nationally. Most of the 27 intercollegiate teams are members of the NCAA Division I Mountain West Conference. The USAFA Falcons compete in sports as varied as swimming, ice hockey, rifle, water polo, gymnastics, and wrestling, as well as football, basketball, soccer, and tennis. The academy maintains heated rivalries with West Point and the Naval Academy, and the schools compete in football for the Commander-in-Chief's Trophy.

To allow for all the required academic, military, and athletic training, daily life is carefully regimented. There are four, 53-minute periods each morning and three each afternoon. Cadets march to breakfast and lunch and (save for those involved in intercollegiate sports) play on intramural teams two afternoons a week, after classes. On the other three afternoons there are squadron military activities or free time. Evenings after dinner are spent studying in one's room or at the library, as are those Saturday mornings not given over to parades and inspections. Saturday afternoons and Sundays are generally free.

During BCT, the doolie may not have visitors or phone calls. During the remainder of the fourth-class year, phone calls and visitors are permitted at set times on weekends. Third-class cadets have limited opportunities to leave the campus. Such privileges increase each year, depending on one's academic and training performance. Only the top two classes may own or drive cars at the academy. Along with summer leave, cadets receive two weeks of Christmas vacation and 10 days during the spring.

Despite all this, there are plenty of activities for social and other leisure events. Arnold Hall, the academy's student union complex, features formal and informal social events, as well as a food court, dancing, television, games, movies, and live performances by popular entertainers. A military reception and ball are featured once a year.

Pride of place among recreational clubs is the Cadet Ski Club, but Amateur Radio, a dramatic club called the Blue Bards, the pistol and rifle teams, equestrian and hunting clubs, an FM radio station, and rodeo are just a few of the many special-interest clubs. There are also choirs, drill teams, and professional organizations. All told, there are more than 80 competitive and recreational clubs cadets can join.

This would not be a military academy if it were not subject to meddling by judges. In 1972 U.S. courts ruled that chapel attendance could no longer be mandatory for cadets. Nevertheless, the cadet chapel remains the architectural crown of the campus. Featuring 17 stunning spires, the chapel has several levels, each serving one of three faith groups (Protestant, Catholic, and Jewish). Mormon cadets attend services in Colorado Springs. There are also special rooms in the cadet chapel for services and ceremonies of other religions such as Buddhism and Islam, and the school even accommodates those practicing paganism/earth-centered spirituality through an outdoor, hilltop stone circle. Catholic Masses are held across the week, while Protestant services are also held on Sunday.

In 1976, at court insistence, women were admitted to all three academies. Now, while there is no doubt of the patriotism or prowess of Air Force alumnae, there is a basic biological fact that the civilian leadership has chosen consistently to ignore: the tendency of people of opposite sexes kept in close quarters to . . . well, fraternize. Every few years a sex scandal emerges at one or another of the academies.

As members of the U.S. Air Force, cadets pay no tuition; in fact, they receive a small salary while attending. As one graduate noted, "USAFA is a tough place to be. However, when you get out, you have a responsible job with good pay and limitless opportunities. I've gotten several interviews on the strength of only the interviewer's curiosity about my background." Another alum boasts, "I make more money than all my friends, and I have zero college debt to pay off."

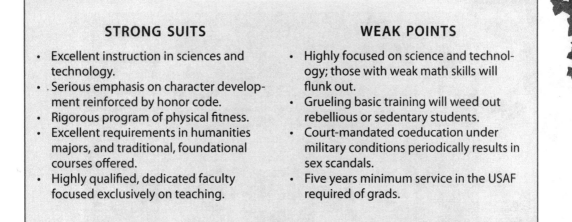

STRONG SUITS	WEAK POINTS
• Excellent instruction in sciences and technology.	• Highly focused on science and technology; those with weak math skills will flunk out.
• Serious emphasis on character development reinforced by honor code.	• Grueling basic training will weed out rebellious or sedentary students.
• Rigorous program of physical fitness.	
• Excellent requirements in humanities majors, and traditional, foundational courses offered.	• Court-mandated coeducation under military conditions periodically results in sex scandals.
• Highly qualified, dedicated faculty focused exclusively on teaching.	• Five years minimum service in the USAF required of grads.

University of Colorado at Boulder

Boulder, Colorado • www.colorado.edu

Red Rock College

The University of Colorado at Boulder was founded in 1876 to educate the citizens of a state that was still very much part of the Wild West. It now comprises nine academic colleges and serves nearly 33,000 students on a stunning 600-acre campus in the heart of the Rocky Mountains.

The campus is spectacular, the faculty is generally respectable, and the curriculum is above average for a state school. The university is large and diverse enough that a student with a strong sense of self-discipline can prosper; if he wishes to pursue a traditional liberal education here, he will find the means to do so but little encouragement.

Academic Life: Skills acquisition

What the University of Colorado calls a core curriculum is merely a rather flexible set of requirements in those dry modern realms of "skills acquisition" and "content areas of study." The student who values a traditional education and finds himself at Boulder can, with diligence, find solid courses to satisfy each requirement, especially in math and science.

The "skills" the school hopes to impart include writing, quantitative reasoning, and a foreign language—in other words, mostly things students used to learn in high school. Several of the seven content-area distribution requirements can be satisfied through politicized courses in gender and ethnicity—indeed, the sheer abundance of such courses at Boulder is depressing. The "human diversity" requirement, for instance, can be fulfilled by "Introduction to Lesbian, Gay, Bisexual, and Transgender Studies." The courses fulfilling the "United States context" requirement include thumb suckers like "America through Baseball" and "Women of Color and Activism." The "contemporary societies" requirement can be satisfied by courses like "The Vietnam Wars" and "Literature and Social Violence." However, there are many excellent classes one could take instead. Even the diversity requirement can be satisfied by an introductory course in traditional Asian American studies, while solid economics classes count for credit in "contemporary societies."

Around 39 percent of Colorado's classes contain fewer than 20 students, and 92 percent enroll fewer than 50. Introductory-level courses for underclassmen are the largest. The university claims that students won't have a problem getting into required courses and will not be prevented from graduating because of limited course availability. To back up this claim, CU has implemented a "Graduation Guarantee," under which students entering with a minimum of academic preparation are guaranteed to get into all the courses they need within four years. If the college cannot meet that promise, additional courses are free.

The honors program at CU–Boulder is one of the strongest in the country, and since a central honors council decides whether a student should graduate with honors, the distinction actually means something. The top 10 percent of incoming freshmen are invited, but other students may request admission. A student in the program can choose honors-level courses in any department and can graduate with honors by maintaining a 3.3 GPA and writing a thesis as a senior. The honors program also offers a number of interdisciplinary courses. Classes are capped at 15 students and range from "Introduction to the Bible" and "Folklore" to " Medical Anthropology"

VITAL STATISTICS

Religious affiliation: *none*
Total enrollment: *32,252*
Total undergraduates: *26,325*
SAT CR/Verbal midrange: *520–630*
SAT Math midrange: *540–650*
ACT midrange: *23–28*
Applicants: *20,506*
Applicants accepted: *87%*
Accepted applicants who enrolled: *44%*
Tuition (general/out of state): *$31,378*
Tuition (in state): *$9,482*
Room and board: *$11,730*
Freshman retention rate: *84%*
Graduation rate (4 yrs.): *40%*
Graduation rate (6 yrs.): *68%*
Courses with fewer than 20 students: *39%*
Student-faculty ratio: *19:1*
Courses taught by graduate students: *5%*
Students living on campus: *28%*
Students in fraternities: *14%*
Students in sororities: *16%*
Students receiving need-based financial aid: *39%*
Avg. student-loan debt of a recent graduating class: *$22,683*
Most popular majors: *biology, business/marketing, social sciences*
Guaranteed housing for 4 years? *no*

Colorado

Blue Collar Ivy

CAMPUS POLITICS: YELLOW LIGHT

This campus in the heart of the Rocky Mountains attracts an environmentally conscious and liberal student population—the school continually has among the greatest number of Peace Corps volunteers. Moreover, its reputation as a school for potheads and politically radical students is merited. One undergrad says the school has been called the "liberal lighthouse of the West." Another says, "Boulder is known for its New Age thinking.... There is a sizable population of hippies, and Greenpeace activists are everywhere." Protests are a common occurrence.

CU isn't quite sure what it wants to be—a bastion for the Left, a football powerhouse, or a haven for pseudo-hippies. As a consequence, it can restrict the freedoms of both its liberal and its conservative students. From forbidding an affirmative-action political-protest bake sale hosted by the College Republicans to informing the leftist Students for True Academic Freedom that they would have to pay $2,000 in security fees to bring Ward Churchill and William Ayers to campus, the university seems always to be stepping on someone's toes.

Trying to remedy its reputation as a party school and leftist breeding ground, the school raised funds to endow a faculty chair for a professor of Conservative Thought and Policy—and in 2013 hired Steven Hayward, a scholar of Ronald Reagan and Winston Churchill. While many criticized its decision to seek out such a scholar, Hayward's qualifications appear to have quieted concerns.

and "Science in the Ancient World." An honors dorm is available for 100 freshman participants.

Several departments at CU stand out. The sciences are generally very good. The aeronautical engineering program is well respected, and NASA recruits many CU students. Boulder has received millions from NASA over the years, and 15 astronauts are CU alums. The physics department is singled out by students and faculty alike as especially strong. From 1989 through 2005, four faculty members won the Nobel Prize in physics or chemistry. These departments are havens for conservative students: "Engineering, physics, and theoretical mathematics are the only subjects [in] which one is not subject to blatant socialist indoctrination," says one student.

Conversely, members of the humanities faculty are unhappy with the disproportionate emphasis they believe CU puts on the sciences. "The scientists support the school with federal grants, so, basically, anything they want, they get," says one professor. Another reports, "There is very little commitment to Western humanities or liberal arts; they've been gutted." Humanities receive much less outside funding and so are starved of funds by the university itself, according to professors. Given the political slant of some of these departments, that may be just as well. One student says, "Most Classics courses do not require students to read Thucydides, Aristotle, or even Homer aside from excerpts here and there. Instead, they seem dedicated to love poems and the desecration of modern culture by elitists who believe that Roman women had more rights than a modern American woman."

Outside the sciences, academic quality varies. (Even within the sciences, geology is bemoaned as inadequately taught.) "There are a lot of people very committed to mainstream teaching in English and American history," says one professor. However, several teachers point to political science as a "radical" department. (It does require its majors to study the American political system, however.)

Two of the most popular disciplines, psychology and environmental studies, are not recommended by more traditionally oriented faculty. Another professor says that sociology, which was once heavily Marxist, is "starting to get better" as retiring professors are being replaced by better scholars. For undergraduate teaching, the foreign languages, especially French, Spanish, and Italian, are quite strong.

English is described as "weak and chaotic" by one professor who admits that "if you're intelligent and resourceful, you can make your way through. Just ask around to find good professors." One English professor says, "If we believed in truth in advertising, we would change the department's name to cultural studies." The requirements of the English department bear out this professor's lament. It's true that majors must take at least one British literature course set before 1660, but another must cover literary theory, genre studies, or popular culture, and still another multicultural or gender studies.

The history department maintains a more traditional approach. Students may choose a broad "geographic distribution" track or a "historical period" approach. All are required to take a lower- and an upper-level course in "World of the Ancient Greeks," European history, and U.S. history. Some students remark that Colorado's advising system entails "a lot of bureaucracy." Students unsure of their majors are shuffled into an "open option" program and assigned an adviser from a pool. Once a student chooses a major, he is assigned to an adviser from his department.

One professor reports: "There is very little commitment to Western humanities or liberal arts. They've been gutted."

Some of the best professors at the university include the approachable and learned conservative scholar E. Christian Kopff in the honors program; David M. Gross in finance; Patricia Limerick in history; Paul W. Kroll in Asian languages and civilizations; Jules Gordon Kaplan in economics; and Thomas R. Cech in chemistry (who shared the 1989 Nobel Prize in chemistry for research on RNA). In 2004 Nobel laureate Carl Wieman was named national Teacher of the Year by the Carnegie Foundation.

UC offers a good array of study-abroad options. Some featured faculty-led seminars include "Justice, Human Rights, and Democracy" (Jerusalem, Israel), the Art History in Rome Summer Program, "Art in Spain" (Madrid), "Art in France" (Paris), "Film and the French Aesthetic" (Paris), "Film and the Italian Aesthetic" (Rome), "Entrepreneurship and Empowerment" (Cape Town, South Africa), "Self Awareness and Images of the Other" (Xi'an, China), "London Finance Seminar," "Venice: Cradle of European Jewish Culture," and the St. Petersburg Language and Culture Summer Program.

CU teaches courses in a wide variety of tongues, including American Sign Language, Arabic, Chinese, Farsi, French, German, Greek and Latin, Hebrew, Hindi, Indonesian, Italian, Japanese, Korean, Portuguese, Russian, Spanish, and Swedish.

SUGGESTED CORE

1. Classics 4110, Greek and Roman Epic
2. Philosophy 3000, History of Ancient Philosophy
3. English 3310, The Bible as Literature
4. History 2170, History of Christianity I: To the Reformation
5. Political Science 2004, Survey of Western Political Thought
6. English 3000, Shakespeare for Nonmajors
7. History 1015, History of the United States to 1865
8. History 4414, European Intellectual History, 1750–1870

Student Life: Party on, dudes

From any campus dorm room, students at CU could have a view of the Rockies, the campus pond, or a mountain meadow. But most CU students flee university housing after their first year. Housing options on campus range from small houses to high-rises. All dormitories are coed, but in some cases, men and women are separated by floor. Coed bathrooms and dorm rooms are available only for married students, who are normally housed in university-owned apartments. There are 14 residential academic programs, which allow students to take small courses with faculty members who live in the same buildings, Oxford-style. The programs offer courses, programs, or cocurricular activities in areas like international studies, leadership, the fine arts, communications, and environmental studies.

Although 30 percent of all CU–Boulder students are members of a sorority or fraternity, it was ranked the number-one party school in the nation by the Princeton Review for several years. The administration has attempted to get tough on drinking, firing lax RAs. However, one student claims that "nearly every student of age" can be found in the bars on any given night. "The university gained the reputation for being a party school for a reason; that is still the culture of the university," says a student. The most egregious event on campus is surely the "smoke fest," which occurs every year as thousands of pot smokers light up on Farrand Field.

The university offers dozens of intramural sports, from basketball to broomball, but students looking for more stringent competition can try out for an intercollegiate club or varsity team. The Buffaloes, represented by their mascot Ralphie, compete in the Pac 10 conference. The Buffaloes have won a number of national and conference championships, excelling particularly in skiing and cross-country. The school competes in six men's and eight women's NCAA Division I sports and has a long history of football successes. The football program has been hit by a number of scandals, including rape accusations against at least nine football players. The university is working to rebuild its football program, and recruits are now supervised by coaches or parents; forbidden to go to bars, clubs, and parties; and subject to an 11:00 p.m. curfew.

Boulder (population close to 100,000), the bohemian capital of the West, boasts that it is home to more than 200 religious congregations. As one Christian student says, "CU is an excellent place for students to grow in their faith. There is a multitude of Christian groups, service groups, and other such activities. Come to CU ready to be challenged in your faith." For Catholics, two parishes in town, Sacred Heart of Mary and St. Martin de Porres, offer Masses; the Aquinas Institute for Catholic Thought provides fairly solid catechism and devotions. St. Aidan's ministers to Episcopalians. There are organizations catering to mainline Protestants, Latter-Day Saints, Orthodox, Adventists, nondenominational Evangelicals, and Jewish, Islamic, Buddhist, and Baha'i students, as well as ecumenical and interreligious organizations. Beware of the group called Campus Crusade for Queers. After some digging, our reporter discovered that it is not, in fact, a chaplaincy.

For the politically minded, College Democrats and Republicans exist, along with the far-left 180 Degree Shift at the 11th Hour activism group and BASE (Building Alliances for Social Engagement) activist journal project. Student-run radio KVCU 1190 provides news and sports and music ranging from Bollywood to Honky Tonk.

When asked to characterize CU's students, one professor says that they "take on a live-and-let-live attitude . . . and have a very strong commitment to looking good and skiing." A student says, "The workload could be heavier. But students are not so tied down by their schoolwork that they can't afford to party midweek or cut class on a Tuesday to ski."

The school's largely wooded campus has won worldwide acclaim for its natural and architectural beauty. Hiking, mountain biking, and skiing are extremely popular. One student warns, "If you don't ski, bike, hike, or climb, you don't belong here." The city's cosmopolitan atmosphere is highly appealing. "It's about a five-minute walk to the mountains," a student says, exaggerating only slightly. "That's probably why a lot of people come here." Some of the top ski resorts in North America, including Vail and Aspen, are within a two-hour drive, along with abundant opportunities for white-water rafting, snowboarding, backpacking, horseback riding, and climbing.

In 2011 campus police reported six forcible sex offenses, five robberies, eight aggravated assaults, 42 burglaries, 10 stolen cars, and one case of arson. The campus has plenty of emergency call boxes and round-the-clock police surveillance. A safety escort service not only helps students get around campus but also escorts students throughout the city of Boulder. All dormitory visitors must present a student ID card or be escorted by a resident.

Boulder is rather a bargain for Colorado residents, who in 2012–13 paid $9,482 in tuition (out-of-state students paid $31,378), and $11,730 for room and board. Admissions are need blind, although the school doesn't promise everyone full financial aid. Only 39 percent of students get need-based assistance, and the average debt of a recent grad is about $22,683.

STRONG SUITS	WEAK POINTS
• Excellent courses in the hard sciences and engineering.	• Heavy drinking and open marijuana use.
• Demanding honors program.	• Humanities are mostly dominated by radical politics.
• A "graduation guarantee" promises a degree in four years (imagine that!).	• Lax requirements for general education and some majors, such as English.
• Many study-abroad and foreign language options.	

University of Connecticut

Storrs, Connecticut • www.uconn.edu

Hoop Dreams

The University of Connecticut began as the Storrs Agricultural School in 1881. A dozen years after its founding, the Connecticut General Assembly admitted women and designated the university as the state's land-grant college. Through most of the country, UConn figures in the common mind more as a basketball team than as an educational institution. With a late start in the land-grant sweepstakes, and the brutal competitive position of a state university in college-rich New England—there are well over a hundred colleges within a hundred-mile radius—UConn has struggled to find its niche in higher education.

UConn's student body is still not of the caliber of those of the top national public universities, though it has grown stronger over the past few years. Over 47 percent of all applicants are accepted, and the midrange of these students' SAT scores (verbal and math) is between 1130 and 1300. Many UConn students are not well prepared for college, though 83 percent do graduate within six years.

Academic Life: UConn choose whatever you want

The heart of the University of Connecticut's academic program had long been its general-education curriculum, which was fairly strong until fall 2005, when these requirements were downgraded.

At least the College of Liberal Arts, to which 62 percent of undergraduates belong, still requires course work in four basic fields (arts, literature, history, and philosophy)—although, as in general-ed requirements, the Western civilization course now must compete for students against 11 other options. The new program renders it possible (though difficult) to graduate from UConn with no "Eurocentric" courses at all. Under the old program, one student says, "it was not possible to construct your schedule so you only have easy courses." Now it is.

Each student must take two writing-intensive courses, most of which are taught by graduate students from various disciplines. One instructor, an English graduate student, says there is no university-wide curriculum for these courses, "So we can pretty much teach what we want—nice, although open to abuses, I am sure, though I don't know of any in particular." Nevertheless, one of the two courses must relate to the student's major.

That said, the requirements for major fields of study at UConn are, on the whole, commendable. English majors, for instance, are required to take a number of specific courses, including survey courses in Shakespeare, Anglophone poetry, British literature, and American literature. In addition to these, students must take a course focusing on a major author. Students can also elect to take an Irish literature concentration, and all students must take one course in the area of "multi-period, multicultural, and ethnic literature" (like "Literature and Culture of the Third World" or "Advanced Study: Lesbian, Gay, Bisexual, and Transgendered Literature"). Students and faculty say the English department is one of the school's best. It often hosts visiting professors from top schools in Great Britain and the United States.

The business school and the sciences are also very strong, with excellent facilities and faculties. A political science major also praises his department, noting that majors face requirements that ensure a broad understanding of the

VITAL STATISTICS

Religious affiliation: *none*
Total enrollment: *25,868*
Total undergraduates: *17,815*
SAT CR/Verbal midrange:
    550–640
SAT Math midrange:
    580–670
ACT midrange: *25–29*
Applicants: *27,247*
Applicants accepted: *47%*
Accepted applicants who
    enrolled: *29%*
Tuition (general/out of
    state): *$26,544*
Tuition (in state): *$8,712*
Room and board: *$11,380*
Freshman retention rate: *92%*
Graduation rate (4 yrs.): *68%*
Graduation rate (6 yrs.): *83%*
Courses with fewer than 20
    students: *42%*
Student-faculty ratio: *18:1*
Courses taught by graduate
    students: *not provided*
Students living on campus:
    73%
Students in fraternities: *9%*
Students in sororities: *11%*
Students receiving need-
    based financial aid: *56%*
Avg. student-loan debt of a
    recent graduating class:
    $23,822
Most popular majors:
    *business/marketing,
    health professions, social
    sciences*
Guaranteed housing for 4
    years? *no*

CAMPUS POLITICS: GREEN LIGHT

While extracurricular life at UConn provides ample opportunity for political expression, political life on campus may best be described as apathetic. One student says that most activist groups on campus make big commotions with only a few participants: "There have been several antiwar demonstrations on campus, but they are sparsely attended. A peace vigil in front of the Congregational Church never draws more than a handful of people." Among the political clubs are the Debate Society, College Democrats, College Republicans, UConn for Youth in Politics, and Queers United Against Discrimination (QUAD). The college is not overtly political, and the student body does not appear to be particularly activist.

It has been eight long years since liberal students brought the college to national attention after "belching" the theme to the TV show *South Park* and blaring Nintendo's *Super Mario Brothers* game from the college sound system in order to interrupt a speech by conservative pundit Ann Coulter. But we couldn't resist mentioning it. An equally uplifting moment came in 2011, when liberal Republican Meghan McCain (daughter of the losing presidential candidate) came to campus to upbraid social conservatives opposed to gay activism as "dangerously out of touch." The *Daily Campus* reported that she told campus conservatives: "I'm scared by people who don't evolve." In 2012 the quite active chapter of UConn College Republicans went as a group to the Conservative Political Action Committee (CPAC) meeting in Washington, D.C., where the messages were presumably friendlier.

discipline. These requirements call for introductory courses in three of four divisions—theory and methodology, comparative politics, international relations, and American politics—in addition to upper-level courses in these areas and in public policy and law, or race, gender, and ethnic politics. Most of the courses that the political science department offers are straightforward, like "Constitutional Law" and "Judiciary in the Political Process." There are a few courses of the ilk of "Black Feminist Politics" but only a few.

History majors must take one course in ancient, medieval, and early modern history, one in modern Europe, one in United States history, and two courses selected from African, Asian, Latin American, and Middle Eastern history. In addition, majors must take a course on historical methodology and complete a thesis seminar that requires extensive writing and original research. Most of the history courses seem solid, and discerning students have little difficulty in gaining a good understanding of Western history and culture. Courses include "Ancient Greece," "Ancient Rome," "The Early Christian Church," "The Reformation," "The Renaissance," "Medieval and Imperial Russia to 1855," and "The Black Experience in the Americas."

Students rank among the best undergraduate teachers David A. Yalof in political science, Sam Pickering in English, and Peter Kaminsky in music.

UConn's Honors Scholar Program does not have separate requirements or a special curriculum; rather, honors students follow the same requirements as do regular students, but they can select more-challenging courses open only to those in the program and are given "the flexibility to craft individualized plans of study during their last three semesters." The university website notes that honors classes are "smaller in size, more interactive, and enroll a high-caliber student." In addition, honors students can "get advice from nationally known faculty members in many disciplines." And there are some other practical benefits as well, such as priority registration for classes, priority housing, and extended library loan privileges.

New liberal arts students are assigned to professional advisers—not faculty members— through the Academic Center for Entering Students. From these staffers they get help planning courses and choosing majors. When students declare majors, they are assigned to faculty advisers in their department. Close faculty-student relationships, it seems, are uncommon. When one student says, "I don't believe in asking an adviser for help, since all the information that I would need I can usually find on my own," he is more or less expressing the view of a majority of students. Another student says that the effectiveness of the advising program depends on which major a student chooses.

> Under the old program, one student says, "It was not possible to construct your schedule so you only have easy courses." Now it is.

UConn's size—more than 17,000 undergraduates—means that some classes are apt to be large. Enrollments for large, freshman-level survey courses can reach the hundreds. The average class size is a hefty 35. One small consolation of the weakened distributional requirements: with broader choices, more classes are likely to be offered, driving down the enrollment in such freshman megamagnets as History 100/101.

Languages offered include Chinese, French, German, Greek and Latin, Italian, Japanese, and Spanish. The school boasts on its website that it offers "over 300 study abroad programs in 65 countries on six continents. You can study as far away as China or as close as Mexico, in a small village in the desert or on a large ship at sea. You might take courses at a university in Ireland, Korea, or Chile; intern at a non-profit in South Africa, Guatemala, or England; conduct field research in Armenia, Mongolia, or the Netherlands; or study with UConn students in Italy, France, or Spain."

Student Life: Little in Storrs

Storrs, Connecticut, is home to approximately 11,000 permanent residents. Located about a half hour east of Hartford, Storrs offers little besides the university, a drugstore, a flower shop, and a few bars. Students spend most of their social lives on campus, or on road trips out of Storrs.

One of the primary focal points of campus life is the Harry A. Gampel Pavilion, home to the aforementioned champion men's and women's basketball teams. With 22 varsity teams, UConn competes in the Big East conference against schools like Pitt, Syracuse, and West Virginia. For the more recreational athlete, Connecticut also offers close to 50 club sports—from cycling to skydiving—and many intramural options. UConn's mascot is a husky perpetually named Jonathan in honor of Revolutionary War hero Jonathan

SUGGESTED CORE

1. Classics 3241W, Greek and Roman Epic
2. Philosophy 2221, Ancient Philosophy
3. Interdepartmental 3260, The Bible
4. History 3335, The Early Christian Church
5. Political Science 3012, Modern Political Theory
6. English 3503, Shakespeare I
7. History 1501, United States History to 1877
8. History 3412W, Intellectual and Social History of Europe in the 19th Century

Trumbull. Today's mascot, cared for by a university fraternity, is the 13th dog to serve in this honorable capacity.

Some 73 percent of UConn students live on campus. They have a number of housing options from which to choose. The university's 17 residential halls range from new and modern facilities to older, more stately buildings. UConn offers single-sex dormitories for both men and women, and in some of the coed halls, men and women are separated by floor. There are no coed bathrooms or dorm rooms. Students can choose to live in alcohol-free dormitories, and all buildings are smoke-free. Students can also opt to live in a residential learning community. Such students take a seminar class together and "have increased opportunities for one-on-one and small group interactions with faculty, staff and peer mentors," according to the college website. Learning community residents also engage in study and social events, attend lectures of well-known speakers, go on field trips, and study abroad.

The university has 16 fraternities and 13 sororities, but membership is small (about 10 percent of students in each).

There are plenty of faith-based organizations to join at Connecticut. Options include the International Christian Fellowship, UConn Students for Christ, All Students Bible Study, and the Alpha Omega Christian Club. There is also the Voices of Freedom Gospel Choir and the United Church of Christ—a student-led initiative based at the Storrs Congregational Church. Jewish groups include the Alpha Epsilon Phi sorority, Hillel, and the Jewish Student Association. The school also hosts a Muslim Students Association, Sikh Student Association, and the intriguing Pagan Organization for Diverse Spirituality.

Social, recreational, and sporting clubs cover the spectrum, from the Paintball Club to the Physics Club, from Dance Team to *Der Deutschklub*, and from the Sailing Team to the Society of Women Engineers.

UConn provides a wealth of cultural opportunities for both students and locals. The Jorgensen Center for the Performing Arts hosts a diverse program of artistic entertainment, including opera, ballet, international symphony orchestras, comedians such as Jerry Seinfeld, and pop music acts such as Ben Folds. The Puppet Festival is held on campus each year—perhaps not a student favorite but an excellent opportunity for those UConn students enrolled in its Puppet Arts Training Program, offered by the drama department—the only such program in the country.

One student says the typical UConn student has "more of a love for alcohol, sex, and music" than for "intelligence, respect, integrity, and success. Apathy overwhelms this campus everywhere except for the party scene." The campus cops would probably agree. A spokesman for the university police department told the school's *Daily Campus*: "Alcohol fuels much of the crime at UConn, especially property damage in dorms, intimidation, simple assaults, and disorderly conduct." The university has recently become stricter in the enforcement of underage drinking laws, symbolically converting one of the campus's most notoriously wild dormitories, known as "The Jungle," into an alcohol-free residence. One UConn official, quoted in the *Daily Campus*, said that students' "extreme drinking...has an incredibly negative effect on the quality of campus life." Statistics show that the number of alcohol-related arrests has declined in recent years, but the university police chief believes that student alcohol use has actually increased—the lower number of arrests simply reflects the thinning of police resources.

Violent crimes are comparatively rare. In 2011 the college reported eight forcible sex offenses, three robberies, three aggravated assaults, three arsons, and 54 burglaries.

UConn is a real bargain for in-state students at only $8,712 tuition for 2012–13; outsiders paid $26,544. Room and board were an additional $11,380. More than 56 percent of students received some form of financial aid, and the average student-loan debt of recent graduates was $23,822.

STRONG SUITS	WEAK POINTS
• Solid majors' requirements in English; students must study Shakespeare.	• Weak gen-ed requirements, even for liberal arts students, with many politicized courses that fulfill them.
• Good programs in the hard sciences and in UConn's business school.	• Required writing-intensive courses are taught by graduate students with little oversight as to subject matter.
• Both the history and the political science departments require foundational courses of majors and offer mostly solid classes.	• Advising seems weak, and close relationships between faculty and students rare.
• Single-sex dorms are available, and there are no coed bathrooms or dorm rooms.	• Students and campus police complain of "extreme drinking" and associated pathologies.

University of Delaware

Newark, Delaware • www.udel.edu

Blue Hens' Blue Collar Ivy

One of the oldest universities in the country, the University of Delaware traces its roots back to 1743; early graduates included George Read, Thomas McKean, and James Smith, each of whom would sign the Declaration of Independence. A state-assisted, privately governed institution, UD offers a range of degrees: three associate programs, 147 bachelor's programs, 119 master's programs, 54 doctoral programs, and 15 dual graduate programs through its seven colleges and in collaboration with more than 70 research centers. It is widely regarded as being among the nation's top 25 state research universities.

The school has long been centrist on the spectrum of public universities, but faculty suggest that it has begun to swing sharply to the left under its current president. One says, "I think the place is moving in a PC direction, adopting things like transgender dorms, thus falling in line with the radical trend in higher education."

Still, the quality of the faculty is generally high, and professors with longevity at the college report that political correctness is not yet overwhelming: most of the faculty are open to dissenting views. As at most large research institutions, the student will have to be his own counselor and take ownership of his educational experience from the very start.

Academic Life: Cherry picking

The University of Delaware's general-education requirements invoke goals that sound lofty enough: students are meant to attain each of a 10-point list of ambitious academic goals, such as "1. Attain effective skills in (a) oral and (b) written communication, (c) quantitative reasoning, and (d) the use of information technology"; "4. Engage questions of ethics and recognize responsibilities to self, community, and society at large"; and "9. Understand the foundations of United States society including the significance of its cultural diversity." In fact, teachers agree that these requirements are vague and inadequate. Students will need to seek out foundational courses themselves.

Class sizes vary from less than a dozen to several hundred at once. Depending on your major, you may end up with graduate students teaching. Still, when you get a real teacher, he will likely be good, students agree. The school places more emphasis on teaching skills (as opposed to research piled up) than most state universities, a professor says. By most reports, teachers stay attentive and engaged with students. "I think the overall quality of undergraduate teaching at Delaware is quite good," a teacher says. "This is a result of an ethos that holds that teaching undergraduates is important." But this teacher adds, "I fear that this ethos is jeopardized by an increasing reliance on adjunct faculty and by the growth of graduate programs." A current student counters that "the school provides ample avenues and opportunities to take responsibility for one's own growth and education. Students who rise to the challenge are met with resources and encouragement from highly qualified faculty, an extensive library and library staff, as well as other campus resources."

UD's distinguished honors program admits 450 students each year. Honors students live together in a living-learning community that provides highly qualified students with many advantages, including interdisciplinary courses geared toward freshmen, smaller class sizes with more opportunities to interact with key faculty members, priority scheduling, special housing options and cocurricular activities to build community, and an advising program for students wishing to compete for prestigious scholarships such as the Rhodes, Marshall, and Truman—of which UD has claimed a high number in recent years. One campus source says the honors program suffers from an excess emphasis on "creative thinking" and "problem solving" over knowledge acquisition but adds that it has the advantage of "introducing gifted students to one another."

Honors degrees are also available in most departments, meeting in small sections with skilled professors. A professor says, "Our [department's] honors program is reasonably successful, but we have not committed sufficient resources; thus, there are not enough true honors courses—too many are merely an extra section of a regular class with an honors component. It's a kind of false advertising."

The university's strongest suit is easily the College of Engineering, where the best department is chemical engineering. Some of the sciences, including biology and chemistry, are also top notch. The physical therapy program is currently ranked second in the world, a teacher says, and the art-restoration department is excellent as well.

Generally speaking, the humanities and social sciences offerings are weak. Ideology intrudes "virtually everywhere except in art history," a professor notes. "Most of the other

VITAL STATISTICS

Religious affiliation: *none*
Total enrollment: *20,737*
Total undergraduates: *17,120*
SAT CR/Verbal midrange:
   540–640
SAT Math midrange:
   560–660
ACT midrange: *25–29*
Applicants: *23,647*
Applicants accepted: *58%*
Accepted applicants who
   enrolled: *28%*
Tuition (general/out of
   state): *$27,462*
Tuition (in state): *$11,192*
Room and board: *$10,196*
Freshman retention rate:
   92%
Graduation rate (4 yrs.): *65%*
Graduation rate (6 yrs.): *78%*
Courses with fewer than 20
   students: *36%*
Student-faculty ratio: *15:1*
Courses taught by graduate
   students: *not provided*
Students living on campus:
   44%
Students in fraternities: *16%*
Students in sororities: *21%*
Students receiving need-
   based financial aid: *48%*
Avg. student-loan debt of a
   recent graduating class:
   $31,002
Most popular majors:
   *business, social sciences,
   education*
Guaranteed housing for 4
   years? *no*

liberal arts programs are mired in political correctness, although there are individual professors and courses that are quite good." Another says, "There are some programs that I would not recommend, as they are too politicized and left wing in their approach—such as women's studies, sociology, and anthropology. One bright spot in the liberal arts is the philosophy department, which has a surprising number of good, thoughtful faculty." In most humanities classes, "the readings are lightweight, the papers casual, and the discussions 'nonjudgmental.' Moral and cultural relativism are absolute dogmas," a teacher warns. Another says that "the faculty in sociology, criminal justice, and political science is uniformly on the left. They go much too far in advocacy during class. But I have never heard of faculty who bully or abuse conservative or religious students."

Majors in English must choose from five concentrations: Literary Studies; Creative Writing; Ethnic and Cultural Studies; Professional Writing; and Drama. There is no common core of classes, although those who specialize in Literary Studies must take classes that cover high points in British and American literature, which means they will encounter Shakespeare and other major authors.

History majors take two breadth classes in world history *or* Western civilization; a course covering history before 1700; and a course in Asian, African, Latin American, or Middle Eastern history; as well as two advanced courses. In addition to a regular major, history students could also concentrate in American, European, or world history. (So U.S. history is optional.) Undergraduate teaching in the department, an insider says, is often preoccupied by the fashionable "emphasis on race and gender." Sources say that a number of solid, more traditional professors remain in the department, however—if you seek them out.

At least 18 credits are required of political science majors. All majors are required to take "Data Analysis for Political Science," "Introduction to International Relations," and "The American Political System," so presumably they will learn something about the U.S. Constitution. Students can pursue a degree in political science or political science education. Through a joint program with the Department of Foreign Languages and Literatures, students may also study political science with French, German, or Spanish.

Highly recommended teachers include Raymond Wolters, Steven Sidebotham, and Jonathan Russ in history; Jan Blits in education; Eric Rise in sociology; Jim Magee and Joseph Pika in political science; Joel Pust, Seth Shabo, Jeff Jordan, and Katherine Rogers in philosophy; Stephen Barr and John Morgan in physics; Raj Varma and Charles Elson in finance; Sheldon Pollack and Burt Abrams in business and economics; Julian Yates and Bernard McKenna III in English; Daniel Sullivan and Gary Weaver in management; and Mike Keefe and Tom Buchanan in mechanical engineering.

Students speak highly of many teachers. "The professors here are all experienced in their field and often become quite close with their students," one reports. Another says, "My professors have been available and willing to help for the most part, just so long as it is clear that I am putting in the time outside of class as well." Class size diminishes as students advance. One current undergrad reports: "Generally, introduction courses will have anywhere from 50 to 150 students. However, as you take higher-level classes, class sizes are much smaller. In my two years at the University of Delaware, I have taken one class with approximately 150 students. The average number of students in all my other classes ranges from 30 to 40." Another student says, "While it is true that one must consciously maneuver courses in order to take advantage of the best the university has to offer, this is not necessarily a weakness of the institution. Brilliant professors inspire comprehensive work in any receptive student who is prepared to actively engage with his own self-development—which to me stands as a strength."

UD offers a good array of languages. Majors include Ancient Greek and Roman studies, Arabic, French, German, Hebrew, Italian, Japanese, Portuguese, Russian, and Spanish.

The University of Delaware launched America's first study-abroad program in 1923, and now the university's Institute for Global Studies coordinates more than 70 study-abroad

CAMPUS POLITICS: YELLOW LIGHT

Like most big universities, the University of Delaware is a mixed bag. A national scandal erupted in 2008 when it was reported that the Residential Life office was conducting a reeducation program aimed explicitly at pushing students to adopt highly specific university-approved views on politics, race, sexuality, sociology, moral philosophy, and environmentalism. The program made mandatory, among other things, one-on-one meetings between students and their resident assistants where students were asked intrusive questions, such as "When did you discover your sexual identity?"

Following coverage on national talk radio and criticism by free-speech advocates, the university quietly eliminated the most intrusive elements of the plan. However, as an insider reports, "the administration, from the very top down, is incorrigible. They have still not removed the Residence Life administrators responsible" for the indoctrination program. What is more, administrators "attack in various ways, including accusations of racism and intimidating legal briefs, those of us who defend the rights of students and faculty." As recently as August 2012, the university was called out by the Foundation for Individual Rights in Education for maintaining a "bullying" policy that banned "teasing," "ridiculing," and the "spreading of rumors."

programs annually. Students can travel to countries as far-flung as the Cayman Islands, Denmark, Hong Kong, and India.

Student Life: Main Street

The idyllic University of Delaware campus in Newark features handsome neoclassical buildings enclosing large open greens. Both academic and student residences comprise the main part of the green, which is classically integrated. There is a range of options for living environments, from single-sex halls to coed by floor or hall. While bathrooms are still single sex, most dorms alternate male and female rooms side by side, leaving little room for privacy or modesty. In 2013 the university opened two new residence halls, bringing together all freshmen in one part of campus. A university official described it as a "first-year student neighborhood" where students could "forge lifelong bonds with their peers and their professors."

Greek organizations are a big presence on campus, as some 20 percent of students at UD pledge one of the 24 fraternities and 19 sororities. Greek life is described as "average. No one will treat you differently if you don't join," a student reports. Another tells us: "There is a wide variety of activities on the weekends. Fraternities, sororities, and bars are in seemingly never-ending supply. However, for those who favor sober activities, the university provides clubs and organizations. Additionally, the University of Delaware is situated around Main Street, which has numerous restaurants, bars, and places for shopping. I rarely have to leave campus to find something fun." Main Street is indeed conveniently located, almost an extension of the campus. In addition to the bars and restaurants, it boasts a variety coffeehouses, bookstores, and shops.

In UD's distinguished honors program, students benefit from smaller class sizes, priority scheduling, special housing options and cocurricular activities to build community, and a strong advising program.

There are more than 450 registered student organizations at UD, including opera, symphony, dance, drama, jazz, model UN, French, and German clubs. The 30 religious clubs include Catholics, Baha'i, Jewish, Methodist, Buddhist, Episcopal, Presbyterian, Lutheran, Muslim, Orthodox, Coptic, Unitarian, and Mormon. A professor says that the "Catholic group on campus has quite an organized program, and the bishop [has taken] a big interest in the university's program."

College Democrats and College Republicans are both active on campus, as are Army and Air Force ROTC. There is a student group called Pro-Life Vanguard, alongside many large progressive organizations. A professor says, "UD is like most major universities in that the faculty is dominated by liberals, Democrats, and those generally on the Left, while there are few conservatives and Republicans. Even so, I have never felt intimidated on campus in any way. I would recommend that any conservative or religious students assert themselves in a polite but firm way." Conservative students should look at the Delaware Leaders Club, which advances knowledge of America's Founding and offers networking opportunities. (The club is sponsored by the Intercollegiate Studies Institute, which publishes this guide.)

The Delaware Fightin' Blue Hens compete in Division I in the NCAA. There are 21 varsity teams at UD, but football is by far the most popular and successful sport. One student warned potential applicants in an online forum: "If you are into any sport except football and maybe lacrosse, go somewhere else." The football team has won six national titles, and in the 2013 Super Bowl, former UD quarterback Joe Flacco and offensive lineman Gino Gradkowski led the Ravens to a victory.

A student reports, "There is a very large party atmosphere at UD. However, if you aren't interested, it is easy to focus on your studies instead. I feel that a good percentage of the students at UD balance having fun and success in their majors." A graduate of the school reminisced in an online forum:

> **SUGGESTED CORE**
>
> 1. Foreign Language and Literature 322, Topics: Classical Literature in Translation
> 2. Philosophy 301, Ancient Philosophy
> 3. English 202, Biblical and Classical Literature (*closest match*)
> 4. Philosophy 311/312, Early/Late Medieval Philosophy
> 5. Political Science 435, Political Thought II
> 6. English 284, Shakespeare for Nonmajors
> 7. History 205, United States History to 1865
> 8. History 356, Modern European Intellectual History

UD is situated in a nice little town where there are plenty of restaurants, a movie theatre, bowling alley, tons of concerts—that is, lots to do. Parents often assume that you can group students into a "drinkers" and "non-drinkers" crowd. I knew plenty of people, including myself, who enjoyed going to alcoholic parties but did not drink. . . . UD does offer substance-free dorms, where residents sign a contract and are generally committed to keeping an alcohol and smoke-free environment. Honors housing (not limited to honors students) is a bit quieter and more sober.

An undergrad praises "the diversity of social groups and types. I have friends of all interests—all of which have found their own place within the community."

As with many large universities, safety is definitely a concern on campus and around town. Students should stay aware of their surroundings, especially if they are walking alone or at night. The University of Delaware Police Department does maintain a presence. The department offers training, events management, building security, messenger service, student police aides, escorts, and the Emergency Care Unit, to name a few. There are also more than 200 emergency phones located on the campus—both inside buildings and outdoors. In 2011 the school reported four robberies, 26 burglaries, three forcible sex offenses, one nonforcible sex offense, three aggravated assaults, one car theft, and one arson.

Tuition in 2012–13 for Delaware residents was $11,192 and $27,462 for out-of-state students. Room and board were $10,196. Forty-eight percent of all undergraduates received some form of need-based financial aid, and the average debt of recent UD graduates was a heavy $31,002.

Blue Collar Ivy

STRONG SUITS

- The College of Engineering is excellent, and its best department is chemical engineering.
- Some of the sciences, including biology and chemistry, are also top notch.
- The physical therapy program is currently ranked second in the world, a teacher says.
- Good departments in philosophy and art history (especially the art-restoration program).
- A strong school emphasis on teaching over research.

WEAK POINTS

- The general-ed requirements are trivial, making core knowledge optional but diversity mandatory.
- Many nonscience programs are politicized (such as sociology, criminal justice, and political science), and several are less than rigorous.
- Women's studies, sociology, and anthropology are so ideological that they should simply be avoided.
- The administration is preoccupied with promoting diversity and sexual radicalism and has punished dissenters in the recent past.

Florida State University

Blue Collar Ivy: Florida

Transformer College

Florida State University has undergone several metamorphoses since its founding in 1857 as West Florida Seminary. After absorbing a college for women, serving briefly as a Confederate military academy, then becoming single sex again for decades, in 1947 FSU was finally founded as a major state university for men and women.

This past decade has marked the most recent period of major growth on the Florida State University campus, "characterized by a renewed sense of heritage, with construction, landscaping, monuments, and signage designed to highlight the university's history," says the school. Amid all the renewal, Florida State has maintained a respectable set of liberal arts programs with solid majors and many excellent teachers. Although there is too much latitude in the core requirements, with a little effort students can construct a very respectable curriculum from the myriad of classes FSU has on offer.

Academic Life: Gulf Stream waters

Florida State's main campus sits on 418 acres in the state capital of Tallahassee. There is also a satellite campus in Panama City, a marine laboratory on the Gulf Coast, and a joint

VITAL STATISTICS

Religious affiliation: *none*
Total enrollment: 40,695
Total undergraduates: 32,171
SAT CR/Verbal midrange:
 550–640
SAT Math midrange:
 560–650
ACT midrange: *24–28*
Applicants: *26,037*
Applicants accepted: *60%*
Accepted applicants who
 enrolled: *38%*
Tuition (general/out of
 state): *$20,080*
Tuition (in state): *$4,916*
Room and board: *$9,912
 (average)*
Freshman retention rate:
 90%
Graduation rate (4 yrs.): *50%*
Graduation rate (6 yrs.): *74%*
Courses with fewer than 20
 students: *35%*
Student-faculty ratio: *22:1*
Courses taught by graduate
 students: *not provided*
Students living on campus:
 20%
Students in fraternities: *15%*
Students in sororities: *16%*
Students receiving need-
 based financial aid: *38%*
Avg. student-loan debt of a
 recent graduating class:
 $20,984
Most popular majors: *crimi-
 nal justice, English, finance*
Guaranteed housing for 4
 years? *no*

engineering program with Florida A&M at Innovation Park. While such resources are worthwhile, they also demonstrate FSU's emphasis on research and the hard sciences—sometimes at the expense of the less remunerative liberal arts.

The university has 16 colleges, offering "more than 275 undergraduate, graduate, doctoral, professional, and specialist degree programs, including medicine and law, covering a broad array of disciplines," the school reports. As far as undergraduate liberal arts studies are concerned, the two most important schools are the College of Arts and Sciences and the College of Social Sciences and Public Policy. Arts and Sciences is made up of 18 departments, 10 institutes and centers, and 10 interdisciplinary programs. Along with the usual programs one would expect to find, it also has some unusual majors like meteorology, English with an emphasis in business, and Latin American Caribbean studies. The College of Social Sciences and Public Policy is home to six departments, including the extremely strong school of economics, and an interdisciplinary African American studies program complete with a culture center. There are also departments that deal with urban planning and public policy, including the Pepper Institute on Aging and Public Policy. (This is Florida, where retirement is a major industry.)

Students in these two colleges, like all undergraduates at the university, are required to take 120 credits of course work to graduate. Acknowledging that an education should be more than something "narrowly focused on acquisition of skills needed to secure your first job," Florida State requires that all students complete the 30-to-42-credit-hour Liberal Studies program, a watered-down core curriculum.

Part of this "core" is a multicultural requirement, with two components: "Cross-Cultural Studies" (the "X-requirement") and "Diversity in Western Experience" (the "Y-requirement"). Students are not fooled and see these courses for what they are: concessions to current leftist trends in academics. "The X and Y requirements are nothing more than indoctrination courses," one student says. "We have to take classes like women's studies, African American studies, and other courses taught from an ideological point of view."

FSU requires that all students demonstrate competency in "oral skills" and "computer skills" by passing with at least a C one course designated as meeting the competency standards for each category. In addition, every returning junior must also pass the College-Level Academic Skills Test (which includes sections on vocabulary and algebra) in order to resume classes their senior year. Students in the College of Arts and Sciences must also demonstrate proficiency in a foreign language at the intermediate level.

"Advising First" is FSU's academic advising program within the undergraduate division. Freshmen choose an academic adviser or "success coach" within their academic unit or department, depending on when they declare a major. Of course, in a school the size of FSU, it is entirely up to the students whether to avail themselves of this service.

Students can expect to do their work in very large classes, especially in their first two years. The student-faculty ratio for underclassmen is a crushing 22 to 1. Class size begins to shrink only in the third and fourth years—and even in the fifth year (which 69 percent of incoming freshmen need to graduate). This generally means that close student-faculty relationships are not forged until late in one's education. And the situation is getting worse. In 2012 FSU president Eric Barron discussed the school's financial straits: "Florida State University has experienced enormous financial stress over the past three years, with the loss of $85 million in state appropriations," Mr. Barron said. "There are no good outcomes when a university budget is cut by 25 percent." According to the *Chronicle of Higher Education,* this has resulted in the loss of as many as 200 faculty positions . . . and counting.

FSU has an honors program open to incoming freshman who had at least a 3.9 GPA in high school and a combined SAT score of at least 1910. Benefits of the program include smaller class sizes; courses taught by the best faculty; the option to live in honors program housing; and honors seminars. The honors seminars are typically limited to 15 students and cover topics unique to their curriculum. Past seminar courses have included "Mysteries of Human Perception and Cognition," "Beethoven as Composer and Icon," and "Living

CAMPUS POLITICS: GREEN LIGHT

FSU has not only College Republicans and Democrats but also College Libertarians and College Independents. The College Republicans are very active, boasting large membership rolls. In recent years the CRs have hosted speakers like Ann Coulter, Michelle Malkin, and 2012 Republican presidential candidate Rick Santorum. The school's conservative student groups definitely have a leg up on those that lean to the left. FSU also has its share of ubiquitous politically correct and radical organizations, such as the Black Student Union and Pride Student Union (a lesbian, gay, bisexual, and transgender group). Truth be told, students at FSU don't care all that much about politics—though in 2010, members of FSU's Federalist Society took part in the local March for Life on the anniversary of *Roe v. Wade.*

In an encouraging move, 2011 saw libertarian billionaire Charles G. Koch pledge $1.5 million "for positions in Florida State University's economics department. In return, his representatives get to screen and sign off on any hires for a new program promoting 'political economy and free enterprise,'" according to the *Tampa Bay Times*—which, of course, deplored such interference in academic freedom.

Green: Theory to Action." Students accepted into the honors program are also eligible for the Honors Medical Scholar Program and the Honors Legal Scholars Program. These preprofessional programs give undergraduates access to the FSU medical school and law school and offer automatic admission upon graduation. Students participating in the Medical Scholars program may even be eligible for early admission to the medical school, making it possible to complete both undergraduate and medical degrees in seven years.

A student who knows his direction can find enough good classes to forge a decent education, according to the professors we consulted. This presumably is not because of the curricular structure but in spite of it. Certain departments and professors are first-rate, and the Classics and economics departments are highly regarded in academic circles.

The English department has excellent degree requirements, including one course in American literature; British literature pre-1660, 1660–1800, and post-1800; world literature; literary criticism; a senior seminar; and four upper-division electives. English majors must also exhibit proficiency in a foreign language. The department's creative writing program, it is worth noting, has been ranked among the top in the nation by *The Atlantic* and is home to Pulitzer Prize winner Robert Olen Butler and nominees for the National Book Award.

> Teachers are mostly fair in class, and student activism is limited, an undergrad says, to "a small but loud contingent of militant gay and minority rights groups that not surprisingly tend to gravitate toward the social science departments."

History majors receive a well-rounded set of requirements, including six hours each in American, European, and world history; six hours of upper-level American history; six of European history; six of Latin American, Asian, African, and/or Russian history (in any combination); and two additional upper-level history courses. Some of these are politicized, but they are easily avoided, as the majority of history classes are solid and informative.

The political science department requires all majors to take at least one class in American government and a choice of two classes from the following: Introduction to Comparative Government and Politics, Introduction to International Relations, Public Administration in American Society, and Introduction to Public Policy. Students must also take six hours each in three of the departmental subfields (American Government, Comparative Politics, International Relations, Public Policy) as well as a senior seminar.

Economics at FSU features a diversity of approaches, including theories ranging from the Chicago School to the Keynesian School.

The Classics department also provides an uncommon educational opportunity for students, explaining on its website: "Some Classics majors go on to become teachers or scholars, but Classics is not primarily a vocational major, [but] an opportunity to receive a comprehensive education in the liberal arts." The courses it offers—including "Greek

Drama," "Greek Poetry," "The Roman Historians and Cicero," and "Literature of the Republic"—have been elsewhere disappearing from course catalogs across the country. The department also has an archaeology program that allows students to travel abroad for several different projects.

Other departments, such as sociology, are not in particularly good shape. The department is divided between technocratic demographers and ideologues who emphasize race and gender relations ad nauseum. A psychology major tells us that "there is a small but loud contingent of militant gay and minority rights groups that not surprisingly tend to gravitate toward the social science departments."

FSU's film school is one of the best in the country. For undergraduates, the school offers a BFA in film production, a minor in film studies, and a non-degree-granting program in which students explore business practices in the film industry. Over the past 20 years, the film students have snagged numerous awards, including the John Templeton Filmanthropy Award for documentaries on philanthropic organizations.

> **SUGGESTED CORE**
>
> 1. Classics 4340, Greek and Roman Epic
> 2. Philosophy 3130/3140, Plato and His Predecessors /Aristotle to Augustine
> 3. Religion 2210/2240, Introduction to the Old Testament/Introduction to the New Testament
> 4. Religion 3505, The Christian Tradition (*closest match*)
> 5. Philosophy of Man and Society 3331, Modern Political Thought
> 6. English 3334, Introduction to Shakespeare
> 7. American History 2010, U.S. History to 1865
> 8. History of Philosophy 3500, 19th-Century Philosophy

Although many classes at FSU are overpopulated, this does not prevent good rapport with professors. One student says, "I believe most professors here truly want to help and see me succeed. They keep very generous office hours and, in my experience, are always willing to make appointments outside of regular office hours if you have a conflict." Most students and professors told us that although the faculty is typically more liberal than the student body, their left-wing views seldom gratuitously intrude into the classroom. A list of recommended professors includes Bruce L. Benson, James D. Gwartney, and Randall G. Holcombe in economics; Roy Baumeister and Jon Maner in psychology; Jeff Keesecker in music; R. Jay Turner in social sciences; and Trevor Luke and Laurel Fulkerson in Classics.

Florida State's study-abroad program is recognized as one of the best in the country. Nearly 2,000 FSU students study abroad each year, many at the school's study centers in England, Italy, Panama, and Spain. Other popular affiliated overseas programs are offered in Argentina, Brazil, China, Costa Rica, Croatia, the Czech Republic, Ecuador, France, Germany, Ireland, Israel, Peru, Russia, Spain, Switzerland, Turkey, and Uruguay.

A few of the many foreign languages offered at home are Arabic, French, German, Greek and Latin, Hebrew, Italian, Japanese, Mandarin Chinese, Portuguese, Russian, and Spanish.

Student Life: RecsportsPlex rex

The school is definitely football crazy—the Seminoles routinely challenge for the national championship and have won it several times in the recent past. The Seminoles field 17 varsity teams that compete in the NCAA Division I Atlantic Coast Conference, including men's football and baseball; women's soccer, softball, and volleyball; and men's and women's basketball, cross-country, golf, swimming and diving, tennis, and track and field (indoor and outdoor).

Intramural and club sports are also numerous. Intramurals on offer change yearly, but in 2012–13, FSU had 22 intramurals, including regulars like flag football, volleyball, and soccer, as well as oddballs like wallyball (volleyball meets wall ball) and tailgate games (horseshoes, washers, bocce, and cornhole). Among the 34 club sports are crew, rugby, and badminton. The school's love of athletics is manifested in the sports complex. The RecsportsPlex has a name like a dinosaur's, which is fitting: it's the largest intramural sports complex in the United States, including 12 football fields, five softball fields, four soccer fields, and a volleyball court—and a zeppelin. (OK, we're kidding about the zeppelin.)

For better or worse, FSU is nationally renowned as a party school. There are 65 fraternities and sororities at Florida State (including "multicultural" and historically black organizations), but only about 16 percent of all students pledge. Most student events are held at the Oglesby Union, which houses a variety of lounges, a bowling alley, movie theater, ballroom, coffeehouse, and several restaurants. The large community supports 550 student groups, including academic societies, religious organizations, and social clubs. Florida State offers an ROTC program as well as its own radio and television stations.

Along with the nearby Gulf Coast beaches, the campus offers three swimming pools and the "FSU Reservation," a lakeside complex that is ideal for picnics, water skiing, and concerts. Florida State has 17 residence halls and four on-campus student apartment complexes, all of which have high-speed Internet; most dorms also require meal plans. There is one women's dorm, Jennie Murphree Hall, but the rest are coed, with some offering the option of single-sex floors. Some of the dorms have limited visiting hours for members of the opposite sex (11 a.m. to midnight during the week and until 2 a.m. on the weekends), while others let roommates determine their own restrictions. The university strongly encourages students to live on campus for at least their first year, offering freshmen several "Living Learning Community" residences. Each community is focused on a different topic, such as "Music" or "Social Justice." The university also offers honors housing and substance-free residences.

Tallahassee is not a terribly safe city, and Florida State's campus-safety statistics reflect this. In 2011 FSU reported three forcible rapes, 10 robberies, and 18 aggravated assaults. *Business Insider* recently listed FSU as the 25th most dangerous college in America.

In-state tuition for 2012–13 was $4,916 (plus a $1,488 fee), with room and board averaging $9,912. Out-of-state tuition was $20,080 (plus a $1,488 fee). In 2011, 38 percent of FSU students received need-based financial aid, and the average student-loan debt of recent graduates was a moderate $20,984.

Florida

STRONG SUITS

- Good programs in science, especially marine sciences.
- Worthy departments in political science, Classics, English, history, economics, and film studies, and a strong honors program.
- Top-notch study-abroad options.
- A wide selection of foreign languages offered.
- Political balance and free expression on campus.

WEAK POINTS

- Far too much latitude in the core requirements, with many politicized or fluff options.
- The school directs most resources to science programs that repay it with research dollars—not to the liberal arts.
- Some of the social sciences, especially sociology and psychology, are heavily ideological.
- Party atmosphere, heavy drinking, significant crime near campus.

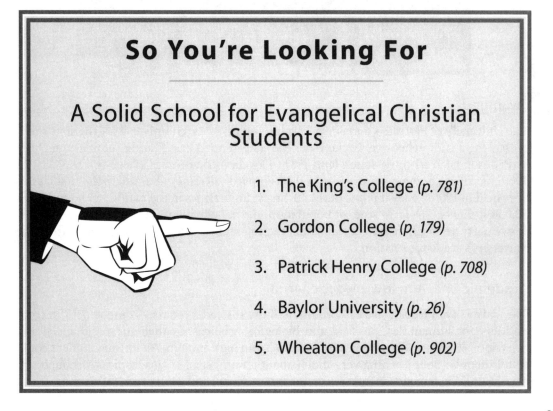

So You're Looking For

A Solid School for Evangelical Christian Students

1. The King's College *(p. 781)*

2. Gordon College *(p. 179)*

3. Patrick Henry College *(p. 708)*

4. Baylor University *(p. 26)*

5. Wheaton College *(p. 902)*

University of Florida

Gainesville, Florida • www.ufl.edu

Swamped

The University of Florida is a major public land-grant research university—the state's oldest and most comprehensive. In the 1860s the state-funded East Florida Seminary in Ocala was consolidated with the state's land-grant Florida Agricultural College in Lake City. In 1905 the college became a university and was moved to Gainesville, where the first classes were held in 1906. Today it is one of the 10 largest universities in the nation, with more than 50,000 students. The large student population, the popularity of Gator football, and a pervasive party atmosphere have a way of distracting many students—and others—from the university's academic mission.

Academic Life: Aim low, sweet chariot

The University of Florida has no core curriculum. Instead it requires competency "in composition, the humanities, physical and biological sciences, mathematics, and social and behavioral sciences." These requirements don't aim high enough. An unwary student could fulfill them without learning very much about a number of critical topics. Although one could fulfill these requirements—even the international and diversity requirements—with substantial courses rooted in traditional academic disciplines, there are also dozens of politicized, trendy, and frivolous choices, such as "Ecofeminism," "Human Sexuality and Culture," "Sex Roles: A Cross-Cultural Perspective," and "Women and Diversity in U.S. History." One professor warns that "students have a broad selection of courses, given the size of the university," which means that while a "student seeking a strong major that promotes critical thinking can blossom," there's nothing to prevent a student from "seeking an easy way through the credentialist system."

"The general-education requirements, in my opinion, dilute the education received in this university," a business student says. "Students take the most vapid courses in the university to meet the requirements, such as 'Wildlife Issues' for a bio credit or 'Astronomy' for physical education credit."

Sometimes students fall into these vapid courses because those they want are not available. One student says that since "there are few electives offered per semester . . . students have to settle for a class they didn't want in order to graduate." This student bemoans the relative paucity of faculty in certain departments. "The extremely low tuition means that a number of courses are large lectures, but junior- and senior-level courses are kept relatively small," a professor says. Another professor is more blunt: UF, he says, "is a large university and, to my mind, only worth attending if you can gain admission to the Honors College."

What about the honors program? It offers smaller classes, special honors sections of large courses, exclusive dorms, program-dedicated advisers, and a unique social and academic community for elite students during their first two years on campus. Sadly, some of the special courses in this program strike us as offering more quirk than core: they include "Modern Masculinities" and "Dude, You're a Fag: The Regulation of Gender and Sexuality in a Working-Class High School." One professor, originally drawn to the school to teach what used to be an "integrated humanities program," is disillusioned. The honors track is now a "hodgepodge." "No longer a balanced overview of the Western humanities tradition," he says, the program has lost its rudder in a sea of fragmentary offerings." Professors propose courses, usually their own

VITAL STATISTICS

Religious affiliation: *none*
Total enrollment: *49,913*
Total undergraduates: *32,776*
SAT CR/Verbal midrange: *580–670*
SAT Math midrange: *590–690*
ACT midrange: *26–31*
Applicants: *27,419*
Applicants accepted: *44%*
Accepted applicants who enrolled: *54%*
Tuition (general/out of state): *$28,448*
Tuition (in state): *$6,170*
Room and board: *$9,370*
Freshman retention rate: *95%*
Graduation rate (4 yrs.): *59%*
Graduation rate (6 yrs.): *84%*
Courses with fewer than 20 students: *45%*
Student-faculty ratio: *20:1*
Courses taught by graduate students: *not provided*
Students living on campus: *23%*
Students in fraternities: *18%*
Students in sororities: *17%*
Students receiving need-based financial aid: *47%*
Avg. student-loan debt of a recent graduating class: *$17,504*
Most popular majors: *psychology, biology, mechanical engineering*
Guaranteed housing for 4 years? *no*

331

CAMPUS POLITICS: GREEN LIGHT

One student says, "The atmosphere on campus lies between [left and right]. For example, a transgender ordinance was passed by the city, and fierce debate arose on both sides of the issue. Students on both sides campaigned before the vote took place. In general, the campus is left leaning, so that could be considered the prevailing orthodoxy, but the education provided to students is not stultified by political correctness."

The school's administration has a tin ear on issues of free speech but seems to respond well to criticism. In 2012 the Foundation for Individual Rights in Education (FIRE) slammed UF for the following Orwellian provision in its "Student's Rights and Responsibilities Policy": "Organizations or individuals that adversely upset the delicate balance of communal living will be subject to disciplinary action." According to *Campus Reform*, when FIRE "announced that University of Florida was sharing the honor of 'Speech Code of the Year' . . . the text of the speech code in question was removed." Still, UF's "Standard of Ethical Conduct" states that "expressions and challenges need to be civil, manifesting respect and concern for others." As *Campus Reform* noted, this policy "essentially requires that students be 'nice' to each other at all times and in all situations."

special interest. At UF the idea of a general, or liberal, education, unfortunately, is long past. The honors program does at least offer an alternative to massive classes and impersonal sections led by sometimes unintelligible TAs.

A quick glance at some key departments shows that they, too, have rather diffuse expectations. English majors, for instance, do not need to read Shakespeare; they must simply take 10 courses in the subject, including several upper-level seminars, whose approaches range from "Victorian Literature" to "Queer Life/Writing." History majors do not need to know anything about America before 1900; only two courses are required in U.S. history, and both could focus on the 20th century. Nor need political science majors study the U.S. Constitution, although a course is required in the U.S. federal government. All students, however, must take at least some math and science.

Students do enjoy flexibility. "Students can enroll in classes offered by other departments with ease," points out an urban planning student. In his specialty, he "can choose from a number of specializations, certificates, and concurrent degree plans, ranging from transportation engineering to sustainable design to historic preservation. Joint engineering or law degrees are often pursued by students. Additionally, [my] college offers several study-abroad programs [Brazil, France]. I was particularly stretched [in a good way] during the summer semester I spent at UF. . . . I enrolled in landscape architecture, environmental science, and history courses outside my discipline. Of these, the environmental science course was the most rigorous and most alien to my previous experiences." The Department of Urban and Regional Planning, he adds, "is ranked in the top 25 in the nation."

Despite UF's size, a psychology major says, "Professors are very accessible, as far as I have seen. Most professors post office hours, and all are required to have office hours at some point during the week." However, students "often do not take advantage of office hours," a professor counters. The trouble may lie in the sheer size of lecture classes. One student in the honors program says that while all her professors have been very friendly, "the larger classes are less 'personal' and therefore there is less contact with the instructor." Another student laments, "I think mentoring is very weak at UF. There are too few professors for the size of the student body."

Another obvious problem is the high percentage of undergraduate courses led by teaching assistants rather than professors. A psychology major says, "The role of the TA depends on the professor. In some classes, the TA is there to answer all questions by the students, grade exams and quizzes, and hold review sessions." Another student says that the role of TAs varies depending on the subject matter. About 20 percent of her classes have been taught by TAs, and sometimes the "system seemed to work very well." However, a student in the business department says that "many students complain about how bad some TAs are with dissemination of information, heavy accents, and lack of communication." Most upper-division courses are taught by professors, sources tell us.

One professor says that UF "is only worth attending if you gain admission to the Honors College." Another counters that Honors has "lost its rudder in a sea of fragmentary offerings."

Where does the undergraduate go to find his way in such a mega-institution? Advising is the responsibility of each college, and therefore the quality varies from college to college. The Academic Advising Center in the College of Liberal Arts and Sciences primarily serves students who need help choosing a major. In some departments and colleges, students must meet with an adviser before they can register for courses, while other departments and colleges have a faculty adviser on staff for students who seek assistance. One PhD student notes: "If students are entrepreneurial, other options for academic advisement and support exist off campus."

In the classroom, professors seem to allow students to express a variety of opinions without fear. And while the faculty leans left, a number of conservative professors can also be found. More important, an atmosphere of freedom seems to prevail. One such faculty member says, "Yes, most of the university is left leaning. But it's not ideological in the sense that there is intolerance of opposing views. It's not so pervasive that it affects instruction in individual classrooms. As a scholar, I never felt any pressure to shape my views to some politically correct standard." One student reports that he and some of his compatriots have felt "unwelcome in the political science and philosophy departments, and in some programs in the College of Fine Arts." Some professors in these programs are said to be very vocal in the classroom about their extra-academic opinions, leaving conservative students feeling it would be imprudent to dissent.

Some of the best academic programs at UF include business, nursing, journalism, psychology, education, engineering, agriculture, and microbiology (in addition to urban planning, mentioned above). Solid professors include Stephen McKnight (emeritus) in history; Sanford Berg and David Denslow in economics; Thomas Auxter (emeritus) in philosophy; Richard Conley and David Hedge in political science; Mary Collins in soil and water sciences; Bonnie Moradi and Carolyn Tucker in psychology; William Marsiglio and Hernán Vera (emeritus) in sociology; and Richard Schneider, Christopher Silver, and Paul Zwick in urban planning.

The intellectual curiosity of the student body is said to flicker, with some bright spots. A faculty member says, "I see the spectrum—village idiots to intensely motivated students." A student in one of the more rigorous departments says, "To be honest, the people I knew who attended UF got more out of the athletics (Gator football) than the academics." Another student says, "UF offers a lot of 'fluff' courses for students looking to meet requirements, such as sports and bartending classes." (At UF, admittedly, the latter could come in handy.) It should be noted, though, that new undergraduates are required to complete an alcohol education tutorial their first semester.

UF offers numerous languages and many short-term, summer-, semester-, or year-long programs in more than 80 countries, such as Australia, China, France, Israel, Peru, Poland, Slovakia, and South Korea. Students can major in Chinese, French, German, Japanese, Portuguese, Russian, or Spanish.

Student Life: No lines for tanning

Gainesville is a college town. A student points out that "the city of Gainesville has made a concerted effort to preserve the trees and landscape within its limits." Parks and preserves (especially Paynes Prairie and Lake Wauberg) prove excellent recreational experiences. Dining in Gainesville is varied and vibrant—ranging from an idiosyncratic pizza joint (Satchel's) to a first-class Mediterranean restaurant (Ti Amo). When there's no football game or other activity to keep them around campus, students tend to go home on the weekends. "There are only two disadvantages to Gainesville: the traffic on game days and the summer heat/humidity," that student adds.

Football is the life of the party at UF. On Saturdays in the fall, the Gators attract some 90,000 fans into Ben Hill Griffin Stadium, otherwise known as the Swamp. UF has a very physically active student body and is consistently ranked among the top five NCAA programs in the nation in overall athletics for both men's and women's sports. In recent years, the revived men's basketball program has become a focal point of school spirit as well, especially with its first National Championship victory. Parties tend to revolve around Gator football and basketball games. "Football games basically shut down the campus on Saturdays, and parties are ubiquitous," a student says.

Gator Growl, an annual pep rally held before the homecoming game, launches a full weekend of parties. "The Gator Growl pep rally is unrivaled in the whole of America," says a student. Another recalls visiting UF "during Gator Growl and instantly knowing I wanted to come here. The school you see with your parents is not always the school you see on the weekend." (Parents take note!) Fortunately, UF is big enough to accommodate students who do not want to concentrate all their extracurricular time on football watching or drinking. "Whatever you like doing, you will find it," a student says. "If you dig the Greeks, we have them; if you like clubs, we have enough to make your head spin; if you like museums and performing arts, we have them; if you like clubbing, we have it—although the quality and variety is debatable."

Athletic students have many options. One reports: "In addition to on-campus gyms and recreational facilities and fields, UF even owns a private lake off campus where students can use rowboats and canoes, or have a picnic or play volleyball." Another student says that many enjoy "lazing about on the grass of the Plaza of the Americas in the heart of campus and watching the bats leave the bat house at dusk and fly out over Lake Alice for an insect meal."

While most freshmen live on campus, only about 23 percent of the student body does. All on-campus residences are coed. However, male and female students are not allowed to share a dorm room and do not share bathrooms. (Actually, Florida law prohibits male and female students from cohabitation in on-campus apartments unless they are married.) With minimal space available on campus, the university does not guarantee housing for all four years. But Gainesville itself offers plenty of options and a welcoming ambiance for students, as the city revolves around student life. Students at UF tend to pay a good bit of attention to their physical appearance, and the Florida sunshine lets them flaunt it. One of the more modest female students says, "I feel a little uncomfortable walking through campus while all of the girls are dressed in practically nothing."

Only 18 percent of men and 17 percent of women join a fraternity or sorority, but there are more than 800 student clubs and organizations, as well as more than 60 intramural and club sports in which to participate, all of which help make this giant university seem a little cozier. Student groups include Gator Free Thought, Fellowship of Christian Athletes, Pro-Life Alliance, Hands Down Hip Hop Dance Sensation, Navy-Marine Student Association, Model United Nations, Union de Estudiantes Puertorriqueños Activos, and Gator Aikido. In addition, there is a remarkably vivid religious presence on campus. Besides the usual Turlington Plaza preachers, thousands of students, and even some faculty, join religious groups, including Baptist Collegiate Ministries, Cru (Campus Crusade for Christ), Catholic Student Fellowship, Islam on Campus, and Jewish Student Union.

Political expression on campus is surprisingly balanced. Students are not activists, but both conservative and liberal perspectives are regularly aired on a range of topics.

The UF campus, a student reports, is "one of the most complex universities in the country; with 21 schools, that makes it a very interesting and large campus. They did a very good job of integrating the newer buildings with the older and more historic ones. It's a very attractive campus."

Crime on campus is not terribly prevalent, given the large number of students. In 2011

SUGGESTED CORE

1. Classics 4340, Greek and Roman Epic
2. Philosophy 3130/3140, Plato and His Predecessors/Aristotle to Augustine
3. Religion 2210/2240, Introduction to the Old Testament/Introduction to the New Testament
4. Religion 3505, The Christian Tradition (*closest match*)
5. Philosophy of Man and Society 3331, Modern Political Thought
6. English 3334, Introduction to Shakespeare
7. American History 2010, U.S. History to 1865
8. History of Philosophy 3500, 19th-Century Philosophy

the school reported six aggravated assaults, 27 burglaries, one robbery, 13 motor vehicle thefts, and nine forcible sex offenses on campus. The university provides free nighttime walking escorts and point-to-point van service for any student; one female student says that usually "an officer will be there within thirty seconds." For the most part, students consider themselves safe, but they report unease about the issue of "date-rape drugs" and some prefer not to walk alone at night. A 2010 incident in which campus police shot a student resulted in many protests. The officer involved was fired for an unrelated offense in 2011.

The University of Florida is generally considered affordable, and for those students seeking aid, plenty of options are available. Tuition for 2012–13 for in-state students was only $6,170 (out of state, $28,448), and room and board were estimated at around $9,370. Says one student, "The good thing about UF is that for many Florida residents with good test scores, [a state merit] scholarship pays full tuition and cost of books. I know many friends who are at UF specifically for this reason." Some 47 percent of students get need-based aid, and the average student-loan debt of a 2011 graduate was $17,504.

STRONG SUITS	WEAK POINTS
• Flexibility—students can study across majors and pursue a wide variety of programs.	• Many massive classes, with too many taught by graduate students who are less than English-fluent.
• Accessible professors who are mostly tolerant of political differences.	• Politicized faculty in political science, philosophy, and some programs in the College of Fine Arts.
• Good programs in business, nursing, journalism, psychology, education, engineering, agriculture, microbiology, and urban planning.	• Many fluff courses offered.
• Single-sex bathrooms and dorm rooms.	• Too many students are preoccupied with parties and sports.

Georgia Institute of Technology

Atlanta, Georgia • www.gatech.edu

Eyes on the Prize

Some say a better name for the Georgia Institute of Technology would be the "North Avenue Trade School." At Georgia Tech, most students enter knowing which career they want to pursue; a degree is just the means of attaining it. The liberal arts sit on the university's back burner, and most engineering students just enroll in them to satisfy curriculum requirements. Even humanities course descriptions are saturated with the words "science" and "technology." But academic life at Tech is rigorous and intense. "One thing I believe about Tech is that they really want you to earn your degree," an engineering student says. "My degree from Georgia Tech will be something of immense pride and satisfaction. I will know that I earned it on my own merits and not anyone else's."

Academic Life: Rigorous careerism

Academic life, as one computer science major puts it, is exceptionally tough, "but it will be well worth the hundreds of all-nighters and stress levels of 'eleven' once I get my degree and am looked at by future employers as one who knows what the heck I am doing because I graduated from such a highly ranked school." The chance to land a good job, not love of

337

VITAL STATISTICS

Religious affiliation: *none*
Total enrollment: *20,941*
Total undergraduates:
13,948
SAT CR/Verbal midrange:
600–690
SAT Math midrange:
660–760
ACT midrange: *28–32*
Applicants: *14,088*
Applicants accepted: *51%*
Accepted applicants who
enrolled: *39%*
Tuition (general/out of
state): *$27,022*
Tuition (in state): *$7,718*
Room and board: *$11,440*
Freshman retention rate:
95%
Graduation rate (4 yrs.): *31%*
Graduation rate (6 yrs.): *79%*
Courses with fewer than 20
students: *41%*
Student-faculty ratio: *17:1*
Courses taught by graduate
students: *6%*
Students living on campus:
56%
Students in fraternities: *25%*
Students in sororities: *29%*
Students receiving need-
based financial aid: *37%*
Avg. student-loan debt of a
recent graduating class:
$23,427
Most popular majors: *archi-
tecture, business/market-
ing, engineering,*
Guaranteed housing for 4
years? *no*

learning, seems to be the primary motivation for most Georgia Tech students. "Purely intellectual curiosity is a luxury most can't afford," one professor says. "Tech's an academic boot camp, and like Marines, most are justifiably proud of surviving it." Another teacher says: "The nature of the institution selects and rewards extreme task focus. Grades are most students' concern, especially in a course not part of their major." With the entire student body out to make the grade and land the job, one student says there is a strong sense of "competing against the system, and a lot of empathy among students. . . . We're all in it together."

Georgia Tech students must go through quite an ordeal before they can embark on their careers. Most engineering students require six years to graduate, and sixth- and seventh-year seniors are not uncommon. The course requirements for the engineering program are so rigorous that they discourage students from taking a wide variety of courses before settling on their majors. A few years ago, Georgia Tech increased the required percentage of hours in the engineering major. As one professor comments on this change, "While training might be better, it's arguable whether people are as well or better educated." One student observes that recently, however, there has been "a shift and an appreciation of broad-based education, even in the colleges of engineering and science." More students than in the past are opting for a bachelor of science in the College of Liberal Arts rather than in the College of Engineering, and some students who choose to major in engineering will minor in history or literature.

"Georgia Tech is not like the typical college people see in the movies; most students show up here knowing what they want to do, and do only that," says a student. "Since engineering is the university's main focus, most people do not take a wide variety of classes." Another engineering student says, "You can't come to Tech and think it will be like high school, where a minimal amount of studying will get you an A. Do that your first semester at Tech and you will flunk out."

Upon entering Georgia Tech, students can choose from among the university's six colleges: Engineering, Computing Sciences, Sciences, Architecture, Management, and the Ivan Allen College of Liberal Arts. Georgia Tech is most renowned for its engineering program, which is among the nation's most difficult. Georgia Tech's nationally recognized engineering facilities include the Manufacturing Research Center, where both undergraduate and graduate students "examine manufacturing processes, applications, and technical solutions," according to its webpage. Undergraduates participate in cutting-edge research that directly supports Tech's academic programs in engineering.

Not all engineering students can compete at this level. "Most engineering majors who do poorly tend to switch to easier course work that can be found in [the] management, industrial engineering, and English majors," says one student. The engineering disciplines, with the exception of industrial engineering, require high-level math and physics skills that professors expect students to master quickly and to use in classes.

The College of Computing Sciences is also highly regarded. It conducts interdisciplinary research and participates in instructional programs within other academic units on campus. Students gain hands-on experience while developing logical and analytical skills in their computer courses. Computer science majors are required to take 23 semester hours of free electives, but many use this flexibility to take courses within their major department rather than to broaden their knowledge in other areas.

The Ivan Allen College of Liberal Arts, which dates only to 1990, does not offer Georgia Tech's most highly touted academic programs. Less than 8 percent of undergraduates enroll in it, and its most popular program is international relations. Even within the liberal arts college, students cannot avoid mathematics and the sciences. For instance, instead of a philosophy department, Georgia Tech has a department of Philosophy, Science, and

CAMPUS POLITICS: RED LIGHT

Surprisingly, given the overall conservatism of most of its tech-savvy students, Georgia Tech has an unexpectedly politicized campus, complete with sit-ins, political rallies, and professors pushing political agendas. Moreover, the school's administration is said to be strongly biased toward the left, offering funding to activist groups like the Women's Resource Center, the African American Student Union, and the pansexual Pride Alliance—while denying student funds to conservative groups such as the College Republicans. Furthermore, Georgia Tech imposes a speech code on conservative students that has drawn fire from free-speech defenders.

As conservative activist (and Georgia Tech grad student) Ruth Malholtra told the Clare Booth Luce Institute: "Georgia Tech's policies restrict the First Amendment rights of all students, with the policies enforced primarily against conservative and religious students. I simply want all students to enjoy equal rights to free speech and religious liberty." According to the Luce Institute, "During her time on campus, Ruth's speech has been censored, her protests have been shut down by campus police, and she has been given lower grades in class—all because she is conservative and wants to advance a different perspective. . . . Even though Ruth is often critical of Georgia Tech's policies and many there have been so brutal to her, Ruth maintains her proud school spirit. She chose Georgia Tech for its 'academic excellence, time-honored traditions, and global impact,' and said that it is her 'love of liberty and love for Georgia Tech' that have compelled her to take a stand for justice."

Technology, replete with courses like "Environmental Ethics" and "Introduction to Cognitive Science." And instead of history, Tech has a history, technology, and society major. It features such courses as "Engineering in History," "The Scientific Revolution," and "Technology and Science in the Industrial Age." Students may take a course in American history, covering the founding and the Civil War, but they are not required to do so.

The English department has just two courses, both in basic composition, which explore technological or political issues. Needless to say, there is no stand-alone English major. Instead of political science, students may major in public policy—where they must take one course that covers the U.S. Constitution. However, most of the program requirements emphasize science and math. "They are not presenting a real liberal arts education," says one professor.

> "Purely intellectual curiosity is a luxury most can't afford," one professor says. "Tech's an academic boot camp, and like Marines, most are justifiably proud of surviving it."

Ivan Allen College's School of Literature, Communication, and Culture offers bachelor of science degrees in science, technology, and culture (STAC) and computational media, with postgraduate degrees in digital media and human-computer interaction. These programs seem to assume that the future of the humanities will be primarily electronic. This school has very few actual literature courses; the emphasis, again, is on science and technology.

Many students and professors inside and outside the Ivan Allen College agree that this college is somewhat politicized. One professor says that Ivan Allen "is a home for liberal activists who confuse advocacy with scholarship. Science it is not." A student says that it is not uncommon, for instance, for students to be graded down by vocally leftist professors for their more conservative viewpoints.

An onerous speech code, unevenly enforced against right-leaning students, led two Georgia Tech undergrads to sue the school in federal court, where judges struck down the school's policies as unconstitutional in 2006. The court victory gave new energy to the College Republicans, who held a First Amendment forum on the four-year anniversary of the ruling. But Georgia Tech continues to resist true freedom of speech. Conservative students and even faculty vocally (as opposed to silently) report a feeling of "persecution" at the hands of the administration.

Tech's College of Architecture, one of the oldest and most highly respected schools of its kind in the country, offers majors in architecture, building construction, and industrial design; the school is a national leader in city and regional planning.

Many students believe the quality of Tech's faculty is its most valuable asset. Almost 60 faculty members have received Presidential, National Science Foundation (NSF) Young Investigator, or NSF Career awards. Professors teach most courses; only a few are conducted by graduate teaching assistants. More often, Tech uses TAs to teach laboratory sections, hold office hours, grade papers, and lead weekly discussion sections.

One student says, "Professors are excellent at what they do, extremely intelligent, and know the subject. They have won high-dollar contracts for the school from huge companies, have tenure at the school, and do major research for which they get recognition." Not surprisingly, then, many professors are interested in their research above all else. One student says that, while faculty members are ready to help if asked, "normally the chain of command is notes, books, Internet, TAs, newsgroups, professors. Professors are generally seen as a last resort. Their line of reasoning is that, in the workforce, you can't just go to the boss and say, 'How do you do this?'"

Freshmen are assigned advisers and required to visit them, but upperclassmen can use their advisers to whatever degree needed. "In my experience, they offer suggestions and help you figure out classes," one student says. "However, they are very willing to let you plan your academic career."

Students name as some of the best professors at the university George F. Riley in electrical and computer engineering; George L. Cain Jr. in mathematics; William Leahy in the College of Computing; Ahmet Erbil in physics; Steve Potter and Eberhard Voit in biomedical engineering; and Charles A. Eckert in chemical engineering. Among active and visible younger faculty

SUGGESTED CORE
1. History 3028, Ancient Greece (closest match)
2. Philosophy, Science, and Technology 3102, History of Ancient Philosophy
3. No suitable course
4. History, Technology, and Society 3030, History of Medieval Europe (350–1400) (closest match)
5. International Affairs 2210A, Political Philosophies and Ideologies
6. Literature, Communication, and Culture 3228, Shakespeare
7. History, Technology, and Society 2006, History of the Old South to 1865
8. History, Technology, and Society 3032, European Intellectual History

are marine biologist and biochemist Julia Kubanek, aerospace engineer and NASA contact Robert Braun, and nanotechnology guru Z. L. Wang.

Georgia Tech offers no majors in foreign languages, but there are degree programs in applied languages and intercultural studies, global economics and modern languages, and international affairs and modern languages. Students can take courses in Arabic, Chinese, French, German, Japanese, Korean, Russian, and Spanish. There is also one Latin course available. Students may participate in a vast array of study-abroad programs in countries such as Argentina, Egypt, Greece, and Singapore. Some departments offer unique faculty-led programs like the Architecture Senior Year in Paris.

Student Life: No time for rambling

Course work at Georgia Tech is tough. Students spend vast amounts of time in the library, in laboratories, and in front of their computers. With only a third of the student population graduating in four years, some students can't afford to "waste time" with extracurriculars. But one student says, "We aren't called 'Ramblin' Wreck' for nothing. We work hard and study lots, then play hard . . . in that order."

Almost a third of women at Georgia Tech join sororities, and a fourth of men pledge fraternities, making the Greek scene an important hub of what social life takes place on

Blue Collar Ivy

campus. Independents sometimes complain that the frats are cliquish and exclusive—keeping nonmembers out of parties, for instance. Those who don't join Greek life are said to make the most of nightspots in the Buckhead neighborhood, which offers a number of opportunities for 18-year-old students who are content to sip Diet Cokes. Given the workload at the school, it's not surprising that it doesn't rank as a party school.

Georgia Tech athletics are popular among students, area alumni, and Atlantans, who often claim a partial ownership of the school—or at least of Tech sports. The Yellow Jackets compete in the Atlantic Coast Conference (ACC), home to such powerhouses as Duke, Florida State, Maryland, and North Carolina. Tech struggles from time to time, but overall its sports programs are strong. In the past decade, Tech saw three of its alumni win Olympic gold medals, sent its basketball team to the Final Four, and won ACC titles in football, tennis, golf, baseball, and women's volleyball. All games are free for students. And despite the workload, Tech consistently ranks among the top 25 schools in the nation in graduating its student-athletes (although it helps that Tech athletes are disproportionately more likely to major in management than in engineering). The university also offers intramural sports, including soccer, sand volleyball, flag football, Ultimate Frisbee, bowling, and Wiffle ball.

Besides sports, Georgia Tech offers plenty of extracurricular activities. Student clubs include those devoted to recreation, leisure, publications, and artistic and cultural productions, as well as honor societies, volunteer groups, and organizations for political, religious, cultural, and diversity purposes. Some of the myriad student clubs are Quizbowl, Rocket Club, Hellenic Society, Future Educators, and Mars Society (they want to settle the planet). Not surprisingly, Georgia Tech also has a number of academic and professional groups, like the Earthquake Engineering Research Institute, the Institute of Electrical and Electronics Engineering, and the *Tower,* a journal of undergraduate research.

Religious groups and ministries on campus include the Fellowship of Christian Students, Orthodox Christian Fellowship, Baptist Collegiate Ministries, Chi Alpha, Catholic Student Organization, Hillel, Latter-Day Saint Association, Muslim Student Association ... and, for the unconvinced, Campus Freethinkers.

Political groups include the College Republicans, Pride Alliance (gay), Students for Life, Student Movement for Real Change, Students in Free Enterprise, Students of Objectivism, and Women's Awareness Month. The *Conservative Buzz* is a campus alternative paper.

Fifty-six percent of Georgia Tech undergraduates choose to live on campus; the rest live in the surrounding area. "To tell you the truth, campus housing is pretty scarce, and many students, after their required freshman year, choose to live off campus or in Greek-life housing," one student says. First-year students have the option of participating in Freshman Experience (FE), which offers a set of traditional dormitories on the east side of campus. Most of the dorms are single sex, and all dorms have an official escort policy for members of the opposite sex. All FE dorms are supposed to be alcohol-free, and all have upperclassmen as resident advisers on each hall, a required meal plan, and 24-hour low-noise rules. Undergraduates who are not a part of FE have limited options for housing. Traditional-style halls typically are single sex with two-person rooms. Some suite-style buildings are available, as well as four apartment complexes originally built for the 1996 Olympics. Apartments are usually the most coveted living options on campus; since housing is decided by lottery and by class, seniors usually snag these prime spots.

Student safety is of great concern at Georgia Tech. In 2011 the school reported three aggravated assaults, five forcible sex offenses, 18 burglaries, five robberies, and 15 stolen cars on campus. Students who seek a Georgia Tech education but would rather not live in Atlanta can attend the school's Savannah campus instead—enjoying all the attractions of a small, lovely old southern city by the sea.

As a state-assisted school, Georgia Tech is considerably less expensive than other universities with comparable reputations. In 2012–13 tuition for Georgia residents was only $7,718, while outsiders paid a more standard $27,022. The housing and meal plans averaged around $11,440. Almost three-quarters of the student body come from Georgia; all in-state students maintaining a B average are eligible for the state HOPE (Helping Outstanding Pupils Educationally) scholarship and the free tuition that comes with it. *Money* magazine consistently ranks Tech as one of the nation's best academic values. The average student-loan debt of a recent graduate was $23,427.

STRONG SUITS	WEAK POINTS
• Offers a world-class education in engineering, with facilities such as the Manufacturing Research Center, where students work alongside teachers. • Excellent classes and facilities in computer science. • First-rate architecture program. • Award-winning researchers lead classes in science and technology. • Reasonable dorm policies, with several single-sex residences.	• Few options in the humanities—mostly classes about the impact of science in those fields. • Strongly politicized faculty in several humanities disciplines. • Significant crime around campus. • Professors delegate student interaction to grad teaching assistants. • Free speech denied to conservatives by administration on several occasions.

University of Georgia

Athens, Georgia • www.uga.edu

Eat a Peach

The University of Georgia was founded in 1785, but for much of its history it has been regarded as little more than a training ground for agriculture students. UGA is now on the rise, drawing better students and more prestigious faculty, largely as a result of the state of Georgia's Helping Outstanding Pupils Educationally (HOPE) scholarship program, through which in-state students can receive full-tuition scholarships, inducing many of the state's top students to stay in Georgia (in 2012–13, 97 percent of in-state freshmen earned the HOPE Scholarship). HOPE students must maintain a B average to keep their scholarships.

UGA's curriculum has quite a bit going for it. Core curriculum requirements for undergrads are comparatively strong, while the honors program is both highly regarded and competitive. One professor praises the sought-after Foundation Fellows Program as a "super honors program that truly offers an Ivy League experience at bargain basement prices." One student reports that she chose UGA over Columbia University when she realized that she could receive a genuine classical education at a bargain price. Throw in a low-key political atmosphere, a fantastic college town, and a strong school spirit, and UGA is clearly one of the better choices for students interested in a southern state university.

Academic Life: Keep HOPE alive

Georgia's curriculum centers on a core that provides students as broad an education as one could hope for at a large state school. While students at UGA have flexibility in choosing their courses, it's impossible for them to get away with taking courses in just one or two disciplines. However, like at many schools, the core curriculum is only as solid as a student wants to make it: Students may choose between "English Composition" II and "Multicultural English Composition."

Many students regard a few course requirements as being insubstantial and easy and of little educational interest. Among these are the "United States" and "Georgia History and Constitution" requirements, which students can easily test out of. Students must also fulfill a cultural diversity requirement that varies by school and department. Most of the courses that fulfill these requirements seem politicized, but courses like "Topics in Romance Languages" and "American Indian History to 1840" are less so. UGA students must also fulfill an "environmental literacy" course requirement. According to a science professor, courses in this area are typically solid. "Ecology here is science rather than politics," the professor says. "Same with agriculture; if you want to talk about the world hunger problem, you go and find agriculture experts who can tell you exactly what's going on."

Since 1996 the university has produced eight Rhodes scholars—not to mention 21 Fulbright scholars in the three-year period leading to 2013. Some alumni remark that they would never get into the school were they to apply now.

One professor who has taught at the university for several years attests to the changes: "University of Georgia students are dramatically better than they were 15 years ago. Large numbers of gifted students who would previously have fled to private universities in the Northeast are now flocking to the University of Georgia."

Perhaps as a result of the influx of these higher-caliber students, the school's honors program has blossomed (honors students in 2012–13 had an average verbal-math combined SAT score of 1466). The strength of this program lies in the rigor of its courses. For nearly

VITAL STATISTICS

Religious affiliation: *none*
Total enrollment: *34,519*
Total undergraduates: *26,259*
SAT CR/Verbal midrange: *560–660*
SAT Math midrange: *580–670*
ACT midrange: *26–30*
Applicants: *18,458*
Applicants accepted: *56%*
Accepted applicants who enrolled: *48%*
Tuition (general/out of state): *$28,052*
Tuition (in state): *$9,842*
Room and board: *$8,970*
Freshman retention rate: *94%*
Graduation rate (4 yrs.): *55%*
Graduation rate (6 yrs.): *83%*
Courses with fewer than 20 students: *39%*
Student-faculty ratio: *18:1*
Courses taught by graduate students: *not provided*
Students living on campus: *8%*
Students in fraternities: *21%*
Students in sororities: *28%*
Students receiving need-based financial aid: *38%*
Avg. student-loan debt of a recent graduating class: *$18,438*
Most popular majors: *business/marketing, social sciences, communications/journalism*
Guaranteed housing for 4 years? *no*

Blue Collar Ivy

CAMPUS POLITICS: GREEN LIGHT

UGA's College Republicans is one of the largest CR chapters in the country and one of the largest student groups on campus. One leader of the club boasts that its members are highly mobilized, bringing conservative speakers and political candidates to campus several times a year. It also provides several internship opportunities during an election year.

Although UGA is described as "friendly" to all groups on campus, conservatives on campus charge favoritism in funding. The university has a ban on political funding but does contribute to the gay activist group Safe Space; the College Republicans receive no funding and have not been given any office space for their expanding and very active group.

For many years, free-speech advocates have objected to the vagueness (and hence arbitrariness) of the school's harassment code. In 2011 a student wrote in the school paper *Red and Black* that UGA's "Acts of Intolerance policy—affecting students living in residential housing—can land students a judicial hearing for making a joke or comment. Writing a sarcastic statement on a dorm door dry erase board that could 'harm or threaten to harm a person' can send a notification letter your way." After such a notification, a student is subject to judgment by a student-run court that can recommend expulsion. "Since harm is vaguely written . . . saying something as simple as 'I don't like your dorm room' or even 'I support Israel' to someone who doesn't can cause 'harm' to sensitive students." The editorialist noted, "Some students even have to hire expensive lawyers to defend them against the student court."

all introductory-level classes, there is a corresponding (and more demanding) honors course, with fewer students and some of the best professors at the school. One Classics student claims that her major is "one of the university's best-kept secrets. . . . For the money you can't beat it—and it is qualitatively better than some Ivy League Classics departments." This same student has found that although UGA overall is more geared toward careerism than the liberal arts, there is a "rich intellectual current" to be found at the school. Some of the students who have caught that wave even enroll in graduate courses, as honors upperclassmen are welcome to do. Yet another perk of being an honors student is the chance to live in the posh quarters of Myers Hall—one of the nicest dorms on campus.

The administration would like to see the school ranked in the same tier as the so-called public Ivies. Before this happens, Georgia must raise the bar in certain areas. For one thing, only 83 percent of students graduate within six years, and a mere 55 percent within four.

Some faculty cite a lack of curiosity among students. "Making the grade is the chief objective of a significant portion of our undergraduates," says one professor. Some students retort that many professors seem uninterested in students' intellectual growth. One student says the university is very good at "grooming young professionals," not scholars. There is also considerable variance in the difficulty of the school's majors. "Education is the most obvious" example of an easy department, says one professor. "If one can get by the university-wide requirements, As and Bs are a sure thing in the College of Education for the rest of one's four years. On the other hand, majors like math, chemistry, physics, and computer science are brutally tough." Agricultural programs and the sciences are particularly strong, in part because they receive more government funding.

Although UGA has become a rather large research university that enrolls some 26,000 undergraduates, most students say their professors are focused on teaching. One says, "I've never run into a situation where my professor has put his own research over his teaching responsibilities." Undergraduate instructors are required to post office hours, and some have an open-door policy. "For the most part, professors are very accessible to students and friendly, too," the student says. "That's what I found so surprising at such a large university: my professors know my name and are happy to talk to students." UGA uses graduate teaching assistants as most big universities do: professors teach large lecture courses twice a week, and TAs lead smaller discussion groups once a week. Upon entering UGA, each student is assigned a professional, nonfaculty adviser who helps him choose a major. Once he has selected a major, a student is assigned a faculty adviser within that department.

Most UGA professors stand well to the left of their students, but a recent study ordered by the Board of Regents showed that only 20 percent of students felt that they needed to agree with the professor to get a good grade, while only 13 percent felt that a professor had inappropriately pushed his opinion on his students. Still, a number of teachers are known for importing liberal politics into the classroom and making conservative students feel uncomfortable. Conservative child- and family-development majors are required to take a "Human Sexuality" course, for instance, where they are pressured to watch films they call "pornographic." However, for each one of these negative anecdotes, we heard several positive accounts of UGA professors.

A professor says, "Large numbers of gifted students who would previously have fled to private universities in the Northeast are now flocking to the University of Georgia."

Faculty members most often mentioned as dedicated to undergraduate teaching include Noel Fallows in Spanish; Charles S. Bullock in political science; James C. Cobb, John C. Inscoe, Stephen A. Mihm, and Kirk Willis in history; Thomas M. Lessl in speech communications; Ronald Blount in psychology; Allen C. Amason in management; Keith S. Delaplane in entomology; John Pickering in ecology; Daniel E. L. Promislow in genetics; and Dwight R. Lee and David B. Mustard in economics.

English majors must complete 10 upper-division courses, including two in British and American literature before 1800, one in British and postcolonial literature after 1800, one in American literature, and one course in Language, Criticism, and Culture. These mandates, on top of the school's relatively strong core curriculum requirements, mean that majors will likely emerge well prepared—although they could, apparently, escape study of Shakespeare.

History majors must choose three upper-division courses from among six geographical areas, a senior seminar, and four courses in general-history electives (options include "The Rise and Fall of the Southeastern Chiefdoms" and "Politics of Gender in United States History"). There seems to be little cohesiveness in the department; students can fulfill these requirements with courses like "United States Women's History to 1865," "The

Blue Collar Ivy

SUGGESTED CORE

1. Classical Culture 4220, Classical Epic Poetry
2. Philosophy 3000, Classics of Ancient Western Philosophy
3. Religion 4001/4080, Old Testament/Hebrew Bible Literature; New Testament Literature
4. Religion 4101, History of Christian Theology (Ancient to Medieval)
5. Political Science 4020, Political Philosophy: Hobbes to Nietzsche
6. English 4320, Shakespeare I: Selected Works
7. History 2111, American History to 1865
8. History 4373, 19th-Century European Intellectual History

Arab-Israeli Conflict," "Wenches, Witches, Damsels, and Nuns: Women in Medieval Europe," or "Premodern Japan: Foundations of Culture and State." University-wide requirements do guarantee a basic understanding of U.S. history and the Constitution.

Political science majors must take eight courses in the department, including two in theory and method (for example, "Political Philosophy: Hobbes to Nietzsche" or "Theories of Political Choice"), two courses in American studies ("Bureaucracy and the Law" or "Judicial Process and Behavior"), and one course in global studies with such choices as "Middle Eastern Political Systems" and "International Political Economy."

The University of Georgia ranks among the top American universities for students studying abroad, with nearly 6 percent of the student body studying abroad each year. UGA offers more than 100 faculty-led study-abroad programs in over 50 countries on every continent, including Antarctica. UGA owns a three-story Victorian mansion in the heart of Oxford, England, as well as two other residential properties in Cortona, Italy, and San Luis de Monteverde, Costa Rica. The school has classes in more than 25 foreign languages, ranging from Latin to Arabic and Sanskrit.

Student Life: Love shack

One couldn't ask for a better college town than Athens, Georgia, with nearly a hundred bars and restaurants, a movie theater, shops, and a renowned music scene.

Athens's appeal probably contributes to UGA's rank (according to the Princeton Review) as one of the top party schools in 2013; UGA has been ranked among the top 20 such schools for most of a decade. Local authorities claim to have increased their efforts to clamp down on underage drinking, and the administration admits embarrassment at this notoriety, but so far efforts have done little to change UGA's reputation.

While a large percentage of the student body hails from Georgia, the university does not typically clear out on the weekends. "It depends on if there's a home football game," a student from an Atlanta suburb says. "If there is, nobody leaves town." The bright lights of Atlanta are within a 90-minute drive, and most students go there at least a few times a year. For outdoorsy students, the Appalachian Mountains are about two hours northeast, and the beautiful beach towns of Savannah and Charleston are both about a four-hour drive.

Talk to any Georgia student and within a couple of minutes your conversation is bound to shift to football. Most students' social lives in autumn revolve around home games. One student says, "The students go crazy during football season and tailgate all day Saturday." (Although it should be noted that university policy now rules that tailgating cannot begin before 7:00 a.m., a late start for die-hard Dawgs.) The Georgia-Florida game is the most coveted ticket of the year. Football may be the center of campus life—indeed, the stadium is located at the very center of campus. Other varsity sports also have been gaining popularity lately, and intramural sports are popular and plentiful.

Many of the student groups—numbering over 600—that receive the most support from the administration are quite liberal, including the Lambda Alliance, a homosexual group, and Safe Space, which promotes a similar agenda. The *Red and Black*, the independent student newspaper, is well known for its liberal tilt. In the university as a whole, says one professor, "there are all perspectives, but overall, people are levelheaded. Tolerance of diverse views is prevalent."

Students living on campus participate in Diversity Awareness Week at Georgia—or DAWG Days—which is sponsored by University Housing and the Residence Hall Association. President Michael Adams has told the *Red and Black* that he stands squarely behind these efforts. The university revised its antidiscrimination policies to include sexual orientation and has rules against harassment and intolerance. Some claim that these rules are so vague that they could be used to hinder the free speech of conservatives.

Around one-third of the student body lives on campus, and the university guarantees housing only for freshmen. Many more students would prefer to live on campus but are denied the opportunity because of a housing crunch, which has been eased somewhat. An upperclassman says, "Dorm life was the best thing about my freshman year. . . . I loved it so much. It is a great way to meet friends and get involved on campus." Residences include huge freshman dormitories, suites in East Campus Village, and other on-campus facilities. The university offers no men-only dorms but several women-only residences. UGA does not have any coed dorm rooms or coed bathrooms.

As important to students as sleep is food, and the UGA kitchen "is extremely popular among students and wins awards yearly," says one student. The UGA dining halls have monthly themed nights that offer unique dishes and decorations.

Rentals in Athens, including nearby houses, downtown lofts, and scattered apartment buildings, are rather pricey. Approximately a fourth of the student body goes Greek, and Greek organizations play a significant role in campus social life for both members and independents. Weekend parties at the houses are popular and generally open to all students.

The campus crime rate is low, but the city of Athens has some dangerous areas. In 2011 UGA's campus saw 53 burglaries, two aggravated assaults, one robbery, five stolen cars, three arsons, and five forcible sex offenses.

For students from Georgia, this school is an amazing value, with 2012–13 in-state tuition at only $9,842 (out-of-state students paid $28,052). Room and board averaged $8,970. Admissions are need blind, and 38 percent of students received aid. However, the school does not guarantee to cover the full need of every student admitted. The average student-loan debt of a recent graduate was $18,438, the school reports.

STRONG SUITS

- A stellar honors program that attracts and challenges Ivy League–caliber students.
- Students report that faculty teach most classes and are very accessible.
- Surveys show that most students find teaching nonpoliticized.
- Math, chemistry, physics, computer science, and agricultural programs are demanding and excellent.
- Reasonable requirements for humanities majors.
- A lively, creative, beautiful college town surrounds campus.

WEAK POINTS

- General-education requirements are lax and can be fulfilled with politicized classes.
- Too few students display intellectual curiosity, faculty report.
- Outside of honors, standards need to be higher in the humanities.
- A party atmosphere and a preoccupation with music and sports distract from studies.

So You're Looking For

A School with Modern Sexual Mores

1. Wesleyan University *(p. 895)*

2. Oberlin College *(p. 702)*

3. Yale University *(p. 923)*

4. Amherst College *(p. 3)*

5. Smith College *(p. 750)*

University of Hawaii at Manoa

Honolulu, Hawaii • manoa.hawaii.edu

Big and Beautiful

Founded in 1907, the University of Hawaii at Manoa rests in a beautiful 320-acre campus, the flagship of the Hawaii University system. A "research university of international standing," UH Manoa offers bachelor degrees in 87 fields and employs 1,306 full-time faculty. The student-faculty ratio is a moderate 14 to 1, but nevertheless there are more than a few very large, somewhat impersonal classes, and graduate assistants teach a fourth of undergraduate courses. About 23 percent of the university's 20,000 students live on campus, while the rest live in nearby apartments or alternative housing. Students will find plenty of lively activity on campus, with more than 200 student organizations to satisfy their "cultural, media, social, service, and professional" interests.

Academic Life: Diverser and diverser

UH Manoa's general-education requirements are divided into two components: Core requirements and Graduation requirements. The Core requirements consist in 12 credits of "Foundations" and 19 credits of "Diversification." Graduation requirements include "Focus" courses and demonstrated competency in Hawaiian or another second language.

VITAL STATISTICS

Religious affiliation: *none*
Total enrollment: *20,426*
Total undergraduates:
14,655
SAT CR/Verbal midrange:
480–580
SAT Math midrange:
500–610
ACT midrange: *21–27*
Applicants: *6,810*
Applicants accepted: *81%*
Accepted applicants who
enrolled: *36%*
Tuition (general/out of
state): *$26,712*
Tuition (in state): *$9,144*
Room and board: *$10,029*
Freshman retention rate:
79%
Graduation rate (4 yrs.): *18%*
Graduation rate (6 yrs.): *55%*
Courses with fewer than 20
students: *60%*
Student-faculty ratio: *14:1*
Courses taught by graduate
students: *25%*
Students living on campus:
23%
Students in fraternities: *1%*
Students in sororities: *1%*
Students receiving need-
based financial aid: *41%*
Avg. student-loan debt of a
recent graduating class:
$20,655
Most popular majors:
*business/marketing, social
sciences, education,*
Guaranteed housing for 4
years? *no*

The "Focus" requirement can be fulfilled with a course at any level in Hawaiian, Asian, and Pacific Issues; a course in Contemporary Ethical Issues at the 300 level or above; a course in Oral Communication at 300 or above; or five Writing Intensive courses, including at least two at the 300 level or above. Each "Focus" course varies from semester to semester. Students can fulfill the language requirement in one of two ways: complete a four-semester sequence in the same language, or demonstrate competence by taking a UH Manoa exam (if available for a particular language).

The Diversification and Foundations offerings range from rewarding to revolting. Students may choose Diversification courses from more than six different areas (such as Literature, Social Science, Biological Sciences, and Humanities), and the immense number of options can be daunting. Navigating through the Literature options alone, students might find such treasures as "Greek Epic" and "The Bible as Literature." On the other hand, a careless student may stumble into less impressive courses like "Race, Ethnicity, and Literature" and "Studies in Literature and Sexuality and Gender."

The average class size at UH Manoa is a cozy 24, but unfortunately about a quarter of courses are taught by grad students. A student tells us that any given "small, introductory course" will "most likely" be taught by a graduate student, while "upper-class specialized courses are mostly, if not all, taught by professors." A professor tells us that the faculty who do the most research are more likely to be given tenure. "Due to the pressure to publish, professors in my department for the past 10 to 12 years have taught fewer courses, a minimum number of courses—in order to use their time for research." Though sometimes hard to contact, professors do "make a point of meeting with you according to their schedules," says one student. "All the professors' office hours are useful." A student reports that he has "really enjoyed" his professors, since they "demonstrate real-life experience." He visits his professors "on a regular basis and will continue to" even after graduation, since he sees them not only as "scholarly references" but as "mentors."

The honors program at UH Manoa is divided by lower- and upperclassman studies, with "Selected Studies" for freshmen and sophomores leading into "Upper Division

Honors" for juniors and seniors. Honors students must maintain a daunting 3.5 GPA and are offered smaller class sizes to facilitate more "in-depth" discussion. The honors curriculum is "inquiry-based," allowing students to self-direct their own education while also fulfilling general-education requirements. These students may also opt to live in exclusive honors dorm floors, with their own reading rooms, honors-only social events, and "personalized academic advising." Honors students may also take "A Section" courses, which are offered in a more intimate and rigorous environment. There are also seminars unique to the honors program, most of which vary from semester to semester, such as "Reacting to the Past: Democratic Athens and Imperial China" and "Public-Policy Making."

Departments and programs recommended by students and faculty include Shidler School of Business; John A. Burns School of Medicine; William S. Richardson School of Law; the School of Architecture; the School of Travel Industry and Management; the School of Ocean and Earth Science and Technology; and the history, American studies, political science, religion, English,

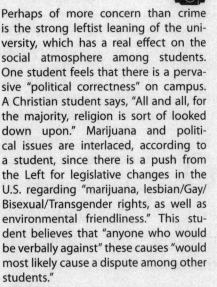

CAMPUS POLITICS: YELLOW LIGHT

Perhaps of more concern than crime is the strong leftist leaning of the university, which has a real effect on the social atmosphere among students. One student feels that there is a pervasive "political correctness" on campus. A Christian student says, "All and all, for the majority, religion is sort of looked down upon." Marijuana and political issues are interlaced, according to a student, since there is a push from the Left for legislative changes in the U.S. regarding "marijuana, lesbian/Gay/Bisexual/Transgender rights, as well as environmental friendliness." This student believes that "anyone who would be verbally against" these causes "would most likely cause a dispute among other students."

There are not many conservative or libertarian groups active at UH Manoa. There is an active Young Americans for Liberty chapter, and students can also take part in the activities of the College Republicans of Honolulu.

and Classics departments. Also commended are the study-abroad and honors programs. "We're very good in astronomy, by the way," adds one professor. "One of the greatest observatories in the country is here in Hawaii." According to one student, the education department is known to be a rather weak one and "ridiculed for its failure to meet testing requirements compared to the rest of the United States."

Some aspects of UH Manoa are much less traditional than one might wish. Courses in Shakespeare are optional even for English majors. Still they must choose a single advanced class in a great author—such as the Bard, Chaucer, or Milton. With many solid offerings, such as "Backgrounds of Western Literature" and "Literary Criticism and Theory," students can put together a good education if they steer clear of courses such as "Studies in Literature and Sexuality and Gender" (not to be confused with "Gender, Sexuality, and Literature") and "Race, Ethnicity, and Literature."

History majors are not required to take any courses covering U.S. history before 1945. Students seeking a degree in history must take 15 credits in a declared "area of focus," which may be United States, Asia/Pacific, European, or World history. The university does offer its share of solid history courses, however, including "Ancient Greece" I and II, "Ancient Rome: The Republic," and "Early Middle Ages 300–900." Or you could blunder into "Gender and Sexuality in the Classical World." It is important to read the course descriptions: the relatively innocent-seeming HIST 379: "American Empire" turns out to be an examination of "social movements and . . . race, gender and class relations."

Admirably, political science majors are required to take either "Constitutional Law" I or "American Politics." Majors must take approximately nine courses in the major, chosen from more than 55 offerings.

Leftism is alive and well in the classrooms of UH Manoa, but fairly tame. "I would say almost all the departments have some sort of classroom negativity toward conservatism," says a student, "seeing how the entire university is quite liberal." But one professor counters that "most scholars . . . are committed to the notion that there is a distinction between political propaganda and the study of political institutions and processes." He feels that the university's faculty are "evenhanded, even if it's not possible to be entirely objective." When professors do show their "political biases," it is usually just "in conversation," and "the issues tend to have less to do with political parties

> One student says that most of his peers "take great pride in their field, and show great interest in investing their time in increasing their knowledge."

and elections than with style of scholarship." According to this professor, the faculty are generally professional enough that if teachers ever were to "favor local candidates or tell people how they should vote," it would "soil their reputation" in the eyes of colleagues. Whatever oppressiveness there may be in the classroom is gentle enough. One Christian student recalls classes in which he "felt it would be best to keep my mouth shut regarding religion, as it may cause a dispute."

Student- and faculty-recommended professors include Peter Hoffenberg, Michael Speidel, Saundra Schwartz, and Karen Jolly (whose specialty is "religion as expressed in popular culture in the Middle Ages") in the history department; Jackie Lindo and Ruben Juarez in economics; and Hugette Montesinos and Keeley Cestare in Spanish.

Students at UH Manoa may have to make a special effort to surround themselves with the right friends. There are a number of students whose interests lie more in social gatherings than in academic achievement. Others are quite motivated. "I would say the intellectual curiosity of the students is high," says a student. "The majority of the students take great pride in their field of specialization, and show great interest in investing their time in increasing their knowledge about their subject." These are the students to seek out. As an undergrad puts it, "It is motivating for me to be around such motivated individuals." A professor recommends that students make the effort to join honor societies, such as Phi Alpha Theta, a club for history majors. "To join, you have to have a pretty good GPA," but it gives students the opportunity of "enjoying the camaraderie and experiences of the other students and participating in our annual meeting and conferences."

UH Manoa offers a broad range of languages, starting with Hawaiian—and including Chinese, Filipino, French, German, Greek and Latin, Hindi, Ilokano, Indonesian, Japanese, Khmer, Korean, Russian, Samoan, Sanskrit, Spanish, Tahitian, Thai, Vietnamese, and many more.

"Our professors teach courses in France or Italy or it could be in Singapore—all kinds of places," a professor says. He reports that students enjoy their experiences abroad. Study-abroad options include programs in Argentina, Australia, China, Denmark, England, Germany, India, Italy, Japan, Spain, and Thailand. A student praises the study-abroad programs as "a great opportunity," especially since "the university has many connections with other universities around the world" that allow UH Manoa "to provide extensive study-abroad options" and "plenty of classes that fulfill degree requirements."

> **SUGGESTED CORE**
>
> 1. History 332, Ancient Greece II (*closest match*)
> 2. Philosophy 211, Ancient Philosophy
> 3. English 322, The Bible as Literature
> 4. History 434, History of Christianity to 1500
> 5. Philosophy 213, Modern Philosophy (*closest match*)
> 6. English 445, William Shakespeare
> 7. History 281, Introduction to American History
> 8. History 338, European Intellectual History (*closest match*)

Student Life: Lost in the weed

UH Manoa is home to the Rainbow Warriors and offers an NCAA Division I athletics program. Popular sports include football, baseball, and volleyball. As one student recently commented in an online forum, "Our sports teams suck, with the exception of Wahine volleyball." Perhaps he is exaggerating, but it does seem that the women's volleyball team is a favorite to many, and quite a few students are more interested in other social (and anti-social) activities.

"Marijuana is almost a culture inside the university," says one student, warning that the drug is used "more than even alcohol." Students may also be exposed to some unsavory activity because of the large presence of gay rights advocates on campus. A student complains that during "Gay Pride Week," gay students engage in "extreme public displays of affection." Unfortunately, some of this wild behavior "is promoted by the university itself," says a student, who tells us that UH Manoa has "an LGBT office in the main campus center."

Greek life, on the other hand, seems to be of little importance. A student tells us that "sororities and fraternities have little to no influence on the atmosphere of the college." One student at UH Manoa tells us, "I have yet to meet one person who is a part of [a fraternity or sorority) during my five years attending the university." A professor mentions instead Greek honor societies—clubs that require serious participation and a high GPA, noting that these groups, too, "tend to be very small."

Both dorms and apartments are available at UH Manoa. Residence halls are contained within two complexes: Hale Aloha Complex and Mauka/Makai Complex. All residence halls are smoke-free, with data ports, cable TV outlets, and Wi-Fi. "Dorm life is fun!" says a student. "Most fun time of my college career," he adds. This student does have his concerns about dorm life, however. All residence halls are coed, and student Housing Services makes room assignments "on the basis of the gender with which the student currently identifies." Students may opt for the Residential Learning Program, where students of similar academic interests are placed together in sections such as the Pre-Law Residential Learning Program, College of Business Residential Learning Program, Honors, or Japanese Language and Culture. "Special Environments" are also available, such as Freshman Only, Sophomore Focused Environment, Gender-Neutral Housing, and Graduate and Family Housing. Some of these housing options may offer refuge to students who wish to escape unhealthy environments. "Promiscuity is highly prevalent," says a student, warning that many undergrads have "no standards" of sexual morality.

In the last year reported, the crime rates at UH Manoa were not particularly high for a student population of more than 20,000. There were 12 forcible sex offenses, two robberies, 16 aggravated assaults, 64 burglaries, and 16 motor vehicle thefts on campus in 2011. The university's security services are constantly active, with campus security officers patrolling the campus "24 hours a day by vehicle and bike and on foot." For any student who feels he or she is in danger, "safety escorts are available after dark, and 68 Emergency Call Boxes are located throughout campus."

Students who hail from the Aloha State could attend it for only $9,144 in 2012–13 (mainlanders paid $26,712), with room and board at $10,029. Some 41 percent of students get need-based aid, and the average loan debt of a recent grad was $20,655.

STRONG SUITS	WEAK POINTS
• Terrific opportunities to study Asian languages and culture. • A beautiful, mostly harmonious environment, with occasional outbursts of pro-libertine activism. • Largely apolitical classrooms. • Good programs in business, architecture, premed, travel management, oceanography, history, American studies, political science, religion, English, and Classics. • A worthy honors option.	• Complex but still lax general-ed requirements that can be knocked off with politicized courses. • Far too many courses taught by graduate students. • Student-professor interaction seems minimal, except for the most motivated undergrads. • Too many stoners, everywhere.

University of Idaho

Moscow, Idaho • www.uidaho.edu

Hope of the West

Founded in 1889, the University of Idaho is a well-funded research institution with stellar agriculture programs. Set on 1,585 acres of rolling countryside campus, UI is home to a largely conservative—but somewhat apathetic—student body increasingly at odds with a left-leaning administration and faculty.

Still, with more National Merit Scholars than all other schools in the state combined, UI remains the pinnacle of higher education in Idaho, the alma mater of numerous state leaders, and the university is overtly conscious that the students of today will be the names of leaders engraved in the Kibbie Dome tomorrow.

Academic Life: With a little luck

Unlike the focused track of most majors at the school, UI's General Education requirements have gotten diluted. They are heavy on cultural and geographic diversity and short on literature and history. An Integrated Seminar is the entry point for first-year students and the foundation of the entire curriculum; recent topics include "Fire, Myth and Humanity" and "Born in the USA: Music and Change in America." From there students bridge

Blue Collar Ivy

VITAL STATISTICS

Religious affiliation: *none*
Total enrollment: *12,420*
Total undergraduates: *9,928*
SAT CR/Verbal midrange:
 480–590
SAT Math midrange:
 490–600
ACT midrange: *20–26*
Applicants: *8,248*
Applicants accepted: *5,020*
Accepted applicants who
 enrolled: *1,585*
Tuition (general/out of
 state): *$17,018*
Tuition (in state): *$4,230*
Room and board: *$7,682*
Freshman retention rate:
 80%
Graduation rate (4 yrs.): *23%*
Graduation rate (6 yrs.): *51%*
Courses with fewer than 20
 students: *25%*
Student-faculty ratio: *18:1*
Courses taught by graduate
 students: *not provided*
Students living on campus:
 39%
Students in fraternities: *17%*
Students in sororities: *18%*
Students receiving need-
 based financial aid: *65%*
Avg. student-loan debt of a
 recent graduating class:
 $24,396
Most popular majors: *busi-
 ness/marketing, educa-
 tion, engineering*
Guaranteed housing for 4
 years? *no*

into the American Diversity and International course requirements, as well as the Humanities and Social Sciences courses.

All these are interwoven with courses in communications, the sciences, and mathematics—UI's Core Requirements, which one professor calls "full employment for the leftist folks." Great Issues seminars during a student's junior year reiterate the themes of the General Education, which narrow into a student's Senior Experience.

A student could, with a little determination and some luck in registering for classes, cobble together General Education classes that included "Literature of Western Civilization," "History of Civilization," "Italian Renaissance," and "Colonial North America, 1492–1763," but could just as easily breeze through with "Dance in Society," "Documentary Film," "Pirates of the Caribbean and Beyond," and "Psychology of Women."

Although Idaho currently enrolls more National Merit Scholars than all the state's other schools combined, one professor tells us he has noticed a definite decrease in the quality of students lately. Certain statistics echo this slide: only 80 percent of freshmen enroll for a second year, and the four-year and six-year graduation rates sit at 23 and 51 percent, respectively.

Engineering, political science, architecture, natural resources, math, business, and the premed programs are all pointed out as superb, but in Idaho, as one professor says, "agriculture is king. Every French fry that McDonald's sells is grown by someone in Idaho." Thus, the College of Agricultural Life and Sciences enjoys massive funding for research and is home to 26 programs, among them Agribusiness, Animal and Veterinary Science: Dairy, and Sustainable Cropping Systems.

English majors can choose one of the following focuses: Literature, Creative Writing, Professional (workplace communication), or Teaching. Most majors will take "Introduction to English Studies" and "The Literature of Western Civilization." All the emphases provide a firm grounding in American and British literature; Shakespeare is required only for Teaching. While the 39-credit Literature emphasis leaves room for a second major or a minor, the others are thick with specialized courses. The "cultural diversity in non-canonical or underrepresented literature" options are unsurprisingly ideological.

The political science department offers both a BA (emphasizing political thought) and a BS (emphasizing methodology and statistics) degree. Both tracks require a course in political theory and research methods and at least two courses in both American and foreign politics. Electives include courses in political philosophy, the presidency, public administration, civil liberties, and the Supreme Court—in other words, a refreshingly traditional approach to political science.

History majors can take a BS (for students planning to pursue a higher degree) or a BA (for those who are not). Each group takes three of the four following courses the first year: "History of Civilization," "Introduction to U.S. History," "Introduction to East Asian History," and "Introduction to Modern Latin American History," as well as "The Historian's Craft." Upper-level electives are a mixed bag; students can choose from classes such as "The Medieval Church: Europe in the Early and High Middle Ages" and "Civilization of Ancient Rome," but also from "American Environmental History" and "History of Sexuality." Students following the BS track must also take several courses of literature in translation (options include "Literature of Western Civilization" and "Literature of Ancient Greece and Rome").

Philosophy majors also have first-year requirements: "Reason and Rhetoric," "Ethics," "Critical Thinking" or "Introduction to Symbolic Logic," and "Belief and Reality." As in the history department, electives run the gamut from solid to fuzzy: "Early Christianity," "History of Ancient Philosophy," "Global Justice," and "Philosophy of Ecology."

The University Honors Program has

CAMPUS POLITICS: YELLOW LIGHT

Idaho's student body is largely conservative, but the administration can come across as heavy-handed leftists. Students have learned, one professor says, to be quiet—to sit down, study hard, and get a good education. This has resulted in a student body that can appear apathetic when it comes to politics and free speech. "Students just go along with the liberals," says one professor. "They know the liberalism is here, and they ignore it. They know they're here to get a good education." A student agrees: "It's not more liberal than any other university, but there is a very secular background to the classes. For instance, in a class on world religions, the professor claimed that a Christmas tree is 'idolatry.' If you have a weak constitution and aren't confident in what you believe, it can easily get overthrown."

Conservative students can find a home here—perhaps even as part of a silent majority—but they must be ever aware of the left-leaning administration and faculty. Just ask former student Alex Rowson what happens if you speak out. In 2010 Rowson was charged by the university with discrimination for saying that "illegal immigration destroyed my home state of California" at a concert celebrating César Chávez Day. He was also charged for harassment in a separate incident when he shouted that "liberalism is destroying America." Charges were eventually dropped, but it took an outcry of national free-speech organizations to help administrators see the light.

consistently been ranked among the best, and with smaller classes, registration perks, leadership opportunities, special Living Learning Communities, scheduled access to professors for lunches and "fireside chats," plus passes to cultural performances, it seems to have earned its accolades. "I've really enjoyed being part of it," says one student. "It can be hard to fit in the credits, but it's worth it." Upper-division seminars for honors students have focused on topics such as "Energy Issues," "Banned Books," "Nanotechnology," "Geography of Conflict," and "The Zombie Apocalypse and International Issues."

"The professors are very accessible and quick to reply to e-mails. Good office hours encourage students to attend," says a student. An 18-to-1 student-faculty ratio means class sizes are standard, but even better are reports that teaching is of preeminent importance. "We probably do more teaching than research," says a professor. "It almost has the feel of private university." Another professor says, "Most universities would say we teach too much. But that's OK—undergraduate education is important here."

One word that came up again and again when describing professors was "friendly." Professors to seek out are Tom Bitterwolf in chemistry; Ruprecht Machleidt in physics; David Paul in exercise science; Holly Dickin, Masaki Ikeda, Paul Joyce, and Frank Gao in mathematics; Robert Dickow and Al Gemberling in music; Rick Fehrenbacher and Eric Greenwell in English; Denim Jochimsen and Scott Minnich in biology; and William Lund in political science.

> "We probably do more teaching than research," says a professor. "It almost has the feel of private university."

Foreign language majors are offered in French, German, and Spanish, plus a foreign language/business course that combines a core of business with a major in French, German, or Spanish. The department also offers courses in Japanese and has a collaboration agreement with Washington State University, which allows students to take courses in Chinese and Russian. Nearly 80 percent of foreign language graduates earn a second degree. Common double majors include international studies, history, political science, English, journalism, public relations, and justice studies.

Foreign language majors are required to spend a semester or year studying abroad. Options include Argentina, Australia, Botswana, Bulgaria, Denmark, Ecuador, France, Fiji, Ghana, Iceland, Indonesia, Japan, Latvia, Malaysia, Mexico, Morocco, New Zealand, and Singapore.

Student Life: All about the outdoors

Outside magazine recently described UI as "a great university to hit the books and backcountry." This backcountry consists of the campus itself and its setting in the rolling Palouse hills near Moscow (pop. 22,000). It is just minutes from skiing, hiking, and whitewater rafting. Don't be intimidated if you're not accustomed to mountain sports; the Outdoor Program, a nonprofit service organization, can help with trip planning and resources. The school offers a wide variety of workshops, trips, and clinics on skiing, snowshoeing, avalanches, indoor kayaking, rafting on the Salmon River, surfing the Oregon Coast, backpacking in the Wallowa Mountains, natural rock climbing, learning to be a wilderness first responder, and white-water kayaking.

The Vandals compete in the Western Athletic Conference in 16 men's and women's NCAA Division I sports: men's and women's basketball, cross-country, golf, tennis, and track and field. Men also play football. Women compete in soccer, swimming and diving, and volleyball.

Even with this focus on activity, there is still a large party segment at the school. A professor reports that bars in Moscow are a big business. The strong Greek system has 33 chapters, whose members make up 35 percent of the student population and almost half of those who live on campus. Maybe, though, it's too large, as students report that "Greek life is huge. If you're not in a dorm or on campus or in Greek, then there's a big separation—you can kind of feel like an outsider. It's hard to get engaged and involved."

Housing options on campus include Theophilus Tower, a coed by floor, freshmen-only residence hall with academic-themed floors; Targhee Hall, a coed, academic traditional community for students interested in or majoring in music, theater, architecture, painting, design, or any other fine arts; McConnell Hall, for returning and transfer students, with both coed and mixed-sex floors and all single rooms; the Living Learning Communities, with housing based on academic interests, social justice commitment, and outdoor/nature interests; and Wallace Residence Center, which has a women's only, substance-free floor and more restrictive policies regarding male visitors, plus two more substance-free floors. Only 39 percent of students live on campus.

Three university apartment residences are available for students. Two of these are specifically geared for single parents, married couples, students over 25, and law students.

Many of the student organizations are academic based. College Republicans, though small, is very active. Special resources exist for the large population of Native American students, including the Native American Student Center. Religious groups on campus include Campus Christian Fellowship, Cru, Chi Alpha Christian Fellowship, Collegiate Reformed Fellowship, Lutheran Campus Ministry, Not by Bread Alone, Refuge Ministries, Sabbath House International, St. Augustine Catholic Center, United Methodist Student Movement, and the Vandals Catholic Club (named for the school team, not modernizing church renovators). The St. Augustine center, reports a student, is right across from Student Union and acts as a "home away from home" for students, with many older people from the community adopting students. "If you're not interested in a more secular lifestyle, it gives you opportunities to step back and focus on prayer and spiritual life, and also on fun opportunities like rafting," says a student.

In 2011 crime on campus included six forcible sex offenses, one aggravated assault,

SUGGESTED CORE

1. Classics 270, Introduction to Greek and Roman Civilization (*closest match*)
2. Philosophy 320, History of Ancient and Medieval Philosophy
3. Religious Studies 375, The Bible as Literature
4. History J442/J542, The Medieval Church: Europe in the Early and High Middle Ages
5. Political Science J426/J526, History of Political Philosophy II
6. English 345, Shakespeare
7. History J411 / J412, Colonial North America, 1492–1763/ Revolutionary North America and Early National Period, 1763–1828
8. History 366, Intellectual and Cultural History of Modern Europe

one motor vehicle theft, and 23 burglaries (a significant increase from the prior year). Still, students feel mostly safe on campus and in the nearby small town of Moscow.

Tuition was a steal for Idahoans at $4,230 per year (outsiders paid $17,018), with room and board at only $7,682 in 2012–13. Some 65 percent of students received need-based financial aid, and the average student-loan debt of a recent graduating class was a middling $24,396.

STRONG SUITS	WEAK POINTS
• Plenty of hardworking students, especially National Merit Scholars.	• General-education options are scattered and often trivial or politicized.
• Faculty committed to teaching more than research.	• Requirements for some key majors are lax, including for English and history.
• Good programs in political science, honors, foreign languages.	• Quality of students said to be declining; 20 percent of freshmen do not return.
• Extensive study-abroad options.	• Powerful Greek system is called exclusive and fuels a party atmosphere.

University of Illinois at Urbana-Champaign

Urbana-Champaign, Illinois • www.illinois.edu

Riding Leviathan

Located some 125 miles south of Chicago, UIUC has a reputation as one of the country's top public universities, attracting to its campus a bevy of bright students and highly regarded faculty and maintaining more than a few excellent academic departments. But undergrads at this state-sponsored behemoth will need to seek out that education amid a vast array of opportunities to waste their time. "This is a research university," says one professor. "We are not a teaching college. People don't come here to get small classes and individual attention. They come for the sports, for the first-rate facilities, and to make contact with some of the best thinkers in their field." Whether many Illini actually exploit such opportunities is an open question.

Academic Life: Diversityland

UIUC has no core curriculum, though its meager set of distribution requirements has become more structured over the past decade. In addition to two-semester English composition and three-semester foreign language requirements, students must now take a total of 10 other courses distributed among broad liberal arts and science categories.

VITAL STATISTICS

Religious affiliation: *none*
Total enrollment: *44,407*
Total undergraduates: *32,256*
SAT CR/Verbal midrange: *540–660*
SAT Math midrange: *690–780*
ACT midrange: *26–31*
Applicants: *28,751*
Applicants accepted: *68%*
Accepted applicants who enrolled: *37%*
Tuition (general/out of state): *$28,570*
Tuition (in state): *$14,428*
Room and board: *$10,322*
Freshman retention rate: *94%*
Graduation rate (4 yrs.): *66%*
Graduation rate (6 yrs.): *82%*
Courses with fewer than 20 students: *34%*
Student-faculty ratio: *18:1*
Courses taught by graduate students: *21%*
Students living on campus: *50%*
Students in fraternities: *21%*
Students in sororities: *21%*
Students receiving need-based financial aid: *46%*
Avg. student-loan debt of a recent graduating class: *$22,975*
Most popular majors: *engineering, business/marketing, social sciences*
Guaranteed housing for 4 years? *yes*

It's easy to get lost in the system at this university, which offers plenty of good courses—and at least as many paths of least resistance. The curriculum is unstructured, and the catalog lists an enormous range of disciplines—more than 150 of them. "Students are pretty much adrift to take whatever they want; there's no real cohesion or body of knowledge they are building," one professor says.

A College of Liberal Arts and Sciences (LAS) professor complains that even in more traditional disciplines, faculty members' interests tend to focus on new, trendy areas of research rather than on more traditional topics. A course in the Old Testament, for instance, may turn out to consist of feminist complaints about Yahweh and patriarchy. The business school is more cautious; one professor says that the school's courses "cover the fundamentals with an eye to the contemporary." Of course, at a school as big as UIUC, it is almost inevitable that a number of serious, well-taught courses will still be offered. UIUC is particularly well known for the quality of its programs in engineering, the sciences, journalism, and business. The College of Agriculture is one of the oldest in the nation, and its programs are widely respected. Other departments with strong programs include economics, labor and industrial relations, geography, and history.

The Classics department has a distinguished history, several world-class scholars, and five majors to choose from: classical archeology, classical civilization, Classics, Ancient Greek, and Latin. The religious studies program sounds surprisingly mainstream for a state university. Religious studies majors are required to take 10 courses, including "Philosophy of Religion" or "Religion and Philosophy"; two courses in Judaism, Christianity, Islam, or any religion of the ancient Near East; two courses in Hinduism, Buddhism, Chinese, or Japanese religions, or indigenous American religions; three courses in a primary area of study; two courses in a secondary area of study; and a capstone project accompanied by a 20-page research paper.

The English department offers three options for majors in English: literature, rhetoric/creative writing, and teaching. Lit majors will take 12 credit hours of courses focusing on British and American literature. They will then have to take 18 more hours of English electives. It will be up to them, ultimately, whether they opt for "Women in the Literary Imagination" over a course on Shakespeare.

The history department's website warns: "Whether you're interested in gender and sexuality, law and society, science and technology, race and diversity, money and power—we have a course for you." Beyond a gateway research-methods course, majors complete six credit hours of U.S. history, six of European history, six of non-Western history, and 12 electives. The highlight of the program comes in junior year, when students take a seminar course and "make history by researching and writing."

The political science major requires three courses in basic political theory, four electives at the 300 level, and six at any level. Students may choose (or skip) courses on the U.S. Constitution.

The university's advising program is anemic. "Teaching professionals," faculty hired by the university to teach introductory courses, serve as departmental advisers. One political science major says that the system is "in dire need of review." The university provides a kind of virtual online "adviser" in the form of an informative webpage, upon which many students rely instead of consulting a teacher. Students are not required to discuss an academic strategy with a human adviser or to hand in a major plan of study until the beginning of their junior year.

CAMPUS POLITICS: YELLOW LIGHT

Politics do not stop at the classroom door at UIUC. As one student says, political bias "usually comes through in the way that course material is presented." A few students report blatantly ideological attempts to punish students who disagree with instructors. "I wrote a paper for my Rhetoric 105 class in which I argued against gay marriage," a student says. "The teaching assistant gave me a D on the paper because 'you can't argue for that sort of position without appealing to hate and religious bigotry.' I had to go to the department chair to get the grade raised to a C, and that's all I could do."

On the other hand, outside the classroom students report a good deal of tolerance for different viewpoints. Says one student: "I have had no problem being an open conservative on campus." In addition to many liberal student organizations, including the left-leaning *Daily Illini* student newspaper, the campus does have a few conservative organizations. The *Orange and Blue Observer* is a rightist paper that takes a vigilant, if not belligerent, approach toward the dominant liberalism of the university. The paper has promoted events such as "Will ObamaCare Kill You?"

The honors program is available to students who maintain a 3.25 GPA. Students in the program can take special, smaller honors courses and register early. The bad news is that a number of the honors seminars deal with the trendiest areas of academia. The English department, for instance, offers honors seminars such as "Race, Ethnicity, and American Fiction" and "Enlightenment Feminism."

In some years, almost a third of classes have been taught by graduate students, though currently it's 21 percent. This is far above the norm, even at state universities. "Many departments have a problem finding faculty to teach basic courses due to the lack of professors carrying a full-time load for whatever reason," a professor says. "The courses that suffer are introductory-level ones." A student says, "My big lecture courses were always taught by professors, but a majority of my classes and all of my accompanying discussion sections were taught by TAs."

Students express a certain ambivalence about UIUC professors—perhaps because they see so little of them. But when professors are good, they are said to be very, very good. The best include Kevin Waspi in finance; Thomas Rudolph in political science; Keith Hitchins in history; Robert McKim and Rajeshwari Pandharipande in religious studies; James Dengate (emeritus) in Classics; and Jose J. Vazquez-Cognet in economics, who has won several awards over the years.

One student says, "In my opinion, some professors often depend way too much on TAs. A lot of times, it is the TA who has office hours that you go to." Another student says, "All professors hold office hours and check their e-mail frequently, but there are a select few who advise you to talk with your TA before seeking advice from them." When in doubt, look up the school's annual "Incomplete List of Teachers Ranked as Excellent by Their Students." Just remember that some teachers may have earned popularity by easy grading.

> "We are not a teaching college," a professor admits. Another says: "I have students who fall asleep or read the newspaper in my class. A lot of them just don't show up."

Like many schools these days, U of I suffers from pervasive grade inflation. "It's notorious," says a professor. "One introductory-level teacher was known for giving half the class As and the other half A-pluses. It's a pact. Students don't harass the professor, and the professor gives them easy grades." Of course, not all professors are willing to compromise, and lazy students sometimes get burned.

Some professors are unhappy with their charges. "I have students who fall asleep or read the newspaper in my class," says one teacher. "A lot of them just don't show up." Another professor says of his students, "Most seem to be interested in graduating and instrumental learning that can aid their careers." A colleague says, "Some students do get very involved, but I would say those are the exception, not the rule." A student says, "If you're smart, that's cool. But a lot of people just try to get by. They don't want to put in the effort."

Professors and students agree that LAS faculty have a heavy leftward tilt. One professor describes this division of UIUC as "highly politically correct." A student agrees: "The College of Liberal Arts and Sciences is exactly what it says: liberal—way left." One professor we spoke to cautioned conservative students to think twice about the school if they were planning on an English major.

One of the school's (scant) general-education requirements is devoted to cultural studies, with options like "Sex and Gender in Classical Antiquity" and "Minority Images in American Film." Academic departments at UIUC are being pressured to "diversify" their course offerings and hire preferred minority candidates. When a British history professor retired recently, he was replaced by a professor who specializes in the history of an indigenous group on a Pacific island. The Classics department reportedly had to argue doggedly to persuade the dean to hire someone who specializes in Roman history. The political science department was ordered to hire an expert in Asian American politics, which barely exists as an academic field. Because of the administration's multiculturalist obsession, "more serious areas get neglected," says a professor. Looking for the most politicized departments at UIUC? Try English, education, history, and women's studies.

The university boasts literally hundreds of study-abroad programs, from engineering in South Korea to ACES in Spain at UPNA in Pamplona (Agricultural, Consumer, and Environmental Sciences). A wide range of language courses are offered at the university, including Arabic, French, German, Italian, Portuguese, Spanish, and various East Asian tongues, with majors in linguistics and even translation studies.

Student Life: Beer in Champaign

This is one of the "wetter" schools in this guide. Few of the almost 45,000 students, however, take advantage of cultural attractions in the area. When they are in town at night, they're usually drinking. There are bars "within fifty paces of the Quad," says one student. Says another, "When you get here, your first priority is to get a fake ID." To get into the bars, one must be only 19 years of age, even though the official drinking age is 21. The university is usually ranked as one of the top 20 party schools in the nation, "but it's not for lack of other things to do," says a student.

No indeed; the university has more than 1,100 registered student organizations. The Student Government Association is large and active, but it tends to throw its weight behind left-wing causes. Politically minded conservative students can find a home with the College Republicans; Illini Collegians for Life; and the Federalist Society for Law and Public Policy, which is a "conservative and libertarian speech and debate club." Church organizations are particularly popular on campus. "There is a very large religious presence here at U of I," says a campus minister. "There is a substantial Catholic presence at the Newman Foundation but also a wide variety of Protestant organizations, such as Christians on Campus and InterVarsity Christian Fellowship."

After drinking, campus life centers primarily on athletics, especially men's basketball and football. UIUC also boasts a strong intramurals program and offers more than 20 club sports, including badminton, basketball, flag football, miniature golf, and Ultimate Frisbee.

The Greek system is enormously popular on campus. More than a fifth of students belong to a chapter, making the UIUC system one of the largest in the country.

SUGGESTED CORE

1. Classical Civilization 221, The Heroic Tradition
2. Philosophy 203, Ancient Philosophy
3. Religious Studies 101, Bible as Literature, or Religious Studies 201/202, Hebrew Bible in English/New Testament in English
4. Religious Studies 440, Early Christian Thought or Religious Studies 108, Religion and Society in the West I
5. Political Science 372, Modern Political Theory
6. English 218, Introduction to Shakespeare
7. History 170, U.S. History to 1877
8. History 350, 19th-Century Romanticism and Politics (*closest match*)

Freshmen are required to live in university residence halls, in a fraternity or sorority house, or in one of the 15 privately owned certified residence halls. More than three-quarters of entering students choose to live in a university residence hall, of which there are several kinds, including a nonvisitation hall, a substance-free hall, and men-only and women-only dorms. There are no coed dorm rooms or coed bathrooms at the university.

In 2011 the university reported four aggravated assaults, five forcible sex offenses, four robberies, 30 burglaries, five stolen cars, and four cases of arson on campus.

Tuition at UIUC keeps edging up. In 2012–13 costs reached $14,428 for in-state students, and $28,570 for out of state. Add to that about $10,332 in room and board. Financial aid is not as widely used here as at other schools—perhaps because it's relatively cheap. Only 46 percent of undergraduates received need-based aid, and the average debt of recent graduates was $22,975.

STRONG SUITS	WEAK POINTS
• Good programs in engineering, the hard sciences, journalism, and business.	• Large classes and little personal attention from professors focused on research.
• The College of Agricultural, Consumer, and Environmental Studies is widely respected.	• Most student interaction is with graduate teaching assistants.
• Worthy departments in economics, labor and industrial relations, geography, and history.	• Many departments are politicized or have shaky requirements for majors.
• Surprisingly good Classics and religious studies courses are offered.	• The school administration seems obsessed with pushing diversity, skewing hiring in many disciplines.
	• Anemic advising leaves students adrift.
	• Serious party atmosphere and heavy drinking.

Indiana University Bloomington

Bloomington, Indiana • www.iub.edu

Here We Go Again . . .

Indiana University is in many ways typical of large state research universities. It has many, many programs—some of them highly ranked—attracts plenty of capable students, sits in an attractive college town, and suffers from a serious case of ideology. Here as elsewhere, administrators and many faculty have carried the concern for "diversity" to shocking extremes, and conservative students sometimes find their voices silenced. Moreover, many IU students seem to be more attracted to the school by its winning basketball tradition or reputation as a "party school" than by a deep love of learning. As at many state universities, one can get a liberal arts education at Indiana, but it takes some careful choosing.

Academic Life: Accepting of all views . . . with some exceptions

Indiana University's degree requirements for a BA are so slack as to be nearly irrelevant. It is possible to graduate from the university without taking a single course in political science or the history and tradition of the West, or in math or a hard science. Interesting as a course in Scandinavian literature (for example) may be, it hardly seems an adequate replacement for a breadth survey of great texts of the Western canon. The university offers more than

369

VITAL STATISTICS

Religious affiliation: *none*
Total enrollment: *38,990*
Total undergraduates:
32,543
SAT CR/Verbal midrange:
510–620
SAT Math midrange:
520–640
ACT midrange: *23–28*
Applicants: *35,218*
Applicants accepted: *72%*
Accepted applicants who
enrolled: *29%*
Tuition (general/out of
state): *$31,484*
Tuition (in state): *$10,034*
Room and board: *$8,854*
Freshman retention rate:
88%
Graduation rate (4 yrs.): *50%*
Graduation rate (6 yrs.): *72%*
Courses with fewer than 20
students: *39%*
Student-faculty ratio: *18:1*
Courses taught by graduate
students: *not provided*
Students living on campus:
36%
Students in fraternities: *16%*
Students in sororities: *18%*
Students receiving need-
based financial aid: *64%*
Avg. student-loan debt of a
recent graduating class:
$19,763
Most popular majors: *busi-
ness/marketing, communi-
cations, education*
Guaranteed housing for 4
years? *yes*

5,000 courses per year, so students do have the resources for a decent education at hand, but they will have to be discerning in their selection of courses. Only a portion of the courses that fulfill university requirements would have a place in a true liberal arts core curriculum.

Yet even students who select their courses with care may find their studies dominated by ideology in the classroom. The university aims to create a "racially and ethnically diverse environment," as well as one where many opinions may flourish. Yet students complain that the diversity policy is, to use the words of one, "almost fanatically enforced." A professor says, "Political correctness rules supreme here and infects discussion and inhibits expression of contrary views throughout the university."

Of course, a plurality of voices and perspectives is not ipso facto a drawback to education. But conservative students will find some of the voices and perspectives too extreme to contribute anything of value to their education. More important, the university appears quite selective in the voices it allows to be heard. One student complains: "Politics definitely intrude upon the classroom." Another student says that "a lot of the professors are really liberal, and to be successful in those classes, you almost need to not tell them your real opinion, but [instead] what they want to hear." Several people report the story of a student who was berated by classmates and a professor for using language common among conservatives; that student later faced the possibility of being thrown out of his program and losing scholarship money. It seems that ideology runs thickest in the School of Education; some students advise prospective students to avoid the humanities in general, while others contend that good, fair-minded professors can be found in those departments.

Recently, some students complained about the appointment of General Peter Pace, former chairman of the joint chiefs of staff, as one of the chairs of the Kelley School of Business, because the general had publicly stated that homosexual acts were immoral. The student newspaper maintained that his appointment was "a powerful stance against the equality of gay people" and that the university should have shown more concern over his comments (and presumably not have made such an appointment).

IU maintains a Gay, Lesbian, Bisexual, and Transgender Anti-Harassment Team to investigate and resolve "homophobic harassment." One graduate student says: "IU prides itself in being an open-minded atmosphere that respects everyone's views. From my experience, this means all views unless they are of the Judeo-Christian variety."

Students with a sufficiently high GPA or SAT score are automatically invited to join the Hutton Honors College, and honors students can live in honors housing and participate in special activities and groups. These students still declare a traditional major but have access to extra courses. The Honors College, with its own set of courses spanning many departments and disciplines, may be a student's best bet for an academic challenge and a slightly better introduction to the tradition of the West. One section of the "Ideas and Experience" course includes a set of texts that have, according to the professor, "challenged norms," "disconcerted readers," and "stretched the imagination": Plato's *Symposium*, Vergil's *Aeneid*, selections from the Bible, and Dante's *Inferno*. Other promising honors courses include "Virgil, Dante, Milton," "Europe: Napoleon to the Present," and "Scientific Controversies." By piling up five or six of these courses, a student could gain a fairly comprehensive foundation in the humanities.

IU is a research university, and it has a vast number of departments and programs. The students with whom we spoke particularly recommended programs in Spanish, music, and the hard sciences; several suggested avoiding liberal arts programs, particularly history. IU's music school is top ranked, as is its Kelley School of Business and its information sciences program. IU is one of the first schools to offer a major in "informatics," a discipline that develops new uses for information technology to solve specific problems in areas as diverse as biology, fine arts, and economics.

In the humanities and sciences, recommended professors at IU include Josep Miquel

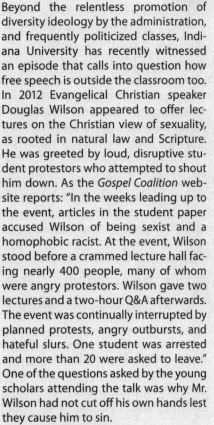

CAMPUS POLITICS: RED LIGHT

Beyond the relentless promotion of diversity ideology by the administration, and frequently politicized classes, Indiana University has recently witnessed an episode that calls into question how free speech is outside the classroom too. In 2012 Evangelical Christian speaker Douglas Wilson appeared to offer lectures on the Christian view of sexuality, as rooted in natural law and Scripture. He was greeted by loud, disruptive student protestors who attempted to shout him down. As the *Gospel Coalition* website reports: "In the weeks leading up to the event, articles in the student paper accused Wilson of being sexist and a homophobic racist. At the event, Wilson stood before a crammed lecture hall facing nearly 400 people, many of whom were angry protestors. Wilson gave two lectures and a two-hour Q&A afterwards. The event was continually interrupted by planned protests, angry outbursts, and hateful slurs. One student was arrested and more than 20 were asked to leave." One of the questions asked by the young scholars attending the talk was why Mr. Wilson had not cut off his own hands lest they cause him to sin.

On the positive side, in 2011 the Foundation for Individual Rights in Education reported that IU had finally removed a policy prohibiting student groups from using their school funding to attend "sectarian" events that involve "proselytizing" for particular religious views. This policy had been used to strip funding from Christian groups.

Sobrer (emeritus) in the Spanish and Portuguese Department; Peter Bondanella (emeritus) in French, Italian, and comparative literature; Aurelian Craiutu and Judith Failer in political science; Robert Ferrell (emeritus), Edward Grant (emeritus), and Noretta Koertge (emeritus) in history; Timothy Long (emeritus) in Classics; Herbert Marks in Jewish studies; Alan Roberts in psychology; and Santiago Schnell in biochemistry.

Research, particularly in the sciences, is one of IU's strengths. The university recently opened new state-of-the-art life sciences labs, and a bioinformatics group at the university just received $1.7 million in grants for life sciences research. One graduate student who teaches in the sciences reports that he was surprised to have three students ask him for letters of recommendation for medical school. He writes: "This was not a role I was expecting, but I can see how students would not develop strong relationships with tenured professors when all their classes are taught by graduate students. . . . This strikes me as a major disadvantage for students at large universities."

Indiana University has gone the way of the virtual university in some respects. Students are only required to see their academic advisers—who may or may not be faculty members—during their freshman year. Afterward, while students are "encouraged" to see their advisers, the online computerized student advising system "monitors" students' progress toward meeting degree requirements. Not surprisingly, students aren't impressed by this hands-off system. One student says, "It's much better to talk to a former student than to your adviser. . . . A lot of times they don't know what's going on." One student also reported that students, faculty, and staff "despise" OneStart, the campus-wide software program that handles student registration, timesheets, advising, financial records, and bills. The student complains: "The entire interface is needlessly complicated . . . arbitrary, not at all intuitive—and no one seems to have the answers about it. My freshman year, online registration took 90 minutes—which was already 60 minutes too long. When they implemented OneStart, it took me three and a half hours to register. . . . It was mind-blowingly frustrating."

A professor admits: "This is not a hardworking university."

The IU student-to-faculty ratio is an unimpressive 18 to 1, but students report that they often find professors within their majors to be accessible and willing to give advice. Students report that freshman survey courses often include 100 to 250 students. IU claims the professors teach "the majority" of classes, but students report that many introductory classes are taught by graduate students; graduate students also often lead discussion sections and give grades in faculty-taught courses. Many students do not take advantage of office hours and extra study sessions. One student recommends teachers who are "somewhat older," saying that, in his experience, professors with tenure care more about teaching and less about their research.

IU has an impressive language program that offers instruction in more than 40 languages, including hard-to-find choices such as Bulgarian, Georgian, and Korean.

On the bright side, it is easy to go abroad for a course of study. IU promises "250 programs in 17 languages (including English) in 52 countries and in nearly every field of study," with school-sponsored programs in countries ranging from Argentina and Belize to Spain, Thailand, Turkey, and Vietnam.

Student Life: Hoosier heaven

"The best part of IU is that there's always something going on," says one student. This includes weekly comedy shows, regular performances such as operas or ballets, free movies in the auditorium, swing dance lessons, a plethora of sporting events, and trips with the IU outdoor club, to name just a few campus amusements. The intramural program is one of the biggest in the country, including more than 20,000 students and offering 27 sports—everything from billiards to euchre to indoor soccer. The student recreational sports center is extolled for its pool, weight room, basketball courts, and track. IU also boasts hundreds of student organizations, including a healthy College Republicans group; a vocal gay, lesbian, bisexual, and transgendered student alliance; the Indiana University Student Foundation, which runs the largest intramural bike race in the country (depicted in the movie *Breaking Away*); and the Student Athletic Board (1,000 members strong), which aims to increase attendance at athletic events, promote school spirit, and coordinate homecoming.

Recent campus events included the week-long "Sexploration" event sponsored by the student health center and Pure Romance (a sex-toy company), which featured a cabaret and burlesque revue, an exhibition of "queer art," and a sex-advice call-in program. Events offensive to conservative students are not uncommon, yet such students are still able to find plenty of wholesome things to do.

Much of student life centers on sporting events at IU, a member of the Big Ten athletic conference. The Princeton Review ranked IU 20th among schools with enthusiastic, loyal student fans. The Hoosier athletic program enjoys a $32 million endowment (the largest in the conference), includes more than 600 student-athletes on 24 varsity teams, and particularly excels in men's swimming and diving, men's soccer, women's tennis—and, of course, men's basketball. Basketball exercises a uniting force at IU; there are more requests for student tickets than can be accommodated. After each big win, "we flood through Sample Gates and onto Kirkwood Avenue to party," says a student.

Unfortunately, major basketball victories are not the only occasion for student drinking. The IU Health Center website encourages students to evaluate and make decisions to change their own alcohol-drinking patterns using the unfortunately named online alcohol assessment test "e-CHUG," a name that seems to reflect the heavy drinking of not a few IU undergraduates. "Drinking is a pretty popular activity here," says another student. The Princeton Review ranked IU as one of the top party schools in the nation, weighing in at number 14 for "best party school," at number 19 for "lots of beer," and number nine for "lots of hard liquor." Students drink throughout the week as well as on the weekends, and there were more than 1,500 students referred for disciplinary action for liquor-law violations in 2007. In response to student complaints about the university's alcohol policy, the school has begun to focus on reforming rather than punishing violators. The Alcohol Alternative Intervention Program allows students implicated in drinking-related incidents to

Blue Collar Ivy

SUGGESTED CORE

1. Classical Studies 311, Classical Epics
2. Philosophy 201, Ancient Greek Philosophy
3. Religious Studies 210/220, Introduction to the Old Testament/Introduction to the New Testament
4. History 208, Pagans/Christians in the Middle Ages (*closest match*)
5. Political Science 382, Modern Political Thought
6. English 220, Introduction to Shakespeare
7. History 105, American History I
8. Philosophy 526, 19th-Century Philosophy

bypass the campus judicial system by voluntarily undergoing counseling.

Given the school's size, the quality of the student body is mixed. Some students complain that the "party school" reputation is undeserved, while others admit that their peers are "more concerned with their social life than with academics," willing only to "do what they have to do to get their degrees." A professor admits, "This is not a hardworking university." Another student says that her fellow students "are going to find the easiest way they can to get to graduation." But others protest the characterization of IU undergraduates as uninterested in their studies. One source insists that "it might bear repeating that IU is a serious research university with excellent professors." An undergraduate says, "I won't lie to you, we do party here, but to say that students are not concerned with getting a good education is absurd." One recent graduate summarizes: "Sure, with a campus as large as IU, many people come to drink and party. However, lots of students are there to get a good education, and they care about doing well." IU is large enough to accommodate a range of intellectual curiosity.

IU has four "neighborhoods" of residence halls grouped together. Different residence halls feature such varied amenities as a music practice room, a game room, an exercise room, a convenience store, a library, and a McDonald's. One residence hall offers a co-op program in which students receive a reduction on rent (up to 40 percent) in exchange for doing such chores as taking out the trash and cleaning the bathrooms. IU offers no single-sex residence halls but does provide single-sex floors for those who would like them—in fact, most floors are single sex, as are all dorm rooms and most bathrooms. Students who do not specifically request limited visitation hours (ending at midnight weekdays and at 2 A.M. weekends) are automatically assigned to residence halls with unrestricted visitation hours. Most upperclassmen live off campus, but they struggle to find adequate parking, according to one student.

IU is relatively safe, given its size. The school reported 11 forcible sex offenses, three robberies, 89 burglaries, and 18 motor vehicle thefts on campus in 2011. The university employs 44 full-time police officers, provides free safety escorts, and offers nightly transportation services. Emergency phones are located across the campus.

One student comments that Indiana state residents can acquire from IU a "decent education at an amazingly low price." In-state tuition in 2012–13 was only $10,034, while out of state was $31,484. Average room and board were $8,854. Admissions are need blind, but the school does not make guarantees about levels of financial aid. Approximately 60 percent of students receive some form of financial assistance.

STRONG SUITS

- A worthwhile set of courses in Western canonical authors offered in the Honors College.
- Good programs in Spanish, music, business, information sciences, and the hard sciences.
- Excellent research opportunities for students working with professors.
- Extensive foreign language and study-abroad offerings.

WEAK POINTS

- Highly politicized classrooms in most of the humanities.
- Huge class enrollments and many introductory courses taught by graduate teaching assistants.
- Weak advising and cumbersome computer-enrollment system that students find infuriating.
- Regularly listed as one of the top party schools in America. Heavy drinking seems pervasive.

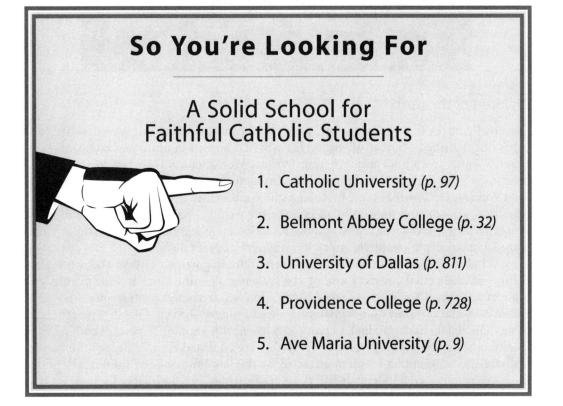

So You're Looking For

A Solid School for Faithful Catholic Students

1. Catholic University *(p. 97)*

2. Belmont Abbey College *(p. 32)*

3. University of Dallas *(p. 811)*

4. Providence College *(p. 728)*

5. Ave Maria University *(p. 9)*

University of Iowa

Iowa City, Iowa • www.uiowa.edu

Children of the Corn

"You really ought to give Iowa a try," goes the old song. And anyone who does try Iowa City's distinguished 173-year-old university will find himself in illustrious company. Flannery O'Connor was a student at its famous Writers' Workshop, and others who either taught or studied there include John Irving, Jorie Graham, Andre Dubus, Wallace Stegner, and Kurt Vonnegut Jr. Iowa has some first-rate faculty and well-regarded programs in medicine, education, science, and the arts in addition to the writing program. Twenty-two of Iowa's programs are ranked in the top 10 among the nation's public universities, and the school is a top-20 university for research, education, and service grant dollars.

What Iowa lacks is a coherent core curriculum, big-name prestige, and a prevalent culture of intellectual curiosity among the students. The university is vast, diffuse, and not very selective. Its pedestrian general-education requirements are far more general than educational and certainly do not guarantee a well-rounded student. Fifty-five percent of its more than 20,000 undergraduates come from Iowa, with another 25 percent coming from adjoining states. A full 80 percent of applicants are admitted. While there are some very fine students among them—often attracted by the low tuition—one professor says that most undergrads "are moderately smart and industrious, but not markedly so. Iowa is so small a state that you don't have to be that smart to get in." Still, says another professor, Iowa is "a fairly intellectual place."

What is true of so many similar schools is true of the University of Iowa: ambitious, motivated students can find a decent educational path among the many available dead ends and bridges to nowhere. But they'll need to use a map and ask directions.

Academic Life: Triage time

Persistent budget cuts over many years have starved UI of professors in the liberal arts, which means larger class sizes and fewer courses. One professor complains that the "faculty and staff numbers are flat, but the bureaucracy has grown threefold." The student-faculty ratio at University of Iowa has gone up in recent years and currently is an unimpressive 15 to 1. There are many, many students at Iowa competing for attention and resources that have been growing scarcer; even so, opportunities abound, and good guidance can be found if sought.

Students are assigned advisers—not faculty but "advising professionals"—at freshman orientation. Students switch to faculty advisers upon choosing a major. A professor says, "Advising is considered a 'service,' which basically means faculty get no credit for doing it. As you can imagine, that means that a lot of faculty don't put any time into it." Nor do many students. As one professor says of his advisees, "I usually have a couple of students who will come in on a regular basis, but most don't bother."

UI's emphasis is emphatically on research in tenure and hiring decisions. A professor says, "The 'secret' is that teaching isn't rewarded at all. Yes, there might be some recognition and small cash awards, but you can be a dreadful teacher and still get huge raises if you publish a lot. If your research drops off, they threaten you with increased teaching load. In other words, teaching is considered a punishment." Says another, "Teaching is important, and it's one of your jobs as a faculty member, but it's hard to measure. So long as your students are not complaining, all is well. Research potential is what gets you hired and what keeps you here."

Students often are intent on doing what they can just to get by, and only 42 percent of

VITAL STATISTICS

Religious affiliation: *none*
Total enrollment: *29,810*
Total undergraduates:
  21,564
SAT CR/Verbal midrange:
  450–630
SAT Math midrange:
  540–690
ACT midrange: *23–28*
Applicants: *18,939*
Applicants accepted: *80%*
Accepted applicants who
  enrolled: *30%*
Tuition (general/out of
  state): *$26,930*
Tuition (in state): *$8,061*
Room and board: *$9,634*
Freshman retention rate: *83%*
Graduation rate (4 yrs.): *42%*
Graduation rate (6 yrs.): *69%*
Courses with fewer than 20
  students: *50%*
Student-faculty ratio: *15:1*
Courses taught by graduate
  students: *not provided*
Students living on campus:
  29%
Students in fraternities: *8%*
Students in sororities: *12%*
Students receiving need-
  based financial aid: *54%*
Avg. student-loan debt of a
  recent graduating class:
  $27,480
Most popular majors:
  *business/marketing,
  communications, social
  sciences*
Guaranteed housing for 4
  years? *no*

Blue Collar Ivy

CAMPUS POLITICS: YELLOW LIGHT

While the faculty leans left, the student body is quite diverse and apparently outspoken. On the right there is an active College Republicans club, a chapter of Young Americans for Liberty, and (at the law school) a Federalist Society chapter. On the left there is a myriad of groups, ranging from the Iowa Public Interest Research Group to the Iowa International Socialist Organization. One student calls Iowa's open atmosphere its best asset. And another says, "I am a conservative and I enjoy this campus; it is a challenge and a wonderful platform for discussions." Students of different opinions tend to get along well, a professor says, adding: "It's the faculty that have gone off the deep end!" Students say that for the most part, classroom indoctrination or intolerance of unpopular ideas is rare. However, according to one professor, conservative students are not vocal about their politics in case their instructors lean left—as many of them do.

Not all the corn is healthy, however. As Townhall.com commented in late 2012: "The University of Iowa does the best job of combining the speech code and the sexual harassment policy into a powerful weapon people can use to destroy just about anyone they don't like: sexual harassment is when 'somebody says or does something sexually related that you don't want them to say or do, regardless of who it is.' Did you get that folks? If you are a student at Iowa and the girl you like has sex with someone else and you get jealous, then guess what? You've been sexually harassed!" The Foundation for Individual Rights in Education has criticized Iowa as having one of the vaguest (and hence most menacing) speech codes in the United States.

them manage to do it in four years. According to one professor, "The main reason students don't get out in four years is because they are just acting dumb: not studying enough and drinking too much." As one student says, "Classes here are manageable. They don't prevent you from having a social life."

There are many planning and advising resources available to students, as well as special first-year classes designed to help them find their way. These include computer programs that map out a four-year graduation plan; first-year seminars on special topics capped at 15 students; Courses in Common, a program through which freshmen can enroll in up to three classes with the same 20 students; and the Pick One program, which encourages involvement in Iowa's hundreds of student organizations. But students must take the initiative, and not enough do.

The approved courses that fulfill Iowa's general requirements can provide a student with a core body of knowledge. They can be fulfilled equally with eccentric, trendy, or agenda-driven classes. The *Daily Iowan* confirms this in a recent article for new students entitled "UI officials: Classes like 'Harry Potter' and 'The Beatles' help engage students." Iowa's first-year seminars, designed to allow freshmen to work closely with faculty members, are capped at 15 students, and faculty members recommend them and enjoy teaching them. But professors are encouraged to design them around their current research, which means the subjects of the courses are frequently narrowly specialized.

Some of the strongest programs at Iowa are traditionally found among the fine arts. The Writers' Workshop is ranked first in the nation. The studio arts and theater programs are also strong, especially printmaking. The university was the first to accept creative work in theater, writing, music, and art on an equal basis with academic research. The English, history, sociology, and political science departments earn high rankings but are uneven.

The English department has recently improved the requirements for its majors, who must take at least one course from each of the following six areas: literary theory and interdisciplinary studies; medieval and early modern literature and culture; modern British literature and culture; American literature and culture; transnational literature and postcolonial studies; and nonfiction and creative writing. The major's requirements are serious and impressive and they guarantee that English majors from Iowa will have a better grasp of literary history than the alumni of many elite colleges.

The history department's requirements are also serious: students need two classes each in American, European, and non-Western history, along with one course studying a period before 1700. Upon declaring a major, they take a small "colloquium" class with other history majors in which "reading, writing, and arguing" are emphasized. Finally, they must submit a portfolio of three graded history papers before graduating.

Refreshingly, political science majors are required to take an introduction to American politics, along with four other introductory courses from a sensible list of 11 choices that includes political communication, political thought and political action, and Russia and Eurasia. The remaining credits are elective.

A professor reveals, "Teaching isn't rewarded at all. You can be a dreadful teacher and still get huge raises if you publish a lot. If your research drops off, they threaten you with increased teaching load. Teaching is considered a punishment."

Recommended professors include Evan M. Fales in philosophy; Michael Dailey and Joe Frankel in biology; David E. Klemm (emeritus) and Jay Holstein in religious studies; Brooks Landon, Garrett Stewart, and Jonathan Wilcox in English; Mitchell Kelly in educational psychology; Chris Brochu in geoscience; Astrid Oesmann in German; and Lawrence Fritts in music.

Iowa's Gay, Lesbian, Bisexual, Transgender, and Allied Union was founded in 1970, making it one of the oldest such campus organizations in the United States. Interestingly, Iowa has come rather late to the game in making diversity an academic requirement, just recently adding a "Values, Society, and Diversity" component to its general-education requirements.

Those seeking off-campus enrichment will also look to Iowa's study-abroad programs; one professor cannot say enough about the "Winterim" program in India. He also recommends anything in the International Writing Program, which brings the world to Iowa. This program lasts for 12 weeks in the fall and is headed by Chris Merrill. Iowa also offers study-abroad programs on six continents in countries ranging from Australia to Uruguay.

Iowa offers a good range of foreign language programs, including Arabic, Chinese, French, German, Greek and Latin, Italian, Japanese, Korean, Portuguese, Russian, Spanish, Swahili, and Zulu.

SUGGESTED CORE

1. Classics 20E:014, Hero/God/Mortal: Literature of Greece
2. Philosophy 026:111, Ancient Philosophy
3. Religious Studies 032:011/032:012, Introduction to the Hebrew Bible/New Testament
4. History 16E:117, History of the Medieval Church
5. Philosophy 026:183, History of Ethics II (*closest match*)
6. English 008:147, Shakespeare
7. History 16A:061, American History 1492–1877
8. History 016:003, Western Civilization III (*closest match*)

Student Life: Flatland, U.S.A.

Iowa City is a community of 67,000 with a metro population of over 100,000, located on the east side of the state on the Iowa River. The downtown area, within walking distance of the university, features a bricked pedestrian walkway lined with stores, restaurants, and coffee shops. Iowa City affords plenty of recreational areas, including a skate park, a walkway by the Iowa River, and a state park a few miles away where students can swim, sun, fish, rent canoes, hike, and bike. "If you are a political junkie, Iowa is one of the greatest places in the country to be once every four years—and the [caucus] season lasts for months," says one professor. Still, a teacher says, "Once you leave Iowa City, you are in the middle of the Corn Belt: a world of hamlets, country towns, and small cities no bigger than Cedar Rapids." Students remain ambivalent about the place. According to one, "When people get here, they can't wait to get out of here. When they leave, they can't wait to get back."

UI has more than 450 student organizations. The largest include Students Today Alumni Tomorrow Ambassadors, University of Iowa Student Government, and College Republicans. More quirky choices are the Iowa Bass Fishing Team and the Society of Composers. Religious students of most faiths will find a group on campus.

One professor notes that it is Iowa and that "most students coming in are Christians," but another adds, "There is substantial religious diversity at Iowa. A number of the Christian denominations have campus ministries. Muslims and Jews are visible on campus as well. The campus ministry groups tend to have student worship meetings on Wednesday or Thursday nights. They provide one of the most useful alternatives to the bar scene." The preoccupations of UI students tend less to the spiritual than to spirits. "We go to football games and we go to bars," a student says. Recently, the *Daily Iowan* reported that "70 percent of UI students engage in high-risk drinking—four or more drinks in one sitting for women, five or more for men—while nationally, 37 percent of students do, according to the National College Health Association." The numbers have been dropping dramatically over the last three years, however, owing to city ordinances that discourage drinking. The university has also increased efforts to combat this problem and recently launched "Ensuring Student Success: Making and Supporting Good Choices," an "orientation program designed to educate students and their parents on making healthy decisions in college."

As one might expect at a Big Ten school, sports are important at Iowa. The front of a newsletter for St. Paul Lutheran Chapel and University Center once announced: "Take Note! On Saturday, Iowa plays Wisconsin in football!" before going on to church news. "Sports are advertised a lot, especially guys' football and basketball," says a student. The wrestling team is famous, having won 20 national team and 31 Big Ten titles. The UI offers 12 varsity teams for women and 10 for men. The school mascot is Herby (short for Hercules) the Hawk. Around 10 percent of students go Greek. For the other 90 percent, there is a lively social scene. "There are tons of bars, and they are full Thursday, Friday, and Saturday nights," says one source. Students hang out at restaurant bars like the Summit, Java House, and Tobacco Bowl. "The worst part of UI is its bar scene," says a student. His lament is borne out by statistics, which show 117 arrests for drug violations in 2011, as well as 777 judicial referrals for liquor law violations. "Partying is pretty big here," a student admits.

Political activity on campus is relatively quiet. Approximately 55 percent of students hail from Iowa and 25 percent from adjoining states—primarily Illinois—and the political leanings of the student body reflect the centrist populism of the region of the country.

Around 90 percent of freshmen live in the 10 residence halls—although students are not required to. UI offers a number of "learning communities" designed to "provide a supportive and engaging environment where students are challenged intellectually and have the unique advantage of bonding with other students who have similar academic goals." Students are selected on a first-come, first-served basis. There is also a "quiet house" option. All halls are officially substance-free—and tobacco is considered a substance. All residence halls are coed, with men and women separated by floor or wing.

If you don't crawl inside a bottle or get hit by a flying one, Iowa City is pretty sedate. A female student reports, "I feel very safe here." In 2011 the school reported 10 forcible sex offenses, six aggravated assaults, and 20 burglaries on campus.

As a state school, Iowa is a sweet deal for residents: in-state tuition for 2012–13 was $8,061 (for nonresidents $26,930), plus $9,634 for room and board. Admissions are need blind, and the school undertakes to cover student need with a combination of grants, work/study, and loans. Some 54 percent of students received some need-based aid. The average student-loan debt of a 2011 graduate was $27,480.

STRONG SUITS	WEAK POINTS
• Good programs in the fine arts, especially the Writers' Workshop, studio arts, theater programs, English, history, sociology, and political science.	• Faculty are uncompensated for advising and hence unenthusiastic.
• Solid, sane requirements for majors in English, political science, and history.	• Research far more important than teaching for tenure.
• Excellent study-abroad and foreign language options.	• Dismal four-year graduation rate (42 percent).
• Good opportunities for students interested in politics, thanks to the Iowa Caucuses.	• Many students unmotivated, just doing enough to get by.

University of Kansas

Lawrence, Kansas • www.ku.edu

No Place Like Home

Founded in 1866 as Kansas's main state university, KU has risen steadily in reputation to become one of the more highly regarded public schools in the nation. Indeed, KU can offer one of the better state-school educations available, largely because it maintains comparatively strong liberal arts requirements and a good honors program. But given the mammoth size of the school and its impersonal approach to teaching, it's not for everyone. "A student who is at high risk for getting lost in a large, bureaucratically inclined institution should stay away from this place," says a professor. But self-directed students who know what they want to study can probably find it here.

Academic Life: Lost in the crowd

The best option at KU seems to be the university honors program. One student insists, "The honors program is the only way to go for students who care about educational quality." Honors students take courses that are more challenging and smaller, at 20 to 25 students, and most live together in special housing. Sadly, honors classes and upper-level courses within their majors are about the only places students will have the opportunity to develop relationships with faculty. Introductory courses enroll more than 100 students. As one student spins it, "There is a beauty to giant lecture halls, in that if you want to remain anonymous, you certainly can." Graduate students teach 22 percent of courses.

Freshmen are assigned professional advisers in the advising center. A student says, "From everything I've heard, these advisers are very impersonal and just want to make sure all the boxes are checked off on your degree plan. I had good experience with the honors advisers, though." Once a student has declared a major, he can visit with a faculty adviser within that department, but he shouldn't expect too much. "Unfortunately, many teachers are not available outside of class," a journalism major says. "Sometimes the size of the school can hinder a student from getting the type of advice and help he needs. KU is not a personal place, and you do not get much individual attention here." Another student disagrees: "To meet with a professor, you simply have to show up during office hours; it's not much harder than going to McDonalds." A professor advises prospective students, "Pick your faculty mentors well and you'll get all the encouragement you need."

As at many research institutions, good teaching is not necessarily emphasized or required for advancement. However, according to a professor, "The Center for Teaching Excellence has established a strong, active, and actually useful presence on campus (encouraged and financially supported by the upper administration). Activity in that center is rewarded, and faculty generally give good reports on the help the center gives for pedagogical training." Just as the quality of instructors varies, so does the quality of students. "There is huge variation in the intellectual ability and curiosity of the KU student body," a professor says. "Our best students can compete with the best students anywhere, but our weakest are pretty weak."

Students majoring in English are required to take one survey of British literature before 1800, one of British literature after 1800, two American literature classes (one before and one after 1865), a Shakespeare course, and an introduction to literary criticism and theory.

History majors must take five courses in one of these two categories, and three courses

VITAL STATISTICS

Religious affiliation: *none*
Total enrollment: *27,939*
Total undergraduates: *19,695*
SAT CR/Verbal midrange: *N/A*
SAT Math midrange: *N/A*
ACT midrange: *22–28*
Applicants: *10,035*
Applicants accepted: *93%*
Accepted applicants who enrolled: *55%*
Tuition (general/out of state): *$22,860*
Tuition (in state): *$8,790*
Room and board: *$8,186*
Freshman retention rate: *79%*
Graduation rate (4 yrs.): *32%*
Graduation rate (6 yrs.): *60%*
Courses with fewer than 20 students: *42%*
Student-faculty ratio: *19:1*
Courses taught by graduate students: *22%*
Students living on campus: *22%*
Students in fraternities: *13%*
Students in sororities: *20%*
Students receiving need-based financial aid: *46%*
Avg. student-loan debt of a recent graduating class: *$22,114*
Most popular majors: *business, health professions, social services*
Guaranteed housing for 4 years? *no*

CAMPUS POLITICS: GREEN LIGHT

On campus, left-wing students are the most vocal. "I would say that liberal elements are much more comfortable on campus, and conservatives just don't speak out enough," says a student. Students differ about the degree to which political ideology affects other classroom instruction. A journalism and political science major says, "The political science courses I have taken remain unbiased." Another student notes that "I never felt uncomfortable because my views differed from the professor's." A recent graduate agrees, "I never felt that my grades would be threatened because I spoke up in class about my conservative beliefs and/or religious/spiritual disposition."

The College Republicans are very active, as are the College Democrats, but both groups usually stick to party politics rather than philosophical issues, often bringing state politicians to speak on campus. Political clubs can obtain financial support through the Center for Campus Life (using student fees), but a representative from the office says most of the funding goes to general expenses like office supplies and flyers for the political clubs. "Controversial funding for speakers or protests, for instance, would have a much harder time finding financial support," he says.

in the other: ancient, history of science, medieval, modern Western Europe, Russia/Eastern Europe, and United States; and Africa, East Asia, Latin America, Native America. While it is impossible to avoid Western history entirely, it would be quite easy to exclude most of it.

Majors in political science must take introductory courses in U.S. politics, and comparative politics or international politics; plus political theory and political science methods of inquiry. The U.S. politics course does cover "basic American governmental institutions, political processes, and policy."

Some of the best departments, professors say, are those in the humanities, political science, journalism, aerospace engineering, preprofessional areas, and music. A proud music major boasts that "KU piano students routinely beat Juilliard and other high-power music school students in competitions. The same is true for organ and voice. . . . For ambitious performance students who can't afford the big-name conservatories, this is a good choice." Journalism majors are also ready to tout their department: "KU has one of the top journalism departments in the country, and it really does live up to the reputation." Recommended professors include Bob Basow, Kerry Benson, Ted Frederickson, David Guth, and Chuck Marsh.

Among highly regarded professors in other departments are Hannah Britton in women, gender, and sexuality studies and political science; Allan James Cigler, Burdett "Bird" Loomis, and Sharon O'Brien in political science; David Katzman in American studies; Douglas A. Houston in business; Stephen Ilardi in psychology; Thomas Lewin, Rita Napier, and Leslie Tuttle in history; Antha Spreckelmeyer in Western civilization; and Thomas Heilke, dean of graduate studies.

During the Vietnam War era, the University of Kansas was wracked by massive student revolts. Some of that spirit still haunts the town. "The state of Kansas is very conservative overall," says a student. "However, Lawrence is very liberal—much like Bloomington, Indiana, or Austin, Texas."

One professor insists that "there are plenty of solid, fair-minded faculty on both sides and the middle of the left-right ideological spectrum." The Hall Center for the Humanities sponsors a series of lectures from diverse perspectives, and the Robert J. Dole Institute of Politics, named after one of KU's most prominent alumni, features speakers from across the political spectrum. Students report that a number of courses—especially those in the social sciences—are politicized. "Certainly there are times when I am afraid to state certain conservative or Christian views," says a student. "However . . . the few times that I felt singled out because of my views, I still received very fair grades." It's no secret that big state schools lean left, and KU is no exception. One student put the case bluntly by saying that "the religious studies department is a good place to study religions, but not if you are in any way religious yourself." Enough said.

> "A student who is at high risk for getting lost in a large, bureaucratically inclined institution should stay away from this place," says a professor.

KU's study-abroad program is excellent, offering programs in various locations in Australia, China, Costa Rica, Denmark, Finland, France, Germany, Ireland, Italy, Japan, the Netherlands, Spain, Sweden, and Switzerland, among other locations. Sadly, only some 19 percent of graduating seniors have studied on foreign shores. One student says that "the university is putting more resources into making study abroad accessible."

Foreign language offerings are plentiful. Choices include all the most popular European tongues and myriad other options, from Cherokee, Croatian, and Haitian to Wolof and Yiddish.

Student Life: Basketball, basketball, *über alles*

The state of Kansas might call to mind huge expanses of flat land, but the city of Lawrence is in one of the few hilly parts of the state, and the campus itself is on top of Mount Oread, making the starting time of that 8:00 a.m. math class only half the battle. KU's limestone campus makes the trek worthwhile. A student says, "The campus is absolutely gorgeous. Sometimes in the winter, my roommates and I drive along Jayhawk Boulevard and stare up at the lighted windows and say, 'How are we so lucky that we get to go to this place?'"

Fewer than one-fifth of students, mostly freshmen, live on campus; however, since that fraction still adds up to about 5,200 students, you are unlikely to feel like an oddball if you join them. Except for two all-women residence halls, dormitories are coed, with separate wings for each sex. One student describes dorm life as crowded, impersonal, and loud: "Fire alarms in the middle of the night happen a lot (usually pranks)," he says. "It can be just overwhelming to live in a tiny room with no personal space and 800 other people on eight floors." However, another student reports, the dorm experience "was wonderful. I made a lot of good friends and didn't have to deal with any of those horror stories that you normally hear about."

Blue Collar Ivy

SUGGESTED CORE

1. Classics 230, Greek Literature and Civilization
2. Philosophy 384, Ancient Philosophy
3. Religious Studies 124, Understanding the Bible
4. History 108, Medieval History (*closest match*)
5. Political Science 301, Introduction to Political Theory
6. English 332, Shakespeare
7. History 128, History of the United States through the Civil War
8. Philosophy 386, Modern Philosophy: Descartes to Kant (*closest match*)

KU requires that a visiting student be escorted by a resident when visiting the opposite-sex wing of a hall. This sounds more impressive than it is. A male student says, "There are supposedly visitation policies in the dorms, but that doesn't really change anything—sleepover guests are the norm." He adds, "Students are sometimes shocked to move out of home and be surrounded by other students having casual sex and attacking anyone who has a problem with that." In the two women's residence halls, where the policies are better enforced, men must be out by 11:00 p.m. on weeknights, but they can stay overnight throughout the weekend. At least you may have to deal with your roommate's boyfriend sleeping in the bunk above you only two nights a week.

KU offers several options for those who wish to live with other students who have interests similar to their own. There are also quiet floors for upperclassmen and scholarship halls, where students share all cooking and housekeeping responsibilities.

About 13 percent of KU undergraduates are members of a fraternity, while 20 percent belong to a sorority, and most members live in the organizations' houses. Fraternities and sororities contribute to KU's reputation as a party school, and drinking plays an enormous role in campus social life. "There is very much a culture of alcohol here, and it can seem at times like the only thing to do here is get drunk," says one student. "If you're afraid that you might party too much, you may want to take that into consideration." Another student insists, "Students at KU can drink as much or as little as they wish. The alcohol is available and accessible to all ages. . . . However, it is not the focus of the university's activities." Lawrence itself provides plenty of other options for weekend and evening entertainment in the form of live music, shops, bars, and restaurants. Students rate it highly as a college town.

One of the best attributes of large state universities is that there are usually other students who share your interests—for instance, in one of the more than 580 student clubs. These range from preprofessional societies—like the Pre-Dental Club and the Public Interest Law Society—to the Philosophy Club, which sponsors lectures and an essay contest, and the KU Federalist Society, which brings conservative legal scholars to campus. Conservative students will also want to check out the KU College Republicans, a vibrant group that is very active in local and national politics and has a great networking base for political internships and jobs. The KU Republicans are countered by quite a number of liberal groups—which accurately reflects the political climate at KU. In fact, the liberal groups tend to swing quite far to the left.

Religious clubs, especially evangelical Christian ones, are also quite popular at KU, and no student should have trouble finding a group that shares his faith: discussion groups, Bible studies, and prayer sessions abound. Some local churches shuttle students to Sunday services. KU is one of the few state schools with a chapel on campus. Danforth Chapel is nondenominational; its webpage says that it is a place for "individual meditation and prayer" as well as weddings, memorial services, and student activities. "A variety of conservative and not-so-conservative Christian student communities thrive here," says one professor. The St. Lawrence Catholic Campus Center is well respected, and one student goes so far as to claim that active involvement with the center "gives you an intellectual and spiritual experience comparable to a good Catholic university."

One of the few interests that nearly every Jayhawk student shares is sports—and basketball above any other. How could they not at this school, where James Naismith, inventor of the game, worked for nearly 40 years? "Basketball is the only university-supported religion on campus," a student says. The legendary Allen Fieldhouse seats more than 16,000 fans, has hosted 37 NCAA tournament games, and is considered one of the best places in the country to watch college basketball. Kansas has been a perennial contender for the NCAA men's basketball championship for decades.

Despite the dominance of basketball at KU, the football team also garners significant attention. The Jayhawks' rivalry with the University of Missouri Tigers is the oldest in college football. Besides varsity athletics, KU offers 16 intercollegiate club teams and many intramural ones, usually organized around residence halls and Greek houses.

Crime is relatively infrequent for a school of KU's size. In 2011 the school reported two forcible sex offenses, one robbery, one aggravated assault, two stolen cars, and 28 burglaries.

Even though it has risen steadily in recent years, tuition at KU is still a bargain, especially if you come from Kansas. Tuition for 2012–13 for in-state students was $8,790; for out-of-state students, it was $22,860. Room and board were $8,186. Almost half of students received need-based financial aid, and the average student-loan debt of a recent graduating class was $22,114.

STRONG SUITS	WEAK POINTS
• Better-than-average liberal arts requirements for a state school.	• Weak formal advising and little personal attention unless you seek it out.
• An excellent honors program—the only way to go, faculty say.	• Very wide range of student interest, energy, basic abilities.
• A top journalism program and good departments in most humanities, as well as political science, aerospace engineering, music, and many preprofessional programs.	• Teaching not emphasized as much as research by school.
	• As a student says, "The religious studies department is a good place to study religions, but not if you are in any way religious yourself."
• Plentiful foreign languages offered and many study-abroad options (too little used by students).	
• Active and solid religious chaplaincies.	

Alice Lloyd College

Pippa Passes, Kentucky • www.alc.edu

The Leaders Are Here

Alice Lloyd College strives to give what it calls "mountain people"—students who live in Appalachia—the skills they need to become leaders in the region. Founded by Boston journalist Alice Geddes Lloyd in 1923, the college is located in the town of Pippa Passes, Kentucky, which is about 150 miles east of Lexington. On a visit, Lloyd had seen a desperate need for educational opportunities in eastern Kentucky.

The small liberal arts college primarily serves students from 108 Central Appalachian counties in Kentucky, Ohio, West Virginia, Virginia, and Tennessee. For qualified students from this region, tuition is covered through grants, scholarships, and participation in the student work program. ALC is one of only seven "work colleges" in America. All full-time students work 10–20 hours a week in jobs that help keep the campus running—such as secretarial, janitorial, food prep, or assisting at the college radio station, WWJD—or at off-campus jobs that help provide needed services in the surrounding communities. The college does not accept direct state or federal funding. The college is led by Joe Alan Stepp, who was the first native Appalachian to become president of ALC when he was appointed in 1999.

Academic Life: A place for teachers

ALC grants degrees in a limited number of majors: biology, business administration, education, English, history, kinesiology, mathematics, social science, sociology, and sports and fitness programs management. The school's general-education requirements seek to give students a good grounding in communications skills and liberal arts, with course requirements in the humanities, social science, natural science, and math. But on their own they do not add up to a traditional humanities education (see our Suggested Core sidebar). Students are also required to pass courses in freshman composition, physical education, public speaking, computer science, and leadership education.

ALC places a heavier emphasis on teaching than on faculty research. There is no tenure system, and professors work on a year-to-year contract basis. Teaching plays an important role in rehiring decisions. "Teaching and working with students is the main focus of our work at ALC," says a professor. " 'Teaching Performance' and 'Advising' are ranked highest on the list of faculty evaluation criteria when requesting promotion." Another reports, "Commitment to teaching is the primary route to keeping a contract. Student evaluations are also important."

Since Alice Lloyd is small, it seems that it's easier for students to develop good relationships with teachers. "Depending on the professor, most of them are helpful," says one student. "As for accessible, almost all the staff live on campus and even eat in the Hunger Din [the campus dining hall] with us." A faculty member adds, "Most of the faculty live on campus, and students can have a close one-on-one and help if needed," says a professor. Another points out that faculty are required to teach five courses a semester, which "doesn't allow us enough time to explore advances or changes in our own fields." ALC does not have graduate programs, so professors, rather than teaching assistants, teach all classes. "Sometimes it feels that we have become grading machines," a professor laments.

Professors are encouraged to "mentor students through close relationships," a one-time teacher reports. The "Senior Seminar" or "Capstone" project are "great

VITAL STATISTICS

Religious affiliation: *none*
Total enrollment: *608*
Total undergraduates: *608*
SAT CR/Verbal midrange: *460–590*
SAT Math midrange: *420–520*
ACT midrange: *20–22*
Applicants: *3,081*
Applicants accepted: *36.6%*
Accepted applicants who enrolled: *24%*
Tuition (general/out of state): *free to qualified students*
Tuition (in state): *$8,500*
Room and board: *$5,140 (free to qualified students)*
Freshman retention rate: *55%*
Graduation rate (4 yrs.): *28%*
Graduation rate (6 yrs.): *37%*
Courses with fewer than 20 students: *44%*
Student-faculty ratio: *16:1*
Courses taught by graduate students: *none*
Students living on campus: *75%*
Students in fraternities: *none*
Students in sororities: *none*
Students receiving need-based financial aid: *76%*
Avg. student-loan debt of a recent graduating class: *$7,729*
Most popular majors: *health sciences, education, business*
Guaranteed housing for 4 years? *yes*

CAMPUS POLITICS: GREEN LIGHT

Politics do not seem to interfere with academics. "I don't feel that any specific department would make a student feel uncomfortable regarding their religious choices," says a professor. "However, this is a culture that self-censors itself in many ways. Individual professors, including myself, frequently engage and encourage students to engage in free and vigorous debates on any topic. Many times these debates fizzle out because the students . . . do not want to participate in them. Anecdotally, students have shared that they feel this is a school where they don't always feel as free to express their opinions in class as they'd like, because of student peer pressure, not from influences from the faculty."

"Probably one of the most explosive political issues in East Kentucky today is coal versus the environment," says a professor. "Recently I asked a freshman class to prepare a debate for a group of donors who wished to visit the classroom. I was very pleased to see my students vigorously defend their positions while also pointing out the strong points of the other side and respecting each other's opinions. The donors were also impressed."

One former professor says the administration is far more conservative than the faculty. "While the faculty try to implement rigorous debate inside the classroom, the administration has its own agenda, a conservative Christian viewpoint not open to debate," he says.

As for the faculty, some may "lean left," he says, but none "glaringly left-wing or right-wing. . . . Most present balanced arguments in the classroom and do not let personal politics interfere."

opportunities for students and their mentor professors to deeply explore issues and trends in their future fields," a professor says.

There are no Honors or Great Books programs at Alice Lloyd, but there are reportedly strengths in the biology, math, natural sciences, business, social science, and education departments.

"The business department prepares students to begin business initiatives to rejuvenate Appalachia," notes another former professor. "The natural science department has an especially high rate of students who continue in graduate and professional schools, especially medical school and pharmacy school."

"The strengths of the social science department include two professors of sociology teaching full time, one social worker teaching part time, and a professor of human geography with half a dozen books in print who is an adjunct," says a professor in that department.

A biology major likes her department because "we get a leg up on the competition. A lot of the classes we take are classes that most students don't take till some form of graduate school."

Likewise, graduates of the premed and prepharmacy programs "have little to no difficulty in being accepted in professional programs," says a professor.

"The strongest parts of my department include the opportunity for students to get great hands-on experience doing all jobs involved in theatrical and music presentations," says a professor in speech and theatre. "We produce plays, choir concerts, and the occasional visual art show. These are guided or led by faculty, but the students do 80 to 90 percent of the work. This allows them to learn on their feet providing them a solid foundation in these art forms."

A former English professor believes his department—and all the humanities—has suffered from an administration decision to bolster the natural sciences and business. The English department offers a literary criticism course in which "approaches may include deconstruction, gender criticism, new historicism, postmodernism, and psychoanalytic criticism." The department also offers a course in Appalachian literature. Shakespeare is an option but not required. Other courses seem solid and traditional, such as linguistics and survey of English literature.

For history majors, a course in U.S. history before 1945 is required. Other offerings in the department seem fairly traditional and sane: history of world civilization, early modern Europe, 20th-century America, and the like.

The college does not offer a degree in political science.

"In all the departments the only other weakness is maintaining stability with faculty retention," says one professor. "In the past several years, too many instructors have not stayed more than five years."

> "The business department prepares students to begin business initiatives to rejuvenate Appalachia," notes a former professor. "The natural science department has an especially high rate of students who continue in graduate and professional schools, especially medical school and pharmacy school."

ALC doesn't fail to capitalize on its location. Its library houses an Appalachian Collection and administers the Photographic Archives and the Appalachian Oral History Project. Various departments offer special courses with Appalachian focuses: economic development in the Appalachian Mountains and the role of coal on the regional and national economy; Appalachian literature, Kentucky history. The college is also home to the renowned Voices of Appalachia choir, which tours the United States annually and shares musically with audiences the pride, hopes, dreams, and sorrows of "Mountain People."

Alice Lloyd herself was keen to instill leadership skills in young Appalachians. "The leaders are here," she was wont to say, and the college's leadership program today combines community service requirements with a minor in leadership classes from several disciplines. The program, starting with a "strong liberal arts academic program," according to the college website, covers leadership philosophy and cultural development. "The institution attempts to infuse leadership education initiatives into all aspects of the educational experience including formal classroom instruction, activities that help students learn to cope with cultures outside of Appalachia, group learning activities, involvement in service to others, opportunities to question their moral, ethical, and religious positions and activities that place them in leadership roles."

The staff at ALC is small, but a few professors seem to stand out: Paul Beasley in history; Charlene Bentley in psychology; Claude Crum and Cynthia Salmons in English; Michael Ware in art; Paul Yeary in chemistry; Sherry Long in education; Denise Jacobs in

SUGGESTED CORE

1. English 201, Survey of World Literature I (*closest match*)
2. Philosophy 105, Introduction to Philosophy (*closest match*)
3. Religion 101 / 102, Old Testament Survey/New Testament Survey
4. History 101, History of World Civilization I (*closest match*)
5. History 321, Early Modern Europe (*closest match*)
6. English 311 / 312, Shakespeare's Tragedies/Histories/Shakespeare's Comedies/Romances
7. History 203, American History I
8. History 322, Europe since 1789 (*closest match*)

business and social science; and Billy Haigler and Janelle Pryor in biology. "There are two of the most helpful and inspiring women on our campus," says one student. "Marsha Neace (who teaches math) and Marylee James (who teaches sociology classes). They are two of the best people I have ever come in contact with."

The only foreign language taught at Alice Lloyd is Spanish. Overseas study opportunities are limited to a Semester in London program.

But ever present is the work ethic that Alice Lloyd wanted to maintain in the consciousness of local young people. "Each student receives a work certificate as well as a diploma at graduation," says a professor. "Students are able to move up through the system to become supervisors of various work groups, and all students receive evaluations and feedback to help them prepare for work after graduation. We also maintain a house on the campus of the University of Kentucky, where our graduates who qualify (based on scholastic records) can stay rent- and utility-free throughout graduate school. Undoubtedly this is one of the reasons that a disproportionate number of our graduates go on to graduate or professional school."

Student Life: Hard work and fair play

While students spend most of their time between studying and working, there are also a number of sports and extracurricular activities they can get involved in. ALC is a member of the National Association of Intercollegiate Athletics and the Kentucky Intercollegiate Athletic Conference. A variety of intramural sports are offered, including basketball, tennis, and touch football.

There is a weekly newspaper and a 24-hour radio station featuring Christian programming. The Eagle Theatre Club produces plays like *Antigone, Much Ado about Nothing,* and *Smoke on the Mountain,* and the Billie and Curtis Owens Literary Society meets to discuss the literature of established authors and new works by students.

The college requires that full-time students live in authorized campus housing—it operates four dormitories—with the exception of students commuting to ALC and living with immediate family members. There are no fraternities or sororities.

ALC would probably never make anyone's list of "party schools." Drinking and "hooking up" appear to be minimal—and discreet at that, due largely to the Christian, conservative atmosphere. Says one professor: "We are a dry campus in a dry county. We are in a conservative part of the state, and that is reflected in the mores of our students and community." There are no coed residence halls. Members of the opposite sex are not allowed within another person's dorm, except on supervised open-dorm nights for about three hours.

"If someone of the opposite sex does come into the building, they are only allowed in the lobby, or once a week (on an appointed day) they are allowed in the rooms; however, everyone's feet must be on the floor and the door must remain open," says a freshman business major.

Nevertheless, "Dorm life is a blast," says a student. "I couldn't imagine living off campus at this point. . . . Most of the resident advisers are really cool—that is a work-study job on our campus."

Though not sponsored by a particular church, the philosophy of the college is based on the Christian faith, and the institution says it tries to integrate Christian principles and values into all aspects of campus life. Apparently the only campus ministry at ALC is Baptist Collegiate Ministries, which one student at least finds a tad exclusive. "We have a Baptist Collegiate Ministries that is supposed to be one of the most inviting groups on campus, but clearly isn't," she says.

Perhaps along with the conservative, religious atmosphere, crime appears to be only of minimal concern. There was a grand total of one robbery reported in 2011, and nothing the previous two years. "The only trouble we really have is theft in the dorm, and alcohol," says a student. "But as long as you know the right people on campus, you can get away with just about anything."

For qualified students from the region the school is meant to serve, Alice Lloyd guarantees financial aid that will cover the cost of attendance, contingent on students' taking part in the extensive (up to 160 hours per semester) work-study program. Some still find that they need extra cash to get by; the average loan debt of a recent graduate was a modest $7,729.

STRONG SUITS	WEAK POINTS
• The school is still true to its founding mission of providing a Christian education that helps poor students get ahead.	• A heavy teaching load keeps faculty from advancing and drives high turnover.
• The work-study program builds character, provides experience, and helps many students graduate debt-free.	• A limited range of majors (for instance, nothing in political science).
• High rates of acceptance in graduate and professional schools.	• Humanities are undernourished compared to more practical disciplines.
• All courses are taught by faculty, who seem to be dedicated to teaching and helping students.	
• A wholesome, upbeat, fun campus environment.	

Berea College

Berea, Kentucky • www.berea.edu

Noble Beginnings

Berea College, a small school in rural Kentucky, was founded in 1855 as a one-room school intended specifically as a place of Christian learning and unity for both blacks and whites. Today the school retains the motto of its founding: "God made of one blood all peoples of the earth" and stands apart from other schools by virtue of its student labor program, its affordability, and its commitment to the underprivileged, particularly of the Appalachian region. The college proudly identifies itself as the first interracial and coeducational college in the South. Today, however, its "Christian mission" might be more aptly identified as a liberal tolerance program.

Still, a school with a real religious commitment, strong teaching, and a program of full-tuition scholarships for every student accepted is nothing to sneeze at and deserves a careful look.

Academic Life: Rigorous classrooms, local goals

Berea College's general-education requirements are fairly broad and open, focused mostly on service to its region, Appalachia; 70 percent of students at Berea College are locals, many from underprivileged families. Mandates are broken down into several categories. First come the writing seminars: "Critical Thinking in the Liberal Arts" and "Identity and Diversity in the United States." The next course requirement is "Understandings of Christianity," which "invites students to imagine and consider Christianity from stances both inside and outside the faith."

Other requirements include a Practical Reasoning course, an Active Learning Experience, and one course in each of six Perspective Areas: Arts; Social Science; Western History; Religion; African Americans', Appalachians', Women's; and International. One Western civilization course offered is "Western Civ II: Studies in Gender," which also includes a focus on Appalachians. The Active Learning Experience (ALE), an opportunity for an internship or service project, is another Berea trademark: students can select from such options as "Middle Grades Student Teaching," "Essentials of Nursing," and "Health in Appalachia."

While this hardly amounts to a real core curriculum, one student says that these requirements "do a good job of honing students' writing skills, as well as exposing us to a wide variety of perspectives. Even though I have a few qualms with it, the program does a good job of exposing students to multiple fields of study, and for this reason I believe many employers and graduate schools favor Berea students."

The college takes learning out of the classroom by requiring, as part of the General Education Program, that all students attend at least seven "Convocations" or campus-wide events featuring speakers, scholars, and performers. But these events are not impartial, and one student reports finding the mandatory attendance oppressive: "These 'convos' are almost always extremely liberal and often attack whites, males, Christians, and Republicans."

"There [have been] some instances where campus politics have entered the classroom," recounts a student. "Though the college is liberally biased, it does respect everyone's views. Berea's religion department can put anyone to the test. Through this department I learned that any student can say anything they want as long as they have good evidence to back up their claims. In fact, the college highly encourages discussion between students."

VITAL STATISTICS

Religious affiliation: nondenominational (*Christian*)
Total enrollment: *1,658*
Total undergraduates: *1,658*
SAT CR/Verbal midrange: *540–660*
SAT Math midrange: *525–625*
ACT midrange: *22–27*
Applicants: *1694*
Applicants accepted: *539*
Accepted applicants who enrolled: *391*
Tuition (general/out of state): *free*
Room and board: *$5,792*
Freshman retention rate: *82%*
Graduation rate (4 yrs.): *48%*
Graduation rate (6 yrs.): *62%*
Courses with fewer than 20 students: *68%*
Student-faculty ratio: *10:1*
Courses taught by graduate students: *none*
Students living on campus: *84%*
Students in fraternities: *N/A*
Students in sororities: *N/A*
Students receiving need-based financial aid: *100%*
Avg. student-loan debt of a recent graduating class: *$7,600*
Most popular majors: *business/marketing, visual and performing arts, education*
Guaranteed housing for 4 years? *yes*

Kentucky

CAMPUS POLITICS: YELLOW LIGHT

Conservatives will certainly be in the minority at this small school, which has a strong progressive culture and tone on campus. A professor writes: "I'm conservative. And Berea College is pretty forthrightly liberal. And I've been here [for decades] and never experienced the least bit of trouble for all that. Nor have I ever observed any students having difficulty: if anything, it tends to work the other way around, since our students tend to come from fairly conservative, fundamentalist backgrounds—they challenge the campus ethos as much as the reverse!" But what this witness refers to is "the usual discomfort that comes from being dunked into a different culture."

A student recounts such an experience: "In one class I had, capitalism was defined as a system where one group of elites controlled the means of production, and another group worked for the first. The ideas of laissez-faire economics were treated throughout the class as a guise for class control, rather than class mobility or individual growth. Very few professors identify as politically conservative, while many are openly liberal."

The College Republicans group on campus is rebuilding itself with a handful of active members after all the previous members left or graduated. Some of the same students are also trying to get a Conservatives in Action group off the ground.

One student has a very different perspective: "Berea College is unbelievably liberal. The administration, faculty, and student body are very liberal and will often times make conservative students feel intimidated or unwelcome. Many Republicans or otherwise politically conservative students and staff will not admit their political beliefs, for fear of retaliation (staff members fear being fired, students fear professors' giving them bad grades on assignments, staff and students fear being harassed by campus members)," he says.

Another student concurs with this assessment: "Yes, the college does have politics consistently intrude into the classroom. Because of a postmodern and liberal bias, students who are conservative or religious often feel uncomfortable and are especially challenged." This student recounts an orientation activity in which students had spelled out for them the college policy that any disapproval or questioning of LGBTQ behavior would be considered ignorant and hate mongering.

A conservative professor disagrees, saying: "I am, in general, quite pleased with the overall quality of our faculty here, and in my experience even the most ideologically left-wing seem to bend over backward to accommodate students of differing opinion."

Students at Berea enjoy close relationships with their instructors and small classes, with a 10-to-1 student-faculty ratio. Classes typically hold 10 to 15 students, and all of them are taught by members of the faculty; no graduate students teach at Berea. One professor said of his department: "Our strength is no doubt individual contact with our students. We all seem to meet with students all day, every day. We work with them constantly." One student says: "Probably because we are such a small college, research, while it is done here, takes a back seat to teaching. Our professors, generally speaking, are awesome instructors. They take time to think their lectures through and help students." Another says, "I love my department [Education] and the faculty there. They can, at times, be unorganized and adopt a 'go with the flow' attitude, which I don't think is a positive quality. Other than that, they are fantastic." Another student attests, "The majority of professors at Berea love to teach. Also, the majority of the classes are small (20 people max), so it becomes a discussion-based style of learning as opposed to lecture."

"Our official standards rank teaching first and scholarship second," another professor explains. "Scholarship has become a little more important lately, but teaching is certainly number one in emphasis for professors and in tenure and promotion decisions. (I know; I have served on that committee.) Teachers teach the right amount: about three courses per term, on average. Everyone I know here is a dedicated teacher."

One professor reports, "In general, most programs seem to be pretty demanding. . . . Our students do well in competition with other Kentucky schools (winning awards at the annual KPSA meeting, for example), and many programs on campus can make similar claims. Various natural science programs, theater, music, art, philosophy, forensics, business, economics, history—all have earned honors off-campus." However, the business school is said to focus excessively on philosophy at the expense of education in entrepreneurship, and the nursing department suffers from a weak faculty.

One student say that Berea's labor program covers full tuition (plus $4–6 per hour) and also gives students an opportunity to work in many different fields before leaving college.

A student says, "The religion department has some definite strengths. It is very academically rigorous and, when cross-compared with other universities, is probably ideologically moderate. But it becomes apparent that the department seems to have an ideological bent. The classes favor a universalist understanding of Christianity and religion in general, in a way that pushes that ideology on students. While Buddhism and Islam are often wrestled with from both the believers' perspectives and higher critical perspectives, Christianity is rarely examined from believers' perspective. [The general-education requirement] on Christianity attacks orthodox Christian beliefs while presenting some parts of Christianity as a postmodernist philosophy. The department lacks what I would consider an orthodox Christian voice. For a college that is so diverse elsewhere, I feel the orthodox or 'conservative' Christian views are usually ignored or blatantly attacked in class curriculum."

The history, psychology, philosophy, political science, and Asian studies programs are praised by insiders, as are the science programs: "Students in science do significant research that one does not always see at a teaching-oriented college," says a professor. Within history, Joshua Guthman is highly regarded. Andrew Baskin, a Berea alumnus and teacher for decades, is a "legend on campus" in African American studies. Mylene Watkins in French is a strict but excellent teacher, and Carol de Rosset, a professor of Spanish, is "a great teacher who loves her students."

English majors, however, are not required to take a course on Shakespeare, although they have the option to take "Intro to Queer Theory." In keeping with the focus of the

SUGGESTED CORE

1. Classics 215, Classical Mythology
2. Philosophy 305, Classical Philosophy
3. Religion 205/207, Introduction to the Old Testament/ New Testament
4. Religion 215, History of Christianity to 1600
5. Political Science 209, Freedom, Law, and the Modern State
6. No suitable course
7. History 161, American History to 1865
8. Philosophy 315, Kant: Philosophical Legacies

college, there are also courses in "African-American Women Writers" and "Appalachian Literature."

History majors do not have to study early American history but have the option of taking "American History to 1865" as one of their major fulfillment courses (the complementary course is "American History since 1865"). Overall, course offerings are scattered and heavy on African American history, with an option for Appalachian offerings.

For political science majors, "American Government" is required, but "American Political Thought" is optional (and not always offered). "American Constitutional Law" is also intermittent and optional. One course entitled "Freedom, Law, and the Modern State" appears to be the only one with an emphasis on classic philosophical thinkers.

Requirements for graduation do not include any work in philosophy or in foreign languages. The language department at Berea is not very strong; availability of courses fluctuates. Courses are offered in Chinese, French, German, Greek and Latin, Hebrew, Japanese, and Spanish.

A strong point of the education at Berea appears to be the hands-on Agriculture and Natural Resources program, which features work and managerial experience on the college's own diversified farm. For students interested in an agriculture program—again, with a local emphasis, as graduates are prepared to go on to farm-related work in the Appalachian region—the program at this small rural college may well be superior to solely research-based learning at a larger school.

Berea does not have its own established study-abroad program; however, the college generously funds students who take initiative to travel. "Berea is unique in that it will, in many cases, pay for huge portions of a study-abroad trip. I would highly recommend that students take advantage of this opportunity while they are attending Berea College," an undergrad says. Another student agrees: "Berea College is definitely one of the best places to go if you want to study abroad. Students can be funded up to a third for summer-abroad trips and up to 75 percent for a semester abroad. On top of that, additional scholarships can be obtained depending on where the student wants to go." A third student says, "Berea covers most of the cost. It also offers students an opportunity to travel pretty much anywhere in the world (having programs in almost any country they choose).

One student advises, "I would recommend our internship opportunities. Berea has a strong connection with its alumni, and almost all students end up going into internships in their fields, thanks to these connections."

Also of note is the student labor program, which, along with generous alumni funding, is the main reason that Berea is able to offer its underprivileged students a tuition-free education. All students are required to work at least 10 hours a week, supporting every department, logistical, and infrastructural element of the school. A student reports, "Not only does the labor program pay us the equivalent of over $24 to $26 an hour ($20 of which defrays our tuition scholarships), but it gives students an opportunity to work in many different fields before leaving college. One of the biggest advantages of Berea is the experience we gain in the workplace outside of academics."

Student Life: Dry campus, dry town

All residence halls on campus are single sex, with a strict visitation policy. Freshmen are not allowed any hall visitation during the first term, presumably to ensure as calm a living atmosphere as possible as they adjust to the freedom and new environment of college life. One reports, "The RAs in the dorms are pretty good at keeping discipline, but the students are good at following the rules. They are coming here basically for free, so I imagine they don't want to mess that up. The visitation, alcohol, and drug policies are enforced."

Another student reports, "Although the college and city of Berea are fairly small, there are things to do and events around campus pretty much every weekend: concerts, movie viewings, particular-interest meetings (such as Anime clubs, musical ensembles, et cetera), and excellent programs offered by residence hall staff. However, this aspect of Berea is experienced mostly by beginning Berea students, because as students progress in Berea, they usually have less and less time for extracurricular and outside activities and need more time for their studies."

Since both the school and the surrounding town are "dry," and students are busy keeping up their grades and earning their tuition scholarships, there is no party atmosphere at Berea. There is no Greek system. There is, however, a lively sports program. The school reports that the Berea Mountaineers "annually send teams to national competitions. As a founding member of the Kentucky Intercollegiate Athletic Conference (KIAC), Berea College competes in the National Association of Intercollegiate Athletics (NAIA). Berea fields teams in 18 intercollegiate sports, as well as a cheerleading squad. During one season of competition in these sports, the participating student-athlete can receive a .25 academic course credit."

There are on-campus living options for married students as well as apartment options for single students. Students with families have the option of living in the Ecovillage, a Berea project made up of 50 apartments, with a Child Development Lab, a Commons House, and facilities relating to studies in sustainability.

As part of Berea's commitment to environmentally sustainable activity, shuttles are provided on the weekends for any students who wish to visit the nearby cities of Richmond and Lexington. "And if you don't feel like leaving Berea," explains a student, "Berea Coffee and Tea is where you can go to talk with fellow students or study. The college itself frequently plans activities for students, such as dancing or concerts. All of these are fairly popular activities."

The Christian ministry on campus is active, but orthodox students will not find it enriching. "[The college] maintains a chaplain in each residence hall, though I feel very few students take advantage of this service," a teacher says. "The Campus Christian Center,

I feel, focuses much more on respecting different religions than it does on promoting Christianity." "I'm a devout Protestant," says one Berea student, "but I have never really used Berea's chaplains. I prefer to talk to my fellow Christian friends for advice instead of someone I don't really know. The churches at Berea, however, are thriving, and I would recommend either Berea Baptist Church or River of Life Foursquare Church." An Evangelical Protestant student recommends seeking fellowship in InterVarsity, Campus Crusade for Christ, and Chi-Alpha Christian Ministries, as well as local churches near campus. St. Clare's is a local Catholic parish.

The town and campus of Berea are fairly safe but not perfect. One student says: "The biggest problem I've personally experienced is the racism among some community members not affiliated with the college. It is not uncommon for drivers by to shout racial slurs at some of my nonwhite friends. If I were to rate the safety of the campus on a scale of 1–10, I would give it a 7.5, with most colleges being a 5.5 or 6." In 2011 the school reported one forcible sex offense, one aggravated assault, 12 burglaries, and one stolen car.

As mentioned, Berea is more than an educational bargain—it's a free ride if you're willing to pull up your bootstraps. Students earn their full tuition scholarships (valued at $21,300), plus $4–6 per hour in spending money working a wide array of campus jobs. Room and board in 2012–13 were a reasonable $5,792. Nevertheless, given how strapped many of these students' families are, some do borrow money to cover necessities. The average debt of a recent graduate is a modest $7,600.

STRONG SUITS	WEAK POINTS
• The school is honestly dedicated to raising up disadvantaged students in a poor region.	• Very strong social-justice tinge to the Christian mission of the school—which undermines orthodox faith, even in religion classes.
• Its full-tuition scholarships make college possible for many who otherwise couldn't go.	• Pervasive leftist ideology in the classroom makes many of its conservative, religious students uncomfortable.
• Professors teach all classes and focus on students rather than research.	• Weak general-education requirements, with little on Western civilization and a lot on race/class/gender.
• The work ethic and experience gained by students build character and provide experience in many fields.	• Shaky majors' requirements in key humanities disciplines.
• Students are ambitious, hardworking, and grateful for the opportunities offered them.	

University of Kentucky

Lexington, Kentucky • www.uky.edu

The Kentucky Promise

The University of Kentucky is the largest and highest-ranked university in the state. In addition to its College of Arts and Sciences, it boasts physical therapy, pharmacy, medical, dental, law, engineering, and architecture programs on its continuous campus. It is currently undergoing an ambitious program of expansion called the "Kentucky Promise," which will include all-new residence halls, a new science building, and renovations to the football stadium and College of Business and Economics building in the near future. UK aims to establish itself as one of the 20 best research universities in the next five years. Such ambitions typically come at the expense of undergraduate teaching, so we hope that Kentucky lawmakers (who subsidize the school) keep a close eye on what's happening in the classrooms.

Academic Life: Assembly is required

The University of Kentucky's General Education requirements, called "UK Core" and revised in the fall 2011 semester, consist of distribution requirements mostly for freshman year. They run along four main lines: Intellectual Inquiry (in the physical and social

VITAL STATISTICS

Religious affiliation: *none*
Total enrollment: *28,094*
Total undergraduates: *20,099*
SAT CR/Verbal midrange: *490–610*
SAT Math midrange: *500–630*
ACT midrange: *22–27*
Applicants: *3,537*
Applicants accepted: *69%*
Accepted applicants who enrolled: *47%*
Tuition (general/out of state): *$19,864*
Tuition (in state): *$9,676*
Room and board: *$10,192*
Freshman retention rate: *81%*
Graduation rate (4 yrs.): *34%*
Graduation rate (6 yrs.): *59%*
Courses with fewer than 20 students: *32%*
Student-faculty ratio: *18:1*
Courses taught by graduate students: *not provided*
Students living on campus: *26%*
Students in fraternities: *14%*
Students in sororities: *24%*
Students receiving need-based financial aid: *43%*
Avg. student-loan debt of a recent graduating class: *$20,579*
Most popular majors: *biology, business, psychology*
Guaranteed housing for 4 years? *no*

sciences, the humanities, and the arts), Oral and Written Communication, Quantitative Reasoning, and Civic Formation. While there are clear strengths to the UK program, the list of subjects it does not require is long and alarming: history, philosophy, and literature. Worse, the school's foreign language requirement makes not even a pretense of requiring proficiency or literacy. Overall, UK seems to expect of students a common set of skills but not a common knowledge base from which to draw; and no attempt is made here to hand down the cultural inheritance of the West.

Most classes are taught by professors, all of whom are required to keep regular office hours; however, some lower-level courses such as science labs are infamous for non-native-English-speaking and uncommunicative TAs. Academic advising is generally considered unsatisfactory. One student laconically describes the overall classroom experience at UK: "Some [professors] are OK; some just Power Point teach." Lower-level and "core" courses are generally "big and boring"; more advanced junior- and senior-level courses tend to be smaller and better.

Perhaps the best detour around the mediocre aspects of UK's academic experience is the university's honors program, in which almost 3 percent of undergraduates are enrolled. Benefits include more intensive classes held in a seminar style with 15–20 students, more intimate academic advising, separate housing for honors students, access to graduate-level courses, and research opportunities with some of the university's scholars and scientists. This program has expanded rapidly in recent years and is now very competitive; straight-A students with strong test scores are known to be baffled when they're not admitted.

UK has a wide variety of subject areas to choose from, though the sciences are generally considered the strongest majors offered (or the "hardest," as some underclassmen complain); more specifically, the College of Agriculture is in the top 10 in the country, and student research opportunities in biology, psychology, and chemistry are plentiful. The Department of Engineering is home to the only college-based NASA control system with a live control room to the International Space Station, right on campus. The College of Design's Architecture program offers the only accredited program in the state.

The English department's faculty and course offerings focus on the modern and familiar but are not radical or polemical. Majors are grounded to a certain extent in the English literary canon with four historical survey courses required; and more intensive courses are available to those interested, including studies in authors such as Shakespeare and Chaucer, and even one called "Ovid in Renaissance Literature." Although it is possible to escape UK with an English degree and avoid Shakespeare entirely, it is more likely that he will serve as mere preparatory reading for the department's main literary experience, which is dozens of credit hours spent with "Women's Literature" and "Major Black Writers." Indeed, while 2012–13's course offerings list eight courses with Zora Neale Hurston's *Their Eyes Were Watching God*—a worthy novel—Shakespeare's *King Lear, Hamlet, Othello,* and *Macbeth* are listed only six times and usually as part of an introductory thematic survey, such as "Depictions of Madness" (*Lear*) or "Family, Home, and Fear" (*Hamlet*). Students will find politicization in all the expected places: for example, one "Intro to Women's Literature" course is subtitled "Reaping the Fruits of a Revised Canon." One major assures that for the most part, the department is very solid and "is very textual in approach."

The history department's course offerings seem a bit more solid, and admirably comprehensive, mostly offering broad overviews of important periods in all major world regions. There are also courses available that cover the state of Kentucky and the surrounding Appalachian region, and the South—including "The Civil Rights Movement in the U.S. since 1930"—alongside a hundred others that examine European political and intellectual history, among other key topics. The major requires at least one course in U.S. history and six credit hours both before and after 1789. Although there is no specific requirement for early American history, the period from the colonization of the New World through World War II is thoroughly surveyed across six separate courses.

CAMPUS POLITICS: GREEN LIGHT

Although a large and secular university, the University of Kentucky is not significantly outside the mainstream politically speaking. If anything, it leans more to the right than most of its kind, perhaps due to the state's largely rural and conservative population; but it is safe to say that religious students will find campus life a bit too libertine. However, "it's easy to find a circle of friends that is clean," one student says.

Finely honed moral standards are not viewed here as "repressive" but politely regarded as archaic and curious. In addition, "there is a big Christian fellowship here," reports one student, "through several denominations." As the largest university in a conservative state, conservatives will not find themselves alone, or their activities or activism restricted, or their voices stifled.

Although not a conservative outlet, the financially independent, student-run *Kentucky Kernel* has a diversity of voices and featured coverage of campus Young Republicans' efforts during the recent presidential elections. Conservative students report that the university "has worked fairly well with" conservative student organizations such as the Fellowship of Catholic University Students and Students for Life and that several such groups are "close knit and passionate about their causes."

403

The political science department emphasizes the mechanics of government in the United States and elsewhere. Political philosophy, though not required of majors, is surveyed in a two-semester sequence that runs from ancient Greece through Machiavelli and on to Marx and Weber. There is also an advanced course, "American Political Thought." Majors must take at least one course in American government, comparative politics, international relations, and political theory. The course "American Government" advertises its "emphasis on the Constitution."

UK's Classics department should be of interest to prospective students for its UK Institute for Latin Studies, which may do more than any other program to revivify the study of Latin and the inheritance of Western culture that comes with it. It is unique and world renowned for its "Living Latin" program, which draws from preclassical sources, all the way through medieval, Renaissance, and even modern Latin, in addition to pioneering the revival of spoken Latin as part of its lively and effective pedagogy. Although the institute is a postgraduate program, undergraduates are sure to benefit from this energy. And even undergraduates, should they so desire, can attend the "*Conventiculum Latinum Lexintoniense*," the department's world-famous workshop in conversational Latin held each summer.

Politics in the classroom are detectable but not stifling. One conservative Catholic student gives a representative and levelheaded summary of his classroom experience: "As it is a secular university, religious students will indeed find in various ways, both in class and on campus, opinions rigorously held by secular professors. Prospective students should in no way be under the illusion that in all their classes they will be comfortable as a conservative or Christian. On the whole, the university is secular and manifestly so. But I can say that I have never felt particularly singled out or insulted because of my faith." One recent graduate affirms that most teachers are "fair" even in departments more prone to be politically contentious; the liberal bias is likely to be more distracting than oppressive.

Although "UK is a secular university, I have never felt particularly singled out or insulted because of my faith," one devout undergrad reports.

Leading faculty include David Bradshaw (a widely published medievalist and philosopher of religion) and Jim Force in philosophy; Frank Walker (the state's poet laureate) in English; Terence Tunberg, Milena Minkova, and Hubert Martin in Classics; Jane E. Calvert (a scholar of the American Founders), Tracy Campbell, and Paul Thomas Chamberlin in history; Patrick Poole, Christine Gobel, and Stephen Gedney in engineering; and Daniel Morey and Emily Beaulieu in political science.

UK offers a satisfactory range of foreign languages that features majors in Chinese, Classics, French, Italian, Japanese, Russian, and Spanish. The developing Islamic Studies department does not yet offer Arabic. UK's opportunities for language immersion abroad, however, are rich and varied, as is their study-abroad program as a whole. Each year UK sends hundreds of students to every major geographical region. The most popular destinations are France, Germany, Spain, and the United Kingdom.

Student Life: Candy, condoms, and coffee

Varsity athletics are a central part of the campus culture at UK. (Collectively, the fans of the Kentucky Wildcats are referred to as the Big Blue Nation.) The men's basketball team, in particular, has both the most all-time wins and the highest all-time winning percentage in the history of college basketball and were national champions as recently as 2012. Says one recent graduate, the impact of "the basketball team is ridiculously huge." For those students who like to play sports in addition to watching them, the Johnson Student Recreation Center has more than 87,000 square feet of recreational and fitness space that includes cardio machines, free weights, a gym, and even a climbing wall; and intramural sports of all kinds have been a staple of campus life for more than 80 years. Besides athletics, there are more than 500 student organizations on campus, and there are clear and easy guidelines in place to allow anyone to start a new one. Most students are involved in at least one, though "it's not like you're weird if you're not in one," says one student.

SUGGESTED CORE

1. Classics 261, Literary Masterpieces of Greece and Rome
2. Philosophy 700, Seminar in Ancient Philosophy
3. No suitable course
4. Philosophy 705, Seminar in Medieval Philosophy
5. Political Science 442G, Modern Political Theory
6. English 340, Shakespeare
7. History 108, History of the United States through 1876
8. Philosophy 513, 19th-Century Philosophy

UK does not have a reputation as an especially wild "party school"; one rowdy upperclassman laments that campus administration is "trying to kill the Greek life off." Students should be aware, however, that nightlife both on campus and off still mostly belongs to the fraternities and sororities and that hard drugs are known to show up at these events. The school also earns a yellow flag for its culture of sexual promiscuity, which is not so much wild as normative: "Abstinence is not encouraged," says one student. "We have programs where they pass out candy, condoms, and coffee." The student center hosts events with names like "The Female Orgasm," a lecture on sexual health designed to "enhance the college experience." However, one recent graduate brags that she "never went to a party that had alcohol" and would assure prospective students that "if you're not interested in that, it's very easy to avoid it."

Approximately 85 percent of students live on campus freshman year, though it is not required. Most residence halls are coed by floor, meaning all students live on a same-sex floor, with the opposite sex living on the floor above and below. All restrooms are strictly single sex. There are currently two all-male and two all-female dorms. It is normal for students to move off campus as upperclassmen.

Religious students give their chaplains mixed reviews but good marks overall. For instance, the Catholic Newman Center on campus has improved considerably in recent years, becoming, according to several students, "much more student-friendly and conservative."

While the city of Lexington has some areas that are more dangerous than others,

students generally feel secure. The university has a system of emergency assistance phones all over campus and sends out text messages whenever there is an incident. The consensus is that if students use their common sense and do not roam alone at night, they should be fine. (Students complain of a "foot stabber" on campus, apparently some student who sneaks under the library cubicles and stabs peoples' feet with a pen.) Despite being situated in a relatively dangerous city, UK's campus is rather safe. Among more than 20,000 students, the 2011 crime statistics reported five sexual assaults, three robberies, four aggravated assaults, 13 burglaries, and 12 motor vehicle thefts.

For Kentucky residents, UK was a bargain compared to private schools, at only $9,676 in 2012–13 for tuition (out-of-state students paid $19,864), plus room and board of $10,192. Only 43 percent of students received need-based financial aid, and students graduated with an average debt totaling $20,579.

STRONG SUITS	WEAK POINTS
• Solid courses offered in most humanities and sciences. • Even typically leftist departments are generally tolerant and tolerable. • A good honors program. • A distinctive Classics program that offers conversational Latin.	• Patchy general-ed requirements. • Very weak foreign language requirement—just one intro course. • Commitment of faculty teaching (vs. research) is quite variable. • Too many graduate students teaching, with limited English proficiency.

Louisiana State University

Baton Rouge, Louisiana • www.lsu.edu

It's the Heat, Not the Humanities

Founded in 1853, Louisiana State was once known as the leading outpost of the southern literary revival, hosting Robert Penn Warren, Cleanth Brooks, and the journal they edited, the *Southern Review*. In political philosophy, too, LSU had a stream of distinguished professors, including Eric Voegelin, Willmoore Kendall, and Charles Hyneman. The *Southern Review* continues to flourish, as do several excellent academic departments. Nevertheless, the intellectual environment at LSU no longer seems so dazzling, and the Agrarians and New Critics who made its English department famous are now held up for scorn in English classes taught by tenured carpetbaggers.

While LSU strives for a national reputation, it must take in a great many students ill prepared by crumbling public schools. Still, there are more good courses and faculty at LSU than at many other state schools, and it has found gold and growth in research. Focused students can find excellent teachers, distinctive academic resources, and hearty fellowship—especially if they enter the school's respected Honors College. The atmosphere in most departments is friendly to patriotism and faith while tolerant of liberalism. The campus is one of the most beautiful in America, though the humid heat—which lasts from April through October—can be brutal.

VITAL STATISTICS

Religious affiliation: *none*
Total enrollment: *30,225*
Total undergraduates: *24,626*
SAT CR/Verbal midrange: *500–620*
SAT Math midrange: *520–630*
ACT midrange: *23–28*
Applicants: *16,169*
Applicants accepted: *76%*
Accepted applicants who enrolled: *46%*
Tuition (general/out of state): *$20,469*
Tuition (in state): *$5,193*
Room and board: *$10,218*
Freshman retention rate: *83%*
Graduation rate (4 yrs.): *36%*
Graduation rate (6 yrs.): *67%*
Courses with fewer than 20 students: *35%*
Student-faculty ratio: *23:1*
Courses taught by graduate students: *17%*
Students living on campus: *27%*
Students in fraternities: *15%*
Students in sororities: *24%*
Students receiving need-based financial aid: *36%*
Avg. student-loan debt of a recent graduating class: *$18,474*
Most popular majors: *biology, business, psychology*
Guaranteed housing for 4 years? *yes*

Academic Life: Honors and others

LSU is foremost a research university, and many of the university's initiatives seem directed at preserving the school's prominence as such—so it's easy to forget that there are more than 24,000 undergraduates hanging about the place, some of them even aspiring toward a liberal education.

The financial situation at LSU is still grim due to the state misappropriating federal stimulus dollars to fund higher education—and becoming addicted to funds that then dried up. Without these federal millions, the Louisiana legislature was forced to institute devastating budget cuts, and for the first time in history less than 50 percent of LSU's operational budget is coming from the state. As Chancellor Mike Martin said, "These cuts and the cuts we face in the future are damaging. They hurt severely. We will fundamentally and structurally [have] to change the university."

Fortunately, LSU's Honors College still offers "the benefits of a small liberal arts environment within a large research university," according to the school. The Honors College describes itself as a "campus within a campus," complete with residence halls, a dining hall, an administration building (the French House, a 1930s-style chateau), and an oak-lined outdoor common area. Honors students can also attend weekly afternoon teas with honors faculty. Students complete a traditional major in one of the regular academic colleges, including fields outside the humanities.

The University College Center for Freshman Year is responsible for the academic advising of each student until he declares a major, at which time he transfers to an adviser in that department. While in the University College, students begin completing the university-wide general-education requirements. One student cautions that survey courses such as these can result "in a disappointingly shallow education," and for that reason, serious scholars should seek out more challenging classes—for instance, by taking the honors sections when they are offered. "LSU is a large state university, so of course there are a thousand ways to graduate while avoiding the most serious matters of study," says one professor. "But there are also some very fine faculty in a number of fields, and the student who wants to look will find them quickly enough."

LSU offers an impressive number of strong academic programs. Within the humanities, English, political science, history, philosophy and religious studies, music, and theater are notable for their quality instruction. The English department's requirements for majors are suspect, though; majors are required to take classes such as "Critical Strategies," "Modern Criticism," and an ethnic or women's literature course such as "Literature and Ethnicity" or "Images of Women." Happily, students must also choose at least one course on Milton, Chaucer, or Shakespeare, and a two-course sequence in either British or American literature. The English department has moved sharply to the left in recent decades; conservative and religious students should be very careful what opinions they express to their Marxist or feminist professors, sources warn.

The LSU geography department is one of the finest in the country. The economics department is free-market oriented, although professors use econometric rather than theoretical approaches to the subject. The political science department is strong in political theory, thanks to the heritage of the great theoretician Eric Voegelin, a former LSU professor. Poli-sci majors are required to take an all-encompassing "American Government"

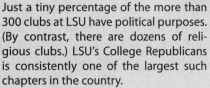

CAMPUS POLITICS: GREEN LIGHT

Just a tiny percentage of the more than 300 clubs at LSU have political purposes. (By contrast, there are dozens of religious clubs.) LSU's College Republicans is consistently one of the largest such chapters in the country.

"Louisiana is a culturally conservative state, and it shows in the student body. There are no hippies, no lovefests on the Parade Grounds," says one student. A professor says, "Generally speaking, I would describe LSU students as conservative and religious but grounded in common sense and decency rather than fanaticism."

The administration, while sensitive to public opinion in this Bible Belt state, sometimes follows its Orwellian, modern-academic instincts into trouble. In 2012 the school took a celebrated photo of a student pep squad, the Painted Posse, and airbrushed out the Christian crosses the students had piously included in their body paint. According to *Campus Reform*, the administrators responsible at first "stood by their decision to edit the photo" to avoid offending non-Christian students. "LSU only issued a formal apology after the controversy made national headlines."

course, but the rest of the curriculum is up to them. Excellent classes are offered, including courses in the U.S. Constitution, American political philosophy, comparative politics, and international politics and law, but none are specifically required. Students interested in learning the history of ideas should seek out the faculty associated with the Eric Voegelin Institute and enroll in their courses, which are among the best theory classes offered anywhere in the United States.

The history department is solid as well. All majors are required to take 12 hours of basic introductory courses in American, European, and world history, as well as an additional 21 hours of electives chosen from an impressive selection of advanced classes in American, European, Asian, and Latin American history.

The mass communications school, while growing in size and reputation, is "soft academically," in the words of one student. Some have called classes in journalism "the easiest [they] have ever taken." Students in the business school are not known for their intellectuality. "Business majors may hardly ever if at all walk into the library," says a student.

Of course, at such a big school, one is bound to find intellectual gems. Among the many fine professors on campus are Gregory Schufreider and Mary Sirridge in philosophy and religious studies; Kevin Cope, Brannon Costello, William Demastes, Michael Hegarty, John Lowe, Elsie Michie, Lisi Oliver, Malcolm Richardson, James Wilcox, and Michelle Zerba in English; Gaines M. Foster, James D. Hardy Jr., Stanley E. Hilton, Paul F. Paskoff, Karl Roider, and Victor L. Stater in history; and Cecil L. Eubanks, Wayne Parent, Ellis Sandoz, and James Stoner in political science.

Professors are said to be remarkably accessible for a school this size. "The teachers are willing to personally help you and take time out for you," a student says. Another student was surprised to find that in most of her honors courses, "the instructor has known the name of every student in the class." Professors are required to hold regular office hours, and most are known to warmly welcome students who need help or want mentoring.

> "LSU is a large state university, so of course there are a thousand ways to graduate while avoiding the most serious matters of study," says one professor.

Outside honors, the advising system is weak. The otherwise excellent history department, for instance, has one undergraduate faculty adviser to handle the academic needs of all majors. One student says the advising program "operates like a factory, and an inefficient one at that."

The foreign languages and literatures department is excellent, offering degrees in Arabic, Chinese, German, Greek and Latin, Hebrew, Italian, Japanese, Portuguese, Russian, Spanish, and Swahili. Students wanting to learn a language immersed in a different culture can take advantage of the more than 300 study-abroad programs offered through LSU, in dozens of countries on every inhabited continent.

Student Life: Fun on the bayou

Baton Rouge has become much more congested since Hurricane Katrina, which thrust tens of thousands onto the streets of a city not known for civic-mindedness, with roads laid out like a bowl of spilled spaghetti, whose public transit system compares quite poorly to that of cities in India. Nevertheless, it's a friendly town with enough cultural attractions—most of them on campus—hosting a school with plenty of potential in one of the most delightful states in the Union.

Student life at LSU is vibrant—if not particularly healthful. Drinking makes up a significant part of social life on campus, as students throng local bars in defiance of the drinking laws—which Louisiana adopted only under enormous pressure from the federal government and does not enforce with any great enthusiasm. Neighboring New Orleans still features drive-through daiquiri shops, and Cajuns to the school's southeast and west tend to take "one for the road" quite literally, flouting bans on open containers. If you prefer eating to drinking, Baton Rouge is a wonderful town to learn the intricacies of Cajun and classic southern cooking; it also hosts a surprising variety of ethnic restaurants.

Among LSU's numerous student organizations are agricultural and equestrian clubs, the usual Greek houses, religious clubs, and ethnic groups. Some of the more unusual include the Wargaming and Roleplaying Society, the Hip-Hop Coalition, and the Poker Strategy Club. A service group called Ambassadors and student government are comparatively popular among students.

There are also many Christian groups. Conservative Catholic students can avoid the bland campus Catholic chapel and take refuge at St. Agnes Church, which offers weekly Latin Masses. New Orleans's Holy Trinity Cathedral, the first Orthodox house of worship established in the New World, has a mission in Baton Rouge. The Baptist Student Union is one of the largest and most active religious centers on campus. Alternatively, the Full Circle Wellness Center serves as a clearinghouse for what they proudly describe as "New Age" organizations and activities. Nearby Jimmy Swaggart Bible College still dispatches young evangelists to preach against the immorality and immodesty at LSU.

> ### SUGGESTED CORE
>
> 1. History, Technology, and Society 3028, Ancient Greek History (*closest match*)
> 2. Philosophy, Science, and Technology 3102, History of Ancient Philosophy
> 3. No suitable course
> 4. History, Technology, and Society 3030, History of Medieval Europe (350–1400) (*closest match*)
> 5. International Affairs 2210A, Political Philosophies and Ideologies
> 6. Literature, Communication, and Culture 3228, Shakespeare
> 7. History, Technology, and Society 2006, History of the Old South to 1865
> 8. History, Technology, and Society 3032, European Intellectual History

The Greek system has a strong presence at LSU. Although only 15 percent of men join fraternities and 24 percent of women join sororities, "their influence is way bigger than those numbers represent. Greek students have a big profile on campus. They're the ones holding office in student government," one student says. Disciplinary actions are taken against the fraternities and sororities quite frequently for violations ranging from alcohol to assault to hazing. "Fraternities keep doing stupid things and getting into trouble here," says a student. "We've had a couple kicked off campus." Indeed, two fraternities were removed from campus and another was put on probation.

Tiger football games are the true center of LSU students' social lives. LSU won its third National Championship in 2007, bestirring its historically fervent football fans to achieve a noise level of 122 decibels, according to ESPN. As one student says, "There is nothing better than to go to an LSU football game and sit in the student section. Everyone around you is so pumped." Tiger Stadium is the sixth-largest college football stadium in the nation, and the third largest in the SEC, holding almost 92,500 fans. Tailgating is extraordinarily popular, as alumni and others fill vast parking lots with pickup trucks containing propane stoves to heat gumbo and barbecue. The city of Baton Rouge clogs with traffic and pretty much closes down on game days as Louisianans converge from all over the state to throng the massive Tiger Stadium. If you don't like football, leave town—well in advance, as many tailgaters arrive on Monday to camp out in the stadium parking lot in anticipation of Saturday's game. LSU's mascot, Mike the Tiger, is a real, live tiger who lives on campus. At past games, he has been paraded in his cage during half-time so he could roar into a microphone.

The LSU athletic program is one of the best in the nation, with strong gymnastics, swimming, baseball, and men's and women's track teams. LSU fields teams in 20 sports (nine men's, 11 women's) and is a member of the Southeastern Conference and NCAA, Division I. The women's and men's basketball teams also have many fans. Students take part in a number of intramural sports, including Ultimate Frisbee, Wallyball, and flag football. At the LSU Union, students can enroll in art instruction or courses in wine tasting and Cajun dancing.

No student is required to live on campus, though many choose to live either in the dorms or in residential colleges—which range from the quaint and traditional (with ceiling fans) to the huge and hideous (which at least are air-conditioned). Happily, students no longer live under the bleachers of Tiger Stadium, as they did well into the '90s. (Huey Long couldn't get legislators to fund a stadium expansion, so he built dorms adjacent to the original stands and put bleachers on the roofs. No, we're not making this up; this guide's lead editor used to live in Tiger stadium.) Some residence halls are single sex, while others separate the sexes by floor or by room.

In 2011 the school reported two sex offenses, nine aggravated assaults, nine robberies, 47 burglaries, 10 car thefts, and three arsons on campus. The LSU Police Department provides awareness and safety training to students, but they are still understaffed. Safety is a more serious problem at LSU than at other campuses of the same size (dangerous slums sit just off campus), and students are well advised to exercise more caution than they might elsewhere.

Like most state schools, LSU is quite a bargain for residents of the state: in 2012–13, the school charged $5,193 in-state and $20,469 out-of-state tuition. Room and board were $10,218. Some 36 percent of students received need-based aid, and the average student-loan burden of a recent grad was $18,474.

STRONG SUITS	WEAK POINTS
• Some excellent faculty and courses in English, political science, history, philosophy and religious studies, music, and theater.	• Mass communications (including journalism) classes are easy, often shallow.
• Renowned programs in geography and foreign languages.	• Business majors are called less than demanding.
• Many options in energy-related fields.	• Aggressive feminism and multiculturalism in English department.
• Excellent Honors College.	• Party atmosphere in dorms, Greek houses.
• Politically balanced campus environment, with many religious options and free speech valued.	• Advising operates like an "inefficient factory."

University of Maine

Orono, Maine • www.umaine.edu

Worth Honors

The University of Maine, a land- and sea-grant university, opened in 1868. While its research is well respected, the school also focuses sharply on teaching, especially in the liberal arts. UMaine students and faculty speak with pride of their engineering, nursing, forestry, and agriculture programs, and the Honors College is truly noteworthy.

Academic Life: Partly cloudy

All students must fulfill a set of general-education requirements within six categories: Science, Human Values and Social Context, Mathematics, Writing Competency, Ethics, and Capstone Experience. There are good courses offered (along with fluff) in each of these categories, so students should choose carefully.

Under Human Values and Social Context, students must take a course in Western Cultural Tradition, with very good options like "History of Ancient Philosophy." In the required Cultural Diversity and Population and Environment subcategories, pickings are slimmer and include "Sex and Gender in Cross-Cultural Perspective." Students can satisfy the Ethics requirement with a worthy class such as "Introduction to the Jewish Bible."

413

Blue Collar Ivy

VITAL STATISTICS

Religious affiliation: *none*
Total enrollment: *10,901*
Total undergraduates: *8,778*
SAT CR/Verbal midrange:
470–590
SAT Math midrange:
480–600
ACT midrange: *20–25*
Applicants: *8,306*
Applicants accepted: *81%*
Accepted applicants who
enrolled: *29%*
Tuition (general/out of
state): *$25,230*
Tuition (in state): *$8,370*
Room and board: *$8,848*
Freshman retention rate:
76%
Graduation rate (4 yrs.): *36%*
Graduation rate (6 yrs.): *60%*
Courses with fewer than 20
students: *55%*
Student-faculty ratio: *15:1*
Courses taught by graduate
students: *not provided*
Students living on campus:
27%
Students in fraternities: *not
provided*
Students in sororities: *not
provided*
Students receiving need-
based financial aid: *60%*
Avg. student-loan debt of a
recent graduating class:
$32,438
Most popular majors: *educa-
tion, health professions,
engineering*
Guaranteed housing for 4
years? *no*

UMaine's student-faculty ratio is a middling 15:1, and more than half of courses have fewer than 20 students. Even the most crowded courses top at around 35 students. "Professors are quite accessible and helpful," says one student. "I have had absolutely fantastic professors." A teacher comments, "One of the things I really like about UMaine is the close balance of teaching and research. The university places a much greater emphasis on teaching than other research universities," with standards "similar to those at very highly ranked liberal arts colleges."

The honors program offers classes no larger than eight to 14 students. Says one, however, "The honors sequence experience varies greatly depending on the professors." A professor praises the Honors College as "the 'jewel in the crown,'" stating that his best students "write very solid senior theses to conclude their BA," followed by a two-hour defense to a faculty committee. The thesis project, a well-chosen adviser, and some of the excellent course material offered (the *Odyssey,* the *Republic,* Greek dramas, the *Aeneid,* Augustine's *Confessions,* Dante's *Inferno,* Renaissance art, the Bible, *The Prince,* Shakespeare's plays, *The Social Contract,* the works of John Locke, Darwin, Freud, Nietzsche, and much more) make the honors sequence the best choice for an undergraduate at UMaine.

Besides the Honors College, students and faculty speak most highly of engineering, chemistry, anthropology, political science, forestry, nursing, history, psychology, biology, marine sciences—as well as the Advanced Structures and Composites Center.

Other programs are weaker. A professor warns against the social sciences, "with the exception of psychology . . . which has a nationally respected doctoral program, especially in family counseling." Though one student calls UMaine's business school "pretty good for a public state university," a professor counters that it has "low standards." This professor also notes that the foreign languages department is "too small" with "too few courses in non-European languages." Another teacher says that UMaine's theater, public administration, and women's studies departments have all been "slated for being phased out due to low numbers of majors."

Though there are courses available on Shakespeare's plays, it is possible for English majors to graduate without ever having read him. Instead, they could take "Literature, Gender, and Gender Theory," "Studies in Gender and Literature," or "Topics and Film." However, the English department is for the most part rather traditional, with solid courses like "Chaucer and Medieval Literature," "The English Romantics" and "The Works of Shakespeare."

History majors must study U.S. history but not necessarily before 1945. Still, there are plenty of valuable courses offered, alongside a few politicized options.

In political science, the very first requirement listed for majors is "American Government." There are well over 50 other courses, most of them solid and worthwhile.

One student remarks that, though he suspects his professors are "largely a bunch of leftists," the school does have "many standout professors in economics and political science with libertarian and conservative leanings." Many of the students also "identify as conservative and independent." According to one professor, the students are largely "more conservative than the faculty, but faculty are generally open to free and vigorous debate." There are a number of "outright conservative faculty" in political science and history, another teacher tells us. "Most of the faculty in engineering, business, and agriculture are fairly conservative Republicans. Not surprisingly, most of those in liberal arts are liberal Dems." One political science professor warns that some departments can be a little unwelcoming to religious and conservative students, including philosophy and "to a lesser extent, history." Another professor says that political science "places a strong emphasis on nonpartisan / nonideological teaching." A student says that when politics come up in classrooms, professors "never stick to one mantra or one belief." Even in philosophy courses, "there's never any religion bashing."

CAMPUS POLITICS: GREEN LIGHT

Students and professors tell us that the political atmosphere on campus is pretty quiet on both the left and the right fronts. A student recalls the "big push for gay marriage to be passed" in Maine. "There was a lot of promotion of that on campus, and I was kind of irritated. . . . I would say that it's probably more of a liberal atmosphere than a conservative one, but it's not conservative bashing." One professor says that students feel "totally free" to express their views. Another professor simply believes that UMaine is "not a particularly politicized campus compared to many other places." In fact, "many students are apathetic about politics, but not our [political science] majors, of course." He also thinks that "students of most any political or religious background would be welcomed to present their views . . . there is almost never any major uproar of a political nature on campus. Activism is much lower than at other schools." Speaking to this point, another professor says that "if one is seeking a fairly quiet campus where one can espouse or practice one's political or religious or other beliefs that might get one into controversy in other schools, UMaine would be a most comfortable place to attend."

There is a vibrant little Young Americans for Liberty chapter at UMaine. There are only seven core members, but they host events regularly and show every sign of growing. Other than the YAL chapter, organized conservative activity is quite low at UMaine. The campus's College Republicans chapter seems to be defunct.

The professors most highly recommended by their colleagues and students are Kyriakos Markides ("a major expert on religion and culture with several bestselling books...and a practicing Orthodox Christian") in sociology; Michael Montgomery in economics; Richard Blanke in history; Mark Brewer (a "widely published [scholar] of American national politics") and Michael Palmer in political science; and Robert Glover, who teaches at the Honors College. Other recommended faculty include Timothy Cole, James Warhola, Howard Cody, Solomon Goldman, Mark Hibben, and Richard Powell in political science; Jessica Miller and Kirsten Jacobson in philosophy; Steven Cohn in sociology; Habib Dagher in advanced structures and composites; Henry Munson ("an expert in world religions") in anthropology; Jan Kristo in reading education; Paul Mayewski and Irv Kornfield in marine sciences; Geoffrey Thorpe, Jeff Hecker, Alexander Grab, and Howard Segal in history; Tina Passman in modern languages and Classics; Richard Brucher, Carla Billitteri, Robert "Tony" Brinkley, Jennifer Moxley, and Leonore Hildebrandt in English; Michael Grillo and James Linehan in art; Karel Lidral and Anatole Wieck in music; Neil Comins in astronomy; Francois Amar and Barbara Cole in chemistry; David Batuski in physics; Stephen Norton in geology; William Bray in mathematics; and Martin Stokes in animal and veterinary sciences.

> UMaine is less politicized and more traditional than most state universities.

A range of languages are taught at UMaine, but some of the language majors programs have recently been suspended for lack of funds. So a student can no longer declare a *major* in French, German, Latin, or Spanish, but he can still be *taught* those languages at beginner, intermediate, and advanced levels. Other languages taught at UMaine include Arabic, Chinese, Farsi, Gaelic Irish, Hindi, Italian, Japanese, Korean, Portuguese, Russian, and Turkish. Some of these languages are offered only at the beginner level.

UMaine offers study-abroad options in many countries, including Bulgaria, Chile, China, Egypt, Germany, New Zealand, and Spain. There are several types of programs, including exchange programs, internships abroad for credit, research programs abroad, and even full-time jobs teaching English around the world.

Student Life: Parties and rumors of parties

UMaine is "a hockey school. Maine has won two national championships and is a perennial hockey power," says a professor. "Many hockey players go on to professional careers. Home hockey games are major events on campus." The school's website boasts: "UMaine is the state's only Division I school . . . so athletics are kind of a big deal here . . . what we're really saying is it's perfectly normal to scream your face off while watching hockey with five thousand of your closest friends at Alfond Arena."

But the fun at UMaine seems tamer than some might think. Though UMaine recently made it into the Princeton Review's top 20 party schools, students disagree. "I don't get the vibe that it's a big party school," says one student. Professors call the school "fairly quiet" and "comfortable," with "a good quality of life." Students seem to spend their time pretty wholesomely. "Mainers are, in my experience, friendly, welcoming, and less pretentious than college students from other locations," says one student, and according to a professor, "Many out-of-state students" are more "attracted to the outdoorsy opportunities" of the university than to partying. "Acadia National Park is about one hour away. The school runs buses to major ski resorts on the weekends, so that is also a popular attraction." The school does not track membership of fraternities (there are 17 on campus) or sororities (of which there are seven), but they do not play a major role at the school, students say.

There are no single-sex dorms or floors at UMaine, but some dorms have single-sex wings, and there are also some single-sex apartments available. All freshmen are required to live on campus for their first year, during which time they can choose to live in a Living Learning Community of their choice. There are eight such communities, including a drug-, alcohol-, and tobacco-free community; an Outdoor Adventure community; a health and fitness community; and even a Great Books community. One resident says that "you feel like you're around the well educated, the people who are here for a reason."

"Dorm life is fantastic," says one student. "First-year residents are gender separated by wing, and bathrooms are not shared." Even in the wings where bathrooms are shared, says another student, "the RAs here are . . . more than willing to help you if you have any issues with other students." With regard to promiscuity, this student remarks that "obviously there are going to be some people who are promiscuous, but I don't see it as very prevalent. . . . I haven't seen anything that could possibly threaten my morality." Another student says that "the culture of promiscuity is . . . nothing outrageous, but it is permitted."

Students can find religious support from a few groups, including UMaine's Cru (Campus Crusade for Christ), which offers Bible studies and other, more social activities, while "[encouraging] participation in a local biblically based church." There is also the "Catholic Community" Newman Center, which holds Sunday Masses and hosts a youth group at a local parish.

Crime is no concern to most students at UMaine. In 2011 (the last year reported) there were nine instances of arson, one aggravated assault, five burglaries, three motor vehicle thefts and six sex offenses. There were also 386 liquor-law violations and 330 drug violations. For a student body of more than 10,000, these crime rates are not alarming. One student feels that "the off-campus police are very good. . . . They're able to crack down on public drinking and stuff like that." He recalls one incident of a female freshman "who got completely trashed . . . but they were able to deal with it quickly and efficiently, and you wouldn't even know about it if you weren't right there at the time." Another student says

SUGGESTED CORE

1. Classics 400, Hero, Myth, and Meaning
2. Philosophy 210, History of Ancient Philosophy
3. Philosophy 220, Introduction to the Jewish Bible (*closest match*)
4. Political Science 302, Medieval Political Thought
5. Political Science 303, Early Modern Political Thought
6. English 253, Shakespeare: Selected Plays
7. History 103, U.S. History I to 1877
8. Philosophy 212, Hegel and 19th-Century Philosophy

that "crime is not a concern at all. The university is located in a very rural area in the state, and the campus community is very safe. There have been no significant incidents lately."

U of Maine is a real bargain for Mainers, who paid only $8,370 in tuition in 2012–13 (compared to $25,230 for out-of-state students) and room and board of $8,848. Some 60 percent of students received need-based aid, but those who borrowed racked up a daunting $32,438 in average student-loan debt.

STRONG SUITS	WEAK POINTS
• Plenty of traditional, solid courses to meet both gen-ed and majors' requirements. • Strong emphasis on teaching, in addition to research. • Very solid programs in sciences, engineering, forestry, nursing, political science, history, psychology. • Humanities departments are less ideological than at most state schools. • Excellent honors program with many serious liberal arts courses. • A Great Books Living Learning Community. • Women's studies department may close for lack of student interest.	• Some departments are "unwelcoming" to religious or conservative students. • Foreign language majors have been cut due to lack of funding. • Several social science departments are subpar. • Few options in theater or the arts.

United States Naval Academy

Annapolis, Maryland • www.usna.edu

Naval Raising

Founded in 1845 in response to a naval mutiny, as the Naval School at Annapolis, what is now the U.S. Naval Academy has expanded from its original 10 acres and 50 midshipmen to 338 acres, and it educates more than 4,000 men and women each year. Since the Naval Academy educates its midshipmen to serve in the Navy and become naval officers, the liberal arts are not the primary focus. But this does not preclude providing midshipmen a good exposure to the liberal arts, not least because the academy puts a great emphasis on the moral and leadership education and formation of its future officers. (Two of the three most popular majors are political science and history.) But students at the academy will also face a solid core of science and engineering.

Academic Life: Seminars and seamen

Since 1933 the Naval Academy has awarded bachelor of science degrees to graduates, some of whom will operate nuclear submarines and guided missile systems. The academy has also become a major source of new officers for the Marine Corps. As at West Point, jealously guarded traditions continue to provide a sense of continuity, year after year.

VITAL STATISTICS

Religious affiliation: *none*
Total enrollment: *4,576*
Total undergraduates: *4,576*
SAT CR/Verbal midrange:
560–670
SAT Math midrange:
600–700
ACT midrange: *25–32*
Applicants: *20,601*
Applicants accepted: *7%*
Accepted applicants who
enrolled: *87%*
Tuition (general/out of
state): *free*
Tuition (in state): *N/A*
Room and board: *free*
Freshman retention rate:
97%
Graduation rate (4 yrs.): *89%*
Graduation rate (6 yrs.): *89%*
Courses with fewer than 20
students: *60%*
Student-faculty ratio: *8:1*
Courses taught by graduate
students: *not provided*
Students living on campus:
100%
Students in fraternities:
none
Students in sororities: *none*
Students receiving need-
based financial aid: *N/A*
Avg. student-loan debt of a
recent graduating class:
N/A
Most popular majors:
*economics, engineering,
political science*
Guaranteed housing for 4
years? *yes*

Admission is highly competitive. To even be eligible, a student must be a single U.S. citizen with no dependents, of good moral character, no younger than 17 and no older than 23, and not pregnant. In addition to scholastic, physical, and leadership requirements, applicants need a nomination from an official source, such as their congressman or senator. Male candidates should be able to run one and a half miles in 10:30, and complete 40 push-ups in two minutes. Female candidates must complete the run in 12:40 and do 18 push-ups.

Annapolis offers each of its midshipmen a core curriculum featuring engineering, science, mathematics, humanities, and social science courses in order to "provide a broad-based education that will qualify the midshipmen for practically any career field in the Navy or Marine Corps," according to the school. Quantitative courses include "Calculus" I and II and "Chemistry" I and II. Humanities classes include "U.S. Government and Constitutional Development," "Preparing to Lead," "Rhetoric and Introduction to Literature" I and II, "Fundamentals of Naval Science," "American Naval Heritage," and "Introduction to Navigation."

Cadets also complete one of 24 majors. Of these, three—English, history, and political science—might be considered liberal arts. (Postgraduate degrees may also be started at Annapolis.) But even liberal arts majors receive a bachelor of science degree, owing to the technical content of the core curriculum. "Middies" (midshipmen) pursue history, English, political science, economics, mathematics, and oceanography; systems engineering majors are eligible for the honors program. Chosen for their "excellent academic and leadership performance," honors students complete a thesis or research project, which they will defend orally in front of a panel of faculty members. If successful, they graduate with honors.

An even more exclusive option is the Trident Scholar Program, through which midshipmen in the top 10 percent of their class in their junior year are invited to submit proposed research projects and programs of study for evaluation. The number of scholars selected has ranged from a low of three to a high of 16, with 13 scholars in the class of 2013. Each scholar is given one or more faculty advisers who are well acquainted with his field of study and serve as research mentors. Trident scholars, according to the academy, "may travel to nearby facilities such as the Naval Research Laboratory or the National Institute of Standards and Technology to use equipment not available at the Naval Academy."

Each company of new midshipmen is assigned two faculty advisers upon admission. After the summer, advising is available on a need basis, and after the new "plebes" (freshmen) have selected majors, they get permanent advisers in those disciplines.

The student-faculty ratio at the Naval Academy is approximately 8 to 1. The faculty consists of officers and civilians in nearly equal numbers. Civilian faculty—nearly all of whom have doctoral degrees—give "continuity to the educational program," the school reports. At the academy, the faculty's first priority is always teaching rather than research. Students especially recommend two professors from the history department: Frederick Harrod and Marcus Jones. "They are just the best of the best," one senior reports. However, most faculty are said to be excellent.

English majors are required to take 10 courses, including "Early Western Literature"; "Anglo-American Literature"; "Shakespeare"; two 300-level literary period courses, for example "Chaucer and His Age" and "The Renaissance Mind"; one 400-level seminar, for example "Literary Theory and Criticism" or "Studies in Literary Figures"; and four additional courses from department offerings. These requirements are better than those at most Ivy League colleges.

CAMPUS POLITICS: GREEN LIGHT

Even though it is primarily (like West Point) an engineering school, Annapolis offers a better grounding in the core subjects of the Western tradition and the American republic than do most civilian colleges, with no incidents reported to us of undue political content in the classroom. In keeping with the American military's nonpolitical tradition, there are no partisan or activist clubs at the academy.

As attractive as the Annapolis experience sounds, it is important to remember that it is first and foremost a naval academy. Its purpose is to train men and women to lead others in combat, whether on sea, on land, or in the air. Anyone with an ethical objection to combat—or moral scruples about which wars of choice the civilians leading the U.S. government might choose someday to launch—should not take the oath "to defend the Constitution of the United States against all enemies, foreign and domestic." Once taken, this oath becomes the cornerstone of the midshipman's, and later the officer's, personal code of honor.

In 2011 Annapolis English professor Bruce Fleming settled a lawsuit he had filed against the academy for disciplining him after he published an article suggesting that affirmative action was lowering standards at the academy.

In addition to the three history courses in the core curriculum, each history major also takes "Perspectives on History" and a "Seminar in Advanced Historical Studies," plus eight electives from four of five distribution areas: American history, European history, regional history, naval and military history, and thematic history. Recent course offerings included "Imperial Rome," "The Age of Chivalry and Faith," "Germany and the Nazi Experience," "Art and Ideas in Modern Europe," "Civil War and Reconstruction," and "America in World Affairs." Again, this is an excellent academic program.

Political science majors must complete 10 courses plus one capstone, with a final thesis supervised by a faculty member. Three courses are required: "American Government," "International Relations/Comparative Politics," and "Political Science Methods." Any graduate would emerge with an understanding of the political system he has volunteered to defend.

The average class size is 18, allowing professors to offer plenty of personal attention. The academy proudly points out that "all courses at the Naval Academy are taught and graded by faculty members, not by graduate assistants."

Given its mission to train officers, the academy also provides professional and leadership training. As plebes, students are introduced to the life and customs of the naval service, where they learn to follow orders and obey commands. As midshipmen (sophomores, juniors, and seniors), they gradually take on positions of responsibility themselves. Students also acquire practical experience from assignments with Navy and Marine Corps units. In the classroom, such courses as "Leadership: Theory and Application," "Ethics and Moral Reasoning for the Naval Leader," and "Fundamentals of Seamanship" round out their education in this sphere.

The strongest memory that graduates of the Naval Academy take with them from Annapolis is Plebe Summer. This is the rigorous, sometimes traumatic, seven-week period in which civilians are molded into plebes. "It's brutal, but it's also a bonding experience. Everyone goes through it, and it just builds an understanding between your fellow plebes. It was the best summer of my life, but I'm glad I only had to do it once," reports a sophomore. On Induction Day, shortly after arrival, the new plebes are put into uniform and taught to salute; indeed, they will salute virtually everyone they encounter—officers and upperclassmen alike. The days start at dawn with an hour of exercise and finish long after sunset. "Plebing" builds a sense of identity with the academy and is the start of the sort of lifelong friendships that only hardship can bring. At Annapolis, Plebe Summer also means an introduction to seamanship, navigation, and combat arms. By the time the school year starts, the plebe is completely familiar with the academy's and the Navy's standards—particularly regarding such intangibles as honor.

As at West Point, the school maintains a strict honor system (here called the "Honor Concept"). Annapolis's Concept states, in part:

Midshipmen are persons of integrity: They stand for that which is right. They tell the truth and ensure that the full truth is known. They do not lie. They embrace fairness in all actions. They ensure that work submitted as their own is their own, and that assistance received from any source is authorized and properly documented. They do not cheat. They respect the property of others and ensure that others are able to benefit from the use of their own property. They do not steal.

Offenses are dealt with by brigade honor committees made up of elected upper-class midshipmen.

All midshipmen majoring in English, history, and political science (as well as economics) are required to take four semesters of a foreign language. A major in Arabic and

Chinese is offered as well as minors in Arabic, Chinese, French, German, Japanese, Russian, Spanish.

Student Life: Such intangibles as honor

The city of Annapolis, the capital of the state of Maryland, is home to the Navy Academy. The academy permits plebes "town liberty" on Saturday afternoons and evenings and liberty within the Naval Academy complex on Saturday mornings and Sunday afternoons. Free time increases as students advance. The academy is home to a number of student organizations, including several national scholastic honor societies. Community service societies include the Campus Girl Scouts, Joy Bright Hancock Group, National Eagle Scout Association, and the Midshipmen Action Group. Musical and theatrical groups include a Gospel Choir club, a Pipes and Drums club, a Trident Brass group, and the famous Masqueraders, who put on one production annually in the academy's Mahan Hall. The academy's radio station and four publications, *The Labyrinth*, *Lucky Bag*, *The Log*, and *The Trident*, offer opportunities for expression.

The old state military colleges, VMI and The Citadel, have already been forced through court action to stop the saying of grace before meals—a subversive practice that suggests allegiance to a power higher than the State. Yet at Annapolis, alone of all three academies, grace is still said before lunch. Thoughtfully, the ACLU has offered to assist any midshipman who might want to sue the academy to stop this. So far, no one has availed himself of this offer, and there's a good reason for that: ultimately, military folk must be willing to die for their country, and without a connection to an even higher duty, this is simply too much to ask.

> The highly qualified faculty holds as its first priority teaching, rather than research. Moral development is encouraged, in part through a strict honor code.

At Annapolis the copper-green dome of the chapel symbolizes this awareness. It serves as the focal point of the Command Religious Program, which tries to "foster spiritual growth and promote the moral development of the midshipmen within the tenets of their particular faith or beliefs." The Chaplains Office conducts worship services and offers counseling. Services are held for members of the Catholic, Christian Science, Jewish, Mormon, Muslim, and Protestant faiths. Eleven religious student organizations contribute to the religious element of a cadet's life. Among them are the Baptist Student Union; Cru (formerly Campus Crusade for Christ); Protestant, Catholic, Jewish, and Muslim Midshipman clubs; and the Officer Christian Fellowship.

The academy's athletic program is intensive, to say the least. Annapolis regards the midshipman's physical growth of comparable importance to his mental and moral development. A physical education curriculum and athletic participation are required of all students, either at the varsity, intramural, or club level. The academy's teams are well supported, both by their mascot Bill the Goat and by the loud crowd, as attested by anyone

Blue Collar Ivy

SUGGESTED CORE

1. English 217, Early Western Literature
2. Philosophy 430, Political Philosophy (*closest match*)
3. English 222, The Bible and Literature
4. History 373, History of Christianity
5. Political Science 340, Modern Political Thought and Ideology
6. English 333, Shakespeare
7. History 346, Revolutionary America and the Early Republic
8. History 216, The West in the Modern World

who has experienced an Army-Navy game. The 18 men's, 10 women's, and four varsity teams play in the NCAA Division I. The academy offers 12 club and 15 intramural sports. Club sports include cycling, triathlon, boxing, and softball. Intramural offerings recently included soccer, wrestling, volleyball, and basketball.

A typical day at USNA is quite regimented, with reveille and watches. All students march to meals and do everything in uniform. Midshipmen live in Bancroft Hall, a massive dorm. The Brigade of Midshipmen is divided into companies. Each company has its own living area at Bancroft, called a "wardroom." Men and women are assigned to same-sex rooms but live on the same floor as the rest of their assigned company. Every bedroom (shared by two or more midshipmen) is wired for computers, Internet access, and phones. The companies are the focus of life at Annapolis, as each midshipman eats, sleeps, drills, and plays with the members of his own company and competes against the other companies. This teaches the small-unit cohesion so integral to warfare and is the source of lifelong friendships. This is also where practical leadership begins—since, as he advances year by year, the midshipman will be expected to assume leadership positions at the company, battalion, and brigade level.

Almost everything a midshipman needs is available on the academy grounds: bookstore, uniform and tailor shop, cobbler shop, snack bar, barber/beauty shop, post office, and recreation rooms. There are also restaurants and an ice skating rink. Members of the brigade eat together at King Hall, where they enjoy such delectables as steak, spiced shrimp, Mexican food, and home-baked pastries. Medical, psychological, and dental care is provided onsite, as well as legal and financial advice. In a word, other than applying himself to his studies and other obligations, the midshipman has little to worry about.

The academy does not report its crime statistics to the government, as is required of civilian schools. However, it seems that the most common offenses have to do with sexual fraternization. For instance, there is a rule forbidding dating between plebes and midshipmen. In 2011 a female student was discharged from the academy, officially for mental unfitness. She charged, according to the *Huffington Post*, that she was being punished for reporting her rape at the hands of another midshipman. In 2011 more than a dozen midshipmen were expelled for using the synthetic drug Spice.

Although the various programs offered by the academy consume more time than the average college student is required to give, midshipmen do get Christmas and summer vacations (leave) plus shorter periods of time off (liberty).

Use of cars is restricted according to class seniority, although no midshipman may have a motorcycle in town. Drinking is forbidden to plebes at the academy. Needless to say, drug use is forbidden for everyone and results in expulsion from the academy. Random urinalysis is conducted.

Women now account for 20 to 25 percent of entering plebes and receive the same academic and professional training as the males. Thankfully, the academy has not tried to butcher the English language with "midshippersons." While the academy has been coeducational since 1976, many still question whether it is a good place for women to study, partly because of the sex scandals that have arisen in recent years. Others ask if a society that sends its young women out to fight its battles is really worth defending.

When accepted to the Naval Academy, the student joins the U.S. Navy. Not only is the education free of charge, but the midshipman earns a salary. Merit, not money, is required of entrants to the service academies.

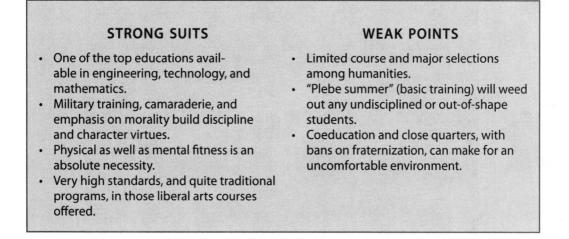

STRONG SUITS	WEAK POINTS
• One of the top educations available in engineering, technology, and mathematics. • Military training, camaraderie, and emphasis on morality build discipline and character virtues. • Physical as well as mental fitness is an absolute necessity. • Very high standards, and quite traditional programs, in those liberal arts courses offered.	• Limited course and major selections among humanities. • "Plebe summer" (basic training) will weed out any undisciplined or out-of-shape students. • Coeducation and close quarters, with bans on fraternization, can make for an uncomfortable environment.

University of Maryland

College Park, Maryland • www.umd.edu

One End of the Table

The University of Maryland offers a number of worthy things: incomparable research and music and arts facilities, school spirit, a lively social scene, and several stellar honors programs. For the bright student who is self-motivated and focused, Maryland presents an option worth considering. Too bad the school does not have a core curriculum or even a decent set of distribution requirements. In 2012 UM unoriginally named its newly revamped general-education requirements "General Education @ UMD," which consists of 40 credit hours divided into three areas: Fundamental Studies, Distributive Studies (with a new sub-catagory called I-Series), and Diversity. We hope the school didn't spend much taxpayer money creating it, because Gen Ed @ UMD is nearly identical to the old CORE program it replaced—which is not saying much. When asked how strong a grounding students get in the basics of a traditional liberal education, one professor responded, "In a word, none."

Academic Life: Salad days

For the fundamental studies requirement, each student must take a basic English composition course in his freshman year and a professional writing course—usually dealing with technical or business writing—in his junior or senior year. A basic mathematics course requirement can be satisfied by taking "Mathematical Models," "College Algebra," or "Precalculus." These are all high-school-level courses. Two new components of this requirement are oral communication and analytical reasoning. A student tells us that "the 'fundamental' classes are ridiculously easy, and frankly a waste of time, but the school no longer allows students to place out of them."

The distributive studies area requires students to take eight courses: two in the humanities; two in the natural sciences (including at least one laboratory course); two in social sciences and history; and two in "scholarship in practice." But a student could take four of the eight required courses from the women's studies department. A new distributive subset called I-Series can be fulfilled with two classes as disparate as "How Safe Is Your Salad?" and "Psychology of Evil." Literally hundreds of courses fulfill the requirements. As one professor says, the Maryland curriculum is "very flexible. Probably too flexible." Another admits that "the University of Maryland is a large university. It makes little to no effort to offer a liberal arts kind of education that one would find in a small college. Rather, it strives to offer students a wide variety of courses that will help them focus on a particular area of specialization, that is, a major field, and then become knowledgeable about that field."

On the subject of diversity, however, the school is taking no chances. Its "understanding plural societies" and "cultural competence" course requirements are intended to "heighten your appreciation of difference itself, and increase your ability to learn from people, cultures, ideas, and art forms different from those you know best." This assumes that you, the student, actually know the literature and history of the West—but since there are no requirements in American history, American or British literature, Western philosophy or civilization, there's no guarantee of that. The "cultural competency" diversity requirement can be satisfied through courses with titles like "Lesbian, Gay, Bisexual, and Transgender People and Communication" and "Fundamentals of Sign Language"—while the "understanding plural societies" component includes such classes as "Race, Crime, and Criminal Justice," "Violence in Families," "International Political

VITAL STATISTICS

Religious affiliation: *none*
Total enrollment: *37,580*
Total undergraduates: *26,775*
SAT CR/Verbal midrange: *580–680*
SAT Math midrange: *610–720*
ACT midrange: *not provided*
Applicants: *26,310*
Applicants accepted: *45%*
Accepted applicants who enrolled: *34%*
Tuition (general/out of state): *$27,287*
Tuition (in state): *$8,908*
Room and board: *$9,893*
Freshman retention rate: *94%*
Graduation rate (4 yrs.): *66%*
Graduation rate (6 yrs.): *82%*
Courses with fewer than 20 students: *35%*
Student-faculty ratio: *18:1*
Courses taught by graduate students: *13%*
Students living on campus: *44%*
Students in fraternities: *10%*
Students in sororities: *15%*
Students receiving need-based financial aid: *41%*
Avg. student-loan debt of a recent graduating class: *$24,180*
Most popular majors: *criminal justice, accounting/economics, psychology*
Guaranteed housing for 4 years? *no*

CAMPUS POLITICS: GREEN LIGHT

The UM administration has a definite leftist bias. According to a report by the *Washington Post*, out of 30 officially recognized political groups on the UM campus, only five were conservative. But overall, politics does not seem to intrude in the classroom, and students aren't "made to feel uncomfortable because of their personal opinions," according to one professor. This is not because there is "free and vigorous debate," however, but "because there is no debate, not because of political correctness or orthodox opinions prevailing." Rather, the answer lies in apathy.

"UM is a liberal campus, but I think the College Republicans and Students for Liberty do a pretty good job holding their own," says a student. The College Republicans sponsor regular well-attended events on campus, such as speaker-writer Christina Hoff Sommers in April 2013 discussing the feminist movement's ongoing "War against Boys."

Relations," and "Does Democracy Have a Future?" "There are really no good options in this arena," a student says. "Even the classes that sound harmless are politically charged."

In the College Park Scholars program, bright students live together in the Cambridge Community and focus on a common theme for two years. About 75 freshmen are invited to enroll in one of 11 interdisciplinary programs each year—which, according to the university, provide "the interpersonal benefits of a small college paired with the intellectual advantages of a major research university." For example, the interdisciplinary program "Global Public Health" is sponsored by UM's School of Public Health, wherein students interact with public and community-based health organizations, including the National Institutes of Health (NIH), and study abroad in disease-infested corners of the world with the United States Agency for International Development (USAID).

The University Honors Program allows the most academically focused undergraduates to interact with other smart students and faculty members. Honors students choose five courses from a list of designated choices, including three honors seminars and a research colloquium. Honors students are housed together, for four years if they prefer. The Honors Humanities program helps give structure to top students in the humanities. The Gemstone program is yet another living-learning community that gives students the opportunity and the direction to integrate science and technology course work with their research projects. Each team in the Gemstone program works for four years on various projects, culminating with a team thesis.

Engineering and science students maintain that their departments are far more demanding than those in the liberal arts. "I will not jump to the conclusion that liberal arts majors at Maryland are cakewalks, but liberal arts friends of mine seemed to have much more free time," says one aerospace engineering alumnus. "My course work took up so much of my efforts that I didn't have lots of time to acquaint myself with much of the school outside of the engineering world." There are certainly bright spots among the humanities and social sciences departments, but the quality of courses can vary dramatically. One professor says, "The smart 'consumer' will take the first year or two to sample different courses in different corners of the campus, find out from other students which departments seem to care about undergraduate instruction, and go for the best teachers." The history and

English departments are "large and well funded," according to one professor; however, they are not well rounded.

History majors are not required to take Western civilization or American history courses, although such classes are offered. The department simply "encourages," but does not require, their majors to take at least two courses in sequence, and "encourages" at least one course both before and after 1500. The only required course is "Historical Research and Methods Seminar," and "at least one course (three credits) must be taken from an approved list of courses on regions outside both Europe and the U.S." In other words, a history major can avoid America and Western Europe but must study non-Western history.

> Core requirements can be met with courses like "How Safe Is Your Salad?" Half could be met with women's studies courses. "There are really no good options," a student says.

English majors can safely avoid Shakespeare but must submit to at least one of the department's more politically correct selections. Required courses include a class in critical methods; literary and cultural history; one course in literary, linguistic, or rhetorical analysis; and a course "in the literature of African Americans, peoples of color, women, and / or lesbians, gays, and bisexuals." In addition, English majors must take two courses focused on writing before 1800, where choices include such classes as "English Literature: Beginnings to 1800" and "Introduction to Literature by Women." Also required is a course in modern British, Anglophone, and / or postcolonial writing (after 1800); a course in American, African American, and / or U.S. ethnic writing; and four electives.

Government and politics majors are only required to take three specified classes: political philosophy; principles of government and politics; and American government. Of the remaining nine courses, at least six must be upper division.

Economics, art history, and the foreign languages are strong at Maryland. The criminology, government and politics, economics, and psychology departments are also said to be relatively solid.

Teachers praised by students include Karol Soltan, Piotr Swistak, and Margaret Pearson in government and politics; Madeline Zilfi, Whitman Ridgway, Peter Wien, and Antoine Borrut in history; Charles Manekin and Christopher Morris in philosophy; and Denny Gulick in mathematics.

Research outweighs teaching at UM. Particularly in the sciences, students say they have problems getting in touch with professors whose research responsibilities are their highest priority. One engineering student says, "In my major, every professor was also deeply involved with research work of his own, so at certain times responses to inquiries were delayed." However, another student says, "When I've taken the initiative to stop in, I've only been met with an open door and willingness to talk and listen on the part of the professor. I've never felt as though I was unwelcome because they were too busy with research."

SUGGESTED CORE

1. Classics 372, Classical Epic
2. Philosophy 310, Ancient Philosophy
3. English 334, The Bible as Literature
4. Religious Studies 341, Europe in the High Middle Ages: 1000–1500 (*closest match*)
5. Government and Politics 742, Modern Political Theory
6. English 304, The Major Works of Shakespeare
7. History 200, Interpreting American History: Beginnings to 1877
8. Philosophy 320, Modern Philosophy (*closest match*)

Academic advising varies based on the school and department but is typically a combination of professional advisers in the Office of Undergraduate Studies and faculty advisers in the department of one's major. The experience seems typical for a state university. "I attended the mandatory orientation advising session to get approval for my four-year plan, but I didn't go back until second semester my junior year just to make sure everything was still in order," says a student. Some departments, however, require meetings with a faculty adviser at regular intervals once a major is declared.

UM is a good place for a self-motivated, focused student—and not for those seeking guidance and interaction with faculty and staff. "In my experience, most professors here are really not that interested in mentoring," a student says. "They will answer specific questions, but only if you're quick and to the point and only during specified office hours." On the other hand, one professor said he was "appalled by the lack of intellectual curiosity of many students and delighted by the depth that others seem to have. This is sort of like the world at large, no?"

On a positive note, Maryland offers the Collegium Musicum for students with a serious interest in early music.

UM's Office of International Affairs sponsors yearlong, semester, and spring- and summer-break study-abroad programs in more than a hundred countries, such as Austria, Bulgaria, China, Cuba, Ethiopia, France, Germany, Hong Kong, India, Israel, Japan, Jordan, Korea, South Africa, Switzerland, Spain, Taiwan, and the United Arab Emirates. Internship, volunteer, and work-abroad opportunities are also available.

At home, students can take Arabic, Chinese, French, German, Greek, Hebrew, Italian, Japanese, Korean, Latin, Portuguese, Russian, and Spanish. Most foreign language courses at UM are offered through the School of Languages, Literatures, and Cultures.

Student Life: Just outside the Beltway

College Park is a pleasant college town with plenty of restaurants, bars, and movie theaters easily accessible by foot from campus. Washington, D.C., is just a few miles away. College Park has its own Metro stop, and a free shuttle takes students there from the center of campus. Many Maryland students intern at government and political organizations and volunteer in service projects in D.C. Still more enjoy the city's nightlife. "There is plenty to do here, on campus and off," a student says, "especially with all the other colleges and universities in the area, there's always something going on."

Students have plenty of options for on-campus housing, from suite-style facilities that house only a few dozen residents to dormitories where 500 of your closest friends live right down the hall. All residence halls are coed except one for women (Cecil Hall), but men and women are always separated by floor or by wing. There are no coed bathrooms or dorm rooms.

Only about 12 percent of students are members of fraternities or sororities, which, as one student says, is "a healthy percentage. Greek life doesn't overpower students' social lives, but it's there if you want to party." A student whose family lives only a few minutes from College Park says that during her freshman year, she rarely went home.

The college currently sponsors 20 varsity sports competing in the NCAA Division I Atlantic Coast Conference, though it is most noted for men's baseball, basketball, and football. (The school's mascot is the terrapin, and students call themselves "Terps.") UM will leave the Atlantic Conference to compete in the Big Ten Conference in 2014. The school eliminated seven varsity teams (men's cross-country, indoor track, swimming/diving, and tennis; and women's gymnastics, water polo, and swimming/diving) in July 2012 due to budget cuts.

There are more than 350 clubs at the University of Maryland, of which more than 30 are religious. These range from the Episcopal Anglican Terps to the Pagan Student Union, and include a number of Christian clubs, such as the Adventist Student Fellowship, Baptist Collegiate Ministry, Cru (Campus Crusade for Christ), Catholic Student Association, Coptic Terps, Jonah Liturgical Dance Ministry, Korean Bible Study, and Lutheran Student Association. Kedma serves Orthodox Jewish students, while the Kesher club caters to the Reformed. Other clubs include the Muslim Students' Association, the Bhagavad-Gita Club, the Sikh Students Association, the Baha'i Club, and the Interfaith Council.

There are plenty of political clubs at the University of Maryland, although most of these range from left-of-center to hard-core Marxist. Political groups include the International Socialist Organization, Model United Nations, and J Street U, the last of which exists to "advocate a just two-state solution to the Palestinian-Israeli Conflict." There are both College Democrats and College Republicans clubs, as well as College Park Students for Liberty, and Republican Women of Maryland, which aims "to increase the effectiveness of women in the cause of good government." There is also a Terrapin Students for Israel and a UMD chapter of the Zionist Organization of America.

In 2011 the college reported the following crimes on campus: four forcible sex offenses, three robberies, four aggravated assaults, 64 burglaries, 37 stolen cars, and a single arson. The school's security service provides a 24-hour escort service for anyone who feels unsafe when walking across campus, maintains "blue light" emergency phones situated throughout the grounds, and provides a heavily lit "preferred path of travel" around campus, which is mapped out on the school's website.

Tuition for 2012–13 was $8,908 for Maryland residents, and $27,287 for nonresidents, with room and board at $9,839. Some 41 percent of students received need-based financial aid. The average student-loan debt of a 2011 graduate was $24,180.

Blue Collar Ivy

STRONG SUITS

- Some worthy honors options that offer living/learning communities.
- Good departments in economics, art history, foreign languages, criminology, government and politics, economics, and psychology.
- Helpful, welcoming faculty in sciences will involve students in research.

WEAK POINTS

- Anemic general-ed requirements leave students to find an education if they can.
- Some time-wasting, cakewalk classes cannot be tested out of.
- Many, many politicized classes and requirements.
- Lax requirements for important majors such as history and English.
- Literally hundreds of courses fulfill the distributive studies requirements.

So You're Looking For

A Good College for Homeschooled Students

1. Princeton University *(p. 721)*

2. College of the Ozarks *(p. 458)*

3. Patrick Henry College *(p. 708)*

4. Grove City College *(p. 190)*

5. Christendom College *(p. 109)*

University of Massachusetts Amherst

Amherst, Massachusetts • www.umass.edu

The Art of Business

The University of Massachusetts at Amherst is the flagship school of the state's five-campus university system. The campus sits on nearly 1,450 acres in the Pioneer Valley of Western Massachusetts—a scenic, rural setting 90 miles from Boston. The university is home to a very strong business program, which provides many internships and vocational opportunities to ambitious students. It is not an ideal place to study the liberal arts.

Academic Life: Sink or swim

The course work at UMass is more oriented toward specialized fields of study and employment than the pursuit of intellectual truth. There are more general-education requirements in the hard sciences than in the humanities. Though the university has an extraordinary number of majors and courses, there seems to be very little overarching structure to the education students receive. Nearly half of the classes have fewer than 20 students, but one professor says he teaches "courses of 250 to 300 students" and doesn't "get to know them very well." He calls the university "a compartmentalized, large bureaucracy. You've got to find your own atmosphere, your own support system." Another professor assures

VITAL STATISTICS

Religious affiliation: *none*
Total enrollment: *28,236*
Total undergraduates: *21,928*
SAT CR/Verbal midrange:
    530–630
SAT Math midrange:
    560–660
ACT midrange: *24–28*
Applicants: *34,326*
Applicants accepted: *63%*
Accepted applicants who
    enrolled: *21%*
Tuition (general/out of
    state): *$26,645*
Tuition (in state): *$13,230*
Room and board: *$9,937*
Freshman retention rate:
    89%
Graduation rate (4 yrs.): *54%*
Graduation rate (6 yrs.): *70%*
Courses with fewer than 20
    students: *44%*
Student-faculty ratio: *18:1*
Courses taught by graduate
    students: *not provided*
Students living on campus:
    61%
Students in fraternities: *6%*
Students in sororities: *6%*
Students receiving need-
    based financial aid: *50%*
Avg. student-loan debt of a
    recent graduating class:
    $27,945
Most popular majors:
    *business/marketing, social
    sciences, psychology*
Guaranteed housing for 4
    years? *no*

us that "students are catered to, and are of the utmost concern."

With more than 28,000 students in all, and a student-faculty ratio of 18 to 1, students may not know where to turn. "Some students may be coming from a small school," the professor observes, "where they used to have everything kind of arranged for them and where they were told what to do." But be warned: "Here you may have to go to five offices to do something; it's such a large place." Only the "self-directed" will thrive, "because it can be challenging to navigate such a large institution." True, the school "has put enormous resources into advising and all kinds of facilities." Students can find some guidance from faculty, according to one undergraduate. "Teachers are all very accessible for the most part. Their office hours are useful when I attend." Another student tells us that "every program that I have expressed interest in I have been able to find on this campus."

Honors courses at UMass are capped at 25 students and offer real-world research experience built into the course work—some of which will bring students overseas for fieldwork and internship opportunities in countries like Brazil, Israel, and Taiwan. The honors program offers an exceptional thesis project in the "Multidisciplinary Honors (MH)" sequence. One professor who directs the MH thesis describes it as "a capstone honors course, a yearlong eight-credit honors thesis where everybody has to do really the equivalent of a *master's* thesis project." During such courses, the professor oversees the students' "collecting original data, analyzing it, and turning it into a full-year thesis project. I have usually eight to 10 students in a class, and those students just blow me away. They do literally grad-program-quality work. Exceptional students."

Students and faculty praise the Isenberg Business School above all other programs, with social science coming in second. Even professors who give lectures to more than 400 students at a time "care about each and every one of [them]," a student says, and "most of the Isenberg staff . . . want nothing more than for their students to do well while also learning as much as possible." Another student agrees, pointing out that "there are lots of different courses, internships, co-ops, and job opportunities." There is variety in the Isenberg Business School. Says one student: "It is world renowned for its sports management department but every program (accounting, finance, hospitality and management, resource economics, etcetera) is very well respected."

Other recommended programs include communications, which one professor tells us is "internationally renowned" and has "a world-class faculty"; political science, which another professor tells us "in particular [strives] for and [has] achieved excellence in teaching, research, and outreach"; and the natural sciences.

English majors are required to take at least one course in Shakespeare on their way to graduation. Some other courses in English seem sound, even traditional, including a course on Beowulf in the original Old English. Another choice is "American Identities," where students learn about "an undemocratic white supremacy inscribed at every level of government."

A history major would find it very easy to avoid a course in U.S. history before 1945. The university offers few such courses, and most view the U.S. through a leftist lens, such as "U.S. History to 1876," which "covers the period from 1450 to 1877" with an emphasis on "the shortage of labor and the abundance of land, slavery, racism, capitalism and 'democracy.'" (Note the irony quotes.) There seem to be no higher-level options covering American history before the mid-20th century.

Political science majors are "required to take one course at the 200 level or above in each of the general fields of American Politics, International Relations, Comparative Politics, and Political Theory." However, one of those courses could be "American Politics through Film." The department offers well over 70 classes, plus several "Experimental Courses" and additional credited opportunities.

CAMPUS POLITICS: RED LIGHT

A professor tells us that "the university as a whole, compared with a lot of other places, tends to be pretty progressive, but not a hundred percent." That's one way of putting it. Some students are less subtle about the political atmosphere on campus. A student says that the school's "weakness" is the "anti-Israel, anti-American bigots who intentionally indoctrinate us to lean toward the left." Another student says that he is often the only conservative in the room. "There has definitely been some hostility from other students in discussion sections." For example, he tells us that when he responded to a liberal TA in class, "playing devil's advocate" for a conservative position, "another student said in reply, 'Who is this a**hole?'" This student says that he is very disappointed in "just how liberal the campus is." The Foundation for Individual Rights in Education gives UMass a "red light" for the restrictions on free speech imposed by its Harassment and Internet Usage.

The Newman Center at UMass is actively pro-life and participates yearly in the March for Life. In addition to some of the more conservative chaplaincies, students will find a few conservative student groups on campus, including a College Republicans chapter and a Student Alliance for Israel. There used to be a conservative newspaper on campus called the *Minute Man*, but it died out with the help of some left-leaning activism by members of the student government.

UMass's strong suit really is the sheer number of opportunities it offers for students to travel and take on internships, fieldwork, and other activities to plump up their résumés and gain valuable experience. A student tells us of "the large availability of internships and jobs," the "[many] study-abroad opportunities available, and opportunities to spend a semester at different schools within the U.S. Everyone I know from UMass that has chosen to study abroad," he adds, "has loved the experience." Though a university with so many specialties can seem impersonal, one student reports that "anyone and everyone can find a home here."

A student warns that "there are certain departments where conservative or religious students would feel unwelcome." In a linguistics lecture, his professor once compared the "propaganda" of President George W. Bush to Nazi rhetoric. There are faculty and TAs in economics who "openly criticize capitalism and lecture as to why socialism is the better option," the student continues, also complaining of a biology professor who taught "that it was foolish not to support stem cell research, but would fail to mention that doing so could kill fetuses." One student says the political science department is "extremely liberal" and reckons that "almost every teacher I've had [at UMass] is clearly liberal, though most welcome arguments and attempt to stay moderate." Another student reports that her "unforgivably liberal" business professor was "encouraging and welcoming of other views [and] never once stopped me from stating my conservative opinions."

> One professor says he teaches "courses of 250 to 300 students" and doesn't "get to know them very well." He calls the university "a compartmentalized, large bureaucracy."

A student recommends political science professor Tatishe Nteta as "by far the best professor I have had at UMass. I had him for 'American Politics,' and he was very passionate and worked extremely hard at presenting both sides of an argument fairly." Other recommended faculty include Edward Voigtman in chemistry; Pamela Trafford in accounting and Donna Spraggon in resource economics (whom one student praises as "definitely two of the best teachers at UMass today"); Kathleen Brown-Perez in the Honors College; and Vinnie Ferraro, Jon Western, and Michael Hanrahan in political science, three teachers whom a student calls "good and fairly moderate."

The UMass atmosphere is not exactly familial, and student involvement can become somewhat perfunctory. "Because of the size of the school," says a student, "a lot of people are very wrapped up in either their own club or organization's mission, or wrapped up in getting homework done and going out to party." There's not much free time, and it's usually not spent in contemplation. Another student complains of the amount of busywork she has to do to keep her head above water. She had entered "hoping to find out a few things about myself through exploratory courses." Once she started her major course work, she realized that "there is no time for that." According to another student, "People tend to be apathetic unless they are pushed (such as [by] a résumé booster or good networking opportunity)."

UMass offers courses in an array of languages, ranging widely from Catalan and Chinese to Swedish and Yiddish.

The university's study-abroad options are truly extraordinary, with more than 400 UMass Amherst-sponsored programs in over 50 countries around the world and 1,000-plus undergraduates going abroad each year. Destinations include Australia, Brazil, China, Denmark, Ireland, Korea, Madagascar, and South Africa.

Student Life: Zoo-Mass Slamherst

One thing that brings students together at UMass is sports. Says a student: "People are very passionate about the hockey team. The basketball team has gained a lot of popularity over the last few years because of their recent exceptional play against top division I teams in the NCAA."

UMass has been ranked one of the top 10 party schools by the Princeton Review, and according to the University's Annual Security Report, there were a total of 1,316 liquor-law violations on campus in 2011. A student says that whatever reputation UMass has as a party school "is honestly a bit overhyped. Though we all have a good time on the weekends and definitely drink and socialize like any typical school, the party scene is mostly house parties." He tells us that students in "the Greek life system . . . are always having house parties of some sort. It costs $5 to get in, and they are typically fun." However, "Greek life is very small here, and being in a fraternity is the exception, not the norm. It doesn't affect the atmosphere of the dorms . . . and you could virtually stay out of Greek life and never know it existed if you truly wanted to."

Greek or not, UMass parties make the news. According to a 2012 article in *BostInno* magazine: "Earlier this year, 13 students from the university were arrested after thousands poured out of their dorms and into the center of campus to riot following the New England Patriots' devastating Super Bowl loss. Students were seen smashing beer bottles, setting off fireworks and chanting 'F*ck the police.' February's riot wasn't the first of its kind, however. Following the Patriots' 2008 loss to the Giants, police made eight arrests after about 500 students formed a mob."

Housing options range from 24-Hour Quiet Floors and Alcohol-Free Halls to Coed Suites and Gender-Free Housing (for students whose gender is "in transition" or who do not wish to "identify" their sex). A student who lives in the South West Residential Area tells us that, in his 22-floor dorm tower, "the floors are single sex and alternate boy-girl every other floor. The RAs in South West are very laid back," he continues, "and will only write someone up if they are blatantly violating a rule, such as playing music so loudly it can be heard from a different floor." This student also tells us that there are "single-sex dorms available in the different residential areas on campus" and that, to his knowledge, "all the bathrooms on campus are single sex." A female student says, "Dorm life is everything one could expect. At times it was loud and crowded, other times it was nice and quiet. Some buildings have coed floors," she warns, and her RAs "didn't really get anything done. . . . Sexual promiscuity is extremely prevalent." Another student is happy with his residence life

---

SUGGESTED CORE

1. English 201/202, Epic
2. Philosophy 320, History of Ancient Philosophy
3. English 203, Bible/Myth/Literature/Society
4. History 100, Western Thought to 1600 (*closest match*)
5. Political Science 271, Modern Political Thought
6. English 221, Shakespeare
7. History 150, U.S. History to 1876
8. History 101, Western Thought since 1600 (*closest match*)

and says the dorms "are awesome. People really do make an effort to make friends freshman year. Most dorms are mixed [sex], however, [and] sex is very prevalent at this school, as with most, though kids are generally responsible about the dangers of pregnancy, rape, and abusive relationships."

Then there are the pleasures of the belly. Students and faculty alike sing the praises of the cafeteria. A professor tells us about the "terrific" food served at the "award-winning dining commons." A student chimes in: "I have been to colleges all across the country, and UMass has the best food. UMass offers an unlimited meal plan, which is very useful for someone like me who eats more than the standard three meals per day."

Thankfully, there are some good chaplaincies and religious fellowship groups at the university, such as Cru (Campus Crusade for Christ), the Catholic Newman Center, and the Orthodox Christian Fellowship. Some groups can sound a little vapid, such as the United Christian Foundation, whose website states, "We are interested in Jesus, social justice, service learning and good beer."

The crime rates at UMass are impressively low. In the last year reported, there were 13 forcible sex offenses, one robbery, five aggravated assaults, 32 burglaries, and one motor vehicle theft on campus. "Crime is not a concern on campus or in the surrounding area," says a student. Whenever he hears about students being arrested, he says it's usually "either for unlawful noise or a minor in the possession of alcohol." A female student recalls that a girl was accosted when leaving a library, and one other girl was nearly raped in her dorm. She says that in response to these incidents, "security was amplified and measures were taken to better protect" students, and she thinks the "UMass Police Department and the Amherst Police Department" are "impressive." Another student says that "crime is almost nonexistent. I feel safe on this campus at all times and have heard of only one instance of rape since I've been here. With a school of over 20,000 kids, I feel comforted by that fact."

Attending UMass is (relatively) affordable for state residents, who paid $13,230 in 2012–13 (outsiders paid $26,645). Room and board were $9,937. Half of students received need-based aid, and the average recent graduate owed a hefty $27,945 in student loans.

STRONG SUITS	WEAK POINTS
• Very good business school, which does well at preparing students to dive into careers upon graduation.	• Trivial general-ed requirements allow for rapid specialization and cultural illiteracy.
• A rigorous honors program that requires a thesis and challenges advanced students.	• Several far-left, politicized departments in the humanities.
• Well-equipped gym and excellent cafeteria.	• Very little coverage of American history before World War II.
• Excellent study-abroad options.	• A bureaucratic and fragmented administration.
	• A serious party atmosphere that has resulted in drunken riots with police.

University of Michigan

Ann Arbor, Michigan • www.umich.edu

Inside Leviathan

The University of Michigan prides itself as "leaders and the best," or at least Michigan's 109,000 football fans like to think so on autumn Saturday mornings as they file into Michigan Stadium to watch the Wolverines (usually) pummel an opponent. The university is a popcorn popper of outrageous ideas, and conservatives face quite a struggle in countering them. The school's sheer size means it can attract some of the nation's best scholars to offer solid and serious classes to America's most talented students. But these good things are hidden, along with many other needles, in one great big haystack.

Academic Life: Behemoth U.

Like most state universities, Michigan has abandoned the core curriculum in Western civilization. Instead, Michigan students must pick from a broad buffet of distributional requirements, many of which can be fulfilled with politicized or overly specialized courses. But students who want a solid education can find one here.

Michigan's honors program is one of the most respected in the country. New students in the College of Literature, Science, and the Arts (LSA) generally join it by invitation

VITAL STATISTICS

Religious affiliation: *none*
Total enrollment: *43,426*
Total undergraduates: *27,979*
SAT CR/Verbal midrange:
610-700
SAT Math midrange:
650–760
ACT midrange: *28–32*
Applicants: *42,544*
Applicants accepted: *37%*
Accepted applicants who
enrolled: *39%*
Tuition (general/out of
state): *$40,302*
Tuition (in state): *$13,625*
Room and board: *$9,752*
Freshman retention rate:
97%
Graduation rate (4 yrs.): *73%*
Graduation rate (6 yrs.): *90%*
Courses with fewer than 20
students: *48%*
Student-faculty ratio: *16:1*
Courses taught by graduate
students: *not provided*
Students living on campus:
37%
Students in fraternities: *8%*
Students in sororities: *12%*
Students receiving need-
based financial aid: *55%*
Avg. student-loan debt of a
recent graduating class:
$19,325
Most popular majors:
*social sciences, biology,
psychology*
Guaranteed housing for 4
years? *no*

only, although interested students with good transcripts may apply. Honors students face a first-rate curriculum: they must take either a humanities course on classical civilizations or the Great Books during their first two semesters, along with two special courses each semester. The honors Literature and Ideas offerings include "Studies in Medieval and Renaissance Literature" and "British Poetry, 17th through 19th Centuries." Some students choose to live in special honors housing. Also look into Michigan's Great Books program, which offers courses in classical and canonical literature from ancient Greece through the present.

The university employs some of the nation's finest scholars, including one Nobel Prize winner. However, as one student says, teaching "always comes second, after getting published." This student charges that although professors dutifully hold office hours and teach the obligatory lecture courses, "in reality, they largely couldn't care less about the classes they're teaching." Another student says that the quality of instruction is uneven: "They know what they are talking about, but do not know how to present it to a class." Upper-level courses often fill up quickly. "You practically have to beg, borrow, and steal to get into any 400-level classes," says one student.

Lectures are generally given and received in the Teutonic style: professors read them and students take notes, sometimes in one of the world's largest lecture halls, "Chemistry 1800," for example, which seats 500 students. One junior reports that she has never actually spoken personally with a professor. During the weekly discussion sections, TAs gloss course readings and delve more deeply into areas about which students have questions. If a student needs individual attention, he has to fight for it.

Michigan is massive and can appear overwhelming, and its advising program does little to remedy that. Advising for LSA students starts with a professional or peer adviser. Once a student declares a major, he can visit an adviser within his department. Students do not have specific faculty advisers assigned to them, and many students never establish academic relationships with faculty members.

Almost every department has its bright spots, but the most respected departments are history, political science, classical studies, anthropology, chemistry, physics, engineering, Judaic studies, Chinese, psychology, economics, business administration, mathematics, Near Eastern studies, neuroscience, art history, and the medieval and early modern studies department.

Students name the following as some of the best undergraduate teachers: Gary Solon (emeritus) in economics; Ejner Jensen (emeritus), John Knott (emeritus), and Ralph G. Williams in English; H. D. Cameron, Ludwig Koenen (emeritus), and Charles Witke (emeritus) in classical studies; Scott Spector in German; John Fine Jr., Diane Owen Hughes, Rudolf Mrázek, and William G. Rosenberg in history; Ronald Inglehart and Greg Markus in political science; and Christopher Peterson in psychology.

Michigan's philosophy department is strong. Majors are required to take courses in formal methods (logic), the history of philosophy, value philosophy, mind and reality, plus three more advanced-level classes. Unfortunately, a course in ancient philosophy is not required. The classical studies department offers concentrations in archeology, classical civilization, classical languages and literature, Ancient Greek and Latin, and Modern Greek.

CAMPUS POLITICS: GREEN LIGHT

Michigan has shaky credentials when it comes to freedom of speech. It evicted the conservative *Michigan Review* from its offices, has limited the time of year and manner in which flyers can be distributed, and implemented a speech code that forbids students from exposing others to "offensive material." Speech-code violations can include teasing someone about his accent, criticizing traditional clothing, or engaging in a Yankee-vs.-Southerner debate.

In 2013, as Fox News reports, the Asian InterVarsity Christian Fellowship "was directed to either revise its constitution—or else be forced off campus. . . . In order for students to be InterVarsity leaders they must sign a statement of faith. But the university said that requirement violated their non-discrimination policy." It seems U. Michigan understands neither freedom of speech nor freedom of association. At least the university's position is consistent.

Michigan imposes a one-course race and ethnicity (R&E) requirement that, says one student, is "basically a course on why the white man is evil." Ideology also appears in many humanities courses—for instance, as one young woman tells us, "when you go into a class on Jane Austen and get a lecture on lesbians." The English department in particular is notorious for forcing feminist and leftist ideology onto students. One student says, "It is often difficult to be the only person in a class to take a conservative stance on an issue and have to defend it against thirty of your classmates. It is even more difficult to write a paper and get a good grade when you disagree with what the professor says. Sometimes you have to sell out your political beliefs for a good grade."

The university also allows creative-expression courses to satisfy distribution requirements. An article in the *Michigan Review*—an independent, right-leaning campus paper—complains that such measures have meant that a "strong classical education has been tossed aside and replaced with a cheaper, dumbed-down, cute and fuzzy, touchy-feely version that churns out moronic alumni who are unable to argue effectively, write profoundly, or think critically." Not to put too fine a point on it. However, the Great Books and the honors program offer a serious, intellectually challenging education—better than many other state schools can promise.

The requirements for English majors at Michigan are middling: students must complete 10 upper-level classes, including three courses on literature before 1830, one of which must focus on literature before 1600, one course in American literature, a "New Traditions" course that "focuses on works by North American and/or British writers/artists of color, world Anglophone writers/artists, or writers/artists of a range of identity categories (involving gender, sexuality, disability, and class) who reflect upon—and are in dialogue about—the differentials of social power and their representation," and one course in poetry. Students could well emerge without having studied Shakespeare.

Political science students choose a concentration within the major. They must take two introductory courses from different subfields (Political Theory, American Politics, Comparative Politics, World Politics, or Research Methods), then complete six more courses (one in four of the five subfields, including the introductory courses already taken, and two advanced courses), as well as two upper-level courses in a discipline related to political science. Thus they could well graduate without having studied the U.S. Constitution or political system.

One student says that teaching "always comes second, after getting published." Another undergrad says she has never spoken personally with a professor.

In the history department, students work with an individual faculty member to customize his or her concentration. Every concentrator must take at least 10 classes in history, five of which must be the 300 level or above. Every concentrator must complete History 202, "Doing History," a course on the foundation of historical research. Of the two remaining courses, one must focus on the period before 1800. Students must also take one course in four of the seven world regions. A junior/senior colloquium enables students to conduct original research. A student could very well graduate having never studied U.S. history.

While each department attempts to provide some structure to its students, it would be all too easy for an undergraduate to graduate with a major in which he has no substantial knowledge—and in which he has simply taken one class per semester. Students would be wise to carefully consider their options to ensure they are pursuing a well-rounded approach to their chosen field.

Study-abroad programs send students throughout Africa, the Americas, Asia, Australia, Europe, and the Middle East. Michigan provides summer-, term-, and yearlong programs for exchange and study-abroad students, as well as field studies as extensions to on-campus courses. More than 60 foreign tongues are taught on campus, and Michigan (laudably) requires students to reach the fourth-term level of a second language in order to graduate. Options range from Bosnian/Croatian/Serbian, Dutch, French, German, and Italian to Ojibwe, Urdu, and Yiddish.

Student Life: Numbers games

Ann Arbor, one of the nation's great college towns, is just a short walk from the dorms. Both on and off campus, Michigan students have a vast number of musical and cultural performances from which to choose, as well as theater, film, and comedy acts. As one student says, Michigan is "a very relaxed place to go to school."

Just under a third of undergraduates—including nearly all freshmen—live on campus. The university guarantees housing for the first year only. Michigan's dormitories include high-rise apartment buildings, old-fashioned houses, and large halls housing more than 9,500 students. Most of the dormitories are coed, separating sexes by floor, but the university does have three all-female dormitories, like the Betsy Barbour house, for women who request them. The Martha Cook Building, a quieter residence with sit-down dinners and teas, is an all-women dormitory that maintains limited visitation hours for men. The Henderson House offers all-female housing in a co-op style. The university offers gender-neutral housing and maintains coed bathrooms in several residence halls. Dorm rooms are single sex, but students can opt to live in a coed corridor, where men and women may live next to each other. Just over one-quarter of the university's residence halls, floors, and rooms are substance-free.

Off campus, rents are generally high; housing should be arranged more than six months in advance (unless you enjoy walking a mile to class). Most students choose to live in the "student ghetto" south of campus, but many other options exist.

Although only about 10 percent of students join fraternities or sororities, some students say the Greek system dominates campus weekends. Especially during their first semester, students often attend house and fraternity parties, usually held in the organizations' off-campus houses. One student says that "beer cans litter Frat Row" and that on the weekends "drunk, skimpily clad individuals can often be seen walking the streets."

Football games at "the Big House" (Michigan Stadium, college football's largest, and the world's fourth-largest, stadium, with a seating capacity of 109,901) are incredibly popular. The atmosphere at men's basketball games is considerably more subdued, with Michigan's Crisler Arena said to be the quietest in the Big Ten Conference. Hockey fans, on the other hand, are known for their out-of-control antics and lewd cheers. The university offers students an extensive intramurals program—more than 20 sports, like broomball, racquetball, basketball, and volleyball—and fields 33 teams for intercollegiate club sports competition, including water polo, rugby, rifle sports, and gymnastics.

To navigate Michigan's size, one student says "the best thing to do is check out a bunch of organizations and groups at the beginning of the year and try to get involved in anything. It is difficult to make friends in class, so if you can become active in a group, you can have a core set of friends and expand from there." Surely one of UM's 1,000-plus clubs will be of interest.

SUGGESTED CORE

1. Classics 385, Greek Mythology
2. Philosophy 388, History of Ancient Philosophy
3. Religion 218, Jesus and the Gospels
4. No suitable course
5. Political Science 301, Development of Political Thought: Modern Period
6. English 367, Shakespeare
7. History 260, U.S. to 1865
8. History 214, Modern Europe (*closest match*)

Michigan

Politically motivated groups include the Model United Nations and Amnesty International. The *Michigan Daily*, the official student newspaper, has impeccable leftist credentials. Students for Choice sponsors a few big-name pro-abortion speakers each year. Conservative students will want to get involved with College Libertarians or College Republicans—the latter an extremely active group that sponsors close to a dozen speakers and events each year, in addition to organizing trips to state and national Republican conventions. The club is exceptional at finding internship opportunities for its members and providing many leadership positions within the organization through its various committees.

For the religiously inclined, Michigan has a variety of organizations, mostly non-denominational or evangelical, including Cru (Campus Crusade for Christ), Intervarsity, Campus Chapel, Christians on Campus, Students in Christ, New Life Church, and Christian Challenge. Other groups consist of Adventist Students for Christ, an Episcopal Center, Hillel, Muslim Students' Association, University Lutheran Chapel, the Catholic St. Mary Student Parish, and the Hindu Students Council.

In recent years crime has decreased on the campus but it is still a cause for concern. In 2011, 14 forcible sexual offenses, four robberies, eight aggravated assaults, four counts of arson, 37 burglaries, and 12 motor vehicle thefts were reported on campus. However, one junior says, "I feel very safe on campus. In a college community, it is pretty easy to spot people who do not belong."

The University of Michigan is undeniably a bargain for in-state students, at only $13,625 in 2012–13. Out-of-state students paid $40,302. Room and board (for a standard double) cost $9,752. Admissions are not need blind, nor does the school guarantee to meet students' full need. Some 55 percent of students received need-based aid. The average student graduated with $27,644 in loan debt.

STRONG SUITS	WEAK POINTS
• Many traditional courses are offered, among hundreds of others.	• Repeated violations of the rights of students to speak and associate freely; Christian groups are ordered to admit nonbelievers.
• An excellent honors and even better Great Books option offers a top-notch education for students who seek it out.	• Massive lecture courses where students mainly interact with graduate TAs.
• Excellent math/science departments, especially chemistry, physics, engineering, neuroscience, mathematics.	• Weak, ineffective system of advising.
• Some solid humanities programs: history, philosophy, political science, classical studies, and art history.	• Politicized English department.
	• "Creative expression" courses can fulfill core requirements.
	• A party atmosphere distracts many students from work.

University of Minnesota–Twin Cities

Minneapolis and St. Paul, Minnesota • www.umn.edu

Fraternal Twins

The University of Minnesota–Twin Cities was founded as a prep school in 1851, before there even was a state of Minnesota. It closed during the Civil War but reopened in 1867 as a land-grant school. Its first bachelor's degrees were awarded in 1873, its first doctorates in 1888. Well regarded in national rankings of large public research institutions, the University of Minnesota is a mixture of disparate elements, offering practically everything—some of it excellent.

The main problem that faces students is how to locate the resources for a real liberal education at a university as enormous as Minnesota where students often get lost academically. Minnesota students are among the smartest in the Big Ten, however, and amid the sheer number of choices offered at UM, a savvy student can find something worthwhile, and at a state university price.

Academic Life: Needling a haystack

Students can study just about anything at the University of Minnesota: there are 180 majors available in the school's 19 colleges, including everything from Latin to urban and

VITAL STATISTICS

Religious affiliation: *none*
Total enrollment: *52,557*
Total undergraduates: *34,812*
SAT CR/Verbal midrange: *540–690*
SAT Math midrange: *610–740*
ACT midrange: *25–30*
Applicants: *39,720*
Applicants accepted: *47%*
Accepted applicants who enrolled: *34%*
Tuition (general/out of state): *$17,310*
Tuition (in state): *$12,060*
Room and board: *$8,000*
Freshman retention rate: *89%*
Graduation rate (4 yrs.): *47%*
Graduation rate (6 yrs.): *75%*
Courses with fewer than 20 students: *41%*
Student-faculty ratio: *21:1*
Courses taught by graduate students: *not provided*
Students living on campus: *21%*
Students in fraternities: *not provided*
Students in sororities: *not provided*
Students receiving need-based financial aid: *54%*
Avg. student-loan debt of a recent graduating class: *$28,407*
Most popular majors: *biology, engineering, social sciences*
Guaranteed housing for 4 years? *no*

community forestry. This may be the only school in America where one could create a double major in, say, interior design and mortuary science. What you can't find at the university is a core curriculum. Minnesota has what it calls the Liberal Education Requirements, a set of distribution mandates that all undergraduates must complete. With few requirements and a broad course selection, they do not guarantee a student a foundational liberal arts education.

Literally thousands of course combinations satisfy the liberal education requirements, and if that's too narrow, students can add to the list through a simple application process. To fulfill his science requirement, for instance, a student can take either "Chemical Principles" I or II or "Geology and Cinema." The range widens in the history and social sciences area. For U of M's purposes, "Sociology of Sexualities," "Anthropologies of Death," "Blood, Bodies and Science," "Principles of Microeconomics," "Intimate Relationships," and "Introduction to GLBT Studies" are the functional equivalents of each other, as well as of classes on ancient Greece, Rome, and American Indians. For arts and humanities, just about any literature is as good as another: Persian poetry, Chinese film, Greek and Roman mythology, or courses like "World of the Bible: Religions, Empires, and Discourses of Power," "Fleeing Hitler: German and Austrian Filmmakers between Europe and Hollywood," and "Reading Culture: Theory and Practice." Our quibble is not that the university offers such a wide variety of icings but that it refuses to distinguish them from the cake.

Most of the university's colleges offer honors programs, and these are usually an improvement over the general curriculum. The aim of the program is a "Latin Honors Degree" (cum laude, etc.), and the appeal is in honors courses taught by "selected teachers," smaller sections, discussion groups, seminars, and "special faculty advisers." Students build honors credits each year through honors course work and an honors thesis or a combination of course work and "non-course honors experiences," such as study abroad, research, or internships. Honors programs are recommended by those on campus as a good way to wring the most out of what could otherwise be a meager general education. "Any student who can get in, should," says one professor. "Class sizes are small, and the instructors mainly excellent."

The quality of advising for nonhonors students varies; professors, upperclassmen, grad students, and professional advisers share advising duties, and many do a good job. As at most big schools, the academic advising becomes more valuable the more effort the student makes to keep in contact with his adviser. Even within the College of Liberal Arts, how much students interact with advisers depends on the department. A freshman interested in economics, for instance, can make appointments with college-wide advisers; once he declares a major, he can meet with a peer undergraduate adviser in the economics department or the faculty member who is the department's designated adviser. With more than 400 students majoring in economics each year, it is undoubtedly hard for students to have extensive one-on-one interaction with the departmental adviser.

Students have ample opportunity to perform research at Minnesota, through the Undergraduate Research Opportunities Program, for example, which gives approximately 800 students stipends to assist faculty members with research or perform their own under faculty supervision.

Students at large state universities should expect some large classes; U of M is no exception, and really could not be otherwise with a student-faculty ratio of 21 to 1. The university reports that 337 of the 3,995 classes it offered (up a percent from our last reporting) in a recent semester had more than 100 students. More than 1,000 classes enrolled fewer than 10 students. Teaching assistants handle the discussion sections in larger classes; faculty members maintain that their TAs are well prepared to teach by the pedagogical courses offered them by each department. One student comments that in some classes professors "rush in, give the lecture,

CAMPUS POLITICS: YELLOW LIGHT

There are outspoken rightist students at U. of Minnesota who sponsor (with College Republicans) an annual Conservative Awareness Week to gain greater visibility on campus. They feel fairly free to speak, thanks to past interventions by the Foundation for Individual Rights in Education, which took their side against a hostile administration. Conservative students have quite a bit to speak up about, it appears.

The university sponsors a Minnesota Gay, Lesbian, Bisexual, Transgender, Ally Programs Office with its own website, support staff, newsletters, and all kinds of programs, such as the GLBT mentor program and the GLBT Cultural Center. The website provides links to support services on and (like the "Butch Project") off campus and sympathetic student groups like "Kinky U," which is a "weekly social and discussion group for those who are interested in . . ." things that modesty forbids us to mention.

In 2013, as *Campus Reform* reported, the school sponsored an official event "designed to help its female undergraduate students achieve more and greater orgasms....The university's official online description of the event, entitled 'The Female Orgasm,' describes it as open to both male and female students."

"Orgasm aficionados and beginners of all genders are welcome to come learn about everything from multiple orgasms to that mysterious G-spot,'" the school's events calendar announced. "Whether you want to learn how to have your first orgasm, how to have better ones, or how to help your girlfriend, Kate and Marshall cover it all . . .' it add[ed]."

and rush off to finish their work, leaving a TA to fend off questions and teach the rest in discussion classes."

Students also sometimes have trouble getting the courses they want or need to graduate. "It's a rarity if undergrads get out of here in four years. And often it is just a matter of the courses they need not being available," one student says. In the Big Ten Conference, U of M ranks ninth in graduation rate, with less than half of students earning the diploma in four years.

Regarding academic quality, one can scarcely generalize about a school so large and varied as Minnesota, as a professor explains: "Colleges are much more autonomous here than at most other schools—the social, political, and intellectual atmosphere differs pretty widely across the various colleges." Another teacher admits that he refers to the local and student papers to keep abreast of what's happening on campus—even in his own department.

Among the best programs at Minnesota are history, economics, philosophy, psychology, political science, chemical engineering, materials science, business, biochemistry, microbiology, the foreign language departments, and the Academic Health Center, which includes the health sciences. Students recommend the following professors: William Grove and Matthew McGue in psychology; Tom Clayton and in English; Bernard Bachrach in history; John Archer in religious studies; Richard Leppert in cultural studies and comparative literature; Marvin Marshak and Oriol Valls in physics; Anatoly Liberman in German; and Ian Maitland in the Carlson School of Management. One professor says, "It is easy for a determined student to find out who has won awards for excellence in teaching, which courses actually teach something, [and] which professors really care about their students."

> Some professors "rush in, give the lecture, and rush off to finish their work, leaving a TA to fend off questions and teach the rest in discussion classes," a student said.

Amid the massive offerings at Minnesota, some politicized disciplines thrive. The gender, women, and sexuality studies department has a GLBT Studies Program. Cultural Studies and Comparative Literature, one program with several tracks, was formed from the rubble of disbanded humanities departments some years ago. The course list includes a hodgepodge of literature (loosely defined), pop culture, and multiculturalism.

The English department's literature program is riddled with politicized offerings but also provides solid courses such as "Historical Survey of British Literature" and "Introduction to Shakespeare." Happily, majors are required to take Shakespeare and American and British literature surveys, and a historical perspectives literature course. One professor says of the department, "It used to be great—the best." There are still good professors, but the department is torn between traditional scholars and cutting-edge theorists. When a professor from the traditionalist faction (who also happened to be a political liberal) won a university teaching award, half the department walked out of the announcement ceremony in protest.

The history department's requirements are less laudable. From a staggering number of choices, a student could put together a major curriculum that is random and eccentric. Required are two survey-level classes, with at least one writing intensive; six upper-division classes, the course "How to Do History," a major paper, and one elective course in history at any level. Further distribution requirements are two classes before 1750 and two after; two unique geographic areas (U.S., Europe, Africa, Asian, Latin America, Middle East, etc.); one world history course; and three "courses in an area of concentration: upper-division courses linked together geographically, chronologically, or thematically." So along with "Urban American History: Race, Class, Gender, and Sexuality in Urban America," one could take the thematically linked "Directed Study" and "Directed Research."

Political science majors also have an alarming freedom from prescription. Students must complete a minimum of eight upper-division classes in political science and must take at least one course from three of the four subfields: Political Theory, Comparative Government, International Relations, and American Government. To say that choices are wide ranging is an understatement.

Foreign language course offerings are impressive, as one would expect. Students can major in French, German, Greek and Latin, Hebrew, Italian, Portuguese, Scandinavian languages (including Finnish), and Spanish, and take classes in others, such as American Sign Language, Arabic, Chinese, Hindi, Hmong, Irish, Ojibwe, Persian, and Swahili. Hundreds of study-abroad programs can place the student wherever these languages are spoken, and almost anywhere in the world, in fact.

> **SUGGESTED CORE**
>
> 1. Classical Civilization 3081W, Classical Epic in Translation
> 2. Philosophy 3101, General History of Western Philosophy: Ancient Period
> 3. Religious Studies 3115/3072, Midrash: Jewish Biblical Interpretation/The New Testament
> 4. Philosophy 3003, General History of Western Philosophy: Medieval Period
> 5. Political Science 5252, Renaissance, Reformation, and Revolution: Early Modern Political Thought
> 6. English 1181W, Introduction to Shakespeare
> 7. History 1301W, Authority and Rebellion: American History to 1865
> 8. History 3282, European Intellectual History: The Modern Period, 1750–Present

Student Life: Where all the children are above average

The campus of the University of Minnesota is split by the Mississippi River. Many of the main buildings and four of the residence halls (concentrated into the Superblock, a compound as big as four city blocks) sit on the east bank of the river, as does the university's medical center, the student union, and the campus's historical focal point—the large green called Northrop Mall.

On the west bank of the river stand most of the school's buildings for the art, music, theater, business, and social science departments, along with the largest single dorm, Middlebrook Hall, and Wilson Library, the main book depository on campus. The business and law schools are also nearby. This campus is perhaps best known for the arts festivals that erupt here each spring.

Less than a quarter of the student body actually lives on campus, and those students are mostly freshmen. The large commuter population creates a rather cold atmosphere at the school—and that's on top of the weather. Take a look around the campus and you'll find students studying alone, walking alone, even eating alone. The library is not the zoo you'd find at some other large state schools; U of M students are here to earn degrees, not to party (although there are some parties).

Students can live in campus dorms, residential colleges, special-interest houses, or private off-campus housing. The university guarantees housing for first-year students and requires everyone living in dorms to have a university meal plan. Three dorms (Territorial, Pioneer, and Frontier), both on the Minneapolis side, are freshmen-only. The Mark G. Yudof Hall (formerly Riverbend Commons) includes suites and some apartments as well as a few language houses. Some residential halls offer discussion seminars for freshmen on a variety of academic topics. There are many "living and learning" communities that are voluntary associations of students with similar interests; these range from speaking Italian or French together to "learning and uncovering the histories and cultures" of sexual dissenters in Lavender House. All dormitories are coed, although men and women are separated by floor or wing, depending on the configuration of the building. There are no coed bathrooms or dorm rooms. Students choose their own quiet hour and visitation policies by wing or hall.

If the extensive list of more than 400 student groups is any indication, Minnesota students' interests are as wide ranging as those at schools with more diverse student bodies. The AB Kilombo Capoeira club, for example, is dedicated to teaching authentic Brazilian *capoeira*. There is Campus People Watchers ("a non-profit, non-creepy organization for those who are into the social, psychological, and analytical aspects of people watching"), Queer Men, Theatre of the Relatively Talentless, Canine Club, Paintball Club, and Zoological, Exotic, Avian and Wildlife Medicine Club, among others. There is also an award-winning paper, the *Minnesota Daily*. Students interested in Greek life can vie for places in 28 fraternities and 14 sororities.

The university also has groups promoting the culture of Afghans, Africans, American Indians, Asian Americans, Greeks, and Hmong. Students of most faiths will find at least one group of fellow faithful: Catholics, Jews, Buddhists, Muslims, Orthodox, and Protestants of many stripes.

All sides of the political spectrum are represented as well, with groups including College Republicans, College Democrats, Amnesty International, the Federalist Society, Socialist Alternative Club, University Pro-Choice Coalition, H20 for Life, and Compassionate Action for Animals.

Gopher sports fields 11 men's varsity teams and 12 women's teams. There are also dozens of club and intramural sports and good facilities for nearly all of them.

Other facilities in the works are a renovation of Northrup Hall, scheduled to be completed in 2013, which will include a cultural and performing arts center with a 2,750-seat multiuse hall. This will draw together several academic programs, including the honors program. In 2009 the university completed a $79.3 million, 115,000-square-foot Wallin Medical Biosciences Building.

The campus is moderately safe for a city-sized school within an urban area, and university police are conscientious about patrolling by bike and car. Nevertheless, in 2011 the university reported 38 burglaries, 12 forcible sex offenses, four robberies, one aggravated assault, and one stolen car on campus.

Tuition for 2012–13 was $12,060 for Minnesota residents and $17,310 for nonresidents, and room and board were $8,000. Admissions are need blind, and the school arranges, with loans, to cover all financial need; 54 percent of undergraduates received some need-based financial aid. The average student-loan debt for recent graduates was $28,407.

STRONG SUITS	WEAK POINTS
• Many opportunities for student research. • Good departments in business and in the sciences: chemical engineering, materials science, business, biochemistry, microbiology, health sciences. • Some strong humanities programs in history, economics, philosophy, psychology, political science, foreign languages departments. • Honors options offer smaller, better classes.	• Core requirements are weak and can be fulfilled with esoteric or politicized classes. • Advising weak unless students proactively seek it out. • Some classes are enormous and offer little interaction with professor (as opposed to graduate students). • Courses are often unavailable, so less than half of students graduate within four years. • Many politicized classes and entire departments in humanities. • School-sponsored orgasm workshops.

University of Mississippi

Oxford, Mississippi • www.olemiss.edu

The New South

The University of Mississippi, affectionately known as Ole Miss, opened in 1848. Today it has grown to more than 18,000 students and is one of the top 30 public schools with the largest endowment per student. Ole Miss celebrated its 25th Rhodes scholar in 2008 and is the proud alma mater to numerous Truman, Goldwater, Fulbright, Marshall, Udall, and Gates Cambridge scholars as well.

It is possible to get a top-notch education at Ole Miss—but it is by no means necessary. The school's wide distribution requirements will not guarantee any such thing. Remarks a professor dryly: "Students can indeed graduate with a narrow knowledge base, particularly by majoring in 'soft' disciplines, which rarely demand more than rote memorization." There are a good many quality courses with excellent professors at Ole Miss—if students are conscientious enough to take them.

Academic Life: Available, not required

While the school encourages students to pursue traditional areas of study, it does not require them—and students can knock off their requirements with courses of wildly vary-

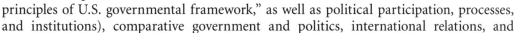

ing quality. For instance, the two-course social science requirement for an English major may be met by any choices from anthropology, economics, political science, psychology, or sociology. And so it goes through most majors.

The University of Mississippi offers 72 bachelor's degrees through the eight undergraduate colleges on the Oxford campus. Degree programs are varied, from Classics and geological engineering to criminal justice, hospitality management, dental hygiene, and elementary education. Should these options not satisfy, the College of Liberal Arts offers a liberal studies degree that allows a student to combine any three minors.

One distinctive degree offered is a bachelor of arts in southern studies. Ole Miss is the home of the Center for the Study of Southern Culture, which for nearly 40 years has been the premier place to study the writings of William Faulkner.

The rigor of major requirements varies. The English department (strong particularly in 19th- and 20th-century American literature, southern literature, and creative writing) requires two composition classes, two intermediate-level survey courses, two upper-level seminars, and one Shakespeare class, as well as seven upper-level electives. The department offers just a few trendy or politicized options. An English major says this department is second to none in quality and variety. "I haven't taken a single boring class," he says. "My biggest problem is having to choose between all of the classes I want to take each semester."

The history department demands 11 classes that "show a reasonable balance between United States and non–United States" history courses. All majors must take a two-course sequence on the history of Europe, two senior seminars, and at least two upper-level courses on the history of non-Western nations. Again, most choices are solid, although students can skip "The History of Ancient Christianity" in favor of "Life After the NFL."

Political science majors are required to take 11 classes in the discipline, including introductory courses in American politics (which cover the "Constitutional principles of U.S. governmental framework," as well as political participation, processes, and institutions), comparative government and politics, international relations, and

VITAL STATISTICS

Religious affiliation: *none*
Total enrollment: *18,224*
Total undergraduates: *15,346*
SAT CR/Verbal midrange: *460–590*
SAT Math midrange: *470–590*
ACT midrange: *20–27*
Applicants: *13,321*
Applicants accepted: *79%*
Accepted applicants who enrolled: *34%*
Tuition (general/out of state): *$16,266*
Tuition (in state): *$6,282*
Room and board: *$9,200*
Freshman retention rate: *81%*
Graduation rate (4 yrs.): *38%*
Graduation rate (6 yrs.): *60%*
Courses with fewer than 20 students: *47%*
Student-faculty ratio: *19:1*
Courses taught by graduate students: *not provided*
Students living on campus: *33%*
Students in fraternities: *35%*
Students in sororities: *36%*
Students receiving need-based financial aid: *52%*
Avg. student-loan debt of a recent graduating class: *$21,393*
Most popular majors: *business/marketing, education, psychology*
Guaranteed housing for 4 years? *no*

CAMPUS POLITICS: GREEN LIGHT

Like many other state schools, a few years ago Ole Miss decided to impose a speech code on its students. Vague enough to be broadly threatening, the school prohibited "hateful" communication on the Internet. While the speech codes are intended to protect students from abuse, they are also open to interpretation, such that an administrator or professor could easily harass or punish a student or group for behavior or speech that is protected by United States law. However, in spring 2012 the university reworded the speech code and the Foundation for Individual Rights in Education certified that its standards now protect free expression.

Ole Miss is one of the few state universities where conservative students feel at home both on campus and in the classroom. While "there certainly are places where leftist and statist ideologies find their ways into the curriculum, particularly in the English, history, and sociology departments," according to one professor, students do not complain to us of professors' political views unduly affecting course content.

Describing her peers, one student uses three words: "Conservative, conservative, conservative." Another student says, "Ole Miss is an extremely conservative southern school, and most of the students value that." While the student body tends toward the right, the student newspaper, the *Daily Mississippian*, has been traditionally dominated by liberal students, according to a professor: "Lip service is paid to 'diversity,' and the homosexual agenda is in full flower on the paper's editorial page."

political analysis. They must also take six advanced-level electives, most of them in traditional areas of study, such as "German Politics," "Mock Trial," and "Political Economy of International Development."

Academic advising is mandatory and its quality varies by school and department. Students in the College of Liberal Arts have different advising options according to their discipline. Some departments offer their own advisers, while others use school-wide resources. Says a student of the Academic Support Center option, "The process usually involves a lot of waiting, but that can be avoided if students take advantage of early advising, appointments, etcetera." A student with an adviser in his department says, "I think the system works very well. . . . Having the same adviser for the entirety of one's undergraduate career is helpful."

Professors at Ole Miss are readily available to students. "In general, the faculty are eager to help when called upon," says a student. "Because Ole Miss is rather small, undergraduates here are much more likely than they are at other public universities to receive instruction from full-time members of the faculty rather than graduate students," says a professor. "Teaching matters here," another reports. "It's not just about publications and research grants." Nevertheless, Ole Miss does make use of teaching assistants, who teach lower-level courses, particularly those that students take to fulfill distribution requirements.

Some schools and departments are known to be more exacting. The School of Pharmacy and the E. H. Patterson School of Accountancy are rigorous, and the economics, English, and physics departments of the College of Liberal Arts are particularly strong. However, one professor says, "The marketing and management majors are widely perceived as easy . . . preparing students for entry-level jobs in the banking, insurance, and real estate industries but failing utterly to equip them with the intellectual tools necessary for a lifetime of learning."

Highly recommended professors at Ole Miss include Jay Watson, Benjamin F. Fisher IV (emeritus), Whit Hubbard, Donald M. Kartiganer (emeritus), and Colby H. Kullman (emeritus) in English; Allison Burkette in linguistics; Gary Long in sociology; William Staton in math; William F. Chappell, John R. Conlon, and William F. Shughart II in economics; Robert B. Westmoreland in philosophy and religion; Alice H. Cooper and John W. Winkle III in political science; Edward Sisson in anthropology; John Czarnetzky in law; and Judith Cassidy, Dale L. Flesher, and Tonya Kay Flesher in the School of Accountancy.

> "Students can graduate with a narrow knowledge base, particularly by majoring in 'soft' disciplines, which rarely demand more than rote memorization," a professor warns.

Students in the university's selective Honors College and the Croft Institute for International Studies are, according to one professor, "the cream of the crop." Honors students take freshman and sophomore seminars, complete a research project undertaken with a faculty mentor, and write a senior thesis. The remaining credit hours come from specially designated honors courses in regular departments, which offer smaller enrollment and more discussion-based classes. Croft students take four core courses, introducing them to international studies and surveying East Asia, Europe, Latin America, and the Middle East. Students have a chance to examine their chosen areas firsthand, as the Croft curriculum includes foreign language training and a required study abroad.

For those outside the prestigious Croft Institute, study-abroad options are still numerous. With more than 60 nations to choose from, including locations like Austria, Botswana, and Mongolia, Ole Miss provides its students with excellent short-term, semester-long, and yearlong options (including a brief January trip on "Environmental Psychology" in Tanzania or "Education, Health, and Child Welfare" in Belize).

Stateside, students may pursue a number of foreign languages. The school offers majors in Chinese, French, German, Greek and Latin, and Spanish. There are also minors in Arabic, Italian, Japanese, and Russian, and courses in Portuguese.

Student Life: Football and cornhole

Oxford, Mississippi, is a charming community of 19,000, just 70 miles south of Memphis. Campus life is peppered with traditions such as the school cheer and lingo like "the Grove" and "the Square." A student says, "By far, the most popular place to hang out in Oxford is the Square, which truly feels like a movie set. There are upward of 30 bars and restaurants around the town square area, so many students opt to spend time there at night." So many students spend time there, in fact, that another student reports, "Lines to get into the most

SUGGESTED CORE

1. Classics 309, Greek and Roman Epic
2. Philosophy 301, History of Philosophy I
3. Religion 310/312, The Old Testament and Early Judaism/The New Testament and Early Christianity
4. History 374, Medieval Church and Empire
5. Philosophy 331, Political Philosophy
6. English 385, Shakespeare
7. History 302–1/303–1 U.S. History, Age of Revolution, 1740–1789/1789–1850: Emerging Nation
8. Philosophy 302, History of Philosophy II (*closest match*)

popular bars can begin around 7:00 p.m. on Thursday nights." Another student says that although it may not compare to New Orleans or Austin, the live music scene has become quite popular in Oxford, "which is great for campus parties, since a lot of really good bands are local now."

Ole Miss is something of a party school. One student calls barhopping an "art" in Oxford. Over a third of students at Ole Miss go Greek, and many students follow family lineages to the university in the hopes of affiliating themselves with the same fraternity or sorority. Says a professor, "Sorority and fraternity activities dominate the social calendar throughout the year, but football is the number one priority in the fall."

Rebel fans support their teams—especially football—vigorously and throw grand parties before, during, and after football season. During that season, "bars are always packed with celebrations," according to a student. "Football is the lifeblood of Ole Miss." Another says, "Game-day attire is very strict: children either have cheerleading outfits or Ole Miss jerseys on, girls have heels and dresses . . . and the guys have suits and ties. If you don't follow these fashion rules, then you're obviously with the visiting team." Another student describes it as "cocktail party meets hard-core tailgating."

Because student life is so enticing, "Ole Miss seems to have a large percentage of fifth-year seniors. Many students choose to spread classes out for a lighter course load each semester," says a student.

Ole Miss offers a variety of student organizations. Student government is popular on campus, as is the student programming board, which brings in musicians and comedians and hosts the annual beauty pageant—something that at other schools would likely be restricted to male transvestites. Otherwise, "few of the professional or special interest organizations seem to be popular or prestigious," says a student. The school boasts nearly 270 organizations, most of which fall along religious, professional, or Greek lines.

Religious groups include Baptist, Episcopal, Catholic, and Muslim associations, as well as evangelical groups like Cru (Campus Crusade for Christ), Fellowship of Christian Athletes, and Young Life. Professional groups include Air Force, Navy, and Army ROTC; the Black Law Student Association; Mississippi Philosophical Association; and the Society for the Advancement of Management. Ole Miss also offers a number of international groups (African Caribbean, Chinese, French, German, Latin American, Pakistani, Russian, Vietnamese, two general international groups, and Sistah Speak for all minority women), as well as sports clubs like badminton, disk golf, fencing, and Ultimate Frisbee.

Special interest groups include an active College Republicans group, gospel choir, Model United Nations, Gay-Straight Alliance, College Democrats, and Financier's Club.

For a school that had to be integrated at gunpoint by federal marshals 50 years ago, Ole Miss is now quite comfortably multiracial—if still rather self-segregated. In 2012 nearly a quarter of the student population was nonwhite. The school has avoided much of the interracial animus (and resulting heavy-handed "diversity" initiatives) that afflict other schools North and South.

Students who do not reside in one of the 24 fraternity and sorority houses can live in university housing. A third of students live on campus, and freshmen are required to, but a tenth of them have commuter status and are exempt from the policy. The halls have set visitation hours, but during the first week of classes in the fall, residents may vote to extend the hours. Residence halls are strictly single sex, which is nearly unheard of at a public university.

Ole Miss is a safe place. The university's 2011 campus crime statistics report 44 burglaries, by far the most in recent years, in addition to one robbery, one aggravated assault, and four forcible sex offenses.

For a Mississippi resident, the school is a real bargain, with 2012–13 tuition at a mere $6,282. Mississippi has, so far, resisted the extreme tuition increases common to other universities. Even Yankees get off lightly: out-of-state students paid $16,266, which reflects a more substantial increase over earlier years. Room and board cost about $9,200. Admissions are need blind, but the school cannot afford to guarantee full financial aid to all. Some 52 percent of students received need-based financial aid. The average debt of recent graduates was $21,393.

STRONG SUITS	WEAK POINTS
• Rigorous programs in pharmacy, accounting, economics, English, physics.	• Undemanding marketing and management majors.
• Very good resources in southern literature and culture.	• Powerful party atmosphere leads many to take light course loads.
• Courteous, friendly atmosphere—and all single-sex dorms.	• Only 38 percent of students graduate in four years (and only 60 percent in six).
• Free discussion of ideas and little politicization of the classroom.	
• Cordial, if somewhat distant, race relations at this once segregated school.	

College of the Ozarks

Point Lookout, Missouri • www.cofo.edu

Hardwork U.

Founded in 1906 as a high school by a Presbyterian missionary, this school has been a college since 1965. And it's a very distinctive one, since students earn virtually the whole cost of their education by working on campus. In exchange for tuition-free classes, they work on the school's cattle and pig farm, bake and sell fruitcakes, and staff the radio station and lodge—among the more than 80 available types of jobs at the school. About 90 percent of students are from low-income backgrounds, and many are first-generation college students. "Other schools may talk about the American dream (though I suspect far too few actually do); we are the American dream," says one professor.

The mountain campus is like a town—with its own hospital, fire department, farm, greenhouses, grain mill, meat-processing plant, gas station, museums, motel, bakery, and restaurant, all manned by student workers. In addition to a solid liberal arts education, students learn lessons about the dignity of labor, personal responsibility, and free enterprise at this impressive blue collar academy.

Academic Life: Educating citizens

The College of the Ozarks imposes a serious core curriculum, which every student must complete, guaranteeing that each graduate has the basics of a true liberal arts education. All students must take two religion courses, "Christian Worldview" I and II. These classes are described by the college as providing "a special focus on understanding and practicing a Christian worldview rooted in the overarching biblical narrative of Creation, Sin, and Restoration, and the development of Christ-like character." For math and science, College of the Ozarks requires only one college mathematics class and a natural science class. Bachelor of arts students must take two semesters of a foreign language, while bachelor of science students choose either an additional laboratory science, mathematics, or computer science course.

An excellent way to enrich the solid educational experience at C of O is by taking courses in its optional Character Curriculum, a Great Books program. The Character Curriculum focuses on ideals of virtue from different eras, including "great authors from Homer to Sophocles, Virgil to Dante, Shakespeare to Milton," says the program description. One student reports, "I enjoyed drinking deeply from literature in 'Medieval/Renaissance Ideals of Character,' where we read Dante's *Inferno* and the *Confessions* of St. Augustine. I highly recommend the character curriculum for those who seek an intense steeping in the Classics, and in other areas as well."

Along with academics and work, the college emphasizes spiritual growth and patriotism. The school is not shy about proclaiming its values—one needs only to drive through the "Gates of Opportunity" at the entry of the campus to encounter the core values for which streets are named: Academic Avenue, Vocational Way, Spiritual Street, Opportunity Avenue, and Cultural Street. "I love that our school is pro-American, that we acknowledge in class and on campus how fortunate we are to live in this country where we are free to live our lives in accordance with our Christian beliefs," a sophomore says. "We are taught not to take these freedoms for granted."

The college offers more than 42 majors in seven divisions: business and communication, education and health, nursing and human services,

VITAL STATISTICS

Religious affiliation: *Protestant (Presbyterian)*
Total enrollment: *1,374*
Total undergraduates: *1,374*
SAT CR/Verbal midrange: *580–630*
SAT Math midrange: *530–560*
ACT midrange: *21–24*
Applicants: *3,299*
Applicants accepted: *9%*
Accepted applicants who enrolled: *95%*
Tuition (general/out of state): *free*
Tuition (in state): *free*
Room and board: *$5,900*
Freshman retention rate: *85%*
Graduation rate (4 yrs.): *58%*
Graduation rate (6 yrs.): *60%*
Courses with fewer than 20 students: *57%*
Student-faculty ratio: *13:1*
Courses taught by graduate students: *not provided*
Students living on campus: *80%*
Students in fraternities: *none*
Students in sororities: *none*
Students receiving need-based financial aid: *94%*
Avg. student-loan debt of a recent graduating class: *$7,062*
Most popular majors: *business, education, nursing*
Guaranteed housing for 4 years? *yes*

CAMPUS POLITICS: GREEN LIGHT

In 2012 both the *Princeton Review* and Young America's Foundation ranked College of the Ozarks in the top 10 among the nation's conservative colleges and universities. Students agree that professors are open about their beliefs but don't try to discourage or stifle debate, nor do they pretend to be final authorities. A professor says, "We are freer to discuss controversial issues than the faculty and students at those campuses which are supposedly more open-minded."

In April 2011 the school invited George W. Bush to speak to the student body at the Character and Leadership Convocation. The event was open to the public and sold out within hours of its announcement.

technical and applied sciences, humanities, performing and professional arts, and mathematical and natural sciences. In addition to traditional liberal arts disciplines, the school offers majors tied to the businesses on campus, including agriculture, conservation and wildlife management, criminal justice, dietetics, family and consumer sciences, hotel and restaurant management, and nursing.

College of the Ozarks offers its students extensive advising opportunities. Upon enrollment, students are assigned an adviser well versed in program requirements for their field of study. "Academic advising is excellent," a freshman says. "There is an open-door policy with most faculty advisers when it comes to students in their care; they take the responsibility very seriously."

Department requirements for English majors are impressive. The department mandates 12 courses: "Foundations of Literary Studies," "Introduction to Grammar," two "Survey of British Literature," two "Survey of American Literature" classes, "Western Literature" (Greek, Roman, and medieval), three English electives, a literary criticism seminar, and a creative writing class. An English major says that the strengths of the department are its "dedicated and passionate faculty members." He notes that while course selections may be limited, teachers are "more than willing to craft special problems or directed reading courses which make up for this lack." Many work assignments in the school's work program reinforce an academic program in English, including positions in the Lyon's Memorial Library, KZOC radio station, *The Outlook* student newspaper, tutoring services, and public relations and academic offices.

History majors at C of O are required to take two Western civilization survey courses, an American history class, and a historiography class. The department calls for seven advanced courses, with at least three in American history and two in modern European history, one course in non-Western (or developing world) history, and one elective. Students also complete a writing-intensive seminar focused on a period or topic in European, American, or developing-world history and an ungraded portfolio class. Students say that while some of the history classes are taught from a liberal perspective, professors treat the Western heritage and American institutions with reasonable respect and welcome opposing viewpoints.

"The political science program is currently under review and not offered at this time," the college informs on its website. This is a good thing, according to a student. "Poli-sci was known as the most liberal department on campus, which apparently did not sit well with some of our big donors, who tend to be extremely patriotic."

A philosophy and religion major has found that the department is more focused on religion than philosophy but adds that professors are "more than willing" to create programs based on student interest and to research new topics for study side by side with students. The full-time faculty members are "extremely student-oriented" and mentor students inside and outside the classroom, he says.

The agricultural programs preserve the agrarian tradition of the school and the region, while the military science programs foster character development, patriotism, and physical fitness. The most popular majors are business administration and early childhood education.

Among C of O's strongest departments are English; philosophy and religion; education; business; military science; and agriculture. Mass communication is considered by students to be the weakest department. They say it suffers from a lack of leadership and too few teachers. One student reports, "There is little opportunity for career development and very little funding. Also, the professors do not offer much in the way of career counseling."

Noteworthy faculty members include Eric Bolger (dean of the college), James Todd, and Mark Rapinchuk in philosophy and religion; Kevin Riley and Rex Mahlman in business; Major James Schreffler in military science; Jeff Elliott in psychology; Dana McMahon and Danita Frazier in education; Daniel Swearengen in agriculture; Jeff Rettig in biology; Leslie Babcox and Hayden Head in English; Gary Hiebsch in speech communication; and C. David Dalton and David Ringer in history.

Students say that professors are actively involved in their lives and that most faculty participate in different organizations on campus. "I believe that the accessibility and the willingness to help of C of O professors is probably one of the institution's strongest traits. Every professor I had at C of O took a vested interest in me; each wanted me to succeed," says a graduate who now works at the college. One transfer student from a large state university says that before Thanksgiving, he went to dinner with his class at a

"I love that our school is pro-American, that we acknowledge in class and on campus how fortunate we are to live in this country where we are free to live in accordance with our Christian beliefs," a sophomore says. "We are taught not to take these freedoms for granted."

professor's home. "Upon leaving [the professor's] house that evening, he inquired about my Thanksgiving plans. I informed him that I was driving to my parents' home for the holiday, at which time he proceeded to ask me if I had enough money for gas. I assured him that I did, three times." Finally, the student says, the professor took his word for it. "This is just one example of how most professors from College of the Ozarks treat their students," he says.

C of O doesn't have a traditional study-abroad department, per se, but does provide a few worthy opportunities for students to travel overseas with specific programs. The most

SUGGESTED CORE

1. English 133CC, Classical Ideals of Character
2. Philosophy and Religion 313, History of Philosophy (*closest match*)
3. Biblical and Theological Studies 273/253, Old Testament/New Testament
4. Philosophy and Religion 333, History of the Christian Church
5. History 163, Western Civilization since 1660 (*closest match*)
6. English 403/423, Shakespeare's Tragedies/Shakespeare's Comedies and Histories
7. History 103, The American Experience (*closest match*)
8. Philosophy 403, Seminar in Philosophy (*closest match*)

impressive is the Patriotic Education Program, which "pairs College of the Ozarks students with WWII veterans, taking them back to the battlefields where they fought," according to the website. Students and veterans have traveled together to England, France, Belgium, Germany, the Netherlands, and Luxembourg to visit sites from D-Day, the Battle of the Bulge, and Berlin, among other battle sites. A recent Holocaust trip took the veterans and students along with Holocaust survivors to Germany, Poland, Austria, the Czech Republic, and the Slovak Republic. There have also been trips to Okinawa, Hiroshima, Iwo Jima, Tokyo, the Philippines, the Solomon Islands, and even China.

The Frances C. Berger Citizens Abroad Program "aims to provide students with an awareness of the world while fostering an appreciation of America and what it represents." This program takes the form of short educational trips rather than the traditional extended stay in a foreign country, but the goal is "to give as many students as possible the opportunity to have a travel-abroad experience." Recent trips included England, China, Rwanda, and Spain.

The foreign language department offers a major or minor in Spanish. Students in education may also pursue a course of study leading to a teaching certificate in a foreign language. Students may take up to two semesters in Hebrew or New Testament Greek through the Department of Philosophy and Religion.

Student Life: Two miles from Branson

The College of the Ozarks sits 40 miles from the city of Springfield, Missouri, and two miles from Branson, Missouri. Each C of O student works 15 hours during the week and two 40-hour workweeks over the course of the academic year. To cover their room and board, students pay cash or work in a summer program. The management of the work-study program is handled by the dean of work education. Students are assigned workstations as they are available on the basis of interest, experience, and ability. Freshmen are usually placed in the cafeteria or the Keeter Center their first semester and then transfer to another job, says a student. Students have supervisors, and grades are given for each work assignment.

Attendance at chapel and convocations is mandatory. Students are required to attend a minimum of five Sunday chapel services and five Christian character-building programs (academic, patriotic, vocational, cultural, and religious) during each semester.

There are no fraternities or sororities, and 80 percent of the student body lives on campus in one of the six single-sex residence halls, where visits between the sexes are limited to the lounge areas. In order to live off campus, the student must be either married, a military veteran, or living with a parent or guardian. The RAs are "very friendly and the housing directors have a vested interest in students' well-being," a student says. Another undergrad says, "My dorm is fairly quiet, which is nice, but there are always plenty of activities planned by the housing staff." Students follow a sensible, work-friendly dress code. Regarding alcohol and drugs, the school has adopted a "zero-tolerance policy." Students say that failure to comply leads to immediate expulsion.

The school accepts only 9 percent of applicants. Ninety percent of the students from each entering class must, by school policy, be from low-income backgrounds—while the other 10 percent consists of children of alumni, scholarship recipients, and international students.

A graduate says that from C of O, he has gained a very large community of friends who are like family. It is a place where "healthy relationships" are the norm and where people "put others ahead of themselves," he says. "The work program weeds out the less-than-serious students," he adds. He adds that the educational experience at C of O is "broad and deep" and understanding the reasons and purpose of work gave him an edge when working on Capitol Hill. The former student has returned to rural Missouri to run for state representative.

Students in Free Enterprise takes on many projects each year and travels internationally to pioneer other SIFE clubs. In addition to academic clubs, some of the other student groups on campus include the Student Alumni Association, Baptist Student Union, Catholic Newman Association, Math-Physics Club, Horticulture Club, Hotel and Restaurant Society, International Student Club, InterVarsity Christian Fellowship, Jazz Band, Jones Theatre Company, Christian Psychology Club, Public Relations Club, Graphic Arts Club, Chorale, Wilderness Activities Club, College Democrats and College Republicans, and ROTC. There are no "diversity" or multicultural clubs, nor are there gay and lesbian, feminist, or pro-choice organizations.

College of the Ozarks Bobcats participate in Division II of the NAIA (National Association of Intercollegiate Athletics) and is a member of the Midlands Collegiate Athletic Conference. It sponsors men's teams in basketball and baseball and has teams for women in volleyball and basketball. The school frequently hosts the Men's NAIA National Basketball Championship.

C of O is one of the quietest campuses in the country. Students say that they leave residence room doors unlocked. "The only crime of which I am aware is the occasional student who tries to hide alcohol in his or her dorm," says a student. Although criminal offenses are quite rare by all accounts—three burglaries in 2011—campus security provides 24-hour foot and vehicle patrols of the campus. There are emergency telephones located throughout.

The college charges no full-time tuition and requires all students to work at an on-campus job. Room and board, however, averaged $5,900 in 2012–13. The college discourages student borrowing and does not participate in federal educational loan programs. Some 94 percent of students received need-based financial aid, and the average student-loan debt of a recent graduate was only $7,062.

STRONG SUITS	WEAK POINTS
• Students develop a solid work ethic by earning their tuition scholarships. • Most emerge with little debt. • Character education is offered alongside solid academic programs. • Wholesome, decent atmosphere in dorms. • Serious atmosphere among these (mostly) first-generation college students. • A worthwhile Great Books option.	• Not much intellectual diversity on campus. • Very limited foreign language offerings. • Heavy work requirements dampen the traditional college experience.

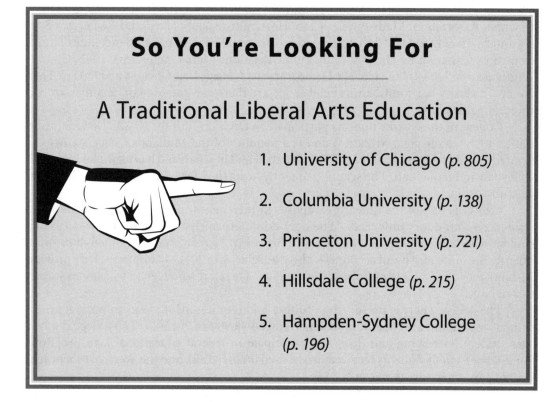

So You're Looking For

A Traditional Liberal Arts Education

1. University of Chicago *(p. 805)*

2. Columbia University *(p. 138)*

3. Princeton University *(p. 721)*

4. Hillsdale College *(p. 215)*

5. Hampden-Sydney College *(p. 196)*

University of Missouri

Columbia, Missouri • www.missouri.edu

Big Brother by the Numbers

The University of Missouri is all about the numbers. The 1,250-acre Botanic Garden campus in Columbia is vast in numbers of students (34,748), degree programs (more than 300, with 50 majors offered online), loyal alumni (262,000), colleges and schools (19), and the variety of clubs and organizations (more than 600). As a major research university, it also brings in big money. As such, it's successful and has been a constant top runner in college rankings since its founding as a land-grant/research university in 1839. But trouble might be on the horizon for Mizzou, with too broad general-education requirements, discontent from both faculty and students, and a Big Brotherish bias-reporting initiative that encourages students to rat each other out for offenses as petty as name-calling.

Academics: Lay low, study hard

The botanic garden campus isn't the only feature to receive accolades at Mizzou. Also praised are the abundance and variety of student groups and the School of Journalism, where the "Missouri Method" facilitates student learning outside the classroom in real-life settings. But complaints on the academic side begin with the general-education requirements.

465

VITAL STATISTICS

Religious affiliation: *none*
Total enrollment: *34,748*
Total undergraduates: *26,996*
SAT CR/Verbal midrange: *510–640*
SAT Math midrange: *530–650*
ACT midrange: *23–28*
Applicants: *20,564*
Applicants accepted: *82%*
Accepted applicants who enrolled: *6,378*
Tuition (general/out of state): *$22,191*
Tuition (in state): *$8,082*
Room and board: *$8,944*
Freshman retention rate: *84%*
Graduation rate (4 yrs.): *45%*
Graduation rate (6 yrs.): *69%*
Courses with fewer than 20 students: *not provided*
Student-faculty ratio: *20:1*
Courses taught by graduate students: *not provided*
Students living on campus: *26%*
Students in fraternities: *22%*
Students in sororities: *28%*
Students receiving need-based financial aid: *59%*
Avg. student-loan debt of a recent graduating class: *$23,588*
Most popular majors: *business/marketing, journalism, health sciences*
Guaranteed housing for 4 years? *no*

Besides the solid basics—algebra, English exposition and argumentation, two writing intensive courses, American history or government, and math reasoning proficiency—the distribution of content requirements, meant to provide "a breadth and depth of knowledge in three areas of study," spread out into so many fields that no two Missou grads are likely to have the same foundation.

However, many of the majors remain strong, in particular those in the science and engineering fields (especially chemistry, physics, and mathematics). Weaker programs are those in the humanities and social sciences. Problems are also reported in the business school.

Many of the large survey and introductory courses are taught by graduate students, or by professors with graduate students leading weekly discussion sessions. There is a push to deliver these classes online, which fits with the university's heavy commitment to research. Since they're at a Carnegie I research university, the school's faculty are under pressure to apply for external grants, and this leads to less time in the classroom. "Teaching takes a backseat to research," one professor complains. "It plays a small role in tenure decisions. The tenure decision is almost entirely based on a candidate's research record." Another professor concurs: "Research and research dollars are the most important key to success. Good teaching is important, but research dollars are more important. Overall, yes, professors teach far too little. Some do not teach at all."

That's not to say Mizzou doesn't have some standout faculty. Professors highly regarded include R. Lee Lyman in anthropology; Norman Land and Kathleen Warner Slane in art history and archaeology; John Adams in chemistry; Michael Podgursky, Jeffrey Milyo, and Myoung Lee in economics; Rachel Harper in English; Robert Collins and John Bullion in history; Dorina Mitrea in mathematics; Michael Budds in music; Etti Naveh-Benjamin and Ines Segert in psychological sciences; Joel Poor in marketing; Holly Higginbotham, Elizabeth Brixey, and Daryl Moen in the School of Journalism; and Justin Dyer in political science.

The history department is also home to exemplary faculty, owning nine of the campus-wide William T. Kemper Fellowship for Teaching Excellence awards. Likewise, the math department is known for excellent pedagogy, particularly in introductory math classes.

Still, weaknesses exist among the faculty. "I wouldn't recommend any professors in the Department of Religious Studies," says a student. "Religious studies is more biased than any other department."

But other disciplines are catching up. "As the older professors are retiring, the new professors tend to be politically correct and intolerant," says a professor. "We have young dumbed-down professors who are now doing the dumbing-down." One student concurs with this assessment, adding, "Younger professors are not as open."

For now, professors and students report that for the most part, the curricula is (surprisingly) nonpolitical. "Even the liberal majority tries to resist pressures from the Left to politicize the curricula," says one professor. That's not to say that departments are entirely free of attempted indoctrination, most notably German and Russian studies, Romance languages and literatures, and women's and gender studies. The education and sociology departments are also criticized as having abandoned Western culture "in favor of political correctness and indoctrination."

Students have their own complaints. "Being a very staunch conservative, it's so tough to be in the journalism school," says one. "They are extremely liberal, and during one lecture my professor made fun of Sarah Palin for almost the entirety of the class. I also took a religious studies course this semester that made my belief in Jesus Christ feel like a minority and one built on myths. One time my professor said my Bible wasn't an accurate source."

CAMPUS POLITICS: RED LIGHT

Don't even think about name-calling at Mizzou. Or sending off-color texts or Facebook postings. You could get reported to the Equity Office through the much-advertised "See It, Hear It, Report It" initiative that encourages students—with abundant flyers around the school and on the university's website—to report any incident of bias. This is all part of the Chancellor's Diversity Initiative, which also hosts forums and seminars on topics such as "African American Women's Efforts to Reshape Gender and Racial Ideologies" and "Chinese Beauty Pageants: Can the Heteronormative Also Be Queer?" But if you want to hold an Affirmative Action Bake Sale, or bring a conservative speaker to campus, or hand out pro-life information, be prepared for furor from your peers and faculty.

"I know there are way more extreme schools than Mizzou, but it has kind of been uncomfortable for me," says an undergrad who has worked with Students for Life. "I feel shunned and unwelcome. Students can be extremely cruel. We've had students sign petitions against us before." Student reaction to the aggressive ideology on campus is muted. "Instead of challenging it in the classroom or elsewhere," reports one professor, "their preferred reaction is to go along."

One positive note is Mizzou's commitment to veterans, with a full-time Veterans Center as part of its Diversity Initiative.

"Campus politics have not been an issue in the political science department," says one professor, "but some students have told me that it is an issue in other classes (particularly English, sociology, and journalism)." Add to that list any course that includes the words "green" or "sustainability," says another professor.

It used to be that the best professors could be found in the Honors College. But these days it seems to be a mixed bag. On the one hand, its 2,000 members enjoy smaller seminars and courses and honors-exclusive extracurriculars (like the Honors Book Club), but its previously strong Great Books component has in recent years been watered down. Another victim has been the Humanities Sequence, which for years featured some of Mizzou's best professors but now has an anemic staff and is under pressure for being, like the Great Books program, Euro-centric and male-centered. "We used to have a fairly decent humanities program, but that has succumbed to the forces of 'social justice' and indoctrination," says a professor.

Students admitted to the Trulaske College of Business should look into the Cornell Leadership Program. Students take field trips to different corporations, receive mentoring from an alumnus and an upper-level business student, participate in a leadership seminar, and attend lectures and presentations by business leaders from around the country as well as luncheons with visiting executives and scholars. English majors are required to take 10 courses, starting with "Writing about Literature." One literature course in each of the following areas is required: Beginning to 1603, 1603 to 1789, 1789 to 1890, and 1890 to the Present. Two courses are required in folklore / oral literature, language, writing and rhetoric, and theory. A senior capstone course is also required. Shakespeare appears only in survey courses and in electives.

> **"Professors teach far too little. Some do not teach at all."** Another teacher says, "We used to have a decent humanities program, but that has succumbed to the forces of 'social justice' and indoctrination."

History students must take 11 courses, including three introductory courses in three of the following areas: United States to 1865, United States since 1865, Europe, and Third World (Africa, Asia, Latin America). In addition, they must take one upper-level course from each of the following areas: Europe, United States, and the Third World. Three upper-level electives are required (examples include "The Ancient World " and "Adoption, Child Welfare and the Family"), as well as one undergraduate seminar and one additional upper-level history course or an undergraduate / honors thesis.

Political science majors must take 10 courses. Requirements include "American Government" and "Introduction to Political Research." Other requirements are one course in comparative government (choices include "The European Union in the Global System" and "Women and Politics"); one course in international affairs ("Genocide, Terrorism and Civil War" and "American Foreign Policies"); and two courses in American politics/public policy ("The Judicial Process" and "Constitution and Civil Liberties"). A course in political theory is recommended but not required.

The vocational opportunities offered by some of the programs are a highlight. Students can help prepare income taxes for families, work at the university-owned TV network affiliate, and cowrite scientific journals. Students in the College of Agriculture, Food, and Natural Resources have the chance to operate a bed and breakfast, or work in the Botanic

Garden, which has 42,000 plants and trees and serves as an outdoor laboratory to professors from 10 academic programs.

There is a surprising lack of foreign language options, given the school's size. Only French, German, Russian, and Spanish are offered as majors. Study-abroad programs are better, with the 60-plus countries including Australia, Brazil, Canada, China, Costa Rica, Ghana, Italy, Japan, Jordan, the Netherlands, Norway, Peru, Rwanda, and the United Kingdom. About 22 percent of graduating seniors have studied abroad.

Student Life: Come to the Zou

The university's hometown of Columbia—pop. 108,500—is in central Missouri and is host to annual events like the Roots 'n Blues 'n BBQ music festival and Art in the Park, a large creative works showcase. Adjacent to campus is the District, a downtown area of shopping and restaurants.

Mizzou's 25 residence halls have a mixture of coed and single-sex floors. Every student living in an MU residence hall is part of either a Thematic Learning Community or a General Learning Community. Mizzou offers more than 100 Freshman Interest Groups, smaller communities within a larger Learning Community. There is agitation on campus to increase the number of unisex bathrooms and to add "gender identity and expression" to MU's nondiscrimination policy.

Football is big. A newcomer to the SEC from the Big 12 Conference—and the only Division I school in the state—the Mizzou Tigers are a home-team favorite at Faurot Field, known as the Zou. Men and women compete in basketball, cross-country, golf, swimming and diving, and track and field. Men also compete in football, wrestling, and baseball. Women compete in softball, soccer, gymnastics, tennis, and volleyball. The multitude of Rec Sports includes four-on-four flag football, basketball, indoor and sand volleyball, racquetball, badminton, soccer, battleship, kickball, inner-tube water polo, and wheelchair relay. The 41 club sports include lacrosse, basketball, soccer, volleyball, Ultimate Frisbee, fencing, dance team, paintball, roller hockey, karate, golf, and ice hockey.

This broad span of activities extends to student organizations. With more than 600 clubs and organizations to choose from, students should have no trouble filling their time. Groups to seek out are College Conservatives Club, College Republicans, and Students for Life.

Religious resources on campus are many and varied. Some are traditional—Catholic Student Association and the reportedly liberal-leaning Newman Center, the Baptist Student Union, Chabad Jewish Student Organization, Episcopal Campus Ministry, Latter-Day

SUGGESTED CORE

1. Classical Studies 3250, Greek and Roman Epic
2. Philosophy 3000, Ancient Western Philosophy
3. Religious Studies 2500/2510, Introduction to Hebrew Bible/Introduction to the New Testament
4. Religious Studies 2630, History of Christian Traditions
5. Philosophy, 4600 Political and Social Philosophy (*closest match*)
6. English 4166, Major Authors, Beginning to 1603 (Shakespeare's Histories and Comedies)
7. History 1100, Survey of American History to 1865
8. History 4580, Intellectual History of Europe, 19th and 20th Centuries

Saint Student Association, Lutheran Student Fellowship—but many more fall in the non-denominational category, such as Cru, *Destino* (a Hispanic-based religious group), Mizzou Students for Christ, Young Life, Mizzou Fellowship of Christian Athletes, and Navigators.

More than 20 percent of students join the school's Greek system—the country's second largest—which comprises 50-plus fraternities and sororities. In recent years troubles have surfaced, with hazing incidents, criminal activity by members, social probation violations, and chapter suspensions.

Nevertheless, Mizzou maintains a largely academic atmosphere. Says one student, "Good academics trump partying for many students." That's not to say Mizzou is overrun by saints. "Sex is very prevalent on campus; you've got thousands of drunk college kids," says another student. "That was also frustrating for me because they hand out condoms and promote sex on campus."

Crime is rare: in 2011 there were 11 forcible sex offenses, 10 burglaries, eight aggravated assaults, and one each of robbery, arson, and motor vehicle theft.

Tuition for native Missourians was a bargain in 2012–13, at only $8,082 (out-of-state students paid $22,191), with room and board of $8,944. Of course, fewer than half of students graduate in four years, so those low prices can be deceiving. Some 59 percent of students get need-based aid, and the average debt of a recent grad is $23,588.

STRONG SUITS	WEAK POINTS
• Good programs in science (especially chemistry, physics, and mathematics) and engineering.	• Options for studying Western civ are few.
• Some fine faculty, especially in history department.	• The best faculty are retiring or retired, being replaced by politicized professors, especially in the humanities.
• Political science department seems non-partisan.	• An Orwellian antiharassment policy strangles free speech.
• Cornell Leadership Program in the School of Business offers real-world experience.	• Ideological faculty dominate some departments, including German and Russian studies, Romance languages and literatures, women's and gender studies, education, and sociology.
• The Botanic Garden is vast and much used by science students.	• Hookup culture prevails on campus.

University of Montana

Missoula, Montana • www.umt.edu

Under the Big Sky

The University of Montana was founded in 1893 and has grown to a midsize institution. The main campus is in an attractive urban setting in Missoula. With 150 student organizations, the NCAA Division I Big Sky Conference athletics program, almost 70 majors, and a strong tradition of participation in outdoor recreation, U of M has much to offer.

Academic Life: Wheat and weeds

At U of M, all students must fulfill requirements in the following categories: English Writing Skills, Mathematics, Modern and Classical Languages or Symbolic Systems, Expressive Arts, Literary and Artistic Studies, Historical and Cultural Studies, Social Sciences, Ethics and Human Values, American and European Perspectives, Indigenous and Global Perspectives, and Natural Sciences (including a lab). The courses that allow students to complete these department requirements vary in quality, but fortunately most of the departments have quite a few solid options, enabling students to build a good foundational education.

The Ethics and Human Values department offers quite a few choices, such as "Roots of Western Ethics," which examines "the origins of Western ethical thinking in the original

VITAL STATISTICS

Religious affiliation: *none*
Total enrollment: *15,669*
Total undergraduates:
13,370
SAT CR/Verbal midrange:
490–600
SAT Math midrange:
490–590
ACT midrange: *21–26*
Applicants: *5,634*
Applicants accepted: *51%*
Accepted applicants who
enrolled: *81%*
Tuition (general/out of
state): *$20,194*
Tuition (in state): *$4,604*
Room and board: *$7,262*
Freshman retention rate:
72%
Graduation rate (4 yrs.): *22%*
Graduation rate (6 yrs.): *48%*
Courses with fewer than 20
students: *47%*
Student-faculty ratio: *20:1*
Courses taught by graduate
students: *not provided*
Students living on campus:
27%
Students in fraternities: *6%*
Students in sororities: *6%*
Students receiving need-
based financial aid: *43%*
Avg. student-loan debt of a
recent graduating class:
$20,532
Most popular majors:
*business/marketing, social
sciences, communications*
Guaranteed housing for 4
years? *no*

writings of Greek and Roman writers," and "Moral Philosophy," which includes "a careful reading of classical texts in the Western tradition." There are also some tares among the wheat, such as "Climate Change Ethics and Policy."

With a comfortable student-faculty ratio of 14 to 1 and moderate class sizes, there is good student-professor interaction. Students comparing notes in an online forum seem to think highly of their teachers. One student writes that she has had "supportive, amazing professors" at U of M, and another says that "the professors are very helpful and extremely available." A student comments that the staff at U of M "have encouraged me to try new things and to take classes that will help me toward figuring out what I want to do." Alarmingly, "The workload in my classes has been relatively light"; however, "most of my teachers have been amazing."

The Davidson Honors College at U of M is open to students of all majors and strives to offer "the intensive learning environment of a small liberal arts and sciences college." With a maximum class size of 20 students, the Honors College allows students to foster a close-knit learning environment and build communication skills through an array of "out-of-classroom experiences" in areas such as Study Abroad, Civic Engagement, Washington Center Internships, and the Wilderness and Civilization Program—up to two of which can be used for honors credit. All honors students must maintain a 3.0 GPA and take a minimum of seven honors courses. Honors requirements include "Introduction to Honors" and "Ways of Knowing," which examines authors such as "Plato, Aristotle, Descartes, Shakespeare, Wordsworth, Darwin, and Freud." With an abundance of material from Joyce, Dante, Aquinas, Augustine, and the Old and New Testaments, it is hard to go wrong. Senior honors students must complete a project including independent research "outside the scope of regular academic courses." The project culminates in a written work and an oral or visual presentation. At this point students will likely be offered scholarship opportunities and the chance to present at local or national conferences.

At U of M, the best offerings are history, geology, biological sciences, psychology, and the liberal studies program. A geography major exclaims, "I love my department! The teachers and TAs are all kind and very helpful. My major offers four different degrees, depending on your interests, and there are lots of opportunities in Missoula and abroad for internships." Another student speaks highly of the journalism department: "The workload can be very tedious sometimes, but I look at it as great experience." Though the work can be demanding, "the classes they require all aid in helping you become successful when you leave this place."

Uneven programs include modern and classical languages, English, and sociology. As one professor tells us, these programs "have mediocre records of research [and] teaching is not strong . . . in the cases of English and sociology, political correctness has run amok."

Requirements for English majors have a good foundational core, including a course on medieval through early modern English lit, a course on American literature, and a course on Shakespeare. One English major says, "I love the English department. Almost immediately, it began to feel more like a family or a group of friends than just class." However, some courses are not so foundational; students are required to take at least one English "diversity" course. Courses that satisfy this requirement are not clearly marked as such, but U of M offers "Native American Literature," "Gay and Lesbian Studies," and "American Women Writers."

CAMPUS POLITICS: GREEN LIGHT

Despite the predominance of left-leaning faculty members and programs, a conservative student can find a place at U of M. As one professor put it, "The campus definitely has a [politically liberal] orthodoxy, but there are outspoken pockets of dissent." Politicized courses are rare, and students typically keep their disputes amicable. One student comments that U of M is "laid back and liberal" and that controversial issues are typically "debated in a civil fashion."

In 2011, after litigation, the university's law school backed down on its policy of forcing religious groups to accept non-believers as members or lose school funding. As *Campus Reform* reports, citing the attorney who represented the Christian group in a suit, "The funding system lacked constitutionally required safeguards to ensure student fees were being distributed neutrally. In fact, the school conceded that the student government had considered the popularity of a group's views. Under the settlement, this will change."

A number of conservative student groups are active, such as the prominent College Republicans chapter, a smaller College Libertarians group, and a chapter of Young Americans for Liberty.

History majors at U of M are required to take either "Western Civilization" I and II or "American History" I and II, depending on the student's chosen track. "American History" I offers a "comprehensive introductory history of Colonial, Revolutionary, and 19th-century America, to 1877." The department has many solid courses from which to choose, and the more politicized choices are not difficult to avoid.

Students majoring in political science are required to take "Introduction to American Government," "Introduction to Comparative Government," "Introduction to International Relations," and "Introduction to Political Theory," along with some eight other classes. Ideologically inclined courses such as "Politics of Social Movements" and "Multicultural

Politics" are outnumbered by strong courses: "Ancient and Medieval Political Philosophy" and "State and Local Government" are among more than 70 options offered.

Politics can intrude into the classroom. Economics, sociology, anthropology, environmental studies, English, and education tend to have more ideological teachers than other disciplines. As one professor puts it, "Some conservative or religious students might feel unwelcome in those departments."

Recommended professors include Linda Frey, Mehrdad Kia, Jeff Wiltse, and Robert Greene in history; Ed Rosenberg in chemistry; George Stanley and Jim Sears in geosciences; and Nat Levtow, Brad Clough, Ruth Vanita, and Stewart Justman in liberal studies. For the most part, students help one another and are generally motivated. As one student reports, "Students here are very driven toward their academics, and there are always people here willing to lend a helping hand if you're having trouble understanding a class."

Students can pursue majors in Chinese, French, German, Greek and Latin, Italian, Japanese, Persian, Russian, Spanish, and Turkish.

U of M also offers a variety of programs and options for students who wish to study abroad. There are faculty-led programs, opportunities offered through partner universities, an International Student Exchange Program, and other opportunities. Destinations include Argentina, Australia, Austria, Belize, Canada, Chile, China, Costa Rica, the Dominican Republic, Fiji, Germany, Greece, India, Ireland, Mexico, New Zealand, Nicaragua, Peru, Russia, Spain, and Vietnam.

Student Life: Live and learn, or party

During downtime, students will find plenty to do on and off campus. One junior says that Missoula has "great local events, like a beautiful weekly farmer's market and 'First Friday,' which is a gallery walk all over the historic downtown, with plenty of free food, wine, and beer." On campus, the student building features "food courts, a game room (also huge with over a dozen pool tables, ping-pong…), a movie theater, and other stuff." Montana is also a great location for wilderness activities and trips through the Outdoor Program.

One student praises her "supportive, amazing professors." Another calls teachers "very helpful and extremely available."

But the central focus is sports. As another student puts it: "Almost everyone turns out to watch the games, and there are huge viewing parties for away games." Another student names football and basketball as "the most popular sports at this university" but notes that "other sports teams and groups are supported, [including] rugby, lacrosse, and volleyball." Writes another student: "If there is a game on that weekend, it is the place to be, and the majority of the students will be cheering in the stands." Additionally, a wide array of other competitive U of M teams exist, including women's soccer, cross-country teams, track and field teams, tennis teams, and a women's volleyball team. Intramural sports include badminton, racquetball, Ultimate Frisbee, soccer, and softball.

There are four sororities and six fraternities at U of M. One student says he finds that Greek life has a beneficient influence: "The chapters at the university of Montana are very respectable and honorable. Each strives to make an impact in the Missoula community...." Members are also "very welcoming to newcomers." Another student commented that Greek students "always put on parties." Though the presence of these Greek partiers "doesn't completely dominate the school," students might need to make an effort to keep on track with their studies. A recent graduate comments that "the party atmosphere is very apparent. It's sometimes hard to stay focused on your education with so much going on in your social life."

Living arrangements offer students both on-campus dorms and off-campus "villages." There are a few different options for on-campus housing, including traditional dorms, four-person suites, and Living Learning Communities that allow students to live near others with similar interests. The Living Learning Communities include Chemistry, Honors, Global Leadership, Intercultural, and substance-free options. There are two single-sex dorms on campus: Elrod for men and Turner for women. Other floors on campus are coed with single-sex bathrooms. While there are no official visiting hours, only guests of the same sex can stay overnight in a student's dorm room. One student suggests being selective when choosing one's housing. Dorm life can be "good, but . . . [it] depends on the dorm you are in . . . no matter what, you will make friends, and the RAs are very helpful and nice." Another student says he finds the dorms "a little cramped" but adds that, "with a few arrangements, you can open the rooms up quite a bit."

There are a number of campus ministries and religious student organizations on campus, including a Catholic campus ministry associated with the local Christ the King Church, a Lutheran student fellowship, an active chapter of Cru (Campus Crusade for Christ), and a number of independent evangelical student ministries.

In 2011 there were nine reported on-campus rapes, five counts of aggravated assault, three motor vehicle thefts, one count of arson, and 36 liquor-law violations. Crime does not seem to be of much concern to students. As one student comments: "I have really no safety concerns, except for theft. A lot of bikes get stolen just because they are not locked up. I have not heard of any crime on campus this year." Another student reports that "U of M's campus has a number you can call and an officer in a golf cart will escort you anywhere on campus so you don't have to walk in the dark alone. . . . I haven't felt threatened by anyone, and the campus police have taken care of several problems in my dorm effectively."

SUGGESTED CORE

1. Classics 155, Survey of Greek and Roman Literature
2. Philosophy 261Y, History of Ancient Philosophy
3. Religious Studies 204/205, Introduction to the Hebrew Bible (Old Testament)/Introduction to the New Testament
4. Religious Studies 335/336, Western Religious Thought I/II
5. Political Science 453, Modern Political Theory
6. English Literature 320, Shakespeare
7. History 101, American History I
8. History 339, European Social and Intellectual History: The 19th Century

University of Montana

The University of Montana is a real bargain for local students, who in 2012–13 paid tuition of only $4,604 (out-of-state students paid more than four times that, at $20,194), with room and board an affordable $7,262. Only 43 percent of students received need-based financial aid, and the average student-loan debt of a recent graduating class was $20,532.

STRONG SUITS	WEAK POINTS
• Most of the classes that fulfill general-ed requirements are fairly solid—and some are excellent.	• Not all classes are rigorous and demanding.
• An excellent Honors College, with some courses focused on the Great Books.	• Weak teaching and political correctness in some departments, such as languages, English, and sociology. Other politicized disciplines include economics, anthropology, and environmental studies.
• Moderate class sizes—and small ones in honors.	• As a student reports, "The party atmosphere is very apparent."
• Good programs in history, geology, biological sciences, psychology, journalism, and liberal studies.	
• A free, open exchange of ideas and limited politics in the classroom.	

University of Nebraska–Lincoln

Lincoln, Nebraska • www.unl.edu

Make It Happen

The University of Nebraska–Lincoln was founded in 1869, just two years after Nebraska became a state. The university has grown alongside its namesake. Today it is the flagship of the University of Nebraska system, with an undergraduate population of just under 20,000, 150 majors to choose from, 40 fraternities and sororities to join, and an NCAA Division I Big Ten Conference athletics program.

Academic Life: The professor's door is open

UNL's general-education requirements are met through a program called "Achievement-Centered Education," or ACE for short. According to the school, this program is "outcomes focused" and strives to equip students with what "all undergraduate students—irrespective of their majors and career aspirations—[should] know or be able to do upon graduation." Students must take "ACE 1" through "ACE 10" to achieve UNL's goals of developing "skills," "knowledge," and "responsibilities," finally "integrating" all three into a final "creative or scholarly product."

Good, strong courses like "Rhetoric as Argument," "Public Speaking," and "Ancient

VITAL STATISTICS

Religious affiliation: *none*
Total enrollment: *24,593*
Total undergraduates: *19,345*
SAT CR/Verbal midrange: *510–660*
SAT Math midrange: *520–670*
ACT midrange: *22–28*
Applicants: *10,022*
Applicants accepted: *59%*
Accepted applicants who enrolled: *69%*
Tuition (general/out of state): *$19,230*
Tuition (in state): *$6,480*
Room and board: *$8,648*
Freshman retention rate: *84%*
Graduation rate (4 yrs.): *32%*
Graduation rate (6 yrs.): *67%*
Courses with fewer than 20 students: *39%*
Student-faculty ratio: *21:1*
Courses taught by graduate students: *not provided*
Students living on campus: *41%*
Students in fraternities: *17%*
Students in sororities: *20%*
Students receiving need-based financial aid: *60%*
Avg. student-loan debt of a recent graduating class: *$21,960*
Most popular majors: *business/marketing, engineering, family/consumer sciences*
Guaranteed housing for 4 years? *no*

Rome" can be found, but useless or harmful courses such as "Introduction to Lesbian and Gay Literature," "Managing Diversity in Organizations," and "Philosophy of Feminism" also count.

The average class size at UNL is 28 students. Most classes are taught by professors rather than graduate assistants. As one alum recalled, "I can't remember more than one or two classes I was in [where] the teacher wasn't a professor." One graduate commented, "If you are involved in campus organizations and make an effort to get to know your professors and grad students, you will receive the individual attention you desire." Another student, a sociology major, wrote that she finds the professors very supportive and accessible: "I enjoy the personal relationships I have developed with the faculty because I know I can ask them questions about anything at any time. The professors at UNL are extremely kind and have an open-door policy. Professors have no problem with students dropping by their office just to talk about how their semester is going or to ask questions about graduate school or about class, for example."

UNL's selective honors program has an average of 18 students per class, its own dormitory and computer lab, and a research requirement culminating in the completion of a senior thesis. The honors program gives students the opportunity to "explore new knowledge through research, to participate actively in a process of discovery, and appreciate and respect a diversity of opinions." Courses vary widely, and most are built around independent research or topics that differ from one semester to the next. Among some slighter courses, such as "Women Making Music" and "Clothing and Human Behavior," better options appear: "Rhetoric and Reading," "English Authors after 1800," "Western Civilization to 1715," "American History to 1877," and "Political Philosophy." If you are attending UNL, honors seems like the only path to a solid liberal arts education.

In online forums, students boast of the computer science, biology, psychology, prenursing, and chemical engineering departments. One senior gives her own list of recommendations: "My favorite classes are always sociology courses, English courses, dance classes— including the history of dance and introduction to dance history, dance injury, and prevention/kinesiology, and I also enjoyed taking the science of food and geography." Another student speaks highly of the music education major, saying, "The instructors are all fantastic, and I'm having a wonderful experience." When it comes to professors, says one student, "I have not met one who is not willing to help students, and multiple teachers are world [renowned] in their fields." Another student reports: "My professors always want to help however they can and encourage students to visit them in office hours."

Another student warns that academic advising at UNL can be arbitrary: "If there are choices to fulfill a requirement, the class is often chosen based on how it will fit into a schedule, as opposed to the content of the course and how choosing such plays a significant role in the path the student wishes to pursue." One student warns against some departments: "The education department is awful. If you're considering attending UNL for the College of Education and Human Sciences, go somewhere else. I wish someone would have told me that four years ago."

CAMPUS POLITICS: GREEN LIGHT

While some of the university's academics may be quite left leaning, UNL is renowned for its protection of free speech on campus. It is one of only 15 universities nationwide to receive the highest rating from the Foundation for Individual Rights on Campus. Students seeking to speak their minds on UNL's campus will find that they have the institutional protection to do so. In addition to the aforementioned student religious groups, conservative students will also find like-minded peers at the university's vital and active College Republicans chapter. For those who are less politically inclined, the Classic Literature Club, a student group dedicated to discussing and promoting the Western canon, might also be of interest.

English majors must complete 12 courses in seven different categories: Introduction to English Studies; Linguistics; Writing and/or Rhetoric; Literary or Rhetorical Theory; Historical Literature Core (period choices include British literature, literature before 1800, and American literature); Literature in the Context of Culture, Ethnicity, and/or Gender; and Capstone Course and Concentration. "Shakespeare" is offered but optional. Indeed, the only obligatory course is the aforementioned "Introduction to English Studies." Some solid options are "British Authors to 1800," "Introduction to Medieval Literature," and "American Literature before 1865." Courses best left alone include "Introduction to Lesbian and Gay Literature" and "Introduction of Women's Literature."

History majors at UNL must take 10 or 11 courses, but one on American history is optional. Required courses include "The Historian's Craft" and "Capstone Seminar." Two classes in American or Canadian history (of any period) are also required, along with two in Latin American, Asian, and/or African history; two in European history; two in the pre-1800 period (anywhere on earth); and several upper-level seminars. There are some fine courses to be found in this department, including "American History to 1877," "Western Civilizations to 1715," and "Early Christianity," alongside "Women and Gender in U.S. History" and "Women and Work in USA History."

Students must take 10 classes in the political science department for a major. Specific courses required are "Power and Politics in America" (an "Introduction to American

Blue Collar Ivy

government and politics"), "International Relations," and a senior capstone course, along with other requirements. Some good choices are "Politics in State and Local Governments," "Political Ideas," and the classically based "Justice and the Good Life." Some courses better avoided might be "Challenges to the State" ("Gendered notions of the state, national security, women's rights, and humanitarian intervention") and "Women and Politics."

Some UNL professors come highly recommended, including Gina Matkin in agricultural leadership, education, and communication; Cheryl Bailey in biochemistry; Thomas "Jack" Morris in biological sciences; Rhonda Fuelberth in music; James Garza and Parks Coble in history and ethnic studies; Amy Goodburn and Joy Castro in English; and Jordan Stump in modern languages and literatures.

> A sociology major wrote, "I enjoy the personal relationships I have developed with the faculty. The professors at UNL have an open-door policy."

Student zeal varies from department to department. One student believes that the student body "is very centered around academics" and another student feels that his classmates are generally supportive of one another: "Students at UNL really are not competitive in classes. . . . If a student has a question, he or she knows they can ask any class member for help and receive assistance without being yelled at or demeaned." This kind of friendliness can be especially important in times of crisis. An upperclassman comments, "I found the curriculum at UNL to be very demanding." This student has "had to work harder than I have ever worked before for good grades (which have always come easy to me)."

UNL has a foreign language requirement and offers majors in French, Classics, and religious studies (one department), German, Japanese, Russian, and Spanish. Courses are also offered in other languages, including Arabic and Portuguese.

Through programs led by its own faculty or in partnership with other schools, UNL offers many locations where students can study abroad, including Australia, Brazil, Costa Rica, France, India, Italy, Japan, Norway, South Africa, and the United Kingdom.

Student Life: Choose wisely

UNL is home to the Cornhuskers, an NCAA Division I competitor and a member of the Big Ten Conference. While UNL's football team is certainly the major attraction, the school also fields competitive teams ranging from men's baseball, basketball, and gymnastics to women's softball, volleyball, and bowling. "Football is the number one priority of this university, at least in my experience," an enthusiastic student reports. "I have lived in Nebraska my whole life, and it still doesn't cease to amaze me the way this state obsesses over the Huskers. If you come to UNL, expect to be a Husker fan or be shunned." Writes a UNL senior: "I love football Saturdays. The excitement on college game day is like nothing else." Besides sports, there are many other clubs and organizations for students to join. This student suggests that "joining an activity is the best way to meet people, especially if you are an out-of-state student." The recreation center, one student reports, "is amazing. They have an indoor football field, lap pool, weight room, rock wall, and tons of other cool stuff, including the injury care and prevention facilities."

While some students call UNL a "party school," others differ. As one sophomore mechanical engineering major puts it, "I think it is grossly inaccurate.... There are plenty of other opportunities." One student even feels that the lack of alcohol on campus "makes for some fairly boring weekends sometimes." Another student comments, "You have to have connections with Greeks or organizations to find parties." Greeks do indeed make their presence known on campus, but mostly in a positive way. Those seeking a university with a vibrant and institutionally embraced Greek life will likely find it at UNL. There are more than 40 fraternities and sororities on campus. As one student put it, "The Greek life is a very positive community at UNL, and I feel like even non-Greeks get [along] very well with Greeks. I am not Greek, but I have plenty of friends who have pledged, and we all get along great!"

Housing at UNL ranges from traditional residential halls to suites and apartments. As one student reports, there are "always events happening in the residence halls. The housing department does a great job in making the buildings more of a community rather than just a place to live." Female students have the option of living in the Love Memorial Co-op, while the rest of the dormitories on campus are coed. In all traditional dormitories, common bathrooms are single sex. While there are no specific visiting hours, each overnight guest must be the same sex as his or her host and may not stay for more than four days in one month. One student reports that "Harper Shram Smith or Abel are the two most social dorms," and another student warns that Abel is often called "the zoo." However," the student adds, "I met many good friends and had many good times there." Regarding promiscuity, one student states: "UNL is not quite as sex-crazed as many other large public universities, but it's not entirely celibate, either. Campus legend says that if a girl goes through her four years at UNL without hooking up, then one of the school's beloved columns will topple. As of today, they're all standing."

By way of antidote, there are a number of campus chaplaincies of various denominations at UNL: Cru (Campus Crusade for Christ), a Catholic student fellowship associated with nearby St. Thomas Aquinas Church, an Orthodox Christian fellowship, a Lutheran student organization, a Presbyterian student organization, a Nazarene student organization, a Latter-Day Saint student organization, a Mennonite student organization, and a number of independent Evangelical student fellowships and ministries.

In the latest crime report (from 2011), there was a total of six forcible sexual assaults, eight on-campus burglaries, three car thefts, and more than 300 liquor-law violations

SUGGESTED CORE

1. Classics 180, Classical Mythology
2. Philosophy 231, History of Ancient Philosophy
3. English 341, The Bible as Literature
4. Philosophy 336, Ethics: Ancient and Medieval
5. Philosophy 221, Political Philosophy
6. English 430A, Shakespeare I
7. History 110, American History to 1877
8. Philosophy 333, History of Philosophy, 19th Century

Nebraska

throughout campus and the residence halls. One junior reports that "at UNL and in Lincoln people just maintain a higher standard of conduct most of the time. . . . I feel safe in Lincoln—the corruption, drugs, gang violence, guns, rapes, and bar fights from other larger cities hasn't come here yet the way it has to other places." Another student agrees: "I don't see the campus police that much on campus, but I feel that it is fairly safe here. In my dorm, I don't always have to lock the door for the fear of people stealing my things. . . . After I finish my night class, I feel safe walking alone back to my dorm. Be on the lookout for bikers: they are everywhere and accidents are prone to happen."

The University of Nebraska is a real bargain for local students, who paid $6,480 in tuition in 2012–13 (out-of-state students paid $19,230), and $8,648 for room and board. Some 60 percent of students received need-based financial aid, and the average student-loan debt of a recent graduating class was $21,960.

STRONG SUITS	WEAK POINTS
• Attentive, helpful professors. • A free exchange of ideas, with very limited injection of politics into the classroom. • Cooperative (not cutthroat) students who lean on each other. • A worthy honors program. • Sane dorm visitation policies.	• Shaky general-ed requirements and silly classes that fulfill them. • Unhelpful advising and a low (32 percent) four-year graduation rate. • Lax requirements for English and history majors who can (respectively) skip Shakespeare and most of U.S. history.

University of Nevada

Reno, Nevada • www.unr.edu

What Happens in Reno . . .

What does the University of Nevada, Reno, want prospective students to know? That it's not Vegas. For one thing, it's only six miles from the California border (and an hour from Lake Tahoe), and about seven hours from Nevada's gambling mecca. Reno is a tourist town, and students at UNR are more interested in skiing and kayaking (okay, and academics) than in playing the slots. And students probably ought to know that it's a Tier I school with a strong academic program full of perks—like one of the largest study-abroad programs in the nation and a fantastic library system—and professors who have won major grants and are more than happy to invite students on research expeditions. And price. Students really, really need to know about the price.

Academics: Solid to the Core

The university's core curriculum will vary somewhat by student (math and writing placement are based on testing) and by individual college requirements, but the basic core is refreshingly traditional and steeped in basic skills as well as the humanities and sciences. The requirements are divided into eight categories: Writing, Math, Social Science, Fine

483

VITAL STATISTICS

Religious affiliation: *none*
Total enrollment: *18,227*
Total undergraduates: *12,415*
SAT CR/Verbal midrange:
 470–580
SAT Math midrange:
 480–600
ACT midrange: *21–26*
Applicants: *7,753*
Applicants accepted: *82%*
Accepted applicants who
 enrolled: *37%*
Tuition (general/out of
 state): *$20,513*
Tuition (in state): *$6,603*
Room and board: *$10,196*
Freshman retention rate:
 79%
Graduation rate (4 yrs.): *17%*
Graduation rate (6 yrs.): *37%*
Courses with fewer than 20
 students: *40%*
Student-faculty ratio: *29:1*
Courses taught by graduate
 students: *not provided*
Students living on campus:
 16%
Students in fraternities: *not
 provided*
Students in sororities: *not
 provided*
Students receiving need-
 based financial aid: *55%*
Avg. student-loan debt of a
 recent graduating class:
 $18,000
Most popular majors: *health
 professions, construction
 trades, business/marketing*
Guaranteed housing for 4
 years? *no*

Arts, Natural Science, Diversity, Core Humanities, and a Capstone.

The Core Humanities requirements are especially impressive: each student must complete "Ancient and Medieval Cultures," "The Modern World," and "American Experiences and Constitutional Change"—all of which are a breath of fresh mountain basin air compared to the humanities at most universities.

Advising is strongly encouraged, and students should meet with their advisors each semester prior to registration. A key facet of the advising program is the concierge service, which can help students remedy registration snafus such as being unable to get a course needed for graduation.

Tutoring, writing, and math centers are available to help students on both a walk-in and appointment basis.

Besides the core curriculum, the university has a lot to recommend itself. Stronger departments include business, chemistry, geography, hydrologic sciences, environmental sciences, nursing (said to be extremely competitive and difficult to gain admission to), psychology, English, biology, history, and political science. Engineering should not be overlooked. "It does a great job preparing you for the workforce," says one student. "You're required to take communications classes that prepare you for interviewing and interacting with colleagues. Plus, the school hosts networking events and interview practice sessions."

Also noteworthy is the Reynolds School of Journalism. A complete curriculum revision to focus on new media technology and a vast renovation has rendered the traditionally solid program even stronger.

The Mackay School of Earth Sciences and Engineering—which includes the popular mining, metallurgical, and geo-engineering degrees—and the College of Agriculture, Biotechnology and Natural Resources deserve accolades as well. Although the latter has only 8 percent of the undergraduate population, it has 25 percent of the university's National Merit Scholars. Researchers in the College of Engineering, home to the large-scale structures laboratory, lead the nation in seismological and large-scale structures testing and modeling.

The university also has 12,500 acres of field laboratories and research areas across the state, used to great extent by professors and students for research. Another stellar resource is the library system, especially the Mathewson-IGT Knowledge Center (don't call it a library), which includes what the university calls "a computer lab on steroids."

The Honors College is also a highlight, according to professors, with benefits including smaller classes, special residential living, and the ability to earn honors credits through service learning or "significant scholarly activities and academic programming." Successful applicants generally have unweighted GPAs of 3.65 or higher and ACT or SAT I scores above 28 or 1220, respectively.

Which brings us to a profile of the average UNR student: SAT scores for Critical/Reading and Math in are the 470–580 midrange, SAT Math in the 480–600 midrange, and the ACT midrange was 21–26. Not terribly low, but not terribly high, either. The good news is that 82 percent of applicants are accepted.

Two troubling statistics emerge from the finer picture of the student body: The four-year graduation rate is only 17 percent, and the student-faculty ratio is a whopping 29:1. Compare that to the national average of 15:1. Despite this, a student says, "If you're willing to go in and talk to professors, they're willing to help you, and even develop friendships with you." Another student commends professors' office hours and willingness to

CAMPUS POLITICS: GREEN LIGHT

The atmosphere at UNR is described as centrist. "For the most part, teachers keep their politics to themselves" says a student. Another student says, "We'll talk politics in classes, mostly in humanities, but it's always a very polite academic discourse."

College Republicans and College Democrats alike are active and come together periodically for debates. The College Republicans especially are reported to be a diverse group with a broad base across campus and well-received events. The Foundation for Individual Rights in Education (FIRE) reported in 2012 that in the past, UNR's policy designated "only four small or remote areas on UNR's campus as 'public forum' areas, and explicitly deemed the rest of the campus a non-public forum. Student activists, working with FIRE and the ACLU of Nevada, protested this unconstitutional policy and proposed a new policy that would open the public university campus to free speech. The students worked closely with UNR administrators, and were able to introduce a policy that designates the entire campus—save the interior of university buildings—as an 'open public forum area.'"

help, and indeed, despite the ratio and seeming dearth of professors, 69 percent of classes have 29 or fewer students. One of the university's long-range goals is to have 70 percent of a student's credit hours taught by faculty with terminal degrees. Given that most schools have higher percentages already, it's not encouraging that UNR sees this as a distant dream.

UNR has a policy that any class with more than 80 students can be counted as two courses for the faculty member. This creates time for research—an increasing piece of professors' lives, although they downplay its significance. "Our department encourages research," says a political science professor, "but not at the expense of teaching."

Recommended professors are Paul Mitchell and Todd Felts in journalism; Robert Metts and Mark Nichols in business; Amit Saini and Charlie Nazemian in math; Dean Hinitz and Holly Hazlett-Stevens in psychology; Kenneth Peak in criminal justice; Vincent

Catalano in chemistry; Jennifer Hollander in biology; Stacy Gordon Fisher, Erik Herzik, and John Marini in political science; Shaun Grekor in philosophy; Barry Peterson in history; Thomas Hertweck in English; and Teresa Wriston in anthropology.

On UNR's weaker side are programs whose funding was hit hard by the state legislature, which funds the university. In recent years, several departments—Classics among them—have vanished. Philosophy and foreign languages were also hurt, and there are reports of administrative turmoil in math and mining.

The English major requires some solid courses. Regardless of specialization (Literature, Writing, Language and Linguistics, and English for Secondary Education), all English majors must take "Introduction to Language" (or "Introduction to Language and Literary Expression"), "Writing about Literature," and "Introduction to Literary Theory and Criticism." "Shakespeare: Comedies and Romances" is just an elective. Literature specialists must also take surveys in transatlantic literature, plus one additional course (options include "Principles of Modern Grammar" and a course on Chaucer). An additional seven electives are required. Writing specialists must also take "Advanced Nonfiction Writing" and eight electives. Language and Linguistics specialists have nine required courses including the aforementioned. Electives include "Drama before Shakespeare," surveys of British literature, "Studies in Postcolonial Literature and Theory," and "Topics in Multicultural Literature."

History majors, who must take 12 courses in the discipline, can construct a focused path through American history underscored by solid courses in European and non-Western history (such as "Renaissance Science and the Secrets of Nature," "Studies in European Intellectual History," and "World War II Goes to the Movies"). However, even with the required two courses in U.S. or European history, it would be all too easy to take an aimless journey that touches on narrow geographical points in time. Cases in point are "Pathologies of Daily Life in Modern China," "Modern Ireland and National Identity," and "History of Sports in America." At least two courses must come from non-U.S. and non-European courses (ancient, African, Asian, Middle Eastern, or Latin American) and the other six from electives.

> UNR's general-ed program "does a great job preparing you for the workforce," says one student.

The political science department is reported as having a small but very solid faculty. Majors are required to take "American Politics: Process and Behavior." Ten courses are required for the major with at least one in each of the following areas: American Government ("Constitutional Law: Separation of Powers and Federalism" and "The American Women's Movement"); Public Administration and Public Policy ("The Judicial Process" and "Identity Politics in the United States"); Political Theory ("Introduction to Political Philosophy" and "Jurisprudence"); Comparative Politics ("Foreign Policies of Major Powers" and "Politics of Sub-Saharan Africa); and International Relations ("Natural Resource Policy").

The university offers majors in French and Spanish, and minors in Japanese studies, Basque studies, international affairs, and Latin American studies.

Another boast of the university is its study-abroad program, one of the nation's largest.

Study destinations include Australia, Brazil, Chile, Costa Rica, Cuba (!), France, Germany, Ghana, Ireland, Israel, Japan, New Zealand, Norway, Scotland, and Thailand.

Student Life: Location, location, location

Some of the highlights of matriculating at UNR aren't on campus at all. As a real estate agent might say, it's all about location—and UNR has a great one. One professor describes the environs by saying, "Start with amazing and go from there." The campus is nestled at the base of the Sierra Nevada mountain range just one hour away from 15 world-class skiing and snowboarding resorts, Lake Tahoe, hundreds of mountain biking and hiking trails including the 165-mile Tahoe Rim Trail, and the Truckee River, home to one of the country's top outdoor white-water kayak parks. A campus Rental Shop makes getting outdoors easy, with rental options for inflatable kayaks, personal flotation devices, wet suits, and cross-country ski equipment.

> ### SUGGESTED CORE
>
> 1. Humanities 201, Ancient and Medieval Cultures (*closest match*)
> 2. Philosophy 211, Introduction to Ancient Philosophy
> 3. English 484A, The Bible as Literature
> 4. Philosophy 212, Introduction to Medieval Philosophy
> 5. Political Science 227, Introduction to Political Philosophy
> 6. English 271, Introduction to Shakespeare
> 7. History 101, United States
> 8. Philosophy 313, 19th-Century Philosophy

UNR is very much a commuter college. Only 17 percent of students graduate in four years, and only 37 percent have graduated at the six-year mark. Nevada also has a large number of part-time students. What this means is that only 62 percent of freshmen, and 16 percent of undergrads overall, live on campus.

Those who do seem happy. "Dorm life was fun—there were lots of events but it was still friendly to academic study, and the RAs were very helpful," says a student. "Dorm living is nice, safe, and comfortable," says another.

If the 13 fraternities and 10 sororities don't feel like home, students have numerous on-campus living options. One of the more unusual ones is Manzanita Hall, a Victorian-style residence for women, especially those who are academically oriented. For hard-studying men there is the turn-of-the-century-style Lincoln Hall. Those looking for a substance-free lifestyle should check out the apartment-style coed White Pine Hall. In coed Sierra Hall—for students in their second year of residence hall living or who are 20 or over—each room has its own bathroom and shower.

The Nevada Living Learning Community houses 320 students in several Living Learning Communities, including Honors Residential Scholars Community, WISE (Women in Science and Engineering), communities for students in business, journalism, engineering, education, prenursing, and science, and a hall open to first-year students with an undeclared major. The university also has family housing options.

Even with so many commuters, the 255-acre campus is reportedly an active place, with nearly 300 student groups—among them College Republicans and InterVarsity Christian Fellowship—and replete with campus activities like movies, lectures, and concerts. Cheering on the Wolf Pack at athletic events are the Blue Crew, a group of spirited—and sometimes wild—students who show up to give UNR teams a home-court advantage in the Lawlor Events Center.

Speaking of athletics, as a member of the Western Athletic Conference, Nevada boasts perennially competitive athletic teams from football to softball. The Wolf Pack competes in men's and women's basketball, golf, rifle, and tennis, men's football and baseball, and women's cross-country, soccer, swimming and diving, track and field, and volleyball.

Intramural Sports include dodgeball, flag football, soccer, softball, basketball, volleyball, and much more. Students can also drop by the Lombardi Recreation Center for an Olympic-size pool, weight room, basketball, handball, and tennis courts, as well as exercise classes including Pilates, kickboxing, boxing, and yoga.

For the religiously inclined, InterVarsity and FCA are popular, active groups. The Catholic Newman Center offers plenty of social activities, but other university-affiliated groups are few. The Mormon church maintains a heavy presence with three facilities in Reno.

Alcohol is allowed on campus only with the permission of Student Life Services, and only at events where all participants are age 21 or older. One's person is mostly safe on campus, if not always your stuff: in 2011, the school reported just one robbery, but 28 burglaries and three stolen cars.

UNR was a bargain for in-state students at $6,603 in 2012–13, but out-of-staters paid more than triple as much, $20,513. Room and board were a modest $10,196. UNR has tuition-reduction programs for students from California and other Western states, but Nevada's legislature wants to restrict these. Some 55 percent of students get need-based financial aid, and the average student-loan debt of a recent graduating class was $18,000.

STRONG SUITS	WEAK POINTS
• Excellent core requirements in the humanities. • Very good study-abroad options. • Extensive opportunities for students to join faculty in research. • Mostly apolitical classrooms and campus. • Solid courses offered in English, history, political science.	• Crushing student-faculty ratio (29 to 1). • Humanities suffering under budget cuts, and administrative turmoil in math and mining. • Mostly a commuter school. • Fewer than half of students graduate in six years.

Blue Collar Ivy

University of New Hampshire

Durham, New Hampshire • www.unh.edu

Snug in the Woods

The University of New Hampshire is a land-, sea-, and space-grant university. It enjoys a comfortable size, with fewer than 15,000 students. At the main campus in Durham, students will find themselves surrounded by the picture-book New England countryside. The small-town atmosphere surrounding the university, together with a relatively moderate student population, provide a good environment for the intellectually curious or professionally ambitious student.

Academic Life: Stay on target

The University of New Hampshire's curriculum consists in a writing course, degree and major requirements, and what is called "The Discovery Program." This medley does not by any means guarantee a good grounding, since UNH's general-education requirements can be fulfilled by a wide variety of courses. But a student can arrange a great education for himself by selecting the excellent courses that can be found buried among the weeds. One student reports that "I have had to work hard to make sure I get the classic liberal arts education I desire, but I am definitely obtaining it."

VITAL STATISTICS

Religious affiliation: *none*
Total enrollment: *15,172*
Total undergraduates: *12,609*
SAT CR/Verbal midrange: *500–590*
SAT Math midrange: *510–620*
ACT midrange: *23–27*
Applicants: *17,344*
Applicants accepted: *74%*
Accepted applicants who enrolled: *23%*
Tuition (general/out of state): *$25,380*
Tuition (in state): *$12,060*
Room and board: *$9,452*
Freshman retention rate: *87%*
Graduation rate (4 yrs.): *64%*
Graduation rate (6 yrs.): *77%*
Courses with fewer than 20 students: *41%*
Student-faculty ratio: *18:1*
Courses taught by graduate students: *5%*
Students living on campus: *59%*
Students in fraternities: *7%*
Students in sororities: *10%*
Students receiving need-based financial aid: *63%*
Avg. student-loan debt of a recent graduating class: *$35,168*
Most popular majors: *business/marketing, social sciences, health professions*
Guaranteed housing for 4 years? *no*

It is also easy to graduate with a poor education. A student warns that there are departments and programs that are merely "centers of ideological reeducation and indoctrination with NO academic substance whatsoever. Conservative or religious students, students interested in critical thought, and students who believe it is important to question their professors" must take care to avoid these options.

With most classes at a cozy size, students can seek guidance from their professors with very little hassle. "With the exception of freshman English seminars," a student writes, "I do not believe graduate students teach any classes." Though the student-faculty ratio is 18 to 1, nearly half the classes at the University of New Hampshire have fewer than 20 students. One student says, "Most professors at UNH are highly accessible...I have been successful in finding professors who take an interest in my life and care about my future."

There is an honors program, which aims at a more in-depth approach to course work, emphasizing independent research and with higher writing intensity. It offers honors-designated housing, special events, smaller classes, its own study-abroad programs—and recruiting for post-graduation academic and employment opportunities.

One student remarks: "In liberal arts, the best departments are easily political science and Classics and sections of communications, history, and psychology." The Department of Political Science is "perhaps the most sensible department within the College of Liberal Arts." A professor says that his department "lacks people in the American government field" and has drifted in focus from "the basics that an undergraduate wanting to learn about...American politics really needs." But "in the American politics side, we do a really good job with the resources we have."

A student tells us that Classics "might be the most [academically] serious in scope" of all the departments, and a professor says it is "really phenomenally good."

One professor remarks that the communications department overall "isn't very good," and a student suggests it "has its fair share of left-wing lecturers devoted to teaching their students how to deconstruct reality television for racist and sexist undertones." There are, however, some communications professors who emphasize the First Amendment in class and who focus on the more traditional merits of "American political rhetoric."

A professor points to the faculty of the history department as "quite good," and a student remarks on the seriousness of several teachers. There are, however, many history courses to be avoided. If a course sounds politicized, it probably is.

Students also speak highly of the psychology department and the Business School, while a professor points to both the business and the engineering schools as the real "bastions of conservatism at UNH."

Some departments are altogether toxic to intellectual growth, and one student warns against "women's studies, queer studies, African American studies, and another interdisciplinary minor program called 'Race, Culture, and Power.'" This student is especially emphatic about avoiding women's studies courses at UNH, "even to fulfill one of the many general-education requirements that the department's courses meet." In these courses, students are graded merely "on the basis of their politics and their ability to regurgitate the opinions of their instructor." Similarly, the student warns that professors in the English department have a tendency to be "more interested in teaching film theory and 'chick lit' than Shakespeare and basic composition."

CAMPUS POLITICS: GREEN LIGHT

The political atmosphere on the campus is said to be mixed. A student observes that, while political debate on campus "is certainly dominated by the Left (in the administration, on the faculty, in the student government, on the student newspaper's editorial board, etcetera)," there are nevertheless "a number of conservatives and libertarians on campus." Students can find a "strong and tight-knit right-wing minority that will only let so much go on before sounding the alarm." A "thick skin" is required of any very "outspoken conservative student," but such a student "will never be short of friends." Even among leftist professors, there are many who will respect their students' conservative opinions.

Groups on campus include the College Republicans, Young Americans for Liberty, and the Catholic Student Organization. The most active of these groups, and the most effective, is probably the Young Americans for Liberty. This group has been active since 2008 and has hosted Rep. Ron Paul as a guest speaker. According to the *New Hampshire*, an independent student newspaper, this group does not mind crossing swords with the UNH College Democrats.

UNH is also developing a new major in sustainability studies, with courses "on the environmental impact of prostitution and the Roman Empire's contribution to climate change," which a student says will only "allow ideologues to indoctrinate students."

Undergraduates studying for an English major can graduate without ever having studied Shakespeare. On the other hand, they are required to take a course that addresses "Race, the Construction of Race, and Race Theory." But there are solid English courses to choose. It might be best to stick with the few Shakespeare and the many British and American literature courses offered.

History majors can graduate with no knowledge of U.S. history before the mid-20th century. The course listing is riddled with investigations of trendy issues such as "American

Environmental History." Solid American history is available, however, and some courses strike us as being particularly strong, including "Through Their Eyes: The History of the Civil War from Primary Sources" and "Revolutionary America, 1750–1788."

Political science majors are required to take 10 courses in their subject, including two classes in American politics and one on America in foreign affairs. Among these requirements is an "Introduction to American Government," in which students are taught the structure and nature of American government and the challenges it has faced since its founding. This department is said to be very strong, regardless of the (leftist) politics of most faculty. One conservative professor tells us that the college "gets a tremendous amount of visibility" in the weeks and months surrounding elections and nominations "because you have the New Hampshire primary here." This historic, recurring event gives faculty a chance to help "students who want to have careers in government." This professor says "our ability to know the people on the campaigns over the years and to get people placed into campaigns has lead to very, very rapid rises of a lot of our students down in Washington. It's an excellent spot for a kid who's interested in getting into government." The department also works closely with the Washington Center, a prestigious internship program in Washington, D.C. "We've sent a tremendous number of students down with the Washington Center," a professor reports. "Students go down for a semester and work either in a legislative office, an agency, or a lobby." He remarks that the Washington Center does "an excellent job of placing people and our students are taking great advantage of that."

One student reports, "I have had to work hard to make sure I get the classic liberal arts education I desire, but I am definitely obtaining it."

When it comes to politics in the classroom, UNH is a minefield—it's hard to know where to step. A professor tells us that "most faculty, particularly the older faculty…don't have a problem with the politics of kids." He does acknowledge that "some faculty members, even some in political science, are 'shorter' with kids who are conservative" but maintains that UNH has "a pretty open environment." Though the university does have its "women's studies and queer studies and those sorts of groups" that "really push particular political agendas on students," the professor thinks of this unpleasantness as "pretty self-selecting," so it can be avoided. New Hampshire is historically a centrist state, so promoting the "inclusiveness-diversity agenda is probably a difficult thing to do."

Activism has nevertheless taken its toll. "On a lot of levels," a preoccupation with diversity has resulted in "students and faculty and administrators that aren't very qualified." However, the professor points out that "because we get little or no revenue from the state, the university has to be really lean." A frustrated student points out that "the university is offering a January term course on Occupy Wall Street and another on the drawbacks of capitalism." He recalls "an anthropology course last fall where one professor urged her students to join the Occupy Wall Street Movement." This student warns that, though "students at the University of New Hampshire can certainly get a solid education, they need to learn how to navigate their way around the faculty and course catalog."

There are plenty of good professors to be found at UNH. In political science, students and faculty speak highly of Susan Siggelakis ("a beloved mentor and teacher") and John Kayser ("the Straussian Lion of the department and one of the faculty's deepest thinkers"). A student claims that those who take Kayser's courses on ancient and modern political thought "receive one of the best undergraduate introductions to political philosophy available." Another standout in this department is Andrew Smith.

Other recommended faculty include Win Watson in marine biology; Stephen Trzaskoma in Classics; Kurk Dorsey and Eliga Gould in history; Dante Scala, Warren Brown, Lionel Ingram (a former U.S. Army colonel), Danielle Pillet-Shore, Lawrence Prelli, and James Farrell in communications; and Neil Niman in economics.

Overall, students exhibit a healthy level of intellectual curiosity at UNH. A female student says that "there is certainly plenty of motivation to learn." She thinks that, "as with any college, there are those who are more academically serious and some who live for the party," but that "most people do care about their academic standing, and UNH has a very strict policy about GPA and academic probation." Another student says that there are more intellectually eager students "in hard science," and "a lot of active student participation in the language departments and in Classics." He thinks that "sociology, political science, psychology" and others of the social sciences are a "mix," while "English majors are more interested in looking inside themselves" than in serious academic work. "The student body might best be described as of above-average intelligence with a lazy streak."

Students interested in language will be glad to hear that UNH offers courses in Arabic, Chinese, French, German, Greek and Latin, Hittite (!), Italian, Japanese, Portuguese, Russian, Spanish, and even Sanskrit.

UNH offers many study-abroad programs, including one at Regents College in London and a particularly popular program in Budapest. There are programs in too many countries to name, from Argentina, Austria, and Australia to China, the Czech Republic, and Switzerland.

Student Life: "Good fences make good neighbors"

The most popular sport on the UNH campus is without a doubt hockey. There are avid sports fans among the students, but the enthusiasm rarely reaches the pitch of a craze or becomes an excuse for excessive partying. One student reports that, when it comes to avoiding binges at UNH, "it really depends on what dorm you're in. Last year I was in Stoke Hall,

---

SUGGESTED CORE

1. Classics 421/422, Major Greek Authors in Translation/Major Roman Authors in Translation
2. Philosophy 570, Ancient Philosophy
3. English 518, The Bible as Literature
4. Philosophy 571, Medieval Philosophy
5. Politics and Society 503, Political Theory and Historical and Social Context
6. English 657, Shakespeare
7. History 405W, History of Early America
8. Philosophy 616, 19th-Century Philosophy

the big freshman dorm with like 600 people and...it was a little bit more of a party dorm, a little louder." The same student tells us that "besides the...fraternities' dorms, there are no fully male...dorms." There are, however, "separate men's and women's facilities even where dorms are mixed sex."

Another student suggests that "female students interested in a more traditional college residential experience might feel inclined to choose Hitchcock, an all-girl dormitory in a convenient location." This is, indeed, the only single-sex dorm available. Students tell us that most "bathrooms are single sex," while one student mentions one bathroom that is "gender neutral" but "located on a floor with three bathrooms, and the other two are single sex."

Students can find dorms that are "much quieter and much smaller," where hookup activities are "minimal." A student reports, "In the dorm I was in last year, there was a bit more of a level of promiscuity, but it happens more in the sororities and fraternities." While UNH does "have a very strict alcohol policy," it is nevertheless a somewhat "wet" school. According to students, raucous behavior "is definitely avoidable if you want nothing to do with it."

One real challenge comes in the form of student aides in the dorms. One student describes Residential Life as "a social justice police state" and advises caution around directors, hall supervisors, and resident assistants. "You need to watch what you say lest you offend someone," this student warns; "they will use every opportunity to teach you their fashionable pieties" and "enforce a far-left worldview on residents."

The school's Sexual Harassment and Rape Prevention Program is unduly restrictive of free speech. According to its website, sexual harassment is defined in part as "statements about sexual orientation or sexuality . . . and other verbal or physical conduct of a sexual nature." According to UNH Residential Life policies, this "behavior may be direct or implied." So tread lightly.

Students tell us that there are a "fair number of practicing Christian students" on campus, and one recommends "the Christian Impact and Catholic Student Organization chapters at UNH" as "positive places for believers to find like-minded peers." Another student makes mention of the "churches and religious services. The Catholic Church is a five-to-ten-minute walk from my dorm. There are other religious associations in the area as well."

UNH students feel safe in their relatively rural setting. In 2011 there were 12 sex offenses, one robbery, five aggravated assaults, and five burglaries reported on the main campus. "There are incidents like any other campus, but UNH has a consistently low crime rate," says a student. There was recently a serious incident that involved the murder of a UNH student, but it did not occur on university property. "It was a town over from us," a student recalls. The university reportedly handled the whole ordeal "in a very sensitive way."

UNH is only comparatively inexpensive—that is, compared to most of New England. Granite State residents paid $12,060 in 2012–13 (outsiders paid $25,380) and room and board charges of $9,452. Sixty-three percent of students received need-based aid, and the average student-loan debt of a recent grad was a crushing $35,168.

New Hampshire

STRONG SUITS

- Excellent political science department, with strong D.C. connections, thanks to the NH primary.
- Classics is "famous."
- Politicized departments are isolated, easy to avoid.
- Mostly fair, open-minded teachers.
- Less bureaucratic and bloated than most state universities.
- A wide array of student religious and political groups.
- Good classes offered in communications and psychology.

WEAK POINTS

- Many ideological courses in the mix with more traditional ones.
- Very politicized programs in women's studies, queer studies, African American studies, and (surprise!) "Race, Culture, and Power."
- Shaky general-ed requirements and weak mandates in some majors (English, history).
- Activist RAs in dorms police student speech.

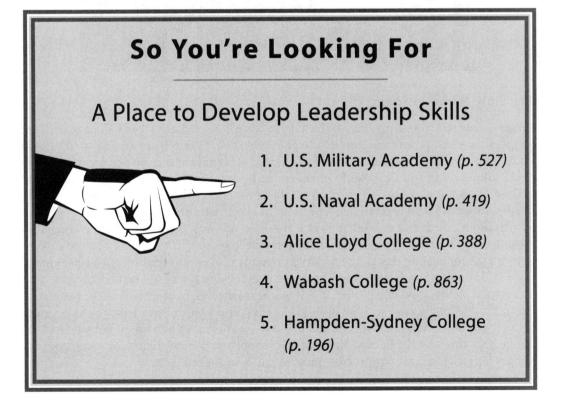

So You're Looking For

A Place to Develop Leadership Skills

1. U.S. Military Academy *(p. 527)*

2. U.S. Naval Academy *(p. 419)*

3. Alice Lloyd College *(p. 388)*

4. Wabash College *(p. 863)*

5. Hampden-Sydney College *(p. 196)*

Rutgers University

New Brunswick, New Jersey • www.rutgers.edu

The Only Game in Town

Rutgers, now the State University of New Jersey, was founded as Queen's College in 1766, and it is the most prominent public college in the state. While there are many top-notch professors offering rigorous courses at Rutgers, the university admits 60 percent of its applicants, allows them to fulfill overly broad general-education "requirements" with a crazy quilt of classes, and makes an effort to retain any student who does his work. Professors attempt to get to know their students personally, keep their office hours faithfully, are glad to help when asked, and are unhappy that more do not seek them out. There is some disappointment, however, that Rutgers isn't more selective, so that the quality of the student body might come up to that of the faculty; too many of New Jersey's best enroll elsewhere.

Still, Rutgers is a "pretty good place for people who don't have capital but have real intellectual ability," says one professor. Rutgers bears the weight of serving as the main state university for New Jersey; in spite of its population and wealth, New Jersey lacks a strong network of public four-year colleges, and this puts an enormous burden on Rutgers. A scandal in 2013 that saw the belated firing of the school's basketball coach for using abusive, antigay language against players cast the school in a jaundiced light.

Academic Life: I got my facts learned

Rutgers University serves more than 58,000 students in three cities. The New Brunswick campus is the largest and oldest, and also the strongest and most selective. The New Brunswick branch is divided into 11 schools for undergraduates and three for graduate students, with liberal arts majors grouped under its School of Arts and Sciences—which is undermined by the school's lax distribution requirements. Rutgers lists more than 4,000 courses in its catalog; most fulfill one of the general academic requirements, and many are overspecialized or politicized. Hence, a Rutgers diploma means something different for each graduate.

The honors program is more thorough, requiring two semesters of honors colloquia (the second semester may be substituted with a study-abroad program or by serving as a peer instructor, among other options) and four designated honors courses, intermediate proficiency in a foreign language, and a six-credit capstone research project.

Advising is available but is not required—to the point where one student tells us: "I am not too sure about advising. I would suspect that would be more in a graduate or higher-level undergraduate setting." Once a student has declared his major, he may visit a professor in his own department for advice—or not, as he likes. This policy is . . . inadvisable, as one professor observes: "A lot of students are alienated, overwhelmed, and confused."

Rutgers has recently instituted programs for motivated freshmen. One is the Byrne Seminar, an offering of more than 150 one-credit pass/fail classes in which top professors from all areas of study in the university introduce themselves and their fields to students. The other is the first-year Interest Group Seminars program in which upper-class mentors give one-credit seminars to freshmen.

At Rutgers there is "a bias toward research over teaching," says a professor. Another says, "In tenure decisions, the ratio of emphasis on teaching to research is at least 30 to 70 percent, although very bad teaching can knock someone out. I also think that professors do far too little teaching, a problem at most research-oriented universities."

New Jersey

VITAL STATISTICS

Religious affiliation: *none*
Total enrollment: *39,950*
Total undergraduates: *31,268*
SAT CR/Verbal midrange: *520–630*
SAT Math midrange: *560–680*
ACT midrange: *not provided*
Applicants: *28,602*
Applicants accepted: *61%*
Accepted applicants who enrolled: *38%*
Tuition (general/out of state): *$23,676*
Tuition (in state): *$10,356*
Room and board: *$11,412 (on-campus)*
Freshman retention rate: *91%*
Graduation rate (4 yrs.): *53%*
Graduation rate (6 yrs.): *77%*
Courses with fewer than 20 students: *39%*
Student-faculty ratio: *15:1*
Courses taught by graduate students: *1%*
Students living on campus: *44.7%*
Students in fraternities: *not provided*
Students in sororities: *not provided*
Students receiving need-based financial aid: *57%*
Avg. student-loan debt of a recent graduating class: *$20,844*
Most popular majors: *social sciences, communications, psychology*
Guaranteed housing for 4 years? *no*

CAMPUS POLITICS: RED LIGHT

A student says that teachers lean "very much to the left, and unfortunately it often does influence the content of the courses. Just last semester, I took a 20th-century history course where the professor was extremely liberal and taught almost every lecture as if conservatives were the problem with society." But another says, "While professors may have had liberal views, I never found it to be a detriment to my education. I've never been punished for offering conservative viewpoints; in fact, professors appreciate the diversity of opinion in the classroom. Professors' views aren't 'preached,' or the focus of the lecture, and they really don't change the classroom atmosphere."

Not everyone is open-minded. Aaron Marcus, a conservative Jewish columnist for the *Daily Targum,* complained in 2012 of violent, anti-Semitic threats he received in response to his writing. As the *Daily Caller* reported, a campus satirical paper stole Marcus's "name, picture, and title of his column, 'Marcus My Words,' to mock him by running an anti-Semitic article that praised Adolf Hitler. The article, which came out Thursday, April 4, with the headline of 'What about the good things Hitler did?' ha[d] Marcus repeatedly praising the genocidal Nazi dictator and attacking Israel."

Rutgers funds a mind-numbing array of diversity programs, and the Office of Social Justice Education and LGBT Communities offers annual student programs like National Coming Out Week, World AIDS Day, "Gaypril," and a month of LGBT awareness activities, and provides career tips such as "locating gay- and lesbian-friendly employers."

Graduate students do a lot of the teaching at Rutgers. An administrator admits that TAs teach courses "frequently"; however, professors lead most lecture courses, and although introductory classes can be as large as 300 students, upper-level classes are much smaller. One political science student says, "In upper-division courses in my major, most classes are small enough that the professor will know your name." All faculty members hold office hours, and "the professors there are helpful if there is a need," says one student.

A recent graduate recommends Rutgers's Camden campus over New Brunswick: "There are no TAs at Camden. This allows students to get to know professors. I was fortunate to get to know almost every professor in my department very well. Regardless of the department, campus, or school, the professors are always willing to spend time with students. I've spoken with students from other large state schools, and they were rather envious."

Rutgers's philosophy department is one of the top-ranked in the world. Rutgers offers an undergraduate medieval studies major, a commendable course of study if rounded out by a complementary minor like Classics, philosophy, or English. One professor adds that math and physics also are highly regarded. He says that "Rutgers is pretty good about trying to build strength in traditional liberal arts disciplines."

The English department boasts some good faculty and an excellent array of courses in all periods. But an English professor laments that his department has gone postmodern: "[Trendiness] is a national disease, but Rutgers has it worse than most places. The tragedy is that Rutgers used to be one of the top 'literary' departments in the nation." He laments the dominance of "identity politics, junior faculty who couldn't make sense of a

Donne poem to save their lives, gender blather, 'gay studies,' et cetera. It is a grim time." English majors are required to take a course in African American, "Ethnic American," or "global Anglophone" literature but not in Shakespeare.

There are some excellent offerings in history, but many of the faculty are leftist. Students can fulfill the American history requirement by taking such specialized courses as "Sport in History" or "Gay and Lesbian History in the United States." History majors must take introductory European or American history classes, but otherwise are free to choose with a minimum of oversight from the department, which requires at least two courses in each of three areas: (1) European, (2) American, and (3) African, Asian, Latin American, or Native American history, and one pre-1500 course.

Political science majors face anemic requirements, which include an introduction to "theoretical approaches to politics"; either "American Government" or "Law and Politics"; either international relations or comparative politics; and at least one 300/400-level course in each of three areas (theory, American, and international). Dubious electives like "Politics of Black America" and "Whiteness and U.S. Politics" fill up the department's offerings.

A professor confirms that faculty and students are largely liberal, but he also says that, given the "gap they are trying to cover between literate and illiterate people, there is an evangelical aspect to teaching at Rutgers that transcends politics."

Due to weak advising, "a lot of students are alienated, overwhelmed, and confused," a professor said. Faculty are judged mostly on research, not teaching.

Classics, art history, and archeology are said to be strong departments. The biological sciences, especially microbiology, are world class. Disciplines that typically have a radical slant at other colleges, such as sociology and anthropology, are more soberly academic at Rutgers. Highly praised professors include David Mechanic in sociology; T. J. Jackson Lears, Paul Clemens, Allen Howard (emeritus), Andrew Shankman, and Michael Adas in history; Bert Levine, John Weingart, Alan Rosenthal, G. Alan Tarr, and Wojtek Wolfe in political science; and William Fitzgerald (Camden campus), William Galperin, and William Dowling in English. Dowling has for years been fighting what he sees as Rutgers's steep decline and runs an iconoclastic website called "WCD at Home," which prospective students should check out.

One professor laments that the "student body generally is not as good as the faculty." Another says, "Rutgers is like any other pretty good state university. Some students are genuinely interested in learning, some only care about grades and/or postgraduation jobs." With social sciences the most popular major, followed by communication/journalism and psychology, there seem to be plenty of careerists. However, a recent alumnus says, "The intellectual life on campus can be described as both challenging and vibrant, if you choose it to be so. . . . Our diverse student body forces you into situations to defend your ideas. For this I am eternally grateful."

Despite its limitations, "incredible bargains and opportunities abound at Rutgers, for

SUGGESTED CORE

1. Classics 01:190:205/ 01:190:206, Greek Civilization/Roman Civilization
2. Classics 01:190:208/Philosophy 01:730:403, Philosophy of the Greeks/Ancient Philosophy after Aristotle
3. Religion 840:201/840:206/ 840:202, Introduction to the Bible I (Torah and Prose)/Introduction to the Bible II (Prophets and Poetry)/New Testament
4. Philosophy 01:730:304/ 01:730:305, The Origins of Medieval Philosophy/Philosophy in the High Middle Ages
5. Political Science 01:790:371/01:790:372, Western Tradition: Plato to Machiavelli/ Western Tradition: Hobbes to Mill
6. English 01:350:221/01:350:332/01:350:323, Shakespeare/Shakespeare: The Elizabethan Plays/Shakespeare: The Jacobean Plays
7. History 01:512:103, Development of the United States I
8. Philosophy 01:730:406, 19th-Century Philosophy

people who know how to use them," says a faculty member. He mentions the Institute for Marine and Coastal Science, a world-class oceanographic research institute; the Aresty Research Center, through which sophomores can apply for paid research internships with a professor from any discipline, leading to a senior thesis and even pay for research trips; archaeological digs; and the Institute for Health, Healthcare Policy, and Aging Research.

Rutgers's study-abroad programs offer myriad opportunities in dozens of locations, from Barbados to South Africa. Rutgers teaches many languages on campus, including Arabic, Aramaic, Armenian, Bengali, Chinese, French, German, Greek (Ancient and Modern), Hebrew, Hindi, Italian, Japanese, Korean, Hungarian, Latin, Malayalam, Persian, Portuguese, Russian, Sanskrit, Spanish, Swahili, Turkish, and Yoruba.

Student Life: Ain't no sin to be glad you're alive

One Rutgers senior says, "New Brunswick is no New York City, but there's plenty to do here." The community surrounding the campus is filled with college students and "New Brunswick has a college town feel, most evident on football game days," notes an alumnus. The campus is sprawling, and auto congestion is acute. "Organizing the day is difficult for students," says one professor, who notes that many have off-campus jobs to make ends meet.

The social scene at Rutgers is . . . lively. "Unfortunately, alcohol does play a big role for a lot of people, especially in the Greek scene," a student says. "But many of us have a great social life without it." One sorority member says that "alcohol is there if you want it, but Rutgers is so large that there's no pressure to conform. There are so many different types of people, that if you don't like something, you can find your own group of friends."

Rutgers University is not residential. No student is required to live on campus, and far less than half the student body chooses to. This could change, however, as Rutgers considers requiring all incoming freshmen to live on campus for their first two years. There are beds to accommodate only about one-third of the students. Most freshmen do live on campus, housed together in traditional hall-style dormitories such as Clothier, a huge building known as a party dorm, or in living-learning communities. Every residence has quiet hours, and most include 24-hour study lounges where students can escape the often chaotic dorm culture. All freshman dormitories are smoke-free, and each dorm has a residential adviser to enforce the rules. Although there are a few single-sex floors and one all-male dorm, men and women are often housed in rooms next to each other. There are no coed bathrooms or dorm rooms, however. And residents of Douglass College (an all-female school absorbed by Rutgers) live in four all-women dormitories. Students can also opt to live in one of many fraternity or sorority houses. There are a number of special houses available for students interested in foreign languages, areas of the arts, sexuality and gender, and academic subjects like history, political science, philosophy, and religion and spirituality.

Spending on and by Rutgers's athletic program is lavish. Rutgers boasts hundreds of intramural teams and nearly 50 NCAA Division I and III varsity sports (each campus fields its own teams). Teams include women's lacrosse, tennis, and basketball, and men's baseball, soccer, and track. Rutgers's Division I football team, the Scarlet Knights, has been called "resurgent" on the university's website. The recent firing of the school's basketball coach for using abusive language (on video) toward students divided the campus.

Religious students of all stripes will find groups of like-minded believers: Catholics, Protestants, Hindus, Orthodox, Jews, Muslims, Buddhists, pagans, even Pastafarians of the "Church of the Flying Spaghetti Monster."

While liberal groups far outnumber conservative ones, College Republicans and Young Americans for Liberty are active. One student says, "I am very much a conservative, and though it is a very liberal campus, I am comfortable being here. It's about making the right friends, taking the right classes, and knowing why you hold your views." A recent graduate adds, "The students—like [at] almost every college in the northeast—lean to the left. But I consider myself fortunate to have the opportunity to study in a diverse classroom; I changed some opinions, clarified others, and formed new ones, largely because of the intellectual conversations I had with left-leaning students."

Conservative students have traditionally rallied around campus alternative paper *The Centurion*—founded by firebrand journalist James O'Keefe, who went on to expose corruption in the "community organization" ACORN and to face charges for a journalistic sting aimed at Louisiana senator Mary Landrieu. Although *The Centurion* stopped circulating in 2010, students are actively planning to bring it back in 2013. Others agree with a recent graduate who scoffs: "*The Centurion* is widely regarded by liberals and conservatives as outlandish and radical. I would say roughly 10 percent read it, and 5 percent believe it to be of any academic value."

Rutgers is not exactly an idyll of peace and order. An annual event called Rutgersfest, held to mark the end of spring-semester classes, had turned into a yearly debacle, with vandalism, street fights, and even shootings raging throughout the night. The *Daily Targum*, Rutgers's student newspaper, reported in May 2010:

> This year's Rutgersfest proved to be more of an ordeal than those of years past when a day of partying turned into a night of violence. We collected a rather impressive pool of anecdotes about the night, all of which were negative. Fights broke out all around New Brunswick. People were driving on sidewalks. Wandering marauders jumped people in the College Avenue parking deck. At least one person had a gun pulled on them near the Grease Trucks. Then there's the physical evidence left

over from the nightlong odyssey, including broken windshields, beer cans, liquor bottles, condoms, and undergarments.

Wisely, the university opted to cancel Rutgersfest in 2012, also canceling all outdoor student events for the weekend when Rutgersfest is traditionally held.

In 2011 Rutgers reported 12 forcible sex offenses, five aggravated assaults, 65 burglaries, seven stolen cars, and three cases of arson on the New Brunswick campus. One campus resident says, "It's a good idea to always lock your door to your room, no matter if you know everybody in the building or not."

If you're a New Jersey resident, Rutgers is a bargain. In-state tuition for 2012–13 was $10,356, while out-of-state students paid $23,676—making Rutgers one of the only universities in America whose tuition rates went down rather than up in the past few years. Room and board were $11,412 for students living on campus. Admission is need blind, but the school does not guarantee to meet every student's financial need. Some 57 percent of all undergraduates received need-based financial aid. The average debt of a recent graduate was $20,844.

STRONG SUITS	WEAK POINTS
• Professors are eager to help students who seek them out. • Good programs in Classics, art history, archeology, the biological sciences (especially microbiology), sociology, anthropology, philosophy, and medieval studies. • Top student research opportunities at the Institute for Marine and Coastal Science, the Aresty Research Center, and the Institute for Health, Healthcare Policy, and Aging Research. • Dozens of foreign languages, including some hard to find, are taught on campus.	• Few students seek out professors. • Heavy emphasis on research over teaching. • Many underqualified students admitted. • Some highly politicized departments in humanities. • Parties can turn into riots that end with shootings.

University of New Mexico

Albuquerque, New Mexico • www.unm.edu

Local Color

The University of New Mexico is right in the center of Albuquerque, the cultural hub of the American Southwest. It is a large commuter school, with 90 percent of students living off campus; and most students (56 percent) do not graduate within six years. Among the pluses of the school is its vibrant, cosmopolitan population. "New Mexico is a melting pot for various ethnicities," one student remarks. It also offers good connections that can lead to careers in the region. Getting a quality liberal arts education here is difficult, but it is possible, sources report. The school's core requirements are strikingly undeveloped, and many majors are shallow and career-oriented. One recent graduate summarizes his college experience this way: "It's decent, but I feel it's mostly a commuter school that has given me an education, but nothing more."

Academic Life: Oases in the desert

UNM's distributional requirements aim not to impart a body of knowledge but to hone students' critical faculties. The school requires classes in seven very broadly defined areas of study: writing and speaking (three courses), mathematics, natural science (two courses),

VITAL STATISTICS

Religious affiliation: *none*
Total enrollment: *28,977*
Total undergraduates: *22,643*
SAT CR/Verbal midrange: *470–600*
SAT Math midrange: *470–590*
ACT midrange: *19–25*
Applicants: *10,743*
Applicants accepted: *64%*
Accepted applicants who enrolled: *52%*
Tuition (general/out of state): *$19,919*
Tuition (in state): *$5,809*
Room and board: *$8,068*
Freshman retention rate: *74%*
Graduation rate (4 yrs.): *12%*
Graduation rate (6 yrs.): *44%*
Courses with fewer than 20 students: *39%*
Student-faculty ratio: *23:1*
Courses taught by graduate students: *not provided*
Students living on campus: *10%*
Students in fraternities: *4%*
Students in sororities: *3%*
Students receiving need-based financial aid: *97%*
Avg. student-loan debt of a recent graduating class: *$19,609*
Most popular majors: *biology, business administration, elementary education*
Guaranteed housing for 4 years? *no*

social science (two courses), humanities (two courses), foreign language, and fine arts. Proficiency in a foreign language or cultural literacy—American, Western, Christian, or any other—are not required.

The school's student-faculty ratio is a crushing 23 to 1, and only 39 percent of its courses have fewer than 20 students. This proportion is partly skewed by many studio and performance art classes, as well as by the low proportion of students who stay for their junior and senior years. Still, only 15 percent of courses have 50 or more students. UNM students praise faculty involvement and enthusiasm above all else; even larger, lower-level courses (and they are large, some with over 300 students) are reportedly taught well, although one student comments online that "some of the professors are not the best, and can often be confusing," and that there are some graduate teaching assistants who do not speak English clearly.

A schoolwide honors program is offered, as well as departmental honors in many disciplines. Such classes are smaller and allow for more intensive interaction among students and faculty. Many remark on how demanding the program is, requiring independent study or a senior thesis. Given the limitations of the university, ambitious students certainly should apply to this selective program. As one student comments, "I think the honors program is great for someone who is ambitious and passionate about learning."

UNM is situated in the center of Albuquerque, emerging from and serving the local community. The strongest programs seem to be the medical and nursing schools; biology and biochemistry, the premed majors, are also praised by undergraduates. One resident says, "Architecture has always been one of those things [for which] UNM has always had a good reputation," with a variety of programs and "a growing emphasis on green design." The strongest department in the School of Arts and Sciences is anthropology, which offers concentrations in the subfields of archaeology and ethnology and focuses on things local, with course offerings like "Cultures of the Southwest," which studies the region's unique combination of Native, Hispanic, and American history and culture.

English majors can choose among several different tracks. Most of the concentration options have career preparation in mind ("Professional Writing") and therefore have fairly sparse literature requirements. Majors should opt for the very solid Liberal Arts track, which requires two literature surveys, a course in Shakespeare, and a course in Chaucer or Milton; or, better, the Pre-Grad track, which requires all three, as well as Early English Literature and an extensive tour through American Lit. Course offerings do not seem influenced by academic ideology so much as the local culture; there is a course called "Writing the Southwest," and the *Blue Mesa Review* (the university's national literary magazine) gets students involved. Happily, most courses are surveys, many of which are rooted in literary classics. The Arthurian tradition even gets some attention.

The history department, too, specializes in local matters (U.S. western and Latin American history), while offering adequate coverage of European and broader U.S. history. A course in America's founding period is not a requirement for the major—indeed, the two-semester survey of American history is merely optional. That said, the course offerings are sound, including 30 courses in U.S. history. As might be expected, there are quite a few studies in colonialism, westward American expansion, and race relations that might invite ideological discussion, but a history major need not dwell in them, opting instead for more conventional options like "History of Christianity to 1517."

CAMPUS POLITICS: GREEN LIGHT

The multicultural origins of New Mexico help promote an organic acceptance of diversity on campus—where many students are either Latino or Native American. So the university doesn't engage in much activism on this front. Students agree that campus culture at UNM leans left. But most students are apathetic, simply trying to get a degree and a job.

The UNM College Republicans are few in number but consistently active and involved in political events on and off campus. There are also several Christian student groups of various denominations, such as the Catholic Apologetics Fellowship and Evangelization; a student pro-life group has recently started up too.

There is the occasional political hiccup. In February 2013 the UNM Student Senate proposed the expulsion of Chick-fil-A from the campus dining hall because of dubious claims from gay students that the restaurant's presence on campus made them feel "unsafe." (The company's founder, you might recall, opposes gay "marriage.") A student poll showed that 85 percent of respondents wished to keep the restaurant, and the resolution was voted down. Not long after, the school's staff council published a brave resolution affirming its commitment to diversity and equality.

The political science major does not offer its students a classically "liberal" understanding of the discipline. It requires a course in American politics but not one grounded in political theory or the Constitution. It also requires courses in American and comparative politics. There is a requirement for political thought, but classical political thinkers and ideas are not offered. The upper-level "American Political Theory" course focuses on the evolution of ideas through "decades of political struggle and experimentation" and assigns *The Autobiography of Malcolm X,* but not the *Federalist Papers*. There are courses in "Community Organizing," "Unpacking the Occupy Movement," and "Hispanics in U.S. Politics." Students should expect not so much a radical or ideological education in this department as a shallow and results-oriented one that merely trains the next generation of local politicians in the wisdom of the present.

The fine arts department at UNM is very strong. The dance department, for example, tries to integrate performance art training and the liberal arts. A student concentrating in flamenco will partake in an internationally acclaimed program that "cultivates critical thinking and analysis as well as helping students build the basic skills for creative expression."

One Albuquerque resident recommends the film department because the region and the city have seen "explosive growth in the number of movies and TV programs filmed here," and "digital media production of all kinds is huge." A media production lab is located near campus and is used by both the UNM arts department and film production companies.

Students studying in humanities departments, such as those in the liberal arts and social sciences, should expect some classroom politics that lean liberal and "multicultural." But UNM is not the product of the academic elite; it is a local institution. Part-time commuters taking a class or two and serious-minded first-generation (or international) students thinking about a future career are the norm at UNM; the culture here is not much informed by the radicalism that has led greater academia in such strange directions in recent decades. That said, the academics are not classically rooted, either. The supply and the demand are both for local and timely matters, and it is not easy to get much of a glimpse beyond these things. As for the classroom experience, professors seem willing to allow for opinions contrary to their own; one student says, "Professors like you to think for yourself and express opinions."

A recent grad reports: "It's decent, but I feel it's mostly a commuter school that has given me an education, but nothing more." One could do worse.

Award-winning and highly praised teachers abound. They include Leslie Donovan and Ursula Shepherd in honors; Christine Sauer in economics; Howard Waitzkin in sociology; Gary Harrison in English; Jane Ellen Smith and Gordon Hodge in psychology; Michael Nakamaye in mathematics; Christopher Mead and Elen Feinberg in art and art history; and Jane Slaughter in history. Other notable faculty include Murray Gell-Mann in physics, who holds a Nobel Prize, and Samuel Truett in history, recipient of a Fulbright award.

UNM offers a fairly strong selection of foreign languages, including some rare and local ones. In addition to standard fare like American Sign Language, Arabic, Chinese, French, German, Greek and Latin, Italian, Japanese, Portuguese, Russian, and Spanish, students can also take Old English, Navajo, and Swahili. What is more, "Tewa, Tiwa, Towa, Keres, and Zuni native speakers are not hard to find," suggests a local resident.

UNM has extensive foreign-exchange and study-abroad programs. Because most American students are commuters, a high proportion of campus residents are foreign students. In addition, the study-abroad program sends students to Australia, Austria, China, Ecuador, Egypt, France, Germany, Kenya, India, Italy, Mexico, Nicaragua, Panama, South Africa, Spain, and Switzerland.

Students need not travel to another continent to get to know another nation; one student reports, "The Native American studies department is very good—and its graduate program is top notch. UNM has one of the best materials collections in the world in its library."

Student Life: Dry in the desert

"Everyone loves the Lobos—especially the basketball program," says one student in an online discussion. UNM's varsity athletics, overall, are the strongest in the state. The basketball team, often nationally ranked, is the main attraction. The soccer team, too, though less popular because they play, well, soccer, is consistently one of the best in the country. On the other hand, the football team, laments one student, "is notoriously bad." It has recently been ranked the worst in the country. Nevertheless, however good or bad the team, fan support is persistent, as seemingly the entire campus gathers to cheer on their Lobos at most events.

> ### SUGGESTED CORE
> 1. Classic Studies 107, Greek Mythology
> 2. Philosophy 211, Greek Philosophy
> 3. English 304, The Bible as Literature
> 4. Philosophy 408, Medieval Philosophy
> 5. Philosophy 371, Modern Social and Political Philosophy
> 6. English 352, Early Shakespeare
> 7. History 161, History of the United States to 1877
> 8. Philosophy 444, 19th-Century Philosophy

Abstinence from drugs and alcohol is promoted aggressively at UNM, and the campus is "dry," with severe penalties enforced after the first offense. One student warns prospective students online that "parties in the dorms WILL get busted." Obviously there is no such thing as a drug-free campus this big, and there is a considerable amount of drinking after hours. The drug of choice seems to be alcohol, with one student commenting that it is a "booze-based campus." Despite all this, UNM is a cleaner campus than most. Most underclassmen commute from home, and a relatively high proportion of campus residents are international or first-generation students who are more likely to be concentrating on their studies and their future. There is comparatively little Greek presence on campus. Students who neither drink nor use drugs report that these things are easily avoided and not a distraction.

Most of the residence halls on campus have been recently renovated and feature computer labs and pool tables. All dorms are coed but separated by floors, suites, or sections of a building. Men and women do not share rooms, bathrooms, suites, or apartments. Students recommend the Casas del Rio apartment complex. One student remarks, "The housing on campus is being renovated and is looking great." Campus dining receives mixed reviews, but there are plenty of restaurants just off campus.

There are student ministries of many denominations. The region is heavily Catholic, and UNM's Aquinas Newman Center is active in charity initiatives, but more traditional students might wish to visit instead San Ignacio Parish, which offers a weekly Latin Mass.

Other chaplaincies include the Canterbury Club (Episcopal), a Baptist student union, a Cru chapter, a Hillel House, a Bahai student group, and a wide variety of other organizations.

Students should be aware that UNM is located right in the heart of a city. "Campus is right on one of the sketchiest streets in Albuquerque, but if you're aware of your surroundings and take the proper precautions, you shouldn't have a problem," a student reports. There is not a strong presence of security or police. Several students report that homeless people are often seen on campus who occasionally harass students. There are streetlights and emergency call buttons all through campus, as well as escorts and a text- and e-mail-based emergency notification system. In 2011 the school reported two sexual assaults, four robberies, 10 aggravated assaults, 19 burglaries, and 57 motor vehicle thefts on campus.

Commuter students from New Mexico find a bargain at UNM, with 2012 in-state tuition at only $5,809 (out-of-state tuition was $19,919); room and board were only $8,068. Some 78 percent of students received grant aid for a further discount, and students graduated with an average debt of $19,609, which is below the national average—although this debt represents an alarming rise of $4,706 since 2009.

STRONG SUITS	WEAK POINTS
• Excellent programs in dance, Native American studies, premed, and nursing.	• Crushing (23-to-1) student-faculty ratio.
• A good honors program—the best option for a solid education here.	• Very few students live on campus.
• An apolitical, nonactivist campus that's open minded and fairly harmonious.	• Low, low (12 percent) four-year graduation rate.
• Little party culture and mostly moderate drinking.	• Students mostly focused on snagging jobs, not exploring ideas.

Brooklyn College (CUNY)

Brooklyn, New York • www.brooklyn.cuny.edu

A Mustache on the Mona Lisa

Founded in 1930, Brooklyn College is one of 11 senior colleges of the City University of New York (CUNY). It gained a reputation for excellence early and kept it until the late 1960s, when open admissions and campus radicalism undermined its standards. A reform policy begun under Mayor Rudolph Giuliani succeeded in further raising admission standards and getting many of the city's better students to apply for admission. In 2005 a Brooklyn College undergraduate received a Rhodes scholarship, and in 2009–10 two masters students received Fulbright fellowships. The school was advancing on many fronts until very recently. To our great disappointment (but not surprise), the solid core curriculum that had guaranteed every Brooklyn College grad a liberal arts foundation was trashed in 2013—and merged with the mediocre distributional requirements that prevail throughout the rest of the sausage factory that is the City University of New York.

Academic Life: Lore among the ruins

Brooklyn's once impressive Core Studies was dumped in 2013, and students now face only the CUNY Pathways program of distributional requirements in English composition, math

VITAL STATISTICS

Religious affiliation: *none*
Total enrollment: *16,524*
Total undergraduates:
 13,099
SAT CR/Verbal midrange:
 490–580
SAT Math midrange:
 520–610
ACT midrange: *not provided*
Applicants: *18,445*
Applicants accepted: *30%*
Accepted applicants who
 enrolled: *21%*
Tuition (general/out of
 state): *$14,550*
Tuition (in state): *$5,884*
Room and board: *$15,085*
Freshman retention rate:
 82%
Graduation rate (4 yrs.): *24%*
Graduation rate (6 yrs.): *48%*
Courses with fewer than 20
 students: *40%*
Student-faculty ratio: *15:1*
Courses taught by graduate
 students: *not provided*
Students living on campus:
 not provided
Students in fraternities: *3%*
Students in sororities: *3%*
Students receiving need-
 based financial aid: *83%*
Avg. student-loan debt of a
 recent graduating class:
 $16,600
Most popular majors: *busi-
 ness/marketing, account-
 ing, psychology*
Guaranteed housing for 4
 years? *no*

and quantitative reasoning, and life and physical sciences, as well as a selection of courses across five areas—World Cultures and Global Issues, U.S. Experience in Its Diversity, Creative Expression, Individual and Society, and the Scientific World. Students who actually seek a solid education will now have to pick among the solid courses that are still being taught at Brooklyn College (see our Suggested Core sidebar).

For now, the college still offers a number of worthy opportunities. The Macaulay Honors College provides students with excellent academic facilities (and a new laptop), along with tuition scholarships and a wide variety of research, internship, academic, and professional opportunities. Admission to such programs is very selective.

The 13,099 students at Brooklyn College can choose from 120 academic programs. Advising works by appointment, but walk-in advising is also available. For the most part, advisers help students schedule their semester and, in small part, advise them in their degrees programs. When a student picks a major, he receives advising from professors in that department.

The English department offers comparative literature, English literature, creative writing, a high school teacher program, journalism, and linguistics majors. The English literature major consists of two literature overview classes, five courses in the fields of study, and a selection of seven areas of English literature, including Middle Ages, Renaissance, 18th century, 19th century and Romanticism, American Literature, modernism, and postmodernism and contemporary discourses. At least two courses must be in Middle Ages, Renaissance, or 18th-century literature. A further six courses must be in electives, one of which must be an English or Comparative Literature seminar. One elective may also be in an "allied discipline," following various cultural studies, art studies, American studies, and so forth. The Renaissance section has many Shakespeare classes and the other classes sport a good array of poetry and prose authors.

The history major consists of 11 courses—an introductory class and eight lower-division courses broken up into five sections: ancient, medieval, and early modern history; European history; transnational and comparative history; U.S. history; and African, Asian, Caribbean, Latin American, and Middle Eastern history. The major requires at least one class in each of those areas. Further, it requires two classes in upper-division courses, one of which must be a colloquium. There are a number of classes permeated with race/class/gender obsessions.

The political science department offers concentrations in political science, international affairs, or urban politics and administration. The two fundamental classes for the major are "Intro to Politics" and "Intro to American Government." Also required are "Analytic Approaches to Political Problems" and "Research Strategies in Public Policy," as well as a senior capstone class. A further five classes count toward the major with a choice of areas: American and urban politics, international politics, comparative politics, political theory, and methodology. Political science majors should graduate with some grounding in American politics.

Strong classes are offered in the Classics and English departments. Classics is very small, but the professors are dedicated, and they, not graduate students, teach most of the classes. A student tells us, "In my experience, all have been very accessible and helpful. The same goes for the English department. Most of its offerings are on the great texts of Western civilization, and there are relatively few courses that are designed for 'multiculturalist' indoctrination. This also applies very much to the history department," he says. Business and education are very popular majors, as are health sciences and psychology.

Some prominent faculty members include Pulitzer Prize–winning historian Edwin Burrows and journalist Paul Moses; historian Michael Rawson and composer Tania León (both Pulitzer Prize nominees); Grammy Award–nominated concert pianist Ursula Oppens; and Kristoff Diaz, a Tony Award–nominated playwright. Current professors that students particularly recommend

CAMPUS POLITICS: YELLOW LIGHT

Brooklyn College's ethnic, religious, and racial composition reflects New York City's diversity, with students from more than a hundred nations. The school is more than 28 percent black, with many students born in all the parts of the Caribbean. It is also more than 13 percent Asian. Many students on campus are religious. The campus is especially accommodating to Jewish students at its Tanger Hillel Center. Yet there are numerous campus organizations devoted to Muslim and Christian believers. There is little radical activism—or activism period—on campus.

A senior reports that "religious students aren't freaks here. They're more apt to be the majority—and most of the faculty know and respect that." The tendentious and strident voices in the faculty can typically be found, however, and a recent decision on the part of the college brought some controversy. An alum claimed that he "disinherited his Alma Mater" when he heard that the college required all incoming freshmen and transfer students to read the book *How Does It Feel to Be a Problem? Being Young and Arab in America*, which profiles the experience of seven young Arabs in the aftermath of 9/11 and was written by a radical pro-Palestinian professor.

In 2013 Brooklyn College featured anti-Israel speakers who argued for an academic boycott of that country, and four pro-Israel students who objected were forcibly removed from the event, with the administration claiming (falsely, it appears) that they were being "disruptive," according to news site *The Algemeiner.* The controversy over this officially sponsored event continues.

include Caroline Arnold in political science, Jennifer Basil in biology, Edwin Burrows in history, and Mark Patkowski in English.

As big as Brooklyn College is, it has a decent student-faculty ratio of 15 to 1, but many of the famous professors either teach in large lecture classes or only to grad students. One undergrad says: "I have yet to get a big name professor." A significant portion of classes are taught by graduate students.

Brooklyn College offers 120 undergraduate and graduate degree programs. Doctoral-level programs are available through the City University of New York Graduate Center in midtown Manhattan, with a number of courses offered on the Brooklyn College campus.

O f professors, a Classics major says, "All have been very accessible and helpful." And in the English and history departments, most "offerings are on the great texts of Western civilization, and there are relatively few courses that are designed for 'multiculturalist' indoctrination."

The colleges of CUNY also offer many study-abroad programs in dozens of countries in both semesters as well as during the summer. Countries include Argentina, Denmark, Germany, Ghana, Ireland, Israel, Italy, Senegal, and Spain. Other programs have particular academic focuses, such as "Mexico–Cooking, Art, Culture," "Religions of India," and "China: Land and People."

Brooklyn offers a good range of modern and classical languages; a student may receive a BA in modern language and literature with an eye toward teaching. Languages offered include Chinese, French, German, Greek and Latin, Hebrew, Italian, Russian, and Spanish.

Student Life: Crossing Brooklyn Bridge

In 2010 Brooklyn College opened its first residence hall for students two blocks from campus, with room options ranging from semiprivate to dorm shares. It also offers a 24/7 doorman and a shuttle to campus. However, living off campus still has its perks, even if it means paying a premium to live in a reasonably safe neighborhood or coping with long commutes on public transportation—for example, free access to the Brooklyn Museum and the Brooklyn Botanic Garden. The college's setting puts students within a subway ride of unparalleled cultural opportunities in Manhattan and Brooklyn itself.

The college welcomed its first building in 40 years in September 2009, a 145,000-square-foot structure doubling as a student center and a state-of-the-art athletics facility. Ground has also broken for a new center for the performing arts, and the college is planning a new state-of-the-art science complex. Of the students at Brooklyn College, a fairly large portion are working adults (almost 30 percent of undergrads are over 24). One student says that "a lot of the students wind up graduating in five, six years, and it's not like they're going to show up at college dances or wear Brooklyn College sweatshirts. There isn't that much school spirit or even dating among students." On the positive side, campus politics and social pressures play a much smaller role in the typical student's career.

Brooklyn College competes as the Bulldogs in NCAA Division III with men's and women's teams in basketball, soccer, cross-country, tennis, swimming, and volleyball. The school also has a coed cheerleading squad and a women's softball team, and offers coed intramural teams in multiple sports.

Although Brooklyn College is a commuter school, there are about 260 undergraduate clubs and organizations. Among these are some 20 sororities and fraternities; groups for black, Hispanic, Chinese, Korean, Jewish, Haitian, Panamanian, Irish, Italian, and Palestinian students; for Roman Catholic, Adventist, Evangelical, Muslim students; for future lawyers, black accountants, Hispanic journalists, and women scientists; for paintball, slow food, and so forth. Students at Brooklyn College do not seem to be too politically active, and there are only a few political groups on campus.

Campus crime has been on a steady decline over the past several years. In 2011 the school reported one forcible sexual offense, two aggravated assaults, and one burglary. However, the train line to the school passes through one or two dicey neighborhoods. The college itself is sufficiently policed and well maintained. The campus is gated, and a strict ID system is used to keep possible intruders out.

For New York State residents, Brooklyn College is an amazing educational bargain, with 2012–13 tuition averaging at $5,884 per year, and out-of-state tuition at $14,550. The school estimates annual room and board to be around $15,085. Some 83 percent of students received financial aid, and the average student-loan debt of a recent graduate was around $16,600.

SUGGESTED CORE

1. Core Curriculum 1110, Classical Cultures
2. Philosophy 3111, Ancient Philosophy
3. English 3183, The Bible as Literature
4. History 3033, Christianity and the Church in Medieval Europe or Philosophy 3113, Medieval Philosophy
5. Political Science 3402, Modern Political Thought
6. English 3122/3123, Shakespeare I/II
7. History 3401, America to 1877
8. Philosophy 3122, 19th-Century Philosophy

STRONG SUITS

- A recent heritage of excellence.
- Mixed political views on campus and in the classroom, and a mostly free debate.
- Some very solid offerings in traditional disciplines, including Classics.
- Good requirements in English and political science.
- Many adult students, with little time for activism or hedonism.

WEAK POINTS

- The once-excellent core curriculum has just been demolished and replaced with tepid distributional requirements.
- Famous professors teach large lecture courses and much use is made of graduate students.
- Recurrent controversies stoked by anti-Western and anti-Israel multiculturalists.

Cooper Union

New York, New York • www.cooper.edu

Free for Now

Cooper Union for the Advancement of Science and Art was founded by self-made philanthropist Peter Cooper in 1859 to be "open and free to all," and right up through 2013 it provided a full tuition scholarship to every student admitted—allowing it to be one of the most selective colleges in the country. Shortly before this guide went to press, however, the school responded to a financial crisis (and its own improvident building spree) by announcing that it would begin to charge tuition. It is unclear how this will affect the culture of the school, which should remain both very generous with financial aid and highly selective.

Cooper Union consists of the Irwin S. Chanin School of Architecture, the School of Art, and the Albert Nerken School of Engineering. Education in each of the three schools is generally described as stellar, although art students we spoke to seemed less impressed with the school than did the architecture and engineering students.

Academic Life: The union of all the liberal arts

Instead of departments such as English or political science, Cooper has a single "faculty of humanities and social sciences." The department requires a set of core liberal arts classes for each student regardless of school, a program that was enacted in the late 1990s. The core humanities courses in the first year are devoted to language and literature; in the second year, the core covers history and political science in the "making of the modern world." In these courses, "through critical examination and discussion of primary materials students develop a broad understanding of the origins of modern society and the conflicts within it."

Freedom to pursue humanities electives is generally limited to the third and fourth years. Although classes required for one's major are guaranteed, lines for enrollment in choice electives can start in the wee hours of the morning. One student reports studying a full array of selections in core curriculum classes from Enlightenment and modern Western philosophers. A freshman says he has already read Hesiod, the *Odyssey, Medea,* the *Aeneid,* the *Inferno,* and several plays of Shakespeare. Even so, one Cooper faculty member we spoke with said that these classes show "a serious decline [of late]. . . . The Western humanities classes are genuinely respectful, but they're not taught with the seriousness that they once were."

That said, it isn't only the "core" classes that look to meaningful texts. The most recent catalog includes a class on morals featuring Hume, Descartes, and Kant, and one class is devoted entirely to an in-depth study of Milton's *Paradise Lost.* A class on American radicalism includes not only leftists such as C. Wright Mills but also thinkers like Dorothy Day, Lewis Mumford, and the founders of the neoconservative movement.

Professors have a reputation for being very engaged. They are often seen on school grounds during weekends, and it's not unheard of for them to respond to e-mail or even phone inquiries on weekends too. Professors work hard to be innovative, and they try to incorporate into the course work the bustling and thrilling environment of New York City. Frequent collaborative projects and generous studio workspaces tend to forge close friendships and lasting relationships among classmates.

The engineering school offers a five-year master's program and bachelor's degrees in chemical, civil, electrical, and mechanical engineering. The architecture

VITAL STATISTICS

Religious affiliation: *none*
Total enrollment: *1,000*
Total undergraduates: *975*
SAT CR/Verbal midrange: *610–720*
SAT Math midrange: *650–780*
ACT midrange: *not provided*
Applicants: *3,500*
Applicants accepted: *8%*
Accepted applicants who enrolled: *not provided*
Tuition (general/out of state): *$19,275*
Tuition (in state): *N/A*
Room and board: *$9,970*
Freshman retention rate: *94%*
Graduation rate (4 yrs.): *63%*
Graduation rate (6 yrs.): *not provided*
Courses with fewer than 20 students: *74%*
Student-faculty ratio: *9:1*
Courses taught by graduate students: *not provided*
Students living on campus: *18%*
Students in fraternities: *not provided*
Students in sororities: *not provided*
Students receiving need-based financial aid: *32%*
Avg. student-loan debt of a recent graduating class *$13,721*
Most popular majors: *fine/ studio arts, electrical engineering, mechanical engineering*
Guaranteed housing for 4 years? *no*

CAMPUS POLITICS: GREEN LIGHT

What political activism exists at Cooper Union tends to lean left. As this book goes to press, student protests against the new policy of charging tuition roil the tiny campus—including a protracted occupation of the president's office by students whose "live-in" includes catered meals.

However, students at Cooper tend to be weighed down with the rigor and volume of their studies, and what free time they have, they devote to recreational activities. Weighty conversation and divisive debates might send this group of driven young adults over the edge. Partisan groups have arisen but not taken root at Cooper Union, and while most conservative students gravitate toward the engineering school, no one interviewed reported feeling any sense of oppressive political correctness among faculty or fellow students.

bachelor's program (which boasts a 5-to-1 student-faculty ratio) takes at least five years to complete—and frequently longer.

The student body includes quite a few Renaissance men and women; you're likely to find them using their free time studying esoteric Asian martial arts or discussing philosophy over chess.

The art school offers a generalist curriculum that covers all the fine arts and promotes an integrated perspective. The school's literature states that "students become socially aware, historically grounded, creative practitioners. They are taught to be critical analysts of the world of contemporary visual communications, art and the culture at large." More than two-thirds of a student's class time is spent in studio courses. The art school's facilities include painting studios, sculpture and printmaking shops, photography studios and darkrooms, a computer studio, and film, video, and animation facilities.

With an impressive commitment to respected texts, Cooper Union struggles constantly to balance a thorough humanities education with the heavy demands of students' technical fields of study. One engineering student complains, "We do interesting stuff in the humanities classes, but, with all we have to do in engineering, I sometimes wonder if we have the time to think through all the stuff we're given."

Consequently, the administration now seems to be evaluating just how much students can handle. Still, the school struggles mightily to make humanities courses more engaging, to keep the interest of students tempted to complain that they didn't come to Cooper to study the Great Books. As a professor comments, "Teaching is taken seriously at Cooper, and it's a serious factor in tenure decisions—and the teaching load is about right." The school's administration wins praise for being "pretty bureaucracy free."

Distinguished humanities professors include the film critic James Hoberman. In art history, classicist Mary Stieber is highly respected and popular. Peter Buckley's and Brian Swann's classes in English literature are also recommended. (The humanities faculty, while excellent, is small—like the school itself.)

Despite Cooper's relative seriousness about Western thought in its core curriculum, leftist critical theory and ideology do have some sway at the school. There is a class offered in "Gender Studies" and a course titled "Women and Men: Power and Politics." But even these left-leaning courses seem to have some intellectual depth: a class on environmental literature includes the writing of Wordsworth and Thoreau; a class on "Love in Western Art and Literature," despite "specific attention to the body, gender, and identity," begins with Plato's *Symposium* and surveys Shakespeare, Keats, Shelley, Austen, before ending up in Derrida.

Other electives currently offered include worthy classes such as "American Foreign Policy," "Russian Art, Architecture, and Literature," "The 'Genius' of the Baroque," "Leonardo, Scientist and Engineer," "History of the Book," and "Macroeconomics."

Study abroad is possible in dozens of countries, through a variety of international exchange programs in which Cooper Union takes part—but we could find no specific programs sponsored by the school. Courses are offered in a range of languages on campus—including French, Hindi, Japanese, and Spanish—while others can be studied at other schools, such as the New School.

Student Life: Nerd heaven

A graduate of Cooper's engineering school says that students here "are known for having very little social life due to the demanding curriculum, which is designed to give the students a master's level of course work in their field by graduation." This graduate says that most social activities at Cooper "center around the standard nerd celebrations: science fiction, video gaming, study groups, and the like." Students admit that their reputation for eccentricity is not entirely unfair. Indeed, they tend to revel in it (still, any jokes about pocket protectors might make you unpopular). The environs of the school are almost unparalleled for live music, quirky bookstores, and countless reasonably priced restaurants of every possible variety.

Even techie students at Cooper Union get a good grounding in liberal arts. "We do interesting stuff in the humanities classes, but, with all we have to do in engineering, I sometimes wonder if we have the time to think through all the stuff we're given," a student says.

Although Cooper is right in the heart of New York and all its attractions, some students say they hardly notice because of the heavy workload. Some insist that only about a fourth of students have a really active social life. On the bright side, this means that drugs are fairly unpopular on campus. It's said that those who do drugs don't last long, and one can hardly imagine how they could, given the rigorous study demands. Put simply, as one professor says, "Students work very hard."

The driven nature of most Cooper Union students is evidenced by the types of clubs they develop. The Punkin Chunkin Club teaches students to use engineering and science skills to convey gourds at high velocity. From the Cooper Culinary Society to an origami club to Battlebots (mission: "to teach students important aspects of robotics by designing, building, and testing fighting robots"), student activities at Cooper differ from the

SUGGESTED CORE

1. Humanities 442, Greek Mythology
2. Humanities 387, The Life and Death of Socrates
3. Humanities 394, World Religions (*closest match*)
4. No suitable course offered
5. Core Curriculum 3, The Making of Modern Society
6. Humanities 450, Shakespeare
7. Social Science 353, American Social History
8. Humanities 343, Decadence and Modernity

typical university's offerings. A number of professional and honor societies are available, from the American Chemical Society to the Society of Women Engineers. Sports clubs include an outdoors club, several dancing clubs, rock-climbing, martial arts, handball, weightlifting, sailing, and Ultimate Frisbee.

Ethnic cultural groups hold popular events: Hillel, the Jewish student association, is quite active, and the South Asia Society is also popular, especially its Diwali (Indian New Year) celebration. The environment at Cooper Union is quite secular; however, New York is replete with busy houses of worship. A devout student will find synagogues and Protestant churches of every denomination within walking distance; nearby New York University is said to have a very active and worthwhile Catholic chaplaincy. A magnificent Ukrainian Catholic cathedral stands right across the street from Cooper's main building, offering reverent liturgies in an exotic tongue.

Dorm housing is apartment-style with three-, four-, and five-person apartments, but only freshmen are guaranteed dorm space. The administration frequently worries about how to mitigate the stress of transition to second year by making more housing available, but there simply isn't space. Currently almost all sophomores from out of town are cast out to fend for themselves in New York's very pricey and sparse rental market. Students also complain that Cooper's facilities are old and dirty and sometimes regret the lack of amenities such as a gym. Nevertheless, there are both intercollegiate and intramural sports, with five intercollegiate men's and women's teams (basketball, tennis, cross-country, soccer, and volleyball), and many intramural coed teams and clubs. Cooper's teams are fairly good despite the lack of both facilities and funding for sports—the tagline on the athletics web page is "No gym, no courts, no fields, no pool, no horses, no time . . . no excuses." For the noncompetitive, a quite cheap, surprisingly good New York City gym, the Asser Levy Recreation Center, is a long walk or short bus ride away at 14th Street and Avenue D, featuring weight machines, exercise classes, and a well-kept pool.

Believe it or not, New York City is one of the safest metropolises in the country, and Cooper Union has an impressive campus security record: from 2009 to 2011, there was no reported crime. Of course, since most students live off campus, Cooper Union undergrads face the typical dangers that attend urban existence.

Until this year, the school has offered full tuition scholarships (valued at $38,550 per year) to every admitted student. Under the new arrangement, need-blind admissions and guaranteed aid will provide needy students a full scholarship, while others will pay $19,275 per year. First-year room and board on campus cost $9,970 in 2012–13, while local rents thereafter can be pricey, and students are responsible for fees, books, general living expenses, and health insurance. The school offers financial aid to help students with that expense, and the typical Cooper Union graduate completed school with $13,721 in debt.

STRONG SUITS

- A worthy core curriculum for every student ensures cultural literacy.
- Very rigorous courses in every subject taught by dedicated faculty.
- Heavy workload, elite students, and a serious work atmosphere.
- A nice range of extracurricular options on campus and off (it's NYC).
- Nonpoliticized teaching and free expression on campus.

WEAK POINTS

- A preprofessional attitude among some students can blunt liberal arts learning.
- Humanities program said to be "in decline."
- Finance shortages seem to have forced an end to Cooper Union's free-tuition policy.

State University of New York at Binghamton

Vestal, New York • www.binghamton.edu

Sinking and Leveling

Binghamton is one of four universities in the State University of New York (SUNY) system. Founded in 1946, it has grown to contain six colleges and almost 15,000 students today. A professor notes that whereas Binghamton used to take pride in being considered a "public Swarthmore . . . in the course of these last 20 years of lack of measured leadership . . . it has begun to approximate a 'public University of Phoenix.'" The professor said the school seems to have decided to "find new and different ways to provide a mediocre education to an increasingly mediocre student body."

Still, if a student is planning to study science, can make his own fun (or doesn't require any), and is willing to seek out exposure to some great research projects, then this school could be a cost-effective academic opportunity.

Academic Life: Cross-listed, crossed up

Binghamton students must satisfy several university-wide general-education requirements, but these are loose enough that each can be met with any of dozens of courses.

Since many courses are cross-listed across disciplines, students often graduate without taking many classes outside their academic areas, says one student. On the other hand, students at the School of Management are noted for taking double majors—with their second major often being in the liberal arts. Explains one student: "I'm not sure how many throughout the school take advantage of double majors, but at the School of Management I can say that, definitely, everybody is in more than one field."

Binghamton needs to focus on making students culturally literate. At the school's liberal-arts-centered Harpur College, even in fundamental courses like "Foundations of Western Civilization," professors have a "great deal of autonomy as far as course material is concerned, which can be a blessing or a curse," a student wrote in one of the campus newspapers. Another student says that many Binghamton students simply ask upperclassmen which courses and professors are easiest and plan their schedules accordingly. Another student replies that course work does present a challenge: "But if you put in the time to study, you will have no problem getting good grades. Everyone here is intelligent and has the potential, if they work hard enough, to find the courses manageable."

Admirably, the curriculum for English majors must include two British literature courses, "American History before 1920," a course in Shakespeare, and "Introduction to Literature Theory/Criticism," plus six more electives, above the introductory level, in literature, rhetoric, or creative writing. Students are advised to choose their professors wisely; at least one member of the English department (like another teacher in philosophy) is listed on the school's website as a "witchcraft expert."

One professor opines that the College of Community and Public Affairs is a particular waste of time, money, and resources, serving, he says, "as a dumping ground for a good percentage of the basketball team." A recent alumnus says that course work is not demanding and that "professors tend to give decent grades for the most minimal effort."

In the political science department, for instance, students report that they can receive a B for almost no work. "Skip the readings, make an uninformed comment in class once or twice a month, and write your final paper the night before, and you are guaranteed at least a B," says a student

VITAL STATISTICS

Religious affiliation: *none*
Total enrollment: *15,308*
Total undergraduates: *12,356*
SAT CR/Verbal midrange: *600–680*
SAT Math midrange: *620–710*
ACT midrange: *27–30*
Applicants: *28,101*
Applicants accepted: *41%*
Accepted applicants who enrolled: *22%*
Tuition (general/out of state): *$16,761*
Tuition (in state): *$7,613*
Room and board: *$12,336*
Freshman retention rate: *90%*
Graduation rate (4 yrs.): *67%*
Graduation rate (6 yrs.): *78%*
Courses with fewer than 20 students: *40%*
Student-faculty ratio: *20:1*
Courses taught by graduate students: *not provided*
Students living on campus: *58%*
Students in fraternities: *10%*
Students in sororities: *12%*
Students receiving need-based financial aid: *72%*
Avg. student-loan debt of a recent graduating class: *$22,634*
Most popular majors: *business, communications, visual and performing arts*
Guaranteed housing for 4 years? *no*

CAMPUS POLITICS: GREEN LIGHT

Students at Binghamton agree that their classmates are quite apolitical. "Out of [more than 12,000] undergraduates, I don't think there are ever more than a few hundred hard-core activist / political types," one student says. "And these few do not get taken seriously by the majority of students." While every year brings a few leftist rallies, teach-ins, and other political events, only a few students— about 20 is typical—attend them, and each event seems to have the same organizers.

In fact, according to one student, the student government is actually more actively conservative in its leanings. "Liberals generally don't get as involved in student government," the student says. "There's College Democrats and College Republicans and a couple of activist groups on both sides, which died down a few years ago. Things have been pretty quiet lately. You hear this from every college, and ours is no different—the students overall are pretty apathetic."

Another student cites the array of speakers the *Binghamton Review* has sponsored—including the late Christopher Hitchens and neocon Dinesh D'Souza—as an indication of the school's enthusiasm for an authentic exchange of ideas in counterpoint to the stale "diversity" offered by their more liberal counterparts. "We attracted a very diverse crowd with very diverse opinions on the speakers," the student says. One professor adds that the average lukewarm student makes for dull classroom dynamics. "As a teacher, I would prefer more radicals and conservatives in my class discussions, but partisans or even proponents of either side are few and far between."

who worked in the campus tutorial center and believes that the other social science departments operate in much the same way. "Just scribble some words on a page, turn it in, and you will get a passing grade. You hardly even need to write in coherent sentences, much less proofread." To its credit, the department requires all majors to take a foundational set of courses in American politics, the American legal system, American political institutions, constitutional law and politics, international law—as well as four advanced electives.

The history department has a substantial set of major requirements, including one course each in United States, European, and world (Middle East, Asia, Africa, or Latin America) history; interregional comparative history; five advanced electives; and a senior seminar. Since the course on U.S. history can come from any period, students are free to study the 1950s and *Father Knows Best* instead of the Founding Fathers.

Bright students can participate in the Binghamton Scholars Program. The four-year honors program allows the top 120 students at Binghamton to take smaller, more rigorous courses, often using collaborative and experiential learning. One faculty member says that the Scholars at Binghamton are "equaled by few and surpassed by none." Another professor, however, is suspicious of the program's lack of academic rigor, noting that "its courses are less academically oriented than oriented toward 'leadership' and community service." The program consists of one class per semester, taken along with the student's regular work. The program fulfills the general-education requirements, freeing up the student's schedule even further.

Freshman Scholars complete a two-semester project-based course ("Scholars" I and II) in which students record in portfolios what they have learned. Likewise, sophomores study two topics, while juniors participate in an experiential-learning class, and seniors complete a capstone project. Apart from this program, every academic department also has a slate of honors courses that are supposed to be more challenging than the regular ones.

According to one professor, Binghamton's weakest departments include sociology ("where the curriculum is devoted to social propaganda and radical philosophy") and philosophy (where the chair specializes in "the study of violence," and several other teachers focus on "postcolonial studies"). This same professor adds, "While the English department possesses a first-rate creative writing program and very good studies in rhetoric, the rest of the department devotes itself strongly to cultural studies, globalization, and the usual radical dispensations." According to one self-described liberal professor, most of the soft sciences are suspect, but the departments most marked by left-leaning identity politics are comparative literature, sociology, and women and gender studies. A teacher notes that when Western civilization does rate a mention among his colleagues, it's more often than not only as "something despicable and to be ranted against."

If you want to get to know grad students really well, this is the school for you. At Binghamton, professors teach the larger lecture courses, whereas graduate teaching assistants lead the weekly discussion sessions. Some lower-level seminars are also led by graduate students rather than by full-time faculty members. Professors normally keep weekly office hours, but how accessible or how willing they are to help undergraduates depends on the professor. "Some of them . . . are great teachers and care about the students' well-being," a biological science major says. "Others are cold and care only about themselves and their research. It's all in the luck of the draw." One student must have good luck indeed: "Almost every teacher I've had has been helpful. They're not here to just do research." He noted that some professors who are attorneys have volunteered to help students resolve personal legal matters.

> A professor said the school seems to have decided to "find new and different ways to provide a mediocre education to an increasingly mediocre student body."

Harpur College has a formal advising program, but otherwise, advising is "virtually nonexistent," says one student, because the only advice professors are instructed to give is on how students can fulfill the university's distribution requirements. Even in that, the student says, "most professors aren't even aware what is going on outside their classrooms or offices, much less of graduation requirements and so forth." Another student sees the advising program as a complete waste of time. "I've never had a positive experience with Harpur advising," this student says. "When I went in for help to finish a five-year course load in four years, they managed to tell me the wrong courses to take. Advising is the bane of every Harpur student."

Students volunteer that the best professors at SUNY Binghamton include Robert Micklus in English; Nancy Tittler in German and Russian studies; Peter Browne in music; Max Pensky (department chair) and Randy Friedman in philosophy; Elizabeth Casteen

SUGGESTED CORE

1. Classics 232/215, Classical Mythology/Ancient Tragedy, Greece and Rome
2. Philosophy 201, Plato and Aristotle
3. Comparative Literature 110, World Literature (Bible as Literature)
4. History 204/205, Early Medieval Europe, 300–1000/Later Medieval Europe 1000–1400 (*closest match*)
5. Political Science 115, Introduction to Ideas and Politics
6. English 245, Shakespeare
7. History 103, Foundations of American Civilization
8. Philosophy 451, Topics in Continental Philosophy

and Thomas Africa (emeritus) in history; and David S. Wilson in biological sciences.

Binghamton's best departments are biology; economics; and philosophy, politics, and law (PPL)—the last of which is especially popular with aspiring attorneys. One professor says, "The course work in this major hammers away at traditional problems in ethics, political philosophy, history, and political science. It seems that PPL comes closer than most to the idea of a basic liberal arts education, staffing its core courses with tenured faculty who have earned a reputation for good teaching." Special-interest majors like Caribbean studies, Africana studies, and women's studies are notoriously weak.

If you need a break from the local color (wintry gray), the school offers an impressive array of overseas programs, and students have access to any of the other overseas programs offered by any of the New York State universities. Programs can either be a semester long or span the entire academic year. Each October, the school holds an Overseas Program Fair that gives students a chance to review all the programs at once. Binghamton sponsors programs in Austria, China, Costa Rica, the Dominican Republic, England, France, Germany, Ghana, India, Ireland, Korea, Morocco, the Netherlands, Nicaragua, and Scotland.

Foreign languages offered at home include Arabic, Chinese, French, German, Greek and Latin, Hebrew, Italian, Korean, Russian, and Spanish, among many others.

Student Life: Not quite a gulag

Most of the 15,308 students share seven residence halls, many of which have been either completely renovated or rebuilt. Mostly constructed in the 1960s, the campus comprises mainly redbrick prison-style buildings separated by more-pleasant lawns of green. Amazingly, demand for on-campus housing at Binghamton is strong, so the university is facing a housing crunch caused by poor planning, in spite of two new halls. Thus, the typically small college dorm room has gotten a little smaller, as many doubles have been converted to triples. The most notorious dorm seems to be Newing; reviews appear repeatedly on various college blogs and are not good. It seems that unless you are a serious partier from Long Island, you may not fit in—nor will anyone get much sleep. As one student says, "The joke on campus is that, at Binghamton, students have a choice of studying, partying, and sleeping—but you can only choose two." In addition, upperclassmen and nontraditional freshmen have the option of living in one of the school's campus apartment complexes: Hillside or Susquehanna. The Off-Campus College program provides lists of available apartments and houses in the Binghamton area. There are no single-sex dormitories at the university, but students do have the option of living on single-sex floors. The school does not have any coed bathrooms or rooms in campus residences.

The university banned alcohol on campus a few years ago, but as one student reports: "That doesn't mean the campus is completely dry. Lots of students drink in their dorm rooms. It's just a matter of not getting caught." Another student says: "Binghamton students go to bars, go to house parties, frat parties, drink, and hook up. There is a lot to do on campus, but very few students participate in those weekend events." Around 10 percent of Binghamton students participate in Greek life, but fraternities are housed off campus, and sororities are not residential. One fraternity member and honors student says that Greek students can find the perfect balance between social life and studies. "[In] our fraternity . . . we recently created the position of Academic Head to deal with advising and study time around midterm week. All fraternities do fairly well, and they also do a lot of community service. Frat life is not throwing kegs out the windows and having D-Day ride up the stairs on a motorcycle—although that would be pretty cool."

"I know plenty of people who will do things other than party, such as spend time relaxing or preparing for a class in the upcoming week," says another student. "While some do take off for the weekends, if there's a paper or a midterm coming up or something like that, you'll find a lot of students studying. Schoolwork doesn't necessarily end on the weekends."

The school has the usual gamut of progressive organizations that haunt almost any college campus, as well as two liberal periodicals, *Prospect* and *Free Press*. The school sponsors the Womyn's Center and the Rainbow Pride Union, alongside more traditional activities such as Ultimate Frisbee and Hillel. The school does have a (Catholic) Newman Center on campus and a number of Protestant ministries. The school also boasts a strong Jewish community, which appears to harbor a group of conservative students. The *Binghamton Review* is the school's student-run right-of-center newspaper.

As one student puts it, "if you like New Yorkers, this is your school. If not, don't apply here." Since the majority of students live so close to home, many are away on weekends, but Binghamton is by no means a suitcase school. The area is surrounded by natural beauty for students willing to pull themselves away from books and beer.

The Binghamton Bearcats (formerly the Colonials) compete in 22 varsity sports in NCAA Division I. Students can also participate in 49 intercollegiate and 18 intramural sports. The football and men's basketball teams get publicity disproportional to their accomplishments owing to regular mentions on alumnus Tony Kornheiser's TV and radio shows.

Crime is not a big problem on campus; in 2011 the school reported six forcible sex offenses, one nonforcible sex offense, 11 burglaries, and one case of arson—not bad for a huge university.

We'll say this for it—the school is dirt cheap, at least for in-state students, who in 2012–13 paid tuition of only $7,613. Nonresidents paid $16,761, and the average spent for room and board was $12,336. Almost half of students received need-based aid, and the average 2012 Binghamton graduate walked away with a manageable debt of $22,634.

STRONG SUITS

- Low, low tuition for NY State students.
- The program in philosophy, politics, and law (PPL) provides a solid education in government.
- English majors must study Shakespeare—not true at many other schools.
- Mostly helpful teachers who care about students.

WEAK POINTS

- Huge classes, lots of grad students teaching.
- Whole departments where grade inflation has gone wild and standards have plummeted.
- Many highly politicized courses and majors.
- Crowded dorms that look like prison blocs.
- Cold weather, geographic isolation.

So You're Looking For

A Party School Where You Can Still Learn Something

1. Washington and Lee (p. 875)

2. University of Hawaii (p. 351)

3. Indiana University (p. 369)

4. Brown University (p. 67)

5. University of Mississippi (p. 452)

United States Military Academy

West Point, New York • www.usma.edu

Duty, Honor, Country

In 1802 Congress enacted the legislation founding the United States Military Academy. Under the command of Colonel Sylvanus Thayer, it was transformed into a rigorous center for civil and military engineering based on France's École Polytechnique. Much of the expansion of the young Republic was facilitated by West Point graduates, who designed the necessary roads, bridges, canals, ports, and railroads. During the Civil War, both sides were commanded by generals who had attended the academy. In every significant conflict the United States has ever engaged in, from the Mexican War to the Persian Gulf wars, products of West Point have led the way. Over the past two centuries, those who have passed through the "Long Gray Line" have gone on to become presidents, ambassadors, generals, engineers, scientists, and intellectuals.

West Point's core curriculum is a very solid introduction to the liberal arts, and the APL major permits an in-depth study of the ideas fundamental to the Western tradition. For the student who desires to combine a liberal arts education with military service, West Point is an excellent choice.

Blue Collar Ivy

VITAL STATISTICS

Religious affiliation: *none*
Total enrollment: *4,624*
Total undergraduates: *4,624*
SAT CR/Verbal midrange:
 560–680
SAT Math midrange:
 590–690
ACT midrange: *25–31*
Applicants: *13,954*
Applicants accepted: *10.6%*
Accepted applicants who
 enrolled: *84%*
Tuition (general/out of
 state): *free*
Tuition (in state): *free*
Room and board: *free*
Freshman retention rate:
 93%
Graduation rate (4 yrs.): *80%*
Graduation rate (6 yrs.): *86%*
Courses with fewer than 20
 students: *94%*
Student-faculty ratio: *8:1*
Courses taught by graduate
 students: *not provided*
Students living on campus:
 100%
Students in fraternities:
 none
Students in sororities: *none*
Students receiving need-
 based financial aid: *N/A*
Avg. student-loan debt of a
 recent graduating class:
 not provided
Most popular majors:
 *engineering, social sci-
 ences, literature/foreign
 languages*
Guaranteed housing for 4
 years? *yes*

Academic Life: *Mens sana in corpore sano*

The formation of West Point cadets aims at creating *mens sana in corpore sano* (a sound mind in a sound body), an Army officer capable of leadership, and a morally upright person who may be trusted in command. All this takes place within a strict system of military discipline. Each cadet takes an oath "to defend the Constitution of the United States from all enemies, foreign and domestic"—that is, to be prepared to fight in this country's wars, near and far. (Conscientious objection after the oath has been administered is viewed as a breach of service contract.) The goal is "to educate, train, and inspire the Corps of Cadets so that each graduate is a commissioned leader of character committed to the values of duty, honor, country." These values are meant to animate "a career as an officer in the United States Army; and a lifetime of self-less service to the nation."

Admission is highly competitive, and candidates must receive a nomination from a member of Congress or from the Department of the Army. Each year the academy admits approximately 1,500 young men and (thanks to activist judges) women, although the male-female student ratio is 84 percent to 16 percent. Upon graduation, cadets receive a bachelor of science degree and a commission as a second lieutenant in the U.S. Army; they must also commit to at least five years of active duty and three years in a Reserve Component. The academy graduates more than 900 new officers annually.

Perhaps because of its intensity, the "West Point Experience" has proved adept at creating bonds of friendship and solidarity. After leaving both the Point and after serving in the Army, the fidelity of alumni both to the institution and to each other is strong. A West Point education can provide unique opportunities for leadership in the civil and commercial spheres, in addition to the military.

Academics at the Point are demanding. To begin with, there is a genuine core curriculum of 26 to 30 courses, depending on the major. The core curriculum "provides a foundation in mathematics, basic sciences, engineering sciences, information technology, humanities, behavioral sciences, and social sciences," according to the school. Combined as it is with physical education and military science, this core constitutes the military academy's "professional major." Although based on the needs of the Army, it is further intended to establish the foundation for a field of study or an optional major. The academy further requires the cadet to complete 10 relevant electives for each major, adding up to 40 academic courses in total. Academic advising during the first two years (called "Fourth and Third Class") is done through "company academic counselors." In his third year (or "Second Class"), the cadet is assigned a counselor in his major.

The United States Corps of Cadets, to which each cadet belongs, comprises 32 cadet companies grouped into battalions, regiments, and finally the corps as a whole. This structure is overseen by the Brigade Tactical Department, led by the brigade tactical officer (BTO), an active-duty colonel. Other, lower-ranking officers and noncommissioned officers (NCOs) are assigned as tactical officers (TACs) to each of the cadet formations. They supervise each cadet's development—academic, military, physical, and moral-ethical. TACs function as commanders of each unit alongside the cadet officers, and they act as mentors, counselors, leaders, motivators, trainers, evaluators, commanders, role models, teachers, and administrators. In addition, the Center for Personal Development, a counseling and assessment center staffed by Army officers trained as professional counselors-psychologists, provides individual and group counseling.

All teaching is done by the professors, and the student-faculty ratio is 8 to 1, with classes usually numbering between 12 and 18 students. Some 55 percent of cadets choose to complete a major in the general fields of engineering, social sciences, or foreign languages and literatures. There are currently 22 optional majors and 24 fields of study, covering virtually all the liberal arts (except Classics), and all science and engineering disciplines found in equivalent highly selective civilian colleges. Each of these fields of study requires a cadet

CAMPUS POLITICS: GREEN LIGHT

As might be expected, life for cadets at West Point is extremely regimented. Of course, given the intensive academic, mental, and physical training undergone, this makes sense. But the academy, anxious to produce good leaders, is not content with mere regimentation. "Moral-ethical development" is important as well: the authorities aim to foster it through "formal instruction in the important values of the military profession, voluntary religious programs, interaction with staff and faculty role models, and a vigorous guest speaker program." But the most important moral element involved is the Cadet Honor Code, summed up in the line "A cadet will not lie, cheat, steal, or tolerate those who do." The Honor Code is supposed to govern cadet life—and to a great degree it does.

However, one consideration for women (and their parents) thinking about applying to the Point is, to be blunt, sexual. Every few years or so there is a sex scandal at one of the service academies. Although no one can fault the patriotism and ability of the academy's female grads, the fact remains that placing young men and women at their sexual peak in intimate proximity and under heavy pressure is a recipe for erotic activity; the fact that such things are reduced to mere pastimes in many high schools does not help. Inevitably, a few commanding officers' careers have ended for such things happening on their watch.

to pursue 10 electives in courses specified by the academic discipline. Cadets who "desire to enrich their academic experiences and pursue disciplines in greater depth" may choose to follow majors with 11 or more electives and complete a senior thesis or design project, the school reports.

Although engineering retains pride of place at West Point, the liberal arts are not neglected. The art, philosophy, and literature (APL) major, for example, offers courses from English, foreign languages, history, law, and social sciences. This major is the best choice for the would-be officer who craves a true humanistic education. It features very solid courses, such as the "Cultural Studies" class, which is mercifully not the politicized piffle it often amounts to elsewhere. Rather, the course "not only acquaints cadets with a particular period and place but also introduces them to various definitions of culture and to recent themes and debates in cultural studies." The course is team taught, and "typical areas of focus include Augustan Rome, Enlightenment France, and Meiji Japan." This fine course is part of the basic requirement for the APL major, together with an art history course ("Eastern Art," "Masterpieces before Giotto," "Topics in Art History," or "Art I: Ancient to Medieval") and an elective ("Criticism" or "Logical Reasoning"), as well as an information technology course, either "Theory and Practice of Military IT Systems" or "Advanced Theory of Military IT Systems," and a senior seminar.

From the Mexican War to the Persian Gulf wars, products of West Point have led the way. For 200 years graduates have gone on to become presidents, ambassadors, generals, engineers, scientists, and intellectuals.

Six electives, either in philosophy or literature, complete the major in APL: four literature or philosophy electives plus one departmental elective and a language elective. This major's literature track offers excellent courses, such as "British Literature" I, "ranging from the Anglo-Saxon period through the eighteenth century"; "American Literature" II, "both traditional and nontraditional writings from the Civil War to the present"; "Shakespeare"; and "World Literature." In many colleges a course in world literature is a sort of random survey; at West Point it teaches students "epics and tragedies of ancient Greece and Rome, Russian novels, works of medieval Islamic literature, haiku of Japan, Continental European novels of the nineteenth century, or postmodern fiction of South America." Cadets are asked to examine works selected for their intrinsic quality and significance without reference to any political agenda. If students choose instead the philosophy track, they'll face courses such as "Philosophy of Mind," which jointly addresses "major topics in the traditional philosophy of mind and questions created by recent developments in artificial intelligence."

History majors may choose the Defense and Strategic Studies or Military track. In either track, students take one of the two above-mentioned IT courses, "Colloquium in History," and in the military track they then take one "integrative experience" course, like "Warfare since 1945" or "Race, Ethnicity, Nation," and seven electives to complete the major—five from the "Military History" section ("War at Sea and in the Air," "Ancient and Medieval Warfare") and two "out-of-stem" history (such as "Medieval Europe"), plus one language course.

Scholars of government may choose among three tracks in the political science major: international relations, comparative politics, and American politics. The American politics major requires one of the two previously mentioned IT courses, one course of four options including "Political Analysis," "Comparative Politics," "Political Philosophy and Policy," and "State and the Economy," and a course in "Advanced American Politics, Policy, and Strategy." Three elective American politics courses, one elective in comparative politics and one in international relations, plus one foreign language course complete the major.

The other side of academia at West Point is the Military Program, which begins on a cadet's very first day. Most military training takes place during the summer. New "plebes" (as first-year cadets are known) undergo cadet basic training—or "Beast Barracks"—in the summer preceding their first academic year. Cadet field training at nearby Camp Buckner takes place during the second year. The third and fourth summers are spent "serving in active Army units around the world; attending advanced training courses such as airborne, air assault, or northern warfare; or training the first- and second-year cadets as members of the leadership cadre." Military science instruction in the classroom is conducted during the school year. The distinct emphasis on military science means that all cadets graduate with a bachelor of science degree, even if they choose a more humanistic major.

The student can choose among the seven languages offered at West Point, which are Arabic, Chinese, French, German, Portuguese, Russian, and Spanish. There are also many study-abroad opportunities, with 140 cadets going abroad every year to 13 countries, and many cadets take part in summer immersion programs, as well, in more than 50 countries.

SUGGESTED CORE

1. History 365, The Ancient World
2. English 388, Ancient Philosophy
3. No suitable course
4. History 361, Medieval Europe (*closest match*)
5. Social Sciences 386, Political Thought and Ideas
6. English 394, Shakespeare
7. History 153, Advanced History of the United States
8. English and Philosophy 376, Kant and 19th-Century Philosophy

Student Life: God, country, and athletics

Despite the many official demands on a cadet's time, he does have plenty of options for the leisure time he gets. Boxing (men's and women's), rock climbing, paintball, rugby (men's and women's), equestrian activities, and water polo are all available, as are a cadet radio station, fly-fishing, sailing, and Big Brother–Big Sister. Cadets produce such publications as the *Howitzer* (a yearbook), the *West Point Calendar, Bugle Notes,* and the *West Point Planner.* Some outsiders may be surprised by the existence of the *Circle in the Spiral,* the literary / art journal of the Corps of Cadets, which features poems, artwork, and stories by cadets.

The Directorate of Cadet Activities sponsors more than 100 clubs, ranging from Amateur Radio, German Language Forum, the Debate Council, the Nuclear Engineering Club, and the Korean-American Relations Seminar to the Inline Hockey Club, the Scuba Diving Club, and the Skeet and Trap Hunting Club. There are no fraternities or sororities.

The academy requires a great deal physically: each semester, every cadet participates in an intercollegiate (NCAA I) club or intramural sport. Intramural sports range from basketball to handball and flickerball. Likewise, the quite successful club teams include such sports as judo, boxing, and equestrian events. West Point is of course renowned for "Army Football"; the entire corps of cadets is required to attend—together with the school's mascot, the Mule—and stand throughout each home game of the "Black Knights." Other intercollegiate sports include men's swimming and rifle and women's soccer and volleyball.

All cadets are housed in the campus barracks. There are generally two or three cadets in a room. Women and men reside on the same floor, but women do room together "in their assigned companies."

From the dawn of warfare, the need for religion to undergird the warrior's resolve has been acknowledged—at least until our own day. In 1972 federal courts ended mandatory chapel attendance at the federal service academies. Nevertheless, until and unless the civilian leadership banishes it entirely, religious life flourishes—on a purely voluntary basis—at West Point.

There are seven chapels at West Point, each of which receives a great deal of use. Gothic Cadet Chapel, the most notable architecturally, was dedicated in 1910. The first pew features silver plates engraved with the signatures of such previous superintendents as Generals MacArthur, Taylor, and Westmoreland. This chapel features Protestant services every Sunday and hosts the Protestant Chapel Choir and the Protestant Chapel Sunday School. Its choir is famous and performs at a number of the academy's traditional ceremonies. The neoclassical Old Cadet Chapel was built in 1836. Originally located near the cadet barracks, it was moved stone by stone to its present location in 1910. Located near the entrance of the cemetery, the Old Cadet Chapel hosts many funerals and memorials and has long been the home for Lutheran services. A third Protestant facility is the Georgian-style Community Post Chapel. Built in 1943, it is occupied now by a Gospel congregation.

Catholics attend the Chapel of the Most Holy Trinity, built in the Norman Gothic style in 1899, enlarged in 1959, and the oldest cadet chapel in continuous use. Among other features, it boasts 22 stained-glass windows showing soldier-saints and memorializing Catholic alumni killed in the service of their country. Masses are held daily at noon, on Saturday evening, and twice on Sunday, with music by the Cadet Catholic Choir and the Catholic Folk Group.

Opened in 1984 the Jewish Chapel contains an extensive Judaica collection, a library, and special exhibits. Sabbath services are held every Friday evening during the academic year, augmented by the Jewish Chapel Cadet Choir. The Eastern Orthodox community worships in St. Martin's chapel downstairs in the Cadet Chapel.

The school does not report its crime statistics; however, apart from occasional sex scandals, there seems to be little criminal activity to speak of.

There is no tuition at West Point. Since all cadets are members of the Army, their education is free, and in addition they receive an annual salary of more than $10,000.

STRONG SUITS

- Exquisite education in engineering, military science, leadership, history.
- Surprisingly extensive, rigorous traditional offerings in most of the liberal arts.
- Broad but serious coverage of foreign cultures, without the politicized lens of multiculturalism.
- Discipline, training, and dead-serious Honor Code combine to provide elite character education.
- Intense physical training that helps provide a sound mind with a healthy body.

WEAK POINTS

- Classics (Latin and Greek) are not offered, nor is a course in the Bible.
- Coeducation in close quarters and military conditions produces sex scandals periodically.
- The intensity of discipline and physical training ensures a certain failure rate. Be sure you're really ready for this.

So You're Looking For

A Place for Good Clean Fun

1. University of Utah *(p. 624)*

2. Patrick Henry College *(p. 708)*

3. Baylor University *(p. 26)*

4. Ave Maria University *(p. 9)*

5. Gordon College *(p. 179)*

North Carolina State University

Raleigh, North Carolina • www.ncsu.edu

Brick by Brick

Founded in 1877 as a land-grant college, NC State now hosts more than 34,000 students pursuing degrees in more than 110 fields spread across 12 colleges. The strongest programs appear in agriculture, science, and engineering. Consistently ranked as a top "best value" public university, NC State maintains an internationally known research university with a modest, yet respectable, liberal arts program.

Academic Life: Box by box

Every student at NC State faces the General Education Program (GEP) requirements for basic competency in humanities, mathematics, natural sciences, physical education and health, and social sciences. There are also "Corequisites" in Diversity, Global Knowledge, and visual and performing arts. Finally, students must meet an "Interdisciplinary Perspectives" requirement, which is often taken care of by one of the corequisites.

NC State hosts a selective honors program, which offers housing in the Honors Village, early registration for classes, advanced advising and study-abroad opportunities, and leadership workshops. The four required honors seminars, however, tend to emphasize trendy topics like "Victims, Vampires, War Dead and Other Corpses: Mediating Death in American Culture."

Another worthwhile program at NC State is the University Scholars Program, available to sophomores with a minimum GPA of 3.25. University Scholars can choose to live in the Scholars Village and must complete four small, seminar-oriented classes chosen from various departments; they are also allowed early registration for classes. They attend cultural events throughout the semester.

Freshmen are assigned advisers and attend a two-semester orientation course, "Introduction to University Education," where they earn one hour of letter-graded credit a semester. NC State does a good job guiding its students toward their majors. Those students already in a declared major will meet each semester with faculty advisers within their departments. Some students complain that in the more popular majors, like engineering, as many as 1,600 students may compete for a 15-minute visit with a single, overworked professor/adviser.

Professors are reportedly dedicated to their students, however. Motivated students find that "professors truly want to ensure that you understand what is being taught in their classes." NC State does make use of TAs, particularly in teaching "gatekeeper" introductory courses, but for the most part they simply help grade tests, supervise labs, and lead discussion groups, leaving the teaching to professors.

Faculty members worry that the intellectual curiosity of their students continues to decline. "We try, but it is tough when students 'know' the way courses should be taught," reports one professor. Students "expect [a] review of upcoming examinations," he says. His colleague affirms: "Their major concern is what will be on the next exam." Yet both students and faculty give a long list of professors they admire: Mindy Sopher in communications; Michael McElroy, Steve Margolis, Walter Wessels, Craig Newmark, Thomas Grennes, Walter Thurman, Charles Knoeber, Rick Stroup, and Michael Wohlgenant in economics; Dudley Marchi in French; Marc Grimmett in psychology; Chau Tran, Gregory Buckner, Herbert Eckerlin, and Kevin Lyons in engineering; Bryce Lane in horticulture; Robert V. Young (emeritus), Soren Palmer, Marvin Hunt, Thomas Hester, Michael Grimwood, John Morillo, Sheila Smith McKoy, and Brian Blackley in English;

VITAL STATISTICS

Religious affiliation: *none*
Total enrollment: *34,767*
Total undergraduates: *25,176*
SAT CR/Verbal midrange: *530–620*
SAT Math midrange: *560–660*
ACT midrange: *23–28*
Applicants: *3,807*
Applicants accepted: *34%*
Accepted applicants who enrolled: *27%*
Tuition (general/out of state): *$20,953*
Tuition (in state): *$7,788*
Room and board: *$8,414*
Freshman retention rate: *90%*
Graduation rate (4 yrs.): *37%*
Graduation rate (6 yrs.): *71%*
Courses with fewer than 20 students: *30%*
Student-faculty ratio: *18:1*
Courses taught by graduate students: *9%*
Students living on campus: *32%*
Students in fraternities: *10%*
Students in sororities: *14%*
Students receiving need-based financial aid: *47%*
Avg. student-loan debt of a recent graduating class: *$18,126*
Most popular majors: *biology, business, engineering*
Guaranteed housing for 4 years? *no*

Blue Collar Ivy

CAMPUS POLITICS: GREEN LIGHT

Like many college systems, the many schools within the University of North Carolina system have implemented speech codes with dubious policies that prohibit "insults" (Appalachian State University), "disrespect for persons" (UNC Greensboro), or "offensive speech" (UNC Pembroke). Despite being the largest school in the UNC system, NC State has avoided adopting significant speech codes. The Free Expression Tunnel (a pedestrian walkway where students are permitted to paint graffiti) allows students to comment on political issues, athletic enthusiasm, and personal views. The school calls it "a robust monument to free speech."

According to the *Raleigh News and Observer*, in 2012 a resident assistant appealed a recently issued school "civility statement requiring residents to 'speak to each other in a civil manner' and prohibiting the display of items that might be 'disrespectful' or 'hurtful.'" The RA argued that legally protected political or religious speech might be threatened, and the university issued a clarification reiterating the importance of free expression.

Bob Patterson in crop science; Walt Wolfram in linguistics; Philip Van Vleck in history; and Andy Taylor and Steve Greene in political science.

With its historic strength, the College of Engineering is clearly the pride of NC State, claiming roughly 23 percent of degrees conferred, but the school is impressive in other areas. The College of Veterinary Medicine is ranked third in the nation, with a 180-acre campus near downtown Raleigh. The College of Textiles seeks to be the "global leader in textile innovation," offering a unique course of study on NCSU's Centennial Campus. While the College of Physical and Mathematical Sciences is also noteworthy, the College of Education is not recommended, having lost its best professors to retirement. The departments of Sociology, Women's and Gender Studies, and Anthropology are dominated by leftist professors who reportedly have little tolerance for opposing views. One former student recounts taking a sociology course, "Social Deviance," in which neither the class nor the professor ever settled on a working definition of what constitutes "social deviance." NC State maintains an excellent English program in its College of Humanities and Social Sciences (CHASS), however, and offers strong programs in architecture, business, and economics.

English majors at NC State are required to complete an impressive course of study beyond their college requirements, choosing from concentrations in Language and Literature; World Literature; Creative Writing; Film Studies; and Language, Writing, and Rhetoric. Teacher Education, Language, and Literature majors have to complete two courses in linguistics, rhetoric, or writing; one course each in British literature from the Middle Ages, the Renaissance, and either the 18th or 19th century; one in pre-20th-century American literature; one in 20th- or 21st-century British or American Literature; a course focusing on an author or a genre; a course in world literature; and three electives in English.

History majors have to take a sophomore seminar, a senior seminar, a non–Western world class, a European history class, an American history class, and five electives, four of which must be at an advanced level. Options for fulfilling the requirements are solid, from

"Rome to 337 AD" and "History of British Cultures and Societies since 1688" to "20th Century U.S. Intellectual History" and "The Italian Renaissance."

Political science majors must take statistics, an introduction to American government, a course in research methods, a class in international politics like "Issues in Global Politics," a course in political theory (either "Introduction to Political Theory" or "American Political Thought"), a class in law and justice or public policy, an intermediate elective, four advanced electives, and a seminar at the senior or graduate level.

NC State students can study in Austria, Brazil, Canada, China, the Czech Republic, Finland, France, Indonesia, Morocco, and New Zealand, among numerous other options. Some programs allow students to work part-time in their host countries or even volunteer or intern for academic credit, including programs in Australia, Ghana, Ireland, Japan, Mexico, and the United Kingdom.

NC State offers study in Arabic, Chinese, French, German, Greek and Latin, Hebrew, Hindi, Italian, Japanese, Portuguese, Russian, Spanish, and Swahili.

Student Life: Back the Pack

Raleigh melds the unique charm of a southern town with the bustle of technological innovation. In 2011 Raleigh was ranked America's best city by *Businessweek* magazine.

More than three-quarters of freshmen live in dorms, and more upperclassmen are electing to continue in dorm life, with 35 percent of all students living on campus or in college-affiliated housing. Nearly all dorms are coed, with the exception of Gold and Welch houses, which are all-male and all-female, respectively, each with just 58 residents (all-women floors are also available to female engineers in the Women of Welch Program). Dorms may be coed by suite or by room, but bathrooms are single sex, and NCSU is careful to try to match roommates by lifestyle preference, religion, and study habits. Most of the alcohol-free dorms (15 out of the 20 dorms) also enforce visitation policies, while dorms that permit alcohol to of-age students typically allow for visitors at all hours. Most upperclassmen live off campus, and the streets that surround NCSU are full of cheap rental properties for students, but the university also offers three apartment complexes for upperclassmen in studio and one- and two-bedroom options.

> The biggest problem is the students, whose quality seems to be falling. One teacher attests: "Their major concern is what will be on the next exam."

Academic student organizations include the Design Council, International Society of Tropical Foresters, Model United Nations, and W. E. B. Du Bois Honor Society. The school also hosts cultural groups like the African American Heritage Society, Arabic Club, Chinese Undergraduate Student Association, and Turkish Language and Culture Club.

The school hosts the *Agromeck,* a yearly historical archive of the university; the *Nubian Message;* the satirical *Wolfpack Lampoon;* the *Windhover* literary journal; Wolf TV student

Blue Collar Ivy

television station; 88.1 WKNC student-run radio; and the *Technician,* NC State's official student newspaper.

NC State is politically inclusive. Clubs like Young Americans for Liberty, Students for Concealed Carry on Campus, Students for a Democratic Society, NC State Students for Life, a chapter of the NAACP, a chapter of Americans Elect (which seeks to promote third-party political options), and active College Democrats and Republicans, are all welcome on campus.

A total of 55 religious groups are available to students, including the Adventist Christian Fellowship; Buddhist Philosophies Group; Hillel, Catholic, and Coptic ministries; InterVarsity; the Navigators; the Self-Knowledge Symposium; a Sikh Student Association; and most popularly, Campus Crusade, which often attracts crowds in the thousands and provides service outlets throughout the year.

The NCSU Wolfpack competes in 24 intercollegiate sports in the NCAA Division I Atlantic Coast Conference and other sanctioning bodies. NC State athletes earned their moniker when their fans were described as behaving like a wolf pack—that intense fandom still springs up when the Wolfpack plays its main rival, the UNC Tarheels. "The Pack" tends to be victorious in football, whereas "The Heels" provide an intense challenge to NCSU's basketball team.

With 33 fraternities and 19 sororities recognized by the university, many Greek students elect to live in Greek housing. Over the past decade, the school and the Greek system have battled over housing issues: in the more crowded fraternities and sororities, students often slept four to a room in run-down homes, while the smaller fraternities shouldered higher rents for space they didn't need. Recently, the school has reached an agreement with the Greek system and decided to allow individual chapters to mortgage and build their own houses. Some 10 percent of men join fraternities, and 14 percent of women join sororities.

Although 68 percent of NCSU students live off campus, student safety is a concern for the school. In 2011 the school reported six robberies, nine aggravated assaults, 41 burglaries, 12 motor vehicle thefts, 234 larcenies, and three hate crimes on campus. The neighborhoods immediately surrounding NC State are mainly very wealthy or very poor. A number of homeless people live near campus, and while their interaction with students is generally friendly, more naive students may find their generosity abused.

For in-state students, tuition was a great deal at just $7,788 for 2012, while out-of-state students paid $20,953. Room and board were $8,414. Although NCSU is well ranked among best-value universities, about half of its undergraduates received need-based financial aid and left school with debt averaging $18,126.

STRONG SUITS

- Excellent programs in the colleges of Engineering, Veterinary Medicine, Textiles, and Physical and Mathematical Sciences.
- Worthy departments in architecture, business, economics, English, history, political science.
- Many dedicated teachers, accessible to students.
- Free and open debate on campus and in most classrooms.
- Located in a charming southern city.

WEAK POINTS

- The College of Education has lost its best professors to retirement.
- The departments of sociology, women's and gender studies, and anthropology are dominated by intolerant leftists.
- Students care more about grubbing grades than learning, professors complain.
- Aggressive homeless people loiter around campus.

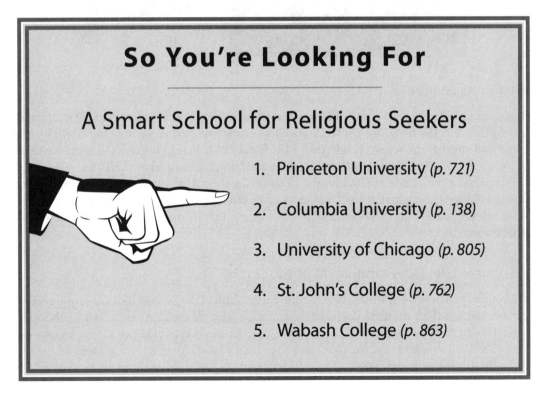

So You're Looking For

A Smart School for Religious Seekers

1. Princeton University *(p. 721)*

2. Columbia University *(p. 138)*

3. University of Chicago *(p. 805)*

4. St. John's College *(p. 762)*

5. Wabash College *(p. 863)*

University of North Carolina at Chapel Hill

Chapel Hill, North Carolina • www.unc.edu

First in Its League

Founded in 1795 the University of North Carolina at Chapel Hill was the first state university founded in the fledgling United States. Its distinctive virtues include the facilities of a large and prestigious research university (in fiscal 2012, research grants and contracts at UNC totaled $759 million, mostly in the sciences), the charm of Chapel Hill's college-town atmosphere, a multitude of student organizations, a strong faculty, and many hundreds of courses. Indeed, a student at the University of North Carolina can certainly graduate with a sturdy foundation in the liberal arts—or waste much of his time. The key is selecting courses wisely.

Academic Life: Queer medieval photography

Although it insists on nothing like a core curriculum, UNC's distribution requirements do a better job than most. Unfortunately, the wide latitude students are given in choosing courses—from "The Medieval Church" to "Queer Latina/o Literature and Photography"—that fulfill requirements means that someone could easily blunder through four years and miss the liberal arts completely. One student sums up the watered-down quality of the general-education curriculum by observing, "U.S. history is not required, and cultural diversity is."

UNC has a highly regarded honors program, which offers separate, smaller sections of existing courses and select interdisciplinary seminars. Each year some 200 applicants are chosen for this program, which carries with it enhanced financial aid. Others can apply to transfer in. Students praise the program for its rigor in liberal arts; however, honors relies for most of its classes on existing undergraduate selections, some of which are trivial or politicized, so it's hardly an intellectual utopia. But students can grapple with the writings of Machiavelli, Descartes, and the American Founders in the honors seminar "The Elements of Politics" or study "Verdi's Operas and Italian Romanticism" and "The Romans," which features readings from Petronius and Virgil. One student says that honors classes "don't seem to be any more rigorous than regular classes, just smaller and more intimate."

Some students report strong relationships with faculty members, who generally maintain open-door policies—while others can't name one who has had an impact on them. As one student explained, "You must take the initiative to seek help from them." Upon enrollment, every student is paired with an academic adviser. He must meet with his adviser at the beginning of his freshman year and when he declares his major, but these meetings can be in a group. One undergrad says, "Academic advising here is exceptional." Others disagree. Advisers, say another student, "will give you 15 minutes before registration, but that's it. And sometimes they can confuse you. . . . Advisers know nothing about course requirements."

Recommended departments at Chapel Hill include business, health care, and "any of the sciences," according to a student. The Kenan-Flagler Business School has an excellent nationwide reputation. The Center for Entrepreneurial Studies has been named among the best in the country and provides students with internships and other opportunities.

The English department is mentioned by some for its attention to teaching and its relatively traditional curriculum. One grad student suggests sticking to the earlier periods taught in the department

VITAL STATISTICS

Religious affiliation: *none*
Total enrollment: *29,137*
Total undergraduates: *18,430*
SAT CR/Verbal midrange: *590–700*
SAT Math midrange: *610–700*
ACT midrange: *26–32*
Applicants: *23,047*
Applicants accepted: *31%*
Accepted applicants who enrolled: *54%*
Tuition (general/out of state): *$28,252*
Tuition (in state): *$7,644*
Room and board: *$9,734*
Freshman retention rate: *97%*
Graduation rate (4 yrs.): *76%*
Graduation rate (6 yrs.): *87%*
Courses with fewer than 20 students: *44%*
Student-faculty ratio: *14:1*
Courses taught by graduate students: *not provided*
Students living on campus: *46%*
Students in fraternities: *17%*
Students in sororities: *17%*
Students receiving need-based financial aid: *64%*
Avg. student-loan debt of a recent graduating class: *$17,525*
Most popular majors: *biology, communications, psychology*
Guaranteed housing for 4 years? *no*

Blue Collar Ivy

CAMPUS POLITICS: GREEN LIGHT

Both students and faculty report an indefinable "mood" of political correctness on the UNC campus, but it appears not to be repressive. Pro-life students catch some heat for their activism and are undersupported by student government compared with events like UNC's semiannual drag show.

In a show of petty political correctness, the school banned the use of the word *freshman* as sexist in 2012. In the same year, the school used student funds to install condom machines in dormitories, reported *Campus Reform*—which pointed with alarm to a story in the *Daily Tar Heel* revealing "illicit sexual activity specific to Davis Library, the University's largest."

A graduate of Chapel Hill wrote in 2011 in a publication of the conservative Pope Center that "liberals dominate the campus dialogue. Their dominance is often revealed as soon as one steps on campus. Admissions ambassadors laud our 'commitment to diversity.' Chants of 'People, not profits!' ring from the frequent leftist protests that disturb our tranquil campus. The blatant lack of support for non-leftist ideas even appears to be official policy. The main lecture series sponsored by the university only brings liberal speakers like Sen. John Kerry or author Kevin Phillips."

Still, conservatives feel free to speak, most teachers are fair, and a lively debate prevails on campus. That's the most one can expect at a state university these days.

(medieval and Renaissance) to avoid politically charged courses. On the other hand, a professor strongly recommends the American literature courses. Southern specialist Fred Hobson is a first-rate scholar and a fair-minded, conscientious teacher, a former student reports. Requirements for the major look excellent: students must take introductory classes in Shakespeare, British literature from Chaucer to Pope, either British literature from Wordsworth to Eliot or a seminar in literary studies, one pre-1660 course, two 1660–1900 courses, and one post-1900 course.

The history major, however, has barely any breadth requirements: students must pick a concentration in ancient/medieval, gender and women, modern European, global, Third World/Non-Western, or United States history and also take one course in Third World/Non-Western history. Beyond that, all bets are off.

Political science majors must take introductory courses in American government and international relations, a lower-level course in comparative politics, and a course in political theory; the rest are electives.

Insiders describe the Department of Classics as "rigorous," and among the best in the country. The School of Journalism and Mass Communication is also highly lauded. The art history department's strength is in teaching, which is made easier by the university's impressive art collection. Disciplines that students are warmly advised to avoid include the African American, sexuality, and women's studies programs.

One professor observed that while discerning and motivated students can cobble together a good liberal arts education from the 77 departments at UNC, they will have more difficulty finding a strong intellectual community. As a remedy he recommends the interdisciplinary studies programs—which tend to be smaller than other departments and provide students with a more cohesive liberal arts program. Particularly recommended are the American and the international studies programs.

Students and professors name the following as among the best teachers at the university: Jean DeSaix, William Kier, and Patricia Pukkila in biology; James Jorgenson in chemistry; Barbara Day in education; Michael Salemi in economics; Robert Cantwell in American studies; Michael McFee, Christopher Armitage, Reid Barbour, Darryl Gless, Philip Gura, Trudier Harris (emeritus), Joy Kasson, Ted Leinbaugh, George Lensing Jr., James Seay, and Jessica Wolfe in English; William Barney, Peter Coclanis, W. Miles Fletcher, Jacquelyn Dowd Hall, John Kasson, Roger Lotchin, and Jay Smith in history; R. Michael Hoefges in journalism; Sue Goodman in mathematics; James Ketch in music; Laurie McNeil and Lawrence Rowan in physics and astronomy; Michael Lienesch, Kevin McGuire, Mark Crescenzi, Georg Vanberg, Terry Sullivan, and Thomas Oatley in political science; Bart Ehrman and Ruel Tyson Jr. in religious studies; Michael Shanahan in sociology; and Daniel Gitterman in public policy.

Almost half of all classes have 20 or fewer students, and 70 percent have fewer than 30—despite a lukewarm student-faculty ratio of 14 to 1. Large classes are broken up into recitation sessions led by graduate teaching assistants. "Most of the introductory-level classes are taught by TAs, but once you move into the more major-specific courses, you usually get professors," says a student.

UNC Chapel Hill is more laissez-faire than liberal, allowing students to use their time well on fundamentals or fritter it away on fluff.

The extent to which politics affects classroom policies and discussion varies. One student comments, "In the classroom, professors are rarely overtly political in my experience, but they are successful in creating an environment conducive to liberal and progressive thought. Right-leaning students can be too intimidated to speak up in class. Including me, every once in a while." A professor says, "My impression is that it is easy for conservative students to feel comfortable here among their peers, though they may feel uncomfortable with some of the faculty's prejudices in certain courses." The student body is indeed more politically diverse than the faculty. UNC's board of governors has mandated that 82 percent of the students in each class be North Carolina residents. This means that many of the students coming from North Carolina's small, rural towns and counties bring traditional and conservative values with them.

UNC has study-abroad programs in locations ranging from Iceland to Togo, and offers courses in Arabic, Bulgarian, Cherokee, Chichewa, Chinese, Croatian, Czech, Dutch, French, German, Greek and Latin, Hebrew, Hindi-Urdu, Hungarian, Italian, Japanese, Korean, Lingala, Macedonian, Persian, Polish, Portuguese, Russian, Serbian, Spanish, Swahili, Tamil, Turkish, and Wolof.

Student Life: Preachers in the Pit

The city of Chapel Hill (population 57,233) is often hailed as a great college town with a vibrant culture, cheap eats, and hopping nightlife. On campus, students hang out at the

SUGGESTED CORE

1. Classics 55, Three Greek and Roman Epics
2. Philosophy 210, Ancient Greek Philosophy
3. Religious Studies 103/104, Introduction to the Hebrew Bible/Introduction to the New Testament
4. History 431, The Medieval Church
5. Politics 271, Modern Political Thought
6. English 225, Shakespeare
7. History 127, American History to 1865
8. History 466, Modern European Intellectual History

Pit, a sunken cement and brick area in the center of campus, where one sees and hears all sorts of people, from pot-smoking hippies to boisterous preachers warning the stoners about the Antichrist. The area is flanked by a dining hall, the campus bookstore, a library, and the student union. Spray-painted signs advertise upcoming events and publicize student groups.

The university boasts about 650 clubs, teams, and student organizations, of almost every kind imaginable. The Young Democrats is one of the university's most active student groups, with more than 700 members. The College Republicans are quite active, and the Students for Life website boasts that it is "one of the most well-respected and active student pro-life groups in the country." The College Libertarians report growing interest in libertarianism on campus. The *Carolina Review*, a conservative journal, is published monthly and also has daily blog entries.

"There is always something going on," a student says. Another student reports, "There are almost always frat parties . . . and the bar scene is very popular." About 17 percent of students join one of the 40 fraternities or 23 sororities. "Greek life is very popular but surprisingly academic. Most fraternities and sororities are highly involved in community service and professional organizations," a student says. A faculty member points out: "Greek students at UNC have a consistently higher GPA on average than non-Greek students." Another student says, however, that the Greek culture is a "fairly isolated sector that the rest of campus pays little attention to."

There are student organizations for Baha'is, Buddhists, Friends, Hindus, Jews, Latter-Day Saints, Muslims, and Zoroastrians, as well as numerous Christian denominations; but houses of worship on campus seem to be a mixed bag. One student found more to praise in the student-run religious clubs than the chapels themselves: "I attended the Newman Catholic Center every Sunday last year as a freshman; there were a lot of student-run programs there. I was happy to see that." But he adds that, in general, "The churches here are more about spirituality and the liberal ideas on social justice and tolerance than religion, God, and duty." Both professors and students note a strong evangelical Christian presence on the campus, with vibrant chapters of InterVarsity Christian Fellowship organizing student missions on and off campus. Students of other faiths should probably seek out more traditional houses of worship in town.

Collegiate sports—led by basketball, of course—are very important to life at UNC (at least when the teams are doing well). The college participates in the Atlantic Coast Conference and the NCAA I division. The men's basketball team won the national championship in 2009. Rameses the Ram is the Tarheels' live mascot, cheering on 13 men's and 15 women's varsity teams. At more than $37 million for 10 years, North Carolina's contract with Nike is the largest of its kind. Students are heavily involved in sports, either by supporting the school's teams or by participating in club or intramural sports. Every October students cram into the 21,750-seat basketball arena for a little "midnight madness" to watch their beloved team scrimmage at the stroke of midnight when the practice season officially begins. There are 40 intramural sports and 50 club teams, ranging from Aikido to squash.

Students speak highly of the more recently built dorms, apartment communities, and family housing at UNC, but one student says, "the dorms are pretty bad," and while recent renovations have made improvements, "a lot of these dorms still have asbestos and other carcinogens in the wall supposedly behind several layers of paint." In 2009 the New North Hall replaced one of the old dorms and houses students and faculty, who praise it highly. There is no distinction between upper-class and freshman housing, and so all undergrads apply for the same slots. UNC does not guarantee housing, but most students who want housing can get it, whether or not they're happy with what they're offered.

Only 46 percent of students live on campus, but those who live off campus tend to reside nearby in fraternity or sorority houses or in apartments. All freshmen are required to live on campus. There are substance-free areas available in various dorms.

North Carolina is southern enough that it still offers both all-men and all-women dormitories, although coed halls are the norm; only six of the 36 halls are single sex. Visitation policies vary from hall to hall; some allow visitors (with roommate consent) until 1:00 a.m., while others permit visitors throughout the night. Says a student, "Visitation policies probably exist, but I am unsure of what they are. Needless to say, they are rarely enforced." On paper, a guest's stay is limited to no more than 72 consecutive hours. Guests of the opposite sex may not use the suite / floor bathroom but rather a public restroom available in the building. "Luckily, there are no coed bathrooms here," says one grateful student. A guest may stay or sleep only in his or her host's room—not on the couch of a common suite, for instance. Three dorms allow 24-hour visitation by the opposite sex.

One UNC tradition is the honor code, a policy that is taken very seriously by students. All students pledge to adhere to the code, which prohibits lying, cheating, and stealing. "Cheating is the most common offense but is by no means taken lightly," says one student. The code, however, doesn't mention public nudity: one frivolous UNC tradition consists of streaking through the library at midnight on the first day of exams.

UNC in 2011 reported 12 forcible sex offenses, three robberies, 365 burglaries, three aggravated assaults, 36 burglaries, and three stolen cars on campus. The university offers an escort service and a shuttle at night. Still, for most students, safety isn't a big concern: "I've always felt safe in each of the three different apartment buildings in which I have lived," one student reports.

Chapel Hill is still a bargain for locals, who in 2012–13 paid in-state tuition of $7,644; the out-of-state rate was $28,252. Room and board were $9,734. These numbers represent a steady increase, which is expected to continue in future years. Admission to UNC–Chapel Hill is need blind, and the college pledges to meet 100 percent of financial need; 64 percent of students received need-based aid. Low-income Carolina residents can graduate from UNC debt-free if they work on campus 10 to 12 hours a week. The average debt burden of a recent grad was a moderate $17,525.

Blue Collar Ivy

STRONG SUITS

- Rigorous programs include English, Classics, journalism, art history.
- Honors classes are more intimate than standard courses.
- Interdisciplinary studies programs (such as American or international studies) offer a more cohesive liberal arts program.
- Other good programs are availabnle in health care, the hard sciences, and the Kenan-Flagler Business School.
- The Center for Entrepreneurial Studies offers students internships and other opportunities.

WEAK POINTS

- Too many politicized or esoteric classes that fulfill core requirements.
- Honors classes are no more rigorous than standard courses.
- African American, sexuality, and women's studies programs are politicized and mediocre.
- Requirements for history major are anemic. (America is optional.)

University of North Dakota

Grand Forks, North Dakota • www.und.org

Home on the Plains

The University of North Dakota began as a one-building college in the middle of a wheat field, six years before the Dakota Territory became a state. Now it is North Dakota's most comprehensive research university, with more than 15,000 students in more than 200 fields of study. And while it is renowned for its aerospace sciences program and its College of Engineering and Mines, it suffers from a low freshman retention rate, low graduation rate, and loose general-education requirements.

Academic Life: The "Harvard of aviation studies"

Overall, UND offers more than 220 academic fields of study, from baccalaureate to doctoral. Its general-education program (called Essential Studies), requires 11 courses chosen from among vast swathes that lump together history, political science, religion, and philosophy into the categories of Arts and Humanities or Social Science. It would be entirely possible for a student to graduate with courses like "Fundamentals of Music," "Oral Traditions in American Indian Culture," and "Introduction to Film" fulfilling his or her Arts and Humanities credits, rather than courses on Shakespeare and history. The latter are

547

VITAL STATISTICS

Religious affiliation: *none*
Total enrollment: *15,250*
Total undergraduates: *11,953*
SAT CR/Verbal midrange:
   N/A
SAT Math midrange: *N/A*
ACT midrange: *21–26*
Applicants: *5,408*
Applicants accepted: *3,984*
Accepted applicants who
   enrolled: *2,334*
Tuition (general/out of
   state): *$15,854*
Tuition (in state): *$5,938*
Room and board: *$6,332*
Freshman retention rate:
   74%
Graduation rate (4 yrs.): *23%*
Graduation rate (6 yrs.): *54%*
Courses with fewer than 20
   students: *39%*
Student-faculty ratio: *17:1*
Courses taught by graduate
   students: *not provided*
Students living on campus:
   31%
Students in fraternities: *8%*
Students in sororities: *10%*
Students receiving need-
   based financial aid: *not
   reported*
Avg. student-loan debt of a
   recent graduating class:
   $31,763
Most popular majors:
   *business, health profes-
   sions, transportation and
   materials moving*
Guaranteed housing for 4
   years? *no*

indeed offered and seem very solid—but it takes a savvy student to select a survey course on Western civilization over, say, "Color Photography." There is no individual foreign language requirement, except in certain departments. While there are some good class offerings, overall, the Essential Studies courses are too broad to be of much educational value.

But for any faults in the general-education scheme, UND makes it up to students when they declare majors. In most departments the requirements are strong. Exceptional departments include the John D. Odegard School of Aerospace Sciences, which offers programs in aviation education, atmospheric research, space studies, and computer science applications. It claims the world's largest nonmilitary fleet of training aircraft and flight simulators on par with those used by the Federal Aviation Administration.

UND's College of Business and Public Administration also earns accolades, especially its entrepreneurship major. Nursing is also strong; *U.S. News and World Report* ranked UND fourth in the nation for rural medicine in 2012. Nor should one overlook the College of Engineering and Mines and its research centers and initiatives.

One premed student praises the biology department ("The teaching goes very in-depth and there is a diversity of teaching styles")—but not so much the chemistry department ("It's very challenging, for one thing, with bigger classes, and the professors don't have the best teaching styles").

Other departments earning low marks are fine arts and theater ("Not quite top drawer," says a professor) and English. One professor notes that the "English department can't sustain enough faculty to have the full range of specialists in their fields…it's not a bad thing, as it has caused the department to become more generally focused, but it is cause for weakness." English requires that majors take 12 courses in the field (with a track also offered for future teachers), and most seem solid enough. Courses must include "Reading and Writing about Texts," "Introduction to Literary Criticism," and either "Survey of English Literature" or "Survey of American Literature." Also required is one course on literature of an earlier historical period (examples include "Studies in

Early Renaissance Literature" and "Studies in Colonial American Literature"—a course on Shakespeare is also among the choices but has no separate requirement), and at least two upper-level courses.

The history department offers two tracks for majors: Option A, with emphasis on upper-level courses and foreign language skills, is for students who plan to enter professional school. Option B, with its slightly greater emphasis on introductory courses and supplemental work in related disciplines, is designed primarily for those who want to enter government service, business, or teaching. Both require 13 credits, including (admirably) "Western Civilization to 1500," "Western Civilization since 1500," "United States to 1877," "United States since 1877," "Historian's Craft," and "Research." Five of the seven electives must be upper level. For Option B students, four courses must form a concentration in either World History or American History. Finally, Option B students are required to take specific courses from other departments, including anthropology, economics, geography, political science, and sociology.

Political science and public administration is equally rigorous, requiring that its majors take "American Government" I, "State and Local Government," "International Politics," "Comparative Politics," "Politics of Public Administration," "Intro to Research Methods," "Intro to Political Thought," and either "Political Behavior" or "Public Policy Making Process," plus four electives at the 300 level, a Senior Colloquium, "Principles of Macroeconomics," and "Intro to Business and Economic Statistics" or an equivalent statistics course. Elective offerings include "American Constitution—Governmental Powers," "International Human Rights," and "Women and Politics." Political science courses seem to focus heavily on the administrative and public policy side (the school also offers a BS in public administration) rather than on political philosophy.

It's not all roses at UND. For one thing, the freshman retention rate is a low 74 percent. Maybe that's directly related to the lower standardized test scores of entering classes: the average ACT score was just under 24 in the class of 2012–13 (few students submit SAT scores). The four-year graduation rate is just 23 percent; the six-year rate is barely more impressive at 54 percent. That's a lot of time and money wasted by students and parents.

CAMPUS POLITICS: YELLOW LIGHT

UND may sit in a conservative state and have a fairly traditional approach to academic disciplines, but it hasn't found the right balance on free speech. First, until the Foundation for Individual Rights in Education (FIRE) brought it to attention, UND defined as punishable harassment actions "which can range from violence and bullying to more subtle behavior such as ignoring an individual at work or study." That part of the definition has now vanished into cold air, but one can still see the university's policies in play—literally. In 2013 a play-by-play basketball announcer was suspended for two games for using the phrase "choke job" to describe a close overtime loss.

More serious is the case of a young man accused of rape and subsequently expelled from UND. Yet even when the police cleared him of wrongdoing—and arrested his accuser for making a false report—the university declined to readmit him. It was only when FIRE intervened on the student's behalf that UND reexamined the case and overturned his expulsion.

Still, class sizes are pleasantly small. Only 3 percent of classes had more than 100 students, and 84 percent had less than 40. "You would never find a class of 200 to 300," says a professor.

There is also a decent balance between research and teaching. One professor reports that he is able to do research while staying in contact with his students. Students echo the sentiment: "There are some bigger classes," says a student, "and in those, you don't get a lot of one-on-one time with professors. But in the smaller classes and labs, it gets a lot more personal: the professors know your name and understand that you're a college student with a lot of work for other classes."

Among the professors named as exceptional are Jim Mochoruk in history; Sharon Carson in English and religious studies; Jeffrey Langstraat in sociology; Douglas Munski in geography; and Jeffrey Carmichael in biology.

Students in UND's honors program fare better than most; they take smaller honors sections of general university courses, with 18 or fewer students per class. They also take upper-level colloquia, which are interdisciplinary specialized courses (like "The Evolution of Environmental Thought," "Politics of Film and Fiction," Genetics and Bioengineering," and "The Coming Plague," to name a few past options). Other honors perks include national and regional honors conferences, participation in cocurricular activities, scholarship opportunities, and residency in a special dorm. Honors students must maintain a 3.2 GPA and complete a senior thesis.

> "There are some bigger classes," says a student, "and in those, you don't get a lot of one-on-one time with professors. But in the smaller classes and labs, it gets a lot more personal."

The Department of Modern and Classical Languages and Literatures offers majors in Chinese studies, classical studies, French, German, Norwegian, and Spanish. An interdisciplinary studies major (with an emphasis on Russia) is also available.

Study-abroad options range from summer to yearlong. Destinations are plentiful and include Australia, China, Finland, Greece, Iceland, India, Japan, Mexico, and South Africa. UND enjoys special ties to Norway and with the American College of Norway (often referred to as "UND in Norway," since students take UND classes taught by UND faculty). In fact, UND has a uniquely diverse flair for a Midwest college, with only 39 percent of its students coming from North Dakota. The rest represent all other states, eight Canadian provinces, and more than 50 countries.

Student Life: Nameless in the penalty box

Grand Forks is a hockey town, and UND is a hockey school. Games are a social occasion, and the team appears in the NCAA Frozen Four more often than not (they also hold seven NCAA Division I titles). Notice they are referred to as "the team"; UND is currently without a sports moniker, having "retired" its controversial Fighting Sioux nickname. Recently, the hockey team joined the National Collegiate Hockey Conference.

The team-*sans-nom* plays at the Ralph Engelstad Arena, one of the diamonds of Grand Forks, a very flat and very cold city in the Red River Valley. The third-largest North Dakota city is also home to the North Dakota Museum of Art and Chester Fritz Auditorium, which host cultural events. University Commons, built on vacant land owned by UND, is a newer commercial and residential district home to retail stores, the $20 million Student Wellness Center, and eventually the expanded UND School of Medicine and Health Sciences.

Tunnels honeycombing the campus help students brave the brutal winter weather. Despite the cold, UND is an active campus; 80 percent of students are reported to use the Wellness Center. From Sunrise Yoga to Noon Cycling, students can take full advantage of the facility's many amenities: a climbing wall, a pool, even the Hopper Danley Memorial Quiet Lounge, where students can "escape from the chaos and demands of everyday life and fulfill their need for silence." Not into sports or silence? Try the center's cooking lessons.

> **SUGGESTED CORE**
> 1. Humanities 102, Introduction to Humanities II
> 2. Philosophy 300, Ancient Philosophy
> 3. Religion 321/331, Jewish Scripture: Old Testament/ Christian Scripture: New Testament
> 4. Philosophy 301, Medieval Philosophy
> 5. Political Science 310, Introduction to Political Thought
> 6. English 315/316, Shakespeare
> 7. History 103, United States to 1877
> 8. Philosophy 303, Kant and the 19th Century

For the outdoorsy types, UND offers skating and skiing trails behind the Wellness Center and an annual road race in the fall. The ice rink is open until late on winter weekends. Intramurals include badminton, pond hockey, indoor Ultimate Frisbee, basketball, soccer, volleyball, broomball, inline hockey, dodgeball, and wrestling. Nineteen teams compete in Division I men's and women's basketball, cross-country, golf, hockey, swimming and diving, tennis, and track and field. Men also compete in football and baseball. Women compete in soccer, softball, and volleyball. Most teams are members of the Big Sky Conference.

Student groups are plentiful, ranging from the professional and academic (American Association of Airport Executives) to service clubs (American Red Cross Club) to the leisurely (Middle Ages Recreation Society). One of the more popular organizations is Students Today Leaders Forever (STLF), which engages students in service projects and takes a spring break whirlwind trip through five cities. Options for religious students include Cru (Campus Crusade for Christ), Fellowship of Catholic University Students (FOCUS), Inter-Varsity Christian Fellowship, and the Lutheran Student Movement (LSM). On the political side are College Republicans, University Democrats, and a fairly active Pro-Choice Voice.

On-campus living arrangements include both all-female and all-male dorms, as well as residences for only upper-class students and apartment-style living. The Conference Center (all-female) has limited visitation hours. Living and Learning Communities include those themed around aviation, the College of Engineering and Mines, Wellness, and Honors. Students can also join one of the six sororities and 13 fraternities (about 8 percent of students live in Greek housing).

Blue Collar Ivy

Crime is low; in 2011 there were only eight reported forcible sex offenses, two burglaries, four motor vehicle thefts, and one arson.

The school is an amazing bargain for in-state students who eventually graduate; in 2012–13 they paid only $5,938 tuition. Out-of-state students paid $15,854. Room and board were $6,332. Despite these low costs, students' average loan burden upon graduation is an alarming $31,763.

STRONG SUITS	WEAK POINTS
• Sound requirements for humanities majors, such as English, history, and political science.	• Scattered, arbitrary general-education requirements (foreign language, philosophy, and religion courses are interchangeable).
• Good course offerings in most liberal arts, with few politicized-sounding courses.	• A limited number of foreign languages are offered.
• Respected departments in sciences, especially aerospace, and in the College of Engineering and Mines.	• Pitifully low (54 percent) graduation rate within six years.
• Worthy programs in entrepreneurship in its business school and in rural medicine.	• Low admissions standards can dumb classes down.

Ohio State University

Columbus, Ohio • www.osu.edu

The "Big" in Big Ten

Founded in 1870 as the Ohio Agricultural and Mechanical College, Ohio State has always been torn between the practical and the liberal arts—and so it resolved the debate by deciding to offer just about every subject under the sun. Among members of the OSU liberal arts faculty, it is a common view that students looking for a serious humanities education would be better served elsewhere. Only "focused, savvy undergraduates" interested in going on for a graduate or professional degree, according to one professor, should choose Ohio State. Another professor says, "A discerning and determined student can gain a good liberal arts education here. The problem is that he or she shouldn't have to struggle against the system to do it."

Academic Life: 50,000 of your closest friends

OSU's general-education mandates give a student plenty of wiggle room so that, although he may have to arrange his schedule so as to incorporate a few requirements, he will surely be able to find a course to his liking—not exactly the goal of a liberal arts curriculum. Student must take at least two courses in "writing and related skills"; three quantitative

VITAL STATISTICS

Religious affiliation: *none*
Total enrollment: *56,387*
Total undergraduates: *43,058*
SAT CR/Verbal midrange: *540–650*
SAT Math midrange: *610–710*
ACT midrange: *26–30*
Applicants: *25,816*
Applicants accepted: *64%*
Accepted applicants who enrolled: *44%*
Tuition (general/out of state): *$25,445*
Tuition (in state): *$10,037*
Room and board: *$10,370*
Freshman retention rate: *92%*
Graduation rate (4 yrs.): *53%*
Graduation rate (6 yrs.): *82%*
Courses with fewer than 20 students: *30%*
Student-faculty ratio: *19:1*
Courses taught by graduate students: *not provided*
Students living on campus: *24%*
Students in fraternities: *7%*
Students in sororities: *7%*
Students receiving need-based financial aid: *not provided*
Avg. student-loan debt of a recent graduating class: *$21,566*
Most popular majors: *area and ethnic studies, business/marketing, social sciences*
Guaranteed housing for 4 years? *no*

and logical skills classes; three courses in the natural sciences, including a lab; three classes in the social sciences; just two courses in the arts and humanities; two additional classes from the natural science, social science, or arts and humanities category; two historical studies; *three* diversity courses; one course on Issues in the Contemporary World; and (admirably) tests or courses to show fourth-semester proficiency in a foreign language.

More substantive is OSU's honors program. Honors students typically come from the top 10 percent of their classes and must have Verbal/Math SAT scores above 1340. Honors students are eligible for merit scholarships and may live in one of four special residence halls. They may also choose from among approximately 500 honors classes taught by elite faculty with smaller enrollments. The Scholars Program is a similar initiative; its 300 participating students live in housing specific to their academic interests, take advanced classes, and enjoy personalized advising and mentoring opportunities. One professor says that both of these programs compare "favorably with a decent, middle-of-the-road Ivy League education."

Outside these programs, the picture is less impressive. History majors take an introduction to the historical method and a senior seminar designed to hone their research skills, as well as 50 hours in their major, including at least 20 in one geographical region and 15 from two or more other regions; and at least 10 credit hours each in history before and after 1750. These are respectable requirements, and many of the departmental course offerings are excellent, but there are also the usual clunkers, like "History of Modern Sexualities." You'll notice that American history is not one of the requirements for the major.

English majors are required to take at least 60 credit hours in English, with a minimum of 35 at the 400 level or above; three survey courses, two in British literature and one in American literature; three writing classes, including one in critical writing; at least two courses set before 1900; one after 1900; a course in an area of English study other than literature; and at least three elective courses at the 300 to 500 level in English. Given the required survey courses, students would not miss encounters with Shakespeare.

Political science majors take at least 50 credit hours, including 35 at the 400 level or above. Major programs must include a four-course focus in one of the department's four fields (American politics, comparative politics, international relations, and political theory) and at least one course in each of the other three. Chances are good that majors will have to study the U.S. Constitution or political system.

Ohio State administrators seem less devoted to liberal arts education than to political purification, pushing various affirmative action policies and sponsored events like "The President and Provost's Diversity Lecture and Cultural Arts Series," which amounts to lectures on topics such as "Strategic Priorities, Strategic Funding," "How the Media Teach about Diversity," "Diversity and the American University Professoriate: National Imperative or Political Correctness?," and "Nine Ways of Looking at a Poor Woman."

Reports about classroom politicization are mixed. According to one political science professor, OSU has "a very open political climate. Liberal and conservative voices are heard. The campus community is very tolerant." She insists that in her department, teachers "pride themselves on being neutral and playing 'devil's advocate' when one political opinion is expressed." A conservative student agrees: "I have had left-leaning, moderate, and conservative professors. I can say that I have never felt uncomfortable in a class, though. As a conservative, I have always been given a chance to voice my opinion, and even encouraged to do so, even when the professor is obviously liberal." Despite these claims, one faculty member maintains that "some topics are relatively taboo." This professor says that at least one "activist Christian" was denied tenure for political reasons. One student complains that in a panel on the Iraq War, "not one of the faculty members on the panel supported the war in Iraq, defended current U.S.

CAMPUS POLITICS: YELLOW LIGHT

Ohio State administrators are dead serious about promoting diversity—and weeding out those on campus who aren't on board with multiculturalist ideology. *Campus Reform* reports that in spring 2013, graduate student Mark Stickle made the mistake of cc-ing one of his professors, Dr. Judy Wu, on a snarky e-mail critical of the Diversity and Identity Studies Collective (DISCO). Realizing his mistake, he sent a hasty apology—which had no effect, apparently. The professor "sent disparaging e-mails about Stickle to university faculty and administrators before reporting the seemingly benign remark to the OSU's Bias Assessment and Response Team (BART).

"'I think it is offensive and unprofessional,' she wrote to one colleague regarding Stickle's e-mail.

"Another professor, Robin Judd, e-mailed Dr. Wu that she was 'just so horrified and saddened' by Stickle's e-mail and that she was 'combing through our handbook . . . to see what policies we set out concerning this kind of behavior.'

"The case against me was judged ludicrous and thrown out—but not before Professors Judd and Wu had engaged in a wide-ranging e-mail campaign, aimed at undermining my character and my reputation as a scholar," Stickle told *Campus Reform*. Further, the site reports, "Wu also contacted the history department at the OSU campus in Newark about Stickle, where he says he was in informal talks about employment. Stickle believes that the correspondence ruined any hopes of him having employment at that campus."

policy, or even offered to play devil's advocate. . . . OSU has a long way to go in terms of academic freedom."

The most politicized departments are said to be the usual suspects (African American, African, and women's studies), along with psychology and English. Says a professor regarding the English department, "Too often I hear from students that they've been ridiculed or even downgraded on their work for their beliefs (whether political or religious), or that they've simply kept their mouths shut or parroted what they knew was party line in order to get decent grades. . . . It's fairly widespread and seems to be worst in classes taught by TAs. Many of our students refer to the 'American Experience' second writing course as 'Indoctrination 101.'" The professor adds that "there are many dedicated teachers in the English department, and as long as students stay away from taboo subjects or don't air their religious views, they find the department surprisingly warm . . . for such a large one."

Currently, OSU is best known for its Fisher College of Business and College of Engineering. The school offers more than 170 degree programs, covering everything from jazz studies to turf grass science.

While none of the departments "specializes in undergraduate education," as one professor reports, nearly all have some excellent teachers, including Janet Box-Steffensmeier in political science; Gene Mumy in economics; Rick Livingston in comparative studies; Edward Crenshaw in sociology; Jay Myung in psychology; Phoebe S. Spinrad (emeritus) in English; and Harding Ganz in history.

Because OSU is such a large campus, it is very important for students to "get connected," says a professor. "It is a big place. To not get lost, one needs to connect with professors." Smart students will generally stand out at OSU. Says a professor: "Those who want to distinguish themselves from the horde at OSU can do so quite easily because most of their undergrad colleagues aren't coming to see their professors and are happy with a C." Once a student identifies the professor with whom he would like to study and "makes a reasoned pitch, works hard, and shows his talent," he will, according to the same professor, receive a "remarkable undergrad education working with some of the top scholars in his field."

> Only "focused, savvy undergraduates" should attend. "A discerning and determined student can gain a good liberal arts education here," a professor says.

Students in the Colleges of the Arts and Sciences are appointed two advisers—one of whom may be a faculty member. Despite this "dual-advising system," OSU stresses students' responsibility to navigate the academic labyrinth. With six-year graduation rates hovering around 82 percent during the past three years, and the four-year rate at 53 percent, this system doesn't seem particularly effective.

Professors at OSU can be surprisingly approachable. One student in a class of 100 says that "the professor went to great lengths to make himself accessible. He ran two separate homework-problem help sessions (in addition to one run by the TA), and he didn't end them until all questions were answered. . . . I have been impressed by the effort he expends in order to serve his students." Students should seek out professors like this—especially since many of their lower-level courses will be taught by graduate students.

One way to avoid OSU's massive lecture classes is to take survey courses at one of the school's regional campuses. According to a student at the Columbus campus, "Many freshman students (myself included) feel that their first year of study is wasteful. . . . If one can avoid coming to the main campus and save money in the process by attending a regional campus closer to home, it would be well worth it." A student at the Newark campus says that "it is much better to take history classes here because the class size is much smaller. Thus, more attention is given to individual students." One exemplary professor at the Newark campus is Mitch Lerner in history.

Ohio State offers a broad range of 32 languages, including Chinese, Latin, Spanish, and Zulu. There are more than 100 study-abroad programs in over 40 different countries and close to a fifth of undergraduates study abroad.

> **SUGGESTED CORE**
>
> 1. Classics 1101, Introduction to Classical Literature
> 2. Philosophy 3210, History of Ancient Philosophy
> 3. English 2280, The English Bible
> 4. History 3230, History of Medieval Christianity
> 5. Political Science 4412, Early Modern Political Thought
> 6. English 2220, Introduction to Shakespeare
> 7. History 1151, American Civilization to 1877
> 8. History 2260, European Thought and Culture, 19th Century

Student Life: It's a riot

Ohio State's campus is located in Columbus, the largest city in Ohio. The prosperous city hosts a substantial arts scene, including museums, a symphony, and a ballet. The city is student-friendly: for example, students can use their university ID cards to ride the local buses free.

In the fall, OSU students tend to be consumed with football. Ohio State has finished first among the Big Ten consistently. Even when the team has suffered a defeat or two, Ohio Stadium, otherwise known as the Horseshoe, is usually packed to its 101,568-seat capacity.

Students gather to party before, during, and after OSU sporting events, especially football games. Unfortunately, students and locals sometimes lose control of their emotions, and "parties" become "riots." Ironically, these mammoth house parties are the direct result of, in one student's opinion, the university's actions. Over the past few years, the university, in collaboration with the city government, used the power of eminent domain to drive out several bars on High Street, ostensibly in the name of revitalization. As a result, the campus drinking scene has moved to less centralized and less watched areas. The closing of close-to-campus bars, says one student, has severely dampened campus nightlife and increased concerns about drunk driving.

OSU hosts an array of male and female Greek organizations, to which 7 percent of students belong. Students say that these groups are more party- than service-oriented and don't play a major role in campus life—apart from hosting events that are usually open to nonmembers as well.

Students at OSU can take advantage of the 550 clubs the university offers, none of which officially sponsor riots. These include some 36 honor societies and nearly 40 religious organizations. The latter include Baha'i, Buddhist, Catholic, Coptic, Jewish, Muslim, and a very wide array of Protestant organizations, as well as a Women and Spirituality Club. "Most students at Ohio State are involved in at least one club or activity," a student says. "There is nearly a club for every ethnic group and language."

Ohio State's intercollegiate sports teams and players are called the Buckeyes, their mascot is Brutus Buckeye, and they participate in the NCAA's Division I in all sports and the Big Ten Conference in most sports. Ohio State's numerous sports offerings include football, basketball, golf, baseball, tennis, and ice hockey. There are also many sports clubs (such as water polo and cricket) and 15 intramural sports.

The College Republicans chapter has a sizable membership. The College Democrats are not as popular, although according to one student, that is only "because there are several smaller liberal clubs on campus representing specific liberal interests." The mainstream student paper, the *Lantern,* is an "unapologetic mouthpiece for the extreme left wing," says one student.

Political fervor is simply absent at Ohio State. As one student says, "Ohio State is generally a conservative campus; students more so than professors. However, since conservatism is the norm, rarely do conservative groups gain a lot of attention."

Nonetheless, one student considers the influence of the gay and lesbian community at OSU pervasive: "Gays and lesbians are a centerpiece of Ohio State's emphasis on 'diversity.'" He points to the FYE seminar called "Guess the Straight Person," as well as to the placards frequently displayed on university buses. The buses carry messages from the Gay, Lesbian, Bisexual, and Transgender Student Services office advertising ways students can work to stop "homophobia." Among the choicer recommendations: "Do not assume everyone is male or female."

The vast majority of students—82 percent—are from Ohio. Only about a quarter live on campus, and relatively few join sororities or fraternities. There are three female-only residence halls, none exclusively for males. The coed dorms house women and men in a variety of ways, sometimes on different floors, sometimes on the same floor but in different wings, and sometimes on the same floor and same wing. All the bathrooms are single sex, and all dorms are smoke-free

The occasional riot is not the only crime about which students at OSU ought to be concerned. The part of Columbus surrounding campus is notable for its high crime rate. In 2011 the school reported 28 sexual assaults, seven robberies, 22 burglaries, eight stolen cars, and six arsons on campus. Still, one new professor says, "I used to live within walking distance of the campus of UT Austin. . . . I planned to live within walking distance here, but it truly is not safe." The campus police department offers both vehicle and walking escorts to students who want them.

Ohio State is quite a bargain for students from the state. While regional campuses are cheaper, even the main campus in Columbus charged only $10,037 in 2012–13. Out-of-state students paid a much heftier $25,445. Room and board averaged at $10,370. The average student-loan debt of a recent graduate who borrowed was $21,566.

STRONG SUITS

- The honors and the Scholars programs offer elite educational opportunities to students selected.
- Requirements for English and political sciences majors are solid.
- Most teachers are fair and don't inject their politics into the classroom.
- Professors are delighted (and surprised) when hardworking students wish to meet with them.
- Regional campuses offer a lower-cost, higher-quality way to gain credits.

WEAK POINTS

- U.S. history and civics are not required; three courses in "diversity" are.
- Administrators push multiculturalism using heavy-handed tactics.
- Most students are happy collecting Cs and going to parties, a teacher reports.
- Heavy drinking and occasional riots occur after sporting events.

So You're Looking For

A Top Great Books Program

1. Yale University—Directed Studies *(p. 923)*

2. Princeton University—Humanities Sequence *(p. 721)*

3. St. John's College *(p. 762)*

4. Thomas Aquinas College *(p. 787)*

5. University of Dallas *(p. 811)*

University of Oklahoma

Norman, Oklahoma • www.ou.edu

Sooner Pride

Located in the city of Norman, the University of Oklahoma (founded 1890) is recognized by the Carnegie Foundation for its "very high research activity." More than 2,600 full-time faculty members teach more than 30,000 students in 21 colleges. The OU Health Sciences Center, located in Oklahoma City, a 20-minute drive from Norman, is one of only four comprehensive academic health centers in the nation.

Academic Life: Well-roundedness

Although the university requires students to complete certain general-education requirements, these do not add up to a true core curriculum. (For that, see our Suggested Core.) On the bright side, teaching has become more important since David Boren became president of the university, says one professor. "At present he requires each faculty member to teach a minimum of 75 students each year," he says. But research is still a significant factor in determining tenure, he adds. One professor we spoke with felt that although OU is a research university, "we do a pretty good job of incentivizing and rewarding good teaching."

Accessibility to professors "depends on the department," an accounting student reports. "Many times the professor teaches the lecture and has graduate students teach the discussion sections and labs. The graduate students are the ones who are best to go to for office hours, not the professors. The only time I have had someone acting as a mentor is either in an actual mentoring program . . . or in my advising appointments." But a student majoring in communication sciences and disorders finds professors extremely accessible: "Most of my classes have been taught by professors. Office hours are very useful, especially in writing classes."

The Honors College has a couple of programs that may be of interest to tradition-minded students. It sponsors informal reading groups of 15 students who meet weekly to discuss works of literature both classic and modern. Recent offerings included Herodotus, Shakespeare, and Tolstoy. Each summer, the college sponsors study abroad at Oxford University.

Another interesting program is the Institute for the American Constitutional Heritage (IACH). One professor says it would appeal to "students who are looking for a strong classical liberal arts education." It's an interdisciplinary center where the U.S. Constitution's philosophical underpinnings, historical context, legal substance, and contemporary relevance are studied. An English-Classics double major says the institute is a "phenomenal program for anyone considering a career in law."

Other strong programs, reportedly, include Classics and letters (whose students regularly win honors in the annual National Latin Exam and the National Greek Exam); constitutional studies; geology; petroleum geology (Oklahoma is an oil-producing state); history of science (the library has one of the three largest collections in the history of science in the world); law; business; and meteorology, which is situated in the National Weather Center building in Norman. That location gives students the opportunity to work for one of the many government meteorological agencies housed at OU "very early on in their education and helps them find jobs after college," says a student who began her studies in the department.

But some students find that while teachers may be smart, there can be problems in getting their messages across. There are Pulitzer Prize winners teaching journalism, for

VITAL STATISTICS

Religious affiliation: *none*
Total enrollment: *27,505*
Total undergraduates: *21,107*
SAT CR/Verbal midrange:
  510–640
SAT Math midrange:
  540–660
ACT midrange: *23–29*
Applicants: *11,650*
Applicants accepted: *79%*
Accepted applicants who
  enrolled: *45%*
Tuition (general/out of
  state): *$20,343*
Tuition (in state): *$8,706*
Room and board: *$8,382*
Freshman retention rate:
  85%
Graduation rate (4 yrs.): *36%*
Graduation rate (6 yrs.): *68%*
Courses with fewer than 20
  students: *38%*
Student-faculty ratio: *19:1*
Courses taught by graduate
  students: *not provided*
Students living on campus:
  32%
Students in fraternities: *22%*
Students in sororities: *28%*
Students receiving need-
  based financial aid: *31%*
Avg. student-loan debt of a
  recent graduating class:
  $23,845
Most popular majors: *nursing, petroleum engineering, psychology*
Guaranteed housing for 4
  years? *no*

CAMPUS POLITICS: GREEN LIGHT

The University of Oklahoma has, since 1994, been led by a conservative Democrat, David Boren, and, as one student points out, the institution is in the heart of the Bible Belt. "But as part of a college town, it does have its fair share of more liberal-minded students," she says. "I see a great mixture of opinions across the campus, and I truly believe students from all viewpoints can find their niche here. I would say that OU makes way for a wide variety of opinions, bringing in a wide variety of speakers with differing viewpoints. . . . I have not personally experienced or heard about classes that are unwelcoming to religious students."

Oklahoma, as one professor acknowledges, is "arguably the most conservative state in the country," and professors "can't really be hostile or condescending toward conservative students." In fact, this professor says that he has "risen through the ranks here without much trouble" in spite of his being "a conservative Republican."

Another student reports that the Norman campus's south oval is the "center of protests and debates on campus. People from within the university and from outside come to the south oval to debate, and the university is open with this as long as it does not get out of hand and nothing is being forced on people."

example, but one major feels that not all of them "have been trained in how to teach." Most of them, she says, are "fairly disorganized, but the skills learned by the end of the courses outweigh the messy classroom structures."

A similar problem arises with foreign teachers with heavy accents, such as in the math department.

As for individual departments, English is troubled by "internecine feuds" and "changing its mission yearly if not hourly," says a professor outside that department. Majors must take a "World literature" course but do not have to take a specific course in Shakespeare. There seem to be enough traditional course offerings, such as "Nineteenth-Century English Literature" and "Shakespeare's Tragedies," but also a good amount of offbeat classes like "Unlikeable Women" and "The Nature of Laughter."

An interesting joint venture between the English and constitutional studies departments in spring 2013 yielded a course called "Shakespeare Moot Court." Students were to prepare to argue a case strictly on the "constitutionality" of a proposition according to "the law of Shakespeare."

Requirements for history majors include a course in U.S. history, either before or after 1865. Other course offerings look fairly traditional but also include titles like "European Women and Gender Relations," "History of the Great Witch Hunt in Early Modern Europe and America," and "Gender and Sexuality in Modern Japan." The university has developed a name for itself as a place of studies about the American West, and courses offered in this area include "The American Frontier since 1828," "America through Western Film," and the history of Oklahoma.

In the political science department, course offerings include "Foundations of American Politics," "American Constitutional Law," "Philosophical Issues in American Politics," "Topics in Political Theory," "Problems in Law and the Constitution," "American Constitutional Development," "Theory of Public Organizations," and "Classical Political Theory." Admirably, all OU students are required to take "American Federal Government." University president Boren, a former Oklahoma governor and U.S. senator, teaches a political science course once a year.

Recommended professors include David Wrobel in history; Linda Zagzebski in philosophy; Allen Hertzke and Donald Maletz in political science; Kevin Butterfield, Ralph Doty, and Kyle Harper, and Samuel Huskey in Classics and letters; James Yoch and Catherine Mintler in English; David Ray and Marie Dallam in the Honors College; Gaye LeBlanc and Ken Stephenson in music; Brian McCall and Michael Scaperlanda in law; David Deming, Michael Soreghan, and Gail Holloway in geology; Krishnan (Ravi) Shankar in mathematics; Michael Strauss in physics; and David Biggerstaff, Frederick Carr, and Susan Postawko in meteorology.

In the field of languages, one can study French, German, Italian, and Spanish—and no fewer than five Native American languages. In fact, OU is a center of Native American studies: the College of Law publishes the only law journal in the U.S. devoted exclusively to Native American legal issues, and OU Press is a leading publisher of books about Native Americans and the American West.

With programs in 100 cities in 50 countries, one in four OU students studies abroad, including at the university's new campus in Arezzo, Italy. "Study abroad is pushed very strongly at OU as President Boren had tried to make it possible for everyone to go," says one student.

Student Life: Serious fun

Sooner football has the third-best record of winning in the nation, after Michigan and Notre Dame. The team has won 27 bowl games and is number four in NFL draft selections. "Sports run this school," says a student. "Fall break is determined by when a football game is."

Off the field, there are more than 450 student organizations, including the American Constitution Society; Air Force, Army, and Naval ROTC; College Republicans; the pro-life Abolitionist Society; the William F. Buckley Society; Young Americans for Liberty; and a number of sports clubs.

A student reports, "The graduate students are the ones who are best to go to for office hours, not the professors."

Fraternities and sororities "are very large and visible around campus by . . . the matching clothing and the sidewalk chalking, but also with the service projects and fund-raisers that they do," said a student. The Greek community "definitely feels dominant on campus, because it's typically those involved in Greek life who are involved in other leadership roles on campus," says another.

All single freshmen under 20 must live in a university residence hall. Living arrangements range from suites, where two double-occupancy rooms share a restroom, to "community style," where up to eight students live in double-occupancy rooms and share a restroom. "There are three different dorm layouts: the towers (Walker, Couch, and Adams),

Blue Collar Ivy

Cate, and the Honors College," says one student. In the tower layout, she says, each floor has female and male sections separated by an elevator lobby and protected by a key card lock. "Neither side has open access to the other side at any time." Among the "special interest" living arrangements is a "quiet lifestyle" floor in one building, where 24 "quiet" hours are observed.

The university has a "faculty-in-residence" program, which puts professors and their families in each of the residence halls. This is meant to foster faculty and student interaction. In addition, a different professor adopts each floor of the residence halls as well as each fraternity and sorority.

Oklahoma doesn't particularly seem to be a "party school." Some students drink and "hook up," as at other universities, but that doesn't appear to be a major problem. Some resident assistants "look the other way when it comes to letting alcohol on the floor, while others are more strict about writing citations," says one student. "After visitation hours end, RAs on duty make rounds going through the halls to make sure males and females are on their own floors." Most bathrooms and floors are single sex, but there are optional coed residence halls for upperclassmen. Mixed genders do not share bathrooms, however. "Sexual promiscuity among freshmen is relatively limited, as the dorm policies are extremely discouraging to this," says a female student.

The number of campus ministries may also help keep students on the straight and narrow. Students can join organizations such as the Baptist Student Union, Brothers Under Christ, the Fellowship of Catholic University Students, and the Hillel Jewish Student Organization. One student highly recommends the annual retreat at St. Thomas More Catholic Church.

There are numerous forums for debate, such as the Society of Fellows, an honor society of 12 students who come together for a regular dinner with a dozen faculty members. Both ends of the political spectrum are represented in both groups, "and we have these awesome discussions about everything from gay marriage to religious freedom," says a professor.

The Honors College and the Religious Studies Club have similar forums. The latter sponsors an event called "Coffee and Conversation," in which students of all religions are invited to spend a few hours in loosely structured small groups discussing religious issues, like the role of their faith in their lives and what they perceive to be misunderstandings of their religions. A student reports that this provides a "comfortable and safe environment for students to civilly discuss religious issues."

Students agree that in general the campus is safe. "Crime is not normally something to worry about," says one. "If you are on campus and do not feel safe walking back to your room, there is a program called Safe Walk where two resident advisers, one male, one female, will come walk to your location and walk you back to your dorm or on-campus apartment." There are also blue easy-to-spot emergency phones around campus. "We had an armed male on campus last semester who was after a female soccer player, but OUPD kept the girl safe," says another student. "We had a sexual assault occur last year, and the school sent out an alert to all students. Because of the incident, we were all required to take an online sexual misconduct module in addition to our alcohol training module." In 2011 there were 29 burglaries on campus, 13 forcible sex offenses, including 11 in student housing, 10 motor vehicle thefts, two arsons, and one aggravated assault.

Tuition is a bargain for native students, at $8,706 (nonresidents paid $20,343) in 2012–13 and room and board of only $8,382. Only 31 percent of students received need-based financial aid, and the average debt of a recent graduate was a considerable $23,845.

STRONG SUITS	WEAK POINTS
• OU's Institute for the American Constitutional Heritage appeals to "students who are looking for a strong classical liberal arts education."	• Weak general-education program.
• A politically balanced, open-minded campus.	• Shaky majors' requirements in history and English—a department wracked by conflict.
• A good Honors College, with a Great Books discussion club.	• Low (36 percent) four-year graduation rate.
• Worthy programs in Classics, constitutional studies, geology, petroleum geology, history of science, law, business, and meteorology. (Oklahoma gets lots of weather.)	• Mixed reviews of teaching in journalism and math departments.
• A relatively modest, wholesome dorm environment.	

University of Oregon

Eugene, Oregon • www.uoregon.edu

Grassroots U.

Founded in 1872 and opened in 1876 with 155 students, the University of Oregon is a big, mixed bag—providing distinctive course offerings and open intellectual pursuits while imposing no significant core requirements. Conservative and religious students are free to speak their minds, mostly, if they're willing to brave peer disapproval. So for undergrads who choose their courses wisely, Oregon might prove a plausible choice.

Academic Life: Quality is an option

The University of Oregon takes a pragmatic approach to general education: students must simply complete two writing courses; either mathematics (for a BS degree) or a foreign language (for a BA); and two courses from the three-component "Multicultural Requirement" of American Cultures; Identity, Pluralism, and Tolerance; and International Cultures.

There is one very solid option at Oregon: the university hosts the Robert D. Clark Honors College, a liberal arts division with about 700 students. First-year students take five intermediate-level history and literature classes: premodern in the first quarter, modern in the second quarter, and an advanced research seminar in either history or literature during the third quarter. As sophomores, juniors, and seniors, honors students take another five colloquia at advanced levels in the arts, sciences, and social sciences. These classes are limited to honors students and intended to offer undergrads from different majors distinctive approaches to a common subject. Honors students must also complete a senior thesis and maintain a 3.0 GPA to graduate.

Clark students have course offerings all their own. Recently available literature classes for freshmen included "Man vs. Food," a class with required readings of *A Modest Proposal*, *The Physiology of Taste*, the British Victorian housewife's Bible *Mrs. Beeton's Book of Household Management*, *How to Cook a Wolf*, and Michael Pollan's *In Defense of Food*, along with fiction excerpts; "Modern Love," a class including readings from Shakespeare, Goethe, Dante, Kierkegaard, Darwin, and Freud; and "Revisions of Empire," which requires students to study *The Tempest*, *Robinson Crusoe*, modern writers, and TV shows like *Gilligan's Island* and *The Simpsons*. History classes include "Disease, Public Health, and the Making of the Modern World," "Architecture and Urbanism in the Modern World," and "Historical Thinking in a Global Framework, 1360–Present." Advanced-level colloquia topics vary from "Hemingway and Film" and "Inventing Confucius" to "Advanced Topics in Leadership" and "Top Mysteries of the Brain."

While students in the Honors College are given special attention when it comes to advising, most undergraduates have to be careful to pursue their advisers. New students must meet with a counselor in the Office of Academic Advising and in their departments. After the initial meeting, the school recommends (though does not require) continuing the relationship throughout a student's academic career.

Nearly half of all courses at the University of Oregon are taught by graduate students. Almost all discussion groups and labs are led by TAs, which is typical in large universities, but 13 percent of seminars and 21 percent of lectures are also TA taught, particularly in lower-level classes. Once students are in intermediate courses, they enjoy developing solid relationships with their professors, who invest significant time in students. "Every professor that I have is very helpful during their office hours," reports one student. His classmate agrees:

VITAL STATISTICS

Religious affiliation: *none*
Total enrollment: *24,396*
Total undergraduates: *20,623*
SAT CR/Verbal midrange: *492–610*
SAT Math midrange: *501–613*
ACT midrange: *22–27*
Applicants: *23,012*
Applicants accepted: *73%*
Accepted applicants who enrolled: *25%*
Tuition (general/out of state): *$28,653*
Tuition (in state): *$9,258*
Room and board: *$ 10,260*
Freshman retention rate: *86%*
Graduation rate (4 yrs.): *44%*
Graduation rate (6 yrs.): *68%*
Courses with fewer than 20 students: *37%*
Student-faculty ratio: *20:1*
Courses taught by graduate students: *49%*
Students living on campus: *19%*
Students in fraternities: *10%*
Students in sororities: *14%*
Students receiving need-based financial aid: *50%*
Avg. student-loan debt of a recent graduating class: *$22,736*
Most popular majors: *business, political science, psychology*
Guaranteed housing for 4 years? *no*

CAMPUS POLITICS: RED LIGHT

Students should approach the University of Oregon with caution. An overwhelming number of courses that meet the cultural requirements are trendy and leftist. Members of the campus pro-life group tell stories about having their promotional materials defaced, and religious and conservative students report that their classmates are often too critical of more traditional outlooks.

In 2011 a sign-language professor was fired from the university under unfair circumstances. Peter Quint asked his students to restrict their classroom communication to sign language—much like a Spanish professor requiring students to speak Spanish in the classroom—but students disobeyed. Professor Quint related a story about a time when, while serving in Pakistan, he faced a gunman with whom he could not communicate. Quint reports that he became frustrated with his students' insolence and asked them, "Do you want me to take a gun out and shoot you in the head so you understand what I am talking about? I had to practice being respectful in Pakistan, otherwise I would have been shot. Can you practice that same respect here?" The professor was told not to come to his classes or to contact any students or employees of the university, denied access to his university e-mail, and placed on leave without pay until the end of his contract. With no criminal charges filed (and with students asserting that they did not feel threatened by Quint) and no chance to defend himself to administrators, Quint was fired for a simple unwise comment.

"I have found the professors to be accessible, communicative, and very helpful." Another adds that professors "are very knowledgeable and easygoing, which makes learning fun and interactive."

Faculty and students alike speak highly of the school's programs in business, the hard sciences (especially physics), religious studies, history, music, and economics. "The math department is one of the school's weakest in my opinion," offers one student, as "teachers seem to know what they are teaching, but they seem very uncaring." Another adds that, while no department itself is weak, inexperienced professors have had a negative impact on various courses he has taken.

As to whether those classes are impartially taught, student opinion varies. Most reports claim that classes are "fairly unbiased" and "an open environment for the free flowing of ideas," although, of course, difficult students do try to provoke their classmates. One student remarks: "Most bias seems to come in the form of passing comments. More often than not, professors try to remain unbiased in formal discussion, tolerating diverse points of view in the classroom." Students do not feel concerned that their grades will be affected if they disagree with their professors, and some welcome the challenge to their ways of thinking: "I just took an introductory sociology course that did not portray the current American political, financial, and social situation in a very positive light. I think that was part of the idea of the class, though, to get the students to think more critically of their own culture." Every syllabus at the University of Oregon provides contacts for the school's Bias Response Team, which helps students who perceive unfairness in the classroom.

Professors at the University of Oregon enjoy good relationships with their students, although political tensions do arise between professors, leaving some more conservative faculty members concerned about their careers.

Students recommend a variety of the professors who have encouraged and challenged them: Stephen Shoemaker, Daniel Falk, and Mark Unno in religious studies; James Mohr in history; Hilary Fisher in French; William Harbaugh and Mark Thoma in economics; and Kendall DeBevoise in political science.

The English department's requirements seem worthy and challenging. English majors must complete a three-course introduction to the discipline; one class in Shakespeare; two classes from a list including a different Shakespeare course; a survey of English or American literature; and courses in folklore, among others. Additionally, advanced classes are required: one in pre-1500 English literature; two in literature from 1500 to 1789 (including options in Spenser, Milton, and medieval drama); two courses in literature from 1789 to the present (options range from teen and children's literature to Native American writers or modern British literature); a class in literary theory or criticism; a course focusing on folklore / ethnic literature / women's literature; and some nine English electives.

History majors at Oregon must complete two advanced courses in pre-1800 history (the long list of options includes "The Crusades," "Samurai in Film," "Classical Greece," and "Colonial American History"); two advanced courses in each of three subjects chosen from the following list: African and Middle Eastern, Asian, European, Latin American, and U.S. History. Courses vary widely, from "Ancient Africa," "Karma and Change," and "Medieval Japan" to "History of France: 1870–Present," "Race and Ethnicity in Modern Latin America," and "Seminar: Oregon History." History majors also have to complete a research paper in an advanced class, six history electives, and two years of study in a foreign language. Students praise the "nearly endless" variety of courses offered by the history department, and nearly all those courses seem serious and pertinent.

> Only half of courses are taught by professors. However, "I have found the professors to be accessible, communicative, and very helpful," says one student.

For the political science major, a similar course of study is required, including a dozen courses in political science (eight of those at advanced levels). Majors must take one class in each of the major's subfields: U.S. politics, international relations, and comparative politics; one in political theory; and one advanced course each in three of these subfields. Unfortunately, the department offers no further guidance for majors. The department does well in offering an ongoing variety of classes on a rotating basis, but more solid courses, available to students consistently, would be helpful in ensuring a solid education. The major is "fairly good," reports a current student, but the "courses could have required more difficult and in-depth assigned reading."

The University of Oregon puts a great deal of effort into its study-abroad programs, and it regularly encourages students to participate. Oregon offers more than 170 programs and internships in more than 90 different countries. The most popular destinations are Argentina, Australia, Chile, China, Denmark, Ecuador, France, Germany, Ireland, Italy,

Blue Collar Ivy

SUGGESTED CORE

1. Classics 301, Greek and Roman Epic
2. Philosophy 421, Ancient Philosophers
3. Religious Studies 222/223, Introduction to the Bible I, II
4. Religious Studies 321/322, History of Christianity
5. Political Science 431, Political Theory: Renaissance, Reformation, and Early Modern
6. English 207, Shakespeare
7. History 201, United States
8. Philosophy 453, 19th-Century Philosophers

Japan, Mexico, Spain, and the United Kingdom. Despite the school's promotion of its program, 25 percent of students elect to study abroad each year.

But students have the opportunity to interact with other cultures without ever leaving campus. Oregon offers classes in Chinese (Mandarin), Danish, Finnish, French, German, Greek and Latin, Hebrew, Italian, Japanese, Korean, Norwegian, Russian, Spanish, Swahili, and Swedish, among others.

Student Life: Granolaville

Since the 1970s, Eugene has been home to many citizens pursuing atypical lifestyles—from the mild-mannered organic grocers, antivaccine activists, and alternative schoolers to hard-core environmentalist radicals. Citizens of Eugene are deeply involved in their community, whether it be preserving natural environments within the city, tending public gardens, or attending community events like the city's First Friday Family Fun Nights, music festivals, or dance classes. Students are drawn to the remarkably green, bikeable property and enjoy living within driving distance of the Pacific Ocean, the Cascade Mountains, and Portland.

More than 250 student organizations are hosted by the university, including a Black Student Union, Multicultural Center, Arab Student Union, Vietnamese Student Association, Women's Center, Native American Student Union, Men's Center, and LGBTQ Alliance. The University of Oregon does host both College Republican and College Democrat groups, as well as Amnesty International and a pro-life group. Students report that the university is careful to fund all groups fairly, whatever their political outlook.

In keeping with Oregon's inclusiveness, an assortment of religious organizations are available to students, from Young Life, InterVarsity, and the Catholic Newman Center to the Baha'i Campus Association, Muslim Student Association, Christian Science Organization, B'nai B'rith Hillel, and Pagan Student Union.

Some students report that dorm life is acceptable, with friendly RAs and a laid-back atmosphere. Dorms are single sex by wing, room, or floor, which suggests mostly single-sex bathrooms. RAs are said to help students become active on campus and generally enforce school policy—although visitation rules are often flouted if roommates don't complain about overnight guests. However, other students have called the living conditions "miserable," pointing to cramped quarters, unhealthy food, loud neighbors, and little privacy. Oregon is working to improve the dorms and currently is renovating its Global Scholars Hall.

While nearly 90 percent of freshmen live on campus, just 7 percent of sophomores do (and 3 and 2 percent of juniors and seniors, respectively). Students can elect to live in special-interest halls, like the Honors Hall, Civic Engagement/Leadership Hall, International House, Quiet Hall, Wellness and Substance-Free Hall, or Gender Equity Hall, geared toward "alternative" students or those who want a roommate of any sex.

For the vast majority of upperclassmen who live off campus, a variety of apartments and houses can be rented near campus for reasonable rates. Students report that many flats are not much farther from classrooms than the dorms, and options vary from townhouses to studios or quads, where rooms are rented individually to four students who share a living room and a kitchen.

For the 12 percent of students who elect to join Greek life, 15 fraternities and 15 sororities are available. Twelve of the fraternities and nine of the sororities have chapter houses that sleep between 30 and 50 members. Oregon is careful to guard against some of the excesses often found in the Greek system, disallowing all alcohol and drugs and requiring an RA in each house.

Regardless of where they live, most University of Oregon students love to cheer on the Ducks, who compete in the PAC-12, Division I Athletics, with men's teams in baseball, basketball, cross-country, football, golf, tennis, and track and field, as well as women's acrobatics and tumbling, basketball, cross-country, golf, lacrosse, soccer, softball, tennis, track and field, and volleyball.

In 2011 the school reported eight forcible sex offenses, three aggravated assaults, 35 burglaries, and three motor vehicle thefts.

Tuition for the University of Oregon in 2012–13 was $9,258 for in-state students (and illegal immigrants) and $28,653 for American students from other states (both rates required $347 in fees). Room and board ran $10,260. Fifty percent of undergraduates received need-based financial aid, and the typical student graduated from the University of Oregon with $22,736 in debt.

STRONG SUITS	WEAK POINTS
• The Honors College Oregon offers solid courses grounded in the Great Books.	• The general-education curriculum is shaky and full of holes.
• Professors, once you reach the classes they actually teach, are helpful and dedicated.	• Almost half of courses (and most of the introductory ones) are taught by grad students.
• Good programs in business, the hard sciences (especially physics), religious studies, history, music, and economics.	• Many faculty are inexperienced.
• Many study-abroad and foreign language options.	• Some students call the dorms "miserable."

Pennsylvania State University

Can You Find the Cheese?

Pennsylvania State University was founded in 1855. The University Park campus is the largest of the 24 Penn State campuses around the state. Penn State is a strong research institution with a wide range of programs for its more than 84,000 undergraduates (over half of them at University Park). As at most large schools, students do best who come in knowing what they want to study—with a map for the maze they will surely encounter. Unlike students at some other massive state universities, Penn State students aren't constantly up in arms about political issues, and the campus politics are usually kept to a dull roar. The university's storied football program is now disgraced, thanks to the cover-up it engaged in of pedophile assaults by assistant coach Jerry Sandusky—which resulted in his prison sentence and the firing of both the legendary head coach Joe Paterno (now deceased) and university president Graham Spanier. A decent education can be found here by students committed to choosing the right courses and staying sober through the endless rounds of sport-related parties.

Academic Life: Not for agoraphobics

Penn State offers over 160 majors through the 11 colleges and nursing school at University Park. The largest colleges for undergraduates are those of engineering, liberal arts, and business. One student warns that the class sizes can be overwhelming; she reports that two of her introductory-level business classes had more than 400 students. Another student complains that some professors are not receptive to student requests for assistance: "The professor comes to teach the class and then leaves. There is little interaction." However, other students report that, aside from limited office hours, teachers are accessible, and one can make "excellent connections with professors" by being sufficiently assertive. The advising program especially is seen as outstanding for a large university—provided that students take advantage of it.

The choices for study at Penn State are vast, but the general-education requirements are scant. Core requirements are called "knowledge domains," with embarrassing explanations such as "developing the skill to communicate by means of the written word is extremely important." It isn't hard to find a course that meets one of these requirements; dozens will do. More than 400 courses satisfy the humanities requirement, ranging from "The Life and Thought of Malcolm X" to "Introduction to Lesbian and Gay Studies" to "Shakespeare." In selecting the core courses, students should get advice from other students and the professors listed below, and use common sense. If a course sounds politicized or fluffy, it probably is.

A good choice is the selective Schreyer Honors College, which includes special honors sections. Another worthy option is the Penn State Washington, D.C., Program, which offers internships in the nation's capital at places such as the ACLU, Nature Conservancy, AIPAC, CNN, NBC, and Pennsylvania congressman Jason Altmire's office. An interdisciplinary program called Classics and Ancient Mediterranean studies (CAMS) is solid and emphasizes primary texts.

One history professor says naming good departments at Penn State is like telling somebody about the

VITAL STATISTICS

Religious affiliation: *none*
Total enrollment: *45,628*
Total undergraduates: *38,954*
SAT CR/Verbal midrange: *530–630*
SAT Math midrange: *560–670*
ACT midrange: *25–29*
Applicants: *45,502*
Applicants accepted: *52%*
Accepted applicants who enrolled: *31%*
Tuition (general/out of state): *$28,746*
Tuition (in state): *$16,444*
Room and board: *$9,690*
Freshman retention rate: *92%*
Graduation rate (4 yrs.): *63%*
Graduation rate (6 yrs.): *87%*
Courses with fewer than 20 students: *38%*
Student-faculty ratio: *17:1*
Courses taught by graduate students: *not provided*
Students living on campus: *37%*
Students in fraternities: *15%*
Students in sororities: *13%*
Students receiving need-based financial aid: *52%*
Avg. student-loan debt of a recent graduating class: *$33,530*
Most popular majors: *business/marketing, engineering, communications*
Guaranteed housing for 4 years? *no*

CAMPUS POLITICS: YELLOW LIGHT

Thanks to the tenor of the student body, campus conservatives keep their heads up; nevertheless, the administration and faculty at Penn State lean heavily to the left and make policies that reflect this fact, according to the Foundation of Individual Rights in Education (FIRE). Penn State's "Principles" speech code is one of the worst in the country—vague, arbitrary, and liable to administrative abuse. The Young Americans for Freedom had their charter revoked by the student government (a decision upheld by the administration) because of a reference to "God-given free will." The student group went to FIRE for aid, and "the day after Penn State [former] President Graham Spanier received a letter from FIRE, he overturned Penn State's decision," YAF reported.

In 2013 students protested when a communications professor, Matthew Jordan, finished a class on the racist film *The Birth of a Nation* with "a montage of news clips criticizing voter ID laws," according to Young Americas Foundation. The course description of the relevant class promises to cover "the role cinema—and, especially, narrative film—plays in relating individuals to the values and assumptions of their culture." In an e-mail to the Young Americas Foundation, Jordan stood by his comparison of Republican Party efforts with the activities of the Ku Klux Klan to disenfranchise freed slaves. This incident confirms the comments of many students, who identified a pattern of political intrusions into classroom teaching.

weather in the United States: "You can't generalize. . . . Penn State is huge, and even within each department there is tremendous variety." This diversity is best exemplified in the English department, where British and American literature is purely optional, as majors "may choose from courses in all the major historical periods and genres of British and United States literature; in the work of individual authors (Shakespeare, Milton, and others); in three genres of creative writing; and in topics of rhetoric, African-American literature and culture, visual culture and media, ethnic studies, gender and sexuality studies, literature and science, and literary and cultural theory."

The history department is solid and has much to recommend it, reports an alumnus; all majors are required to take two Western civilization courses and two American heritage classes. "I switched from an undecided liberal arts major to history my sophomore year and I am very happy with my decision," a student says. "Every class I've taken so far has been excellent and free from indoctrination."

The political science department is a bit weak, as majors are not required to take any courses on the U.S. Constitution or American political philosophy. The business, agriculture, and engineering programs at University Park are well regarded both on campus and nationally, and Penn State's geography department is also among the best at the university, offering a balanced combination of hard science and social science courses.

The William Randolph Hearst Foundation gives high ratings to several journalism programs at the school. The education department is rated highly by several students enrolled in it. A professor on the Penn State faculty highly recommended by students was author Philip Jenkins (emeritus), Jens Guettel, Jason Strandquist, and Anthony Kaye in history and religious studies. Other recommended faculty include Sean Brennan, Kostadin Ivanov, Thomas Litzinger, Timothy Simpson, and H. Joseph Sommer III in engineering; Herman Bierens (emeritus) and Neil Wallace in economics; James P. Lantolf in linguistics; Rosa A. Eberly and J. Michael Hogan in communications; Jonathan Brockopp and Gerald (Gary) Knoppers in religious studies; David Rosenbaum, Jeff Love, and Andrew Peck in psychology; and Paul Amato in sociology.

According to a student, "politics intrude directly into the classroom" on a regular basis. Outside of the sciences, courses vary widely in terms of how infused they are with ideology. One PSU student says, "Obviously, classes are ideologically polarized, if not politicized. In (one) political theory class, we read extremist feminist authors, John Rawls, and Foucault, and this is considered a good cross section of contemporary theory." Another student says, "Some professors do not blatantly push their ideals on you, but their politics are usually obvious, and speaking from the right in a political conversation can be uncomfortable, if not terrifying. It is possible to voice other perspectives, but be prepared for at least a gentle rebuttal and possibly something more disconcerting."

Students who want to perform research at Penn State have many opportunities, even as undergraduates. The university is consistently among the top recipients in the nation of research funding. Some tenants of the university's Innovation Park research complex also take Penn State interns.

> With classes of more than 400 students, it's not surprising that, as one student says, "the professor comes to teach the class and then leaves. There is little interaction."

Students can expect to find teaching assistants leading the discussion sections of large courses—although professors do teach most classes, and generally teach well, students say. Even those professors wrapped up in their research tend to pay attention to their undergraduate teaching, students report. "Surprisingly, even some of my huge introductory classes were taught by professors, not TAs," a student says. "But those same professors were very elusive outside of the classroom." One faculty member says that some students, especially in the humanities, genuinely enjoy learning and visit professors during office hours—not just to contest a bad grade, but to talk about ideas. One student reports that office visits to graduate teaching assistants are more helpful than visiting professors themselves. "It's a big school," says a student, "and, like all big schools, it is what you make it. You can either become a number in the system or take advantage of its benefits."

Students point to the African and African American studies programs as among the most politicized on campus, alongside women's studies.

Most of the conservative students we consulted report that they feel unable to voice their opinions in class, and one describes being forced to read materials that clearly had a political agenda unrelated to the stated subject of the class. Another says: "It takes a strong person to not be swept onto the (liberal) bandwagon, because this faculty, with perhaps a few exceptions, is composed of fantastic intellectuals. That being said, there are many ways in which a conservative can find common ground without giving way to their rhetoric."

Blue Collar Ivy

SUGGESTED CORE

1. Classics and Ancient Mediterranean Studies 001, Greek and Roman Literature
2. Philosophy 006, Philosophy and Literature in Western Culture (closest match)
3. Religious Studies 110/120, Hebrew Bible: Old Testament/New Testament
4. Religious Studies 124, Early and Medieval Christianity
5. Political Science 435, Foundations of American Political Theory
6. English 444, Shakespeare
7. History 020, American Civilization to 1877
8. No suitable course

She continues, "There are numerous opportunities, and many great professors to work with if you can work around the politics."

The university offers a wide variety of opportunities to study abroad, on six continents in dozens of countries, such as China, Costa Rica, the Czech Republic, Denmark, Ecuador, Egypt, England, France, Greece, Hungary, India, Ireland, Israel, Japan, Kenya, Mexico, Russia, Scotland, Spain, and Tanzania, among others.

The school offers classes in Arabic, Chinese, French, German, Greek and Latin, Hebrew, Hindi, Italian, Japanese, Korean, Polish, Portuguese, Russian, Serbo-Croatian, Spanish, Swahili, and Ukrainian.

Student Life: They don't call it Happy Valley for nothing

Happy Valley is isolated and surrounded by mountains—scenic, but not exactly cosmopolitan. The university requires freshmen to live on campus, but only about 20 percent choose to stay after that; Penn State has room for only a little over 13,000 of its almost 46,000 students. There are four university apartment complexes and the residence halls are clustered in five groups. Most are coed by floor (each floor is single sex), though one student reports that several dorms have coed floors as well. Students must use their ID cards to open outer building doors. Students say housing is in high demand, and more is being built, mainly for upperclassmen and graduate students. Off-campus students live in nearby apartments in the town of State College.

With a large percentage of the student body in the Greek system, residential fraternities and sororities play a large role in solving the school's housing problem—and in social life on campus. That may be one reason why Penn State has earned the dubious distinction as one of the country's leading party schools. "Many students take advantage of little aside from the bars and fraternity or sorority parties," reports one student. "Drinking is a serious problem." Another student insists that "there is usually a party in process it seems, but they do not always include alcohol."

The *Daily Collegian* newspaper has been run by students for 116 years. It has a very left-leaning editorial page, which one student characterizes as "sometimes vicious." Nevertheless, students maintain that many of their peers are "fairly conservative," and campus speakers appear to be fairly balanced in their views. Conservative groups on campus include the Young Americans for Freedom, Students for Life, the College Libertarians, and the Conservative Coalition.

The school's 15 varsity teams are known as the Nittany Lions. The word Nittany, derived from an Indian word meaning "single mountain," is the name of a peak near campus. The Nittany Lions compete in NCAA Division I in 15 men's and 14 women's sports, including baseball, basketball, football, soccer, cross-country, fencing, golf, gymnastics, lacrosse, ice hockey, softball, swimming, tennis, track, volleyball, and wrestling.

In 2012 former assistant football coach Jerry Sandusky was convicted of 45 counts of sexual abuse, most of which occurred in the Penn State athletic facilities. During the trial it was revealed that top university officials knew of the abuse and covered it up. They were subsequently charged with perjury and fired. The NCAA imposed a series of inadequate sanctions, including a $60 million fine, revoking and limiting football scholarships through 2017, and stripping the football team of all titles from 1998 to 2011. In 2013 Pennsylvania governor Tom Corbett filed an antitrust lawsuit against the NCAA in protest of even these sanctions. The student response has been bizarre and troubling. There was an almost immediate cry for President Spanier's head, but when Coach Paterno (who knew about the abuse for years and was the most responsible for Sandusky's continued access to young boys) was forced to resign, there was a protest of almost 10,000 students and alums. Maybe a course in ethics should be added to the gen-ed requirements.

The Penn State University Police is a full-time police agency granted the same powers as the municipal police by city law, employing close to 250 police officers, security officers, police interns, and student officers who provide round-the-clock service. Still, students are advised to exercise caution around campus. In 2011 the university reported 24 forcible sexual assaults, 112 burglaries, two robberies, six aggravated assaults, one stolen car, and 11 arsons. "I feel relatively safe on campus most of the time," says a female student. "But I try not to be out alone at night."

Tuition in 2012–13 for Pennsylvania residents was $16,444, and $28,746 for out-of-state students. Room-and-board rates vary by dorm and meal plan, but averaged $9,690. Fifty-two percent of full-time undergraduates received financial aid of some kind, and the average student graduated with a looming loan debt of $33,530.

STRONG SUITS	WEAK POINTS
• The selective Schreyer Honors College offers smaller, more rigorous classes.	• General-education requirements are worthy of a middlebrow high school.
• Departments are so big that good courses and teachers can be found.	• Hundreds of courses, many politicized and/or trivial, fulfill core mandates.
• In the history department, requirements are solid and classes mostly apolitical.	• Shaky mandates for English and political science majors.
• Business, agriculture, engineering, geography, journalism, and education programs are highly praised.	• Grad students do much of the teaching.
	• Many classes are politicized by professors.
• A good range of religious and conservative groups are active on campus.	• Nationally "famous" as a party school.
	• An administration still clouded by its cover-up of sex abuse in football program.

Temple University

Philadelphia, Pennsylvania • www.temple.edu

Bare, Ruined Choirs

Founded in 1884 and named for the historic Baptist Temple, Temple University is now affiliated not with a church but with the state. It is renowned as one of the most "diverse" universities in the nation, boasting more than 36,000 students from 120 countries and all 50 states. Temple has diverse locations and courses of study, with nine campuses, more than 100 degree programs, 17 schools and colleges, and five professional schools. Templetons consider their cosmopolitan origins a major attraction of the school. "It's big yet small," says one student. "I love how colorful we are." Sadly, the school in recent years demolished its once-solid core curriculum, and has pursued a senseless romance with multicultural-ism. Still, there is much left of value for those who know where to look.

Academic Life: Temple of doom?

Temple's once outstanding Intellectual Heritage program "is history," mourns a professor. "A new program, weirdly called 'Mosaic,' was created to fill the void." Another professor explains: "The Intellectual Heritage courses within the Mosaic have undergone total revi-sions. Each of our two courses (one on 'journeys, self and others, community, and faith,' and the other on 'science, power, money, environment/city') offers students four core texts, plus a supplementary book (selected from approved options) for each core text." Perhaps the greatest change is the approach, which one professor says is "thematic rather than sequential or chronological, and reaches further beyond the classic 'canon' than in the past."

All freshmen receive academic advising from their particular school's advising office until they declare a major, when they are assigned a faculty or staff adviser in their department. The quality of advising varies, since students decide how often (if ever) to consult their appointed mentors. The Liberal Arts school has a fully staffed advising center open on weekdays during regular business hours. Appointments are recommended, but same-day advising is still available on a first-come, first-served basis.

Within its undergraduate colleges, Temple is said to be renowned in areas such as business, communications, education, art, music, and the hard sciences.

The English department is quite good, requiring all majors to complete an introductory English survey course; British literature to 1660 and British literature from 1660 to 1900; two American literature classes; six electives; and a senior capstone course.

The history department uses a "step approach" for undergraduate majors. The 12 required courses are two introductory classes; three intermediate; four advanced, one of which must be writing intensive and taken junior year; one senior capstone class; and two electives at any level. The department admits these are "broad requirements," with the only solid mandate being that students complete a minimum of two classes each in American and European history, and three courses in Asian, African, Latin American, or Global/Comparative history.

The political science major requirements are respectable, including "The American Political System," "Foreign Governments and Politics," "International Politics," "Introduction to Political Philosophy," a senior capstone, and six upper-level electives.

Students speak effusively of their favorite professors, such as Reginald White in business and accounting. Says one student, "Dr. White is a great teacher. He's in-depth and really understands the work." Je-Wei Chen in mathematics

VITAL STATISTICS

Religious affiliation: *none*
Total enrollment: *36,744*
Total undergraduates:
27,567
SAT CR/Verbal midrange:
490–600
SAT Math midrange:
510–610
ACT midrange: *21–26*
Applicants: *18,731*
Applicants accepted: *67%*
Accepted applicants who
enrolled: *22%*
Tuition (general/out of
state): *$22,832*
Tuition (in state): *$13,006*
Room and board: *$10,276*
Freshman retention rate:
87%
Graduation rate (4 yrs.): *36%*
Graduation rate (6 yrs.): *68%*
Courses with fewer than 20
students: *36%*
Student-faculty ratio: *15:1*
Courses taught by graduate
students: *not provided*
Students living on campus:
17%
Students in fraternities: *4%*
Students in sororities: *4%*
Students receiving need-
based financial aid: *68%*
Avg. student-loan debt of a
recent graduating class:
$24,730
Most popular majors: *business, communications,
visual and performing arts*
Guaranteed housing for 4
years? *no*

CAMPUS POLITICS: YELLOW LIGHT

In the past decade, Temple University has gotten in trouble several times for policies that were skewed against conservatives. A graduate student (and decorated veteran) who was vocally conservative got thrown out of his program—and had to embark on a multiyear litigation against the university (he won). Temple tried to gouge conservative sponsors of an anti-Islamist speaker for extra security costs, then backed down when its demands went public. In 2010 the president of a student group admitted that Temple's student government maintained "an unwritten discriminatory policy" designed to "deny funding to student groups for speakers who are 'offensive'—or not 'inclusive' and 'friendly,'" according to the Foundation for Individual Rights in Education, which still gives Temple a "yellow light" rating because of "at least one ambiguous policy that too easily encourages administrative abuse and arbitrary application."

Temple University changed its grievance procedures after Pennsylvania legislators investigated charges of campus indoctrination and discrimination. The revised policy called on officials to report all grievances to the school's Board of Trustees. Students should be informed, it said, of what to do if they believe that professors have violated their rights, including how to lodge grievances. Students who want to file complaints, said the new rules, should be able to do so with someone outside their departments. This policy seems to have improved things; there have been no high-profile cases of student abuse since it was adopted.

is "able to explain everything in such a manner that it all just clicks." Edith Saltzberg in music is known as "the most understanding professor at Temple . . . she makes the class interesting and truly loves to teach." Other recommended professors include Susan Bertolino, Richard Libowitz, and Richard Orodenker in liberal arts; Michael Bradley in English; Joseph Soler in education; and Daniel Tompkins in Classics.

The average class size at Temple is a moderate 27, but the student-faculty ratio is a discouraging 15 to 1. It's unclear whether this has anything to do with the school's anemic four-year graduation rate of just 36 percent.

Temple maintains campuses in Rome and Tokyo. Exchange programs with Germany, Puerto Rico, and the United Kingdom are also available. A shorter visit abroad is possible with one of the many summer-study programs in Brazil, Costa Rica, Germany, Ghana, India, Jamaica, and Senegal, to name a few.

Foreign languages offered include Chinese (Mandarin), French, German, Greek and Latin, Hebrew, Italian, Japanese, Russian, and Spanish.

Student Life: Urban youths

If you like city life, you'll love Temple. The Temple environs have all the flavor of fascinating Philadelphia, one of America's most beautiful, public-spirited cities. Trolleys, subway lines, and a campus shuttle traverse the nearby town, providing several ways to get about. The university is close to the arts, music, culture—and crime. The architecture is nothing to write home about. One insider notes wryly: "It's interesting that they put the social sciences department in a complex of minimalist and brutalist architecture and there presume to give insight on the human condition. It's like sending a great chef to Ethiopia."

Temple prides itself on its innovation and progressiveness. With 85 percent of its campus offering Wi-Fi, Temple has the distinction of being one of the most connected campuses in the United States. Most professors have gotten "current" and use Blackboard—an online learning system—to post assignments, lecture notes, grades, and announcements. This commitment to advanced technology is evidenced in the TECH Center, a 75,000-square-foot state-of-the-art facility said to be "the largest of its kind in the nation." It is purportedly filled with "'e-sources' that cater to current learning styles" and "a variety of workspaces to enable students to work collaboratively or individually."

Temple is hardly a sanctuary. Situated in crime-blighted downtown Philly, it has to struggle to keep students safe. One student says, "People are constantly being shot right down the street."

Dorm life for the more than 6,800 resident students takes place primarily in the high-rise residential halls and apartment-style residences on the Main Campus. A few of the oldest residences feature single-sex floors, but the majority sport newer, coed halls with private bathrooms. Students can choose between suburban and city campuses and are generally pleased with their options. "The dorm I've lived in is pretty nice," says one undergrad of James White Hall. "We have shared bathrooms, but a full kitchen . . . it's great for getting to know the student body."

Temple boasts that its activities are "as diverse as the student body." Temple provides more than 300 clubs and organizations, including juggling, snowboarding, knitting, chess, musical theater, Habitat for Humanity, and yoga, among numerous others. One of the school's largest student organizations is the *Temple News*, Temple's noted twice-weekly community newspaper, which features nearly 200 student writers, photographers, editors, and business employees, coordinated by a staff of 20. Temple also has a competitive political debate club (Temple is a member of the competitive National Parliamentary Debate Association) and a variety of community-service opportunities. There are also College Republicans, College Democrats, Temple Libertarians, Temple Democratic Socialists, ACLU, and a Planned Parenthood affiliate.

Temple University was among the first institutions in the United States to sponsor extracurricular athletic activities for its students; both the football and basketball programs were inaugurated back in 1894 under the direction of Coach Charles M. Williams. The school's sports teams are called the Owls, harking back to the days when Temple was a night school. The Owls participate in the NCAA's Division I as members of the Atlantic Ten Conference (A-10), with the exception of football, which moved to the Mid-American Conference. The school's most popular teams are men's and women's basketball; men's soccer, baseball, and lacrosse; and women's volleyball.

Greek life at Temple is small but growing. There are 20 recognized fraternities and 15 sororities. Their memberships have doubled in the past five years, to comprise about 4 percent of the student population.

SUGGESTED CORE

1. Greek and Roman Classics 3396, Classical Epic
2. Philosophy 2161, History of Philosophy: Greek
3. Religious Studies 2496, Introduction to the Bible
4. Religious Studies 3501, History of Christianity I
5. Political Science 2431, Modern Political Philosophy
6. English 2297, Shakespeare
7. History 1101, U.S. History to 1877
8. Philosophy 2165, Hume, Marx, Darwin, and Freud

Crime is a real issue in the surrounding neighborhoods. Temple's campus is tightly packed into a somewhat hostile city. Says a student, "The worst aspect of being here is the environment. The neighbors are sick of us expanding and don't like us in general. People are constantly being shot 'right down the street,' although I've never run into stuff personally." On the campus itself, students seem fairly secure. In 2011 the school reported a decline in incidents on campus, noting three forcible sex offenses (down from six the year before), four robberies (down from nine), three aggravated assaults, and four burglaries.

Tuition costs are moderate, and financial aid is available. As the school website states: "The founder of Temple University, Dr. Russell H. Conwell, believed that education should be available to anyone on the basis of their intellectual and personal motivation, regardless of their income. In this spirit, we are eager to assist all Temple students to afford a college education." Tuition for a full-time undergraduate from out of state in 2012–13 was $22,832; in-state tuition was a much more moderate $13,006; room and board were $10,276. Some 68 percent of undergraduates received need-based financial aid, and the average student-loan debt of a recent graduating class was $24,730.

STRONG SUITS

- Good departments in business, communications, education, art, music, English, political science, and the hard sciences.
- Very cosmopolitan student body.
- Many opportunities for study abroad.
- Situated in a beautiful city full of history and culture.

WEAK POINTS

- The once fine core curriculum has been replaced by weaker thematic, multiculturalist courses.
- The four-year graduation rate is very low (36 percent).
- Advising is uneven and largely optional.
- The neighborhoods around the school are ridden with crime.

University of Rhode Island

Job Camp

The University of Rhode Island is a land-, sea-, and urban-grant public research institution. It was chartered in 1888 and still maintains the "old farmhouse" that housed its first researchers. The university has some very strong vocational opportunities to offer, and the faculty are quite personable with their students. Unfortunately, the political atmosphere of the university is oppressively leftist, and Greek life can take a fairly heavy toll on students' brains and livers.

Academic Life: Teacher! Leave those kids alone!

There is no core curriculum at URI, and the general-education requirements are of no real help. The university has a "policy of allowing the greatest latitude possible in course selection." Though all bachelor of arts majors are expected to fulfill the requirements, the university "offers a wide choice to fill its general-education requirements and encourages students to select free electives that cross departmental and college lines." While all students must complete courses "selected from the same list of approved courses, there are possible variations based on the student's major" as well.

VITAL STATISTICS

Religious affiliation: *none*
Total enrollment: *16,317*
Total undergraduates: *13,219*
SAT CR/Verbal midrange:
 490–590
SAT Math midrange:
 500–610
ACT midrange: *21–26*
Applicants: *20,012*
Applicants accepted: *76%*
Accepted applicants who
 enrolled: *21%*
Tuition (general/out of
 state): *$25,912*
Tuition (in state): *$9,824*
Room and board: *$10,767*
Freshman retention rate:
 82%
Graduation rate (4 yrs.): *41%*
Graduation rate (6 yrs.): *63%*
Courses with fewer than 20
 students: *33%*
Student-faculty ratio: *16:1*
Courses taught by graduate
 students: *not provided*
Students living on campus:
 43%
Students in fraternities: *11%*
Students in sororities: *13%*
Students receiving need-
 based financial aid: *65%*
Avg. student-loan debt of a
 recent graduating class:
 $25,973
Most popular majors:
 *business/marketing,
 health professions,
 engineering*
Guaranteed housing for 4
 years? *no*

Two-thirds of courses have fewer than 30 students. Students report that very few classes are taught by graduate teaching assistants. One student says that she has never had any TAs in class at all. Another says, "I haven't had many graduate assistants, but when I did, they did not hinder my learning. They were a little easier to understand." A student says that TAs "teach recitations sometimes but they tend to be only in large classes." A professor tells us, "Teaching is pretty central here. We're not a very high-powered research place. I think there are some very good parts to the research, but teaching is still a very important aspect to a career here."

The selective honors program at URI offers courses with 15 or fewer students in the upperclassman level, 20 or fewer in underclassman courses. To graduate with honors, students must complete at least 18 credits in honors, including the Honors Seminar, Colloquium, Tutorial, Senior Seminar, and Senior Project. Besides smaller classes and the opportunity to complete a senior thesis with a faculty mentor of the student's choosing, the honors program offers a few solid classes like "Legal and Environmental Ethics of Business," which covers the United States Constitution and "its application to historical and current business issues," and "Art History, Ancient–Medieval." Unfortunately, there are perhaps more classes like "Class and Social Justice," which "focuses on four issues of social justice: Poverty, Race, Sexual Orientation, and Health Care." The strongest point of the program might be the vocational help to be found in the Administrative Internship it offers. A professor recommends the honors program, however, saying that "it's not particularly large, but I think it does offer a number of advantages to bright students if they want to dig into the different fields."

Faculty and students recommend the pharmacy, engineering, business, nursing, education, individual education, political science, and history departments. The pharmacy program is especially praised by students and professors. One student says that it is "well respected, with many illustrious alumni," while a professor tells us that it is "growing by leaps and bounds, and just had a new building constructed for it."

Some departments are thought to be weaker, including English, communications

("There are not many people in those majors," says a student), chemistry, and economics. A student says that the chemistry faculty "are notorious [teachers]." He believes that the department is poorly run, "having experienced it firsthand. Nothing gets done, and when it does, it takes weeks." Another student warns that some professors in political science "can have a hard time seeing nonliberal perspectives." Economics is said to be a "small department" that "does not offer a lot of classes or specializations."

English majors must take at least one course from each of five different historical periods. Though there are two Shakespeare courses that can fulfill the "1500–1660" period requirement, students could opt for other options and graduate without ever having studied Shakespeare at all. Many English courses seem quite solid, such as "The Epic," which covers "epic literature from Homer to the modern period," and "U.S. Literature and Culture from 1865 to 1914." However, the department also has its share of classes like "Foundational Texts in Modern Gay and Lesbian Culture" and "Contemporary Women Novelists of the Americas."

Though courses in U.S. history before 1945 are offered at URI, they are not required for majors. The courses offered in the history department look pretty solid overall, including "American Colonial History to 1763" and "The American Revolution and Confederation: 1763–1789." There are a few trendier, more politicized courses that students might be well advised to avoid, such as "Women in the United States, 1890–Present," which studies "changes in sexuality, reproduction and work" and "images of women in popular culture."

Political science majors are required to take "Introduction to American Politics," which covers the "basic principles of the government of the United States: constitutionalism, separation of powers, federalism, civil

CAMPUS POLITICS: RED LIGHT

According to current undergraduates, URI's political scene is not a pretty picture. "It's a very dumbed-down campus. I'd say the vast amount of diversity-focused training…is to blame," a student complains. Another says that "when voicing conservative views on campus," one should "be prepared to be crucified." In 2011 a piece was published by *The Good 5¢ Cigar*, the daily student-run URI newspaper, which mocked conservative students for "crying" about ideological and liberal professors. The article slammed all conservative thought as unworthy of classroom discussion, stating that "faculty will never change their curriculum for a small group of loud-mouths. . . . Conservatives are never going to have power here and nothing can possibly be done about it. At the university, conservatives will never be allowed to sit at the cool people's table in the cafeteria."

Following the mass murder at Sandy Hook Elementary school in Newtown, Connecticut, URI history professor Erik Loomis "tweeted" some very violent language aimed at the NRA, as the *American Thinker* reported. "I want Wayne LaPierre's head on a stick" was his initial reaction to the shootings. "It looks like the NRA has murdered some more children," he added. When his comments drew fire from the Right, he tweeted "Dear right-wing morons, saying you 'want someone's head on a stick' is a metaphor. I know metaphor is hard for you to understand." In March 2012 Loomis had called for a "decades-long fight to the death [against conservatives]. That's the nation's only hope."

liberties; politics; legislative, executive, and judicial organization; functions of government." Once students declare their major, they often choose either an American or a World Politics focus, which would require either "American Politics Theories and Applications" or "World Politics Theories and Applications." Also required are a minimum of 32 credits in the department. Most courses are worth four credits, and more than 80 political philosophy and political science courses are offered at URI.

Students looking to boost their résumés will find some great opportunities at URI. As a student puts it, "The internships and opportunities given to students are exceptional." Students will be given occasions to "network with companies" before they graduate. One student says that the Department of Human Development and Family "offers a lot of internships for students," and another praises the Naval War College Internship. A student also praises the International Engineering Program, which is an opportunity for promising engineering students to get some on-the-job training overseas.

Students warn that most classes at URI are "dumbed down by political correctness" and that many faculty are "not welcoming toward conservatives." One student remarks that in science courses, "We're too busy talking about molecules and reactions to think about politics. All sciences are pretty free of biases." A politics student says, "I feel very unwelcome in the department, as though my professors look down on me as a conservative." Another major adds that "the same applies [with regard to religion]." A professor points out that Rhode Island is "the most liberal state in the Union," and that "there are a lot of Democrat students at the university. We try to *find* conservative students, in fact. It's much more lively and interesting to have some debate." This professor says that, despite the liberal majority, "Some of the brightest students are conservative, and I would hope that they think it's a balanced presentation. . . . I don't see that there's anybody that I know that's an ideologue in their teaching."

> S tudents warn that classes at URI are "dumbed down by political correctness."

Students and faculty recommend professors Sheryl Foster in the philosophy; Marc Hutchison, Shanna Pearson-Merkowitz, William Dolan, and Nicoli Petro in political science; Michael Honhart and Lori Bihler in history; Diane Kern, Bill Malloy, and Mary Hoyt in education; Judy de Olivera in language; Sean O'Donnell, Paul Larrat, and Stephen Kogut in pharmacy; Barbara VanSciver in biology; Michael McGregor in chemistry; Gordon Dash in business; and Phil Clark in nursing/gerontology.

Students report that the intellectual curiosity of students at URI is "overall . . . above average," though it "varies by department." Some students are not very academically serious. "The toughest majors, pharmacy followed by engineering, are those that have the most dedicated students," sniffs a student. "They aren't like the fashion majors, who take a 100-level communications class and claim it's hard." A professor tells us that some of the students in the honors program are very "bright" and "[recommends] the honors program as a bright spot in the university."

URI offers courses in many languages, including Arabic, Hebrew, Japanese, Modern

Greek, Portuguese, and Russian. There are also majors and minors available in a few languages, including Chinese, French, German, Italian, and Spanish.

Student Life: Beware of Greeks bearing Trojans™

Rhode Island offers 18 intercollegiate sports, and the university is a member of the Atlantic 10 Conference and NCAA Division I (Division I-AA for football). A student says that basketball is the most popular sport at URI, "even though they are not very good at the moment." Says another student, "The teams we have aren't that great (notably basketball and football). Here people aren't that concerned about the teams, because they are well aware that they are not competitive." In her opinion, "Hockey is becoming very popular very fast…and will most likely be made a Division I team next year." However, as one student puts it, sports at URI simply "aren't quite as popular as at [other universities]. It seems like URI has to bribe the students to go to a basketball game."

> **SUGGESTED CORE**
>
> 1. Classics 391, Ancient Laughter: The Comic Tradition in Greece and Rome/396, Myths of Rome/397, Greek Myth and Tragedy
> 2. Philosophy 321, Ancient Philosophy
> 3. Religious Studies 125, Biblical Thought
> 4. Philosophy 322, Medieval Philosophy
> 5. Political Science 342, Political Theory: Modern and Contemporary
> 6. English 280, Introduction to Shakespeare
> 7. History 414, History of the United States to 1877
> 8. Philosophy 324, Recent European Philosophy

So what do students like to do with their time? "Greek life is pretty big on campus," a student warns. "That is where the parties take place." We are told that "URI is a big Greek school. Like half the population is in Greek life," so watch out for "major parties and alcohol." (In reality, 12 percent of URI students are members of fraternities/sororities.) The "very prevalent" Greek system "negatively affects the atmosphere," according to one student. Another student says her fellow students in the Greek system "create a party-like atmosphere. They also have a history of hazing, even though it is banned." However, one student thinks differently about Greek life: "It's there, but you can reasonably ignore it." In his opinion, Greek groups "don't detract from the atmosphere" at all, as long as you don't join them.

But this student is not so easy on student morals. "Campus in general is quite promiscuous," he says, and "Barlow Hall is the most sexually active dorm in America, FYI. There are some gender-neutral bathrooms in Adams Hall, home of the LGBT Center." Another student says that "there are no enforced visitation policies" between men and women, adding that "there are coed floors in the dorms and suites. Rooms themselves are single sex." When it comes to bathrooms, we are told that some are "primarily female or male. It depends on the dorm…but promiscuity is a must among URI students. All RAs are fully loaded with bags of condoms." At the beginning of each semester, contraceptives are handed out to all students who want them and bowls of condoms are available on the desks of every RA at the school, along with candies. The candies are there to keep students from feeling embarrassed—if they want a condom, they need only ask for a chocolate, reach in the bowl and discreetly take a Trojan™.

Students can take refuge in the university's Catholic Center, which a student calls "an awesome place to go for support and prayer." She also praises the Newman Club, a Catholic student organization. "The Catholic Center is really great," says another. "Several participants in the Catholic Center are members of the College Republicans." Another place to go for prayer and fellowship is the new Rhody Christian Fellowship, which holds regular Bible studies, encourages daily Scripture reading, and will even give Bibles to students who wish to participate.

Students at URI report that the university's crime rates do not worry them. "Crime is not a concern on campus," says one student, "though if there were a shooter on campus we would all die, because our URI police are not allowed to carry guns." Another student adds that "the dorms are not very protected. Pretty much just anyone can walk in. I would feel safer if our police were allowed to carry guns." But one student points out that "there's nothing surrounding URI, so it's pretty safe." Not that safe. In the last year reported, there were 17 forcible sex offenses, one robbery, three aggravated assaults, 49 burglaries, two motor vehicle thefts, and one arson committed on campus.

URI was a bargain for residents of that tiny state with tuition at only $9,824 in 2012–13 (outsiders paid $25,912) and room and board at $10,767. Some 65 percent of students received need-based financial aid, and the average student-loan debt of a recent graduating class was $25,973.

STRONG SUITS	WEAK POINTS
• Mostly small classes, with faculty largely focused on teaching. • Good programs in pharmacy, engineering, business, nursing, education, individual education, political science, and history. • Excellent internships.	• Students criticize programs in English, communications, chemistry, economics. • Shakespeare and early U.S. history are optional for English and history majors, respectively. • Randy, drunken dorm life is fueled by overweening Greek organizations.

College of Charleston

Charleston, South Carolina • www.cofc.edu

Palmetto Bucks

In 1785, two years before statesmen ratified the U.S. Constitution, another group of founders in South Carolina created the College of Charleston. Most of today's popular majors certainly would not have appeared on any late-18th-century class schedule. Nowadays, students at the College of Charleston can major in hospitality and tourism management, studio art, and athletic training, among 52 options. Yet many traditional areas of study remain, and if students are willing to look, they'll find excellent professors able to guide them.

Academic Life: One from column A . . .

The school's mission statement claims the college "retains a strong liberal arts undergraduate curriculum." However, excepting for a few general-education requirements, students are free to choose their own slate of courses—and few are prepared to do so, because . . . they haven't yet been educated. Moreover, depending on teachers' whims about reading material, students can take "core" courses that fail to teach the traditional core. For instance, "core" history courses typically offer only a sampling of each era, requiring students to

VITAL STATISTICS

Religious affiliation: *none*
Total enrollment: *11,649*
Total undergraduates:
10,461
SAT CR/Verbal midrange:
560–650
SAT Math midrange:
560–640
ACT midrange: *23–27*
Applicants: *11,086*
Applicants accepted: *73%*
Accepted applicants who
enrolled: *28%*
Tuition (general/out of
state): *$25,304*
Tuition (in state): *$9,918*
Room and board: *$10,461*
Freshman retention rate:
83%
Graduation rate (4 yrs.): *52%*
Graduation rate (6 yrs.): *63%*
Courses with fewer than 20
students: *31%*
Student-faculty ratio: *16:1*
Courses taught by graduate
students: *not provided*
Students living on campus:
32%
Students in fraternities: *13%*
Students in sororities: *21%*
Students receiving need-
based financial aid: *45%*
Avg. student-loan debt of a
recent graduating class:
$22,449
Most popular majors:
*business, education,
communications*
Guaranteed housing for 4
years? *no*

cram information from textbooks into their heads rather than ideas from primary sources.

As at all public universities, the quality of students can vary tremendously, and academic life at the College of Charleston is no exception. In 2012 scores for the Critical Reading portion of the SAT ranged from as low as 400–499 for the bottom 4 percent of students to as high as 700–800 for the top 10 percent. The math portion showed similar variations.

The best option for a serious student at Charleston would be to enroll in the selective Honors College by applying as a high school senior. The 200 honors students accepted each fall must maintain at least a 3.4 GPA at Charleston. The Honors College offers three residence halls for honors students (including an all-female house), where lectures, seminars, and social activities are plentiful. Most departments also offer courses available only to honors students. Along with their honors-level course requirements, honors students must also participate in a Western-civilization history class as sophomores, take an academic writing course, two semesters of mathematics, and an independent study as juniors, and must complete a senior thesis.

Charleston students have the option to earn the school's original bachelor's degree—*Artium Baccalaureatus*—which requires them to take, in addition to the requirements for their major, 18 hours in Greek or Latin language courses, and six hours (with a 2.5 average grade) in approved courses in classical civilization. We recommend this option highly to anyone who can handle the workload.

If students (or parents) find Charleston's general-education requirements too flexible, they may find a little more structure within the disciplines. Students pursuing an English major must take two courses on major British writers, a survey of American literature, and an introduction to English studies course. Students must also take one "Difference in Literary Tradition" or "Film and Cultural Studies," a writing, language, or rhetoric course, a theme- and/or genre-centered course or an author-centered course and three surveys in British or American literature pre-1700, 1700–1900, and post-1900. Two electives and a capstone are also required. Thankfully, the classes offered are typically strong, such as "The British

South Carolina

Novel" for a theme-centered class and "Modern English Grammar" to fulfill the writing requirement.

The philosophy major is less structured, with only four required courses: history of ancient philosophy, history of modern philosophy, symbolic logic, and a senior seminar in philosophy. Students are free to choose as their remaining classes such topics as "Ethics and Sports," "Environmental Ethics," and "Feminist Theory."

The history department requires all majors to take one class from five areas of distribution: premodern (before 1500); modern Europe (since 1500); modern Asia, Africa, or Latin America; United States; and comparative/transnational. Additional requirements include a writing course called "The Historian's Craft" and a research seminar that entails writing a substantial paper. History majors must also take three electives, from which they may choose such classes as "Ancient Rome" and "Women in Europe."

The political science major "is intended to allow students to sample broadly from the variety of subfields that make up the discipline," the school reports. Students are required to take courses in American government, world politics, or world regional geography, and two classes in political thought and research. Beyond their introductory classes, students must take one course each from three of these subfields: American politics and process, global politics and spaces, and politics of ideas. Classes range from traditional to trendy; "Constitutional Law" and "LGBT Politics" both fulfill the American politics and process requirement.

CAMPUS POLITICS: GREEN LIGHT

Even though the College of Charleston is nestled in the heart of the South, the student body is more moderate than conservative, and there are significant contingencies of libertarians, independents, and "apathetics" as well. Students openly participate in pro-life events such as 40 Days for Life, and the campus's most active political group is the Americans for Informed Democracy, a moderate group seeking to educate Americans about world issues and to discuss U.S. politics on a global scale. The group brings in congressional candidates as speakers and focuses on supporting charitable causes rather than stirring up controversies.

Indeed, the academic atmosphere at the College of Charleston is decidedly apolitical, even though the faculty tends to veer left of center. At Charleston, departments like political science, African American studies, and even women's and gender studies are remarkably tame and free from any outrageous and offensive course titles. We've heard no reports of discrimination against conservative students. For the most part, the free exchange of ideas and forthright classroom discussions are encouraged by the College of Charleston faculty. It seems students' greatest navigational challenge is learning how to avoid doing the "Charleston Shuffle" when they trip on the school's old cobblestones.

Academically, the College of Charleston is best known for its business and marketing program, science departments, and education school.

The School of Sciences and Mathematics touts a distinctive major called Discovery Informatics, which integrates math and computer science. Students first take a foundational set of math, computer science, and organizational and management courses, then may choose a "cognate" in which to specialize—such as biomechanics, e-commerce, customer-relationship management, exercise physiology, psychology, or "geoinformatics," among others. The science departments have strong academic relationships with the Medical University of South Carolina (MUSC), also in Charleston, and students and faculty sometimes work with MUSC for internships and research projects.

Other useful majors—although they may not be what the school's founders had in mind when they toasted to the "liberal arts"—include Jewish studies, historic preservation and community planning, special education, arts management, and urban studies. Historic preservation and community-planning majors find the city of Charleston a prime spot for learning this worthy craft.

Students say that professors are generally willing to help when asked but that few students take advantage of office hours, except right before exam time. One recent alumnus told us: "How much time professors are willing to give you depends on the department. My physics professors—I know they were busy, but they would always go out of their way to help." But he adds: "I can't say the same for my psychology professors. Research and publishing seemed to take precedence."

> Many faculty are eager to mentor, if students will seek them out. "My physics professors—I know they were busy, but they would always go out of their way to help," an alum says. However, "I can't say the same for my psychology professors."

The college does have a formal faculty-student advising program, but this is also only as effective as the student makes it. One student told us that he forged much stronger relationships with other faculty members than with his adviser.

The College of Charleston is particularly strong in foreign languages, offering courses at least to the intermediate level in Arabic, Chinese, French, German, Greek, Latin, Hebrew, Hindi, Italian, Japanese, Portuguese, Russian, and Spanish.

The college sponsors semester-long trips to Santiago, Chile; La Rochelle, France; Buenos Aires, Argentina; Havana, Cuba; and Trujillo, Spain. For students who can't bear to be away from Charleston during the academic year, various departments at the school also offer summer programs in foreign countries. For instance, the biology department takes students to the British Virgin Islands, Indonesia, Panama, and Germany; the Classics department leads students to Italy; and the elementary education department takes interested students to Ecuador. Additionally, exchange programs are available in locations as diverse as Austria, Brazil, and China.

Student Life: Location, location, location

Many college campuses in this country will leave you impressed, but the College of Charleston will leave you enchanted. The architecture perfectly fits the university's surroundings.

Each Charleston student begins his studies by walking through the arch at Porter's Lodge in the school's main square, Cistern Yard. Above it is carved in Homeric Greek "Know Thyself." Graduating seniors—the women decked out in white dresses and men in white dinner jackets—walk through that same arch out into the world again. The gorgeous, oak-lined Cistern Yard bordered by the Classical and Roman Revival buildings is a favorite spot on campus, and students enjoy reading books, sunning themselves, and chatting in the grassy areas. The nearby Fountain Walk adds to the ambiance.

Lovely as the campus is, it's hard to find a place to live there. Just a third of Charleston students live on campus, and the school can guarantee housing for students in their freshman year only (and 93 percent of freshmen avail themselves of this opportunity). Residence halls provide those freshmen (and honors students) single-sex, coed-by-floor, and coed-by-room accommodations. Most charming are the school's historic houses, providing rooms to a small number of students in gracious older mansions. To compensate for the lack of on-campus housing, the college's housing department provides a list of rentals each semester and helps sophomores and upperclassmen secure one of the many off-campus apartments nearby. One student says there is no shortage of rentals, but many are exorbitantly priced. Although most students live in the general area, the College of Charleston is not exactly a commuter school, but the housing situation does move most of the weekend social activity (drinking) into private houses and apartments. Such events are *(ahem)* unchaperoned.

In 2012, 37 percent of all Charleston students (and 45 percent of freshmen) came from outside South Carolina; last year, Charleston boasted of having students from 71 foreign countries and every state in the country, many from the Northeast. The demographics here are certainly interesting, even if they are not exactly typical of the state of South Carolina. To start with, the student body is just under 6 percent black—making it much whiter than at the University of South Carolina and about the same shade as Clemson. (The state is 28 percent black.) Nevertheless, the race issue does not seem to be as pressing as at many other universities. The Office of Institutional Diversity is a small department that sponsors educational, cultural, social, and outreach events such as Martin Luther King Jr. Day. The school also boasts a Jewish population of 7 percent, along with corresponding organizations and areas of study. Like many schools nowadays, the College of Charleston is female dominated; male students make up just under 38 percent of the school's population.

Charleston students are not immune to the joys of a cheap can of beer; tourists visiting the historic area of old Charleston often complain about the throngs of students from the College of Charleston and from other area universities who move through the streets from bar to bar. "There's definitely a prevalent bar scene around here," one student says, as

SUGGESTED CORE

1. Classics 253, Ancient Epic
2. Philosophy 201, History of Ancient Philosophy
3. Religious Studies 201/202, The Hebrew Bible/The New Testament
4. No suitable course
5. Political Science 150, Introduction to Political Thought
6. English 301/302, Shakespeare: The Early/Later Period
7. History 201, United States to 1865
8. Philosophy 304, 19th–Century Philosophy

"the bars are only a block from campus." While the school does offer courses in Ancient Greek, the real Greek life is with the school's 13 fraternities and 13 sororities. Though they are a minority—only 13 percent of men and 21 percent of women join them—they add much to the party atmosphere here, particularly during Greek Week and Homecoming. But Greek life does not dominate social life, as it might in smaller colleges, and independents can certainly find a niche of their own.

The college fields 21 Division I NCAA athletic teams, but football isn't one of them. Charleston students vent their school spirit on the college's basketball team, which has fared well on a national level in recent years. A 5,000-seat basketball arena, the TD Convention Center, opened in November 2008. The sailing team (whose headquarters is located just across the water on Charleston Harbor) consistently ranks nationally and boasts several recent national championship trophies; the Cougars also excel at baseball and women's volleyball.

But Charleston students don't spend all their time drinking and watching basketball. The city offers plenty of opportunities for volunteerism and community service, and Charleston students enthusiastically respond to these needs. The Center for Civic Engagement provides students with the opportunity to work at a food bank, perform service projects during Homecoming week, and participate in alternative breaks teaching English or environmental sustainability in rural Appalachia. Over a recent winter break, students traveled to Atlantic City to help the victims of Hurricane Sandy. During Hunger and Homelessness Awareness Week, students challenge themselves to live on the average food stamp allotment for one week. There is Charleston's annual Dash for Cash, where a little litter collection quickly turns into a highly competitive scavenger hunt for garbage, cleaning up the streets in the process. By the end of both days, the city is considerably tidier. Since 2007, students have raised more than $200,000 for a local children's hospital by dancing for "17 hours and 70 minutes" straight in the school's Dance Marathon. The College of Charleston is the number-two Peace Corps recruiter among medium-sized schools in the Southeast.

The college offers many clubs and organizations for student involvement: the Historic Preservation Club; the Association for Computing Machinery; and the Anthropology/Sociology Club; along with organizations devoted to belly dancing, real estate, archaeology, and Arabic. Athletic clubs include crew, cricket, golf, soccer, and running. The college also hosts 16 faith-based student organizations, including an atheist-humanist alliance and a Pagan club, as well as the much more popular Baptist Collegiate Ministry, the Catholic Student Association, and Cru (formerly Campus Crusade for Christ). This is a school in the South, and religious life is strong here. The city of Charleston is known as the "Holy City" because of its numerous churches, many of which cater to students.

You can't beat Charleston for location. With its historic houses, gorgeous Battery Walk, and Spanish moss-draped streets, Charleston has consistently been named one of the country's most scenic cities, and one etiquette expert has also ranked it the "best-mannered city" in the United States. Charleston is always ready to welcome tourists with its many hotels and bed-and-breakfasts—so if all else fails, at least the College of Charleston is a great place for mom and dad to visit.

Crime at the College of Charleston is modest, at least for a campus of more than

10,000 students. In 2011 the university reported six forcible sex offenses, one robbery, and seven burglaries. Although the area immediately around the university is quite safe, students should certainly be cautious when venturing past the touristy area, particularly at night. The university has helped to curb crime with its 24-hour patrols, late-night escorts, emergency telephones, lighted sidewalks, and secure dormitory access. Public safety officers teach regular Rape Aggression Defense classes for students.

As a public university, Charleston charges low tuition for in-state students—just $9,918 in 2012–13, cheaper than the other top universities in South Carolina. (Carpetbaggers pay $25,304.) Room and board were $10,461. The college is often touted as a "best buy" school: "You get a lot for what you pay," says an alumnus. Forty-five percent of Charleston undergraduates received need-based financial aid, and the average graduate accumulated $22,449 in college debt.

STRONG SUITS	WEAK POINTS
• Honors College and *Artium Baccalaureatus* options offer a solid, even elite educational experience to qualifying students. • Solid programs in business, marketing program, premed, science departments, and education. • Innovative options such as "Discovery Informatics" offer good math and information science training. • Good programs in tourism, historic preservation, Jewish studies, foreign languages. • Mostly apolitical campus and classroom atmosphere. • One of the most beautiful campuses in the country.	• General-education requirements are lax, and even "core" classes sometimes barely skim the surface. • Advising quite uneven, not always useful. • Some politicized classes, though they don't dominate offerings. • Hard to find housing on campus.

University of South Dakota

Vermillion, South Dakota • www.usd.edu

Territory Trending Left

A smaller school with solid courses and bargain tuition, the University of South Dakota in Vermillion has been around since the region was still a territory. Today it is the state's only public liberal arts university and home to an expanding list of programs and degrees. Its academic offerings are not the only things expanding; a $100 million campaign recently renovated much of the campus. Not so exciting is a trend one professor notes in the largely conservative student body: a "thickening constituency on the left."

Academic Life: Bang for your buck

The education begins with the four-stage Framework for Liberal Learning. In the first stage, Foundations, the university recognizes that "necessary foundational skills include proficiency in writing, reading, communication, information literacy, and quantitative literacy" and as such requires basic courses in those areas. The second stage, Investigations, broadens a student's educational exposure by requiring courses under the headings Community and Social Interaction (history, anthropology, psychology, political science), the Human Experience (humanities and fine arts), the Natural World, and the Aesthetic Experience. Most of the course offerings are traditional and on target without veering off into the fields of political correctness. From there a student branches into Expertise and Integrations. Focused mostly on degree requirements, this stage also requires an Intensive Writing course that expands students' research-based critical-writing skills. For the Globalization requirement, a student can take courses such as "Art Theory and Criticism," "World Religions," any of several history courses, or foreign language courses. Study abroad also fulfills this requirement.

Noted undergraduate programs are psychology, political science, education—and business, which has earned a highly regarded accreditation from the Association to Advance Collegiate Schools of Business. "Undergraduate education is the primary focus," says one professor. "It's traditional, intellectual, it offers a well-rounded view of different areas, and it trains students well for law school or an MBA."

Weaker programs are those in science and engineering, which one professor diplomatically says "could be enhanced." Hindered by low enrollment are sociology and Classics.

Nursing is traditionally a popular program for associate's degrees, but the recent addition of a bachelor's track has produced some complaints from students about changes in methodology and pedagogy.

English major requirements include two courses in American literature, two courses in British literature, "Introduction to Criticism," and a senior capstone. Students can choose to specialize in either Creative Writing or Secondary Teaching. Both require 12 courses. For Secondary Teaching, a Shakespeare course is required, as is either "Introduction to Linguistic Science," "Modern English Grammar," or "History of the English Language," plus an additional nine elective courses. Students who specialize in Creative Writing must choose two playwriting or creative writing courses, plus nine electives. Solid options abound, with plenty of courses focused on great writers (Milton, Chaucer, Shakespeare) as well as survey courses on Western and world literature, the Heroic Age, Romantic and Victorian literature, colonial literature, and mythology.

As with English, the history major's requirements are solid and focused. History majors take 12 courses, including "United States History" I and II, "Historical Methods

VITAL STATISTICS

Religious affiliation: *none*
Total enrollment: *10,284*
Total undergraduates: *7,690*
SAT CR/Verbal midrange: *460–610*
SAT Math midrange: *460–620*
ACT midrange: *21–26*
Applicants: *3,443*
Applicants accepted: *49%*
Accepted applicants who enrolled: *73%*
Tuition (general/out of state): *$5,843*
Tuition (in state): *$3,897*
Room and board: *$6,648*
Freshman retention rate: *74%*
Graduation rate (4 yrs.): *27%*
Graduation rate (6 yrs.): *23%*
Courses with fewer than 20 students: *51%*
Student-faculty ratio: *17:1*
Courses taught by graduate students:
Students living on campus: *28%*
Students in fraternities: *17%*
Students in sororities: *9%*
Students receiving need-based financial aid: *62%*
Avg. student-loan debt of a recent graduating class: *$26,629*
Most popular majors: *nursing, business, psychology,*
Guaranteed housing for 4 years? *no*

CAMPUS POLITICS: GREEN LIGHT

Given that South Dakota is a conservative state and that the majority of students hail from small, rural towns, it's no surprise that the study body is described by one professor as "middle-of-the-road conservative." But this same professor also notes a "thickening constituency on the left."

"There are a lot of campus politics—I'd say it's equal on both sides—but there's no hostility between the two," says one student. She adds, "Some professors do lean, but they would never look down on you. Some are obviously more strong in their viewpoints, and students always know who's conservative and who's liberal, but it doesn't come through in their teaching."

A nonpartisan Political Science League hosts debates without hostility from both sides.

Says another student: "Being a school in South Dakota, you tend to get more conservative viewpoints because so many people come from small towns, so you do see that in your classes. But there's a big push for diversity on campus, even if there's not a lot of it." This is evident in the number of administrative offices and committees focused on diversity. Chief among them are the Campus Diversity Enhancement Group, charged with planning, implementing, monitoring, and evaluating diversity initiatives across campus. Also, students report increasing momentum of the 10% Society, which promotes awareness and understanding of homosexual issues.

Native American students are well served in both course offerings and through Native Services. Conservative students should check out College Republicans.

and Historiography," and either "World Civilizations" I and II or "Western Civilizations" I and II. Of the remaining electives, two courses must be in American history and two in non-American history. History majors may select an emphasis for their degree among: Ancient Studies (examples include "Greek Art and Archaeology" and "Early Church"); Diplomacy ("History of Russia Under Tzars" and "America: From Great Depression to the New Frontier, 1933–1963"); Great Plains ("Early American Indian History and Culture" and "US West History in Film"); Military History ("American Civil War and Reconstruction" and "European Military History"); and Pre-Law Studies ("American Legal Issues" and "Constitutional Law").

Political science majors must take 10 courses, including "American Government"; either "Introduction to Political Theory" or any other upper-level political theory course; "Introduction to Research Methods"; "Governments of the World" or "World Politics"; and "State and Local Government" or "Public Administration." The remaining courses are chosen from electives, and once again the offerings are strong, mostly lacking the usual mishmash of grievance studies. Examples include "Political Geography," "Constitutional Law," "Courts and Judicial Politics," "United States Congress," and "Advanced Problems in International Relations." The department is also strong in its administrative offerings; courses on the application of politics, such as "Introduction to the Nonprofit Sector," "Public Policy Analysis and Program Evaluation," and "Local Government Administration and Politics," are plentiful.

A perk of the political science department is the Farber Fund, which provides more than $170,000 each year for poli-sci, criminal justice, and international studies majors to attend conferences, participate in study tours, complete internships, travel abroad, and conduct research.

The psychology department also commands praise. "The faculty interaction is great. The professors are willing to work with you and work on research," says a psychology major. "The upper level has a wide variety of classes."

The honors program has its own core curriculum that fits within the university's Framework for Liberal Learning. The first two years of the curriculum are built around an interdisciplinary theme such as "Freedom, Responsibility, and the Self" or "Knowledge and Belief." The last two years of honors courses present a variety of academic experiences. Honors students also enjoy individualized academic advising and participate in a wide spectrum of special events and opportunities. Many students choose to live on the honors floor. Additionally, honors students receive priority registration. The typical honors student has a 3.7 unweighted GPA and an ACT score of at least 27.

Another praised program is the First Year Experience, designed to help freshmen integrate into university life. Options for this include Living-Learning Communities, orientation events, academic skill presentations, cultural events, and the Coyote Mentor Program, where a student is paired with USD faculty or staff based on personal and academic interests. Students here will learn to read, write, and think on their feet," says a professor.

> "Being in South Dakota," says one student, "you tend to get more conservative viewpoints because so many people come from small towns."

Any review of USD would be incomplete without some hat tossing to professors. Across the board, students praised their elders, particularly Scott Breuninger and Steve Bucklin in history; Mary Pat Bierle, Chad Newswander, Eric Jepsen, and Matt Fairholm in political science; David Carr in economics; Nick Curry in music; John Dudley, Dennis Sjolie, and Emily Haddad in English; Sara Goldammer in mathematics; Timothy Heaton in geology; Brennan Jordan in science; Dave Moen in business; Aimee Sorensen in communications; Barbara Yutrzenka in psychology; and Joseph Vitt in chemistry. Mike Roche in criminal justice received uniform accolades and has received numerous teaching awards.

The faculty's popularity perhaps comes at a deficit of research. "Research is secondary," says a professor. "Interacting with students is the primary focus."

With a very manageable 17:1 student-faculty ratio, students find that professors' doors are open and office hours are plentiful. Introductory classes are in the 100-to-200-student range and mostly taught by professors. Math sections are usually taught by graduate students. Fifty-one percent of courses have fewer than 20 students.

Foreign language options are minimal. Only French, German, and Spanish are offered as majors. Latin is only a minor. The study-abroad program is more developed; it sends students to six continents for ranges of two weeks to a full academic year, including destinations such as Argentina, Australia, China, Costa Rica, the Czech Republic, Egypt, France, Ghana, India, Japan, Morocco, South Africa, and Spain. Recent examples of the

SUGGESTED CORE

1. Classical Humanities 418/440, Ancient Rome/Ancient Greece
2. Classical Humanities 411, Ancient Philosophy
3. Religion 224/225, Old Testament/New Testament
4. Philosophy 413, Medieval Philosophy
5. Philosophy 462, Modern Political Philosophy
6. English 431/432, Shakespeare I/II
7. History 151, United States History I
8. Philosophy 141, Modern Philosophy (*closest match*)

shorter, faculty-led programs include a two-week excursion to England to study Comparative Counterterrorism in Ireland and the United Kingdom, and a three-week study of the Greek Isles.

Student Life: Scenic and serene

The closest town, scenic Vermillion, has a quiet population of 10,000 and is walking distance from campus. If you're in the mood for a drive, Sioux Falls and Sioux City are an hour away. Minneapolis is five. Luckily for campus-bound students, USD, nestled on 321 acres along the bluffs above the Missouri River, boasts a friendly population and plenty to do. "It takes only about five minutes to get across campus," says one student, "and you'll run into plenty of people you know, but the great thing is you'll always see new people, too. It's the perfect size." To go along with the quaint campus are the friendly people. "I grew up in a small South Dakota town," says another student. "USD fits the small-town atmosphere but is large enough to have opportunities and good programs."

Because the campus is small, almost everything is close and convenient. In the heart of campus is the newly expanded Muenster University Center, where students can dine, study, play, or watch any of the 15 big-screen TVs. Speaking of expansion, USD's recent $100 million plan has brought enhancements to the athletic and fine arts facilities, laboratories and schools, and the residence halls.

Residence halls are also convenient. First-year students are required to live on campus, and housing includes North Campus and Coyote Village—two very different living styles. The four halls that comprise North Campus are all double-occupancy and have both coed and single-gender floors. The newer Coyote Village has single-student, apartment-style rooms organized around a common living area and kitchen. Burgess and Norton Halls are coed and focus on smaller student communities (58 students per floor in single and double rooms). McFadden Hall is another apartment-style complex with 25 four-person apartments. These apartments can be coed or single gender.

Specialty floors include single-gender floors, an honors floor, and quieter, academically focused floors.

The Greek system is another option. Seventeen percent of men join fraternities, and nine percent of women join sororities. Students in the Greek system tend to populate campus leadership roles—either a boon or a bane, depending on one's perspective.

The Coyotes compete in the NCAA's Division I as members of the Summit League, except football, which competes in the Missouri Valley Football Conference. Men and women compete in basketball, cross-country, golf, track and field, and swimming and diving. Men also play football, and women play soccer, softball, tennis, and volleyball.

An active intramural league features 19 sports, including flag football, cross-country, trap shoot, racquetball, and coed softball, volleyball, and basketball. Club sports include baseball, cycling, fencing, ice hockey, paintball, and men's and women's rugby, soccer, and tennis.

Religious life at USD could be considered a weak point. "There's not a lot of campus ministry," says one student, "but Cru (formerly Campus Crusade for Christ) is very large and active." There is a small smattering of other nondenominational groups. Religious resources include the Lutheran Student Fellowship and the Luther Center, and the Catholic St. Thomas More Newman Center.

For a small school, USD has a lot of on-campus cultural resources, such as the National Music Museum (14,500 instruments from every historical period), a gallery of the American Indian artist Oscar Howe, the University Art Galleries, and the Warren M. Lee Center for the Fine Arts, a state-of-the-art facility that hosts dozens of concerts and events each month.

Safety is not a large concern for students. In 2011 there were four forcible sex offenses and seven burglaries.

For a risible 2012–13 tuition of $5,843 (out-of-state) and $3,897 (in-state), students get an education steeped in comprehensive basic courses, widened through classic disciplines, and solidified in focused major requirements. Room and board in 2012–13 were $6,648. Sixty-two percent of students received need-based financial aid, and the average student-loan debt of a recent graduating class was $26,629.

STRONG SUITS	WEAK POINTS
• Low, low prices, even for out-of-state students.	• Programs in science and engineering lack funds and facilities.
• Good programs in psychology, political science, education, and business.	• Low enrollment hinders some humanities and social sciences programs, such as sociology and Classics.
• Solid, traditional departments with good major requirements in English, history, political science.	• Nursing program undergoing major changes, irritating many students.
• A sane, nonpartisan campus atmosphere.	• Limited foreign language offerings.

University of Tennessee

Knoxville, Tennessee • www.utk.edu

Think Big

Knoxville is the flagship campus of the Tennessee university system. With an undergraduate enrollment of more than 21,000, and an even larger family that flocks to campus for the weekly rituals of Big Orange sports, students will always be in the heart of bustling activity. Campus culture at this research institution is defined by a southern enthusiasm for football and an insatiable school spirit, but the opportunity for rigorous academics exists for those who are willing to seek it out.

Academic Life: Dig in or get left out

The freshman entering the general-education program at UTK will find that entry into academic life requires sitting through a number of large "survey" courses, taught by graduate students and less rewarding for their size and the lack of student participation. In the honors tracks or as the student rises to higher-level classes, the education will become considerably more demanding and rewarding, involving closer contact with professors. "Beyond the survey level, students are very bright and very engaged. In some places, the public option is considered a 'back-up school,' but that is simply not the dynamic in Tennessee. Some of the brightest students in the state aspire to go to the flagship campus."

The general-education program is twofold: "building basic skills"; then a sort of diversity training, identified by the university as a system for "developing broadened perspectives." The array of options for fulfilling general-ed requirements is extremely wide and loose. However, the discerning student may find that he can navigate the system to his advantage by selecting interesting, traditional courses and researching professors. Every student is required to take three courses in Communication through Writing, including English 101 and 102 (students can test out), as well as a writing-intensive study. Options for the writing-intensive course are varied and include "Agricultural Leadership," "Hotel, Restaurant, and Tourism," "Medieval Studies," and "Philosophy."

Next is one course in Communicating Orally. Some options for this requirement include either a course in Communications Studies or the student's choice from a variety of approved courses, including "Aerospace Engineering" or "Animal Science."

The requirement for the "Quantitative Reasoning" component of general education is two courses, either in mathematics or statistics or from a selection of approved courses in other departments, including architecture, computer science, or, for example, "Interior Design: Lighting for Interior Design" or "Music Technology: Sound Recording Techniques." For "Developing Broadened Perspectives," two courses are required in each of the fields of natural sciences, arts and humanities, social sciences, and cultures and civilizations. In arts and humanities, the student may select courses from among the departments of Africana studies, architecture, art history, Classics, English ("Introduction to Shakespeare," "British Lit 1: Beowulf through Johnson," "Major Black Writers"), musicology, philosophy ("The Human Condition: Values and Reality," "Environmental Ethics," "Bioethics"), religious studies ("Religious Studies: Professional Responsibility"), Russian literature, and theater.

For the two social sciences courses, there is a broad spectrum of offerings, including "Agricultural Economics: Economics of the Global Food and Fiber System," "Political Science: United States Government and Politics," "Sociology:

VITAL STATISTICS

Religious affiliation: *none*
Total enrollment: *27,018*
Total undergraduates: *20,829*
SAT CR/Verbal midrange: *530–64*
SAT Math midrange: *530–65*
ACT midrange: *24–29*
Applicants: *14,398*
Applicants accepted: *67%*
Accepted applicants who enrolled: *43%*
Tuition (general/out of state): *$27,580*
Tuition (in state): *$9,092*
Room and board: *$8,752*
Freshman retention rate: *85%*
Graduation rate (4 yrs.): *39%*
Graduation rate (6 yrs.): *66%*
Courses with fewer than 20 students: *39%*
Student-faculty ratio: *17:1*
Courses taught by graduate students: *not provided*
Students living on campus: *37%*
Students in fraternities: *15%*
Students in sororities: *10%*
Students receiving need-based financial aid: *45%*
Avg. student-loan debt of a recent graduating class: *$22,860*
Most popular majors: *business/marketing, social sciences, psychology*
Guaranteed housing for 4 years? *yes*

603

CAMPUS POLITICS: GREEN LIGHT

UTK is large enough that any student should be able to find like-minded peers, and its background is traditional enough that conservative students should not expect to encounter a hostile atmosphere overall. Nevertheless, there exist attitudes among much of the student body, faculty, and administration that characterize most public research institutions. The main student paper, the *Daily Beacon*, offers a mix of views but seems predominantly liberal, and the university is set to launch a Sex Week modeled after the event of the same name at Yale and Harvard; yet such trends coexist with a campus predominantly southern in character, where sporting events are opened with a prayer.

"There is a range of opinion here on campus," explains a professor. "Being in the South and in the Bible Belt, there is certainly a conservative dimension to the student body, but also, as a big university, it is a meeting place for the more liberal-minded. In my experience, students are open, engaged, and eager to talk out the controversial issues."

According to one student, "Campus politics can intrude sometimes, but it is pretty rare. I wouldn't say there are departments that would make anyone feel uncomfortable, but they will make you think about cultures other than your own, for sure. UT seems to be a pretty free campus in my opinion. The culture of our campus is pretty diverse."

Some organizations that students may want to look into joining include the American Constitution Society, Young Americans for Freedom, College Republicans, Pro-Life Collegians, the UTea Party, Students for Liberty, and Students in Free Enterprise.

Social Justice and Social Change," and "Women's Studies: Marriage and Family, Roles and Relationships."

The final two courses in Cultures and Civilizations can be fulfilled either in a foreign language, with two courses in a foreign language at an intermediate level or one intensive foreign language course; or the student may select from a list of departments, from anthropology and Classics to global studies or medieval studies.

The faculty-to-student ratio is 15:1. However, it may take some time—perhaps a whole year—before students begin to enjoy close contact with their professors in class, unless they make a concerted effort upon arrival to seek out excellent faculty and attend their office hours. In such popular majors as psychology and English, however, students are more likely to be taught largely by graduate students in the context of very large lectures. According to one student, "I think there is a little bit of both teaching and research going on. I make sure to research all my teachers before I take them. I have been stuck in lecture classes where I have literally learned nothing and suffered from a lack of participation by my classmates. Some teachers are incredibly engaging and wonderful, and others, not so much. I think that as you get further along in your major, you begin to have teachers who really care about their subjects, instead of grad students teaching gen-ed classes because they have to."

Ambitious students wishing to reach the inner academic circle have excellent opportunities to do so through the various honors programs in place. Almost every field of study can be enhanced by seeking out its particular honors offerings. More important, there are several honors tracks that are either available upon matriculation for top applicants or to which current students can apply. Features of the programs include enriched/enhanced course work, undergraduate research, and special housing options.

The College Scholars Program is "the oldest, most selective, and most prestigious honors program" at the university. It includes an option for students to design their own majors if their interests are not sufficiently served by the programs offered: "once admitted to the program, a Scholar is exempt from all the course distribution requirements for undergraduates in the College of Arts and Sciences." Scholars are required to complete the general-education program and 120 credit hours of course work, with at least 42 of those hours at a 300 course level or higher. In addition, every scholar must complete a demanding senior project.

The Chancellor's Honors Program, which also features a specialized curriculum, can be entered as a matriculating freshman. Haslam Scholars, a group of a mere 15 students selected from among the chancellor's students, enjoy a "premiere specialized honors program," a complimentary laptop, $4,000 in study-abroad funding, and $5,000 in thesis research funding. Haslam Scholars are expected to be leaders on campus and to have ambitious postgraduate plans. All honors students enjoy special library privileges and opportunities to compete for dedicated scholarships. Most important, honors courses are of a much higher caliber. "Students in honors classes have small classes—usually no more than 15 students. It's an excellent program, and the classes are as lively and as intimate as they would be at any small liberal arts college," a student reports. "I love taking honors classes and would *highly* recommend them. They are honestly one of the best-kept secrets at UT. The teachers are delightful and excited to teach, and the class is generally easier because the students genuinely want to be there. I have taken many different honors classes over the years and have loved them."

A student says, "I have been stuck in lecture classes where I have literally learned nothing and suffered from a lack of participation by my classmates."

Students interested in history will find a strong faculty with a strong emphasis on medieval scholarship. Jay Rubenstein, a medievalist, is a highly regarded scholar and excellent teacher. Lynn Sacco, whose specialization is not traditional, might nevertheless be of interest, as she is extremely beloved by students. Requirements include a course in European history, one in U.S. history, as well as a senior research seminar. For the most part, the courses offered to fulfill these requirements—particularly the European and United States courses—are quite solid.

The English major is divided into four concentrations: Literature, Creative Writing, Rhetoric and Writing, and Technical Communications. According to the school, all majors have five basic requirements: one course in pre-1660 literature; one in literature written from 1660 to 1900; one class in post-1900 literature; one in language, theory, folklore, cultural, ethnic, gender, or film studies; and one special topics, major authors, or senior seminar. An English major could graduate without studying Shakespeare, although his work is offered for students who seek him out.

Blue Collar Ivy

SUGGESTED CORE

1. Classics 253, Greek and Roman Literature in English Translation
2. Philosophy 320, Ancient Western Philosophy
3. Religious Studies 311/321, Introduction to the Hebrew Bible/New Testament and Early Christian Origins
4. Philosophy 322, Medieval Philosophy
5. Philosophy 391, Social and Political Philosophy
6. English 206, Introduction to Shakespeare
7. History 221, History of the United States
8. Philosophy 326, 19th- and 20th-Century Philosophy

The political science major at UTK is not strong on political philosophy: there is only one theory course required, and only four courses are currently being offered. The curriculum is divided into four areas: United States Government and Politics / Public Administration; Comparative Government and Politics; International Relations; and Political Theory. Prerequisites are "U.S. Government and Politics" and "Introduction to Political Science." Every major is required to take at least one course in all four areas. Some examples of the kinds of classes offered are "State Government and Politics," "United States Constitutional Law: Sources of Power and Restraint," "Western European Politics," "International Political Economy," "American Political Thought," "Ancient and Medieval Political Thought," and "Modern Political Thought."

The engineering, nursing, and business programs are all highly regarded and popular. Students interested in psychology may suffer from lack of access to the strong faculty and overcrowded classes, and students looking to major in education will have to go elsewhere; UTK offers only a minor in this discipline.

UTK puts a heavy emphasis on aiding students in the process of adapting to university life, probably in response to a low graduation rate. The Office of First-Year Studies orchestrates programs for freshmen, including a required online summer course before arrival. The Freshman Seminar Program offers a wide variety of small, one-credit courses for students to select in addition to their regular course work. Topics are random, for example, "Sailing: Learn to Sail," "Understanding Obesity," "Capitalism and Freedom: America's Strength," and "Sex on Campus." While the majority of the options may sound frivolous, the program is apparently very popular among students, who find that it is a fun and engaging way to connect with faculty and meet peers in an intimate class setting.

The span of languages offered is not particularly strong and indicates that student fluency in foreign languages is not a high priority. The languages offered are Arabic (Modern Standard), Chinese, French, German, Greek and Latin, Italian, Japanese, Hebrew (Modern), Persian, Portuguese, Russian, and Spanish. Levels in these do not advance beyond I and II. Intensive language study is available in French, German, Italian, Portuguese, and Spanish.

For students interested in study abroad, the Programs Abroad Office handles a variety of options, from university-sponsored exchange programs to applications to third-party programs, as well as faculty-led tours during breaks. The office offers research and support on a wide array of these opportunities, but they are handled on a case-by-case basis. Potential student trips range from Argentina and Australia to Malta, Morocco, Sweden, Thailand, the U.K., and Vietnam.

Students who are looking at the various options for affordable education in Tennessee might want to consider the University of Tennessee at Chattanooga, the system's second largest school. Although slightly more expensive and lacking the glamorous sports program, UTC offers an interesting alternative. "UTC is set in an exceptionally attractive, cohesive, and vibrant city that is widely regarded as one of the nation's jewels of urban revival. It boasts distinguished faculty like historian Wilfred M. McClay and economist J. R. Clark, both of whom hold endowed chairs, and its School of Education is a rare bastion of strong scholarship and sensible reform-minded thinking." Other remarkable faculty include David Carrithers in political science; Phil Giffin, Bruce Hutchinson, and Leila Pratt in economics; and M. A. McCoy, John Freeman, and Lucien Ellington in education.

Student Life: Bleed orange

Extracurricular activities primarily revolve around the high-caliber "Big Orange" sports program, which fields 18 men's and women's NCAA Division I teams and includes more than 500 student athletes. The men's football team is the top attraction, with men's and women's basketball a close second. "It is surprising how intense the passion is for the football team and how energetic the support is for the basketball team." On game days, Neyland Stadium (capacity: 102,455) is routinely filled with a crowd composed of students, family, alumni, and faithful Tennesseans.

Given the enthusiasm for their nationally recognized teams, it is no surprise that UTK is known for a party atmosphere. The Princeton Review ranked UTK as 2013's number 20 "party school" in America, a dubious distinction that, one professor confesses, "one must regretfully admit is not undeserved." With the emphasis on school spirit, the regular sporting events preceded by tailgating parties and populated by crowds of locals and alumni—all in festive orange—and a vivacious Greek life, the typical UTK undergrad is expected to have plenty of fun.

"Most of the partying takes place off campus or at the bars on the strip [in Knoxville]," a student says. "People will usually hold pregames in their apartments before heading off to Cumberland Avenue to spend the rest of the night at the bars on the strip. Occasionally frats will have [parties], but as you get older, you don't usually attend those things as much as the freshmen and sophomores do."

Another reports: "We certainly are a football school, and a lot of people come because they have a great passion for sports and the entertainment side of big college life. But those students, sadly, eventually weed themselves out. The quality of entering students goes up every year."

Greek life is a major part of campus culture, with the Dean of Student's Office of Sorority and Fraternity Life dedicated to its support and oversight (while the office provides a laundry list of strict rules governing Greek behavior, it is unclear whether all the stipulations are followed). There are 25 fraternities located on campus at "Fraternity Park" (capacity: 500), and 13 sororities situated in "Sorority Village" (capacity: 590). Many freshmen will be recruited and may rush to join, but must wait a year for live-in privileges. The university performs a safety-code inspection once per semester in the Greek houses. "There is a lot of Greek life here," one student attests, "but it is definitely not a necessary thing in order to 'fit in.'"

Residence life consists of 7,500 students in 12 residence halls with standard accommodations. Several of the halls are single sex and they vary as to setup (suite-style vs. community bathrooms). A student reports that "dorm life at UT isn't bad. I would definitely suggest living in Presidential Court freshman year because all those buildings are next to each other and close to the cafeteria. Plus, you get your bathroom cleaned every week for you!" Visitation is limited for freshmen, but upperclassmen may find that, unless they choose their roommates wisely, they may have unwanted visitors overnight, as the policies loosen considerably.

"The dating here is sparse," explains one student. "I feel that most college kids are not here to attain a meaningful relationship. I would assume [that there is sexual activity in the dorms]; dorm rules are pretty easy to get around." As far as campus safety, students feel comfortable on campus, by and large, as long as they use safe conduct. "The off-campus neighborhood, Fort Sanders, can be pretty shady. This is where the majority of people live after their freshman year, and it is definitely a trouble spot." The university has basic precautions in place—for example, more than 100 emergency 911 phone stations on campus, and over 500 security cameras, including in residence halls and garages. Every residence hall is staffed 24 hours a day by Housing Department personnel, including a live-in hall director and at least one live-in assistant hall director, in addition to RAs on every floor. There is also a fairly extensive bus transport system to get around campus and to the sporting venues. In 2011 the school reported four forcible sex offenses, one robbery, 28 burglaries, and 10 stolen cars.

This is one of those schools that is a genuine bargain for local students—who paid tuition of only $9,092 in 2012–13 (out-of-state students paid triple that, or $27,580), with room and board a moderate $8,752. Less than half (45 percent) of students received need-based aid, and the average debt burden of a recent graduate was a comparatively modest $22,860.

STRONG SUITS	WEAK POINTS
• Several excellent honors programs.	• Shaky general-education requirements.
• History department is very good and specializes in medieval studies.	• Lax mandates in English and poli-sci; little political philosophy offered.
• Highly praised programs in engineering, nursing, and business.	• Psychology and education programs called "anemic."
• Balanced campus politics and mostly nonpoliticized teaching.	• Heavy party atmosphere with lots of drinking.

Texas A&M University

College Station, Texas • www.tamu.edu

Marching Orders

Texas A&M University at College Station has undergone rapid changes during the past 50 years—none greater than in 1963, when the school converted itself from an all-male military academy to a full-fledged coeducational university. But Texas A&M has retained much from its military-school past. The university still sponsors the Corps of Cadets, which, with 2,000 members, is the largest uniformed body of students outside the three main U.S. service academies. Although A&M still excels in agriculture and mechanics, the university is actively attempting to improve its liberal arts programs.

The Texas A&M student body is primarily responsible for maintaining the deep traditions and sane conservatism of the campus. In a recent school-sponsored report describing the incoming freshmen, 25 percent of the new class consisted of first-generation college students. A student explains, "This is not a crowd that worships academia like the East and West coasts. These are people that place relationships with God, country, and family out in front." We wish that the liberal arts curriculum at the school did more to gently encourage a love for the genuine goods of academic life in this wholesome environment mostly free of contemporary toxic trends. Instead, recent administrations have seemed intent on smuggling in the strange gods of multiculturalism and feminism. We hope that resistance

Blue Collar Ivy

VITAL STATISTICS

Religious affiliation: *none*
Total enrollment: *49,861*
Total undergraduates: *39,867*
SAT CR/Verbal midrange: *510–650*
SAT Math midrange: *570–670*
ACT midrange: *24–30*
Applicants: *25,949*
Applicants accepted: *64%*
Accepted applicants who enrolled: *60%*
Tuition (general/out of state): *$25,035*
Tuition (in state): *$8,505*
Room and board: *$8,400*
Freshman retention rate: *92%*
Graduation rate (4 yrs.): *50%*
Graduation rate (6 yrs.): *84%*
Courses with fewer than 20 students: *19%*
Student-faculty ratio: *21:1*
Courses taught by graduate students: *11%*
Students living on campus: *13%*
Students in fraternities: *6%*
Students in sororities: *13%*
Students receiving need-based financial aid: *41%*
Avg. student-loan debt of a recent graduating class: *$22,716*
Most popular majors: *agriculture, business, engineering*
Guaranteed housing for 4 years? *no*

among alumni, faculty, students, and (most important) state legislators frustrates these efforts.

Academic Life: Room to grow

Like other state universities in Texas, A&M requires undergraduates to complete a set of distribution requirements that, depending on the courses chosen to fulfill them, need not be particularly demanding.

Roughly 14 percent of the undergraduate population majors in some type of engineering, and the programs are among the finest on campus. Virtually every engineering program offered, from aerospace to petroleum, ranks among the top 20 in the nation, and several are among the top five. The Mays College and Graduate School of Business also receives high marks, with programs in accounting, management, and marketing ranked among the top 25 in the nation in popular surveys. The College of Architecture, with more than 1,900 current students, is one of the largest in the United States.

The university's offerings in the College of Agriculture and Life Sciences are extensive, including fields like agricultural communications and journalism, poultry science, and wildlife and fisheries. The College of Veterinary Medicine and Biomedical Sciences is widely considered to be one of the most advanced in America. The school continually makes national headlines, most notably when the cloning program replicated several kinds of small animals.

The College of Liberal Arts enrolls about 16 percent of all undergraduates. The course offerings don't stand out as academic challenges, but at least they have not morphed into the ideological circus acts seen on many "progressive" campuses. Degree requirements are prescribed by each department and there may be some overlap with the college-wide distribution requirements. Students majoring in a liberal arts discipline must take extra courses required by the College of Liberal Arts, including two literature, two additional humanities, one additional social and behavior sciences, and two intermediate-level foreign language courses.

Classical studies is available as one of the college's several minors, as are religious studies, women's and gender studies, comparative cultural studies, and 21 other selections.

The PhD program in American politics ranks among the top 20 in the country, and the economics department consistently appears in rankings of the top 40 programs. According to its website, the political science department offers courses in all facets of the discipline: American politics, comparative politics, international relations, methodology, normative political theory, public administration, public law, and public policy. Poli-sci majors must take classes in the Constitution and American political thought, and most of the department's course offerings are solid and traditional.

The English department offers three bachelor degree tracks: literature, rhetoric, and creative writing. All tracks are quite good, requiring solid courses, including Shakespeare and American literature as well as several writing components.

The history department is solid as well, requiring Western civilization and American history courses, and offering many worthwhile classes ranging from ancient to modern history.

One of the university's former presidents, Ray Bowen, made several moves that some alumni thought were aimed at conforming A&M to the progressivism often characteristic of elite public universities. One recommendation was to "diversify and globalize the A&M community," which could be accomplished partly with a "plan that will require students to take six hours of international or cultural diversity classes," one alumnus says. Conservatives contend that the plan was implemented merely to pacify critics who say that A&M students suffer from provincialism. "[The new requirement is] just one step in a larger plan to sacrifice the values that make A&M special" says a student, going on to make the most damning accusation one can make against an A&M president: "He wanted to make us just like the University of Texas."

CAMPUS POLITICS: GREEN LIGHT

It won't surprise the reader that an A&M school in Texas is fairly traditional. One professor describes the average faculty member as "at least moderately conservative" and the average student as "pretty conservative." This same professor says that "some, maybe even many, midlevel administrators are hostile to the views of the [typical] A&M student and consequently seek to transform the largely Christian, conservative student body into something more 'representative.' Consistent with this, faculty now undergo a mandatory diversity class in which orthodox Christian and conservative beliefs are treated essentially as the root of bigotry and, by implication, inconsistent with the diversity thrust at A&M."

The administration is also at odds with the average A&M student. The school endorses a Gay Awareness Week and sponsors an annual performance of the ubiquitous *Vagina Monologues*. Various activist groups push for the nontraditional programming offered at most universities. Alternative radio exists for students interested in bucking the crew-cut crowd: KEOS-FM offers a mix of music and agitation courtesy of programs like *Democracy Now*, an activist organization funded by MoveOn.org. The administration's attempts at "diversity education" seem likely to encourage partisanship and divisive politics on campus, but these dragon's teeth have not yet borne fruit. In April 2013 the student government voted to let students withhold their portion of student funds from gay activist groups—but the resolution was vetoed by the student government president.

Bowen's successor, former secretary of defense Robert Gates, followed in Bowen's footsteps in ways many students and alumni found disturbing. "He seemed to be pushing the same Vision 2020 that Bowen had," says a professor. Despite state budget cuts, Gates established a new vice president and associate provost for institutional diversity—the only VP-level provost who reports directly to the president. This provost was tasked with implementing a campus-wide program to support diversity, including compulsory diversity training for members of the Student Government Association and the campus daily, the *Battalion*. "You have to understand that around here, diversity still means cultural diversity, not sexual diversity; regardless, it's a politically charged word," insisted a source on campus, noting that this is still a school at which the president introduces himself with a "howdy." Gates's successor, Elsa Morano, was the worst yet in pushing the "progressive" agenda, but mercifully she lasted just a little over a year. We hope that her replacement, current president R. Bowen Loftin, will focus on accentuating the university's traditional strengths instead of trying to turn A&M into a pale copy of the leftist research factories that so many state universities have become.

A student says of his peers: "This is not a crowd that worships academia like the East and West coasts. These are people that place relationships with God, country, and family out in front."

Texas A&M is a large state school, so it isn't surprising that graduate teaching assistants teach some courses, but more commonly they lead weekly discussion sections for large lecture classes or laboratory sections for science courses. "Professors are accessible to students [during] office hours," says a student. However, an undergrad warns, "The advising program is not well advertised, so students need to be aware of the services on their own." Underclassmen who have not yet decided on a major can speak with professional advisers in the General Studies Program, the "keynotes" of which are, according to the program, "exploration and flexibility." More often, students visit their major advisers (either faculty members or professional advisers), who help the students choose courses, fulfill degree requirements, and prepare for graduation and careers.

Noteworthy professors include Robin Smith in philosophy; David Vaught in history; Dan Lineberger, Tracy Rutherford, and Jodi Sterle in agriculture and life sciences; Roel Lopez in wildlife and fishery sciences; and David Bergbreiter, James Pennington, Michael Rosynek, Eric Simanek, and Gyula Vigh in chemistry.

The school does offer an honors program. Honors students, who must maintain a 3.5 GPA, apply for the program within their area of study. Students pick and choose from the 300-plus honors-level courses offered throughout the university. An honors student can also enroll in one of the honors study sequences: the Engineering Scholars Program, the Business Honors Program, the College of Liberal Arts Honors Plan, or the College of Science. The liberal arts plan begins with a freshman honors seminar; seminar offerings include "More than the Bomb: How Radioactivity, Nuclear Power, and Nuclear Weapons Define

Your World" and "Pathways to Health and Happiness." Then they take two sophomore courses, "Foundations of the Liberal Arts: Humanities" and "Foundations of the Liberal Arts: Social Sciences." This is where students will find politically correct courses, a teacher reports, commenting that "the first stages of rot appeared in the honors program. This is where you will find the queer studies and the feminism."

Texas A&M offers a wide array of study-abroad opportunities all over the globe, including Australia, Beijing, Belgium, Croatia, Fiji, Iceland, Qatar, Rwanda, Samoa, and hundreds of others.

At home, students can study Arabic, Chinese, French, German, Greek and Latin, Japanese, Russian, Spanish, and several more foreign languages. A foreign language component is not a university core requirement for graduation, but quite a few departments insist on several semesters or demonstrated proficiency to earn degrees in certain majors.

SUGGESTED CORE

1. Classics 372, Greek and Roman Epic
2. Philosophy 410, Classical Philosophy
3. Religious Studies 211/213, Hebrew Scriptures/New Testament
4. History 418, European Intellectual History from Ancient Greece to the Early Middle Ages (*closest match*)
5. Political Science 350, Modern Political Thought
6. English 212, Shakespeare
7. History 105, History of the U.S.
8. Philosophy 414, 19th-Century Philosophy

Student Life: Shout it out

Texas A&M is a member of the Big 12 athletic conference and so sports—especially football—are a high priority. In addition to the 18 varsity teams, students have 34 club sports and dozens of intramural teams from which to choose—including, for sedentary nerds, a sports trivia tournament. The athletic facilities are staggering: a soccer stadium, a softball complex, a golf course, a tennis center, an arena for volleyball, two track stadiums (indoor and outdoor), the Brazos County Expo Complex (the 70,000-square-foot home of the equestrian team), Kyle Field (the enormous state-of-the-art football stadium), and several other large venues.

Instead of cheerleaders, the Aggies have "yell leaders." If the Aggies win, the Corps of Cadets throws the yell leaders into a campus fountain (aka the Fish Pond). If A&M loses, students and alumni stay in the stands to practice school yells for the next game. Midnight yell practices, held the night before every home game, often attract as many as 30,000 people. Another remnant of Texas A&M's past is the tradition of kissing one's date after each touchdown, extra point, or field goal.

Only some 10 percent of Texas A&M students are involved in Greek life. Instead, Texas A&M boasts the largest student-union program in the nation, with more than 800 university-recognized clubs and organizations. If you can't find one that interests you, then you aren't looking: the groups cover all interests, from Aggieland Mariachi and the Philosophy Club to a group dedicated to fashion.

The list of student organizations includes dozens of religious groups, most of them Christian, including Philadelphia Sisters, ReJOYce In Jesus Campus Fellowship, and

Christian Business Leaders. One student says, "I'd have to say that a lot of A&M students turn to religion-based recreation, such as Bible study, praise and worship groups, and other religious social activities." St. Mary's Catholic Center on campus seems vibrant and orthodox, featuring traditional devotions, pro-life activities, and significant intellectual support; it's refreshing to be able to say that about such a campus ministry. There has been an explosion of Catholic devotion on campus, resulting in a wave of priestly and religious vocations from A&M, meriting national media attention. A 2011 A&M football game against rival UT-Austin featured dozens of nuns and priests in the stands on the A&M side, leading commentators to remark that UT didn't stand a chance. (It didn't.)

Many students join the Corps of Cadets because of its prestige on campus. Almost all of Texas A&M's many traditions have their genesis in the school's military past, to the extent that the corps even serves a vital role at football games. For example, to be a member of the Fightin' Aggie Band, one must first be a member of the Corps of Cadets, as the band wears military uniforms and marches military style.

There are fewer than 8,000 on-campus housing spaces available for noncorps students. Eleven residence halls are single sex, and the coed dorms split men and women by floor. There are no coed bathrooms or bedrooms in the residence halls.

College Station is an extremely safe town, and the campus within is no different. In 2011 A&M reported 29 burglaries, one robbery, three forcible sex offenses, three car thefts, and one arson on campus.

Considering the school's many virtues, A&M is an amazing bargain for students from Texas, who paid just $8,505 in 2012–13 (out-of-state students paid $25,035), with room and board at $8,400. Only 41 percent of students received need-based financial aid, and the average debt of a recent grad was a moderate $22,716.

STRONG SUITS	WEAK POINTS
• Engineering programs among the best in the U.S.	• Honors program is being infused with ideological content.
• The liberal arts much more foundational, less ideological, than at other state schools. Political science and economics are especially good.	• Liberal arts programs less prestigious, rigorous than science and business disciplines.
• Accounting, management, and marketing are highly ranked nationally.	• Administration is trying to push the school to conform to secular leftist national norms—with mixed success.
• Agriculture, biomedical, and veterinary programs are large, well-funded, and innovative.	
• A wholesome campus environment with a strong religious life.	

University of Texas at Austin

Austin, Texas • www.utexas.edu

Walmart U.

Founded in 1883 on just 40 acres, with a single building, two departments, eight teachers, and a little more than 200 students, the University of Texas at Austin is now one of the largest public universities in America. The main campus, just a quarter mile from the Texas State Capitol, has grown to 424 acres, with more than 21,000 faculty and staff, 17 colleges and schools, and over 50,000 students.

If the typical large university is a mall, then, as one student says, the University of Texas at Austin is "the Walmart of higher education." With more than 350 undergraduate degree programs on offer, it's a one-stop shop where all political ideologies, oddball hobbies, and career interests are nurtured or, in some cases, pandered to. The good news is that a first-rate classic liberal arts education is available to enterprising students who seek it out. One graduate student reports, "Overall, the campus is a hotbed of political correctness, but if a student is smart and does research into which classes to take and what professors in those classes teach, he can still get a solid education. It just takes a little effort."

Perhaps the most salient political issue on the UT campus is race and its use in admissions. After a Supreme Court decision permitted the reinstatement of the use of race in admissions, the university has been doing so aggressively since the entering class of 2005.

VITAL STATISTICS

Religious affiliation: *none*
Total enrollment: *52,186*
Total undergraduates: *39,955*
SAT CR/Verbal midrange: *550–670*
SAT Math midrange: *580–710*
ACT midrange: *25–31*
Applicants: *35,431*
Applicants accepted: *47%*
Accepted applicants who enrolled: *49%*
Tuition (general/out of state): *$33,128*
Tuition (in state): *$9,790*
Room and board: *$10,946*
Freshman retention rate: *93%*
Graduation rate (4 yrs.): *51%*
Graduation rate (6 yrs.): *79%*
Courses with fewer than 20 students: *39%*
Student-faculty ratio: *18:1*
Courses taught by graduate students: *not provided*
Students living on campus: *19%*
Students in fraternities: *13%*
Students in sororities: *17%*
Students receiving need-based financial aid: *45%*
Avg. student-loan debt of a recent graduating class: *$22,478*
Most popular majors: *biology, business, psychology*
Guaranteed housing for 4 years? *no*

Given that state law since 1997 has required UT to automatically admit all high school graduates in the top 10 percent of their classes who wish to enroll, these policies have combined to put an extraordinary strain on the university. Texas lawmakers make noise every year around election time promising to repeal or alter this crippling law, but the outrage subsides and the promises are forgotten after election day, only to be resurrected with the same furor when reelection campaigns resume.

To add insult to injury, current UT president William Powers Jr. instituted a "four-point strategic plan" to ensure that race is paramount in determining admissions and new hires. One UT student claims that "diversity of skin color, diversity of national origin, etc., are valued, but diversity of thought, in general, is not." The term "diversity" itself is frequently a code word for outright hatred of Western culture and all its works; the religious pursuit of this unholy grail has ruined other universities. Texans, stay tuned.

Academic Life: Dislocated and quirky

In keeping with its home state's ethos, that "everything's bigger in Texas," UT has more than 170 fields of study and 120 majors, and the sheer quantity of choices on offer demands that students have some help in making wise ones. Yet academically, most UT students go it alone. "What we can't do at a place like UT is maintain any serious quality control," a professor says. "That someone has 'earned' a BA at a large state university means nothing." What universities like UT do instead, this professor says, is "magnify the dangers that are inherent in the modern elective system—they offer a smorgasbord of dislocated and quirky courses on a far larger scale. They also offer the raw materials for a classic liberal education, if you know how to find them and put them together."

The flip side of an abundance of choice is that there's a niche for everyone, a situation most students praise. Rapidly locating and scurrying into that niche is critical at such a massive school. While UT students are not unfriendly, the vast majority of faces will be unfamiliar as you're hoofing it across the sprawling campus from class to class. "I feel about as much camaraderie with my fellow students at UT as I do with someone off the street who wears the same brand of shoes I do," one student says.

At many colleges it is easy to be a science or an engineering major and never encounter the great works of the West; at UT that is also possible for liberal arts majors. "Play your cards 'right' in UT's liberal arts college and watch yourself learn nothing toward a classical education," a student says. "All in all, you can get a liberal arts degree from UT and really have no education at all."

Happily, a group of distinguished faculty at UT rose to the occasion and developed a serious initiative that addresses the curriculum's civilization gap. Lorraine and Thomas Pangle, professors of government and directors of the Thomas Jefferson Center for the Study of Core Texts and Ideas, stepped forward as leaders for the revival of a Great Books canon. The program hopes to offer students throughout the university the opportunity of satisfying the core curriculum requirements with courses that include "major works of philosophy, religion, history, and literature; seminal writings in the sciences and social sciences; works of art; and major political documents and speeches, with special attention to the development of ethical, political, and religious ideas as reflected in works of enduring value." The Thomas Jefferson Center describes its Certificate Program in the Core Texts and Ideas as an "introduction to the liberal arts through the study of the great books . . . open to all UT undergraduates to complement any major with an integrated sequence of six courses that can also meet the UT general-education requirements." Students interested in a less structured alternative to the Core Texts and Ideas program may take either a six-course concentration in Western civilization or a four-course minor in Core Texts and Ideas. The Jefferson Center also sponsors a book club, a lecture series, and an executive seminar series for local professionals and community leaders.

Other ways students can improve on UT's inadequate general distribution requirements are through programs that serve as challenging interdepartmental options for advanced students. For example, Plan II Honors, a major in itself, is a core-like sequence designed for students who show high proficiency in both language and mathematics. Plan II students are very bright, with average combined verbal and mathematics SAT scores of over 1400. Acceptance into the program is highly competitive; in 2012 it received more than 1,300 applicants for its 178 slots. Plan II seeks to foster a tight community through common course work and small class sizes. Freshmen begin with a yearlong English literature course and a semester of logic. That is followed in the sophomore year by "Problems of Knowledge and Valuation," a two-semester philosophy session. Freshmen and juniors take seminars of varying quality and relevance. Spring 2012 selections ranged from "Myths of War and Violence " to "Law, Ethics, and Brain Policy."

Most Plan II seminars and sequences are heavy on writing, and in their fourth year students write—and probably rewrite—a thesis of 7,500 to 15,000 words. (Outside Plan II, only honors-track students write theses.) Virtually anything can be a "thesis," including artwork (accompanied by a paper), performances, and scientific studies. "Morale in Plan II is high, and rightly so, both for students and teachers," says a professor. "However, it does not have its own faculty and depends on the departments. Individual faculty members are usually eager to teach and offer courses in the program, but the departments are not always happy to see

CAMPUS POLITICS: YELLOW LIGHT

A student says of the political climate at UT, "Any outspoken conservative thought is generally regarded as unenlightened, racist, and narrow-minded. Intelligence is gauged by how few convictions students hold, how often they 'experience' other cultures, and how quickly they denounce traditional moral values." One professor agrees, "Lots of students drop my course when I tell them I am conservative and Republican. . . . I have over the years been called a Nazi, UT's Rush Limbaugh, and so on, although my evaluations are very good. . . . Students have told me about being penalized [in other courses] for their conservative writings or about having to write what the professor wants, not what they really think."

Also disturbing is an incident reported by *Campus Reform*. A UT journalism professor, Robert Jensen, conducted an interview with the *Huffington Post* in January 2013 in which he blamed recent mass shootings on . . . white privilege. "Why are the men who commit mass murder disproportionately white?" Jensen asked rhetorically. "My guess is that it has something to do with the sense of entitlement that most white people feel. . . . When the world doesn't deliver what those men feel they deserve, violence is seen as a reasonable response," continued Jensen.

their best faculty drawn off to teach a course that has a maximum enrollment of 15."

Like Plan II students, if to a lesser degree, students who enroll in the College of Liberal Arts Freshman Honors Program benefit from smaller class sizes and honors sections of introductory courses during their first two years. In addition, these students receive helpful advice concerning their academic schedules and broader career goals. Liberal arts students with 60 hours of completed course work and a UT GPA of at least 3.5 may apply to the Liberal Arts Honors Program (Upper Division), which provides special seminar-type classes and an honors diploma.

Other schools and departments also offer special programs. The McCombs School of Business has the Business Foundations Program, directed toward students who are completing a nonbusiness major but desire more courses applicable to the "real world." The College of Natural Sciences offers the Dean's Scholars Program, which facilitates undergraduate research projects and interaction between students and faculty. The Turing Scholars Program in computer science does the same for young programmers.

Majors in the business school, including the professional program in accounting and the Business Honors Program, are considered some of the best in the country. Many other UT departments rank highly; philosophy is excellent, as are psychology, Classics, and linguistics. In the natural sciences, physics, math, and chemistry are all solid, as is the computer science department.

Majors to which the least-prepared students gravitate are education and English. These are also two of UT's most left-leaning departments, students report. English majors are not required to take a Shakespeare class but must choose a multicultural course from among such titles as "Gay and Lesbian Literature and Culture" and "Mexican American Literature and Culture." The communications department is very ideological, according to a student we consulted. He says it "mostly comprises far-left liberals determined to use the media to drive conservative ideas out of the public sphere altogether. . . . That department made the English department look moderate by comparison." (See our Yellow Light for confirmation.)

The history department is politically charged, and the requirements reflect this. Majors must take two U.S. history classes, but the choices range from "United States, 1492–1865" to "History of Mexican Americans in the U.S."

The government department does not require majors to study the American Constitution, and an American political theory requirement can be fulfilled with such classes as "Racial and Ethnic Politics." Religious studies is not a road to salvation, UT insiders report. "Students should be cautioned that most religious studies courses are hostile to religion," says a professor, "though a growing number of courses that treat religion with respect, unaffiliated with that program, are springing up."

Budding journalists at UT have access to a unique resource—the original notes made by reporters Bob Woodward and Carl Bernstein from their investigation of Watergate. The Harry Ransom Humanities Research Center holds these notes and recently received additional materials that had been withheld to protect the (now-exposed) identity of "Deep Throat," the reporters' principal source. Those interested in another presidency should visit the Lyndon Johnson Presidential Library, located on the other side of campus.

A grad student says, "Overall, the campus is a hotbed of political correctness, but if a student is smart and does research into which classes to take and which professors teach them, he can still get a solid education."

As might be expected of a school its size, the academic advising at UT is mediocre except in very small majors and special freshman programs. The average student is best off educating himself in detail on degree requirements and interests and acquainting himself with the inches-thick book of course offerings, and only then meeting with an adviser to double-check. "You get as much out of the advising process as you put in," one student says. "Advisers are just happy if you have your act together ahead of time so they can move down the list. However, advisers are generally knowledgeable, and when prompted can be quite helpful in helping you determine what courses and instructors best fit your needs. But they don't waste time providing this support if you don't ask for it." A professor says that advising is better in some of the less populated departments, like Classics and philosophy.

Some assistance may come from faculty and graduate teaching assistants, who hold regular office hours. Students commend faculty for reaching out to those who show up. "I've never met a professor who wasn't more than happy to receive students for one-on-one tutelage," a student says. A professor notes, "There is an overall atmosphere and opportunity that should not be shortchanged. I think the brighter students who already have some sense of their own interests and direction really have a good time here and get a good education."

619

Because UT is so large, it is difficult to characterize the general intellectual character of students. One professor says that students are "less curious than in the past," but another says that students "in the past year or two have begun showing more interest in academic studies than I've ever seen here." In this, as in everything else at UT, both curious and apathetic students can find a niche.

With a student-faculty ratio of 18 to 1, UT relies heavily on graduate students to teach everything from massive lecture courses to small seminars. "Too much of the burden of teaching still rests with graduate students," says a professor. "Unfortunately, financial support for graduate students has not kept pace with support in a given field available elsewhere, and this means that UT is not competitive with universities of similar or higher rank. The quality of graduate students inevitably suffers."

UT can boast of many professors known for their excellent teaching and advising. Among them are J. Budziszewski, Roderick Hart, Thomas and Lorraine Pangle, David Prindle, Alan Sager, Devin and Dana Stauffer, David Leal, and Jeffrey Tulis in government; George Forgie, Brian Levack, and William Louis in history; David Hamermesh and Dale Stahl in economics; John Ruszkiewicz and Jeffrey Walker in rhetoric and composition; Randy Diehl, Phillip Gough (emeritus), Joseph Horn (emeritus), Robert Josephs, Peter MacNeilage (emeritus), James Pennebaker, and Del Thiessen (emeritus) in psychology; in Classics, Karl Galinsky, Thomas Palaima, Stephen White, and Robert Hankinson (also in philosophy); Jean-Pierre Cauvin (emeritus) in French; Michael Starbird in mathematics; Larry Carver, James Garrison, Ernest Kaulbach, Martin Kevorkian, and Wayne Rebhorn in English; Daniel Bonevac, Robert Kane (emeritus), Robert Koons, A. P. Martinich, Alexander Mourelatos, Stephen White, and Paul Woodruff in philosophy; Michael Harney, Stanislav Zimic, and Madeline Sutherland-Meier in Spanish; John Butler, Christopher Ellison, Mark Regnerus, and Robert Woodberry in sociology; and Samer Ali, Hina Azam, and Harold Liebowitz (emeritus) in Middle Eastern studies.

UT offers degrees in a wide array of foreign languages, including Chinese, Czech, French, German, Greek (Classical and Modern), Hebrew, Hindi, Italian, Japanese, Malayalam, Persian, Portuguese, Russian, Sanskrit, Spanish, and Turkish. In addition, UT has one of the largest study-abroad programs in the world, offering more than 700 programs across the planet.

Student Life: Keeping it weird

Though they may agree on little else, nearly all of UT's more than 50,000 students confess to one thing: Austin is the perfect college city. It's a place where offbeat people are known to congregate, and conventional people have a tendency to "go native." There's even an active community group called "Keep Austin Weird"—it seems that many longtime locals haven't exactly been delighted to see their bohemian city steered toward normalcy by Silicon Valley types and assorted other yuppies who have migrated to Austin's technology industry in recent years. But Austin is not Dallas or Houston, at least not yet. Formalities are rare: in Austin, "dressing up" still simply means wearing your Ropers instead of your flip-flops. The city is renowned for unpretentious intellectuality in a region full of down-home pleasures such as the annual Wiener Dog Races in the nearby town of Buda, which attracts fanatical dachshund owners from around the country.

Just as the city of Austin's politics are unrepresentative of the state of Texas as a whole, so is its remarkable natural beauty, as seen in the nearby Texas Hill Country. To cool off after a rigorous run or ride on one of the city's many hike-and-bike trails, students can paddle a canoe down Barton Creek or take a chilly dip in spring-fed Barton Springs Pool, both of which are situated within Zilker Park, a downtown beauty that spans 351 acres.

As the state capital, Austin provides many opportunities for students to release their political energies; the capitol building is within walking distance of campus. Hundreds of student organizations fit almost every need or interest; all that's necessary to start another group is three interested students. The all-male Longhorn Hellraisers (women can join the Hellraiser Honeys) paint their faces burnt orange and white, take off their shirts, and scream at football and basketball games.

UT's 35 fraternities and 27 sororities are lively, though unable to exert control over the raucous campus social scene. Just two sorority houses (and not a single fraternity) are actually located on campus, and their off-campus location at a school of this size means the Greeks are not much of a social focal point at UT; in fact, they actually have a good reputation on campus for their involvement in the community. UT is known as a party school, but the partying usually takes place in the city of Austin, not on campus.

UT students can participate in almost 1,000 clubs and organizations. Language clubs, film series, and discussion groups abound. The most award-winning daily student newspaper in the nation, the *Daily Texan*, rivals many midsized city newspapers in its professionalism. Alternative publications come and go, but the largest college humor magazine in the nation, the "loud, lewd, and totally inappropriate" *Texas Travesty*, is always good for a laugh. UT has many religiously oriented student organizations. Christian students wishing to remain so should generally avoid the churches adjoining campus, sources tell us. Catholic students, for instance, should skip the Catholic Student Center, perhaps in favor of Mass at a local parish like Sacred Heart.

University clubs and organizations include the American Constitution Society, College Republicans at Texas, Libertarian Longhorns, Young Conservatives of Texas, Blanton Museum of Art Student Guild, Hook 'Em Arts, UT Concert Chorale, Christian Legal Society, Fellowship of Christian Athletes, Cru (Campus Crusade for Christ), Young Life College Fellowship, Habitat for Humanity, Gigglepants Improv Comedy Troupe, Longhorn Cricket Club, Texas Triathletes, UT Dance Team, University of Texas Cycling, University French Club, Chess Club, Spirit of Shakespeare, and Willie Nelson Center Students.

Football is king in Texas, and in an age of mushy sentimentality it is refreshing to see the healthy, hearty hatred that persists between the Longhorns and the Texas A&M Aggies. UT participates in the NCAA I conference, where the Longhorn football team is consistently ranked in the top 10, and the UT men's and women's basketball teams are usually among the nation's best as well. The men's baseball, cross-country, golf, swimming, tennis, and track teams also participate in the conference, as do the women's crew, cross-country, golf, soccer, softball, swimming, tennis, track, and volleyball. Intramural sports are quite popular, though some of the playing fields are unfortunately situated a couple miles north

Blue Collar Ivy

SUGGESTED CORE

1. Classical Civilization 322, Ancient Epic
2. Philosophy 301K, Ancient Philosophy
3. English 358J, The Bible as Literature
4. Philosophy 349, History of Medieval and Renaissance Philosophy
5. Government 314, Competing Visions of the Good Life
6. English 321, Shakespeare: Selected Plays
7. History 315K, United States, 1492–1865
8. History 329L, Early Modern Philosophy: Descartes to Kant (*closest match*)

of campus. Teams include men's and women's basketball, golf, lightweight football, racquetball, soccer, softball, swimming, tennis, Ultimate Frisbee, volleyball, team handball, and outdoor track and field.

Residence-hall living is not the norm at UT. The university's 14 residence halls have a combined capacity of just over 7,100, even with the mammoth Jester Hall, which holds just shy of 3,000 residents. The vast majority of students dwell off campus, many in private dormitories adjoining the campus, but most students live in the thousands of apartments surrounding the school; the farther from campus, the cheaper the rent. For those who do live on campus, single-sex dormitories are available for both men and women. There are no coed dorm rooms or bathrooms.

Freshman orientation on campus is available but not required. Much of the programming is suspect, so incoming students may want to give it a miss. One student recalls attending an orientation program on diversity. "We were told to accept everything and be open-minded to all. Those who did not would be considered intolerant, racist, and close-minded," she says.

Famous nationwide for its offbeat and often radical, if not large, protests, the West Mall steps beneath UT's famed clock tower are as active as ever. On the West Mall and in other university-designated "free-speech zones," students are allowed to hold sound-amplified events between 11:30 a.m. and 1:30 p.m. The Young Conservatives of Texas have been tastefully rowdy in recent years, and socialists and Greens are always protesting something. The Campus and Community Involvement Office, while notorious for its bureaucracy, is the institutional backbone behind the 37 political groups on campus.

In 2011 the school reported two forcible sex offenses, six aggravated assaults, 51 burglaries, two stolen cars, and three arsons. Students report feeling reasonably safe on and around campus, and given the size of the school, the incidence of serious crime on campus does not appear to be alarmingly high. There are, however, occasional incidents on Guadalupe Street (the "Drag"), which borders the west side of campus and tends to collect runaways, vagrants, and the weirdest of the weird. (Ever seen the cult movie *Slacker*? It's set at UT, provides a pretty accurate picture of this side of campus life, and makes the school seem oddly appealing.)

UT is attractive to Texas residents, with 2012–13 tuition at $9,790 or $33,128 (out of state) and room and board at $10,946. The school practices need-blind admissions, and while it can't fulfill all requirements, it claims to meet "the need of most students, and particularly those with higher needs," according to the financial-aid office. Around 45 percent of students got need-based aid, with 2012 graduates owing an average of $22,478.

STRONG SUITS

- The Thomas Jefferson Center for the Study of Core Texts combined with Ideas and "Plan 2" yield an Ivy-level education grounded in the Great Books.
- Excellent majors in the business school, as well as in philosophy, psychology, Classics, linguistics, physics, math, chemistry, and computer science.
- Honors and tutoring options in business, computer science, and natural sciences are very rigorous.
- Lively, creative, politically diverse campus atmosphere.

WEAK POINTS

- Distributional requirements inadequate. Hundreds of courses fulfill mandates.
- Less demanding majors include education and English.
- Politicized departments in history, religious studies, communications, and various grievance studies.
- Anemic advising, except in certain departments (such as Classics).

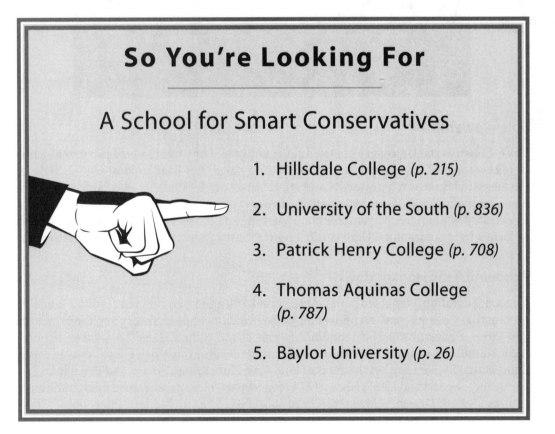

So You're Looking For

A School for Smart Conservatives

1. Hillsdale College *(p. 215)*

2. University of the South *(p. 836)*

3. Patrick Henry College *(p. 708)*

4. Thomas Aquinas College *(p. 787)*

5. Baylor University *(p. 26)*

University of Utah

Salt Lake City, Utah • www.utah.edu

Solar Powerhouse

Once known as the University of Deseret, the University of Utah received its current name in 1892—some 42 years after students first matriculated. It is Utah's oldest school. Today it is a major public research university and attracts over 31,000 students who can choose from 83 undergraduate majors and 90 graduate degrees (including Utah's only medical school). Even if students and faculty grumble about parking and the sheer size that makes it difficult to form a tight community, Utah is still a powerhouse of sports, research, and academics.

Academic Life: Hunker down

General education starts with the American Institution requirement, which laudably ensures that students "have an understanding of fundamentals of history and the principles and form of government and economic system of the United States." A writing requirement solidifies a student's expository skills. Students also must delve into what is called "Intellectual Exploration" in the areas of Fine Arts, Humanities, Social, and Behavioral Sciences, and Physical and Life Sciences. For the most part, these appear to be solid, traditional courses ("Greek Drama," "Masterpieces of World Art," "Early Modern Philosophy," "Rise of Civilization"), with a few less intensive choices (like "Geography, Yoga, and a Sense of Place"). Students seeking a bachelor's are also required to complete a language requirement and two quantitative intensive courses, one course in diversity, an upper-division writing/communication course, and a course that fulfills the international requirement.

Advising is mandatory for first-year students. So is hard work: one student advises, "If you're not accustomed to studying hard, learn how to study before you get here."

Of course, its location in a mining state affects the university; the College of Mines and Earth Sciences is among the strongest and most popular departments on campus. Other noteworthy majors include chemistry, biology, English, nursing, communications (including journalism), psychology, biomedical engineering, political science, and business. Creative writing and dance are also considered strong.

Incoming freshmen can sign up for LEAP (Learning, Engagement, Achievement, and Progress), a two-semester learning community. Most LEAP students take two LEAP courses in the fall (social science and writing) and one in the spring (humanities). Staying with the same professor and classmates throughout the year could go a long way toward making the large campus feel a little smaller.

Speaking of size, more than 3,000 students enrolled in the latest class, swelling the ranks to almost 29,000 undergrads. Numbers don't add up? That's because only 17,518 of those undergrads are full-time students; the rest are part-time or some other form of "degree seeking." The good news is that 82 percent of first-year applicants gain admission and that 88 percent of freshmen return for a second year. The not-so-good news is that tuition for out-of-state students stands at $22,642 (for those in state it's $7,139).

As a student at Utah, you stand a much better chance than just about any student in the nation at inventing something that makes you money. That's not just due to the fact that Utah is a massive research university that commands $410 million in research funds each year. It also boasts the Technology Venture Development office, which helps with licensing

VITAL STATISTICS

Religious affiliation: *none*
Total enrollment: *32,388*
Total undergraduates: *24,840*
SAT CR/Verbal midrange: *510–620*
SAT Math midrange: *510–650*
ACT midrange: *21–27*
Applicants: *11,118*
Applicants accepted: *82%*
Accepted applicants who enrolled: *3,079*
Tuition (general/out of state): *$22,642*
Tuition (in state): *$7,139*
Room and board: *$7,155*
Freshman retention rate: *88%*
Graduation rate (4 yrs.): *22%*
Graduation rate (6 yrs.): *36%*
Courses with fewer than 20 students: *43%*
Student-faculty ratio: *13:1*
Courses taught by graduate students: *not provided*
Students living on campus: *14%*
Students in fraternities: *3%*
Students in sororities: *4%*
Students receiving need-based financial aid: *46%*
Avg. student-loan debt of a recent graduating class: *$20,796*
Most popular majors: *social sciences, business/marketing, communication/journalism*
Guaranteed housing for 4 years? *no*

CAMPUS POLITICS: GREEN LIGHT

The overall political atmosphere trends conservative, as one might expect, but students report that there is actually an even mix in the student body. The conservative groups like College Republicans pull large numbers—more than 100 at weekly meetings—but so do groups dedicated to gay activism. A student involved with College Republicans has seen his share of intolerance. "I've been called a bigot and a hater," he says. "If you want real conservatives, go to BYU."

"While almost all of the teachers that I have encountered have liberal mindsets, due to a decent portion of the classes being LDS it sort of balances out, and the professors seem to be more conscious of being open to all viewpoints," says a student. "You do not see campus politics at all in the classroom." But another student disagrees, saying that English and theater lean to the left, while business leans right.

and commercializing faculty inventions and educating students. In 2011 it helped start 18 new companies that grew out of university research—second only to MIT.

The university also supports more than 80 research-based centers and institutes, like the Keck Center for Tissue Engineering, the Petroleum Research Center, the American West Center, and the Energy and Geoscience Institute.

If you're not much of an inventor or engineer, there's always the English program, known for engaging faculty and smaller classes than other departments. Majors are required to take 13 courses, with just three specified as requirements: "Critical Introduction to Literary Forms"; "Introduction to Critical Theory"; and one literary history course (pre- or post-1800). Through electives students can narrow their focus by period (one course is required in literature, ranging from the Middle Ages through modernism) or by form and genre (selections include courses in poetry, creative writing, studies in drama, children's literature, and studies in rhetoric and style). Literary-history options are plentiful and focused: options include courses on Shakespeare, Chaucer, Milton, and Victorian literature. The Studies in Methods and Theories options show a less traditional bent, with selections including "Theories of Gender and Sexuality" and "Ecocriticism."

History majors can select from a host of useful courses. Among the required 13 are "U.S. History to 1877" and "U.S. History since 1877." They must also take three broad lower-division survey courses (examples include "Western Civilization to 1300" and "Latin American Civilizations to 1820s"). Seven upper-division courses are required, including one from Asia, Europe, Latin America, Middle East, and the United States. There is a wide selection of courses in ancient history, followed by just as many on the Renaissance and more modern times. The United States, too, is the subject of a good share of courses.

Political science majors take 12 courses plus another four in allied fields (anthropology, communication, economics, ethnic studies, family and consumer studies, gender studies, geography, history, Middle East studies, philosophy, psychology, sociology, and city and metropolitan planning). "U.S. National Government" is required, and students must take two of the three introductory courses to international relations, comparative politics, and political theory. For electives, students can choose from among a good number of U.S.-centered courses (such as "Constitutional Law" and "Federalism"), although courses from non-Western nations have a heavy showing: "Islam and Politics," "Politics of Revolution in Latin America," "Politics in China," and "Government and Politics of Japan," to name a few. Likewise, political theory classes have their share of gender-based courses, including "Feminist Political Theory." But as one professor says, the department offers a good breadth and "covers the discipline broadly, from traditional theory through American politics to world politics."

Speaking of professors, Utah beats the national student-faculty ratio with a healthy 13 to 1. But with several lecture halls and auditoriums in the 300-to-400-student range, first-year students shouldn't expect to benefit from this faculty attention too soon. However, smaller classes in the upper-class years bring down the average class size, so that overall more than 40 percent of classes have fewer than 20 students.

Recommended professors are Barry Weller, Anne Jamison, and Kathryn Stockton in English; Mark Button, Steven Lobell, and Ella Myers in political science; Ilya Zharov and Holly Sebahar in chemistry; Mark Nielsen in biology; Abe Bakhsheshy in business; Anne Yeagle in economics; Ray Gunn in history; Richard Ingebretsen in physics; David Hawkins and Aaron Phillips in writing; David Sanbonmatsu in psychology; Victor Camacho in mathematics; Andrew Jorgenson in sociology; and Larry Coats in geography. One student named the entire biomedical engineering faculty as his favorite professors.

Of the physics department, one student says, "It seems like many of the professors are getting very old and uninterested in students. This does seem to be changing, however, as they seem to be getting new professors who are very good teachers."

One place to find the best professors is the Honors College. Classes are capped at 30 students and taught by faculty actively engaged in research that is often integrated into the classroom. The centerpiece is an experiential-based program called Engaged Learning Opportunities; the university describes these as "signature experiences that bring students and community partners together in collaboration that results in real-world applications." Juniors and seniors should consider the Honors College Think Tanks—yearlong, for-credit courses in which students and faculty design original solutions to pertinent social issues.

Foreign language majors are offered in Chinese, French, German, Greek and Latin, Japanese, Russian, and Spanish. Study-abroad options, which range from spring-break trips to full-year programs, include Armenia, Brazil, China, Costa Rica, Denmark, Ecuador, Egypt, England, Finland, Ghana, India, Italy, Japan, and Peru.

> One student advises, "If you're not accustomed to studying hard, learn how to study before you get here." When it comes to student life, the Mormon church "tends to be the primary outlet for student involvement and activities—not Greek life, not student government," notes a professor.

Blue Collar Ivy

SUGGESTED CORE

1. Classical Civilizations 2790, Ancient Epic
2. Philosophy 1000, Intro: Survey of Philosophy
3. English 2030, The Bible as Literature
4. Philosophy 5110, Ancient Medieval Philosophy
5. Political Science 3700, Political Philosophy
6. English 2300, Introduction to Shakespeare
7. History 170, American Civilization
8. Philosophy 4130, 19th-Century Philosophy

Student Life: Not as dry as you think

It's hard to discuss student life at the university without a nod to the impact of the Church of Jesus Christ of Latter-Day Saints (LDS). Roughly 50 percent of the student body are Mormon, and adjacent to campus is the LDS Institute of Religion, which holds religious education classes for students but is not affiliated with the university. "The LDS tends to be the primary outlet for student involvement and activities—not Greek life, not student government," notes one professor. It also affects student behavior, suppressing the party culture that captures so many schools. "It's not as big a deal here," says the same professor. "There just isn't much drinking and drugging."

While powerful, the LDS influence is not overbearing. There are still parties every weekend on Greek Row. Utah might technically be a dry campus, but exceptions are doubtless made. Another effect of the strong LDS presence is the lack of other religious groups on campus. "There are great churches close to the school," says a student, "but there don't seem to be many on-campus groups for Christian students."

There are a smattering of New Age and humanist groups (Mindfulness and Meditation Group and Secular Humanism, Inquiry, and Freethought) and non-Christian groups (like the Buddhist Humanism Club), as well as several groups for minority students (Chinese Student Christian Fellowship, Korean Christian Student Fellowship, and the Muslim Students Association). But traditional Christian groups are few; the main ones are Cru and The Edge (both nondenominational). If you seek a true denomination, you'll need to venture out into Salt Lake City.

Which isn't that bad, thankfully. Just take TRAX, the light-rail system that has saved many a student's sanity, since parking on campus is so incredibly tough. Students are issued free passes for TRAX, the train, and the bus system, and combined with the free campus shuttle that runs every 15 minutes, students should have no problem getting to where they need to go.

If your destination is Salt Lake City (pop. 189,000), it's just a three-mile trek. You'll find the Historic Mormon Temple Square, the home of the Jazz and the Grizzlies, the Mormon Tabernacle Choir, plus tons of shops, restaurants, and art galleries. Salt Lake is the gateway to some of the best skiing in the country—a fact that is not lost on Utah's student body of outdoor enthusiasts.

"By far the coolest thing about the U is the outdoor mind-set that the entire university has," says a student. "We have one of, if not the biggest ski club in the country, and everyone is involved in some sort of outdoors. Whereas at a lot of other colleges, the weekends are simply a time to party; at the U it is time to ski, snowboard, hike, fish, rock-climb, backpack, go to the trampoline gym (and then party, of course). Utah is one of the best places in the world for outdoors and being within 30 minutes of it all really changes the mind-set of the school."

You could also visit the 2002 Winter Olympic venues. In fact, it's a legacy of those Olympic Games that is one of the best things about campus life—the dorms. All buildings in Heritage Commons (except for Officers Circle) were built for the 2002 Winter Olympics and were used by the athletes during the Games. In 2012 the university added the Donna Garff Marriott Honors Residential Scholars Community—and these, reportedly, are even nicer than the others, with full kitchens and suite-style living.

Residence options for first-year students are the suite-style, coed Chapel Glen; the suite-style, single-sex-by-floor Gateway Heights; and the six Living Learning Communities in Sage Point (Honors, Go Global, Green/Sustainability, Leadership and Service, Outdoor Leadership, and Engineering). Residents of these halls may not host an opposite-sex guest overnight.

Within the 10 houses that make up the Officers Circle (where all houses are based on students' academic, social, or civic interests) are the Fine Arts House, the Crocker Science House, and the Alliance House (residents are allowed to select a space without consideration of "gender identity/expression" or sexual orientation). The university also has apartment communities for students.

However, only 40 percent of freshmen and 14 percent of undergrads overall live on campus. And just 3 and 4 percent of students go Greek. "Utah seems to have much more of a commuter campus than most schools because of demographics," says a professor. "Undergrads are older and more likely to have families and jobs."

But this isn't too much of a wet blanket on campus life, because when your campus is as big as Utah's, that means there are still a lot of people doing things. Political student groups include the Constitution Club, College Republicans, and Young Americans for Liberty. College Democrats and College Libertarians are both huge, reports a student. Social and academic groups abound. Whether you're a gamer, a ballerina, or fascinated by meteorology, Utah has a group for you.

Especially if you like athletics. The MUSS is the university's student fan club for football, men's basketball, and women's soccer, volleyball, and gymnastics, and was named one of the Top Five Student Sections in the country by ESPN. The Utes, members of the NCAA Division I (FBS for football) and the Pacific-12 Conference, also field teams in men's and women's swimming and diving, basketball, tennis, golf, and skiing, as well as cross-country and softball for women, and football and baseball for men. In 2009 its football team won the Sugar Bowl. Besides all the off-campus opportunities, students can join intramural leagues for soccer, basketball, racquetball, kickball, tennis, volleyball, bowling, softball, and a variety of others.

Crime is of low concern for students. On campus in 2011 there were five forcible sex offenses, 90 burglaries, and three aggravated assaults—low numbers for such a large school. "I would feel completely comfortable walking anywhere around the entire city of Salt Lake by myself at night, let alone the campus itself," says a student. The low incidence of crime is attributable in part because the area around the university is mostly middle-to-upper-class neighborhoods, and partly because of the LDS influence.

But there could be another reason: guns. Unlike universities, Utah lets students carry guns on campus, and students considering this school ought to be aware that many of their classmates could be packing. Says one student who takes advantage of his concealed carry permit: "Knowing that at any time in a lecture hall there are probably a relatively large percentage of people carrying a gun makes me more confident that a Virginia Tech incident could not escalate to the point that it did." Although an emergency alert system has been installed to address this type of situation, it has mainly been used as a rattlesnake-on-campus alert.

The school is an amazing bargain for native students, with tuition at $7,139 and $7,155 for room and board in 2012–13 (out-of-staters paid $22,642). Some 46 percent of students got need-based financial aid, and the average student-loan debt of a recent graduating class was $20,796.

STRONG SUITS	WEAK POINTS
• Excellent program in the College of Mines and Earth Sciences.	• Few religious options for non-Mormon Christians.
• Worthy departments in chemistry, biology, English, nursing, communications, psychology, biomedical engineering, political science, business, creative writing, and dance.	• Some massive (300–400 student) courses.
• Nonpoliticized courses in most disciplines.	• Physics department said to have weak teaching.
• Solid, traditional classes on offer, even in humanities departments.	• A dry campus, which is not for everyone.
• Many opportunities for students to engage in cutting-edge research.	

University of Vermont

Burlington, Vermont • www.uvm.edu

Land-Grant Elite

Chartered in 1791, the same year in which Vermont became a state in the Union, UVM is the fifth-oldest university in New England, after Harvard, Yale, Dartmouth, and Brown. The University of Vermont enjoys the status of a "public Ivy" because of its reputation for elite "educational experiences at much lower public university tuition." As a land-grant institution, it is renowned for its research, but that doesn't keep faculty from being extraordinarily personable teachers. Their students have a reputation for successful careers that begin directly after graduation.

Academic Life: I'm OK, you're OK

Although the overall character of UVM is distinctly "progressive," the general-education requirements at UVM allow for some solid course options, especially in such broad requirement categories as Arts and Humanities, Social Sciences, and Language and Literature. Undergraduates are also required to take six credits in "Diversity and Racism in the U.S." and "Human and Societal Diversity," but that is over and done with fairly quickly.

Despite a student-to-faculty ratio of 17 to 1, professors at UVM are very available and

631

VITAL STATISTICS

Religious affiliation: *none*
Total enrollment: *13,097*
Total undergraduates: *11,211*
SAT CR/Verbal midrange:
  540–640
SAT Math midrange:
  550–650
ACT midrange: *24–29*
Applicants: *21,808*
Applicants accepted: *77%*
Accepted applicants who
  enrolled: *14%*
Tuition (general/out of
  state): *$33,672*
Tuition (in state): *$13,344*
Room and board: *$10,064*
Freshman retention rate:
  85%
Graduation rate (4 yrs.): *65%*
Graduation rate (6 yrs.): *76%*
Courses with fewer than 20
  students: *50%*
Student-faculty ratio: *17:1*
Courses taught by graduate
  students: *3%*
Students living on campus:
  50%
Students in fraternities: *7%*
Students in sororities: *6%*
Students receiving need-
  based financial aid: *57%*
Avg. student-loan debt of a
  recent graduating class:
  $27,725
Most popular majors: *social
  sciences, natural resources
  and conservation,
  business/marketing*
Guaranteed housing for 4
  years? *no*

helpful to all their students. Half of courses have fewer than 20 students in class, and the average class size is 30, which is outstanding for a school of this size. "Professors are very accessible and very helpful," says a student. "There are many professors who I've met who are very willing to meet outside of class. They'll hand out their e-mails and oftentimes even their cell phone numbers for emergencies." Another student has been very impressed with the in-class performance of faculty, whom she describes as "really passionate about it, and you really learn the material." A professor tells us that "virtually all the primary instructors for our courses are faculty, and we do not rely on doctoral candidates for instruction to the degree that many other research universities do. Based on recent information," he adds, "I would estimate that no more than 2 to 3 percent of our courses (and probably even fewer) are led by graduate assistants."

"The Honors College is really strong here," says a student, citing the study-abroad options tied to the honors track. The Honors College offers a more focused track for students who wish to avoid the rather limpid general-education requirements of the university at large. Keep in mind, however, that honors course work ranges from traditional to trendy. In their first year, students will read "texts such as Descartes's *Meditations*, Hume's *Inquiry Concerning Human Understanding*, V. S. Ramachandran's work on neuroscience, Anne Fadiman's *The Spirit Catches You*, and Mary Shelley's *Frankenstein*." Throughout their undergraduate careers, students will be confronted with material "often involving race and culture in the U.S. and beyond." Among courses for Spring 2013 were "Mixed: Multiracialism in U.S. Culture," "Imagining Race and Region in Early New England," "Ethnolinguistic Identities," and "The Social Construction of Disability."

Students and faculty speak highly of the environmental science department. "We're well known for that, and they've put a lot of energy and focus into it," says a student. "Engineering and computer science are the strongest departments I can think of," says another. One student says that "UVM is really strong in physical sciences like physics and biology, and they have a really good research department." She says that students in the sciences are "involved in a million different research labs and . . . they have a really high reputation of getting jobs after

Vermont

graduation." Another student says that in the College of Education and Social Services, "the faculty and other students I was engaging, whether in class or in the field, wanted to help people and valued the dignity of each person, with the desire to give them either the best education possible or improve their circumstances." A professor believes that "environmental studies is quite strong, and engineering and mathematics are increasingly strong." He is excited about the new "Complex Systems Center, which is an interdisciplinary program" and recommends checking out "some of the energy courses where students travel to China for fieldwork."

A student suggests avoiding "anything in social sciences and the arts. I don't think it's a very good decision to go to UVM for an English major of all things." Another student agrees that "the English department here isn't very strong." One student, who has "spent a lot of time with students and faculty of the history department," says that this is "where I faced the most discrimination and negativity" for voicing conservative views.

English majors at UVM are not obliged to read the works of Shakespeare. Courses are available, such as "Shakespeare" and ENGS 320, which is a seminar on "a major author" (sometimes the Bard), offering "in-depth study of the works, critical reception, and context of an author writing in English." Other courses in English range from "Chaucer" to "Gender and Sex in Lit Studies," which addresses "writing by women and LGBT authors and/or literary representations of gender and society."

History majors are not required to take even one course in the history of the United States before the mid-20th century. The History Major Checklist includes requirements in the histories of Europe, Africa, Asia, the Middle East, Global History, and the history

CAMPUS POLITICS: RED LIGHT

A student warns that "any kind of public profession of" a conservative view, "whether it be a political or a religious" one, "is usually followed up by a question like, 'Why do you think it's OK for you to impose your beliefs on me?'" He says that he doesn't feel like he should talk about his beliefs and that it is best to keep a low profile as a Christian conservative. "But I would say there is a great desire to tolerate everyone and be open to everyone," yet "at the same time that creates a very uncomfortable situation, and it's fake. I would say it's very fake." Another student says, "The majority of discrimination I faced was on the part of other students. In this regard I faced almost complete dismissal of opposing or different perspectives and mockery." She goes on to say that "there is no question that UVM is quite liberal and pro-abortion. The biggest obstacle UVM has standing in its way is that students pride themselves on being inclusive and accepting but in reality are only so to those who agree with them. . . . More often than not this does not include a Christian perspective."

Although the Foundation for Individual Rights in Education gives UVM a "yellow light" speech code, and there have been some rather explosive confrontations between conservatives and liberals on campus in the past, it is fair to say that UVM is pretty peaceful now—if only because the fight is over. It is probably best for conservative students to keep their views to themselves and do their best to select the best courses available. There have been only two politically conservative student organizations at UVM in the past five years, both of which have apparently disbanded.

of "the Americas." There is no mention of the history of this nation in the requirements. For those who get their hopes up about the requirement in "the Americas," the checklist states that "those concentrating in the Americas must include three (3) hours of Canadian or Latin American History." Other courses include "History of Women in the US/Women's and Gender Studies 161." Although American history is somewhat marginalized within the history department, students will find some solid courses such as "Ideas in the Western Tradition," which covers "great books of Western civilization in their historical setting," such as "Classical Greek" and "Classical Roman Civilization."

Political science majors must complete four "core courses," one of which is "American Political System," covering the "institutions, processes and problems of American Government." For a more in-depth study of the U.S. Constitution, majors may also take "Constitutional Law." There are more than 80 political science courses offered at UVM and several internships that offer credit, though they do not count toward a major.

The school atmosphere can be "really welcoming," says one student. "Anybody from any different background or political affiliation" can benefit from the opportunities available at UVM. She tells us that "Career Services, which is part of the Study Abroad office, is really, really helpful. They always hold events, like lessons on how to make a résumé." She recommends the staff of the Study Abroad programs. "They can answer any question on demand." Another student says that the faculty are "outstanding" and "not only open to discussion but supportive in one's pursuit of academic excellence."

The faculty at UVM lean heavily left. But do they impose their views on students? "Every once in a while you get that one professor," says a student, "but not very much." He thinks that the students who focus their studies on science will have little trouble with politics in class. One student says that political correctness is "not really prominent" in classes and that faculty are "not at all" unwelcoming of conser-

O ne student says, "There's a great deal of what I would call false tolerance" at UVM. Conservative ideas meet with benign neglect. So do other activities. Another student says: "There definitely is a lot of pot smoking on campus, and it's not discouraged by campus police."

vative views. But conservatives only "feel welcomed in an extremely weak sense," another student counters. "There's a great deal of what I would call false tolerance" at UVM. A history minor says that "for the most part, the faculty was amazing, but I did have two professors who were blatantly anti-Catholic and discriminated against those with a different view." She says that she has known many Catholic students within the college of Arts and Sciences who "faced discrimination and intolerance at a much higher level. Anti-Catholic and liberal views were built into lectures and if challenged, one was met with ridicule and disgust."

Students and faculty have recommended many professors at UVM, including Joan Rosebush in mathematics (who has been "an inspiration and mentor"); Lesley-Ann

Dupigny-Giroux in geography (who "plays a huge role" in her department); Peter Dodds and Chris Danforth in mathematics; Terence Cuneo in philosophy (whom a colleague recommends as "an excellent Christian philosopher"); Steve Titcomb in electrical engineering; Maggie Ebbsein and Josh Bongard in computer science; Donna Rizzo in technical engineering; and Mandar Dewoolkar and Eric Hernandez in civil engineering.

UVM offers courses in a great range of languages, including Chinese, ESL, French, German, Greek and Latin, Hebrew, Italian, Japanese, Portuguese, Russian, and Spanish.

The university also offers study-abroad options with destinations as diverse as Australia, Finland, Japan, Mexico, and Russia, to name a few. Students can make arrangements through UVM to study for full credit at foreign universities, and there are various exchange programs offered as well.

> ### SUGGESTED CORE
>
> 1. Classics 24, Myths and Legends of Trojan War
> 2. Philosophy 101, History of Ancient Philosophy
> 3. Religion 23, The Bible
> 4. Philosophy 105, History of Medieval Philosophy
> 5. Philosophy 140, Social and Political Philosophy (*closest match*)
> 6. English 135, Shakespeare
> 7. History 011, U.S. History to 1865
> 8. Philosophy 160, Continental Philosophy

Student Life: Dude . . . wait, what?

"UVM has a beautiful campus" says a student. And it truly is a scenic place, sitting as it does on the shore of Lake Champlain between the Adirondack and the Green Mountain Ranges. Campus life can be loads of fun. A student tells us that "in the warmer months, everything from Zumba to meditation groups are on the green . . . cultural events are well attended. Also there are quirky things like campus yard sales outside the Bailey Howe Library. And always free food, hot chocolate, coffee . . . all the time!" One student "just joined ROTC and would highly recommend it."

The dorms are all mixed sex, with housing options that include "Residential Life special-interest" communities "such as the Rainbow Cottage, S.A.F.E. Program, or a Living and Learning Center program (creative and performing arts, diverse cultures, wellness, professional interests, and more)." A student complains that the RAs make it their business to indoctrinate residents with a "very relativistic sense of tolerance" that is "hammered in" to students. "Political correctness, 'never imposing your beliefs about something on someone else,' that's emphasized greatly since day one."

One belief that is not imposed is compliance with local drug laws. A student says: "The biggest thing about UVM that could either attract or repel students would be pot—there definitely is a lot of pot smoking on campus, and it's not discouraged by campus police." Another student remarks that "UVM is really loud, 'cause people party a lot." She believes that this is because the resident assistants are so "laid back. . . . They don't really do anything." She goes on to tell us that, "On the final day of classes, a bunch of people—I mean like a large majority of people on campus—get naked, go outside, and run around central campus for hours. It's been going on for a couple of years."

Greek life is not much of a presence on campus, we are told. "There are frats / sororities, but they are a minority" and mostly "do a lot for charities," a student says. "The campus is very into social activism, protests, that type of thing. Environmental events" are popular, and "student government is very active."

A student tells us that "hockey is very popular" at UVM, "although our team isn't very good. Basketball is also big." UVM is home to the Catamounts, with eight varsity teams for men and 10 for women. The Catamounts compete at the NCAA Division I level and are members of the America East Conference, the Hockey East Association, and the Eastern Intercollegiate Skiing Association. And these kids are no dumb jocks. UVM took home the "Academic Cup" for seven straight years from 2005 to 2011 in recognition of their student-athletes' high GPAs. But for many students, sports are not central to social life.

At least not public sports. Promiscuity on campus is said to be pretty extensive, but students don't seem to be too flamboyant about it. "As much as college students hook up, I haven't had any issues," says a female student, "none of my roommates have been particularly promiscuous. It's not outrageously bad." Another student says that at least "people go to their rooms for that. It's not like, *in your face.*"

There is a very active Catholic Center at UVM, which one student describes as "the best thing UVM has going for it. It is a thriving community that encourages and provides students with the tools and means to strive for the pursuit of holiness and academic excellence." Unfortunately, there are few other Christian organizations on campus. There are some that have ceased to be active, and others that, though active, strike us as rather insubstantial, like the Cooperative Christian Ministry, which "works collaboratively with UVM's Residential and Student Life Departments, ALANA Student Center, Women's Center, the LGBTQA Center, the Center for Cultural Pluralism, and the Center for Health and Well-Being to sponsor programs of mutual interest."

The crime rate at UVM is quite low, with five forcible sex offenses, one robbery, 36 burglaries, and four cases of arson reported in 2011 (the last year reported). A student tells us, "I've heard statistics about Burlington being one of the safest cities in the country. The university has a kind of alert system; they use text messages, calls, e-mails—it's very effective. I've always felt very safe." Crime "happens rarely," says one student. "Even stuff going around town like burglaries in apartments—the school makes sure everyone knows about it." Another student recalls that "someone got stabbed on campus a couple of days ago, which is really rare, and it was regarding a drug deal, like somebody didn't pay for their drugs or something." But she says "that was a pretty big deal. As for downtown, it's not as bad as most cities. I mean, every once in a while we get e-mails from the school saying 'don't go down this street because someone got mugged' or something." She tells us that even "teachers inform you about [any crimes], so there's no way you could not know about it."

By New England standards, the school is inexpensive for Vermont residents, with 2012–13 tuition at $13,344 (outsiders paid $33,672), and room and board $10,064. Only 57 percent of students get need-based aid, but the average student-loan debt of borrowers was an alarming $27,725, according to the Project on Student Debt.

STRONG SUITS

- Good programs in engineering, computer, physics, biology, and environmental sciences.
- Excellent opportunities for students to engage in research.
- A strong and very helpful study-abroad office.
- Mostly nonpoliticized teachers who don't impose their ideology (almost univocally leftist) in the classroom.
- Extensive internship opportunities.

WEAK POINTS

- Shaky, vague distributional requirements.
- Lax majors' requirements in humanities such as English and history.
- Extremely politicized courses offered and virtually no conservative faculty.
- Extensive pot smoking and promiscuity on campus.
- Few religious options on campus, except for Catholics.

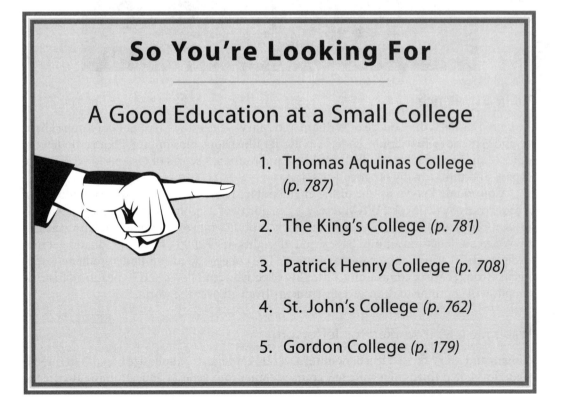

So You're Looking For

A Good Education at a Small College

1. Thomas Aquinas College *(p. 787)*

2. The King's College *(p. 781)*

3. Patrick Henry College *(p. 708)*

4. St. John's College *(p. 762)*

5. Gordon College *(p. 179)*

College of William and Mary

Williamsburg, Virginia • www.wm.edu

Public Excellence

Chartered in 1693, the College of William and Mary created the first Phi Beta Kappa chapter and America's first honor code. Among its illustrious alumni are Thomas Jefferson, James Monroe, and John Marshall. William and Mary has scores of reasons to be proud of its past, and unlike many other colleges, it is.

Commonly known as one of the eight "public Ivies" for giving a superior education at comparatively little cost, W&M reserves a majority of its slots for state residents. And no wonder. The school has the highest Fulbright acceptance rate of all top research universities (50 W&M students and alumni have won Fulbrights since 2000), and its graduates get into medical school at twice the national average. The college's focus on undergraduate teaching, its strong sense of community, its highly selective admissions, and its beautiful historic campus will continue to draw serious students from all over the world.

Academic Life: It worked for Jefferson

William and Mary revised its curriculum several years ago, to emphasize breadth of knowledge. Now equal thirds of a student's courses come from general-education requirements, electives, and a student's concentration. One recent alumnus says that students "must learn something of both the humanities and the sciences—although various paperwork games can be played to avoid a few things. However, the education requirements are established so that not too much can be worked around."

W&M's academic departments generally provide solid, rigorous courses for the requirements, but they certainly do not constitute a core curriculum. A history major says that while the courses at W&M are "well taught," he also complains that he "consistently" has trouble registering for courses because preferred classes "are very scarce in most majors due to state budget cuts."

English majors take 36 credits, with at least one course in British literature of the Middle Ages and Renaissance; one in British literature from 1675 to 1900, with classes in Augustan satire, Romantic and Victorian poetry, and the Victorian novel; one course studying a single author; an American literature course; and a research seminar.

W&M is well known for its American history program; its doctoral program in colonial history ranks among the top four in the country. One history major says that his early American history course was surely among the best offered in the country. A broad survey of courses shows a more sober list than that found at many universities. History majors must complete a course on Europe before or after 1715; two American history survey courses; one non-Western history; and a colloquium described as "intensive reading and writing on a carefully defined historical topic or period."

According to faculty and students, the college's strongest programs are biology, classical studies, economics, history, anthropology, geology, physics, religion, and the School of Business.

Government has some excellent professors, but it has become increasingly ideological in recent years. A government major says, "William and Mary is definitely more liberal than conservative." But this rarely gets in the way of learning. "The students tend to know that people have those leanings; it doesn't mean the teachers are wholly partisan in the classroom," a student says. Majors must take 33 credits, including introductory classes in American government, comparative politics, and international relations; one course on political theory;

VITAL STATISTICS

Religious affiliation: *none*
Total enrollment: *8,258*
Total undergraduates: *6,171*
SAT CR/Verbal midrange: *630–740*
SAT Math midrange: *620–720*
ACT midrange: *28–32*
Applicants: *12,109*
Applicants accepted: *32%*
Accepted applicants who enrolled: *33%*
Tuition (general/out of state): *$37,344*
Tuition (in state): *$13,570*
Room and board: *$8,600*
Freshman retention rate: *95%*
Graduation rate (4 yrs.): *83%*
Graduation rate (6 yrs.): *91%*
Courses with fewer than 20 students: *48%*
Student-faculty ratio: *12:1*
Courses taught by graduate students: *not provided*
Students living on campus: *75%*
Students in fraternities: *25%*
Students in sororities: *29%*
Students receiving need-based financial aid: *29%*
Avg. student-loan debt of a recent graduating class: *$24,344*
Most popular majors: *business, interdisciplinary studies, social sciences*
Guaranteed housing for 4 years? *no*

Virginia

Blue Collar Ivy

CAMPUS POLITICS: GREEN LIGHT

With the exceptions noted above, classrooms seem mostly nonpoliticized at William and Mary. It is one of the minority of colleges to show a devotion to free expression on campus, according to free-speech advocates at the Foundation for Individual Rights in Education. No incidents of student expression being suppressed have come to light in recent years.

William and Mary students do react to threats to what they see as their "rights," however. *The Informer* reported on an administration proposal to ban "items used predominantly for drinking games (e.g., pong tables and beer bongs)" and came out strongly in defense of students' rights to possess and use these tools: "Do we wish to be the poor man who can only say, 'First they came for beer pong, and I did not speak up because I did not play. Then they came for beer bongs, and I said nothing because I did not own one. Finally, they came for my Solo cups, and no one was inebriated enough to speak out for my drink?' No, surely we do not. Now is the time for action. Restore Honor. Restore Sanity. Restore Beer Pong."

We are glad there aren't worse things to complain about at William and Mary.

a course on research methods; and a 400-level seminar.

Departments where students say that professors' political leanings influence learning include sociology, religion, and economics. A student says that conservative students are not routinely targeted by faculty members. "There are obvious exceptions, but this is generally not a major issue." Regarding the political atmosphere among the student body, one undergraduate feels that "apathy is worse on campus than bizarre political stances."

Professors seem to care about their charges. One student says, "Professors are very accessible, and they teach almost all the classes I take," noting that some teachers take on more of a mentoring role for students. Another student says that faculty are proactive with their students. "All the professors are required to have office hours, of course," the student says, "but even beyond that, they're willing to talk with you outside of class and get to know you."

The student-faculty ratio is 12 to 1, which is excellent for a public university (and better than many private colleges). An administrator says, "When you walk into a classroom, that person in the front is a professor. What a novel idea!" Students say that professors teach all their courses, while graduate teaching assistants lead weekly discussion sections for the largest lecture courses.

Incoming students get a premajor faculty adviser whom they must meet with three times in the first semester. Later on, students get faculty advisers from within their major departments. A student says, "We're able to get whatever we need from the process."

For all its emphasis on teaching, William and Mary does place pressure on faculty to publish, and the occasional beloved teacher doesn't get tenure because he has failed to produce articles. Still, a professor says that the college makes it clear that faculty focus should be on the students—in the classroom and the laboratory: "W&M doesn't have a 'Research First' policy."

Some of the best professors mentioned by students include Phil Kearns in computer science; George Greenia in modern languages and medieval and Renaissance studies; Clay

Clemens and George Grayson in government; Charles Johnson in mathematics; Sarah Stafford in economics, public policy, and law; Hans von Baeyer and Robert Welsh (both emeritus) in physics; and John Conlee and Kim Wheatley in English.

William and Mary has respectable foreign language offerings and many opportunities for international study. At W&M, one can take Arabic, Chinese, French, German, Greek and Latin, Hebrew, Italian, Japanese, Russian, and Spanish. The college sponsors more than 30 study-abroad programs in 23 countries and gives students access to hundreds more through other schools. Perhaps most interesting is a new joint-degree program beginning in 2011 with the University of St. Andrews in Scotland. Admitted students will spend two years at each school and earn a diploma bearing the insignia of both.

Student Life: Nerds who know how to relax

The 1,200-acre William and Mary campus is located just off the grounds of colonial Williamsburg. The main part of the William and Mary campus—the part where guides naturally spend the bulk of the tour—is an extension of the colonial style of the surrounding town.

Three-quarters of the student body live on campus. William and Mary guarantees housing only for freshmen and seniors, and seniors often prefer to live off campus anyway. Students who want campus housing tend to get it. Freshmen live together in all-first-year dorms. Campus dormitories are coed by wing or floor, but Greek housing remains single sex. One benefit of the school's honor code is that at the beginning of the year, students and their RAs make their own decisions about campus living spaces—voting on when quiet hours are, visitation rules, etc. The dormitories are generally nothing to write home about; the coveted lodges, cottage-style houses in a central campus location that each house seven people, are always the first to be chosen in the housing lottery. "The new Jamestown dorms and the renovated Bryan complex are now quite popular," remarks one student. The off-campus

An administrator says of William and Mary: "When you walk into a classroom, that person in the front is a professor. What a novel idea!"

Ludwell apartments are growing in popularity as well, housing mostly juniors and seniors.

The Department of Women's Studies is active on campus, and one of its pet projects is Mosaic House, a full wing of the Jamestown Dorm. W&M's Office of Diversity and Community Initiatives oversees programs such as the Celebration of Cultures and talks entitled "What's Your Gay Point Average?" In general, the most active political groups on campus are on the left, including the LAMBDA alliance, which holds a Gay, Lesbian, Bisexual, and Transgender Awareness Week. (Some more conservative Virginians are known to call the school "William and Larry" because of its supposedly high Gay Point Average.) There is a branch of the NAACP as well as a group called the African American Male Coalition, which "focuses on black empowerment." Student publications include *jump!*, the *DoG Street Journal*, the *Winged Nation*, and the *Flat Hat*.

SUGGESTED CORE

1. Classical Studies 316, The Voyage of the Hero in Greek and Roman Literature—The Classic Epic
2. Philosophy 231, Greek Philosophy
3. English 310, Literature and the Bible
4. Religion 332, Religion and Society in the Medieval West
5. Government 304, Survey of Political Theory: The Modern Tradition
6. English 205, An Introduction to Shakespeare
7. History 121, American History to 1877
8. History 392, Intellectual History of Modern Europe

Conservative groups are in a distinct minority. These include the Students for Life and the popular College Republicans—but they are generally "quiet," says one student. Not so the *Virginia Informer,* which frequently battles with the administration and was named the 2009 best paper of the year by the Collegiate Network. Another student notes that the law-school-student-led John Locke Society on campus also garners respect among conservatives. "The JLS is a conservative and classical-liberal philosophical group that seeks to inform the intellectual and political debate on the W&M campus," a student explains.

Fraternities at William and Mary are mostly residential. About a quarter of students participate. But students say Greek life has an even stronger presence on campus than this statistic indicates. Weekend frat parties are popular and are open to the entire student body. Greek organizations host fund-raisers for charity, says one student, "that often take the form of laid-back Saturday afternoon sports tournaments." Another student speaks of Greek life on campus, explaining that "ongoing incidents related to alcohol consumption or property destruction have led to several fraternities losing their housing or charters in the past few years." The school has increased its efforts to stem underage drinking. Yet, by banning alcohol at regular events, the college has inadvertently driven many students to resort to private binges. One student notes, however, that underage drinking is usually addressed immediately by authorities. "The campus police deal with a heavy hand," the student says. Currently it is a matter of policy that a fraternity must report to the administration whether it intends to have a "wet" or "dry" party; if the party is "wet," the revelers can expect a heavy police presence.

Religious activities are fairly popular on campus, with interdenominational groups remaining the largest. There are more than 30 religious clubs, ranging from Quaker to Catholic, Hindu to Hillel. A student says, "A lot of the major religious denominations are about as close to campus as you can get without actually being on campus. Some students will drive a distance for services they might prefer elsewhere, but for the most part worship is easily accessible." Another says, "There is a really vibrant religious community within Williamsburg and William and Mary, especially if you are Christian; Catholicism is the largest represented religion here; Catholics are very active and do a lot in the college community." Some 75 percent of students are involved in community service projects.

A student says that support for the athletic program is generally good. W&M athletes, the Tribe, have some of the highest graduation rates in NCAA Division I sports. Aside from the 23 varsity sports programs, W&M also has plenty of club and intramural teams, with a high percentage of the student body participating in sports.

According to one student, the typical William and Mary undergrad is "nerdy and dedicated to his studies but able to relax." Students report that because of their workload, they must be driven to have a social life. One student acknowledges that the curriculum's rigor has led to the perception that W&M students are bookworms. "There's a reputation at W&M, I guess, that on any given Saturday soon after classes begin, you'll find students packing the libraries to study," the student admits. "That's a little exaggeration, but I think students generally try to keep up with their studies." He adds, "I would not say that W&M is a party school—we have more of a scholarly focus. But if people want to come here and have an active social life, there are plenty of opportunities."

William and Mary boasts a low crime rate, mostly because of its setting but also because of the honor code and the prevailing atmosphere of trust. "I don't walk by myself at night at three in the morning on the weekend," a female student says, "but we're no better or worse than any campus. I've never felt unsafe." The college reported in 2011 eight forcible sex offenses, one robbery, one aggravated assault, seven vehicle thefts, and 29 burglaries on campus.

For a school of its caliber, William and Mary is an excellent value for Virginians, who in 2012–13 paid only $13,570; out-of-state students paid $37,344. Room and board averaged $8,600. Some 29 percent of students get need-based aid. The college covers most Virginia residents' demonstrated financial shortfalls, and the average graduate of W&M owed a moderate $24,344 in student loans. Undergraduates can also take advantage of a financial-aid program called Gateway William and Mary. This program is a combination of institutional, state, and federal grants for students from low- and middle-income families who display academic promise.

STRONG SUITS

- Strong general-education requirements for a public university.
- Mandates for English, history, and government majors are solid.
- Good programs in biology, classical studies, economics, history, anthropology, geology, physics, religion, and the School of Business.
- Excellent student-faculty ratio; only professors teach.
- Good, helpful advising program.
- Accessible professors and mostly hardworking students.

WEAK POINTS

- Ideological teachers in political science, sociology, religion, and economics.
- Budget cuts have made some important courses hard to get into.
- Strong gay activist and feminist contingent on campus.
- Some alcohol problems have led to strict policies that have driven drinking underground.

George Mason University

Fairfax, Virginia • www.gmu.edu

Freedom U.

George Mason University was founded in 1957 as a branch of the University of Virginia and became independent in 1972, thriving in the sciences and technical fields, especially in serving the graduate students who constitute almost 20 percent of the student body.

The school has amassed an impressive faculty, including some of the country's leading free-market economists. For such a young university, it is quickly reaching a critical mass, attracting students who seek both a fairly traditional education and college environment, even as they mingle with an ethnic cross section of the Global Village.

Academic Life: Back to basics

GMU has an impressive economics department, sufficient solid courses for students to obtain a sound liberal arts education, and some state-of-the-art facilities. All this is available to Virginia students at a relative bargain, despite recent increases in tuition. The university is governed by the surprisingly powerful and traditionally conservative GMU Board of Visitors, which has often been at odds with the school's faculty senate. Precisely because of limited input from faculty, GMU has retained a moderately strong general-education program. One student says, "The general-education program at George Mason is superb. It ensures that dedicated students will be exposed to a wide variety of disciplines, producing well-rounded, informed individuals with global perspective and proficiency in subjects outside the specialized fields."

Students who want more structure may opt for one of the university's alternative educational paths. One of these tracks, Mason Topics, directs freshmen through the general-education requirements according to a particular theme. On-campus students stay together on "living/learning" floors in the residence halls. They attend films and lectures together and form study groups. Each group has its own theme, such as the Global Village, the American Experience, the Information Society, or the Classical Presence. Another path is the interdisciplinary New Century College. One who followed it says, "I encourage all students, especially conservatives, to avoid New Century College. It remains politicized and out of touch with reality." But others speak favorably of New Century, with one student saying, "Its discussion-based environment is definitely the most informative and enlightening. . . . It has caused me to stretch my learning beyond my major and to integrate the different areas of my learning into cohesive projects," such as crafting an academic website.

Upon arrival, students are appointed professional advisers, moving on to faculty members upon choosing their majors. The advising process is a mixed bag. "Professors tend to be very accessible and warm," says one student. But another complains, "I don't feel like my adviser cares about my success. . . . I am pretty sure that if he saw me walking on campus, he wouldn't even be able to tell you that I was one of his students." Professors, for their part, complain of students who don't take advantage of opportunities for interaction. One professor says, "I have office hours every week, and fewer than 10 students come to see me during the semester."

Elite students may fulfill their general-education requirements through the honors program (offered by invitation only), which offers smaller classes and greater access to top faculty. Students are given access to the best resources and faculty on campus, as well as their own lounge and computer lab, priority registration, and their own floor in university residences. Through an integrated curriculum

VITAL STATISTICS

Religious affiliation: *none*
Total enrollment: *24,004*
Total undergraduates:
20,653
SAT CR/Verbal midrange:
520–630
SAT Math midrange:
530–630
ACT midrange: *23–28*
Applicants: *17,621*
Applicants accepted: *55%*
Accepted applicants who
enrolled: *28%*
Tuition (general/out of
state): *$25,154*
Tuition (in state): *$9,620*
Room and board: *$9,250*
Freshman retention rate:
86%
Graduation rate (4 yrs.): *41%*
Graduation rate (6 yrs.): *66%*
Courses with fewer than 20
students: *32%*
Student-faculty ratio: *16:1*
Courses taught by graduate
students: *not provided*
Students living on campus:
28%
Students in fraternities: *8%*
Students in sororities: *9%*
Students receiving need-
based financial aid: *61%*
Avg. student-loan debt of a
recent graduating class:
$25,822
Most popular majors: *business/marketing, English, social sciences*
Guaranteed housing for 4
years? *yes*

CAMPUS POLITICS: GREEN LIGHT

Students report that outside of a few unduly politicized departments, professors strive for balanced teaching and an atmosphere of genuine tolerance. Another student says, "George Mason is one of the most diverse campuses in the world. There is a wide range of professors in all political spectrums and religious backgrounds. From my experience, the classroom has always been one of free and vigorous debate." Another student concurs: "George Mason, although being one of the most conservative schools in the country, still makes all students feel welcome and is still relatively liberal compared to the nation as a whole."

With numerous outlets for libertarian interests, including various institutes, think tanks, the economics department, and the mostly conservative board of visitors, one professor reports: "Openness to conservative ideas in areas such as law, economics, and public policy make George Mason an unusually good fit for students with rightward leanings and practical policy interests." A student agrees: "I have noticed more vocal conservative students and a comparatively open environment toward all political viewpoints." GMU houses the Institute for Humane Studies, which promotes the study of freedom in the conviction that greater understanding of human affairs and freedom fosters peace, prosperity, and social harmony. IHS offers scholarships, grants, internships, and seminars to students at GMU and across the country.

of interdisciplinary courses, honors students "learn to probe the foundations of knowledge, develop new skills in addressing complex issues, and think independently, imaginatively, and ethically." Unfortunately, many of the recent honors courses seem infused by multiculturalism or other postmodern fads.

The faculty is especially impressive at GMU. One student claims, "Mason is effective at recruiting top talent, as evidenced by the experts representing us in fields such as economics, neuroscience, conflict resolution, and politics. They are attracted to GMU's spirit of creativity, exploration, and independence." But some of the more than 60 majors offered by George Mason attract better scholars than others. The English department, for instance, has garnered criticism for, in the words of one student, "replacing courses that examine individual genius with those that examine culture (for example, African American literature) in a sad, egalitarian effort." The course descriptions for English, and a faculty that includes a number of experts in gender studies, minority literature, and pop culture, support this assessment. Still, the department has left room for interesting courses in writing and rhetoric as well as solid literature courses. Novelist Alan Cheuse, who teaches creative writing, is among the most esteemed of the English department faculty.

Once students declare their majors, they face varying departmental requirements. Political science majors, fittingly, must take an American constitutional theory class. English majors must take a survey course on writing and literature and at least one class in literature before 1800; in literature before 1915; in popular, folkloric, or minority literature and culture; and an upper-level elective. Unfortunately, it is possible for English majors to avoid Shakespeare and British literature altogether. History majors must take two courses in U.S. history; two in European history; two in global, Latin American, African, Asian, and/or Middle Eastern history; a course titled "Introduction to the Historical Method"; a senior seminar in history; and four electives. As in English, students can avoid important areas of the discipline if they really want to.

Most of George Mason's politicized departments can be found in the social and behavioral sciences, from which students must take one course; this area includes sociology, psychology, anthropology, and women's studies. And in a different sense, politics is present in George Mason's economics department—which is staunchly free market. One of its faculty says proudly, "The economics department is clearly the best freedom-oriented department in the world. It also houses many of the leading econ bloggers." There are a number of big guns on staff. Led for years by chairman Donald Boudreaux, who just stepped down, the department includes leading theorists of the Chicago, Austrian, and Public Choice schools of free-market economics. The faculty, according to another professor, "deliberately ignores political correctness and the conventional economic wisdom." One student says, "The most impressive thing about our school is, hands down, the economics department." The resulting curriculum is described by one student as "diverse and challenging but also fun." Besides Boudreaux and Nobel laureate James Buchanan (emeritus), other excellent professors in the department include James Bennett, Peter Boettke, Bryan Caplan, Tyler Cowen, Garett Jones, Dan Klein, Peter Leeson, David Levy, Thomas Rustici, Alexander Tabarrok, Gordon Tullock (emeritus), Richard Wagner, and Walter Williams. Many of these are nationally known as cutting-edge scholars heavily invested in their research—an investment that actually transfers into the classroom: "The best aspect of emphasizing research at GMU is that it translates directly into teaching material," says a graduate student.

> "The general-education program at George Mason is superb. It ensures that dedicated students will be exposed to a wide variety of disciplines, producing well-rounded, informed individuals."

Other top teachers at George Mason include Robert Ehrlich in physics; John Orens in history; Hugh Sockett in public and international affairs; and Charlie Jones and Steven Weinberger in linguistics.

GMU does sponsor many trips and study-abroad programs, including ongoing opportunities to visit Belize, Cambodia, Costa Rica, eastern Europe, Ecuador, Egypt, England, Greece and Turkey, India, Ireland, Israel and Palestine, Italy, Kenya, Mexico, Nicaragua, South America, Switzerland, Spain, and Syria. As for foreign languages, students may minor in Chinese, classical studies, French, German, Japanese studies, Russian, or Spanish. Students may major in foreign languages, with a concentration in either French or Spanish.

Student Life: Achieving critical mass

The GMU campus lies only 15 minutes by rail from downtown Washington, D.C., which offers all the nightlife, social opportunities, and historical interest any student could wish

SUGGESTED CORE

1. Classics 340, Greek and Roman Epic
2. Philosophy 301, History of Western Philosophy: Ancient
3. Religion 371 / 381, Classic Jewish Texts / Beginnings of Christianity
4. Religion 316, Christian Thought and Practice
5. Government 324, Modern Western Political Theory
6. English 322, Shakespeare
7. History 121, Formation of the American Republic
8. History 102, Development of Western Civilization

for. Once mainly a commuter school, GMU is today, as a professor notes, "the largest residential college in Virginia." A transfer student from out of state says, "New residential buildings are popping up all over campus, and it is becoming a more friendly place for traditional full-time college students. . . . Also opening in this same area was a new dining hall and a 24-hour Starbucks. Southside, the new dining hall, was a major upgrade from the old one that was located in the ugliest building on campus. In addition, two new fitness centers equipped with basketball courts, weight rooms, treadmills, and the like opened this past year to accommodate the increasing number of residential students. More campus housing is scheduled to open this fall, equipped with new dining options that include a New York–style pizzeria."

As the living environment blossoms, so does student life. "The Housing Office at GMU does an excellent job of promoting community for the students who live on campus," says one of these students. "There are events going on every day in residential areas. All the resident advisers are required to do at least three or four events a month for their floors alone. There are so many housing events going on that they often overlap—these events are specifically for resident students. I've personally seen residents on the same floor get very close with each other by attending the different programs on campus."

Still, three-fourths of students live off campus. For them, a student says, "there are other Mason-wide events going on almost every single day. GMU is such a fun campus, with so many things going on that one would have a hard time feeling like he/she does not belong." Less than 10 percent of students belong to Greek organizations, which nevertheless, according to students, form the hub of a burgeoning social life on campus. As one freshman wrote in an online forum, "If you are an out-of-state student, you're going to want to make friends right off the bat. It really becomes like a ghost town around here on the weekends. If you're a guy, join a frat or else parties are going to be almost impossible for you to get into." Campus parties tend to center around pre- and postgame celebrations of the school's popular basketball team.

Much of student life organizes itself around a network of more than 200 organizations. Economics-related organizations are highly rated, including an Adam Smith reading group, led by Professor Dan Klein, and the GMU Economics Society. Says a member of the latter: "I personally discovered all of my best friends in it."

Religious ministries range widely, including Muslim, Jewish, Catholic, and a wide variety of other Christian chaplaincies. Conservative-minded believers should investigate the Fellowship of Catholic University Students (FOCUS), Chi Alpha Christian Fellowship, Christians on Campus, or Cru (formerly Campus Crusade for Christ).

Political groups include the (far-left) Students for a Democratic Society, Animal

Rights Collective, College Democrats, College Republicans, Feminist Student Association, and the gay-oriented Pride Alliance.

Some of the most visible groups are nonpolitical organizations directed at students from specific countries, such as the Indian Student Association, and almost every conceivable religion is represented on campus. However, not all celebration of ethno-religious diversity at GMU is spontaneous and student driven. In addition to the Office of Equity and Diversity Services, the school spends money on an Office of Diversity Programs and Services, a Multicultural Research and Resource Center, a Black Peer Counseling Program, and a Women's Studies Research and Resource Center—all of which engage in the same hodgepodge of counseling, workshops, sensitivity training, and lectures devoted to feminism, racism, sexism, classism, homophobia, and other varieties of contemporary groupthink.

The university has several athletic fields, and the Patriot Center seats 10,000 for indoor sports (and rock concerts), an impressive number given that only 250 athletes compete in the 20 men's and women's NCAA Division I sports programs. Mason's Patriots men's basketball team is the star athletic attraction, one of the top-ranked teams in the country; it made the Final Four in 2006, and in 2007–8 it went as champion of the CAA conference to the NCAA tournament. Other varsity teams include baseball, cross-country, golf, lacrosse, rowing, soccer, softball, swimming and diving, tennis, indoor and outdoor track and field, volleyball, and wrestling—but no football. Many intramural sports are also available. The 26 club sports encompass everything from underwater hockey to bowling.

Crime is not unknown on the George Mason campus. In 2011 the school reported eight forcible sex offenses and 31 burglaries. Such security problems have led to an on-campus escort service and "lots of police." Despite that, one professor says, "Everyone here feels quite safe." Students agree. Says one young woman: "I never get worried walking around at night."

GMU's undergraduate tuition for the 2012–13 term was $9,620 for Virginia residents and $25,154 for out-of-state students. Room and board averaged $9,250. Admissions are need blind, but the school does not guarantee to match each applicant's need. The average student-loan debt of a 2012 graduate was $25,822.

STRONG SUITS	WEAK POINTS
• For a public university, quite solid general-education requirements. • Nationally renowned, free-market-oriented economics department. • A strong honors option. • Largely apolitical classrooms, with free discussion of many viewpoints.	• Advising is called anemic and unhelpful. • Ideological content infuses English, sociology, psychology, anthropology, women's studies, and many recent honors classes. • Students rarely seek out professors for advice.

University of Virginia

Charlottesville, Virginia • www.virginia.edu

So Long as Reason Is Left Free

Thomas Jefferson founded the school known as UVA (just "VuhGINyuh" in the South) in 1819 and designed the stately grounds himself. Thanks in part to a $4.7 billion endowment, UVA has withstood funding decreases better than many institutions. And despite the ubiquitous diversity and sustainability concerns that seem to preoccupy every major institution of higher learning today, it is still true that at Mr. Jefferson's university, many top-notch professors busy themselves with the "enduring questions," and bright students take academics (or at least their grades) very seriously.

Academic Life: Eschew the SWAG

The intellectual quest envisioned by Jefferson is best represented today at his university by the Echols Scholars program. Students in this honors program comprise almost 10 percent of undergraduates in the College of Arts and Sciences; elite incoming freshmen are invited to join. Echols Scholars live together in their first year, register early for classes, and are exempt from distribution requirements. Echols scholars are usually high-achieving, career-oriented students, and their natural affinity for learning coupled with regular advising generally prevents them from misusing this complete curricular freedom. Yet some report being bored: "I didn't have to take any required classes, so I was never 'stretched'" intellectually, says one recent graduate.

Another choice for ambitious students is the bachelor of arts with honors program. UVA, unlike other universities, does not award honors to graduating students based on grade point average. Rather, students must apply to pursue a course of independent study for their third and fourth years of college, during which time they study under departmental tutors. Candidates are evaluated by visiting examiners from other colleges and universities and may receive degrees with "honors," "high honors," or "highest honors" as the only grades for two years of work, or else they may be recommended for an ordinary BA—or no degree at all. Students who wish to be considered for a degree with distinction must apply to the distinguished major program of their departments. A senior thesis is usually required, and admission to these programs is selective in most departments. Achievement of a 3.4 GPA and completion of the program requirements result in the award.

Still another option, for those students seeking a liberal arts education in a smaller setting, is the University of Virginia's College at Wise, whose course offerings and general-education requirements are better than those on the university's main campus. Classes in the English department at Wise include "Western Literary Tradition," "Arthurian Literature," and "Shakespeare: The Early Plays." Instead of a feminism course, there is one on "Intellectual History of the United States."

The university does not have a core curriculum, and its distribution requirements are so vague that a student would have to work hard not to fulfill them by graduation. Even the 12 credits (three or four classes) of natural sciences and mathematics are difficult to miss, given that the departments under that rubric range from astronomy to economics to environmental sciences.

More structure is provided within the majors. The top-ranked English department, for example, requires its students to take two pre-1800 courses, a 400-level seminar, and a three-course sequence on the history of literature in English. An English professor says, "We're full of postcolonial theory, currently very fashionable, but we're also

VITAL STATISTICS

Religious affiliation: *none*
Total enrollment: *24,297*
Total undergraduates: *15,762*
SAT CR/Verbal midrange: *610–720*
SAT Math midrange: *630–740*
ACT midrange: *28–32*
Applicants: *23,587*
Applicants accepted: *33%*
Accepted applicants who enrolled: *48%*
Tuition (general/out of state): *$38,018*
Tuition (in state): *$12,006*
Room and board: *$9,419*
Freshman retention rate: *97%*
Graduation rate (4 yrs.): *87%*
Graduation rate (6 yrs.): *93%*
Courses with fewer than 20 students: *53%*
Student-faculty ratio: *16:1*
Courses taught by graduate students: *not provided*
Students living on campus: *43%*
Students in fraternities: *33%*
Students in sororities: *33%*
Students receiving need-based financial aid: *33%*
Avg. student-loan debt of a recent graduating class: *$20,951*
Most popular majors: *business/marketing, economics, psychology*
Guaranteed housing for 4 years? *yes*

CAMPUS POLITICS: GREEN LIGHT

"UVA is itself liberal, but it is located in the Bible Belt with a large Christian contingent," reports one professor. "It also has a tradition of civility. The broader political climate and the tradition of civility mean that the institution is fairly tolerant toward conservatives on the faculty and in the student body."

The school has become more tolerant of free speech. The Foundation for Individual Rights in Education (FIRE) gives UVA its "green light" rating for having cleaned up its speech codes. A FIRE press release says, "While more than two-thirds of the nation's colleges maintain policies that clearly and substantially restrict freedom of speech, UVA is now a proud exception, having fully reformed four speech codes."

The administration is prone to a treacly kind of piety. One of Teresa Sullivan's first university-wide events as president was a Day of Dialogue decreed in response to a 2010 off-campus murder of a UVA student. The event included faculty, students, and staff in "discussion groups," as well as a "public art project" for the university community. An art and architecture professor designed a work that she said "expresses movement from the darkness of mourning to the lightness of healing and change." As the school website reports, "It begins with the Rotunda's columns being veiled in black, diaphanous fabric in the days leading up to [the Day of Dialogue]. 'This represents the university community's shared experience of grief and loss,'" said the artist. "When the veils are rolled back, the gleaming white columns once again will reveal all that they symbolize about Thomas Jefferson's learning community."

very strong in traditional areas such as Shakespeare and medieval literature." Another professor notes that "while the department is quite strong, it offers comparatively very little in the way of theory compared to Michigan or Duke." High praise indeed.

In religious studies, students must take three courses in a single religious tradition, two courses in another creed, one course in a third, and a senior-level majors' seminar. With 33 full-time faculty members and nine joint members, the department is the largest of its kind among public universities in the United States. Its undergraduate program has been highly rated for years.

History majors must take one course in pre-1700 Europe; one in post-1700 Europe; one in U.S. history, which could be as specialized as "History of the Civil Rights Movement"; two courses in a choice of African, East Asian, Latin American, Middle Eastern, or Southeast Asian history; and a major seminar. Five courses remain to complete the major, but no more than six courses can be from any one field of study.

The 30-credit requirements in the political science major include (in the government track) one class in American politics; one in comparative politics; one in international relations; and one in political theory; in addition to 12 credits in related disciplines such as history, philosophy, and social science.

Well-regarded disciplines at UVA besides English and religious studies include history, art history, economics, and Classics. However, one professor did warn us that "the humanities are overwhelmingly liberal" and "do not take seriously" the Great Books and ideas of the West. A student adds, "The problem is that, in the liberal arts, the syllabi largely determine the class conversation, and sometimes you can't help but 'talk liberal' when you're reading liberal rhetoric." Another adds, "Generally, I'd stay away from SWAG (Studies in Women and Gender), education, sociology, and African studies."

The McIntire School of Commerce is solid; one recent Echols scholar calls it "probably the best department," and it was recently ranked second in the nation among undergraduate business schools by *Bloomberg Businessweek*. On the other hand, the mathematics department, an insider says, "is mediocre nationally. Majors will learn very well but won't be working with the nation's leading scholars."

Professors highly recommended by students include Steven Rhoads, John M. Owen, and Larry Sabato in politics; James D. Hunter and William Bradford Wilcox in sociology; Edwin Burton and Kenneth Elzinga in economics; Paul Barolsky in art history; Jenny Clay and John Miller in Classics; Charles Robert Marsh Jr., Vanessa L. Ochs, Robert Wilken (emeritus), Vigen Guroian, and William Wilson in religious studies; Gordon Braden and Paul Cantor in English; Gary Gallagher, Michael Holt (emeritus), and Jon Lendon in history; David Herman in Slavic languages and literatures; and Louis Nelson in architecture.

The UVA advising program is described by students as rather meager. Each student is appointed an academic adviser before he arrives on campus, whom he can replace after choosing a major; all advisers are teaching faculty.

UVA students do tend to be serious, the type who worry that a 15-hour course load makes them look like underachievers and who haggle with professors over B-pluses. Grade inflation is consequently a problem. Bias is also an issue, as one student tells us: "I have heard of students in the politics departments having papers marked down for their conservative views." Still, "economics is taught from what may be a slightly right-of-center viewpoint," according to a recent graduate. One student reports that political biases "certainly do" affect course content in some departments. Students recommend a close reading of course syllabi and using the two-week trial period each semester to drop a class if necessary.

> A professor warns that "the humanities are overwhelmingly liberal" and "do not take seriously" the Great Books and ideas of the West.

Students are highly career oriented. "Everyone's pretty keyed up here about grades. It's a pretty intensely success-centered environment," says one. Another notes, "There is a high percentage of 'go-getters' who are often arrogant." One professor says that UVA students are "more careerist" than those he taught at two other esteemed public universities. Another faculty member reports, "Most students do not seem to be interested in the material for its own sake." On the other hand, another professor states that many of his students "are more grounded than their peers at other universities. They tend not to get carried away."

Introductory courses are large. They are taught by professors, but the smaller discussion sections are usually taught by graduate teaching assistants. Once students reach the sophomore and junior levels, class sizes shrink significantly to 20 or 30 students. Even in large courses, professors endeavor to be friendly and accessible, particularly to students

SUGGESTED CORE

1. Classics 204, Greek Mythology
2. Philosophy 2110, History of Philosophy: Ancient and Medieval
3. Religious Studies 1210/1220, Hebrew Bible: Old Testament/New Testament and Early Christianity
4. Religious Studies 2050, The Rise of Christianity
5. Politics 3020, Modern Political Theory
6. English 2550, Shakespeare
7. History 2001, American History to 1865
8. History 3802, Origins of Contemporary Thought

who exhibit an eagerness to learn. University Seminars (USEMs) are offered to freshmen as a way to connect students with faculty. These once-weekly courses are kept to about 20 students and taught by esteemed professors. Unfortunately, they can be highly specialized and politically biased, since they are often used to introduce students to the professor's current research.

Reportedly, professors really are concerned about their students, but as one teacher says, "When only 10 to 15 percent of the students care about what they are learning, it is tough." Another student adds, "A lot of our professors do care, and in fact complain that not enough students visit their office hours. Professors almost always teach classes, with very rare exceptions."

UVA can arrange for students to study practically anywhere in the world through the International Studies Office. The school sponsors its own programs on five continents. Foreign language programs offered include Asian and Middle Eastern, Classics, ESL, French, German, Italian, Portuguese, Slavic, and Spanish.

Student Life: Tippling with the wahoos

First-years are required to live on campus in dorms. The dorms are generally grouped into "old" and "new," the former being closer to central campus, with the latter offering more amenities. Housing in the first-year dorms is sex segregated by floor or by suite. Upperclassmen residential assistants run first-year orientation, which is mostly a recounting of university regulations but does include a sensitivity-training program.

UVA has three residential colleges. Hereford is the largest and houses about 250 students, most of whom live in single rooms. The 200 residents of Brown College—who are said to be quirky—live closest to the central "grounds" (UVA lingo for campus) but have to share their rooms. The newest residential college, IRC, is organized along the lines of parliamentary government, with elected officials. All the colleges are modeled on the residential experience at Yale, Oxford, and Cambridge. They offer community meals and house faculty members alongside students. Upperclassmen may move off campus, and many do.

UVA offers more than 980 active student organizations. Popular groups include Madison House, a center for various service projects; University Guide Services, students who give tours of UVA; singing groups; First-Year Players, a theater troupe; student government; Honor Committee; and a wide variety of Christian and other religious groups. Catholic students attend the nearby parish of St. Thomas Aquinas—whose webpage, we note with alarm, features folks playing guitars in church. There is a group called Catholic Student Ministry associated with the church; do not confuse it with the group called "Catholics United," which is for LGBT Catholics.

The school boasts a number of "secret societies," most of which are philanthropic in nature. (If any are misanthropic, they aren't telling.) The school's official newspaper is the *Cavalier Daily*. Student-run publications include some on the left, such as the *Yellow Journal* and the *Declaration,* as well as the conservative *Virginia Advocate.*

The Queer Student Union and Queer and Allied Activism are among UVA's several highly active gay groups on campus. One student informs us, "There are some conservatives on campus, but the racial groups and Queer Alliance groups are gaining enough power to silence many of them." Minority and ethnic organizations are abundant. According to one student, "The Far Left learned that 'de-Westernization' of the curriculum doesn't get far, so it started peddling 'internationalization.' There is also massive institutional support for groups like the Muslim Students Association, whose members can be anti-American. Conservative students are not as fearful here as they are at schools like Columbia, but being openly conservative is not the norm." The university has a handful of conservative or classically liberal organizations, including the Liberty Coalition, an umbrella group of libertarian-leaning clubs, and the College Republicans. One student suggests that, overall, UVA "is a school with an immense silent conservative faction . . . who are more engaged in Greek life, the Commerce school, et cetera."

UVA's persistent preservation of its single-sanction Code of Honor in the face of periodic challenges is another indication of a deference for tradition and perhaps even an innate conservatism, at least in the student body. The Honor Council is a student-run manifestation of the Code of Honor, established in 1842. If a student is convicted of lying, cheating, or stealing, the only possible penalty is expulsion from the university. Some students recently have had their degrees revoked after graduation. Most students take the code seriously, and exams are often unproctored.

At UVA, there has been a great emphasis on "diversity," mostly focused on race. Multiple diversity centers are located in the Student Union, and the administration has pushed a "black ribbon of tolerance" ("like the red ribbon for AIDS," says a student) campaign. According to one student, "there is definitely pointless diversity for diversity's sake." While the administration seems concerned about race relations, most of the students do not. Students admit that self-segregation is an issue on campus; the lower, older part of campus is 90 percent white and is the location for most of the Greek activity. The upper campus is much more diverse, and since foreign students tend to gravitate to that location, the ethnic clustering has taken on a self-perpetuating quality.

Sports, especially in the South, are considered a big part of the college experience, and this is true at UVA. The Cavaliers won NCAA championships in women's rowing and men's soccer last year and consistently field strong teams in tennis, lacrosse, field hockey, and women's basketball and soccer. Performance in the big-time sports of men's basketball and football has been less stellar in recent years. The university sponsors 12 varsity sports for women and 11 for men. The university recently built a $130 million basketball venue, the John Paul Jones Arena, even as "our academic buildings fall down around our ears," according to one professor.

In the old days, UVA was famous up and down the East Coast as a party school, and though the administration has done much to change that, UVA students manage still to have a lot of authorized and unauthorized fun. Students call themselves Wahoos, after the fish that supposedly can drink twice its weight. Although a third of the student body goes Greek, parties on Rugby Road are the center of attention on weekend (and some weekday) nights. One professor tells us "that the hookup culture is alive and well at UVA. Very little 'dating' in its proper sense actually occurs." Except, surprisingly, at football games, where the men show up looking like Virginia gentlemen in orange coat and ties, and the women don sundresses and pearls.

Charlottesville, a relatively small city, has experienced some high-profile crimes. One student informs us that "at least a few students get assaulted each year by people in the ghetto right next to school." Another student adds, "Programs to help students get rides at night are a big help." In 2011 the school reported 13 forcible sexual assaults, 54 burglaries, 16 automotive thefts, and one robbery.

If you're from Virginia, UVA is a real bargain: 2012–13 in-state tuition was only $12,006. For out-of-state students, tuition was $38,018, with room and board $9,419. Admissions are need blind, and the school commits to covering the needs of any student who enrolls—and 33 percent of those determined to have financial need received aid. The average student left the school with $20,951 in debt.

STRONG SUITS	WEAK POINTS
• A unique, highly respected honors program subjects students to the highest standards.	• Some programs are heavily politicized, including the prestigious English department, plus studies in women and gender, education, sociology, and African studies.
• Excellent programs in the School of Commerce as well as in English, religious studies, history, art history, economics, and Classics.	• Distributional requirements are far too lax, easy to fulfill.
• A venerable honor code that students treasure and obey.	• Students complain of politically biased grading.
• Students tend to be serious, even overachievers.	• Math department is not nationally prominent.
	• Advising is not very helpful.

University of Washington

Seattle, Washington • www.washington.edu

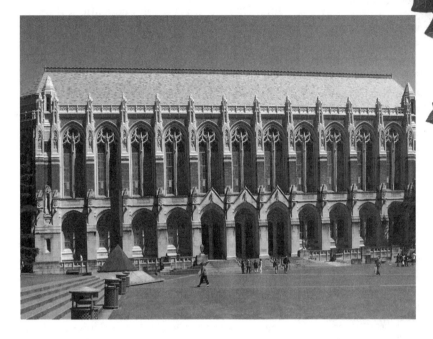

A Niche in Red Square

Founded in 1861, the University of Washington is the largest university in the Northwest and one of the oldest on the West Coast. UW has all the usual advantages of state schools—including affordable in-state tuition and a national reputation—along with all the deficiencies of a large state research university—uneven teaching, a weak core curriculum, inadequate advising, and insufficient housing.

Also predictable are the UW students and faculty who are outspokenly political and politicized, and not just when participating in protests on Red Square, a central campus location where radicalism flourishes. (And yes, it actually is named Red Square.) However, in a school with almost 30,000 undergraduates, there is a niche for everyone, including conservative students desiring a solid liberal arts education.

Academic Life: Classical Greece = lesbian lives

The behemoth known as the University of Washington includes 16 schools and colleges, 12 of which offer degrees for undergraduates. The College of Arts and Sciences, the largest, houses 46 departments, with 868 faculty members offering more than 7,000 classes to more

657

VITAL STATISTICS

Religious affiliation: *none*
Total enrollment: *42,568*
Total undergraduates:
28,933
SAT CR/Verbal midrange:
520–650
SAT Math midrange:
580–700
ACT midrange: *24–30*
Applicants: *26,138*
Applicants accepted: *59%*
Accepted applicants who
enrolled: *39%*
Tuition (general/out of
state): *$28,860*
Tuition (in state): *$11,305*
Room and board: *$9,969*
Freshman retention rate:
93%
Graduation rate (4 yrs.): *56%*
Graduation rate (6 yrs.): *80%*
Courses with fewer than 20
students: *35%*
Student-faculty ratio: *12:1*
Courses taught by graduate
students: *6%*
Students living on campus:
13%
Students in fraternities: *6%*
Students in sororities: *5%*
Students receiving need-
based financial aid: *37%*
Avg. student-loan debt of a
recent graduating class:
$20,800
Most popular majors:
*psychology, biochemistry,
political science*
Guaranteed housing for 4
years? *no*

than 25,000 undergraduates annually. In a school this size, it is not surprising that a student can graduate from U-Dub—as the university is called—with exposure to only a very narrow field of knowledge and a transcript filled with unserious classes taught by mediocre instructors. Or he can get a solid education, if he knows where to find it.

The graduation requirements in the arts and sciences program are vague and unstructured. Hundreds of courses satisfy these requirements, and many courses suit more than one category at the same time. Consequently, the magic word *flexibility* appears frequently in university literature. For instance, to satisfy the Individuals and Societies requirement, students can choose either "Classical Greece" or "Lesbian Lives and Culture."

UW students face entirely too much flexibility. The course catalog is the size of an old-fashioned, big-city phone book. Ideally, an incoming freshman would seek advice from a faculty member on how to make the most of his time at the university, but some students graduate from UW without ever having received advice regarding courses, majors, or their careers after college. The university offers one-size-fits-all advising on selecting courses and majors. Students who have not declared majors can visit the Center for Undergraduate Advising, Diversity, and Student Success, where they make 30-minute appointments with professional advisers, not faculty members. There are upward of 6,000 new students starting each autumn quarter and only 12 premajor advisers. Once students have declared a major, they are assigned departmental advisers, who, according to a specialist in the advising center, are either full-time professional advisers or, more likely, graduate students.

According to a recent graduate, to flourish at the University of Washington, "students must be independent, self-motivated, and ambitious. At UW, you can go to class, go back to your room and play video games for the rest of the day . . . or you can be involved intellectually, socially, and in extracurricular events. It's up to the student."

Because UW has such a large student body, many classes—especially at the introductory level—are huge. These are taught by professors, graduate teaching assistants, or both. In a typical intro-level course, the professor teaches the class two days a week, and students break up into smaller discussion groups led by TAs once a week. "TAs normally grade most papers and exams and generally have a lot more contact with students than the professors do," says one student. Foreign TAs without a working knowledge of English is a common complaint among students. Thankfully, as students begin to specialize in their majors, class sizes grow smaller and students have more opportunities to create relationships with faculty members.

In an effort to ease the transition from high school to an enormous state university, UW offers an option to freshman, the Freshman Interest Group program, which includes optional housing and adds structure to the curriculum while providing a smaller academic community. There is also a Freshman Seminar Program that offers first-year students access to small, discussion-oriented classes, according to the program's website. The seminar topics vary each year, as do their quality. The entering class of 2012 had several seminar options, including "What Makes a Leader?" and "Rock the Archive: Music, Gender, and Digital Archives."

The College of Arts and Sciences has many strong departments. For instance, the philosophy department is solid, emphasizing the philosophy of science, an area in which it has several eminent scholars. Majors take a course in logic; one in modern philosophy, modern political philosophy, or modern ethics; and one in ancient philosophy, ancient political philosophy, or the history of ancient ethics, as well as four other upper-level courses

The history department is said to be more committed to teaching than are some other majors, but the requirements are too broad. History majors must take an "Introduction to History" class; one course each in European, American, and non-Western history; two courses each in premodern and postmodern history; and one senior seminar in historiography or history colloquium.

Students claim there is not much political indoctrination in the classroom unless you are taking courses in one of the more politicized departments. Students say that in addition to the ethnic studies programs and the women's studies department, political science and international studies—particularly Middle East studies—are particularly left wing. A political science major says, "As a conservative Republican, I find myself in the decided

CAMPUS POLITICS: YELLOW LIGHT

A campus journalist at UW once quipped that "15 percent of the student body is liberal, while 10 percent is conservative. Everybody else is pretty much waving in the wind—apathetic or indifferent. The institution, but not necessarily the campus as a whole, is obliging to liberal views." Part of "the institution" is the student government, a group of usually liberal students who nominate their own successors and thus are able to perpetuate their own power and views. One student says that the official campus newspaper, *The Daily*, is an "unabashedly and poorly edited liberal mouthpiece."

Although it is true that the majority of students and faculty are politically and socially liberal, there is a growing conservative presence on the UW campus—including the Young Americans for Liberty, which has steadily grown in the past couple of years. Our sources also tell us that the conservative Greeks exert a disproportionate influence on campus as well.

minority." The political science major covers five broad fields: American politics, comparative politics, international relations, political theory, and political methodology. Majors need to take courses in only three of these subfields. In addition to these classes, poli-sci majors must take three introductory classes and four final courses from the upper-division electives. Economics and business are said to have less ideological faculties.

Every humanities department offers the usual trendy and trivial choices. An English professor says that his department is among the worst in this regard. In his department, students can take courses in "Introduction to Cultural Studies," "Experimental African American Literature," "Dirty Sexy Money: Studies in American Realism and Naturalism," and "American Intersections: The Cultural Production of Race/Gender/Sexuality in 20C U.S."

English major requirements were revised for classes entering after August 2012, and the formerly excellent requirements have become seriously watered down. Students must take an introductory writing course and an introduction to the major, followed by one course each in "theories and methodologies," "forms and genres," and "histories" of language and literature. There is also a required Critical Practice course and a senior capstone course, in addition to 20 credits of required electives. Course options range from "Shakespeare" to "Studies in Popular Culture."

Happily, a cultural and ethnic diversity course requirement has been proposed and rejected several times over the years by UW faculty. An arts and sciences administrator says, "It's still in the works," and the director of the Task Force on Diversity in the Curriculum says she is attempting "to enhance the number of courses on race, ethnicity, gender, class, etc. on campus" even without faculty backing for a diversity requirement. The task force evolved into a full-fledged Center for Curriculum Transformation Project, a university-funded program operating out of the Office of Minority Affairs and Diversity that seeks to develop "courses and curricula that include the study of race, gender, ethnicity, nation and nationhood, class, disability, sexuality and religion and their intersections." The project leads workshops for faculty members on how to incorporate diversity issues into their courses. Topics in 2013 included "Race in the Classroom," "Diversity in the Classroom," and "Infusing Global Learning Goals into the Curriculum," and faculty seminars focus on "diversity pedagogies."

An alternative to the standard Arts and Sciences curriculum is the Interdisciplinary Honors Program, a four-year track during which students take at least one designated honors course per quarter, participate in two experiential learning projects, and keep an ongoing learning portfolio. Eligible students may also choose to participate in Departmental Honors or College Honors—the latter a particularly ambitious program requiring the simultaneous completion of both the Interdisciplinary and Departmental Honors programs in at least one of their majors.

One student in the Interdisciplinary program says, "Honors professors as a breed tend to be a little stranger and some are decidedly better than others." Many of the courses are rigorous—especially the science courses, which are much better than the usual "science for nonscience majors" fare. Another student describes the program as "very intense, with only the most serious students." According to its website, the program offers many perks, including "personalized and comprehensive" academic advising; small classes; special seminars; aid in finding internships and research opportunities; special study-abroad programs; peer mentoring; a designated computer lab; designated residence-hall floors; and several other benefits exclusive to the honors programs.

Recommended professors at UW include Jon Bridgman (emeritus) and James Felak in history; Gerald Baldasty in communication; Keith Leffler (emeritus) in economics; G. Alan Marlat in psychology; David Thouless in physics; Daniel Weld in computer science; and Jonathan Mercer in political science. One upperclassman advises students to check online evaluations before registering for courses; from these, students can often find out how past students have rated faculty and choose their classes accordingly.

UW's Office of International Programs and Exchanges provides guidance for students participating in the university's more than 300 study-abroad programs, on all inhabited continents. At home, students may study any of a long list of languages, from Arabic and American Sign Language to Uygur and Ukrainian.

Student Life: Living in the Emerald City

The University of Washington is too large for stereotypes. With so many students, it is a truly diverse place, including a number of international students, fraternity and sorority members, arts aficionados, environmentalists, and athletes. There is certainly a niche for everyone, with more than 500 registered clubs and organizations, including almost 60 campus ministries (the Muslim Student Association, InterVarsity Christian Fellowship, Baha'i Student Association, Young Life College, Catholic Newman Center, and Hillel, among many others); College Republicans and Young Democrats. Sources say that the student body is overwhelmingly politically and socially liberal, especially when it comes to homosexual and minority entitlement issues.

> As an undergrad at UW, "you can go to class, go back to your room, and play video games for the rest of the day . . . or you can be involved. It's up to the student."

As one professor notes, "The best thing about UW is the location. Seattle is a wonderful town, and the campus, though in a city, is safe, has lots of greenery, and its buildings are readily accessible." Since the school is enormous and most UW students live off campus, some undergrads still find it difficult to attain a comfortable sense of community. As one student reported, "I can walk through the middle of campus and not necessarily see anyone I know." As a result, many students—more than 3,000—opt to join one of UW's 45 fraternities or sororities. Although the Greek residences are private housing facilities, the administration has every fraternity and sorority sign a recognition agreement in which they submit to "certain well-defined rules" (in particular, a pledge to keep residences alcohol-free). Any Greek group that does not abide by the agreement is not officially recognized by the university. In any case, Greek life has kept some students from becoming

Blue Collar Ivy

SUGGESTED CORE

1. Classics 210, Greek and Roman Classics in English
2. Philosophy 320, Ancient Philosophy
3. English 310, Bible as Literature
4. Ancient and Medieval History 360, Medieval Christianity (*closest match*)
5. Political Science 310, The Western Tradition of Political Thought: Modern
6. English 225, Shakespeare
7. History of the Americas 301, Foundations of American Civilization
8. Modern European History 406, European Intellectual History: 19th Century

just a number. "If I had to do it over again, I would have joined a fraternity," says an upperclassman. "They provide a sense of community."

Housing on the UW campus is not guaranteed, even for freshmen. The student housing office attributes this policy to the high demand. In fact, housing is difficult to find off campus, too, because Seattle's cost of living has been rising steadily. The student housing office confesses that "UW is primarily not a residential campus"; only 13 percent of undergraduates live in the university's 16 residence halls and off-campus apartments.

Married couples and same-sex domestic partners are allowed to live together in UW's family housing buildings. In the residence halls, the university offers single, double, and triple units, but there are no single-sex dorm options for undergrads, but students can choose men-only or women-only floors. In many of the residence halls, men and women live next door to one another. However, there are no coed dorm rooms or bathrooms.

Athletics are a fundamental element of student life at UW. The nine men's and 11 women's varsity teams compete in NCAA Division I-A and the Pacific Twelve Conference. Huskies football dominates the fall semester with the unique tradition of tailgating by boat, as UW's Husky Stadium is built on the shores of Lake Washington. In fall 2012 UW began a $250 million remodeling and renovation on the stadium—the most expensive in NCAA history. In 2009 the men's rowing team and the women's softball team won their national championships. The same year, the university's athletic department discontinued the men's and women's swimming programs due to budget cuts.

UW also hosts 19 men's and women's intercollegiate teams and more than 25 intramural and club sports. The Intramural Activities Building houses top-quality athletic facilities, including a state-of-the-art fitness center, five gyms, squash courts, climbing walls, an indoor track, a swimming pool, racquetball/handball courts, multiactivities studios, saunas, an indoor cycling studio, a health food café, outdoor sports fields, 13 tennis courts, and running and walking trails.

UW has a relatively safe campus, despite its large size and urban location. However, the area surrounding UW is not as safe; in fact, according to the *Seattle Times*, nearby University Way is one of the most crime-ridden areas in Seattle. The campus police, an accredited state police force, provides around-the-clock security and surveillance, and the school also offers several escort and shuttle services at night. In 2011 UW reported five forcible sex offenses, three robberies, three aggravated assaults, 40 burglaries, and one car theft.

University of Washington is a bargain for in-state residents, with 2012–13 tuition at $11,305 (out-of-state was $28,860), and room and board $9,969. Thirty-seven percent of UW undergraduates received some form of need-based financial aid and graduated with an average debt of $20,800.

STRONG SUITS	WEAK POINTS
• Philosophy and history departments are notable. • Departmental and college honors programs offer a beefed-up education. • Many foreign language and study-abroad options.	• Sketchy, lax distributional requirements can be fulfilled with politicized fluff. • Outspokenly politicized faculty and student body. • Advising is impersonal and ineffective. • Administration is fixated on diversity. • Graduate teaching assistants—many with halting English—see more of students than professors do.

West Virginia University

Morgantown, West Virginia • www.wvu.edu

Country Roads

West Virginia University is a large land-grant research university founded in 1867. Head-quartered in the small city of Morgantown, the university has several regional campuses and offers more than 185 degree programs at the undergraduate, graduate, and first profes-sional levels. It maintains a medical school and a law school, as well as large programs in engineering and agriculture, and enrolls more than 29,600 students.

Academic Life: Chinese menu

The university does impose a set of general-education requirements for all students to com-plete in addition to their major courses. Students could study classical (Greek and Roman) literature in translation and ancient (Greek) philosophy, but the plethora of options also allows students to meet the requirements with courses on popular movies or "Science Fic-tion in East and West."

Most classes on campus have between 20 and 29 students in them. Some students report that graduate teaching assistants lead lab sections, while professors teach the lec-tures. Still, teachers seem to be approachable and committed to students. "The professors are extremely accessible due to smaller class sizes," says one student. Another says, "The ones I have seem very intent to make sure students understand what needs to be learned. Professors are definitely there in office hours and are helpful," he says.

Every student is assigned a counselor, usually a professor in his own major. "Every time we go through scheduling, they meet with us," a student says. "You have to meet with your adviser before you can register for next semester's classes, so they know you're on track to meet the requirements for your major."

A professor in the College of Business says the university's research and teaching emphases are balanced. "In the finance area, in particular, good theory and good practice go hand in hand," he says. Also, the finance area "provides a rigorous education with caring and thoughtful faculty." This area, he says, is "analytically challenging, with a direct connection to real-world applications in all the areas of finance. It is not an area where casual students will do well with limited effort. Serious students will receive an excellent education and resultant job prospects."

Engineering, forensics, and criminology are said to have excellent departments. "Students from WVU are some of the most recruited by the FBI," says an undergrad. "The engineering department is rigorous, challenging, and almost guarantees students a job after graduation."

"TV journalism is headed by an award-winning lecturer, Gina Dahlia, who works very hard and sincerely to keep up the reputation of the program," says a student in the Perley Isaac Reed School of Journalism. "The PR program has a very active set of students who participate and involve themselves in the school's community. Many graduating from this program gain a lot of experience in the PR field during school." Says a public relations major: "The strongest points of my major are the resources provided to all students in the School of Journalism and the teachers who strive to know each student personally and push them to succeed."

Another student, who is majoring in biology and biochemistry and plans to enter medical school next year, feels there "should have been more human anatomy and physiology courses available to the students."

VITAL STATISTICS

Religious affiliation: *none*
Total enrollment: *29,617*
Total undergraduates: *11,742*
SAT CR/Verbal midrange: *470–570*
SAT Math midrange: *480–590*
ACT midrange: *21–26*
Applicants: *15,815*
Applicants accepted: *85%*
Accepted applicants who enrolled: *37%*
Tuition (general/out of state): *$22,320*
Tuition (in state): *$7,080*
Room and board: *$9,808*
Freshman retention rate: *78%*
Graduation rate (4 yrs.): *33%*
Graduation rate (6 yrs.): *59%*
Courses with fewer than 20 students: *33%*
Student-faculty ratio: *23:1*
Courses taught by graduate students: *not provided*
Students living on campus: *25%*
Students in fraternities: *7%*
Students in sororities: *7%*
Students receiving need-based financial aid: *36%*
Avg. student-loan debt of a recent graduating class: *$24,113*
Most popular majors: *business/marketing, engineering, interdisciplinary studies*
Guaranteed housing for 4 years? *no*

CAMPUS POLITICS: GREEN LIGHT

The Foundation for Individual Rights in Education warns that WVU has policies that "both clearly and substantially restrict . . . freedom of speech." The school made headlines in 2013 when, as the *Daily Caller* reported, a professor prohibited his students from citing Fox News (along with *The Onion*) as sources in papers for his class: "The tagline 'Fox News' makes me cringe. Please do not subject me to this biased news station. I would almost rather you print off an article from *The Onion*."

But students and professors we interviewed said the political environment is relatively open and that there isn't a pervasive atmosphere of self-censorship. "Our environment is very open to the professional, candid, and cordial exchange of ideas," says one professor. "I don't think conservative or religious students would feel unwelcome," says a student. "You see both sides of a liberal, free environment and political correctness. Right out of our student center, the Mountain Lair, is the 'free-speech zone.' Twice last semester I saw a man with a Bible in his hand, preaching. People were there asking questions. Maybe the next day someone would be there for gay rights or the Democratic or Republican party. There's a pretty even mix."

"I think WVU fosters an open-minded atmosphere that is nonjudgmental and open to all different cultures, religions, and ways of life," said another student. A different student added: "I think that WVU is more on the free-thinking and vigorous debate side. . . . However, personally I feel a lot of students at WVU come from a more religious background than, let's say, do students in New York."

English majors were formerly required to take at least one course in Shakespeare. Now, however, a course on the Bard is an option to fulfill the "Study of a Major Author" requirement. Required for the major is a course in "Gender / Multicultural / Transnational" studies. In addition to traditional course areas, the department offers courses ranging from the sound (Appalachian, Southern, Native American writers) to topics in gay and lesbian studies.

A course in U.S. history before 1945 is not required of history majors. A historical research project is. Course offerings seem largely solid, however, including "Western Civilization," "Greece: From Troy to Alexander," "History of the American Revolution," "Antebellum America," along with "Women, Gender and Kinship in Pre-Modern Europe."

Political science majors are required to take an introductory course in American government and politics, as well as intermediate courses in the subfields of Public Policy and Public Administration, Comparative Politics, International Relations, and Political Theory. A political philosophy course, "History of Political Thought," is rightly required, and several others are offered: "Modern Political Thought," "American Political Philosophy," and "Civil Society in Context."

Professors who are most highly recommended by colleagues and students include Brian Luskey in history; Gregory Noone, Robert DiClerico and James Whisker in political science; Rita Colistra and Gina Dahlia in journalism; Barton Cowan and Thomas O. Patrick in law; Kevin Lee and William Peterjohn in biology; Mingming Xu in chemistry; Harry Turtle in business; Steve Kite ("very informed individual who has a lot of experience") in geology; James Pappajohn (who "went the extra step and had review sessions after class . . . students were able to ask questions and he'd thoroughly go over problems and make sure they knew what was going on") in math; and Nicholas Perna in music.

At West Virginia, a student can major in Chinese, French, German, Italian, Russian, or Spanish—or minor in Chinese studies, foreign literature in translation, Japanese, linguistics, or ESL education. In 2012 the university introduced a new program in Latin American Studies, an interdisciplinary program involving language, culture, history, geography, politics, economy, religion, and society.

WVU has exchange programs with universities in 28 countries, including Botswana, China, Estonia, South Africa, and Turkey. And there are faculty-led study-abroad programs in the areas of law, political science, languages, medicine, social work, and more. "The school is big on encouraging study abroad for students through departments as well as in general," says a student.

Student Life: Party hardy

West Virginia University is a member of the NCAA and competes in the Big 12 Athletic Conference at the Division 1-A level in 17 intercollegiate varsity sports. "The club sports offered at the university have made my and others' collegiate experience tremendously more enjoyable through competitions and friendships forged," says a student. The university's rifle team is first in the nation.

WVU holds another distinction, though. It is consistently rated by the Princeton Review and other outlets as one of the nation's top "party schools," if not *the* top. The university has tried to combat the trend by sponsoring alcohol-free activities.

But one student says the school's party reputation is overblown. "We've had a bad rap for being a party school," he says, admitting that the hedonist option is there for anyone seeking it out. But, he adds, "If you're not really a party student, I don't think it bothers you a lot academically because you're not really involved in that stuff. I've seen almost no effect on my academic pursuit."

> "The professors are extremely accessible due to smaller class sizes," says one student.

Says one student: "The best thing about my school is the energy and school spirit. You can be who you want to be at WVU, but you know you're still part of a giant Mountaineer family that you can't help but to love. It doesn't matter where you come from when you arrive at WVU—when you leave, you'll always consider yourself a Mountaineer."

There are some 350 student organizations, including the Mountaineers for Life, Christian Pharmacists Fellowship, Christian Legal Society, Republican Law Caucus, and College Republicans. Religious organizations and ministries include Baptist Campus Ministry, Cru (Campus Crusade for Christ), Campus Light Ministries, Chabad Jewish Center, Christian Student Fellowship, Fellowship of Christian Musicians, Lutheran Campus Ministry, Newman Club (St. John University Parish), and Hillel.

If Greek life is your thing, WVU has 28 fraternities and sororities, involving some

Blue Collar Ivy

SUGGESTED CORE

1. Classics 231/232, Greek and Roman Civilization and Culture/Greek and Roman Myths
2. Philosophy 244, History of Ancient Philosophy
3. English 235, The Bible as Literature
4. Philosophy 351, Topics in Medieval Philosophy
5. Political Science 371, History of Political Thought 2
6. English 263, Shakespeare I
7. History 152, Growth of the American Nation to 1865
8. Philosophy 354, Themes/Continental Philosophy

1,500 students. For those who don't wish to live in a fraternity or sorority, there are 11 residence halls on campus. With a few exceptions, all unmarried freshmen are required to live in university housing. Most of the residence halls are coed, though one is for female students only. "We have a variety of bath and shower facilities," says a university spokeswoman. "Some are community bath and some are suite-style. All bath, shower, and toilet areas, however, are single sex." The university also owns several apartment buildings for students. "Just recently, the dorms started allowing opposite sexes to sign in to stay overnight in most dorms," reports a student. "Sexual promiscuity is very evident on campus."

Another student says resident assistants are "helpful, especially if you are looking to get more involved in the dorm community. They're not too intrusive or prying."

Crime often seems to stem from the drinking culture, based on what students report, as well as street fires and rioting in Morgantown after major sporting events. "Our campus is known for burning couches, but the university and local police have issued mandates to curb these incidents," said a student. "There is crime every so often in downtown Morgantown, where students gather for nightlife and partying," says another. "I believe they are typically a result of drunken fights or battery." A student admits, "There are some alcohol-related accidents." According to public records, burglary leads the way in crime on campus, with 22 in 2011, along with seven aggravated assaults, four forcible sex offenses, four motor vehicle thefts, one arson, and one robbery.

The school is quite affordable for natives, with 2012–13 tuition at $7,080 ($22,320 for out-of-staters), and room and board at $9,808. Only 36 percent of students received need-based financial aid, and the average loan debt of a recent graduating class was $24,113.

STRONG SUITS

- Good programs in business (especially finance), journalism, public relations, engineering, forensics, and criminology.
- Largely apolitical teaching.
- Engaged, available faculty and small classes at most levels.
- Many study-abroad options.
- Solid requirements in political science.

WEAK POINTS

- Shaky general-ed requirements—offering both solid fare and fluff.
- Weak mandates for English and history majors, though good courses in both.
- Insufficient anatomy and physiology courses for biology students.
- Rampant party atmosphere: "Our campus is known for burning couches."

University of Wisconsin–Madison

Madison, Wisconsin • www.wisc.edu

The State of *The Onion*

Founded in 1848, the gargantuan University of Wisconsin–Madison is known as one of the best public universities in the country. UW–Madison has a long history of scientific innovation; the first stem cells were isolated on its campus, using primates in 1995 and later embryonic humans. (Maybe it's time for a required course in ethics.)

Academic Life: Area student lacks curriculum

While the quality of UW students has improved as the university has become more selective over the past decade or so, a professor says, "A high percentage of students are intellectually curious, but there are also quite a few who just coast through because we are so large. It would be wrong to say that a majority of students demonstrate true intellectual curiosity. But a large percentage does." One teacher says he teaches a course that often touches upon the writings of Plato and Karl Marx—two authors most of his students have never read before. "This is just basic literacy, but my students don't have any reference," he says. "We've created a college environment that deemphasizes academics for socialization and being good citizens; very little here is related to disciplined learning."

VITAL STATISTICS

Religious affiliation: *none*
Total enrollment: *42,441*
Total undergraduates: *30,367*
SAT CR/Verbal midrange: *550–670*
SAT Math midrange: *620–740*
ACT midrange: *26–30*
Applicants: *28,983*
Applicants accepted: *51%*
Accepted applicants who enrolled: *40%*
Tuition (general/out of state): *$26,628*
Tuition (in state): *$10,379*
Room and board: *$8,080*
Freshman retention rate: *94%*
Graduation rate (4 yrs.): *53%*
Graduation rate (6 yrs.): *83%*
Courses with fewer than 20 students: *44%*
Student-faculty ratio: *17:1*
Courses taught by graduate students: *not provided*
Students living on campus: *24%*
Students in fraternities: *9%*
Students in sororities: *8%*
Students receiving need-based financial aid: *61%*
Avg. student-loan debt of a recent graduating class: *$24,000*
Most popular majors: *social sciences, engineering, business/marketing*
Guaranteed housing for 4 years? *no*

Instead of a core curriculum, however, UW–Madison hopes to encourage students to widen their knowledge through breadth requirements. But it might startle you to find out just how *lame* those mandates are. "The breadth requirements are very weak and have been that way ever since 1970," one professor says. Another observes, "A new core curriculum was introduced in the middle 1990s, but it was too weak to produce any significant change in what students are learning."

But even these vague requirements, which can be fulfilled by hundreds of choices, are seen as a burden by some Madison students. One teacher warns that any student "interested in a solid education . . . needs a strong sense of independence and determination to find the right classes and seek out the quality faculty members."

Certainly the most onerous requirement for UW–Madison students is the ethnic studies requirement. Classes that satisfy this requirement are blatantly politicized, such as "Race, Ethnicity, and Inequality in American Education," and "Women in Ethnic American Literature." Students who'd rather escape such toxic politics should look into the short list of worthy courses that meet this requirement, like "Studies in Folk and Ethnic Genres in Performance" and "The American West to 1850."

One program that takes the business of learning seriously is the Integrated Liberal Studies (ILS) program, whose courses are wide-ranging and mostly excellent. A professor reports that many students in ILS double major in political science, history, philosophy, or sociology. The ILS program is affiliated with the Bradley Learning Community, which brings together 250 serious students to live as a group in a residence. Bradley offers students reserved spots in high-demand courses, seminars, and noncredit courses and greater access to the university's top professors.

Wisconsin's College of Letters and Science (L&S) is the largest division in the university, comprising 39 departments and five professional schools. Over half of UW–Madison students are enrolled at L&S. The best departments in L&S, according to professors, include sociology, political science, economics, philosophy, Slavic, and German.

History offers a decent range of courses but does not require its majors to graduate with a solid grasp of major historical eras. For instance, history majors can fulfill their United States history requirement with courses like "Asian American History: Settlement and National Belonging " or "History of American Capitalism." One professor explains that the department has been steadily declining in quality for at least a decade. He diagnoses the problem as "narrow specializations that concentrate research of trivialities, rather than on matter of great consequence." However, a student does tell us that the department "has great resources."

The political science department is well-respected nationally. Ten poli-sci classes must be completed, with at least one each in political theory ("Introduction to Political Theory" or "Ancient and Medieval West Thought"), American politics ("Introduction to American Politics" or "Introduction to State Government"), comparative politics ("European Union: Politics and Political Economy" or "Political Narrative of Contemporary China"), and international relations ("Principles of International Law" or "Conflict Resolution").

The English department has more traditional requirements. Students on the literature track (the other two tracks are Creative Writing and Language and Linguistics) must complete 10 intermediate- or advanced-level classes, including a four-credit writing-intensive course in either "British Literature before 1750," "British and Anglophone Literature from 1750 to Present," or "American Literature"; a Shakespeare class; an additional pre-1800 non-Shakespeare course; and five electives. Although the electives may be trendy classes like "Introduction to Children's Literature," "Chicana/o Literature," or "Gender and Language," the required classes are mostly solid literature surveys. The department offers a surprising number of respectable classes on the major literary figures of the Western canon.

CAMPUS POLITICS: YELLOW LIGHT

Wisconsin likes to assert its commitment to free speech, but in practice the school administration has revealed a pattern of hostility to religious student groups, which has landed it in court. From banning an antiwar discussion panel to denying religious student groups the same funding offered to other student organizations, UW–Madison has found itself embroiled in controversy. Particularly targeted seems to be any group associated with the Catholic Church. The campus chapter of the Knights of Columbus was refused recognition by the school unless it admitted women and non-Catholics as members. In a truly Orwellian moment, former chancellor John Wiley claimed that the group must open membership to all students in order not to "violate the separation of church and state." The university had also derecognized InterVarsity Fellowship and a Lutheran group. It took the Wisconsin Board of Regents to enact a new policy forcing all institutions within its system to let religious student groups choose their members based on their beliefs.

Despite the resolution of the issue, a few years later, UW yanked student funding and campus recognition from the campus Catholic group for hosting events focused on evangelism, prayer, and religious instruction (like a retreat that included Mass and prayer). The judge in the case that followed noted that among those activities sponsored by the group are spiritual counseling sessions and a leadership retreat and that the university has no right to selectively discriminate against religious groups—or the particular activities of religious groups it deems undesirable—in its funding.

The university's weakest departments are, predictably, gender and women's studies, Afro-American studies, and the global culture programs. Unless you enjoy political sermons in the classroom, just avoid them.

In part because of its sheer size, Wisconsin ranks second only to Harvard in the number of professors who have won prestigious awards and grants. "Research is king at Wisconsin," says a professor, "but many departments also stress teaching, and the College of Letters and Science has made many efforts to inculcate a culture that encourages good teaching." Another professor agrees, saying, "Student evaluation of teaching is a major input into the annual merit-pay increase exercise."

Among many excellent teachers, students single out the following: Rebecca Koscik in the School of Medicine and Public Health; John Witte (emeritus), Howard Schweber, Donald A. Downs, and Charles Franklin in political science; Jean Lee (emeritus), Robert Frykenberg (emeritus), and William Cronon in history; and Mary Anderson (emeritus) in geology.

> A teacher says, "We've created a college environment that de-emphasizes academics for socialization and being good citizens; very little here is related to disciplined learning."

Incoming freshmen are assigned not to faculty members but to professional advisers. After choosing a major, each is assigned an adviser (usually a faculty member but sometimes a graduate student or staff member) within that major. Students tell us that their advisers are not so much interested in helping them plan their education as making sure they graduate on time. Despite their efforts, just over half of students graduate in four years.

While the average class size is 29, at a school as large as Wisconsin, many introductory courses are the size of a high school graduating class. Large lectures are usually supplemented by discussion sessions that include up to 30 students and are led by graduate teaching assistants.

All professors interviewed for this essay lament the fact that grade inflation is a serious problem at Wisconsin. "What is needed is an institution-wide policy so one does not penalize one's own students by grading them tougher than others do," one professor says. "There should also be some sort of national policy, as we do not want to penalize UW students in relation to those at other schools."

The university has other strengths, including a popular study-abroad program (UW–Madison ranks ninth among U.S. colleges in the number of students who venture to foreign lands) and a variety of internship opportunities in the state legislature, criminal justice institutions, Washington, D.C., internationally, and more. Study-abroad options include most of South America and Europe, as well as many destinations in Asia, Africa, and Central America. There are more than 150 programs to choose from.

Among more than 80 options, students can study languages (living and dead) from across the globe. From Akan (Twi) or Zulu to Old Church Slavic, Old High German, or

Ottoman Turkish, numerous obscure languages are taught at UW–Madison, along with the more conventional choices.

Student Life: Beer me

The University of Wisconsin–Madison is pleasantly situated in a vibrant location, though some students complain about the long, harsh winters. "Bascom Hill is a major pain in the winter," says a UW–Madison graduate. "Walking down that hill is a serious challenge, especially for the less coordinated loaded down with books. At least it helped us stay in good shape." A favorite student custom is sledding on cafeteria trays down the local hills after the first snowfall. "It is a great way to take a break," says a student.

> **SUGGESTED CORE**
> 1. Classics 568, Topics in Classical Literature
> 2. Philosophy 430, History of Ancient Philosophy
> 3. Religious Studies 333, Early Christian Literature: Matthew–Revelation
> 4. History 200, Topics in Medieval Europe (*closest match*)
> 5. Political Science 502, The Development of Modern Western Political Thought

Madison has been known for its student activism ever since the 1960s and radical student groups still often dominate campus debate, but most students are uninterested in politics. A professor says that conservative students have "made their presence felt." However, a student tells us that the "general feeling is that conservatives shouldn't say what they think. Pressure is from the students, not the professors."

One professor says that the university tries to restrict free-speech rights with "climate" and "professional conduct codes." The campus has hired a vice-provost for diversity and climate. "This fellow promotes himself as the campus's chief diversity officer (CDO)!" says a professor.

The most active campus groups on the left are the Wisconsin Public Interest Research Group (WISPIRG), and MEChA (a Chicano racialist movement). On the right, the College Republicans are active, and one alumnus says the campus paper, the *Badger Herald*, has become more libertarian of late. Although the independent conservative paper, the *Mendota Beacon*, ceased publication, another, the *Daily Cardinal*, has taken its place. One conservative student told us he is happy to have the opportunity to confront different worldviews. "This is a very political campus, and you have the opportunity to become politically involved," the student says.

A professor says, "Conservative students are not afraid to speak up and challenge the liberal orthodoxy of the campus, and there are now four student newspapers that represent a diversity of intellectual opinion. There is a dedicated group of faculty . . . who have been very active politically in favor of free speech and discourse and have won many free-speech victories over the years. Students are active in politics . . . which adds real energy to the institution—especially because student voices are much more diverse intellectually than they were several years ago. Conservative students should definitely consider Wisconsin, as they will find a vibrant niche, and they will find it challenging to counter the conventional liberal wisdom of the campus." However, one graduate cautions incoming students: "UW–Madison is a place for someone grounded in his belief system. Make no mistake, someone will question who you are, what you believe, and why."

Not all at Wisconsin is protest and counterprotest, though. Two undergraduates in 1988 launched *The Onion*, a must-read weekly satirical paper with its own TV series on IFC. *The Onion* may well be the state university's (and even the state's) proudest achievement.

For the spiritually minded, UW–Madison supports (and at times, refuses to support) a broad variety of religious organizations and clubs. From the Yoga, Empowerment, and Service Plus (YES+) to the Social Work Student Union, and the Muslim Students Association to Calvary Lutheran or Chabad Jewish associations, a number of religious outlets exist, including the Atheists, Humanists, and Agnostics @ UW–Madison interfaith discussion group.

With 750 clubs and organizations in all, the temptation for new students is to become overcommitted and spend an inordinate amount of time on extracurricular activities. "There is a wide variety of activities available for students during the week and on the weekends as an alternative to partying," one student says. Union South, the university's student center built in the late '60s, was replaced by a more architecturally inviting building of the same name in 2011.

And then there are the myriad pleasures to be found inside a bottle. Wisconsin has a well-deserved reputation as something of a school for tipsy smart kids. It won dubious distinction as the 13th-best party school according to the Princeton Review in 2013 and the fifth-best according to *Playboy* in 2012. Wisconsin has the highest percentage of binge drinking of any state in the union, with nearly 26 percent of adult residents admitting to binge drinking in the last month.

Such accolades forced the administration to admit that there is a campus-wide drinking problem. Under pressure from the school, local bars agreed to eliminate drink specials on Friday and Saturday nights, an effort that backfired when other Wisconsin patrons sued the participating bars for antitrust violation in a case that went to the state supreme court. The bars now offer drink specials again. Despite the school's efforts, alcohol abuse at Madison has not abated much in the past two decades—although the school has seen "sustained decreases" in the rate of "frequent" binge drinkers.

As a member of the Big Ten, the university fields several high-profile athletic programs. The Wisconsin Badgers, with mascot Bucky Badger, are main rivals with the University of Minnesota. The two teams compete for the Paul Bunyan's Axe trophy in their football games. Fans from the university and around the state are extremely loyal to the Badger team (whose football stadium, the fourth-oldest in the nation, underwent extensive renovation that expanded seating capacity to 80,000). Basketball games are well attended, too (the school cultivates a rivalry with Michigan State), and hockey has always been popular. Men and women compete in basketball, cross-country, golf, hockey, rowing, soccer, swimming and diving, tennis, and track and field. Men also wrestle and, of course, play football, while women can compete in lightweight rowing, softball, and volleyball.

Less than a quarter of undergraduates live on campus, although 90 percent stay there for their freshman year. The undergraduate residence halls are divided into smaller "houses" of 50 to 80 residents. Dorms are as diverse as the students who inhabit them. Some dorms, especially those abutting campus on University Avenue, are well known as party halls. Quieter spots are Chadbourne Residential College or the Lakeside Dorms on

Lake Mendota. The school's formerly all-women dorm, Elizabeth Waters Hall, has gone coed. The university has no coed dorm rooms or bathrooms, and even in the dormitories, men and women are separated by floor or wing. One current student says, "I despised the dorms. Rooms were too small, food was terrible, it was too loud, and I felt like I was in jail. I got out ASAP."

For its size, UW–Madison is relatively safe. In 2011 the school reported 24 forcible sex offenses, two robberies, three aggravated assaults, 32 burglaries, three motor vehicle thefts, and one arson.

For a state school, UW–Madison is pricey. Tuition in 2012–13 ran $10,379 for in-state students and $26,628 for out-of-staters. Room and board were $8,080. The university granted need-based financial aid to 61 percent of students. A typical UW–Madison student graduated with more than $24,000 in student-loan debt.

STRONG SUITS	WEAK POINTS
• Respected programs in political science, sociology, political science, economics, philosophy, Slavic, and German.	• Lax, easy to complete general-education requirements.
• A solid humanities education is offered through the Integrated Liberal Studies program of the Bradley Learning Community.	• Diversity course required—and most choices are ideological.
• Teaching evaluations play a real role in tenure decisions—so teaching is valued, along with research.	• Conservative groups targeted by administration and must protect themselves in court.
• Many varied study-abroad options and a vast array of languages (many hard to find) are offered.	• Very politicized programs in gender and women's studies, Afro-American studies, and global cultures.
	• Grade inflation rampant.
	• A campus-wide drinking problem.

University of Wyoming

Laramie, Wyoming • www.uwyo.edu

A Privilege

Though located in Laramie, Wyoming, a town with more than 30,000 residents, the University of Wyoming has a quiet and even rural charm. The school's 10,000 undergraduate students make up a vibrant community, with more than 200 clubs and organizations and an energetic student government. The only four-year university in its state, UW enjoys particularly high state funding both for its nationally recognized research and for the many internship opportunities it makes available to students. Students can also take advantage of the many study-abroad programs, which, thanks to the patronage of native son former vice president Dick Cheney, are very well funded.

Academic Life: Faculty take top honors

The general-education requirements at the University of Wyoming do almost nothing to guarantee that students emerge with a liberal arts education. The University Studies Program consists of 10 to 12 classes—with choices of varying quality—in required areas like Intellectual Community ("Intellectual Community in Cinema"), Oral Communication ("Public Speaking"), and Quantitative Reasoning ("Finite Mathematics"). Students must also take one course each in Physical Activity and Health; the U.S. and Wyoming constitutions; and in Arts, Humanities, Social Science; and something called Integrated Cultural Context. U.S. Diversity and Global Awareness elements are incorporated into the above classes. After this, the Arts and Sciences Core (for students in that division) requires two four-hour courses in a foreign language, a non-Western course, and three courses from a different division within the school from one's major—hence, science courses for an English major.

The average undergraduate class size at UW is 29 students, and faculty make themselves fully available to students. One student reports that no graduate student has ever taught any of her undergraduate classes in all her four years at UW. She added that her situation was typical for the university: "I think it's something like only 10 percent of classes are taught by graduate students campus-wide." A professor says that graduate students are mainly "responsible for discussion sections."

One student reports that professors are very accessible and committed to the students. "Professors offer lots of one-on-one time and easy access to their time. I think they do an excellent job for undergraduates." Another student reports that "professors are extraordinarily accessible. I'm in contact with many of my professors regularly because I've gotten to know them so well. A lot of the professors have an open-door policy and put their cell phone numbers on syllabi so you can contact them directly." One professor believes that students could make much more use of their professors' time. "I mean we have regular office hours and students sometimes just don't visit us. There's not as much in-person interaction as there used to be."

UW has an honors program that offers "innovative courses taught by award-winning faculty," honors housing, priority registration, unique scholarships, and honors-specific study-abroad options in Glasgow, Scotland, or London, England. Honors students also complete a senior project and specific honors classes. The senior project results in a "substantial piece of work" presented to professors, friends, and family at the end of senior year. The honors courses offered at UW vary by semester.

Unfortunately, the current honors lineup offers little in the way of traditional liberal

VITAL STATISTICS

Religious affiliation: *none*
Total enrollment: *12,903*
Total undergraduates: *10,194*
SAT CR/Verbal midrange: *480–610*
SAT Math midrange: *500–630*
ACT midrange: *22–27*
Applicants: *4,181*
Applicants accepted: *96%*
Accepted applicants who enrolled: *40%*
Tuition (general/out of state): *$12,390*
Tuition (in state): *$3,180*
Room and board: *$9,084*
Freshman retention rate: *76%*
Graduation rate (4 yrs.): *23%*
Graduation rate (6 yrs.): *53%*
Courses with fewer than 20 students: *41%*
Student-faculty ratio: *14:1*
Courses taught by graduate students: *not provided*
Students living on campus: *23%*
Students in fraternities: *5%*
Students in sororities: *4%*
Students receiving need-based financial aid: *47%*
Avg. student-loan debt of a recent graduating class: *$21,241*
Most popular majors: *nursing, elementary education, psychology*
Guaranteed housing for 4 years? *no*

CAMPUS POLITICS: GREEN LIGHT

There seems to be very little political antagonism in the atmosphere of the student body itself, and there are no uproars to report among students and faculty. In fact, one student reports that she "never had a professor" who made her think "I better not say this" or "I'd better tailor what I write" to fit his desires. "I never had that problem." Another student states that, even though politics can be brought up in the classroom, he "never felt uncomfortable" about it.

One student reports that in some classes, "I felt the discussions got a bit more like personal attacks, but always from fellow students, and usually the teachers were pretty good about keeping it under control or saying something after class to rectify the situation." A faculty member comments, "Overall, I think our faculty are pretty good about just emphasizing that students should be looking at the different sides and why people have different viewpoints on the different sides of politics."

An active College Republicans chapter has hosted Ann Coulter as a speaker and, according to one student, has had "great success" influencing students. Other student groups friendly to conservative ideas are the Student Veterans Organization and the Federalist Society.

arts. Instead, students will investigate their "personal and cultural identities through the making of any art/project/writing of their choosing" in "Investigating Cultural Identity," or discussing "concepts relating to gender, ethnicity, economics, politics, health, education and sports" in "Game of Sports." Other options include "Spirituality and Hunting," "HIV/AIDS: Disease and Dilemma," and "The Empire Writes Back," a course about "literature and film created in former colonies." Still, the honors program offers more than the standard state university education, so one student says that "the program is something I would recommend."

Other departments and programs lauded by current students and faculty include Cheney International (for study abroad), which is "really strong," according to students; the education program; and the engineering, political science, psychology, and criminal justice departments.

English majors face reasonable requirements. They must take one of the following: "Shakespeare and Renaissance Literature," "Shakespeare: Romantic Comedies and History Plays," "Shakespeare: Tragedies and Romances," or "Early English Renaissance Literature: 16th Century." They also need two courses in upper-level literature courses from two different periods before the 20th century. Most of those options are quite solid, such as "English Drama: Restoration and 18th Century," "Chaucer," "Middle English Literature," "Milton," and "American Prose: Early through Mid-19th Century." Majors must take one from another list of trendier-sounding courses like "Non-Western Women Writers," "Gender: Humanities Focus," or "Women's Studies."

At UW, the aim is to allow history majors to "tailor the major" to their own interests. Only two courses are specifically required: "the third-year History Methods and fourth-year Proseminar courses." Besides those, students can pick any four courses at the 1000–2000 level and five courses at the 3000–4000 level. Good options include "Western Civilization" I, "United States History" I, and "Medieval Christianity." Less impressive are "European Gender and Women's History," "The Multicultural West," and "Agriculture: Rooted in Diversity."

As for political science majors, they are required (with all other undergrads) to take "American and Wyoming Government." Beyond that, a degree requires some 11 courses specific to the major. But majors "are required to complete at least one class in each of the five political science subfields: American politics, comparative government, international relations, political theory, and public law." The more than 130 course choices include "United States Presidency" and "Political Philosophy: Ancient and Medieval."

One graduate student recommends involvement in student government, which "enabled me to see a lot more of the campus than I otherwise would have." Another student says: "We have an excellent student government. A lot of students get into it." Many also join some of the many other "societies and student groups on campus. They're very well managed." A faculty member tells us that "there are a lot of opportunities here."

> A faculty member says students have told her "they can't tell if a faculty member is a Democrat or a Republican."

Besides student groups, a professor suggests that students take advantage of internship opportunities. "There's the Washington semester program where students go to Washington, D.C., and work at one of the congressional offices there for an entire semester; there's also work in Wyoming congressional offices."

One student reports that "politics definitely come into courses" and that "political correctness does affect the classroom." He says that there's "a lot of talk about things like climate change and the impact that Americans have on the planet." Despite this, this student says he never felt uncomfortable. "There's certainly a welcoming atmosphere." Another student says, "I wouldn't necessarily say that in individual classes students would be made unwelcome for conservative views, but in certain areas of study," conservatives may feel like part of a "minority" and "outnumbered." This discomfort is not inflicted by professors, but by "other students in class." A faculty member says students have told her "they can't tell if a faculty member is a Democrat or a Republican." This is "a good indication that faculty are able to stay in the middle and not push one view or the other onto the students. I was always impressed that I've heard the students say that over the years."

Some departments may be a bit more politicized than others. Liberal arts courses, for instance, are more likely to be problematic, with biases stultifying classroom discussions. "I hear lots of stories about that kind of stuff from my conservative friends," he says, but "in engineering, for instance, there's less of a platform."

Student- and faculty-recommended professors include Paul Dellenback, Connel Frick and Dennis Coon in mechanical engineering; Ryan Kobbe in civil and architectural engineering; James King and Andrew Garner in political science; Cary Heck in criminal justice; Duncan Harris and Diane Panozzo in English; Heather Rothfuss in agricultural and natural resources; Susanna Goodin in philosophy; Ruth Bjorkenwall in global and area studies; and Noah Miles in honors.

SUGGESTED CORE

1. Classics 4270, Classical Epic Poetry
2. Philosophy 3120, Ancient Greek Philosophy
3. English 2170, The Bible as Literature
4. Religious Studies 3235, Medieval Christianity
5. Political Science 4650, Political Philosophy: Modern
6. English 4110, Shakespeare: Romantic Comedies and History Plays
7. History 1210, United States History I
8. History 4170, Europe in the 19th Century

One professor tells us that her students are very motivated. "Their interest level is very high." A student agrees, "I would say on the whole that students are quite motivated. Most of my peers are very hardworking students." Another student has a similar account: "I personally didn't experience much apathy among my classmates. They get involved in different intellectual clubs, and they seem to really dedicate themselves to their academic careers."

U Wyoming offers a broad range of languages, including Chinese, French, German, Greek and Latin, Japanese, Russian, and Spanish.

The university's foreign options are very extensive, including exchange programs, formal study abroad, and faculty-led programs. Exchange locations range very widely, from Austria to Taiwan. There are study-abroad options in Australia, Israel, Italy, Korea (South), New Zealand, Russia, and Wales. Faculty-led trips have gone to Benin, China, and the Galapagos Islands, among other choice locations.

Student Life: Growing up

Aside from honors housing, U Wyoming's campus has six residence halls. Sophomores and up can live in Crane Hall, in single rooms, or in student apartments. For the most part, men and women reside in separate wings of the same floor, with separate bathrooms for men and women in their respective wings. As one student puts it: "It's coed in the sense that one wing of a floor is all-female and one wing is all-male." This student says she "enjoyed the dorms" during her freshman year. "I met a lot of people really fast."

There are also several special housing options for students who wish to share a space with others who have similar interests or values. Options include the Freshman Interest Group, the Substance-Free Living Community, an Engineering Community, an Honors Community, a Coed Community, the Female-Only Community, the Male-Only Community, 21 Years and Older Community, Upper Division Students Crane Hall, and the Army ROTC Community.

There is some promiscuity to be found in the dorms, but it can be avoided. One student remembers being much more exposed to sexual activity during his first year, but said that overall, "It really isn't that prevalent. I never found that to be too much of an issue at this school." Another student adds: "I think it's a very modest campus, just because of the cultural norms and values out here."

Students can join the Cowboys and Cowgirls, who are level I-A in the NCAA Division and compete in basketball, cross-country, golf, soccer, swimming, track, tennis, volleyball, and wrestling. Athletic students who want to stay out of the big leagues will find plenty of opportunity for sport on campus: 45 intramural sports, 19 club sports teams, and a half-acre of recreation facilities. "Sports are definitely big" says a student. "Football's huge. Basketball as well. We don't have a very good football team—but we have an excellent women's basketball team." Another student adds that "students go to athletic events for free since they're covered in the student fees that we pay, so sports are always huge. Probably the biggest events are football, and our girls' basketball team is phenomenal!"

When it comes to partying, a student tells us that the campus used to be much worse than it is now. As a member of a fraternity, "There was some wild partying and that's why I quit. But I know that the school has cracked down on a lot of it." So while there "is still a party atmosphere" among some students, "we're blessed with a university that has a pretty low tolerance for anything too wild or illegal."

A student tells us that "Greek life is definitely big at the university, and I encountered a lot of Greek students in our student government." This student feels good about the presence of fraternities and sororities. Another student says that the Greek system "on the whole positively affects the atmosphere of the campus. They do good stuff."

A member of the Fellowship of Christian Athletes called it "an excellent organization," adding that "there are a number of really great campus ministries," naming the Navigators and Campus Venture as groups that "bring in Christian pastors from around town, or even athletes give talks." He also recommends the Laramie Valley Chapel, a downtown church that "does a great job of catering to college students" and sends "a bus from the dorms to their church before their morning service." He also recommended Emmaus Road Community Church, stating that "there's a good college student community there."

The crime rate at U Wyoming is remarkably low, with four sex offenses and 13 burglaries in 2011. One female student says, "I'd say it's a very safe campus. We have 911 emergency call boxes all over campus, and it is reported yearly how many times they were used. I don't ever feel unsafe walking across campus regardless of what time it is, and our university police are great. If you do feel uncomfortable, they do personal escorts to wherever it is you're going."

Tuition for state residents in 2012–13 was a scant $3,180 (out-of-state students paid almost four times that, at $12,390), while room and board were $9,084. Almost half (47 percent) of students got need-based aid, and the average student-loan debt of a recent graduating class was $21,241.

STRONG SUITS	WEAK POINTS
• Good programs in engineering, political science, psychology, and criminal justice. • Mostly nonpoliticized teaching and open-minded faculty. • Well-funded, plentiful study-abroad programs. • Extensive internship opportunities. • Muted, sane atmosphere in dormitories.	• Shaky, overly flexible general-ed requirements. • Honors program courses more esoteric and trendy than traditional. • Students make little use of office hours, though professors are available. • Dismal four-year (23 percent) and mediocre six-year (53 percent) graduation rates.

Mount Holyoke College

South Hadley, Massachusetts • www.mtholyoke.edu

Designing Women

Founded in 1837, Mount Holyoke is a small, highly selective, nondenominational college for women. The school offers plenty of solid course offerings—among a host of less promising ones—and faculty members who genuinely care about their students' academic progress. Students choosing Mount Holyoke would do well to avoid courses that the college calls "innovative" and "experimental," since they are likely to be steeped in leftist politics.

Academic Life: Girls who wear glasses

Mount Holyoke's academics are rigorous and innovative, its focus is strenuously global, and its graduates often go on to do great things. Famous alumnae include Emily Dickinson, playwrights Suzan-Lori Parks and Wendy Wasserstein, Frances Perkins (first female cabinet member in U.S. history), and Julia Phillips, the first female movie producer to win an Academy Award.

It is unfortunate that the school imposes no rigorous core curriculum. Instead, students are free to choose from an overly wide range of courses in a series of loosely defined intellectual categories. The school's foundational goals—a comprehensive knowledge of

VITAL STATISTICS

Religious affiliation: *none*
Total enrollment: *2,322*
Total undergraduates: *2,322*
SAT CR/Verbal midrange:
    610–720
SAT Math midrange:
    610–700
ACT midrange: *28–31*
Applicants: *3,876*
Applicants accepted: *42%*
Accepted applicants who
    enrolled: *31%*
Tuition (general/out of
    state): *$41,270*
Tuition (in state): *N/A*
Room and board: *$12,140*
Freshman retention rate:
    92%
Graduation rate (4 yrs.): *78%*
Graduation rate (6 yrs.): *81%*
Courses with fewer than 20
    students: *64%*
Student-faculty ratio: *9:1*
Courses taught by graduate
    students: *not provided*
Students living on campus:
    93%
Students in fraternities: *N/A*
Students in sororities: *none*
Students receiving need-
    based financial aid: *65%*
Avg. student-loan debt of a
    recent graduating class:
    $19,187
Most popular majors: *biol-
    ogy, English, international
    relations and affairs*
Housing guaranteed for 4
    years? *yes*

Western history, music, and arts—have suffered here (as elsewhere) under the assault of trendy academic theories and practices.

However, many students seem happy with the school's curriculum. One student says, "Our distribution requirements are enough, I think, to make sure every student intellectually expands herself 'out of the comfort zone.'" Another says, "We are very international, we have a macro, global focus, we are socially active, we have causes, and we want to do something with our careers that will make a difference."

The 287 faculty members of Mount Holyoke are impressive teachers dedicated to their students. They have also proved themselves to be busy scholars, research scientists, and artists. Well over half the faculty are women, and more than 90 percent have doctorates. Students speak very highly of the school's teaching, one-on-one support from professors, and the fairness in grading. Six months after graduation, 86 percent of the class of 2008 were working or in advanced study. Of those students, 17 percent were attending graduate/professional schools. Typically, over 75 percent enroll in graduate or professional schools within 10 years. Alumnae attend graduate school at institutions like Harvard, Yale, Stanford, and Georgetown, and the college has among its ranks Fulbright fellows and other award-winning scholars.

Students at Holyoke choose from among 48 departmental and interdisciplinary majors, or design their own programs. In addition to the standard programs such as physics and French, newer fields of study include interdisciplinary offerings like African American and African studies, Asian studies, Latin American studies, and gender studies—many of which are, predictably, politicized.

Students are assigned faculty advisers in their first year and may later change them when they settle on majors. Faculty keep long office hours and are reportedly very accessible. Many students speak warmly of teachers who welcome students seeking direction, intellectual answers, or "just to chat about life." Other Mount Holyoke women report that they visit their teacher's homes, meet their families, and eat with them in student dining halls. One student says, "I have formed at least ten to twelve substantive relationships with professors who I would/could/do go to for anything."

Mount Holyoke has long prided itself on its small classes; its student-faculty ratio is a strong 9 to 1. Professors teach all courses, although assistants sometimes lead laboratory sections. Students do, however, report frustration with frequent changes on the faculty, and the number who are off on leave. "There is a lot of professor turnover, and a lot of sabbaticals happen at odd, overlapping times," one student says, "This means that it is tricky for students of smaller majors to fulfill course requirements and for students to find willing or knowledgeable thesis advisers."

While many students report working extremely hard for their grades, one student remarks, "You don't have to lock yourself away in the library tower, stoking your internal fires with caffeine and hard labor to be a success here. You really just have to have an open mind, a willing heart, and a disciplined manner."

The politics of Mount Holyoke are decidedly leftist, and some students report that dogmatic professors are known to preach their views in the classroom. Although some students find the situation overbearing, one says that she avoids such classes through word of mouth and by carefully reading course descriptions. Other students point to a genuine commitment on the part of the faculty to encourage opposing discussion and debate. One student says, "Conservative students may feel that they are a minority in some departments, but they won't feel unwelcome."

Some of the disciplines taught on campus where students of a traditional bent might feel left out include critical social thought, politics, international relations, and gender studies. Others that enjoy a more neutral reputation include economics, humanities, mathematics, and the science departments. One student describes her major as having "more Marxist, proto-feminist [and] leftist . . . professors than not. While they don't force their views on the students, the slant is immediately apparent," she says.

Professors at Mount Holyoke noted for their teaching include Kavita Khory in

CAMPUS POLITICS:
RED LIGHT

One might wish that political, philosophical, and intellectual diversity were valued as highly at Mount Holyoke (and elsewhere) as are crude demographic differences among elite students and scholars. A conservative student told the Clare Booth Luce Institute (a national group for conservative women) about her experience at Mount Holyoke: "It wasn't until college, when I was surrounded with extreme liberalism from my classmates and professors, that I really became concrete in my conservative beliefs and was able to stand up and articulate my conservative position to my peers, professors, and friends. Every day I am challenged and tested in my conservative beliefs . . . whether it's a professor making an unfair generalization about conservatives, classmates professing untruths about conservatives to the class, or friends making jabs."

Mount Holyoke has been criticized by the Foundation for Individual Rights in Education for its vaguely worded ban on "harassing" speech, which could punish free discourse on key moral issues (such as sexuality), while *Campus Reform* has noted an "indefensible" imbalance in the choice of campus speakers at Mount Holyoke. In 2010 two out of three visiting speakers invited by the school's Weissman Center for Leadership and the Liberal Arts were outspoken progressives—and no conservatives were invited.

international relations; Joan Cocks, Penny Gill, Vinny Ferraro, and Chris Pyle in politics; Don Cotter in chemistry; Jonathan Lipman in history/Asian studies; Stephen Jones in Russian; and Bill Quillian in English. Jim Hartley in economics is also lauded for his introductory class, "The Great Books of Western Civilization." Says one student: "It was the perfect balance of criticism and justification/explanation." The school is also home to Joseph Ellis, author of the popular history *Founding Brothers*.

Holyoke made SATs optional for prospective students in 2001.

Because Mount Holyoke belongs to the Five College consortium, its students are welcome to attend classes and events at Amherst, Hampshire, and Smith colleges, and the University of Massachusetts—offering them a much wider choice of courses (some 5,300 in all) and access to all the schools' libraries. They are linked by a high-speed fiber optic network, and a free bus travels among the schools, which lie within a 12-mile radius of each other.

English majors are required to take an introductory course, two courses in literature written before 1700—which are generally straightforward, apart from some cross-listed gender studies classes. A course covering Shakespeare in particular is not required, though students are likely to encounter him in the pre-1700 classes.

History majors are required to take courses covering three of the following regions: Africa, Asia, Europe, Latin America, and North America. They must also take five 300-level courses, a research seminar, and one course that studies history before 1750. It is quite possible to fulfill these requirements without taking a single course on European or American history.

O ne Mount Holyoke student says, "We are very international. We have a macro, global focus, we are socially active, we have causes, and we want to do something with our careers that will make a difference."

Politics majors must take one course each in American politics (which could be filled by "Environmental Politics in America"), comparative politics (such as "Chinese Politics"), international politics, and political theory (which could be filled by "Invitation to Feminist Theory"). Majors must also take three additional 300-level courses. No course in the U.S. Constitution is required.

Despite the school's small size, Mount Holyoke students have many worthy academic programs available, on campus and elsewhere. Among these are its Junior Year Abroad; Community-Based Learning programs; the Speaking, Arguing, and Writing Program; the Miller Worley Center for the Environment's programs; study abroad through the McCulloch Center for Global Initiatives in countries like Costa Rica, Chile, France, Germany, Hong Kong, Japan, South Korea, Spain, and the United Kingdom; and a variety of internships.

Language departments offer degrees in Chinese, French, German, Greek and Latin, Italian, Japanese, Russian, and Spanish, and other language courses are offered as part of degrees such as African, Asian, Jewish, Latin American, and Middle Eastern studies.

Student Life: South Hadley country club

The school is situated in the center of South Hadley, Massachusetts. About 93 percent of students live on campus, in 18 residence halls. Most halls house freshmen through seniors, nicely mixing the classes and encouraging mentor relationships.

Each hall has a living room area with a piano and a grandfather clock, as well as a dining room with a kitchenette or full kitchen where students have the option of preparing their own meals. Each room has Internet access, a phone line, and a cable-ready outlet. The college also offers kosher/halal dining facilities. Milk and crackers (affectionately known as "M and Cs") are traditionally served in each residence hall during the evenings on Sunday through Thursday. Most bathrooms are single sex, but each hall does have at least one coed bathroom for guests, who are allowed overnight stays. Ham Hall, Mount Holyoke's language hall, hosts Chinese, French, German, Italian, and Spanish language fellows, exchange students who help teach their own language in exchange for a stipend and a year in America. Each language has its own table in the dining hall and occasionally holds private banquets.

Students may choose from more than 150 active student organizations, including the ACLU, Mount Holyoke Koinonia Fellowship (Christian), Amnesty International, Coalition for Gender Awareness, Classics Society, College Democrats, College Republicans, Economics Club, Environmental Action Coalition, The F-Word (formerly known as the Feminist Collective), Jewish Student Union/Hillel, Multi-Faith Council, Model United Nations, Newman Association (Catholic), Pagan Wiccan Collective, Protestant Council of Deacons, Sisters of Hinduism, Reaching Inwards, Student Coalition for Action, Muslim Student Association, Youth Action International, and a number of study groups and sports clubs. The College Republicans have a Facebook page (last updated in 2009), but we could not find much more evidence of their activities. An attempt was made to start a pro-life group, but it never got off the ground, sources tell us.

One in three students is foreign or is African American, Asian American, Hispanic, Native American, or multiracial. Students report that women from given ethnicities usually stick together at first. However, an undergrad reports that "once people grow intellectually, they branch out and the cliques go away."

One attribute of MHC that deserves comment is its growing reputation as being a "lesbian school." One student says that campus lesbians are a vocal minority. "For some, being a lesbian is cool," she says. "Some girls think it's the thing to do for support on a

---

SUGGESTED CORE

1. Classics 211s/212, Gods and Mortals: Ancient Greek and Roman Myth/Greek Tragedy and Film
2. Philosophy 201, Philosophical Foundations of Western Thought: The Greek Period
3. Religion 203f/204s, Introduction to the Hebrew Bible/Introduction to the New Testament
4. History 129f, The Middle Ages: 300–1300
5. Politics 212f, Modern Political Thought
6. English 211fs, Shakespeare
7. History 170f, The American Peoples to 1865
8. Critical Social Thought 250f/Philosophy 252, Introduction to 19th-Century Critical Social Thought/Philosophical Foundations of Western Thought: The 19th Century

single-sex campus." Another student says that "a homophobic student will not survive on the MHC campus, where alternative sexual lifestyles are very visible and their proponents outspoken." Other students point out several coed opportunities at some of the campus events, including dances with men from neighboring colleges. One student says, "You can party and have a crazy, youthful, coed time at another of the five colleges, but then come home to sweet, peaceful MHC without worrying that you'll wake up to a mess in your own hallways."

The college holds religious services on campus; on a given weekend, one might celebrate Sunday or Shabbat. Catholic and Protestant services take place weekly in the Abbey Chapel, while Shabbat services are held at the "Eliot House," a campus spiritual center. The Eliot House also has daily call to prayer for Muslims, space for weekly gatherings, and a Japanese meditation tea house. The Abbey Interfaith Sanctuary, a renovated Christian chapel, holds sacred objects and texts from the various faith groups represented on campus. Five chaplains work on campus: Muslim, Protestant, Jewish, Catholic, and a Japanese tea-mistress. Together they call for "an inclusive community working towards spiritual depth, moral development, and social justice," while seeking to broaden the interfaith community, the school's website reports. Students who find campus religious activities to be too liberal should look into congregations in nearby towns.

Mount Holyoke students have enviable choices when it comes to extracurricular activities, many of which have a distinctly country club character. The college maintains one of the finest equestrian centers available for students, which includes more than 60 boarding stalls, a large outdoor all-weather footing show arena, a permanent dressage arena, two indoor arenas, and a cross-country course through 120 acres of woods, fields, and streams. The college manages "The Orchards," an 18-hole championship golf course designed by Donald Ross. Within walking distance of the golf course is the state-of-the-art athletic and dance complex, which houses a 25-meter, eight-lane pool; an indoor track; numerous tennis, racquetball, volleyball, basketball, and squash courts; and weight training and cardiovascular fitness areas. The Mount Holyoke Lyons boast NCAA Division III teams in basketball, crew, cross-country, field hockey, golf, lacrosse, riding, soccer, squash, swimming and diving, tennis, indoor and outdoor track and field, and volleyball. Participation in extracurricular arts such as dancing and singing are equally popular.

Mount Holyoke seems particularly concerned about security. The Department of Public Safety patrols the campus twenty-four hours a day. The campus is well lit and campus phones are always nearby. In 2011, there was one forcible sex offense on campus and one motor vehicle theft (later explained as the "unauthorized use of a golf cart"). Students report feeling very safe, and benefit from safety training such as free RAD (Rape Aggression Defense) courses.

If Mount Holyoke is an oasis of learning, its prices mirror those of a resort. Tuition in 2010–11 was $41,270, with room and board at $12,140. However, 65 percent of undergraduates received need-based financial aid, while other students got merit scholarships. The average debt of a recent graduate who borrowed was only $19,187.

STRONG SUITS

- Rigorous classes that have produced many famous graduates.
- A high percentage of alumnae go on to advanced or professional education.
- Close relationships between students and teachers.
- Extensive study-abroad options.
- Lovely campus and dorms.

WEAK POINTS

- Lax curriculum allows students to over-specialize or flounder.
- Rigid leftist ideology pervades many departments, sometimes emerging in biased classroom presentations.
- Extensive faculty turnover and sabbatical travel makes some necessary courses hard to enroll in.
- The college's growing reputation as a "lesbian school" will make some uncomfortable.

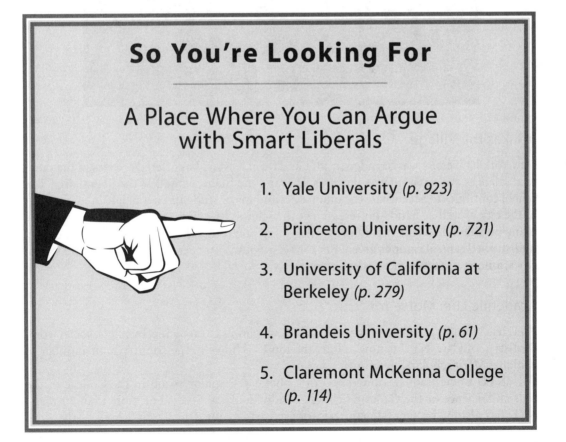

So You're Looking For

A Place Where You Can Argue with Smart Liberals

1. Yale University *(p. 923)*

2. Princeton University *(p. 721)*

3. University of California at Berkeley *(p. 279)*

4. Brandeis University *(p. 61)*

5. Claremont McKenna College *(p. 114)*

New York University

New York, New York • www.nyu.edu

It Takes the Village

New York University was founded in 1831 and from its start has offered courses in the practical sciences and arts, such as business, law, and medicine, as well as the liberal arts. The school continues to accentuate the pragmatic, and many students participate in internships in the city as well as hands-on research at the school. By going to NYU, students sacrifice many traditional college experiences—tailgating and football, for instance, and a bucolic, undisturbed central campus green. But they gain four years spent in one of the world's great cities, among its future movers and shakers.

Academic Life: Morse for "core"

NYU has 11 undergraduate programs, including schools of medicine, business, social work, dentistry, and law. NYU is now among the top 15 schools in the country in its number of National Merit scholarship winners.

NYU undergraduates interested in a liberal arts major enroll in the College of the Arts and Science or the Gallatin School of Individualized Study. For more than 40 years, NYU has also had a separate conservatory for arts majors, the Tisch School of the Arts, which attracts would-be actors, film and TV directors, playwrights, screenwriters, animators, and composers.

Arts and Science students must meet the requirements of the Morse Academic Plan (MAP). One professor says the school's curriculum "is better than nothing, but it's half what it should be. The best classes are probably the required science classes. The Foundations of Contemporary Culture program, which is supposed to be our Core . . . is really more like a Chinese menu." Arts and Science undergraduates must take a class in Western civilization, called "Texts and Ideas," and the class descriptions boast a good array of primary sources, albeit with a special emphasis on the 19th century and thinkers like Marx, Darwin, and Nietzsche. Some professors assigned to teach these classes have an agenda and will present the Bible as mythology, sources say. The other three classes in the Foundations of Contemporary Culture are on non-Western topics.

One professor says that "the program was developed when the school had a poorer average caliber of students than it does now, and they made up requirements that they knew these less bright students could consistently meet. Now, professors . . . inject some of their ritualistic political correctness into the thing."

One alternative offering smaller classes and a different curriculum is the Gallatin School of Individualized Study, home to about 1,200 undergraduate students. It offers many internships and private lessons in the arts. Most notably, the Gallatin School teaches many seminal, primary works of the Western tradition from the ancient and modern worlds. While NYU has a fairly weak advising system for its College of Arts and Sciences, the Gallatin Division places a great deal of emphasis on its advisers' helping students develop their academic plans. Hundreds of faculty members serve as Gallatin advisers.

Outside Gallatin, advisers are available for students who ask for help, but as is typical of NYU, students have to take the initiative. One student reports that "my adviser was very nice, but she didn't seem to know which classes were worth taking. Often she would just shrug."

While NYU is a giant school, classes are not necessarily large—at least in the humanities. The average class size is under 30 students. In the sciences, one student says, most courses are "huge

VITAL STATISTICS

Religious affiliation: *none*
Total enrollment: *43,911*
Total undergraduates: *22,280*
SAT CR/Verbal midrange: *650–750*
SAT Math midrange: *630–730*
ACT midrange: *29–31*
Applicants: *41,243*
Applicants accepted: *32%*
Accepted applicants who enrolled: *36%*
Tuition (general/out of state): *$40,878*
Tuition (in state): *N/A*
Room and board: *$16,133*
Freshman retention rate: *100%*
Graduation rate (4 yrs.): *77%*
Graduation rate (6 yrs.): *84%*
Courses with fewer than 20 students: *55%*
Student-faculty ratio: *11:1*
Courses taught by graduate students: *not provided*
Students living on campus: *52%*
Students in fraternities: *1%*
Students in sororities: *2%*
Students receiving need-based financial aid: *65%*
Avg. student-loan debt of a recent graduating class: *$36, 351*
Most popular majors: *business/marketing, social sciences, visual and performing arts*
Guaranteed housing for 4 years? *yes*

CAMPUS POLITICS: YELLOW LIGHT

Undoubtedly, NYU is a left-leaning campus, at least in the arts, humanities, and social sciences. The school does boast a strong, active College Republicans chapter that claims to be "the most publicized and influential group of students on any American campus," with appearances on ABC, CBS, NBC, MSNBC, CNN, FOX News, BBC, and other networks. Articles about them have also appeared in the *New York Times*, the *New York Post*, the *New York Daily News*, the *Chicago Sun-Times*, and *Rolling Stone*. "Challenging the political bias imposed upon us in the classroom . . . we spread a powerful message of independence and social responsibility absent from much of NYU and the perceptions of our peers," the CRs boast. The group brings in speakers such as Ann Coulter and Michelle Malkin and hosts an annual debate with the College Democrats. There is also a College Libertarians group. Occasional controversies arise—for instance, when students wanted to host a display of cartoons depicting Muhammad, and the university outraged free-speech activists by banning it—but it's fair to say that most NYU students are too career oriented to care very much about politics.

lectures with professors," and graduate teaching assistants actually do more of the teaching. Some students say that the professors can be surprisingly accessible. One says, "I had profs who gave out their home numbers and others who changed their office hours in response to e-mail requests." But there are certainly NYU students who found the faculty less than welcoming. "If you're in a big class with a big name professor, they're never going to know who you are," says one recent grad. This seems to be a particular difficulty with the sciences. "Most of my classes have had at more than 100 students, with a few having as many as 250 or 300. The professor is unlikely to recognize you. . . . Graduate students teach far too many classes, even upper-level courses." Furthermore, "teaching is definitely second to research," reports one professor. Graduate TAs also teach lower-level foreign language classes and the mandatory freshman writing course, as well as many of the weekly discussion sessions for the larger introductory courses.

Philosophy majors must complete a strict core that ensures students will graduate with a broad knowledge of the discipline, including logic, ancient philosophy, modern philosophy, ethics or political philosophy, metaphysics or epistemology, the philosophy of mind or language, and upper-level seminars. There are very few "philosophy of feminism," "eco-ethics," or other such courses at NYU.

The English, Spanish, Judaic studies, Middle Eastern studies, Italian, and math departments are said to be strong.

History is less highly regarded, and it houses a number of tenured radicals (as do the anthropology, sociology, and women's and black studies departments). History course offerings include few ancient or medieval options, a wide selection in modern and contemporary history, and too many "gender issues" classes. One student says "There are decent professors. But it's like everything here. You've got to ask around and find out who's good." The history major consists of nine classes, six of them upper level, with two courses in each of three geographical areas (U.S., European, and non-Western) and one advanced seminar. Students need only take one course set before 1800 and could easily miss any study of the American Founding or Civil War.

The math department attracts many of the school's best students. A good number of these students are from the city's population of Russian immigrants, and the department has become a significant feeder of foreign-born actuaries seeking out lucrative positions in the city's large insurance industry.

The program in undergraduate English requires four core courses—British literature (two terms), American literature, and a class in literary interpretation—plus one course in critical theories and methods, one in British lit before 1800, then three English electives, and an advanced seminar. Courses in Shakespeare aren't technically required, but they are offered each year, and his work would be hard to miss.

Politics majors take two seminars in economic principles, one in international relations, one in statistical methodology and a senior thesis, among 10 total classes, two of which are core courses. Further, one course must be taken from three of five subject areas: analytical politics, political theory, American government and politics, comparative politics, and international politics. Political theory throughout is weighted heavily toward the modern and contemporary. It is possible for a politics major to get through without taking a serious course covering the U.S. Constitution—and there are many ideologically charged options worth avoiding.

Undergrads report some huge classes and research-obsessed professors—but few mind much because "NYU has direct access to major employers and operates a brilliant career center," as one student declares.

Given its location, it is no surprise that NYU is widely recognized for its film and television, theater, and business schools. One student there says Tisch School of the Arts "is competitive. But it's in a mostly healthy way. They give you equipment and let you work. If you want to be in TV and film, it's a great place to get experience." One way that students get internships and part-time jobs is by attending events at which alums turn up on campus. Students also pound on the doors of nearby employers in finance, entertainment, advertising, and fashion.

One student notes that "NYU has, with its location, direct access to major employers. NYU operates a brilliant career center that hosts fairs, recruiting receptions, et cetera, as well as providing walk-ins with advisers who specialize in career development."

Some of the best teachers at NYU, according to students, are Simon Bowmaker in economics; Chris Chan Roberson in film; Nicola Cipani and Chiara Marchelli in Italian; Pádraig Ó Cearúill in Irish (language); Nils Froment in French; Paul W. Glimcher in neuroscience; Evelyn Birge Vitz in French; Michael Tyrell in English; Michael Peachin and Roger S. Bagnall, first director of the Institute for the Study of the Ancient World; David Engel in Judaic studies; Jorge Castañeda and Shinasi Rama in politics; and Anne Lounsbery in Russian and Slavic studies.

NYU's weakest departments are in the sciences, music technology, and in fields like sociology, women's studies, and African studies. The journalism department is said to have become more politicized over the past few years, and the education department has been positively radicalized.

Students should ask for advice on classes from older students whom they respect. However, most sources told us that classroom politics at NYU are more often implicit, and therefore tolerable. "Most professors, at least all I encountered, were liberal but reasonable. There is a sort of assumption that everyone is liberal, so no one asks," says one student. Another, majoring in chemistry, said her experience was that "politics generally didn't intrude into the classroom." Students at the school are said to be more politically "apathetic" than activist.

NYU encourages students to study abroad for at least a semester. According to the Institute of International Education, NYU has more students studying abroad than any other school in the country. Destinations include Argentina, China, the Czech Republic, England, France, Germany, Ghana, Italy, and Spain.

NYU offers more than 25 foreign languages, ranging from Greek and Latin to Irish, Japanese, Swahili, and Turkish. Through an agreement with Columbia University, NYU students can take a vast array of other languages uptown.

Student Life: Bright lights, big city

NYU sits squarely in one of the most interesting parts of America's most cosmopolitan city. Perhaps consequently, fraternities and sororities are not a big part of student life—only 1 percent of men join NYU's 17 fraternities, and only 2 percent of women join the 11 sororities on campus. As one student puts it, NYU students consider themselves Manhattanites who just happen to be taking classes.

There are dozens of churches of every denomination, as well as historic synagogues, within walking distance. The school maintains vibrant chaplaincies and religious clubs, including Cru (formerly Campus Crusade for Christ) and the Bronfman Center for Jewish Student Life, along with Lutheran, Episcopalian, and Islamic ministries. The Catholic Student Center is said to be especially active and faithful.

The school sports more than 350 student groups and organizations, including the College Libertarians, Gentleman of Quality, Finance Society, Amateur Astronomers Association, Objectivist Club, Fine Arts Society, Break Dance Club, Gallatin Photography Club, Habitat for Humanity and several other community service groups, Women in Computing, Polish Club, Organization of Black Women, and Toastmasters at NYU.

One student shares, "Many times while walking around Manhattan, I'll experience a strange sense of pride coming across a random NYU building in an unlikely place (always designated by a purple flag outside). It's something hard to describe . . . but NYU just seems exciting because it's growing."

Tight housing, like high pressure, comes with the downtown territory. The university has five traditional dormitories—one of which is exclusively for freshmen—plus a number of row houses, apartments, and suite-style residence halls. More than half of undergrads live on campus, and 90 percent of freshmen. Each dorm is coed, but "all student rooms have their own bathrooms, which is a huge plus," one student says.

Athletic facilities exist at NYU, and sports teams as well, although no one seems to care about them, except when there is the occasional high-profile victory. One student said, "I don't know anyone who's ever been to a NYU athletic event," before amending her opinion to allow that she knows one male student "who'd been to a women's basketball game . . . once." Even so, NYU does field 10 men's teams and nine women's varsity teams—but no varsity football team. Intramural sports include bowling, volleyball, basketball, tennis, football, softball, and something called Quikball.

Many NYU students are in preprofessional programs, and their ambition leads them to work extraordinarily hard. Students also tend to be ferociously independent. Says one student, "With such a large student body, NYU tends in general to be pretty stark in terms of personal attention. Many things are relegated to bureaucratic process and the ubiquitous 'NYU ID number.' The college can be impersonal, and sometimes overwhelming."

Crime is occasionally a problem, but one student said he does not worry about coming home at "any hour," and crime stats bear this out. In 2011, with over 40,000 students, NYU reported one forcible sexual assault, 28 burglaries, and 193 drug-related disciplinary actions.

NYU costs as much as any of the Ivies, with a 2012–13 tuition of $40,878 and room and board of $16,133. Some 54 percent of students received some aid, but the university is not notably openhanded and does not practice need-blind admissions. The average student-loan debt of a recent graduate was a heavy $36,351.

STRONG SUITS	WEAK POINTS
• Bright, highly ambitious students. • The Gallatin School offers numerous courses focused on the Western tradition. • Excellent programs in media and entertainment, with many options for internships throughout Manhattan. • Apolitical classes in most disciplines, with fair-minded teachers. • Good programs in English, philosophy, math, Spanish, Judaic studies, Middle Eastern studies, Italian.	• Teachers put research first and don't always get to know students. • Teaching in freshman writing, sciences, and foreign languages relies too heavily on graduate students. • Some ideological departments, including history, journalism, sciences, music technology, sociology, women's studies, and African studies. • Housing is tight and all dorms are coed.

Northwestern University

Evanston, Illinois • www.northwestern.edu

Growing Ivy in Evanston

About 160 years ago, Northwestern University was founded to serve students in what was then the Northwest Territory. Today Northwestern is a national university with an international scope. The administration continues to make admission more selective as the school boosts its profile as a research university. Among the six undergraduate schools, over half of all students are enrolled in the Weinberg College of Arts and Sciences. On campus, religion and spirituality are considered "a personal thing," a student tells us, and while the campus political climate is decidedly left of center, it is mostly respectful of opposing views.

Academic Life: Freedonian studies

Northwestern has no required core curriculum, and degree requirements are decided individually by each of Northwestern's 11 schools and colleges. Besides its main undergraduate division, the Weinberg College of Arts and Sciences, Northwestern's Evanston's campus includes the Medill School of Journalism, the School of Communication, the School of Education and Social Policy, the McCormick School of Engineering and Applied Science, the School of Continuing Studies, and the Bienen School of Music, as well as a graduate school, the Kellogg School of Management, and the Garrett-Evangelical Theological Seminary. Northwestern's impressive law and medical schools are located in nearby Chicago, allowing some students and faculty to take advantage of both campuses. The university also has a campus in Doha, Qatar.

Weinberg College of Arts and Sciences enrolls almost 52 percent of Northwestern's 8,475 undergraduates. In it students find some 29 departments, 37 majors, 10 adjunct majors, and 54 minors. All Weinberg freshmen are required to take two thematic writing seminars, which include no more than 15 students. Students should be especially careful in choosing freshman seminars because their seminar instructors are also their premajor advisers and the evaluators of their writing proficiency.

The school offers no core curriculum but does have a decent set of distribution requirements. Students choose two courses from each of the following areas: natural sciences; formal studies; social and behavioral sciences; historical studies; ethics and values; and literature and fine arts, in addition to demonstrated proficiency in a foreign language. Although the majority of course offerings appear to be solid, some do appeal to grudge-driven identity politics. Despite the lax curriculum, Northwestern students typically have the foresight to choose courses from a variety of disciplines. One professor says few students graduate from NU without taking a broad range of classes.

Some majors, such as American studies, integrate different fields of study within the major in order to gain a broader understanding. There are also ad hoc majors created by students, who can initiate their own courses under the supervision of a faculty member.

Northwestern is one of just a few universities using the quarter system (three quarters plus a summer session), which means students face exam periods no fewer than six times a year, counting midterms and finals. "I always feel like I'm studying for some final or another," one student says. Time management is one key to success here; the other is course selection.

Northwestern seems to strike a reasonable balance between its commitments to research and to teaching. One humanities professor says there is keen pressure to "publish or perish" and that faculty members are supposed to spend 45 percent of their time on research,

VITAL STATISTICS

Religious affiliation: *none*
Total enrollment: *19,968*
Total undergraduates: *8,475*
SAT CR/Verbal midrange: *670–750*
SAT Math midrange: *690–780*
ACT midrange: *30–33*
Applicants: *32,065*
Applicants accepted: *15%*
Accepted applicants who enrolled: *42%*
Tuition (general/out of state): *$43,380*
Tuition (in state): *N/A*
Room and board: *$13,329*
Freshman retention rate: *97%*
Graduation rate (4 yrs.): *87%*
Graduation rate (6 yrs.): *95%*
Courses with fewer than 20 students: *73%*
Student-faculty ratio: *7:1*
Courses taught by graduate students: *2%*
Students living on campus: *65%*
Students in fraternities: *32%*
Students in sororities: *38%*
Students receiving need-based financial aid: *42%*
Avg. student-loan debt of a recent graduating class: *$22,130*
Most popular majors: *economics, engineering, journalism*
Guaranteed housing for 4 years? *no*

CAMPUS POLITICS: YELLOW LIGHT

Insiders speak of Northwestern as "liberal" but "nonaggressive." While the majority of professors seem to be politically liberal, they were described as largely "fair." The faculty certainly spans the political spectrum to include former terrorist Bernardine Dohrn; Holocaust denier Arthur Butz; leftist columnist Garry Wills; Templeton Prize winner Charles Taylor; and Nobel laureate economist Dale Mortensen. But for the most part, political issues don't enter the classroom unnecessarily.

The *Northwestern Chronicle* offers news and commentary from a somewhat conservative viewpoint. The main student paper, the *Daily Northwestern*, is more liberal. The College Republicans sponsor speakers a few times a year—though they rarely pack the house.

Sadly, according to the Foundation for Individual Rights in Education, Northwestern's policy on "Hate Crimes and Bias Incidents" is so broadly written, it could be used to suppress conservative views (for instance, on social issues).

In 2013 Northwestern announced an even more accelerated push to promote diversity, unveiling a multipronged initiative backed by the following: "the Assistant Provost for Diversity and Inclusion, Director of Equal Opportunity and Access, Assistant Dean for Student Life and Multicultural Affairs, Director of Community and Inclusion (Student Affairs), Executive Director of Multicultural Student Affairs, Director of the Women's Center, Director of Diversity and Inclusion—Kellogg, Director of Minority Affairs—Feinberg School of Medicine, and the Director of Diversity Education and Outreach—Law School." Your tuition dollars at work.

45 percent on teaching, and 10 percent on administrative projects. Professors in the sciences, where the pressure to publish is perhaps greatest, tend to have lighter teaching loads.

One benefit of the strong emphasis on research is that undergraduates can take part in it and get paid to do so. The university supports this through several funds. To reward those professors who are actively working with their students in their endeavors, the university offers an award for excellence in "mentoring undergraduate research." Despite the emphasis on research productivity, however, one student says that "professors seem generally interested in students. I haven't had one yet that wasn't concerned with my academic soul." Some professors focus more on research than teaching, but one faculty member notes that since Northwestern prides itself on its many superb instructors, "there is a teaching culture here by tradition and so it's pretty good."

The admissions office boasts that NU faculty members teach more than 90 percent of courses. However, in larger lecture courses, professors typically teach twice a week, with students breaking up into smaller discussion groups, taught by graduate teaching assistants, once a week. Professors are described as "available" to those who "take the initiative," although, as one student puts it, "they are not going to hold your hand." A professor describes his students as "very curious" and adds that they "respond to good teaching and make it very rewarding." Students looking for professor reviews can access the CTEC (Course and Teacher Evaluation Council), which collects and records student evaluations of faculty.

Students and faculty have identified the following as particularly strong teachers: Gary Saul Morson, Andrew Baruch Wachtel, and Irwin Weil (emeritus) in Slavic languages and literature; Joel Mokyr, T. H. Breen, and Edward Muir in history; Kenneth Seeskin in religious studies; Charles Taylor in philosophy; Mary Kinzie in English; Robert Gundlach in linguistics and the Writing Program; Sandra L. Hindman (emeritus) in art history; Andrew Koppelman in political science and law; Martin Mueller and Robert W. Wallace in Classics; and Robert J. Gordon, Mark Witte, and 2010 Nobel Prize winner Dale Mortensen in economics.

Northwestern's Medill journalism program is regarded as a leader in the field nationwide, with a long list of graduates who have won the Pulitzer Prize. The School of Communication's theater program boasts graduates such as actors Charlton Heston, Warren Beatty, Julia Louis-Dreyfus, and producer-director Garry Marshall. The McCormick School of Engineering and Applied Science is consistently strong, which is not surprising since its faculty includes 26 members of the National Academy of Sciences and 21 members of the National Academy of Engineering.

D espite the emphasis on research at Northwestern, one student says that "professors seem generally interested in students. I haven't had one yet that wasn't concerned with my academic soul."

The presence of the Kellogg School of Management helps boost the undergraduate economics program, which is consistently ranked in the top five in the nation by *Bloomberg Businessweek*. Other strong departments, according to students and teachers, include English and Slavic languages and literature. Within the English department, students may choose to major in either literature or writing. English majors are not required to take a Shakespeare class, although such courses are offered, but they must take at least three courses of literature written before 1798 and three written after. Only one class must be in American literature.

The political science department is solid, requiring students to acquaint themselves with Plato, Aristotle, Machiavelli, Hobbes, Locke, Rousseau, Madison, Mill, and Marx, among others. An American political philosophy class is a required course, although one in the U.S. Constitution is not.

History is a popular department at Northwestern, although the major requirements are quite weak: students are not required to take basic Western civilization or American history classes unless those topics fall under the rubric of their concentration.

The comparative literary studies, international studies, Latino studies, gender studies, and race and ethnicity studies programs are predictably leftist in tone and course content, but the economics department features several noteworthy free-market economists. Of Weinberg College's 29 departments, a few could fairly be described as "politically correct," students report, including Asian American studies, Latin American and Caribbean studies, Jewish studies, and African American studies. A professor in the social sciences calls the profusion of ethnic studies departments a "waste of university resources." One teacher who has sat on hiring committees says that ideology "has not undermined things viciously," but in his own department he has seen candidates eliminated for their political views.

Beware Northwestern's courses on human sexuality. In 2011 the campus was sickened by the following turn of events, as reported by the *Weekly Standard:* "A tenured professor, teaching a heavily attended undergraduate course on human sexuality, decided to bring in a woman, who, with the aid of what was euphemistically called 'a sex toy' (uneuphemistically, it appears to have been an electric dildo), attempted to achieve a climax in the presence of the students."

In case that makes you want to skip town, Northwestern is known for its many opportunities for study abroad, with its overseas programs receiving enthusiastic reviews from students. The Study-Abroad Office coordinates more than a hundred programs on six continents. Students can study abroad for just a summer or up to a full year. Since 2008 Northwestern has operated a satellite campus in Qatar, which offers bachelor's degrees in journalism and communications. At home, students may study Arabic, Chinese, French, German, Greek and Latin, Hebrew, Japanese, Korean, Persian, Polish, Portuguese Swahili and Turkish.

Student Life: North by Northwestern

Although Northwestern students spend most of their time studying, there are many attractions nearby to lure them outside the library. The university's attractive 240-acre campus is located in the Evanston suburb, a few blocks from Lake Michigan and just 10 miles north of downtown Chicago. The School of Music features frequent performances on campus, and the school sometimes hosts musicians from Chicago's jazz venues.

One student says NU is "definitely not a party school." Students are said to be heavily career oriented. More than a third of undergraduates are members of the 39 recognized fraternities or sororities, but even these organizations are not especially focused on partying. Besides the Greek system, student life at NU offers a full range of more than 400 student groups and organizations, including 64 Squares (a chess club), Boomshaka (percussion-dance performance), Lovers and Madmen (a theater group devoted to Shakespeare), the Outing Club, College Republicans, and College Democrats.

There are several Christian groups on campus: Campus Crusade, Catholic Undergrads, and InterVarsity Christian Fellowship, to name a few. NU is also home to the Buddhist Study Group, the Rainbow Alliance, Northwestern Students for Life, Hillel, For Members Only (a black student group), and a long list of other ethnic, cultural, and religious organizations.

One professor notes a "dramatic improvement in the quality of athletics" in recent years. The Northwestern men's and women's Wildcats play 19 varsity sports, from football to fencing, in the Big Ten Conference. In 2009 a total of 184 athletes received Academic All-Big Ten honors. But Northwestern isn't known for its sports success or student enthusiasm; the stands only fill up when teams are winning. Still, NU students have achieved excellence in a few sports. The women's lacrosse team won five consecutive NCAA I national championships beginning in 2005. The football team, in spite of holding the all-time record of Division I-A losses, went to the Outback Bowl in 2010. (The last bowl game Northwestern won was the 1949 Rose Bowl.)

Intramurals at Northwestern range from equestrian sports to aikido and Ultimate

Frisbee, while club sports such as tennis, billiards, and dodgeball provide a break from classroom pressures. Northwestern's high-quality recreation centers allow students to participate in swimming, racquetball, aerobics, and other sports. The Sailing Center maintains a fleet of boats and provides instruction in how to sail them on Lake Michigan.

Nearly 70 percent of NU's approximately 8,475 undergraduates live in the 15 university residence halls. Residents choose from a wide variety of living arrangements, from small houses to huge dormitories to residential colleges. Students also have the option of single-sex or coed residences and can take their meals at any of the dining halls, which are located in the residences. All bathrooms are single sex. The 11 residential colleges at NU are intellectual living communities organized around different interests, such as engineering, community service, and the arts. Activities and special programs relate to each residence's theme. Masters and fellows are professors who are actively involved in each college.

Northwestern has managed to keep campus crime down. However, as one student says, "At night, most girls I know don't walk alone." In 2011 Northwestern reported 46 burglaries, two liquor law arrests, and five motor vehicle thefts on its Evanston campus.

Northwestern stands with other well-known schools in charging a hefty tuition—$43,380 in 2012–13, with $13,329 for room and board. Financial aid is based on need, and the school guarantees to meet the full financial needs of students. Forty-two percent received need-based aid, and the average indebtedness of a recent NU grad was 22,130.

SUGGESTED CORE

1. Classics 211, Ancient Athens: Democracy, Drama, and Civilization
2. Philosophy 210, History of Philosophy: Ancient
3. Religion 220/221, Introduction to the Hebrew Bible/ New Testament
4. Religion 340–1, Foundations of Christian Thought
5. Political Science 201, Introduction to Political Theory
6. English 234, Introduction to Shakespeare
7. History 210–1, History of the United States: Precolonial to the Civil War
8. Political Science 303, Modernity and Its Discontents

STRONG SUITS

- A healthy balance between teaching and research among faculty.
- Many opportunities for students to earn money for conducting research.
- Highly praised programs in journalism, Slavic languages and literature, English, management, and political science.
- Mostly fair-minded teachers and apolitical classes.

WEAK POINTS

- Ideological courses in some departments, such as comparative literary studies, international studies, gender studies, and most ethnic-based studies.
- Faculty report conservative job candidates being rejected.
- Occasional outrages, such as a masturbation demo in a human sexuality course.

Oberlin College

Oberlin, Ohio • www.oberlin.edu

Boundless, Desolate Fields

In 1833 two Yankee ministers founded Oberlin to train "teachers and other Christian leaders for the boundless and most desolate fields of the West." Since then, Oberlin has grown considerably in reputation and influence and has left its original Christian mission far behind. The college has "progressed" to a curriculum soaked in ethnic, class, and gender obsessions. Oberlin students are known both for their intellectual firepower and for their leftist social activism.

Academic Life: Lasting relationships

Oberlin College has neither a core curriculum nor a decent set of distribution requirements. With such a minimalist curriculum, students can—and sometimes do—avoid intellectually substantive courses and devote themselves instead to grievance-based disciplines such as women's and ethnic studies.

The College of Arts and Sciences (there is also a music conservatory) offers 46 majors. Some of these provide little more structure than the basic college requirements. Others, though still fairly weak, have improved somewhat over the years. Oberlin English majors must take one course in English literature before 1700, one in literature between 1700 and 1900, and one in literature from 1900 to the present. They are also required to take one course designated as American, one as British, and one as "Diversity"—not a bad balance. Courses in poetry and drama are also recommended. English majors also have the option of selecting interdisciplinary "concentration majors."

History majors can also avoid basic courses, although in 2010 the requirements were expanded a bit: majors must now take two introductory survey courses covering two different geographical areas, one premodern course, and one from each of the three following areas: Europe and Russia; United States and North America; and Asia, Latin America, and Africa.

The politics department's only breadth requirement is to take intermediate courses in three of these four fields: American politics, comparative politics, international politics, and political theory; students could easily avoid foundational courses.

Oberlin's Conservatory of Music is the college's finest academic offering. Enrolling a little more than 600 students, the conservatory offers bachelor of music degrees in performance, composition, technology in music, jazz studies, music history, and music theory (as part of a double major only). Oberlin also offers an undergraduate performance diploma and a graduate artist diploma, as well as four master's degrees. The music conservatory boasts 150 practice studios, around 230 Steinway grand pianos, 40 music studios, five concert halls, a music library, and rare electronic and computer musical instruments. Says one student, "Because of the conservatory, there are a lot of musical performances, most of which are fun and showcase excellent talent."

The sciences are also very strong at Oberlin. One professor says, "I think natural science at Oberlin is a little-known jewel—it has a crucial function in maintaining [Oberlin's] academic caliber and does attract some of the best students." In fact, three Oberlin graduates have won Nobel prizes, all in the sciences.

Other strong departments at the college include Classics, philosophy, politics, and mathematics. Excellent professors include Paul Dawson in politics; Jeffrey Witmer in mathematics; David Benzing (emeritus), Yolanda Cruz,

VITAL STATISTICS

Religious affiliation: *none*
Total enrollment: *2,944*
Total undergraduates: *2,930*
SAT CR/Verbal midrange: *640–740*
SAT Math midrange: *620–720*
ACT midrange: *28–32*
Applicants: *7,172*
Applicants accepted: *31%*
Accepted applicants who enrolled: *33%*
Tuition (general/out of state): *$44,512*
Tuition (in state): *N/A*
Room and board: *$12,120*
Freshman retention rate: *93%*
Graduation rate (4 yrs.): *73%*
Graduation rate (6 yrs.): *86%*
Courses with fewer than 20 students: *68%*
Student-faculty ratio: *11:1*
Courses taught by graduate students: *not provided*
Students living on campus: *91%*
Students in fraternities: *none*
Students in sororities: *none*
Students receiving need-based financial aid: *70%*
Avg. student-loan debt of a recent graduating class: *$20,000*
Most popular majors: *biology, music performance, political science*
Guaranteed housing for 4 years? *no*

703

CAMPUS POLITICS: RED LIGHT

Several students complained to us about the pervasive climate of political correctness on campus. Meanwhile, the social atmosphere will probably be enough to make traditionalist students feel extremely unwelcome. Safer Sex Night and the Drag Ball are not just student parties but institutionalized traditions that students passionately defend and prospectives always hear about (sometimes looking forward to them, sometimes fearing them). One student boasts: "Nothing is unusual here, from nudity in the quad to puking contests in the name of 'art' to men wearing dresses around campus. We are the social conservative's nightmare."

In 2013 Oberlin was treated to a campus-wide orgy of sensitivity training when a few incidents of vulgar, racist graffiti were followed by a purported sighting of someone in Klan costume—which later turned out, campus sources say, to have been a student going home from a party wrapped in a blanket. Instead of fully investigating this "sighting" first, the school canceled classes to gather students for solemn discussions of tolerance and a series of anti-hate events that went on for weeks. Such self-congratulatory hand-wringing is par for the course at Oberlin, as columnist Michelle Malkin (an alumna) has noted—recalling outright "racist" hoaxes perpetrated during her college days by minority students eager to focus attention on racism.

and Roger Laushman in biology; and Martin Ackermann (emeritus) in chemistry and biochemistry.

Unfortunately for students, a good deal of Oberlin's political activity occurs within the classroom, where teachers lean overwhelmingly to the left. One professor says segments of the Oberlin faculty are "ideological and aggressive." A student sees things differently: "I wouldn't say that politics intrude in the classroom; they just make for some interesting debate." A professor says, "The whole public atmosphere is pretty much confined to the Left. In the rhetoric that is constantly used at this place, in questions of sexual orientation and racial divides, there is a real balkanization that has taken place in recent years." One member of the College Republicans reports suffering verbal abuse for her political stance, and another "one of our members got beat up last year before the election, and although there is nothing to prove it was politically motivated, a lot of us have our doubts." He goes on to say, however, that he recommends Oberlin to conservative students and finds the teachers "respectful."

All classes are taught by professors, since Oberlin has only a few graduate students. Upon entering, each Oberlin student is assigned an academic adviser to help choose courses, majors, and future careers. The First Year Seminar Program offers several colloquia each year for freshmen and sophomores, with enrollments limited to just 14 students. "Many of those courses are excellent due to the small class size and their interesting subject focus," a student says.

Oberlin has study-abroad programs in almost two dozen countries on every inhabited continent. The college offers courses in Arabic, Chinese, French, German, Greek and Latin, Hebrew, Italian, Japanese, Korean, Russian, and Spanish.

Student Life: *In loco dementis*

Oberlin has no fraternities or sororities, and instead offers cooperatives. The several on- and off-campus cooperatives house about 20 percent of Oberlin students and offer dining services. Nine of these co-ops are for dining only, and four are residential. Each cooperative is based on a particular theme and identity, ranging from the Kosher House to the Third World Cooperative.

Other housing options at Oberlin include traditional dormitories and theme houses. In order to foster community, Oberlin requires all students to live and eat in dorms or co-ops, but recently it has run out of room, so it's allowing certain seniors to live off campus. Off-campus housing appears quite affordable, and the small town of Oberlin seems fairly safe. There are 11 dorms, "village housing" in college-owned apartments and houses, and nine program houses, themed by language or culture. The college no longer has single-sex dormitories, but it does section off various areas of dorms to be all-women or all-men, by student vote. There are a few coed bathrooms on campus, also by student ballot. Students must choose among the following options: "females only," "males only," "everyone," "just me," "just females (/males)," "female (/male) bodied persons," and "female (/male) identifying persons," whatever these might mean. Even more "open" is the recent option to room with someone of the opposite sex. Or, we guess, of neither.

> A professor laments, "The whole public atmosphere is pretty much confined to the Left. In the rhetoric that is constantly used at this place, in questions of sexual orientation and racial divides, there is a real balkanization that has taken place in recent years."

Extracurricular clubs cover a wide range of interests; they include an Anime Club, student radio (WOBC), and a Zionist club. Besides campus performances, cooperative activities, studying, and heading into Cleveland, students "otherwise go to the Feve (the only bar) or to the Oberlin Inn for pitchers night," says one student. Every year, one of the most popular and controversial events is Safer Sex Night, run by the Sexual Information Center. At one Safer Sex Night, education videos were broadcast on monitors throughout the buildings, and students arrived at the event scantily clad—some in nothing more than a bumper sticker. Faculty members performed demonstrations on how to safely use condoms and other contraceptive devices. This school-sponsored event is much anticipated on campus by students who enjoy games like "Sexy Twister," "safer oral sex" demos, and demonstrations like "Sex Toys 101." The night encourages sexual release, both with or without a partner, and shows students how to do this "safely," although "safely" in this case includes various sadomasochistic activities. After publicity and safety problems, the college banned the sale of alcohol at Safer Sex Night, stopped showing pornographic films, and closed the "Tent of Consent," which two students could enter for two minutes and do whatever they liked—as long as they had discussed their intentions beforehand.

Oberlin's brand of political radicalism is aimed primarily at the liberation of desire. As *FrontPage Magazine* has written, "Oberlin embodies a far-left paradise of agitation, Marxist activism, and sexual licentiousness." Students eager to "make a difference in the world" seem to thrive here and organize around groups such as the Peace Activists League and the Oberlin Action against Prisons.

There is a slow-growing contingent of students with more conservative viewpoints. Back in 2005, an alumnus stepped in to reorganize the long-defunct Oberlin College Republicans—much to the chagrin of the college. The CRs have hosted conservative speakers such as William Kristol and Karl Rove and boast on their website, "We have established ourselves as one of the most active student organizations on campus." A CR member says that the conservatives on campus realize all too well that they are a minority but are guardedly hopeful that students are ready for a change.

An Oberlin College Republican says, "During my time here, I have perceived a growing sense of discontent with the traditional liberal bent at Oberlin. I hear more and more people, while generally liberal themselves, complain of closed-mindedness in the political sphere." The Oberlin pro-life group dissolved about 15 years ago, and the libertarian group has been inactive for several years. Another student says that while Oberlin is predominantly liberal, she had never experienced any hostility toward the conservative minority.

Health concerns seem not to extend to the use of liquor and other drugs. Students say that many Oberlin students are drug users and heavy drinkers. An *Oberlin Review* article reported that students, speaking anonymously, found drug use to be widely popular. One student says it is "really, really easy" to obtain drugs at Oberlin.

Conservative religious students are a clear minority at Oberlin. One source says, "The number of students who don't associate with any religion at all is probably the largest group." One Catholic student notes that there are over a hundred Catholics on the mailing list, but only around 30 go to weekly Mass. The Jewish community boasts the most students attending services.

Perhaps it is telling that on the Oberlin website for student organizations, faith-based clubs are listed under the same category as identity organizations such as La Alianza Latina and the Lesbian, Gay, Bisexual, and Transgendered Union. Still, there is a Christian fellowship, a Hillel, and a Muslim students association, as well as a Queers and Allies of Faith group. Local houses of worship include a Lutheran church, several evangelical and Pentecostal denominations, a Friends meeting, a Unitarian Universalist fellowship, and a Catholic church (though students should probably drive to Cleveland's Immaculate Conception, St. Rocco, or St. Stephen parishes for Latin Mass on Sundays). Jewish religious services are held weekly either at the Hillel center or at Talcott Dining Hall. The campus is also home to weekly Catholic, Muslim, Protestant, and Friends services.

Campus publications include the *Oberlin Review,* the weekly student newspaper; the *Grape,* a magazine focused on world affairs and opinion; *Scope,* a student publication dedicated to artistic endeavor; *Oberlin on Oberlin,* "an online publication chronicling student life and student concerns"; the *Plum Creek Review,* Oberlin's literary magazine; and *Nommo,* focusing on issues relevant to blacks at Oberlin.

Although John Heisman began his coaching career at Oberlin, the college hasn't seen the likes of him lately. Athletics are not a major draw on campus. But that may be changing; according to one professor, "Athletics are more of a priority with the college than they have been in the past." Oberlin is a member of the North Coast Athletic Conference, an NCAA Division III group, and offers 22 varsity sports and between 10 and 15 intramural sports, depending on the year. Students can also participate in any of 12 club sports, including rugby, fencing, and tumbling and circus performance. In 2009–10 Oberlin's Yeomen took third place in cross-country and All-NCAC second-team doubles and singles in tennis. The Yeowomen were All-NCAC first-team singles and doubles and second-team singles.

Crime statistics in 2011 showed 10 forcible sex offenses, 42 burglaries, two motor vehicle thefts, and two robberies on campus.

With 2012–13 tuition at $44,512 and room and board at $12,120, Oberlin makes for an expensive trip out to left field. Nor does the school practice need-blind admissions. However, students admitted will find their full financial need met. Seventy percent of the student body receives need-based financial aid from the college, and the Oberlin Access Initiative provides students eligible for Pell Grants with enough financial aid to avoid having to take out any student loans. Still, the average debt of a recent graduate was around $20,000.

STRONG SUITS	WEAK POINTS
• World-class music performance program and resources.	• No core curriculum or even a decent set of distribution requirements.
• All courses taught by professors, not graduate students.	• One professor calls some leftist colleagues "ideological and aggressive."
• Most classes are small.	• Coed dorm rooms and official school options for "female (/male) bodied persons" and "female (/male) identifying persons."
• Rigorous freshman courses.	• Many radical activist groups with administration support.
• Good programs in the hard sciences.	• Widespread use of drugs.

Patrick Henry College

Purcellville, Virginia • www.phc.edu

Clarity Begins at Home

Patrick Henry College is part of a David and Goliath story that started more than 30 years ago. In the 1970s, thousands of American parents became alarmed by the deteriorating academic and moral quality of public education and turned to homeschooling as an alternative. This was a risky venture. Despite its long history, the practice had become rare, and in many states and localities homeschooling was actually illegal—as it still is, for instance, in Germany (where Nazi-era laws forbid it).

Thirty years later, homeschooling borders on the mainstream. In what is perhaps the greatest monument to its successful coming of age, the Christian homeschooling movement catalyzed the establishment of Patrick Henry College: a four-year undergraduate school offering a complete liberal arts education and preparation for careers in government, politics, media, and education for homeschooled young adults as well as graduates of private and public schools.

This ambitious vision began to take concrete form with the founding of Patrick Henry College in 2000 in Purcellville, Virginia. PHC is dedicated to the difficult and delicate task of harmonizing three things that many today think are in tension with each other: a liberal arts education, worldly success, and an evangelical Christian lifestyle.

Academic Life: A home for schooling

The school now hosts 320 students, a healthy student body for a school that has existed for 13 years, and PHC grads have already made their mark in the world. PHC students are in high demand in congressional offices, government agencies, public policy foundations, and news media outlets as interns. Under the Bush administration, PHC students were a conspicuous presence in the White House (at one point, seven out of a hundred White House interns were PHC students).

That mission is anchored solidly in the school's academic program, which requires of students a strong liberal arts core curriculum and then complements the academic majors they choose with practical apprenticeship programs. The core curriculum introduces students to the principles of the Western intellectual tradition, while the majors give both theoretical and practical grounding in particular fields such as politics, journalism, and the humanities. The apprenticeship program is especially valuable in helping students begin a professional career while still in college.

Once students complete the significant core curriculum, Patrick Henry College offers majors through two departments. The department of government confers bachelor's degrees in journalism and government, while the department of classical liberal arts offers BAs in literature, history, and classical liberal arts. This relatively narrow range of disciplines is actually an advantage, since the school is able to concentrate its resources in a handful of programs.

Students are assigned an academic adviser based on their anticipated major. Advisers assist students with major declarations, course planning, and academic concerns.

The most popular and well-developed major at PHC is government, which offers four different tracks: political theory, American politics and policy, international politics and policy, and strategic intelligence. The political theory track is headed by Mark Mitchell, probably the most well-liked teacher on campus. Its students get a thorough training in classical political philosophy, studying thinkers from Plato and Aristotle to

---

VITAL STATISTICS

Religious affiliation: *nondenominational (Christian)*
Total enrollment: *320*
Total undergraduates: *320*
SAT CR/Verbal midrange: *630–740*
SAT Math midrange: *560–660*
ACT midrange: *29–34*
Applicants: *239*
Applicants accepted: *79%*
Accepted applicants who enrolled: *45%*
Tuition (general/out of state): *$24,352*
Tuition (in state): *N/A*
Room and board: *$9,768*
Freshman retention rate: *93%*
Graduation rate (4 yrs.): *58%*
Graduation rate (6 yrs.): *72%*
Courses with fewer than 20 students: *65%*
Student-faculty ratio: *11:1*
Courses taught by graduate students: *none*
Students living on campus: *95%*
Students in fraternities: *none*
Students in sororities: *none*
Students receiving need-based financial aid: *35%*
Avg. student-loan debt of a recent graduating class: *$30,000*
Most popular majors: *communications, literature/ foreign languages, social sciences*
Guaranteed housing for 4 years? *no*

CAMPUS POLITICS: GREEN LIGHT

Patrick Henry College is an extremely conservative school, politically and religiously. (There is said to be only one Democrat on campus.) Nevertheless, PHC has a great deal of intellectual diversity. One student calls it "a melting pot of conservatism." The idea that PHC is "cranking out Karl Roves is untrue," says another. Almost every conceivable variety of right-of-center thought and sentiment is present on campus. There are *National Review*– and *Weekly Standard*–style neoconservatives, traditional conservatives, libertarians, "small is beautiful" localists, and Constitution Party supporters. Patrick Henry College buzzes with debate at all levels of political discourse, from horserace-type punditry about particular campaigns to the airy heights of political philosophy. When a new freshman steps onto campus, he will most certainly be forced to reexamine his political beliefs or inclinations in this atmosphere that promotes debate and critical thought. Furthermore, although PHC offers students many opportunities to get involved in practical politics, it is not an activist factory. "The school is not a place to make activists, but it is a comfortable place for activists," says a student.

After extensive interviews with students and faculty, we found no free-speech issues at Patrick Henry College—except for an occasional prudishness on the part of some students that makes it difficult to discuss some of the racier bits of Western history. A student who transferred out of PHC after converting to Catholicism reported that the atmosphere on campus is overwhelmingly Protestant, and students who object to that should look elsewhere.

Tocqueville, Eric Voegelin, and E. F. Schumacher. Political theory classes often reach the level of a graduate school seminar, sources say. An offshoot of the theory program is the Alexis de Tocqueville Society, which publishes an excellent student journal featuring articles such as "Ancient Views of the Body in Homer, Plato, and St. Augustine."

The policy tracks (both American and international) focus on the empirical and practical details of governmental decision making. The policy programs seem to give students a solid introduction to political praxis. One professor says that students are hampered by Patrick Henry's lack of emphasis on statistics and economics—although a student disagrees, arguing that the "policy track is solid. You delve into statistics that fuel research." An offshoot of the policy tracks is Libertas, a student organization that lobbies in Congress. Policy majors, says one student, are concerned with "how to make biblical worldview and policy match. How do we prepare legislation that's biblical and attractive to society?"

The strategic intelligence track in the government department, the largest government track, is an exciting program that is distinctive to PHC. Students learn to become intelligence analysts and undergo training that will give them a security clearance by graduation. One student says that graduates are "getting really great jobs. Government agencies and private contractors are snapping them up."

The government department also offers a journalism program directed by journalist Leslie Sillars, whom students describe as an "extremely good" teacher. Journalism majors have a choice between two curricula: a government track that prepares them specifically for political and government coverage, and a classical liberal arts track that is aimed at journalism covering cultural and religious issues and topics. Says one student: "Journalism is really good at placing its students." One recent graduate landed a writing position with *Slate*.

Within the classical liberal arts department are three majors. Of these, the literature major is the most well established. Headed by Steve Hake, whom students describe as "dedicated," the major offers courses in both critical interpretation and creative writing. Says one professor, "What I see every day are writers, very creative ones. Writers outnumber critics three to one. . . . I believe that some of the literature that is read in the twenty-first century will be written by some of these students." Students majoring in literature study the great works of European and American literature.

The history major offers strong instruction in European, American, and contemporary world history. David Aikman, an award-winning journalist formerly with *Time* magazine, peppers his lectures on contemporary world history with anecdotes of his own experience as an eyewitness to world events, from Israel to Tiananmen Square. All history majors are required to take core courses in U.S. history, the history of Western civilization, and the philosophy and methodology of history. There are also electives in the history of Russia, China, and the Middle East, and electives on thematic topics like Islam. In the senior year, two major projects cap a history major's curriculum: a year-long senior thesis based on primary source research, and a faith and reason integration project.

A student says, "Professors are really personable, not aloof. It's just like talking to your neighbor. A professor will say, 'Here, let me pray for you.' They care about you as people."

Paradoxically, the weakest major in the classical liberal arts department is the one called classical liberal arts. For a long time, teachers report, it was unclear as to what this major was even about. It has recently been settled that the major exists primarily as an education department, preparing students for careers as teachers in the rising movement of classical elementary and secondary education. The recent hiring of Laura McCollum as professor of education and academic dean has breathed life into this major, and there are plans for its expansion.

All of PHC's departments are said to have dedicated faculty and practical apprenticeship programs, and the college is so small that students describe their professors as very accessible. None of the classes are taught by teaching assistants. "I have the home phone numbers of two of my professors," one student remarks. "Some of my best memories are lunches with teachers." Another student says, "Professors are really personable, not aloof. . . . It's just like talking to your neighbor. A professor will say, 'Here, let me pray for you.' They care about you as people." Some more exceptional teachers at PHC are Stephen Baskerville in government; Gene Veith in classical liberal arts; Robert Spinney in history; and Michael Kucks in physics. Says one student, "I'm not good at physics, but I didn't want to miss a class because Professor Kucks teaches it."

In addition to working closely with faculty, all the majors offer hands-on opportunities

SUGGESTED CORE

The school's required core curriculum suffices.

for working in their respective professional fields. Journalism majors intern with print, radio, or newspaper companies. Literature majors can find internships with presses or policy foundations or work with outside professional writers and academics, such as Catherine Pickstock, Patricia Wrede, and Peter Leithart. History majors can intern with historical archives, and classical liberal arts majors find internships with local Christian private schools.

The overarching framework for all these majors and the core curriculum is the college's Evangelical Protestant faith. Patrick Henry's Evangelical commitments are summarized in its two-part Biblical Foundations Statement, a bare-bones assertion of Protestant orthodoxy that would be hard for a conscientious Catholic or Orthodox Christian believer to sign on to.

Faculty, but not students, must subscribe to the Statement of Biblical Worldview, a more detailed theological statement. It goes into somewhat more depth on doctrines such as biblical inerrancy and the Trinity and applies them to particular questions—such as biblical creation, the structure of family life, and the "biblical basis" for democratic government.

There are no science or math majors at PHC, so the courses in physics, biology, and Euclid's geometry are designed to be especially intelligible for students who do not have great aptitude for math or science. Patrick Henry College does stand out from other liberal arts schools through its position on creationism. PHC is not merely skeptical of evolutionary theory. The school's Statement of Biblical Worldview categorically rejects evolution in favor of special creation and declares that all classes must adhere to an understanding of creation in six 24-hour days—something St. Augustine questioned in the fourth century. However, PHC confers no BAs in biology, much less in anthropology or geology.

The absence of a philosophy or theology department may make the course offerings in those disciplines relatively weak compared with the rest of the curriculum, but such courses are well integrated into the political theory track of the government major, and the core curriculum contains both philosophy and theology requirements. There are three biblical studies requirements, two courses in the "Theology of the Bible," and one in the "Principles of Biblical Reasoning." Prominent Christian apologist John Warwick Montgomery spends each fall semester teaching core courses in apologetics.

With its emphasis on politics, Patrick Henry College stresses forensic reasoning and debate ability. A sign of this is the success of Patrick Henry students in debate. PHC's moot court team has repeatedly won the American Collegiate Moot Court Association national tournaments and even in past years has bested Balliol College, Oxford. PHC's newest debate team participates in the National Forensic Association, and it has already claimed top 10 speaker awards and team rankings at every tournament.

All PHC graduates must demonstrate intermediate-level proficiency in a foreign language. Government majors on the strategic intelligence track must study a modern foreign language. Classical liberal arts, history, and literature majors must choose a classical language. Aside from taking one of the languages PHC offers (currently, Greek, Latin, and Russian), students frequently choose to complete their language requirement by going overseas, although Patrick Henry does not offer a formal study-abroad program.

Student Life: Getting "Bob-tized"

Patrick Henry students are generally serious about their studies, and the campus atmosphere is fairly quiet and sedate. Drinking parties and dormitory bacchanals are absent. Alcohol use is forbidden (on and off campus), and students must follow a "business casual" dress code during school hours, Monday through Friday. Chapel service, held three times a week, is mandatory, and while attendance is now enforced by the honor system, the services are still well attended.

As on all college campuses, romance is an important part of student life. Patrick Henry students are said to abide by the college prohibition on sex outside of marriage, but they do date. While at first it was somewhat paternalistic, the administration now takes a more relaxed approach to students' private lives. So long as they observe the school's ethical standards (for example, no cheating, drinking, or fornication), students are treated as adults.

Almost every day there is an Ultimate Frisbee pickup game. There are active intercollegiate men's and women's soccer and basketball teams. In 2009 the Sentinels, the basketball team, qualified for the Shenandoah Valley Athletic Conference. There is also intramural volleyball, basketball, football, soccer, softball, tennis, and table tennis. Residential areas in dormitories are sex segregated, but dormitory lounges are coed, and students frequently socialize and watch movies in the lounges. There are no foreign language immersion houses.

There are only a handful of student organizations (only about 15 are officially recognized), but they offer a diverse array of choices. The Titan Society explores the world of finance; the Student Media Network produces and distributes student publications; *Sans Frontières* promotes a better understanding of foreign cultures; the International Justice Mission Club raises awareness of global human slavery, trafficking, and exploitation; the *Patrick Henry Herald* is a weekly newspaper, and *Cuttlefish* is a monthly literary publication. Other groups include the Student Chorale, Strings Ensemble, fencing club, yearbook committee, and mixed martial arts club. There are no fraternities or sororities.

Minor pranks are frequent occurrences. Male students who get engaged are given Bobtisms. This means they are dunked in the campus's Lake Bob, even in the middle of winter.

Altogether, there is a very cohesive spirit at PHC. One undergrad remarks: "It's a tight-knit community. Be prepared to know everybody, and have everybody knowing you." Another student says: "You're friends with everybody, but gossip can be a problem. Spiritual life on campus is very good. Almost every guy in my dorm wing is a very zealous (in the good sense) Christian and genuinely striving to follow God's will in life. There's a lot of encouraging going on and a high percentage of enthusiastic Christians."

The close-knit religious community on campus exerts a powerful effect on students. One says that he learned at PHC that "a lot of people are hurting, dealing with their own sets of issues and headaches. Realizing that has given me a better understanding of people and more of a concern for their well-being." Originally, this student wanted to run for higher office, but now he feels called to seminary.

The school's campus is isolated and extremely safe. While the school does not report annual crime statistics, there have been very few incidents since it was founded.

Tuition at PHC was $24,352 in 2012–13, and room and board averaged $9,768. The average student-loan debt of a recent graduating class was $30,000. The school reports that 35 percent of students received need-based financial aid, while more than 90 percent received merit-based aid.

STRONG SUITS	WEAK POINTS
• A solid grounding in the Western tradition from a traditional, American Protestant perspective. • Excellent programs in government, writing, history, and journalism. • Mandatory internships in every major prepare students for the world of work. • Friendly, committed teachers who form strong mentor relationships with students. • A wholesome (if insular) campus environment with traditional mores.	• Little instruction in math or science. Biology classes teach "young Earth" creationism. • The education program has long been weak, though new hires are trying to strengthen it. • The intense evangelical atmosphere is likely uncomfortable for non-Protestants. • Ironically, very limited offerings in theology and church history.

Pepperdine University

Malibu, California • www.pepperdine.edu

Beach Boys for Jesus

Founded in 1937 by Christian entrepreneur George Pepperdine and affiliated with the United Churches of Christ, Pepperdine University remains remarkably true to the aspirations of its founder. Its brand of higher education is essentially aimed at cultivating a pragmatic—rather than an intellectual—graduate who embraces Christian values, is conservative in disposition, and is poised for a life of leadership and purpose. Pepperdine brings together a relatively sound liberal arts curriculum, a religious orientation, and a warm, friendly atmosphere situated in one of most beautiful campuses of the United States.

Academic Life: Preprofessional, plus a core

Pepperdine's interdisciplinary curriculum with a small core is much better than most. Its three-course core sequence, "Western Heritage," takes students briskly from 30,000 BC up through the present. By adding a few courses, a student can construct a traditional liberal arts education, especially through the school's Great Books Colloquium. In it, students will find support from a serious and accomplished faculty, small classes, ample opportunities for close instruction, and an emphasis on teaching, rather than research. The colloquium has

715

some of Pepperdine's "most engaging scholars," says one professor, and there are often 20 or fewer students in each class, meaning students can develop a good working relationship with a professor. One professor says, "If a student wishes to get a solid liberal arts education at Pepperdine, he or she must be involved in the Great Books program."

Every student is assigned an adviser from the Academic Advising Center and a first-year seminar adviser—or major adviser, if he has chosen one. The Career Center and Academic Advising Center provides additional assistance.

Pepperdine's small undergraduate population in Seaver College makes it fairly easy to get to know professors. "If you are a motivated student and you find professors with whom you hit it off," a professor says, "you can do a lot of one-on-one." Says a student, "The faculty members are extremely accessible. I really feel spoiled. All my teachers know my first name."

Professors are primarily teachers, not researchers. Graduate students do not teach classes. While research is valued, two out of the four standards used to determine tenure and promotion have to do with teaching. "Here at Pepperdine, teaching is the priority," a faculty member says. "Teaching is still the primary responsibility," another confirms.

Only a few courses—primarily in religion and the humanities—are taught in large lecture halls. Most courses at Seaver College are quite small.

Pepperdine University comprises Seaver College (for undergraduates); the School of Law; the George L. Graziadio School of Business and Management; the Graduate School of Education and Psychology; and the School of Public Policy, which opened in 1997. Pepperdine is well known for its programs in business administration and sports medicine, and it offers a sound economics program as well. Students may also pursue a BA through the Center for International Studies and Languages, with concentrations offered in Asian studies, international management, European studies, political studies, and Latin American studies. Less popular divisions at Seaver are natural science (a BA designed for students who intend to enter the dual-degree 3/2 engineering program), religion, and art.

Several faculty named philosophy as one of the weaker departments, with one suggesting that the discipline is almost ignored. Pepperdine largely regards philosophy as "integrated into other fields," as one professor put it. Required courses include "Introduction to Philosophy," "Logic," "Ancient Philosophy," "Modern Philosophy," "Ethics," and a "Major Philosophical Problems Seminar."

Speech restrictions and classroom politics are generally not an issue at Pepperdine. In September 2010, Pepperdine's College Libertarians sponsored a "free-speech wall" in honor of Free Speech Week at the university. The wall contained comments and statements by fellow students, which one undergraduate complains was filled with "racist and sexist" stuff—while another said that though she did not agree with certain comments, she would "still protect your right to say them." The paper wall was torn down by a lone protestor who disagreed.

The English department at Pepperdine offers three concentrations: writing, literature, and education, with different requirements. The literature focus prescribes 10 courses: one introductory class; four in British lit (one of which must be pre-1800 and another post-1800); four American lit courses; a literary theory course; two electives (one designated as multicultural); and one senior seminar.

The major in history requires, among other things, "History of the American Peoples" from precolonial times to the present

CAMPUS POLITICS: GREEN LIGHT

Pepperdine is a politically balanced university, and while there may be some slight variation in the atmosphere of some classes, from center-left to center-right, conservative as well as more liberal students should feel at home here. True to the vision of George Pepperdine, the school has integrated religion and religious themes into its curriculum and teaching. As one professor says, "The undergraduate and graduate faculty take faith seriously. Pepperdine has an active Christian worldview, which is both optimistic and highly affirming." Another teacher suggests that Pepperdine is "one of very few schools where the Christian emphasis has actually increased over the last twenty years." Perhaps the most serious challenge to the vision of Christian education at Pepperdine is the business ethos that prevails at the school, which diverts resources away from the teaching of subjects such as philosophy that appear to have few eventual professional possibilities.

In 2012 libertarians were rankled when a political science major was told she could not gain academic credit for an internship with a group seeking to legalize marijuana use, because that organization's goals were incompatible with the university's mission.

(two courses); "Historiography"; an introduction to research; and a senior thesis. Students may concentrate on American, European, or global history.

Political science is divided into five subfields: methodology, political theory, American government and politics, international relations, and comparative government. All political science majors must take "American People and Politics," one introductory course in four of the five fields, a research methods course, and a writing-intensive course.

Pepperdine's religion requirements can be fulfilled by taking one out of several three-course sequences, with titles like "The History and Religion of Israel" or "The History and Religion of Early Christianity."

There are a number of truly outstanding professors at Pepperdine—although many, including Ted McAllister and James Q. Wilson in the School of Public Policy—generally do not teach undergraduate courses. Some of the best undergraduate faculty at Pepperdine include Ronald W. Batchelder in economics; Michael G. Ditmore in English; Paul Contino, Michael D. Gose, and Mason Marshall in Great Books; Don Thompson in mathematics; J. Christopher Soper in political science; and Ronald C. Highfield in religion.

Students can participate in one of Pepperdine's many international study programs. Seaver College offers six year-round residential programs in Buenos Aires, Florence, Heidelberg, Lausanne, London, and Shanghai, along with summer programs in these countries as well as in East Africa, Fiji, Russia, Scotland, Spain, and other locations.

Seaver College requires its students to take one language course in Chinese, French, German, Hebrew, Italian, Japanese, or Spanish, and offers majors in French, German, and Italian.

Student Life: Reading at Canyon Ranch

Pepperdine has one of the most beautiful campuses in the nation. Located about 30 minutes from Los Angeles in Malibu, the school overlooks the beach. A student says, "The Malibu campus feels insular. Besides the ocean and beautiful beaches, there is not much activity in the vicinity. Malibu is a hideout for stars and is prone to quietude and privacy."

The university, as one faculty member says, has no "town-gown relationship." For one thing, there's not much of a town; students have to drive most anywhere they want to go off campus. But Pepperdine offers many activities to keep students occupied—perhaps more than it should. "Sometimes there are too many social distractions, along with the beach, which keep students from studying," says one professor.

Pepperdine lists more than 70 registered student organizations in addition to a national Greek system of seven sororities and five fraternities. Examples include the Model UN, Military Service Club, Dance Team, and the Asian Student Association. Pepperdine operates TV-32 and KWVS FM 101.5. The Student Journalism Program produces a weekly printed newspaper, *The Graphic*; an online newspaper, the *Online Graphic*; and a biannual news magazine, *Currents*. The Young Democrats, College Libertarians, and College Republicans are active on campus, though the student body leans Republican.

> "Sometimes there are too many social distractions, along with the beach, which keep students from studying," says one professor. Another agrees, "If a student wishes to get a solid liberal arts education at Pepperdine, he or she must be involved in the Great Books program."

Housing at Pepperdine is limited, but freshmen and sophomores under 21 and not living with their parents must live on campus. Seaver College provides on-campus housing for approximately 1,900 unmarried students. The school imposes some rules—no alcohol, no firearms, no candles, no pets, no smoking in dorms, and no one from the opposite sex in your living area except during specified hours. As students share their accommodation with a roommate, they are also requested to keep guests to a minimum.

Pepperdine's religious commitment draws many of its students, and Pepperdine expects its students to pursue religious interests. Even so, one student says, "the relative conservatism of the student body is not evident in the way the girls dress. I have never seen such short skirts in my life." The college strongly encourages students to join a church, and it offers Seaver-wide worship assemblies, devotionals, small-group Bible studies, student-led ministries, monthly missions meetings, and an on-campus ministry (University Church of Christ). The University Church of Christ holds Bible study groups and conducts services on Sunday mornings. "Collide," a student-run devotional group, also meets every Wednesday. Besides these, there are a number of small groups that meet on campus. One professor says that there is a "healthy mix between the devout and the not-so-devout" among Pepperdine students. For Catholics, the rather liberal Our Lady of Malibu parish is close by.

Pepperdine's convocations, of which students must attend 14 per term, "are usually religious, sometimes political, and [the latter] always liberal in nature," according to a student. "If there are conservative speakers, they never talk about politics, only religion."

Pepperdine University is a member of the West Coast Conference, the Mountain Pacific Sports Federation, and Division I of the National Collegiate Athletic Association. Pepperdine has a number of competitive athletic programs. The Waves are well known in water polo, tennis, and volleyball circles, and field teams; other varsity sports include golf, cross-country, basketball, baseball, track, soccer, swimming, and diving. "The homecoming basketball game is huge—everyone from the school goes, packing the Firestone Fieldhouse, and the camaraderie is amazing," a student says.

Pepperdine has 22 suite-style residence halls, which are designated either "Freshmen Only" or "Standard." The latter are open to all class levels, but usually house only freshmen and sophomores. Each hall contains a double bathroom, a common living area, and four double bedrooms. The suites are clustered six to a hall surrounding a main lobby with a fireplace, television, and laundry room. The Rockwell Towers Residence Hall is reserved for 275 sophomores and upperclassmen; it has two wings for men and four for women,

---

SUGGESTED CORE

1. Great Books Colloquium 121, I (Greeks and Romans)
2. Philosophy 300, Ancient Philosophy
3. Religion 101/102, The History and Religion of Israel/The History and Religion of Early Christianity
4. Religion 531, Christian History and Theology I: Ancient and Medieval
5. Great Books Colloquium 123/Philosophy 310, III (17th to early 19th Centuries)/Modern Philosophy
6. English 420/Great Books Colloquium 122, Shakespeare/II (Early Christianity to Renaissance)
7. History 520/521/522, Colonial America, 1492–1763/The American Revolution and the New Nation, 1763–1815/Jacksonian America and the Civil War, 1815–1877
8. Great Books Colloquium 324, IV (19th Century to Present)

separated by the main entrance and lounge. The tower has double rooms, and each pair of doubles shares a bathroom.

The Lovernich Residential Complex houses nearly 300 students, all over the age of 21. The complex is composed of three blocks that overlook a landscaped courtyard. The blocks' apartments are made up of two bedrooms, one bathroom, a living area, and a kitchen, although two students share each bedroom. Apartments are designated for both men and women.

Pepperdine also hosts around 250 public-arts and musical events each year. The fine arts department has a number of performing ensembles—including a chamber music ensemble, jazz band, guitar ensemble, and wind instrument ensemble—and students may catch their performances at the college's intimate theaters. Equipped with a three-manual Rogers organ and acoustically redesigned in 2004, Stauffer Chapel hosts a number of vocal and instrumental chamber concerts.

Pepperdine is one of the safest campuses in the nation, and violent crime is rare. In 2011 the school reported one forcible sex offense, and 14 burglaries on campus.

It is not cheap to study in Malibu. Pepperdine's 2012–13 tuition was estimated at $42,772, and room and board at $12,600. Approximately 75 percent of Pepperdine students received some form of financial assistance each year. Some 57 percent of students got need-based aid. The average loan debt of a 2011 grad was a stiff $32,238.

STRONG SUITS	WEAK POINTS
• Liberal arts students call teachers dedicated, and accessible if one takes the initiative. • No classes led by graduate students, and most are small. • Renowned programs in business administration, sports medicine, economics. • Free speech and a mostly balanced, open political atmosphere, with many religious groups. • The school is on the beach in Malibu.	• Weak program in philosophy. • Religion and humanities classes are among the largest, most impersonal. • Many of the "name" faculty don't actually teach undergraduates. • Students face many diversions from study in this spa-like environment.

Princeton University

Princeton, New Jersey • www.princeton.edu

The Undergrad's Ivy

Founded in 1746, Princeton University is the fourth college established in the U.S. It has historically been a competitive, elite institution—and now, often tying with Harvard, it's almost always rated the first or second best college in America. Princeton prides itself as being the "undergraduate's Ivy." One professor describes it as being "as close to the intellectual ideal for undergraduates as one can find in a top research university." With its small graduate program and student faculty ratio of 6 to 1, Princeton sends its big-name professors out to teach. One student says that professors are "very accessible and helpful, overall." According to a student, "Princeton encourages students to pick smaller majors where they can get more attention from profs."

The school has expanded its campus recently and extended its residential college system.

Out of all the Ivies, Princeton is the one most friendly to conservatives and people of faith. It's also near or at the top when it comes to academic excellence. Anyone who can get in should be thankful and attend.

VITAL STATISTICS

Religious affiliation: *none*
Total enrollment: *7,859*
Total undergraduates: *5,249*
SAT CR/Verbal midrange: *690–790*
SAT Math midrange: *710–790*
ACT midrange: *31–35*
Applicants: *27,189*
Applicants accepted: *8.4%*
Accepted applicants who enrolled: *57%*
Tuition (general/out of state): *$38,650*
Tuition (in state): *N/A*
Room and board: *$12,630*
Freshman retention rate: *98%*
Graduation rate (4 yrs.): *90%*
Graduation rate (6 yrs.): *96%*
Courses with fewer than 20 students: *71%*
Student-faculty ratio: *6:1*
Courses taught by graduate students: *not provided*
Students living on campus: *97%*
Students in fraternities: *N/A*
Students in sororities: *N/A*
Students receiving need-based financial aid: *90%*
Avg. student-loan debt of a recent graduating class *$5,330*
Most popular majors: *biology, engineering, social sciences*
Guaranteed housing for 4 years? *yes*

Academic Life: No pain, no gain

Like most universities today, Princeton lacks a core curriculum, although its students typically get a well-rounded education. The school requires AB (Bachelor of Arts) undergrads to take a range of courses, covering seven distinct areas, including epistemology and cognition, ethical thought and moral values, historical analysis, quantitative reasoning, two science and technology courses (one with laboratory), two social analysis courses, and two literature and the arts courses. Students must also complete one to four terms of a foreign language, depending on the language and the level at which they start.

For those who want to get a serious education in the foundations of Western thought and civilization, we recommend the highly rated Humanities sequence—a yearlong set of four courses that focus on Western literature, philosophy, religion, and history. While this is essentially a Great Books course, it is interdisciplinary, with reading complemented by museum visits, film, and discussion. A sophomore calls Humanities "one of the defining experiences of my intellectual life." This much-praised sequence, as a student remarks, is meant only "for the highly motivated who are seriously interested in developing a thorough grounding in the great literature and philosophy of the West." Another comments that "one of the best aspects for me came from the amazing students."

The Writing Seminars required for freshmen are relatively new to Princeton. The university offers over a hundred each year to compensate for the unfortunate fact that few high schools—even good high schools—teach analytical writing and reasoning skills.

Seminars are the smallest classes at Princeton, with no more than 12 students in each, but lecture classes aren't massive. Students meet twice a week for 80 minutes, which may not sound like much—but, as with other courses, these are supplemented by "precepts," small group discussion sessions. Although these are often led by graduate students, professors will usually act as preceptor for at least one session, even in the larger classes. One student notes that although English is generally considered "one of those majors where it's easy to get lost in the shuffle," lectures in the department "are small enough so that the professor takes all of the precepts.... I've been incredibly impressed with how easy it is to develop truly meaningful relationships with some of the top professors in the country." Students have plenty of access to their professors, if they want. One undergrad says, "I find that most students don't use office hours, but that professors are consistently urging students to seek them out. I find it's always very easy to make appointments—and that professors are extremely accommodating."

Princeton's freshman academic advising system has been known to leave freshmen floundering in classes that are over their heads. For 2012 a new pilot program has been introduced to improve the system and to make it more useful. Also, this teething problem is usually resolved after freshman year, when "knowledgeable departmental advisers take over," as one student explains.

Students choose a major at the end of their sophomore year. In their third year, they write in-depth "junior papers," which often serve as the basis for a senior thesis—a requirement at Princeton. These independent research projects are both challenging and rewarding for students. "I think the combination of the junior papers and the senior thesis

CAMPUS POLITICS: GREEN LIGHT

The faculty at Princeton is overwhelmingly left of center, but politics rarely enters the classroom to any significant degree, and different viewpoints are welcomed. As one student says, "As long as I do top-notch work, professors (even very liberal ones) respect it. I've never had a professor penalize me for voicing a different opinion; if anything, professors mark students down if they feel the student is merely parroting back what he has been told."

Princeton is one of the few U.S. universities with a solid, intellectual conservative presence (the James Madison Institute), and its effect is noteworthy. Conservative and religious students will find a welcoming environment, far more open to conservative viewpoints than most secular schools. One student says that, at Princeton, students have "the very best arguments for conservative social and political ideals and beliefs, but also (from peers and professors) some of the sharpest liberal critics of those views.... The country's future conservative leaders are coming from Princeton."

means that Princeton undergraduates do more serious, independent work than students almost anywhere, and they provide extensive opportunities for working one-on-one with faculty," says one professor. Scientists perform original research while creative writing students craft novels. Public policy students design new public and private programs: For instance, 1989 graduate Wendy Kopp's senior thesis became the basis for the volunteer program Teach for America.

Academics at Princeton are rigorous. Grade-deflation policies are in place to ensure honest evaluations.

A Princeton tradition is the honor code. Exams are unproctored, and students must sign an honor pledge on their tests. Violations are tried by tribunal, and punishments include suspension and expulsion.

Literary types should apply for seminars in the creative writing department, where bestselling writers Joyce Carol Oates and Paul Muldoon critique student papers. A student says that English is "one of the strongest programs in the country, [with] an incredibly dedicated group of professors who are passionately interested in getting to know students one on one." As to faculty, the same student recommends "flamboyant Victorian Lit professor" Jeff Nunokawa and "brilliant Spenser/16th-century lit professor" Jeff Dolven.

Departmental requirements are solid; majors take "British Literature from the 14th to the 18th Centuries" and an introductory genre course; two courses in pre-1800 British literature (only one can cover Shakespeare); a pre-1865 American literature class; a post-1800 literature course; a class in "Anglophone or U.S. minority literatures"; a class in theory and criticism; and a junior seminar. Students may opt to concentrate on tracks such as comparative literature, creative writing, or British literature.

The history department is renowned for its strong faculty, with Harold James, Stephen Kotkin, Anthony Grafton, and lecturer Paul Miles singled out for special praise. A retired Army colonel, Miles is a popular lecturer, with "impeccable manners and a lecture style that students find most illuminating and informative," says one professor. His balanced, respectful, and nondogmatic approach to American civic and military history has made his course, "The United States and World Affairs," one of the most popular at the university. Majors must complete two prerequisite classes and a course each in European, U.S., non-Western, and premodern history, as well as a junior seminar and four history electives. Students are required to choose a concentration (like the Near East; women and gender; or war, revolution, and the state) and pass a comprehensive exam.

> "I think the combination of the junior papers and the senior thesis means that Princeton undergraduates do more serious, independent work than students almost anywhere, and they provide extensive opportunities for working one-on-one with faculty," says one professor.

Classics is another strong department, where professor Harriet Flower is highly recommended. One faculty member says, "The best humanistic education continues to be in the Classics, but the liberal arts, engineering, and the natural sciences are very strong as well."

In the politics department, Robert P. George is described as "a great mentor, highly involved despite having one of the busiest schedules of anyone at Princeton." In fact, George was singled out repeatedly by students and faculty alike for his contribution to academic life. George is the director of Princeton's James Madison Program in American Ideals and Institutions—described by one student as "a must-join for conservatives." Politics majors must take two prerequisite classes and one in systematic analysis, like "Mathematical Models in the Study of Politics" or "Social Statistics." Students decide to concentrate in American politics, comparative politics, international relations, or political theory, and will write a senior thesis and complete a senior examination in the subject. Three classes in the primary field, two in another field, and one in a third are required as well.

The math and physics departments are well respected at Princeton, and science generally has a good name here. Computer science teacher Brian Kernighan, one student says, "is particularly great to work with." The math department, says another, "is the top in the country. One of the greatest professors is Nicholas M. Katz, followed by Robert C. Gunning."

The German department came in for much praise, with one professor saying that "the German program is one of the country's best, led by a senior lecturer who specializes in secondary-language acquisition." One student singled out the teaching of senior lecturer Jamie Rankin, who is also known for "cooking an eleven-course reproduction of the last dinner on the *Titanic* for freshmen."

SUGGESTED CORE

Humanities 216-217-218-219, a four-course sequence on the history of Western culture, may be supplemented with the following:

- Religion 230, Hebrew Bible and Ancient Israel
- Religion 251, The New Testament and Christian Origins
- History 373, The New Nation

Many students take Econ 101 and 102, and almost all the professors for these courses are excellent, from libertarian Elizabeth C. Bogan to boisterous left-winger Uwe Reinhardt.

Princeton offers a number of study-abroad programs, from summers, years, or semesters to research work, postgraduate programs, volunteer work, and international internships. Particular programs around the world are affiliated with Princeton, like the University of Queensland in Brisbane, Australia; a program in British literature at the University College in London; a science program in Paris; and an architecture exchange program with the University of Hong Kong, among others. Despite Princeton's extensive offerings, just about 14 percent of students study abroad.

Languages offered on campus include Ancient or Modern Greek, Arabic, Chinese, French, German, Hebrew, Hindi, Italian, Japanese, Korean, Latin, Russian, Spanish, Swahili, and Turkish.

Student Life: Parnassus in New Jersey

The Princeton campus is considered beautiful and harmonious, with most buildings constructed in some form of the "collegiate gothic" style that Princeton helped make famous. Even the school's newest buildings are being constructed in a compatible style.

Princeton boasts more than 200 student-run organizations—and according to one student, proposals for new organizations come in weekly. Students read a bevy of publications, including the *Daily Princetonian*, a humor magazine called the *Tiger*, *Business Today* (the U.S.'s largest student publication, with a circulation of 200,000), the artsy *Nassau Weekly*, and others. There is also a campus radio station, WPRB.

Even those not studying theater have a chance at acting. As one student says, "A school has to be pretty amazing to have an open-audition Shakespearean theatrical troupe that puts on four to five theatrical productions a year—and that gets quite excellent and appreciative audiences." Musicians and singers can join the Princeton University Glee Club, the

Princeton Chapel Choir, the Lux Choir (which specializes in Anglican sacred music), the Princeton University Orchestra, Jazz Ensemble, Band (one of fewer than a dozen "scramble" bands in the U.S.), or Opera Theater, among others. There are also numerous a cappella groups, chamber music ensembles, and dance groups.

A number of students also join community service organizations, entrepreneurial clubs, multicultural groups—and ROTC, which offers merit-based scholarships that pay full tuition and fees. Founded by Princetonians James Madison and Aaron Burr, the American Whig-Cliosophic Society (Whig-Clio) is the oldest college political, literary, and debating club in the United States.

Princeton students have long had a reputation for heavy reading, but one student added that "they are very athletically inclined; they also like to exercise hard." Over 25 percent of the student population plays varsity and junior varsity sports. The Princeton Tigers compete in orange and black on 36 varsity teams and are particularly strong in lacrosse and rowing.

In recent years Princeton has earned a reputation for being one of the more faith-friendly elite universities in the U.S. There are several prayer groups and religious groups on campus, which, as one professor notes, "often draw sizable numbers of the religiously devout to their regular meetings." Religious organizations range from the Baha'i Club and Athletes in Action to the Orthodox Christian Fellowship and Muslim Students' Association. There is also the Anscombe Society, named for the British analytic philosopher and Catholic convert G. E. M. Anscombe. The society puts on a number of lectures throughout the year, and has occasional "Pro-life, Pro-family" receptions and coffee evenings. Connected to the official campus ministry are a number of clergy of various denominations. These include David Buschman (Baptist), B. Keith Brewer (Methodist), and Fr. Tom Mullelly, the Catholic chaplain who heads the very active Aquinas Institute on campus. The institute sponsors a number of lectures throughout the year and offers pilgrimages to places like Rome and Assisi—as well as rather more lighthearted weekend beach retreats. A Mormon temple is located less than a mile from campus, and the "young, dynamic" Rabbi Eitan Webb attracts the more traditionally minded Jewish students to Chabad.

Conservative groups on campus include *The Tory* (a moderate / conservative journal), College Republicans, College Libertarians, Princeton Pro-Life, the aforementioned Anscombe Society, and the "Clio" side in the regularly scheduled Whig / Clio philosophical and policy debates. Rightist students also tend to network through events of the James Madison Program.

Nearly all Princeton undergrads live on campus, as do 70 percent of its graduate students. Several housing options are available to Princeton undergrads, including "close-knit residential college communities" (each with its own dining hall) and individual dormitories. All bathrooms are single sex, and although the majority of halls are coed, students can request single-sex housing.

"The eating clubs are one of the biggest and best traditions that Princeton has to offer," says a student. Membership in these clubs is one of the more expensive dining options for students (and the clubs have been criticized for promoting elitism), but joining comes with many benefits, and both juniors and seniors can receive some financial aid based on the cost of a club's meal plan. About 75 percent of Princeton students enter a club.

The surrounding borough of Princeton is beautiful if pricey, but town-gown interactions are few. Students report that they are not concerned about crime—and indeed, no crimes were reported on campus in 2011.

Like most top-tier universities, Princeton isn't cheap. In 2012–13 tuition was $38,650, with room and board at $12,630. But Princeton boasts of offering "the strongest need-based financial aid program in the country" and encourages applications from outside the elite. Admissions are entirely need blind. Princeton has eliminated loans from its financial aid packages. Princeton students almost never graduate with debt; less than a quarter took out loans averaging $5,330. One reason the school can afford to be generous is that alumni are unusually giving, since most look back fondly on their time at "Ol' Nassau."

STRONG SUITS	WEAK POINTS
• Top tier faculty in every field. • A strong emphasis on teaching as well as research. • Extensive demands for writing from all students. • A Humanities sequence that grounds students who choose it in Western civilization. • A politically tolerant atmosphere with many religious and conservative groups that enjoy free expression.	• Graduate students lead many discussion sections. • Students rarely make use of office hours to meet with teachers. • Advising is still weak, though a new program is in place.

Providence College

Providence, Rhode Island • www.providence.edu

Trust in Providence

The country's leading college run by Dominican friars—St. Thomas Aquinas's order—Providence College has revitalized its historic religious and academic mission and attracted a cadre of talented faithfully Catholic faculty and brought a new sense of vitality to the school. The school's rediscovered focus on faith-filled liberal education is drawing better students and teachers and drawing more national attention. With its emphasis on the liberal arts and its substantial core curriculum, especially the Development of Western Civilization program, which takes the student through the intellectual history of the West, Providence College is a highly attractive choice.

Academic Life: Hounds of heaven

When most of America's colleges and universities were pitching those pesky core humanities requirements, PC was initiating its Development of Western Civilization (DWC) program. Begun in 1971 and revised for the first time in 2012, the DWC is a mandatory, 16-credit sequence of courses. Team taught by 62 faculty from 11 different disciplines, the DWC program guides students through a chronological and interdisciplinary examination of the major developments that have shaped Western civilization. The first three semesters feature seminars on major texts, with the fourth semester a team-taught colloquium. The remainder of the core curriculum includes two theology classes, two philosophy, one natural science, one social science, one quantitative reasoning, and one fine arts.

Absent from the core curriculum is any required writing course. Outside of what is offered through the DWC program, students can avoid writing-intensive courses throughout their four years at Providence. Instead, students are "encouraged to fulfill proficiency requirements in the major, Core Foundation, Core Focus, or free electives." Proficiencies include Intensive Writing (I and II), Oral Communication, Diversity, and Civic Engagement, and may be fulfilled by taking various electives specific to the major.

Ambitious students should enroll in the Liberal Arts Honors program, which entails taking honors sections of six core requirement classes. Honors classes are slightly smaller in size, require more reading and writing and are often conducted in a seminar style. Select freshmen—approximately 500 per year—are invited, and 125 typically enroll. Others may apply for the program after one or two semesters of superior work.

Most classes at Providence are quite small, thanks to a student-teacher ratio of 12 to 1. More important, the teachers are actually professors and not graduate assistants. Teachers at PC are quite available to students, as one student says: "I feel like my professors not only know who I am but care about who I am—they want me to succeed." Adds another student, "All teachers have office hours, and many allow you to come visit anytime; their doors are always open." Before choosing a major, students have faculty advisers appointed to them. They may choose new ones after selecting a major.

Most disciplines are solid, serious, and traditional, and departmental requirements are—for most majors—impressive.

The English department requires 10 courses: "Introduction to Literature," four courses in literature before 1800, four in literature after 1800, and one elective from either of these two fields. Options are solid, such as "Shakespeare: Tragedies

VITAL STATISTICS

Religious affiliation: *Roman Catholic*
Total enrollment: *4,448*
Total undergraduates: *3,852*
SAT CR/Verbal midrange: *520–640*
SAT Math midrange: *530–640*
ACT midrange: *23–27*
Applicants: *9,652*
Applicants accepted: *61%*
Accepted applicants who enrolled: *17%*
Tuition (general/out of state): *$36,730*
Tuition (in state): *N/A*
Room and board: *$12,440*
Freshman retention rate: *90%*
Graduation rate (4 yrs.): *82%*
Graduation rate (6 yrs.): *85%*
Courses with fewer than 20 students: *50%*
Student-faculty ratio: *12:1*
Courses taught by graduate students: *not provided*
Students living on campus: *78%*
Students in fraternities: *none*
Students in sororities: *none*
Students receiving need-based financial aid: *86%*
Avg. student-loan debt of a recent graduating class: *$21,500*
Most popular majors: *history, business/marketing, health professions*
Guaranteed housing for 4 years? *no*

CAMPUS POLITICS: YELLOW LIGHT

College Republicans dwarf the struggling College Democrats on campus, reflecting the politics of the student body overall. All groups host speakers and get involved in local and national politics, but "students here are pretty apathetic," says one we spoke with.

Most faculty avoid injecting politics into the classroom. However, in 2012 the *Conservative Daily News* (CDN) site expressed alarm at a memo released by the college in response to a single incident of racist graffiti in a dorm. The school is considering creating a Bias Response Protocol that would "provide ongoing training and education" in diversity and sensitivity. A senior at Providence told the CDN, "Chasing down every incident of bias or intolerance could certainly lead to the hindrance of free speech. Most importantly, how the school decides to define 'bias' and 'intolerance' will determine whether . . . the BRP will target conservative groups on campus."

Worse still, in March 2013, as *Campus Reform* reports: "Renowned anti-racist activist Tim Wise claimed that the Catholic Church is in part responsible for the slaughter of Native Americans in a speech funded by and hosted at a Catholic university on Wednesday. 'The Church was directly implicated in slaughtering the indigenous people on this continent,' said Wise, in his speech at Providence College. . . . 'It was directly implicated in sending indigenous children to boarding schools to strip them of their culture, to cut their hair, to kill the Indian and save the man for Jesus.' Wise's speaking event was cosponsored by a variety of student groups as well as the Student Multicultural Activities, the Black Studies, Women Studies, Political Science, and Sociology Departments."

and Romances," "The Victorian Age," and "American Literature to 1865." The absence of the esoteric, and the emphasis on canonical authors, is noteworthy in the English department.

The same can be said for the history major, which also has rigorous requirements. Students are required to take multiple courses in both American and European history, like "History of the United States: From the Beginnings to 1815," and so on. Refreshingly, the history department professes to train students in "doing the work of history with the greatest possible objectivity, resisting personal and social prejudice and ideology," a teacher says.

Political science majors must take 11 courses, including "Politics" and "Introduction to Empirical Analysis"; one course in each of these four fields: comparative government and politics, international relations, political theory, and American politics; a capstone senior seminar; and four electives, chosen from solid options.

The philosophy and theology departments are quite strong. One student says that the "philosophy faculty has undergone a transition from Dominican friars to predominantly lay professors over the past fifteen years" but nevertheless has become "more committed to the school's Catholic mission. Perhaps because of this, the department enjoys a very strong relationship with its upstairs neighbor, the theology department. Students and faculty from the two disciplines compete in a friendly but competitive softball game every semester." Providence requires its theology department members to swear an oath of fidelity to church doctrine—a Vatican requirement few other Catholic colleges obey.

According to students and faculty, business, marketing, and management are among the weaker programs at the college. (A shame, since they are also among the most popular.)

The school's library is somewhat small, but one recent alumnus says that the college did a "great job in providing resources" any time they were needed.

Top teachers include Steven Lynch and Anthony Esolen in English. Says one student, "English has some great faculty. On my 'Development of Western Civilization' team, Dr. Robert Reeder is the English professor; he's young, energetic, and really loves to teach. I also have Dr. Brian Barbour for a Shakespeare course, and he is excellent! He is incredibly knowledgeable about what he teaches and he really has a passion for it." Also recommended are Michael O'Neill and Patrick Macfarlane in philosophy; Mario DiNunzio (emeritus), Fred Drogula, and Patrick Breen in history; and Liam Donohoe in mathematics and computer science.

> Professors in the history department do "the work of history with the greatest possible objectivity, resisting personal and social prejudice and ideology," a teacher says.

Providence offers engineering students a 3+2 program, moving after three years of engineering at Providence to two years of studying an engineering concentration of their choice at either Columbia University or Washington University of St. Louis. Providence has a comparable 3+4 Optometry Program with the New England College of Optometry and a 4+1 BS/BA/MBA.

Providence students can choose from more than 14 countries in Europe, 17 in the Middle East and Africa, five in Asia and Oceania, and 10 in Central and South America. The school requires no foreign language courses—although it does offer majors in Classics, French, Italian, and Spanish, and a minor in German.

Student Life: Red-brick Dominican

Nearly 70 percent of students come from New England and about 90 percent hail from the Northeast. One student recalled that "when I first came here, it seemed like everyone came from New England and a lot of them already knew each other."

The vast majority of PC students live on the 105-acre campus, which sits on a hill in the Northwest of the city. Notable among the buildings on campus are Harkins Hall—the original campus building—and St. Dominic Chapel. Providence has 15 dormitory and apartment buildings. Of these, nine are traditional dorms (four all women, four all men, and one coed by wing), five are apartments that are single sex by apartment, and one building of suites—aptly named Suites Hall—that is coed by floor. Underclassmen generally live in traditional dormitories with suites and apartments reserved for juniors and seniors. Housing is not guaranteed for all four years.

According to the student handbook, dorm residents "are expected to adhere to the norms and values associated with Catholic teaching." Hence, the college limits visiting hours for guests of the opposite sex in rooms. Violations are punishable by the school—although enforcement is up to the resident assistant in each dorm. Rules are interpreted more strictly in the all-female dorms.

SUGGESTED CORE

The college's 16-credit inter-disciplinary program, "Development of Western Civilization," suffices.

Almost every dormitory on campus is home to at least one Dominican friar. "It's good for students," says one RA, "They think twice before stepping out of line in front of a member of the order that perpetrated the Spanish Inquisition." More than 50 Dominican friars and sisters live on campus, serving as professors and advisers. The friars are a major fixture at PC; you can't miss the guys wearing the white habits and the black *cappas* striding across campus. "Pasta with the Padres," an annual event at the start of the school year, gives students an opportunity to meet and interact with the friars.

The campus ministry offers Theology on Tap and a number of service opportunities in Boston. Some students complain that campus ministry is preoccupied with social justice, referring to it as "Catholic Lite." The school offers students Mass three times a day during the week and five liturgies every Sunday (including the Saturday Vigil). The Center for Catholic and Dominican Studies, which was founded in 2006, is meant to maintain, enhance, and promote the distinctive Catholic and Dominican mission of Providence College. The center offers multiple lectures each semester.

The events with the largest draw at PC are certainly the men's basketball games. Like most of the other 19 men's and women's varsity sports programs at the college (including men's ice hockey, swimming and diving, and soccer, as well as women's ice hockey, tennis, and volleyball), the men's basketball team is Division I and plays in the Big East Athletic Conference—a tough conference for such a little school. Men's hockey, which plays in the elite conference Hockey East, also draws large crowds of students to their games against some of the best teams in the country.

Providence has more than a hundred active student groups or organizations. Notable among these are the Cowl, the student newspaper, and the famous Blackfriars Theater group. Active political groups on campus include College Democrats, College Republicans, and Libertarians.

The city of Providence boasts five other schools, including Brown University. Students can shop at the city's downtown mall Providence Place, or on Thayer Street, which boasts vintage clothing shops, bookstores, music, and restaurants. Providence's Federal Hill—the city's Little Italy—is another popular student destination, with more than 20 restaurants in a quarter-mile radius. A student bus runs a dedicated loop throughout the neighborhood surrounding PC during the later hours of the day and into the evening. PC students are not allowed to have cars on campus until their junior year.

For years the college has struggled with a sobriety problem. Some shocking statistics in past years have led the school to crack down, hard. All hard liquor is banned from residence halls and apartment complexes, with the exception of McPhail's, the on-campus bar.

Apart from underage drinking, crime is fairly infrequent. In 2011 there were five burglaries, two sex offenses, and one motor vehicle theft on campus. Campus police responded well to a recent uptick in crime, bolstering their presence on campus and in the surrounding community and working with the Providence Police Department.

Tuition for 2012–2013 was $36,730 (which will rise to $41,350 in 2013–14) and room and board $12,440. Admission is need blind, but the school is unable to guarantee full funding to students. The school does offer various need- and merit-based assistance. Some 86 percent of students received need-based financial aid, and the average student-loan debt of a recent graduate was $21,500.

STRONG SUITS

- A very solid, worthy core curriculum guarantees all grads have a foundation in Western civilization.
- The school is solidly committed to its Catholic identity and liberal arts mission.
- Many highly qualified, nonpoliticized faculty.
- Small classes taught by faculty, not graduate students.
- Solid, traditional departments in most areas.
- Friars or sisters reside in almost every dormitory.

WEAK POINTS

- Not enough emphasis on writing in core curriculum.
- Business program, among the most popular, is said to be weaker than others.
- Drinking problem persists on campus, despite strict school rules.
- Administration now pushing aggressive diversity initiatives that may target conservative student groups.

Rice University

Houston, Texas • www.rice.edu

Against the Grain

The Rice Institute, which later became Rice University, was founded in 1912. It became a small school of the highest quality where students lived in residential colleges and faculty-student relations were warm and intense. Although Rice is now much larger, those attributes still characterize the university. Teaching is still emphasized, and with Rice's outstanding student-faculty ratio of just 5 to 1, no one need fall between the cracks. Socially, Rice University is very comfortable: its residential college system offers students the close-knit community atmosphere of a smaller school, alongside the resources of a larger one.

Rice is comparatively affordable, has an excellent academic reputation, a top-notch student body, and a $4.42 billion endowment. No wonder some consider it Texas's alternative to the Ivy League. It's a shame that a weak curriculum and troubling policies on free speech keep Rice from being a slam-dunk choice for traditionally minded students.

Academic Life: No way of knowing

Rice's distribution requirements are pretty weak, mandating just four courses in each of three groups: Group I, which includes more than 200 courses in the departments of art, art history,

English, philosophy, medieval studies, Classics, theater, women's studies, foreign languages, and many others. Group II is a catchall for the social sciences, and Group III covers "analytical thinking and quantitative analysis," covering the "various disciplines of science and engineering."

One professor defends this system as superior to its rigidly structured predecessor, in which students had no choice but to take politically charged subjects. The professor says, "Anybody has the right to take courses in queer theory, postmodern interpretations of everything, etc. But nobody is required to take them." Despite their academic liberty, even students recognize the weakness of Rice's curriculum. One comments, "Rice does not require any specific courses, and a student could easily graduate without taking any history or English course." Still, "when our graduates write back from graduate school, they tell us it is easier—and professors at those universities . . . commend us for the preparation of our students," a professor says.

The sciences, engineering, and social sciences, according to one professor, appear to "have nonideological faculties and tolerate believers of all stripes quite readily." The same professor says that "the humanities departments are definitely getting a lot more politicized." Another professor adds, "There are no strong departments in the humanities. They are uniformly postmodern." For example, the history department lost its two medievalists in 2000 and has not replaced them. Another professor called the atmosphere in the department "stiflingly present-minded."

At Rice students traditionally had ample opportunities to develop relationships with their professors, who are said to be very accessible during office hours and outside class. With a student-to-faculty ratio that bests any of the Ivies', Rice enjoys a median class size of 14 students. "Professors are associated with a residential college and serve as advisers to entering students from those colleges until they declare a major," says one student. "These advisers, especially the older professors, are extremely accessible; they eat lunch in their residential colleges frequently." But as "old guard" professors retire, many who replace them exhibit a different ethos, insiders say. A faculty member says, "One problem with the younger faculty is that they have little patience, if any, for the claims of undergraduates."

VITAL STATISTICS

Religious affiliation: *none*
Total enrollment: *6,082*
Total undergraduates: *3,708*
SAT CR/Verbal midrange: *650–750*
SAT Math midrange: *690–790*
ACT midrange: *30–34*
Applicants: *12,393*
Applicants accepted: *21%*
Accepted applicants who enrolled: *36%*
Tuition (general/out of state): *$36,610*
Tuition (in state): *N/A*
Room and board: *$12,600*
Freshman retention rate: *89%*
Graduation rate (4 yrs.): *79%*
Graduation rate (6 yrs.): *92%*
Courses with fewer than 20 students: *69%*
Student-faculty ratio: *5:1*
Courses taught by graduate students: *not provided*
Students living on campus: *77%*
Students in fraternities: *N/A*
Students in sororities: *N/A*
Students receiving need-based financial aid: *91%*
Avg. student-loan debt of a recent graduating class: *$13,944*
Most popular majors: *engineering, natural sciences, social sciences*
Guaranteed housing for 4 years? *no*

CAMPUS POLITICS: YELLOW LIGHT

Rice may boast a more conservative student body than most schools outside Texas, but many of its major liberal arts departments are ideologically slanted. In the words of one professor, "I would not recommend Rice for humanities. . . . No department in the School of Humanities would be comfortable for a conservative student."

Rice's speech code includes a prohibition against sending unsolicited "material which explicitly or implicitly refers to sexual conduct" or that "contains profane language or panders to bigotry, sexism, or other forms of prohibited discrimination." While Rice has affirmed that it has no intention of punishing protected speech (i.e., a mass "e-mail from a conservative student organization advertising a speech by an opponent of illegal immigration"), the policy certainly allows it to do so. Opinions vary on what effect administrative policies or campus politics have on student expression. One professor says, "I think students are rather free to express their views on anything." However, another professor reports that "free speech by students is completely stifled. The previous president, Malcolm Gills, hired a senior administrator just to keep the student newspaper in line." One student adds, "We may have a fairly decent number of conservatives at Rice, but it's hard to know. Many of us are afraid to voice our opinions in class or in papers for fear of being shot down by the almost monolithically liberal faculty."

Science professors who actually teach tend to be more involved in research than are humanities professors, but one student says that they at least "try to involve undergraduates" in their work. "There are many opportunities for engineering/science students to work in a professor's lab," says an undergrad. However, he pointed out, "Most full professors in science and engineering teach no more than one course per term."

According to students, some of the best teachers are J. Dennis Huston in English; Richard J. Stoll and Rick Wilson in political science; Baruch Brody, Tristram Engelhardt, and George Sher in philosophy; John S. Hutchinson, James Tour, and Kenton Whitmire in chemistry; Richard Baraniuk and Don Johnson in electrical engineering; Stephen Wong in bioengineering; Raquel Gaytan in languages; James Thompson and David Scott in statistics; well-known conservative scholar Ewa Thompson in German studies; and Steve Klineberg in sociology.

Teaching assistants, who at Rice are undergraduates, help with review sessions; graduate students, sometimes called instructors, teach some introductory courses. The formal advising program "is a bit subpar, especially the general advising before declaring a major," says one student. Upon entering college, every student is assigned a faculty adviser based on his area of interest. Once he declares his major, he is assigned to the designated adviser for his major. Because there are usually just one or two official advisers assigned to a department, it's hard for students to get much time with them. "The adviser in your major department usually understands the issues of that department quite well but typically just rubber-stamps your decisions," a student says.

Rice's strict honor code is vigilantly enforced by students. Cheating on an exam, besides resulting in an automatic course failure, could lead to a three-semester suspension. For falsifying data on a lab report, a two-semester suspension is not unusual.

Rice advertises itself as a research school. It has traditionally been strongest in the sciences and engineering, and many students are in premed, a program that can be intense. One premed student says, "At Rice, most people are very serious about their work, but I've never felt threatened by any competitiveness among my peers. There's no competition in a cutthroat way, and many students study together, helping each other learn the material." Rice premed students typically have some of the highest MCAT scores in the country.

The School of Architecture is highly regarded. Students in the program must complete additional distribution requirements, foundation courses in architecture, and a "preprofessional sequence" in their junior and senior years. The Shepherd School of Music is excellent in music theory, history, and performance.

Distribution requirements for the English major include three advanced-level classes in writing before 1900 (two of which must be from pre-1800 periods), only one of which may be a class on Shakespeare, as well as one class on "non-canonical traditions, such as courses in women, African American, Chicano/a, Asian American, ethnic, global, and diasporic writers."

> "A student could easily graduate without taking any history or English course," a professor laments. Nevertheless, "when our graduates write back from graduate school, they tell us it is easier—and professors at those universities commend us for the preparation of our students."

History majors must take 10 courses distributed over premodern, European, United States, and Asian/Latin American/African history. Sadly, the requirement for U.S. history may be fulfilled by courses like "Caribbean Nation Building" or "U.S. Women's History."

Political science majors only have one required class: "Introduction to Statistics." A student could easily graduate without any substantial knowledge of the American political system or philosophy; in fact, Rice's dearth of political philosophy classes in general is troubling.

Rice offers a number of study-abroad opportunities, in semester- or yearlong programs in Australia, Denmark, England, France, Hong Kong, Hungary, India, and Korea, among others, including programs at New York University and the American University in Cairo. The school teaches Arabic, Chinese, French, German, Greek and Latin, Hebrew, Hindi, Italian, Japanese, Korean, Portuguese, and Spanish. Foreign language majors are available in French, German, and Hispanic studies.

Student Life: Houston calling

Rice's residential college setup, modeled after the Oxford system, organizes nearly every aspect of social life at the school; some students choose Rice precisely for this reason. The 11 colleges mix students of various races and temperaments. Rice students self-segregate much less than at other schools—there are no ethnic-awareness halls, for instance, or political-issue or gender-issue dormitories. Rice students are very loyal to their individual colleges. "People will do almost anything for their college. Your college is your family," says one student. In the words of one student, "It creates a small community for each student, and college activities are the center of social life. College spirit and intercollegiate rivalries add an element of fun to the Rice experience."

Unfortunately, Rice University's residential colleges do not have enough room for its 3,000-plus undergraduates, and a quarter of them have to live off campus, missing the benefits of the college system

A student's closest friends usually come from his own college. "With the residential college system, as opposed to the Greek system, Rice students get to know a much more diverse group of people. Freshmen are living in the same halls with upperclassmen. Varsity athletes are living next to math nerds," a student reports. All dormitories are coeducational, but each college offers a few single-sex floors, and all bathrooms and shower areas are single sex. Students in the newer colleges enjoy suite-style living, while those in the older buildings enjoy nicer architecture. A faculty master lives in a house next door to the residence halls of each college and serves as a live-in adviser.

"We work incredibly hard, but students know how to leave work behind and have a good time," says one student.

Special interest clubs range broadly from the National Society of Black Engineers, Community of Rice Entrepreneurs, Proud Past (the "Queers and Allies" group), Low Keys Female a cappella, and the Chess Club to the Legalese Pre-Law Club.

Churches of almost every denomination stand near campus, and many are accessible on foot. InterVarsity Christian Fellowship and Campus Crusade for Christ are the largest and most active religious groups on campus. One professor says that Rice "has active private support groups for Catholics and Evangelicals. Rice's anticlericalism is of long-standing vintage, but the conservative Christians have managed to obtain on-campus support." Conversely, in an opinion piece in the student newspaper, the *Rice Thresher,* an atheist complained, "As a non-Judeo-Christian at Rice, I appear to be in the minority." Other traditions at Rice are represented by clubs like Canterbury (the Episcopal Student Association), the Baptist Student Ministry, Progressive Christians at Rice, Interfaith Dialogue Association, Rumi Sufi Islamic club, a Mormon group, and Lutheran, Catholic, and Jewish chaplaincies.

Political views are voiced in columns or letters to the *Rice Thresher* student paper, rather than in demonstrations. "The student body is largely apathetic," an undergrad says. An independent student magazine, the *Rice Standard,* gives voice to conservative views (among others)

and space for literary contributions. Many students were enthusiastic about Ron Paul's campaign for the Republican nomination in 2012, in part because Rice sits in congressman Paul's former district. Political clubs offer outlets for libertarians, a Rice branch of the ACLU, and a pro-Israeli group, as well as Young Democrats and College Republicans.

One thing more popular than politics at Rice is drinking. "Rice is a wet campus with a relatively relaxed alcohol policy, so plenty of students drink," a student says. "There is a lot of drinking on campus, but there are also a lot of things to do for those who don't drink. I've never felt any pressure to drink," says another.

Five miles away stands Houston's revitalized downtown, replete with theaters, concert halls, and the city's best nightlife. With Houston's city sprawl—and the beaches of Galveston just an hour away—many students recommend having a car. About half of upperclassmen do, and for a fee students may park in the stadium lot.

In 2010 Rice athletes had the highest student-athlete graduation rate in NCAA Division I, with men and women competing in basketball, cross-country, tennis, and track and field. Men's sports also include football, golf, and baseball, while women compete in soccer, swimming, and volleyball. The Rice Owls, whose colors are blue and gray, have found success with their baseball team, which finished well in the 2003, 2006, and 2007 College World Series. The women's teams have consistently competed in NCAA tournaments for soccer, basketball, track and field, and tennis.

Rice is a reasonably safe place; it has seen a recent drop in crime. In 2011 Rice reported two forcible sex offenses and 10 burglaries. However, bike thefts are common. "I've never felt at risk," says one student, "but you have to remember you're in Houston."

Rice University is midpriced for a private school, with tuition in 2012–13 at $36,610 and room and board at $12,600. Admission is need blind, and the school does not impose loans on students with family incomes of less than $80,000. Some 90 percent of students received some sort of financial aid, but a substantial amount still borrowed money to pay for college, and the average student graduated with $13,944 in student loans.

STRONG SUITS	WEAK POINTS
• Abundant resources and many skilled teachers.	• Patchy, ideological departments in most of the humanities.
• A cadre of (mostly older) faculty who serve as willing mentors to students.	• Weak advising.
• Significant research opportunities for science and engineering students.	• Few courses in political philosophy.
• Good programs in sciences, architecture, and music.	• New faculty tend to be ideological and preoccupied with research.
• Hardworking students who are collaborative, not cutthroat.	• Shortage of dorm space undermines otherwise worthy residential college system.

Sarah Lawrence College

Bronxville, New York • www.slc.edu

Boutique

Most of what people think they know about Sarah Lawrence isn't true. It isn't a women's college; it has been coed since 1968. It was never one of the prestigious "Seven Sisters," nor is it a venerable institution; the college was founded in 1928. And while its post office address is that of the handsome and pricey Westchester suburb of Bronxville, its 44-acre campus sits entirely in the depressed industrial city of Yonkers, albeit in its fanciest section.

So what makes Sarah Lawrence so unusual, beyond the fact that it is currently the most expensive college in the United States? The answer lies in a unique method of organizing the curriculum and in the close relationship between teachers and students, one that seeks to imitate the teacher-student relationships for which Oxford and Cambridge are famous. Whether this method provides a thorough education depends entirely on the seriousness of the student.

Sarah Lawrence is not a comfortable place for politically conservative or religious students. Nor is it a school for the typical premed or prelaw student, and serious engineering and hard science majors might wish to look elsewhere too. But it does offer something distinctive, and the abundance of famous graduates the school has produced provides some strong testament in its favor.

Academic Life: The Sarah Lawrence system

Sarah Lawrence's teaching system does not assure students—or prospective employers—that they will graduate with any specific base of knowledge. There is neither a core curriculum nor a Great Books program. There are also no majors and no letter grades. (Indeed, applicants need not take the SATs or ACTs.) Instead, students may if they wish declare what the university calls a "specialization" in a subject. The only requirements for graduation are to complete 120 credit hours, meet some very minimal distribution requirements, take a foreign language, and pass a noncredit physical education requirement that does not include a swim test. Lab science is not required. At the end, all students graduate with the same degree: a bachelors of arts in liberal studies.

Students typically take just three courses per term, instead of the four or five they would take at most colleges and universities. However, more than 80 percent of the classes offered are 85-minute, twice weekly seminars. Along with these, professors are obliged to meet separately with each student in their seminars at least once a week for 45 minutes of one-on-one meetings and discussions. During this encounter, students work with the faculty member to develop a notion of what they will produce from the class, their so-called conference work. This is a Sarah Lawrence term for what might be a pair of papers, a performance (in a dance or theater class, for example), or a 40-to-60-page paper that might be comparable to a senior thesis at another school. The faculty member teaching the class is called its "don." As one student puts it, "This is an incredibly supportive place. You really talk with your professors. It's all about letting people develop their own style." This high level of attention is made possible by a student-faculty ratio of 9 to 1 and an average class size of 13.

To further facilitate the principle of openness, classes are usually in rooms with circular tables, and students are encouraged to express their opinions on an equal basis with the instructor. (Of course, if the student's views are on a par with the professor's, one must wonder why there is a professor, or why the school does not permit graduate students to teach classes.)

This system does inspire student enthusiasm about the faculty, and the school's proximity to New York City and higher than normal pay for adjunct professors has allowed

VITAL STATISTICS

Religious affiliation: *none*
Total enrollment: *1,744*
Total undergraduates: *1,413*
SAT CR/Verbal midrange: *N/A*
SAT Math midrange: *N/A*
ACT midrange: *N/A*
Applicants: *2,012*
Applicants accepted: *61%*
Accepted applicants who enrolled: *30%*
Tuition (general/out of state): *$45,900*
Tuition (in state): *N/A*
Room and board: *$13,844*
Freshman retention rate: *89%*
Graduation rate (4 yrs.): *63%*
Graduation rate (6 yrs.): *70%*
Courses with fewer than 20 students: *94%*
Student-faculty ratio: *9:1*
Courses taught by graduate students *none*
Students living on campus: *85%*
Students in fraternities: *none*
Students in sororities: *none*
Students receiving need-based financial aid: *60%*
Avg. student-loan debt of a recent graduating class: *$18,360*
Guaranteed housing for 4 years? *yes*

CAMPUS POLITICS: YELLOW LIGHT

We did not turn up horror stories of classroom bias or restrictions on free speech. Nevertheless, if you're looking for a place where students and teachers stand at all points of the political spectrum, and all feel free to express their opinions, Sarah Lawrence might not be the place. We couldn't put it any better than Sarah Lawrence's official college magazine, which ran a feature admitting:

"There's an easy way to pick a fight at Sarah Lawrence College: proclaim yourself a Republican. . . . By all impressions the ratio among teachers is similarly lopsided, and at the big table in the faculty dining room—where colleagues gather for lunch, conversation, and debate—you'd have to listen long and hard to hear a conservative opinion. Sarah Lawrence is overwhelmingly pro-choice and pro-gay marriage, antiwar and anti-enhanced-interrogation techniques. It may be true that, as former dean of the College Barbara Kaplan wrote . . . Sarah Lawrence emphasizes 'individuals finding and defining roles and values that are appropriate to themselves—and often bucking convention,' but this self-definition takes place within a liberal framework that is itself seldom bucked."

One student in 2011 wrote in *Sarah Lawrence Speaks:* "I've sat through many classes and conferences and heard professors and classmates take countless shots at Republicans, Tea Partiers, President Bush, and capitalism. Not all jokes were unfounded and most were expectedly quite brilliant. I was never angry that the jokes were made, but more disheartened by the attitude with which they were delivered and accepted, as if never to be questioned."

it to attract many famous instructors. In past decades, the likes of choreographer Martha Graham and novelist E. L. Doctorow have taught at the school.

Sarah Lawrence does not have majors, but it does have academic departments, although some of these may have only one or two full-time faculty. Among the school's 41 disciplines are such politicized choices as Africana studies, ethnic and diasporic studies, and lesbian, gay, bisexual, and transgender studies. Classes offered include "Queer Theory," and "The Invention of Homosexuality."

The departments that today seem to generate the most student enthusiasm are dance, theater, and literature—each of which displays the school's preoccupation with remaining "cutting edge." The dance program has just one class focused on classical ballet among its more than two dozen offerings; theater is definitely oriented toward avant-garde productions; and the literature department leans heavily on eclectic courses such as "Contemporary African Literatures: Bodies and Questions of Power" and "Giles Deleuze and the Composition of Living" (while still offering a number of solid, traditional choices).

Certainly, Sarah Lawrence has produced an astonishing number of famous graduates in the arts, especially for such a small school: Jane Alexander, Jill Clayburgh, Carrie Fisher, Robin Givens, Lauren Holly, Tea Leoni, Julianna Margulies, Holly Robinson Peete, Kyra Sedgwick, and Joanne Woodward. Its alumni also include directors Brian De Palma, J. J. Abrams (Creator of *Lost*), and Joan Micklin Silver. Among the school's other illustrious grads are former White House chief of staff Rahm Emanuel; singer-songwriters Carly Simon and Lesley Gore; *The View* cohost Barbara Walters; playwright David Lindsay-Abaire; novelists Allen Gurganus, A. M. Homes, Ann Patchett, and Alice Walker; choreographer Meredith Monk; and fashion designer Vera Wang. Beatle wives Linda McCartney and Yoko Ono each attended Sarah Lawrence.

Among the current faculty members whom students and faculty most highly recommend are Fred Smoler in history and literature, outspokenly conservative Jefferson Adams in history, Mike Siff in computer science, Scott Calvin in physics, and Melissa Frazier in literature.

A colleague describes Smoler, who teaches a class on modern warfare, as "witty, fast, bright, and popular." Siff, who offers a class on cryptography that can be taken by both serious math geeks and nonmajors, is said to be "energetic and able to teach to multiple levels." This student also calls Frazier, who teaches a class on the Russian novel, "someone who will push you and from whom you'll learn as much as you will from anyone you'll ever study with."

Along with its emphasis on individualized instruction, Sarah Lawrence strongly encourages its students to enroll in term- or year-abroad programs, and it reports

SUGGESTED CORE
1. Classics, The Greco-Roman World (*closest match*)
2. Philosophy, Ancient Philosophy
3. No suitable course
4. History, Christianity and Classical Culture: An Enduring Theme in European Thought
5. Politics, Modern Political Theory
6. Literature, Shakespeare and Company
7. History, The Founders and the Origins of American Politics
8. No suitable course

that more than 50 percent of its students will receive some of their instruction overseas. To this end, it offers study-abroad programs in Italy (Florence and Catania), Oxford, and Paris, as well as an acting program in London. Sarah Lawrence is one of the few American colleges to offer study abroad in Cuba. Sarah Lawrence offers language instruction in French, German, Greek and Latin, Italian, Japanese, Russian, and Spanish.

A vant-garde Sarah Lawrence, the most expensive college in America, is a very cozy environment. As one student puts it, "This is an incredibly supportive place. You really talk with your professors. It's all about letting people develop their own style."

Student Life: You can't take the A train

The Sarah Lawrence campus is just a five- to 10-minute stroll from Bronxville's main street and, perhaps more significantly, the Bronxville train station. The station provides a quick means to get into New York City. The city therefore serves as a lure for students, and on the weekends many students can be found there.

Reflecting Sarah Lawrence's founding as a finishing school for upper-crust young women, the school remains overwhelmingly female. The class of 2014 will be approximately 70 percent female, and that's a more evenly balanced sex ratio than most Sarah Lawrence classes have had. And though the school is small—it still has incoming classes of fewer than

350—it has been growing. Consequently, the dorm rooms, which were once a selling point, are no longer so spacious.

Freshman dorms are either coed by floor or all-female, and girls may request to be on a female floor. However, upper-class students are typically in coed dorms with coed bathrooms, and they may even request to be in a coed suite. Many seniors and some juniors can get single rooms. There are no sororities or fraternities at Sarah Lawrence, although students may ask to live as upperclassmen in the school's "sustainable living" house, which features composting.

Sarah Lawrence is not a member of the NCAA; its athletics teams compete with other schools in a small-school grouping called the Hudson Valley Athletic Conference, which includes colleges like Concordia and Marist. Sarah Lawrence has men's and women's teams in swimming, softball, tennis, basketball, equestrian, and crew, plus some intramural sports like squash.

At least half the school's undergraduate organizations fall into three categories: groups concerned with white, male, heterosexual oppression (for example, the Alliance for White Anti-Racist Action, the Asian Pacific Islander Coalition for Action and Diversity, and Queer People of Color), arts groups (Student Filmmaker's Coalition), and singing groups (Vocal Minority).

Along with these clubs are an odd mix of others devoted to subjects like chess and bicycling. However, there are also some politically incorrect factions, including a group devoted to carnivorous eating, and the Christian Union. That said, this is Sarah Lawrence; hence, the campus has a Voices for Palestine club but no College Republicans. A Princeton Review survey placed Sarah Lawrence in the top-five least religious colleges in America. Even so, Sarah Lawrence does have both a Hillel Group and a Muslim Student Association, and each has weekly meetings. Catholic students at Sarah Lawrence should seek out a local parish, such as Yonkers' St. Eugene Parish, where a weekly Latin Mass is offered.

The school is quite safe. In 2011 it reported 14 burglaries, one forcible sex offense, and three arsons on campus.

Sarah Lawrence is the most expensive college in America. Tuition for 2012–13 ran $45,900, and room and board cost $13,844. About 60 percent of students received financial aid, and the school says it aims to provide aid packages competitive with those provided by schools like Middlebury and Haverford. The average school grants for financial aid students ran to just under $35,080 for four years. The average student in 2011 graduated with a relatively modest debt of $18,360.

STRONG SUITS	WEAK POINTS
• Intense personal attention with highly qualified faculty members. • Professors take students and their individual interests very seriously. • Many opportunities for theater and performing arts, and famous alumni/ae. • Extensive study-abroad options.	• Absurdly lax curricular requirements. • Weak programs in hard sciences. • Univocal leftist politics in and out of the classroom. • One of the most secular schools in the U.S.

Seton Hall University

South Orange, New Jersey • www.shu.edu

Which Turnpike Exit Is Rome?

Long a working-class, pragmatic university, Seton Hall has recently won praise and new acclaim for rediscovering its focus on liberal arts "core" education and its Catholic identity. A newly revised core curriculum, a reinvigorated Catholic Studies program, and a major in liberal studies give students meaningful exposure to the Great Books as seen through the eyes of the Faith—making Seton Hall one of the first places that serious Catholic students ought to consider.

Academic Life: Taking up a collection

In 2008 Seton Hall drastically improved its core curriculum. It requires six classes "rooted in questions central but not exclusive to the Catholic intellectual tradition," in which students read many of the great texts of the ancient world and the Christian West: the Bible; the works of Augustine, Aquinas, Dante, Plato, and Aristotle; and a sampling of works from other religious traditions and from the modern period. One student advises taking the core courses early "so you can be exposed to all the disciplines before you lock yourself into a major." That's good advice at any school.

745

VITAL STATISTICS

Religious affiliation: *Roman Catholic*
Total enrollment: *9,800*
Total undergraduates: *5,300*
SAT CR/Verbal midrange: *500–600*
SAT Math midrange: *500–600*
ACT midrange: *24*
Applicants: *10,851*
Applicants accepted: *85%*
Accepted applicants who enrolled: *17%*
Tuition (general/out of state): *$32,700*
Tuition (in state): *N/A*
Room and board: *$11,550*
Freshman retention rate: *81%*
Graduation rate (4 yrs.): *52%*
Graduation rate (6 yrs.): *66%*
Courses with fewer than 20 students: *45%*
Student-faculty ratio: *14:1*
Courses taught by graduate students: *2%*
Students living on campus: *42%*
Students in fraternities: *7%*
Students in sororities: *11%*
Students receiving need-based financial aid: *77%*
Avg. student-loan debt of a recent graduating class: *$37,724*
Most popular majors: *behavioral sciences, communications, criminal justice*
Guaranteed housing for 4 years? *no*

There is still some fluffy course work in majors like communications, but "the university has made a conscious commitment to weed out easier courses and majors and to strengthen the intellectual rigor of all programs," a business professor says. "We're on a 'quality' kick."

Seton Hall's honors program offers a rigorous curriculum, close interaction with faculty members, and intellectual camaraderie. As freshmen and sophomores, honors students take colloquia in "Classical Civilizations" (beginning with Genesis and Plato's *Republic* and *Timaeus*), "Medieval Civilizations," "Early Modern Cultures," and "Contemporary Civilization." A student explains: "The honors program is one of the strongest academic features of the campus. Its heavy focus on primary sources, while examining thought from the beginning of history through the present day, encourages critical thinking, and the discussion-based nature of classes ensures that students become proficient in making their cases verbally as well as in writing."

Seton Hall boasts many excellent professors. Some of the best include Angela Weisl in English; Deirdre Yates in communication; Martin Edwards, Assefaw Bariagaber, Philip Moremen, and Ann Marie Murphy in international relations; and Msgr. Richard Liddy in religious studies. Notable history teachers include Dermot Quinn, William Connell and James McCartin. The philosophy department is anchored by Robert Mayhew, David O'Connor, and Fr. John Ranieri.

A professor who has served on tenure committees says: "Nobody has ever asked a question about a candidate's political views or whether he or she is 'liberal' or 'conservative.' I can also honestly say that I've never heard of a faculty member being sanctioned or ostracized." The course catalog explains that the women's studies program "is established in the spirit of St. Elizabeth Ann Seton, whose life of activism, spirituality, and leadership serves as an inspiration to our community."

The student-faculty ratio is a middling 14 to 1. A professor notes that the university has improved this ratio by hiring many more adjunct professors—despite a stated commitment to reduce reliance on part-timers. A few courses utilize graduate teaching assistants.

The school assigns each freshman a "professional mentor." Once he picks a major, each student is assigned a department adviser for that major.

Seton Hall's best departments include classical studies, international relations, Catholic studies, and some of the humanities. The English department, which includes among its teachers poet Jeffrey Gray, actually focuses on English literature, not theory or politics. Majors are required to take an "Introduction to Literary Studies," and six-credit, yearlong sequences in the Great Books, American literature, and British literature—then seven electives from several different areas, and a senior seminar.

The history department is strong in American social and constitutional history and in European intellectual history. The history major also requires breadth in the discipline, including courses in American, European, and non-Western history, and a requirement for a class in pre-1750 history from a largely sensible-sounding list.

The political science major requires basic surveys of both United States politics and Western political thought, and in comparative politics, international relations, and research methods.

CAMPUS POLITICS: GREEN LIGHT

A student says that "on campus, it is the general perception of politically active students that the university strives to discourage particularly overt activism… simply out of a desire to avoid controversy. The most noted cases of this have been the denial of speakers; the university has prevented both John Kerry and Tom DeLay from speaking on campus on separate occasions, and it is an immense hassle to get politicians on campus with the university's red tape."

In 2010 the school underwent a bruising presidential search that saw liberal faculty effectively veto a well-qualified conservative priest who had been selected for the position. The job was given to another faithful Catholic, but conservative commentators expressed concern about the resistance of many teachers—including one longtime gay activist with tenure—to the Catholic revival at the school. Still, most are hopeful that Seton Hall will continue to deepen its commitment both to its religious mission and to the liberal arts.

The theology department is a mixed bag. Courses fulfilling the school's philosophy and religion requirement range from "Introduction to Catholic Theology" to "African Cultural Philosophy," "Buddhist World of Thought," and "The Black Church."

Seton Hall's program in Catholic studies is much stronger, requiring of majors "Introduction to the Catholic Vision," "The Catholic Classics and Interiority," and an Integrating Seminar. Students also take six electives such as "Catholicism and Literature," "Catholic Social Teachings," and "Christian Belief and Thought."

The Hall has many options available for study abroad, including faculty-led tours to places like China, France, Japan, Italy, Spain, and the U.K.; exchange programs in Germany, Ireland, Japan, South Korea, and the U.K.; and third-party-provider programs. Foreign languages offered are Arabic, Chinese, Filipino, French, German, Greek and Latin, Italian, Japanese, Portuguese, Russian, and Spanish.

SUGGESTED CORE

1. Classics 2301, Epics and Novels of Greece and Rome
2. Philosophy 2020, Ancient Philosophy
3. Religious Studies 1102/1104, Introduction to the Bible/Introduction to the New Testament
4. Religious Studies 1202, Christian Belief and Thought
5. Political Science 1401, Western Political Thought
6. English 3312, Shakespeare
7. History 1301, American History I
8. English 3250, Western Europe in the 19th Century

Student Life: OK, so we're in Newark . . .

South Orange is on the outskirts of Newark, a blighted northeastern city, but Seton students need walk only a few blocks to grab a train to New York City, half an hour away. The campus is alive with movie nights, salsa dance lessons, self-defense sessions, game nights, lectures, concerts, and open-mic nights. Student-run WSOU-FM is usually ranked among the top student stations in the country. Students also run *The Setonian*, a weekly newspaper, and Pirate TV.

Seton Hall recognizes more than 100 student organizations, including résumé-boosting outfits like the Economics Club and the Brownson Speech and Debate Union, cultural and religious organizations, and drama, art, and musical groups. One student says that while there are activities on campus every day, "You get so comfortable just hanging out with your friends, doing nothing, that you miss out on more enriching activities," he says. Seton Hall has fraternities and sororities, though few join them.

Political groups active on campus include College Republicans, College Democrats, Seton Hall University Students for Individual Liberty (SHUSIL), Seton Hall United for Life, Amnesty International, and Young Socialists for Democratic Change.

Worthy institutes on campus include one devoted to G. K. Chesterton, and one to Bernard J. Lonergan. The campus ministry program is firm in its Catholic position on moral issues. The university administration does, however, permit the airing of alternative views, even concerning Catholic doctrine.

Seton Hall has an active campus ministry, with three Masses daily and four on Sundays. Immaculate Conception chapel has been stripped of all the junk installed during the '70s and made Gothic again. One professor comments that this renovation was "a kind of symbol, if you will, of the university's conscious effort to rediscover its Catholicism." One non-Catholic student says the university's religious mission, while important for Catholics, is not intrusive: "It's there if you want it, but it's never pushed on you."

The Pirates compete in NCAA Division I's Big East conference in baseball, basketball, soccer, volleyball, swimming, and cross-country, and women's volleyball, softball, tennis, and golf. There is no space on the crowded campus for varsity football, field hockey, or lacrosse teams, though the university offers fine facilities for intramurals and pickup games, as well as for personal fitness.

Half of all students live off campus. Only seniors are allowed to have cars on campus. Students who manage to get a room have few complaints; they are comfortable enough, with bathrooms for every other room. Some dorms also offer "living and learning" voluntary communities, and Turrell Manor has a servant leadership and academic excellence program. All dormitories are coed except for the third floor of Neumann Hall (women only); the coed dorms have several single-sex floors and wings. One student says, "Dorm life has been excellent for me. My RAs have always had a very hands-off approach, leaving you free to do your own thing so long as you didn't make trouble." Overnight guests of the opposite sex are forbidden, but otherwise visitation policies seem relatively liberal.

A professor reports, "The university has made a conscious commitment to weed out easier courses and majors and to strengthen the intellectual rigor of all programs. We're on a 'quality' kick." Another teacher points to "the university's conscious effort to rediscover its Catholicism."

Seton Hall's 58 acres are wisely locked behind metal fences, with four gates—only two are commonly used. Students coming home late at night can call for an escort service, and emergency call boxes were recently set up. Crimes reported on campus in 2011 were three forcible sexual offenses, two burglaries, and two stolen cars. Given the school's location within a few miles of urban slums, these numbers are remarkably low. Still, the campus was stunned in 2010 when a shooting spree at "an off-campus house party...left a Seton Hall University student dead and four other people wounded," as Fox News reported.

Seton Hall is one of the cheaper private colleges. Tuition and fees for 2012–13 totaled $32,700. Room and board, for those who could get into a dorm, came to $11,550. In a competitive push within New Jersey, the university just announced that students enrolling at Seton Hall directly from high school in September 2012 can receive the Rutgers in-state tuition rate. Admissions are need blind, although the school does not guarantee to meet every student's need. Seventy-seven percent of all undergraduates received need-based financial aid, but the average indebtedness of recent graduates was a hefty $37,724.

STRONG SUITS	WEAK POINTS
• An administration committed to reclaiming the school's Catholic identity and liberal arts mission. • An excellent core curriculum and an honors program with a Great Books focus. • Solid departments in classical studies, international relations, Catholic studies, English, history, and political science. • A wide variety of political , religious, and social options on campus.	• Still some shaky disciplines, including communications. • Theology department considered "a mixed bag," inferior to Catholic studies program. • Campus is situated in crime-ridden city of Newark, New Jersey.

Smith College

Northampton, Massachusetts • www.smith.edu

Amazons.com

Founded in 1871, Smith College is the largest private women's college in the United States. The college is famous for producing independent and ambitious women competent in their chosen professions. However, a conservative or religious student might find her independence tested by the school's thoroughgoing commitment to radical feminism, which pervades both classroom and campus.

Academic Life: Fill in the blank

Liberal arts have been a priority at Smith since its founding, but today the college places more of an emphasis on technology and the sciences, as well as majors such as education. Indeed, the traditional liberal arts curriculum no longer prevails at Smith—which, since 1970, has had no distribution requirements for graduation. None. (The only mandatory course is a writing-intensive class for first-time students.) This blank space, to be filled with the personal preferences of teenagers, has replaced Smith's once impressive curriculum.

Thus, Smith students must carefully structure their own programs if they wish to obtain an authentic liberal education. Nevertheless, academics at Smith are described as "competitive," and students actively participate in class discussions. "They are an ambitious lot," says one faculty member. Currently, the most popular majors include psychology, government, art, economics, biology and English. A student may also design her own major, subject to approval.

Requirements for the majors provide some structure. English majors, for instance, are required to take two courses out of four "gateway" options: "Methods of Literary Study," part I or II of a British literature survey, or "American Literature before 1865"; two courses on literature before 1832; a seminar; courses on two of three major literary figures (Chaucer, Shakespeare, or Milton); two upper-level literature seminars (one taken in the senior year); and four additional courses within the department. One can take classes as traditional as "What Jane Austen Read: The Eighteenth-Century Novel" or as trendy as "Victorian Sexualities."

History majors must take five courses in their field of concentration and achieve "geographical breadth" by taking courses in three of the following areas: Africa, East Asia and Central Asia, Europe, Latin America, the Middle East and South Asia, and North America. Thus, a history major can graduate without ever learning anything about ancient or medieval history, the American Revolution, or the Civil War.

The government department requires majors to take courses in American government, comparative government, political theory, and international relations. This is one of the more leftist and politicized departments as evidenced by courses such as "Seminar in Political Theory: Religion and Democracy," a hysterical denunciation of the "Religious Right" in America. The class draws consistent parallels between conservative Christians in America, intolerant Muslims in the Middle East, and Hindu nationalists in South Asia.

A rigorous interdepartmental major and minor in medieval studies are also offered at Smith. This may be the option at Smith that comes closest to a traditional liberal arts education. All students enrolled in the major are required to achieve a working knowledge of Latin and to gain in-depth knowledge of the history, religion, and art of European civilization. A major in classical studies is also offered.

VITAL STATISTICS

Religious affiliation: *none*
Total enrollment: *3,212*
Total undergraduates: *2,664*
SAT CR/Verbal midrange: *610–720*
SAT Math midrange: *600–710*
ACT midrange: *27–31*
Applicants: *4,341*
Applicants accepted: *42%*
Accepted applicants who enrolled: *35%*
Tuition (general/out of state): *$42,840*
Tuition (in state): *N/A*
Room and board: *$14,410*
Freshman retention rate: *93%*
Graduation rate (4 yrs.): *78%*
Graduation rate (6 yrs.): *85%*
Courses with fewer than 20 students: *67%*
Student-faculty ratio: *9:1*
Courses taught by graduate students: *none*
Students living on campus: *95%*
Students in fraternities: *N/A*
Students in sororities: *none*
Students receiving need-based financial aid: *62%*
Avg. student-loan debt of a recent graduating class: *$24,484*
Most popular majors: *economics, political science, psychology*
Guaranteed housing for 4 years? *yes*

CAMPUS POLITICS: RED LIGHT

Smith has leaned heavily to the left for a very long time. A decade ago, a faculty member was denied tenure (he got it after a national uproar) for writing for a conservative magazine. The atmosphere has gotten no better since. As the beleaguered College Republicans wrote in a group letter published in the campus newspaper:

Conservative students at Smith face extreme adversity from their peers if they make their opinions public. During last year's Conservative Coming Out Day, an annual event held by the Smith Republicans to encourage Smith students to come out as conservatives or moderates, several Smithies said that they would join the club, but were afraid of the social ramifications: being taunted, ridiculed and ostracized by their housemates and friends.

This is a valid concern. . . . In the heat of the last presidential election, girls in one member's house posted vicious messages on her door. Additionally, it has been nearly impossible to advertise our club's events because flyers are torn down within hours. If they do remain up, they are vandalized. . . .

The liberal bias penetrates the classrooms as well. In one club member's American government class, during the most recent presidential primaries, only the liberal candidates' platforms were discussed. The professor made little effort to include conservative candidates, such as John McCain and Mitt Romney, in the classroom dialogue.

Smith does have a strong advising program. Each freshman is assigned a faculty adviser who helps direct her path until she declares a major, usually during her sophomore year. Then she chooses her own adviser within her department.

The student-faculty ratio at Smith is an excellent 9 to 1, and student-faculty relationships are reportedly strong. Classes are usually small—two-thirds of them have fewer than 20 students—and, although there is a small population of graduate students on campus, professors teach all the classes and grade all exams. Students rate the accessibility of Smith's faculty as one of the school's finest points.

Smith's extensive internship program, "Praxis: The Liberal Arts at Work," gives every student the opportunity to take part in a summer internship funded by the school. As one professor states, "With little financial investment, students have fabulous resources and opportunities at Smith; the internships they complete make for great experiences and 'get ahead' résumés."

Recommended faculty at Smith include Gregory White, Donald C. Baumer, J. Patrick Coby, and Marc Lendler in government; James Miller, Roisin O'Sullivan, Randy Bartlett, Roger Kaufman and Mahnaz Mahdavi in economics; Marnie Anderson, Ernest Benz, and Richard Lim in history; Craig Davis, Bill Oram, Jefferson Hunter, Dean Flower, and Douglas Lane Patey in English; Dana Leibsohn in art history; Kevin Shea and Shizuka Hsieh in chemistry; John Brady in geology; Borjana Mikic and Glenn Ellis in engineering; Jocelyne Kolb in German; Justin Cammy in Jewish studies; and Andy Rotman, Suleiman Ali Mourad, and C. S. Lewis specialist Carol G. Zaleski in religion and biblical literature.

The school's outgoing president, Carol

Christ, said that one of her main focuses is diversity and that she intends to explore how the campus can be even further "diversified" via admissions. And she seems to be getting her wish; the current student body is 12 percent Asian, 5 percent black, 9 percent Hispanic, and 11 percent "other / unknown." Christ sought even more community-wide discussions and debates on issues of race, class, gender, and sexual identification. It is unclear whether her incoming successor, Kathy McCartney, shares this preoccupation.

One professor praises the abundance of library resources: "Smith's Rare Book Collection is the finest of any college in the country, containing materials from cuneiform tables through incunabula to contemporary small press-work. Many classes make use of these materials, and the Curator of Rare Books, a member of the art department, teaches a range of courses on the art and history of the book."

Almost 50 percent of students participate in a study-abroad program during their time at Smith. Smith is well known for its junior-year-abroad program, with choices including Florence, Geneva, Hamburg, and Paris. The college maintains a formal affiliation with programs in Japan, Mexico, Spain, and southern India. If those options aren't enough, more than a hundred other study-abroad programs have been preapproved by the school. Although a foreign language is not required at Smith, it is a distribution "suggestion," and the college offers a number of languages: Arabic, Chinese, French, German, Greek and Latin, Italian, Japanese, Korean, Portuguese, Russian, and Spanish.

A professor says, "Students have fabulous resources and opportunities at Smith; the internships they complete make for great experiences and 'get ahead' résumés." But conservative students fear "being taunted, ridiculed and ostracized by their housemates and friends."

Student Life: LUGs on the Mill

Northampton is located right outside Smith's gates, but the school's semirural setting means students are only a five-minute walk from the countryside. Near campus, the Mill River flows, where students go for picnics and relaxation.

In one telling incident, in April 2003 by a campus-wide vote, Smith students decided to eliminate the words *she* and *her* from their student government's constitution, according to the *Chronicle of Higher Education*. Er, why? To avoid offending those Smith students who don't identify as women. Apparently, a small contingent of students consider themselves "transgender," and this all-female school feels constrained to placate them. In response to similar initiatives, Smith administrators have hired a part-time gender specialist "to provide counseling services and consultation to the college to support transgender students." Smith's Campus Diversity board works closely with the administration's Office of Institutional Diversity and the diversity committees associated with each campus residence.

Smith has an active lesbian community that is loud and proud. The group runs its own student organization, not to mention special committees for lesbians of color, bisexuals,

SUGGESTED CORE

1. English 202, Western Classics in Translation, from Homer to Dante
2. Philosophy 124, History of Ancient and Medieval Western Philosophy
3. Religion 162/215, Introduction to the Bible I/II
4. Religion 231, The Making of Christianity (*closest match*)
5. Government 262, Early Modern Political Theory 1500–1800
6. English 256, Shakespeare
7. History 264, Colonialism in North America, 1492–1830
8. Government 263: Political Theory of the 19th Century or History 250: Europe in the 19th Century

and transgendered folks. Smith also offers health insurance benefits to domestic partners. Some students claim that a number of Smithies are merely "LUGs"—lesbians until graduation.

Smith has more than a hundred student clubs of all types. Arts and performing arts clubs include Celebrations (a multicultural dance company), Crapapella, Handbell Choir, the Wailing Banshees, and a *Vagina Monologues* group. German, Italian, Russian, astronomy, and anthropology clubs exist, along with the Minority Association of Prehealth Students and the Union of Underrepresented Students in the Sciences. Asian, black, Chinese, South Asian, Indigenous, Korean, Latina, African and Caribbean, and Vietnamese students all have their own associations.

Most numerous are Smith's social and political action groups, which range from Amnesty International, College Republicans, and AWARE (Activist Women Advocating Rape Education) to Prism: Queer Students of Color, Size Matters (an "anti-sizeism" organization), Transcending Gender, and the Global AIDS Campaign. Students also have a weekly paper, *The Sophian,* and a campus radio station. A $23 million, 60,000-square-foot campus center was dedicated in 2003.

Several religious groups are represented at Smith, like the Association of Smith Pagans, Al-Iman, Hillel, Newman Association, Unitarian Universalists, and the Radical Catholic Feminist Organization at Smith. Students call Smith Christian Fellowship "very strong," but in 2010 Smith laid off its three chaplains (one Protestant, one Catholic, and one Jewish), since fewer "than a hundred students were actually participating in regular religious services provided by the college. Maybe close to fifty total, to be honest," a dean reported.

Most Smithies live in one of 36 self-governing houses; these accommodate between 10 and 100 students, drawn from all four classes. A limited number of seniors are allowed to live off campus with their families, but just 6 percent do so. Each campus house has its own unique traditions and style. Smithies should have no complaints regarding home accoutrements, which often include complete kitchens, dining rooms, pianos, and sometimes an in-house cook. Each bedroom has high-speed Internet access. Special-interest housing includes a French house, a senior house, and the Ada Comstock house for "non-traditional aged students." Family-style meals are served in some houses on Thursday nights, and students may invite faculty or staff to join them at dinner. Smoking is banned in every building at Smith; those wishing to light up must stand at least 20 feet away from any Smith facility.

Freshmen are well cared for. Before a student arrives on campus, one of the "heads of new students" contacts her to explain various campus details. Once at Smith, she helps the student during orientation. A Big Sister/Little Sister program puts new students in contact with seniors within the same "house" who leave gifts and clues about themselves for a week. First-year students are also offered a variety of seminars that emphasize writing, public speaking, group work, and library and quantitative skills.

Sports are a big part of life at Smith, and the Pioneers play in blue and white or blue and yellow uniforms (each class has its own school color). The school even offers an exercise and sports studies major. Smith's 14 varsity teams compete in the NCAA Division III in basketball, crew, cross-country, equestrian sports, field hockey, lacrosse, skiing, soccer, softball, squash, swimming and diving, tennis, track and field, and volleyball. Intercollegiate club sports include fencing, rugby, kung fu, tae kwon do, ice hockey, synchronized swimming, golf, and Ultimate Frisbee.

Though there aren't any sororities, keg parties still find a place on campus. Plenty of young men from nearby colleges stay the weekend at Smith, and a bus system that runs until 2:30 a.m. gives easy access to coeducational colleges in the area. Smith has a large counseling department to help students deal with such issues as depression and eating disorders. According to the school's website, about 25 percent of the student body avails itself of these services each year.

One of many Smith traditions is this: on the day before commencement, alumnae escort graduating seniors, who parade around campus wearing white dresses and then plant ivy to symbolize the connection between the school and its graduates. That night the entire campus is lit with colored paper lanterns, providing a soft glow to the grounds that is perfect for reminiscing about bygone days and long-lost LUGs.

Smith is relatively safe compared to other schools; 2011 crime statistics listed three forcible sex offenses, two motor vehicle thefts, and seven burglaries. Students declare they feel "extremely safe" on campus.

All these privileges come at a hefty price. Tuition for 2012–2013 was a steep $42,840, and room and board $14,410. Sixty-two percent of Smith's student body received financial aid averaging $39,120 from the college, but the average student-loan debt of a graduate was, nevertheless, a heavy $24,484.

STRONG SUITS	WEAK POINTS
• Students are ambitious and competitive. • Elite professors teach small classes and are quite accessible to students. • Good resources for freshmen and advising. • A rigorous program in medieval studies offers a chance for a traditional liberal arts education.	• No curricular requirements at all beyond a single writing intensive course. • An intense focus by the administration on diversity. • An almost unquestioned acceptance of leftism. • Religion of so little interest, the school laid off several chaplains for lack of work. • Aggressively visible lesbian community on this all-female campus.

Southern Methodist University

Dallas, Texas • www.smu.edu

Oh Lord, Won't You Buy Me . . . a Presidential Library

Southern Methodist University is known as one of the leading schools in the Southwest—and as a finishing school for children of the Texas business elite. There are probably more Mercedes-Benzes with Jesus fish parked here than anywhere in the world. (One professor notes wryly, "It's easier to find the Mercedes than the Jesus fish.") Yet the school has been steadily attracting serious scholars, not only in business and fine arts, but also in political science, history, psychology, and engineering. The $300 million George W. Bush Presidential Library sits on its campus, attracting and employing scholars and policy wonks to SMU. Says one teacher: "SMU combines many of the best features of liberal arts colleges and big research universities. It has the intellectual resources of a big school, with relatively small classes and a personal focus, a happy medium that offers the advantages of both."

Academic Life: That education business

The school's curricular requirements are weak. Says one professor: "We don't have a very strong core. There's a lot of choice for students—as in 'one from Column A or B.' If you don't want a grounding in the classical Western tradition, you don't have to get it. You could fulfill your requirements through a hodgepodge of fluff or entirely non-Western courses. Still, it's very possible to get that grounding if you're motivated to get it." The competitive University Honors program invites about 600 students to take intimate seminars on special topics with enrollment in each course capped at 20 students. Teaching assistants rarely preside over such classes.

Students majoring in the humanities, mathematics, the natural sciences, and the social or behavioral sciences study in Dedman College. Others apply to the Cox School of Business, the School of Engineering, the Simmons School of Education and Development, or the Meadows School of the Arts. One graduate student says that his sense "is that, if so inclined, an undergraduate could successfully carve out a substantive 'classics' curriculum at SMU." However, among many students one finds a "disturbing utilitarian mentality, where people are looking to check off the boxes and move off to a pre-professional program. A little too much of a tendency to ask, 'What am I going to do with this?'" says a professor.

SMU is the principal training ground for Dallas professionals, and the Cox School of Business offers the most popular majors—business and finance. According to a professor, the school "is considered one of the top twenty in the U.S. It's selective—you need a good GPA to declare a major there." One special opportunity for select business undergraduates is the BBA Leadership Institute, a seminar program taught by outside business leaders and professionals, addressing real-life business situations.

Entering freshmen at SMU take a "wellness program." One student says, "I think that the part about making good life choices is great, but the part that basically says that 'no one is ever wrong' really bothers me." The university administration is known as being highly solicitous of the personal needs of individual students.

Professors are considered easily accessible and often show an unusual degree of willingness to give one-on-one attention to freshmen. The university also provides what it calls an "academic safety net" for its students in the form of the Learning Enhancement Center, where students can take seminars on time and stress management, receive writing tutorials, or enroll in an elective that builds study skills.

VITAL STATISTICS

Religious affiliation: *Protestant (United Methodist)*
Total enrollment: *10,982*
Total undergraduates: *6,221*
SAT CR/Verbal midrange: *580–680*
SAT Math midrange: *600–690*
ACT midrange: *26–31*
Applicants *10,338*
Applicants accepted: *55%*
Accepted applicants who enrolled: *25%*
Tuition (general/out of state): *$41,750*
Tuition (in state): *N/A*
Room and board: *$13,539*
Freshman retention rate: *89%*
Graduation rate (4 yrs.): *60%*
Graduation rate (6 yrs.): *75%*
Courses with fewer than 20 students: *59%*
Student-faculty ratio: *11:1*
Courses taught by graduate students: *2%*
Students living on campus: *33%*
Students in fraternities: *32%*
Students in sororities: *43%*
Students receiving need-based financial aid: *40%*
Avg. student-loan debt of a recent graduating class: *$26,297*
Most popular majors: *business/marketing, social sciences, communications*
Guaranteed housing for 4 years? *no*

The SMU student body is moderately conservative. Many note that the professors are generally more liberal than either the "decidedly Republican" student body or the larger community, although one professor called his colleagues "more conservative than that of most major American research universities. There is ideological diversity, with conservatives and Republicans on the faculty. I've heard of very few incidents of political intimidation in class—most of them in rhetoric classes in the English department taught by instructors," he said.

One student states that the campus "is located in an extremely conservative community and surrounded by a [relatively] conservative urban area. Occasionally I've observed some liberal groups who have placed flyers around campus. The school newspaper seems to be more to the left." Some students have noticed elements of political correctness they find irksome. The Office of New Student Programs requires its student leaders to take part in a diversity exercise that one student says "demeans every white, rich male who happens to be fortunate enough to be born with a mom and a dad in the home." Privileged treatment of "designated victim" groups can occur. One freshman reports that recently the school axed the debate team for not having enough members, while leaving intact the homosexual organization, which had fewer members.

The university has a solid academic reputation in the humanities that continues to improve. English and history are well regarded at SMU, and its theater and arts programs are nationally recognized. Psychology "has built itself into quite a good department," says a professor. "It used to be one of our weaker ones. The faculty made the major more challenging and did a lot of hiring of more productive research faculty." Anthropology offers excellent training in archaeological research, particularly in the Americas. "We have someone doing cutting-edge work in Mayan spots, and a campus facility and summer program in Taos, New Mexico," says a professor.

The history department shines in the study of the American Southwest, thanks to a special endowment from former governor Bill Clements. The department is mostly solid if you make it a point to avoid the ethnic studies and women's studies programs and their course offerings. History majors are required to take classes in American history before and after 1865 and are offered a fair amount of traditional Western civilization courses as well. Majors must also complete a rigorous junior seminar in research and writing.

A student describes the university's English department as "professionally distinguished" and has high praise for some of its professors. There is an annual literary festival on campus, and the university also publishes the famous *Southwest Review*. English majors must study medieval, early modern, and modern literature, as well as poetry and literary criticism. Shakespeare is not specifically required, but he would be hard to miss.

SMU offers some exceptional opportunities for political science majors. The department has a strong focus on American government and politics, and in political theory—"especially in Enlightenment and modern political thought," says a professor. All poli-sci majors must complete courses on the U.S. Constitution and American political philosophy as well as classes in international politics and political theory. The department is bolstered by a prestigious political studies institute, the John Goodwin Tower Center for Political Studies, which focuses on international relations and comparative politics. The center offers competitive internships in Washington, D.C., and a limited number of research fellowships for undergraduates.

The hard sciences are not as strong as the social sciences, a teacher tells us. "Those departments are mostly fairly weak, smaller than they should be. SMU has somewhat underinvested in those areas. I also hear negative reports on teaching in those departments—for instance, grad students not fluent in English," he says.

However, the university's Meadows School of the Arts is highly esteemed. Its facilities include the Bob Hope and Greer Garson theaters. The Meadows School has earned a prominent place nationally among American art schools and offers diverse programs—visual arts (art and art history), performing arts (dance, music, and theater), and communications (advertising, cinema/television, corporate communications and public affairs, and journalism), as well as an excellent program in arts administration.

> While SMU is a balanced campus with ample resources, students show a "disturbing utilitarian mentality, where people are looking to check off the boxes and move off to a preprofessional program. They ask, 'What am I going to do with this?'" says a professor.

Highly recommended SMU professors include John Lamoreaux in religious studies; Robin Lovin in ethics; Joseph Kobylka, Michael Lusztig, Dennis Simon, and J. Matthew Wilson in political science; Willard Spiegelman and Bonnie Wheeler in English; and Jeremy Adams, Edward Countryman, and Dan Orlovsky in history.

For students looking to study abroad, SMU offers more than two dozen summer-, semester-, and yearlong study-abroad programs to places all over the globe, from Australia to Vietnam. SMU offers majors in French, German, Italian, and Spanish—area studies or simply in foreign languages. Minors are offered in Greek and Latin, Hindi, Japanese, and Russian.

Student Life: Greek envy

SMU is located in the Park Cities, an affluent section of Dallas. The stereotypical SMU student is an affluent Texan or southern preppy. At the same time, many students emphasize that the climate is basically upbeat, open, and friendly, with little snobbery publicly evident.

A third of all students live on campus, where the facilities are excellent and "feature a variety of room types, bathroom styles, and community areas," according to the school's website. The 11 residence halls, four apartment halls, and nine theme houses are all coed and nonsmoking and have high-quality, state-of-the-art accommodations. Single, double, and triple occupancy are available in the residence halls, and each hall has both a resident assistant and a hall director, who are in charge of resident life and manage a support staff of students. All halls observe a minimum of 10 quiet hours a day. There are no visitation hours, but all guests must be escorted at all times by the hall residents whom they are visiting. SMU also owns several unfurnished efficiency, one-bedroom, and two-bedroom apartments adjacent to campus that are available for a monthly rental rate.

More than a third of all undergraduates are also in fraternities and sororities, and most of their upperclassmen live in the Greek houses. Although students involved in Greek life frequently go out of their way to insist that the social atmosphere at SMU is open, friendly, and nonexclusive, there's no denying the heavy social dominance of the fraternities. Social life revolves around the weekly fraternity parties. It's said that the weekend begins on Thursday night, to the degree that Friday has the greatest manifestation of class-skipping. Friday night is devoted to relentless revelry, Saturday to recovery, and Sunday to cleaning up and gearing up for the week ahead. Campus parties continue to draw seniors and juniors who have moved off campus.

Special-interest-club social activities are lively during the week, and theater and political groups are popular. Social and student government "leadership development" activities, such as the Leadership, Education, Activities, and Development (LEAD), Program Council, Student Foundation, and Student Senate are also unusually prestigious at SMU. The university is traditionally a launching pad for careers in politics—especially if you're a Republican. However, the local atmosphere is changing: in recent years, Democrats have swept most local offices in Dallas, a city that has been written up nationally as both increasingly liberal and "gay friendly."

The student newspaper, the *Daily Campus,* has a fairly healthy reputation for vigorous debate between contributors of various viewpoints. One provocative exchange involved a proponent of the "intelligent design" critique of Darwinian evolution, biologist Michael Behe, and SMU professor John Wise. This exchange was notable for the newspaper's willingness to give Behe's views a serious hearing in the first place.

"SMU has a strong group of ethicists, including Robin Lovin at the Perkins School of Theology," says one student. "There is a core of religiously committed students, but overall the campus is pretty secular," says a professor. "There is no hostility to religion. Christian students won't encounter opposition, but SMU doesn't have a genuine Christian flavor. It's about as palpably religious as Georgetown. Religious programs are there, but students would have to seek them out." Still, a student observes that there seem to be "a large number of students involved in on-campus Christian ministries." Cru (Campus Crusade for Christ) alone draws roughly a hundred students to its weekly meetings. There are many local churches and other houses of worship available in Dallas—and the more devout students should probably seek them out. The conservative St. Thomas Aquinas Catholic parish is a short drive away, as is Park Cities Presbyterian, a solid Protestant congregation.

SMU's 16 sports teams, the Mustangs, compete in the NCAA's Division I, and the school's 19 club sports and more than 30 intramural teams are very popular with students. The state-of-the-art fitness and recreation center was recently completed, and the athletic facilities are second to none, including the spectacular Gerald Ford football stadium.

There is ample police presence on campus, and female students say they feel quite safe; however, in 2011 the school reported two forcible sex offenses, three aggravated assaults, 11 burglaries, one case of arson, and three stolen cars on campus. Dallas is one of the more dangerous major cities in America, so students are advised to exercise caution.

With 2012–13 tuition at $41,750 and room and board at $13,539, SMU is fairly expensive. Only 40 percent of students received need-based financial aid, and the average student-loan debt of a recent graduate was $26,297.

STRONG SUITS	WEAK POINTS
• The Cox School of Business is a regional leader, producing many successful executives. • Professors are accessible and, like the administration, take a real interest in student well-being. • A politically balanced school, with free expression of many viewpoints. • Good programs in English, history, political science, anthropology, and psychology. • The Meadows School of the Arts is highly acclaimed.	• Weak curriculum, with requirements that can be fulfilled through "fluff" courses. • Rampant preprofessionalism among students undermines intellectual curiosity. • Hard sciences weaker than social sciences, with undergrads taught by graduate students not fluent in English. • Party atmosphere fueled by a dominant Greek system.

St. John's College

Annapolis, Maryland• www.stjohnscollege.edu

Battle of the Books

Founded as King William's School in 1696, then chartered in 1784 as St. John's College, St. John's was for most of its history an unremarkable regional school. The college was about to close during the Great Depression when some pioneering educators offered a bold plan to save the school by making it distinctive. And thus was born the first "Great Books" college in America. Within a few years, school supporter Mark van Doren of Columbia was telling his colleagues of St. John's model: "Until it is accepted everywhere in America, we shall lack the right to say that liberal education exists among us." The divide between St. John's and most other colleges has only grown in subsequent decades, as it has held firm to its self-hallowed canon and they have thrown their curricula to the winds.

St. John's is one college on two campuses, which share the same program of study and many of the same characteristics. The teachers are called tutors, and students and faculty all refer to each other by their last names—always preceded by "Mr." or "Miss." Classes are always taught by the tutors, never by graduate students. Grades are not routinely reported to students; many do not know their GPAs. Very few students are to be found playing on computers, watching television, listening to iPods, or texting on cell phones; they talk to each other. In that conversation, they help each other to live the life of the mind.

Academic Life: From Plato to NATO

Reading and discussion stand at the heart of academics at St. John's. A current student says: "I went to a large public research university for my undergraduate studies and found that although I had constant stress and work to complete, I did little in the way of genuine learning. Being at St. John's has given me that experience." Another student observes, "It is probably impossible to find another school in the U.S. with more reverence for Western civilization and the Great Books than St. John's. It's practically the campus religion." (That would make it the only one; though it's named for an Apostle, the school is utterly secular.)

Every course in the curriculum is required, and students at both campuses follow essentially the same program of study. Classes are small, about 20 or fewer students, and conducted using the Socratic method of discussion rather than lecture. The excitement of students is palpable. One says, "We study Ptolemy intensively, then in two years we study Einstein. . . . Sometimes we make connections across thousands of years, and the whole room has mutual understanding of all questions discussed for each. This is not restricted to math but is true in every subject."

In the twice-weekly seminar, students break into groups of 20 or so and enter discussions led by pairs of tutors. Some students note that seminars are dictated by the students, who are deemed equal to tutors—so the meetings can vary in quality. Works are studied chronologically, from the origins of civilization to the present. As one student says, "We are here to engage books in their own right, not to blindly accept what each subsequent author posits." These seminars give an overview of the greatest works of the Western world and discuss subjects such as philosophy, theology, political science, literature, history, economics, and psychology. Much depends here on the quality of the tutor, and several students report an insistence on lockstep thought in the supposedly free-flowing seminars. "Question all you like, but don't declare a particular opinion," warned one.

Besides the seminar, students participate in labs and take language, math, and music tutorials. The language tutorial takes place all four years and covers Attic Greek in the first two years and French in the last two. One junior says that her favorite classes have been ones

VITAL STATISTICS

Religious affiliation: *none*
Total enrollment: *968*
Total undergraduates: *850*
SAT CR/Verbal midrange: *620–730*
SAT Math midrange: *560–690*
ACT midrange: *25–30*
Applicants: *433*
Applicants accepted: *78%*
Accepted applicants who enrolled: *49%*
Tuition (general/out of state) *$44,554*
Tuition (in state): *N/A*
Room and board: *$9,994–10,644*
Freshman retention rate: *90%*
Graduation rate (4 yrs.): *60%*
Graduation rate (6 yrs.): *69%*
Courses with fewer than 20 students: *100%*
Student-faculty ratio: *8:1*
Courses taught by graduate students: *not provided*
Students living on campus: *82%*
Students in fraternities: *N/A*
Students in sororities: *N/A*
Students receiving need-based financial aid: *70%*
Avg. student-loan debt of a recent graduating class: *$27,672*

CAMPUS POLITICS: GREEN LIGHT

The prevailing political attitude at St. John's is liberal, but the school is not highly politicized. Students with more conservative views, morally or politically, are readily accepted in the classroom and in the campus community. A student at the Annapolis campus writes:

"One of my favorite things about this college and the people who attend it is their acceptance of and respect for people of all walks of life. There is an unwritten rule of respect on this campus that everyone is expected—and wants—to follow. It is what makes our small community such a rich atmosphere for learning and growing, as well as a safe and friendly place to voice opinions and have serious discussions about the important things in life. The majority of St. John students have been raised by or are familiar with Judeo-Christian beliefs, but for whatever reasons do not currently choose to live by them. There are, however, a fair number of practicing Jews and Christians on campus who have formed student-run clubs and organize trips to temples and churches to worship together. Although they are a minority on campus, they enjoy their time here just as much as anyone else and have no trouble making friends."

in which the entire period was spent in discussion of one phrase or sentence, quibbling over students' choices of various words in their translations. The math tutorials require students to work through proofs themselves, and music instructs them to sing and compose so they understand how music functions.

St. John's students don't do quite all their learning through seminars. Every week the school sponsors a substantive Friday Night Lecture, which students are expected to analyze carefully. There follows a lively Q&A, which can go on for hours.

Students are awarded conventional letter grades but mostly so they may later apply to graduate school. Their main feedback comes in "Don Rags," during which tutors critique each student's work in his presence, and he replies. In the junior year, the Rags may be replaced by conferences where the student speaks first, giving a self-evaluation, and then the tutors share their remarks. Grades are not discussed.

For upperclassmen, "preceptorials" are as close as students get to electives, and the choices differ every year. Students will often approach a tutor and ask to have certain subjects or authors treated.

To cap off the program, seniors write a substantive essay under the guidance of a faculty adviser. On the night that essays are due, the dean "stops time" for an hour before midnight so tardy students can hand in their essays. Each student must give an hour-long oral defense of the essay, which is open to the public.

There are no majors at St. John's, but according to the school, a student who has successfully graduated can be viewed as having the equivalent of a double major in philosophy and the history of math and science, along with a double minor in classical studies and comparative literature.

Although the curriculum is set, this doesn't mean students only read and discuss the texts assigned. "Johnnies" (as students are called) have inquisitive natures and a broad interest in accumulating knowledge; they're the kind of kids who edit Wikipedia. Anywhere you go at St. John's, you will find students and tutors talking about anything and everything. Students often put together "guerrilla seminars," which are just a group of students (and very likely tutors) who get together in their free time to discuss topics of interest. These informal discussions are vital to the life of St. John's. The college also offers a "take a tutor to lunch" program, at the school's expense; students are well-advised to take the college up on this, since most tutors do not hold posted office hours.

One undergrad says: "Tutors are very accessible and generally helpful. All a student needs to do is to schedule an appointment with a tutor—no need to worry about long lines during 'office hours.' The shortest meeting I've ever had with a tutor, one on one, was twenty minutes, and the longest was three hours of intense intellectual discussion. Probably nowhere else in the U.S. can a student get that much individual attention and mentoring from tenured instructors."

> A student says, "It is probably impossible to find another school in the U.S. with more reverence for Western civilization and the Great Books than St. John's. It's practically the campus religion."

Students choose who they take to lunch but not who to study under. So the faculty we recommend for lunch are as follows: At Annapolis, the much-loved veteran Eva Brann, who received the National Endowment for the Humanities Medal in 2005; Dylan Casey, Paul Ludwig, Robert Williamson (emeritus), Jon Lenkowski, Carl Page, Michael Grenke, Walter Sterling, Stewart Umphrey (emeritus), Peter Kalkavage, Jim Beall, and Henry Higuera. At Santa Fe, Jorge Aigla, Grant Franks, Peter Pesic, J. Walter Sterling, and Edward Cary Stickney. As one undergrad observes, "Just as students are required to take all classes, faculty are expected to teach across the curriculum and have to learn Ancient Greek and astronomy and Baudelaire no less than the students. This is all part of the culture of St. John's." On the down side, at John's, a poor tutor (and there are some) can be a real handicap for his students.

About 70 percent of graduates go on to some sort of postbaccalaureate study. A surprisingly large number go on to work in medicine and the sciences. Many enter law, teaching, and the arts. Successful alumni include film directors (Lee David Zlotoff, *The Spitfire Grill;* Jeremy Leven, *The Legend of Bagger Vance*); journalists and editors (Lydia Berggren of the *New York Times;* Nancy Miller of Bloomsbury U.S.A. Publishing; Timothy Carney, columnist, the *Washington Examiner;* Ray Cave, retired editorial director of *Time*); broadcasters (Lisa Simeone, host, NPR's *World of Opera;* Seth Cropsey, former director of the International Broadcasting Bureau); and luminaries in many other fields.

Because of the unique program that builds upon itself over four years, transfer students must start as freshmen. Similarly, while students can transfer between the Annapolis and Santa Fe campuses, there is no study abroad. All Saint John's students spend a full four years (or more) studying at one of the Saint John's campuses. The only languages taught on campus are Ancient Greek and French.

Student Life: A school of two cities

St. John's decided to grow, while maintaining an intimate sense of community, by establishing a faraway second campus in New Mexico. Each campus has around 450 students. A certain friendly rivalry exists between the campuses. One Annapolis student says, "Santa Fe is for the weed-smoking hippies to hang out in the mountains." A Santa Fe student counters, "Annapolis is full of limousine liberals."

The Santa Fe campus has townhouse-style buildings that students say can be a bit uncomfortable; however, the city of Santa Fe offers many more options than Annapolis, and many students move off campus in their sophomore year. A new residence center is soon to be built with a $5 million donation by an alumnus couple, and named for them. The Winiarski building will provide housing for many students as well as common rooms, seminar rooms, and faculty offices.

The unofficial mascot of St. John's is the platypus, which seems entirely fitting. There are student newspapers, drama clubs, film societies, religious organizations, political clubs, and parties. The school sponsors many dances throughout the year for students through the Waltz Committee. Swing and contemporary dance are also popular. Each campus has an extensive intramural program but no intercollegiate one.

Politics plays only a small role at St. John's. As one student writes, "Most students on campus are of the liberal mind-set, but this certainly does not get in the way of friendships or classes. I have not found there to be much political discussion on campus . . . but there are plenty of people to discuss politics with if one is interested in doing so. There is a St. John's Republicans group as well as a St. John's Democrats group on campus, both student-run and organized. Again, the opinions of others are accepted and/or tolerated by everyone—so long as those opinions do not harm anyone."

The school requires all freshmen to live on campus. In Annapolis there are eight dorms, the oldest of which was built in 1837 and the newest in 2006. Upperclassmen aren't guaranteed student housing, and in years past, many moved off campus as soon as they could. Maryland rents are keeping more of them on campus these days. According to one student, "Dorm life is in many ways similar to that at other schools. Students can be loud at odd hours, and sometimes there are disagreements among the students. On the whole, students are respectful of one another and interested in maintaining a happy and fun community. RAs have all been impressive, in my experience. There are a few single-sex floors, but most dorms are mixed, with single-sex bathrooms." There are no restrictions on intervisitation, the bathrooms offer condoms, and one undergrad reports feeling uncomfortable at St. John's because of the expectation that casual sex was routine. Pressure at St. John's may be intense, and there have been a few suicides in the past two decades.

St. John's appears to have something of a problem with drug use. Students say that the Santa Fe campus reeks of weed. More serious are reports of harder drugs on the Annapolis campus in past years. Most students only tipple, but enough drink to excess on a regular basis to raise concerns. Sober students can choose a substance-free dorm, but enforcement is said to be spotty.

St. John's is a secular institution, and religious life must be pursued off campus. But both Annapolis and Santa Fe offer many, varied options for worship.

Both campuses are rather safe. In 2011 the Annapolis campus reported two burglaries and five thefts; the Santa Fe campus reported four forcible sex offenses.

St. John's is pricey, with tuition for 2012–13 at $44,554, and room and board some $9,994–10,644. Admissions are need blind, and about 70 percent of students received aid. All aid is need based, although it may differ by campus. The average student-loan debt of a recent St. John's graduate was $27,672.

STRONG SUITS

- Small, academically intense classes centered exclusively on the Great Books.
- Enthusiastic discussions of ideas that extend outside the classroom.
- Close personal attention from widely educated "tutors" (professors).
- Absence of political activism of any stripe; an atmosphere open to hardworking students of any worldview.

WEAK POINTS

- Very secular atmosphere, with social mores to match.
- The "great ideas" discussed can come to seem of equal value, leading to a highbrow relativism.
- The quality of each class depends very much on the "tutor," whose quality can vary.
- No majors and little or no preparation for any career in particular—apart from academia.

Stanford University

Palo Alto, California • www.stanford.edu

Make Yourself Useful

Businessman Leland Stanford, founder of this university, once said that "technically educated boys do not make the most successful businessmen." Leland Stanford's insight appears to have been lost on those who now look after his patrimony. Stanford University's reputation as a leader in both the sciences and the liberal arts began to fade in 1987, when it abandoned its Western civilization requirement—after a storm of student protest directed by Jesse Jackson, who led the infamous chant, "Hey hey, ho ho, Western Civ has got to go."

Today, instead of Western civilization, Stanford requires courses in global community, American "cultures," or gender studies. Perhaps as a result, Stanford students have found little to entice them to explore the liberal arts and have increasingly turned toward technical fields such as computer science and engineering, which are two of the university's most popular majors.

Yet Stanford continues to attract the "best and the brightest." Its graduates are found on the U.S. Supreme Court (Justices Breyer and Kennedy, as well as the retired Sandra Day O'Connor and the late William Rehnquist). Seventeen Stanford graduates, including Sally Ride, have served as astronauts. Stanford is second only to Harvard in the number of graduates serving in Congress.

Academic Life: The decline of Western Civ

Students who are mature and savvy enough can find good liberal arts courses at Stanford. As one conservative student wrote, "Stanford definitely has its share of politicized courses with their multicultural dogma. But the courses which form a foundation in Western civilization, although not mandatory, are readily available for the taking." The best option is the Program in Structured Liberal Education (SLE), a "yearlong, residential, rigorous writing and literature course that intensely covers the canon of Western civilization along with some material on Hinduism and Buddhism," says a past participant. An alumnus warns, "It's not exactly super-friendly to conservative Christian viewpoints. But fortunately, a Catholic SLE alumnus started a program a few years back of 'SLE talks' explaining the Christian perspective on various issues SLE covers, and we've kept it alive."

Students say that professors are accessible to undergraduates. "I've yet to have a professor, of any rank or stature, not return an e-mail," one student says. "In terms of access to professors, you really can't beat Stanford." Graduate teaching assistants rarely teach courses, but they do often lead discussion or laboratory sections for larger lecture classes.

Each freshman is assigned a "pre-major" adviser with whom he must meet before he can register for classes. Advisers or "academic directors" are also located in each freshman dorm. After choosing a major, each student is assigned (or chooses) a faculty adviser. One student warns that "quality varies dramatically, and the good advisers are in high demand. Professors really do act as mentors." Another adds that he has "access to a pool of conservative professors who are eager to help like-minded students and who aren't in high demand from the rest of the student body."

Stanford's humanities departments are riddled with politically correct programs, such as the Center for Comparative Studies in Race and Ethnicity, African and African American studies, urban studies, and feminist studies (which now includes "LGBT/Queer Studies"). This last program has, as one student puts it, "a huge" presence on campus, sponsoring lectures, activist workshops, and essay contests.

VITAL STATISTICS

Religious affiliation: *none*
Total enrollment: *18,217*
Total undergraduates: *7,063*
SAT CR/Verbal midrange: *680–780*
SAT Math midrange: *700–790*
ACT midrange: *31–34*
Applicants: *36,632*
Applicants accepted: *7%*
Accepted applicants who enrolled: *73%*
Tuition (general/out of state): *$41,250*
Tuition (in state): *N/A*
Room and board: *$12,721*
Freshman retention rate: *98%*
Graduation rate (4 yrs.): *80%*
Graduation rate (6 yrs.): *95%*
Courses with fewer than 20 students: *68%*
Student-faculty ratio: *5:1*
Courses taught by graduate students: *not provided*
Students living on campus: *91%*
Students in fraternities: *24%*
Students in sororities: *28%*
Students receiving need-based financial aid: *53%*
Avg. student-loan debt of a recent graduating class: *$16,458*
Most popular majors: *computer science, human biology, engineering*
Guaranteed housing for 4 years? *yes*

CAMPUS POLITICS: YELLOW LIGHT

A number of conservative undergraduates tell us that while Stanford is predominantly liberal and secular, they are still relatively comfortable there. One traditional Christian undergraduate says, "I have not had personal experience with a particular department being consistently unwelcoming to conservative or religious students. It is much more common for a particular professor, TA, or even student to make his or her (usually liberal) political ideas known to the class. In general, campus is lively and open to political debate, as there is a strong minority of conservatives here."

Not every student feels comfortable speaking up, as a 2011 commentary in the *Cardinal Principle* noted:

> Perhaps the clearest and most dramatic indication of the way that conservatives are intimidated on this campus is the fact that five conservative writers for this newspaper, *The Cardinal Principle,* have chosen to publish only under pseudonym. This is more than 20% of the conservative staff. No liberal author has ever made such a request. The conservative writers told me they did not want to have their names attached to their articles for two reasons. First, they feared that their professors and/or TAs would learn of their conservative leanings and that this would negatively affect their grades, although their articles had no direct relation to their class material. Second, some did not want the broader Stanford community to know that they had conservative views for fear of social isolation and ostracism.

According to one history student, "It's fairly easy to avoid the 'politically correct' classes and still fill your requirements. So far, such classes have fairly obvious clues regarding their nature.... But there are a lot of them." Another student says, "Many of the political science classes are liberal and PC, but if you look you can find some classes that are taught by conservative professors," a student says.

A number of Stanford faculty members are tabbed by students as outstanding teachers, including Judith L. Goldstein in political science, international political economy, and trade politics; Robert Sapolsky and William James Nelson in biology; Philip Zimbardo (emeritus) in psychology; David Kennedy (emeritus) and Norman Naimark in history; Jack Rakove in history, American studies, and political science; Scott Hutchins in English; Jack Baker in civil and environmental engineering; Kathleen M. Eisenhardt in management; Alyssa O'Brien and John Peterson in writing and rhetoric; Brad D. Osgood in electrical engineering; Douglas D. Osheroff (emeritus) in physics; George Springer (emeritus) in aeronautics and astronautics; Mark Lucianovic in mathematics; Eric Roberts and Mehran Sahami in computer science; Michael Bratman in philosophy; Roger Noll (emeritus), Michael Boskin, and Robert Hall in economics; and William Hurlbut in bioethics.

Political science, especially, is reputed to have excellent undergraduate teaching, with several professors having filled key administrative positions in Washington. Condoleezza Rice, former secretary of state, is back at Stanford, based at the Hoover Institution and on the political science faculty. Majors must declare two concentrations, one primary and one secondary, in the following fields: international relations, American politics, "justice," or comparative politics, and take six courses in a primary and three courses in a secondary concentration. All majors must also take a "methods" course and complete at least one advanced undergraduate political science seminar. One of the courses taken toward the major must entail "sustained research and writing." A major could easily miss any courses addressing the American Constitution and political system.

To major in English, a student needs three methodology courses: one each on Poetry and Poetics, Narrative and Narrative Theory, and Critical Theory; four historical courses: "Literary History" I, II, and III and a "panoramic" course; and one senior seminar. Shakespeare makes an appearance in one of the survey courses and appears in some of the electives.

History majors at Stanford must complete one survey course each on Europe and the United States; one sources and methods seminar (course titles include "Forbidden Desires in China from Daoist Devotees to Dr. Sex"); two undergraduate colloquia; a writing seminar; and at least one other small group course. They may choose to concentrate in one of four areas—The Americas, Africa/Asia/Middle East, Europe/Eastern Europe/Russia, or history pre-1700—or stick to the "general history track."

The strength of Stanford now resides in its science and engineering programs. Over the years Stanford has been able to attract a core group of premier physicists and physical scientists, including several who have been awarded the Nobel Prize. Scientists develop and conduct research at the Stanford Linear Accelerator Center, a world-renowned center for physics that offers a number of educational programs to the public. Despite the school's stellar reputation in engineering and science, students majoring in other disciplines can graduate without a very rigorous experience in math or science, given the broad "general education" requirements.

Students can study Arabic, Catalan, Chinese, French, German, Greek and Latin, Italian, Japanese, Korean, Portuguese, Slavic, Spanish, and Tibetan languages, as well as some other languages by special arrangement. Stanford students can study abroad in virtually any corner of the globe, and generous financial aid policies help make this possible for all students.

Student Life: Silicon implants

Most students live on campus all four years, as Bay Area housing prices are exorbitant. Housing is guaranteed for four years. In general, students enjoy living on campus; as one student says, "Stanford's on-campus housing is wonderful." There are many different styles of living, from apartments to house-style units, dorms, and co-ops. Except for one all-female residence, dormitories and even dorm rooms are coed, with some single-sex floors, but fraternities and sororities provide single-sex options. One student states that bathrooms are usually single sex. A pilot program begun largely to meet demands of "transgender" students has now resulted in permanent implementation of "gender-neutral housing" in a number of student residences. There are no male/female visitation rules. A student notes that "RAs are immensely helpful on all fronts. I, however, do lament the very lenient policy regarding alcohol in dorms."

About 13 percent of undergraduates belong to the 11 fraternities and 13 sororities (a new sorority was added in January 2011), which provide a significant source of social life as well as single-sex housing, albeit often in a party atmosphere. (Greek houses are periodically placed on suspension for alcohol violations.) Nine of the Greek organizations have residential houses on campus, while the rest are unhoused. The frats don't have a monopoly on the campus party scene, however; Stanford allows alcohol in some of its dorms, and students say that nearly everyone drinks, although there is no evident peer pressure to do so, and that alcohol and drug use are no more prevalent than at comparable California schools.

> Stanford humanities are riddled with leftist programs, such as race and ethnicity, African and African American studies, urban studies—and feminist (including "LGBT/Queer") studies, which one student says has "a huge" presence on campus, sponsoring lectures, activist workshops, and essay contests.

Undergraduate students are not the only ones living on campus—57 percent of graduate students and 30 percent of faculty also reside on "the Farm," the nickname for Stanford's scenic 8,180-acre spread.

Stanford is what the student makes of it. As one undergrad says: "Between the entrenched *Stanford Review* and the Stanford Conservative Society, I'm fairly confident that conservatives and moderates can find a home away from the propaganda." The Conservative Society serves primarily as a forum for conservatives to gather socially rather than for in-depth discussion. A student does tell us, however, that "the Veritas Forum and some good, truth-probing multifaith panels are also increasingly active on campus," providing lively discussion and conservative and faith-based viewpoints on various topics.

Another place where conservatives might find solace is the Hoover Institution, a public-policy research center housed on Stanford's campus. Hoover frequently sponsors lectures, has an active internship program, and is a resource for reasoned scholarship on issues of considerable public interest. Three current Hoover affiliates are Nobel laureates: economists Gary S. Becker, Michael Spence (emeritus), and Douglass North. The *Stanford Review* sponsors "Hoover lunches" with institution fellows, open to the entire campus.

Some conservatives report feeling that they need to hide their views from peers. One undergrad student tells us that she received hate mail after writing an article favoring California's Proposition 8, a successful legislative initiative to preserve traditional marriage. A writer for the *Stanford Review* says that it is "a popular target of casual mockery among most students."

While Memorial Church is certainly a masterpiece (its splendid mosaics are world famous), the services there may disappoint believers in anything in particular. According to the church's website, its Sunday morning service is entirely ecumenical, including male and female ministers and a rabbi. The Catholic presence on campus is strong, with "a very solid core of students who are quite orthodox in their beliefs and practices. The preaching and teaching is typically quite faithful to church teachings, and the entire ministry staff is wonderfully and admirably dedicated to the spiritual welfare of the community." More conservative Catholic students frequent Our Mother of Perpetual Help parish in nearby Santa Clara, which offers Latin Masses. There is a joint Episcopal and Lutheran ministry at Stanford, so more orthodox-minded Episcopalian/Anglican believers should seek out Christ the King Church in Campbell, a more traditional parish. Evangelical Christians have a number of active groups on campus, and InterVarsity Christian Fellowship holds weekly Bible studies in all freshman dorms.

Stanford appears to offer a student club or society for nearly every interest, with more than 650 organizations, ranging from academic to preprofessional to athletic to religious to multicultural, are available. Clubs include Chabad and Hillel for Jewish students; Israeli Student Organization; a number of publications, including the *Stanford Daily* and the conservative *Cardinal Principle,* humor magazines, and an undergraduate philosophy journal; career and preprofessional clubs; music, dance, and drama groups; Stanford Dragonboat, an "on-water paddling" team; a radio station; Women and Youth Supporting Each Other; Reformed University Fellowship; and the ReJOYce in Jesus Campus Fellowship. Beside the *Review* and the Conservative Society, there are other worthy groups, such as Stanford Students for Life. The Haas Center for Public Service provides numerous opportunities for students.

Palo Alto "just isn't a college town, and there isn't much there for Stanford students," says one student. Another student says Palo Alto is a pleasant enough place but "is somewhat pricey. A better bet is Castro Street in Mountain View [five miles from campus].... The area is more middle class and less yuppie, the food is cheaper, and there aren't as many crazies around."

Cardinal athletics are an important part of student life at the university. Stanford is a Division I school, fielding teams in baseball; football, softball; men's and women's basketball, rowing, water polo, and soccer: and many other sports. Since 1980 the Cardinal (not Cardinals; the name refers to the school color) have won almost 99 NCAA team championships and 114 national championships. Tiger Woods, Mike Mussina, and John Elway are three former Cardinal athletes who have gone on to stardom.

In 2011 the school reported 12 forcible sexual assaults (down from 21 the previous year), 101 burglaries, 20 stolen motor vehicles, two robberies, two aggravated assaults, and five cases of arson on campus. Directly off campus, students say Palo Alto attracts many homeless people, who, one student notes, "may threaten to kill you."

SUGGESTED CORE

1. English 314, Epic and Empire
2. Philosophy 100, Greek Philosophy
3. English 201, The Bible and Literature *(closest match)*
4. Philosophy 101A, Medieval Religious Philosophy *(closest match)*
5. Political Science 131L, Modern Political Thought
6. English 373a, Shakespeare from Script to Stage
7. History 150A, Colonial and Revolutionary America
8. Modern Thought and Literature 136A, European Thought and Culture in the 19th Century

Stanford offers a world-renowned education and charges a commensurate tuition, which in 2012–13 was $41,250, with $12,721 for room and board. It is the school's policy to provide grant-only aid and not require students to take loans. Of students who did borrow, however, the average debt of a recent grad was $16,458.

STRONG SUITS	WEAK POINTS
• Good liberal arts courses, including a number covering Western history and civilization, are still offered—if you know where to look.	• The core curriculum requiring study of Western civilization was demolished long ago, replaced by vague distribution requirements.
• The Program in Structured Liberal Education offers a traditional liberal arts curriculum.	• Many, many courses and entire departments are heavily politicized.
• Professors are accessible to and interested in students.	• Requirements in some majors, such as political science and English, are anemic with scant foundational material.
• Very good teaching offered in political science, engineering, and the hard sciences.	• Crime on campus is an ongoing concern.
• A dogged, if embattled, conservative subculture exists and publishes a newspaper. The Hoover Institution conducts worthy programs on campus.	

Swarthmore College

Swarthmore, Pennsylvania • www.swarthmore.edu

Quaker Roots and Cash

Founded during the Civil War by Quakers, Swarthmore College has been nonsectarian since 1908. Set on picturesque land 30 minutes from Philadelphia, Swarthmore has a huge endowment and high academic reputation, but it's less than the sum of its parts. The school's curriculum has deteriorated into a Chinese menu of choices, some sound, but many politicized and shallow. Swarthmore has traveled even further down the path of radical chic than most other East Coast liberal arts schools—and that's a long journey, indeed.

Academic Life: A trip to Sam's Club

Swarthmore students do pull their weight. "We have some genius types here, but more than that we have a lot of very hardworking people," says one student. The school is self-conscious about the fact that its classes are rigorous and high grades comparatively more difficult to obtain. "Anywhere else, it would have been an A," reads one popular T-shirt. One student describes the general atmosphere as "the revenge of the nerds." Another says that the best thing about Swarthmore is the quality of the intellectual environment: "You're surrounded by . . . brilliant people."

VITAL STATISTICS

Religious affiliation: *none*
Total enrollment: *1,545*
Total undergraduates: *1,545*
SAT CR/Verbal midrange:
    680–780
SAT Math midrange:
    670–770
ACT midrange: *30–33*
Applicants: *5,575*
Applicants accepted: *14.2%*
Accepted applicants who
    enrolled: *40%*
Tuition (general/out of
    state): *$42,744*
Tuition (in state): *N/A*
Room and board: *$12,670*
Freshman retention rate:
    97%
Graduation rate (4 yrs.): *86%*
Graduation rate (6 yrs.):
    91.6%
Courses with fewer than 20
    students: *72%*
Student-faculty ratio: *8:1*
Courses taught by graduate
    students: *none*
Students living on campus:
    93%
Students in fraternities: *14%*
Students in sororities: *none*
Students receiving need-
    based financial aid: *54%*
Avg. student-loan debt of a
    recent graduating class:
    $20,020
Most popular majors: *eco-
    nomics, biology, political
    science*
Guaranteed housing for 4
    years? *yes*

Sadly, Swarthmore's distribution requirements exert only marginal influence on students' choices. As one says: "The requirements are designed not to encourage some sort of grounding in the basics, but a diversity of perspectives. . . . This is good, but not enough." One professor says that "there is so much choice among introductory courses and departments that . . . one can't count on common background in respect to anything. We don't teach enough survey Western civilization" courses.

Of the modern languages and English departments, one professor says, "It's a classic case of third-rate minds studying second-rate minds." The English department, says one student, seems to cater to the "political interests" of the student body. Swarthmore English majors must take at least nine "units of credit" in the department, including three in literature written before 1830—not necessarily including any Shakespeare, or any specific time periods within that range—and three in literature written after 1830, along with writing a senior essay. Courses in multicultural, feminist, or queer theory are not required, although the department abounds in them, and many of the eligible courses are taught through such ideological filters.

One student calls the history department "infamously partisan" and another conservative student agrees that the department shows a "strong leaning" to leftist viewpoints. A history major must complete nine credits in the department, including at least one course addressing the period prior to 1750 and at least one covering Africa, Asia, Latin America, and the Near East, and a senior research seminar. There is no requirement that the student study the history of the United States or of the Western world.

Swatties majoring in political science must take the equivalent of at least eight courses in the department and complete a senior comprehensive exercise. Courses must include at least one each in political theory, American politics (not necessarily addressing constitutional theory or American political philosophy), and comparative and international politics.

The sociology and anthropology major may not be quite as politically charged as the English major, but it is widely acknowledged to be one of the easiest. Students do not regard mathematics as particularly well taught.

Like most schools, Swarthmore has departments devoted to various races and a single sex, but these are not particularly extensive; the majority of their faculty and courses are drawn from other departments. One student warns that "religious students may feel a bit unwelcome in the philosophy department, which is typically very secular. Indeed, the religion department too has a few bizarre views on Christianity, but is generally open to debate/discussion."

There are some very good departments at Swarthmore. Engineering, economics, political science, biology, and physics all receive high marks from faculty and students, and there are pockets of strength in psychology and philosophy. Some highly recommended professors include the stellar conservative scholar James R. Kurth (emeritus), Benjamin Berger, and Kenneth Sharpe in political science; Barry Schwartz in psychology; Richard Eldridge, Hugh Lacey (emeritus), Hans Oberdiek, and Richard Schuldenfrei (emeritus) in philosophy; John Boccio in physics; Rosaria Munson and William Turpin in Classics; Larry Westphal in economics; Amy Cheng Vollmer in biology; and painter Randall Exon in studio art.

Thanks to Swarthmore's stellar 8 to 1 student-faculty ratio, the easy accessibility of teachers is "one of the best things about the school," says one student. When they enter, students are assigned faculty advisers; when they choose majors, they get faculty advisers within their departments. In general, students report, the best advice on what courses to take (and to avoid) comes from other students.

At Swarthmore the political atmosphere in class can be "oppressive and hostile" for those who don't conform, says one student. Another says that he purposely avoids English

---

CAMPUS POLITICS: YELLOW LIGHT

A left-liberal worldview is taken as a given at Swarthmore. Rebecca Chopp, a scholar of "progressive religious movements," was named the first female president of Swarthmore in 2009. In her commencement address to the Class of 2010, Chopp described worldwide disasters that occurred during the graduates' college years, but reassured her listeners that "the news has not been entirely bleak during your tenure with us—far from it. Two years ago we witnessed—and many actively participated in—the election of our country's first African-American president, who has since appointed the first Latina justice of the Supreme Court. And this past year brought the passage of a health insurance reform bill that was a hundred years in the making."

All forms of sexual activity are broadly accepted as worthy of being celebrated. The college sponsors an annual symposium on "a current topic for the lesbian, gay, bisexual, transgender, and queer community." Students do say that those with a more traditional religious approach to nonmarital sexuality are accepted and not pressured. They must, however, have strong stomachs.

Conservative students seem to concur with other Swatties that "this is a…nurturing environment where people care intensely about each other." Students occasionally express concerns about being penalized academically for their conservative views but generally agree that in most cases they are given a fair hearing. One student says that "the campus is very tolerant, but it is expected that people are willing to get along with those who disagree."

courses because of the "tacit assumption that everyone is a liberal. . . . Professors don't really encourage debate about that." A third student says, "There's definitely some tension from some of the more radical elements on campus, who feel that it's a place for liberals." But, he says, "most Swatties are open to new, different ideas."

A professor confirms the overwhelming impression that the Swarthmore faculty and administration is "self-consciously . . . self-confidently, and self-assertively left-liberal." The general feeling, says this professor, is that "non-leftists have something wrong with them." According to another teacher, "Being professional means being biased." However, in class, "one can occasionally evoke a minority of articulate conservative voices." Students report that they usually feel as if they must censor themselves in the classroom; there is pressure "not to offend," and conservative students "are not terribly keen on admitting it." One student admits that "the real issue is simply one of numbers: There are far more liberal students and professors than conservative ones."

> Swatties discuss others' ideas smoothly and sometimes brilliantly but are not "intellectual," in that they do not tend to develop their own ideas.

The Left is given pride of place at Swarthmore. One student was praised for taking a yearlong college sabbatical to work on a campaign to promote the legalization of gay "marriage," and the college website features articles praising students for campaigning for environmental sustainability and showcasing a library "peace collection" of "bumper stickers, buttons, and flags" which it calls a "renowned resource."

Swarthmore's agenda goes well beyond education—and extends into leftist activism. The college has employed its status as a shareholder to pressure any company in which it holds even a $2,000 investment—squeezing such companies as Lockheed Martin, FedEx, Dover, and Masco corporations to add the category of sexual orientation to their nondiscrimination policies, for instance.

About 40 percent of Swarthmore students study abroad, often in their junior years. Study in virtually any corner of the world is possible through a wide range of programs. The less adventurous can spend time at various high-ranking colleges throughout the United States through exchange programs. Swarthmore also belongs to the Tri-College Consortium with Haverford and Bryn Mawr Colleges. Students may take courses at these schools, participate in their social activities, and use their libraries. A free shuttle bus provides transportation.

Foreign language offerings are broad for a small school, including Arabic, Chinese, French, German, Greek and Latin, Japanese, Russian, and Spanish.

Student Life: Organization kids

Swatties are ambitious achievers who have been "checking the boxes since they were kids," one professor says—young men and women who are "academic" in that they can study and discuss others' ideas smoothly and sometimes brilliantly, but not "intellectual," in that they do not tend to develop their own ideas. However, this professor continues, Swarthmore students "are even better than they were ten, twenty years ago. There really are an amazing number of insightful, proficient, innovative students. I learn from my undergraduates."

The town of Swarthmore is tiny (population under 7,000), safe, and wealthy. For students, the town provides only a few basics. (For one thing, it is "dry.") But with the train stopping just a couple of hundred yards from the dorms, Philadelphia's Center City and points in between are just a few minutes away. But in their free time, most students tend to stay on campus. The college generously funds student parties—although it insists that college money not be spent on alcohol.

Students are required to live on campus only for their first two semesters, but in fact 93 percent stay in college housing throughout their years at Swarthmore. Dorms range in size from eight to 218 occupants. Juniors and seniors generally have singles. Most students subscribe to the college meal plan. In 2000 the college changed its policy to allow coed rooming for upperclassmen. Two dorms remain all female and one dorm has all-male and all-female wings; beyond that, none of the housing is single sex. In addition, students are petitioning to increase the numbers of "gender-neutral" bathrooms on campus.

SUGGESTED CORE
1. No suitable course
2. Philosophy 102, Ancient Philosophy
3. Religion 003/004, The Bible: In the Beginning . . . / New Testament and Early Christianity
4. Religion 014, Christian Life and Thought in the Middle Ages
5. Political Science 012 or 101, Introduction to Modern Political Theory/Modern Political Theory
6. English Literature 020 or 101, Shakespeare
7. History 005A, The United States to 1877
8. History 003A, Modern Europe, 1789 to 1918: The Age of Revolution and Counterrevolution

There are two fraternities that rent lodges on campus and provide a social outlet for the relatively few Swattie men (about 13 percent) who join. However, the frats do not offer residential or dining facilities and are not a major force in campus life. There are currently no sororities, but a group of female students are planning to reinstate Greek life after a 79-year ban.

The political climate at Swarthmore is conventionally leftist. For instance, the school newspaper refers to the college's Republicans as being "in the closet," which students in past years turned into a joke by referring to themselves as "closeted conservatives" and holding an "It's Ok to Come Out" as a College Republican campaign. When that group proposed a Veterans' Day memorial service, leftists protested. "People here are soldier-hating, fascist liberals," says one embittered student. Swarthmore's alternative, conservative student newspaper, *Common Sense*, suspended publication some years ago for lack of editorial staff.

Student groups abound, ranging from Queer Peer Counselors, Feminist Majority, War News Radio, Swat STAND (addressing violence in Sudan), and Voices for Choice, to a knitting club known as the Knit-Wits, a number of a cappella groups, a folk dancing club, Apple Pie (a philosophy discussion club), a drama club, and several comedy troupes. A Swarthmore College Republicans website has not been updated since 2000. Swarthmore Students Supporting

Life is said to be fervent during those semesters when it has any members. (The Protestant campus chaplain was, however, unable even to recall the name of the group in a recent interview.) Students also produce a number of publications, including *Ourstory*, which, according to its editors, is "a publication centered on the idea of diversity" and seeks to "engage and connect our campus" on issues like "race, class, gender, sexuality, and politics."

A number of religious groups meet on campus, including both a more secular (Ruach) and a more conservative religious (Chabad) Jewish group meeting under the umbrella of Hillel, and two Protestant groups, a "progressive" one and a chapter of InterVarsity Christian Fellowship, which hosts regular Bible studies, prayer meetings, and other activities. Catholic Mass is offered on campus on Sundays and midweek under the auspices of the Catholic Newman Community, which does not seem to be particularly active. Several people reported that there has been an upsurge of interest in religion and that the administration has become "more open to spirituality on campus."

The Swarthmore Garnet Tide teams, whose mascot is Phineas the Phoenix, include 22 intercollegiate varsity sports in NCAA Division III. Intramural and club sports are said to be fairly popular, especially Ultimate Frisbee. One professor speculates that the demise of football some years back was driven by the school's affirmative-action policies, which ate up so many admissions slots. Other Swatties suggest that losing the team was a way of ridding the school of an undesirable symbol of traditional masculinity. Many Swarthmore types "definitely do not like the traditional jock," says one student.

Crime at Swarthmore and in the adjacent neighborhoods is not quite as low as one might guess. The school reported six forcible rapes, eight burglaries, one car theft, and one aggravated assault in 2011. Still, in general, students feel quite comfortable walking the campus and adjoining neighborhoods at night.

Swarthmore isn't cheap, but aid is generous. In 2012–13, tuition was set at $42,744 and room and board $12,670. About 54 percent of undergraduates received need-based scholarships, and starting in 2008–2009 grants replaced all student loans, which were previously offered in aid packages. Still, the average debt burden of a student borrower was reported as $20,020.

STRONG SUITS	WEAK POINTS
• Hardworking students. • Good programs in engineering, economics, political science, biology, and physics. • Accessible, highly qualified faculty, who teach all classes. • A mostly supportive, even "nurturing" campus environment.	• Several humanities departments have weak requirements and politicized courses. • Not enough classes covering Western civ. • Shaky curricular requirements. • Classroom discussion heavily skewed by a leftist faculty and student body. • A minimal, and minimally active, presence of conservative or religious students.

The King's College

New York, New York • www.tkc.edu

God, Money, and Power

Founded in 1999, taking the name of a former Christian college in the Hudson Valley, The King's College was started by the Campus Crusade for Christ in Manhattan, with the lofty mission of "preparing exceptional students for principled leadership." It combines fervent Evangelical faith with a serious respect for the life of the mind and the duties of citizenship in a democratic society. The school's ambition to make an impact was made clear when, in August 2010, the college appointed as president the neoconservative writer and filmmaker Dinesh D'Souza. He resigned in October 2012 amid a personal scandal that the school handled in a forthright and principled way. Andrew Mills is serving as interim president as a professional committee searches for a new leader for the school.

Academic Life: Art Deco Oxbridge

The King's College began in the basement of the Empire State Building but has recently moved to the Wall Street area, and if this suggests that the founders intend to engage the culture—well, they do. The tiny school (only 465 students so far, and 21 permanent faculty) was founded to serve the following mission: "Through its commitment to the truths

781

VITAL STATISTICS

Religious affiliation: *nonde-nominational (Christian)*
Total enrollment: *465*
Total undergraduates: *465*
SAT CR/Verbal midrange: *580–670*
SAT Math midrange: *520–610*
ACT midrange: *24–28*
Applicants: *3,388*
Applicants accepted: *67%*
Accepted applicants who enrolled: *21%*
Tuition (general/out of state): *$29,240*
Tuition (in state): *N/A*
Room and board: *$11,600*
Freshman retention rate: *71%*
Graduation rate (4 yrs.): *46%*
Graduation rate (6 yrs.): *51%*
Courses with fewer than 20 students: *48%*
Student-faculty ratio: *15:1*
Courses taught by graduate students: *not provided*
Students living on campus: *76%*
Students in fraternities: *none*
Students in sororities: *none*
Students receiving need-based financial aid: *81%*
Avg. student-loan debt of a recent graduating class: *$20,957*
Most popular majors: *liberal arts, general studies/humanities, business*
Guaranteed housing for 4 years? *yes*

of Christianity and a biblical worldview, The King's College seeks to prepare students for careers in which they will help to shape and eventually to lead strategic public and private institutions, and by supporting faculty members as they directly engage culture through writing and speaking publicly on critical issues."

In practice, this means taking a body of largely Evangelical Christian students and introducing them to a level of academic engagement that many have never before encountered.

One key element in the King's College education is its solid core curriculum. A professor at TKC said of these courses:

> Our introductory classes in Western civilization and American history and politics are deeply respectful of the heritage they present. Among the distinctive features of Western civilization we emphasize are the dignity of the individual, the capacity of Western civilization to reform itself (it alone abolished slavery), and its quest for scientific knowledge. We teach the American Founding as one of the signal events in Western history and pay particular attention to the rule of law, the separation of powers, freedom of religion and speech, and the protection of property rights.

Beyond its wide-ranging core, The King's College limits its mission, offering just two degrees in four programs: a bachelor of science in business management and a bachelor of arts in a program called Politics, Philosophy, and Economics (PPE)—the latter modeled on famous programs at several Oxford colleges that trained numerous generations of British cabinet ministers. The PPE degree offers concentrations in literature, theology, media, and education. Said one student of the PPE major: "Very few schools offer this unique degree, but I believe it to be valuable because it speaks to the three most influential areas of human interaction with God, money, and power." Another said that "the strongest aspect of this major is the philosophy portion, and in particular political philosophy. You come away from this course being able to think very critically about issues and also (hopefully) being able to write well. The economics portion is somewhat weak in my opinion, but I know that the school is working to develop this end of the major."

According to a faculty member, "The emphasis in economics had been very free market. It could have been described as 'all Hayek all the time,' but that's changing." In one economics class, a professor integrates his free-market approach with the school's biblical inspiration—for instance, by using the parable of the Prodigal Son to illustrate the U.S. trade deficit and profligate federal spending. The political science program bears a heavily philosophical stamp, in part because the school's former chancellor, J. Stanley Oakes, and several of its faculty were trained by followers of Harry Jaffa, the constitutional theorist most influential among neoconservatives.

Students seem to appreciate being held to a high standard. According to one, "In a recent student satisfaction survey conducted at King's, the aspect of the school most valued by students is academic rigor. King's students work hard for their grades, and most are, of necessity, 'awakened' intellectually." At The King's College, faculty foster such awakenings through small classes with an emphasis on the Great Books and great ideas, trips to the innumerable artistic and cultural treasures of one of the world's great cities, and

CAMPUS POLITICS: GREEN LIGHT

The political atmosphere at King's College "is by no means monolithic," one teacher insists. As one student says, "People often joke that King's is a cookie-cutter school of right-wing Republicans from Middle America. The student body is actually quite diverse— King's has many international students and students from all over the country. Divergent opinions are well tolerated." Another agreed, saying, "Debate is quite vigorous on campus, especially on issues such as . . . gay rights. A big campus-wide debate concerns to what degree religious morality should enter the American political arena. As TKC is a Christian college, religious students are quite welcome, and on the flip side, more-liberal, less-religious students are also very welcome. Non-Christians have come to King's and loved it. They said they didn't feel oppressed by religion in the classroom." A self-described "progressive" student told *New York* magazine in 2011: "The students and most of the professors are totally smart and open to argument. I would hate to see King's written off as a right-wing breeding ground, but there's definitely potential for that."

work in local soup kitchens as part of theology class. Since the school's emphasis is on that "mere Christianity" shared by most broadly orthodox believers, it attracts as students and faculty both Catholics and Protestants—although the latter, unsurprisingly, predominate. Renowned Catholic philosopher Peter Kreeft has for several years come down each week from Boston College to teach philosophy classes, while other distinguished professors come in from points much farther south and west. However, the school is building its permanent faculty and will probably diminish its reliance on visiting professors.

By all accounts, members of the permanent faculty work closely with students outside the classroom—and even visiting professors make sure to schedule extensive office hours. "King's professors are for the most part extremely accessible," a student says. Furthermore, "many professors are involved as faculty advisers in the House system. Through this channel and others, professors get very involved in students' lives. From frequent meals or coffees in between classes, to sharing home-cooked meals, to just walking about the city discussing the pressing issues that our country and world face, the professors go out of their way to extend the education experience beyond the classroom," reports the student.

Favorite teachers include Kreeft in philosophy; David Tubbs in politics; Henry Bleattler in media; and Robert Jackson in English. One undergrad singled out Steve Salyers in communications, praising him for the care he shows students: "He spends almost all his time on campus and frequently has students to his home for dinner or parties. He really extends the process of learning beyond the classroom." Theology teacher Robert Carle is said to be "incredibly knowledgeable, [with an] incredible grasp of material he teaches—whether it's civil rights, church history, writing, or comparative religions."

"**O**ur introductory classes in Western civilization are deeply respectful of the heritage they present," a professor says. "We teach the American Founding as one of the signal events in Western history."

The school's library is small and full of conservative and religious classics, and the texts used in classes. Some of the acknowledged weak points at TKC are areas the school has not found time to address in all the flurry of starting up a college and crafting a focused program to serve its stated mission. The school teaches no hard sciences and no foreign languages except Latin. The college hopes to roll out a number of study-abroad options in the near future; presently, International Ventures allows students and faculty to study for up to three weeks in venues including Albania, Bulgaria, the Caribbean, China, Central Asia, France, Kenya, Israel, Turkey, and Uganda.

Student Life: Jonah in Nineveh

As one might expect of a Christian school located in what many believers might consider the heart of Mammon, The King's College takes a more laissez-faire approach toward student life than many religious colleges. The school is not "value-neutral," of course, and it maintains a reasonable set of rules for a Christian college. But rather than build up an elaborate structure for discipline, TKC has emulated American military academies and older religious schools in crafting an honor code, which students adopt and enforce themselves. "We see that as more suited to young adults living in a major city," said an administrator. "We want the students to take ownership of these values and internalize them—not look at a list of imposed, detailed rules which they're immediately tempted to try to circumvent. That's just (fallen) human nature," he observes. One student reports, "The school's location in New York City is a huge boon. King's students are not in a 'Christian bubble' but in an extremely worldly city that is 'the center of the universe.' The school's location is strategic for cultivating leadership in the secular national institutions of government, business, media, education, et cetera."

SUGGESTED CORE

The Common Core, which consists of 20 required courses, suffices.

There are no dorms per se but rather blocks of apartments in four buildings. All male students live in the Ludlow Residence, and female students reside in Herald Towers or The Vogue. The newest housing facility, Clark Street Residence, is in the heart of Brooklyn Heights. The residences are divided into 10 "Houses" with two faculty advisers and a five-member core leadership team consisting of a president, a helmsman (responsible for new House members), a chamberlain (resident assistant), a scholar (responsible for cultivating intellectual life), and a vicar (responsible for cultivating spiritual life). According to the college, "a House consists of 25 to 30 students who live, study, and work together. Each House is named after a great historic leader who left his/her mark on our world . . . and carries with it the values and traditions particular to that House." The student Houses compete in debates, contests, sports, and projects for missionary outreach.

Said a student, "It's an interesting environment for college life, because we share those buildings with hundreds of other tenants. Our rooms are spread throughout the buildings, so we're not really clumped into one big party hall. Students spend a lot of time studying with each other in the various apartments. Because they all have kitchens, group meals are also a frequent part of 'dorm life.' Every apartment has four students (typically), and each apartment has its own bathroom." Said another student, "The residence director lives with his family in the girls' buildings. All visitors are announced by the buildings (they check in at the desks and are buzzed up). All overnight guests must be reported to a chamberlain. Guys cannot be in girls' rooms and vice versa past 1:00 a.m." Of these arrangements, a student says, "housing rules are actually very limited. King's wants to treat its students as adults and let them make their own decisions. You can smoke or drink, if you are of age, but not in the apartments themselves—out of respect for your roommates (and New York laws). And there are 'privacy hours.' This is not so much a curfew but a way to make sure two or three roommates don't dominate the apartment over the others."

Infractions of rules are handled by student committees, in accord with the school's honor code. Said one student: "Dorms are dry, and most students don't drink. But if students do come back to the dorm really drunk, they're likely at most just to be questioned."

Current clubs and organizations at King's include Financial Services Club, TKC Theatre, The King's Debate Society, Mock Trial, The King's College Republicans, King's Dancers, Tent (Monday evening worship services), running, skiing, and outdoor clubs, and the school's paper, the *Empire State Tribune* (named for the school's first campus).

King's became a member of the National Christian College Athletic Association (NCCAA) in 2012 with men's baseball, basketball, cross-country and soccer, and women's basketball, volleyball, and soccer. Intramural sports offered are basketball, flag football, and Ultimate Frisbee. Recreation sports for students with common interests include cycling, swimming, snowboarding, and skiing.

The King's College's crime statistics do not yet appear in the Department of Education database.

As private colleges go, TKC's costs are midrange, with 2012–13 tuition at $29,240 and housing at $11,600. No board plan is offered; students have kitchens, and there are literally hundreds of eateries within walking distance. The school works hard to help students financially; 81 percent of full-time undergraduates received need-based financial aid, but the average debt of recent graduates was still $20,957.

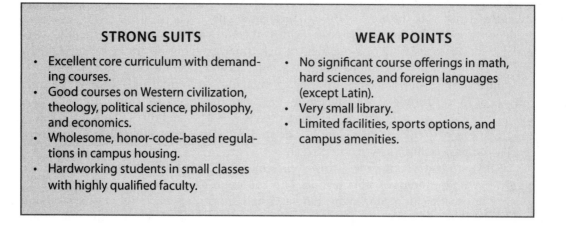

STRONG SUITS	WEAK POINTS
• Excellent core curriculum with demanding courses. • Good courses on Western civilization, theology, political science, philosophy, and economics. • Wholesome, honor-code-based regulations in campus housing. • Hardworking students in small classes with highly qualified faculty.	• No significant course offerings in math, hard sciences, and foreign languages (except Latin). • Very small library. • Limited facilities, sports options, and campus amenities.

Thomas Aquinas College

Santa Paula, California • www.thomasaquinas.edu

Baptizing Socrates

In 1971, in response to the shock-secularization of Catholic colleges in America, a small group of scholars in California envisaged an education built on the Great Books of the Western world, viewed through the lens of the greatest thinker in Catholic history, St. Thomas Aquinas. They named the college for him and built a remarkably successful school.

Academic Life: No textbooks, lectures, or majors

At TAC, there are no majors, minors, electives, or concentrations. All students take the same four-year program and earn the same bachelor's degree in liberal arts. The course of study features theology, philosophy, natural science, and mathematics. Students take Latin during their freshman and sophomore years, as well as a music class during their junior year. "Seminar," an evening class for discussing literary, philosophical, historical, and political works, starts with Homer and Plato in the freshman year and concludes with works such as the Lincoln-Douglas debates and, in senior year, the writings of Henrik Ibsen and Flannery O'Connor. In each of their four years students have regular recourse to the works of the school's namesake, St. Thomas Aquinas.

VITAL STATISTICS

Religious affiliation: *Roman Catholic*
Total enrollment: *370*
Total undergraduates: *370*
SAT CR/Verbal midrange: *620–700*
SAT Math midrange: *560–660*
ACT midrange: *25–29*
Applicants: *165*
Applicants accepted: *81%*
Accepted applicants who enrolled: *63%*
Tuition (general/out of state): *$24,500*
Tuition (in state): *N/A*
Room and board: *$7,950*
Freshman retention rate: *85%*
Graduation rate (4 yrs.): *72%*
Graduation rate (6 yrs.): *76%*
Courses with fewer than 20 students: *100%*
Student-faculty ratio: *12:1*
Courses taught by graduate students: *not provided*
Students living on campus: *99%*
Students in fraternities: *N/A*
Students in sororities: *N/A*
Students receiving need-based financial aid: *81%*
Avg. student-loan debt of a recent graduating class: *$15,685*
Guaranteed housing for 4 years? *yes*

Textbooks are used rarely; instead, students are in "conversation" with Great Books authors. Permanent faculty members with one or even two PhDs take the title "tutor." Each class session is dedicated to understanding and evaluating a great text through the give-and-take of formal but friendly conversation. Some students admit that they don't always end up with a conclusion or final answer after a seminar class but add that the contents of the texts stay with them. "Seminar classes allow students to meditate on the texts and learn how to think rather than what to think," one tutor explains. "They teach students to concentrate and puzzle through the real value of the text on their own, making these perennial ideas and questions their own."

One alumnus says, "The intense study of mathematics truly stretched my mind. I thought in ways I never had before—in ways I hadn't known I could think—and it was amazing how much I felt I gained in sheer mental ability from the years of studying geometrical proofs." Students are expected to master the general theological and philosophical principles that govern various disciplines, from literary interpretation to chemistry to biblical studies.

Students read a wide range of authors—from the likes of Newton and Einstein, to Karl Marx, St. John Damascene, Tocqueville, Cervantes, and Archimedes—who are central to understanding diverse areas of knowledge.

The courses are highly interdisciplinary. During a discussion of Newton's *Principia*, for example, students may cite examples or raise issues from Shakespeare, Aristotle, or Dante. This is possible not only because all students are taking the same courses according to the same schedule but also because all tutors are expected to be able to teach all courses. A new faculty member might teach Euclid, Latin, and freshman Seminar, and the next year teach philosophy, laboratory science, and sophomore Seminar.

Most important, students are initiated into the encyclopedic breadth of Aristotelian philosophy and Thomistic theology. Students take four years of philosophy, and although they study the major dialogues of Plato, the emphasis is on Aristotle's works. Graduates of the college will have completed intensive study on all of Aristotle's most important philosophical works: the *Organon, Poetics, Rhetoric, Physics, Nicomachean Ethics, Politics,* and *Metaphys-*

ics. The theology course is more varied, with freshman year dedicated solely to reading the whole biblical canon; sophomore year to saints Augustine, Athanasius, John Damascene, and Anselm; and junior and senior years to Aquinas's *Summa Theologiae.* Still, the emphasis is on the essential principles of Thomas's theology, as well as his interpretation of Aristotle.

As one student puts it: "Seminar encourages you to think. You're not just expected to sit there and take notes. In it, we set our own pace—which is often faster than in a lecture course."

Students report excellent relationships with their tutors, a significant number of whom are returning students. Perennial favorites include John F. Nieto and Paul J. O'Reilly. "The tutors are very helpful," says one student, "not only with questions or problems arising from class but also concerning graduate schools, career choices, your spiritual life, sports, and even dating."

Some disciplines, such as statistics and sociology, are not covered at all. Other fields are only treated in a cursory fashion; students read Adam Smith and Karl Marx, but they do not cover the basic principles of modern economics. Some sciences are only partially covered. Students read and discuss Gregor Mendel but do not read about modern genetics. Students read Einstein on relativity but no authors on quantum mechanics. In the humanities, history is treated in a hit-or-miss fashion. Students read some of the greatest historians of the classical world, such as Thucydides and Gibbon; influential philosophers of history, such as Vico and Hegel; and some foundational American political documents. There is comparatively little treatment of literature. "We just don't have time," says one student simply.

Some cite the relative infrequency of writing assignments as a weakness of the program, particularly in considering it as a preparation for graduate school. "I wrote less as a

CAMPUS POLITICS: GREEN LIGHT

The overall atmosphere at TAC is reminiscent of a rural small town. Innocence and order are maintained by a fairly strict set of rules—perhaps not as rigorous as those of some evangelical schools but certainly stricter than at most Catholic colleges. Drinking on campus is forbidden under pain of expulsion, even for those who are of age. The latter, however, may store liquor with prefects and may drink off campus. They are also served wine and beer at some school functions. The use of drugs is also grounds for expulsion. Every few years TAC expels a few students for such offenses. Still, students are generally supportive of off-campus drinking, so long as moderation is observed.

The atmosphere at TAC is not politically charged. Some students attend conferences sponsored by groups such as the National Young Republicans, Young America's Foundation, and the Intercollegiate Studies Institute (the publisher of this guide). The Tocqueville Society is a student-run club that exists primarily to consider political issues from a philosophic point of view. It coordinates lectures and hosts forums for students. In recent years a number of students have attended the "Walk for Life," a large annual pro-life march in San Francisco. A college donor usually charters a bus or students drive their own cars for the six-hour drive to the event. TACers for Life also arranges weekly vigils outside an abortion clinic.

student at Thomas Aquinas College than I did as a high school student," says an alumnus. Freshmen craft five short papers, one each in math, language, theology, philosophy, and the literature seminar. Sophomores write four longer papers, and juniors write two 1,500-word essays in theology and philosophy. Seniors do write a thesis (about 60 pages) on a question raised by the curriculum, working with an adviser over the course of the senior year and finally defending it in an oral examination conducted by three tutors.

The use of secondary sources in papers, excepting the thesis, is discouraged. "More of the thoughts in my college papers are originally my own than is typical for college writing assignments, I think," a student says.

> "The tutors are very helpful," says one student, "not only with questions or problems arising from class but also concerning graduate schools, career choices, your spiritual life, sports, even dating."

Students report that faculty members are extremely accessible; most tutors live close to campus, and all dine in the same refectory with students. It is not uncommon for tutors to continue a class discussion over meat loaf or tacos with a group of students. Beyond office hours, students visit tutors in their homes for informal dinner-seminar symposia, and for holidays.

To strengthen teacher-student relationships, the college holds "Don Rags," allowing each student to meet with his tutors to discuss the student's performance. The tutors review the student in question and allow him or her to listen in, respond, and ask questions. "Don Rags principally allow teachers to improve class conversations," says one tutor. "They help a tutor to adjust or give pointers on a student's class participation." Students report that despite some nervousness, they enjoy these rags and benefit from them.

TAC has no study-abroad program and teaches no modern languages—sola Latina. Every graduate must complete the full four-year program, so the college accepts no transfer credits.

Student Life: A very small town

Santa Paula is a small, rural, oil-and-citrus town in Santa Clara valley. The campus accommodates up to 370 students (TAC's maximum enrollment) in California Mission–style buildings, with red tiled roofs and white walls. Its central building is the new chapel, the fruit of 10 years' planning and building.

Students say that their time at Thomas Aquinas College is spent in a "close-knit community." According to one graduate, "You don't spend every meal drawing math diagrams on napkins, or every evening in the dorm talking about proofs for God's existence. But the seminar classes, the common curriculum, and the small community lead to significant personal discourse. Because of this, there are many opportunities for friendships with people who are, at least superficially, very different from you or from the kind of people you usually hang out with."

A student says, "It is nearly impossible to come here without meeting and becoming very good friends with amazing, interesting, and very charitable people. It is simply a life that is the envy of any other place I can imagine." This kind of community, of course, is not for everyone. Says one student: "Everybody knows everything about everybody. There's a real small-town mentality."

There are six single-sex dormitories on campus. Ninety-nine percent of students live on campus. Each dorm room houses two students. Sophomores through seniors are encouraged to select their own roommates. The center of each dorm is a large, spacious lounge, equipped with a billiards table and other amenities.

Peace and order are maintained by student prefects, whom one student characterizes as "mostly people I could respect—not too uptight or rigid, just honest people with good judgment." Each male dormitory traditionally elects a "dorm tyrant" who is a ceremonial and social figurehead, like a rowdy constitutional monarch. The dorms play pranks on each other, and every school year opens with "dorm wars," with water balloons, wrestling, and competitive feats of strength.

Although students have computers and cell phones, dorms do not have Internet access or television sets. Full Internet access is available in the library and student mailroom. Smoking is also forbidden inside the dorms, so many students smoke and talk on balconies, porches, or just outdoors. These last areas are also sites for parties. Students also socialize in "the commons" (the large dining area) and at the campus coffee shop.

Dorm visits by members of the opposite sex are grave violations. A nightly curfew is in effect at 11:00 p.m. on weeknights and 1:00 a.m. on weekends—except on first Fridays for 24-hour Eucharistic adoration and during final exam week. Students who break curfew without permission will receive disciplinary sanctions, such as community service or suspension of privileges.

The school insists on a professional dress code and modesty regulations. Inside classrooms, the chapel, and "the commons" during school hours, men must wear slacks and collared shirts, and women must wear skirts or dresses that reach the knee. Public displays of affection, such as holding hands or romantic embraces, are also forbidden.

There are ample sporting opportunities at Thomas Aquinas College. TAC does not participate in intercollegiate sports, but the school does have two part-time athletic coordinators (one for men and one for women) and various intramural teams. Students also play in local county leagues. Sports on campus include flag football, soccer, and basketball (which are the most organized), as well as volleyball, hockey, and tennis.

Students also develop their artistic sides. The sporadically published student journal *Demiurgus* features essays, caricatures, poetry, and humor by students and tutors, while the *Aquinas Review* is a vehicle for more formal writing. The Schola is an all-male choir that sings Gregorian chant; the St. Genesius Players is an on-campus Shakespearean troupe. Students also practice their creativity with Trivial and Quadrivial Pursuit, a "stump the student" contest. Informal groups meet over meals for the study of Ancient Greek, Hebrew, Latin, French, and German. Musically inclined students are encouraged to enter the college choir or join the cast of the musicals produced each year. In recent years many students have taken an interest in filmmaking, and they have produced amateur films that are shown in on-campus film festivals.

Thomas Aquinas College is a deeply devotional school. In this college of 370 students, there are three full-time chaplains and three Masses per day, with confessions before and after. One of the daily Masses and one of the three Sunday Masses are in Latin, and the Sunday Mass is accompanied by Gregorian chant, polyphony, or classical music. Just about all Catholics on campus (some 90 to 95 percent of the student body) attend one of these three Masses—and many take part in other devotions.

Priests dine in "the commons" with students and are very accessible. Some students go on to develop their own religious vocations. A large number of students and alumni have gone on to priestly, religious, or monastic life. TAC grads can be found in monasteries from Switzerland to Oklahoma.

Although Thomas Aquinas is a Catholic college, several non-Catholics also attend, as they are attracted to the rigorous liberal arts program and the class format. There are no mandatory chapel requirements, however, and students are perfectly free to follow their own religious or philosophical convictions.

The school is extremely safe; the only crime reported on campus between 2009 and 2011 was one burglary. The campus has its own security.

In terms of cost, Thomas Aquinas stands in the middle rank of private colleges. Tuition in 2013–14 is $24,500, with room and board coming in at $7,950. The college receives no federal subsidies, funds, or contracts. A majority of students receive aid by working campus jobs in the school's work-study program. Some 81 percent of students received need-based financial aid, and the average student-loan debt of a recent graduating class was $15,685.

STRONG SUITS	WEAK POINTS
• Stellar core curriculum covers Western civilization and Catholic thought in great detail.	• Not enough instruction in or practice of writing/rhetoric.
• Exclusive engagement with the Great Books as primary texts.	• Little attention to literature or history; ideas hover in a timeless Platonic "heaven."
• Intense classroom discussion, using purely Socratic method, teaches students to read closely and argue tightly.	• Some human sciences are scanted—such as statistics, sociology, economics—and hard sciences offer no lab time.
• High-minded, intellectually ambitious student body.	• The range of acceptable opinion is narrow; those who aren't conservative Catholics (or considering conversion) might feel quite out of place and under pressure.
• Wholesome dorm and campus environments.	

Tufts University

Medford, Massachusetts • www.tufts.edu

Acting Globally

Over the past 150 years, Tufts has grown from a small Universalist college into a flourishing research university. Today the science and engineering departments, along with numerous preprofessional programs, are Tufts's particular strengths. Tufts has a global focus, laying heavy emphasis on foreign language and study-abroad programs, with many on-campus cultural events. Alas, Tufts's globalism goes beyond cosmopolitanism into the anti-Western ideology of multiculturalism, while affirmative action directs hiring and admissions decisions. But somewhere in the midst of the political correctness hides an opportunity for the discerning to find a genuine liberal arts education. Students will just have to seek it out.

Academic Life: Tuft enough

Tufts has no core curriculum but instead maintains a set of foundational and distribution requirements. A student could fulfill a number of these requirements with arcane choices such as "America/National Pastime" (a course about baseball) and "Sex and Gender in Society" for social sciences. "Undoubtedly, students can get away with it," one senior says. "With primary majors in women's studies, American studies, peace and justice studies, and the like, the arts and sciences curriculum can be easily manipulated so that a student might never take anything more difficult than introductory math and 'Women in Native American Culture.'" Happily, as another insider reports, "This is a good school with lots of smart students" who know better than to cheat themselves out of a good education.

Students can still study the foundations of Western civilization at Tufts in classes like "Western Political Thought" I and II, which cover the Great Books, and "Plato's Socrates," which teaches the majority of the Platonic dialogues. Any Tufts undergrad should seek these courses out and look into our suggested core curriculum (see sidebar), to complete his education.

Students must meet further requirements within their majors, and certain majors are quite demanding. The international relations major comes with an eight-semester language requirement and 12 other courses, including an introduction to international relations, "Principles of Economics," a course in international economics, a course focusing on "the historical dimension," and another on "theories of society and culture." Majors also take seven additional courses in a specific thematic cluster, such as "Regional and Comparative Analysis" or "Global Health, Nutrition, and the Environment."

Unfortunately, Tufts offers little guidance to its English majors. They must take one survey course; two pre-1860 and two post-1860 nonsurvey courses in British, American, or Anglophone literature; and five electives. Students could easily skip Shakespeare and Milton in favor of "Un-American Activities," "Postmodernism and Film," "The Politics of Reading," and "Nonwestern Women Writers."

History majors must complete a foundation seminar; a pre- or early-modern class; one course each in U.S., European, and non-Western history; and a "concentration core" of four related courses. Students may determine their own concentrations along thematic or geographic lines.

Political science majors must take two "foundational" courses in American politics, comparative politics, political theory, or international relations, as well as another class in each of those fields. Finally, a "methodology" class like "Political Behavior of Young People" is required, as is one upper-level seminar.

Despite the looseness of its curriculum, Tufts puts a high priority on teaching. Professors, not teaching assistants, teach nearly all classes. However, the mandatory freshman writing courses are taught by graduate students from various departments. Graduate students also lead most of the weekly discussion groups in large lecture courses.

With most classes small, students do get the opportunity to form relationships with professors, whom students consider "accessible." Professors in the sciences often use student assistants on research projects.

Students have a number of options when they need course advice. Freshmen can enroll in small-group seminars in which their professors will serve as their advisers. One student says, "This program was worthwhile because I met people in an academic setting, so I was guaranteed to get to know them better through the class." Another student says, "It was fun but the advising wasn't helpful at all." Freshmen who don't use these seminars are appointed a faculty adviser and two upperclassmen as peer advisers, any of which they are free to change.

One student reports that some freshman English classes are politicized wastes of time, for instance, "Films about Love, Sex, and Society," a seminar which in the past has assigned students to watch a porn movie. The more politicized departments are the interdisciplinary programs, such as Latin American studies, Africa in the New World, and urban studies. The courses that fulfill the world civilizations requirement are also notoriously ideological. Some students also complain of a partisan slant in political science classes.

At Tufts, professors' political views are often obvious; many post political cartoons and slogans on their office doors, and their opinions often permeate classroom discussion. One philosophy and political science major says, "They do more than seep into the discussion—they *are* the discussion." This is not universally true, however. One student praises a philosophy professor who "takes a vote on what students think on a certain issue in class. One time,

CAMPUS POLITICS: YELLOW LIGHT

Tufts is a challenging place for conservative students. A student sums up the political atmosphere at Tufts by saying, "We're a northeastern liberal campus. That's no secret." Another says, "I can see how it would be difficult to be conservative here, because most people are liberal. If you're actively conservative, people will actively dislike you and try to engage you in an antagonistic dialogue." Another student says, "For the average student who just wants to have his own opinion without being assailed for it—I feel bad for that kid."

In 2006 and 2007, the Tufts conservative newspaper the *Primary Source* published satirical pieces aimed at race-based affirmative action and Islamist activism on campus. The school took disciplinary action against the newspaper, finding it guilty of "harassment," and the *Primary Source* has since ceased publication. An array of free-speech organizations spoke up for the students, to no avail. In 2010 the Foundation for Individual Rights in Education wrote Tufts's president, explaining why it had added the school to its "red alert" list of colleges that suppress free speech: "We find it especially disappointing that Tufts has continued to stand by its unjust actions and willingly imperil the free expression of its students." There is currently no conservative paper at Tufts.

a student asked him what his thoughts were on the issue. He says, 'Wait to ask me until after the semester.'"

The 750-student College of Engineering is held in high esteem on campus. A student says of engineering majors, "I'm living with two engineers and they are always working; they have to work so hard, but when they come out they have so many job opportunities—they're set, they are ready for anything."

Students say the best departments at Tufts are international relations, history, biology, child development, English, political science, economics, and philosophy. Outstanding professors at Tufts include Robert Devigne and Vickie Sullivan in political science; Nan Levinson and Christina Sharpe in English; Joseph Walser in comparative religion; David Denby in philosophy; and Eric Todd Quinto in mathematics. In child development, students praise Donald Wertlieb and Calvin (Chip) Gidney, who is known as being "incredibly well spoken and knowledgeable." One student praised Gregory Carleton's Russian literature courses as "fascinating. He always sat down with his students to go over their writing."

> "The curriculum can be easily manipulated so that a student might never take anything more difficult than introductory math and 'Women in Native American Culture,'" says one undergrad.

Tufts strongly encourages students to study abroad, and more than 40 percent of all undergraduates do. Options are many, including London, Madrid, Paris, sites in Japan, Chile, China, Ghana, or a semester spent on a ship at sea. Tufts also offers a summer study-abroad option in Talloires, France, that is highly praised by students who have participated. One student calls this program in the French Alps "a jewel."

Tufts offers courses in Arabic, Chinese, French, German, Greek and Latin, Hebrew, Italian, Japanese, and Spanish.

Student Life: The elephant in the ashtray

Seventy percent of Tufts students live in university residence halls, and Tufts offers an abundance of options. Special-interest houses allow students to base their residential life on a particular theme, including Africana, Asian American, Jewish, and Muslim culture, arts, foreign languages, and the "gay-friendly" Rainbow House.

Freshmen can choose to live in one of four all-freshman dorms, two of which feature live-in faculty members or "scholars-in-residence," while all four feature upperclassman tutors in addition to the regular resident assistants. Tufts offers several single-sex options for women, but fraternities are the only single-sex option for men. Most dorms have young men and women living as next-door neighbors, although some separate the sexes by floor. A few halls have coed bathrooms, but they are single-use with lockable doors. Dormitories usually offer substance-free and "healthy living" floors, though alcohol can certainly be found in plenty at other dorms and at the fraternities. Dorms range in age from brand new to vintage 1957. Haskell and Wren Halls were built in the 1970s as "riot-proof" dorms. Says one resident, "It's terrible for meeting people."

Weekend social life for Tufts students revolves around Boston and its many colleges rather than around the campus. Tufts's Greek system is under great pressure from the administration, but more than 10 percent of Tufts students still pledge. Overall, the Tufts campus has become much less raucous, mostly due to more stringent drug and alcohol rules. According to one student, "They used to knock on your door if they smelled pot and ask you to stop. Now they call the police." Once allowed to use their discretion in reporting student infractions, RAs are now required to report everything.

Town-gown relations are reportedly very strained. Tufts students who live off campus have complained that residents resent the college kids who live in apartments in their communities. One student says, "A lot of neighbors are really obnoxious to the students. There was a noise complaint because students were merely talking in their apartment."

> **SUGGESTED CORE**
>
> 1. Classics 31/32/140, Classics of Greece/Classics of Rome/Classical Epic
> 2. Philosophy 151, Ancient Philosophy
> 3. Religion 21/22, Introduction to the Hebrew Bible/New Testament
> 4. Religion 35, Introduction to Christianity (*closest match*)
> 5. Political Science 42, Western Political Thought II
> 6. English 50/51, Shakespeare I/II
> 7. History 24/25, Revolutionary America, 1763–1815/Antebellum and Civil War America, 1815–1877
> 8. Philosophy 55, The Making of the Modern Mind

In the early 2000s, Tufts appropriated $500,000 per year for diversity programming. Its commitment to diversity remains strong today, seen in the university's "Group of Six" culture centers: the Asian American Center; the Africana Center; the International Center; the Latino Center; the Lesbian, Gay, Bisexual, and Transgender (LGBT) Center; and the Women's Center. Students say, "There is a great diversity here, with people from all over the world." Tufts is at least consistent and comprehensive in its definition of diversity; the "economically disadvantaged" are listed as a separate minority group. Tufts students have been heard to complain that there are too many "rich kids" on campus.

Alongside left-leaning student groups stand the Tufts Republicans—which is very active. That's a good thing for students. Says an undergraduate: "It is difficult to be a conservative on campus, but we get enough respect that it's not that bad." However, others assert, "Groups with right-wing opinions are small and shunned; no one cares what they think. It's very liberal here."

The Granoff Family Hillel Center is reportedly one of the most welcoming buildings on campus. The student body is around 25 percent Jewish, which makes Hillel "a huge presence." A rainbow of faiths are represented at Tufts, including Baha'i, Buddhist, Hindu, and Muslim. The Tufts Christian Fellowship, Protestant Student Fellowship, Unitarian Universalist, Eastern Orthodox, and Catholic Community at Tufts serve students.

Tufts boasts some more venerable traditions. It seems that the famous circus owner P. T. Barnum donated $50,000 to Tufts in the late 1800s and threw in the stuffed hide of his most famous elephant, Jumbo, as a bonus. The animal was destroyed in a fire in 1975, but some of his ashes are kept in a jar, which Tufts athletes rub before games for luck. The appropriately named Tufts Jumbos compete on nearly 30 varsity teams in NCAA Divisions I (squash and sailing) and III (basketball, cross-country, lacrosse, and so forth), as well as in the New England Small College Athletic Conference.

A number of club and intramural teams are also available and popular. Says one student: "There's plenty of room to be who you are, and plenty of groups to join." A second enthusiast states, "There are an incredible number of activities, clubs, and organizations to get involved with at Tufts." Club sports include rugby, tae kwon do, Ultimate Frisbee, baseball, and fencing, while intramural teams play Wiffleball, floor hockey, and flag football.

Tufts was surprised to find itself at the top of the *Daily Beast*'s 2010 report on the nation's most dangerous campuses. The *Beast*'s statistics were disputed by Tufts, which claims that most of the reported crimes were committed off campus on properties adjacent to campus. The school's 2011 report listed two forcible sex offenses, two robberies, three aggravated assaults, and 18 burglaries in that year. Safety phones are located all over campus, a police force is present, and the grounds are well lit, but students would do well to be aware of the dangers of the surrounding areas.

Tufts' 2012–13 tuition was a hefty $41,998, with room and board at $11,512. "It's way too expensive," says one student. Tufts meets the full demonstrated need of all admitted aid candidates. Forty-three percent of students received need-based aid, with 22 percent having received more than $48,000. For students who plan to work in nonprofit organizations or in the public sector, Tufts offers to pay off loans, since these jobs usually tend to pay less than do the more popular professional choices for Tufts grads. Still, the typical Tufts student who borrowed graduated with $17,000 in debt.

STRONG SUITS	WEAK POINTS
• Good programs in engineering, international relations, history, biology, child development, English, political science, economics, and philosophy.	• Lax curriculum, with plenty of politicized, time-wasting courses.
• Many opportunities to work closely with faculty, especially in research in the sciences and engineering.	• English major heavy with ideological classes.
• Very good study-abroad options.	• Politicized programs in Latin American, African, and urban studies.
• Professors teach most classes, and are said to be quite accessible.	• Courses that fulfill the world civilizations requirement are notoriously partisan, as are some political science classes.
	• Lots of administration money sloshing around in "diversity" initiatives on this heavily left-leaning campus.

Tulane University

New Orleans, Louisiana • www.tulane.edu

Coming Up for Air

Founded in 1834 as the Medical College of Louisiana, it closed during the Union occupation of New Orleans. In 1884 it was reorganized as the private Tulane University of Louisiana and grew into one of the country's leading private research institutions. Much of the credit for Tulane's rapid comeback after the devastation of Hurricane Katrina in 2005 goes to President Scott Cowen, who toughed out the disaster himself. A massive restructuring created a smaller but stronger university, with a respectable set of distribution requirements, mandatory public service, a residency requirement, and more opportunities for interdisciplinary studies.

Academic Life: Learning to serve

The Newcomb-Tulane College oversees the undergraduate schools of architecture, business, liberal arts, public health and tropical medicine, and science and engineering. In addition to the requirements of the individual schools, all students must complete the distribution requirements, which are worthy but fall far short of a real core curriculum.

Students seeking a broad liberal education would do well to apply to the school's

VITAL STATISTICS

Religious affiliation: *none*
Total enrollment: *13,359*
Total undergraduates: *8,338*
SAT CR/Verbal midrange:
620–710
SAT Math midrange:
620–700
ACT midrange: *29–32*
Applicants: *37,767*
Applicants accepted: *25%*
Accepted applicants who
enrolled: *17%*
Tuition (general/out of
state): *$45,240*
Tuition (in state): *N/A*
Room and board: *$12,040*
Freshman retention rate:
90%
Graduation rate (4 yrs.): *63%*
Graduation rate (6 yrs.): *72%*
Courses with fewer than 20
students: *68%*
Student-faculty ratio: *11:1*
Courses taught by graduate
students: *not provided*
Students living on campus:
44%
Students in fraternities: *10%*
Students in sororities: *16%*
Students receiving need-
based financial aid: *43%*
Avg. student-loan debt of a
recent graduating class
$31,177
Most popular majors:
*business/marketing,
social sciences, biology/
biomedical sciences*
Guaranteed housing for 4
years? *no*

honors program, where "everyone works hard—students and professors," according to a teacher. Honors students must complete four hours of graduate-level courses before their senior year and maintain a GPA of 3.6 or higher. Courses are taught by full-time faculty members and are generally limited to 20 students. A recurring honors course offering is the two-semester "Community, Polity, and Citizenship," which includes readings from Homer, Plato, Virgil, the Qur'an, Dante, Teresa of Avila, and the Bible during the first semester, then Machiavelli, Rousseau, Dostoevsky, and Nietzsche (among others) in the second. Honors seniors complete a thesis or research project of around 70 pages.

Tulane InterDisciplinary Experience Seminars (TIDES) include some of the school's most distinguished faculty. Students choose from more than 80 topics, ranging from "Law and Order," "New Orleans Cities of the Dead: Cemetery Architecture and Its Cultural Legacy," and "The Physics of Baseball" to "Sex, Drugs, Rock and Roll, and Disease." These courses offer only one credit hour and meet in small groups of about 15 to 20 students.

Tulane recognizes that it has an important role in rebuilding the city, so it added a public-service requirement to its curriculum and inaugurated the Center for Public Service (CPS) to oversee its implementation. "Memories of Katrina are going to be there to shape our thinking here at Tulane," a professor says. "We're tied to our city more closely as a result of Katrina." Another professor notes that the stronger emphasis on community service at Tulane is also attracting a new kind of student—one "who is academically talented and intellectually curious but also possesses strong interests in public service and the community."

To graduate, students must participate in one approved CPS program. Sociology students, for example, may assist the New Orleans city attorney's office in rehabilitating a neighborhood, while seniors in biomedical engineering may participate in a yearlong design project.

Tulane is noted for its programs in architecture, international development, philosophy, political economy, Latin American studies, and economics. "The political economy major is particularly distinctive," says a professor. Students report that the economics department is largely free market in orientation, a rare thing these days. Students in this field can participate in a summer internship program and a study-abroad program at the Institute for Economic and Political Studies in London and Cambridge. In this department, students particularly recommend Professor Mary Olson.

The political science department is "filled with young and enthusiastic teachers that make classes very enjoyable," a student says. The department regularly offers a course called "Political Thought in the West," which covers Western thinkers such as Plato, Aristotle, Locke, Berkeley, and others. Political science majors must take one class each in American politics, comparative politics, political methodology, international politics, and political theory, as well as a statistics class. They must also demonstrate proficiency in a foreign language and select six electives in political science. However, one could choose to study the U.S. Constitution in "American Government" class or dabble in "Environmental Politics and Policy." One's theory course could be "Greek Foundations of Western Political Thought" or the tiresome "Feminist Political Theory." Political science students recommend teachers Brian Brox, Thomas Langston, and Gary Remer.

Much more rigorous is the political economy division, which "provides an integrated interdisciplinary education in which majors take core courses in the field of political economy and other courses from related disciplines, including economics, political

CAMPUS POLITICS: GREEN LIGHT

"A political environment at Tulane exists, but it must be sought out," says one student. "Tulane sponsors organizations of different political leanings; the Tulane College Democrats and the Tulane College Republicans are the largest. Most of their political meetings and events, however, are conducted in private. There are very few open protests or demonstrations. For this reason, some go so far as to say that Tulane is politically apathetic. I don't believe this to be true. I think a good political debate is readily available at Tulane, but there is very little in-your-face politics."

Says another student: "It is a real struggle to get anyone but a core few on either side of the aisle interested. Faculty struggle to get students to debate in class and are often pleased when conservative and libertarian students express their views on a legal subject matter." Tulane itself "encourages debate" and even "went out of its way to ensure that the College Republicans' Ann Coulter event went off without a hitch," he says.

Still, the Tulane administration doesn't hide its preferences. In 2012 the online resource *Campus Reform* noted that the ratio of liberal commencement speakers invited to Tulane to conservative or centrist speakers was an overpowering 19 to 4.

science, history, and philosophy," a teacher reports. In this program, students recommend Martyn Thompson and Mark Vail.

The history department is also strong. A student says, "The history department boasts some of the best teachers at the school. . . . I also appreciate that the history department at Tulane takes a classic approach." According to one professor, there's almost a built-in preference for the Western tradition at Tulane. "The (history) curriculum as a whole has made a huge investment in the Western tradition. That's the way the liberal arts were structured in the 1950s and 1960s, and that's the way it pretty much remains today." Majors must take at least 10 classes in three of the department's six geographic fields, which include the United States, ancient and medieval Europe, the Middle East/North Africa, modern Europe, Latin America, and Africa. Recommended professors include George L. Bernstein, James Boyden, Emily Clark, Kenneth Harl, Colin M. MacLachlan, Larry Powell, Samuel C. Ramer, and Randy Sparks.

The English major at Tulane offers little in the way of real requirements, only calling for 10 courses that include the introductory "Literary Investigations" class, an introduction to British or American literature, a pre-1800 literature class, a course in American literature, and a senior capstone. Although the department does offer two Shakespeare classes (one per semester) and one in Chaucer, most of the courses are lighter fare. "Place-Based Storytelling in New Orleans," "Hip Hop Feminism in Black Women's Writing," "Literary London," and a great number of creative writing classes fill the roster of available English classes. Students recommend Michael Kuczynski, who teaches British literature (including Chaucer) and a bibliography class.

> A history professor says that his department's "curriculum as a whole has made a huge investment in the Western tradition. That's the way the liberal arts were structured in the 1950s and 1960s, and that's the way it pretty much remains today."

Tulane's student-faculty ratio is an impressive 11 to 1, and most teachers are said to be eager to assist students. One grad student says, "In my experience, the professors have been extremely accessible and helpful." Another student says, "Tulane is an undergraduate-oriented school. This means that most undergraduate classes are taught by full professors, not teaching assistants. I have made friendships and worked on a close basis with full professors." A professor says, "Tulane students are as competent and serious as the best students at the best places in the country. They have a real seriousness about studying." A student says, "Everybody could have gone to an Ivy or a more selective school, but they came to Tulane—not because of the money, just for the experience, the town, the life."

Some of Tulane's best teachers in other departments, students and faculty say, are Ronna Burger, and Eric Mack in philosophy; James McGuire in physics; and Harvey and Victoria Bricker in anthropology (both emeritus).

For those interested in study-abroad programs, Tulane offers semester-, summer-, and yearlong programs. Study-abroad options span the globe, from Ghana to Singapore. Tulane provides a number of foreign language options. Both majors and minors are offered in French, German, Greek and Latin, Italian, Portuguese, Russian, and Spanish. Classes are also available in Arabic, Chinese, Creole French, Hebrew, Japanese, and Vietnamese.

Student Life: Love in the ruins

Tulane is located in a part of New Orleans that was built above sea level and hence was not as heavily damaged as other parts of the city. Just across St. Charles Avenue, which borders the campus, is the exquisite Audubon Park, which includes a public golf course, jogging and walking trails, and lagoons. Across Magazine Street at the opposite end of the park is Audubon Zoo, one of the nation's finest.

Tulane was long notorious as a party school whose students somehow found time to do a little homework. Students still say alcohol plays a tremendous role in most of their social lives. The university has tried to steer students away from the hard stuff by banning alcohol on campus for underage students. One junior says that the prevalence of drinking has decreased some and mostly moved off campus, where alcohol is easy to obtain. Other students insist that drinking doesn't get in the way of class work. "Tulane has students that do nothing but party," says one student, "but also a lot of students who live in the library. Although the party-going students are better known because they are louder, students wishing to spend long nights in study will not go unaccompanied. I think this mix is healthy."

SUGGESTED CORE

1. Classical Studies 4060, Classical Epic
2. Philosophy 201, History of Ancient Philosophy
3. Jewish Studies 2100/Classics 2200, Introduction to the Hebrew Bible/New Testament: An Historical Introduction
4. History 303, Early Medieval and Byzantine Civilization from Constantine to the Crusades (*closest match*)
5. Political Science 4780, Modern Political Theory
6. English 446/447, Shakespeare I/II
7. History H1410, History of the United States from Colonization to 1865
8. Philosophy 310, 19th-Century European Philosophy

Just a small percentage of Tulane's students join one of 20 Greek organizations, and few live with their fraternities or sororities. While this doesn't stop the Greeks from throwing large parties, New Orleans itself tends to offer more alluring social options.

Tulane provides more political organizations than the typical university. College Democrats and Republicans are represented, as well as a Socialist Organization, pro-Israel club, pro-life club, an Environmental Action League, and chapters of Amnesty International and the ACLU. Tulane also provides the chance to get involved in media, including the *Hullabaloo* newspaper, a literary society, and WTUL 91.5 FM. The late media genius Andrew Breitbart was a Tulane alum.

Tulane offers religious support to its students as well. The university plays host to a Muslim student association, as well as a Hillel group and a Chabad Jewish Student Center. Christian organizations include Cru (Campus Crusade for Christ), Chi Alpha, Fellowship of Christian Athletes, Impact (a black Christian group), and InterVarsity, as well as Baptist, Episcopal, Presbyterian, Catholic, and Methodist centers or groups. Beyond the campus, New Orleans has historic churches and synagogues all around the city, including the gorgeous downtown St. Patrick's parish—one of the few places on earth where the Latin Mass was continuously celebrated after Vatican II.

Tulane's Green Waves compete in NCAA Division I with six men's and nine women's teams. Although Tulane is committed to its sports, no team has achieved real success in recent years. Prospective students may enjoy the school's intramural or club sports programs. Intramural offerings are considerable, from basketball, tennis, biathlon, and racquetball to flag football, Ping-Pong, and soccer. Club sports include aikido, ballroom dancing, boxing, cricket, gymnastics, lacrosse, rugby, and running, among many others.

All freshmen and sophomores are required to live on campus—although students may apply for exemption if they are older than 21, married, or live locally with a parent or guardian. Students are assigned to a residential college to which they belong throughout their undergraduate years. These colleges help to provide a community and extracurricular activities. Tulane offers a number of on-campus housing options, including coed dorms (the sexes are separated by floor), suites, and apartments. The all-women Josephine-Louise Hall is a bastion of southern propriety, with a security guard at the front desk 24 hours a day registering all guests; male visitors must be escorted at all times.

Per capita, post-Katrina New Orleans is among the most violent cities in the nation and has a murder rate nearly double that of the next most dangerous U.S. cities, like Detroit. Students should not avoid Tulane for fear of crime, but they should be extremely careful and remember that in New Orleans dangerous neighborhoods sit right next to safer ones. On-campus offenses in 2011 included three forcible sex offenses, one aggravated assault, 19 burglaries, one incidence of arson, and two stolen cars. Not bad for a school in New Orleans.

Tulane charged Ivy League–level tuition of $45,240 and $12,040 for room and board for the 2012–13 school year. Loans are not required of students with family incomes of less than $75,000. Some 42 percent of students received need-based aid, and the average student-loan debt of a recent grad was a stiff $31,177.

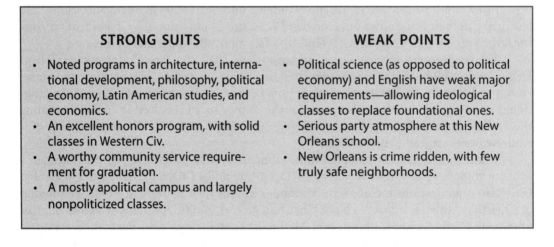

STRONG SUITS	WEAK POINTS
• Noted programs in architecture, international development, philosophy, political economy, Latin American studies, and economics.	• Political science (as opposed to political economy) and English have weak major requirements—allowing ideological classes to replace foundational ones.
• An excellent honors program, with solid classes in Western Civ.	• Serious party atmosphere at this New Orleans school.
• A worthy community service requirement for graduation.	• New Orleans is crime ridden, with few truly safe neighborhoods.
• A mostly apolitical campus and largely nonpoliticized classes.	

University of Chicago

Chicago, Illinois • www.uchicago.edu

Old School

Chartered in 1890, Chicago's campus has been home to 87 Nobel laureates, more than any other American university. Chicago scientists were the first to split the atom and to measure the speed of light. As part of a research university, the college offers both breadth and depth of learning and provides students with an almost unparalleled academic experience. One student describes Chicago as "a scientific and economic powerhouse." Students have the valuable opportunity to work in some of the same classes as advanced graduate students, while their core classes ground them in the essentials of perhaps the best liberal arts curriculum in the world.

Academic Life: Midwestern monastic

Chicago is one of the only well-known schools in America whose core curriculum is worthy of the name. With the help of an academic adviser, students navigate through the core and begin taking classes in their chosen major. Chicago grants the bachelor of arts or bachelor of science degree in 50 fields in the arts, humanities, natural sciences, social sciences, and in such interdisciplinary areas as biological chemistry, environmental studies, and cinema and media studies. Along with its tradition of academic excellence, Chicago has a well-deserved reputation as a deeply serious, intense, and rigorous school. Well-organized and prepared students will flourish. Others might flunk. The school imposes a very serious curriculum, grounded in some of the great works of the West. We highly recommend the humanities sequence "Human Being and Citizen." In this sequence, students read the most important works of the Western tradition, beginning with Homer and continuing into the 20th century. Another excellent humanities sequence is "Greek Thought and Literature." Faculty advisers "are very available to those who seek them out," a student says.

Another tells us, "Nearly all of my classes have been taught by professors. They are, by and large, eminently approachable." Another student tells us, however, that "professor and student interactions are more formal. As a student, you are a dime a dozen, and everyone wants a professor's time." Professors teach between two-thirds and three-fourths of the classes—a good thing, since "when TAs grade, because they are inexperienced, they are not always the most judicious graders," a student complains. Many of Chicago's best professors still teach undergraduate classes. These include Rachel Fulton Brown, Constantin Fasolt, and Hanna Gray (emerita) in history; Paul J. Sally Jr. in mathematics; James Redfield in Classics; John Mearsheimer, Charles Lipson, and Nathan Tarcov in political science; Nobel winner Gary Becker and James Heckman in economics; Jonathan Lear and Robert Pippin in philosophy; Ralph Lerner (emeritus) in social sciences and the Committee on Social Thought; Michael Fishbane in Jewish studies; Isaac Abella in physics; and Jean Bethke Elshtain, Jean-Luc Marion, and David Tracy in the Divinity School.

Concentrations (the Chicago term for a major) are grouped into five collegiate divisions: Biological Sciences, Humanities, New Collegiate, Physical Sciences, and Social Sciences. We particularly recommend that students who want an intensive liberal arts curriculum explore the New Collegiate concentration "Fundamentals: Issues and Texts." Students in this major (which is dubbed "Fundies") choose six classic texts to study in detail in light of one overarching question. One Fundies student testifies, "I spent time at Oxford later on and found myself to be so much better prepared than my peers, both British and American. I attribute this to the Chicago core and Fundamentals." Students concentrating in Fundamentals write a research paper in their junior year and must take in their senior year a comprehensive exam on each of their texts. If a student cannot find a major that suits him, the New Collegiate Division allows him to create his own through Tutorial Studies. It is difficult to find a professor, however, who is willing to commit to being a tutor.

On the down side, it is surprising to learn that English majors at Chicago need not take a class in Shakespeare, history majors are not required to study America, and political science majors need not take a course in U.S. constitutional theory. Nevertheless, the excellence of Chicago's core and the intense rigor of its faculty make it unlikely that students will emerge without having read the key texts in their disciplines. Sharply politicized classrooms are essentially nonexistent at Chicago. As one student says, "Although the administration may be introducing diversity and trying to get rid of the Great Books program, when professors teach what they teach, they are pretty evenhanded. We tend to attract the kind of people who are interested in what books are saying. . . . I call myself a conservative, and I've never been bothered by the political atmosphere in the classroom."

Some departments are more ideological than others. According to one student, "Here, as elsewhere, there seem to be a lot of bad and politicized classes, but you are not required to

---

CAMPUS POLITICS: GREEN LIGHT

The University of Chicago has, in the words of a student, "one of the least politicized campuses I've seen." Students are not themselves especially concerned with politics. This generally reflects the intensely focused and rigorous nature of the Chicago experience. Right-leaning intellectuals should check out the Edmund Burke Society, based at the university's law school, for Oxford-style debates on both political and philosophical topics. Both College Republicans and College Democrats are active on campus. Conservative students should also check out the nonpartisan political quarterly *Midway Review*. There are at times various leftist protests on campus, but they are almost always ignored by people on campus or are sometimes answered by satirical counterprotests.

The university recently established the Becker Friedman Institute to build on its strengths in economics and to honor the contributions of conservative economist and current professor Gary Becker and the late libertarian professor Milton Friedman, both Nobel Prize–winning economists with long histories at Chicago. This institute's founding outraged leftist faculty, some 170 of whom submitted a petition to the university president demanding that its name be changed, according to the *Chronicle of Higher Education*.

---

take any, and I have not." The departments of English, social administration and public policy, Near Eastern languages and civilizations, and sociology get relatively poor marks in this regard. One professor says that the English department in particular is "full of methodologists and ideologues." One member of the economics department says it is less political than in the past and characterizes the faculty as "heterogeneous . . . devoted to a wider range of theoretical and empirical issues, including game theory, auction theory, long-term economic growth, et cetera."

Conservative professors can be found in a number of other departments as well, from political science to the Committee on Social Thought. Academic life at Chicago can be challenging in several senses. One student says, "As a Christian, I have encountered innumerable people that disagree with me, but this has not made me timid: it has only required me to defend my beliefs against skepticism, which can hardly be anything but healthy. . . . I have no desire to be surrounded by people who think precisely like me. People who come here need to be willing to defend all of their beliefs, regardless of their ideology."

The intensity and rigor of academic life have tended to give Chicago a reputation for asceticism. Students who come to Chicago should be prepared to enjoy their immersion in the life of the mind and their academic work. As one student noted, "The key to a good undergraduate experience seems to be the capacity to get the vast majority of one's personal satisfaction from academic work. . . . While others might play Frisbee or beer pong, we argue about the niceties of Kantian metaphysics."

Chicago sponsors its own study-abroad programs. Destinations include Athens, Barcelona, Berlin, Bologna, Cairo, England, Ireland, Cape Town, Freiburg, Jerusalem, Kyoto, Oaxaca, Paris, Pisa, Rome, St. Petersburg, Toledo, and Vienna. The university's newest center abroad is in Beijing.

Chicago offers more than 50 foreign languages. Related majors are classical studies, East Asian languages and civilizations, Germanic studies, Jewish studies, linguistics, Near Eastern languages and civilizations, Romance languages and literatures, Russian studies, Slavic languages and literatures, and South Asian languages and civilizations.

Thanks to its daunting core curriculum, U. of Chicago educates all students deeply and thoroughly. Says one: "I spent time at Oxford later on and found myself to be so much better prepared than my peers, both British and American."

Student Life: Talking shop

The school's Gothic buildings recall the High Middle Ages, though not all students appreciate them: "They have a few new buildings that are really nice, but why does the school not have air conditioning in a lot of places? The place is pretty, but some of the buildings are dilapidated." Still, with plenty of cafés, high-end condos, and new landscaping, the university's campus and once-blighted Hyde Park neighborhood have probably never looked so posh. Students do throw parties and alcohol does appear, but both the drinking and the "hookup" culture found on most campuses are more subdued here. Chicago undergraduates attend graduate workshops and lectures in their spare time and talk philosophy in the campus's numerous coffee shops. There are no Greek organizations.

There are many university-sponsored activities—for example, 17 men's and women's varsity sports teams, 33 intramural sports, and 39 active club sports, out of more than 350 student organizations, including a large number of religious groups. The Catholic Students Association, based at Calvert House just off the main quadrangle, offers Mass, Bible study, prayer, and social and charitable work. In town is the gorgeously restored church of St. John Cantius on Carpenter Street, which offers Mass in Latin with Gregorian chant. InterVarsity Christian Fellowship and Cru (formerly Campus Crusade for Christ) both have chapters at the university. The Chabad Jewish Center provides kosher Shabbat and holiday meals to all Jewish students, regardless of affiliation or observance. The Orthodox Christian Fellowship holds weekly vespers services on campus. The Hyde Park Vineyard Church two blocks north of the campus holds regular evangelical worship services and organizes smaller "house groups" for prayer and study.

The university guarantees housing for four years for every student. Freshmen are required to live in on-campus housing. The 11 undergraduate residence halls are divided (most often by floor) into "houses" composed of 40 to 100 students. Resident heads (advanced graduate students or university staff) and resident masters (faculty members) organize programs of social and cultural events that may include guest lecturers, dinners, residence-hall special events, and trips for opera, theater, and sporting events—usually for very low prices. One student told us that "I lived in a [house] for two years and found the resident assistants to be very nice; they made an effort to foster a real sense of community among the students." Freshmen are assigned same-sex roommates, but upperclassmen can opt for coed dorm rooms. Residential students may eat at any of three dining commons, 12 cafes, or two on-campus retail locations. According to one student, "Crime is probably the one major drawback to this university." Another adds that the surrounding neighborhood is "consistently populated by too many socially undesirable individuals." In 2011 the school reported seven burglaries, two aggravated assaults, two robberies, five forcible sex offenses, and two stolen cars. One student tells us, "If you want to be here, you will want it so badly that you will ignore the crime rate."

Chicago is as expensive as it is excellent, with 2012–13 tuition at $44,574 and room and board at $13,137. Admissions are need blind, and Chicago guarantees to meet the need of any student it accepts. Some 47 percent of students received need-based aid. The average student-loan debt of recent graduates was $22,663.

SUGGESTED CORE

1. Humanities 12000, Greek Thought and Literature
2. Philosophy 25000, History of Philosophy I: Ancient Philosophy
3. Biblical Studies 31000 /32500, Jewish History and Society I: Introduction to the Hebrew Bible/Introduction to the New Testament
4. Philosophy 26000, History of Philosophy II: Medieval and Early Modern Philosophy
5. Philosophy 21600, Introduction to Political Philosophy or Social Sciences 15100/15200, Classics of Social and Political Thought I/II
6. English 16500/16600, Shakespeare I: Histories and Comedies/II: Tragedies and Romances
7. Laws, Letters, and Society 20603, Early America to 1865
8. Philosophy 27000, History of Philosophy III: Kant and the 19th Century (closest match)

STRONG SUITS

- Famous for both the sciences and the humanities, the school attracts top scholars from around the world.
- Students come here to work, hard. Some call the atmosphere "monastic."
- A core curriculum that creates broadly cultured graduates, regardless of major.
- A diverse and tolerant political atmosphere, with some prominent conservative scholars and programs on campus.
- Set in thriving, arts-rich Chicago—for those students who find time to leave the library.

WEAK POINTS

- Students who aren't well prepared, disciplined, and dedicated will simply flunk out.
- Many famous professors are preoccupied by scholarship; most interaction (including grading) involves teaching assistants.
- Crime in Chicago is high, winters are awful, and the school is in a bad neighborhood.

University of Dallas

Irving, Texas • www.udallas.edu

Keeping the Liberal Arts Alive

Founded in 1956, this otherwise unremarkable regional college in a sprawl town outside of Dallas has made a name for itself among thoughtful Catholics by holding fast to two attributes that other, more conventionally prestigious schools have shed: its religious identity and its rigorous core curriculum. Students and teachers who could otherwise have found themselves at better-funded schools with greater name recognition in secular (and secularized ex-Catholic) academia go instead to Irving, Texas, where they find like-minded people eager to immerse themselves in the Great Books of the Western world, read through the lens of sophisticated Catholic orthodoxy.

Academic Life: Seeds from the core

All students at Dallas must take its excellent two-year core. This gives undergraduates a common bedrock of texts, authors, and ideas from which to approach their majors—and their lives. "My friends who went to more prestigious universities didn't have to study nearly as much as I did," says one recent graduate. A professor adds: "The core curriculum is the strength of the school, period. All departments live off its strengths, its commitment to truth, its way of exposing students to the best in the Western tradition, its commitment to that tradition."

Upon enrolling in the university, each entering freshman is assigned a faculty adviser who helps to guide the student through the ins and outs of the core curriculum. After the first year, a student may select a new adviser from among the faculty in the major department or the university at large. Advising is also available through the Academic Success Office.

Students and faculty alike consider English, politics, theology, and philosophy to be strong departments. English boasts, according to one teacher, "superb professors who have a deep commitment to reading texts as revealing truth about the human condition (rather than as fashionable postmodern meaningless play with signifiers, or Marxist embodiments of race, class, and gender), and who have a deep commitment to the students through their teaching."

Theater students also will encounter a solid program. As one professor reports: "Drama is an unusual strength here because of the core: The drama students can see modern and contemporary drama in the light of their strong backgrounds in classical Greek drama and Shakespeare, and—unlike drama students almost anywhere else—have serious grounding in history, philosophy, and theology."

"Philosophy is strong, and theology is strong both in scholarship and in its commitment to intellectually exploring yet remaining faithfully Catholic," says one teacher we consulted. "Departments like these do not hide from controversy or difficult questions, but they all do believe that truth exists and that the human is designed to seek it, find it, and live it." Beware of the recently created (and highly unpopular) major in pastoral ministry, where some longtime faculty members were public dissenters from Catholic doctrine and that in 2012 invited the theologically radical (and scandal-tainted) Cardinal Roger Mahony to speak.

One professor says that the economics department "has a strong commitment to the ideas of classical liberalism in the strain of Adam Smith, and of Austrian economics in the strain of Hayek. It's a small department, but they do good things."

The medical school acceptance rate for Dallas graduates is 85 percent, indicating that the science departments are excellent and that spending two years on core classes does nothing to prohibit students from pursuing a plan of study outside the liberal arts.

Dallas students may augment their introduction to the liberal arts by participating in the Rome program at Due Santi, the university's campus located about 10 miles from the heart of the Eternal City. About 80 percent of Dallas students participate in the program, typically during their sophomore year.

In addition to the bachelor of arts degrees offered through the Constantin College of the Liberal Arts, the university also offers a BA in business through the College of Business and a BA in pastoral ministry through the (still controversial) School of Ministry. In addition to traditional majors, students may complete a preprofessional or dual-degree program (for example, predentistry or a joint BA/MBA program). Additional concentrations (for example, journalism or medieval and Renaissance studies) may also be pursued.

CAMPUS POLITICS: GREEN LIGHT

One teacher sums up the atmosphere at UD as follows: "This is a place founded on conservative and religious principles, and the practice of both is vigorous, thoughtful, and critical. We are not a 'safe little Catholic school to which to send your children,' if by that one means keeping them safe from challenging ideas. Yet all is done with a real eye to truth, respect, and decorum. Religious life is not predicated from above; in fact, students have several options and freely seek them out, and so the spiritual life of the campus often bubbles up from below, from the students themselves. Political correctness is an object of great scorn here."

Teaching at Dallas is strong. Some of the best undergraduate teachers include John Alvis, Andrew Moran, Rev. Robert Maguire, Gregory Roper, David Davies, and Gerard Wegemer in English; Richard Dougherty in politics; Rev. James Lehrberger in philosophy; Susan Hanssen, Thomas W. Jodziewicz, and Francis Swietek in history; Alexandra Wilhelmsen in Spanish; William Doyle in economics; Richard Olenick in physics; and Frank Doe in biology. Professors generally take an active role in university social events and extracurricular programs. Students give them high praise: "The professors really live what they teach," says one student. "They write what they think, and they behave the way they preach."

Class sizes remain moderate. Graduate students who hold a master's degree may teach undergraduate classes—and an increasing number of them do, sources tell us. About half the freshman classes offered in the English, theology, politics, and philosophy departments are taught by instructors or adjunct or visiting teachers. Business, history, foreign languages, the arts, and education also rely heavily on non-PhDs, but the sciences and the humanities retain more professors.

Foreign languages offered on campus include French, German, Greek and Latin, Italian, and Spanish.

Student Life: Air conditioned rectitude

Perhaps the least attractive thing about the University of Dallas is its location, in a relatively joyless patch of sprawl called Irving, adjoining the Dallas–Fort Worth monsterplex. The university's Dallas Year program tries to overcome the place's limits by organizing outings for freshmen to the opera, museum, concerts, and sporting events. There is a bus stop in front of the school and a light rail station that connects students to most of Dallas. Most students do not feel trapped at the school and believe they have plenty to do on campus with the various clubs and activities, such as music in the quad every weekend. Still, it's a good idea to own a car.

Overall, students and faculty seem impressed with their experience of the school. One professor says that the students are "hard working, respectful, and bright. I certainly do not see our students as closed-minded or set in their ways and thinking. They are, I think, truly open and unafraid. Many of them are devout Catholics, and that does provide a standard for their judgments. They are open to anything compatible with authentic Catholicism."

> A teacher says, "The core curriculum is the strength of the school, period. All departments live off its strengths, its commitment to truth, its way of exposing students to the best in the Western tradition, its commitment to that tradition."

The fundamental agreement among Dallas students on core beliefs is an important contribution to the school's community atmosphere. "You are surrounded by kids who will enforce the school's ideas that there is truth, it can be known by man, and it is unchanging," a student says. As another student puts it, "There's always someone who has common ground with you, and it's easy to find them." However, some students have reported that it can be difficult to find a place between the conservative, homeschooled cliques and the rowdier, beer-drinking crowd.

Students often attend Mass at the beautiful Cistercian monastery nearby or the Dominican priory on campus. On campus, Mass is said twice daily at the university's ultramodern Chapel of the Incarnation; many students attend, but there is little pressure, if any, for them to do so. It is possible to "get through UD and not learn anything about your faith," says one student. "But if you want to practice and grow in your faith, there is opportunity to do so and you would never be ridiculed for it." Students seeking a more traditional liturgy should investigate the Latin Mass or Eastern Rite Catholic parishes just down the road in Irving.

As Catholic as UD is—about 82 percent of its undergraduates identify themselves as such—students and faculty report that non-Catholics generally feel comfortable at the school. Says one professor about non-Catholics, "Those I have spoken with have expressed some surprise that no one ever approached them about becoming Catholic."

One teacher cited "what I like best about UD students—what I call 'playful seriousness and serious playfulness.' As a colleague said to me once, 'you almost never get that world-weary "whatever" from a UD student.'"

And students are involved at University of Dallas. With almost 50 student organizations to choose from and a very active student government, the school offers a broad variety of activities throughout the year. Those looking to strengthen their Romance languages may choose French, Italian, Classics, or Spanish clubs. Swing club and a dance team provide an outlet for the agile, while sailing and Ultimate Frisbee organizations allow for athletic endeavors. The academically minded might join the economics, education, math, prehealth, chemistry, physics, or psychology clubs. The university also offers College

SUGGESTED CORE

The school's required core curriculum suffices.

Republicans and Democrats and the Knights of Columbus. The *University News* provides a clear take on campus issues, as well as commentary on social, political, and religious matters.

Students do not generally attend UD for its sports programs, though the school offers 14 NCAA Division III sports programs for those interested in playing for the Crusaders (their unofficial mascot is the Groundhogs), and in fall 2008 the university became an associate member of the North Eastern Athletic Conference. (But even though this is Texas, there is no football team.) Some intramural sports are also offered, including flag football, soccer, basketball, volleyball, and softball, and they are popular. Rugby is a club sport with a good-sized student following. The school has completed a $2 million expansion of its fitness center.

All but the newest dorms are single sex, and even the new hall does not include coed floors or bathrooms. Visitation hours for members of the opposite sex are quite restricted, and students entertaining members of the opposite sex must keep the door propped open. Some 63 percent of students live on campus; most students are required to do so until they are 21. Many students find off-campus housing just across the street from the campus; other apartments are relatively easy to find in nearby neighborhoods. While Dallas has become one of the more dangerous large cities in America, the campus is very safe. In 2011 the school reported two forcible sexual assaults and three burglaries on campus.

Undergraduate tuition in 2012–2013 was $29,140, and room and board were $9,890. As at most universities, financial aid is offered in the form of loans, grants, scholarships, and work-study programs. Merit-based scholarships are available, and some 94 percent of the undergraduate population received financial aid. The average debt of a recent grad was $28,500.

STRONG SUITS	WEAK POINTS
• A solid, rigorous curriculum ensures that every student, regardless of major, gets a true liberal arts education.	• Despite its long presence, UD has a very low profile in Dallas, which doesn't help graduates find jobs.
• The school is strongly committed to its religious identity and the intellectual tradition that accompanies it.	• Many freshman courses taught by adjuncts, visiting professors, or non-PhDs.
• Most majors are serious and traditional. Especially good departments are English, political science, and theology.	• High average student debt for a nonelite diploma may be a burden to graduates.
• Campus life is wholesome and fun, with single-sex dorms, sound visitation rules.	

University of Notre Dame

South Bend, Indiana • www.nd.edu

Land O' Lapsed

The University of Notre Dame has long been one of the most visible Roman Catholic universities in the United States. But the Catholic identity of the school began to be undermined in 1967, when a group of Catholic university officials, gathering at Notre Dame's retreat in Land O' Lakes, decided that a firm Catholic identity was a liability in an increasingly secular age. Following Notre Dame's lead, these educators seceded from church authority, and as a result few Catholic colleges in the United States are, well, Catholic.

At Notre Dame, a healthy core of faithful Catholic students and many of the faculty have persisted in fighting for the school's religious identity and tradition of liberal arts education. However, the leadership of the university, especially its governing board and president (Rev. John Jenkins, CSC), has largely supported the ongoing secularization of the school and its moves toward emphasizing research over teaching. Notes an insider: "People thought that Fr. Jenkins would tilt things back toward a traditional outlook, but he has allowed *The Vagina Monologues* and alienated conservatives on campus. He also inaugurated a campus-wide yearly 'forum' centered on some big, liberal hot-button issue such as health care, immigration, or global warming." However, Notre Dame can still offer a solid education in a comparatively wholesome atmosphere. For how much longer this will be true, we cannot say.

Academic Life: Under the Golden Dome

ND has long had a solid commitment to undergraduate education. There are still professors at Notre Dame who hail from an era when research did not matter at all, and they still do not publish. But the newer hires are very interested in publishing and do so as often as they can, churning out prodigious amounts of scholarly work. Despite this, says an insider, "I've never heard any complaints about students being unable to get attention from their professors." For now, tenure and promotion decisions include a lot of attention to teaching evaluations. However, with the president's new emphasis on research, this may be changing. In 2009 Notre Dame opened "Innovation Park," a research park next to campus designed to further commercial applications of university research.

"ND is very ambitious to be regarded as a 'top tier' research university," one teacher says. "There is a lot of money being put into these projects. I have heard of at least one case where a theology professor was a great teacher but was essentially forced out for not doing enough research." This professor glumly concludes, "While many say that the focus of the school is teaching of students, the jury is still out."

Education at Notre Dame begins with the First Year of Studies Program, which requires a total of 11 courses. Thanks to admirably small classes, students find getting into a first- or even second-choice seminar sometimes difficult. The composition courses are particularly demanding, culminating in a final writing portfolio.

Despite the lack of a core curriculum, most students we talked to were optimistic about the chances of getting a solid education at Notre Dame. Says one insider, "Even a student who does not care about the liberal arts in any way probably would get a fair amount of a traditional education by choosing the required nonmajor philosophy, theology, et cetera, courses at random." A faculty member muses, "The professors can be hit or miss. The education you receive, regardless of the school, largely depends on the classes and professors you choose to take." A student remarks that Notre Dame is "very large and intellectually diverse. While there are some Catholic theologians in the department who are famously

VITAL STATISTICS

Religious affiliation: *Roman Catholic*
Total enrollment: *12,004*
Total undergraduates: *8,452*
SAT CR/Verbal midrange: *650–760*
SAT Math midrange: *680–750*
ACT midrange: *32–34*
Applicants: *14,357*
Applicants accepted: *24%*
Accepted applicants who enrolled: *50%*
Tuition (general/out of state): *$42,971*
Tuition (in state): *N/A*
Room and board: *$11,934*
Freshman retention rate: *97%*
Graduation rate (4 yrs.): *91%*
Graduation rate (6 yrs.): *96%*
Courses with fewer than 20 students: *55%*
Student-faculty ratio: *12:1*
Courses taught by graduate students: *9%*
Students living on campus: *80%*
Students in fraternities: *none*
Students in sororities: *none*
Students receiving need-based financial aid: *45%*
Avg. student-loan debt of a recent graduating class: *$20,833*
Most popular majors: *finance, political science, psychology*
Guaranteed housing for 4 years? *yes*

CAMPUS POLITICS: YELLOW LIGHT

In a decision that outraged Catholics nationwide, in 2009 Notre Dame invited fervently pro-choice President Barack Obama to give the commencement speech at graduation and receive an honorary degree. Protests arose not only from student groups and faculty but also from pro-lifers and church officials around the country, including more than 60 bishops—Notre Dame's local bishop among them. The philosopher Ralph McInerny, who was retiring after 54 years of teaching at Notre Dame, called the invitation "an unequivocal abandonment of any pretense at being a Catholic university." More than 80 protestors from outside the college, including an elderly priest, were arrested and faced criminal charges that President Jenkins refused to drop.

In 2010 Notre Dame fired associate vice president for residence life Bill Kirk, a 22-year employee who was the only senior administration member to take part in a protest rally against Obama's visit. Professor David Solomon of the Center for Ethics and Culture told *National Review* that a "number of other administrators have told me that in light of Bill Kirk's treatment, they will in the future keep their heads down rather than dissent from the policies of the central administration."

Perhaps the school is trying to tack again toward the Catholic center; in 2012 it joined other Catholic employers in suing the Obama administration over the contraceptive/abortifacient mandate included in Obamacare; in 2013 Notre Dame invited as its commencement speaker the popular (and thoroughly orthodox) Cardinal Timothy Dolan.

heterodox, there are more and more orthodox professors." Another advises, "I think the key is to avoid certain professors rather than to avoid departments entirely." Most classes (except in foreign languages) are taught by faculty rather than by TAs—who instead help with grading and discussion sections.

There are many students, sighs a professor, who come to Notre Dame merely "motivated to be in business or watch football." In contrast to this, however, "there is a serious minority of students who are hungry for knowledge and to discuss ideas." It's also fortunate that "the professors . . . always seem to add more to the education than just the basic facts and consider the larger implications by getting students intellectually involved."

Freshmen are assigned professional advisers—17 of whom serve a freshman class of around 2,000. Once students pick majors, some departments match faculty advisers with a small group of students, while others have one faculty member serve the entire department. In sophomore year, students enroll according to their majors in one of five colleges (School of Architecture, Arts and Letters, Science, Engineering, or the Mendoza College of Business). Also available to the Notre Dame student is the Law School, the Graduate School, and six major research institutes.

In the College of Arts and Letters is the justly renowned Program of Liberal Studies (PLS). Known around campus as the Great Books major, PLS offers a three-year sequence of seminars and tutorials. Starting with the *Iliad* and ending with *The Brothers Karamazov,* the reading list in the Great Books Seminar is impressive and should attract any Notre Dame student serious about a liberal arts education; indeed, many choose it as part of a double major. The program's excellent faculty includes Walter J. Nicgorski, Phillip Reid Sloan (emeritus), and Mary Katherine Tillman (emerita).

The philosophy department is particularly strong. Highly respected nationwide, it includes Alasdair MacIntyre (emeritus), Alvin Plantinga (emeritus), and William David Solomon. As an insider states, "We have everyone from conservative Thomists to raging feminists here."

Another strong department is architecture, whose graduate program is world famous for its embrace of neoclassical forms. Says a teacher, "All of the students study the masterworks firsthand in Rome during their third year." Notable faculty in this department include neoclassicist Duncan Stroik, who has designed buildings for several of the schools listed in this guide.

Political science is another outstanding department; its recommended faculty include Patrick J. Deneen, Mary M. Keys, Daniel Philpott, Michael Zuckert, and Catherine Zuckert. Students are admirably required to take eight courses—either two introductory and six advanced or four introductory and four advanced—with at least one course each in American politics, international relations, comparative politics, and political theory, plus two writing seminars. One poli-sci major observes that there are "great courses, such as Professor [Donald] Kommers's 'Constitutional Law,' Professor [John] Roos's class on Congress, and Professor [Dan] Lindley's foreign policy course."

Engineering benefits from expansive and up-to-date facilities and is said to be mostly composed of conservative students. Similarly, the Mendoza College of Business gets "ridiculously" high rankings. Relates a veteran: "The students get hired right away." One student says, "The business school portion of the faculty has not only the strongest conservatives but also some of the most devout Catholics." Recommended in this department is Carolyn Woo, the college's dean and a "very solid individual, committed to the Catholic mission of the university." In 2009 the business school opened the Center for the Study of Financial Regulation.

> "ND is very ambitious to be regarded as a 'top tier' research university," one teacher says. "I know one great teacher was essentially forced out for not doing enough research."

Undergraduate history classes at Notre Dame are "very good," says a teaching assistant. "They usually make primary texts their focus and encourage the students to wrestle with their implications in discussion." Students recommend the class "The World of the Middle Ages," taught by Thomas Noble. Other "all-stars" of this department are Mark Noll and John Van Engen.

The history major requires 10 courses: one introductory workshop; four area courses, one of which must be pre-1500, from four out of five categories (Africa, Asia, and the Middle East; ancient and medieval Europe; modern Europe; Latin America; and the United States); three courses in a chosen concentration (ranging from Middle Eastern history to intellectual history to women's history); one seminar in the chosen concentration; and one elective. A history major could theoretically avoid studying any American history; he could also take a different track and study America but avoid any courses on ancient or medieval Europe.

Students and alumni have long griped about the theology department, home to well-known dissidents from church teaching. But it seems, as one degree seeker puts it, to be "undergoing a renaissance." Like the philosophy department, the theology department is big enough, a student says, "to include wackos and solid professors." Another agrees: "While each does have professors that might be considered embarrassments to their department, the overall quality of the courses and scholarship is definitely top notch." Theology professors who were highly recommended include Rev. Michael Baxter, CSC; Brian Daley, SJ; David Fagerberg; John Cavadini; Eugene Ulrich; James VanderKam; Gary Anderson; Robin Darling Young; Blake Leyerle; Joseph Wawrykow; Ann Astell; J. Matthew Ashley; Cyril O'Regan; and Randall Zachman.

Other outstanding faculty members at Notre Dame include Thomas Werge in English; John T. McGreevy and James Turner in history; Charles K. Wilber (emeritus) in economics and policy; Adrian Reimers, John O'Callaghan, and Alfred Freddoso in philosophy; Rev. Wilson (Bill) Miscamble, CSC, in history; William Kirk in accountancy; and David Veselik in biology.

The English department has the reputation of being rather weak and "very divided along ideological lines." Complains an undergrad: "One English course I took on Hemingway was particularly bad. It essentially taught that the West and all men were evil." A new Catholic professor was said to have quit in disgust over the inanity in this department. English majors do face decent requirements, which were recently beefed up: one writing-intensive introduction; one research seminar; one course in pre-1500 literature; one in 1500–1700; two in 1700–1900; one after 1900; one course in British literature; one in American; one in either American ethnic-identity literature or English-language literature outside the United States or Britain; one course in poetry; and two in fiction, drama, film, or critical theory.

Devout or conservative students should be leery of sociology, film, and (surprise!) gender studies, sources say. Perhaps the greatest danger to Notre Dame's identity lies in the careerist emphasis that dominates many departments. One teacher warns of "white-collar vocational education" and the craving for prestige as "the engine of secularization. We hire faculty whom we see as qualified not because they add to the catholicity of the school but because they help in our quest for momentary greatness."

Students should check out the programs offered by the Cushwa Center for the Study of American Catholicism, the Erasmus Institute, the Center for Ethics and Culture, the Jacques Maritain Center, and the Medieval Institute. Each fall, the Center for Ethics and Culture holds an annual conference that is highly regarded by students.

Notre Dame has a variety of outstanding study-abroad programs, in locales on every inhabited continent. The school offers courses in Arabic, Chinese (Mandarin), French, German, Greek and Latin, Irish, Italian, Japanese, Korean, Portuguese, Quechua, and Russian.

Student Life: Touchdown Jesus

There are 30 dorms, none of them coed, and a priest or a nun lives in most of them. Each hall has a chapel and its own intramural sports teams. Intervisitation is restricted to certain hours, but most dorms also have lounges where the sexes can mingle 24 hours a day. On the whole, dorm life seems pretty wholesome for a large university. Hard liquor is officially prohibited in the dorms, for example, but students differ over how widely this ban is observed. (Students observe in online forums that RAs regard a closed dorm-room door as sacrosanct.) Eighty percent of undergraduates live on campus, and students are encouraged to stay in the same residence hall for all four years. Notre Dame student government provides resources for finding affordable and safe off-campus living, as well as social resources.

The party scene is said to be somewhat subdued, thanks more to the heavy ND workload than any strict enforcement of policies by the school. Still, students host on- and off-campus parties, and there is a knot of bars near campus that cater to students of age—although students complain about the absence of clubs with live music or other entertainment.

Masses are held several times daily in ND's beautiful basilica, and they are well attended. Dorms have their own chapels, each offering weekly liturgies. The university's Campus Ministry directs students to choirs, retreats, eucharistic adoration, Bible studies, plus an orthodox introduction to Catholicism for non-Catholics. It helps Protestant, Orthodox, Buddhist, Muslim, and Jewish students find local resources and places of worship.

One student says that ND has a strong "Catholic circle…a network of several devoutly Catholic student groups. It includes the Militia Immaculata, Children of Mary, Orestes Brownson Council, Notre Dame Right to Life, Knights of Columbus Council (the nation's oldest chapter), the *Irish Rover,* and a few others. These are groups that, while separate, have many close connections and shared members that create a network for the most orthodox of Catholics to find a great home." The conservative student newspaper, the *Irish Rover,* wages an ongoing campaign to keep Notre Dame true to its liberal arts roots and Catholic identity. An active pro-life movement on campus generates multiple initiatives, including conferences and fund-raisers for mothers in need.

Says one student, "On campus you can generally pick your own fate: if you want to be a serious Catholic, go to Mass somewhere between weekly and daily, and study a lot of medieval philosophy, you can do that. On the other hand, if you want to take a bunch of women's studies classes and donate your pocket change to Planned Parenthood, you can do that too."

The administration, sources say, is actively moving the school closer to the secular model of elite eastern schools. For years, amid protests from campus groups such as the Knights of Columbus, there was a campus production of *The Vagina Monologues,* a trendy, toxic play that celebrates, among other things, lesbian statutory rape. The school's assistant vice president for student affairs has helped form the Core Council for Gay, Lesbian, Bisexual, and Questioning Students.

The College Republicans are active in grassroots campaigning. A small, informal libertarian group hosted 2008 Libertarian presidential candidate Bob Barr on campus. The

SUGGESTED CORE

1. Classics 10100 01, Ancient Greece and Rome (*closest match*)
2. Philosophy 30301 01, Ancient and Medieval Philosophy
3. Theology 40101 01/40108 01, Introduction to the Old Testament/New Testament Introduction
4. Theology 40201 01, Christian Traditions I
5. Political Science 10600 01, Political Theory
6. English 40226, Essential Shakespeare
7. History 10600, United States History to 1877
8. Philosophy 30303 01, 19th- and 20th-Century Philosophy

College Democrats, however, are reported to be "one of the strongest College Democrat chapters in the country."

The spiritual center of campus, some admit, is not the basilica but the football stadium. As one of many students would say, "The ND football spirit is phenomenal. All the students are guaranteed tickets to all the home games, and the student section remains standing and on fire with spirit throughout the game." Athletics—as well as many other social activities—revolve around the sport, which the school started playing back in 1887. The school gets precious national exposure thanks to an exclusive contract with NBC to carry all its home football games.

Notre Dame competes in NCAA's Division I and captured the 2010 Big East Conference title in women's swimming and diving, women's rowing, women's soccer, women's tennis, and men's indoor and outdoor track and field. There are 13 men's and 13 women's varsity teams, as well as 30 club teams and 57 intramural teams. The school's mascot is the leprechaun.

Campus crime is pretty infrequent. In 2011 the school reported one robbery, five aggravated assaults, 43 burglaries, and five stolen cars. Notre Dame Security Police patrol the campus, and there are emergency call stations as well as free walking escorts at night. Monitored security gates limit car access to campus, and residence halls are locked at all times.

Notre Dame may have started out as a school catering to blue collar immigrant kids, but it isn't cheap today. Tuition for 2012–13 was $42,971, and room and board were $11,934. However, admissions are need blind, and the school pledges to meet accepted students' full need. Over 45 percent of undergraduates received need-based aid, and the average debt of a recent graduate was $20,833.

STRONG SUITS	WEAK POINTS
• General-education requirements in traditional liberal arts are extensive.	• Dissenting Catholics also teach theology; students must choose carefully.
• First Year courses are small and demanding, with significant writing required.	• A push toward research emphasizes publishing over teaching among new hires.
• Most classes are taught by professors, not teaching assistants.	• Many students are mainly interested in preparing for jobs and watching football.
• The Program of Liberal Studies serves as a Great Books option that any ambitious student should take.	• Some departments, especially English, sociology, film, and gender studies, are partly or wholly politicized.
• Excellent programs in philosophy, political science, history, architecture, business, engineering—and many good professors in theology.	• An upswing in gay activism on campus, with some support from the school's administration.

University of Pennsylvania

Philadelphia, Pennsylvania • www.upenn.edu

All about the Benjamins

The University of Pennsylvania was founded by Benjamin Franklin more than 272 years ago to teach both the practical and the theoretical arts. Some insiders worry that pragmatism has largely trumped liberal education at Penn. As one professor puts it, "Three of the four undergraduate divisions, Wharton, Engineering, and Nursing, don't pretend to cultivate the life of the mind but rather aim primarily to prepare one for a career."

While the campus leans far to the left, that doesn't seem to affect classroom behavior as badly as it does at many schools. A good number of faculty express independent views, and the school has been responsive to defenders of political free speech. Still, the weakness of the school's curriculum, the preprofessional spirit that prevails, and the tragicomic episodes of political correctness that have taken place on campus are troubling.

Academic Life: Penn is mightier than the word

Like most elite schools, the University of Pennsylvania has traded a core curriculum for distribution requirements. "The trend has been away from a 'traditional' education," an insider says. Students at the School for Arts and Sciences must now take a course in U.S.

823

VITAL STATISTICS

Religious affiliation: *none*
Total enrollment: 21,329
Total undergraduates:
    10,301
SAT CR/Verbal midrange:
    670–780
SAT Math midrange:
    690–790
ACT midrange: *30–34*
Applicants: *31,218*
Applicants accepted: *12%*
Accepted applicants who
    enrolled: *63%*
Tuition (general/out of
    state): *$43,738*
Tuition (in state): *N/A*
Room and board: *$12,368*
Freshman retention rate:
    97%
Graduation rate: *95%*
Courses with fewer than 20
    students: *72%*
Student-faculty ratio: *6:1*
Courses taught by graduate
    students: *not provided*
Students living on campus:
    65%
Students participating in
    fraternities or sororities:
    25%
Students receiving need-
    based financial aid: *43%*
Avg. student-loan debt of a
    recent graduating class:
    $17,891
Most popular majors:
    *business/marketing, engi-
    neering, social sciences*
Guaranteed housing for 4
    years? *no*

cultural diversity. Diversity courses "focus on race, ethnicity, gender, sexuality, class, and religion," and almost all choices are heavily politicized. Says a campus source: "The university instituted the 'diversity' requirement—in my cynical opinion—to boost enrollments in otherwise unsuccessful 'oppression studies' courses. One has to seek out the more traditional courses, as fewer and fewer are actually required."

Advising, according to students, is somewhat anonymous; one calls it "a joke," saying that professors are unfamiliar with course requirements and, in general, unhelpful. Before declaring a major, underclassmen are assigned premajor advisers (not necessarily faculty members), but after that they are given faculty advisers within their departments. Reports a professor: "Penn is a big university. Some students work very hard and do very well. They become known to the faculty and have plenty of access. But others just drift along." Drifting along is entirely possible, students report, saying that no one would really notice unless a student started failing courses.

Happily, most Penn students have enough intellectual ambition to choose foundational courses on their own. Says a professor, "The students are certainly very engaged and curious. The stronger departments tend to attract the best students." However, he warns, "In order not to lose students, some departments have started to lower grading standards. I have heard that in some classes, TAs cannot give grades below B-." The School of Arts and Sciences (SAS), called on campus "the College," typically attracts 60 percent of some 10,301 undergraduates. Other students are divided among the School of Engineering and Applied Science, the School of Nursing, and the Wharton School for business students. Undergraduates can take classes in any of the four schools. Penn also has 12 graduate and professional schools that annually enroll another 13,057 students.

The serious-minded student will find ample opportunities at Penn. One graduate recommends that students do a senior thesis (which is optional) and that they look into the honors program called the Benjamin Franklin scholars Integrated Studies Program: "These seminars tend to attract the best students and the most talented professors. The classes are very rigorous," he said. Other recommended departments include chemistry, politics, philosophy and economics (PPE), religious studies, and economics. An insider adds, "Based purely on reputation, I think the business school (Wharton) and the joint degree program in Business and International Relations are among the strongest."

Penn has its share of high-profile professors, including seven MacArthur Award recipients, five National Medal of Science recipients, five Nobel Prize winners, and five Pulitzer Prize winners. Stars in their field, as at many other elite colleges, these faculty members are encouraged to value research and publishing over teaching. As one professor says, "The only thing more important than getting published is getting famous." Another insider counters, "Overall, there's a good balance. Students get enough contact with the faculty." One student suggests that "humanities students, by and large, should have no problem getting to know their professors. It's the science and other pre-professional classes that are too large for that."

While students seem to agree that all Penn departments lean at least a little to the left, there are several in which more traditional professors and respect for honest intellectual discourse are present. One source says that "history and classical studies are the strongest programs in the humanities. They have some excellent professors and most faculty members teach at least three courses a year."

All history majors must take a course each in four out of five geographic areas and two courses in history before 1800. This means it would be easy to skip the founding years of U.S. history. Still, says one history major, "the history department at Penn has one of the strongest intellectual history programs. The professors who teach medieval and early modern intellectual history are world class scholars and great pedagogues. . . . It is easy to

CAMPUS POLITICS: YELLOW LIGHT

Nearly every department at Penn has a few politicized courses, but students can sidestep these pretty easily if they wish, says an undergrad: "Most professors avoid politics." However, there are certain departments that contain more politically charged classes—such as English, psychology, sociology, and political science. Says one teacher, "It depends on who the professor is. Many are indeed very critical of both Western and American institutions. Most criticisms are respectful, but others border on the vitriolic. Capitalism receives particularly sharp attacks from most faculty members, in my experience." "On the whole," sums up another professor, "Penn seems rather hostile to the right-of-center."

Penn's president, Amy Gutmann, has taken very public stances in favor of euthanasia, and in 2007 she established the Institute of Regenerative Medicine at UPenn for the promotion of stem cell research, which entails the destruction of embryonic human beings. Penn is known for relative freedom of expression, perhaps thanks to the presence of Professor Alan Charles Kors, who cofounded the Foundation for Individual Rights in Education (FIRE) in response to political correctness he encountered at Penn. Kors has remained a devoted champion of student liberty at UPenn, and the university has generally responded well to FIRE's criticism, even changing certain policies that could infringe on student rights.

Although UPenn's guidelines aren't perfect, the university continues to stress its commitment to intellectual freedom, reaffirming that "the content of student speech or expression is not by itself a basis for disciplinary action."

find good teachers." On the negative side: "Like many departments, history has a fair number of professors who are ideologically driven. They care less about teaching history and more about teaching their political views. In history, it has also become popular to attack the notions of objectivity and of objective truth—a tactic that allows some faculty members to justify their own tendentious and ideologically driven teaching," the student says.

Another student warns, "Based on my personal experience I have found the sociology and the anthropology departments to be very tendentious. The departments are very ideologically driven and have set agendas. The English department has many professors with similar problems."

> For teachers, "the only thing more important than getting published is getting famous."

In English, majors pick among a wide variety of courses, many of them burdened with leftist ideology focused on the unholy trinity of "race, class, and gender." However, the department does require a substantial core for majors, one class in literature before 1660; one in literature from 1640 to 1832; and one in 19th-century literature. Majors could still graduate without having studied Shakespeare, though few probably choose to. The department also requires one diversity class in "difference and diasporas."

Political science is the most popular major in the SAS. Majors must also take at least one course in each of four subfields: American Politics, Comparative Politics, International Relations, and Political Theory.

The list of recommended faculty must begin with Alan Charles Kors, a professor of history who cofounded the admirable Foundation for Individual Rights in Education. Other worthies include Robert A. Kraft in religious studies; Martin Seligman in psychology; John J. DiIulio Jr., and Stephen Gale in political science; Michael Gamer, Al Filreis, and Anne Hall in English; Thomas Childers, Walter A. McDougall, Ann Moyer, Edward Peters, Jonathan Steinberg, Roger Chartier, and Arthur Waldron in history; Gary Hatfield in philosophy; Philippe C. Met in French; and Rita Copeland and Jeremy McInerney in classical studies. In 2006–7, Penn added 40 new professors to its standing faculty of arts and sciences. According to one undergrad, "The new professors tend to get rave reviews from students."

One teacher says, "Conservative opinion is represented, though as anywhere else, the dominant worldview is a rather archaic and romantic liberalism." However, the level of political "intrusion" into the classroom depends on the particular faculty member. Admits one Penn insider, "Obviously, the various minority studies and gender studies departments tend to be hostile to religious and conservative students. There is some debate on campus, but liberal and left-wing opinions tend to be more prevalent and more accepted. The student newspaper used to have a token conservative voice, but they do not even bother to pretend anymore."

Many students point to its dual-degree programs and the school's interdisciplinary majors as the best part of Penn. The school's many study-abroad opportunities also earn praise, and it has one of the highest percentages in the U.S. of students who spend semesters in other countries. The university offers study-abroad programs in almost 50 countries, and every year about 600 students travel internationally to study, research, train, or volunteer. Destinations include Australia, Chile, China, Denmark, Egypt, France, Ghana, Japan, Russia, and just about everywhere in between. Short-term, semester, and yearlong programs are available.

Penn offers a wide variety of languages, including Cantonese, Dutch, French, German, Greek and Latin, Hindi, Italian, Judeo-Spanish, Mandarin, Modern Greek, Old Egyptian, Russian, Sanksrit, Sumerian, and Swahili.

Student Life: Throwing toast to the team

More than 60 percent of Penn's undergraduates live on campus, and those who don't usually stay nearby. Most students live on campus for two or three years, then move to one of the rental houses around campus—which, students say, seem to be owned and managed by a near-monopoly called Campus Apartments. As a result, one student says, "It is very hard to find safe, affordable housing in University City."

Those 6,000 undergraduate students who stay on campus can choose from 11 houses and two high rise towers. Off-campus properties owned by the university include Domus, an eight-story apartment complex, and the Hub, a 10-story, mixed-use apartment and retail building. In the dorms, "gender neutral" housing is now available, allowing roommates of both sexes. Although residents are given the final vote on whether to allow them, coed bathrooms are found in many dormitories.

For recreational activities, Penn has over 200 student groups, half of them academically oriented. Penn is noted for its arts scene, which includes award-winning a cappella groups ranging from the traditional Counterparts to groups like Penn Masala, a Hindi singing group. Of course, the great city of Philadelphia offers countless riches, and getting downtown is "not hard to do at all, and there's tons to do and see down there," says one student.

Cultural groups include everything from the Jewish Heritage Program to Canadians at Penn and the Black Student League. UPenn has a number of environmental groups as well as several political groups like Amnesty International, College Democrats and Republicans, and Penn for Life.

A popular news publication on campus is the *Daily Pennsylvanian*, which receives prestigious national awards on a regular basis. Conservative students should also look into the well-written alternative campus paper, the *Pennsylvania Independent*.

Athletically, Penn has a set of respectable teams. The sports teams are called the Quakers, and their colors are red and blue. UPenn participates in the NCAA's Division I (Division I-FCS for football) and in the Ivy League conference.

SUGGESTED CORE

1. Classical Studies 26/27, Ancient Greece/Ancient Rome
2. Philosophy 003, History of Ancient Philosophy
3. Religious Studies 125/135, Introduction to the Bible (Old Testament)/Introduction to the New Testament
4. Religious Studies 433/434, Christian Thought from 200 to 1000/Christian Thought from 1000 to 1800
5. Political Science 181, Modern Political Thought
6. English 535, Shakespeare
7. History 020, History of the United States to 1865
8. History 343, 19th-Century European Intellectual History

Penn has a large Jewish student population, and cultural activities sponsored by Penn Hillel and other Jewish organizations are frequent. Other faiths are represented by the campus Newman (Catholic) Community and various Protestant, nondenominational Christian, Islamic, and Hindu groups. The real color of Penn is green: "While I have met people from all over the world, of all different nationalities, most people were relatively well off," one student says.

At Penn, "there is a lot of room to express your opinion," says one student. Another agrees that, in general, the atmosphere of Penn is "one of vigorous debate," where both sides are usually given a chance to be heard. Another student characterizes the environment as "very centrist, perhaps slightly rightward leaning." However, some conservative students report that they felt silenced in classes during the most recent presidential election season when their professors made their own political affiliations known.

The Greek system dominates campus events: frat parties are the favorite activity for those too young to hit the bars. Drinking on campus is much more prevalent than drug use. Says one student, "Penn definitely lives up to its reputation as the 'Party Ivy.' . . . Penn is not very serious about stopping underage kids from drinking. All of my RAs have said something to the effect of, 'If you're going to drink, just don't cause any trouble on the hall.'"

Crime is a serious issue in west Philadelphia. In 2011 there were 12 forcible sex offenses, nine robberies, two aggravated assaults, 17 burglaries, one stolen car, and one arson on campus.

With tuition mounting to $43,738 in 2012–13 and room and board costs of $12,368, Penn is pricey. However, some 43 percent of students received need-based aid. Considering the cost of the school, the average debt of a graduating class was a relatively low $17,891.

STRONG SUITS	WEAK POINTS
• Mostly ambitious, hardworking students.	• No core curriculum, and many distribution requirements can be met with politicized courses.
• Many highly qualified, well-known professors.	
• A solid liberal arts education is offered through the Benjamin Franklin Scholars Integrated Studies Program.	• Serious grade inflation, imposed by departments' fear of losing enrollment.
• Excellent course offerings in intellectual history, chemistry, Classics, religious studies, business, international relations, and politics, philosophy, and economics (PPE).	• Faculty under pressure to publish, which can diminish attention to teaching.
	• Politicized departments, including English, sociology, and anthropology—in addition to various "grievance" or ethnic studies majors.
• Worthy dual-degree programs and interdisciplinary majors.	• Significant crime in west Philadelphia, site of the school.

University of Southern California

Los Angeles, California • www.usc.edu

Believing Its Own Press

Founded in 1880, when Los Angeles was a provincial backwater of some 11,000 inhabitants, USC is now big, rich, and intensely preprofessional. USC has a number of truly world-class programs, and it more than adequately prepares its students in these programs to compete in the outside world. Classes are inviting, with 26 students on average, and despite its size, the school offers a true sense of a close-knit community. But, as with all schools, certain parts of USC are stronger than others. In other words: caveat emptor.

Academic Life: Ready for my close-up

Many of USC's strong professional programs are known throughout the world, especially the School of Cinematic Arts—which regularly produces top-flight screenwriters, editors, and directors—the Viterbi School of Engineering, the Thornton School of Music, and the Marshall School of Business. Sure enough, at USC the high achiever will find that the sky is the limit. However, the basement is also an option. As one student says, "You can just slide through one of the easier schools . . . and get no education."

Of the school's pallid distribution requirements, another student says, "I don't know anyone who didn't just consider them a thing that you have to do." In fact, he says, the prevailing attitude toward the requirements is "just get an A and get it over with." Even if students aren't serious about these courses, it seems that USC is; one professor notes that the school has grown stricter about which courses fulfill these mandates. What is more, some of them with offbeat titles are in fact good classes, poorly named—it's a marketing thing. "In many departments and among many faculty, there is an effort to avoid looking traditional or canonical," the professor says. "The titles look like conference titles." However, notes a grad student, "The composition program is highly advanced—a forerunner in the field, a model that many other universities base themselves on. This is incredibly important because learning to express yourself well is one of the best ways to get ahead in the workplace."

Students must complete one class each in "Western Cultures and Traditions," "Global Cultures and Traditions," "Scientific Inquiry," "Science and Its Significance," "Arts and Letters," "Social Issues," and two writing classes: "Critical Reasoning" and the advanced "Writing 340."

In addition to the school's distribution requirements, students face a mandatory diversity requirement—one course selected from a list of many that don't offer much meaningful learning, even for those dedicated to learning about other cultures. For instance, American studies offers a course on "Race and Class in Los Angeles." Such a course should be of interest only to future diversity enforcement officers or civil rights ambulance chasers.

The Honors Core, or "Thematic Option," offered by the College of Letters, Arts, and Sciences, is the best way to complete the school's requirements. "I doubt that there is any Ivy League school that has as tough an academic challenge," says one honors student. According to USC, the honors curriculum "is arranged around four core courses which focus on the history of Western civilization through the close reading of primary literature and philosophical texts." It is heavy on reading and writing, and it focuses on all the right things. Unfortunately, the program admits only 200 students each year, and the typical enrollee has a high school GPA of 4.0 and a 2100 SAT score—which suggests that this program is slightly harder to get into than Harvard.

Another worthy initiative at USC is its Renaissance Scholars award, which is given to select students who combine study in two widely divergent fields—physics and theology, or computer science and poetry, for instance. These scholars compete for a $10,000 award upon graduation "for the purpose of post-baccalaureate study."

While USC students have a reputation of being more conservative than those at most other West Coast schools, there is no denying that both students and faculty with traditional views have experienced problems when it comes to expressing themselves in the classroom. "The politicization of speech in the classroom is clearly confined to certain humanities departments—English, comparative literature, and somewhat in political science and history," says a professor. Some students would add the religion department to that list. "One student says, "I would characterize the Western humanities courses as critically respectful of Western ideals and American institutions, but rarely agreeing with them. Often, I find that these classes acknowledge their presence, but resent them."

Yet another undergrad rues the lack of actual instruction in the Western canon and in American institutions. "The founding fathers would have never known what hit them here. I was the only one in class who had read *The Federalist* and the Constitution, and the Declaration of Independence.... The emphasis here is on 'non-Western traditions.' This is fine, but, there is a decidedly strong bent against learning about the philosophical underpinnings of our laws and government. We need stronger work that honestly addresses our history and traditions and culture respectfully, instead of assigning pejorative terms to dismiss it."

CAMPUS POLITICS: YELLOW LIGHT

"USC is a little more conservative than UCLA or the University of Washington or UC Berkeley," says one student. Another notes that the Unruh Political Student Association "is meant to foster political discussions and events through this student-based group sponsored by the Unruh Institute of Politics. So far, they have encouraged events from both sides politically." According to one student, because of the dynamic Christian religious groups on campus, "a lot of Christians on other campuses look to us and say, 'That's what we want on our campus.'"

Such students might not envy USC's classroom atmosphere, however. One undergrad says, "If a student wishes to discuss religion, and he does not agree with the professor, that student will be made to look like a fool." Another student says, "I think you can see a humanistic, liberal secularism [in] everything on campus." Says one teaching assistant: "As a graduate student who teaches a class and takes English courses, I am by far in the minority in terms of political and religious views. My boss frequently goes on anti–fundamentalist/ evangelical Christian rants in front of the entire department of eight assistant lecturers. No one objects, although the content is quite inflammatory. And the requirement for students to write essays for the 'Academic Community' is often just shorthand for kowtowing to left-leaning ideas."

As one professor notes, "things are uneven" at USC, and "a lot can depend on what faculty you get, and what departments and what courses." A student says, "USC, in a lot of ways, is really school by school." Another student reports, "Unfortunately there is no continuity in teaching ability. Many professors are primarily researchers who are obligated to teach a course every semester, often quite begrudgingly. Very few professors at USC will equip students to be citizens, to be financially wise, to be discerning, or to be good. This simply does not happen. There is no consensus about what constitutes knowledge or what constitutes a noble life."

Even so, an undergraduate can get a good education at USC. According to a student, "I found it transformative on quite a few levels. . . . I was taught to think for myself. I was taught to be critical, even if my colleagues in classes were not. (And many weren't. It was like they worked so hard to get here and all they wanted to do was party and do minimal work.)"

Finding the right professor can help students achieve a real education. Among the outstanding faculty at USC are Gene Bickers in physics and astronomy and vice provost for undergraduate programs; Peggy Kamuf in French and comparative literature; Leo Beal Braudy in English; Paul Wendell Knoll (emeritus) in history; Sharon Anne Lloyd in philosophy; John Ellis Bowlt in Slavic languages and literature; Don Hall in the School of Cinematic Arts; Howard Gillman and Janelle Wong in political science; and Juliet Ann Musso in the Sol Price School of Public Policy. One student says, "The best professor on the USC campus is Dallas Willard in the philosophy department. He has been at USC for over 30 years and is an excellent resource for guidance about what professors and courses to take. He goes out of his way to care for his students in every dimension."

The university also offers opportunities for undergraduates to get involved in both the hard and the social sciences. "The president and the provost have continually pushed faculty" to include undergraduates in research, a professor says. Among other programs, thematic-option students can participate in an annual undergraduate research conference. Undergraduate opportunities abound in the Summer Undergraduate Research Internship Program at the Southern California Earthquake Center.

> A student complains: "Many professors are primarily researchers who are obligated to teach a course every semester, often quite begrudgingly. Very few professors at USC will equip students to be citizens, to be financially wise, to be discerning, or to be good."

USC's music program is excellent. There is a fine program in linguistics, and the Slavic department is well regarded. So is the history department. One professor says, "Learning history is something USC values highly, and the faculty has responded. The intellectual rigor and attention to analysis even in first- or second-year classes is impressive. It forces one to think."

To major in history, a student must complete three survey courses, as well as "Approaches to History," and six upper-division classes. Students must take one course each in Asia and Eurasia, Europe, and North and Latin America or comparative histories; one pre-1300 class, one 1300–1800 class, and one post-1800 class to present; and three of their courses in one area of concentration like "the Middle Ages," "visual and popular culture," or "history and international relations." Apparently, the history of the American Founding and Civil War are not required.

English majors must take the following classes: two pre-1800, one 19th-century, and one American literature class are required, along with three upper-level English classes. Thus they could miss Shakespeare if they aren't careful.

For the political science major, two introductory courses (from "Theory and Practice of American Democracy," "Ideology and Political Conflict," "Comparative Politics," and "Law, Politics and Public Policy") are required. Students must then choose one class each from the fields of American politics, comparative politics, law and public policy, and political thought, as well as two upper-level electives and another elective. The U.S. Constitution and American political philosophy might well slip through the cracks.

USC's School of Cinematic Arts is perhaps the best in the world. As one student says, "I'm twenty-one. Give me $40 million and I could make a feature film better than the one I saw last week in the theater. I realize how well prepared I am." At the very least, the program teaches self-confidence. And where else could you find something called the "Hugh M. Hefner Chair for the Study of American Film"?

> ### SUGGESTED CORE
>
> 1. Classics 325, Ancient Epic
> 2. Philosophy 315, History of Western Philosophy: Ancient Period
> 3. Religion 111g/121g, The World of the Hebrew Bible/The World of the New Testament
> 4. Religion 509, Early and Medieval Religious Thought in the West
> 5. Political Science 371, European Political Thought II or Philosophy 101g, Philosophical Foundations of Modern Western Culture
> 6. English 430, Shakespeare
> 7. History 100gm, The American Experience
> 8. History 420, European Intellectual and Cultural History: The 19th Century, 1790–1870

Class sizes at USC are generally on the small side, typically including fewer than 30 students in upper-division courses. However, students are concerned about the quality of teaching. "Some professors I've had have made me question the tenure program," a student says. "At a university like USC, tenure is mostly based on research and not teaching. Sometimes, unfortunately, it shows." Another student says, "It is vital that you not rely on your academic adviser when choosing courses or professors," because he or she is likely to steer advisees "toward the most popular or most professionally decorated teachers" regardless of teaching ability or course content.

But there is no dearth of excellent professors at USC, and while some courses are larger—especially the lower-level intros—many professors are quite reachable. "They're accessible," says a student. "You can send an e-mail to a professor and get an answer within an hour." A professor say, "The administration tells us to be there for our students."

The university also offers plenty of chances to study abroad: from Cape Town and Taiwan to Chile and Italy, and recommends overseas programs based on major.

Students are required to demonstrate competency in a nation's language before they study abroad if classes in that language are offered by USC. Language options are Arabic, Chinese, French, German, Hebrew, Hindi, Italian, Japanese, Korean, Persian, Portuguese,

Russian, and Spanish. (The school explains that students begin learning other languages like Czech, Modern Greek, or Swahili "upon arrival in the host country.") Although USC offers solid language options, it has no language requirement.

Student Life: Have your people call my people

Student life at USC is a motley assortment of activities, undertaken smack-dab in the heart of Los Angeles, with all its diversions. "It is L.A., you know," a student says. "There are unlimited options." Another student says that those attending USC can try "anything and everything." One student complains, "There isn't too much of a night life around USC. So students with cars flee campus for Westwood, Hollywood, Santa Monica, Pasadena, and Huntington Beach." However, "the campus itself is pretty uninviting for general hanging out," a student says. "It's easy to feel trapped at USC. The campus is essentially a two-square-block island dropped into a horrible area of downtown Los Angeles."

USC sits near the center of U.S. popular culture—Hollywood—so students can expect to be exposed both on and off campus to the whole panoply of postmodern weirdness. On campus, there are more than 750 student organizations catering to nearly every interest. Students recommend Troy Camp and Spirits in Action, two of USC's prominent philanthropic organizations. More than 400 academic groups include Chicanos for Progressive Education, Theatre Forum, and Critical League Studies Association.

USC hosts a Russian Trojans club, ALIVE, Jewish Alliance for GLBTs and Straights, among a few hundred others. Political groups include the Student Coalition against Labor Exploitation, SC Students for Israel, UNICEF, and Creating Just Communities, as well as College Democrats and College Republicans. USC is also home to several law organizations among the 38 registered political groups on campus.

The school is known for having an extremely active contingent of religious groups, from the Hillel Center for Jewish Life at USC, Alliance for Inquiry and Reason, and Seventh-Day Adventist Chinese Student Community to the Sikh Student Association and the Catholic Student Association. The campus hosts multiple "Places for Reflection and Worship," like the Little Chapel of Silence; the Fishbowl multifaith chapel; the Reverend Thomas Kilgore Jr. Chapel of the Cross ecumenical Christian space; the Muslim Prayer Space; and the United University Church, which is a progressive Christian congregation. Currently, Hindu devotee and religion scholar Varun Soni acts as the dean of religious life.

Despite being broadly available, not all the chaplaincies on campus have a record of orthodoxy, so students might prefer to seek houses of worship off campus. There are plenty of options.

Athletics play a big role in campus life. USC's principal rival—hated crosstown foe UCLA—is always a welcome target for Trojan partisans. "Even if you are not a major sports fan, it's hard to avoid being pulled into Trojan pride and whipping out your victory sign when USC beats UCLA or Notre Dame," a student says. Things can get ugly: two football fans were stabbed as they tailgated before the USC-UCLA football game in December 2010. Police officers reported that the brawl involved some 40 to 50 people and included assaults on two officers who attempted to calm the situation.

USC also has a well-entrenched Greek system, with 60 recognized Greek organizations on campus. Greek life is mostly confined to Fraternity Row along 28th Street, just north of campus. "The Row is generally open only to people in the Greek system," says a student. "They only very infrequently have open parties to which everyone is invited." Getting into fraternity parties is easy for pretty girls, students report, but nearly impossible for non-Greek men. Another student calls it "a world unto itself," but he also notes that it does carry weight around the college: "The Greek system is huge at USC."

Non-Greek housing at USC is primarily coeducational, although men and women are assigned to different wings or floors of certain buildings and bathrooms are single sex. Ten residence halls are primarily for freshmen, who make up the vast majority of the dorm population, although many of USC's school-run apartments are also set aside for first-year students. Students say rooms are sometimes hard to come by. "There are some nice dorms on campus, and none of them are infested or particularly dirty," a student says.

"Diversity" at USC seems to involve less the mixing of cultures than their self-segregation, says one student: "Unfortunately the Koreans all hang out with other Koreans and the African Americans all hang out with other African Americans. There is no USC community—there are tiny communities that often fail to interact."

Students differ on the impact of crime on campus, though many point nervously to the dangerous surrounding neighborhood, known for homelessness and gang activity. In 2011 the school reported seven forcible sex offenses, five robberies, one aggravated assault, 50 burglaries, one motor vehicle theft, and two incidences of arson on campus. "I feel very safe on campus, even at night, because we have a good Department of Public Safety here," a female student says. However, another considers "the area outside USC to be incredibly dangerous" and states that "all Metro buses are to be avoided, especially as a female." Says one student, "Let me be unequivocally clear: the surrounding area of the school is extremely dangerous. Muggings, hit-and-runs, and knifings are common in the blocks surrounding our area."

One thing many students have in common is money—a lot of it. The 2012–13 tuition was $44,463, and room and board $12,440. However, admissions are need blind, and the school commits to meet the full need of any student who enrolls. One needy student says that USC "has one of the best financial-aid programs in the country." Some 42 percent of students got need-based aid, and the average loan debt of a recent grad was $30,217.

STRONG SUITS	WEAK POINTS
• World-class programs in cinema, engineering, music, and business. Good departments in history, linguistics, and Slavic languages.	• Lax general-education requirements.
	• Slack mandates for majors in political science, English, and history.
• A selective honors program that's as good as any in the Ivy League.	• Politicized courses predominate in several humanities disciplines.
• Highly qualified faculty.	• A party atmosphere catches up too many students.
• Extensive research opportunities.	• Serious crime in nearby neighborhoods.

University of the South

Sewanee, Tennessee • www.sewanee.edu

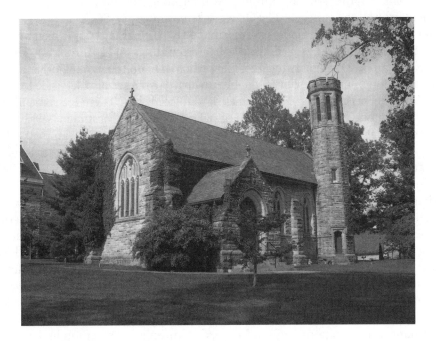

Mind of the South

The University of the South, commonly called Sewanee, is unique. The Domain (as the campus is called) is adorned with beautiful buildings and 13,000 acres of forest and fields. Refounded after the Civil War in 1868 with nine students and four professors, Sewanee became a seat of learning and maturation for generations of southerners. If it can avoid shedding its traditions to placate the insatiable devotees of multiculturalism, Sewanee will remain in the best sense a university of the South.

Academic Life: Tradition by popular demand

"The approach to education here is intellectual, not mechanical," says a professor in the sciences. "Some students think about the practical so little that they're scrambling for jobs the last semester they're here."

The school requires an introductory "English 101" composition class and one course designated as "writing intensive," with a second "writing intensive" course to be completed in the student's major. The best option on campus is the Interdisciplinary Humanities track. The four chronologically arranged courses begin with "Tradition and Criticism in

Western Culture: The Ancient World" and continues with courses in the medieval and early modern periods, then "The Modern World, Romantic to Postmodern."

Despite its small size, Sewanee has educational opportunities across the curriculum, even in its smallest departments. The philosophy department has just four faculty members and one visiting professor, yet it offers a major and a minor.

The English department—the most popular major on campus—has been home over the years to many literary figures of national note, including William Alexander Percy, Andrew Lytle, Allen Tate, and Caroline Gordon. Home to the nation's oldest and most prestigious literary quarterly, the *Sewanee Review,* the English department is traditional in focus. Its requirements are excellent, including two Shakespeare courses and at least two courses in English literature before 1750.

The history major has taken a laxer turn in recent years. Formerly required to declare a concentration, as of 2012 history majors now work with a faculty adviser to "devise a program that best suits the student's interests." They are still, however, required to take at least one course each on the period before 1700, the period after 1700, and on an area outside Europe and the United States.

The political science department is excellent, although its courses have also been watered down. All majors were formerly required to study American political philosophy and the U.S. Constitution. Now they are only required to take classes in American politics, political theory, comparative politics, and world politics.

The environmental studies program, which offers four majors (environmental policy, ecology and biodiversity, natural resources and the environment, and environmental chemistry) and a certificate in watershed science, is also said to be excellent; the university's immense land holdings are an asset to the program.

One freshman says, "Among my friends there is a general feeling of being overworked. Sewanee prides itself on preventing grade inflation." In the past few years, however, some lowering of standards has been alleged. The school now offers minors in women's studies and gender studies, and other majors are changing for the worse, too. "New faculty members are often allowed to

VITAL STATISTICS

Religious affiliation: *Protestant (Episcopal)*
Total enrollment: *1,507*
Total undergraduates: *1,469*
SAT CR/Verbal midrange:
580–680
SAT Math midrange:
560–650
ACT midrange: *25–30*
Applicants: *2,920*
Applicants accepted: *61%*
Accepted applicants who
enrolled: *24%*
Tuition (general/out of
state): *$34,442*
Tuition (in state): *N/A*
Room and board: *$9,916*
Freshman retention rate:
91.5%
Graduation rate (4 yrs.):
78.3%
Graduation rate (6 yrs.):
83.2%
Courses with fewer than 20
students: *69%*
Student-faculty ratio: *10:1*
Courses taught by graduate
students: *not provided*
Students living on campus:
95%
Students in fraternities: *41%*
Students in sororities: *40%*
Students receiving need-
based financial aid: *42%*
Avg. student-loan debt of a
recent graduating class
$23,721
Most popular majors:
*English, social sciences,
psychology*
Guaranteed housing for 4
years? *yes*

CAMPUS POLITICS: GREEN LIGHT

"Sewanee's students are for the most part rich kids from traditional, conservative, southern families," says a faculty member. "That's just the nature of the place." Generally, students are "moderately right leaning," says a student. "There tends to be a strong majority of students who favor conservative social positions. . . . However, there is a large minority of center-left students as well." Many of the student political groups are issue-focused rather than partisan, although there are both College Republicans and College Democrats on campus. Both conservative and liberal students generally feel comfortable voicing their views. According to another undergrad, "School officials encourage debates, but they are not well attended, with the majority of students being conservative, and the debates more often focused around liberal-leaning topics."

Sewanee is that rare thing, an Episcopalian college. So its mores are dictated by the debates within the divided Anglican Communion. In 2012 the campus chaplaincy announced that it would perform same-sex "marriages" in the college chapel.

teach courses that they create, and the coherence of many majors in the humanities has been lost or severely damaged," a professor says. "There is no sense among the younger faculty of what a major should consist of, and the older members of the faculty seem willing to let the young have their way. Sewanee is experiencing ten years late what other liberal arts colleges have experienced."

Most students still report positive experiences at the school. As one student tells us, "I have had great experiences in many areas of study. One of the best was the independent study that was created for seven students who wanted to study biblical Greek. It opened a whole other reading of the New Testament for everyone in that class."

Academic fetishes like "multiculturalism" and "diversity," says one professor, "are seldom heard and affect the curriculum in minor ways if at all. Most efforts to import cultural diversity actually originate with the students involved in a handful of extracurricular groups." But another faculty member disagrees, insisting that "the ideas behind the words are having an impact."

"Our liberal arts curriculum is still strongly oriented toward the cultural legacy of Europe and toward canonical texts in most disciplines," a professor insists. "This is a campus where the most popular major is English and where the two most popular classes in that major are Shakespeare and Chaucer." According to one student, "The strongest points of the English major are the emphasis on writing and scholarly knowledge over a wide base of literature. The weakest point would be the lack of direction provided to students about what to do with their knowledge after graduation."

One professor says, "We see students outside the classroom all the time. Interaction with students is not only common; it's expected." Another professor says that Sewanee has "enough serious students who are grateful for the leisure to study to make teaching here rewarding." Freshmen are assigned faculty advisers by dormitory, so small groups of hallmates normally share both faculty advisers and an upperclassman proctor. After the first year, students are welcome to choose a faculty adviser and to change advisers at any time.

One undergrad says, "Student-professor relationships are one of the best things about

Sewanee. . . . It's not unusual to meet a professor at the local coffee shop just for a talk, or to have dinner in his home with a couple of other students, or to run into him at the basketball game, or to babysit his kids. All classes are taught by professors, never graduate students. I definitely consider a couple of professors my mentors." Another undergrad agrees: "It is hard to single out just one professor because they have all been helpful in any way possible. They love the students—and that is why they are here."

Students recommend among teachers John Palisano in biology; Donald Potter in forestry and geology; Harold Goldberg, Charles Perry, Woody Register, and Susan Ridyard in history; James Peters in philosophy; Gayle McKeen in political science; Timothy Keith-Lucas in psychology; Gerald Smith in religion; and Thomas Carlson, Pamela Macfie, Wyatt Prunty, and Dale Richardson in English.

Sewanee teachers are said to be more politically liberal than students, but not across the board. While most faculty members are genuinely fair-minded, one instructor is known to penalize a grade if a student refuses to use neutered, feminist English. "I'm not sure that any Sewanee department is 'politicized' in that it is dominated by an intolerant leftist agenda," says a faculty member. But much is in transition; many of the more traditional senior teachers are retiring. One faculty member says, "A great deal could change very quickly after that, and I might be giving very different answers. . . . But for now, Sewanee is a good and valuable place."

"**O**ur liberal arts curriculum is still strongly oriented toward the cultural legacy of Europe and toward canonical texts in most disciplines," a professor says.

One student says, "My experience has been that Sewanee is truly a community. Instead of political correctness, there is concern for people; diversity is accepted because people are accepted as they are. The general attitude toward different opinions (political, religious, or otherwise) in the classroom is that any position is welcome as long as it is well thought out, and pretty much any germane discussion is welcome as long as it is respectful." Adds another, "Most of my classes stay away from politics. It enters in where necessary, such as in political science, economics, et cetera. However, there are some places where politics would not be expected, but are present, such as education courses and biology."

The university offers opportunities for study abroad through its own programs and through partnerships with other colleges and universities. Students enrolled in the European studies program choose one of two study options, "Ancient Greece and Rome: The Foundations of Western Civilization" or "Western Europe in the Middle Ages and the Renaissance," and spend three weeks at Sewanee before heading overseas to York or Durham and six weeks at Oxford, followed by five weeks of travel on the Continent and in London.

Students in all majors are required to reach the intermediate, fourth-semester level in a foreign language. Sewanee offers majors in Chinese, French, German, Greek and Latin, Italian, Japanese, and Russian.

SUGGESTED CORE

1. Classics 351/353, Greek/ Latin Literature in Translation
2. Philosophy 203, Ancient Philosophy from Homer to Augustine
3. Religion 141/142/143, Introduction to the Bible/ Introduction to the Bible I (Old Testament)/Introduction to the Bible II (New Testament)
4. Religion 321, Christian Theological Paths
5. Political Science 302, Recent Political Theory
6. English 357/358, Shakespeare I/II
7. History 201, History of the United States I
8. Humanities 202, Tradition and Criticism in Western Culture: The Modern World, Romantic to Postmodern

Student Life: Masters of their Domain

Perched on a flat-topped mountain, Sewanee is a good distance from any urban center. Still, "there are a lot of options if you need to get 'off the Mountain' for a day or a weekend," says a student.

The school provides so many extracurricular options that four years isn't enough to sample them all. "The joie de vivre is remarkably similar to what I remember" from a generation ago, says one alumnus. "So many events are scheduled during the weekends that we are not likely to become a suitcase college," a professor says. In fact, another professor says the residential-life office faces problems each Christmas and spring break in getting students out of their dorms. "And many of the students do anything they can think of to remain on campus during the summer," she says.

For politically minded students, Sewanee is home to College Republicans, College Democrats, and College Libertarians, as well as a Model UN group. The school has three student-run publications: the *Cap and Gown*, the annual publication of the student body recounting the year's activities; the *Mountain Goat*, a literary magazine published once a semester; and the *Sewanee Purple*, a bimonthly student newspaper.

Greek life is very popular with 60 percent of students counting themselves as members. The 12 fraternity and nine sorority houses are on campus, and most parties are open to nonmembers. "There is a strong frat scene, and little else," says one student. "However, there is very little pressure on those who do not want to drink. Many people participate in the social scene and do not drink." Of course, for those who do, help is at hand: "BACCHUS is an organization that encourages responsible drinking behavior within the campus community by providing safe rides on campus," the school reports. "The Greek system is very large at Sewanee, but all the parties are 'open'; you don't have to belong to the fraternity or sorority to go to the party and to be welcomed," a student says.

Sewanee fields 11 men's and 12 women's NCAA III varsity sports teams and hosts the men's and women's intercollegiate club sports of canoeing, lightweight crew, and rugby. Students also participate in the intramural sports of climbing, cycling, martial arts, and fencing, among others. The university also has an equestrian center that offers a riding program for all experience levels and for which students can earn Physical Education credit.

Ninety-six percent of students reside on campus, with only a limited number of seniors allowed off campus. The university mostly offers coed living spaces but retains four single-sex dormitories, two men's and two women's, and has a policy that roommates may be neither of the opposite sex nor same-sex partners. Most dorms are arranged in suites with a common bathroom for every one or two students. Emery Hall, once a morgue and recently converted to a women's dormitory, is now a "starting place" for "'theme' housing," the latest trend in universities.

"The life of Sewanee revolves around the dorms," reports an undergrad. "All students gather in them, study in them, live, work, play in them. The student aides, called 'proctors' and 'assistant proctors,' are dedicated to their dorms and want them to be the best places to both play and work, and they strive to make sure that their dorm maintains a great reputation during their time as proctors. Visitation ends at midnight during the week and at 1:00 a.m. on the weekends. Depending on the specific dorm, this may or may not be strictly enforced. Many dorms are not single sex, but they divide the sexes by floor."

Although the school is officially Episcopalian, other faiths are supported. Baptist Collegiate Ministries and the Sewanee Catholic Community are active student groups, as are Fellowship of Christian Athletes and the Presbyterian Campus Ministry. As the school is owned by the Episcopal Church, "there is a heavy influence of that denomination, and students are presumed to have a working knowledge of the Bible, especially when used in class to explain allusions, et cetera. There is no pressure placed on the students, however, and all students are encouraged to worship if and how they choose," observes one student.

Crime is remarkably low. In 2011 the school reported three forcible sex offenses, one arson, and 33 burglaries on campus. Says one student, "Crime is of very little concern. If there is any criminal activity, the police send out an e-mail warning students, and then (normally) thefts cease quickly. Many doors remain unlocked."

Tuition in 2012–13 was $34,442, and room and board $9,916. Some 40 percent of students received need-based financial aid, and the average student-loan debt of a recent grad was $23,721.

STRONG SUITS	WEAK POINTS
• The Interdisciplinary Humanities track offers a traditional liberal arts education.	• Younger faculty more caught up in academic trends, while many traditionalists are retiring.
• Excellent programs in English, political science, environmental studies.	• Some departments, such as philosophy, are very small—with few faculty choices.
• Courses are all taught by professors, not graduate students.	• New, politicized programs such as gender studies may be setting a trend.
• Small classes, which form close mentoring relationships with faculty.	• The campus is isolated, and there are few off-campus options.
• Magnificent campus, with comparatively wholesome dorm policies.	

Vanderbilt University

Nashville, Tennessee • www.vanderbilt.edu

Putting on a Yankee Hat

Originally endowed by a New York rail tycoon, Cornelius Vanderbilt, after the Civil War, Vanderbilt University produces many leaders in business and academia and has a higher national profile than most southern schools. In all, two alumni and three faculty members have been awarded Nobels, and Vanderbilt has bragging rights as the alma mater of more than two dozen Rhodes scholars and two vice presidents of the United States.

Unfortunately, the school has done much to shed its southern heritage and weaken the emphasis on Western civilization in its liberal arts curriculum. Worried faculty and students see the school remaking itself on the model of northeastern academies, thereby losing what made it distinctive.

Academic Life: Goodbye, Great Books

In the absence of a liberal arts core curriculum, students in Vanderbilt's College of Liberal Arts and Sciences must fulfill a set of broad distribution requirements. An admissions officer explains that the Vanderbilt curriculum aims to teach students "life skills"—that is, competency in areas like quantitative reasoning, "problem solving," and communication. "Majors don't decide what you do," the admissions officer says.

For the writing requirement, students must demonstrate "basic competency in English composition" through SAT or test scores or by taking a basic class, English 100. Beyond that, students must take at least three writing-intensive courses. Students must also complete three classes in the humanities or arts and three classes in international cultures, which can range from foreign language classes to international music or literature courses. Additionally, Vanderbilt students take a class in the "history and culture of the United States," three mathematics and natural science classes (one of which requires a lab component), two social science classes, and a "perspectives" class that gives "significant attention to individual and cultural diversity, multicultural interactions, sexual orientation, gender, racial, ethical, religious, and 'Science and Society' issues."

A history major says that some students view distribution requirements as a chore, a hurdle to jump before reaching the real goal—one's major. But another student says, "If you graduate from Vanderbilt with a degree from Arts and Sciences (perhaps excluding women's studies), you will have a great deal of knowledge and be prepared to enter the workforce."

The gen-ed requirements allow for so much flexibility that core areas of knowledge—American history, ancient philosophy, European intellectual history, and the like—can easily be avoided. Students could knock off their U.S. history and culture requirement with courses like "Women, Health and Sexuality" or "Rhetoric of the Mass Media." One economics major says, "My course load is quite rigorous by choice, but you could create an easy schedule for yourself with a little research."

Vanderbilt has eliminated its dedicated humanities department, along with courses it used to offer, such as "Great Books of the Western Tradition." What humanities courses remain have been absorbed by the religious studies department. The best alternative still at Vanderbilt covering the Western tradition appears to be the European studies major.

The school has also implemented a new history curriculum, which now offers such gems as "Sexuality and Gender in China." To major in history, students must take five

VITAL STATISTICS

Religious affiliation: *none*
Total enrollment: *12,836*
Total undergraduates: *6,817*
SAT CR/Verbal midrange: *670–770*
SAT Math midrange: *710–790*
ACT midrange: *32–34*
Applicants: *28,348*
Applicants accepted: *16%*
Accepted applicants who enrolled: *41%*
Tuition (general/out of state): *$42,118*
Tuition (in state): *N/A*
Room and board: *$13,818*
Freshman retention rate: *97%*
Graduation rate (4 yrs.): *87%*
Graduation rate (6 yrs.): *92%*
Courses with fewer than 20 students: *62%*
Student-faculty ratio: *8:1*
Courses taught by graduate students: *5%*
Students living on campus: *86%*
Students in fraternities: *35%*
Students in sororities: *50%*
Students receiving need-based financial aid: *47%*
Avg. student-loan debt of a recent graduating class: *$18,543*
Most popular majors: *engineering, interdisciplinary studies, social sciences*
Guaranteed housing for 4 years? *yes*

CAMPUS POLITICS: RED LIGHT

The Vanderbilt administration wants high national rankings, and so recent years have seen the university attempt to conform more closely to the academic establishment. This has meant more courses with obvious political agendas and increased funding for "diversity" programming, liberal speakers, and leftist campus groups. In 2011 pro-life groups protested Vanderbilt's policy of requiring nursing students to take part in abortions, but to no avail.

In 2012 *Religion Today* reported that Vanderbilt is applying its nondiscrimination policy to Christian groups on campus—allowing nonbelievers to join and even seek to run those groups. Four campus Christian clubs were targeted by the university: the Christian Legal Society, the Fellowship of Christian Athletes, Beta Upsilon Chi, and the Graduate Student Fellowship. One other group that expects to run afoul of the policy is the widely known InterVarsity Christian Fellowship—but it could have an impact on groups of every denomination.

But Vanderbilt isn't hard on every religion. It supported Awadh Binhazim, chaplain to Muslim students, when in a public forum in 2010 he affirmed the position of Islamic law that demands execution of homosexuals. Binhazim claimed, "I don't have a choice as a Muslim to accept or reject teachings." Vanderbilt said that the "university is dedicated to the free exchange of ideas. It is the belief of the university community that free discussion of ideas can lead to resolution and reconciliation."

Should gay non-Muslims try to take over Binhazim's Muslim group, it is unclear how Vanderbilt administrators would react. Their heads might simply explode.

classes in a concentration like Asian, global and transnational, comparative, or European history. They must also complete a history workshop or junior seminar, one or two capstone courses, and two to four electives. Students may also elect to concentrate in economics and history or English and history, which provide unique interdisciplinary paths. They could easily skip all study of the American Founding or Western civilization.

The English student at Vanderbilt must choose to concentrate in literary studies, creative writing, or specialized critical studies. Literature majors must first take an introductory class in poetry, literary criticism, or literature and cultural analysis, followed by three classes in pre-1800 literature and one class in "ethnic or non-Western literature." Additionally, students must complete five electives. While the department offers a variety of classes, it fails to acknowledge any kind of literary canon—or require the study of Shakespeare.

One of Vanderbilt's best departments is philosophy, which emphasizes American philosophy, Continental philosophy, and the history of philosophy. Philosophy majors at Vanderbilt are required to take a course in logic, one in ethics, and at least six hours in the history of philosophy. John Lachs, a distinguished scholar of American philosophy, teaches an interdisciplinary course (together with a historian and an economist) covering the history of the idea of liberty.

In contrast, students view the political science department as having a few good scholars but still suffering from the lingering effects of a war between proponents of a heavily statistical approach and those who favor qualitative and theoretical methods. The political science major calls for two introductory courses, choosing from American government, comparative politics, international politics, and political theory. Students must complete an intermediate-level class each in political theory, comparative politics, international politics, and American government and politics, as well as four electives.

Vanderbilt's women and gender studies department was recently absorbed into the department of sociology. But never fear: such courses as "Women's Rights and Women's Wrongs" will still be offered, as will "Gender and Sexuality: Feminist Approaches" and other recondite topics viewed through the lens of toxic ideology.

The Margaret Cuninggim Women's Center presents lectures and conferences such as "Gender and Sexuality" sponsored by the Warren Center for the Humanities. Other featured cocurricular programs include studies and activism about sexual health, body image, domestic violence, and brown bag lecture series like "Genderism: Transgender Students, Binary Systems, and Higher Education."

Vanderbilt's religious studies department offers a wide array of traditional-sounding courses such as "Themes in the New Testament" and "Christianity in China." These come alongside "Ethics and Ecology" and "Marriage in the Ancient Near East and the Hebrew Bible," which ponders the "institution" of marriage (their quotes) to "shed light" on and "reveal its complexities."

> Says a student: "My favorite aspect of Vandy is all the opportunities I have to be involved in the extras—like music and athletics."

Vanderbilt's best professors include the aforementioned John Lachs in philosophy; Michael D. Bess, David L. Carlton, and Joel F. Harrington in history; Camilla Persson Benbow in psychology; Roy Gottfried, Mark Jarman, and John Plummer in English; Robert W. Pitz and Greg Walker in mechanical engineering; Lori A. Troxel in civil engineering; Douglas P. Hardin in mathematics; Stephen Buckles and John Vrooman in economics; David A. Weintraub in physics and astronomy; Professor Emeritus Robert Innes in human and organizational development; Susan Kevra in French; and Carol Swain in political science.

Vanderbilt still places a good deal of emphasis on close relationships between professors and students. Students are very likely to know at least one of their professors from their freshman seminars, which are limited to 15 students and mostly taught by senior faculty members. "In my experience, the professors are quite approachable," says a student, "I've eaten dinner at the homes of some professors. They give advice if you ask for it, and nine times out of ten, the professors are quite understanding and helpful to students."

On the other hand, other students have complained that "some classes are so big, it's hard to get help when you need it." Professors, not graduate teaching assistants, teach 95 percent of undergraduate courses. Graduate students usually lead the weekly discussion sections attached to large lecture courses and grade most tests and papers.

The formal advising program is weak. Each entering freshman is assigned a faculty adviser who is supposed to help him choose courses and, eventually, a major. Once the student has declared a major, he is assigned to a faculty member within that

SUGGESTED CORE

1. Classics 130/146, Greek Civilization/Roman Civilization (*closest matches*)
2. Philosophy 210, Ancient Philosophy
3. Religious Studies 108/109, Themes in the Hebrew Bible/New Testament
4. Religion 140, Great Books of Literature and Religion
5. Political Science 203, History of Modern Political Philosophy
6. English 209a/209b/210, Shakespeare I/Shakespeare II/ Shakespeare: Representative Selections
7. History 139/140, America to 1776: Discovery to Revolution/U.S. 1776–1877
8. Philosophy 228, 19th-Century Philosophy

field. Unfortunately, many students do not meet with their advisers as often as they should—though they are now required to do so before they can register.

As for the courses themselves, a junior says, "My favorite aspect of Vandy is all the opportunities I have to be involved in the extras—like music and athletics—along with my classes. I can do well in my classes and still participate." Another agrees: "The course load here is not so rigorous that students can't find time for extracurriculars and socializing, but succeeding here does take work. The administration pressures departments to avoid the grade inflation that occurs at other schools." But one engineering student complains that "liberal arts majors don't have anywhere near the workload carried by engineers or premed students." (He shouldn't worry; they likely won't earn the same salaries either.)

Vanderbilt encourages students to study abroad, providing month-, summer-, semester-, and yearlong programs in 26 countries. Students may study in Chile, China, the Dominican Republic, Hungary, New Zealand, Russia, South Africa, and Spain, among other countries. Just under a third of students choose to study abroad in 100 preapproved programs.

Embarrassingly, there is no foreign language requirement, but interested students can take courses in French, German, Greek and Latin, Italian, Japanese, Portuguese, Russian, and Spanish.

Student Life: A night at the opry

Nashville is an entertainment paradise, at least for country music fans, but once outside of Nashville, students must drive a ways to get anywhere. Memphis is three hours to the west, and the Great Smoky Mountains are four hours to the east.

Vanderbilt guarantees students housing for four years and requires all unmarried students to live on campus unless they live with their parents or guardians. Students live in any of 29 residence halls, which include singles, doubles, efficiency apartments, one- or two-bedroom apartments, suites for six, and lodges that hold 10 students. A tour guide claims that in recent years there hasn't been enough interest among students in single-sex dorms for the university to create any new ones, but many of the newer residences have single-sex floors. There are some coed dorm rooms and bathrooms.

Dorm life at Vanderbilt is comfortable, as many students enjoy such amenities as music practice rooms, laundry facilities, study rooms, 24-hour convenience stores, and common social areas. Freshmen live apart from upperclassmen.

Many students say that campus life revolves around the Greek system; there are 16 sorority houses and 20 fraternity houses, and over 42 percent of men and half of women join. Not long ago an article in *Seventeen* portrayed Vanderbilt as having a student body composed of materialistic rich kids. Lately, as the university has tried to bring in a more diverse student body, some faculty leftists have attacked the Greek system as a bastion of elitism. One senior says that the typical Vanderbilt student is "wealthy, conservative, attractive, well-dressed, drives a BMW, and is Greek." (No wonder their teachers are appalled.) A student complains that "Vanderbilt is a very hierarchically based institution, and people who are not comfortable displaying their wealth and size-two figures should go someplace else."

The Black Graduates' Recognition Ceremony, held the day before the university commencement, "is designed to honor all black graduating students." Similar attempts are made to help Asian and other minority students feel at home through groups like the Korean Undergraduate Student Association, Turkish Student Association, and the Masala-SACE (South Asian Cultural Exchange). Perhaps more might be done to accommodate "majority" students from less affluent backgrounds.

For the politically minded student, clubs like Dores for Israel, Amnesty International, and College Republicans are available. The Vanderbilt *Torch* is a student periodical published by conservatives and libertarians on campus. A variety of special interest groups like the Alternative Energy Club, Law and Business Society, Chess Club, Model United Nations, Toastmasters, Fashion for a Cause, and American Constitution Society all provide extracurricular outlets for students.

A number of spiritual and religious groups further enrich student life. The university supports chaplains for Muslims, Catholics, the Reformed University Fellowship, Jews (Hillel and Chabad), United Methodists, Presbyterians, and Episcopalians. All these religions have associated student groups, as do various other Protestant organizations.

As a member of the Southeastern Conference, the Vanderbilt Commodores compete against such football powerhouses as Florida, Auburn, and Georgia. The school maintains membership in the conference even while retaining strict educational requirements for its players—a policy that doesn't always translate into the most successful team. However, in 2008, Vandy enjoyed a winning season and played a bowl game—the Music City Bowl—for the first time in 53 years. The basketball team is competitive, and intercollegiate club sports and intramural sports are also popular with students. Club sports range from cycling and field hockey to triathlons and jiu-jitsu.

Crime is becoming a concern. On-campus crime in 2011 included 11 forcible sex offenses, two robberies, 19 burglaries, three motor vehicle thefts, and one case of arson.

Vanderbilt is expensive, with 2012–13 tuition at $42,118. Room and board added $13,818. Vanderbilt pledges to meet all demonstrated need with institutional grants, scholarships, and work-study projects (rather than loans), and 47 percent of students received an average of $39,892 in need-based financial aid. Vanderbilt works to reduce the financial burden on students and families, and the typical student graduated with a relatively modest $18,543 in debt.

STRONG SUITS

- Solid, mostly traditional programs in philosophy, religion, and political science.
- Freshman seminars are taught by senior faculty, allowing students to form working relationships with them.
- The administration has taken serious steps to fight grade inflation.
- A varied social environment, with abundant religious groups and a politically diverse student body.

WEAK POINTS

- Weak curriculum for general education and shaky major requirements in key fields such as English and history.
- No humanities or Great Books option. To learn Western civilization, students must be savvy enough to take European studies.
- Some courses are huge, and much of the grading is done by graduate teaching assistants.
- Advising is said to be weak and not much used by students.
- Students of limited means complain of class consciousness and snobbery.

So You're Looking For

A Good Education at a Large University

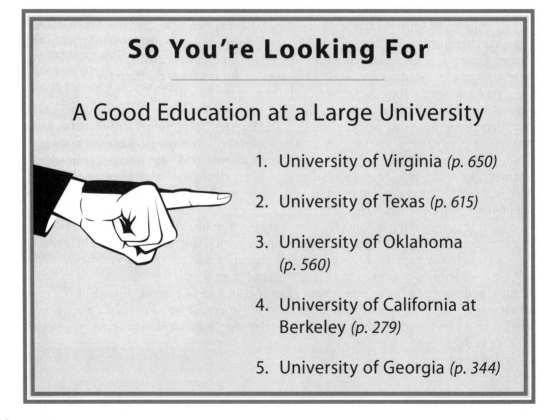

1. University of Virginia *(p. 650)*

2. University of Texas *(p. 615)*

3. University of Oklahoma *(p. 560)*

4. University of California at Berkeley *(p. 279)*

5. University of Georgia *(p. 344)*

Vassar College

Poughkeepsie, New York • www.vassar.edu

Challenge the Status Quo

Vassar College opened in 1865 to offer women an education equal to that available to men at Yale and Harvard. Though Vassar is now coed, it still retains the self-styled "progressive spirit" that animated its founding. It claims a mission based on "toleration and respect for diversity," a "commitment to social justice," and "a willingness to challenge the status quo." One liberal student characterizes Vassar as "liberal without doubt." Students and faculty at Vassar who are skeptical of "progressive" dogmas tend to keep a pretty low profile.

Academic Life: Our advice is . . . get advice

Vassar does little to ensure that students actually receive a true liberal arts education. Vassar's curriculum is quite unstructured, giving students virtually free rein to overspecialize or dabble aimlessly. A professor comments, "There's no core, really no distribution requirements, so it is up to the adviser to give good advice and for the student ultimately to create his own program. But if you don't want to take a literature course, you don't have to."

Finding what is most useful at Vassar could be difficult, but advising at the school is said to be strong. Entering students are assigned premajor faculty advisers. Once they

Vassar College

declare majors, they are assigned to faculty members in their own departments. The dean of freshmen oversees the premajor advising program and new student orientation. In 2010 the school established an online peer-advising network, connecting freshmen to upperclassmen before they declare a major. Students must consult with their advisers before registering.

Requirements kick in when students start work within their majors. Students majoring in history, for instance, must take 11 courses in that discipline, including at least one in each of four areas: European history; American history; and two courses each in pre-1800 history (courses such as "Renaissance Europe," "From Tyranny to Terror: The Old Regime and the French Revolution," or "Colonial America"); and Asian, African, Middle Eastern, or Latin American studies. Finally, history majors complete a senior thesis. No study of the American Founding or Civil War is required of majors.

According to a professor, political science is "a large department—about fourteen professors." The teaching is solid, and there are "courses on almost all areas of the world." Yet there is a "lack of ancient and medieval political theory courses. Generally (and as with many Vassar departments), the courses do not so much survey the field as focus on important aspects of the topic." Political science majors must take 10 courses, including one in each of four major fields of study: American politics, comparative politics, political theory, and international relations. The political theory requirement is an uncommon one and a definite strength. Students need not necessarily study the U.S. Constitution, although most probably do.

The English major was recently bulked up—without really adding much beef. Students who enter Vassar now need 12 English classes to complete the major, at least four of which must be at the 300 level. In their senior year, English majors must complete a 25-page paper in one of those 300-level courses. Students must also take two courses in literature written before 1800 and one additional course in literature written before 1900, as well as a course on race, gender, sexuality, or ethnicity. It is quite possible for an English major to graduate without taking a course in Shakespeare.

Classes at Vassar are small: just three Vassar classes enroll more than 50 students, and two-thirds have fewer than 20. The student-faculty ratio is an excellent 8 to 1, and the average class size 17. One professor says, "You can't get tenure unless you're a good teacher. But you also need some scholarship—a few articles, a book, and evidence of scholarly commitment, and some service to the college." Adds an undergrad: "The professors offer lots of office hours, and they're very accessible. And they're also really good about getting back to you by e-mail if you want to get into a class. Generally they're very responsive."

Vassar's strongest programs include philosophy, biology, and art. English is considered "excellent in spots," and the programs in the Romance languages provide fine opportunities for study abroad. A student describes the history department as "small but with really great professors." The economics department offers a respectable range of courses, including introductory and advanced classes on Marxist economics along with a couple on neoclassical (free market) and game theory. A unique major at Vassar is Victorian studies, a program that combines history, literature, and sociology.

Students and faculty praise the following teachers: Nancy Bisaha, Robert K. Brigham, James Merrell, Leslie Offutt, and Michaela Pohl in history; Mark C. Amodio, Beth Darlington, and H. Daniel Peck in English; Nicholas Adams, Eve D'Ambra, Susan D. Kuretsky, Brian Lukacher, and Molly Nesbit in art history; Robert Brown in Classics; Giovanna Borradori, Mitchell Miller, and Douglas Winblad in philosophy; Peter G. Stillman in political science; and Alexis Klimoff in Russian. Vassar's website also offers a student-run ranking of the faculty (for students' use only).

The required Freshman Writing Seminar is a small-group practicum designed to

CAMPUS POLITICS: RED LIGHT

Vassar's reputation for radical, and sometimes bizarre, politics is as strong as its reputation for academic rigor. The college offers many explicitly politicized courses, the administration seems genuinely exhilarated at the prospects of promoting its own leftist agenda, and many students become activists.

But when nonleftist students try to get in on the game, not all faculty members are willing to let them take the field. According to the free-speech watchdog publication *The Torch*, when the Moderate, Independent, and Conservative Alliance (MICA) got approval in 2010 from the student government for its start-up publication the *Vassar Chronicle*, several Vassar professors protested the decision to allow nonleftist students a campus voice. Professor Boyd Gardner objected this way: "My opposition, and the opposition of several of my colleagues, was grounded in the fact that the decision to create a new publication, especially one that will address such emotional topics as national and local politics, should not be entered into lightly." Be very, very careful about what you say and how you say it, kids. We're listening . . .

A student, Rachel Anspach, responded to the faculty concerns: "As a liberal, I think that it is unfair that conservative groups are being targeted for discrimination when it occurs within most campus clubs. A college education should be about discovering your opinions and learning how to defend them. Only hearing one point of view defeats the purpose of going to a liberal arts college."

introduce students to the "Vassar experience" and to promote the effective expression of ideas in both written and oral work. A recent listing included an Africana Studies course entitled "The Fire This Time: Hip Hop and Critical Citizenship" and an English class on "The Symbolic Quest," which included readings from *Sir Gawain* and *the Green Knight* and *Paradise Lost*. The school's writing center recommends research books and looks over student draft papers.

The school's introductory courses are often interdisciplinary and typically fascinating. Nearly every department offers a freshman course; a recent catalog lists about 20, including the Classics / philosophy / history class "Civilization in Question," which required readings from Homer, the Bible, and (alas) Foucault; the history course "The Dark Ages: 400 to 900"; and "The Art of Reading and Writing" in English composition. Most students say these classes are an excellent place to learn the art of clear, concise expression. (Though they won't learn that from Foucault—a sex-obsessed culture critic who lauded Chairman Mao from a safe academic perch in France.)

A professor says that, at Vassar, "There's no core, really no distribution requirements. If you don't want to take a literature course, you don't have to."

Outside of class, academic opportunities are numerous, despite campus budget problems, and interested students should comb the catalog and discuss with faculty and other students the unique internship, research, and study-abroad possibilities that are available. There are also research opportunities in the sciences working under faculty. Vassar participates in the Twelve College Exchange Program, so students may spend a semester or a year at schools such as Amherst, Bowdoin, Dartmouth, Wheaton (the one in Massachusetts), or Williams.

Dilettantes and ideologues have plenty of choices at Vassar—the women's studies program being a good example, offering courses like "Transnational Queer: Genders, Sexualities, Identities." The urban studies program takes a kitchen-sink approach. It claims to introduce students "to a temporal range and spatial variety of urban experience and phenomena" and to engage them "experientially in a facet of the urban experience." This might prove helpful to students who have never actually visited a city (Poughkeepsie doesn't count).

Almost half of Vassar students study abroad at some point during their four years, and the college sponsors (or cosponsors with other colleges) study in Australia, China, Ecuador, England, France, Germany, Italy, Russia, Scotland, and Spain. Vassar students may also study abroad through another school. The education program sponsors a teaching internship at primary and secondary schools in Clifden, Ireland. Students majoring in international studies are actively encouraged to study in a foreign country. "Junior Year Abroad is huge," one senior reports.

Languages offered include Arabic, Chinese, French, German, Greek and Latin, Italian, Japanese, Russian, Spanish, and Hebrew.

Student Life: Shiny happy people

The Vassar campus is peaceful, and residential life is pleasant. Throughout winter, the area's average temperature hovers in the 20s, but in more temperate months, students can take advantage of Vassar's 500-acre farm, complete with hiking and jogging trails.

Four Gothic residence halls, housing about 150 students each, form a typical quad. The college has five other student residences off the main quadrangle, and approximately 20 percent of Vassar students (all upperclassmen) live in apartments or townhouses further from the center of campus. One residence hall is reserved for women only, but all other halls are coed and do not separate men and women by floor. Many bathrooms are coed, and students can share suites (though not individual rooms) with members of the opposite sex.

Sixty percent of Vassar's students are female. The school's admission department points out that women are 55 percent of all college students nationally, so Vassar is really not so unbalanced.

Each house at Vassar is self-governed, meaning that students make most of the decisions; there are no resident advisers in the buildings, so "student fellows" do most of the counseling and community programming that RAs oversee at other schools. Some floors in each dormitory are set aside as "wellness corridors" or substance-free areas. Smoking is prohibited in residence halls unless residents decide to designate a specific smoking location. Houses also maintain quiet hours between 11:00 p.m. and 10:00 a.m.

About 94 percent of Vassar students live in college-owned housing. Housing is guaranteed (and required for full-time students) for all four years, but upperclassmen may have to live in double- or triple-occupancy rooms originally meant for one or two residents. Although Vassar did approve sex-neutral housing in 2008 to accommodate its vocal LGBTQ students, the university has not fully incorporated the policy, and suites or upperclassman apartments are the only way to live with members of the opposite sex.

Vassar was founded by a wealthy brewer, and its students do drink—a lot. Drug use is also popular on campus: mostly marijuana, but students claim that anything is available, and that the administration often doesn't step in with budding alcoholics or addicts until it is too late. Raunchy Vassarites enjoy the pages of *Squirm*, the student-run campus porn magazine, sponsored by an approved organization that has hosted a movie night featuring two pornographic films.

SUGGESTED CORE

1. Classics 216/217, History of the Ancient Greeks/History of the Ancient Romans
2. Philosophy 101a, History of Western Philosophy I: Ancient
3. Religion 125/127b, The Hebrew Bible/The New Testament and Early Christianity
4. Medieval and Renaissance Studies 246a, Medieval and Early Modern Europe: The Power of Church and Court
5. Political Science 270b, Modern Political Thought
6. English 240 or 242, Shakespeare
7. History 274a/275b, Beyond Jamestown and Plymouth Rock: Revisiting, Revising, and Reviving Early America/U.S. History's Greatest Mystery: Revolutionary America, 1750–1830
8. Philosophy 205b, 19th-Century Philosophy

More traditional students should contact the Moderate, Independent, and Conservative Alliance of Vassar, a puckish and independent-minded organization that has weathered faculty resistance to publish its magazine, the *Vassar Chronicle*.

Athletic Vassarites can participate in one or more of the school's 25 NCAA Division III varsity teams. The Brewers compete in the Upstate Collegiate Athletic Conference against nine other small New York colleges in sports like basketball, fencing, rugby, soccer, volleyball, and swimming and diving. Intramurals allow students to choose competitive or recreational play in soccer (indoor and outdoor), volleyball, tennis, softball, or basketball, as well as tournaments in squash, flag football, golf, and badminton.

Religious students will find a number of organizations on campus. The Catholic Community pledges to cultivate "religious life through faith, community, and social justice." In other words, skip it, and go to the Latin Mass at St. Joseph's parish in town. The Vassar Christian Fellowship promises that membership is "open to all Vassar students regardless of race, color, sex, ethnicity, nationality, political or sexual orientation, marital status, or handicap" (does that cover everybody?), and its main event is a twice-yearly book table offering publications and information on concerts and speakers. The Vassar Jewish Union offers fellowship to students of varying degrees of orthodoxy, "regardless of their backgrounds or form of Jewish expression," while the Vassar Pagan Circle "works to provide a space for all those who identify with or would like to learn more about Paganism." For those who cannot commit to many gods (or even One), the Unitarian Universalists offer a "liberal, non-creedal religious tradition that values the inherent worth and dignity of ALL people." Students who find that too constraining might prefer to join the Barefoot Monkeys, a club for jugglers.

Students can participate in 91.3 WVKR, the college radio station, the *Miscellany News* student paper, or in *The Vassarion* yearbook.

Most of Vassar's other student organizations are politically minded or focused on activism. Many are devoted to issues of sexuality (TransMission, which welcomes "transgender, genderqueer, and intersex people," ACT OUT, Queer Coalition, Intersextions dialogue group, and the aforementioned Squirm "sex-positive forum"). Other groups include UNICEF, PEACE, Vassar Greens, and the Vassar Green Party. Racial and ethnic groups include *Poder Latino*, the Feminist Majority Leadership Alliance, the Women of Color Alliance, Council of Black Seniors, African Students Union, Caribbean Students Union, or Black Students Union. Vassar has other issues-based groups, like the Animal Rescue Coalition and the Vassar Prison Initiative, which is "committed to raising awareness about issues related to the prison industrial complex").

To judge by crime statistics, Vassar is a very safe campus. A female undergrad says, "Crime might be a concern off campus but not on. I wouldn't go out after midnight in Poughkeepsie, but there's not much reason to really." In 2011 the school reported 13 forcible sex offenses, six arsons, and 18 burglaries on campus.

Tuition for the 2012–13 school year at Vassar was $45,580, plus $10,800 for room and board. Financial aid is readily available and admission is need blind. More than 66 percent of students received financial aid, and the average first-year student received about $40,390 in 2012. Vassar awards more than $25 million in scholarships in addition to federal and state aid. The college has thus far resisted cutting financial aid in the midst of its current budget crisis, and the typical Vassar student graduated with a modest $17,234 in student-loan debt.

STRONG SUITS	WEAK POINTS
• Highly qualified, accessible professors focused on teaching.	• Lax curriculum allows students to over-specialize or focus on politicized courses.
• Respected programs in history, political science, philosophy, freshman writing, biology, and art.	• Virtually no courses in ancient or medi-eval political philosophy; thought begins with Machiavelli.
• Small classes taught by professors, not grad students.	• Many aggressive, leftist activist groups as opposed to small, embattled conserva-tive clubs and tepid religious ministries.
• Good study-abroad options, especially through Romance languages department.	• A student-run porn magazine, *Squirm*, gets school funding and has shown porn films on campus.
• Fascinating introductory, interdisciplinary classes.	• Significant drinking and drug use among students.

Villanova University

Villanova, Pennsylvania • www.villanova.edu

Guiding Spirit

Founded in 1842 by the Order of St. Augustine, Villanova University is named for St. Thomas of Villanova and is still run by the Augustinians, though few of them teach. Villanova's liberal arts requirements and programs remain comparatively strong. The campus is relatively apolitical, and there is a large and vibrant pro-life group on campus. Compared to many of the nation's other Catholic universities, Villanova seems to be a solid intellectual and spiritual option for academically serious and community-minded students.

Academic Life: Getting more from the core

When Villanova introduced its new "core" curriculum 20 years ago, "reading Catholic literature and discussing it seriously became the norm on campus," says one professor. Indeed, Villanova's curriculum is better than most. One student says that Villanova "teaches students to be well-rounded people both inside and outside of the classroom," while another student characterizes the curriculum as "stretching." Students still need to make wise choices to avoid ideologically driven courses, and one professor laments that there are too few "intrusions" of Catholic faith into student life or the classroom.

One professor reports that Villanova's 32nd president, the Reverend Peter M. Donohue, OSA, has a "vivid and personal style—and has fostered enormous loyalty among alums, students, faculty, and staff. His personal touch has energized the campus."

Of the student body, one student says, "I think we're getting noticeably more dynamic, interesting, and intellectual." A professor agrees: "The students get better every year. We're really starting to attract more intellectual, conservative, and genuine students." One student reports that her peers are "well-read before they get to college" as well as "determined and motivated."

The faculty is a mixed bag. While one professor worries that "there is a fair amount of focus by some faculty—especially new hires—on trendy, superficial subjects," others are more hopeful. One teacher points to several recently recruited professors who seek "to educate their students by opening their 'minds and hearts' to the whole truth." Says another, "We have an excellent faculty, and it's getting better every year. . . . Some of us are on the left in our personal politics, some on the right, but we're all serious about liberal education." He continues, "The [introductory freshman seminar] course we teach . . . reflects Villanova's ever-greater seriousness about its intellectual mission. In the first semester, students take 'Traditions in Conversation,' which is on the ancient, medieval, and Renaissance periods, and places Augustine's thought in dialogue with the other roots of the Western tradition." Other professors voice similar optimism.

For students who want a real liberal education, Villanova's Department of Humanities may be as good an option as they are likely to find at many elite institutions. The humanities major at Villanova offers students a new way to explore the timeless wisdom of the Western tradition. The curriculum combines a rigorous series of required courses—God, Person, Society, World, and the Senior Seminar—along with a wide range of electives, including seminars on the Catholic novel; the nature of truth, goodness, and beauty; the idea of classical statesmanship; the history of capitalism; and the role of forgiveness in human life.

Humanities at Villanova seeks to reintegrate all the branches of humanistic learning,

VITAL STATISTICS

Religious affiliation: *Roman Catholic*
Total enrollment: *10,626*
Total undergraduates: *6,584*
SAT CR/Verbal midrange: *590–680*
SAT Math midrange: *620–710*
ACT midrange: *30–33*
Applicants: *14,901*
Applicants accepted: *45%*
Accepted applicants who enrolled: *24%*
Tuition (general/out of state): *$42,150*
Tuition (in state): *N/A*
Room and board: *$11,393*
Freshman retention rate *94%*
Graduation rate (4 yrs.): *88%*
Graduation rate (6 yrs.): *91%*
Courses with fewer than 20 students: *42%*
Student-faculty ratio: *11:1*
Courses taught by graduate students: *not provided*
Students living on campus: *70%*
Students in fraternities: *19%*
Students in sororities: *33%*
Students receiving need-based financial aid: *53%*
Avg. student-loan debt of a recent graduating class: *$38,055*
Most popular majors: *business/marketing, engineering, social sciences*
Guaranteed housing for 4 years? *no*

CAMPUS POLITICS: GREEN LIGHT

Villanova students and professors report some intrusions of ideology into the classroom and occasional pressure to conform paper and test content to please a professor's particular intellectual bent—usually liberal. Although the degree and regularity of these intrusions varies, it is clear that the conservative student must choose his classes, professors, and major wisely, as liberalism is the norm in most departments.

However, conservative students have plenty of opportunity outside the classroom to express their views. For example, a popular student group is Villanovans for Life, which organizes an annual Respect Life Week, promotes pro-life causes and demonstrations throughout the year, and participates in the annual March for Life in Washington, D.C. Pro-abortion groups are not allowed on campus, and the student health center does not offer contraceptives or abortifacients.

The university has two student newspapers: *The Villanovan* (on the left) and the *Villanova Times* (on the right), but *The Villanovan* garners more support from the administration and is able to publish more frequently.

restoring philosophy and theology to their role as guiding lights in that integration. According to faculty, the department's courses call into question the prejudices of an age that assumes "modern is always better," even as it seems incapable of asking, "Better for what?" From Plato and Plutarch, to Dante and Aquinas, and on to Tolkien and T. S. Eliot, humanities courses explore the richest answers to fundamental human questions—not merely the most recent ones.

One attractive program is the Matthew J. Ryan Center for the Study of Free Institutions and the Public Good, which "promotes inquiry into the principles and processes of free government and seeks to advance understanding of the responsibilities of statesmen and citizens of constitutional democratic societies." (The Intercollegiate Studies Institute, the publisher of this guide, is a cosponsor of this program.) The Ryan Center conducts small reading groups for faculty and students and sponsors campus-wide events and seminars. A 2012 event topic was "Human Scale and Human Politics: Fostering Civil Society and an Ethos of Gratitude."

Villanova's competitive honors program, under the direction of Thomas W. Smith, has implemented several first-rate academic sequences that provide a three-semester experience combining integrated humanistic learning with a strong leadership emphasis. Along with its flagship Interdisciplinary Scholars Program, Villanova honors now offers a Politics, Philosophy, and Economics sequence that culminates in a study-abroad experience at Cambridge University; a Humanities Independent Scholars Program that culminates in a semester abroad at Scotland's St. Andrews University; and a promising sequence entitled "The Good, the True, and the Beautiful."

In addition to Irish studies and the aforementioned humanities major, strong departments include astronomy and astrophysics (separate from the physics department) and the other hard sciences, the Center for Liberal Education, economics, political science, philosophy, and English. Weaker departments at Villanova reportedly are history, education, and communications.

English majors do not have to take a course in Shakespeare, although it is offered, as are many worthy classes in the history of literature, such as "Chaucer," "Dryden, Swift, and Pope," "American Short Story," and a solid course on the Catholic novel.

History majors must take two American and two European classes as well as one world history course. Western civilization is not required, unfortunately, nor is American history before or after 1865. (No wonder this is known as one of Villanova's weakest departments.)

The political science department is both popular and rigorous, requiring majors to take courses on the U.S. Constitution and American political theory, as well as comparative politics and international relations.

> A professor says: "We're really starting to attract more intellectual, conservative, and genuine students." But another laments few "intrusions" of Catholic faith into student life or the classroom.

The Villanova School of Business is one of the university's best-known programs, and the College of Engineering has a strong advising program and several excellent professors, though one engineering student admits, "You'd be better off going to Penn State or a similarly big school with bigger labs and more money to throw around. That's really the only program that suffers from being too small, and that's just the nature of engineering."

Villanova enrolls about 4,000 graduate students, but generally only students in the Villanova doctoral program in philosophy are allowed to teach undergraduate courses. Professors are said to be intent on their students' learning the material. "Many professors do care about their students and devote lots of time to them," reports a faculty member. A student agrees: "Professors are always readily available and unusually willing to help." Faculty are required to hold office hours each week, and many students say they take advantage of them—and not just right before exams (though some faculty say the students do not avail themselves of this opportunity as often as they could). Some faculty members give out their home phone numbers at the beginning of the semester and encourage students to call with questions. Villanova's largest classrooms, typically used for introductory biology and chemistry classes, hold approximately 100 students. Faculty members are also dedicated to helping students make good choices in selecting their courses; students say the advising program is strong.

The best faculty members at Villanova include Richard Jacobs in education and human services; Andrew Bove, Peter Busch, Chris Daly, Greg Hoskins, and Catherine Wilson in the Center for Liberal Education; Jesse Couenhoven, Margaret Grubiak, Kevin Hughes, Anna Moreland, Mark Shiffman, Thomas Smith, Michael Tomko, and James Matthew Wilson in humanities; David M. Barrett, Lowell Gustafson, Robert Maranto, Colleen Sheehan, A. Maria Toyoda, and Craig Wheeland in political science; Christopher Haas in history; Charlie Zech in economics; Earl Bader, Karen Graziano, James Kirschke, and Hugh Ormsby-Lennon in English; Tom Busch, John Doody, Daniel Regan, Michael Waddell, and Jim Wetzel in

SUGGESTED CORE

1. Classics 2032/History 3011, Classical Mythology/Greek Civilization (*closest matches*)
2. Philosophy 3020, History of Ancient Philosophy
3. Theology and Religious Studies 2000/2050/2300, Introduction to the Bible/Old Testament Survey/New Testament Survey
4. Theology and Religious Studies 2725/1000, Christian Classics I/Christian Faith and Life, or Philosophy 3030, History of Medieval Philosophy
5. Political Science 6100, Modern Political Theories
6. English 3250, Shakespeare
7. History 2000, Investigating U.S. History I
8. Philosophy 3050, Kant & 19th-Century Philosophy

philosophy; Randy Weinstein in chemical engineering; Kevin Hughes in classical studies; Tony Godzieba, Martin Laird, Bernard Prusak, and Darlene Weaver in theology; Paul Lupinacci in statistics; John Santomas in math; and Sayed Omran in Arab and Islamic studies.

Villanova's Office of International Studies currently coordinates full-year and semester programs in Ireland, England, Australia, and Italy. On campus, the university offers Arabic, Chinese, French, German, Greek and Latin, Hebrew, Italian, Japanese, Portuguese, Russian, and Spanish.

Student Life: Vanillanova

Villanova guarantees housing on campus for the first three years; most seniors live in off-campus apartments. Villanova manages 18 residence halls and eight apartment buildings. Students can choose to live in either single-sex or coed dorms, but even the coed dorms are segregated by floor, which means students never live next door to a member of the opposite sex. Many freshmen opt for the Villanova learning communities, in which students live together in a dorm and share a core humanities seminar. There, one student says, "usually people get to know their hallmates a little faster." Recent themes included "Nature and the World" and "Mind, Body, Spirit."

One student characterizes the typical Villanova student as "an Irish or Italian upperclass Abercrombie clone from the suburbs." Another student says a common nickname for the school, whose student body is around 73 percent white, is "Vanillanova." This is rapidly changing. The administration embarked on an extremely aggressive diversity campaign a few years ago, resulting in the Caucasian population plummeting 12 percent in just six years. The Villanova Intermediary Persons program pairs volunteers with incoming minority freshmen to serve as first friends on campus. In an example of "diversity gone wild," Villanova also provides gay, lesbian, bisexual, and transgendered clubs and support groups on campus.

Thirty-three percent of women and 19 percent of men are members of Greek organizations, but because they do not have their own houses, Greeks are less exclusive and more service oriented than at other schools. Students will find plenty of activities on campus to occupy their free time: publications, dances, some music and theater recitals, concerts, and free cultural and popular films in the student center. In addition, there are more than 250 student groups and organizations, as well as 44 club and intramural sports.

Villanova maintains a Peace and Justice Center, which offers courses such as "Eco-feminism" alongside classes in real Catholic social teaching. The center supports student groups such as Villanovans for the Ethical Treatment of Animals, Bread for the World, Villanovans for Life (a very active group on campus that regularly puts up pro-life displays), and Villanova Partnership with Catholic Relief Services. The Center for Liberal Education website maintains a library of work by Dorothy Day and Thomas Merton on how to integrate faith and economics, and Professor Charlie Zech has also contributed to such efforts to integrate Catholic thought with socioeconomic realities.

The school has a real "focus on service," reports a student proudly: "We have the largest Habitat for Humanity program in the nation and participation is huge in similar programs." One student summarizes the tension that sometimes occurs between the oft-invoked but ill-defined "Spirit of Saint Augustine" and the concrete teachings of the church: "There is . . . a sense that campus ministry is striving to be inclusive and tolerant of any lifestyle or opinion that is averse to the traditional doctrines within Christianity."

The Villanova NROTC program includes about 150 midshipmen and has produced more admirals and Marine Corps generals than any other school except for the U.S. Naval Academy. Says one parent of an NROTC student: "The dedication and determination of the NROTC midshipmen is unparalleled." Lately, several NROTC students have chosen to minor in Arab and Islamic studies, another strong program at Villanova.

There are 24 NCAA Division I sports teams at Villanova and more than 500 student athletes. A large portion of the student body also participates in the school's more than 40 intramural and intercollegiate sports. The Pavillion is the university's 6,500-seat multipurpose recreational facility and arena and home to the wildly popular men's and women's Wildcat basketball teams. It is also used for concerts, trade shows, college and job fairs, Advanta International Tennis Championship games, NCAA Championship events, and the Villanova Law School graduation.

The Sunday Masses for students are largely student-run and are often standing-room only. One student reports that at both the Masses and in-campus ministry in general there is a tendency "to use inclusive language to the point that one can no longer distinguish Christianity from self-help manuals." More traditional students might wish to investigate one of the Latin Masses offered in nearby Philadelphia, for instance at the Our Lady of Consolation and Our Lady of Lourdes parishes.

Most students are Catholic, but all agree that religion "is never really in your face," as one student says. "We don't try to downplay Christianity," says another Catholic student, "but we are accepting of all faiths. . . . My best friend here is Buddhist." Popular organizations for non-Catholic students include Hillel and a Muslim student group. Despite the Catholic ethos of the university, one student cautions that "the average student does not take Catholic ideals completely to heart. Issues like sex before marriage, abortion, and general morality" are not necessarily approached according to Catholic teaching. "In that sense the average Villanova student is not too much different from the average public university student." Excessive drinking is the favorite weekend activity of students, according to one professor.

Mostly as a result of student complaints, the university loosened its visitation policy to allow students to entertain visitors (including those of the opposite sex) until midnight on school nights and until 2:00 a.m. on Fridays and Saturdays. Upperclassman dorms can have these hours extended if all residents attend a session on "roommate rights and responsibilities." The student handbook talks the talk of Catholic modesty and chastity—however, Villanova rarely enforces restrictions on intervisitation, students report. RAs are "pathetic," says one student, because they rarely take note of violations or an active part in organizing activities and getting to know their hall members.

The campus is secluded enough from the outside community that it suffers little crime. During 2011 Villanova reported five sexual offenses, one aggravated assault, 18 burglaries, two cars stolen, and one arson.

Villanova's tuition in 2012–13 was $42,150, and room and board $11,393. Admissions are need blind, but the school does not come close to meeting every student's full financial need. Only 53 percent of undergraduates received need-based financial aid, and average indebtedness of recent graduates was a hefty $38,055.

STRONG SUITS

- Good courses in Irish studies, humanities, economics, political science, philosophy, English, astronomy, and astrophysics and other hard sciences.
- Reasonable distributional requirements, with some coverage of the Western tradition.
- The academic preparation and intellectual curiosity of students seems to be consistently improving.
- A good number of traditional professors focused on core material in their disciplines.
- Conservative and religious students seem comfortable and free on campus.

WEAK POINTS

- Some disciplines are shaky, faculty and students report, including history, education, and communications.
- New faculty hires reportedly trendier, more ideological.
- Campus Catholic liturgies insert feminist language into services.
- Engineering facilities not competitive with those in better-funded schools.

Wabash College

Crawfordsville, Indiana • www.wabash.edu

A Few Good Men

There's only one rule at Wabash: The student will "conduct himself at all times, both on and off the campus, as a gentleman and a responsible citizen." The rule tells you a lot—for instance that the school aims to form gentlemen, not ladies. Wabash, founded by Dartmouth men in 1832, is one of only a few all-male colleges left in America. The school seems poised to carry on its traditions and distinctive mission for decades to come.

Wabash is a good choice for young men in pursuit of the liberal arts. The college does take seriously the ideal of the liberal arts—the education and development of the person. Moreover, destructive political correctness, with a few exceptions, is absent from campus and classes alike, and conservative students will find an environment that both supports and challenges their ideas.

Academic Life: Half Great Books, half . . .

The Wabash curriculum is better than at many liberal arts colleges. The faculty has an unusually clear idea of what undergraduate education is all about. The smallness of the place discourages self-indulgent specialization, and the single-sex student body means that students can "say what they think, without worrying about trying to impress girls" or "adjusting their remarks to placate feminist or other current orthodoxies," according to a professor. Wabash's common requirements include a freshman tutorial and a worthy freshman colloquium entitled "Enduring Questions." Alarmingly, the school has eliminated its long-standing sophomore course in "Culture and Traditions" (C&T), which was traditionally presented as a two-semester Great Books course.

"The college leans toward a Great Books ethos without actually claiming it," says one professor. "There are some of the typical courses you will find elsewhere, on film, masculinity, race, and feminism, for example, but the college is actually fairly conservative in its attitude toward topical classes geared toward contemporary concerns." Says another: "Writing is of prime importance. This is true across the board." A recent graduate agrees: "What particularly impressed me about Wabash is the premium it places upon writing. In most classes, students regularly are assigned 10-to-15-page reports; tests are in essay format, almost never multiple choice." Classes are small: 77 percent enroll fewer than 20 students and all but five classes have fewer than 40 students.

Whatever the imperfections of the school's common curriculum, the requirements for majors and even minors are mostly quite strong.

English majors on the literature track (there is also a creative writing option) take three survey courses chosen from the following: "Introduction to Medieval and Renaissance Literature"; "Introduction to Shakespeare"; "English Literature 1660–1800"; "Introduction to English Literature 1800–1900"; "Introduction to British Literature after 1900"; "Introduction to American Literature before 1900"; and "Introduction to American Literature after 1900." Majors also take "Introduction to the Study of Literature" and four additional courses, including at least two "Studies in . . ." and one "seminar" course. Options range from a seminar in "Sexualities, Textualities, and Queer Theory," "Studies in Historical Contexts: King Arthur, Romance and Chivalry," "Studies in Individual Authors: George Bernard Shaw," and "Studies in Literary Genres Science Fiction." Majors also take comprehensive exams—a rare and worthy requirement.

History majors take one course in world history either before or since 1500; another course in the philosophy and craft of history; a research seminar; and six more courses (including two advanced courses) such as "Topics in American History," "America to 1877," "Topics in Latin American History," "Topics in Asian History," "Classical and Imperial China to 1911," "Topics in African History," and "Advanced Topics, Medieval and Early Modern Europe." This means that one could emerge having studied little or no American or European history. Students must also maintain a portfolio of papers, the evaluation of which is part of the senior comprehensive.

The major in political science requires four introductory surveys—of American politics, comparative politics, political theory, and international politics. He takes two advanced courses in one area of specialization chosen from the four areas above, for example, "History of Political Thought: Ancient and Medieval," "Military Institutions in Domestic and International Politics," "Economic and Political Development," or "Topics in Constitutional Law," plus at least two additional political science courses and a senior seminar with a research paper. One conservative student, however, laments that "there is not a single Republican—let alone a conservative—on the staff of the political science department. In my comparative politics course, I start out the morning with a (on a good day) 10-minute harangue about Republicans, conservatives, or why Scandinavia is 'God's country.'" He adds, however, that "the department grades fairly despite their obvious biases."

Best known nationally is the religion department, which is home to the Center for Teaching and Learning in Theology and

CAMPUS POLITICS: GREEN LIGHT

Conservative and religious students will find Wabash a warm and tolerant place, but this doesn't mean that the professoriate is on the whole sympathetic to conservative or libertarian ideas. It does mean that teachers are unusually tolerant and really do believe that disciplined study and open discussion advance the cause of truth—on which they do not believe they have a monopoly. "While Wabash attracts a conservative student population, the faculty, which like most academic institutions leans more to the left than to the right, is not overtly political inside the classroom," a student says. "Professors have reputations for political bias, but I think they reserve their activism mainly to academic publishing, public speaking, and one-to-one informal conversations with students."

Of course, not all Wallys (as Wabash students are affectionately called) play on the same team. shOUT (short for "Wabash OUT") has official recognition and funding for meetings, lectures, and an "alternative"—that is to say, drag—party that attracts many from other colleges. Wabash was one of the first in the region to stage Tony Kushner's homo-Marxist drama *Angels in America*.

In 2012 the Wabash *Phoenix* published a reasoned critique of a proposal that has gained some traction on campus: to add to the Wabash curriculum a required course on gender studies—in this case, a class on masculinity. *The Phoenix* expressed the fears of many students that such a class would inevitably be taught from a feminist point of view. Stay tuned.

Religion and hosts an annual summer institute for professors of religion from other colleges. The program is strong on Christian scripture, history, and theology, and is unusually encouraging to traditional understandings of the faith, although students are required to take at least two course in non-Christian religions. One professor of religion told us how pleased he was at the number of "devout Roman Catholics" teaching in other departments and their contribution to the spiritual and intellectual ethos of the campus community. Stephen Webb, whose writings appear in *Touchstone, First Things,* and *Books and Culture,* is one of the stars of the Wabash religion faculty. A student tells us that all the professors in this department are fair and approachable teachers. "Even the resident liberal theologian (once affiliated with the Jesus Seminar) grades fairly essays that critique his positions."

English, history, and the Classics are also strong. One student says that the English faculty "knows how to engage students and elicit vibrant class discussions" and that the department is seen as "one of the more dynamic academic programs" on campus.

Wabash tends to attract top-notch professors who are revered among students. A recent graduate says that, "They come to Wabash, many of them at least, because it's a place that espouses cutting-edge academic research as much as it does excellence in teaching and student mentorship. Students are encouraged to seek out their professors and to use them as resources in their academic and personal lives. . . . By my senior year, I had dined or had drinks with most of my professors. . . . Wabash professors, especially Warren Rosenberg and William Placher, mean the world to me. . . . I graduated with the feeling that I knew my professors not merely as scholars or intellectuals, but as people." Another student agrees, "Many of the faculty do spend a great deal of time with students and attend student activities such as athletic events, concerts, and lectures."

> The smallness of all-male Wabash discourages self-indulgent specialization, and students can "say what they think, without worrying about trying to impress girls" or to "placate feminist or other current orthodoxies," says a professor.

Wabash students particularly recommend teachers Jon Baer and David Blix in religion; David Krohne (emeritus), John Munford (emeritus), and David Polley in biology; and David Kubiak in Classics.

Wabash College offers 22 majors, including joint "3–2" programs in engineering with Columbia University, Washington University, and Purdue.

Through the Great Lakes Colleges Association and other means, Wabash men are able to study abroad in such exotic locations as Japan or Senegal. Indeed, each year about 40 Wabash men go abroad to one of more than 140 countries, and their student-aid packages travel with them. And if a student comes up with a meritorious research proposal that doesn't seem to fit in anywhere, Wabash will do its considerable best to find funding for it. Wabash also encourages internships and collaborative student-professor research projects throughout the academic year and during summer breaks. Some destinations include Uganda for folk music, Mexico to San Cristobal for volunteering at an NGO, and

Washington, D.C., for an annual conference on neuroscience.

Foreign languages offered at Wabash include French, German, Greek and Latin, Russian, and Spanish.

Student Life: The Sphinx and the village

Crawfordsville is only 45 miles from Indianapolis. The nearest coeds are an hour away, at DePauw, Butler, Purdue, and the University of Illinois; Indiana University is even farther. But women are for the weekends, and so is drinking, that last refuge of the dateless; one hears little of drug use. Without women, there is no need to dress to impress, and while there are students of considerable means, they don't stand out. Indeed, the student paper warns that the Wally who wants to get a job had better learn to dress up for it.

College life centers on its 10 fraternities and the elite Sphinx Club, dedicated to "promoting campus unity, spirit, and togetherness among all students of Wabash through traditional and philanthropic events." About 50 percent of the student body are fraternity men, all of whom, including pledges, live in frat houses. Fraternities seem to dominate campus life. Independents say that the school caters more to Greeks and often ignores the concerns of others.

> **SUGGESTED CORE**
>
> 1. Classics 105/106, Greek Civilizations/Roman Civilizations (*closest matches*)
> 2. Classics 140, Philosophy of the Classical Period
> 3. Religion 141/162, Hebrew Bible/History and Literature of the New Testament
> 4. Religion 171, History of Christianity to the Reformation
> 5. Political Science 335, History of Political Thought: Renaissance and Modern
> 6. English 216, Introduction to Shakespeare
> 7. History 241, America to 1877
> 8. Philosophy 345/History 231, Continental Philosophy/19th-Century Europe (*closest matches*)

Wabash has more than 70 Student Senate–recognized clubs and organizations, including the Progressive Students Movement, shOUT (the official organization for gay, bisexual, questioning, and supportive students), and a number of music and theater groups, such as the Wabash Chamber Orchestra and the annual Studio One-Acts, written and directed by theater students. *The Phoenix* is published by Wabash's Conservative Union. Other student-run newspapers include Wabash's *The Bachelor*, "the voice of Wabash since 1908," and *Callimachus*, an arts journal.

One of the most impressive things about Wabash College, says one student, is "the quality of outside speakers that the college and clubs bring in to lecture. Though we are a college with fewer than 1,000 students in a small town in the middle of nowhere, the college consistently attracts big-name and high-quality speakers and performers." In fall 2010, Princeton professor Robert George spoke at Wabash on natural law.

The political atmosphere at Wabash in general, says one student—and many agree—is "one of free and vigorous debate. While the professors are overwhelmingly leftists, the student body leans more to the center-right." College Republicans are active on campus, as is the Conservative Union.

Wabash competes in NCAA's Division III, so there are no athletic scholarships, and sports practice is kept to two hours a day at most. Men who wouldn't get to play varsity elsewhere make the team here; indeed, nearly half do. Much enthusiasm goes into the traditional football rivalry with DePauw, with the freshman class keeping night watch against invading pranksters on the eve of the big Monon Bell game. Beside football, Wabash competes in 10 other varsity sports—cross-country, soccer, golf, basketball, indoor track and field, outdoor track and field, wrestling, tennis, swimming and diving, and baseball—as a member of the North Coast Athletic Conference. Twenty-four intramural sports—including canoeing, cycling, cross-country, golf, disc golf, horseshoes, indoor track, outdoor track, pocket billiards, racquetball—and four club sports (rugby, crew, lacrosse, and volleyball) round off the active sports life at Wabash. Eighty percent of Wabash students participate in at least one intramural or club sport.

Crime is not much of a problem at Wabash. The only crimes reported on campus in 2011 were seven burglaries.

Tuition in 2012–13 was $33,600, and room and board varies by meal plan and housing situation (fraternity housing is slightly cheaper than dormitory housing), but the average was $8,300. Roughly 80 percent of students received some need-based aid, and the average debt of a recent graduate was $29,897. The good news is that the college gives an unusually large number of generous merit scholarships to students. As one student says, "Personally, I could not have gone to Wabash if it weren't for the merit scholarships it provided me."

STRONG SUITS	WEAK POINTS
• High morale and sense of mission. • Solid, traditional requirements for majors like English, history, political science. • A welcoming place for students of every political persuasion and religion. • All-male student body helps focus attention on schoolwork, except on weekends.	• Core curriculum recently weakened to drop Great Books requirement. • Some departments are uniformly leftist, with no dissenters. • This small, all-male school (1,000 students) in "the middle of nowhere" offers limited social options.

Wake Forest University

Winston-Salem, North Carolina • www.wfu.edu

Sleepers, Wake!

Founded by Southern Baptists in 1834, Wake Forest has found it useful to back away slowly, hands in the air, from its founders' religion. As one student says, "Wake Forest's current connections to its Southern Baptist heritage are little more than lip service." Wake Forest has followed other academic trends by replacing its once-strong distribution requirements with a weaker regimen. But the university still maintains a number of outstanding academic departments, and it draws a good number of intelligent and morally serious students. Wake Forest's faculty members understand that they are teachers first and researchers second, and the school does a good job of balancing the two facets of the university.

Academic Life: Waking the dead

The university recently cut the number of required courses by a full semester, and many of the classes that can be used to satisfy its distribution requirements are introductory. One professor laments, "Students take the most popular courses and often repeat what they took in high school." One student says many fluff classes are available, especially in the communications, sociology, and political science departments. "A liberal arts student can truly

VITAL STATISTICS

Religious affiliation: *none*
Total enrollment: *7,351*
Total undergraduates: *4,775*
SAT CR/Verbal midrange:
610–700
SAT Math midrange:
620–700
ACT midrange: *28–32*
Applicants: *9,869*
Applicants accepted: *40%*
Accepted applicants who
enrolled: *31%*
Tuition (general/out of
state): *$42,700*
Tuition (in state): *N/A*
Room and board: *$11,700*
Freshman retention rate:
94%
Graduation rate (4 yrs.): *82%*
Graduation rate (6 yrs.): *88%*
Courses with fewer than 20
students: *56%*
Student-faculty ratio: *11:1*
Courses taught by graduate
students: *not provided*
Students living on campus:
71%
Students in fraternities: *35%*
Students in sororities: *42%*
Students receiving need-
based financial aid: *40%*
Avg. student-loan debt of a
recent graduating class:
$35,070
Most popular majors:
*business/marketing, biol-
ogy, political science*
Guaranteed housing for 4
years? *yes*

graduate knowing very little beyond a limited scope," he says. This is evident in the English department, where a Shakespeare course is still required, but many of the core classes have been watered down. For instance, a student claims that "the basic American and British literature courses are becoming less substantive, in my opinion. A quick glance at their reading lists would reveal that these classes are not filled with the great authors but rather works of radical chic with perhaps a play of Shakespeare or some Hawthorne thrown in." One student warns, "The liberal arts are increasingly becoming subject to political correctness and are drifting from traditional texts and subjects."

Fortunately, while Wake Forest offers a broad spectrum of majors, most of the trendy interdisciplinary areas such as women's studies, ethnic studies, and urban studies are offered only as minors—and therefore do not have the power or popularity that they do at other universities.

The history department is solid, requiring majors to take classes in American, European, and world history. Western civilization courses are offered but not required.

Although some complain that the political science department tends to promote the views of the Left, it is one of the university's strongest academic departments—and one of the largest at the school. As one professor says, "This is due in large part to the quality of the faculty, many of whom are widely published and well regarded in their fields and are also excellent teachers who work closely with students." Poli-sci majors are required to take one course each in American politics, political theory, international politics, and comparative politics.

The business school program is reputedly very challenging, as are the hard sciences (chemistry, biology, and physics). Outside the business school and the hard sciences, Wake's better departments include economics, mathematics, and the foreign language programs, including Chinese, French, Greek and Latin, German, Italian, Japanese, Russian, and Spanish. A classical languages major says that his department is "one of the few liberal arts departments at Wake Forest that still avoids being politicized."

"Philosophy remains a bastion of good, solid academic tradition," a professor says. "They're unwilling to go along with faddish multiculturalism." Wake offers a distinctive minor in early Christian studies, in which students take courses on the New Testament, the age of Augustus, and the Greco-Roman world, and select relevant courses in the art, history, religion, and philosophy departments.

The religion department includes courses such as "Feminist and Contemporary Interpretations of the New Testament" and is said to take a dim view of traditional Christianity, Baptist or otherwise. "That department is highly politicized and heavily influenced by liberal theologies," a student says. "For instance, a student I know who wishes to become an Episcopal priest has majored in Greek and avoids most religion classes because of their content." A student reports that in his sociology class on deviant behavior, the "correct" answer on an examination identified religious objections to homosexuality as bigotry. Well, that settles things, doesn't it?

The school's honors program allows Wake's most academically talented upperclassmen to take small-group seminars together. Those who take at least four honors seminars can graduate with distinction. In the English department, the honors courses are mostly specialty courses in topics like Chaucer, Milton, Victorian poetry, and the literature of the South. Topics for honors seminars in other disciplines vary by semester.

The close relationships between faculty and students often touted by the Wake Forest administration appear genuine. Admissions literature says that the school "maintains its high academic standards by ensuring that undergraduate classes, lectures, and seminars are taught by faculty members, not teaching assistants." (TAs teach only the lab sections of science and language courses.) Wake Forest faculty members do generally value teaching over research, and one professor says, "It is difficult to come up with schools that are truly analogous to Wake Forest in their teaching/research balance, and this is one of the most attractive features of the school."

Students say their professors are accessible and almost always welcome students, even outside scheduled office hours. Freshmen are assigned faculty members as advisers, but a student says he "typically asks upperclassmen for advice" when selecting classes for his major.

CAMPUS POLITICS: GREEN LIGHT

Wake Forest has come a long way from its Baptist roots. The college pays employee benefits to same-sex lovers of faculty and staff, and the school's Wait Chapel now solemnizes same-sex "commitment ceremonies." One of the most influential political groups on campus is the Gay-Straight Student Alliance, which passes out rainbow stickers to faculty members and encourages them (with great success) to display them on their office doors.

However, overall, the Wake Forest student body is notable for being apolitical. A true spirit of tolerance is expressed in the university newspaper—where, a student reports, "there are a good number of conservative columnists, and they maintain a vigorous debate with their liberal counterparts, and in no sense would I say that there is any stifling of debate." The same student notes that conservative and religious students are in the majority at Wake Forest and that campus religious organizations are active.

Some of the best professors at Wake include Charles M. Lewis in philosophy; Robert Utley in humanities; William Moss and Eric Wilson in English; Roberta Morosini and M. Stanley Whitley in Romance languages; J. Daniel Hammond and Robert M. Whaples in economics; Richard D. Carmichael and James J. Kuzmanovich in mathematics; Kevin Bowen, Stewart Carter, Brian Gorelick, and Dan Locklair in music; Helga Welsh in political science; James P. Barefield in history (emeritus); and James T. Powell in classical languages.

> Once an old-fashioned Baptist college, Wake Forest is rapidly modernizing. One student warns, "The liberal arts are increasingly becoming subject to political correctness and drifting from traditional texts and subjects."

Wake Forest is one of the dwindling number of colleges that still has an honor code. Entering freshmen attend an honor assembly in which a professor delivers a sermon on being honest and forthright. Students then sign a book, agreeing to the code and acknowledging the consequences for violating it—possible expulsion.

Wake Forest puts a good deal of emphasis on international studies (though most are offered only as minors), including Asian, East Asian, East European, German, Latin American, and Russian studies. In addition, certificates are offered in Italian studies and Spanish studies. The school runs its own study-abroad programs in Argentina, Chile, England, France, Morocco, and Spain. There is a residential language center for students who wish to speak Russian or German on a regular basis. More than 60 percent of Wake Forest undergraduates study abroad during their college years, and the college's domestic Wake Washington (D.C.) program has won national recognition.

Student Life: If a beer falls in the forest . . .

Wake Forest is situated in the old tobacco town of Winston-Salem, North Carolina, a city of about 232,000 people. The school is only a short drive from downtown, but it is separated from the city by a wooded area.

Despite the headlong secularization of the university, one of the most popular groups on campus is the Baptist Student Union—a social and spiritual group that sponsors summer missions, prayer groups, local ministries, intramural sports teams, and other social events. The Campus Kitchens group distributes food from dining halls to the needy in Winston-Salem. Musically inclined students can choose from a large number of groups, most of them Christian in nature. The InterVarsity Christian Fellowship hosts prayer and discussion groups on campus, and the Wake Forest Baptist Church holds services in Wait Chapel every Sunday morning. The Wake Forest Catholic Community has daily and Sunday Masses in Davis Chapel; a local Latin Mass is offered at the parish of St. Benedict the Moor. There is also an Orthodox Christian Fellowship and a Hillel on campus.

Wake Forest has more than 200 registered clubs and organizations, including ballroom dancing, the Brian Piccolo Cancer Fund, a chess club, a comedy troupe, Habitat for Humanity, a handbell choir, Ultimate Frisbee, and Volunteer Service Corps.

Politically inclined students can join the College Republicans, which hosts a speaker series and plans campus events, and Democracy Matters, an organization that gets involved in local and national elections.

Wake Forest's Office of Multicultural Affairs, a university-funded department, sponsors many activities for ethnic minority students, including new minority student orientation, the Martin Luther King Jr. Celebration, Black History Month, Asian Awareness week, Multicultural Summits, and minority tutoring and scholarships. The office also advises the Black Student Alliance—one of the more active political groups on campus.

Living off campus is the exception, not the rule. While all the residential halls are within close walking distance of the campus's center, the coveted rooms are on the Quad, central to Wake's academic and social life. Most of the dormitories have men and women divided by floor; the university did away with its all-women residence hall a few years ago. Theme houses allow students to live with friends with shared interests in the languages or the arts. There are no coed dorm rooms or shower areas on campus, although some theme houses do have coed bathrooms. Substance-free (no smoking or alcohol) dormitories for freshmen and upperclassmen offer an escape from one's more Dionysian peers.

And substance use, particularly of alcohol, is heavy at Wake Forest. In the past decade or so, the community has seen fraternity parties become much more widespread. Students say that every weekend is a party weekend. Binge drinking is a genuine problem, with students frequently sent to the emergency room for detox. A popular tradition at Wake Forest calls for seniors, at the last home football game, to drink a fifth of liquor (750 ml) within 24 hours. The university has attempted (with mixed success) to counter this lethally stupid custom.

Wake Forest offers plenty of things to do on campus in the evenings and on weekends, often attracting lecturers and cultural performances to its halls. One student says, "At least once at Wake, one should attend a performance of the Lilting Banshees, a satirical student comedy group." Wake Forest athletics are probably dearer to students than anything else. The Demon Deacons compete on eight men's and eight women's intercollegiate teams in NCAA Division I, and the men's basketball team is usually a contender in the powerful Atlantic Coast Conference. Students also have plenty of nonvarsity options, including 36 intercollegiate club teams. Intramural teams include basketball, bowling, dodgeball, inner tube water polo, tennis, and many others.

SUGGESTED CORE

1. Classics 255, Classical Epic: *Iliad, Odyssey, Aeneid*
2. Philosophy 232, Ancient Greek Philosophy
3. Religion 102, Introduction to the Bible
4. Philosophy 237, Medieval Philosophy or Religion 372, History of Christian Thought
5. Political Science 276, Modern Political Thought
6. English 323, Shakespeare
7. History 251, The United States before 1865
8. Philosophy 352A, 19th-Century European Philosophy: Hegel, Kierkegaard, and Nietzsche

Wake Forest has become more dangerous in recent years. In 2011 the college reported 81 burglaries, five forcible sex offenses, four car thefts, four aggravated assaults, and one arson on campus.

Wake Forest is Ivy priced, with a 2012–13 tuition of $42,700 and estimated room and board at $11,700. However, admission is need blind, and all students who enroll are guaranteed sufficient financial aid; 40 percent of Wake Forest students received need-based aid. The average indebtedness of a recent graduating student was $35,070.

STRONG SUITS	WEAK POINTS
• Good programs in history, political science, business, and philosophy. • Honors options in various departments are rigorous. • The school's honor code is still in place, governing academic conduct. • Extensive and widely used study-abroad options.	• Trendy, politicized classes proliferating in humanities departments. • Religion department seems hostile to traditional Christianity. • Heavy drinking is common on campus. • Gay activism (and "weddings") a troubling presence at this Baptist-founded school.

Washington and Lee University

Lexington, Virginia • www.wlu.edu

White Columns and an Honor Code

Washington and Lee is the nation's ninth-oldest university. Now named for two great statesmen, the school was founded in 1749 as Augusta Academy. When the first U.S. president intervened to save the school from bankruptcy in 1796, it took his name in gratitude. After Appomattox, General Robert E. Lee took off his uniform to lead the school until his death in 1870. Lee's ethos profoundly reshaped the school, which soon added his name to Washington's.

Since Lee's tenure as president, W&L has earned recognition as one of the South's outstanding liberal arts institutions. However, in recent years administrators have shown their dissatisfaction with the school's reputation as a bastion of regional elites and have strived to recruit a more diverse student body and a more "progressive" faculty. An increasing emphasis on "diversity," some say, threatens to overwhelm what makes the school unique. New and ideologically infused programs, the politically correct tone of campus publications, and a trend toward hiring what one alumnus calls "radicals" as teachers could mean that W&L is changing inexorably—in the same way that many once-distinctive religious and regional schools have already done. Lovers of learning hope that the virtues long treasured at W&L survive the pressures of politics "unto all generations of the faithful heart."

VITAL STATISTICS

Religious affiliation: *none*

Total enrollment: *2,193*

Total undergraduates: *1,790*

SAT CR/Verbal midrange: *650–740*

SAT Math midrange: *660–740*

ACT midrange: *29–32*

Applicants: *6,487*

Applicants accepted: *18%*

Accepted applicants who enrolled: *44%*

Tuition (general/out of state): *$43,362*

Tuition (in state): *N/A*

Room and board: *$11,006*

Freshman retention rate: *94%*

Graduation rate (4 yrs.): *88%*

Graduation rate (6 yrs.): *93%*

Courses with fewer than 20 students: *74%*

Student-faculty ratio: *9:1*

Courses taught by graduate students: *not provided*

Students living on campus: *60%*

Students in fraternities: *86%*

Students in sororities: *79%*

Students receiving need-based financial aid: *40%*

Avg. student-loan debt of a recent graduating class: *$24,716*

Most popular majors: *business/marketing, economics, political science*

Guaranteed housing for 4 years? *no*

Academic Life: Connecting the disciplines

Washington and Lee's Foundation and Distribution requirements are better than most—largely because nearly all the courses that fulfill them are solid and serious. "I have gained a great deal of experience in diverse disciplines," says a student. Notes another: "Some of my favorite classes have been a result of general-education requirements." These requirements take up more than one-third of the credits required for graduation. Indeed, as one professor remarks, "It is difficult to graduate from WLU and not get a liberal arts education."

Taking classes in diverse disciplines alone does not a liberal education make, however. Students can graduate from W&L having little or nothing to do with what has traditionally been called the canon or with a study of America's founding or political institutions.

Major requirements impose more curricular discipline. For instance, the English department requires its majors to take at least three courses in each of three areas: earlier British literature, later British literature (including world literature written in English), and American literature. Students could well miss Shakespeare.

History majors must take 36 credits, 15 of which must come from one of three areas of emphasis: European and Russian, American, and global. There is no required American history or Western civilization sequence.

Politics students, on the other hand, are required to take "American National Government"; they also face a hefty 41-credit requirement. One student says that politics professors masterfully articulate the "complex current political and economic phenomena. . . . We not only learn about current political events but are challenged to think about what Machiavelli or Locke would have said about them." A faculty member adds, "Politics is truly first rate. We are perennially one of the top three or four majors, and we offer a wide range of courses."

Academic advising helps students navigate requirements. Freshmen are assigned an adviser, and after choosing a major, they are paired with someone from their field. Students may register for classes only after obtaining their registration password from their advisers. Another option for freshmen seeking guidance is enrolling in a small first-year seminar. These classes, which are capped at 15, introduce the student "to a field of study by way of a special topic, issue, or problem of interest." Options include "Fictions of Vietnam in France and the U.S.A." and "Hard-boiled L.A.: Film Noir and the City of the Angels."

Offering 40 undergraduate majors, W&L is proud to be the only top-tier liberal arts college with a fully accredited business school and a fully accredited journalism program. The English, philosophy, history, business, accounting, economics, and pre-med programs are widely considered the best on campus, and are thus among the most popular.

The student-faculty ratio is an outstanding 9 to 1. All classes are taught by professors. (Language departments make use of native-speaking assistants who do lead some sessions, though faculty teach the class itself.) Teachers are said to be accessible to students. "The professors' influence extends beyond the classroom, however, and they often become akin to good friends," says one undergrad. Another student lauds his teachers for their hard work: "They manage to teach three classes, schedule several hours' worth of office hours (which attract lines of students), advise

CAMPUS POLITICS: GREEN LIGHT

Conservative-leaning groups are the most active and vocal on campus. There is a small gay and lesbian group, but that is about the only active organization that could be called radical. "Students are able to express any views they may have," one says. "W&L is likely one of the most conservative college campuses in the country. Despite this, no one is ostracized for having differing ideas." One College Republican suggests that W&L is labeled as conservative merely because it has a more balanced political atmosphere. In 2012, at a debate cosponsored by a gay group at W&L law school and by its Federalist Society, columnists clashed over the question of same-sex "marriage." Andrew Sullivan spoke in defense of the innovation, while Maggie Gallagher opposed it. The fact that such divergent groups could work together to organize a civil dispute on such a hot-button issue speaks well for the cordial and respectful atmosphere at Washington and Lee.

students on everything from classes to careers, and complete their own research projects. As a result, students often develop very close personal and professional relationships with professors." Teachers often ask students to help with research work, giving them training in areas that are often available only as graduate study in other universities.

"Professors teach all classes," one student says. "And when I say teach, I mean *teach*. They don't just get up in front of a class and dictate for an hour." Some 74 percent of classes have fewer than 20 students, and few report problems getting into the courses they want.

When it comes to the classroom, teachers tend to be more left-leaning than the student body. On the whole, however, conservative or religious students and their ideas are welcome. "Even the most liberal professors and left-leaning courses enthusiastically welcome disagreement and discussion from the conservatives," says a professor. A real diversity of thought within the classroom—too rare on today's college campuses—often gives rise to lively discussions. Says one liberal student, "One of my economics professors, who's clearly left-leaning, had us reading Milton Friedman the other day." A faculty member says, "The best antidote to political correctness is a faculty committed to learning, by which I mean a faculty who still want to learn and not just teach. This sense of wonder preserves fairness. I am happy to say that I have colleagues with just this disposition."

Remarks another: "The faculty are uniformly superior and conscientious. They are outstanding scholars and teachers. There may be examples of faculty at some institutions who choose not to teach and instead simply do research and writing. That is not the case here. The beauty of our faculty is that they represent and manifest the ideal combination: they are active scholars who use their research and writing to inform their teaching; they can produce knowledge as well as disseminate it."

Students list many praiseworthy professors, including William F. Connelly Jr., Tyler Dickovick, Robin Le Blanc, Lucas Morel, Robert Strong, and Eduardo Velásquez in politics; Marc Conner, Edwin Craun, and Suzanne Keen in English; Miriam Carlisle and Kevin Crotty in Classics; George Bent in art history; Timothy Diette and Arthur Goldsmith in economics; and Lad Sessions in philosophy. One undergrad praises all his professors for

> "The professors' influence extends beyond the classroom. They often become akin to good friends," says one undergrad. Another says: "They manage to teach three classes, schedule several hours' worth of office hours (which attract lines of students), advise students on everything from classes to careers."

being "superb and fair." Remarks one contented professor, "You can judge the success of a school by how long its faculty stick around. Faculty at W&L are here to stay."

One popular option on campus is Spring Term Abroad, which in 2011 included trips to Argentina, Brazil, the Caribbean, China, Denmark, France, Italy, Spain, Tanzania, and the U.K. (London). Washington and Lee students can enroll in longer study-abroad programs, most of which are sponsored by other institutions with which W&L has agreements.

Languages offered at the university are Chinese, French, German, Greek and Latin, Italian, Japanese, Portuguese, Russian, and Spanish.

Student Life: Drinkers yes, slackers no

Many students find W&L's atmosphere intoxicating. "Washington and Lee is all about the little things that can't be measured by *U.S. News and World Report*," says one. "Teachers who really care. A campus that's beautiful. Friendly people with character and integrity. A killer social life. If studies took into account all the little things that really make schools what they are, Washington and Lee would be number one."

As a longtime W&Ler relates, "W&L is located in a beautiful part of the world, the Shenandoah Valley. This is the best and worst of small-town, small-college life. For some, that is intimate. For others, that can be claustrophobic. Along with the smallness comes a domination of the social scene by the sororities and fraternities. Again, if that is what a student wants, she or he will thrive here. But if you need the trappings of a bigger city—ethnic foods, sports, museums—then this probably is not the place."

The relative isolation makes for an atmosphere in which students study hard and then relieve stress over a glass (or a six-pack) of beer. But not everyone parties every night. "For every student who drinks four nights a week, there is a student who doesn't," says one student, who considers himself a moderate tippler.

One student warns, "Prospective students should know that if they are not at all interested in the Greek system when they come here, they are in for a very long four years." About 86 percent of men and 79 percent of women belong to the 15 fraternities and eight sororities on campus. Although Greek organizations do their share of community service activities, they are also a center of student inebriation. "Partying is a major social activity at W&L," one student says. A teacher admits, "We suffer our issues with Greek life and drinking as any university, but we do a pretty reasonable job of managing them." However, a professor says that "hazing is another worrying reality at W&L. There was an egregious case . . . that resulted in the suspension of a fraternity for a full year."

> ### SUGGESTED CORE
>
> 1. Classics 203, Greek Literature from Homer to the Early Hellenistic Period and Classics 204, Augustan Era
> 2. Philosophy 110, Ancient Philosophy
> 3. Religion 101/102, The Hebrew Bible: Old Testament/New Testament
> 4. Religion 250, Early Christian Thought: Orthodoxy and Heresy
> 5. Politics 266, Modern Political Philosophy
> 6. English 252, Shakespeare
> 7. History 107, History of the United States to 1876
> 8. History 226, European Intellectual History, 1880 to 1960 (*closest match*)

Still, classrooms are competitive, and "the workload can be daunting," says a student. "Most people here intend to succeed and take classes seriously." Still another reports that "intellectual discussions can occur anywhere at any time . . . in places you wouldn't expect, such as locker rooms." A faculty member finds that "academic life is very impressive here. Our students are highly motivated, increasingly diverse, and more international. Our typical student is extremely active, engaged in many pursuits, and on a 26-hour clock." A second professor agrees, "Our students are W&L's greatest strength. They are honorable, decent, ambitious, smart, and friendly. Many are intellectually serious."

Traditionally, the student body at W&L has been generally rather conservative—unsurprising, at a school where Robert E. Lee and his family are buried below the campus chapel and museum. (Lee's horse, Traveller, is buried outside the chapel.) Lee's presence is still palpable at the university. One student considers him "the physical embodiment of what all W&L students aim to be: honorable, of integrity and character."

Generous scholarship offerings, a major outreach to attract international students, and the addition of "diversity" programs on campus have begun to chip away at the school's southern identity. We just hope that all this diversity doesn't homogenize the school, rendering it as sanitized and politically correct as certain other colleges formerly known as southern.

Most students are involved in more than one of the 125 clubs and organizations on campus, including a student newspaper, a radio station, and a cable television station.

Religious organizations include the (Episcopalian) Canterbury Club, Baptist Campus Ministries, Catholic Campus Ministry, Generals' Christian Fellowship, Reformed University Fellowship, Orthodox Christian Fellowship, and a Hillel club.

There are politically active groups across the spectrum, with College Democrats and College Republicans, and Students for Life and Students for Choice. The one gay group is the GLBT Equality Initiative. The feminist group Knowledge Empowering Women Leaders (KEWL) combines course work in women's and gender studies with programs outside the classroom.

W&L is an NCAA Division III school—which means its athletic program cannot offer scholarships, and student play is restricted to fewer games. A high percentage of students play varsity sports—there are 11 for men and eleven for women—or intramural sports such as soccer, tennis, flag football, billiards, and big pink volleyball.

Fittingly, "the honor code established by General Robert E. Lee remains a strong force in the W&L community. It is taken very, very seriously and is extremely effective," according to a student. Incoming students pledge to abide by this honor system, which is run by their peers. Offenses against honor include lying, cheating, stealing, and other breaches of trust. For students found guilty, there is only one punishment—expulsion. The honor system is a manifestation of General Lee's "one rule" at the university: that every student be a gentleman. The Speaking Tradition, for instance, dictates that when people pass each other, they say "hi," even if they are strangers. One undergrad says simply, "The Honor System works, and the speaking tradition really does promote a friendly atmosphere."

Students are required to live on campus for their first two years, beyond which the university does not guarantee housing. About 60 percent of the student body lives on campus. All residence halls are coed, but men and women are separated by floor, and there are no coed bathrooms or dorm rooms. On-campus housing includes fraternity and sorority houses, where many students live as sophomores. There is a limited number of substance-free housing options. Resident advisers live in freshman housing.

Crime on campus is rare, though the school did run several years of "sexual assault summits" to address sexual misconduct on campus and in off-campus housing. In 2011 the school reported five burglaries, one case of aggravated assault, two forcible sex offenses, and one case of auto theft.

Tuition for 2012–13 was $43,362, with room and board $11,006. Students are encouraged to apply for both need-based aid and merit-based aid to best avail themselves of the more than $28 million in financial aid and scholarships. The school meets all demonstrated need. The average recent graduate emerged owing $24,716.

STRONG SUITS

- Solid, worthy (instead of fluff) classes fulfill distribution requirements.
- Devoted teachers who really mentor students.
- Excellent departments in English, philosophy, history, business, accounting, economics, and premed.
- A courtly, friendly southern ethos prevails on its beautiful campus.
- Significant research opportunities for students.

WEAK POINTS

- New hires are said to be pushing diversity courses and trendy approaches to disciplines.
- Insufficient requirements for English and history majors.
- Significant heavy drinking culture of long standing.
- Problems with hazing in the dominant Greek system.

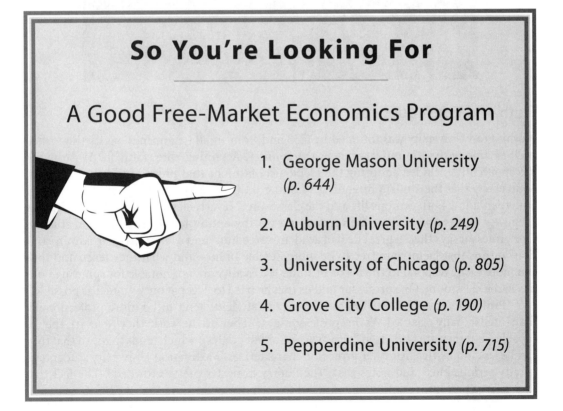

So You're Looking For

A Good Free-Market Economics Program

1. George Mason University *(p. 644)*

2. Auburn University *(p. 249)*

3. University of Chicago *(p. 805)*

4. Grove City College *(p. 190)*

5. Pepperdine University *(p. 715)*

Washington University in St. Louis

St. Louis, Missouri • www.wustl.edu

Truth and Consequences

Washington University was founded in 1853 and from small beginnings has distinguished itself as among the top universities in the country. Attaining elite status for Washington has apparently included adopting the ideological fashions that prevail in like institutions. Sources say that the student attending Washington University will face a multiculturalist ethos pervading both campus life and the classroom. Nevertheless, there is a lot of scholarly firepower at this university, which makes it a worthy option for the self-directed student. One professor says that "a great deal of academic freedom" and a "nonintrusive administration" means that faculty are free to be more flexible in how and what they teach and thus can more easily respond to the needs of students. Faculty are not notable for spouting politics in the classroom. One professor told us that he tried to "keep it out as much as possible."

Professors say that Washington University students tend to be more professionally than intellectually oriented. As one professor says, "They do the work; they're smart; they're capable," but they are also often "very worried about grades," which tends to mean that they can be less inquisitive. Another professor characterizes Washington University students as "pretty serious kids" and notes that "the library is always pretty crowded." The fact that such a large percentage of freshmen intend to become doctors and that the business school is so popular suggests that most students enter Washington University having already chosen a career.

Academic Life: Harvard of the Midwest

Students can get a traditional liberal arts education at Washington but only if they seek it out. The school's distributional requirements are not particularly strong, nor are its science mandates (only one course in "applied numeracy" is mandated for the BA in arts and sciences).

Students who want a broad, humane education should explore "Text and Tradition" (T&T), one of seven optional First-Year Academic Programs. In this interdisciplinary program, "students explore the classic texts and intellectual traditions upon which American and European culture has been built." Reading lists "are chosen with care from the best of Western thought," says one student, but "the T&T faculty seem to have no conception of the physical limits on reading." The same student says that Text and Tradition is "no substitute for a true liberal arts education," but that it "is absolutely essential if you go to Washington University, because it might very well be the only engagement to be had in the Great Books style."

Another noteworthy freshman option is FOCUS, a yearlong seminar program that explores one major topic from the perspective of a variety of disciplines. These courses are limited to 14 to 16 students each. "We want to encourage students to think more deeply about issues and to get into discussion with the faculty and with their peers," says one professor. Nine seminar topics were offered in 2013, including "Law and Society," "Literary Culture of Modern Ireland," "Phage Hunters and Bioinformatics," and "Women in Science."

A worthy major that builds on the Text and Tradition program is the Interdisciplinary Project in the Humanities (IPH). One member of faculty says that there is "a lot of intellectual energy in the department." The faculty has a "high level of scholarship" with "a lot of publications" among professors. And students, says the same professor, "can get a lot of individual attention from the very beginning." The IPH major consists of an introductory core, which introduces students to "the American and European philosophical, religious, and literary traditions." The project's cultural calendar, called the Lyceum,

VITAL STATISTICS

Religious affiliation: *none*
Total enrollment: *13,908*
Total undergraduates: *7,239*
SAT CR/Verbal midrange: *690–760*
SAT Math midrange: *710–780*
ACT midrange: *32–34*
Applicants: *28,823*
Applicants accepted: *17%*
Accepted applicants who enrolled: *31%*
Tuition (general/out of state): *$43,705*
Tuition (in state): *N/A*
Room and board: *$13,580*
Freshman retention rate: *97%*
Graduation rate (4 yrs.): *86%*
Graduation rate (6 yrs.): *93%*
Courses with fewer than 20 students: *68%*
Student-faculty ratio: *7:1*
Courses taught by graduate students: *not provided*
Students living on campus: *78%*
Students in fraternities: *25%*
Students in sororities: *25%*
Students receiving need-based financial aid: *39%*
Avg. student-loan debt of a recent graduating class: *not provided*
Most popular majors: *social sciences, engineering, pre-med/medical sciences*
Guaranteed housing for 4 years? *yes*

CAMPUS POLITICS: GREEN LIGHT

As with many other colleges, the Washington University campus and student body leans to the left. The college recently showed its commitment to political correctness when it canceled a traditional orientation event hosted by a large corporation after it came out that the company had donated $150,000 to a Minnesota political action committee supporting a candidate opposed to gay "marriage."

However, the vast majority of students are too focused on grades and career to sign up for the latest rally or protest, or even to discuss politics. Consequently, political ideology generally does not intrude into the classroom. The College Republicans and the Conservative Leadership Association are both active on campus, though political groups are probably less obtrusive here than at many colleges.

allows students to attend a wide range of cultural events, including concerts, theater, operas, and exhibitions.

The university assigns advisers to freshmen, but they seldom become close to the students. One says that "students are best served by seeking out for themselves professors whom they would like to advise them," since adviser assignments are usually "random and sometimes wholly inappropriate." Premajor advisers are not necessarily faculty members, but after declaring a major, a student is assigned a faculty adviser within his discipline.

Professors, not grad students, lead most courses. As at all research universities, there exists at Washington a tension between teaching and research. Commitment to teaching varies from instructor to instructor. A student says, "Most departments make it a priority to allow professors time to teach. . . . I doubt you'll find it better anywhere else, unless you go to a school where professors do nothing but teach." One professor says, "Most of the (science and nonscience) faculty I know take their teaching very seriously and put a great deal of time into it. On the other hand, there is very strong pressure to get research grants."

In the humanities, "professors are extremely accessible to students," but science professors remain much more aloof, an undergrad reports. A graduate student says that "older faculty teach far more than they publish, while newer faculty have considerable workloads in both teaching and publishing." This means that the otherwise impressive student-faculty ratio of 7 to 1 is misleading.

Opportunities abound for student research. The school's world-renowned medical center attracts many premed students. One student claims that most entering freshmen intend to be doctors, but after realizing how intense the program is, only a fraction of them actually finish as premeds. The premed program and the other sciences together constitute the "university's crown jewel," says another student. Engineering is also outstanding, with a recent graduate remarking, "For an engineering undergraduate, there are no truly 'weak' programs." Another well-respected program is philosophy-neuroscience-psychology (PNP), an interdisciplinary concentration that studies the mind and brain.

A professor says the Classics department shows a "willingness to work individually with students." Classics students can take a semester to study in Athens, Rome, or Sicily, or take part in an archaeological project in the Mediterranean, such as the Athenian Agora and the Iklaina Archaeological Project at Pylos.

With Nobel laureate Douglass North (emeritus—he still advises undergraduates), the economics department is also strong, as are the School of Fine Arts and the School of Architecture.

The School of Engineering and Applied Science attracts some of the nation's very best faculty and students. One engineering major says, "Professors [in engineering] tend to be very accessible." Many students say the business school is less rigorous than the rest of the university, although it has improved in recent years.

Some departments are weaker than others. The philosophy department, which places a heavy emphasis on interdisciplinary crossover with psychology, linguistics, and cognitive science, offers no medieval philosophy courses and only in recent years added ancient philosophy.

Professors most often mentioned as particularly strong teachers include Eric Brown and Claude Evans in philosophy; Lee Benham (emeritus) and Stephanie Lau in economics; Gerald Izenberg (emeritus), David Konig, and Mark Gregory Pegg in history; Robert Lamberton, George Pepe, and Susan Rotroff in Classics; and Richard Kurtz (emeritus) in psychology. Another student says that those who take one class with professor of Russian language Mikhail Palatnik will "stay in Russian for the rest of their time in school. He's just that good." Other outstanding faculty include Paul Stein in biology, Dewey Holten in chemistry, Gary Jensen (emeritus) in math, and Barna Szabo in mechanical engineering.

A professor says of Washington students: "They do the work; they're smart, they're capable," but they are also often "very worried about grades," which tends to mean that they can be less inquisitive.

Students who major in English will most likely study Shakespeare, but it is not required. Besides a course in American literature and a course in a major author—for example, Jane Austen or Chaucer—the major further requires two courses in literature before 1700 and two courses before 1900.

Faculty in the history department are said to be excellent. Courses range from the traditional ("Western Civilization") to the trendy ("Sports and Culture: Fair Play?: Race, Gender, and Nation in American Sports"). Requirements for the major are thin and can be fulfilled without taking either American history or the history of Western civilization. Still, many solid courses are offered by worthy teachers.

One student says that the political science department isn't theoretical enough, focusing on "electoral minutiae, never political philosophy." Departmental requirements permit majors to avoid the study of the U.S. Constitution or American political thought. Students must select courses from three out of five subfields: American politics, comparative politics, international relations, political methodology, and political theory.

Washington University offers a great number of study-abroad options. However, these options vary according to one's department. Thus, English majors can study in the U.K. and Ireland—as can political science majors, who also have options in Chile, Croatia,

India, Israel, Jordan, Kenya, Nicaragua, and Switzerland, among many others.

The school offers majors in Arabic, Chinese, French, German, Greek and Latin, Hebrew, Italian, Japanese, Persian, and Spanish, and courses in many other languages.

Student Life: Under the arch

The city of St. Louis offers a wonderful variety of cultural activities. There is considerable university interaction with the surrounding neighborhoods (with residents of University City sometimes complaining of "gentrification"), and many of the 7,200 undergraduate students volunteer in the city, building houses, feeding the poor, teaching English to immigrants, and tutoring disadvantaged children.

Washington University boasts 332 student organizations, and the Student Union's Student Group Directory lists seven separate categories of clubs. For instance, artsy students will enjoy the Washington University Pops Orchestra, the Aristocats (a coed all-Disney a cappella group), and More Fools than Wise (a small chamber vocal ensemble).

The university is very politically engaged. Active groups include the College Democrats, College Republicans, and the College Libertarians. The school also has a Conservative Leadership Association that is "nonpartisan and nonsectarian, but all conservative." The official college paper is titled, unimaginatively, *Student Life.*

The Washington University Bears compete on NCAA Division III teams in every major sport. The university particularly excels in women's sports. In 2011 the women's cross-country team claimed the championship, and in March 2010 the women's basketball team won its fifth national championship. The men's basketball team won the title in 2009. Plenty of intramural sports are also available, including racquetball, billiards, swimming, bowling, cross-country, volleyball, flag football, and men's and women's arm wrestling.

Fraternities and sororities attract about one-quarter of the student body. Students say that Greek life dominates the weekend social lives of students, especially freshmen. "For the first two years, if you don't like frat parties, or frat-like dorm parties, then you probably have good friends but nowhere to go with them," says one student. However, Washington University students deny that it's a party school. One professor says, "The university has become much more conscious of drinking problems in recent years." In response, administrators have been imposing ever more regulations on alcohol at parties, particularly the massive, all-campus Walk In, Lay Down (WILD) outdoor party held each semester.

Speaking of spirits, there is a surprisingly strong religious presence at Wash U., with several active Christian groups, including the Baptist Student Union, Association of Christian Truth Seekers, and One Voice Christian Fellowship—plus Jewish groups and a great many clubs for members of other religious faiths. The Catholic Student Center works too hard at being popular, according to Catholic students. A better choice is the local Oratory of St. Francis de Sales, which features the Latin Mass with Gregorian chant.

Almost two-thirds of the undergraduate population—including all freshmen—live on campus in one of the 10 residential colleges in an area known as South Forty. Each of these residential colleges includes one to three buildings and gives students the feel of a smaller university community. The university guarantees housing only for freshmen, most of whom live in all-freshmen dormitories. All residential halls are coed. There are no coed bathrooms or dorm rooms, but one student says that on his floor, "the line between sexes in the bathrooms was often blurry." The same student also says that students on his floor also "openly drank" and that dorms were not policed properly. Substance-free ("sub-free") housing, however, is available to freshmen. The residential-life office offers an apartment-referral service for students who choose to live off campus, and the university also owns apartments near campus that in some cases are closer to classroom buildings than are the dormitories.

Campus crime statistics list few incidents. In 2011 there were eight forcible sex offenses and 11 burglaries on campus.

Undergraduate tuition for the 2012–13 academic year was $43,705, with room and board averaging $13,580. Admissions are not need blind, but about 39 percent of undergraduates received need-based financial aid.

STRONG SUITS	WEAK POINTS
• Highly qualified faculty and hardworking students.	• Philosophy department too dependent on cross-listed courses, especially in psychology—and offers little in ancient and nothing in medieval thought.
• Text and Tradition, a freshman option, focuses on Western civilization—and leads into the excellent Interdisciplinary Project in the Humanities.	• Business school less rigorous than the rest of the university.
• Highly regarded programs for premeds, engineers, and hard-science students.	• Few courses in political philosophy—as opposed to the minutiae of election campaigns.
• Extensive opportunities for research alongside faculty members.	• An ongoing problem with campus drinking, despite strict school regulations.
• Good departments in Classics, economics, history, fine arts, and architecture.	

Wellesley College

Wellesley, Massachusetts • www.wellesley.edu

More than a Hen Party

Wellesley College was founded in 1875 and has earned a glowing academic reputation. Today it is considered by many to be the crown jewel of the "Seven Sisters," the most prestigious and selective women's colleges in United States. "Students come fairly ambivalent about the single-sex aspect of the college and simply fall in love with the beauty of the campus," says one faculty member. "It works its magic on them." Wellesley has a distinguished alumnae network that is nonpareil among American colleges and access to seemingly unlimited funding sources, both internal and external.

In the past, Wellesley prided itself on the well-rounded liberal arts education it provided its students. While Wellesley's curriculum is still grounded in the liberal arts, much of that material is viewed through the jaundiced lens of multiculturalism—a political ideology intrinsically hostile to the very civilization that created and sustains the liberal arts.

Academic Life: Serious classroom environment

In lieu of a core curriculum, the school imposes some distribution requirements, of which one student says, "They can be as serious or as easy as you make them. But I like the idea that everyone has to be at least familiar with all fields of study." However, Wellesley is no longer a liberal arts school in the true sense. "There were too many classes at Wellesley where I did readings, went to lectures, wrote the papers, and in the end still knew nothing about the topic I couldn't have discovered on Wikipedia," an otherwise contented alumna says. Students are also required to take at least one course with a multicultural focus.

Every new student is initially advised by a class dean—an administrator assigned to their entire class—and a faculty adviser. After selecting a major, the student can change advisers or keep the one she has. Fortunately, advisers at Wellesley really are advisers, professors who actually guide students through college and aren't there just to make sure students satisfy course requirements. The First-Year Mentoring Program pairs 15 freshmen with a junior or senior who lives in the same dormitory complex and leads weekly meetings. Since Wellesley does not have graduate students, professors—not teaching assistants—conduct all courses.

"The best aspect of Wellesley is the serious classroom environment," says one Wellesley woman. "Students come for the academic experience. They have high expectations for themselves and their learning and come prepared to work. Classes are very engaged; we have a good time and learn a lot."

Unfortunately, students point to classes, professors, and entire departments where the rainbow of opinion has been squeezed by political uniformity into a few narrow shades of purple and pink. They nod at the usual suspects, such as peace and justice studies and women's studies, but also at certain courses in German and Spanish—complaining for instance that one professor in a foreign language course was "outspoken on socialist views and did not deal well with conservative students." Other students note that Africana studies, religious studies, and even chemistry held some minefields for women with more traditional views, and they complain of an economics course taught from a dogmatically Marxist perspective.

In the English department, majors are required to take one class each in critical interpretation, Shakespeare, pre-1800 lit, and pre-1900 lit. Their remaining six classes must be at intermediate

VITAL STATISTICS

Religious affiliation: *none*
Total enrollment: *2,481*
Total undergraduates: *2,481*
SAT CR/Verbal midrange: *650–740*
SAT Math midrange: *640–740*
ACT midrange: *29–32*
Applicants: *4,478*
Applicants accepted: *30%*
Accepted applicants who enrolled: *43%*
Tuition (general/out of state): *$41,824*
Tuition (in state): *N/A*
Room and board: *$13,032*
Freshman retention rate: *97%*
Graduation rate (4 yrs.): *84%*
Graduation rate (6 yrs.): *92%*
Courses with fewer than 20 students: *72%*
Student-faculty ratio: *7:1*
Courses taught by graduate students: *not provided*
Students living on campus: *93%*
Students in fraternities: *N/A*
Students in sororities: *none*
Students receiving need-based financial aid: *60%*
Avg. student-loan debt of a recent graduating class: *$14,189*
Most popular majors: *literature/foreign languages, social sciences, visual and performing arts*
Guaranteed housing for 4 years? *yes*

CAMPUS POLITICS: YELLOW LIGHT

While Wellesley has been open to a diversity of ideas—even traditional ones—it seems that remaining a conservative at Wellesley can make your professors sad. A history professor spoke of an "exceptionally bright" student in his class whom he felt he had not served well because, at the end of the class, "she was still conservative." The head researcher for the Wellesley Center for Women claimed in a speech that conservative women should be pitied because they've been used by men to work against their own interests. She was quoted as saying of Wellesley conservatives: "And to think these women are highly educated!" One person who attended the speech recalls that the speaker went on to "lament the failure of higher education to weed out or change traditional women."

One Wellesley graduate wrote in 2012 in the *Washington Examiner*, "As a political science major, I was offered seminars such as 'Marxism, Anarchism and Fundamentalism,' 'Feminist Political Theory' and 'Race and Political Theory,' but an equivalent course on conservative theorists such as Edmund Burke or Michael Oakeshott was nonexistent." However, she wrote, "I never experienced a hostile classroom environment as a conservative at Wellesley. Aside from requisite Paul Krugman readings in economics and political science classes, my professors were fair.

"Largely as a result of off-campus experiences and internships, I grew the confidence to speak up in class and voice my disagreement with assigned readings or with my peers. Professors welcomed this debate because class discussion is far more interesting when everyone is not in agreement."

or advanced levels, and they can take no more than two creative writing electives. While the major requirements could certainly be stronger, Wellesley offers excellent classes like "Milton," "Renaissance Literature," "Southern Literature," and "Colonial and Post-Colonial Literature," alongside race- and gender-obsessed courses that should be avoided.

History majors must complete a class in the history of Africa, Latin America, or Asia, and one class in the history of the U.S., Europe, or Russia. Of their seven electives, one must come from premodern history, and the department urges (but does not require) students to concentrate on a field, time, nation, or theme, like "the history of women" or "the ancient world." Course offerings are impressive.

More substantial are the requirements for a major in political science. Students are recommended to take an introductory course and one intermediate- or advanced-level class each in American politics and law, comparative politics, international relations, and political theory, as well as an additional advanced-level course in two of the fields. Finally, students complete three electives, such as "The First Amendment," "Political Economy of Development and Underdevelopment," "Gender and Conflict Resolution in South Asia," "International Environmental Law," "Race and Political Theory," and "Power and Politics."

The school has many virtues. Says one undergrad: "I like the small classes, and how everyone gets along. The professors are considerate to us." Inside the classroom, students say they generally feel comfortable sharing their own ideas and opinions, regardless of whether their thoughts align with those of their professors. "I knew my professors were generally very liberal, but I never felt looked down upon for my views," says one conservative student. "Wellesley's near worship of tolerance has, for the most part, also been afforded to conservative students both in and out of the classroom," a student says. "When I quoted the Bible in an English class to emphasize a literary point about Dante, it was praised and not ostracized. After disagreeing strongly with a professor in my final essay about *Roe v. Wade*, where I preferred using 'baby' and she preferred 'fetus,' she gave the paper an A, writing that I was to be applauded for maintaining my conservative beliefs on a campus like Wellesley."

Another student disagrees, saying, "It is virtually impossible for a free marketplace of ideas to exist at the college, especially within the administration." She adds, "There is definite pressure to conform to political correctness here at every level. Certainly the faculty is asked to join the party line. Students should know this about Wellesley before deciding to come here."

Despite a number of opinionated departments, the alumnae, overall, are supportive of their picturesque alma mater, as are many current students. "I do enjoy Wellesley; I've received a good education from fantastic professors," says one. Teachers recommended by current and former students include Marion Just and Edward Stettner (emeritus) in political science; Thomas Cushman and Jonathan Imber in sociology; Karl "Chip" Case (emeritus) in economics; Kathleen Brogan and Larry Rosenwald in English; Andrew Webb in biology; Mary Kate McGowan, Nicolas de Warren, and Catherine Wearing in philosophy; Tracy Gleason, Beth Hennessey, and Paul Wink in psychology; Stephen Marini in religion; Jerold Auerbach (emeritus) and Guy Rogers in history; and Ray Starr in Classics.

> "Wellesley's near-worship of tolerance has, for the most part, also been afforded to conservative students both in and out of the classroom," a student says.

Students are very vocal about their favorite instructors and make their opinions available to fellow students in an online server called "First-Class," where such matters are discussed in forums not accessible to faculty. "The only rules on that forum are that they must be respectful of the professor and cannot comment about whether they are an easy or hard grader," says a student.

Some introductory courses enroll more than a hundred students, but these classes divide into small discussion groups. However, as one student complains of humanities and social sciences seminars, "Discussion-based classes often turn into self-help groups, with each student . . . offering a personal example or story that might touch the theme of the reading but doesn't fully relate." Nonetheless, students say "there is no such thing as an easy A" at Wellesley, and anything lacking in class time is made up for with copious amounts of homework.

Wellesley is also proud of its science program. In the Science Center, students have access to state-of-the-art instrumentation, including a confocal microscope, two NMR spectrometers, microcalorimeters, and a high-power pulsed tunable laser. The adjacent

Whitin Observatory boasts sophisticated telescopes. The greenhouses and botanical gardens are used for study and are open to the public.

Wellesley students can register for courses at MIT, so science-minded students should have no problem finding classes they need. There are a number of exchange programs in which students may cross-register at MIT, as well as at Brandeis University, Babson, and Olin College of Engineering. Through the Twelve College Exchange Program, students may opt to study for up to two semesters at one of the participating schools, such as Amherst, Bowdoin, Dartmouth, Vassar, Smith, and Mount Holyoke.

Several hundred students take advantage each year of the many study-abroad options. The college administers programs in Aix-en-Provence, France, and Vienna. Wellesley is also a member of consortia that offer programs and exchanges in many different colleges and universities abroad.

Wellesley offers classes in Arabic, Chinese, German, Greek and Latin, Hebrew, Hindi, Italian, Japanese, Korean, Russian, and Spanish.

Student Life: Too much to do

Wellesley's proximity to Boston means there are plenty of opportunities for students to socialize with colleagues from the area's numerous other schools—both on and off campus grounds. The college funds two bus services, and commuter rail runs within easy walking distance of campus.

Wellesley maintains an Office of Religious and Spiritual Life for students—although it's not picky about which spirits are invoked. The school chapel is beautiful, though much of what made it peculiarly "Christian" has been removed. It is now a "multifaith space" rather than a church. The college website pledges to "support the celebration" of Baha'ism, Buddhism, Christianity, Hinduism, Jainism, Humanism, Judaism, Islam, Native American and African traditions, Paganism, Sikhism, Unitarian Universalism, and Zoroastrianism. The larger faiths have associated chaplaincies or student groups.

However, students cannot be sure that all these chaplains or programs will present their respective faith traditions in unadulterated form. For example, the Catholic chaplaincy sponsors Dignity (a gay-advocacy organization officially condemned by the church) and invites abortion-friendly speakers to campus. Religiously orthodox students should take the hint and attend services off campus—for instance, at one of the more conservative congregations in Boston or Cambridge.

At least the school's tolerance has begun to include conservative students; heretofore Wellesley has been at best a challenging environment for those with more traditional views. Despite a stubbornly leftist faculty, conservative students do report a growing curiosity and appreciation in their peers for other points of view. "I find that my classmates are becoming less ideological . . . and more curious about what is true," one student says. A professor concurs: "Now any person could find a niche in Wellesley; it is becoming a much more open place than it was. People are now taking great pains to allow for differences of opinion." Another student assures incoming freshmen that "Wellesley is slowly but surely changing for the better." There is a chapter of College Republicans, a pro-life group, and a range of

Christian organizations on campus, which are "small, but active."

Students interested in service will find opportunities like Campus Girl Scouts, Sexual Health Educators, and Habitat for Humanity, as well as the Best Buddies program, which pairs students with mentally handicapped buddies. A number of cultural and ethnic clubs are available, from the Hellenic Society, Spectrum GLBTQA association (which hosts the school's annual Dyke Ball), and Hui O'Hawaii to the Wellesley Arab Women, Canadian Club, and Wellesley Asian Alliance. Literary and media outlets include *Counterpoint* journal, *The Legenda* yearbook, the Science Fiction and Fantasy Society, Wellesley College Television, and WZLY radio.

Fourteen varsity sports are offered, as well as instructional programs in fitness, athletics, and dance. Wellesley Blue athletes compete in the NCAA Division III and are affiliated with several other athletic associations, like the New England Women's and Men's Athletic Conference. The school offers club sports like soccer, equestrian, skiing, and water polo, and intramural kickball, mini-marathon, badminton, and dodgeball teams.

SUGGESTED CORE

1. Classical Civilizations 202/204, Crisis, Drama, Classical Athens/Latin Literature
2. Philosophy 201, Ancient Greek Philosophy
3. Religion 104/105, Study of the Hebrew Bible—Old Testament/New Testament
4. Religion 216, Christian Thought 100–1600
5. Political Science 241, Modern Political Thought
6. English 112, Introduction to Shakespeare
7. History 203, Out of Many: American History to 1877
8. Philosophy 230, 19th-Century Philosophy

Wellesley is almost entirely a residential college, with 93 percent of students (and all freshmen) living in 14 dorms ranging in size from 38 to 300 students. A small-community atmosphere is preserved through the residence halls, where first-year students share both dorms (if not rooms) and meals with members of other classes. Specialty housing includes the Lake House independent living cooperative for upperclassmen, with a huge kitchen and no residential staff; the Instead feminist cooperative; and Casa Cervantes and La Maison Francaise language halls. Other language halls are located within larger dorms, and a Multifaith Living and Learning Community and Sustainability Co-Op are also available.

Wellesley women maintain an extensive social life with men from the many colleges around Boston, and men are welcome visitors on campus. "The official rule for guests is that they may stay over for three nights a week, but this is never enforced," one student says. "However, Wellesley women are vigilant about men in the dorms and will stop to ask [one] who he's with." The alcohol policy of the college is that a student must be of age and drinking in a private space, that is, not a hall or living room. Students are pleased with a "Good Samaritan Policy" that prohibits disciplinary action against any individual who seeks medical attention for alcohol-related illness. "This keeps everyone extremely safe," says one source.

In 2011 the school reported six burglaries and one forcible sex offense. The college's police force promotes campus safety by providing blue-light emergency phones all over campus and an escort service and shuttle van for students out late at night, although the school makes it clear that the van is for safety and not transportation to and from social events.

Wellesley is a pricey pleasure, with tuition for 2012–13 at $41,824 and room and board at $13,032. However, 60 percent of undergraduates received financial aid, and Wellesley meets 100 percent of demonstrated financial need. The average Wellesley student carried a modest $14,189 in student-loan debt.

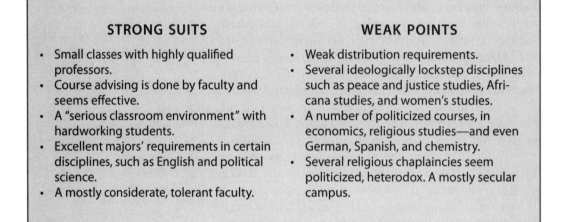

STRONG SUITS	WEAK POINTS
• Small classes with highly qualified professors. • Course advising is done by faculty and seems effective. • A "serious classroom environment" with hardworking students. • Excellent majors' requirements in certain disciplines, such as English and political science. • A mostly considerate, tolerant faculty.	• Weak distribution requirements. • Several ideologically lockstep disciplines such as peace and justice studies, Africana studies, and women's studies. • A number of politicized courses, in economics, religious studies—and even German, Spanish, and chemistry. • Several religious chaplaincies seem politicized, heterodox. A mostly secular campus.

Wesleyan University

Middletown, Connecticut • www.wesleyan.edu

Do Not Enter

Wesleyan University was founded in 1831 by the Methodist Church to educate ministers. Since then, Wesleyan has assiduously abandoned most of its traditions, its last ties with Methodism—and, some assert, any contact with reality.

Wesleyan is rich in physical and intellectual resources. Classes are usually small, professors care about their students, and the school is one of the top 10 liberal arts colleges in terms of sending students on to complete PhDs. But there is little intellectual or political diversity in the classroom or elsewhere. And reading about current practices at Wesleyan makes one want to take a shower (with the door closed—see below).

Academic Life: Less than the sum of the parts

Wesleyan does not have any core requirements, and the set of "general education expectations" it "strongly encourages" are weak, allowing many students to graduate without any exposure to several major disciplines. Says one faculty member: "The students tend to be quite curious and, at times, adventurous. The relatively loose curriculum can create many opportunities to pursue one's bliss. However, the same curriculum can fail to force students to reintegrate their diverse studies or confront the larger debates that have been central to the Western tradition. Seniors routinely mourn the fact that all their courses, when taken as a whole, failed to achieve sufficient coherence. The whole was far less than the sum of the parts."

One undergrad isn't troubled: "I suppose students (if they really tried) could graduate through 'puff' courses, but people come to Wesleyan to learn. Taking easy courses at a school like Wesleyan seems like a waste of money." The problem, of course, is that what some 18-year-olds see as foundational really isn't. For instance, in the approved general-education "The Biology of Sex," the course description promises to "debate the age-old topics such as whether sexual reproduction is sexist." The primary textbook is *Dr. Tatiana's Sex Advice to All Creation.*

A professor complains: "The university has created a host of interdisciplinary programs that are weak and overly politicized: the African American Studies Program, the American Studies Program, the Science in Society Program, and Feminist, Gender, and Sexuality Studies are particularly weak and often indistinguishable with respect to their offerings." In fact, Wesleyan offers a vast array of controversial and academically questionable courses. Most of these classes even fulfill the distribution guidelines— for example, "Key Issues in Black Feminism," "Queer Literature and Studies," and "The Making of American Jewish Identities: Blood, Bris, Bagels, and Beyond."

Wesleyan's system is exacerbated by its emphasis on research. According to a professor: "Teaching is less important than research at tenure and promotion time, and this fact shapes the decisions faculty members make regarding the use of their time. After tenure, some professors scale back dramatically on their research and could doubtless teach more. However, these are generally the very professors who should not be teaching anymore, either because they are no longer interested in scholarship or view the classroom as a context for political (re)education." The administration fails to deliver for different reasons: "Heavy university investments in fashionable studies have led to a systematic underfunding of core departments."

In the First-Year Initiative Program (FYI), freshmen are offered optional special classes that are designed to improve their writing and rhetorical skills. There is no English composition requirement; instead, the school asserts that writing skills are emphasized and developed throughout the curriculum.

Students receive faculty advisers upon entering the university and department-specific advisers after declaring their majors. As one student says, "The quality of advising is heavily dependent on the advisers. Some students love and praise their advisers," while others find them to be useless.

A professor reports: "The English, government, and economics departments routinely attract the largest enrollments and for good reason: they tend to be the best departments, in each case characterized by strong research and quality teaching. The history and philosophy departments are also quite strong." However, "The English department at Wesleyan—like at many institutions—seems to have a strong leftist bias, and conservative students bemoan the heavy political content of many of the courses." English majors concentrate in one of five areas: American; British; race and ethnicity; creative writing; or theory and literary forms. Study of Shakespeare is not required, and course offerings include "Toni Morrison" and "Black Power and the Modern Narrative of Slavery."

History majors at Wesleyan are not required to take any broad survey courses in history or indeed any class on the United States or Europe. The department calls for eight courses within an area of concentration—Africa, South or East Asia, and Latin America; Europe; gender and sexuality; intellectual history; religion and history; or the United States—and two courses outside the concentration. Students must also complete three seminars and a final research project.

"The social science departments—with the notable exception of sociology—offer a less politicized curriculum regardless of the political orientations of the individual professors. There is a strong department norm—shared with economics—against ideological proselytizing," says a professor. Government majors choose from one of four concentrations: American politics, comparative politics, international politics, or political theory.

The College of Social Studies is held up by some on campus as the school's venue for a "classical" education—if you can credibly use that word for courses that mostly assign

CAMPUS POLITICS: RED LIGHT

We're tempted to replace our "Red Light" here with a brightly painted "Do Not Enter" sign. The items cited are merely the tip of a very dark iceberg.

In an effort to cater to diverse student tastes, Wesleyan currently offers a number of special-interest houses. The Womanist House is for students "who are committed to the issues of Wesleyan women, regardless of race, class, sex, sexual orientation, or cultural background," while the Open House is "a safe space for lesbian, gay, bisexual, transgender, transsexual, queer, questioning, flexual, asexual, genderf**k, polyamourous, bondage/disciple, dominance/submission, sadism/masochism (LGBTTQQFAGPBDSM) communities and for people of sexually or gender dissident communities." Yep, they use all the letters.

Then there is the student-run "C**t Club." The club is about "celebrating vaginas" and came under attack from community members when it sold a button reading "Vagina Friendly" to a first-grader attending a student activity fair. This sort of crassness may not be as shocking to Wesleyan students as it is to outside observers. One's sensibilities can grow dull over time.

authors who date back only to the 19th century. "The College of Letters tends toward a more politicized curriculum as exhibited by the fact that it was the home of the much celebrated course on pornography in which students were encouraged to make their own porn flick as a final project," says a teacher.

Some of the more worthwhile departments include medieval studies, art history, Classics, molecular biology and biochemistry, biology, and physics. Wesleyan also has a strong literary tradition, reflected in the presence of its own university press and a series of prestigious summer workshops for writers.

Politics is omnipresent at Wesleyan, inside and outside the classroom. "Most of the humanities, most of the interdisciplinary programs, and some of the social sciences are highly politicized and uniformly on the post-Communist left. Conservative and religious students would likely find them to be inhospitable unless they were willing to go 'under cover,'" says a faculty member. "I have found it to be a rather isolating environment for anyone who has conservative or libertarian inclinations."

> A student reports, "Although the majority of students are on the left, they tend to be far more willing to consider alternative arguments than the professors, many of whom are strident and dogmatic in their political positions and show little toleration for conservative or religious students."

"Interestingly, although the majority of students are on the left, they tend to be far more willing to consider alternative arguments than the professors, many of whom are strident and dogmatic in their political positions and show little toleration for conservative or religious students," says a student. "It would not be a stretch to describe the average student as a career-minded New Yorker interested in building a decent résumé." One professor notes that there is growing tolerance on campus for conservative (or at least libertarian) viewpoints. "I have found that even students who have cut their teeth on the classic Wesleyan curriculum (an odd amalgam of Toni Morrison, Noam Chomsky, and Michel Foucault) are open to consider the arguments made by the likes of Russell Kirk, Friedrich Hayek, and Murray Rothbard," says the teacher.

Students enjoy ample opportunities to interact with their peers and professors in and out of class, and graduate teaching assistants do not teach undergraduates. Standout faculty members include Andrew Szegedy-Maszak in Classics; Martha Crenshaw, Marc Eisner, and John Finn in government; Ronald W. Schatz in history; John P. Bonin in economics; and Will Eggers and Richard S. Slotkin (emeritus) in English. Peter Rutland, who teaches Russian and Eastern European studies in the government department, is a notable scholar of Soviet economics.

Almost half of all Wesleyan undergraduates study abroad for at least a semester. The university runs programs on every inhabited continent. At home, Wesleyan offers American Sign Language, Arabic, Catalan, Chinese, French, German, Greek and Latin, Hebrew, Hindi, Italian, Japanese, Korean, Portuguese, Russian, Spanish, and Swahili, and also contains two state-of-the-art language labs for student use.

Student Life: *Goat Boy and the Potato Chip Ritual*

Wesleyan is definitely a residential school, with 98 percent of the undergraduate student body living on campus. The nature of residential life probably contributes most to the "progressive" character of the Wesleyan experience. While the current university policy assigns first-year students roommates of the same sex, upperclassmen can choose coed dorm rooms and coed bathrooms. It is not unusual for students in these coed bathrooms to shower with the doors open. A housing official says, "The hall makes the decision [whether to have coed bathrooms] at the beginning of the school year, after they get to know one another."

The Wesleyan Student Assembly is constantly pressing the administration to implement gender-neutral housing for all students. A WSA resolution states that since "gender and biological sex are separate and distinct concepts" and "the historical rationale for same-sex roommate assignments is based upon antiquated heterosexist assumptions and obsolete concerns," all students, including incoming freshmen, should not be excluded from the right "to define their own gender and make housing decisions, irrespective of that definition." Mercifully, there are still a handful of single-sex residences for those who request them, and substance-free options are also available. Housing is guaranteed for four years; upperclassmen who wish to live off campus have to petition for permission. Male students may opt to live in a limited selection of Greek housing; there are no houses for sororities.

One conservative student complained of heavy social pressure from activist groups to adopt the most radical linguistic experiments in support of sexual diversity, citing a university-wide memo sent out by a student organization, the Wesleyan Trans/Gender Group, insisting that students replace he/she/him/her with "ze (subjective) and hir (objective and possessive). For example, 'I was talking to my friend Kris earlier. Ze told me that hir paper was due tomorrow, and it was stressing hir out.' Some students prefer to be referred to with gender neutral pronouns, and many students prefer to use gender neutral pronouns in papers instead of the universal he." Got that?

As you might guess, Wesleyan has gone to enormous lengths to promote multiculturalism and ethnic (not intellectual) diversity on campus. The Queer Resource Center serves an active and noisy homosexual student population. In its library, students have been

SUGGESTED CORE
1. English 251, Epic Tradition
2. Classical Civilization 217, Philosophical Classics I: Ancient Western Philosophy
3. Religion 201/212, Introduction to the Hebrew Bible/New Testament
4. Philosophy 261, Christianity and Philosophy (*closest match*)
5. Government 338, Modern Political Theory
6. English 205, Shakespeare
7. History 237, Early North America to 1763
8. History 216/Philosophy 258, European Intellectual History since the Renaissance/Post-Kantian European Philosophy

offered videos like *Goat Boy and the Potato Chip Ritual, Dress Up for Daddy, Female Misbehavior, Party: A Safer Sex Videotape for Black Gay Men, Stop the Church,* and *Two in Twenty: A Lesbian Soap Opera.* Along with pornography, the Queer Resource Center library serves up "free condoms, oral dams and gloves."

Among the other student organizations at Wesleyan are the Black Women's Collective, the Wesleyan Christian Fellowship, Step One ("a confidential resource for students questioning their sexuality"), several a cappella groups, Wesleyan Film Series, Clinic Escorts (which chivalrously provides escorts for women heading to abortion clinics), Wesleyan Democrats, Woodrow Wilson Debate Society, and Wheatgrass Co-Op. Second Stage is a student-run group overseeing Wesleyan's student theater. The company produces dance and theater shows that are entirely designed, directed, teched, and performed by Wesleyan students.

There are religious resources on campus for those students interested in them. There are resident Muslim, Jewish, Catholic, and Protestant chaplains, as well as groups associated with Buddhism, Unitarian Universalism, Christian Scientists, Quakers, Hindus, and other faiths. In addition to religious-themed program houses, the university sponsors several faith-based student groups—the majority of which are Jewish, to serve approximately 20–22 percent of Wesleyan's undergraduate student body.

Wesleyan's professors and administrators are not alone in their embrace of the radical academic Left. Students themselves are no slouches when it comes to leftist activism. Among the more politically oriented student organizations are the Environmental Organizer's Network, Ethnic, Trans/Gender Group, the black student group Ujamaa, Amnesty International, an ACLU group, Wesleyan Democratic Socialists, and Promoting Human-Animal Relations and Liberation at Wesleyan.

Underage drinking is pervasive at Wesleyan. Drinking is permitted openly, often accompanied by liberal drug use, during the annual outdoor music festivals: Uncle Duke's Day, Buttstock, and the Spring Fling.

Wesleyan sports teams compete in the New England Small College Athletic Conference (NESCAC), a division of the NCAA Division III. Committed primarily to academics, the conference does not permit member schools to recruit off campus, to hold out-of-season practices, or to grant athletic scholarships. Among the men's and women's 29 available intercollegiate sports, interested students should find ample opportunities to compete. Wesleyan varsity teams once competed as the "Methodists," but today Wesleyan athletes are known as "Cardinals." The Freeman Athletic Center features ice skating, swimming, track, and basketball facilities; a fitness and strength-training center; and an exercise room. The center includes a gymnasium with seating for 1,200, a 7,500-square-foot fitness center, and eight squash courts.

In 2011 the university reported 24 burglaries, seven forcible sex offenses, and one aggravated assault.

Going to Wesleyan is a costly excursion into parts unknown; in 2012–13 tuition was $45,628, with room and board for underclassmen $13,434. The school currently offers need-blind admission and commits to meeting 100 percent of a student's demonstrated financial need. However, the school has a mixed record of being able to meet this commitment, since its endowment is about half the size of peer schools. Only 49 percent of the undergraduates who applied for financial aid for the 2011–12 academic year received a need-based award. The average Wesleyan student graduated with $25,864 in student-loan debt.

STRONG SUITS	WEAK POINTS
• Respected programs in English, government, economics, history, philosophy, medieval studies, art history, Classics, molecular biology and biochemistry, biology, and physics.	• Pervasive, often suffocating leftist bias in classrooms in many departments.
• Social sciences, apart from sociology, tend to be academic rather than politicized.	• Aggressive, radical sex activism on campus supported by the administration and pushed by student government.
• A long literary tradition and a well-known college press on campus.	• Coed bathrooms and dorm rooms.
• Some single-sex residences still exist (use them!).	• Vapid core curriculum and weak requirements in many majors.
• Good foreign language and study-abroad options.	• The C**T Club.

Wheaton College

Wheaton, Illinois • www.wheaton.edu

Socializing the Gospel

Wheaton, founded in 1860 by abolitionists, prides itself on being "the Harvard of the Evangelical world." For 150 years, Wheaton has positioned itself as the bulwark of intellectual Christianity, inculcating both knowledge and wisdom. And while Wheaton still has a reputation as a conservative school, over the past several years there has been a decidedly leftward shift. For example, over 60 percent of Wheaton's faculty polled in the *Wheaton Record* claimed to have voted for pro-choice Barack Obama in 2008. (To put that in perspective, imagine that, in another election, 60 percent of the faculty at UC Berkeley had voted for Pat Buchanan.) That was four years ago (nobody surveyed in 2012), but life is short and tenure is long, so the same professors are mostly still teaching at Wheaton—and there has been no sign of a social conservative upsurge since.

In addition, Wheaton's once-solid core curriculum now includes two mandatory, politically driven diversity courses designed to promote "races, genders, ethnicities, religions, and cultures other than Anglo-American and white majority European," according to the school's website. Not surprisingly, "students come in very hard-line conservative," says one professor, and while "few leave as liberals, many [become] moderates." It appears to some that this 150-year-old bastion of orthodox Christianity is inching down the road of the Social Gospel, which has secularized so many Christian institutions (and entire denominations).

Academic Life: Illinois roundheads

Although Wheaton's general-education requirements have been diluted in recent years, one student declares, "I believe the general-education requirements are wonderful. . . . We get to dabble in subjects we might not have even known we would be interested in without those requirements." A professor says, "The core requirements are not as tight as they were a quarter of a century ago, and students must take the initiative. Still, Wheaton has all the resources for grounding yourself as deeply as possible in the liberal arts, through the courses in biblical and theological studies, English, philosophy, art history, history of music, political philosophy, and foreign languages."

Wheaton students choose from about 40 undergraduate majors in the arts, sciences, and humanities. One of Wheaton's biggest disciplines is biblical and theological studies. Very close to it in popularity and reputation is the psychology department. These are the only departments at Wheaton that also offer doctoral degrees.

Biblical and theological studies is the "crown jewel" of Wheaton. It is the largest department in terms of both faculty and students. Most professors are published, but the department's main professional standard is quality of teaching. Although each biblical studies professor specializes in one of the two testaments, the department as a whole gives equal weight to both canons. Theologically, the department is doctrinally conservative, although in methodology it is moderate or left of center, and one can find a fairly wide range of views represented.

The English department is very strong in both scholarly reputation and teaching. All majors must take two courses each in British and American literature, both pre- and post-1800, and may opt to concentrate in writing or secondary-school education. The English writing concentration offers very close working relationships with professors. "The classes are a lot smaller," says one student, "and professors pour a lot of effort into your writing." The department's Wade Center houses papers of C. S. Lewis, J. R. R. Tolkien, Dorothy Sayers, and others,

VITAL STATISTICS

Religious affiliation: *nondenominational (Christian)*
Total enrollment: *3,034*
Total undergraduates: *2,508*
SAT CR/Verbal midrange: *600–720*
SAT Math midrange: *610–700*
ACT midrange: *30–36*
Applicants: *1,950*
Applicants accepted: *68%*
Accepted applicants who enrolled: *44%*
Tuition (general/out of state): *$30,120*
Tuition (in state): *N/A*
Room and board: *$8,560*
Freshman retention rate: *96%*
Graduation rate (4 yrs.): *76%*
Graduation rate (6 yrs.): *88%*
Courses with fewer than 20 students: *54%*
Student-faculty ratio: *12:1*
Courses taught by graduate students: *not provided*
Students living on campus: *90%*
Students in fraternities: *none*
Students in sororities: *none*
Students receiving need-based financial aid: *50%*
Avg. student-loan debt of a recent graduating class: *$24,067*
Most popular majors: *liberal arts, social sciences, theology*
Guaranteed housing for 4 years? *yes*

CAMPUS POLITICS: YELLOW LIGHT

There is an ongoing struggle raging for Wheaton's soul. For some years, all faculty of the education department had to endorse a "Conceptual Framework" that instructed future teachers that they must be "agents of social change" and cited among its sources the Brazilian Marxist Paulo Freire and retired Weather Underground terrorist Bill Ayers. In a wholesome development, concerned alumna Julie Roys reports: "When Dr. Philip Ryken became president...he reviewed the document and vowed to oversee a complete revision. [The] revision unveiled today shows a heartening return to correct biblical thinking....The new document also encourages teachers to 'embody justice.' But, instead of drawing on Marxist models, it points to Christ."

One student says, "Politics have intruded into the classroom, especially during...presidential elections. As a large majority of faculty supported Barack Obama for president, teachers would often make subtle to not-so-subtle comments....One anthropology professor even subtly hinted that Barack Obama was the only candidate with 'true Christian principles.'"

One Wheaton grad recounted at the online journal *Values and Capitalism*: "In four years at Wheaton, I read Chinua Achebe's *Things Fall Apart* in three different general-education courses and not a single word from Burke, Bastiat, Tocqueville, Smith, or Hayek."

Not all is amiss at Wheaton; the school did join other Christian colleges in 2012 in suing the Department of Health and Human Services over its mandate that religious institutions provide contraceptives and abortifacients to employees.

and is a major international research center. Classroom discussions are especially intense and engaging. According to one professor, students often have a "Protestant angst" that leads them to explore texts with intensity. "Reading books and poems are deeply engaging activities, often involving the states of their souls or emotions."

The department offers a summer program, Wheaton in England, which leads students to London, Stonehenge, and other culturally important locations, as well as Stratford-on-Avon, John Milton's cottage, and various C. S. Lewis sites. The program includes such courses as "Literature and Place in Romanticism" and "Medieval Literature." Another opportunity is the Scholar's Semester in Oxford, sponsored by the Council for Christian Colleges and Universities. Opportunities at Oxford are not restricted to English and literature, however. This program also offers in-depth studies in Classics, theology and religious studies, philosophy, and history.

The "rising star" at Wheaton is the politics and international relations department. This department has been growing in prominence at Wheaton, thanks to the school's increasing focus on international issues (a significant number of students are children of overseas missionaries) and its majors' dominance of student government. Over the past few years, the department has become one of the most popular at Wheaton. All poli-sci majors must take courses in American political philosophy and the U.S. Constitution in addition to mandatory internships with governmental and nongovernmental agencies.

The history department is said to be mediocre, not requiring a Western civilization course but offering several world history classes instead. American history before 1865 is offered but not required of majors, alongside "History, of Women in the U.S." and

"Women's Voices in U.S. History. " Students must take at least one course each in American, European, world (Asian, African, or Latin American), and Christian history.

The sociology and anthropology department is politically left of center, but it's still one of the few sociology departments in the country that attempts to place academically rigorous research within a context of biblical ethics. The geology department is described as "small but good," and Wheaton's Conservatory of Music has a strong national reputation, offering six degrees in music. The business and economic program is also well established. Overall, the humanities tend to be stronger than the sciences at Wheaton, although the pre-med program has been successful in getting students into medical school. The philosophy department covers all areas of modern philosophy and is very popular with students.

Physics is the weakest science department, and apart from music, the fine arts at Wheaton are small and underdeveloped. The theater is excellent but small, and students cannot major in drama, except as a concentration within the communication department.

> Wheaton students often have a "Protestant angst" that leads them to explore texts with intensity. "Reading books and poems are deeply engaging activities, often involving the states of their souls," a teacher says.

Wheaton is building an $80 million science center, with eight new teaching labs, research space for every faculty member, research labs that open up into teaching labs, new state-of-the-art equipment (electron microscope, DNA sequencer, anatomy lab with cadavers), and a planetarium/observatory.

Wheaton's faculty is well regarded by students for its quality and accessibility. "Across the board," says one student, "professors are interested in you, without exception. They spend extra time to be available in office hours, especially for giving help for papers. It's a real consistent ethic." Many students take advantage of Wheaton's "Dine with a Mind" program, which pays for one-on-one on-campus lunches between professors and students. Wheaton has traditionally placed its biggest emphasis on teaching, although the school "has begun encouraging faculty to integrate research into teaching, " says one professor. "And the school has been making an effort to free up professors' time to do research, especially with undergrads. But in making hiring and other decisions, the balance is overwhelmingly in favor of teaching."

Recommended professors include Roger Lundin, Brett Foster, and Leland Ryken in English; Robert Lee Brabenec and Terry Perciante in mathematics; Michael Graves, Timothy Larsen, George Kalantzis, John Walton, and Daniel Treier in Bible/theology; William Struthers in psychology; Mark Amstutz, Sandra Joireman, and P. J. Hill in economics; Sarah Borden and W. Jay Wood in philosophy; L. Kristen Page in biology; E. John Walford in art; Brian Howell in anthropology; and Paul Robinson of Human Needs and Global Resources (HNGR).

SUGGESTED CORE

1. English 101, Classics of Western Literature and Classics 258, Tales of Troy
2. Philosophy 311, History of Philosophy: Ancient and Medieval
3. Bible and Theology 211/213, Old Testament/New Testament Literature and Interpretation
4. Bible and Theology 315, Christian Thought (*closest match*)
5. Political Science 347, Renaissance and Modern Political Philosophy
6. English 334, Shakespeare
7. History 351, American History to 1865
8. Philosophy 312, History of Philosophy: Modern and Contemporary (*closest match*)

Wheaton's student body is in one important sense homogenous. As one student puts it, "There are different denominations, but there is one faith there, the Christian faith. And the school is predominantly Protestant. There may be a few Catholic students here or there, but I haven't met any in my three and half years." There are no speech restrictions at Wheaton, but its doctrinal outlook does impose limits that have caused controversy. All professors must sign a statement of faith that the school regards as compatible with most Protestant tenets but incompatible with Roman Catholicism (when a professor crossed the Tiber in 2006, he was fired). A controversy arose when an English professor, Dr. Kent Gramm, resigned after the college demanded an explanation for his divorce, drawing national criticism for its actions and prompting calls for a reexamination of its strict lifestyle standards. Students and faculty overwhelmingly supported the administration's decision. Says one undergrad: "The professors sign on to this when they take a faculty position with the college. . . . Our professors are not just teaching us . . . they mentor and disciple us. It is of the utmost importance that they are practicing what they 'preach,' if you will."

Wheaton has several study-abroad programs. Its largest is Human Needs and Global Resources (HNGR), a program that offers a certificate in fighting world hunger. Students enter a six-month internship with a nongovernmental organization undertaking development work in a Third World country while also completing course work. There are also various "Wheaton-in" programs (for example, Wheaton-in-Spain, Wheaton-in-France), generally led by foreign languages faculty. The school runs many overseas ministries that give Wheaton students a chance to travel. Moreover, as one student puts it, "The overseas ministries allow students to both travel and serve. Service/evangelism is the main focus of these ministries abroad."

Foreign language studies have grown in recent years. This department offers the traditional majors in French, German, Spanish, and Ancient Language (Classics), and classes in Hebrew, and Mandarin Chinese. Students can take Arabic at the nearby College of DuPage for transfer credit.

Student Life: Clean and sober

The leafy suburb of Wheaton, Illinois, is only 25 miles from Chicago. "Wheaton is a very well-rounded campus, " says one student. "I have participated in informal sports, great conversations, movies, campus concerts, trips to Chicago, and a discipleship/Bible study group."

According to the *Chronicle of Higher Education*, Wheaton ranks second only to Brigham Young University in campus sobriety. Students are required to pledge to refrain from tobacco, alcohol, and gambling during the academic year. "There's not much of a party scene," says one student, "but don't worry, you'll make great friends and have a good time." Many students go dancing at the University of Chicago on Friday nights or attend concerts and movies in the Windy City.

The centers of Wheaton freshman and sophomore community life, however, are the dorms. Most juniors and seniors live in campus-owned houses and apartments. For them, these are the centers of community life. Each dormitory is structured as a residential community and is designed to support all areas of a student's campus life. Dorms are either single sex or coed; however, even the coed buildings have sex-specific floors with strict intervisitation rules. Each dorm has an upperclassman as a resident assistant, who ensures compliance with rules and arranges for weekly recreational activities. Of the RAs, an undergrad observes, "The resident assistants for the freshman/sophomore and upperclassman dorms are selected through a competitive application and interview process to ensure that they are serious about serving other students and aren't just looking for a free rooming budget." Each dorm and floor has its own traditions, activities, and rivalries, and sponsors Bible studies and fellowship groups.

Wheaton students can participate in more than 70 clubs and organizations, including drama, model UN, musical theater, Christian Feminists Club, College Democrats, College Republicans, Earthkeepers, German Club, Orphan Helpers, Pre-Law Society, Men's Glee Club, Student Global Aids Campaign, Tikvaht Israel Club, Wheaton Film Society, Women's Chorale, and 13 honor societies.

Sports are a unifying force on campus, as Wheaton's teams are very good, and most students show interest and enthusiasm. More than 50 percent of students participate in intramurals, including badminton, basketball, bowling, water polo, golf, nontackle football, tennis, Ultimate Frisbee, track, and soccer. A full 25 percent of Wheaton's student body takes part in varsity or club sports like baseball, basketball, soccer, tennis, swimming, water polo, cross-country, golf, and wrestling. In addition, Wheaton is a Division III school with highly ranked soccer, football, and swimming teams, and competitive baseball, cross-country, basketball, golf, tennis, track, volleyball, water polo, and wrestling teams as well.

Three times a week, all undergraduates are required to attend services in Edman Chapel, and they agree to attend church on Sunday off campus as part of their signature of the school's Covenant. Most are also involved in some kind of active mission work during school, assisted in their efforts by the Office of Christian Outreach.

Wheaton is an extremely safe college. In 2011 the only crimes reported on campus were eight burglaries, one motor vehicle theft, and two cases of arson.

As private colleges go, Wheaton College is quite reasonable. Tuition for the 2012–13 academic year was $30,120, with room and board $8,560. Half of all undergraduates received need-based financial aid, and the average student-loan debt of a recent graduating class was $24,067.

STRONG SUITS

- Better-than-average distributional requirements.
- A solid commitment to its Christian mission and excellent Bible and theology classes.
- A thriving program in politics and international affairs.
- Very highly regarded English and music departments.
- Wholesome, sober campus life with many social activities.

WEAK POINTS

- A big dose of politicized diversity courses in many disciplines.
- Anemic departments in history, the hard sciences, and most of the arts.
- A growing Social Gospel consensus among faculty that demotes traditional moral issues in favor of economic "justice" and "social change."

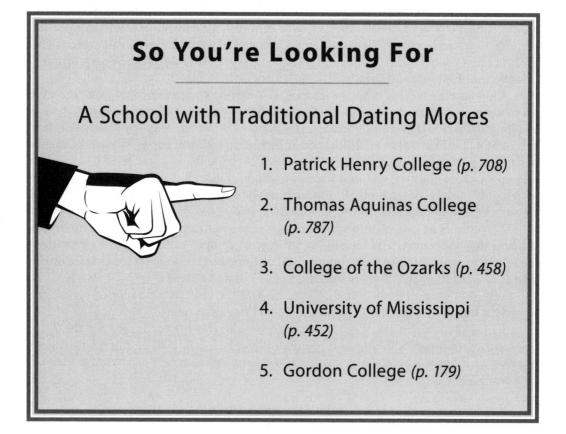

So You're Looking For

A School with Traditional Dating Mores

1. Patrick Henry College *(p. 708)*

2. Thomas Aquinas College *(p. 787)*

3. College of the Ozarks *(p. 458)*

4. University of Mississippi *(p. 452)*

5. Gordon College *(p. 179)*

Whitman College

Walla Walla, Washington • www.whitman.edu

Walden West

Whitman College was established in 1882 by Cushing Eells, in memory of Christian missionaries Marcus and Narcissa Whitman—but it was chartered as a secular, not a religious school. Whitman is known for being independent from sectarian and political control; however, a default liberalism certainly pervades the campus. One professor explains that although there is no "direct silencing of any particular groups," one can joke about the political Right "without raising an eyebrow, but joking about the absurd hyperbole of liberal activists would require a detailed defense." One student says, "It would be hard to be a conservative here," but another reports, "I was blessed with an intellectually aggressive class that wanted to discuss, debate, out-and-out argue, and then go to lunch together afterward."

Academic Life: Antiquity and modernity

Whitman's worthy General Studies Program requires all freshmen to take a two-semester course, "First-Year Experience: Encounters," which is an "introduction to the liberal arts and the academic construction of knowledge" and is "organized around a variable theme."

VITAL STATISTICS

Religious affiliation: *none*
Total enrollment: *1,596*
Total undergraduates: *1,596*
SAT CR/Verbal midrange:
    610–740
SAT Math midrange:
    610–700
ACT midrange: *28–32*
Applicants: *2,982*
Applicants accepted: *54%*
Accepted applicants who
    enrolled: *28%*
Tuition (general/out of
    state): *$42,106*
Tuition (in state): *N/A*
Room and board: *$10,560*
Freshman retention rate:
    93%
Graduation rate (4 yrs.): *80%*
Graduation rate (6 yrs.): *89%*
Courses with fewer than 20
    students: *62%*
Student-faculty ratio: *9:1*
Courses taught by graduate
    students: *not provided*
Students living on campus:
    75%
Students in fraternities: *36%*
Students in sororities: *27%*
Students receiving need-
    based financial aid: *48%*
Avg. student-loan debt of a
    recent graduating class:
    $17,711
Most popular majors:
    *economics, psychology,
    biology*
Guaranteed housing for 4
    years? *yes*

In 2012–13 that theme was "Encounters: Transformation." Students meet in small-group seminars of no more than 16. A third (optional) general-studies course entitled "Critical Voices" is less promising. The course warns that it "will call into question the dominance of traditional Western world views by critically examining the historical and ideological roles played by 'others.'"

A music major says that "as a liberal arts school, Whitman really forces you to stretch intellectually with all its general-education requirements (two courses each in the humanities, social sciences, and the fine arts). While I wasn't thrilled at the prospect of taking a biology course, it was good to have a class that forced me to learn something about the environment and to think more concretely about the Earth."

The requirements at Whitman don't go far enough. One teacher explains that "it is possible to get a strong liberal arts education at Whitman if the student chooses wisely from the potpourri of diverse offerings, and if the student gets solid direction from his/her adviser." For example, because there are so many options offered, English literature majors could possibly "avoid hundreds of years of English lit, traditional major authors, and important periods." Another teacher points out that only so much can be achieved in two semesters. It is possible to receive a grounding in a traditional liberal arts education by supplementing what the core lacks throughout one's next three years of study. However, students are not required to take these courses, making it possible to easily miss receiving a real liberal arts education if they don't choose their courses very carefully.

Upon submitting an application, students are given a premajor adviser, a faculty or staff member. After four semesters at Whitman, students choose a major and receive an adviser in that department.

Whitman offers 45 majors and 32 minors. Students may also enter double majors (most commonly combining environmental studies with another program) or an individually planned program. Past examples include political philosophy, peace and conflict studies, American studies, environmental studies, creative writing, and astrophysics.

Popular majors at Whitman include biology, BBMB (biochemistry, biophysics, and molecular biology, a program unique to Whitman), English, politics, psychology, sociology, environmental studies, and history. One teacher comments that biology, chemistry, and geology are among the strongest departments, with "dedicated faculty members and good opportunities for undergraduate research." Both teachers and students told us that there isn't a single weak department at Whitman. However, there are some that "could use more professors or space," says a teacher.

English majors must take "Approaches to the Study of Literature," four period courses in English and American Literature with at least two courses in English and one in American literature ("Studies in Renaissance Literature," "Studies in British Literature," or "The American Literary Emergence, 1620–1920"). They also take one single-author course ("Chaucer," "Shakespeare," or "Milton"); one seminar in English and American literature ("Medieval Literature: Humans, Gods, and Monsters in Medieval Literature," "Studies in Renaissance Literature—Sex, Love, and Power in the English Renaissance," or "Romantic Literature: Romantic Poetry"); and two additional advanced courses ("Colonial and Anti-Colonial Literature," "Reading India"). Admirably, all seniors must pass a written comprehensive and an oral examination. Shakespeare would be hard to miss, and he's almost certainly on the test.

History offers courses in seven geographical areas: ancient Mediterranean, East Asia, Europe, Islamic world, Africa, Latin America, and the United States. A major must take at least one course in each of three of these areas, at least one course treating a period before 1500 AD, and "two related courses within one geographic field" ("Topics in Middle East History," "Alexander the Great and the Hellenistic Kingdoms"). Courses include "Topics in Comparative History"; a "comparisons and encounters" elective ("The Roman Empire," "Modern European Imperialism,"

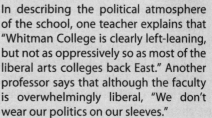

CAMPUS POLITICS: YELLOW LIGHT

In describing the political atmosphere of the school, one teacher explains that "Whitman College is clearly left-leaning, but not as oppressively so as most of the liberal arts colleges back East." Another professor says that although the faculty is overwhelmingly liberal, "We don't wear our politics on our sleeves."

Out of all the departments at Whitman, the politics department is known as farthest left. However, one conservative teacher defends department faculty, saying that "they intentionally aim to prevent their own politics from entering into the classroom, and several [professors] have said that they far prefer a thoughtful conservative student to a run-of-the-mill liberal student. In fact, because the pedagogical goal in these classes involves using classic texts of the Western tradition to challenge students' preconceptions, and because many students come with left-of-center preconceptions, even liberal politics professors end up articulating and defending important conservative perspectives."

Students don't entirely agree. One new student told the *Whitman Pioneer* in 2012 that she "has been surprised by the one-sided nature of political discussions. There's no political diversity. I'm sure any conservatives are more closeted conservatives because it can be awkward here."

The school administration seems fixated on racial and ethnic diversity and practices what critics call discriminatory policies. A teacher says, "Although the college maintains that it does not discriminate in hiring for . . . 'diversity' positions, the record shows that it is difficult or impossible for a white male to be offered a 'diversity' position, unless he shares the position with a nonwhite spouse."

"The United States in the World"); and one seminar ("Special Topics in Ancient History: Egypt and the Amarna Age" or "Special Topics in Ancient History: Sicily, 800 BCE—800 CE"). It seems that students could emerge without taking classes in the American Founding and Civil War.

The politics department's requirements are less concrete, with no common introductory requirements. The students choose seven courses, take one senior seminar, and write a senior thesis. Worthy course offerings recently included "Introduction to Ancient and Medieval Political Theory," "Introduction to Modern European Political Theory," "The Politics of Globalization," "Political Ecology," and "American Political Theory."

Seniors must complete senior assessments with a passing grade in the major field they have chosen. The examination may be completely oral or a combination of both written and oral. Some individual majors are also expected to complete an extensive project of a written or multimedia thesis, or presentation.

> One student says, "It would be hard to be a conservative here," but another reports, "I was blessed with an intellectually aggressive class that wanted to discuss, debate, out-and-out argue, and then go to lunch."

Whitman provides many excellent teachers: Timothy Kaufman-Osborn (who recently assumed the office of provost and dean of the faculty of Whitman College), Paul Apostolidis, Phil Brick, and Jeanne Morefield in politics; Nina Lerman and David Schmitz in history; Pete Crawford, John David Earnest, Lee Thompson, and Susan Pickett in music; Bob Carson, Kevin Pogue, and Pat Spencer in geology; Delbert Hutchison and Paul Yancey in biology; Leroy Wade Jr. in chemistry; Dana Burgess in Classics; Jonathan Walters and Walter Wyman Jr. in religion; Michelle Janning in sociology; and Jan Crouter in economics. "Teaching excellence is a top priority," says one teacher, although another laments that "research is becoming more important in decisions regarding tenure and promotion."

Students may participate in the college's urban-semester study and internships in Philadelphia and Washington, D.C. In addition, students have the opportunity to apply for many science research internships available through the college. Whitman also offers a Semester in the West program, where environmental majors study "public lands conservation and rural life in the interior American West."

Whitman also provides combined programs where students can receive an advanced degree and specialized training from another school that specializes in a given field. These cooperative programs include engineering and computer science with Caltech, Duke, Columbia, the University of Washington, and Washington University in St. Louis; forestry and environmental programs with Duke; oceanography and biology or geology programs with the University of Washington; law with the Columbia School of Law; and education with the University of Puget Sound. The University of Washington confers degrees in both oceanography and computer science. Engineering and computer science degrees are a 3+2 program, meaning that students spend their first three years at Whitman and the next two at a sister school. Law with Columbia University is a 3+3 program, while the education program with Puget Sound is a 4+1 program.

Whitman keeps a low student-faculty ratio of 9 to 1. "Professors are incredibly helpful and available—and you don't even have to be a student," exclaims one undergrad, recalling her visit as a prospective student. Faculty at Whitman are known to collaborate with students on research projects, join them on the intramural sports field, serve on committees with them and bring them home for dinner. It is generally agreed on campus that "teaching has always been the central responsibility at Whitman College."

Since Whitman is an undergraduate college, there are no graduate assistants teaching classes. However, "There are a significant number of adjuncts teaching regular courses at Whitman, especially in the first-year core," says a faculty member.

One teacher speaks highly of Whitman's study-abroad programs, which "are offered in many countries around the world (China, Japan, France, Scotland, and Australia, to name a few). About half of all students spend some time studying abroad." Students may choose from 42 programs and have the option of studying on five continents.

Foreign languages taught at Whitman include Chinese, French, German, Greek and Latin, Japanese, and Spanish.

SUGGESTED CORE

1. Classics 227, Greek and Roman Epic
2. Philosophy 201, Readings in Western Philosophical Tradition: Ancient
3. Religion 201/202, The Hebrew Bible/The New Testament and Early Christianity
4. History 202, European Intellectual History, 386–1300
5. Politics 122, Introduction to Modern European Political Theory
6. English 351/352, Shakespeare
7. History 105, Development of the United States (1607–1877)
8. History 277, 19th-Century Europe, 1815–1914 (*closest match*)

Student Life: Nature and culture

Whitman College is located in the town of Walla Walla, in the southeastern corner of Washington State. Geographically, it is surrounded by mountains, with the Snake and Columbia Rivers nearby. Whitman offers boundless opportunities to enjoy the great outdoors in close proximity. Students say that everything in Walla Walla is bike-able—but many students have cars, which are helpful for escaping the immediate vicinity.

Whitman College provides approximately 113 student organizations, which include honor societies (Phi Beta Kappa, Sigma Delta Pi, the Order of Waiilatpu); religious organizations (Whitman Christian Fellowship; Hillel-Shalom; Unitarian Universalist Community; and Atheists, Humanists, and Agnostics); minority organizations (Club Latino, Club for the Recognition of Cultures of Minorities, Wakilisha Afrika, and Black Student Union); and a wide variety of liberal organizations like Feminists Advocating Change and Empowerment, Voices for Planned Parenthood, Young Democrats, the inevitable homosexual advocacy groups, Coalition against Homophobia, and GLBTQ. One student reports, "The problem at Whitman is that there is too much to do. Any given night offers five different lectures, movies, presentations, parties, and dances."

There is but a single politically conservative organization on campus, the Campus Conservatives, which strives "to bring speakers to campus, educate our fellow students about conservatism, cultivate an atmosphere of healthy political discussion, and ensure that the campus gives fair voice to the conservative end of the political spectrum," according to the group's website.

Religious students who come to Whitman should "seek out a faith community on or off campus and become as active as possible," one professor says, noting that "only a minority of students are religiously active." Walla Walla provides places of worship for both Catholics and Protestants, as well as a small but active synagogue. While historic St. Patrick's parish in Walla Walla is very beautiful, tradition-minded Catholics may choose to drive an hour to St. Joseph Catholic Church in Kennewick, which hosts regular Latin liturgies.

Whitman proudly fields 22 varsity athletic teams for men and women, for example alpine and Nordic skiing, cycling, rugby (men and women!), and three "coed" sports: water polo, tae kwon do, and triathalon. The school is affiliated with both the National Collegiate Athletic Association (NCAA-III) and the National Association of Intercollegiate Athletics (NAIA-II). Whitman's ski team competes in the U.S. Collegiate Ski Association. Of the club sports present, the "fighting missionaries" cycling club team can boast four DII National Championships within the past six years. More than 70 percent of Whitman's student body chooses from a dozen intramural sports (20 percent in varsity sports). For noncompetitive students, there is a plethora of physical education classes. Whitman also provides excellent outing programs that take advantage of the school's idyllic location.

More than 75 percent of Whitman students live on campus; all students under 21 must live on campus for at least four semesters. The campus offers residence halls arranged in both traditional dormitory style and in suites. All dorms are coed, except for one that houses freshman women and some sorority members. Members of the four fraternities live in separate houses and enjoy separate dining services. Douglas Hall houses a few single rooms and suites of eight students and is an option for upperclassmen. A housing official says that each year a handful of students opt for coed dorm rooms (they must have parental approval). Almost all dorm rooms, however, are single sex. Except for those in the "interest houses," all residence hall bathrooms are single sex. Whitman's 11 interest houses include La Casa Hispana, La Maison Française, Tekisuijuku (Japanese House), Das Deutsche Haus, Asian Studies House, Environmental House, Fine Arts House, Community Service House, MECCA (Multi-Ethnic Center for Cultural Affairs), Global Awareness House, and Writing House. The Glover Alston Center, completed in 2010, serves as a "resource to facilitate Whitman's commitment to sustaining a diverse community," the college announced.

In a small town like Walla Walla, you wouldn't expect much crime—but there is a little, and some of it takes place on campus. In 2011 the school reported one forcible sex offenses, one burglary, and one motor vehicle theft.

Whitman is not cheap. For the 2012–13 academic year, tuition alone cost $42,106, while room and board were $10,560. However, Whitman provides a very comprehensive and diversified financial aid program, including grants, scholarships, employment opportunities, and loans. Some 48 percent of students received need-based financial aid during the 2012–13 school year, and the average student-loan debt of a recent graduate was $17,711.

STRONG SUITS	WEAK POINTS
• Much better than average general-education requirements encourage broad learning. • Especially worthy English, biology, chemistry and geology departments. • Many opportunities for student research in the hard sciences. • Diverse and worthwhile dual-degree programs in preprofessional studies. • All classes are taught by faculty, not grad students. • Beautiful location, with many outdoors opportunities.	• Significant use of adjunct faculty in some departments. • Lax majors' requirements in political science and history, despite worthy courses. • Some coed dorm rooms. • Minimal religious or conservative presence on campus.

Williams College

Williamstown, Massachusetts • www.williams.edu

If Every College Were Thus Located

Founded in 1793, Williams College is a richly endowed liberal arts school in the gorgeous Berkshires of western Massachusetts—about which Henry David Thoreau calculated that the scenery was worth at least the equivalent of one endowed professorship. Top-notch applicants have been drawn to Williams since the beginning. Williams students are rather a privileged bunch: less than 60 percent are graduates of public high schools. However, in recent years the school has increased the number of students receiving financial aid, now up to 53 percent. The school's high-minded, genteel liberalism is secure enough to be tolerant of intellectual dissent.

Academic Life: Diversity and tutorials

Williams students face only vague distribution requirements, which can be fulfilled by quirky or politicized courses if they do not choose carefully. They could easily graduate without having studied the basic texts of Western civilization. Recently added requirements for one course in quantitative or formal reasoning and two courses designated as writing-intensive added some backbone to a curriculum that might otherwise allow a student to earn a degree without ever having to answer a question with a right and wrong answer. Some students say they appreciate the flexibility in the relaxed curriculum. "It allows the student to take courses in areas that interest him or her while exposing the student to different departments," a history major says.

Not every undergrad likes the system or the attitudes it enables. One says that too many of his fellow students "tend to be focused on career paths that lead to high-paying jobs rather than opportunities to discuss events that occurred in the past. They only want to know enough about Thucydides to quote him in an argument on current events." Another agrees: "The study of Western civilization is given no special place in the curriculum. Sure, the courses in history, literature, and philosophy are often there—or at least seem to be—but it is entirely possible to leave here without reading any really great books or learning any history beyond that of race and gender."

While the requirements for particular departments at Williams are by no means trivial, they are sometimes too loose fitting to be useful. For instance, English majors need simply take two courses set before 1700; in other words, Shakespeare is optional. They must also take two courses set between 1700 and 1900, one course set after 1900, an analytical writing "Gateway" course, and a class on literary criticism. The department strongly recommends that students study classical and modern languages, along with foreign literature, but falls short of actually demanding either.

Likewise, the history major simply requires that students take courses from three different geographical or temporal areas. They may choose from Africa, Asia, Europe and Russia, Latin America and the Caribbean, the Middle East, and the U.S. and Canada, or premodern history. The seminar "Approaching the Past" is required, and students much take at least three courses "linked by common themes, geography, or time period" in order to develop a concentration within their major. Since the concentration is self-determined, anything from "Military History" or "Women in Asia" to "Colonial Cultures" could satisfy—and a student could major in history at Williams with "Latinas in the Global Economy" as his only American history course.

VITAL STATISTICS

Religious affiliation: *none*
Total enrollment: *2,109*
Total undergraduates: *2,053*
SAT CR/Verbal midrange: *660–770*
SAT Math midrange: *650–760*
ACT midrange: *30–32*
Applicants: *7,030*
Applicants accepted: *17%*
Accepted applicants who enrolled: *49%*
Tuition (general/out of state): *$44,660*
Tuition (in state): *N/A*
Room and board: *$11,850*
Freshman retention rate: *97%*
Graduation rate (4 yrs.): *89%*
Graduation rate (6 yrs.): *95%*
Courses with fewer than 20 students: *71%*
Student-faculty ratio: *7:1*
Courses taught by graduate students: *not provided*
Students living on campus: *94%*
Students in fraternities: *none*
Students in sororities: *none*
Students receiving need-based financial aid: *53%*
Avg. student-loan debt of a recent graduating class: *$9,448*
Most popular majors *economics, English, social sciences*
Guaranteed housing for 4 years? *yes*

CAMPUS POLITICS: YELLOW LIGHT

Williams is one of the few liberal arts colleges that hasn't completely given itself over to political correctness and leftist posturing. With reasonable student conduct policies, an outstanding faculty, and a strong athletic program, the school retains the respect of academic circles and the world at large. As far as politics go in the classroom, most faculty members at Williams are said to be fair-minded liberals. "I have yet to take a class where I thought the professor's ideology influenced the course or my evaluation in it," a student says. "If anything, the course I took that had the strongest ideological tilt (a very slight one) was from a conservative professor in a course on American imperialism. . . . I even had [a different] professor regularly ask me if I thought the course was leaning to the left, as he knew I was a conservative."

A recent president of the Garfield Republican Club, which was defunct before he revived it, told the *Williams Record* in 2012: "Even though people at Williams are intelligent and well-read, they have an aversion to speaking their mind for fear of having their whole class descend upon them. And at a small school, nobody wants that reputation." The group seems to be more libertarian than traditionalist, sources report. One professor recalled that "in the mid-2000s there were some active social conservatives associated with Williams for Life and Williams Catholic . . . but this activism seems to have completely disappeared in recent years."

Political science majors have the option of choosing a "traditional subfields" or "individual concentrations" approach to the subject. The more traditional route requires an introductory course and capstone class, plus two electives in American politics, international relations, political theory, or comparative politics. Additionally, these students must take two classes in other subfields. Those who opt to determine their own concentrations simply take five classes on a theme, as well as two classes in another area. Previously approved concentrations include "Justice in Theory and Practice," "Politics of Disempowered People," or "Environmental Politics and Policy."

An article in the *Williams Record*, the student newspaper, indicates that there is some student frustration with the obsession with diversity and the effect it has on the curriculum. The author notes that many traditional courses have been eliminated to make room for more politically correct material, resulting in choices that have become homogenized. He bemoans the proliferation of "classes about minorities" over "classes about stuff deemed important for the last hundred years." Or the past 2,500 years, for that matter.

Though there is no Western civilization requirement, entering students must take at least one Exploring Diversity course. Categories include "Comparative Study of Cultures and Societies," "Empathetic Understanding," "Power and Privilege," "Critical Theorization," and "Cultural Immersion." The courses must "promote a self-conscious and critical engagement with diversity." Thankfully, a number of worthy courses do fill the requirement, so students can skip "Feminist Bioethics" in favor of "Traditional Chinese Poetry" or "cultural immersion" in a study-abroad program.

Students select from a list of 36 majors, with economics, English, political science, psychology, art, and biology the most popular—while departments like Classics, computer science, women's and gender studies, and foreign language studies each produce fewer than 10 majors per year. The student-faculty ratio is an excellent 7 to 1.

Williams puts a great deal of emphasis on tutorials; it has recently increased the number it offers and opened them to underclassmen. A tutorial typically enrolls 10 students grouped into five pairs, which meet for an hour each week in the presence of the professor, who observes as one student presents a short paper and his partner critiques it. One faculty member told the *Chronicle of Higher Education* that his tutorials were "without a doubt, the single best teaching experience I ever had." More than half of graduating seniors have taken at least one of the school's 60 tutorials.

Students who seek attention from professors will readily receive it. "The key is finding and working with the best professors," says one student. "They're out there, and you can usually build a strong major around one or two of them." Another student says, "Professors are definitely accessible to students. Every professor provides plenty of office hours, and many give you their home phone numbers to call them any time. . . . Many professors I've had enjoy meeting outside the classroom for coffee or a meal."

One student admits that his peers "tend to be focused on career paths that lead to high-paying jobs rather than opportunities to discuss events that occurred in the past. They only want to know enough about Thucydides to quote him in an argument on current events."

The best departments at Williams are in the sciences—especially biology, chemistry, physics, geology, computer science, mathematics, and neuroscience. The Chinese and Japanese departments are strong, and the art history program is said to be extraordinary. Students can take advantage of the Williams College Museum of Art and the nearby Clark Institute of Art. In political science, the international relations program is described as "excellent." Highly praised professors include Eugene Johnson, Michael Lewis, and Sheafe Satterthwaite in art; Stephen Fix in English; Charles Dew and James Wood in history; Joseph Cruz in philosophy; James McAllister and Darel Paul in political science; and Robert Jackall and Jim Nolan in sociology.

Advising at Williams appears to be moderately strong. Freshmen are advised by members of the general faculty. Students are assigned departmental faculty advisers after they declare a major; this normally occurs after their sophomore year. Individual departments determine their own advising policies.

Williams maintains an honor code that administrators and students take very seriously. Students broadly adhere to it and faculty report that they feel safe in leaving exams unproctored and even allowing students to "self-schedule" tests as take-homes.

Williams operates on a two-semester schedule, with a four-week Winter Study Program between semesters, during which professors have the chance to test-teach new classes or materials or to concentrate on a smaller subject that can be covered in less than a semester.

SUGGESTED CORE

1. Classics 101, The Trojan War
2. Philosophy 201, History of Ancient Greek Philosophy
3. Religion 201, The Hebrew Bible (*no suitable New Testament course*)
4. History 324, The Christianization of Europe
5. Political Science 232, Modern Political Thought
6. English 201/201F, Shakespeare's Other Worlds/ What Shakespeare's Heroes Learn
7. History 252, North American History to 1865
8. History 227, A Century of Revolution: Europe, 1789–1917 (*closest match*)

Study abroad at Williams is encouraged during the junior year. Students may elect to spend an entire academic year or a semester literally anywhere in the world; the college lists hundreds of approved programs, but Williams students may submit a request to study at any foreign university. Additionally, the college's Wilmers, World, and Lawrence Fellowships fund international travel. Another excellent opportunity is the Williams-Oxford program at Oxford University's Exeter College.

Despite the school's commitment to "Exploring Diversity" and providing study-abroad opportunities, Williams imposes no foreign language requirement. It offers foreign language majors in Arabic studies, Chinese, French, German, Greek and Latin, Japanese, Russian, and Spanish. It also provides instruction in Italian and self-study courses with native speakers of Hebrew, Hindi, Korean, and Swahili.

Student Life: Amherst *delenda est*

The college is remote and bucolic, some 145 miles from Boston and 165 miles from New York City. The campus itself adds much to the landscape, with the older buildings designed in traditional academic style. Each member of every graduating class since 1862 has planted a sprig of ivy next to some building or wall.

Almost all students live on campus due to the college's eight-semester residency requirement, and more than 90 percent of upperclassmen have single rooms. "The living space has recently been divided into four 'neighborhoods' that are meant to be self-governed. Students are expected to remain in the same community for all four years," reports the school housing office. Williams has no frats, sororities, or special-interest housing. Housing is guaranteed for all four years, and first-year students are housed together in "living groups" of 22, with two junior advisers per living group.

Upperclassmen can live in mansions confiscated from campus fraternities in 1962. The dorms are coed. A Web description of Williams and Sage halls says the bathrooms are "usually single sex and are shared by [four to six] people." Still, living conditions at Williams inspired conservative alumna Wendy Shalit's heartfelt manifesto *A Return to Modesty,* which Shalit published when she was only 23.

Much of students' out-of-class activity takes place on campus, with many involved in sports, student organizations, and social events. The campus proper is 450 acres, but the college also owns the 2,200-acre Hopkins Memorial Forest and maintains a top-notch golf course on campus. The athletic program is one of the strongest in the nation in the NCAA Division III; the school almost always wins the division's Sears Directors' Cup, a national award based on the aggregate success of a school's teams. The school mascot is a purple cow, and teams are called the Ephs after college founder Ephraim Williams. About 44 percent of students participate in intercollegiate athletics, 36 percent in varsity athletics. However, because athletes are academically strong, students report that cliques do not tend to develop along team lines, and student-athletes are as much students as they are sportsmen.

The Ephs compete in purple and gold in nearly every major sport, from basketball and baseball to crew, volleyball, skiing, field hockey, and swimming and diving. Club sports include rugby, sailing, equestrian, water polo, gymnastics, cycling, figure skating, cricket, fencing, and several martial arts.

In 1821 a Williams president nearly depopulated the college by leaving to found Amherst College—taking with him most of its faculty and students. Since then, the schools have been bitter rivals, and Williams generally stomps Amherst in their annual football game. Williams played Amherst in 1859 in the world's first intercollegiate baseball game.

Newer "traditions" include the raucous Coming Out Days in October, with opportunities for a Queer Bash, a Sex Jam, and viewing gay pornography. Spring ushers in "V-Week," which features the inevitable production of *The Vagina Monologues.* While the default position at the school is distinctly Blue State liberal (students receive a free subscription to the *New York Times*), student discourse on matters political typically remains civil and high-minded. Students who dissent from the left-liberal line may find the atmosphere a bit stifling. However, one undergrad says that Williams "has not proved to be the liberal hippie bastion that I was told it would be, though it has its share of leftist activism." He went on to opine that "attending a school like Williams, known for both its academic rigor and liberal political leanings, will better serve conservative students than seeking out a college with like-minded students." Right-of-center students should seek out fellow travelers, of course—for instance by joining the college's recently revived Garfield Republican Club (which is mostly libertarian).

The Williams Literary Circle gives budding writers a chance to critique one another's work, while Springstreakers gives budding exhibitionists the opportunity to honor and catalog one another's "achievements." Other groups include the numerous a cappella choirs, the Public Health Alliance, Queer Student Union, Tap Ensemble, Photography Club, Gospel Choir, Habitat for Humanity, Voice for Choice, and Zambezi Marimba Band.

Those interested in media may consider writing for the ad-supported *Williams Record,* which circulates 3,000 copies of its broadsheet paper weekly. Smaller journals include the *Williams Telos* (a Christian journal), the *Literary Review,* and the *Mad Cow* humor magazine. Any student of Williams College—or adult member in the surrounding community—may host a program on 91.9 WCFM.

The college has a multicultural center that hosts a number of speakers and events per year. It offers a preorientation program intended to create a "network of support" for incoming minority students through a variety of social events and forums. The college reports its "U.S. minority enrollment" as 38 percent (a recent jump from 23 percent). Spirituality persists amid the uplifting natural vistas of Williams, which hosts active religious communities in a variety of Christian student groups, including a Catholic Newman Center, along with Jewish and Islamic organizations—as well as a spirituality group and a secularist community.

Williams is a safe campus; burglary is the most commonly reported offense, with eight incidents in 2011. Seven forcible sex offenses were also reported that year, along with two aggravated assaults, and one arson.

Williams is one of the costliest schools in the country, with tuition, room, and board weighing in at more than $56,510 for the 2012–2013 academic year. However, because it is also rich, it can afford to be generous. Admissions are need blind, and the college promises to meet 100 percent of demonstrated need for every student. About 53 percent of the students received some aid in amounts that averaged $40,185, and the average Williams student graduated with a student-loan debt of just $9,448—which may reflect the fact that many students come from wealthy backgrounds and don't need to borrow.

STRONG SUITS

- Abundant tutorials (with only 10 students) with highly qualified professors intensify learning.
- Teachers are accessible and very interested in students; no graduate teaching assistants.
- Good programs in hard sciences (biology, chemistry, physics, geology, computer science, mathematics, and neuroscience), Chinese, Japanese, art history, and international relations.
- An honor code that is taken seriously governs student behavior.

WEAK POINTS

- Flaccid general-education requirements.
- Shaky mandates for English and history majors; Shakespeare and Lincoln are optional.
- Many traditional courses have been dropped to make room for diversity classes.
- Some coed bathrooms.
- A diversity course requirement for all students—but none in Western civ.

Yale University

New Haven, Connecticut • www.yale.edu

Stained Glass and Gargoyles

Based in a battered but recovering New England city, Yale University is the second-oldest university in the United States. Its campus, as one student boasts, is "a Gothic wonderland with a dash of Georgian stateliness." Students arriving at Yale will find not only crenelated buildings, but a vibrant intellectual life, the best political clubs in the nation, a vast array of artistic opportunities, and a high-minded respect for ideas. Yale, however, is not for the faint of heart. Those with conservative or religious convictions will find themselves in the minority and will certainly be challenged and sharpened by debate with some of the best and brightest liberal opponents. They will also study under the leading scholars in the world.

Academic Life: Direct your studies

While Yale's commitment to undergraduate education is stronger than that of many other schools, it nevertheless leaves students completely free to define their own education—before they know enough to do so. The distributional requirements call for two course credits in: arts and humanities, sciences, social sciences, foreign language skills,

VITAL STATISTICS

Religious affiliation: *none*
Total enrollment: *11, 875*
Total undergraduates: *5,349*
SAT CR/Verbal midrange:
700–790
SAT Math midrange:
710–790
ACT midrange: *not provided*
Applicants: *25,689*
Applicants accepted: *8%*
Accepted applicants who
enrolled: *66%*
Tuition (general/out of
state): *$42,300*
Tuition (in state): *N/A*
Room and board: *$13,000*
Freshman retention rate:
99%
Graduation rate (4 yrs.): *89%*
Graduation rate (6 yrs.): *97%*
Courses with fewer than 20
students: *75%*
Student-faculty ratio: *6:1*
Courses taught by graduate
students: *none*
Students living on campus:
88%
Students in fraternities: *not
provided*
Students in sororities: *not
provided*
Students receiving need-
based financial aid: *50%*
Avg. student-loan debt of a
recent graduating class:
$9,254
Most popular majors: *eco-
nomics, history, political
science*
Guaranteed housing for 4
years? *yes*

quantitative reasoning, and writing. Each entering fresh-man is assigned a faculty member or administrator to serve as a first-year adviser.

For Yalies who do seek an education in Western civilization, the college offers a marvelous resource: the Directed Studies program, which several conservative students agree is "the shining star of Yale academic programs." After admittance to Yale, interested students must apply (again!) for this program; only 125 students each year are admitted, about 10 percent of the average freshman class. Students in the program spend their entire freshman year taking three two-semester courses studying literature, philosophy, and historical and political thought through the close reading of primary sources in the Western tradition. According to one student, "They stick to the canon quite well, so it's worth doing just for the sake of what you read." This includes Homer, Sophocles, Virgil, Dante, Petrarch, Cervantes, Shakespeare, Goethe, and Tolstoy in literature; a survey of thinkers from Plato through Aquinas and then from Descartes through Nietzsche in philosophy; and sources like Herodotus, Plato, Livy, Aquinas, Machiavelli, Burke, and Hamilton in the history and politics course. Directed Studies immediately immerses undergrads in "small classes with brilliant professors," says one student. A professor adds that "kids in these classes are studying with a good proportion of the elite in their freshmen classes."

Students and faculty list the following programs as particularly strong: art history, biology, biochemistry, economics, genetics, mathematics, music, neuroscience, physiology, psychology, and religious studies. History and humanities are the two departments most praised by students. One said, "I know of no departments that are terribly weak, though the sciences in general are often perceived as weaker simply because they don't quite measure up to Harvard or MIT, whereas our humanities and social science departments do." History has "top notch" professors, according to students, among them being Joanne Freeman, John Lewis Gaddis, Donald Kagan, Paul Kennedy, and Jay Winter.

Other highly praised teachers include Gregory Ganssle, John Hare, and Karsten Harries in philosophy; Ian Shapiro and Steven Smith in political science, Miroslav

Volf, Carlos M. N. Eire, Bentley Layton, and Harry Stout in religious studies; David Quint, and Ruth Bernard Yeazell in English language and literature; Charles Hill in international studies; Dante scholar Giuseppe Mazzotta in Italian; Eric Denardo in operations research; Maria Rosa Menocal in Spanish and humanities; Paul Bloom, Kelly Brownell, and Laurie Santos in psychology; Vladimir Alexandrov in Slavic languages and literature; Brian Scholl in cognitive science; Sidney Altman in molecular, cellular, and developmental biology; and Stephen Stearns in ecology and evolutionary biology.

Yale English majors must take 14 courses in the discipline, including an introductory survey course on English poetry (or four separate classes on the major British poets) and either a survey course on tragedy or a drama course covering roughly the same material. In addition, majors must take at least three courses in literature before 1800, one in literature before 1900, and one course in American writing, and complete a senior essay. If a careful student is able to filter out the ideological emphasis on race, class, and gender, he will receive a thorough literary education.

History majors need take only 12 courses, and while they must take at least two classes in U.S. or Canadian history and two more in European history, there is no reason to think that a graduate with a degree in history will have learned about the founding of the American republic, the U.S. Constitution, the Middle Ages, or ancient Greece and Rome. The department does require that students take three classes in "preindustrial" history, but this could be fulfilled with non-Western courses or the study of Byzantine or early Russian history. Moreover, a major could skip the central path of U.S. history entirely by choosing classes focused on Canada, the slave trade, or American medical regimens.

Yale's popular political science department permits students to meet requirements with many courses from other disciplines or through combined majors (the most common

---

CAMPUS POLITICS: YELLOW LIGHT

Despite Yale's many virtues, at the institution's heart there is a moral hollowness—which sometimes seems to extend up to its head. The squishiness was demonstrated in March 2010, when the dean's office announced it was "inviting students to submit anonymous essays about their campus sexual experiences for a new online collection called 'sex@Yale,'" according to the *Chronicle of Higher Education*. In 2012, in response to Sex Week, Undergraduates for a Better Yale College was organized "to openly challenge the prevailing libertine culture. In our events and activities, we try to present a vision of sexuality that takes love and intimacy, not the individual search for pleasure, as the starting point," said one of the founders.

Despite the leftist orientation of most of the campus, Yale is a mostly tolerant place. While conservative students may be regarded as slightly gauche, professors generally treat them fairly. One student recalled that the only pressure he felt was about his social and religious conservatism, and that "there have been a couple of times in class or in discussions with friends that I have hidden the fact that I oppose gay marriage and abortion." Most intolerance faced by conservatives on campus seems to originate with students, who are quick to ostracize outspoken traditionalists. But nobody who overcame all the barriers to getting into a place like Yale is likely to quail in the face of a little old-fashioned shunning.

is political science/economics). Dividing the field into five distinct areas—American government, comparative government, international relations, analytical political theory, and political philosophy—the department asks students to take two classes in each of at least three of these fields, write a senior seminar essay, and complete 11 courses in the major. But a major could easily graduate having never read *The Prince* or *The Federalist Papers.*

Yale students are very positive about their professors. Not only are they serious scholars, deeply involved in research, they are warm mentors and devoted teachers. "Professors are generally extremely accessible, and office hours are very helpful, especially when it comes time to write papers," says one student. He also adds, "One of my friends was even given the keys to the apartment of one of his professors when he was leaving the country so he could study a rare book." Another student says, "You won't have trouble talking to your professors—even the ones in the big lecture classes will meet up with you if you're up to asking them."

> **"The focus is on undergraduate teaching at Yale—unlike at Harvard," one professor says. One student comments: "You won't have trouble talking to your professors—even the ones in the big lecture classes will meet up with you if you're up to asking them."**

"The focus is on undergraduate teaching at Yale—unlike at Harvard," one professor says. There are few if any genuinely mediocre professors at Yale, but some are better at teaching than others, while a few have trouble keeping their personal politics out of the classroom. Hence, students reading Yale's "Blue Book" should seek out the professors and programs recommended by this guide, trusted faculty advisers, and sensible peers.

There are many graduate student teachers at Yale, called teaching fellows or TFs. Students report that they enjoy the energy TFs bring to the small sections that supplement lecture courses with professors. "In my experience, the TFs are fantastic," said one undergrad. However, teaching fellows—especially those in the social sciences—are more likely than the faculty to infuse their pedagogy with radical politics.

Class sizes are small at Yale, and the student-faculty ratio is an outstanding 6 to 1. Grade inflation, a national problem, is found in some courses.

Like most colleges, Yale has greatly expanded its study-abroad programs recently, so much so that 1,335 students studied overseas for some or all of last year. Yale-in-London and a partnership with Peking University in Beijing are special programs offered by the Center for International Experience. Yale offers study-abroad programs in dozens of countries across the six inhabited continents.

Yale offers course instruction in more than 50 foreign languages, with some study overseas. Languages on campus include such obscure dialects as Ancient Egyptian, Coptic, Hittite, Nahuatl, Pali, Sumerian, and Syriac. Major programs of study are offered in Classics, East Asian languages and literature, French, German (and various Scandinavian tongues), Italian, Near Eastern languages and civilizations, Portuguese Slavic languages and literature, and Spanish.

Student Life: Sex week and Gregorian chant

Student life at Yale College centers on the residential college system, designed in imitation of the much more extensive college system at Oxford and Cambridge. In June 2008, Yale University decided to boost its undergraduate enrollment by 15 percent by adding two additional colleges, for a total of 14 residential colleges.

Every college, headed by a residential master and dean, has developed its own personality over the decades. As one student says: "Each college is like a microcosm of campus with its own dining hall, courtyard, administrative apparatus, and other amenities." All freshmen and sophomores must live on campus, and most undergraduates choose to live in their colleges throughout their four years at Yale; 88 percent of undergrads live on campus. After freshman year, students can pick their suitemates but only from within their college. Unfortunately, Yale just began a pilot program, starting with the class of 2011, to allow coed suites for seniors.

Privacy is not always to be expected, although seniors, juniors, and even many sophomores get single rooms. All individual suite bathrooms are single sex, as are most freshman bathrooms. In many residential colleges, floors are coed, and, as one student acknowledges, "The makeup of the floor determines whether the bathroom is single sex." Students wishing to avoid floors with coed bathrooms can generally do so, but this will substantially limit their choice of rooms.

There are several Greek houses off campus, and they are known for having some raucous parties. With party themes like "CEOs and Corporate Hoes" and the alleged sexual targeting of freshmen women, some fraternities are accused of creating a climate of incivility on campus. There is a campus-wide "hookup culture," and according to one survey a high percentage of students are sexually active. Institutional concern and attention was accelerated by a scandal in 2010 concerning a Yale fraternity whose members marched around campus chanting jokes about rape and necrophilia.

Students report a significant prevalence of frat-house drinking, but say no one is pressured to drink if he wishes to abstain. As for drugs, "there is a very small (almost nonexistent) group of drug users who largely keep to themselves," a student says. One college dean says, "Generally the demands of the courses are such that you can't do a lot of drinking and smoking weed. Most people realize that the demands are too great, after a brief period of

SUGGESTED CORE

1. Classical Civilizations 254a, Introduction to Greek Literature
2. Classical Civilizations 125a, Introduction: Ancient Philosophy
3. English 395a/Religious Studies150, The Bible as Literature/New Testament in History and Culture
4. History 226, Jesus to Muhammad: Ancient Christianity to the Rise of Islam
5. Philosophy 128a, Introduction to Political Philosophy
6. English 200/201, Shakespeare: Comedies and Romances/Histories and Tragedies
7. History 124J, Colonial American History
8. Humanities 293, Roots of Modernity or Humanities 302, Foundations of Modern Social Theory

experimentation." Yale's campus culture does offer many intellectually rewarding ways for students to use their time. In particular, Yale has perhaps the most vigorous undergraduate political scene in the nation. "Even though maybe three-fourths of the kids vote Democrat, there are actually a lot of active conservative groups on campus. They're not in the closet," a professor says. Campus conservative groups focus more on high-minded discussion than on activism, and members often forge lifelong friendships.

As a microcosm of America's degenerating social elite, the school makes room for every kind of postmodern madness known to man. The college's annual Sex Week has evolved from academic discussions of sexuality to a more hands-on approach to the "interaction of sex and culture and manifestations of sex in America," reports the conservative *Yale Herald*. The unsavory quality of the affair may also be indicated by its principal sponsor—a company selling sex aids whose logos and "toys" are prominently displayed.

There are many campus ministries. "Some of the larger and more active student groups are the evangelical Yale Christian Fellowship and Yale Students for Christ. Jewish students, too, have a remarkable variety of more or less Orthodox options through the Slifka Center for Jewish Life at Yale, Yale Friends of Israel, and such," says a student. More traditional Catholic students tend to attend St. Mary's on Hillhouse Avenue, where liturgies feature an exquisite Gregorian chant and polyphonic choir, rather than St. Thomas More chapel on campus.

The Yale Political Union (PU) is the nation's oldest and most respected student debating society. It is the largest undergraduate organization at Yale, and several conservative students pointed to the PU as one of Yale's best assets—a place for "free and vigorous debate," said one student.

Campus publications include the conservative *Yale Free Press*; the *Yale Record* (a humor monthly); and the notoriously liberal *Yale Daily News*. Many Yale students also volunteer in the New Haven community and in the public schools.

Yale fields intercollegiate teams in all the major sports. Like other Ivy League schools, it requires that its athletes maintain high academic standards and does not award athletic scholarships. This often results in hilariously lopsided contests against more athletically inclined schools. Fifty percent of students participate in one or more intramural sports.

New York City, the shore, and the New England countryside are all within easy reach by train or car.

New Haven was once regarded by Yalies as "notoriously seedy," with crime kept at bay by the moats, wrought-iron gates, and turreted walls of the college. But thanks in large part to Yale's largesse, the town is recovering nicely. Crime is still a concern, however, and new students should learn their way around before straying too far. In 2011 the school reported 18 forcible sex offenses, four robberies, three aggravated assaults, 27 burglaries, three motor vehicle thefts, and three arsons. To keep students safe, Yale has an extensive campus security system.

A Yale education does not come cheap. The tuition for 2012–13 was $42,300, plus $13,000 for room and board. Admissions are need blind, and the school guarantees to meet the full demonstrated financial need of admitted undergraduates. All financial aid is need based, and 55 percent of undergraduates received it. The school is phasing out student loans, and the average recent graduate emerged with a modest $9,254 in student-loan debt.

STRONG SUITS

- The optional freshman Directed Studies program provides a solid core curriculum and intense practice in writing across disciplines.
- Top scholars, most of whom are skilled teachers, despite their focus on research.
- World-class programs in art history, biology, biochemistry, economics, genetics, history, humanities, mathematics, music, neuroscience, physiology, psychology, and religious studies.
- Mostly excellent teaching assistants, who lead discussion sections of lecture courses.

WEAK POINTS

- Anemic distribution requirements allow for overspecialization and dilettantism.
- Some teaching assistants are politicized, and grade accordingly.
- Aggressively raunchy sex activism pervades campus.
- Coed bathrooms are hard to avoid.
- Significant crime near campus.

Get a Real Education from ISI

Choosing the Right College has been produced by the staff of the Intercollegiate Studies Institute (ISI). Founded in 1953, ISI is a nonprofit, nonpartisan educational organization whose mission is to "educate for liberty"—to inspire college students to discover, embrace, and advance the principles and virtues that make America free and prosperous.

Even after you've chosen the right college, you need to make sure you get the education you deserve.

Tens of thousands of students across America look to ISI to help navigate the college experience. The reason is simple: no other organization can provide the attentive guidance, top-flight programming, educational resources, and close relationships that ISI does.

Though it costs you nothing to join ISI, what you gain is invaluable.

join.isi.org